# STEVENS' HANDBOOK OF EXPERIMENTAL PSYCHOLOGY

# STEVENS' HANDBOOK OF EXPERIMENTAL PSYCHOLOGY

**Second Edition**

## VOLUME 2: Learning and Cognition

*Edited by*

**RICHARD C. ATKINSON**
**RICHARD J. HERRNSTEIN**
**GARDNER LINDZEY**
**R. DUNCAN LUCE**

98-303

WILEY

**A Wiley-Interscience Publication**
**JOHN WILEY & SONS**
New York / Chichester / Brisbane / Toronto / Singapore

**Library of Congress Cataloguing in Publication Data:**

Handbook of Experimental psychology.
    Stevens' handbook of experimental psychology.

    Rev. ed. of: Handbook of experimental psychology
edited by S.S. Stevens. 1951.
    "A Wiley-Interscience publication."
    Includes bibliographies and index.
    Contents: v. 1. Perception and motivation —
v. 2. Learning and cognition.
    1. Psychology, Experimental.   I. Stevens, S. S.
(Stanley Smith), 1906–1973.   II. Atkinson, Richard C.

III. Title.   [DNLM: 1. Cognition.   2. Learning
3. Motivation.   4. Perception.   5. Psychophysiology.

WL 102 H2355]
BF181.H336   1988          150          87-31637
ISBN 0-471-04203-X (v. 1)
IBSN 0-471-04207-2 (v. 2)

# CONTRIBUTORS

PETER D. BALSAM, Ph.D.
Associate Professor, Department of Psychology
Barnard College of Columbia University
New York, New York

NELSON BUTTERS, Ph.D.
Professor, Department of Psychiatry
University of California, San Diego
School of Medicine
La Jolla, California
Chief, Psychological Services
San Diego V.A. Medical Center
San Diego, California

JOHN B. CARROLL, Ph.D.
William R. Kenan Jr. Professor of
   Psychology Emeritus
L. L. Thurstone Psychometric Laboratory
Department of Psychology
University of North Carolina at Chapel Hill
Chapel Hill, North Carolina

NELSON H. DONEGAN, Ph.D.
Assistant Professor, Department of Psychology
Yale University
New Haven, Connecticut

WILLIAM K. ESTES, Ph.D.
Professor, Department of Psychology
Harvard University
Cambridge, Massachusetts

BARUCH FISCHHOFF, Ph.D.
Professor, Departments of Social and Decision
   Sciences, and Engineering and Public Policy
Carnegie-Mellon University
Pittsburgh, Pennsylvania

SAM GLUCKSBERG, Ph.D.
Professor, Department of Psychology
Princeton University
Princeton, New Jersey

HAROLD GOODGLASS, Ph.D.
Director, Boston University Aphasia Research
   Center
Professor, Department of Neurology
Boston University
School of Medicine
Boston V.A. Medical Center
Boston, Massachusetts

JAMES G. GREENO, Ph.D.
Professor, School of Education
Stanford University
Stanford, California

ELIOT HEARST, Ph.D.
Distinguished Professor of Psychology
Department of Psychology
Indiana University
Bloomington, Indiana

DAVID G. LAVOND, Ph.D.
Postdoctoral Research Associate
Department of Psychology
Stanford University
Stanford, California

SARAH LICHTENSTEIN, Ph.D.
Research Associate
Decision Research
Eugene, Oregon

GEORGE A. MILLER, Ph.D.
James S. McDonnell Distinguished University
   Professor of Psychology
Department of Psychology
Princeton University
Princeton, New Jersey

DONALD A. NORMAN, Ph.D.
Professor, Department of Psychology
University of California, San Diego
La Jolla, California

CONTRIBUTORS

RICHARD W. PEW, Ph.D.
Principal Scientist, Experimental Psychology
Bolt Beranek and Newman Inc.
Cambridge, Massachusetts

DAVID A. ROSENBAUM, Ph.D.
Associate Professor, Department of Psychology
University of Massachusetts
Amherst, Massachusetts

DAVID E. RUMELHART, Ph.D.
Professor, Department of Psychology
Stanford University
Stanford, California

RICHARD M. SHIFFRIN, Ph.D.
Professor, Department of Psychology
Indiana University
Bloomington, Indiana

HERBERT A. SIMON, Ph.D.
Richard King Mellon University Professor of
  Computer Science and Psychology
Department of Psychology
Carnegie-Mellon University
Pittsburgh, Pennsylvania

PAUL SLOVIC, Ph.D.
Research Associate
Decision Research
Professor, Department of Psychology
University of Oregon
Eugene, Oregon

RICHARD F. THOMPSON, Ph.D.
Professor, Department of Psychology
University of Southern California
Los Angeles, California

BEN A. WILLIAMS, Ph.D.
Professor, Department of Psychology
University of California, San Diego
La Jolla, California

# PREFACE

Stanley Smith Stevens' original *Handbook of Experimental Psychology*, published in 1951, comprised 36 chapters in six sections, all in one large volume. Here, the number of chapters has shrunk to 27, the sections to four, and the whole made more manageable as two volumes. The shrinkage is not in experimental psychology, for what has vanished are mainly importations into psychology from other disciplines. The original *Handbook* had chapters on the neuron, on synapses, on neural maturation, on the mathematics of growth curves, and on the anatomy of motor systems. Also missing are topics that now seem less pertinent to experimental psychology than they did right after World War II, such as engineering psychology, equipment design, and manpower training. As experimental psychology developed, it grew less dependent on other sciences and focused more sharply on its own territory.

Experimental psychology has grown differentially. What was a single chapter on Cognitive Processes has become a section of nine chapters in the present edition, a full third of the entire undertaking. The section on Sensory Processes has been transformed into Perception, a shift away from the physical and physiological to the more purely psychological. Physics and physiology remain, as they must, but the hope is that they make more meaningful contact with psychology's variables. The section on Motivation has grown from three chapters to five, almost all of the growth owing to the enriching convergence of behavioral biology and experimental psychology. The section on Learning and Adjustment changed its name to Learning and ceded Cognitive Processes and Speech and Language to other sections. It abandoned a mixture of substantive and methodological chapter topics that has become unwieldy, and it now presents four fundamental issues of simple learning: conditioning processes, stimulus discrimination, response strength, and the physiology of learning and memory.

This work is not so much a revision of Stevens' *Handbook* as it is a tribute to its editor. Although the present editors had quite different relations with our predecessor, all of us were significantly influenced by him in our work, and we are unified in our admiration for him as a scientist, scholar, and person. It is difficult to say anything about Smitty without saying a great deal. Here space permits us only to point to his distinguished contributions to sensory psychology and measurement, and to his Harvard presence for four decades, where in his highly individual manner he molded generations of experimental psychologists. So, too, did his *Handbook* shape experimental psychology in its time. Readers who are not familiar with him and his work may wish to consult his fascinating autobiography, which says much of interest about him and about our science (S. S. Stevens, *Autobiography*. In G. Lindzey (ed.), *A History of Psychology in Autobiography, Vol VI*. New York: Appleton-Century-Crofts, 1974, pp 395–420).

Conversations among the editors about a possible new edition of Stevens' *Handbook* began in the fall of 1977. The old edition was out of date and out of print, but the question was whether a new one of so comprehensive a scope would be useful at a time when fine handbooks in perception, learning, and other specialized areas of experimental psychology have become available. Or were the fissures within experimental psychology so deep, we wondered, that it was pointless to try to span them in a single work. We came to believe that the very fractionation of our subject that almost deterred us could be blamed in part on the lack of a contemporary *Handbook*. Experimental psychology has more coherence than is reflected in the specialized textbooks, handbooks, journals, and monographs of our time, or so we thought. Wiley, publisher of the original *Handbook*, agreed. The next step was to try to discover whether colleagues elsewhere agreed as well.

In the summer of 1978, a tentative outline, drafted by the editors, was sent to several dozen psychologists and other scholars. They were asked for advice on the idea of a new edition, on our outline, and on possible authors. Their answers helped mold our tentative plan into the present *Handbook*. Because of their generous response to our inquiry, the outline was extensively revised, a list of prospective authors drawn up, and, most significantly, the editors felt encouraged to proceed with the project. We acknowledge, but cannot fully repay, our debt to these consultants by listing their names.

Authors were recruited to write chapters of a level of scholarship sufficient to serve the needs of scholars and a level of clarity to serve those of beginning graduate students in experimental psychology. That was Stevens' conception of his *Handbook*, as it is the present editors'. All who were asked accepted or provided advice, about the outline of the *Handbook* or about alternative authors. Soon we had the assemblage here represented. Only the enduring and versatile George A. Miller turns up as author in both editions, although several others of the original authors helped as consultants.

Also enduring is Geraldine Stone Stevens, whom Stevens gratefully acknowledged in his Preface. We are grateful to her, too, for allowing us to grace this edition with "Stevens" in its title, for advice about how to put a handbook together, for editing about one-third of the chapters, and for her enthusiasm and encouragement.

The editors needed further help as the chapters came in. The reviewers listed below provided expertise where the editors' expertise fell short. Their criticisms and suggestions were often detailed, and occasionally fundamental. We know we speak not just for ourselves but also for the authors when we express most earnest thanks to these reviewers for accepting the largely thankless task of careful editorial reading and commenting. Much, though not all, of this edition's long delay from conception to publication is accounted for by the slow pace of the successive exchanges from reviewer to author and back again, always via an editor.

But the delay would have been worse, perhaps infinite, had it not been for the efforts of Susan Herrnstein, of whom we write, as Stevens wrote of Geraldine Stone Stevens in his Preface, that "she did more work on this handbook than anyone else." Detecting a vacuum, Susan Herrnstein took administrative command—organizing, advising, and keeping the communication and paper flowing among editors, authors, publisher, and, at last, printer. Despite a schedule already too busy, she found the time and energy to do the work that needed to be done when the rest of us did not. We cannot begin to repay our debt to her, but our profound gratitude we can at least acknowledge here.

R.C.A.
R.J.H.
G.L.
R.D.L.

*29 January 1988*
*Cambridge, MA*
*La Jolla, CA*
*Stanford, CA*

## Consultants

Jack A. Adams
Abram Amsel
S. Howard Bartley
William H. Batchelder
Frank A. Beach
Robert C. Bolles
Robert M. Boynton
J. Douglas Carroll
Russell M. Church
Charles N. Cofer
F.I.M. Craik
Robert G. Crowder
M.R. D'Amato
Hallowell Davis
James Deese
Victoria A. Fromkin
Wendell R. Garner
Norman Geschwind
James J. Gibson
Bert F. Green, Jr.
Sebastian P. Grossman
Norman Guttman
Eliot Hearst
Ernest R. Hilgard
Robert A. Hinde
Earl Hunt
Tarow Indow
Paul A. Kolers
John I. Lacey
Alvin A. Liberman

Frank A. Logan
George Mandler
Lawrence E. Marks
A.A.J. Marley
Edwin Martin
George A. Miller
Thomas O. Nelson
Allen Newell
Irwin Pollack
Michael I. Posner
J.O. Ramsay
Floyd Ratliff
Robert A. Rescorla
Lorrin A. Riggs
Rudolph W. Schulz
Charles P. Shimp
B.F. Skinner
Richard L. Solomon
Norman E. Spear
J.E.R. Staddon
Saul Sternberg
N.S. Sutherland
Philip Teitelbaum
Garth J. Thomas
Richard F. Thompson
Endel Tulving
William Uttal
Bernice M. Wenzel
Wayne Wickelgren

## Reviewers

Norman Anderson
Phipps Arabie
Elizabeth Bates
Ursula Bellugi-Klima
Gordon Bower
Robert Boynton
Herbert Clark
Michael Domjan
Richard L. Doty
Trygg Engen
E. Bruce Goldstein
Isidore Gormezano
James L. Gould
Bruce P. Halpern
Katherine S. Harris
Julian Hochberg
J.A. Scott Kelso
Walter Kintsch
Michael Kubovy
Herschel Leibowitz
Steve Link
John C. Loehlin
George Mandler
James L. McGaugh

William J. McGill
Donald R. Meyer
Jeffrey Miller
Richard Millward
John A. Nevin
Donald Norman
Carl Pfaffman
Leo Postman
Howard Resnikoff
David Rumelhart
Richard Shiffrin
Edward Smith
Larry R. Squire
Saul Sternberg
Patrick Suppes
Delbert O. Thiessen
Garth J. Thomas
Richard F. Thompson
William Vaughan, Jr.
Allan R. Wagner
Wayne Wickelgren
Thomas Wickens
Frederic L. Wightman

# CONTENTS

# CONTENTS

# CONTENTS FOR VOLUME 1

# LEARNING

# Chapter 1

# FUNDAMENTALS OF LEARNING AND CONDITIONING

**Eliot Hearst,** *Indiana University*

## INTRODUCTION

Together with the study of vision and audition, experiments on conditioning and learning constitute a large part of the laboratory research performed during the first century of scientific psychology. To uncover basic mechanisms of sensation and perception, rigorous psychophysical techniques with both animals and humans

The writing of this chapter was supported by National Institute of Mental Health Research Grant MH 19300 and a James McKeen Cattell Fellowship. I thank the many students and colleagues who read and criticized versions of the manuscript. Particularly valuable was the help of Robert Rescorla, who generously supplied constructive suggestions and detailed commentary at various stages of the work. I acknowledge both Rescorla's and Herbert M. Jenkins's specific influence on my organization of the chapter and on my thinking about many topics covered here. For example, the classification of learning procedures derives mainly from Rescorla and Holland (1976). Useful reviews of the final draft of the manuscript were furnished by Abram Amsel, James Dinsmoor, Ralph Miller, Charles Perkins, Michael Rashotte, Herbert Terrace, and Allan Wagner; I am sorry I could not incorporate even more of their suggestions into the published version and I hope they will forgive me for deciding to omit some points about which they felt strongly. Finally, Dexter Gormley, Jim Hull, Susie Hull, and Sheryl Mobley deserve great credit for providing expert assistance in preparation of the manuscript and illustrative material.

have proved invaluable. Similarly, students of classical and instrumental conditioning have adopted objective methods and measurements to determine principles of learning and memory in animals and humans. As in other biological sciences, which also rely heavily on model systems involving convenient infrahuman organisms, the study of learning has depended on rats, pigeons, dogs, cats, and monkeys as subjects, in the hope that consistent results would emerge, revealing basic laws with substantial generality across situations, response classes, and species.

The domain of animal behavior and conditioning can easily justify its own separate existence. However, in the long run an understanding of "simple" processes of learning is also assumed to be important, either for its direct application to human behavior or, perhaps more realistically, for its establishment of the degree to which various conditioning mechanisms participate in complex human activities. These crucial questions can be settled only after we attain a reasonably complete knowledge of animal learning mechanisms—which, as this chapter will demonstrate, are not so simple after all.

Besides their inherent appeal and potential

implications for human behavior and cognition, experiments on animal learning have furnished specific tools and models for studying many topics of general psychological significance, including the workings of the brain, the analysis of development and aging, and the nature and evolution of intelligence. The use of surgical, pharmacological, and electrical stimulation techniques can rarely be ethically justified with healthy human beings; therefore basic research on the biological foundations of behavior must rely, at least initially, on animal work that permits measurement of phenomena resembling as closely as possible aspects of human learning and memory. And even experimental psychologists concerned with less molecular issues— such as social interactions, pedagogy, personality, or psychopathology—have found techniques or analogues from the animal learning laboratory useful in their research and theorizing.

This chapter concentrates on the most important procedures, findings, and theoretical accounts that have guided the study of learning in infrahuman organisms. Human laboratory research and practical implications will not be disregarded, however (see also Estes, Chapter 5, and Pew & Rosenbaum, Chapter 7, in this volume). The chapter emphasizes work performed and new directions taken since the earlier edition of this handbook, which highlighted the topic of animal learning in four relatively disparate contributions (Brogden; Hilgard; Miller; and Spence; all 1951). First I offer a bit of history, sketching the major intellectual paths that converged in the modern study of learning. Then a discussion of some definitional issues follows and previews the three general kinds of learning procedures that have captured experimental interest. Next, in the main parts of the chapter, there is a survey of relevant methods, results, and theories for each of the three paradigms.

Throughout the chapter the reader should detect the increasing liberalization of views and the broadened scope of topics that characterize contemporary research in the field. Many concepts and themes prominent in today's experimental psychology of human cognition and memory appear in work with animals too—for example, discrepant information, causal attribution, context dependency, short-term retention, inference and representation, cognitive maps, selective attention, priming effects, patterning and organization. And discernible also

in current animal research are the influences of sociobiology, ethology, and developmental neurobiology toward heightened recognition of evolutionary specialization, genetic determinants of behavior, and species differences.

## HISTORICAL BACKGROUND

Excellent general accounts of the intellectual and experimental precursors of modern research in learning and conditioning can be found in several sources, including Anderson and Bower (1973), Bower and Hilgard (1981), Cofer (1979), Gottlieb (1979), Hilgard and Marquis (1940), Jenkins (1979), Keller (1973), and Kimble (1967). Aside from its intrinsic interest, a historical perspective helps one to understand and appreciate (1) why conditioning experiments were so readily accepted as bearing significance for numerous psychological processes and (2) why such experiments have typically been conducted in certain ways. The following short look at the heritage of the past emphasizes influential beliefs and methods, rather than the individual scientists who proposed and championed them. The various routes are not easily separable, and some complex issues had to be glossed over to keep this summary brief.

### Empiricism-Associationism versus Nativism-Rationalism

Associationism remains a central theme in current accounts of animal learning, which typically appeal to association between events as the main basis for learned changes in behavior. Proposals concerning the elementary laws of association—contiguity, similarity, and contrast—can be traced back at least as far as Aristotle (384–322 B.C.). Philosophers interested in the origins of knowledge and the nature of the human mind have expressed many views on the topic, but the British associationist-empiricist philosophers of the seventeenth to nineteenth centuries (e.g., Hobbes, Locke, Berkeley, Hume, Hartley, James Mill, John Stuart Mill, and Thomas Brown) receive major credit for propagating the belief that sensation and association are the two most basic mental processes. For the empiricist, past experience is the main if not the only source of human knowledge; complex ideas (like justice or psychology) that are not directly sensed arise somehow from the association of simpler ideas. This type of doctrine differs from more rationalistic and nativistic views, which grant the mind a variety of innate or intrinsic perceptual and relational mechanisms that actively constrain or structure incoming sensory data. For example, Descartes (1596–1650) claimed that certain ideas are innate, like geometrical axioms and the concept of the self.

In contrast to Descartes, the British empiricists viewed the mind of the newborn infant as virtually a blank tablet (tabula rasa) on which only experience makes inscriptions. Relying not on experimentation but on shrewd introspection and logical analysis, these philosophers propounded certain primary laws, corresponding to those of Aristotle, that controlled the formation of associations between different ideas and could determine our judgments of causality. Contiguity of such ideas or elements (that is, their temporal or spatial proximity) was the most important principle, but similarity and contrast between elements were also thought to facilitate their association. Thomas Brown took a valuable step forward by proposing a number of secondary laws that govern associative strength, which included the duration, frequency, vividness, and recency of the associations (see Cofer, 1979). However, in opposition to the analytical approach of the early associationists and foreshadowing the concepts of organization and hierarchical structure used later by Gestalt psychologists and cognitive scientists, J.S. Mill argued in the 1840s that simple ideas may often combine into a more complex idea whose properties are not predictable from the properties of its elements.

The work on human learning and memory performed in the 1870s and 1880s by H. Ebbinghaus brought the associationistic tradition into the laboratory (see Estes, Chapter 5, this volume). Later on, the behaviorists, while shunning the mentalistic, introspective approaches of most predecessors, still retained a strong emphasis on association and analysis and on nurture over nature in determining human and animal behavior.

This long tradition helps to explain why laboratory research on associative processes in animals and humans was so quickly accepted as a worthwhile topic for psychologists to study. Conditioning experiments provided an objective way to investigate associations, not between ideas but between different stimuli or between stimuli and responses. Furthermore, because tabula rasa theory was not only philosophically respectable but also in harmony with democratic principles, the study of learned responses was favored over the analysis of innate behavior patterns, particularly in North America. The associationistic tradition also tended to bias researchers against the study of what were considered nonassociative modifications of behavior. Continuing to reflect these emphases, Mackintosh's *The Psychology of Animal Learning* (1974)—a definitive survey of the field—stated at the outset that phenomena like habituation (the waning of response to a single, repeated stimulus) would not receive much attention and that the book would cover the "analytic study of the associative processes underlying learned modifications of behavior" (p. 1).

## Reflex Action versus Voluntary Behavior

Despite some of these beliefs about the role of experience in human knowledge, nature obviously endows all organisms with responses that are evoked in machinelike fashion by specific stimuli. In the seventeenth century Descartes had proposed a rudimentary physiological theory, said to hold for all animal behavior and some human behavior, that anticipated conceptions of reflex action that were widely discussed and analyzed experimentally by biologists in the eighteenth and nineteenth centuries (see Fearing, 1930/1964, for an exhaustive review). During those centuries a distinction was often made between voluntary and reflex muscular responses, with the former arising spontaneously and the latter instigated by appropriate environmental stimuli.

Physiologists originally applied the reflex concept only to inborn connections or correlations between stimuli and responses, and usually studied them in special "preparations" like frogs or cats with brains sectioned at various levels. Habituation of these reflexes after repeated stimulation was reported. However, at the beginning of the twentieth century I.P. Pavlov began to regard normal, behaving organisms as aggregates of both inborn and learned reflexes that could be released by more-or-less interchangeable stimuli. He found that salivary "psychic secretions" developed in response to features of the surroundings where harnessed dogs received periodic feedings. Pavlov devised a specific technique for studying the acquisition of such responses in a reliable, objective manner. When a stimulus—for example, the ticking of a metronome, the conditioned stimulus (CS)—that did not initially elicit salivation was repeatedly paired with one that did —the unconditioned stimulus (US)—the CS itself soon came to evoke many drops of saliva. Pavlov viewed conditioning in relation to his particular hypotheses about brain function, which postulated interacting excitatory and inhibitory processes in the cerebral hemispheres. Unlike many later experts in conditioning, who considered physiologizing premature or misleading, Pavlov always attributed his findings to specific nervous-system actions.

The Pavlovian tradition encouraged the use of visceral and glandular behavior and of isolated skeletal responses (for example, eye blinks, finger or paw flexions) in the experimental study of associative mechanisms—responses that were originally triggered by particular USs. Pavlov's principle of *stimulus substitution*, whereby a new stimulus comes to substitute for another in evoking a response, helped foster views of learning phrased in terms of objective stimulus-response (S-R) linkages and transfers. However, as this chapter will reveal, contemporary Pavlovian research is much more flexible regarding the variety of response assays it employs. These include certain directed movements of the whole organism and behaviors not originally evoked by the US.

In the second half of the nineteenth century, Alexander Bain and Herbert Spencer had provided a useful context for interpreting voluntary behavior, as opposed to involuntary reflexive responses. They suggested that specific accidental movements may be followed by gratification involving the production of pleasure or the avoidance of pain, and that such movements therefore become more likely. The writings of these two men contained some of the first explicit proposals that sensorimotor (S-R) associations could be acquired or eliminated on the basis of their pleasurable or painful consequences. Even before Pavlov developed his own procedures, E.L. Thorndike independently began research more closely related to Bain and Spencer's proposition. Thorndike constructed wooden puzzle boxes from which various species, by per-

forming some response such as pulling a string, could escape and reach a piece of food located outside. Like Pavlov, Thorndike attached importance to reactions that an inexperienced animal makes to a situation (e.g., scratching, pushing anything loose or shaky, exploring objects). These instinctive reactions provided the raw material from which a particular response emerged in the situation—an S-R bond selectively strengthened by its "satisfying consequences" (Thorndike's influential *law of effect*).

Two-process learning theories (e.g., Skinner's 1938 account of respondent versus operant conditioning), which view the processes involved in Pavlovian and Thorndikian conditioning as fundamentally different, developed from subsequent work with both of them. Obviously, a basic distinction between involuntary and voluntary action is deeply embedded in our everyday thinking about behavior and personal responsibility, and is specifically embodied in our legal and moral systems. For example, it underlies the difference between manslaughter and murder as well as the criteria for deciding whether a person should be sent to a prison or mental hospital. However, in this chapter voluntary behavior is described as obeying certain laws and thus cannot literally be "free" (see also Williams, Chapter 3, this volume).

## Evolutionary Theory and Comparative Psychology: Species Similarities versus Differences

Although various aspects of animal behavior had been described by resourceful naturalists for centuries (see Barber, 1980; Diamond, 1974; Singer, 1981; Thorpe, 1979), the greatest force promoting the use of infrahuman organisms in the experimental psychology of learning was the general belief of Charles Darwin and his followers that "there is no fundamental difference between man and the 'higher' mammals in their mental faculties" (Darwin, 1871, p. 35). The idea of mental continuity between species—paralleling evolutionary views about the continuity of physical characteristics and stressing the principles of random variation and natural selection —was the watchword of the early comparative psychologists, who presumed that the most notable features of organismic evolution involved progressive changes in learning ability or behavioral plasticity ("intelligence"). The survival value of these changes was obvious and they seemed correlated with the growth and differentiation of the brain. Even study of the behavior of lower vertebrates like fish and amphibians was thought likely to reveal principles of learning helpful in understanding the behavior of higher animals. Some details about the beginning of this movement—its initial emphasis on anecdotal reports of animal intelligence, its distinctions between instincts and habits, and C.L. Morgan's plea for careful experiments and clear, parsimonious definitions of crucial concepts—can be found in Bitterman (1979), Boakes (1984), and Gottlieb (1979).

Given this enthusiastic start, it is surprising how little work was accomplished along the lines envisaged by early comparative psychologists. Jenkins (1979) perceptively comments that during the early 1900s a knowledgeable observer would certainly have predicted the inevitable and intensive study of a wide variety of species, examined in many different behavioral tasks and in the context of theories of evolutionary specialization. However, nothing of the sort happened. The comparative point of view was more or less suspended, and experiments on conditioning and learning focused on just a few, presumably representative, organisms and just a few arrangements for analyzing learning. The examination of species differences —one of the hallmarks of any energetic and complete comparative psychology based on evolutionary principles—garnered little attention.

The reasons behind this neglect are varied and include difficulties, still unresolved today, in devising fair yardsticks by which to rank or rate the learning ability and intelligence of different organisms; but it is probably more important that many experimentalists had come to believe that the basic phenomena of learning could be explained by principles or laws that hold broadly across species. So there was no urgent need for simultaneous study of many kinds of organisms, responses, and stimuli. Except when taken to an extreme, this opinion is justifiable, and it reappears later in this chapter. However, in the last 10 to 20 years, partly because of the increasing influence of ethology and sociobiology, and partly because of findings concerned with so-called biological constraints on learned behavior, the original themes of comparative psychology have regained a place of

deserved importance in the study of animal learning. Work on behavioral differences among species is one significant aspect of current research. (See also Baerends, Chapter 14, and Rozin & Schull, Chapter 10, of Volume 1).

## Behaviorism versus Gestalt Psychology

The second decade of the twentieth century marked the explicit beginning of the behavioristic movement. Though it had many clear antecedents in psychology and other disciplines, it is usually dated from J.B. Watson's keynote article in the 1913 *Psychological Review*. Watson contended that psychology must be viewed as a purely objective, experimental branch of natural science, with the theoretical goal of predicting and controlling behavior. This aim would presumably be achieved by using the concepts of stimulus and response, habit formation, habit integration, and so forth; if Watson's strategy were adopted, work "on the human being [would] be comparable directly with the work upon animals" (1913, p. 170). Although the objective study of behavior could proceed in other ways, Watson favored the conditioned reflex technique developed by Pavlov and his Russian contemporary, V. Bekhterev (Watson frowned on Thorndike's law of effect, because the notion of strengthening or weakening S-R bonds by means of subsequent satisfaction or discomfort seemed mentalistic to him). Like Pavlov, and in the tradition of associationism, empiricism, and analysis, Watson believed that complex habits were basically combinations of simpler ones. He stated boldly that "on account of its bearing upon human training, learning in animals is probably the most important topic in the whole study of behavior" (1914, p. 45).

Research with young children could also be objective, in Watson's opinion, and his best-known experiments—not very carefully performed—concerned the conditioning and removal of preschool childrens' emotional (fear) responses to small animals. There he followed procedures that combined aspects of the Pavlovian and Thorndikian paradigms (see Watson, 1924). A famous subject in the history of psychology— 11-month-old Albert B.—was conditioned to fear a white rat by associating it with the loud sound created by striking a metal bar with a hammer. Soon the mere sight of the rat caused Albert to whimper, cry, and move as far away as he could. In addition, this fear reaction transferred itself to other furry objects, like a rabbit or a Santa Claus mask.

The objective, no-nonsense approach of the behaviorists had a huge effect on methodology in psychology. Most of today's experimentalists still employ techniques for stimulus control and response measurement that do not depart radically from those acceptable to a disciple of Watson. However, contemporary workers often deplore early behaviorism's weak theory development and its relative neglect of processes intervening between stimulus and response.

Eventual dissatisfaction with the oversimplified nature of Watson's framework engendered two different courses of action: (1) attempts to reshape or improve the whole general approach by more sophisticated theoretical strategies and more careful analytic experimentation, and (2) a rejection of the behaviorist's stress on animal work, its strong associationistic bias, and its emphasis on analysis. In the first category of these post-Watsonian views, neobehaviorists like C.L. Hull, E.C. Tolman, E.R. Guthrie, and B.F. Skinner found themselves in general agreement with Watson that animal learning was probably the single most important topic in psychology. Except perhaps for Tolman, they shared Watson's view that psychologists should think mainly in terms of stimuli and responses. The years from approximately 1930 to 1960 represented the golden age of behavior theory, with relevant articles and controversies filling the pages of journals of general experimental psychology (see Spence, 1951, for part of the story).

The second post-Watsonian course of action was antedated by writings of the Gestalt psychologists, who published their first attacks on prevalent atomistic views of psychology at about the same time that Watson unleashed his own very different criticisms of the leading psychologies of the 1910s. Although the Gestaltists' work focused on human perception, Köhler's studies of *The Mentality of Apes* (1925) used chimpanzees and other species who were required to solve a variety of problems: discovering a detour to reach some goal, putting hollow sticks together to rake in otherwise unobtainable bananas, stacking boxes to climb on and pluck food attached to the ceiling. Köhler was impressed by the sudden appearance and immediate repeat-

ability of the solutions. But workers with opposing views pointed out that much unsuccessful behavior typically preceded the so-called moment of insight, the time when a subject presumably grasped the essential relations between crucial aspects of its environment. Nevertheless, the Gestalt psychologists continued to describe everyday learning and problem solving as primarily flexible and intelligent—not characterized by trial-and-error and gradual increments in stimulus-response connections, but by abrupt restructurings of the perceptual field. This process was governed by the same basic laws of organization as the Gestaltists stressed in accounting for various phenomena of perception.

The Gestalt psychologists also maintained that past experience had been overemphasized in explaining animal or human learning and behavior. The innate organization of the nervous system, the present context in which the subject finds itself, and the intrinsic nature of the events presented to the subject all merited more attention, in their opinion. Contiguity and repetition, they thought, acted only indirectly in forming associations. Their effectiveness depended upon the inherent properties of the events involved, so that, for example, not all CSs and USs should be equally easy to associate (Köhler, 1947, pp. 152–156).

Contemporary cognitive approaches to learning and memory, which stress organization, structure, and the perception of relations, reflect the influence of their Gestalt antecedents as much as the basic techniques bequeathed by the behaviorists. The student of history notices that today many pertinent issues still appear again and again: the question of appropriate levels of analysis in various situations (molar versus molecular); the suitability of knowledge-centered (representational, perceptual, more centralistic) as opposed to response-centered (more peripheralistic) approaches; the role of biological constraints and intrinsic factors in associative learning; the problem of whether learning can be interpreted as a succession of discrete stages or states, rather than as gradual changes in response strength or associative value. Although not novel from a broad historical perspective, these themes will recur in this chapter's discussion of specific research in learning and conditioning.

# LEARNING: DEFINITION AND CLASSIFICATION

## Definitional Issues

Learning is a theoretical process whose occurrence is inferred from changes in an organism's observable behavior (performance) as a result of certain environmental experiences. Besides learning, many other factors affect performance. Therefore, serious attempts to define learning have usually specified which types of performance changes and which kinds of experiences qualify. In view of the limits of our present knowledge, lengthy discussion of such details is not fruitful. However, most proposed definitions are phrased so as to exclude from the domain of learning certain modifications of behavior that seem intuitively not to belong. Performance changes resulting from motor fatigue, sensory adaptation, brain damage, disease, temporary motivational or emotional states, old age, poor diet, the ingestion of some drug, and various maturational factors are typically excluded. Although these conditions may influence what and how we learn, the general behavioral effects to which they refer are not themselves ordinarily considered instances of learning, nor will they be in this chapter.

To eliminate some or all of these possibilities, as well as to provide a more positive definition, various authors have suggested that learning should be conceived as a relatively permanent change in behavior or that the experiences producing this change involve practice or reinforcement. Such definitions run into difficulties for several reasons. Among them is the point that learning can obviously occur in the absence of overt changes in behavior, although subsequent detection of what has been learned always requires some meaurable behavioral effect. Students in a classroom may learn important facts or techniques while merely observing or listening to their instructors, and appropriately-exposed animals may learn about the location of inaccessible food, or the patterning or sequencing of external stimuli, without the occurrence of any detectable relevant behavioral change during the actual learning experience. An experimenter's job, like a teacher's, often demands the development of sensitive tests to assess whether and what a subject has learned because of some prior experience; this chapter describes several comparatively new methods, some of which prove more revealing than classic techniques. Because learning can sometimes be demonstrated after a single trial, or when the target response is physically or pharmacologically prevented, the necessity for practice is unclear. And reinforcement is itself a theoretical term, which has come under especially severe attack in recent years.

An adequate characterization of learning in terms of necessary and sufficient experiences and decisive behavioral effects will be possible only when successful general theories of learning become available. In the meantime it seems best to classify experiments on learning into three types, according to objective procedural criteria that do not entail a specific kind of behavioral outcome or a commitment to any particular underlying process or theory.

## Experiences that Produce Learning

In experiments on learning, subjects receive some experience at time $t_1$, and then at a later time ($t_2$) their behavior is assessed. If their performance at $t_2$ depends on having had the experience at $t_1$, we can seriously pursue the possibility that learning has occurred. Laboratory studies of learning may be classified according to three kinds of treatment or experience that an organism might receive at $t_1$. Each involves a different way of presenting some stimulus $S_1$.

First of all, the experience at $t_1$ may simply consist of single or repeated exposure to $S_1$, which might be a discrete stimulus (e.g., food, shock, noise) or a general setting. The $S_1$ is delivered independently of the subject's responses or the presentation of any other stimulus. As a result of such exposure, changes in behavior often appear at $t_2$. For instance, a noise presented several times at $t_1$ may subsequently evoke a smaller startle response at $t_2$ than if no preexposure or less preexposure had been given. This type of outcome, usually labeled *habituation* and characterized by a decrement in some natural response to a stimulus after numerous presentations, illustrates one possible effect of such prior experience.

Preexposure produces other results too, occasionally facilitating rather than weakening the subsequent effectiveness of a stimulus; either kind of behavioral effect at $t_2$ can provide evidence that something was learned about $S_1$ at $t_1$.

Although experiments examining this sort of $t_1$ treatment are frequently performed by both physiologists and psychologists, many textbooks on learning neglect or completely omit mention of the procedure and its outcomes. The topic may have been slighted because the organism's experience at $t_1$ does not explicitly include the occurrence of two or more discrete events that can be associated, or because the outcome of the treatment is most often indexed as a decline in some *unlearned* response (e.g., startle) to a stimulus. In fact, the procedure has commonly been used as a control treatment to aid in the analytic study of "true" learning, which many workers believe associative in nature—no surprise in view of the above-outlined historical perspectives.

A second type of experience at $t_1$ involves the presentation of two different stimuli, $S_1$ and $S_2$, in some relation to each other. The standard example of this paradigm is Pavlovian (classical) conditioning, in which $S_1$ is a biologically significant event (e.g., food or shock) consistently preceded by a more neutral event $S_2$ (e.g., a light or tone). In this arrangement $S_1$ is called the US or reinforcer, and $S_2$ the CS. The effect of such an experience has traditionally been assessed in terms of a change in response to the CS (the conditioned response—CR) at $t_2$. The measured response has typically been similar to the one initially elicited by the US (the unconditioned response—UR), for example, salivation to food. However, other assays of performance at $t_2$— including changes in responses unlike or even antagonistic to the UR—may provide valuable indices of the extent to which the relation between $S_1$ and $S_2$ has affected the subject. Moreover, changes in additional properties of the CS, such as its ability to act as a reinforcer for new stimuli (higher-order conditioning), can also serve as $t_2$ indexes that learning has occurred at $t_1$. And recent experimentation has paid special attention to other relations between stimuli that may produce learning at $t_1$, for example, (inhibitory) arrangements in which presentations of the CS signal absence of the US.

A third kind of treatment at $t_1$ entails presentations of a stimulus $S_1$ that depend on the occurrence of some response by the subject. This paradigm comprises the standard procedures of instrumental (Thorndikian, operant) conditioning, in which, for example, a subject's response produces food or prevents shock. In successful operant conditioning experiments the establishment of such a response-stimulus dependency at $t_1$ increases the probability of that response at $t_2$, compared, for instance, to the performance of subjects given no prior experience, or whose experience involves occurrences of $S_1$ at $t_1$ regardless of their behavior. Again a wide range of response-$S_1$ relations can be established at $t_1$, and a variety of different behavioral measures at $t_2$ can be accepted as indicating learning about those relations.

Although classification of experiments on conditioning and learning into these three categories is a useful organizing device, in practice it is impossible to study one type of experience in complete isolation from the others; the three procedures are inevitably mixed together. For example, the second and third types always include exposure to individual stimuli or to a general setting, the first type of experience. And exposure to discrete individual stimuli does not occur in an environmental vacuum; the stimulus always appears in a general setting or context, and thus some relation is implicitly arranged between that stimulus and its setting, or between that stimulus and behaviors normally exhibited by subjects in the situation. Insofar as possible, experimenters attempt, by means of appropriate comparison groups, to assess the relative contributions of each of the three kinds of experience.

This chapter stresses similarities in the phenomena and findings that result from the three types of treatment. The many close parallels that characterize their effects will suggest that similar basic processes or mechanisms are operating in all three types. However, it must be emphasized that the classification is based on procedures, and the question of commonality of processes can only be resolved in the context of specific theoretical and perhaps physiological analyses. Similar procedural outcomes do not necessarily imply close correspondence between underlying mechanisms.

To isolate the particular aspects of the experience at $t_1$ that are responsible for the behavioral effects measured at $t_2$, data are gathered from comparison (control) groups treated differently at $t_1$ (in the simplest cases, merely left in their home cages or placed in the apparatus without any stimulus presentations). Sometimes the comparison condition involves preconditioning performance baselines obtained from the same individual. The selection of appropriate control groups or individual baselines is not a simple, mechanical, purely objective decision—as textbooks on experimental design often imply—but rather a judgment that reflects the experimenter's theoretical views about which aspects of the experience at $t_1$ are crucial for producing the behavioral changes at $t_2$.

In what follows (see also Hearst, 1972; Hearst, Besley, & Farthing, 1970; Rescorla, 1967, 1969; Rescorla & Holland, 1976, 1982) there is the suggestion that our choice of control groups and response assays may have been too limited in the past. Students of learning want to discover the circumstances that produce learning at $t_1$, in what form this learning is retained or represented until $t_2$, and how learning is displayed in actual performance. A greater variety of comparison groups, baseline conditions, and measures of behavior can aid in pursuing these goals.

## LEARNING FROM EXPERIENCE WITH INDIVIDUAL STIMULI OR SITUATIONS

### Preview and Examples

A few illustrations and general comments can help set the scene for discussion of basic methodology and findings connected with this learning procedure. One of the first behavioral studies of repeated stimulus exposure was conducted almost a century ago. Exploring the mental powers of spiders—which were apparently not vast—Peckham and Peckham (1887) found that a spider dropped quickly from its web on the first occasion when a nearby tuning fork was vibrated. However, the response diminished with repetitions of the stimulus on a given day, recovered somewhat on the next day, but eventually stopped completely. This study is mainly of historic interest. Today's researchers would apply less primitive techniques and concentrate on such outcomes as a baby's progressive reduction in eye fixation time to a repeated visual stimulus, or a rabbit's decreasing vasoconstriction response to a recurring tone.

As noted earlier, the term *habituation* is ordinarily applied here. The stimulus seems to attract attention at first, but eventually loses this power. Found in organisms ranging from protozoa to adult human beings (see Thorpe, 1963),

the phenomenon has obvious adaptive value; it implies the existence of mechanisms that enable organisms to learn to ignore or minimize the impact of insignificant stimuli.

On the other hand, repetitions of a stimulus sometimes produce an augmentation of the initial response to it. Such *sensitization* of behavior is exemplified by the increasing strength of the respiratory-funnel withdrawals that are elicited in the (invertebrate) sea slug *Aplysia* by repeated electric shocks (see Castellucci & Kandel, 1976). The mobbing response of chaffinches to certain predators undergoes a 1- or 2-min increase after the predator is presented, followed by a decline (Hinde, 1954). These kinds of facilitative effects are often short lived and prominent only during the early stages with a repeated stimulus, but sometimes they are more-or-less permanent (see Castellucci & Kandel, 1976; Hinde, 1966, pp. 213–218; Razran, 1971). Unlike habituation, response sensitization seems to be instigated by strong stimulation and is apparently correlated with high levels of overall excitability in the subject, such as the states produced by powerful noxious USs. Sensitization has clear survival value, but in a direction opposite to habituation. It involves heightened general responsiveness to stimuli and suggests the operation of biological mechanisms that facilitate attention to dangerous or other important events and encourage appropriate approach and withdrawal tendencies to them.

Besides producing facilitation or reduction in naturally evoked responses, repeated presentations of a stimulus frequently alter its subsequent effectiveness as a CS or reinforcer in Pavlovian or instrumental conditioning. If a tone is repeated alone many times before being used as a Pavlovian CS, conditioning is generally retarded. This phenomenon is known as *latent inhibition* because stimulus preexposure hinders (inhibits) later conditioning, even in the absence of overt behavioral changes to the stimulus during the preconditioning phase of the experiment (Lubow, 1973; Lubow, Weiner, & Schnur, 1981; Siegel, 1972). Although responses to the prospective CS could be measured during that phase (as in studies of habituation), the experimenter rarely bothers to do so. When the *US-preexposure effect* occurs, there is also a retardation of subsequent conditioning, but here subjects are preexposed to the US of a forthcoming learning procedure rather than to the CS. Repeated presentations of electric shocks, injections of illness-producing agents, or deliveries of food interfere with later conditioning that uses these events as reinforcers. Like latent inhibition, this phenomenon has been the subject of much recent empirical and theoretical treatment (see Randich & LoLordo, 1979).

Subjects preexposed to complex stimuli or general situations, rather than to discrete simple stimuli, may display some change in their overall ability to learn and perform various tasks, or to discriminate among stimuli that are constituents of the original setting. Infant rats placed until two or three months of age in an "enriched" environment containing a variety of visual and manipulable objects ("toys") learn maze and discrimination tasks better than subjects raised in isolation or under normal rearing conditions (see Greenough, 1976; Rosenzweig, 1971). White-crowned sparrows that are exposed to the songs of their own species during a critical period after birth develop normal ("full") song, whereas birds isolated during the critical period eventually sing atypical songs (Marler, 1970; see also Marler & Peters, 1981, and Mason & Lott, 1976). Studies of so-called *perceptual learning*—in which mere exposure to fairly complex stimuli increases the subsequent discriminability and recognizability of the stimuli and their features —show that rats preexposed to different shapes (circles, triangles) on the walls of their home cages often learn discriminations between these shapes more quickly than other subjects that receive no preexposure to them (Gibson, 1969; Hall, 1980).

These facilitative effects occur even though various behaviors decline in strength during exposure to a particular setting; the amount of activity or exploration usually decreases as the situation loses its novelty, an outcome often considered a form of habituation (Berlyne, 1960; Fowler, 1965). Nevertheless, increased familiarity with situations or stimuli often affects positively their hedonic value. Familiarity is said to breed contempt, but the opposite seems more frequently true, especially when long-term preferences are measured. Reactions resembling attraction or affection develop to familiar objects or sensory events in most mammals, including man (see Hill, 1978). Taste preferences and certain social attachments conform to this outcome, which some writers consider related to imprint-

ing—the phenomenon whereby the young of precocial birds begin to follow some conspicuous, moving visual stimulus to which they are exposed during a limited period soon after birth. Normally the stimulus is their mother, but even the ethologist Konrad Lorenz has been pursued over land and water by appropriately imprinted geese.

These examples show that behavioral effects of exposure to individual stimuli or situations are widespread and have important implications for a variety of phenomena in conditioning. Surely bird-song development, imprinting, enrichment effects, and perceptual learning are complex matters and are regarded by many workers as special forms of learning, not easily fitted into any standard paradigms and different from each other (see Marler & Terrace, 1984; Baerends, Chapter 14, Volume 1). But they, as well as the effects of exposure to discrete simple stimuli, deserve more attention in research and theory on the psychology of learning than they have received up to now.

## Behavioral Techniques and General Methodology

Conclusions about the effects of prior exposure to a particular stimulus or setting may differ, depending on details of the assessment procedure, the application of relative versus absolute response measures, the analysis of group versus individual data, and so forth. All these methodological points arise during examination of different general methods for determining the effects of such preexposure, but since similar problems apply throughout the chapter, their early inspection is advisable, even if they involve a short digression from the major topic of this section.

### *Elicitation Power*

The most common and direct way to evaluate the influence of repetitions of a particular stimulus is through changes in the frequency or magnitude of a response elicited from the outset by the stimulus. Some findings from Marlin and Miller's (1981) work with the startle response of rats to a 90-dB tone are shown in Figure 1.1. During phase 1 the number of startle responses to the tone declined in the group receiving tone presentations. On the other hand, startle movements happened infrequently in the control

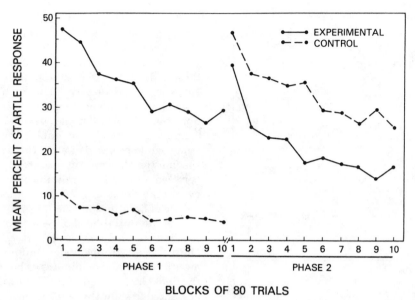

**Figure 1.1.** Habituation of rats' startle responses to a loud tone. For the experimental group 800 tones were presented in phase 1 and, after a 1-hr break, there were another 800 presentations in phase 2. Tones were presented to the control subjects in phase 2 only; during phase 1 their likelihood of a startle response was measured at times when tones were presented to the experimental group. (Redrawn from Marlin & Miller, 1981.) From "Associations to Contextual Stimuli as a Determinant of Long-Term Habituation" by N.A. Marlin and R.R. Miller, 1981, *Journal of Experimental Psychology: Animal Behavior Processes*, 7, p. 319. Copyright 1981 by the American Psychological Association. Adapted by permission.

group, which was not given tone presentations. In phase 2, which occurred one hour after the end of phase 1, all subjects received tone presentations under the same conditions as for the experimental group in the first phase. The control group's habituation curve in phase 2 was indistinguishable from the experimental group's in phase 1; this outcome demonstrated that the between-phase decrement in the experimental group was due to prior tone exposure and not merely to previous placement in the experimental setting. The data also reveal that habituation was not a short-term effect in the experimental group. Despite some initial recovery, the curve for the experimental group obtained one hour after habituation remained lower than at the start.

In many species initial orientation movements toward biologically significant stimuli (e.g., inaccessible prey) habituate much less rapidly than do actual approach or withdrawal responses (Hinde, 1970). Consequently, habituation curves with different slopes appear for different responses to the same stimulus. Similarly, Leibrecht and Kemmerer (1974) found

little or no correlation among rates of habituation in chinchillas for activity, respiratory, and head-shaking responses to an air puff.

There are several methods for comparing rates of habituation resulting from the elicitation technique. Unfortunately, conclusions may differ depending on the index selected, a problem that has caused confusion in interpretation of past results. Sometimes the experimenter counts the number of trials until the original response disappears, whereas on other occasions the crucial measure is the absolute or relative decrease in response strength from its initial level. The hypothetical curves of Figure 1.2 demonstrate the inconsistent conclusions that could be drawn from the same set of data because of the index of habituation (see Hearst, 1972, pp. 31–33, and Hearst & Koresko, 1968, for examples of a similar problem in another area of animal learning research). The results depicted in Figure 1.2 could have been obtained from the same group of subjects tested under different conditions on three separate occasions, or from three separate groups of subjects tested only once (each under a different condition).

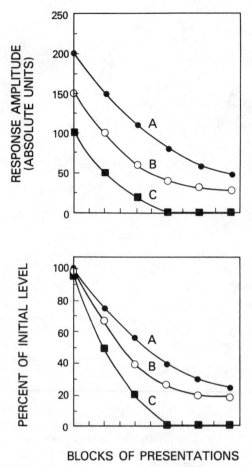

**Figure 1.2.** Hypothetical habituation curves for the same data plotted on the basis of an absolute (top) or relative (bottom) measure.

Using one criterion (time to cessation of response), the experimenter would conclude that curve C showed more habituation than either curve A or curve B; however, curve A and curve B could not be distinguished from each other on the basis of this index. An absolute index (top set of curves) would suggest that the conditions generating curve A produced more habituation than occurred for curve B, which in turn showed more habituation than did curve C (the absolute decrements from the first to the last presentation block are 150, 120, and 100 units, respectively; of course, this outcome may partly reflect the presence of a floor effect, since the response measure cannot go below zero). On the other hand, a relative index (bottom set of curves) would suggest the opposite ordering of

the three groups (decrements of 75%, 80%, and 100%, for A, B, and C, respectively, over the course of habituation).

How can an experimenter decide which of these indexes is the most appropriate or valid? No wholly satisfactory answer exists for this kind of question, and an experimenter can only hope that all the different indexes converge on a single conclusion. Preferably, the particular study would be based on some theory that makes specific testable predictions about the relation between absolute and relative measures. In any event, the point is that the evaluation of the degree of habituation usually entails consideration of the initial level of responding as well as the final level. However, an alternative would be to test all groups under uniform conditions after a rest period of minutes or hours following the final block in Figure 1.2. Data will shortly be presented to show that assessment procedures of this kind may reveal the specific lasting effects of a prior habituation period more clearly than would measures of performance obtained during the different group treatments of original habituation.

One problem that affects data interpretation throughout this chapter is often ignored, rationalized, or simply unrecognized. When findings from individual subjects are grouped together and averaged, the results are frequently not representative of the functions obtained from the individuals themselves. Averaging over many subjects or over blocks of trials makes learning curves smoother than trial-by-trial data from individual subjects. Many workers believe that such averaging is justified because it minimizes the effects of uncontrolled factors and reveals the true nature of the underlying phenomenon or relation. However, Hinde (1970) noted that fluctuations are "almost ubiquitous and are too easily regarded as experimental artefacts and conveniently submerged in grouped data" (p. 10). Konorski (1972, p. 349) reached a similar conclusion, declaring that averaged curves falsify reality by concealing irregularities inherent in the very nature of learning. And B.F. Skinner, one of the most vocal proponents of the use of individual data, argued that "an averaged curve seldom correctly represents any of the cases contributing to it" (1966, p. 21).

These critical comments are in the spirit of Claude Bernard's similar arguments, favoring a strong reliance on individual phenomena, that helped establish the science of experimental medicine (Bernard, 1865/1957, particularly pp. 129–140). Sidman (1952, 1960) was one of the first to discuss explicit problems in the treatment of group versus individual data from animal learning studies. In his influential textbook Kimble (1961, pp. 114–116) demonstrated, in perhaps the simplest possible way, how the averaging of a set of stepwise individual learning curves produces the false picture of gradual (not stepwise) learning. Given the incontestable fact that group curves often fail to supply an accurate representation of what happens in individual subjects, Estes (1956; see also Spence, 1956, Chapter 3) suggested several methods of handling the general problem, especially within the context of well-established principles of statistical inference and hypothesis testing. In any event, because habituation, Pavlovian and operant conditioning, perception, memory, attention, and virtually every topic of interest to experimental psychologists involve processes that occur in individuals—not groups—researchers can help their audience by indicating, if possible, whether a particular group curve does or does not faithfully represent outcomes or functions that are characteristic of individuals.

In this chapter data from individual subjects are sometimes presented to illustrate a phenomenon or effect, but more frequently a conventional group curve is given—primarily because most experiments in animal learning have involved group comparisons, with individual differences taken into account by statistical analysis. However, in the absence of explicit ·knowledge about the individual data constituting any group curve, the reader should be somewhat skeptical of the significance or appropriateness of group presentation. Remember that such pioneers in animal learning as Pavlov and Thorndike regularly presented typical data from individual subjects to demonstrate basic phenomena—a method that has also characterized much physiological and pharmacological research since the inception of those sciences.

Now that these general methodological digressions are out of the way, we can return to the specific use of elicitation power as an index of the consequences of stimulus repetition. Several important variations of the elicitation technique concern the effects of preexposure to one stimulus on responding elicited by new stimuli. Three possibilities deserve consideration: (1) if the new stimulus has many features or dimensions in common with the preexposed one, it may naturally evoke similar responses; (2) even if the new stimulus is quite different, it may come to evoke responses like those to the preexposed stimulus; and (3) again though the new stimulus is quite different, various preexisting responses to it may be magnified by prior exposure to another stimulus.

As an example of case 1, habituation to a tone may be followed by tests in which the tone's frequency or intensity is changed. Such a manipulation often yields a gradient of stimulus generalization, in which high levels of responding are elicited by stimuli far from the preexposed (habituated) value, and low levels of responding by nearby stimuli (see also Balsam, Chapter 2, this volume). Some graded effects of this kind, as well as revival of responding to the preexposed stimulus when presented in a new context, help weaken alternative explanations of the original response decrement in terms of peripheral sensory or motor effects. That is, if both increases and decreases in the intensity of a habituated tone produce an immediate recovery of the elicited response, neither sensory adaptation (lowered sensitivity of auditory receptors because of their repetitive stimulation) nor effector fatigue (lowered responsiveness due to repeated elicitation of the target behavior) is likely to be a major determinant of response decrements that experimenters want to classify as habituation (see also Hinde, 1970, p. 3, for other ways to analyze or rule out adaptation or fatigue as alternatives).

Assessment of recognition memory or perceptual ability in human infants often involves changes in the features or dimensions of a stimulus to which the subject has been repeatedly exposed (see Olson, 1976). For instance, after the cardiac response of five- to six-month-old infants had been habituated to a particular speech sound, a different speech sound frequently reinstated cardiac deceleration (Moffit, 1971).

In case 2, mere exposure to certain stimuli, especially strong aversive USs, may cause neutral stimuli to evoke responses resembling the response to the US—responses that would not otherwise occur with these new stimuli. For example, lights and tones of moderate intensity do not normally elicit flexions of the finger, startle responses, or eye blinks, but they may do so after exposure to electric shocks, loud noises, or air puffs to the eyelid. And in case 3, simple exposure to certain stimuli may affect the magnitude of various preexisting responses or reflexes to other stimuli; for example, after receiving a series of shocks, subjects may display a much larger startle response to a bell than they would typically.

These second and third kinds of preexposure effects are not easily separable and create potential interpretative problems in standard Pavlovian conditioning. The question is whether CRs to a CS would have appeared or grown in magnitude had there been no pairing of the CS and US, but only the USs delivered. Often characterized as nonassociative effects that presumably must be assayed via special control groups before the actual degree of Pavlovian conditioning can be determined, these phenomena receive attention in discussions of pseudoconditioning, alpha conditioning, and sensitization (see Burstein, 1973; Harris, 1943a; Hilgard & Marquis, 1940; Kimble, 1961; Kling & Stevenson, 1970; LoLordo, 1979a; Mackintosh, 1974; Razran, 1971; Rescorla, 1967). Of course, as kinds of behavioral change due to experience, they may justifiably be considered forms of learning, despite the label pseudo that has become attached to some of them.

### Training Power

Stimulus-exposure effects may be assessed not only by recording changes in the power of stimuli to elicit specific responses, but also by examining their capacity to serve effectively as signals or reinforcers in new learning tasks. In the latent inhibition paradigm mentioned above, a preexposed stimulus like a tone proves hard to establish as an effective CS in subsequent Pavlovian conditioning. The stimulus somehow resists association with virtually any US and therefore the assessment procedure is called a test of retardation of learning (Rescorla, 1969, 1979) or of resistance to reinforcement (Hearst, 1972). Analogously, such preexposure retards training of a stimulus as a positive or negative signal in an instrumental task (Halgren, 1974; Lubow, 1973).

As noted earlier, repeated presentation of a US alone hinders later Pavlovian conditioning with that US (the US-preexposure effect). Simi-

larly, when presented as a consequence of responding in an instrumental paradigm, various preexposed stimuli may be relatively ineffective reinforcers (e.g., Butler, 1957; Glanzer, 1953). However, not all preexposed stimuli tend to lose their capacity to serve as operant reinforcers. Witness the power and permanence of an imprinted object to reward various operant responses (Hoffman & Ratner, 1973).

Prolonged exposure to relatively complex stimuli or settings, such as the enriched environments or geometric shapes referred to earlier, is almost always evaluated by means of the subjects' subsequent capacity to acquire certain discriminations or chains of behavior. Because these early experiences are rather indefinite, their facilitative effects prove more difficult to analyze experimentally and characterize theoretically than those produced by repetitions of specific discrete stimuli.

### Control of Choice or Preference

The consequences of exposure to particular stimuli or situations can also be measured by offering subjects the choice of exploring, consuming, approaching, initiating, or terminating a variety of stimuli in comparison to the preexposed one (Hill, 1978). Performance on choice tests constitutes a popular way to investigate the development of taste preferences: repeated exposure to saccharin, for example, leads rats to increase their consumption of it relative to simultaneously available water. In this type of research rats normally display initial neophobia for unfamiliar smells or tastes, an avoidance tendency that ordinarily habituates with continued exposure and no aversive consequences. The selection of appropriate stimuli as alternative choices to the target taste often presents problems; if strongly positive or negative alternatives are supplied, it is difficult to decide whether the target stimulus has itself become more positive or negative. That is, the selection of a neutral alternative and the determination of a psychological zero point are hard to achieve. Consequently, simple changes in choice or consumption of the target stimulus provide the principal means of assessing effects of preexposure with this type of assay (see also Hearst et al., 1970, pp. 398–403, and Zeaman, 1976).

All three of these general techniques—elicitation power, training power, and choice or preference—can provide evidence that stimulus exposure modifies the subsequent behavior of a subject. For organisms that do not show a definite capacity for conditioning by Pavlovian or instrumental procedures, the elicitation technique may be the only practical method to apply. Occasionally, the administration of certain drugs (see, e.g., Carlton, 1963, 1969), or the removal of certain parts of the brain (see, e.g., Moore & Stickney, 1980) may be used along with the above techniques to test theories of, say, habituation, sensitization, or latent inhibition.

## Basic Phenomena and Influential Variables

Considerable data have been accumulated concerning experience with individual stimuli. Reviews and bibliographies of this work can be found in many places (Fantino & Logan, 1979; Groves & Thompson, 1970; Harris, 1943a, b; Hinde, 1966, 1970; Horn & Hinde, 1970; Humphrey, 1933; Leibrecht, 1972, 1974; Lubow, 1973; Peeke & Herz, 1973; Randich & LoLordo, 1979; Ratner, 1970; Razran, 1971; Rosenzweig & Bennett, 1976; Thompson & Spencer, 1966; Thorpe, 1963; Tighe & Leaton, 1976). The present discussion centers on a set of parameters and phenomena that parallel those to be stressed for the other two major learning paradigms in later sections of this chapter. Little explicit consideration is given here to such factors as type of species, individual differences, motivational state, and developmental level. Because habituation has been studied the most, it captures more attention than other relevant phenomena.

### Conditions of Initial Experience
One aspect of any exposure treatment is the number of presentations of the target stimulus $S_1$. In studies of habituation, latent inhibition, and US preexposure, increasing the number of presentations of $S_1$ regularly yields more and more pronounced effects. For instance, the amount of decrement in the probability of a startle response to a loud sound in rats is an increasing function of the number of prior presentations of that sound (see Figure 1.1 above); the degree of retardation of eyelid conditioning to a tone CS increases as the number of prior presentations of the tone increases (Siegel, 1972); and the interfering effect of previous injections of a toxic drug on learning

later to associate saccharin with that drug is directly related to the number of prior injections (e.g., Cannon, Berman, Baker, & Atkinson, 1975). On the other hand, with a relatively intense $S_1$ the relation between number of presentations and response magnitude may not be monotonic (see some of the empirical curves in Figure 1.6).

The rate of presentation of $S_1$ also influences its behavioral effects. Thompson and Spencer's (1966) list of parametric characteristics of habituation, which they argued can serve together as an operational definition of the phenomenon, includes the statement that "the more rapid the frequency of stimulation, the more rapid and/or more pronounced its habituation" (p. 18). In support of this conclusion, Thompson and Spencer reported that hind-limb flexion responses of spinal cats (decerebrate cats with spinal transection) attained a much lower amplitude after 2 min of stimulation once per second than after 2 min of stimulation once every 3.2 sec—a result that, unfortunately though instructively, later proved to reflect the greater number of stimulations in the once-per-second case, rather than the higher stimulation rate (see Thompson, Groves, Teyler, & Roemer, 1973). An informative experiment by Davis (1970; see also Wagner, 1976) also showed that characterization of the general effect of stimulus presentation rate is not so straightforward as Thompson and Spencer concluded. Figure 1.3 summarizes the results of Davis's study of interstimulus interval (ISI). On trial 1 of habituation training (not itself shown in the middle panels of the figure) there was no difference in the number of startle responses between the 2-sec and 16-sec ISI groups; but over the course of 1000 trials of training, the 2-sec group exhibited much more response decrement than did the 16-sec group, seemingly in agreement with Thompson and Spencer's summary statement.

However, a different conclusion emerged when each habituated group was retested after a 1-min (top right panel) or a 24-hr (bottom right panel) period of no stimulation. Subjects in the 16-sec group showed lower levels of responding at all the ISIs tested (including 2 sec and 16 sec). Two types of effects are apparently involved— one a short-term, refractory-like local effect produced by proximity to preceding instances of $S_1$ (middle panels), and the other a long-term effect produced by spaced presentations (right panels). Castellucci and Kandel (1976, pp. 11–12) also concluded that long-term retention of

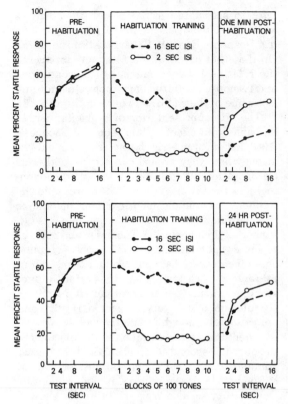

**Figure 1.3.** Startle responding in groups of rats, all of which were first tested at each of four interstimulus intervals (ISIs) during prehabituation, and then habituated for 1000 trials with a constant ISI of either 2 sec or 16 sec. After a 1-min (top) or 24-hr (bottom) break, all subjects were retested at each of the four ISIs. (Redrawn from Davis, 1970.) From "Effects of Interstimulus Interval Length and Variability on Startle-Response Habituation in the Rat" by M. Davis, 1970, *Journal of Comparative and Physiological Psychology, 72,* p. 180. Copyright 1970 by the American Psychological Association. Adapted by permission.

habituation was better after spaced than massed training. Paralleling this conclusion within a latent inhibition design, the findings of Lantz (1973) indicated that spaced preexposures to a tone (30-sec or 150-sec ISIs) produce more retarded subsequent learning of a tone-shock association (conditioned suppression) than do massed preexposures (2-sec and 10-sec ISIs). Schnur and Lubow's (1976) results were similar: the amount of latent inhibition in an escape-avoidance task was a direct function of the ISI during preexposure.

The intensity of $S_1$ is another widely studied

variable. Thompson and Spencer stated that "the weaker the stimulus, the more rapid and/or more pronounced is habituation. Strong stimuli may yield no significant habituation" (1966, p. 19).[1] Castellucci and Kandel (1976) illustrated this type of effect in their observation of greater decrements in the amplitude of the gill-withdrawal response in *Aplysia* with weak than with strong tactile stimulation.

However, conclusions about the effects of $S_1$ intensity depend on the method of assessing the degree of habituation. A weaker stimulus initially produces a weaker response, and if one's criterion of habituation involves the number of stimulus presentations before the response disappears, or the absolute level of responding after a certain number of trials, habituation may almost necessarily prove greater to weaker stimuli (see discussion of Figure 1.2 above).

Davis and Wagner (1968) questioned Thompson and Spencer's general statement about intensity effects, along lines like those that encouraged Davis to perform the ISI study in Figure 1.3. After standard habituation of the startle response to different tone intensities (108 or 120 dB) presented every 8 sec to two separate groups of rats, Davis and Wagner tested each subject 1 min later with five intensities (96, 102, 108, 114, and 120 dB). Test responding to all these sounds was greater in the group habituated to the low (108-dB) than to the high (120-dB) stimulus. According to this type of test, habituation is more pronounced after exposure to a high- than to a low-intensity stimulus. Analogous results have been found in the latent inhibition experiments of Crowell and Anderson (1972) and Schnur and Lubow (1976), as well as in most US preexposure research (Randich & LoLordo, 1979).

The use of common test stimuli to evaluate habituation after a long series of presentations to various groups under different conditions—as in Davis and Wagner's studies—avoids the confounding of intensity differences at both the time of original habituation and the time of assessment that characterizes research on this topic. It also provides a potential technique for isolating learning (i.e., relatively long term) from performance effects. In rebuttal, Thompson

[1]Thompson et al. (1973, p. 251) later added that "repetition of very strong stimuli tends to yield increased response (i.e., response sensitization) rather than response habituation."

et al. (1973) argued that the alteration of stimulus intensity between preexposure and testing creates stimulus generalization effects that are hard to interpret.

An interesting variable that influences stimulus-exposure effects, but has not received enough attention is the degree of stereotypy of $S_1$. Kimble and Ray (1965) repeatedly evoked the wiping response of frogs to a bristle applied to the skin. When the stimulus was delivered to the same spot every time, the response waned (habituation); but when the place of stimulation varied somewhat from trial to trial, the wiping response actually increased over trials (sensitization). Shalter (1975) suggested that the continuously changing temporal and spatial contexts of natural situations may explain why there is relatively little loss of response to recurring predators and alarm calls; this failure to habituate is very adaptive. He cited Hartshorne's comment that "what stimulates animal organisms is change; what deadens response is sameness or persistent repetition" (1956, p. 176). Furthermore, in classical conditioning nonmonotonous CSs (e.g., with irregularly changing intensity) yield stronger and more durable CRs than do very uniform CSs, a point noted by Konorski (1967) and Pavlov (1927). Logan and Gordon (1981) have described analogous effects of varied reinforcement and stimulation on the durability of instrumental responses, and Amsel's (1972a) general theory of persistence implies such outcomes.

Although no one has apparently performed a conventional habituation study assessing levels of evoked responding to a compound stimulus after exposure either to the compound itself or to its separate elements, Holland and Forbes (1980) compared single and compound presentations of $S_1$ in a latent inhibition design. One group of thirsty rats drank salt and sucrose separately in tap water, whereas another drank only a combination of the two; control subjects received only tap water. Then the salt–sucrose compound was paired with illness-inducing lithium chloride in all subjects. Greater latent inhibition occurred in subjects preexposed to the elements than to the compound. This result parallels findings from studies of Pavlovian conditioning (Rescorla & Wagner, 1972), to be described later, because a compound CS usually produces stronger CRs after conditioning of its individual elements than after its own conditioning.

Contrast effects appear in studies of stimulus exposure. As usually applied to Pavlovian and operant conditioning, this phenomenon refers to an exaggeration of the effect of some treatment or condition when it is interspersed with one or more different conditions rather than presented alone. Lipsitt and Kaye (1964) observed that human newborns displayed more sucking to a nipple when it was alternated with a less effective stimulus for sucking (a rubber tube) than when only the nipple was offered. Using rabbits, Whitlow (1975) found that presentation of a sequence of two 1-sec tones of different frequencies (separated by 30 or 60 sec) led to greater vasoconstriction to the second stimulus than when the two tones were of the same frequency. The above effects regarding the weaker response levels produced by uniform as compared with variable conditions of exposure in habituation studies may also involve outcomes analogous to contrast phenomena in conditioning.

As an unusual final example of a factor that affects response to stimulus repetitions, consider the serial position of $S_1$ within a fixed sequence of several different preexposed stimuli. Using the vasoconstriction response in rabbits and presentations comprising a regular series of auditory, visual, vibrotactile, and electrotactile stimuli, Wagner and Pfautz (1978) found that after 8 or 16 repetitions of a particular sequence the greatest habituation had occurred to items at the beginning and end of such "lists", and the least habituation (poorest retention) to items in the middle. Such effects are especially provocative because they mirror one of the most general findings in studies of human memory (see Estes, Chapter 5, this volume).

### Post-Exposure Phenomena
Superficially at least, the waning of response following repetitions of a particular stimulus seems quite similar to behavioral decrements obtained in conventional Pavlovian or operant arrangements—in particular, the loss of behavior that occurs during experimental extinction (see, for example, Kling & Stevenson, 1970). In addition, several parallel phenomena are observed in the different arrangements. One of these is *spontaneous recovery*: if the stimulus is not delivered for some time after the original habituation series, a new series of stimulus presentations ordinarily yields a partial recovery of the response, which wanes again as stimulation

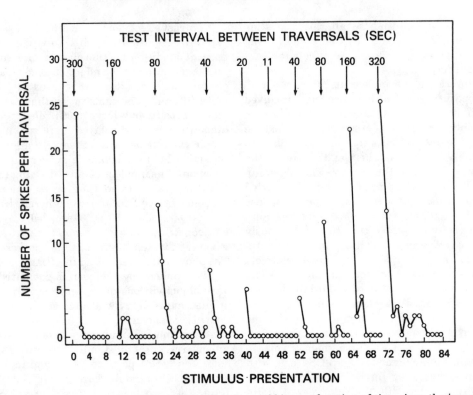

**Figure 1.4.** Spontaneous recovery and rehabituation in a rabbit as a function of time since the immediately preceding habituation period. The stimulus was the experimenter's movement across the animal's visual field (a traversal), and the response was the number of spikes emitted from a neural unit in the subject's midbrain. Except when the time between stimuli was varied between 11 and 320 sec (top scale, corresponding to gaps in the record), the interstimulus interval was always 4 sec. The 11-sec interval produced no recovery after presentation 45. (Redrawn from Horn & Hill, 1966.) From "Responsiveness to Sensory Stimulation of Units in the Superior Colliculus and Subjacent Tectotegmental Regions of the Rabbit" by G. Horn and R.M. Hill, 1966, *Experimental Neurology*, *14*, p. 210. Copyright 1966 by Academic Press. Adapted by permission.

continues (*rehabituation*). Figure 1.4 (see also Figure 1.1) illustrates this kind of reinstatement effect and indicates that its magnitude is a direct function of the time that elapsed since responding dropped to zero. Tests for spontaneous recovery offer one way to assess the permanence of the original effects of exposure; if recovery is complete after a brief interval without stimulation, it may be unwarranted to consider the previously achieved decrement as a form of learning (cf. Marlin & Miller, 1981).

With lower organisms or relatively simple responses of higher organisms, total recovery may occur in a few seconds, but in some cases it can take at least 5–30 min (see Hinde, 1970, who also points out several technical problems in devising meaningful indexes of the amount of recovery). For various behaviors, especially complex responses of higher animals, there is

often little recovery over intervals of considerably more than a day. In discussing these memory effects, Leaton and Tighe (1976) remarked that retention of habituation may last up to 21 days in *Aplysia*, 4 days in the earthworm, 42 days in the rat, and 7 days in man; and "there is no reason to assume that these data represent the limits of retention for these species" (p. 326). Similarly, in a latent inhibition paradigm, the retardation of learning produced by preexposure to the CS is often not diminished even after a lapse of several days (Crowell & Anderson, 1972; Holland & Forbes, 1980; Lubow, 1973).

If subjects are given a series of uniform rehabituation sessions, the amount of recovery is generally smaller each time, and habituation takes place more and more rapidly (called the *potentiation of habituation* by Thompson and Spencer, 1966). Of course, this outcome may

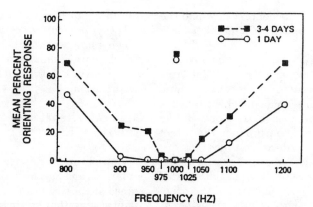

**Figure 1.5.** Stimulus generalization gradients obtained immediately following habituation of the orienting response of chicks to a 1000-Hz tone. Separate gradients are displayed for two age groups, 1 day and 3 to 4 days old. The isolated symbols in the center of the figure indicate baseline responding to 1000 Hz during the first four original habituation trials with that tone. (Redrawn from Rubel & Rosenthal, 1975.) From "The Ontogeny of Auditory Frequency Generalization in the Chicken" by E.W. Rubel and M.H. Rosenthal, 1975, *Journal of Experimental Psychology: Animal Behavior Processes, 1,* p. 291. Copyright 1975 by the American Psychological Association. Adapted by permission.

sometimes reflect merely the lower response strength at the start of each new rehabituation session; there is less distance for responding to fall before minimal levels are reached (see the discussion accompanying Figure 1.2). The phenomenon of *habituation below zero* (also called subzero habituation, silent habituation, or overhabituation) has also been reported occasionally. If, during a habituation session, the subject's elicited responses have either disappeared or reached a low, stable level, the continued presentation of the stimulus (which now produces no further measurable change in the response) can still have demonstrable effects. It often leads to less recovery of responding in a later session than if the extra presentations had not been given (Thompson & Spencer, 1966). Such an outcome suggests that the general phenomenon of habituation is not primarily based on changes in simple peripheral (effector) mechanisms, but on more central processes.

The stimulus generalization of decremental effects due to preexposure has been explicitly investigated in several studies. Figure 1.5 presents an example of a generalization gradient from habituation research (Rubel & Rosenthal, 1975). For the two groups of chicks, an orienting response (measured by opening of the eyes) was lowest at the original habituated stimulus (1000 Hz) and increased gradually as test stimuli increasingly different from the original stimulus were presented (but see Davis &

Wagner, 1968, for gradients of different shape along an intensity dimension). Siegel (1972) has reported an analogous stimulus-frequency effect from a latent inhibition experiment: auditory stimuli differing greatly in frequency from the preexposed value were established faster as effective CSs in subsequent eyelid conditioning than stimuli similar to the preexposed one.

A change in the place or context of $S_1$ exposure may reverse the prior effects of stimulus repetition. Shalter (1975) found that domestic and jungle fowl, already habituated to a black ball or a warning call, showed renewed responsiveness when the location of either stimulus was changed. This kind of result seems to depend on the biological significance of the stimulus (Evans & Hammond, 1983). An important experiment by Lubow, Rifkin, and Alek (1976) attempted to integrate the findings from perceptual learning studies (in which stimulus preexposure enhances subsequent learning) and latent inhibition studies (in which stimulus preexposure retards subsequent learning). In children and rats, these experimenters obtained (1) an enhancement of instrumental discrimination learning when a new stimulus was presented in an old environment or an old stimulus in a new environment, but (2) a retardation of such learning with the presentation of either a new stimulus in a new environment or an old stimulus in an old environment. Thus the consequences of prior stimulus exposure depend on the relative novelty of the context in which the effects are assessed (see also Channell & Hall, 1981).

The phenomenon of *dishabituation* involves the temporary reinstatement of a habituated response to $S_1$ as a result of the recent or simultaneous presentation of some novel, extraneous stimulus. The stimulus is extraneous in the sense that it does not itself produce the target response. For most writers, instances of dishabituation are considered operationally distinguishable from increases in some habituated response that occur when features of the original stimulus are changed (just discussed as examples of variations in stimulus generalization). In dishabituation, responding to the original stimulus (e.g., a light) is restored by presentations of an additional stimulus (e.g., a sound or touch) that is very different from the original one and does not itself evoke the target response. On the other hand, in stimulus generalization the habituated response also reappears, but to a new stimulus that would itself normally evoke the response and that has many features in common with the original stimulus (see Leaton & Tighe, 1976, p. 331, and Pavlov's, 1927, concept of disinhibition, to be discussed later in this chapter). Demonstrations of dishabituation provide another potential way of eliminating sensory adaptation and effector fatigue as plausible explanations of response decrements during a habituation procedure, because the subject still seems fully able to sense $S_1$ and to make the target response.

Lantz (1973) reported dishabituation in her studies of latent inhibition. The interfering effect of prior tone presentations on later learning of a tone-shock association in rats was weakened when a red light was illuminated between the habituation and conditioning phases. Rudy, Rosenberg, and Sandell (1977) too found that latent inhibition in a taste aversion paradigm was disrupted by exposing rats to a novel stimulus (a black box) just prior to conditioning with a preexposed taste.

According to Harris (1943b) and Thompson and Spencer (1966), virtually all responses of mammals that can be habituated can also be dishabituated. Furthermore, experimenters have reported the habituation of dishabituation; as the dishabituator is repeated, its effectiveness in reinstating responses to $S_1$ declines. Findings about dishabituation have played an important role in definitions and theories of habituation and other preexposure effects. As will shortly be shown, many workers believe that instances of dishabituation should be viewed not as a direct disruption of habituation but rather as a case of sensitization.

## General Theories of Stimulus Exposure Effects

In view of the abundance of data, the variety of situations and organisms examined, and the presumed simplicity of the subject's experience, it is surprising that so little theoretical progress has been made concerning the consequences of exposure to individual stimuli or settings. Biologically oriented workers have contributed more to theory development in the area than have researchers on learning and conditioning. Attitudes are changing, however, and students of learning now find it valuable—even necessary—to consider the possible effects of mere stimulus exposure in their general accounts of conditioning and learning. As noted earlier, experience with individual stimuli or settings is always embedded in the other two learning arrangements identified in this chapter. A deeper understanding of the products of any one of the three arrangements should inevitably sharpen our comprehension of the others.

Three kinds of theoretical approaches have arisen to deal with the typical phenomena produced by stimulus exposure. The first two are basically nonassociatve, whereas the third attempts to integrate the findings with suitable principles or accounts of associative learning. However, despite functional similarity, all examples of phenomena like habituation and sensitization in different organisms and experimental situations are hardly likely to result from operation of the same underlying mechanisms. Therefore the generality of any of the interpretations remains a key issue.

### Biological Models

The most reductionistic, molecular approach to analysis of the behavioral impact of repeated stimulation is taken by theories that seek to explain the phenomena in terms of underlying physiological or biochemical processes. The more elegant tests of these kinds of accounts entail the use of experimental preparations that are characterized by relatively simple responses and nervous systems, with as few synapses as possible to complicate matters. Thompson, Donegan, and Lavond (Chapter 4, this volume) review such techniques and interpretations in detail, and there is no need to repeat much of their description and summary. Kandel's work with *Aplysia* is a fine example (Kandel, 1976; Kandel & Schwartz, 1982). Thompson's own extensive research with hind-limb flexion responses in spinal cats has provided substantial empirical and logical support for a dual-process theory comprising independent decremental and incremental factors that presumably interact to yield many of the phenomena described above.

So far in this chapter, the terms habituation and sensitization have referred to specific experimental outcomes. Dual-process theory treats them as inferred processes, both of which are believed to involve interneuronal rather than afferent or motor changes. Habituation is assumed to be a purely decremental process,

affecting specific S-R pathways and steadily weakening particular responses elicited by a given stimulus; the process presumably reflects the build-up of some form of synaptic depression that gradually recovers after cessation of stimulation. On the other hand, sensitization is viewed as a more transient process, at first increasing with repeated stimulation but eventually returning to a relatively low or neutral level as repetitions continue or time passes without stimulation. Unlike habituation, sensitization is conceptualized as a nonspecific process, influencing the organism's general state of responsiveness and raising the probability that additional weak stimulation will be effective in eliciting many different responses. Sensitization becomes important when stimulation is intense.

The algebraic interaction of these excitatory and inhibitory processes is the primary determinant of a subject's performance, but dual-

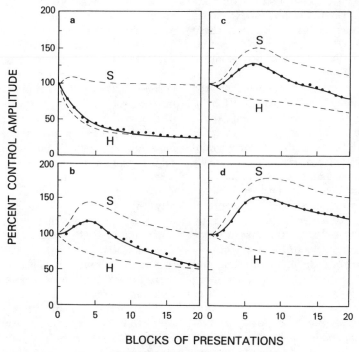

**Figure 1.6.** Hypothetical interaction of habituation (H) and sensitization (S) in dual-process theory. Dots connected by solid lines represent actual group data from hindlimb flexion responses in acute spinal cats. Dashed lines indicate inferred changes in the two theoretical processes that presumably interacted to produce the data obtained. The intensity of the shock stimulus, increased from low to high in panels (a) through (d), yielded pronounced response decrements in (a) and increments in (d). (Redrawn from Groves & Thompson, 1970.) From "Habituation: A Dual-Process Theory" by P.M. Groves and R.F. Thompson, 1970, *Psychological Review*, 77, p. 422. Copyright 1970 by the American Psychological Association. Adapted by permission.

process theory does not supply explicit quantitative rules for mapping the resultant of the competing processes into actual performance. Figure 1.6 presents a schematic representation of the theory, illustrating hypothesized effects of changes in stimulus intensity on the growth and decay of habituation and sensitization; the theoretical curves (dashed lines) were constructed so as to conform to actual data points (solid lines) obtained from spinal cats. Although not indicated in the figure, short-term effects of variations in stimulus frequency, or of the addition of a novel stimulus (presumably producing dishabituation via added sensitization), can easily be handled by the theory.

The generality of dual-process theory remains open at present, not only as applied to complex nervous systems and behaviors but also to very simple systems without synapses. The overall account has proved useful for analyzing results from work on such diverse responses as gill withdrawal reflexes in *Aplysia* (Groves & Thompson, 1970; Kandel, 1976) and startle reactions in active rats (Davis, 1972, 1974). However, sensitization is more enduring in both these cases than dual-process theory would predict. Furthermore, the theory does not smoothly account for the differences between short-term and long-term response decrements demonstrated by Davis and Wagner (1968) and Davis (1970). Except for a few special preparations, application of the theory entails completely inferred rather than actually measurable electrophysiological or biochemical processes. The theory's current value is more as a heuristic guide than as a precisely testable model, and it has encouraged some fairly unconventional interpretations for the success of several behavior-therapy techniques (see Watts, 1979). Along with other biologically oriented views of habituation phenomena (e.g., Carlton, 1963), evaluation and extension of dual-process theory require more knowledge of the short- and long-term effects of repeated stimulus exposure on behavioral output. One exciting development is the application of Kandel's cellular model of habituation and sensitization to various phenomena of classical conditioning (see discussions in Marler & Terrace, 1984).

### Perceptual-Attentional Processing

A second type of explanation centers on mechanisms by which sensory information is specifically analyzed for novelty by the nervous system. Evolution equips organisms with the capacity to detect newness or change, which is often a sign of danger. According to Sokolov's (1963, 1976) account, successive presentations of a particular stimulus help to establish an increasingly complete internal representation (model) of the stimulus in the nervous system. A given input is compared with its current neural representation, and the magnitude of the subject's response is directly determined by the discrepancy between the input and the representation. When the discrepancy is small, that is, novelty is slight, responses to the stimulus will be weak so long as it does not signal anything of importance. Such an interpretation parallels accounts that make extensive use of the concept of attention: frequent repetitions are said to weaken attention to a stimulus, or to lessen its salience, and thus to reduce behavioral output. A stimulus that at first attracted attention fails to hold it.

In both these general views, distinctive changes in the stimulus should reinstate responding—because there is in one case a mismatch with the internal model, and in the other a restoration of attention. Thus, if the frequency or duration of a tone is altered, or the stimulus is presented in a different context, various behaviors ought to reappear. Upward sloping generalization gradients (e.g., Figure 1.5) and dishabituation are explained in this manner. Even the omission of some stimulus from a regular sequence of events should and often does lead to a revival of responding.

This type of account is historically and logically linked to Pavlov's emphasis on the importance of the "investigatory" or "what-is-it?" reflex that typically occurs to novel CSs (Pavlov, 1927; see also Konorski's, 1967, notion of the targeting reflex). A dog pricks up its ears and turns toward the source of a new sound, but this reaction disappears as the stimulus is repeated without reinforcement. When the investigatory reflex to some potential CS was weak or absent, Pavlov stated, conditioning proceeds more slowly than usual. Similarly, Sokolov and his colleagues recorded the so-called orienting reflex (OR) to repetitive stimulation, as indexed by a variety of behaviors including the galvanic skin response (GSR) and changes in the electrical activity of the brain. Sokolov (1963) reported that the GSR diminishes to low levels after repeated tone presentations, and that subsequent conditioning with that tone as a CS is retarded. Conditioning begins only when the OR reappears strongly to the tone.

Perceptual-attentional accounts of this kind can encompass the phenomena of habituation, latent inhibition, and perhaps US preexposure. However, such interpretations have difficulty handling incremental effects like response sensitization. In addition, they do not make clear predictions about the consequences of manipulating various parameters of $S_1$ presentation (e.g., frequency, intensity).

### Associative Learning

Although meriting more consideration than they received, initial attempts to subsume various stimulus-exposure phenomena within principles or theories of Pavlovian and operant conditioning were restricted in their applicability and testability. Wickens and Wickens (1942) suggested that preexposure to USs may produce apparent CRs to novel CSs (pseudoconditioning) because of stimulus generalization between features of the CS and already experienced properties of the US (e.g., they both have sudden onsets). Stein (1966) assumed that an inhibitory rebound automatically follows the neural excitation evoked by a repeated but unreinforced stimulus. The conditioned form of this inhibitory reaction gradually moves backward in time and counteracts the regular excitatory effect produced by stimulus onset. Expressing a more response-centered view, Ratner (1970) argued that the waning (or intensification) of behavior to a recurring stimulus is created by interference (or facilitation) from reactions elicited by other stimuli in the situation. These other stimuli may have different effects on, say, general activity or consummatory behavior, depending on whether they are intermittently or continuously present. And Amsel (1972a) interpreted habituation in terms of Pavlovian counterconditioning—a mechanism to be described later in this chapter—in which a new response replaces the one originally made to $S_1$.

In one way or another, all these approaches reflect the point that, even in the apparently simple case of mere exposure to a stimulus, the potential always exists for the development of associative learning. Subjects in habituation research, for example, are ordinarily transported to some special apparatus to receive the appropriate treatment. Consequently they may learn about features of the general context as well as about properties of the target stimulus. Temporal or spatial contiguity should foster the establishment of associations between the periodic stimulus and different features of the general situation, or between various elements (e.g., frequency, location, intensity) of the target stimulus itself. Because particular behaviors are typically elicited by the target stimulus and by aspects of the situation, the possibility for associations involving responses also exists.

Several analyses of stimulus preexposure effects have evolved from approaches of this kind. Because an introduction to the main findings and theories of Pavlovian and operant conditioning has been reserved for later in the chapter, this is probably not the best place to discuss the details of these interpretations. However, general aspects of the most influential account ought to be mentioned here. Readers may prefer to return to the material after reading the rest of the chapter.

Wagner (1976, 1978, 1979, 1981) developed an explicit theory of habituation that embraces many of the phenomena outlined above. His main idea is that a surprising event will be more effectively processed than an expected one. The better processed a stimulus is, the more likely it will be to elicit its own URs and to support associative learning between it and other events. Events are expected or primed if they are already represented in the subject's short-term memory (STM) at the time they occur. Priming may result from either a recent presentation of the stimulus itself (self-generated) or the presentation of cues that predict the stimulus (retrieval generated or associatively generated). Within-session decrements in responding, produced by frequent repetitions of the same stimulus, take place mainly because the representation of a recent stimulus is still likely to be active in STM whenever a new presentation occurs. The new stimulus is therefore not well processed, and responding to it is weak. Thus short-term habituation is basically nonassociative.

On the other hand, long-term habituation, which would refer to a loss of responding that lasted minutes, hours, or days after the last presentation of the stimulus, is considered primarily associative. Reintroduction of the subject into the old experimental context causes associatively generated recall of the target stimulus, which hinders its effective processing. To speak somewhat causally, a second or third placement in the test situation calls up memories of the stimuli encountered there, which blunt the impact of the actual presentations of these stimuli.

Wagner's general account makes the predictions that habituation should be (1) context specific (disrupted if the target stimulus is presented in a new setting) and (2) removed or diminished by leaving the subject in the original context without presentations of the target stimulus—as compared, for example, with leaving it in its home cage for an equivalent period of time. The second prediction about the extinction of habituation is not made by nonassociative accounts. Wagner has accumulated evidence confirming these and other related speculations. Furthermore, he has suggested or implied how context-generated priming can also help to explain latent inhibition and the US preexposure effect (for other pertinent material about contextual influences, see Hall, 1980; Hinson, 1982; Lubow et al., 1976; Randich & LoLordo, 1979; and Siegel, 1979). However, Marlin and Miller (1981) failed to support several important predictions from Wagner's general interpretation—at least concerning its applicability to acoustically evoked startle responses of rats. Marlin and Miller offered an alternative account of long-term habituation that includes contextual influences but is basically nonassociative.

Several attempts to explain the phenomenon of latent inhibition have relied on associative mechanisms of a different kind. One possibility, viewed as tenable a few years ago, assumed that a preexposed stimulus would come to evoke some active inhibitory reaction because the stimulus is never associated with any important event. However, this type of explanation has been ruled out by experiments (Halgren, 1974; Reiss & Wagner, 1972; Rescorla, 1971a) demonstrating that prior exposure to a stimulus retards not only excitatory but also inhibitory conditioning to that stimulus. (If some inhibitory reaction had been conditioned to the stimulus during previous exposures, its transformation into a signal for nonreinforcement should be *easier*.) These results suggest that preexposure somehow affects the overall salience or associability of the target stimulus, rather than the acquisition of particular behaviors to it

(see also Lubow et al., 1981). Such a loss of salience or associability might be interpreted in terms of subjects' learning that the stimulus either is uninformative and can be ignored (learned irrelevance or noncorrelation), or is not associated with impending danger (learned safety). In contrast to Wagner's account, these explanations focus more on what might follow the target stimulus than on what might precede it and make it expected or surprising. So far, experimental separation of these alternatives has been difficult. To be noted shortly is an analogous quandary that is related to certain phenomena of Pavlovian conditioning, which can be interpreted by changes in either the predic*ted*ness or the predic*tive*ness of events.

In summary, exposure to individual stimuli or settings has multiple and often complex effects. Up to now, the most influential accounts of these phenomena have been nonassociative, either (1) postulating decremental and incremental neural processes triggered by repetitive stimulation or (2) proposing attentional mechanisms that automatically detect stimulus novelty and modulate appropriate responses. However, while not denying the involvement of such factors, several current interpretations have assigned a bigger role to associative mechanisms—especially in explaining effects that are retained over rather long time periods.

Worth reiterating is the disclaimer that no single set of behavioral or physiological mechanisms is likely to handle the broad spectrum of outcomes generated by stimulus exposure. Because habituation clearly occurs in primitive organisms lacking a central nervous system, the inevitable involvement of complex associative learning seems implausible. Nevertheless, effects of stimulus exposure in simple species may reflect biological precursors of more complicated forms of learning and selective attention, and consequently they deserve serious analysis by students of Pavlovian and operant conditioning. This ubiquity of various stimulus-exposure phenomena across the animal kingdom and the embedding of that kind of treatment in more complex arrangements provide strong justification for accelerated development of integrative theories on the topic, including those based on evolutionary considerations. We know something about the circumstances of stimulus exposure that produce different outcomes, but very little about the underlying content or representation of this learning and how it is translated into actual behavior. Facilitation versus weakening of specific responses may imply differences not so much in what the organism has learned about a particular stimulus, but rather in how that learning generates certain behavioral changes.

## LEARNING FROM EXPERIENCE WITH RELATIONS BETWEEN STIMULI

### Preview and Examples

Psychologists have been much more interested in how organisms learn about dependencies between two or more stimuli than in how they are affected by the presentation and repetition of a single stimulus. Standard Pavlovian conditioning exemplifies the case in which two explicit stimuli occur in some definite relation to each other, regardless of the subject's behavior. Most often, a relatively neutral stimulus signals the arrival of a biologically important stimulus, but there are other possibilities too. Some remarks on the range of stimuli, responses, and experimental settings used in past and current research can smooth the way for examination of specific methodological, empirical, and theoretical issues.

In accordance with Pavlov's choices, a variety of visceral and glandular responses have served in conditioning experiments over the past 75 years. More popular in America than salivary conditioning have been arrangements with aversive USs and such behaviors as the galvanic skin response (GSR; believed to reflect mainly a change in sweat gland activity), vasomotor reactions, or alterations in cardiac rate or pattern—all presumed indicants of emotional learning. Russian work with implications for human psychosomatic illness (see Bykov, 1959) has revealed that secretions from many internal organs are susceptible to conditioning. For example, an external CS, such as a tone associated with delivery of acid into a dog's stomach (US), comes itself to evoke bile secretion from the liver, a response that is a UR to excess stomach acidity.

Besides these autonomic responses, many studies have used reflexes involving local undirected skeletal behaviors—such as paw flexions to electric shock in cats and dogs, knee jerks to tactile stimulation in human beings, jaw movements to liquid food delivered directly into the oral cavity of rabbits, and eye blinks to shock, loud sounds, or air puffs. Indeed, until recently, eyelid conditioning in human beings and rabbits, along with salivary conditioning, provided the main source of data for theorizing about associations based on pairings of two stimuli. Details concerning the different appetitive and aversive unconditioned reflexes employed in conventional Pavlovian experiments, as well as a further indication of the wide range of organisms used in such studies, can be found in Corning, Dyal, and Willows (1973a, 1973b, 1975), Fantino and Logan (1979), Kimble (1961), Mackintosh (1974), Razran (1971), and Thompson, Donegan, and Lavond (Chapter 4, this volume).

Three arrangements, each relatively neglected prior to the 1960s but much simpler to implement than most of the standard preparations, furnish the bulk of contemporary data on learning that results from relations between stimuli: (1) fear conditioning (also called *conditioned suppression* or the conditioned emotional response, CER); (2) *autoshaping*; and (3) *food aversion learning*. The first is historically linked to Watson's analysis of emotional behavior, which achieved experimental expression in his research with the infant, Albert B. (see pp. 7–8). Watson and many later behaviorists wanted to demonstrate that Pavlov's paradigm applied not only to "spit and twitches," but also provided a plausible basis for understanding personality development, emotion, and other complex psychological processes. Introduced by Estes and Skinner in 1941, the CER technique measures the effect of a CS by presenting it while the subject performs some regular, ongoing behavior—usually a well-established instrumental response, for example, lever pressing for food in a rat. Because most organisms become inactive when afraid, a stimulus paired with shock will suppress ongoing behavior. The amount of suppression presumably indicates the magnitude of fear evoked by the CS. Reviews and discussions of the voluminous literature on the CER technique appear in Blackman (1977), Campbell and Church (1969), Davis (1968), and Lyon (1968).

The second currently popular arrangement was labeled autoshaping by its discoverers, Brown and Jenkins (1968). In the standard setting with pigeons, illumination of a circular key serves as the CS and the availability of grain in a nearby food hopper as the US. After a number of CS-US pairings, virtually all birds approach and peck vigorously at the illuminated key, even though grain would arrive regardless of their behavior.

Brown and Jenkin's discovery fascinated students of learning because the key peck was a directed action of the whole organism—the type of response that had been for years considered a form of behavior trainable only by operant and not Pavlovian conditioning. Later work showed that both lever pressing in rats and key pecking in pigeons, the most studied responses in operant conditioning, are susceptible to autoshaping. Obtained with various species, stimuli, and settings since 1968, autoshaping is now generally regarded as a manifestation of the widespread tendency of organisms to approach (or, under certain circumstances, to withdraw from) significant environmental stimuli (see Dickinson & Mackintosh, 1978). Hearst and Jenkins (1974), Locurto, Terrace, and Gibbon (1981), and Schwartz and Gamzu (1977) review the topic.

Food-aversion or taste-aversion learning is the third technique now extensively used to study learning based on stimulus relations. (Flavor-aversion learning, which suggests either taste or smell, may be a preferable name; conditioned toxicosis is another term used for this phenomenon.) It was initially recognized, analyzed, and popularized by Garcia and his collaborators (see Garcia & Ervin, 1968; Revusky & Garcia, 1970). On this procedure the ingestion of a flavor (CS), say, saccharin, is paired with some illness-inducing experience (US), for example, administration of lithium chloride (LiCl), x-irradiation, or rapid rotation of the subject's body. When later offered different liquids, organisms that have experienced such CS-US pairings avoid substances possessing the flavor associated with illness. Like autoshaping, this phenomenon at first excited attention because it apparently contradicted certain widely held beliefs about conditioning. Since taste-aversion learning often required only a single CS-US pairing and was successful with CS-US intervals that were hours long, it seemed biologically preorganized compared with other forms of associative learning.

The acquisition of food aversions has been reliably observed and carefully analyzed in numerous species since 1970. It entails probably the simplest method for investigating exposure to stimulus relations: no expensive automatic equipment is required and the experimenter needs only graduated water bottles, syringes, and a supply of tasty substances and nausea-producing agents to perform methodologically acceptable research. The immense literature on food aversion learning can be penetrated by reference to reviews and bibliographies in Barker, Best, and Domjan (1977), Domjan (1980), Logue (1979), and Milgram, Krames, and Alloway (1977).

Pavlovian research has been extended to instances in which both associated events are relatively neutral at the start of a study. Sensory preconditioning arrangements examine the consequences of presenting, say, a tone and a light in some positive relation, then following the light by a standard US, and ultimately checking on whether the tone will have effects similar to those of the light in the prior phase. A type of inference by the subject is presumably involved; that is, if A then B, if B then C, therefore, if A then C. And second-order conditioning, whereby some new stimulus is paired with an established CS rather than with a US, has served not only as a fruitful subject of investigation but also as a sensitive tool for detection of other learning.

Finally, the most widely investigated phenomena of classical conditioning during the 1970s involved compound or multiple CSs, for example, lights and tones presented simultaneously. The control exerted by the separate components of the compound depends on an interesting set of factors, whose effects yield important implications about the selectivity of attention and learning. Current theories of Pavlovian conditioning focus on this arrangement, often including as another crucial component the overall context in which the CS and US are presented.

Instead of being a restricted, primitive form of learning, Pavlovian conditioning has proved quite broad and flexible. Infrahuman organisms seem surprisingly sensitive to the "causal texture of their environments" (Tolman & Brunswik, 1935) and are controlled by patterns or configurations of stimuli as well as by simple stimulus elements. Animals can detect a wide variety of dependencies among external events —even rather innocuous, biologically insignificant stimuli—and they reveal these capacities not just in reflex responses but in many other behaviors. The range of stimuli whose relations produce learning appears much greater than suspected several decades ago. Furthermore, important practical implications of Pavlovian findings have materialized; one fine example is Siegel's (1979) analysis of drug tolerance and addiction. For these and other reasons, the main emphasis in the psychology of learning during the 1970s and 1980s shifted from operant conditioning to classical conditioning.

## Behavioral Techniques and General Methodology

### Control and Comparison Groups

In research on Pavlovian conditioning the experimenter has to demonstrate that the arrangement of a particular relation between two stimuli is responsible for the behavioral changes observed at a later time $t_2$. There must be evidence that the outcome at $t_2$ would not have occurred if there had been no previous relation between the CS and US, or if the two stimuli had been presented in some different relation. For instance, mere exposure to the CS or US—as described in the foregoing discussion of habituation, sensitization, and pseudoconditioning—might have been sufficient to generate increases or decreases in the likelihood of certain responses to the CS at $t_2$.

To rule out alternatives of this kind, experimenters have often included various comparison groups that receive the same number of presentations of CS or US or both as the experimental group, but in single, unpaired, or independent fashion. The selection of specific comparison treatments depends strongly on the CS-US relation that a particular worker thinks is crucial for conditioning. Until fairly recently, simple contiguity of the CS and US was viewed as most critical. Therefore, control groups were usually added that did not permit close temporal proximity between the two events. In these explicitly unpaired groups (sometimes misleadingly called random procedures) the CS and US occurred as often as in the standard paired group but were always kept far apart in time. The experimenter would then evaluate the amount of "true" associative learning by comparing differences at $t_2$ between the paired and unpaired treatments.

However, in the 1960s strong arguments (see Rescorla, 1967) were raised against this type of comparison, mainly on the grounds that a CS never followed by the US does not really bear a random relation to it. Instead, the CS supplies definite information—that the US is not coming. An explicitly unpaired CS should therefore become a signal for nonreinforcement (that is, a presumed conditioned inhibitor), whereas the standard paired procedure would establish a signal for reinforcement (a conditioned excitor). Learning based on a CS-US relation would be assumed to occur with both paired and unpaired stimuli, but with unpaired the learning would be negative, and with paired, positive; thus, some new comparison or baseline treatment would be needed to allow separate assessment of the two outcomes, positive and negative. According to this general view, the crucial factor in conditioning is how informative or predictive the CS is about the US—in other words, what type of overall correlation there is between them. This correlation can be explicitly defined in terms of the likelihood that the US will occur during or just after the action of the CS as compared with the likelihood that the US will occur in the absence of the CS.

If Pavlovian conditioning is so conceived, a logical comparison group would be one in which the CS supplies no information about occurrences of the US. This goal can be achieved, procedurally at least, by making CS and US occurrences independent of each other. The correlation between them would be neither positive—in which the probability of occurrence of US with the CS, p(US/CS), would be greater than without the CS, p(US/$\overline{CS}$)—nor negative [p(US/$\overline{CS}$) > p(US/CS)]. Instead, the correlation would be zero; the two probabilities are arranged to be equal. This zero-correlation or truly-random-control treatment has been widely used recently as a baseline against which to assess both excitatory and inhibitory learning. The approach has encouraged the study of conditioned inhibition as an active form of learning, a possibility not readily handled by simple contiguity accounts.

The concepts of contiguity and informativeness recur in the pages ahead. The reader should keep in mind that the appropriate comparison group specified by one theory of associative learning may be inappropriate in the context of another theory. Consequently, the most defensible policy may entail concurrent assessment and an attempt to disprove a variety of alternative explanations—not merely the experimenter's favorite—by including several different control groups, along lines suggested by the general scientific strategy of strong inference (Platt, 1964) or converging operations (Garner, Hake, & Eriksen, 1956).

### Assays of Conditioning

Methods for assessing the effects of exposure to relations between stimuli correspond closely to the three techniques already described for measuring the behavioral products of exposure to individual stimuli. These assays involve changes in the power of a stimulus (1) to evoke or modulate specific responses, (2) to participate effectively in new training arrangements with the stimulus serving as a signal or reinforcer, or (3) to affect performance when choice and preference among various continuously available stimuli are evaluated.

Alterations in the evocation power of the CS, measured primarily in terms of the latency, amplitude, rate, probability, or resistance to extinction of responses evoked by the CS—or by related stimuli in studies of generalization—have historic priority as assays of Pavlovian conditioning. (Since the word elicitation, used earlier in this chapter, implies stimulus-produced reflex behavior, as in Catania, 1979, the more general term, evocation power, is used here.) A sufficient number of CS-US pairings yields increases in the amount of salivation or the probability of an eye blink to a CS that did not initially produce those responses. When the CS and US occur in very close contiguity, CRs may be difficult to separate from URs. For that reason, occasional CS-only trials are sometimes interspersed with regular CS-US pairings to permit measurement of CRs uncontaminated by overlapping behavior elicited by the US.

The more traditional approaches to Pavlovian conditioning insist that the behavior produced by the CS at $t_2$ meet certain requirements of response type and form: "True" conditioning, it is said, results in UR-like behavior to the CS. This criterion is linked to Pavlov's notion of stimulus substitution and his own observations of a clear similarity between the CR and UR. Moreover, largely to rule out nonassociative incremental processes like sensitization and pseudoconditioning, some writers have demanded that Pavlovian conditioning generate a response

to the CS that is different from any original responses to it—thus distinguishing the outcomes of conditioning experiments from those described previously for cases in which the original response to a repeated stimulus changes. Other investigators have stated that the CR must be chosen from the same effector system as the UR and that receipt of the US must not entail any "instrumental" activity, such as reaching out or moving somewhere to obtain food (see Amsel, 1972b; Gormezano & Kehoe, 1975).

However, such strictures about response topography have begun to disappear. Many students of learning would now accept as evidence for conditioning any behavioral changes to the CS at $t_2$ that can be demonstrated to depend on the prior relation between the CS and US. For example, in taste-aversion learning and conditioned emotional response (CER) arrangements the behaviors measured to the CS at $t_2$ are normally different from those directly elicited by the US. In another type of setting, Holland (1977, 1980a) found that a light paired with food elicits one pattern of anticipatory response in the rat (e.g., rearing of the body), whereas a tone paired with food comes to elicit another set of behaviors (e.g., head jerking). Neither of these CRs resembles the UR to food, but each is similar to behavior observed when the CSs are first presented.

Frequently, Pavlovian conditioning can be demonstrated with some but not other UR-related behaviors. For example, the probability of eye-blink CRs does not seem to increase with repetitions of a tone followed 7 sec later by shock to the outer eyelid of rabbits, although the same paired stimuli result in clear changes in heart rate CRs as training progresses (Vandercar & Schneiderman, 1967). Sometimes certain emotional or aggressive behaviors develop to signals of nonreinforcement, but at other times such stimuli do not evoke any definite reactions. However, even with such "behavioral silence", there are certain assays, to be mentioned in a moment, that can reveal effects of the subject's exposure to a negative CS-US relation. Because the form of a CR depends on so many factors, including the properties of the CS and the CS-US relation, it seems overly restrictive to insist that the development of UR-like reactions to the CS should serve as a defining feature of Pavlovian conditioning.

Summation or combined-cue tests are valuable assessment techniques, particularly in studies of conditioned inhibitory stimuli. Such CSs presumably involve tendencies or processes opposite those of conditioned excitors, but they may generate little or no overt change when presented alone (behavioral silence). Summation tests use evocation power as an index (Hearst, 1972; Rescorla, 1969). For instance, a suspected inhibitory stimulus could be combined with a CS that is already known to produce appreciable responding (e.g., a bell paired with food or shock). If the effect of the combined stimuli is considerably lower than that of the bell itself, then the inference that the other stimulus is inhibitory receives support. However, the experimenter would also have to demonstrate that the decrease required the subject's prior exposure to some relation between the suspected inhibitor and the US. This is necessary to eliminate the possibility that the response reduction is due to mere novelty of the combination—that is, an unconditioned effect created by generalization decrement (stimulus change) or by interfering processes that Pavlov labeled "external inhibition" (see p. 36).

In parallel fashion, another way to measure the excitatory capacity of a CS would be to combine it with a known excitor and to determine whether behavior in response to the latter stimulus is elevated. Note also that variations of the summation technique are being applied whenever a Pavlovian CS (1) is superimposed on some operant baseline—as with the CER procedure—or (2) in another type of assay, is combined with an effective US to examine its incremental or decremental influence on URs. In both instances, CS-evoked changes in far-above-zero behavioral effects are used to assess the CS's power, rather than any products of its own isolated presentation.

Besides measuring the power of stimuli to evoke or modulate particular behaviors, an experimenter can assess effects of the subject's prior exposure to some relation between stimuli by examining the subsequent training power of the stimuli. Does prior experience with a particular $S_2$–$S_1$ relation facilitate or retard new learning involving those events as CSs or reinforcers? In practice, the new learning task could be either Pavlovian or operant. For example, compared with untreated groups or groups placed on a truly-random-control procedure, subjects previously exposed to explicitly unpaired instances of CS and US show slower conditioning when the CS is later paired with the US. This type of retardation is similar to but normally more pronounced than that described earlier for studies of latent inhibition. Furthermore, according to the logic of second-order conditioning, a stimulus that has been paired with a US should subsequently serve as a Pavlovian reinforcer in training new CSs that are merely paired with that stimulus rather than with a US. Rescorla (1980) noted that second-order conditioning is often successful even when no definite CRs to the first-order CS develop in the initial phase. Thus the ability to condition new CSs sometimes proves a more sensitive index of the power of a CS than does measurement of any overt responses it comes to evoke.

When subsequent instrumental training provides the new learning task, responses will normally be acquired that remove or prevent CSs previously paired with shock or the absence of expected food (escape or avoidance responses: Daly, 1974; McAllister & McAllister, 1971). Behaviors that produce CSs previously paired with the presence of food or the absence of shock tend also to increase in probability (Dinsmoor & Sears, 1973; Fantino, 1977; Gollub, 1977; LoLordo, 1969). In such cases the CS is usually said to have acquired conditioned or secondary reinforcing powers, so that it can contribute to the training of new operant behavior.

After a CS has occurred in some relation to a US, its hedonic value may change, as reflected in performance on tests involving choice of or preference for a set of continuously available stimuli. Food containing a taste previously paired with illness is less likely to be selected for consumption from a group of rewarding substances than a food of novel taste or one that has been paired with removal of some nutritional deficiency (Zahorik, 1977). Analogously, subjects tend to remain in certain locations in preference to distinctive places where they have been shocked, and to choose places where they have been fed. In these and other test arrangements (see Hearst et al., 1970; Hearst, 1972), the impact of prior exposure to certain stimulus relations is assessed by subjects' preferences among different events or objects, rather than by specific evaluation of evocation or training power.

## Basic Phenomena and Influential Variables

This section reviews the best documented findings and phenomena from studies of learning based on explicit relations between stimuli. First, important aspects of the CS and US themselves are considered and then the nature of the relation between them. Readers will find other sources useful for more details, for example, Black & Prokasy (1972), Boakes and Halliday (1972), Dickinson and Mackintosh (1978), Gormezano and Kehoe (1975), Gormezano and Moore (1969), Hilgard and Marquis (1940), Kimble (1961), LoLordo (1979a–c), Mackintosh (1974), Moore and Gormezano (1977), Prokasy (1965a), Razran (1971), Rescorla and Holland (1982), and Terrace (1973).

### Conditions of Initial Experience

The basic outcome of a conditioning experiment is the behavioral change from $t_1$ to $t_2$ that is taken as an indication of learning. Pavlovian arrangements yield progressive, monotonic changes in the index of conditioning as the number of exposures to the CS-US relation increases. Figure 1.7 includes acquisition curves for salivary, eyeblink, CER, autoshaping, and taste-aversion conditioning. Taste aversions are generally acquired in one trial with strong USs, but Garcia, Ervin, and Koelling's (1966) use of a relatively weak US, among other details, permitted detection of changes in drinking behavior over successive trials. Like most curves in Figure 1.7, typical acquisition functions are negatively accelerated. Performance eventually reaches some stable asymptotic level—an outcome predicted by various formal models of learning but probably often attributable to an artificial ceiling or floor on the response index (the percent eyeblink and CER suppression measures, for example).

Sometimes a positively accelerated segment appears early in conditioning, which generates an overall learning curve that is S-shaped (sigmoidal). Various theorists have interpreted this initial trend differently: (1) the response measure is assumed to be an insensitive reflection of learning until associative strength attains some threshold value, below which CS-US learning may occur though it is not yet apparent in performance; (2) a number of trials are presumed necessary before CS-US learning can begin, a lag traceable to several possible sources: (a) habituation of fear and exploratory responses to the general apparatus must first occur, (b) so-called latent inhibition produced by CS familiarity must be overcome in some cases, or (c) rapid conditioning to the experimental context interferes at first with learning about the discrete CS; (3) learning is hypothesized to involve not a gradual process but a succession of sudden transitions from one state to another, for example, unconditioned–intermediate–conditioned, as certain quantitative (Markov) models would imply. However, because acquisition curves vary so greatly in the presence and magnitude of this initial positive acceleration, the relative merit of all these interpretations is moot. Often the divergent outcomes may merely reflect the use of group versus individual data, the averaging of scores over trials or blocks versus sessions, or the type of performance index, continuous or discrete. At any rate, the question of appropriate mapping of learning into performance is a problem that still arises repeatedly in theoretical analyses of acquisition.

Speed of acquisition generally differs between various Pavlovian procedures. For conditioned suppression and taste aversion, learning is usually complete within 10 trials, whereas it can last hundreds of trials for eyelid conditioning and autoshaping. Even so, changes in certain parameters can reduce or reverse such differences. For example, a decrease in the rate of presentation of CS-US pairings (that is, extension of the intertrial interval, ITI), under otherwise standard conditions, leads to acquisition of autoshaping in a mean of 10 or fewer trials, rather than 50 to 100 trials (see Gibbon, 1981; Gibbon & Balsam, 1981). Therefore, global statements about the rapidity of conditioning for different arrangements are very difficult to make.

The degree of prevailing motivation affects acquisition, too. Hungrier and thirstier subjects show stronger Pavlovian appetitive CRs. The more anxious human subjects display higher levels of eyelid and startle conditioning. Discussions of these kinds of results, and their relation to whether drive level affects learning or performance, can be found in Cofer and Appley (1964) and Kimble (1961).

### NATURE OF THE US

The choice of a US affects both the speed and eventual asymptote of conditioning. Uncon-

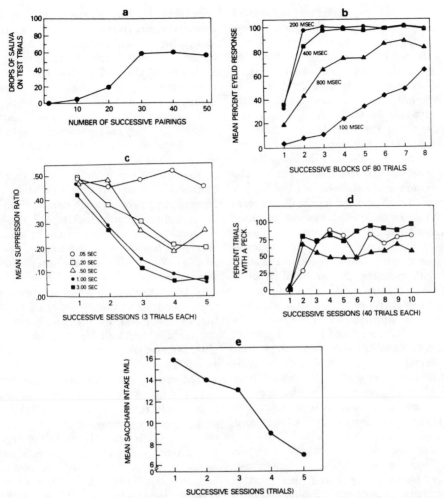

**Figure 1.7.** Sample acquisition curves from some common Pavlovian procedures involving CS-US pairings (trials). (a) Increases in the amount of salivation as tone-food pairings progressed in one dog (redrawn from Anrep, 1920.) From "Pitch Discrimination in the Dog" by G.V. Anrep, 1920, *Journal of Physiology, 53,* p. 380. Copyright 1920 by the Physiological Society. Adapted by permission; (b) Increases in the probability of an eyelid (nictitating membrane) response with more and more tone-shock pairings in four groups of rabbits, each trained with a different interval between the CS and US (redrawn from Smith, Coleman, & Gormezano, 1969.) From "Classical Conditioning of the Rabbit's Nictitating Membrane Response at Backward, Simultaneous, and Forward CS-US Intervals" by M.C. Smith, S.R. Coleman, and I. Gormezano, 1969, *Journal of Comparative and Physiological Psychology, 69,* p. 229. Copyright 1969 by the American Psychological Association. Adapted by permission; (c) Increases in conditioned suppression as a function of the number of light-shock trials in five groups of rats exposed to different shock durations during training; suppression is strongest as the response index approaches .00 (redrawn from Riess & Farrar, 1973.) From "UCS Duration and Conditioned Suppression: Acquisition and Extinction Between-Groups and Terminal Performance Within-Subjects" by D. Riess and C.H. Farrar, 1973, *Learning and Motivation, 4,* p. 370. Copyright 1973 by Academic Press. Adapted by permission; (d) Increases in autoshaped keypecking for three individual pigeons that received 40 daily pairings of key illumination and grain (redrawn from Wasserman, 1972.) From *Auto-Shaping: The Selection and Direction of Behavior by Predictive Stimuli* (p. 47) by E.A. Wasserman, 1972. Bloomington, IN: Indiana University. Copyright 1972 by Dr. Edward Wasserman. Adapted by permission; (e) Development of an aversion to saccharin over trials on which saccharin drinking was followed by the injection of apomorphine in a group of rats (redrawn from Garcia, Ervin, & Koelling, 1966.) From "Learning with Prolonged Delay of Reinforcement" by J. Garcia, F.R. Ervin, and R.A. Koelling, 1966, *Psychonomic Science, 5,* p. 121. Copyright 1966 by the Psychonomic Society. Adapted by permission.

ditioned stimuli can be classified in several ways. One division is into exteroceptive versus interoceptive, determined by whether the US is presented externally or internally. However, no important systematic differences in conditioning seem to exist between these kinds of USs (Bykov, 1959; but Mason & Lott, 1976, p. 149, and some students of taste-aversion learning might argue about this conclusion). Another common categorization designates USs as appetitive or aversive (or, in Eastern Europe, alimentary and defensive). The two classes conform to what the layman would call desirable and undesirable events, and they are technically (operationally) defined by their effects in instrumental conditioning situations. An appetitive US such as food will increase the probability of a response that produces it, whereas an aversive US such as shock will increase the probability of a response that prevents or removes it.

Although some writers (e.g., Konorski, 1967) have argued that appetitive and aversive USs differ in their motivational and temporal properties, the two types of US seem to produce analogous empirical phenomena and activate similar but antagonistic associative processes. Their reciprocal affective properties have been examined in both Pavlovian and instrumental settings (see Dickinson & Dearing, 1979; Dickinson & Mackintosh, 1978; and Rescorla & Solomon, 1967). For instance, although a signal of shock usually facilitates shock-avoidance responding, it suppresses operant responding for food; the latter effect is the standard CER phenomenon.

As embodied in Pavlov's law of strength, the intensity and duration of the US affect Pavlovian conditioning. Conditioning is superior when more intense, concentrated, or longer USs are employed. Several years ago serious attempts were made to distinguish between the effects of US strength on learning and on performance. In general, familiar statistical (factorial) designs were used. Groups of subjects experienced different US values during original conditioning and then were further subdivided into groups that received tests with either their original US or a different one. Comparison of test scores from groups *trained* at different intensities provided a measure of the effects of US intensity on *learning*; comparison of groups *tested* at different intensities supplied information about effects on *performance*.

Applied also to other parameters of conditioning besides US intensity (e.g., motivation level), these attempts to separate learning and performance have been inconclusive. Most relevant variables probably affect both learning and performance, or their effects seem to vary with the particular response system and experimental arrangement involved. Explicit testable theories concerning the translation of learning into behavior on various tasks appear to be required if the general issue is ever to be truly illuminated or resolved.

Related to the topic of US strength is the diminution of the UR that sometimes occurs as conditioning progresses (Kimmel, 1966; Wagner, 1981). Control groups lacking CS presentations show that this outcome is not simply an example of reflex habituation. As implied above (pp. 26–26), Wagner's (1979) interpretation of this phenomenon presumes that a US is less effectively processed when expected (primed) than when unexpected. Donegan (1981) found that the likelihood of conditioned diminution of the rabbit's eyeblink UR is directly related to US intensity, which supported Wagner's overall analysis.

The novelty of the US influences the rapidity of Pavlovian conditioning. Speed of acquisition is inversely related to number of prior US presentations. In surveying this US-preexposure effect, Randich and LoLordo (1979) decided that the phenomenon can reasonably be handled in terms of either (1) growth of some kind of centrally mediated habituation of emotional responses to the US, or (2) blocking of the effectiveness of the nominal CS by strong associations between the US and the general experimental context—an explanation pursued later in this chapter. The most popular current views include provision for both nonassociative (1) and associative (2) factors.

NATURE OF THE CS

Conditioned stimuli have typically been selected for their neutrality; if a stimulus does not initially elicit much behavior, the experimenter can more readily detect conditioning to that stimulus. On the other hand, the stimulus must obviously be discriminable by the subject, and events that do not originally evoke some definite orienting or attentional response often prove to be relatively weak CSs. In general, the same factors that enhance the effectiveness of a US act correspondingly for a CS: intensity or

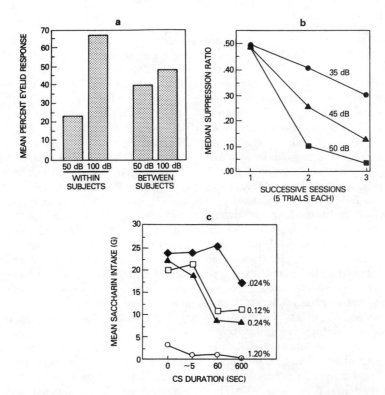

**Figure 1.8.** Illustrations of the general relation between CS intensity and CR strength. (a) Differences in probability of the human eyelid CR to a CS, as dependent on whether a tonal CS of low (50 dB) or high (100 dB) intensity was used and whether different groups received only one intensity level (between subjects) or a single group received both intensities on interspersed trials (within subjects) (redrawn from Grice & Hunter, 1964.) From "Stimulus Intensity Effects Depend Upon the Type of Experimental Design" by G.R. Grice and J.J. Hunter, 1964, *Psychological Review*, *71*, p. 249. Copyright 1964 by the American Psychological Association. Adapted by permission; (b) Group differences in rats' acquisition of conditioned suppression as a function of the intensity of the auditory CS; maximum suppression would be .00 (redrawn from Kamin, 1965.) From "Temporal and Intensity Characteristics of the Conditioned Stimulus" by L.J. Kamin in *Classical Conditioning: A Symposium* (p. 126) by W.F. Prokasy (Ed.), 1965, New York: Appleton-Century-Crofts. Copyright 1965 by Appleton-Century-Crofts. Adapted by permission; (c) Saccharin aversions produced by pairing saccharin with ionizing radiation, as a function of the duration of access (sec) to saccharin and the concentration (%) of the saccharin solution given to different groups of rats (redrawn from Barker, 1976.) From "CS Duration, Amount, and Concentration Effects in Conditioning Taste Aversions" by L.M. Barker, 1976, *Learning and Motivation*, *7*, p. 270. Copyright 1976 by Academic Press. Adapted by permission.

salience, and novelty. Recent work has added localizability and sensory modality to the list of influential CS properties.

The greater the intensity or amount of the CS, the higher are the conditioning levels typically achieved. This conclusion is illustrated for eyelid, CER, and taste aversion learning in Figure 1.8. Novel stimuli make better signals than do familiar stimuli, as is shown in latent inhibition. Furthermore, once conditioning has become fairly well established, trial-by-trial variations in features of the CS—say, irregular

changes in its intensity—seem to maintain CRs better than do stereotyped presentations (Konorski, 1967; Pavlov, 1927, Chapter 14). Perhaps variability of stimulation interferes with habituation to the CS. This may be related to the common finding that larger behavioral differences often appear when single subjects rather than separate groups are exposed to several values of some independent variable (see Figure 1.8a).

However, in one important sense, novel stimulation can impair Pavlovian CRs. If some unusual extraneous stimulus—that is, a stimulus that does not normally generalize much with the CS and does not evoke similar responses —is presented just before or during the CS, it may weaken the CR by a process Pavlov called indirect or *external inhibition*. Thus the sudden appearance of a novel odor in the laboratory or the entry of an unfamiliar guest might temporarily reduce or eliminate CRs. Pavlov explained this effect in terms of competing reflexes: "Any new stimulus immediately evokes the investigatory reflex . . . and the conditioned reflex is in consequence inhibited" (1927, p. 44).

Species differ widely in their sensitivity to changes in various stimulus modalities. Not surprisingly, CSs from modalities that are especially important in view of the subject's particular ecology and evolution—for example, visual stimuli for food in birds and taste or odor stimuli in rats—are generally most effective, although some conditioning seems attainable with virtually any CS that the subject can discriminate. Noted above was the finding that qualitatively different CSs often produce dissimilar CR topographies; auditory and visual signals for food in rats or pigeons yield different patterns of anticipatory behavior (Hearst & Jenkins, 1974; Holland, 1977). Furthermore, the ease with which stimuli from the same modality are localized affects conditioning of directed movements toward them (Holland, 1980a; Wasserman, 1973). Until recently, work on Pavlovian conditioning neglected this possibility; physical restraint of subjects had inadvertently prevented detection of CS-approach behaviors.

As with the US, a theoretical question has concerned whether CS parameters affect degree of learning or whether they merely influence performance generated by associations of essentially equivalent strength. Pertinent research has centered on CS intensity, primarily because of Clark Hull's use of the concept of *stimulus intensity dynamism* (see Champion, 1962; Gray, 1965; and Mackintosh, 1974). After conditioning with one intensity of CS, presenting more intense CSs often produces stronger CRs—in contrast to the outcome expected on the basis of stimulus generalization (because novel test stimuli actually yield *higher* levels of behavior than does the original CS). This result suggests that the main effect of CS intensity is on performance. However, training with more intense CSs sometimes produces stronger CRs when all subjects are subsequently tested under identical conditions. Thus CS intensity appears to affect both the formation and exhibition of Pavlovian associations. An interesting methodological possibility is thereby raised: on occasion, an experimenter may only be able to detect learning by means of tests at $t_2$ with stimuli more intense than the original CS.

A pertinent matter is whether the absolute or relative intensity of the CS is responsible for the effects just described (Levis, 1971; Logan, 1954; Perkins, 1953). Intense CSs are not only stronger than weak CSs on some absolute scale, but they are also more discriminable from the constant background. Such discriminability probably does contribute substantially to the influence of CS intensity; the higher the background noise level is, the less effective are CSs of the same absolute auditory intensity. Furthermore, a CS that involves reduction of background noise becomes a more powerful signal in direct proportion to the change from the background level (Kamin, 1965). However, other experiments have shown that an upward shift in intensity from the prevailing background level yields a more effective CS than an equivalent downward shift—some evidence for the importance of absolute intensity level. Among other reasons, work on CS intensity is important because an understanding of its effects may permit us to treat variations in many CS parameters (novelty, localizability, modality, etc.) in terms of modifications in one factor: the perceived intensity of the CS.

For simplicity, CSs have been discussed here as if they were isolated, elementary, individual events. Naturally occurring CSs are typically much more complicated than that; they are objects composed of many different features and they usually involve simultaneous stimulation from more than one sensory modality. Current Pavlovian research and theory stress compound stimuli, a topic that receives consideration later.

EXTRINSIC RELATIONS BETWEEN STIMULI

Rescorla and Holland (1976) have suggested that we distinguish between two general kinds of stimulus relations, extrinsic and intrinsic. Extrinsic (arbitrary) relations can be specified without reference to the particular events that serve as CS and US. For example, regardless of the stimuli selected for study, an experimenter can arrange for: (1) the CS onset to be separated from US onset by 5 sec, (2) the US to occur three times more often in the absence of the CS than

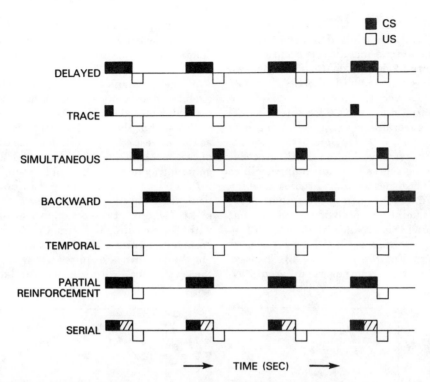

**Figure 1.9.** Schematic diagrams of the most widely studied temporal relations between CSs and USs in Pavlovian conditioning. The striped bar in the bottom (serial) arrangement designates an extra CS, different from the one used in the other procedures.

in its presence, and (3) the US delivery to follow only 25 percent of the CS presentations. On the other hand, specification of intrinsic relations between two stimuli always entails identification of the events themselves. They are naturally or inherently related in a way that does not hold for other CSs and USs (a notion reminiscent of some aspects of Gestaltist or cognitively oriented approaches to learning). An example is the relation known as similarity; one can decide whether a CS and US are similar only if one knows exactly what the stimuli are. Do they both have a gradual or sudden onset? Do they both come from the same sensory modality? Historically, students of Pavlovian conditioning have concentrated on extrinsic relations. They are discussed first, but recent research confirms the importance of intrinsic relations as well.

(1) TEMPORAL CONTIGUITY. The temporal relation between the CS and US—their order and the time interval between them—has been the most widely studied of the extrinsic relations that influence conditioning (see Gor-

mezano & Kehoe, 1981, for a penetrating review and analysis). For many years close temporal proximity of the CS and US was viewed as almost a defining characteristic of Pavlovian conditioning—not surprising when one considers the old assumption in philosophy and psychology that contiguity is the indispensable ingredient for association of events or ideas. Various temporal relations between the CS and US are listed and diagrammed in Figure 1.9.

When the CS begins before US delivery and continues at least until the onset of the US, the arrangement is called *delayed conditioning.* When the CS begins and ends some time before US delivery, the procedure is called *trace conditioning* (presumably some persisting trace of the CS mediates conditioning, because the CS itself is no longer physically present when the US appears). In *simultaneous conditioning* CSs and USs overlap exactly in time, whereas in *backward conditioning* the CS follows US offset. *Temporal* (or *time*) *conditioning* involves no explicit CS presentations, but USs occur every *x* sec or min. *Partial reinforcement* refers to procedures in which the US is delivered after some but not all CS trials. For completeness, *serial conditioning* is included as a basic paradigm in Figure 1.9 despite its use of at least two CSs, which regularly precede the US.

Though most widely explored for eyelid conditioning, variation in the CS-US interval (ISI) has similar general effects on the strength of conditioning in all Pavlovian arrangements. Conditioning is strongest when the CS precedes the US, and the degree of conditioning declines when the ISI becomes too long. Studies in which very short intervals (e.g., shorter than 2 sec) have been examined in detail often indicate that extremely brief ISIs produce weaker conditioning than some longer, optimal interval. Figure 1.10 (see also Figures 1.7 and 1.13) displays sample ISI functions from several different Pav-

lovian preparations—rabbit's eyelid response, rat's licking behavior, cat's paw retraction, rat's conditioned suppression, and rat's taste aversion.

In the 1950s and 1960s, mainly on the basis of eyelid studies, many writers stated that the optimal ISI is probably about 0.5 sec. However, now we know that the most favorable value, as well as the longest effective ISI, depends on the type of response, the intertrial interval (ITI), and the general way of assessing conditioning. Successful eyelid or finger-flexion conditioning is difficult to achieve with ISIs longer than a second or two, whereas taste-aversion learning occurs with ISIs measured in hours. Conditioned activity in anticipation of food, autoshaped behavior, and the CER can be acquired somewhere between these extremes—with ISIs of several minutes or

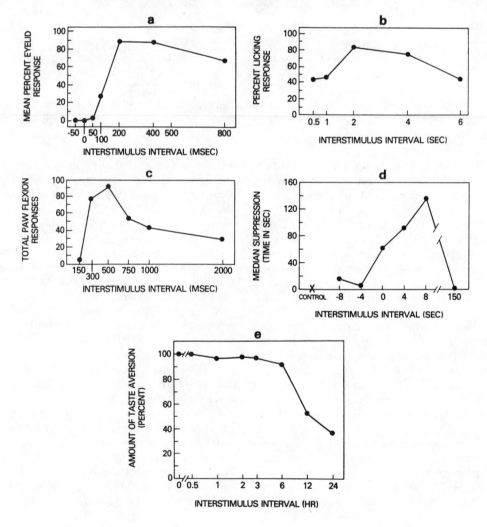

longer. Konorski (1967) viewed such differences as mainly reflecting the development of two kinds of CRs, preparatory and consummatory, one of which involves fairly diffuse behaviors and the other discrete, brief reflexive responses (see also Dickinson & Boakes, 1979; Dickinson & Mackintosh, 1978). Long duration CSs support the former, and short CSs the latter.

Delayed conditioning is consistently superior to trace conditioning when the time of CS onset is the same, especially at relatively long ISIs. Some conditioning is usually observed with simultaneous presentation of the CS and US; this outcome is best documented for the CER arrangement (see Figure 1.10d and Heth & Rescorla, 1973). Backward excitatory conditioning has been demonstrated in a few preparations—particularly when aversive USs and a small number of trials are involved—although its effectiveness is modest (see the review by Spetch, Wilkie, & Pinel, 1981). In fact, rather than producing excitatory CRs, a backward procedure often leads to the development of conditioned inhibition. Apparently, initial conditioning is excitatory, but because the CS signals a relatively long US-free period it usually acquires inhibitory properties.

In temporal conditioning, the passage of time —discriminated by means of unknown internal cues—is the presumptive CS; behavior is weak immediately after delivery of each US but accelerates as the time approaches for the next US (an example of Pavlov's *inhibition of delay*). Daily activity rhythms are probably established in this fashion, on the basis of regular feeding times. Temporal conditioning procedures resemble habituation paradigms, because only a single event is presented repeatedly. However, anticipatory CRs are the focus of interest in temporal conditioning, and URs in studies of habituation. The other two arrangements in Figure 1.9, partial reinforcement and serial conditioning, will be discussed later.

As noted above, conditioning is better when the periods (ITIs) between individual CS-US pairings are lengthened. Recent work on autoshaping has demonstrated that the effectiveness of a given ISI depends in a clear way on the ITI used in the experiment. When the ISI/ITI ratio is small, autoshaping is rapid and performance is well maintained; but if this ratio is too large autoshaping may be weak or nonexistent. Thus the absolute values of the ISI and ITI are not so crucial as their relative values. This

**Figure 1.10.** Sample functions resulting from variation of CS-US contiguity. (a) Percent nictitating-membrane CRs during acquisition for groups of rabbits exposed to different intervals between the onset of the tone CS and shock US. The − 50 value was a backward conditioning procedure, and the 0 value a simultaneous conditioning procedure (redrawn from Smith, Coleman, & Gormezano, 1969.) From "Classical Conditioning of the Rabbit's Nictitating Membrane Response at Backward, Simultaneous, and Forward CS-US Intervals" by M.C. Smith, S.R. Coleman, and I. Gormezano, 1969, *Journal of Comparative and Physiological Psychology, 69*, p. 230. Copyright 1969 by the American Psychological Association. Adapted by permission; (b) Conditioned licking responses during three 90-trial sessions in which the onset of a visual CS preceded delivery of water US by varying time periods in different groups of rats (redrawn from Boice & Denny, 1965.) From "The Conditioned Licking Response in Rats as a Function of the CS-UCS Interval" by R. Boice and M.R. Denny, 1965, *Psychonomic Science, 3*, p. 94. Copyright 1965 by the Psychonomic Society. Adapted by permission; (c) Total number of paw withdrawal CRs in extinction after conditioning of different groups of cats with different CS-US intervals (redrawn from Wickens, 1973.) From "Classical Conditioning, as It Contributes to the Analysis of Some Basic Psychological Processes" by D.D. Wickens in *Contemporary Approaches to Conditioning and Learning*, (p. 217) by F.J. McGuigan and D.B. Lumsden (Eds.), 1973, Washington, DC: V.H. Winston. Copyright 1973 by the Hemisphere Publishing Corp. Adapted by permission; (d) Conditioned suppression of rats' licking produced by a 4-sec tone paired only once before with a 4-sec shock, but separated from the shock by different intervals in different groups. Minus values indicate backward conditioning, and the 0 value refers to simultaneous conditioning. The control group received a shock but no tone. The longer the latency, the stronger the suppression (redrawn from Mahoney & Ayres, 1976.) From "One-Trial Simultaneous and Backward Fear Conditioning as Reflected in Conditioned Suppression of Licking in Rats" by W.J. Mahoney and J.J.B. Ayres, 1976, *Animal Learning and Behavior, 4*, p. 359. Copyright 1976 by the Psychonomic Society. Adapted by permission; (e) Saccharin aversion, measured by rats' percentage of choice of plain water over saccharin 24 hr after one pairing of saccharin ingestion (CS) and x-irradiation (US). The interval between CS and US was manipulated in different groups (redrawn from Smith & Roll, 1967.) From "Trace Conditioning with X-Rays as an Aversive Stimulus" by J.C. Smith and D.L. Roll, 1967, *Psychonomic Science, 9*, p. 12. Copyright 1967 by the Psychonomic Society. Adapted by permission.

observation underlies one currently influential quantitative theory of temporal effects in conditioning, the scalar expectancy model (Gibbon, 1981; Gibbon & Balsam, 1981). Moreover, the general findings suggest that many examples of ISI curves—though presumed to reveal the minimum, optimal, and maximum CS-US intervals for conditioning—depend so greatly on the ITI in force during their determination that they have little or no overall applicability.

(2) CONTINGENCY AND INFORMATIVENESS. Recent years have seen important challenges to traditional beliefs about the central role of CS-US contiguity in Pavlovian conditioning. Organisms seem to learn about CS-US relations not simply because the two events are contiguous but also because one event helps predict the other. Such concepts as informativeness or predictiveness have generated novel data and guided the development of theories of Pavlovian conditioning.

Almost always, Pavlov and his followers studied events that were both paired and correlated. That is, not only were the CS and US contiguous but USs never occurred in the absence of the CS. But perhaps this lack of US delivery in the ITI is as critical for conditioning as is pairing of the CS and US. It seems intuitively obvious that conditioning should fail or be much less successful if USs occur with approximately equal frequency in the presence and absence of the CS. And yet the implications of this possibility were not appreciated or pursued until the 1960s.

Besides this argument on the basis of logic, several robust findings and phenomena have led researchers to question the necessity for and sufficiency of temporal contiguity in Pavlovian conditioning. Studies in which the contingency (correlation) between the CS and US was varied, while their contiguity was held constant, demonstrate that contiguity is not sufficient for conditioning. Such variation of the CS-US correlation is based on consideration of the dependencies outlined in the contingency space of Figure 1.11. When the probability of US delivery during the CS—which would include the presumed neural trace of the CS—is much greater than during absence of the CS (upper left sector of the space), excitatory conditioning should occur because onset of the CS informs the subject that USs are much more likely than before

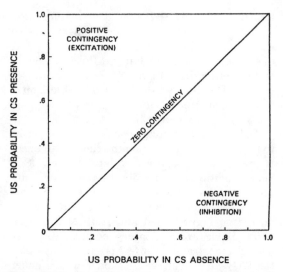

**Figure 1.11.** Pavlovian contingency space determined by variations of US probability in the presence versus the absence of the CS.

(positive contingency or correlation). When the opposite relation holds (lower right sector), inhibitory conditioning should occur because onset of the CS signals a marked decrease in the likelihood of USs (negative contingency or correlation). When the two probabilities are equal (diagonal line, corresponding to the truly random control of Rescorla, 1967) the CS is uninformative and no conditioning should result (zero contingency or correlation).

Rescorla (1968) found that even when the likelihood of shock delivery during the CS (i.e., the number of contiguous CS-US pairings) is held constant, the amount of conditioned suppression to the CS varies inversely with the probability of the US in non-CS periods. The top panel of Figure 1.12 displays some of his results, indicating the suppression produced during test sessions by a 2-min tone. The tone had previously been paired with shock on 0.4 of the trials, while the probability of shock in equivalent non-CS periods had varied among different groups. When the two probabilities were equal at 0.4, no conditioning developed to the CS (but see LoLordo, 1979b, for a review and interpretation of studies that have apparently yielded some evidence of behavioral change to the CS within that kind of treatment).

A similar finding from a signtracking (autoshaping) experiment (Hearst, Bottjer, & Walker, 1980) is depicted in the bottom panel of Figure

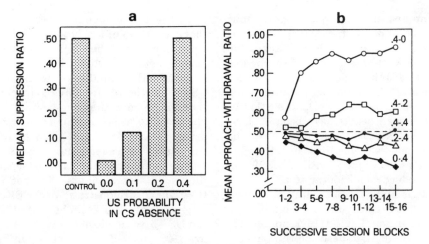

**Figure 1.12.** Effects of variation in US probabilities during the presence versus the absence of the CS. (a) Amount of postacquisition conditioned suppression in rats (maximum suppression = .00) when the p(shock/tone) was the same (0.4) for all four experimental groups during acquisition, but the p(shock/no tone) varied from 0.0 to 0.4; the control group received tones but no shocks (redrawn from Rescorla, 1968.) From "Probability of Shock in the Presence and Absence of CS in Fear Conditioning" by R.A. Rescorla, 1968, *Journal of Comparative and Physiological Psychology*, *66*, p. 4. Copyright 1968 by the American Psychological Association. Adapted by permission; (b) Approach-withdrawal toward a keylight CS during acquisition in groups of pigeons that received various probabilities of grain US during the CS and during an equivalent non-CS period (the first value on each curve's label is the p(US/CS) and the second is the p(US/no CS).) Approach-withdrawal ratios above .50 indicate conditioned approach to the CS, and below .50, conditioned withdrawal (redrawn from Hearst, Bottjer, & Walker, 1980.) From "Conditioned Approach-Withdrawal Behavior and Some Signal-Food Relations in Pigeons: Performance and Positive vs. Negative 'Associative Strength'" by E. Hearst, S.W. Bottjer, and E. Walker, 1980, *Bulletin of the Psychonomic Society*, *16*, p. 185. Copyright 1980 by the Psychonomic Society. Adapted by permission.

1.12. The arrangement used by Hearst et al. yielded overt trial-by-trial measures not only of excitatory conditioning (indexed by approach to the keylight CS, ratios above 0.5) but also of inhibitory conditioning (indexed by withdrawal from the keylight CS, ratios below 0.5). With the probability of grain delivery held constant at 0.4 per CS presentation, decreases from 0.4 in the probability of grain during equivalent non-CS periods produced increments in CS-approach behavior. On the other hand, with the probability of grain during the absence of the CS held constant at 0.4 per standard time period, decreases from 0.4 in the probability of grain during the CS produced increments in CS-withdrawal behavior. When the two probabilities were both 0.4, neither approach nor withdrawal was observed.

A second finding—that demonstrates the insufficiency of CS-US contiguity for conditioning and further encourages an informational type of account—developed from analysis of a procedure, anticipated by Lashley (1942) and later studied

extensively by Kamin (1969). The basic phenomenon, certainly the most widely explored Pavlovian paradigm of the 1970s, is known as *blocking*. Kamin presented two groups of rats with a CS composed of a simultaneous noise and light (NL), followed by a shock US. However, prior to the NL-shock pairings, one of the groups had been exposed to simple pairings of only the noise with the shock. For this group, the light in the subsequent NL-shock phase was redundant; the shock weas already completely predicted by the noise. In the other group—not given prior lights, noises, or shocks—the light and noise were equally informative. In a final phase of the experiment, Kamin tested the light by itself for the first time. He found that it suppressed behavior substantially more in the subjects that had not experienced initial N-shock pairings. The prior conditioning of the noise had blocked conditioning to the light in the other subjects, despite the fact that both groups received an equal number of contiguous light-shock pairings.

Blocking has since been obtained in different

arrangements and species. A good deal is known about factors that determine its magnitude (see Dickinson & Mackintosh, 1978; Mackintosh, 1978; Rescorla & Holland, 1982). The phenomenon has provided the main impetus for several new theories of Pavlovian conditioning, and relations between animal work and stimulus selection in human beings have been explored (Rudy, 1974; Trabasso & Bower, 1968). Nevertheless, the most important implication of the effect is that regular contiguity with a US is not enough to produce conditioning to a CS.

A few other findings that question the sufficiency of CS-US contiguity for conditioning also deserve mention. Pavlov (1927, pp. 141–143, 269–270) was the first to describe the phenomenon of *overshadowing*, which refers to the greater conditioning that accrues to a stimulus, say, a light, paired with a US than accrues to the same US-paired stimulus when it is always presented in combination with another stimulus, say, a noise. If either of the two stimuli is particularly intense or salient, individual tests of both CSs after their joint pairing with the US may reveal little or no conditioning to the weaker one, which is said to be overshadowed by the other stimulus—even though the weaker stimulus would show substantial conditioning if it were the only stimulus paired with the US. Once again, the most important point is that a stimulus contiguous with a US may become strongly conditioned under some but not other circumstances.[2]

Along similar lines, Wagner (1969) and his colleagues have demonstrated that a light paired with the US 50 percent of the time will acquire different degrees of conditioning, depending on whether either of two tones randomly presented in combination with the light is a better predictor of the US than the light. If each tone is followed by the US 50 percent of the time, the light will be an effective CS when presented alone; but if one tone occurs only on reinforced trials and the other tone only on unreinforced

trials the light will gain little or no strength. In that case the reinforced tone is a relatively more valid predictor of the US than is the light (100% versus 50%) and overshadows it.

Besides these challenges to the sufficiency of CS-US contiguity for Pavlovian conditioning, there are results that question its necessity in any absolute sense. Learning can occur over surprisingly long ISIs. One such outcome is the ease with which aversions can be established to a taste even when the taste is separated from illness by several hours. Another is Kamin's (1961, 1965) demonstration of CER trace conditioning with 1 or 2 min between CS offset and the US—a value close to that reported by Pavlov (1928, pp. 93–94) for trace conditioning of the salivary CR. Recently, Kaplan and Hearst (1982) and Rescorla (1982) found that substantial temporal gaps (at least 1 min) between CS offset and the US can be bridged in autoshaping experiments—that is, strong conditioning occurs to the CS—if other stimuli are appropriately placed in the ITI or ISI (see the serial conditioning procedure of Figure 1.9), or if the ITI is lengthened appreciably (Kaplan, 1984). These results dispute the existence of any absolute temporal gradient, mediated by persisting regular neural traces of the specific CS, that would inevitably limit conditioning. The data support a more relativistic action of contiguity.

All these results indicate that the crucial factors responsible for Pavlovian conditioning are much more complex than implied by simple, traditional notions of contiguity (see also Rescorla, 1972). Close contiguity between the CS and US undoubtedly promotes conditioning, but what the CS tells the subject about the US must somehow enter into any full account. This goal is attainable in several ways, as will be seen in the discussion of general theories of conditioning.

(3) VARIATIONS OF THE BLOCKING DESIGN. Some of the most interesting Pavlovian phenomena arise from modifications of the standard paradigm for blocking. The paradigm can be schematized as a three-stage experiment in which the blocked group is exposed to the following sequence of experiences: (1) A-US; (2) AX-US; (3) test X. In this design A and X refer to separate stimuli, such as a light and tone. As noted above, control subjects for which stage 1 is omitted display substantial evidence of

---

[2]Some recent studies involving taste-aversion learning (e.g., Durlach & Rescorla, 1980; Garcia & Rusiniak, 1980; Lett, 1980) have yielded an effect opposite to overshadowing. That is, the simultaneous presentation of another stimulus augmented excitatory conditioning to a CS. This outcome may result from the formation of associations between the two elements themselves, rather than from associations with the US. The specific circumstances that produce overshadowing as opposed to potentiation have not yet been identified (see also Domjan, 1983).

excitatory conditioning to X in the third stage—in contrast to the weak or zero conditioning to X that occurs in the blocked subjects. The best analyzed variations of the standard design comprise alterations in either the kind of stage 1 treatment or the consistency of the US event between stages 1 and 2 (that is, the reinforcer following A may not be the same as that following AX).

For example, if stimulus A receives inhibitory training in stage 1 by being made a signal of nonreinforcement, then X becomes an especially strong excitor as a result of being combined with A and followed by the US in stage 2—an outcome that has been termed *superconditioning* (Rescorla, 1971b; see also Kaplan & Hearst, 1982). Together with results from the standard blocking and control treatments, this finding suggests the operation of an important general rule: if X is reinforced in combination with another stimulus A, it becomes a stronger and stronger excitatory stimulus as A changes from being excitatory to neutral to inhibitory. Stimuli A and X seem to share in the excitatory power that can be generated by association with the US; to the degree that A already possesses excitatory power, X will not be able to gain it. Any theory of Pavlovian conditioning must handle this outcome.

Another way of changing the treatment in stage 1 is to pair both A and X individually with the US—that is, to have separate trials of A-US and X-US. When this is done, tests of A and X in stage 3 after the standard AX-US treatment in stage 2 usually reveal less excitatory conditioning to each element than would have occurred if stage 2 had been omitted (Kremer, 1978; Wagner & Rescorla, 1972). This outcome has been attributed to *overexpectation* of the US in stage 2: the associative strengths of A and X at the start of stage 2 presumably add to a value exceeding the level that the US can support. Consequently, the AX compound undergoes a decrement in conditioning during stage 2, which is shared among its elements.

If USs but no CSs are presented in stage 1, and X is then paired with the US in stage 2, the design for experiments on the US-preexposure effect is fulfilled. The usual outcome is that X acquires excitatory strength slowly. One plausible view interprets the situational context as stimulus A in the standard blocking paradigm; excitatory conditioning to the context in stage 1 blocks conditioning to X in stage 2 (see Hinson, 1982; Randich & LoLordo, 1979; and Tomie, 1981).

The second major variation of the blocking design—changing the US event from stage 1 to stage 2—has also produced interesting and theoretically significant results. For instance, if a more intense US follows AX in stage 2 than follows A in stage 1, excitatory conditioning of X is less successfully blocked. Another example of so-called *unblocking* occurs when a single shock comes after A in stage 1 but two shocks after AX in stage 2. Kamin (1969) interpreted these results in terms of the surprise value of the US event in stage 2. That is, if the added element X is followed by an unexpected event (higher shock, extra shock), conditioning to X does occur. On the other hand, expected events are not effective in conditioning new stimuli that precede them.

Alternatively, after standard stage 1 treatment, a milder US or no US might follow AX in stage 2. Under these conditions, X may become a conditioned inhibitor, as revealed by summation or retardation tests. Here the new US event is surprising too, but its effect is to transmit inhibitory rather than excitatory properties to X. However, one cannot conclude that (a) presenting unforeseen but *more* aversive events after AX then after A would lead to unblocking and the growth of *excitatory* strength to X, or (b) presenting unforeseen but *less* aversive events would lead to unblocking and the growth of inhibitory strength to X. Dickinson, Hall, and Mackintosh (1976) found that if two shocks follow A in stage 1 and one shock follows AX in stage 2, unblocking still occurs and X demonstrates excitatory strength when tested alone in stage 3. This result is of obvious theoretical interest and will be mentioned later (see Dickinson, 1980a; Dickinson & Mackintosh, 1978; Randich & LoLordo, 1979; Rescorla & Holland, 1982).

(4) COMPOUND CONDITIONING: CONFIGURATIONS VERSUS ELEMENTS. A historically important issue concerns the degree to which a compound stimulus functions as a unitary, organized event rather than as a mere aggregate of its individual elements. Although some accounts of learning have assumed that conditioning to a compound can be fully understood in terms of separate conditioning to its elements, the data

render such views too simplistic (see Baker, 1968; Kehoe & Gormezano, 1980; and Razran, 1971, for reviews). Perhaps the strongest counterexample is provided by *negative patterning*, which involves a discrimination among three types of trials: A-US, B-US, and AB-no US. Organisms can learn this kind of discrimination under a variety of circumstances. They eventually respond to A or B, but not to their compound. In contrast, other subjects pretrained only with the elements (A-US, B-US) respond substantially to presentations of AB. Because the two groups react similarly to A and B, but not to AB, the compound must somehow be different from its elements. This possibility is strengthened by the ability of animals to acquire *positive patterning* (A-no US, B-no US, AB-US), as well as *conditional discriminations* of the form AB-US, CD-US, AD-no US, BC-no US.

Characterization of the manner in which a compound is unique—that is, distinct from its components—has been difficult. The compound may best be considered a different stimulus from its elements, but one that generalizes to those elements because of common features. The issue is related historically to the Gestalt psychologists' belief that the whole is different from or greater than the sum of its parts. Such a view is consistent with the opinion of many contemporary cognitive psychologists (see Estes, Chapter 5; Rumelhart & Norman, Chapter 8; and Shiffrin, Chapter 11, this volume), that organization and structuring of elements were neglected by early students of learning and memory, who focused on simple associations among components (but cf. Hull's 1943 concept of afferent neural interaction and Tolman's 1932 concept of the sign-Gestalt). There is now a vast animal and human literature supporting claims for the importance of organizational, holistic factors.

(5) DEPENDENCIES BETWEEN NEUTRAL STIMULI (CSs). Whenever a Pavlovian conditioning experiment includes more than one CS, the subject may learn something not only about the relation between the US and each of these stimuli but also about dependencies between the CSs themselves. Studies of *second-order conditioning* and *sensory preconditioning* enable a fairly direct look at CS-CS learning. There are two training stages in each of these conditioning arrangements, followed by a test phase. In second-order conditioning one stimulus $CS_1$ is first presented

in some relation to the US; then another stimulus $CS_2$ is presented in some relation to $CS_1$; and finally the effect of $CS_2$ is assessed. To be specific, the pairing of a light with food in the first stage should permit the light to serve as a reinforcer when paired with a tone in the second phase; the result is excitatory conditioning of the tone.

The sensory preconditioning procedure (Brogden, 1939) closely resembles the design for second-order conditioning, except that the two training stages are interchanged: first, $CS_2$ is presented in relation to $CS_1$; then $CS_1$ is presented in relation to the US; and finally the response to $CS_2$ is measured. In neither of the two conditioning paradigms is $CS_2$ ever actually presented along with the US. Therefore any conditioning of $CS_2$ can be attributed to its relation to $CS_1$, provided explicit controls are included for simple stimulus generalization between $CS_1$ and $CS_2$ and for certain other nonassociative effects such as mere familiarity (Rescorla, 1980).

One justification for interest in CS-CS associations is that such relations capture the essence of everyday learning better than does standard first-order conditioning; biologically significant events like food and shock USs are rarely involved in real-life situations. Nevertheless, until fairly recently, the existence of second-order conditioning and sensory preconditioning was viewed with skepticism, owing to the lack of well-controlled and robust laboratory demonstrations. Such evidence is now available, however; among other developments, adoption of the CER, autoshaping, and taste-aversion procedures has led to many convincing reports of both phenomena (see Rashotte, 1981; Rescorla, 1980; and Thompson, 1972).

In general, experiments on CS-CS relations reveal essentially the same phenomena and laws as those based on relations between CS and US. For example, second-order conditioning is better with forward than with backward temporal relations and with a $CS_2$ that is highly informative about the imminent presence or absence of $CS_1$. Blocking, overshadowing, and conditioned inhibition occur in studies of CS-CS relations. The degree of excitatory second-order conditioning is directly related to the strength of the $CS_1$, as established by variation of US magnitude (O'Connell & Rashotte, 1982). However, in sensory preconditioning, simultaneous rather than forward presentations of $CS_2$ and $CS_1$ frequently produce maximal learning (Fudim, 1978; Holman, 1980; Rescorla, 1980)—unlike the outcome from standard first-order conditioning.

In addition to their significance as mechanisms of associative learning and as potential devices for the study of complex inferential processes in animals (see Dickinson, 1980b), second-order conditioning and sensory preconditioning also offer more flexibility in the selection of stimuli than is available in first-order conditioning. For example, the similarity of $CS_1$ to $CS_2$ can be more easily and objectively manipulated than the similarity of $CS_1$ to the US. Consequently, the procedures allow study of certain otherwise intractable problems.

(6) PARTIAL REINFORCEMENT. One way to change the correlation between the CS and US, as well as the number of pairings between them, is to deliver the US after only a certain proportion of the scheduled CS presentations. Pavlov (1927, pp. 384–386) reported fragmentary data indicating that acquisition of salivary CRs proceeded satisfactorily on a 50 or 33 percent schedule, but was greatly weakened when the percentage was reduced to 25 percent. However, Humphreys's (1939) work awakened great interest in the topic, which was further advanced by Skinner's research on operant reinforcement schedules. Humphreys found little or no difference in the acquisition of eyelid conditioning for human subjects reinforced on either 100 or 50 percent of the trials. He commented that the "lack of effect from non-reinforcement . . . is indeed paradoxical" (p. 146). His further finding (see Figure 1.14) that resistance to extinction was greater after partial than after continuous reinforcement was even more provocative (and replicable).

Since the 1940s numerous studies have examined the effects of partial reinforcement on acquisition and extinction of Pavlovian and instrumental CRs. Most of the work has involved instrumental procedures, and the topic will arise again when those procedures are discussed. Some writers (for example, Amsel, 1972b; Amsel & Stanton, 1980; Gray, 1975; Kimble, 1961; and Terrace, 1973) have argued that the basic effects of partial reinforcement on acquisition and extinction in animals are not the same for simple classical conditioning as for other forms of learning. But the case is not overwhelming. Mackintosh (1974, pp. 72–75) offers a

concise, and balanced general review, and Gibbon and Balsam (1981) discuss the relevant autoshaping literature. In any event, overall comparisons of classical and instrumental conditioning are equivocal because of the many differences in detail between the pertinent experiments (see also Hearst, 1975a).

The fact that partial reinforcement does not always weaken Pavlovian conditioning still represents a theoretical challenge. It is worth noting that almost every relevant study has involved no presentations of the US in the absence of the CS. Therefore a high positive contingency between the CS and US is characteristic of the most widely investigated schedules of partial reinforcement. That correlation may often be large enough to offset any weakening effects of nonpairings.

(7) SPATIAL CONTIGUITY. Although Pavlovian research has focused almost exclusively on temporal factors, spatial relations between stimuli should also have definite effects. Whether CSs and USs are located close to or far from each other could make a difference. In the context of conventional experiments—employing restrained subjects, relatively diffuse CSs, and USs delivered directly to the subject's skin or mouth—it is understandable why the study of spatial relations was neglected. For a long time investigation of this topic was limited to instrumental conditioning situations, such as the maze. However, modern techniques like autoshaping, the CER, and food-aversion learning use subjects that are free to move around in the test situations, which permits more meaningful manipulation of the relative location of specific CSs and USs. For example, Peden, Browne, and Hearst (1977; see also Holland, 1980a; and Karpicke, Christoph, Peterson, & Hearst, 1977) reported that pigeons' approach to a visual signal for food was stronger when the CS and US were close together than far apart. Testa and Ternes (1977) suggested that the associability of a stimulus with an illness-producing food depends on the spatial proximity between the two. Galef and Dalrymple (1981) found support for this prediction and argued that spatial relations between cues and food, rather than modality-based differences, may be implicated in many findings relating to taste aversions.

One new way to analyze variations of the spatial contiguity between stimuli exploits the advantages of second-order conditioning procedures—in which, for example, competition between unconditioned and conditioned approach or withdrawal tendencies can be minimized. The experimenter is able to endow two CSs with virtually any spatial features. Using such methods, Marshall, Gokey, Green, and Rashotte (1979) and Rescorla and Cunningham (1979) have identified effects of spatial contiguity that do not seem reducible to differences in temporal contiguity.

## INTRINSIC RELATIONS BETWEEN STIMULI

When two events are related intrinsically, they bear some natural preexperimental affinity to each other—unlike the arbitrariness that characterizes extrinsic relations. The biological bases for such affinities are often difficult to isolate or describe in any simple, objective way. They involve properties of events whose relatedness depends on the particular inherited structure of a species: the perceived similarity of the events, their inclusion in the same sensory modality, or their mutual participation in some well-organized, inborn bodily system. Although the relevant findings are capable of several interpretations, factors of this kind affect associability in Pavlovian conditioning.

The historical section of this chapter mentioned some early nonbehavioristic approaches that stressed the role of natural, organizational factors in learning and perception. In addition, the originators of comparative psychology wanted to investigate how species specialization via evolutionary processes was reflected in measures of animal intelligence. Until the 1970s, however, little attention was devoted to intrinsic relations between events because most learning theorists (for example, Edwin Guthrie, Clark Hull, & B.F. Skinner) had committed themselves to a search for abstract principles that presumably would have broad application regardless of the specific stimulus, response, and organism involved. Consequently, research centered on a few representative situations and animals. Biological science normally proceeds this way; since it is not feasible to examine simultaneously a great variety of organisms and arrangements, several convenient model systems are chosen for extensive analysis. A persistent question is the overall applicability of the conclusions to other settings and species.

Viewed against this historical context, the dramatic results of John Garcia and his colleagues had a big impact on the field of learning and conditioning. In an important study Garcia and Koelling (1966) gave rats experience with a compound CS consisting of a flavor component (saccharin) and an audiovisual component (light and noise). In different groups of subjects, exposure to this multiple CS was followed by either a US that produced illness or a standard electric-shock US. When shock was the US, subjects developed an aversion to the audiovisual component and not to the flavor. However, when the US involved illness, an aversion developed only to the flavor. A plausible conclusion from this study—the one stressed by Garcia and Koelling—is simply that the relative associability of a particular CS depends on the US employed; the experiment had demonstrated that each type of CS would become aversive under certain circumstances, and thus the results could not be due to large differences in their overall salience. Work that revealed strong taste-aversion learning, even after a single flavor-illness pairing, and with CS-US intervals that lasted minutes or hours, was viewed by many researchers as additional evidence that evolution has equipped organisms with specialized predispositions—to form certain associations easily and quickly, perhaps in a different way from those normally established by a laboratory psychologist.

One proposed corollary to this view was that it should be difficult or impossible to form associations between external features of the environment, such as spatial locations, lights, or tones, and subsequent illness. This pessimism has proved unwarranted; after as few as two pairings, such associations can unquestionably be established (see, for example, Dickinson & Mackintosh, 1978; Krane, 1980; Willner, 1978). Furthermore, conditioning in which very long time intervals occur between cue or response and consequence is not confined to the taste-illness paradigm. It also happens in instrumental settings with conventional food reward (D'Amato, Safarjan, & Salmon, 1981; Lett, 1975).

Besides these specific points, skepticism greeted the view that specialized biological constraints may invalidate the generality of much prior research. Two criticisms merit particular attention. First, the taste-aversion experiments were censured on methodological grounds; critics claimed that the regular omission of important control groups meant that nonassociative effects such as pseudoconditioning or sensitization could explain the results (see Bitterman, 1975, and Schwartz, 1974). However, most of these criticisms have been answered, as summarized by LoLordo (1979d) and Revusky (1977a). More constructively, attempts have been made to develop complex experimental designs that could rule out such alternative explanations. One of these strategies involves exposure of all the subjects to separate trials with all the individual CSs and USs under investigation. For example, some subjects would receive pairings of $CS_1$–$US_1$ and $CS_2$–$US_2$ and other subjects pairings of $CS_1$–$US_2$ and $CS_2$–$US_1$; events with the same subscript are presumed to be qualitatively related in some way. The few experiments that have employed variations of this design generally reaffirm the influence on conditioning of particular intrinsic relations (see Domjan, 1983).

LoLordo (1979d) has presented a critical analysis of designs, results, and varied interpretations of research on the topic. He remarked on the possibility that several examples of so-called biological constraints on learning may only reflect the insensitivity of various assessment techniques. One index, say, power to suppress a certain response like drinking, may reveal little or no learning to a particular CS after it is paired with a specific US. However, measurement of the subsequent ability of the CS to serve as a signal or reinforcer in another setting might yield evidence of considerable learning in the earlier phase.

A second major reaction to the proposed uniqueness of phenomena such as taste-aversion learning centered on a more fundamental issue: whether the principles of associative learning that govern certain sets of CS-US relations differ from those for other sets. Seligman (1970) argued that the laws of learning established via traditional experimentation, with arbitrarily selected stimuli and representative organisms, may not hold for stimuli that the subject is biologically prepared to associate. This challenge generated much soul-searching and debate, both emotional and appropriately reflective (see Hinde & Stevenson-Hinde, 1973; Seligman & Hager, 1972; Shettleworth, 1972). Despite initial claims to the contrary, the general laws and phenomena of conditioning do appear similar for all kinds of CSs and USs (but, for counterclaims,

see Kalat, 1977; and Johnston's 1981 article and the remarks on it).

Like every other conditioning arrangement, taste-aversion learning is promoted by increases in the magnitude and novelty of the CS and US and is facilitated by close CS-US contiguity. Furthermore, it is characterized by the phenomena of monotonic acquisition, extinction, retention, blocking, overshadowing, sensory preconditioning, stimulus generalization, discrimination learning, second-order conditioning, and conditioned inhibition (see Domjan, 1980; Logue, 1979; Revusky, 1977b; Testa & Ternes, 1977). Although the absolute temporal limit in the taste aversion paradigm is much longer than for other conditioning arrangements, there is wide variation in the latter preparations also. For instance, CER conditioning occurs with CS-US intervals hundreds of times longer than those effective for eyelid conditioning.

In response to Seligman's challenge, some authors attempted to demonstrate how different physical characteristics of tastes, illnesses, lights, tones, and shocks might explain their supposed selective associabilities; this approach would not need to posit unique biological predispositions. For instance, taste CSs and illness-inducing USs are typically long lasting and have a gradual onset, whereas shock and food delivery are abrupt and brief. Krane and Wagner (1975) reported that when a shock US follows a taste CS by 30 or even by 210 sec, the taste proves more aversive than when the CS-US interval is as short as, say, 5 sec. This finding in itself would not satisfactorily explain the much longer CS-US intervals that can be bridged if the US is the administration of a poison. However, it does suggest that stimuli from different modalities may have their maximal physiological effects at considerably different intervals after initial presentation. The actual degree of CS-US contiguity and contingency would obviously be affected by such CS and US properties. Eventually, some intrinsic relations may be reducible to relations between extrinsic attributes of this kind, rather than to CS and US belonging together.

In any event, these controversies have encouraged the specific study of intrinsic relations. Testa (1974, 1975) and Rescorla and Furrow (1977; see also Rescorla, 1980) found that physical similarity of the stimulus events in first- or second-order conditioning—for example, their intermittent versus continuous nature, their membership in the same sensory modality—promotes their associability. Such demonstrations could be considered analogous to the finding of easier associability of tastes with illnesses than of tastes with shocks; the former seem more perceptually similar. Like various extrinsic relations, intrinsic relations may well promote conditioning, though they provide no overwhelming reasons to question the generality of the laws and phenomena discovered using arbitrary CSs and USs. Certainly, the biological heritage of our subjects will probably never again be neglected as it was for many years. On the other hand, the flurry of activity in the 1970s concerning constraints on learning has not led to any dramatic reorientation of work on animal learning and behavior. The critical comments of the movement have spurred specific new kinds of studies, which are now incorporated into the general stream of research in animal conditioning (Domjan, 1983; Domjan & Galef, 1983).

## Contrast and Induction

The effects of conditioned excitors (CS + s) and conditioned inhibitors (CS − s) are magnified when they are interspersed (contrasted) with one or more other CSs rather than presented alone. Already mentioned is the general facilitative influence of CS variability on performance of conditioned responses, but the terms contrast and induction apply to more specific phenomena. Pavlov (1927) reported that an established CS + elicited more salivation when it was closely preceded by one or several CS − trials than by another CS + trial. He also determined that responding was more suppressed (inhibition was greater) to a CS − that closely followed one or several CS + trials than one following another CS − trial. Pavlov called these two outcomes *positive* and *negative induction*, and he related them to transient rebound effects like those observed in physiological reflexes (Sherrington, 1906). That is, removal of an inhibitory stimulus is automatically followed by a brief period of heightened excitability, and removal of an excitatory stimulus by enhanced inhibition—thus amplifying the effects of CS + s and CS − s presented during those respective periods. Transient and sustained contrast have been extensively examined in instrumental conditioning arrangements (see ahead and Mackintosh, 1974, chapter 7).

## Experimental Neurosis

In his later years Pavlov devoted much effort to the development of animal analogs of human psychopathological conditions. Earlier, one of his colleagues had discovered that a dog trained to salivate during presentation of a circle (CS + ) but not of an ellipse (CS − ) showed definite signs of disturbed behavior when the circle and ellipse were gradually made very similar. The dog squealed and barked, became excited, attacked the apparatus, and performed poorly even when easy discriminations were reinstated. It is noteworthy that aversive USs were not involved and that the subject had no control over food delivery; because the procedure was Pavlovian, a food US occurred on approximately half the trials, regardless of the dog's behavior (that is, the program amounted to a 50 percent schedule of partial reinforcement).

Pavlov tried to isolate factors responsible for this and other examples of "experimental neurosis". His theoretical analysis was phrased in terms of a clash between excitatory and inhibitory brain processes (Pavlov, 1928). He studied the temperamental variations that seemed implicated in the susceptibility of different dogs to experimental neuroses—a research strategy resembling current explorations of links between personality factors and vulnerability to mental illness in studies of human psychopathology. Several therapies were assessed in Pavlov's laboratory—for example, drug treatment and rest—and the relation between sleep, hypnosis, and inhibition was pursued, because his neurotic dogs frequently displayed lethargic behavior. This work was the precursor of modern research on animal models of human psychosis and neurosis, reviewed by Dinsmoor (1960), Gray (1980), Keehn (1979), Maher and Maher (1979), and Maser and Seligman (1977).

## Conditioning and Individual Development

In the 1970s there was a proliferation of research on the role of ontogenetic developmental factors in the acquisition and performance of Pavlovian CRs—particularly, CER suppression and taste or odor aversions. Adaptation of these techniques for use with organisms of almost any age has permitted elegant studies of learning and memory even in newborn animals. Chapters in Spear and Campbell's (1979) volume summarize aspects of this work. There is also evidence that taste and odor aversions can be acquired by rat fetuses receiving *in utero* injections of the CS and US (Stickrod, Kimble, & Smotherman, 1982).

### Post-Acquisition Phenomena

After Pavlovian conditioning has been established, changes in the properties of and relations between CSs and USs can have pronounced behavioral effects. This section describes some research on extinction, counterconditioning, and stimulus generalization.

EXTINCTION

When an organism is shifted from one CS-US relation to another, the animal at first persists in its earlier behavior and then somehow adjusts to the new relation. Since Pavlov's time, students of learning have been interested in how and why CRs disappear during extinction. In the most typical case, a CS and US are first paired, generating excitatory conditioning. Then the CS is presented alone and performance weakens. However, some alternative extinction procedures have received attention—such as continuing the CS and US presentations, no longer paired but independent of each other (that is, a zero correlation between CS and US).

Unfortunately the term extinction has been used in several different ways. Sometimes it refers to an experimental procedure, particularly

the removal of the US, whereas at other times it describes the consequences of that procedure, that is, the loss of behavior. The term is also employed in a more theoretical fashion, to designate the process that is presumably responsible for the response decrement. Much confusion can be avoided if these various usages are kept distinct.

Many effects on CRs produced by US removal after Pavlovian conditioning bear a surface resemblance to effects observed for URs in standard habituation experiments (see Figure 1.13). There is usually a more-or-less gradual, negatively accelerated decline in responding. If the subject is then removed from the apparatus for a period of minutes, hours, or days—or if the subject is allowed to remain in the apparatus for a long period without any CS or US presentations—subsequent reintroduction of the CS leads to a partial but temporary revival of responding, which again weakens as trials continue. The term *spontaneous recovery* refers to this type of phenomenon in both the habituation and extinction arrangements. As in habituation experiments (see Figure 1.4 above), the amount of spontaneous recovery of a CR increases as a function of time since original extinction (Grant, Hunter, & Patel, 1958). Successive extinction sessions that are separated by rest periods yield progressively less spontaneous recovery.

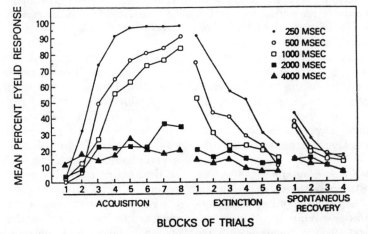

**Figure 1.13.** Acquisition, extinction, and spontaneous recovery of the rabbit's eyelid (nictitating membrane) CR for groups trained with different CS-US intervals (250, 500, 1000, 2000, and 4000 msec). The effects of variation of the interstimulus interval may be compared with those in Figures 1.7b and 1.10a, obtained under similar conditions. (Redrawn from Schneiderman & Gormezano, 1964.) From "Conditioning of the Nictitating Membrane of the Rabbit as a Function of CS-US Interval" by N. Schneiderman and I. Gormezano, 1964, *Journal of Comparative and Physiological Psychology*, 57, p. 192. Copyright 1964 by the American Psychological Association. Adapted by permission.

*Extinction below zero* (also called silent extinction) is another phenomenon that corresponds to an effect observed in research on habituation. Continued presentation of the CS after cessation of responding to it produces less recovery of behavior to the CS in a subsequent session than if the extra CSs had not been given (Pavlov, 1927, pp. 55 ff.). One interesting effect was named *disinhibition* by Pavlov (the "inhibition of an inhibition"). After responding has virtually stopped in extinction, the introduction of a novel stimulus—altogether unlike the original CS and not itself capable of evoking the conditioned response—often causes a temporary revival of responding to the CS, an effect that dissipates with repetitions of the novel stimulus. This type of behavioral restoration is analogous to the dishabituation mentioned earlier in this chapter. However, unlike one popular account of dishabituation, disinhibition cannot easily be attributed to some kind of general sensitization effect. That is because stimuli that produce disinhibition during extinction often weaken the same response when presented during conditioning—as described above in discussing Pavlov's external inhibition. Discussions of external inhibition and disinhibition can be found in Bottjer (1982), Brimer (1972), and Hearst, Franklin, and Mueller (1974).

It is noteworthy that a few presentations of the US, in the absence of CSs, will temporarily reestablish extinguished behavior to the CS. This outcome may involve an effect like sensitization or disinhibition. However, an alternative interpretation emphasizes reinstatement of the general context in which original learning occurred. By reintroducing some important features of that context (i.e., periodic USs), this procedure may lower the threshold for responding to the CS. Or it may restore the subject's internal representation of the US (Rescorla, 1979).

The well-known *partial-reinforcement-extinction effect* (PREE) aroused wide experimental interest after its description in a Pavlovian conditioning situation involving the human eye blink (Humphreys, 1939). Skinner (1938) had earlier reported similar effects for operant conditioning. Figure 1.14 presents a summary of Humphreys's findings. The two groups that had received CS-US pairings on every trial during acquisition (96 in Group I, 48 in Group III) extinguished more rapidly than a group given 96

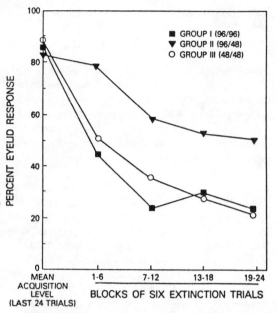

**Figure 1.14.** Humphreys's classic demonstration of the effect of partial reinforcement during acquisition on the amount of extinction responding. Human subjects received either 48 or 96 trials of eyelid conditioning. The 96/96 and 48/48 groups (I and III, respectively) received 100 percent reinforcement, but only a random half (96/48) of the trials were followed by the US in Group II. Then all groups were given 24 trials of extinction. (Redrawn from Humphreys, 1939.) From "The Effect of Random Alternation of Reinforcement on the Acquisition and Extinction of Conditioned Eyelid Reactions" by L.G. Humphreys, 1939, *Journal of Experimental Psychology*, 25, p. 148.

acquisition trials but with reinforcement on only 48 of them. Considered in the context of prevalent learning theories of the 1930s and 1940s, which tended to view resistance to extinction as a suitable measure of habit strength, Humphreys's result presented a paradox: how could fewer pairings of CS and US ever produce greater habit strength and why did interspersed trials of extinction fail to weaken the CR? Today reviewers of the literature often comment that the PREE is generally easier to obtain in instrumental conditioning arrangements than in Pavlovian settings. Nevertheless many examples of the effect occur in Pavlovian arrangements (see Gormezano & Moore, 1969, p. 166; Hall, 1976, p. 137; Mackintosh, 1974, pp. 72–75).

Since Pavlov's time, theoretical interpretations of the response decrements produced by extinction have fallen into two major categories. The effect of the original experience with reinforcement is thought to be either (1) removed and possibly replaced by some new kind of learning, or (2) preserved relatively intact but counter-balanced by some antagonistic, super-imposed reaction or process. In Pavlov's opinion, the phenomena of spontaneous recovery and dis-inhibition demonstrated that the original effect (so-called excitation) was preserved after extinc-tion, because it is restored by the passage of time or by novel stimulation. He believed that extinc-tion established an opposing process, inhibition, that acted to prevent the expression of excita-tion. Spontaneous recovery and disinhibition presumably occurred because rest periods and novel stimuli disrupt the currently dominant (inhibitory) process.

Recent findings in which, for example, respond-ing to a CS was eliminated by removal of the correlation between the CS and US (a truly ran-dom procedure), but subsequently reappeared strongly when CS-alone trials were presented, also suggest that effects of past excitatory train-ing are well retained (see Lindblom & Jenkins, 1981). However, these and other experiments do not tell us whether there was any loss of the prior training effects, nor do they uniquely sup-port an account of extinction based on inhibi-tion. In fact, an originally excitatory but later extinguished CS does not ordinarily show con-ditioned inhibition via summation and retarda-tion tests (Rescorla, 1969, 1979). No satisfactory general theory of extinction is available, though Mackintosh (1974) presents some approaches to specific findings.

### COUNTERCONDITIONING

The effects of a particular CS-US relation may be reversed or altered by pairing the CS with some new US, especially one of opposed motiva-tional or affective value. Fear responses to a CS for shock can be greatly reduced by feeding the subject during the CS (Klein, 1969). Countercon-ditioning procedures resemble popular tech-niques to break habits by ensuring that another response will occur in the presence of the usual stimulating circumstances. Especially consis-tent with Guthrie's (1952) views on learning, these kinds of schemes have many practical implications for behavior therapy—in Masters and Johnson's (1966) treatment of sexual dysfunc-tion, for example, and Wolpe's general method of systematic desensitization (Wolpe & Lazarus,

1966; see also Wilson & Davison, 1971). Counter-conditioning also figures in Amsel's (1967, 1972a) highly influential account of the PREE, to be described later. Dickinson and Dearing (1979) report some important recent work on counterconditioning in Pavlovian settings.

### GENERALIZATION

Once acquisition is achieved with a particular

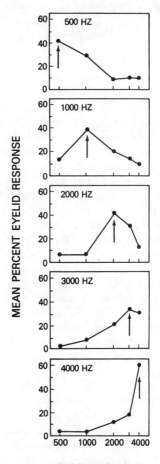

FREQUENCY (HZ)

**Figure 1.15.** Mean percentage of total eyelid CRs to various tone frequencies during tests of generaliz-ation to new stimulus values after conditioning to a particular CS (indicated above each curve, and by an arrow below the CS). (Redrawn from Siegel, Hearst, George, & O'Neal, 1968.) From "Generalization Gradients Obtained from Individual Subjects Follow-ing Classical Conditioning" by S. Siegel, E. Hearst, N. George, and E. O'Neal, 1968, *Journal of Experi-mental Psychology, 78*, p. 172. Copyright 1968 by the American Psychological Association. Reprinted by permission.

CS, the effects of other similar stimuli will also have been modified. Generalization gradients with a peak at the previously reinforced value have been obtained in postconditioning test sessions in which the features of an excitatory stimulus are varied. On the other hand, gradients with a minimum at the value of a CS negatively correlated with US appear with variations in features of that inhibitory stimulus. Figure 1.15 provides examples of excitatory gradients from the rabbit (nictitating membrane) eyelid conditioning preparation (Siegel, Hearst, George, & O'Neal, 1968).

A review of work on stimulus generalization may be found in Balsam (Chapter 2, this volume). Although no single theory of generalization is accepted by students of learning, it has long been popular to conceptualize similarity in terms of shared common elements: generalization occurs because some elements present in the original CS are also present in the test stimuli. Recent accounts derived from such an assumption are given by Rescorla (1976) and Blough (1975).

Strong generalization between two CSs may be overcome by arranging for them to occur in different relations to a US. For example, standard discrimination procedures entail pairing only one of the CSs with the US. The eventual appearance of differential behavior to the two stimuli indicates that the subject can distinguish between them—something not necessarily revealed by standard tests for stimulus generalization. Conversely, physically dissimilar stimuli may come to generalize strongly in various new tasks and situations after they have all been paired with equivalent USs. Such mediated generalization has been offered as one mechanism for certain aspects of language learning in human beings. Studies of semantic generalization are relevant to the issue: words or objects that are physically different may gain much the same meaning because of similarity of the events with which they are commonly associated (for reviews, see Gormezano & Moore, 1969; Kalish, 1969).

## General Theories of Pavlovian Conditioning

Theoretical accounts of Pavlovian conditioning are hard to classify. In the heyday of behaviorism the most popular interpretations naturally centered on observable responses and attempted to explain the acquisition, transfer, and topographical modification of CRs by means of widely accepted principles like contiguity and reinforcement, or by compatible notions like Pavlov's concept of stimulus substitution. These kinds of theories still command adherents (see Gormezano & Kehoe, 1975; Kimmel & Burns, 1975), but they have generally been superseded by new sorts of explanations. Evidence demonstrating the ineffectiveness of mere contiguity—derived mainly from such phenomena as blocking, overshadowing, and conditioned inhibition—has spurred the growth of accounts that stress changes in the subject's processing of CSs and USs.

These new approaches interpret the obtained behavioral changes primarily as a reflection of the operation of various mechanisms for perception, attention, memory, or representation. Therefore they have much in common with recent cognitive or information-processing views of human memory and performance, in which subjects register information about environmental events or relations, process details of that information to varying degrees, and act on the basis of these encoded sources of knowledge. The old distinction between learning and performance is a significant feature of these contemporary accounts, whose application to animal learning and behavior employs relatively simple associative principles, as revealed in Bolles (1975) and the separate contributions to the Hulse, Fowler, and Honig (1978) volume.

Several major themes of traditional and contemporary theories have been anticipated in the foregoing discussions of habituation, sensitization, and Pavlovian conditioning. All the accounts have something to say about the circumstances that produce learning, the contents of the associations that are formed, and the way in which the relation between learning and performance should be conceived. Detailed evaluations of relevant theories appear in Bower and Hilgard (1981), Dickinson (1980b), Dickinson and Mackintosh (1978), Gormezano and Kehoe (1975), Mackintosh (1974), Pearce and Hall (1980), Rescorla and Holland (1982), and Spence (1950, 1951). The older, response-centered approaches are examined here, before the currently popular event-processing models.

### Response-Centered Theories
In the Thorndikian (S-R) tradition some accounts

have postulated that associations between the CS and particular responses form the content of Pavlovian conditioning. Either simple contiguity of these elements or, according to other theorists, contiguity plus reinforcement define the circumstances that produce learning. For example, Guthrie (1935, 1952) argued that classical conditioning takes place simply because CS-US pairings ensure that the UR occurs shortly after the CS. Such close contiguity of a stimulus and response creates an association between them so that the CS comes to evoke a response resembling the UR—provided the CS is repeated fairly precisely each time and no other strong interfering behaviors happen during the CS or US.

Hull (1943, 1952) agreed with Guthrie that the basic associations in Pavlovian conditioning are S-R and that CS-UR contiguity is a necessary circumstance for successful conditioning. However, like his colleagues and intellectual descendants (e.g., Spence, Miller, Amsel, Logan), he stressed the role of motivational factors; Hull maintained that the US must also involve reduction of some drive or drive stimulus. For him, effective reinforcers were drive reducers, and responses followed by reinforcement were strengthened (a law-of-effect interpretation; see Williams, Chapter 3, this volume). Thus Hull treated Pavlovian and instrumental conditioning in essentially the same manner, with the Pavlovian arrangement merely supplying a way of forcing occurrence of the response to be strengthened by reinforcement. However, theoretically at least, any response that happens to appear during the action of the CS should also increase in probability, owing to its conjunction with the US (like Konorski's 1967 notion of parasitic reinforcement or Skinner's 1948 superstitious conditioning of irrelevant behaviors).

Other writers pointed out that certain Pavlovian CRs might modify the value of the US directly. Anticipatory salivation could increase the palatability of food and freezing behavior reduce the severity of an imminent shock—a possibility that, if valid, would convert many instances of Pavlovian conditioning into examples of instrumental learning (for reviews and discussion of this view, see Gormezano & Kehoe, 1975; Perkins, 1968). Although the idea cannot account for the initial appearance of a specific response to the CS, it does suggest that the topography and latency of a CR should change during conditioning until the response produces a maximally positive effect on the US. For example, short-latency CRs ought to weaken in settings where longer-latency CRs overlapping the US would receive the most reinforcement. Some accounts of changes in the form of eye-blink CRs during conditioning have been based on this response-shaping principle. Gormezano and Moore (1969), Kimmel and Burns (1975), and Prokasy (1965b) amplify the point.

Skinner (1938, 1953) cannot accurately be labeled an S-R theorist, but his analyses of classical conditioning were certainly response-centered. He accepted the validity of Pavlov's principle of stimulus substitution—"a previously neutral stimulus acquires the power to elicit a response which was originally elicited by another stimulus" (Skinner, 1953, p. 53)—but he asserted that Pavlovian CRs constitute only a small part of the total behavior of an organism. According to Skinner, Pavlovian conditioning can add "new controlling stimuli, but not new responses" (1953, p. 56). Therefore, he emphasized operant conditioning, which presumably generates novel, complex behaviors from available but simpler responses.

These response-centered theorists took behavior as their starting point and offered accounts of conditioning that inevitably included some response as a basic associative element, with contiguity by itself or together with reinforcement providing the circumstances necessary for learning. The learning-performance distinction was either ignored (Skinner) or employed to handle the important behavioral effects of certain "nonassociative" factors like drive level or CS intensity (Hull). Critics devised several techniques to test the implication that an overt response was a necessary part of Pavlovian conditioning. Blockage of the UR during original CS-US pairings, by means of surgical procedures or the injection of drugs (e.g., curare, which paralyzes skeletal muscles), did not prevent conditioning; when the blocked response later became physically possible, the CS evoked it. Successful sensory preconditioning experiments also indicated that definite responses need not be elicited by the stimuli originally paired (which did not reduce any obvious drive, either). And an appeal to the conditioning of specific peripheral responses cannot explain the effects of Pavlovian CSs on instrumental responding, because, for example, a shock signal reduces appetitive operants (such as bar pressing for food in the CER procedure) but typically increases bar pressing to avoid shock. Furthermore, Pavlovian conditioning sometimes fails even though the US evokes a reliable overt UR (Mackintosh, 1974, pp. 92–93).

Such results generally rule out very peripheralistic, response-centered explanations of Pavlovian conditioning. However, most behaviorists were willing to broaden the definition of a response to include various covert reactions, central nervous system activities, and emotional states; that is, specific unknown CRs may often be conditioned—responses that the experimenter unfortunately does not or cannot measure. This kind of reasoning allowed maintenance of response-centered views, despite loss of some objectivity and testability.

Pavlov's principle of stimulus substitution does not necessarily imply a response-centered view of conditioning. In fact, Pavlov's (1927) physiological theory of conditioning has usually been interpreted as attributing learning to the establishment of connections between contiguously-activated CS and US centers in the brain—which seems to implicate S-S associations as the basic contents of learning (see Konorski, 1967; Mackintosh, 1974). On the other hand, response-centered theorists often take the substitution principle to mean that the CS becomes directly associated with the UR and thus will evoke CRs closely resembling URs (and in some of his writings Pavlov himself said that CSs get connected with the salivary center, e.g., 1928, p. 56). But many reports of CR-UR dissimilarity create obvious difficulties for an unembellished substitution account. For instance, the CR may lack features of the UR, as in swallowing; it may include behavior that is not part of the UR, as in activity changes or withdrawal behavior; it can be virtually the reverse of the UR, as with numerous pharmacological USs (the basis for Siegel's 1979 analysis of drug tolerance and addiction); and it can be directed at a different object or location from that of the UR, as in autoshaping. Besides, CR form depends on the type of CS that signals a given US.

Thus, despite their longevity, traditional response-centered theories have suffered from offering too simple and restricted a view of Pavlovian conditioning. Critics like Tolman (1932) and Woodworth (1958) favored alternative accounts that stressed stimulus–stimulus learning and introduced such concepts as the "causal texture of the environment" (Tolman & Brunswik, 1935) and the "reinforcement of perception" (Woodworth, 1947). In a rudimentary way, those accounts anticipated current ideas about stimulus selection, informativeness, and relational learning.

### Event-Processing Theories

Many contemporary approaches can be viewed as attempts to explain the frequent failure of simple CS-US contiguity to produce conditioning to a CS. These theories preserve contiguity as an important contributor to learning, but identify possible reasons why the stimulus events presented to the subject may be poorly processed; that is, the CS or US may not be strongly attended to and registered in the first place, or may not be maintained long enough in memory. Regardless of the specific bases for these processing deficits, the important point is that an effective contiguity between the two paired events is not established. The theories are designed to handle the numerous demonstrations that Pavlovian conditioning depends not only on the particular CS-US relation but also on relations between USs and other cues, including the general experimental context in which the organism is placed.

VARIATIONS IN US EFFECTIVENESS:
THE RESCORLA–WAGNER MODEL

Kamin (1969) suggested that the blocking of conditioning to a new but redundant CS resulted from the lack of surprise provoked by presentations of the US; a reinforcer was presumably ineffective to the degree that a subject expected it. Kamin's work showed that neither CS-US contiguity nor a positive CS-US contingency was sufficient to condition a CS, and his findings therefore encouraged changes in how theorists viewed the behavioral effects of variations in Rescorla's molar index of contingency (see Figures 1.11 and 1.12 above). This contingency approach was handicapped by its inability to predict details of trial-by-trial changes in the excitatory or inhibitory strength of CSs during training. After all, organisms would presumably require considerable exposure to differential US probabilities in the presence versus absence of the CS before their behavior could adjust appropriately. Animals would have to possess the abilities of an expert statistician to integrate all this information. This seemed implausible.

Consequently, Rescorla and Wagner (1972; see also Wagner & Rescorla, 1972) developed a formal model based on the idea that the capacity of a US to support associative learning to a contiguous stimulus is not constant. The effectiveness of a US varies depending on how well anticipated the US is on any given trial—on the basis not only of the nominal CS but also of all other stimuli acting on the subject during the trial. Learning with a particular US reaches its asymptotic value when that US is wholly expected. The Rescorla–Wagner theory contains three basic equations, similar in their overall conceptualization to the linear-operator models used in several prior quantitative treatments of learning (see Estes, Chapter 5, this volume); but now the equations are applied to compound stimuli. When two stimuli are presented in a compound (AX) and followed by a particular US, any changes in associative value of the stimuli ($\Delta V_A$ or $\Delta V_X$) as a result of a single trial—that is, the theoretical amount of conditioning accruing to each element of the compound—are determined by:

$$\Delta V_A = \alpha_A \beta_1 (\lambda_1 - V_{AX})$$

$$\Delta V_X = \alpha_X \beta_1 (\lambda_1 - V_{AX})$$

$$V_{AX} = V_A + V_X$$

Here $\alpha_A$ and $\alpha_X$ represent the salience of A and X, $\beta_1$ is a learning-rate parameter dependent on the properties of the US, and $\lambda_1$ is the fixed asymptote of associative strength supportable by that US. A strong US sustains high maximum levels of conditioning, and a weak US low levels (nonreinforcement is assigned a $\lambda$ of zero). The surprisingness or unexpectedness of the US is embodied in the parenthetical quantity $(\lambda_1 - V_{AX})$, which represents the discrepancy between the maximum possible associative strength and the current strength (V) of the stimulus compound AX. The smaller that quantity is, the less surprising is the US and the smaller the change in the separate associative strengths of A and X on that trial ($\Delta V_A$ and $\Delta V_X$). When the US is altogether surprising, the parenthetical quantity is equal to $\lambda_1$ and, depending on their respective saliences, $V_A$ and $V_X$ will gain relatively large increments on that trial.

The crucial point—that all signals on a trial contribute to the amount of surprise a US provokes—is indicated by the term $V_{AX}$, which participates in the determination of separate acqui-sition functions for A and X, and is assumed to equal the current sum of their associative strengths. Negative V values signify the accrual of conditioned inhibition to an element or compound; inhibition is not conceived as a special process distinct from excitation. The model does not make precise quantitative predictions, but the theoretical terms $V_A$, $V_X$, and $V_{AX}$ are presumed to be ordinally (monotonically) related to standard dependent variables in Pavlovian research, such as magnitude, probability, or latency of response (see Rudy, 1974, for applications of the model to the data of paired-associate verbal-learning studies).

Of course, when a single stimulus A announces the US, as in standard Pavlovian conditioning, the model predicts a negatively accelerated acquisition curve; the US is increasingly less effective as $(\lambda_1 - V_A)$ approaches zero. But, more important, the model makes clearcut predictions that embrace many known facts about complex phenomena such as blocking, overshadowing, conditioned inhibition, and CS-US contingency variation. When X is introduced for the first time in a blocking experiment, the prior conditioning of A means that $V_{AX}$ already approximates $\lambda_1$; because the associative strength of X is assumed to begin at zero, it should remain there or hardly increase at all. In other words, X may be noticed but is not associated with the wholly expected US. However, if US intensity is increased when AX-US trials are initiated, the higher value of $\lambda$ should produce some excitatory conditioning ($\Delta V_X$) to X. On the other hand, if US intensity is decreased at that time, $\Delta V_X$ will be initially negative and X should reveal inhibitory conditioning.

Overshadowing that is assessed after several trials of compound (AX) conditioning is easily handled by the theory as an example of mutual blocking of A and X. When these two stimuli are of equal salience, their individual associative strengths grow in equal increments and achieve equivalent asymptotes, which are half those attained when either A or X is conditioned alone. However, as the salience of A is made stronger than X, A should increasingly overshadow X, while X loses its ability to overshadow A. With respect to extinction and conditioned inhibition, the Rescorla–Wagner equations predict that simple nonreinforcement of a previously excitatory stimulus A would not convert it into an inhibitor, because $V_A$ can never be forced below zero. But if reinforced A trials are followed by a series of unreinforced AX trials, X should become an inhibitor; $V_A$ and $V_X$ both lose strength until eventually $V_A = -V_X$. The greater the excitatory strength of A before the start of unreinforced AX trials, the stronger should be the inhibition later developed to X. Support for these predictions, as well as other applications to inhibition, appear in Wagner and Rescorla (1972).

This molecular, contiguity-based model is also capable of accounting for the molar effects of manipulations of CS-US contingency (mentioned with respect to Figures 1.11 and 1.12 above). The invariant experimental context (its lighting, ambient noise level, etc.) would be viewed as a stimulus itself (say, A), and X would represent the discrete CS that is compounded with A on conditioning trials. Positive X-US contingencies would yield above-zero $V_X$ values (excitation to X) and negative X-US contingencies would yield below-zero $V_X$ values (inhibition to X). The truly-random or zero-contingency procedure would eventually lead to zero-associative strength for X, and a high level of excitation to the unchanging background. Characterization of the context as a critical CS allows a related explanation of the US-preexposure effect, described earlier. That phenomenon would occur because conditioning to the discrete stimulus X would be blocked by prior excitatory conditioning of the background stimulus A.

Despite its recognized heuristic value, testability, and capacity to account for many facts of Pavlovian conditioning—some of them counterintuitive—the Rescorla–Wagner model has proved vulnerable on several counts. A number of these weaknesses were pointed out later by Rescorla (1979) and Wagner (1978, 1979) and by the authors of alternative event-processing accounts to be reviewed shortly. The original theory had difficulty dealing with the phenomena of latent inhibition and learned irrelevance, because the associative strength of a novel stimulus should not be reduced by being presented in isolation or by occurring in a random relation with US. The fact that the unexpected *omission* of a shock produces unblocking (i.e., leads to excitatory conditioning of X in the blocking paradigm) also created problems for the theory; if anything, X should develop inhibitory proper-

ties. And though the model predicted that conditioned inhibition should extinguish when USs are eliminated, Zimmer-Hart and Rescorla (1974) failed to obtain this result. In addition, recent work of Gibbon (1981), Jenkins, Barnes, and Barrera (1981), and Lindblom and Jenkins (1981) challenges other fundamental tenets of the model. Overall evaluations of the Rescorla–Wagner approach are available in Dickinson (1980b), Dickinson and Mackintosh (1978), LoLordo (1979c), Pearce and Hall (1980) and Rescorla and Holland (1982).

## VARIATIONS IN CS EFFECTIVENESS: THE MACKINTOSH AND PEARCE–HALL THEORIES

An alternative general account of stimulus selection in Pavlovian conditioning stresses experience-produced changes in the processing of different CSs. An influential early version of this kind of approach was contained in Sutherland and Mackintosh's (1971) interpretation of discrimination learning phenomena in terms of selective attention. Organisms were assumed to possess a limited attentional capacity that prevents full processing of all stimuli presented on a trial; each element of a compound stimulus must compete for the fixed amount of attention available. Applied to blocking, this view presumes the growth of such strong attention to stimulus A in the initial phase that little or no attention can be given to X in the second, compound-training phase. Thus processing of X is weak and an effective X-US contiguity impossible. An obvious problem with this approach derives from evidence that pretraining A as a signal for one US (e.g., food) enhances rather than blocks later conditioning to X when AX signals a different outcome (e.g., shock or absence of food: see Dickinson & Mackintosh, 1978).

Mackintosh (1975) offered an account of stimulus selection in Pavlovian conditioning that stressed changes in the degree of attention to and processing of different stimuli as determined by their relative ability to predict important new information. Blocking was attributed to active learning by the subject to ignore the redundant stimulus X, which is useless because it predicts no change in the US compared to that already predicted by A. In contrast to the Rescorla–Wagner theory, in which the α value (salience) of a stimulus always remains the same, Mackintosh's approach assumed that α increases if that stimulus predicts the US more accurately than other stimuli in the situation. Conversely, $\alpha$ decreases if the stimulus proves to be a relatively invalid or redundant predictor of the US.

This theory handles the findings that (1) sometimes no blocking occurs on the first AX trial (the subject must learn that X is redundant, which leads to a decline in $\alpha_X$), (2) a shift from two USs to one US during the second stage (AX) of a blocking paradigm produces excitatory conditioning to X (the surprising change in the US makes X informative), and (3) a CS presented originally in isolation proves harder to associate with a US than does a novel stimulus (in the latent-inhibition design, as well as when there is zero CS-US contingency, the subject initially learns that the CS is irrelevant). In contrast to the Rescorla–Wagner model, losses of US effectiveness are not particularly important in the Mackintosh account; they only explain why acquisition attains a certain asymptote. But one obvious problem with Mackintosh's approach is its neglect of conditioned inhibition.

Pearce and Hall (1980) also assumed that the effectiveness of a CS varies on successive trials according to its predictive power. However, unlike Mackintosh, Pearce and Hall postulated that a stimulus is more likely to be processed when it does not consistently predict some upcoming event; a well-conditioned CS, evoking a maximal CR, possesses near-zero associability. Nevertheless, unexpected events can restore the associability of such a stimulus, although subsequent acquisition to it will generally take longer than with appropriate controls.

Pearce and Hall's approach has intuitive appeal, because one might suppose that processing will be devoted to events whose consequences are uncertain. Their view is also consistent with some findings reported above: that stereotyped, well-established CSs often lose their ability to evoke strong CRs and may need to be varied somewhat from trial to trial to maintain their effectiveness. Pearce and Hall's account (cf. Lubow et al., 1981) describes alternatives that parallel the difference between controlled and automatic strategies in human information processing (see LaBerge, 1975; Schneider & Shiffrin, 1977; Shiffrin & Schneider, 1977). Subjects employ the controlled strategy when a stimulus or context is unfamiliar; it presumably allows them to learn about the features and relatedness of different events. Subjects use the automatic strategy when they are quite familiar with the

task; it supposedly bypasses the central mechanisms involved in associative learning. The loss of associability of highly predictive CSs signifies a transition from controlled to automatic processing.

Thus the event-processing models spawned in the last decade are already surprisingly diversified. Besides the foregoing accounts, Wagner (1978, 1979, 1981) has presented an approach to Pavlovian conditioning that entails changes in the processing of both CS and US; but each is mediated via the same type of mechanism. He treats the CS as a signaled event too—normally predicted by the experimental context—and expected (primed) CSs are not well processed for the same reason that unsurprising USs are weakly processed. In support of Wagner's view, CRs to a CS are reduced by prior presentation of a signal for the CS (e.g., Holland & Ross, 1981). And, as noted above (p. 26), presentation of a preexposed stimulus in a new context, or re-placement of the subject in the old context without presentations of the preexposed stimulus, weakens the degree of habituation to it. Wagner's conception differs from Mackintosh's and Pearce and Hall's in that for Wagner the processing of the CS varies as predicted by prior events, rather than as predictive of subsequent events.

Extensive evaluation of all these approaches is beyond the scope of this chapter. Each has particular virtues and defects, but with certain modifications or additions may handle the principal facts of blocking, overshadowing, and inhibitory learning, as well as of contextual conditioning, a major research focus in the 1980s (see Balsam & Tomie, 1985). Probably the processing of both CS and US is changed by past experience. Some theory encompassing these two kinds of effects ought eventually to prove the most powerful and fruitful. Finally, mention should be made of a very promising recent attempt to synthesize the Rescorla–Wagner model with the major assumptions of Amsel's frustration theory. This new model (Daly & Daly, 1982) handles many phenomena of Pavlovian and instrumental learning with appetitive USs and is available in precise form for computer simulation.

### Content of Learning or Association
The circumstances that may produce learning —contiguity, reinforcement, surprise, lack of redundancy, changes in attention—have been

stressed so far. A related but somewhat independent topic concerns the nature of the associations formed during learning. What, if anything, becomes associated with what, when the individual elements in a conditioning experiment —stimulus, response, and reinforcer—are considered as possible candidates for linkage? Which aspects of these events does the subject encode during learning? Discussion and analysis of these issues has a long history, instigated in the 1930s and 1940s by the battle between two supposedly distinct types of theories, S-R and S-S. The major differences between these accounts are well reviewed in Bower and Hilgard (1981) and Spence (1950, 1951). Many problems and phenomena explored during the height of that controversy remain important today, but current phrasing of the theoretical alternatives is much less extreme. Even though Pavlovian procedures differ from operant procedures in their explicit specification of only two events—stimuli and reinforcers—the possibility of S-R associations cannot be ignored, because USs are normally events that evoke strong, reliable reactions.

Two major sets of techniques have been developed to analyze what is learned in Pavlovian conditioning. One set examines initial learning under special circumstances, and the other introduces certain manipulations after standard learning is complete. In the first set the question of whether CS-US or CS-response associations underlie Pavlovian conditioning has been pursued by attempting to eliminate either the sensory properties of a US or the responses elicited by it. If removal of either one interferes greatly with conditioning, then the eliminated aspect is deemed an important associative element.

"Stimulus-free" reinforcers have mainly involved direct stimulation of the motor cortex, which elicits certain movements via the central nervous system but does not possess the afferent qualities of conventional USs. Extending back to the 1930s, such research has yielded equivocal results; but recently Pavlovian conditioning of the rabbit's nictitating membrane response via pairings of a tone CS and stimulation of the abducens nucleus was obtained in a series of well-controlled experiments (see Mis, Gormezano, & Harvey, 1979, who also provide references to past work on the topic). Thus central motor stimulation can apparently serve as the US in Pavlovian conditioning.

"Response-free" reinforcers supposedly charac-

terize (1) sensory preconditioning studies, in which no definite responses occur to the paired neutral stimuli, and (2) research in which overt URs are prevented by drugs, for example, curare. As noted earlier, neither (1) nor (2) precludes learning from CS-US pairings.

These kinds of studies indicate that Pavlovian conditioning does not require a US that acts via afferent pathways or evokes some explicit UR during training. However, the work has been demonstrational and not penetrating. Even though the manipulations may not prevent conditioning, they could reduce or modify it; the methods do not assess the magnitude and nature of any such disruption.

The second major set of techniques for exploring what is learned in Pavlovian conditioning is more analytical and has received wider usage. The strength or significance of the US is changed after the completion of training—say, by satiation, habituation, or a series of presentations of more intense or less intense USs—and responding to the CS is then redetermined. If clear alterations in behavior occur after such modifications of the US, it is inferred that features of the original US participated in the earlier learning; that is, some kind of S-S association was involved. However, if CS-evoked behavior is unaffected by subsequent changes in the US, the implication is that an (S-R) association has been formed between the CS and the response elicited by the original US. Rozeboom (1958) first suggested this approach. Its most effective application employs second-order conditioning ($CS_2$–$CS_1$) because the value and properties of a $CS_1$ can be more easily altered than those of a US, for example, by separate nonreinforced presentations of $CS_1$, or by pairing $CS_1$ with a new US.

Unfortunately, results from this technique have not yielded any definite general conclusions. Sometimes gross changes in the reinforcer produce no effect on responding to the CS, whereas on other occasions there seems to be considerable encoding of the particular features of the reinforcer. Experimental outcomes depend on the type of Pavlovian arrangement used and, apparently, on the degree of similarity between the CS and the original reinforcer. A skeptic could argue that changing the US might also change the UR and therefore the CR—an S-R, not S-S interpretation. Reviews of this work appear in Dickinson & Mackintosh (1978) and Rescorla & Holland (1982).

On the basis of such research, Pavlovian conditioning cannot simply be characterized as S-S or S-R; if anything, it usually seems to generate both types of associations. Years ago, Spence (1950) pointed out that the two alternatives are not mutually exclusive. Nowadays a consensus exists that the whole question of what is learned is inappropriately phrased in S-S versus S-R terms. A more profitable approach would entail a search for rules controlling which features or aspects of reinforcers are encoded by organisms in different situations. As Dickinson and Mackintosh (1978) comment, classical conditioning may best be conceived as the formation of associations between some internal representation of the CS and a representation of information about events related to, as well as properties of, the US. Events related to the US would include motor responses or emotional reactions reliably evoked by it. At any rate, new techniques are being developed for analyzing the nature of CS and US representations (see Dickinson, 1980b, Chapter 3; Marler & Terrace, 1984).

There is also a large literature, related mainly to autoshaping, that focuses on the issue of whether subjects are more controlled by the CS-US relation than by the response-US relation (S-S versus R-S associations). Because birds persist in pecking the CS even when the response prevents food, and because they seem to learn about the CS-US relation even when they are physically blocked from approaching and contacting the CS and US, the S-S relation seems more important in that setting. Results, problems, and extensions of these analytic methods have been discussed by Jenkins (1977), Hearst (1979), and various authors in Locurto, Terrace, and Gibbon's (1981) volume.

### From Learning to Performance

The relation between the hypothetical process of learning and the specific behavioral changes generated by learning has not been a major problem for response-centered theories of Pavlovian conditioning in the reflex tradition. Governed by mechanisms like stimulus substitution or S-R contiguity, the emergence of a particular type of CR is anticipated. In fact, most research performed by theorists with these views has focused on measurement of CRs selected for study because they involve the same effector system as do certain strong, reliable URs produced by the reinforcer. Gormezano and

Kehoe (1975) present a clear rationale for this approach, which entails a rather restricted definition of Pavlovian conditioning.

In contrast, the currently popular event-processing models are theories of association, not behavior. Numerous responses and techniques are presumed to be plausible indicators of the CS's associative strength. Nevertheless, these newer theories of Pavlovian conditioning must eventually handle the question of why learning is revealed by changes in only some responses. Historically, the translation of learning into actual performance has been a problem for the more cognitive types of theories. It triggered Guthrie's oft-cited complaint that Tolman's theory provided no basis for action and merely left the subject "buried in thought."

Resolution of the difficulties experienced by response-centered and event-processing theories in treating performance is currently unattainable. Still, a number of points merit discussion. Clearly, many CS and US aspects influence the type of behavioral change that occurs during learning—complications that did not surface when Pavlovian conditioning was limited to a few highly standardized arrangements with subjects that could not move around freely.

The foregoing description of response-centered theories mentioned evidence that challenged the view that CR-UR resemblance is a necessary outcome of successful Pavlovian conditioning. The same conclusion emerges from studies showing that CR form is determined by properties of the CS. The topography of paw flexion in cats, eyelid closure in rabbits, and freezing in rats differs as a function of the CS's modality, duration, or contiguity with an aversive US (see Rescorla & Holland, 1982). In a series of studies Holland (1977, 1980a, b) demonstrated that anticipatory appetitive CRs in rats depend on a number of similar variables. Although the simple principle of stimulus substitution can be carried quite far (see Dickinson & Mackintosh, 1978; Mackintosh, 1974; and Moore, 1973), it fails to embrace these kinds of effects smoothly. A reflex response does not merely get transferred from its original elicitor to a new stimulus.

However, liberalizing the stimulus-substitution idea could help salvage it as an important principle to account for performance. First of all, certain discrepancies between CRs and URs may be attributable to interference from behaviors generated via instrumental sources, as was mentioned above (p. 53). Various responses preceding USs could receive superstitious reinforcement because of their chance pairing with the US, or particular reactions could actually modify the hedonic value of the US. However, the numerous studies demonstrating persistence of specific responses in the CS-US interval even when they prevent an appetitive US suggest that such instrumental effects may not be too widespread (for a review of the omission procedure, see Peden et al., 1977).

Secondly, some failures of the stimulus-substitution principle might be traceable to interactions or dominance relations between responses naturally evoked and supported by the CS—for example, components of the investigatory or orienting reflex to it—and responses generated by pairing the CS with the US. Holland (1980a) has offered this possibility to account for the emergence of different CR patterns to auditory and visual signals in rats. Timberlake and Grant (1975) found that rats come to approach and engage in social contact with another rat whose automatically programmed periodic entry into the chamber is a signal for food US. Subjects do not bite or devour their visitor.

Finally, the US may best be viewed as a complex event that evokes a sequence or pattern of behaviors, some more contiguous with the CS than others. For example, even though swallowing is elicited by a US, it may fail to transfer to a CS because it occurs too long after US delivery. In fact, when milk is delivered directly to a dog's mouth through a tube in its cheek, conditioned swallowing does appear to the CS—in contrast to what happens when a dog laps the liquid from a bowl; then, Konorski (1967) reports, the CR consists mainly of the "posture of expectation." In addition, the sequence of behavioral changes induced by a US (e.g., administration of various drugs) may include both upward and downward changes in some response index. Using related facts, Solomon and Corbit (1974; see also Solomon, 1980) developed an opponent-process theory of motivation that attributes successive primary and secondary (opposing) effects to a single US. The interaction between these processes complicates predictions about the types of responses that should occur to CSs (see Eikelboom & Stewart, 1982; Siegel, 1979).

Some recent accounts of CR origin that are especially relevant to Pavlovian settings involving unrestrained subjects deemphasize the importance of behaviors triggered by the US itself. Instead, they focus on the intriguing possibility that organisms are endowed with certain biologically preorganized action patterns that appear in anticipation of certain kinds of reinforcers. These reactions could be viewed as complex URs that precede USs. Dogs display activities that resemble begging and hunting during a CS for food (Jenkins, Barrera, Ireland, & Woodside, 1978). Rats bury a prod associated with electric shock (Pinel, Treit, & Wilkie, 1980). Animals approach signals positively correlated with food or negatively correlated with shock, and withdraw from signals positively correlated with shock or negatively correlated with food (Hearst & Jenkins, 1974; LeClerc & Reberg, 1980; Wasserman, Franklin, & Hearst, 1974).

The idea is appealing that, besides reactions originally elicited by CSs and USs, there are also inborn forms of anticipatory behavior. Laboratory CSs serve as substitutes for the natural signals evoking these response patterns. The possibility conforms not only to certain aspects of response-centered approaches (unconditioned behaviors can transfer to rather arbitrary stimuli) but also to several features of expectancy theories (subjects will reveal their anticipations in appropriate ways). Furthermore, the general notion is compatible with strongly biological approaches to learning (see Timberlake, 1983a). The range of applicability of the *natural-anticipation* interpretation is uncertain, but it deserves serious attention.

Hollis (1982) has focused on the biological function of Pavlovian conditioning in her recent analysis of CRs, which she views as batteries of responses enabling animals to optimize their interaction with the forthcoming US. According to this view, conditioned reflexes are basically preparatory and possess a selective advantage; they allow the organism to deal better with the coming biologically significant event. Pavlovian conditioning renders it more likely that food and water, mates, predators, and rivals are predictable events for which the animal can prepare efficiently. Siamese fighting fish that receive a discrete signal of the approach of an intruder show superior aggressive defense toward the intruder (e.g., number of bites). Courtship patterns and copulatory behavior in male quails are initiated more quickly when the female's appearance is signaled than when it is not. Hollis presents a variety of data, many from natural settings, to support her basic hypothesis of *prefiguring*, which would at some times predict signal-directed behavior and at others standard glandular, visceral, or motor anticipatory CRs, as well as differences in CR form from one situation to another or with added experience. Although the idea of a CR as a preparatory response is in itself not new, Hollis's attempt to relate this notion of Pavlovian conditioning to current ethological, evolutionary, and ecological knowledge provides valuable insights into potential response rules governing the topography, frequency, and timing of CRs.

Finally, widening the choice of behavioral indexes has permitted the rapid development and evaluation of event-processing theories, though the new findings are not qualitatively unlike those obtained when very strict criteria govern the choice of a Pavlovian CR. However, a bothersome problem arises when quantitative measures of specific behavior are affected by variations in the nature of the total CR. For instance, if components of the CR change differently when the degree of CS-US contiguity or partial reinforcement is varied, it is no easy matter to assess how these factors influence theoretical associative strength. This problem highlights the need to base conclusions about Pavlovian conditioning on other measures besides standard CRs—that is, the CS's capacity to serve as a signal, reinforcer, and so forth. So long as these assays yield inconsistent conclusions, theories of association will remain tentative and imprecise. However, comparison of results from many assays should eventually lead to a better understanding of relations between learning and performance, as well as to a firmer knowledge of the conditions that produce learning and of the nature of CS and US representations.

## LEARNING FROM EXPERIENCE WITH RELATIONS BETWEEN BEHAVIOR AND STIMULI

### Preview and Examples

A third type of procedure completes the possibilities identified above for producing learning. This paradigm was first studied experimentally in Thorndike's puzzle boxes and in the complex mazes constructed by psychologists around 1900. There the presentation of $S_1$, a highly valued event such as food delivery or access to an escape route, depended on the emission of some prior behavior. In contrast to Pavlovian conditioning, $S_1$ occurred if and only if the appropriate response had been made. Thus the response was *instrumental* for the outcome. Similarly, Skinner's (1938) new term, *operant*, referred to conditioning in which a response operated on the environment to produce a particular consequence. Although writers sometimes quibble about usage of the two terms, they are employed interchangeably in this chapter.

Until the 1970s, research on animal conditioning in the West stressed instrumental arrangements. A common justification for this emphasis involved the presumed practical importance of these kinds of behavior-environment relations. Furthermore, parallels exist between (ontogenetic) mechanisms of individual response modification in instrumental learning and the (phylogenetic) action of random variation and natural selection in evolution. Because of an organism's innate endowment and past experience, it emits a variety of behaviors in any situation; those behaviors that produce favorable environmental consequences are selectively strengthened or maintained and those that produce unfavorable consequences are eliminated or weakened (see Skinner, 1981).

Although we soon see that acceptable comprehensive definitions of favorable and unfavorable consequences are virtually impossible to formulate, the type of distinction Thorndike made in 1913 can help organize the relevant material. Thorndike called an event *satisfying* when an animal does nothing to avoid it and will often do something to attain or preserve it, whereas an event was called *annoying* when an animal does nothing to maintain it and will often do something to avoid or escape it. If consequential stimuli $S_1$s are divided into two such categories with, say, food delivery and noxious electric shock serving as instances of the positive and negative classes, respectively, instrumental conditioning procedures can be partitioned into several different types. Examples of these procedures, together with an indication of the range of responses and stimuli used in actual research, provide a preview to the details covered in the sections ahead.

When $S_1$ is absent, a response may produce it, prevent its onset, or prolong its absence; and when $S_1$ is already present, a response may terminate it, prevent its cessation, prolong its presence, or increase or decrease its current value (e.g., by changing its intensity or accessibility). Although all these alternatives merit investigation, only some of them have been examined extensively in controlled studies of operant conditioning. Furthermore, as Cohen (1969), Tryon (1976), and Woods (1974) pointed out, there are several interesting additional possibilities, based mainly on the consequences of *not* responding, that seem distinguishable from the foregoing alternatives. Nevertheless, the focus here is on the more widely studied arrangements.

A response that produces a positive $S_1$ will generally increase in strength (as measured by, say, response probability or speed), relative to appropriate control treatments. A pigeon pecking a key for grain, or a rat traversing a runway for food pellets, illustrates this response-contingent arrangement, often labeled *reward* training (see Kimble, 1961; Mackintosh, 1974; and Rashotte, 1979a). On the other hand, a response that produces a negative $S_1$ will normally weaken, provided of course that the response initially occurs often enough for decrements to be detected. This arrangement is called *punishment* training (see Azrin & Holz, 1966; Mackintosh, 1974; Overmier, 1979a; and Walters & Grusec, 1977), and is exemplified by the effects of response-dependent shock on a gerbil's digging or of a teacher's rebukes on a student's likelihood of commenting in class.

When a response terminates a positive $S_1$ or prevents its delivery, the behavior is generally reduced or eliminated. *Withdrawal* training, the term most frequently applied to the stimulus-termination procedure, is illustrated by a situation in which ongoing cartoons are turned off whenever thumb sucking occurs in young children (Baer, 1962). In *omission* training, which refers to the stimulus-prevention procedure (see Dickinson & Mackintosh, 1978; Konorski, 1948; Peden et al., 1977; and Sheffield, 1965), prior thumb sucking would cancel a currently absent but upcoming cartoon program. In everyday life the application of withdrawal or omission is clearly preferred to punishment for suppressing or reducing unwanted behavior. Penalties, fines, and cancellation of scheduled recreations are obvious examples.

Finally, a response that terminates or prevents a negative $S_1$ usually increases in strength. Numerous studies involving *escape* or *avoidance* training exemplify these arrangements (see Brush, 1971; Dinsmoor, 1977; Mackintosh, 1974; and Overmier, 1979b). A dog may have to jump over a hurdle to terminate (escape) shock or to forestall its imminent delivery (avoidance). We can escape the noise of the clock's morning alarm by pushing the control button after the alarm has awakened us, though some fortunate people can avoid the noise by waking up a few moments beforehand to push the button.

Positive and negative reinforcers have typically been defined in rather specific ways by workers in the field of operant conditioning. Because the literal meaning of the word reinforcement entails the notion of strengthening, these definitions embody a response-facilitating outcome. Thus a positive reinforcer is an event that strengthens a response producing it (i.e., reward training), and a negative reinforcer is an event that strengthens a response removing it (i.e., escape training). As far back as Thorndike's formulation of the law of effect, such definitions have been criticized as circular or tautological —they are said to construe learning in terms of reinforcement and reinforcement in terms of learning. There have been several noteworthy attempts to redefine or reconceptualize the nature of reinforcement so as to overcome or minimize the potential problem of circularity. The theoretical section ahead mentions the relevance of approaches (1) that propose some unitary basis for the effectiveness of all reinforcers (e.g., drive reduction), (2) that presume "transsituational" generality for reinforcers, or (3) that offer empirical methods for specific advance predictions about whether reinforcement-like effects on performance will occur.

Instrumental conditioning has been studied in numerous situations, involving many different types of signaling stimuli, responses, reinforcers, and species. Organisms ranging in size from fruitflies and honey bees to elephants and baboons have found their way through mazes, learned to approach one stimulus and not another, or pushed against panels, buttons, and other devices to produce some favorable outcome or terminate an unfavorable one. In addition to conventional positive reinforcers like food and water, animals have acquired responses to obtain electrical stimulation in certain brain areas; to produce simple stimulus changes such as presentation of lights and sounds; and to gain the opportunity to explore a new environment, spend time with a sexual partner, or engage in special activities such as running in a wheel. Bright lights, loud noises, electric shocks, and stimulation of specific parts of the brain have served as negative reinforcers. Human beings have had their behavior modified by subsequent presentation of money, flashing lights, the addition or subtraction of points on a counter, the words "right" and "wrong," or expressive gestures from another person. Stimuli from all sensory modalities have served as cues that particular responses will be reinforced or extinguished. Some studies of this kind have centered on determination of precise psychophysical functions in nonhuman organisms (see Balsam, Chapter 2, this volume).

Most responses used in instrumental conditioning experiments with animals have been directed movements of the whole organism, which require either the animal's manipulation of some external object or its locomotion from one place to another. However, in the past 20 years researchers have frequently asked whether various visceral and glandular (involuntary) responses can be facilitated or suppressed by favorable or unfavorable consequences—in experiments on so-called biofeedback. In addition to its practical import, this work is of systematic significance, because some theorists had maintained that autonomic responses were conditionable mainly if not exclusively by Pavlovian procedures. In general, these writers had also argued that directed movements were conditionable mainly if not exclusively by instrumental techniques—a conclusion challenged by the discovery of autoshaping.

The acquisition of complex motor skills and the creation of new behavioral repertoires have occupied many students of instrumental learning who view the training of such acts as going far beyond the principles of Pavlovian conditioning. Because of the great diversity of behaviors made possible by operant procedures, the methods have found widespread interdisciplinary and technological application in such areas as psychopharmacology, space flight, programmed instruction, and behavior modification. Coverage of instrumental conditioning in this chapter follows the general pattern adopted above for the other two learning procedures. However,

because Williams's and Balsam's contributions to this volume focus on closely related data and issues in the field, the present discussion is more selective than for the other procedures.

## Behavioral Techniques and General Methodology

### Arrangements, Procedures, and Assays

Specific situations for studying instrumental conditioning can be classified in several ways. Most frequently, they are subdivided into *discrete-trial* and *free-operant* procedures. Of the two, the discrete-trial arrangement is a clearer counterpart to Pavlovian paradigms, because the experimenter controls the occurrence of definite trials that alternate with time intervals (ITIs) during which response measurements are not normally taken. Any immediate effects of the reinforcer itself on the target response are thereby minimized. For instance, opportunities to traverse a maze are separated by periods during which subjects are placed in a waiting chamber. In a free-operant task, on the other hand, ITIs are not included and the subject remains in a place where a certain response is always available—as in the standard Skinner box, which yields a continuous measure of performance (e.g., rate of lever pressing).

Both discrete-trial and free-operant procedures can be further characterized in terms of stimulus and response complexity. Stimulus conditions may be uniform or varied throughout a session. External cues enable discrimination of reinforcement opportunities in varied but not in uniform conditions; for instance, during one sound (S+) the response produces a given outcome, but during another sound (S−) it does not. These cues are most often called *discriminative stimuli* (Skinner's term). In addition, the experimenter may demand either a single response or multiple responses; the inclusion of choice points in a maze (as opposed to a simple straight alley), or of extra levers to be activated in a Skinner box, are multiple arrangements. And in some tasks definite sequences of different behaviors are required.

In addition to the puzzle box and the Skinner box, several other settings for performing relevant experiments are illustrated in Figure 1.16. The runway or straight alley is essentially a maze that lacks any choice points. The standard shuttlebox comprises a two-section chamber where a light or a sound signals an impending shock that can be avoided or escaped only by movement to the other side of the box. In the delayed-reaction apparatus a restrained subject is permitted to observe some brief stimulus designating which one of several nearby compartments contains food; but time passes after termination of the signal before the subject is released to choose among compartments. This situation was one of the first devised to study animal memory capacities (Balsam, Chapter 2, this volume, covers research on infrahuman memory).

Subjects placed on the Lashley jumping stand (Figure 1.16g) must leap across a spatial gap to dislodge the correct visual stimulus,

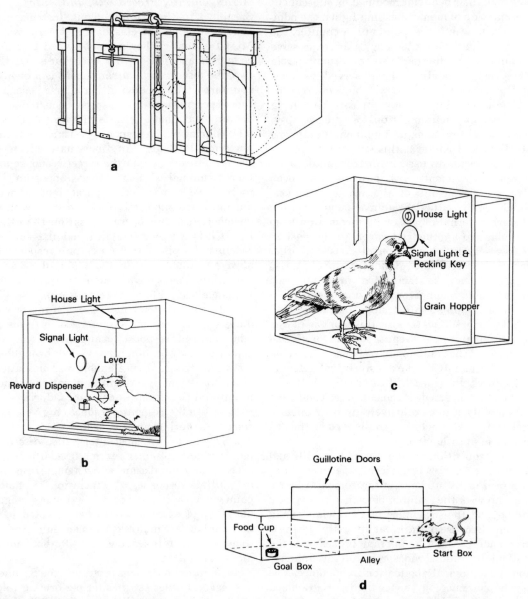

**Figure 1.16.** Schematic drawings of various arrangements for studying instrumental learning, performance, and discrimination. (a) Thorndike's puzzle box; (b) Skinner box for small mammals; (c) Skinner box for pigeons; (d) Runway (straight alley); (e) Shuttlebox; (f) Delayed-reaction apparatus; (g) Lashley jumping stand; (h) Wisconsin General Test Apparatus. See text for further details.

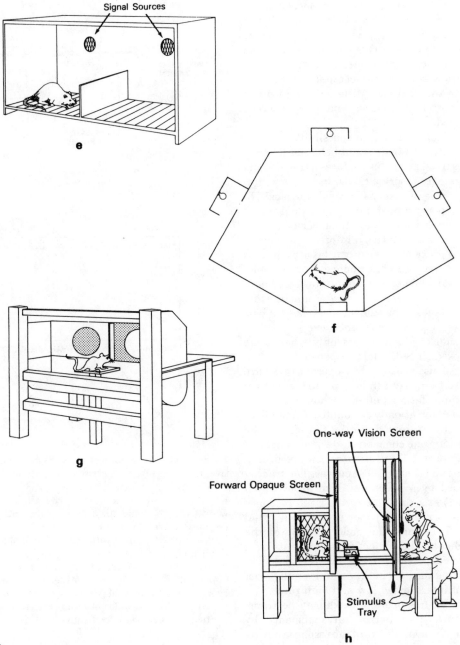

**Figure 16** Continued

which has food behind it; the wrong stimulus remains fixed in place and a leap at it ends with a tumble into the net below. The Wisconsin General Test Apparatus (WGTA) is a flexible piece of equipment that allows presentation of several different objects to the subject. If the

subject picks up the correct one, a piece of food hidden underneath is uncovered.

Discrete trials may be massed fairly close together or spaced minutes, hours, or even days apart. When no choice is required among alternative responses, response speed (or a reciprocal measure, the latency between trial onset and the initiation or completion of the response) is the most common index of performance. However, response magnitude can also be employed in the runway, by means of a harness detecting the force with which the subject pulls toward or away from the goal (see Miller, 1959). In other arrangements, both accuracy and speed of choice are recorded.

According to Skinner, the possibility of uninterrupted, moment-by-moment behavioral measures gives free-operant procedures a tremendous advantage over discrete trials. In his view, frequency or rate of response provides a sensitive index of response probability in individual organisms during brief or long time periods. Like methods based on positive reinforcement, shock-avoidance procedures also can be arranged to yield uninterrupted performance. For example, on the popular Sidman avoidance task (Sidman, 1953)—also known as continuous or nondiscriminated avoidance—the subject must make a particular response at least once every $x$ sec to prevent shock, which occurs only when $x$ sec have elapsed since the last response.

The responses used in free-operant tasks are selected so that they can be repeated numerous times without fatigue, often for hours, and can easily and automatically be counted. Cumulative response curves, introduced by Skinner in the 1930s, provide one common mode of data presentation. Figure 1.17 illustrates the recording equipment and some typical curves. The tracing is produced by a revolving drum from which paper feeds at a constant speed. Each response moves the pen up the paper a small but equal distance. Therefore, the general slope of the curve indicates the subject's response rate over any selected portion of the session, and fine-grained irregularities in the tracing signify brief periods of interspersed low and high rates.

Of course, free-operant tasks may be transformed into discrete-trial arrangements by restricting the availability of the response during sessions—say, with rats by use of a lever that can be removed and reinserted. Conversely, many discrete-trial arrangements can be converted into free-operant procedures by allowing some response of the subject to initiate successive trials: returning to the start box or pushing a switch. And as noted earlier, discrimination and choice procedures are possible with both kinds of tasks. Thus the procedural distinction

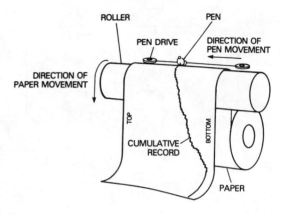

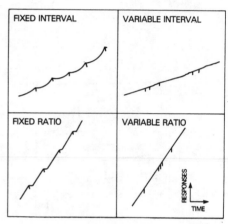

**Figure 1.17.** The major features of Skinner's cumulative recorder (above; redrawn from Catania, 1979) (From A.C. Catania, *Learning,* © 1979, p. 70. Reprinted by permission of Prentice-Hall, Inc., Englewood Cliffs, NJ) and some hypothetical cumulative response curves (below; redrawn from Millenson & Leslie, 1979) (Reprinted with permission of Macmillan Publishing Company from *Principles of Behavioral Analysis* by J.R. Millenson and J.C. Leslie, p. 91. Copyright © 1979 by J.R. Millenson) resembling closely those that would be obtained on the four most widely studied schedules of reinforcement (see p.77). Vertical ticks indicate food delivery.

between discrete-trial and free-operant training is somewhat artificial and may be of little significance.

In practice, however, investigators who favor free-operant techniques are less interested in the acquisition of behavior. They prefer to analyze factors affecting performance after the target response has reached a steady state or asymptote. For example, they want to assess the effects of amount, delay, and schedule of reinforcement on response rates in individual subjects exposed to different values of these variables. In contrast, experimenters favoring discrete-trial procedures are more likely to plot average learning curves and study the factors influencing original acquisition, as revealed in separate groups of subjects. The Skinnerian preference for employing data from a few individuals deemphasizes study of variables affecting initial learning, because there is no uncontaminated way of comparing simple acquisition curves in the same subject under different conditions.

Analysis of changes in the target behavior itself may be either molar or relatively molecular and detailed. For example, speed of running in a straight alley can be timed on each trial from the opening of the start box until the animal enters the goal box; or the response may be analyzed further into initial, middle, and terminal components by photocells that are triggered as the animal completes successive thirds of its total route (see Figure 1.16d). In a free-operant task, response rates over fairly long time periods provide molar measures of performance, but can be decomposed into rates over brief intervals (e.g., as a function of seconds since the last reinforcement), or into distributions including the frequencies of different interresponse times (IRTs)—divided up, for instance, into intervals of 0 to 2 sec, 2 to 4 sec, and so on, between successive responses. Certain general approaches to instrumental behavior stress molecular characteristics, and dimensions of responding such as force or duration can be separately reinforced (Notterman & Mintz, 1965; Skinner, 1938; Zeiler, 1977). Proposing a broad (micromolar) theory based on such considerations, Logan (1960) viewed, for example, fast running as a different response from slow running—rather than as a stronger version of the same response.

Although studies of instrumental learning have focused mainly on the measurement of the response selected for reinforcement, examination of other behaviors can also be valuable. The target response may not change very much, or may actually fall below its baseline levels; but facilitation of other reactions can still be pronounced. For example, subjects placed on omission procedures requiring restraint of a particular response often display regular, stereotyped sequences of various kinds—responses that may have occurred

rarely, if at all, during initial exposure to the situation (Kramer & Rilling, 1970; see also Staddon, 1977). Given appropriate control results, the finding demonstrates that something has been learned as a consequence of instituting a specific behavior-reinforcer relation.

The strength of operant behavior may be assess by its persistence when conditions are altered. In fact, Nevin (1979) suggested that resistance to change is often a more sensitive indicant of operant conditioning than some standard measures such as response rate. Altered conditions might involve extinction, punishment, satiation, or increased amount or delay of reinforcement. However, Amsel (1967) views persistence as a different dimension of behavior from vigor, choice, or rate of response. The PREE (above, p. 50) and other paradoxical effects of reinforcement led him to conclude that resistance to extinction is not a simple measure of operant strength.

By offering the subject other response alternatives, the experimenter might detect modifications of a response that otherwise appears unaffected by a particular response-reinforcer relation. For instance, mild punishment after every key peck may not appreciably affect pecking in a pigeon, but the bird often switches completely to an unpunished but equally reinforced alternative key if the option is made available (see Azrin & Holz, 1966). Arrangements for studying choice and preference among different responses are the focus of much contemporary research and theory in operant conditioning. Williams (Chapter 3, this volume) concentrates on this topic.

### Control and Comparison Treatments

The question of appropriate control groups or comparison baselines for instrumental conditioning raises issues that parallel those for Pavlovian conditioning. How much of the response change that results from making $S_1$ contingent on a prior response is due to their contingent or contiguous relation? Mere presentations of $S_1$ could themselves increase (or decrease) the likelihood of various responses, especially responses similar to (or competitive with) URs elicited by $S_1$. As in Pavlovian conditioning, choice of comparison treatments depends largely on an experimenter's theoretical preferences about the nature of instrumental learning. No baseline or control measure is ideal from everyone's point of view.

Until fairly recently, researchers usually assessed the effect of instituting an R-$S_1$ relation by comparison with the so-called operant level of the behavior—its original probability of occurrence in the complete absence of $S_1$. Lever pressing in rats has an above-zero but low operant level in standard conditioning chambers, but key pecking in pigeons hardly ever occurs. Therefore shaping of these conventional operants, by successive approximations to the required response, constitutes a first step in many studies. Shaping is normally accomplished in an informal way, so that specific factors affecting acquisition of the target behavior are difficult to isolate (however, cf. Platt, 1973, and Platt & Scott, 1981). In contrast, when such behaviors as eating, drinking, or wheel running are the instrumental responses, shaping is not needed because levels are naturally high.

The more complex "omission" and "yoked" control arrangements are now often employed to evaluate the effects of introducing a particular R-$S_1$ dependency. With omission, a separate group of subjects (or individual subjects exposed at separate times to the different treatments) receive $S_1$ only when they have omitted the target response for $x$ sec. That is, the target response and $S_1$ are explicitly unpaired. Differences in behavior between the omission and regular conditioning groups presumably expose the role of R-$S_1$ contiguity. So long as the two groups receive approximately equal numbers and distributions of $S_1$ presentations (not so easy to achieve), consistent group differences rule out explanations based on simple effects of delivering $S_1$s in the situation. However, the omission procedure permits superstitious reinforcement of any behaviors that happen to occur just before $S_1$. These behaviors could replace or interfere with the target response and complicate analysis of the action of contiguity.

On the yoking procedure, each yoked subject receives $S_1$s (or the opportunity to produce $S_1$s by an operant response) whenever its partner, a matched master subject, obtains them during standard instrumental conditioning. Thus the temporal pattern of $S_1$ presentations or availabilities is the same for any paired subjects. Church (1964) and Dunham (1977) have noted some deficiences of this control procedure, which has also been applied to isolate differences between Pavlovian and instrumental conditioning (see Gormezano, 1965). The yoked (Pavlov-

ian) subject receives a schedule and pattern of CS-US pairings that are determined by the behavior of the (instrumental) master subject, who must emit appropriate CRs, say, to produce food or avoid shock.

Besides being yoked, $S_1$ can be delivered independently of the target response by a treatment that parallels the truly random control in Pavlovian conditioning. That is, the probability of $S_1$, given the response p(US/R), would be explicitly set equal to the probability of $S_1$, given no response p(US/$\bar{R}$) (see, for example, Hammond, 1980). Both this and the yoking procedure allow conjunctions of the target response and $S_1$, and therefore might be criticized by researchers whose theoretical views about contiguity require control treatments involving no pairings. In any event, as Williams (Chapter 3, this volume) reports, the rate of free-operant behavior typically declines when noncontingent reinforcers are delivered in addition to contingent ones.

New control baselines have been fostered by Premack's (1965) probability-differential hypothesis of instrumental performance—further developed, modified, and refined by other theorists interested in how the relative values of various activities can be altered by limitations on their availability (see Timberlake, 1980, for a review). In many relevant studies the instrumental activity (e.g., licking a solution of 0.1% saccharin) occurs frequently at the outset and is often similar to activities elicited by the particular $S_1$s used (e.g., licking 0.4% saccharin). Reflecting the emphasis of these theories, a reward is typically described in response terms (what others call a reinforcer now means an opportunity to engage in the contingent response). On what are termed paired baselines both the instrumental and contingent response are permitted to occur freely; on single baselines, only the instrumental response is available. Data from these baselines are compared with results obtained when a certain amount of the instrumental response is required to gain access to the contingent response. To assess certain quantitative models of performance, Timberlake (1979) used some other comparison treatments that seem preferable to the paired or single baselines.

## Basic Phenomena and Influential Variables

The extreme heterogeneity of instrumental conditioning arrangements hampers a satisfactory

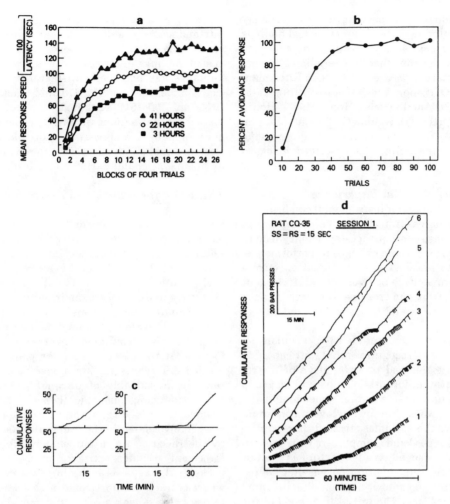

**Figure 1.18.** Sample acquisition curves from some common instrumental learning situations. (a) Increases in running speed along an elevated platform over successive blocks of trials with food reinforcement. Different groups of rats were trained at different food deprivation levels—3, 22, and 41 hr (redrawn from Davenport, 1956.) From *Choice Behavior as a Function of Drive Strength and Rate of Learning* (p. 28) by J.W. Davenport, 1956, Iowa City: University of Iowa. Adapted by permission; (b) Acquisition of avoidance behavior for a group of rats trained in a shuttlebox. A movement to the other side of the box terminated the warning signal and avoided the scheduled shock (redrawn from Kamin, 1957.) From "The Effects of Termination of the CS and Avoidance of the US on Avoidance Learning: An Extension" by L.J. Kamin, 1957, *Canadian Journal of Psychology, 11*, p. 51. Copyright 1957 by the Canadian Psychological Association. Adapted by permission; (c) Cumulative response curves for four individual rats during their first session of operant conditioning in a Skinner box. Each lever press was reinforced by food (redrawn from Skinner, 1938.) From *The Behavior of Organisms: An Experimental Analysis* (p. 68) by B.F. Skinner, 1938. New York: Appleton-Century-Crofts. Adapted by permission; (d) Acqui-sition of Sidman avoidance in a rat whose lever pressing continuously postponed shock for 15 sec (RS = 15 sec). If the rat did not respond at all, it received a shock every 15 sec (SS = 15 sec). The six successive hours of the first session of training are separately placed above each other. Vertical ticks indicate the delivery of shocks (redrawn from Sidman, 1966.) From "Avoidance Behavior" by M. Sidman in *Operant Behavior: Areas of Research and Application* (p. 453) by W.K. Honig (Ed.), 1966. New York: Appleton-Century-Crofts. Copyright 1966 by Appleton-Century-Crofts. Adapted by permission.

organization of the important results. Nevertheless, presentation of the major empirical findings and phenomena closely parallels the coverage given above for the other two paradigms. Extensive general reviews are available in Bitterman, LoLordo, Overmier, and Rashotte (1979), Catania (1979), D'Amato (1969), Honig (1966), Honig and Staddon (1977), Kimble (1961), and Mackintosh (1974). Williams's chapter in this volume discusses many points not described in depth here.

### Conditions of Initial Experience

Acquisition curves for instrumental conditioning show that increases in the number of exposures to the response-consequence dependency lead to systematic, monotonic changes in performance. Figure 1.18 presents a few acquisition curves involving appetitive or aversive reinforcement in discrete-trial and free-operant settings with groups of rats (a and b) and individual rats (c and d).

Because so many factors affect acquisition, everyone now recognizes that attempts to characterize the real or true curve of instrumental learning, for either individual or group data, are unwarranted—the same conclusion that was drawn earlier for Pavlovian conditioning. Besides the variables stressed there, differences in the speed and asymptote of instrumental conditioning depend on such factors as the target response's preconditioning baseline, effort requirements, complexity, prior shaping, and intrinsic feedback. The initial likelihood of the target response is influenced by phylogenetic factors and by general features of the experimental situation—often related to the number of alternative responses available and to the prevailing motivation. Animals flee locations where they have been shocked, and hungry rats repeatedly traverse a runway even though no reward is ever given (Timberlake, 1983b).

In addition, many appetitive instrumental experiments begin with the subject's exposure to the general apparatus (habituation to the situation) and with "magazine training" to eat or drink quickly from the reinforcement dispenser whenever it operates. Though hardly studied as a specific variable, this preliminary experience undoubtedly affects the speed of later instrumental learning (and not always positively, as experiments on latent inhibition and the US-preexposure effect suggest).

The curves in Figure 1.18a suggest that the rate and asymptote of instrumental acquisition are directly related to drive level. Interpretation of such findings in terms of learning versus performance has not been satisfactorily resolved (see Kimble, 1961, pp. 411–416, and Mackintosh, 1974, pp. 150–151). Although Hullian theory viewed drive as a (nonassociative) general energizer of habits, increases in motivation seem also to establish stronger or different original habits (e.g., Capaldi & Hovancik, 1973).

NATURE OF THE REINFORCER AND SIGNAL OR CUE

Both the rate of learning and asymptotic instrumental performance typically bear a positive relation to the amount, the intensity, and the duration of the reinforcer. Several examples of such results are presented in Figure 1.19 for appetitive and aversive conditioning.

The quality, the type, and the location of the reinforcer also affect instrumental learning. For example, using semiliquid rewards, Hutt (1954) found that their sweet, sour, or plain quality yielded differences in rats' responding for the rewards, presumably of unequal palatability. Interestingly, pigeons typically peck a key more frequently for food than water reward, which is most likely related to the different URs elicited by the rewards. As in autoshaping, food reinforcement produces strong, brief, open-beak pecks at the key—as if the bird were eating—whereas water reinforcement yields weak, sustained, closed-beak pecks, and muscle movements like those involved in drinking (see Hearst & Jenkins, 1974; Jenkins & Moore, 1973).

Electric shocks are sometimes more effective when delivered to certain parts of the body than elsewhere. An instructive experiment of Fowler and Miller (1963) revealed that shocks to a rat's hind paws speeded up running toward a food-baited goal box, whereas shock to its front paws decreased speed. This outcome was attributed to the degree of compatibility between running and responses directly elicited by the shock.

The effectiveness of a specific reinforcer also depends on its novelty. For example, animals adapted beforehand to mild shocks often show little effect when such shocks are applied as punishers. Rats can tolerate relatively strong punishing shocks if exposed previously to gradually increasing levels. These kinds of results, which have analogues involving appetitive

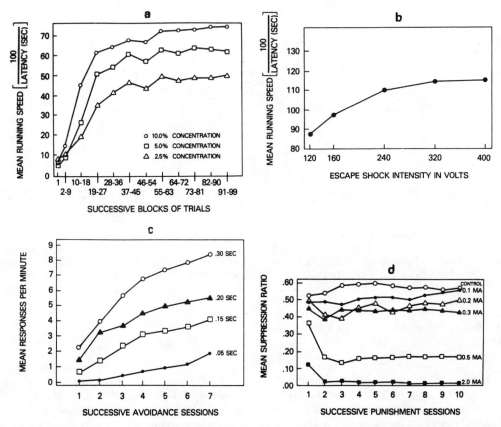

**Figure 1.19.** Illustrations of the effects of variation in characteristics of the reinforcer on instrumental learning and performance. (a) Differences in acquisition of running in a straight alley between groups of rats that received different amounts of sucrose (% concentration) in the goal box (redrawn from Kraeling, 1961.) From "Analysis of Amount of Reward as a Variable in Learning" by D. Kraeling, 1961, *Journal of Comparative and Physiological Psychology, 54*, p. 561. Copyright 1961 by the American Psychological Association. Adapted by permission; (b) Asymptotic running speeds of five groups of rats that had to run to a nonshocked goal box to escape shocks of various intensities (redrawn from Trapold & Fowler, 1960.) From "Instrumental Escape Performance as a Function of the Intensity of Noxious Stimulation" by M.A. Trapold and H. Fowler, 1960, *Journal of Experimental Psychology, 60*, p. 325. Copyright 1960 by the American Psychological Association. Adapted by permission; (c) Acquisition of Sidman avoidance behavior in five groups of rats that received different durations of shock for failure to press a lever at least once every 20 sec (redrawn from Riess & Farrar, 1972.) From "Shock Intensity, Shock Duration, Sidman Avoidance Acquisition, and the 'All or Nothing' Principle in Rats" by D. Riess and C.H. Farrar, 1972, *Journal of Comparative and Physiological Psychology, 81*, p. 349. Copyright 1972 by the American Psychological Association. Adapted by permission; (d) Differences in the suppressive effects of response-contingent, immediate shocks as dependent on the intensity of the punisher, which was delivered intermittently for rats' food-reinforced lever pressing (redrawn from Camp, Raymond, & Church, 1967.) From "Temporal Relationship between Response and Punishment" by D.S. Camp, G.A. Raymond, and R.M. Church, 1967, *Journal of Experimental Psychology, 74*, p. 117. Copyright 1967 by the American Psychological Association. Adapted by permission.

reinforcement, can be related to various findings about habituation and sensitization, as well as to contrast effects.

When instrumental behavior is placed under explicit stimulus control, so that particular consequences occur only when certain stimuli are present, parameters of these cues have fairly consistent effects. The available findings parallel those produced by variations of CSs in Pavlovian conditioning (above, pp. 34–36). For

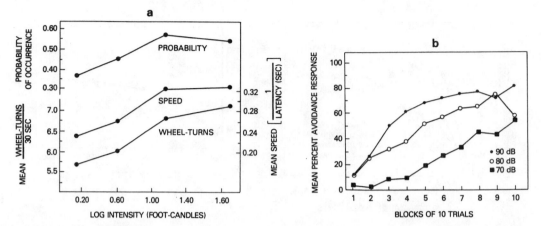

**Figure 1.20.** Effects of discriminative stimulus intensity on instrumental learning and performance. (a) Several measures of behavior over 42 acquisition trials in five different groups of rats that had to rotate a wheel during lights of different intensities (footcandles) to avoid shock (redrawn from Kessen, 1953.) From "Response Strength and Conditioned Stimulus Intensity" by W. Kessen, 1953, *Journal of Experimental Psychology, 45,* p. 85; (b) Acquisition of shuttlebox avoidance in three groups of rats, each trained with a white noise of a different intensity as the warning signal (redrawn from Bauer, 1972.) From "The Effects of CS and US Intensity on Shuttlebox Avoidance" by R.H. Bauer, 1972, *Psychonomic Science, 27,* p. 267. Copyright 1972 by the Psychonomic Society. Adapted by permission.

example, increases in cue intensity, novelty, or salience usually improve measures of acquisition and performance. Figure 1.20 presents some relevant data concerning stimulus intensity in aversive tasks. The phenomena of latent inhibition, external inhibition, stimulus intensity dynamism, overshadowing-blocking, and configuring-patterning appear in instrumental learning experiments that expose, train, and test cues in a manner like that already described for Pavlovian conditioning (see Gray, 1965; Haddad, Walkenbach, Preston, & Strong, 1981; Haggbloom, 1981; Hearst et al., 1974; Kehoe & Gormezano, 1980; Lubow, 1973; Wagner, 1969; and Winnick & Hunt, 1951).

EXTRINSIC RELATIONS BETWEEN BEHAVIOR AND STIMULI

Relations between responses and stimuli can be classified like the relations in Pavlovian conditioning: extrinsic versus intrinsic. An extrinsic relation can be specified without regard to the particular response, reinforcer, or cue. For instance, occurrence of the target response during a cue will be followed 5 sec later by the reinforcer; every 10 instances of the response will produce the reinforcer; the response will procure the reinforcer on only half the trials. In contrast, an intrinsic (nonarbitrary) relation

demands identification of the stimuli and responses involved. Does the effectiveness of instrumental conditioning depend on the similarity between the specific target response and natural behaviors elicited by the specific reinforcer? Historically, the analysis of instrumental learning has stressed extrinsic relations and they are discussed first here.

(1) DELAY OF REINFORCEMENT (TEMPORAL CONTIGUITY OF RESPONSE AND REINFORCER). Corresponding to Pavlovian investigations of CS-US contiguity are experiments varying the time between instrumental response and reinforcer (for reviews, see Renner, 1964, and Tarpy & Sawabini, 1974). Acquisition and asymptotic performance of food-rewarded or shock-escape responses are inversely related to the delay between the required response and the occurrence of the reinforcing event. Likewise, both the degree of suppression produced by punishment and the rate of free-operant avoidance (Sidman, 1966) are lowered by increases in the time between the response and actual or imminent shock. Figure 1.21 displays sample delay-of-reinforcement gradients.

The classic studies of delay gradients in appetitive instrumental learning, which include the data in Figure 1.21a, led many researchers (see

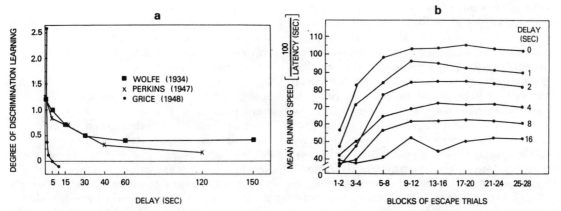

**Figure 1.21.** Sample delay-of-reinforcement gradients for appetitive and aversive instrumental tasks. (a) Degree of learning as dependent on the delay between response choice and delivery of food in three classic studies using groups of rats (redrawn from Grice, 1948.) From "The Relation of Secondary Reinforcement to Delayed Reward in Visual Discrimination Learning" by G.R. Grice, 1948, *Journal of Experimental Psychology, 38*, p. 12; (b) Acquisition of escape behavior in six groups of rats reinforced by shock termination after varying delays following subject's entry into the goal box of a charged runway (redrawn from Fowler & Trapold, 1962.) From "Escape Performance as a Function of Delay of Reinforcement" by H. Fowler and M.A. Trapold, 1962, *Journal of Experimental Psychology, 63*, p. 465. Copyright 1962 by the American Psychological Association. Adapted by permission.

Kimble, 1961, pp. 150–153) to infer that successful acquisition at response-reward intervals longer than a few seconds requires the mediation of some conditioned reinforcer during the delay —for example, the distinctive visual cues that are consistently present while the subject is waiting in the goal box of a runway. When Grice (1948) seemingly eliminated or minimized the possibility of conditioned reinforcement, little learning was observed beyond a 3-sec delay (Figure 1.21a). Researchers now agree that the appearance of such cues during the delay can help subjects bridge long gaps between response and reinforcer (see analogous comparisons between trace and serial Pavlovian conditioning, p. 42 above). However, Spence's (1956) argument that delayed reinforcement permits strengthening of any other behavior that happens to occur during the interval—behavior more contiguous with reinforcement than the target response—indicates another, perhaps more important reason why delayed reinforcement may often be ineffective. Revusky (1971) contended that prevention of such interfering associations would probably lead to successful learning over long delays (say, beyond an hour), even in the absence of any conditioned reinforcement. Evidence consistent with his prediction will be noted shortly.

(2) CONTINGENCY AND INFORMATIVENESS. Although the case is currently not so persuasive as for parallel issues in Pavlovian conditioning, the belief that response-reinforcer contiguity is necessary or sufficient for instrumental learning has weakened in recent years. No one questions the generally facilitative effects of contiguity, but there is increasing acceptance of the idea that a response must provide information about (i.e., predict) the reinforcer in order to gain strength (see Harzem & Zeiler, 1981). Early studies of instrumental conditioning neglected the possibility that frequent, apparently optimal contiguity of response and reinforcer might be relatively ineffective if reinforcers occurred at other times during sessions.

Several results and phenomena argue against the necessity or sufficiency of response-reinforcer contiguity in instrumental learning. Some parallels with Pavlovian findings are striking. In studies in which the number of temporal conjunctions (pairings) between response and reinforcer remain relatively constant or even increase, much weaker levels of operant behavior have resulted when the contingency between response and reinforcer was altered by the delivery of extra reinforcers (USs) than when the extra USs were withheld (see Catania & Keller, 1981; Hammond, 1980; and Zeiler, 1977). However, little or none of this work has examined the effects of $p(US/R)$ versus $p(US/\bar{R})$ during initial acquisition; instead, changes in $p(US/\bar{R})$ are typically introduced after the target response is well established. Therefore, the research suggests but does not demonstrate that response-reinforcer contiguity is insufficient for original instrumental learning. Furthermore, the free reinforcers may, via contiguity alone, strengthen unspecified behaviors that compete with the target response and indirectly lower its probability. This possibility is related to interpretations of Herrnstein's matching law, which treat the relative strengths of various responses as dependent on their different frequencies of reinforcement (see de Villiers, 1977; Williams, Chapter 3, this volume). Similarly, in Pavlovian conditioning the view that extra USs affect performance, not learning, is embodied in the approach of Gibbon and Balsam (1981).

Examples of blocking and overshadowing of response-reinforcer associations also imply that mere contiguity of the two events is insufficient for learning their relation. By analogy to Pavlovian research, if the reinforcer is well predicted by some previously established or particularly salient stimulus, instrumental conditioning of a contiguous response ought to be hindered or blocked. St. Claire-Smith (1979) examined the effects of intermittent response-contingent shocks on rats' stabilized bar pressing. Each shock was immediately preceded by either (a) a brief pre-established signal for shock or (b) the same stimulus when it was novel. Suppression of bar pressing in the first group was significantly weaker.

In other research, reviewed by Mackintosh and Dickinson (1979) and Rescorla and Holland (1982), associations between responses and appetitive reinforcers have been blocked or overshadowed by analogous procedures. Although alternative explanations of specific results exist, the data agree with the notion that mere response-reinforcer contiguity is insufficient for instrumental learning. To become strongly conditioned, the response may need to be the best predictor of the reinforcer.

On the other hand, Skinner's (1948) classic experiment on superstitious conditioning has long been regarded as a clear demonstration of the sufficiency of simple response-reinforcer contiguity in operant conditioning. In that work pigeons received grain every 15 sec regardless of their behavior, but still showed acquisition of consistent movements in the situation. For instance, one pigeon pecked repeatedly toward the floor between food presentations and another hopped from side to side. When food was no longer given, these kinds of responses persisted for a considerable time but eventually disappeared (extinction). Skinner contended that mere accidental pairings of a response with grain were sufficient to strengthen and maintain the response, despite its irrelevance for food delivery and despite the intermittency of the response-food conjunctions. Skinner's explanation was so straightforward, and his extensions to human superstitions so graphic, that it was easily accepted and widely applied.

However, the work of Staddon and Simmelhag (1971; see also Staddon, 1977) cast doubt on the generality of Skinner's results and interpretation. In a systematic replication of his experiment, Staddon and Simmelhag found that the behaviors (e.g., circular movements, wing flapping, head bobbing) that occurred frequently at the time of reinforcement during the subjects' early exposure to the procedure disappeared eventually or became confined to periods not long after grain delivery (interim activities). After 20 or 30 sessions most subjects were pecking at the front wall as the scheduled reinforcer arrived (terminal activities), even though this pecking response had been relatively rare during the initial sessions.

There is no easy way to explain Staddon and Simmelhag's results as superstitious conditioning. On that basis, asymptotic behaviors should not be so uniform from subject to subject, and the initial behaviors that happened to coincide frequently with grain delivery should predominate. Staddon and Simmelhag's finding seems related to autoshaping, in which a signal (here, temporal) for grain produces a particular type of response—displaying great intraspecies consistency rather than variation. Pecking is an important element of natural appetitive behavior in pigeons.

Besides these challenges to the sufficiency of response-reinforcer contiguity in instrumental learning, several lines of research dispute the necessity for contiguity. Lett (1979) reported that rats can acquire a correct choice response in a T-maze even when food reward is delayed for at least an hour after the response. In her work subjects were removed from the maze immediately after their choice, returned to their home cages to spend the delay interval, and then fed in the start box if the choice had been correct. Furthermore, D'Amato and his colleagues (see D'Amato et al., 1981) have reported one-trial acquisition of long-delay conditioned preferences in rats left in the distinctive arm of a T-maze for up to 40 min and subsequently given sucrose in a location outside the maze after a 2-hr delay. Compared approximately two days later with previously exposed but unreinforced animals, the subjects rewarded with sucrose spent substantially more time in the distinctive arm. In addition, the learning of such conditioned preferences was found to be a monotonic increasing function of the amount of exposure to the distinctive arm of the maze. D'Amato et al. concluded that one-trial long-delay learning is not limited to the acquisition of taste aversions.

The findings described in this section (see also Mellitz, Hineline, Whitehouse, & Laurence, 1983) point toward general conclusions like those drawn above for Pavlovian conditioning. Simple response-reinforcer contiguity apparently cannot be assigned the overriding role it was usually given in earlier interpretations of the acquisition of instrumental behavior, since such contiguity seems neither necessary nor sufficient for learning. However, compared with theoretical work in Pavlovian conditioning, the postulation of notions such as informativeness and predictiveness has been relatively sparse in instrumental conditioning.

There remains the issue of whether subjects can actually learn that their responses and the delivery of reinforcers are unrelated, that is, $(p(US/R) = p(US/\bar{R})$, with R normally referring not to a single response but to a broad range of behaviors. Learning such a general relation should retard later acquisition of various instrumental responses. In a parallel vein, Pavlovian research has indicated that exposure to uncorrelated CSs and USs interferes with subsequent conditioning to the CS; but this work on "learned irrelevance" (see Baker & Mackintosh, 1979) encounters alternative explanations in terms of the potential additive effects of latent inhibition to the CS and preexposure to the US. The instrumental analogue, learned helplessness, has generated many experiments in both animals and human beings: subjects that first receive aversive events (e.g., signaled or unsignaled shocks) regardless of their behavior often fail to acquire easy escape or avoidance responses in a subsequent phase.

In addition to Maier and Seligman's (1976) hypothesis, which postulates the subject's acquisition of some such cognition as "Nothing I do matters," other accounts of learned helplessness have been based on changes in general activity, development of certain competing behaviors, and neurochemical reactions. There is now a consensus that the overall phenomenon has no single explanation; Maier and Jackson (1979), for example, have evaluated alternative, more response-centered interpretations and listed failures to obtain the basic effect. Practical implications for human coping behavior and depression have been pursued by Seligman (1975).

(3) DEPENDENCIES BETWEEN RESPONSES AND NEUTRAL STIMULI. Subjects placed in any new situation may learn not only about certain spatial relations among various environmental features, but also about how certain of their different behaviors modify the succession of external stimuli. They probably become familiar with what happens if they move to the left or right, back up rapidly, or push against a particular environmental feature. Associations of this kind can occur even if a definite reinforcer is not delivered in the setting.

Several major areas of research seem especially pertinent to learning about relations between behavior and presumably neutral aspects of some context or surroundings (CSs). The first of these concerns latent learning, in which unrestrained subjects are first exposed to situations—in most experiments simple or complex mazes containing distinctive goal boxes—without any apparent reinforcement. Then in the next phase a standard reinforcer (US) is supplied in the goal box (CS). A final series of test trials assesses whether subjects that had previously had the chance to explore the entire situation reach the goal box faster and more efficiently than subjects not given that opportunity. Many studies have yielded positive results (see MacCorquodale & Meehl, 1954; Mackintosh, 1974, pp. 207–213; and Rashotte, 1979b), but there are enough negative reports to satisfy the skeptics.

The procedure parallels that of sensory preconditioning; there, too, relations among neutral events are presumably learned in the first phase, but are only revealed by later association of reinforcement with one of the events and subsequent changes in the effectiveness of the other event or events. In a study of response preconditioning, St. Claire-Smith and MacLaren (1983) first allowed lever presses to produce a light or noise and then (with the lever removed from the chamber) paired the light or noise with food in one experiment and shock in another. Subsequent test sessions revealed that lever pressing was facilitated by the food-paired stimulus and suppressed by the shock-paired stimulus, compared to appropriate control groups.

Another relevant research area involves work on conditioned reinforcement. A secondary or conditioned reinforcer is a formerly neutral stimulus (CS) that gains reinforcing power by association with a US or an established conditioned reinforcer. One technique for assessing this capability is to see whether the stimulus can itself support instrumental learning. The resemblance of the procedure to second-order Pavlovian conditioning is close, because in both cases a neutral event is first associated with a reinforcer and thereby acquires subsequent training power: to condition new excitatory CSs in Pavlovian arrangements, or to build up new behaviors in instrumental procedures.

The strength of conditioned reinforcers is determined by basically the same factors that govern simple Pavlovian conditioning: for example, the number of pairings of the neutral stimulus with the US, the magnitude of the US, the delay between the stimulus and the US, and the information conveyed by the stimulus about the US. Conditioned reinforcers can be negative or positive; the behavior that terminates a tone associated with shock is strengthened. Surveys of the general topic, along with theoretical evaluations, are contained in books by Hendry (1969) and Wike (1966), and in analytical reviews by Fantino (1977), Gollub (1977), Kelleher and Gollub (1962), Mackintosh (1974), and Nevin (1973a). Of course, students of learning frequently employ conditioned reinforcement to analyze many complex aspects of human behavior, which can hardly be attributed to primary reinforcers like food, water, or shock. Token economies illustrate the practical application of principles of conditioned reinforcement.

(4) SCHEDULES OF REINFORCEMENT. The relation between behavior and a subsequent stimulus can be varied by presenting the stimulus after some but not all occurrences of the response. In discrete-trial arrangements the study of schedules of intermittent reinforcement normally involves manipulation of the percentage of trials on which the reinforcer is given for making the target response (that is, p(US/R). For example, different groups of rats may find food in the goal box of a runway on 25, 50, or 100 percent of the trials. Research of this kind is analogous to parametric investigations of partial reinforcement in Pavlovian conditioning, in which p(US/CS) is varied (p. 45). Although initial acquisition is usually slower under partial than under continuous reinforcement, asymptotic performance and resistance to extinction may be as high—or even higher— after partial as after continuous reinforcement (see Rashotte, 1979a, 1979d).

In discrete-trial settings, the patterning of successive reinforced and unreinforced trials has received much attention. The findings have influenced accounts of animal memory, as well as theories of the advantage of partial reinforcement in extinction. Reliable differences in behavior usually emerge when reinforced (R) and nonreinforced (N) trials always occur in some simple but fixed sequence. For instance, when R and N trials are alternated in a runway with food reward (that is, RNRNRN), rats eventually run faster on R trials than on N trials. This result demonstrates the formation of a discrimination between trials on which reward will or will not occur.

The most comprehensive analysis of such sequential learning is that of Capaldi (1966, 1967, 1971, 1978), who hypothesizes that the outcome of an immediately preceding trial—via its representation in memory and its subsequent reactivation when the subject is replaced in the experimental context—can serve as an effective cue for the event due on the current trial. Capaldi's account implies that lengthening the ITI should weaken acquisition and performance of patterned behavior, a prediction supported many times. Nevertheless, significant evidence of learned patterning appears with ITIs of 30 min or longer—even as long as 24 hr (Capaldi, 1967, 1971; Jobe, Mellgren, Feinberg, Littlejohn, & Rigby, 1977; but cf. Amsel, Hug, & Surridge, 1969). Such results supply extra support for the idea that, for various kinds of learning in infrahumans, close temporal contiguity of important events is not necessary.

Despite the interest in partial reinforcement displayed by students of Pavlovian conditioning and discrete-trial instrumental learning, schedules of reinforcement have been most widely explored by investigators using free-operant procedures. In fact, self-proclaimed operant conditioners typically maintain that reinforcement schedules are a critical factor, perhaps the most influential single variable, in the generation and practical control of behavior. The classification of intermittent schedules made by Skinner (1938) and extended by Ferster and Skinner (1957) still underlies much contemporary work. Skinner based his classification on two types of criteria; (1) time elapsed since delivery of the last reinforcer, and (2) number of responses required for the reinforcer. The time-based arrangements are called interval schedules and the response-based arrangements ratio schedules. Thus, on fixed-interval (FI) schedules the subject receives the reinforcer for its first response after passage of $x$ sec or min since the prior reinforcer, whereas on fixed-ratio (FR) schedules the subject receives the reinforcer each time it completes $y$ number of responses. On variable-interval (VI) schedules the time between reinforcement availabilities is aperiodic rather than fixed. Likewise, when the number of responses required for reinforcement is irregular, a variable-ratio (VR) schedule operates.

Figure 1.17 displays portions of cumulative response curves representing typical asymptotic performance on Skinner's four basic schedules. Records of FI behavior are scalloped in appearance; responding is minimal right after a reinforcer but normally shows a positive acceleration as the time for the next reinforcer draws near. Behavior under FR is characterized by periods of high, steady responding, with pauses immediately after receipt of a reinforcer; these postreinforcement pauses increase as a direct function of FR length (see Davey, 1981; Nevin, 1973b; and Zeiler, 1977). Because the time for reinforcement is unpredictable on both VI and VR schedules, linear curves, with relatively few irregularities, are the usual outcome.

The research on reinforcement schedules performed from the 1950s to the 1980s has centered on (a) analysis of the factors contributing to differential response rates and patterns between these basic schedules, as well as combinations or variations of them; (b) investigation of the effects of different parameters (e.g., drive level, amount or delay of reinforcement) on performance within a particular type of schedule; and (c) quantitative treatment of choice behavior on complex procedures that involve two or more schedules acting simultaneously (concurrent schedules). In the third arrangement (c), Herrnstein's well-known matching law predicts—with certain limitations of schedule and procedure—that the relative rates of responding on the different schedules should match the relative rates of reinforcement obtained on the schedules.

Some points related to topic (a) will be considered here. The other topics are extensively pursued in the reviews and reports in Williams (Chapter 3, this volume), Honig (1966), Honig and Staddon (1977), Nevin (1973b), Schoenfeld (1970), and the pages of the *Journal of the Experimental Analysis of Behavior*.

The primary facts to be explained in the comparative analysis of simple interval and ratio schedules concern (i) the much higher response rates obtained on ratio schedules than on interval schedules with similar overall patterns and frequencies of reinforcement, (ii) the appearance of pauses in behavior immediately after consumption of a reinforcer (particularly on FI and FR schedules; see Figure 1.17), and (iii) the direct relation between frequency of reinforcement and response rate on interval schedules. Unfortunately, more than 40 years of research demonstrate that performance on even the simplest schedules is complexly determined in ways that relate to these three facts. Furthermore, what have masqueraded as theories of schedule effects are often mere redescriptions of empirical relations.

First of all, the delivery of a reinforcer presumably has not only a strengthening but also a selective function. On both interval and ratio schedules the baseline behavior is generally strengthened (increased in frequency) by delivery of reinforcers, but on FRs and VRs rapid bursts of responding are shaped or selected because they are more likely to be followed by a reinforcer than are slowly-paced groups of responses. The faster a subject responds on a ratio schedule, the more frequently is the reinforcer delivered during a given time period. On the other hand, rapid responding on interval schedules is not preferentially reinforced; so long as the subject maintains some minimal rate of responding, the reinforcers will follow at approximately their scheduled times. In fact, on interval schedules relatively long waits between responses (interresponse times, IRTs) are more likely to be followed by a reinforcer than are short IRTs—a point recognized and stressed by Skinner back in 1938. For example, any IRT greater than 2 min is always reinforced on an FI or VI schedule with a maximum of 2 min between reinforcer availabilities. Thus, by an analysis in terms of differential reinforcement of various IRTs, instead of accounts based on reinforcement of other behavioral properties like response rate, clarification of some basic schedule effects has been achieved, although not to everyone's satisfaction (see Reynolds & McLeod, 1970; Shimp, 1981; and Zeiler, 1977).

Analysis of IRTs has led to the study of schedules that explicitly reinforce particular IRTs. Schedules using differential reinforcement of low rates (DRL) reinforce the subject only when a specific long IRT (i.e., a wait of at least 10 sec between successive responses) has been attained. Those with differential reinforcement of high rates (DRH) provide reinforcement for a single, very short IRT or a group of short IRTs (e.g., three responses in 1 sec). As intended, DRL schedules yield slow rates (see a review by Kramer & Rilling, 1970) and DRH schedules give fast, steady rates (provided the requirement is gradually approximated and never set so high that responding extinguishes as a consequence of sparse reinforcement). The DRL schedule has often served as a sensitive baseline in studies of brain lesions or drugs suspected to affect timing behavior—or to have facilitatory properties, requiring a relatively low output for their detection.

Interpretation of the second general finding —the postreinforcement pause that occurs on FI and FR schedules—is not especially controversial. It parallels Pavlov's analysis of "inhibition of delay" (p. 39) and Skinner's (1938) disussion of "temporal discrimination from the preceding reinforcement." The delivery of the reinforcer comes to function as a negative stimulus (S−) signaling a period of nonreinforcement. Even though ratio schedules do not impose direct temporal restrictions, the interval between reinforcers on large FR schedules is necessarily long because of the time needed to complete the ratio. Thus pausing after reinforcement on FI and FR

schedules is apparently caused by similar temporal discriminations. The pause is absent on most VI and VR schedules, which indicates that it is not a mere aftereffect of consuming the reinforcer (cf. Harzem & Harzem, 1981).

Catania and Reynolds (1968) explored many aspects of the third fact about reinforcement schedules mentioned above. Figure 1.22 summarizes one major result: as frequency of reinforcement increases on VI schedules, response rate increases in negatively accelerated fashion. Various molar and molecular determinants have been proposed to account for relevant complexities (see, for example, Davey, 1981; Mackintosh, 1974; and Zeiler, 1977).

Types of schedules, reinforcers, responses, and stimuli can be combined in innumerable ways, often producing very complicated behavioral repertoires that simulate those encountered in everyday life—at least in the opinion of many students of operant behavior. Lists or descriptions of the major types of complex schedules are supply by Catania (1979, pp. 185–187), Ferster

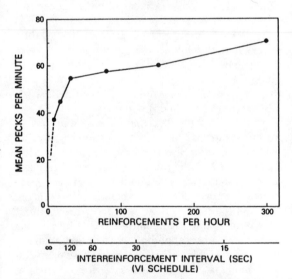

**Figure 1.22.** Asymptotic rates of key pecking as a function of rate of variable interval reinforcement for a group of six pigeons, each exposed to several different schedule values (redrawn from Catania, 1979, and Catania & Reynolds, 1968.) From "A Quantitative Analysis of the Responding Maintained by Interval Schedules of Reinforcement" by A.C. Catania and G.S. Reynolds, 1968, *Journal of the Experimental Analysis of Behavior, 11,* p. 370. Copyright 1968 by the Society for the Experimental Analysis of Behavior, Inc. Adapted by permission.

& Skinner (1957), and Zeiler (1977). A few common varieties deserve mention here. Subjects may be trained on two or more simple schedules, each of which is in force during different parts of a session: say, FR, FI, and Sidman avoidance. When distinctive stimuli (for example, different colored lights) designate which of the simple schedules is currently operating, the overall procedure is called a multiple schedule. However, when no distinctive stimuli are provided, a mixed schedule is in effect (the subject can detect the current schedule only by discriminating differences among the schedules in the frequency, patterning, or type of reinforcers).

Sometimes schedules are sequentially linked together so that completion of the requirement for one schedule (e.g., VR) does not itself produce primary reinforcement, but instead initiates a second, different schedule (e.g., FI) during which, say, food is possible. When differential external stimuli accompany these separate schedules, the procedure is a chained schedule; and conditioned reinforcement (that is, the change to the external stimulus present during the final link) presumably maintains responding in the first link. On tandem schedules, the same succession of simple schedules is involved, but no stimulus change marks the switch to the second schedule.

On the complicated but widely investigated concurrent-chain schedule, two responses are simultaneously available at the start of a given trial. For instance, in this initial link the left and right keys may be illuminated in a pigeon's Skinner box. Pecks at these keys produce a stimulus change (e.g., illumination of the center key) according to the particular schedule assigned to each side key. After the stimulus change occurs, primary reinforcement in the form of grain is available on a schedule (terminal link; pecking the center key) that depends on which response (left or right) produced the stimulus change. Choice and preference among different schedules, amounts, delays, and so on, of primary reinforcement in the terminal link of the chain can be assessed by analysis of relative response rates in the initial link. The general procedure has been widely used for studying conditioned reinforcement, which presumably plays an important role in the control of responding during the initial link.

Finally, a few other aspects of work on inter-

mittent reinforcement merit comment. Schedules of aversive control have been studied both separately and along with schedules of appetitive reinforcement. Pertinent research on punishment, avoidance, and escape is reviewed in Honig (1966), Honig and Staddon (1977), Mackintosh (1974), and Overmier (1979a, 1979b). Another important topic that is closely connected with intermittency of reinforcement concerns *adjunctive* or *schedule-induced behaviors*. These reactions are observed mainly at times during an appetitive schedule when the reinforcer is improbable. The behaviors include polydipsia (excessive drinking in food-rewarded animals that are not deprived of water: the volume drunk is sometimes as much as one-half the total weight of the animal); aggression toward other organisms or objects; wheel running; ingestion of wood shavings; licking of an air stream; and even self-injection of certain drugs. No full account of these by-products of reinforcement periodicity is available, but Davey (1981), Falk (1971, 1977), Roper (1981) and Staddon (1977) have reviewed relevant data and theory.

Although some investigators still believe that the analysis of reinforcement schedules is fundamental to the understanding of learning and performance, since 1970 there has been a shift away from study of the schedules themselves. Mackintosh (1974, p. 181) characterized free-operant schedules as "frighteningly complex," and in an oft-cited passage Jenkins (1970) portrayed them as technical inventions that might not mirror too closely what happens in natural environments. "Neither men nor animals are found in nature responding repeatedly in an unchanging environment for occasional reinforcement" (p. 107). Whether or not such schedules form a separate subject matter, they have been useful as tools or baselines for illuminating many Pavlovian and instrumental phenomena, as well as for assessing the effects of drugs, brain lesions, and other psychophysiological manipulations. The stable, reliable behaviors created by various schedules have impressed researchers from other biological sciences, who are often surprised by the high degree of day-to-day and moment-by-moment control a psychologist can produce over animals' voluntary responses. Thus schedule technology has fostered the interdisciplinary appeal of animal learning research.

(5) SPATIAL CONTIGUITY. A number of studies, mainly with primates, have examined the role of spatial proximity of cue, response, and reward locations in instrumental discrimination learning (see a review by Cowey, 1968). This work demonstrates that spatial separation of the cue from the response or the cue from the place of reward is less favorable for discrimination learning than when the sites of the cue, the response, and the reward are close together. Although the evidence is not overwhelming, it seems to do more harm to separate the cue from the response than to separate it from the reward (e.g., Miller & Murphy, 1964).

Hearst and Jenkins (1974; see also Hearst, 1975b) discussed such findings in terms of their relation to autoshaping. That phenomenon also seems to be implicated in Grastyán and Vereczkei's (1974) observation that an auditory signal produced poorer performance when it came from the start box than the goal box of a runway (in both cases the signal indicated trials on which food was in the goal box). Apparently, approach to the CS for food facilitated or interfered with appropriate instrumental behavior, depending on whether the CS and food were in the same or a different location.

## INTRINSIC RELATIONS BETWEEN BEHAVIOR AND STIMULI

Although lacking the dramatic impact of work on taste aversions, research on cue-response-reinforcer interactions in instrumental learning has also led students of conditioning to reassess their confidence that general principles of behavior can emerge from relatively arbitrary, standard experimental arrangements. How much does the particular choice of stimulus, behavior, and consequence matter, and to what extent do species-specific factors intrude? It turns out that a response readily trainable with one type of instrumental consequence may be unaffected by some different consequence, even though the latter serves as an effective reinforcer for other responses. Such results suggest that particular response-reinforcer relations are inherently easier to learn than others.

Ease of instrumental conditioning seems to depend on the compatibility of the target response with behavior that the subjects emit naturally in pursuit of a specific goal or under certain motivational states. Shettleworth (1975) found that face washing, scent marking, and body scratching with the hind foot in golden hamsters were little affected by contingent food delivery. On the other hand, digging and rearing behaviors were elevated when food was produced. Significantly, the readily conditioned responses increase when hamsters are food-deprived or expect to be fed, whereas the responses that resist conditioning tend to decrease in hungry animals.

Vivid examples of the "misbehavior of organisms," described by Breland and Breland (1961, 1966), relate to the same theme. While training many species to perform tricks for various commercial enterprises, Breland and Breland discovered that certain unnatural responses were difficult, if not impossible, to maintain. The behaviors tended to drift toward "instinctive" responses appropriate to the type of reinforcer. Otters trained to place a wooden ball in a chute for food eventually began to paw the ball or chew it like food. These intrusions delayed their receipt of food but nevertheless increased in frequency as training continued.

In the domain of aversive conditioning, Bolles (1970) presented evidence that species-specific defense reactions (SSDRs) naturally evoked by the occurrence or anticipation of aversive events—responses like running or fighting in rats—are more easily conditioned as avoidance responses with an electric shock US than are responses like lever pressing. Incidentally, several writers have suggested that the choice of lever pressing or key pecking as standard operants with food reward may not be so arbitrary as once thought—because rats bite and lick levers predicting food, and pigeons peck food signals (autoshaping). Failure to consider species-specific responses of cats when in the presence of other organisms, including human beings, apparently led Guthrie and Horton (1946) to conclude that learning to rub a pole had occurred; Moore and Stuttard (1979) found that stereotyped "greeting rubs" would have occurred without any reinforcement, so long as the experimenters were visible to the cat—as was true in the famous Guthrie studies.

One simplistic conclusion from all these findings is that the ease of instrumental learning depends on the particular combinations of response and reinforcer selected for conditioning. However, the results may not reflect an inability to learn some response-reinforcer association, but rather the interfering effects of other highly probable responses on the performance of the target response in situations involving specific motivational states and US expectancies. At any rate, no one can now say which response-reinforcer relations an organism is "prepared" to learn. Until criteria for such decisions are made explicit and not invoked in post hoc fashion, much relevant theorizing will remain fairly circular.

The presence of an external cue or discriminative stimulus in many instrumental conditioning experiments raises the issue of whether certain dimensions or modalities foster the learning of some specific response-reinforcer relations better than others. In a series of studies along these lines, LoLordo and his colleagues found, for example, that visual cues overshadow auditory cues when pigeons press a treadle for food, but the reverse is true when the treadle is pressed to avoid shocks. Such differential stimulus control presumably has evolutionary significance: visual cues are believed to be particularly important to the natural appetitive behavior of birds, and auditory cues to their natural defensive behavior (the latter seems less plausible than the former). LoLordo (1979d) presented a careful analysis of relevant possibilities. Other useful commentaries on intrinsic factors in the acquisition of instrumental responses are by Domjan (1983), Domjan and Galef (1983), Dunham (1977), and Shettleworth (1979).

## Contrast Effects

Students of instrumental learning have long been interested in how prior or simultaneous exposure to other conditions of reinforcement (e.g., amount, frequency) affects a subject's reaction to one particular condition. A reward of four pellets may lead to strong instrumental behavior if the subject usually receives few or no pellets for that response, but to weak instrumental behavior if the subject customarily receives a reward of eight pellets. Parallel research on habituation and Pavlovian conditioning has been mentioned above (pp. 19 and 48). In instrumental conditioning, *positive contrast* refers to augmented performance under a particular condition when the subject also receives exposure to a less favorable condition. *Negative contrast* refers to decrements in performance under a particular condition when the subject is also exposed to a more favorable condition. The most common arrangements for studying contrast involve (1) shifts to a different reinforcement condition after prolonged experience with only one condition (successive or nondifferential contrast), or (2) shifts between different reinforcement conditions during the same session (simultaneous or differential contrast).

Despite extensive analysis, no tidy set of principles has emerged to integrate the varied results of research on contrast. Measurement problems often intrude (for example, ceiling effects that hinder detection of positive contrast); findings are frequently inconsistent from one task to another; and there is disagreement about whether certain phenomena are transient or long lasting. Thus, even though positive and negative contrast can be readily demonstrated under some conditions, most experimenters do not feel confident about the generality of the results.

Many workers believe that progress on the topic will arise only from fresh conceptualization of the pertinent issues. Initial work on successive contrast during the 1930s and 1940s had a strong impact, because it indicated serious deficiencies in early versions of Hullian theory, which had implied that reinforcers merely strengthened S-R associations. Instead, the contrast data showed that subjects acquiring instrumental responses were also learning about features of the reinforcer; their performance often displayed rapid changes when the reinforcer was altered, as if the subjects' expectancies had been violated. Consequently, Hull and Spence developed the notion of incentive motivation, based on the acquisition of fractional anticipatory goal responses (see Spence, 1956). Reviews of research and theory on contrast include those of Black (1968, 1976), Dunham (1968), Flaherty (1982), Mackintosh (1974), McSweeney, Ettinger, and Norman (1981), Rashotte (1979c), and Schwartz and Gamzu (1977).

## Conflict

Because of their potential implications for understanding certain forms of human maladaptive behavior, experimental arrangements that produce strong incompatible responses have frequently been examined in studies of animal instrumental learning. Conflict situations can be classified in several ways: approach–approach conflict (in which the incompatible responses lead to different rewards; acceptance of one means sacrifice of the other); avoidance–avoidance conflict (in which the incompatible responses both lead to negative events, as suggested by the expression "between the devil and the deep blue sea"); and approach–avoidance conflict (in which a particular action has both positive and negative outcomes, like food and shock).

The approach–avoidance arrangement has been widely explored in the laboratory, stimulated by Neal Miller's (1944, 1959) classic analysis of conflict and displacement in terms of interacting generalization gradients for the response tendencies of approach and avoidance. His account has been influential in clinical research and has generated attempts to reduce the negative effects of such conflict through the administration of certain drugs. However, recently discovered weaknesses of the model have rendered its status uncertain (see Mackintosh, 1974, pp. 521–524). Pavlov's paradigm for producing experimental neurosis (above, p. 48) is somewhat similar to instrumental arrangements for studying conflict; it also produces strong opposing response tendencies.

### Post-Acquisition Phenomena

Once the performance of an instrumentally conditioned response has stabilized, there are many ways to modify its strength. The most widely studied procedures involve changes in the response-reinforcer relation or in the stimuli present when the response has been reinforced. Because Balsam (Chapter 2, this volume) concentrates on operant generalization and discrimination, the focus here is on studies of extinction. Investigation of the effects of nonreinforcement has obvious practical implications for the elimination, recovery, and persistence of habits.

### EXTINCTION

When the target response is no longer followed by the reinforcer, performance declines—usually in a gradual but rather irregular manner. Other less common ways of extinguishing the response destroy the relation between response and reinforcer by delivering reinforcers independent of behavior (see, for example, Boakes, 1973; Lindblom & Jenkins, 1981, experiment 4; Rescorla & Skucy, 1969). The phenomena of spontaneous recovery, silent extinction, disinhibition, and behavioral reinstatement by "free" USs, have all been observed after removal of the instrumental

reinforcer. In general, the existence of these effects implies that nonreinforcement does not erase the neural record of prior conditioning but somehow sets up a process that prevents its current expression.

A host of factors affect resistance to extinction (see summaries in D'Amato, 1969; Kimble, 1961; Mackintosh, 1974; and Rashotte, 1979d). For example, increments in the number of continuously reinforced trials normally enhance response output and persistence in extinction, except under certain circumstances involving sizable rewards and a relatively large number of training trials (for this overtraining extinction effect, see Mackintosh, 1974, pp. 423–427, and Rashotte, 1979d, pp. 242–244). The more varied the conditions of reinforcement (e.g., amount, delay) during acquisition, the greater the number of responses in extinction. Massed trials produce faster extinction than spaced trials, but this outcome depends on the kind of trial distribution in force during original acquisition. Varying the strength of the relevant drive during acquisition does not seem to affect extinction behavior assessed under equivalent drive conditions for all groups. Changing the circumstances of aversive stimulation after punishment, avoidance, or escape conditioning has had interesting consequences (see summaries by Brown & Cunningham, 1981; D'Amato, 1969; and Overmier, 1979a, 1979b). Some cases show self-punitive (masochistic) behavior and exceptionally strong resistance to extinction.

The partial reinforcement–extinction effect (PREE) in instrumental conditioning has been the major focus of extinction research. General theories of instrumental extinction and response persistence draw much of their empirical support from studies of the PREE, which as noted above (p. 50) were instigated by results from a Pavlovian conditioning experiment of Humphreys (1939) and from Skinner's (1938) work on intermittent operant schedules. The magnitude of the PREE depends on many factors that are conscientiously reviewed by Mackintosh (1974, chapter 8) and Rashotte (1979d). Instead of listing those variables and commenting on the inconsistency and complexity of their effects, it seems preferable to describe briefly the two most prominent theories devised for the PREE. One account derived from Amsel's (1967, 1972a) influential and comprehensive analysis of frustration as a motivating emotional reaction produced by nonreward; besides several other behavioral phenomena, this theoretical framework encompasses various paradoxical effects observed in extinction (see also Amsel & Stanton, 1980). The second approach views reward and nonreward as two kinds of distinctive stimuli whose memories endure for some time. This type of interpretation has been most fully developed by Capaldi (1966, 1967), though it was foreshadowed by Hull (1952) and Sheffield (1949).

Amsel's theory is based on the notion that unexpected absence of reward (e.g., after a series of regularly rewarded trials) elicits a frustration reaction, which has specific stimulus properties and typically induces a variety of behaviors that compete with the target response. During acquisition under partial reinforcement the subject often receives reward for making the target response in the presence of (intratrial) frustration-associated cues. Stimuli that evoke anticipatory frustration reactions eventually become signals that the response may be rewarded, and thus they help maintain the behavior when reward is terminated in extinction. After continuous reinforcement, on the other hand, the elimination of reward produces frustration for the first time—which evokes strong competing behavior and leads to the rapid disappearance of the instrumental response. In this case frustrating stimuli have never been associated with rewarded responses (that is, counterconditioned) and cannot support the target response.

Capaldi's account of the PREE does not rely on assumptions about motivational processes. As in his work on patterning of reinforcement (above, p. 76), Capaldi stresses the importance of (intertrial) sequences of and transitions between nonrewarded (N) and rewarded (R) outcomes, which are assumed to produce discriminably different memory traces. Under partial reinforcement subjects learn that recent experience with N is often followed by R; on the other hand, under continuous reinforcement no positive conditioning to aftereffects of N trials is possible, because N trials do not occur. The explanation of the PREE follows directly. Capaldi and his colleagues have also demonstrated that resistance to extinction after partial reinforcement is enhanced, for example, by increasing either the number of consecutive N trials prior to each R trial during acquisition or the variety of N-lengths to which subjects are exposed during acquisition. Simple accounts of extinction phenomena based merely on percentage of prior partial reinforcement cannot handle these results.

Most researchers in the field think that both Amsel's and Capaldi's accounts have definite, unique strengths and that a theory of extinction and persistence will eventually emerge that integrates the two—which are in many details more similar than different. Today, however, we are, as Rashotte (1979d) concluded, "far from a full answer" to the question of why responding persists or weakens in extinction.

## General Theories of Instrumental Conditioning and Performance

The occurrence of certain events after a particular response will increase or decrease the probability or other characteristics of that response. The problem is how to interpret this empirical or weak law of effect: when and why do certain consequences produce behavioral changes? A satisfactory answer to this question has eluded learning theorists, but not for want of trying. Many writers have attempted to specify the nature of reinforcement and its mechanisms of action.

Until the 1960s the most popular accounts viewed reinforcers as drawn from a set of stimuli possessing some absolute, unitary power to strengthen responding—usually attributed to their capacity to reduce or induce drives and thereby to return the overall biological state of the organism to minimally disturbed or optimal levels. On the other hand, several recent approaches treat reinforcement in a relativistic manner, as involving behavioral activities whose availability affects the likelihood of other activities on which such availability depends. Rather than strengthening prior behavior, these dependencies are said to regulate or rearrange the time and effort devoted to various responses in the subject's repertoire, thus maintaining an inherent equilibrium among the responses. Depending on the circumstances, any activity in which organisms engage is a potential reinforcer.

Still other treatments try to reduce most if not all instances of instrumental learning to the action of the same basic mechanisms as those that govern Pavlovian conditioning. The most modern of these accounts have a cognitive flavor and suggest that subjects form associations between representations of responses and reinforcers on the basis of the informativeness of the response. Finally, a variety of old and new approaches interpret reward, punishment, and avoidance in terms of interactions between two processes assumed separately to underlie Pavlovian and instrumental conditioning.

This brief outline reflects the diverse nature of theoretical approaches to instrumental conditioning. Furthermore, particular theories may center on positive reinforcement and neglect negative reinforcement, and vice versa. As with theories of Pavlovian conditioning, the present discussion will focus on different views of (1) the circumstances producing instrumental learning, (2) the associations or representations established during such learning, and (3) how learning is reflected in specific measures of performance. Undue scrutiny of topics covered by Williams (Chapter 3, this volume) is avoided. Good general references include Bower and Hilgard (1981), D'Amato (1969), Honig and Staddon (1977), Jenkins (1979), Kimble (1961), Mackintosh (1974), Mackintosh and Dickinson (1979), Overmier (1979c), Rashotte (1979b, 1979c), and Timberlake (1980).

### Classic Theories

Because current accounts echo certain themes of their predecessors, a short survey of pre-1950 approaches is useful. Pavlov maintained that there was no basic difference between classical and instrumental conditioning, despite the arguments of Konorski and others (see Dickinson & Boakes, 1979). Pavlov's final thoughts on this matter stressed that neural representations of any two paired events could transmit excitation in both forward and backward directions. Accordingly, in instrumental arrangements discrete CSs or situational stimuli would come to activate a neural representation of the US, which in turn would generate representations of any responses that consistently preceded it. These response representations would trigger corresponding overt behaviors. As described and evaluated by Dickinson (1980b, pp. 110 ff.), Gormezano and Tait (1976), and Mackintosh and Dickinson (1979), this bidirectional hypothesis calls to mind Brogden's (1962) work on circular conditioning. A neutral auditory stimulus that was originally presented only after a particular response would itself later evoke that response.

Pavlov's account has not been very influential,

and of course Thorndike's law of effect spawned the popular interpretations of instrumental conditioning as an incremental, strengthening process controlled by the consequences of a response. Although Thorndike admitted the existence of other forms of learning, he overwhelmingly emphasized the role of satisfying outcomes in establishing S-R bonds. The reinforcer was not itself a part of the learned association; it merely acted as a catalyst in forging bonds between situations and actions. Spence (1951, p. 696) noted that Thorndike's view of a satisfying state as a retroactive strengthener differed from Pavlov's concept of reinforcement. Pavlov used reinforcement in its simple physiological sense—a facilitator of activity.

Hull (1943) thought that, as a theoretical principle, the law of effect governed all learning (see above, p. 53). His original account paralleled Thorndike's in its assumption that S-R connections are gradually strengthened by positive outcomes, which themselves are not elements of associative learning. Unlike Thorndike, however, Hull offered need reduction or drive-stimulus reduction as the biological basis for reinforcement.

Skinner's law of operant conditioning also resembled Thorndike's familiar principle: "If the occurrence of an operant is followed by presentation of a reinforcing stimulus, the strength is increased" (1938, p. 21). However, this statement carefully avoids any implications, physiological or otherwise, about why a reinforcer possesses this power. Skinner believed that no circularity is created by defining a reinforcer in terms of its strengthening power: "some stimuli are found to produce the change, others not, and they are classified as reinforcing and non-reinforcing accordingly" (1938, p. 62). Significantly, and in contrast to Thorndike and Hull, Skinner thought that reinforcement strengthened prior responses and not S-R bonds. Any external stimulation correlated with reinforcement of the operant was said to "set the occasion" when the response would be reinforced, not to elicit the response or to become directly linked with it. Thus Skinner's emphasis was on the response-reinforcer (R-S) dependency, but he did not neglect the occasion-setting function of correlated (discriminative) stimuli.

For Guthrie (1935) all conditioning resulted from S-R contiguity, followed by some kind of distinct stimulus change that prevented any interfering responses from becoming attached to the original S. The presentation of food after a lever is pressed ensures that the stimulation following the pressing of the lever is different from stimulation before it; thus the original S-R association is preserved. However, the question of what kinds of stimulus change preserve the original S-R link is logically equivalent to the question of what kinds of events are effective reinforcers.

Tolman believed that correct S-R associations do not get "stamped in," nor do incorrect ones get "stamped out." Instead instrumental learning involves the organism's discovering or refining the various types of stimulation that alternative responses lead to (Tolman, 1932, p. 364). Organisms learn *about* features of the reinforcer, not really *because* of the reinforcer. Tolman considered reinforcers to be especially salient events that, depending on motivational demands, affected the subject's performance—not its learning about features of and relations between stimuli. Tolman's theory is characterized as S-S, in contrast to the S-R theories of the first half of this century, as mentioned earlier.

### Later Approaches

#### ABSOLUTE, BIOLOGICALLY ORIENTED THEORIES OF REINFORCEMENT

It would simplify matters greatly if effective reinforcers were limited to events that possess single or very few common properties. The search for such absolute markers has persisted for a long time, without great success. Most of these approaches can be described as homeostatic, with reinforcement restoring some imbalance between ideal and actual organismic states or external stimulation. They are theories of biological equilibrium or tension reduction; without correcting certain deficiencies caused by deprivation, or various excesses caused by powerful continuous stimulation, organisms could not long survive. Hull's need-reduction account fell into this category: thirsty animals acquire responses that lessen states of dehydration, and organisms suffering persistent pain emit behavior that eliminates it. However, many physiological need states such as hunger or thirst require considerable time for their reduction— far longer than the few seconds presumed to be the effective limits of the delay-of-reinforcement gradient. Therefore Hull and in particular N.E.

Miller (1951) eventually favored drive-stimulus reduction as the crucial condition for reinforcement. Hunger pangs or a dry mouth are strong, specific stimuli impelling action that rapidly reduces their intensity.

As reasonable as these statements appear, they do not provide a solid basis for predicting the reinforcing power of various events. Even though need reduction or drive-stimulus reduction is presumably absent, the presentation of mild sounds and lights, the opportunity to explore a novel environment or to manipulate certain objects, and the electrical stimulation of specific brain areas can function as instrumental reinforcers. Defenders of the Hullian approach answered by invoking additional drives, like curiosity or exploration, which they argued are also controlled by deprivation and satiation. However, successful conditioned reinforcers do not seem to reduce needs for the primary reinforcers from which their strength derived (Kimble, 1961, pp. 169 ff.). Furthermore, instrumental learning does not necessarily occur even when tissue needs are explicitly reduced by a response (Richter, 1942–1943).

For other theorists, increases as well as reductions in arousal or drive could be reinforcing. These writers, basing their arguments on physiological discoveries concerning the brain's reticular activating system (e.g., Moruzzi & Magoun, 1949), viewed reinforcers as events that shift general arousal toward optimal, preferred levels. Consequently, Hebb (1955), Malmo (1959), and Berlyne (1967) described reinforcement in terms of an inverted-U function. Below the point of optimal arousal, increases in drive were reinforcing, but above that point it was drive reductions that were reinforcing. Unfortunately, specification of optimal arousal levels proved impossible to achieve in practice.

Related to the notion that increases in arousal may prove reinforcing was the observation that various kinds of external stimulation seem to induce drives and yet continue to act as strong reinforcers (Sheffield, 1966). Novel objects to be explored or manipulated fall into this category, as well as sweet tastes and gentle strokes. Male rats will continue to respond to the sexual stimulation of a female by engaging in copulatory activity, even though they are not allowed to ejaculate, that is, are not permitted drive reduction (Sheffield, Wulff, & Backer, 1951). Apparently, certain drive-inducing external stimuli (incentives) are inherently reinforcing, provided their intensity is not excessive. Sheffield also suggested that the vigorous behaviors evoked by such stimuli—rather than their sensory aspects —could explain their reinforcing ability. The responses of drinking a sweet solution, chewing, or copulating might furnish the main source of reinforcement. In support of this proposition, some (but not all) relevant studies have reported high correlations between the vigor of instrumental and consummatory responses (see Hall, 1976, and Kimble, 1961).

However, partly because consummatory behavior seems unnecessary for successful reinforcement—a rat learns to make correct choices even when food is injected directly into its stomach (see Miller, 1963, for comments)—an alternative, less peripheralistic hypothesis of Glickman and Schiff (1967) has received favorable attention, though little empirical validation. They suggested that reinforcement entails the selective facilitation of species-specific motor patterns preorganized in the central nervous system. The capacity of goal objects to trigger certain neural centers was presumed crucial for their reinforcing effects (see also Bindra, 1976, 1978).

Currently, attempts to describe reinforcers in terms of one or two simple attributes have been virtually abandoned by students of learning. A revival of such efforts may require the impetus of new discoveries in physiological psychology.

RELATIVISTIC, BEHAVIORALLY ORIENTED
THEORIES OF REINFORCEMENT
Several influential theories of instrumental behavior avoid speculation about the biological bases of reinforcement. They try to escape the potential circularity of the law of effect, not by searching for a common property linking all reinforcers or by arguing that reinforcers effective in one situation will work in almost all other situations (Meehl's 1950 principle of transsituationality; see Schnaitter, 1978, for one review and assessment of the principle). Instead, the new approaches discard standard law-of-effect explanations and view reinforcers mainly as activities that organisms freely display when certain stimuli are present. The general framework is empirical. Baselines of various behaviors (e.g., drinking, eating, running) are initially determined without any instrumental contingencies. Then, depending on relative response preferences displayed during baseline determi-

nation, predictions are made about whether the opportunity to engage in one activity will facilitate a second activity required for that opportunity.

Premack (1959, 1965, 1971) originated this general kind of approach in a version that is often labeled prepotent-response theory or probability-differential theory. Premack's fundamental principle is that "for any pair of responses, the more probable one will reinforce the less probable one" (1965, p. 132). There is no fixed, universal set of reinforcers; any activity can be a reinforcer, depending on the experimental conditions—in particular, the relative probabilities of the instrumental and other responses. For example, nonthirsty rats will increase their drinking in order to run, but not the converse (wheel running is more probable than drinking during baseline sessions); and thirsty rats will increase their running in order to drink, but not the converse (drinking is now the more probable baseline response). That is, either drinking or running can be a reinforcer (an instance of Premack's "reversibility principle"). The drinking of water, a standard reinforcer, can serve as an instrumental response, just as running, a standard instrumental response, can serve as a reinforcer.

Experiments with human beings by Premack (1959) revealed that children who prefer eating candy to playing a pinball machine increase the amount of their machine playing over baseline levels in order to obtain candy. However, their baseline level of candy eating could not be increased (and at times even decreased) if machine playing became contingent on eating candy. The converse effects were obtained in children who originally preferred playing the machine to eating candy.

According to Premack's account, punishment involves cases in which opportunities to engage in less probable responses are made contingent on more probable responses. Looked at broadly, the theory assumes that activities are reallocated by imposition of a schedule that disrupts baseline outputs—a behavioral disequilibrium that organisms work to remove.

An obvious practical problem with Premack's approach arises when the responses under study are not commensurate (see Dunham, 1977). Response rate or total time devoted to an activity may be an appropriate index for some but not other behaviors. A sexual episode is a highly preferred but relatively brief and infrequent activity; how is it to be compared to, say, drinking during baseline sessions, so that the two behaviors can be ranked in terms of their relative probabilities? Sometimes, simple measures of trial-by-trial choice among alternative responses during baseline phases, or other assays of "momentary" probabilities, may provide acceptable ways to compare disparate behaviors.

Despite such difficulties and other later theoretical developments, Premack's view of reinforcement has remained influential because of its emphasis on baseline assessments of response hierarchies, its encouragment of novel research involving advance predictions about reinforcement value, and its common-sense appeal. Every parent knows that highly preferred activities, such as opportunities for children to play outside or watch television, constitute the most effective rewards for completion of less welcome behaviors, such as cleaning up rooms or eating vegetables.

Related to Premack's account is the response-deprivation theory of Timberlake and Allison (1974; see also Timberlake's 1980 molar equilibrium model of learned performance). This approach is based explicitly on the notion that instrumental performance springs from resolution of a conflict between the freely occurring (baseline) behaviors of subjects and the constraints imposed by a particular contingency between responses. In a typical experiment within this framework, after determining stable response baselines (above, p. 68), the experimenter arranges that if one response is performed at only its baseline level, the other response will not reach its own baseline level. The subject is said to be deprived of the latter (contingent) response, and the former (instrumental) response normally increases above its baseline level. The fundamental principle of response-deprivation theory is that any response can serve as a reinforcer if the contingency schedule deprives the subject of the response.

Therefore, unlike Premack's theory (and contrary to most people's intuitions), Timberlake and Allison's account predicts that a less probable response can reinforce a more probable one. Studies have yielded outcomes of this kind (Timberlake, 1980, pp. 30–33). For example, Konarski (1979) and Konarski, Johnson, Crowell, and Whitman (1980) found that, under appropri-

ate response-deprivation conditions, children increased their amount of coloring behavior in order to engage in the lower probability response of solving math problems.

Prominent contemporary developments along related lines involve the testing of particular quantitative models that scale the value of different behaviors in various ways and take into account certain limitations on action. Some of these models represent explicit attempts to integrate behavioral accounts and principles with theories and concepts used by economists analyzing supply, demand, utility, income, leisure, and so forth (see Allison, 1979, 1981, 1983; Hursh, 1980; Lea, 1978; Rachlin, Battalio, Kagel, & Green, 1981; and Staddon, 1980). Rewards are viewed as economic commodities. These approaches are basically theories of asymptotic performance, not of original associative learning. Williams (Chapter 3, this volume) assesses these models, especially in relation to competing interpretations of Herrnstein's matching law. The accounts have been profitably applied to foraging in wild animals, predatory and mating strategies studied by ethologists, and token economies.

PERCEPTION-CENTERED "COGNITIVE" THEORIES
Some writers (e.g., Bindra, 1976, 1978; Moore, 1973) believe that instrumental conditioning can best be understood in terms of the learning of relations between stimuli, a view that combines Pavlovian and Tolmanian themes. Besides eliciting conventional CRs involving autonomic and isolated skeletal reflexes, predictive Pavlovian CSs also evoke directed approach and withdrawal movements of the whole organism, as described in discussions of autoshaping. Such responses are typical actions studied in instrumental conditioning, which ordinarily involves localized areas or objects (maze units, levers, keys) to traverse or contact, consistent goal sites, and spatial stimuli that bear an unvarying relation to each other. Tolman believed that a rat in a maze learns about such relations and sites and that these representations (cognitive maps: see Menzel, 1978, and Olton, 1979) underlie emergence of the correct response when reward is available. This view puts the burden of explaining instrumental behavior on the correlation between certain external stimuli and the reinforcer, rather than on the correlation between certain responses and the reinforcer. The Pavlovian contingencies embedded in instrumental

tasks evoke movements toward or away from CSs.

However well this kind of account may apply in many standard arrangements (see Dickinson & Mackintosh, 1978, and Mackintosh & Dickinson, 1979), it is hard pressed to handle, say, both the increased and decreased CRs obtainable during operant conditioning of autonomic responses (biofeedback; see Hearst, 1975a, and Miller, 1969), the facilitation of undirected skeletal behaviors (wheel running, grooming), and the learning of precise motor skills. For these reasons, new approaches to instrumental conditioning that focus on learning of specific response-reinforcer relations have received more attention and amplification.

Along these lines, Dickinson (1980b) and Mackintosh and Dickinson (1979) have pursued implications of the view that representations of responses are directly associated with representations of the reinforcer in successful instrumental learning—unlike the S-R theories outlined earlier. This approach assumes close parallels between the laws of Pavlovian and instrumental conditioning; actions are associated with USs in about the same way as CSs are linked with USs. Several experiments have shown that (1) different behavior patterns (e.g., washing versus scratching, high versus low response rates) can serve as effective positive and negative cues in discrimination learning situations, and (2) overshadowing, blocking, and relative validity-salience effects occur when a response replaces an external CS in standard designs for such phenomena (pp. 41–42). Such findings suggest that responses can indeed be conceptualized as potential predictive signals, in the modern parlance of Pavlovian conditioning. However, empirical support for this view of the circumstances producing instrumental learning is not yet impressive or easy to amass.

## Two-process Theories.[3]
One general account of the acquisition and per-

[3]Although not all writers distinguish between "two-factor" and "two-process" theories, some writers have used two-factor to identify theories that make a fundamental distinction between classical and instrumental conditioning (e.g., Konorski's or Skinner's), and two-process to identify theories that merely assume frequent and important interactions between the effects of the two conditioning procedures. Much of the later research performed in the Hull–Spence framework, involving incentive motivation and fractional anticipatory goal responses, invokes two-process theory by this criterion, as does Amsel's analysis of the drive-versus-cue features of incentives (see Amsel, 1967).

sistence of instrumental behavior assumes the existence and interaction of two distinct kinds of associative processes. Anticipated in many ways by Miller and Konorski (1928), Schlosberg (1937), and Skinner (1938), it was Mowrer (1947) who offered the first well-developed treatment based on the notion that Pavlovian conditioning is fundamentally different from but still underlies instrumental conditioning. Mowrer argued that Pavlovian CRs provide the motivation or "problem" solved by the instrumental reaction. In other words, emotional states established by Pavlovian conditioning mediate instrumental responses.

This approach has been most extensively applied to avoidance learning and punishment. Previously the nature of the reinforcement for successful avoidance behavior had appeared elusive—because nothing followed a correct response—and the motivation sustaining the behavior also seemed unclear. Mowrer proposed that, early in training, the general situation or the discrete CS correlated with shock comes to evoke fear responses via Pavlovian processes (CER conditioning, as we would call it today). This conditioned fear state supplies the basic motivation that is diminished or removed by the avoidance response. Thus fear reduction or termination provides the reinforcement for making the instrumental response. Furthermore, response-produced proprioceptive stimulation can also serve as a CS. The subject's initiation of a previously punished response should evoke fear, which would lead the subject to emit other behavior. This process presumably accounts for the effects of punishment (see Dinsmoor, 1954).

There are many variants of two-process theory, and its basic theoretical features can be related to conditioned reinforcement, incentive motivation and the Hull–Spence mechanism (see Spence, 1956) of fractional anticipatory goal responses ($r_G - s_G$), as well as the expectancy notions of cognitive theories. Surveys of two-process theories can be found in Gray (1975), Mackintosh (1974), Overmier (1979c), Rescorla and Solomon (1967), and Trapold and Overmier (1972). Some comments on influential recent research pertinent to modern two-process theory seem necessary to update the matter.

Rescorla and Solomon (1967) proposed that the laws of Pavlovian conditioning are "probably the laws of emotional conditioning or laws of acquired drive states" and these states "can serve either as motivators or reinforcers of instrumental responses" (p. 172). If Pavlovian CRs do instigate or reinforce instrumental behavior, then concurrent measures of the two presumed types of behavior—for example, records of salivary CRs during operant conditioning of lever pressing for food, or of fear CRs (heart rate, respiration) during instrumental avoidance learning—should reveal close correspondences between the acquisition curves for each type and between the sequences in which they appear on a given trial after acquisition is complete.

Evidence is inconsistent on these points (see Overmier, 1979c; and Rescorla & Solomon, 1967). Sometimes autonomic CRs reliably precede the instrumental response on each trial, sometimes the opposite effect occurs, and sometimes no reliable sequence is observed. In several experiments autonomic CRs were acquired first and then the instrumental response, but in other studies the outcome was the reverse. Prevention or blockage of peripheral autonomic (fear) responses by means of surgery or drugs does not have an important effect on avoidance performance. Thus there is no strong empirical support for the notion that some peripheral (Pavlovian) CR is necessary for the maintenance or guidance of ongoing operant behavior.

In any case, technical and logical problems plague concurrent-measurement studies of this kind. Separation of different emotional states on the basis of autonomic indexes is virtually impossible. Skeletal instrumental behaviors can themselves affect autonomic measures directly, for example, heart rate. Attempts to determine whether certain autonomic responses precede or follow the operant responses that they presumably mediate are surrounded by difficulties. Different response systems have different intrinsic properties (latency, recovery time) and incommensurate units; initiation and completion of different responses are hard to specify when continuously-expressed behavior (e.g., heart rate) is compared with relatively discrete reactions (e.g., lever pressing); and in any case it may be that some unknown correlate or consequence of the measured response is really the crucial mediator. Because of the interpretative obstacles and empirical inconsistencies, tests of two-process theory via the concurrent-measurement technique have more or less ceased.

Many provocative and consistent findings have resulted from a more fruitful strategy, which assumes the existence of classically conditioned central representations as mediators but discards the use of specific autonomic or other measurable responses to detect these representations (see reviews by Overmier, 1979c; and Rescorla & Solomon, 1967). Pavlovian CSs are presented while subjects perform some instrumental response. If Pavlovian conditioned emotional states do mediate instrumental behavior, they should have predictable effects on ongoing operants. Numerous results confirm this general hypothesis. Pavlovian signals of shock facilitate avoidance behavior, whereas Pavlovian signals of safety (conditioned inhibitors of fear) depress avoidance behavior. Readers are familiar with the suppressive effect of Pavlovian shock signals on appetitive instrumental behavior (the CER phenomenon). Thus Pavlovian CSs can clearly modulate instrumental learning and performance.

But does such evidence of transfer and interaction demonstrate that the operationally distinct Pavlovian and instrumental procedures generate their effects via fundamentally different processes? Analogous experiments performed within a single category would reveal that either two Pavlovian or two instrumental responses also interact with each other. The postulation of different processes seems justifiable only if different principles, findings, or mechanisms are shown to underlie instances of Pavlovian and instrumental conditioning. The literature on this point, which still divides learning theorists, was reviewed by Hearst (1975a), who concluded that no proposed difference convincingly distinguishes the two types of conditioning: learning of visceral-glandular (autonomic-involuntary) versus skeletal (somatic-voluntary) reactions; arbitrariness of the relation between CR and reinforcer; "eliciting" CSs versus "occasion-setting" cues; kinds of effective reinforcers and drives; general laws and phenomena. As noted above, both procedures yield extinction, spontaneous recovery, stimulus generalization and discrimination, blocking and overshadowing, contrast and induction, conditioned inhibition, disinhibition, and so forth. Miller and Balaz (1981) and Overmier (1979c) agreed basically with Hearst's conclusions. However, Overmier maintained that the apparent necessity of an intact neocortex for instrumental though not for classical conditioning offers some solid support for two-process theories. In rebuttal of Overmier's point, Ralph Miller (personal communication, 1983) argued that ultimately there is some neural localization of all behavior. Arm movements use different circuits from leg movements, but this does not mean they necessarily obey different principles of learning.

### Content of Learning or Association

The matter of what is learned during instrumental conditioning has been anticipated in the foregoing discussions of the necessary and sufficient circumstances presumed to govern it. Just as for Pavlovian conditioning, the student of learning wants to determine (1) which of the explicit events occurring during instrumental conditioning are associated with each other, and (2) which features, dimensions, or aspects of these individual events exert primary control (that is, are strongly encoded by the subject). Although much effort has been expended on questions of whether learning is basically S-S, S-R, R-S, or some combination of these possibilities, no strong overall conclusions exist. Therefore, the value of surveying some significant methods and results is largely heuristic—to inform the reader of the reasoning behind certain kinds of experimental designs. The techniques correspond in some important ways to those described earlier for studying what is learned in Pavlovian conditioning.

Some procedures for analyzing the content of instrumental learning expose subjects to different experiences before original instrumental training, whereas others compare the efficiency of original learning under different conditions. A third kind of procedure involves experimental manipulations after instrumental training for a particular reinforcer; these changes may involve (1) the type or value of the reinforcer or of stimuli paired with it or (2) the availability of the original response. This last technique, entailing postconditioning modification of elements of the original learning situation, has been the most popular approach.

Latent-learning studies (see above p. 75, and Rashotte, 1979b) supply one example of the first method. In the successful experiments subjects that are initially allowed to explore a maze without receiving any apparent reinforcement —owing either to the absence of, say, food or water or to prior satiation of subjects for any available reinforcers—display good instrumental performance as soon as reward is introduced in the goal box and they are appropriately motivated. Preexposed subjects of this kind may do as well as subjects that have received reward on every previous trial. The classic S-S theorists used latent learning as evidence that the formation of associations among various environmental stimuli is the main basis for instrumental learning. They considered neither reward nor the actual emission of the correct sequence of responses a crucial ingredient. Besides the issue of learning, Timberlake (1983b) has argued that reward is not even necessary for good performance by rats in mazelike environments.

Another variant of the first general technique, originally suggested by Thorndike, involves preliminary reinforced sessions in which rats are transported through a maze in a little basket, trolley, or raft. Here, too, the correct set of responses is not made before placement in the standard instrumental situation. Nevertheless, subjects with such prior experience often run or swim through the maze efficiently when they are later required to do so (see Dodwell & Bessant, 1960; Gleitman, 1955; and McNamara, Long, & Wike, 1956).

An analogous overall design is shown in studies of perceptual learning (above p. 12) and learning by observation of proficient subjects (vicarious reinforcement: see Bandura, 1977; Chance, 1979; and Mackintosh, 1974, pp. 200–202, for relevant studies and critical comments). The general findings, when positive, have also been used to argue that S-R associations are not the basis of instrumental learning.

The second major technique for examining the contents of instrumental learning involves variation of the original training itself. A well-known example compared place with response learning (Tolman, Ritchie, & Kalish, 1946, 1947). Can subjects learn more easily where the reinforcer is located than what response (e.g., a left or right turn) is required to reach it? A variety of ingeniously designed mazes were employed to examine this possibility (see Olton, 1979). Tolman and his colleagues concluded that forming associations between environmental stimuli (cognitive maps) is easier than attaching specific responses to particular stimuli. However, in an important paper Restle (1957) demonstrated that the results depend on the relative salience of place and response cues in different tasks. He also presented a mathematical model whose predictions about relative learning rates were widely confirmed.

The final technique for analyzing the content

of instrumental learning provides all subjects with the same original instrumental training. Then either the reinforcer or the required response is changed in some way. From the effects of these manipulations the experimenter attempts to infer which features of the original arrangement have been encoded by the subject and have formed elements of associative connections.

Tinklepaugh's (1928) famous study was one of the first of this type, but similar findings have often been obtained. While a well-trained monkey watched, a piece of banana was concealed under a particular container. A few seconds later, the monkey was permitted to make its choice of containers. On crucial test trials, however, a lettuce leaf was secretly substituted for the banana during the delay interval. After lifting the container and finding the lettuce, the subject exhibited disruption, surprise, and searching behavior. Lettuce was an acceptable but less preferred food, so that the experiment approximates the paradigm used later to explore successive negative contrast (above, p. 81). The immediate change in its behavior was indisputable evidence that the subject had encoded some representation of the reinforcer, just as perception-centered expectancy theories predict. Although early simplistic versions of S-R theory could not handle such a result easily—because they viewed the reinforcer as a mere catalyst in strengthening S-R bonds—the theories of neo-Hullians like Spence and Amsel incorporated and developed, more than Hull (1943) did, the idea that subjects anticipate particular consequences of responses.

A useful variant of this third technique—one that does not confound shifts in the nature of the reinforcer with concurrent measurement of the instrumental response—entails a postconditioning change in the value of the reinforcer or reinforcer-associated stimuli during a phase in which the instrumental response is itself not possible. Such experiments have often been called studies of inference or reasoning (see Jenkins, 1979). After an animal has learned that, in situation A, performing response X will lead to reinforcer Y, it experiences an altered Y (that is, Y') without the opportunity to perform X. If, when returned to A, the animal immediately shows a change in the likelihood of X that conforms to the change from Y to Y', it has demonstrated an appropriate inference. A positive outcome indicates that the subject encoded a representation of Y during original training.

Examples of such experiments involve training a rat to run to food located in a distinctive goal box, and then placing it directly in that goal box without reward (latent extinction), or with a larger or smaller reward or some kind of punishment. During a subsequent test the animal is returned to the start box and its speed or choice behavior is measured. Although not always successful in demonstrating complex inferences, the relevant studies provide reasonable evidence that stimuli associated with instrumental rewards are encoded by subjects and guide their performance (see Mackintosh, 1974, and Rescorla & Holland, 1982).

Some recent experiments have employed inference-type designs that involve actual changes in the value of the reinforcer rather than cues associated with it. For instance, Adams and Dickinson (1981) and Chen and Amsel (1980) found that instrumental behavior for a particular reinforcer is weakened by later, separate training in which the reinforcer is paired with a poison. However, other experiments employing this taste-aversion procedure have yielded negative results (see Rescorla & Holland, 1982). Moreover, attempts to change the value of a reinforcer by satiating the subject for it frequently lead to surprisingly little change during tests of established instrumental responding. Consequently, Adams and Dickinson proposed that instrumental behavior may often become automatized and relatively independent of its usual reinforcing supports. This is basically a form of S-R explanation, like Rescorla's (1977) suggestion that (1) much of the motivation for instrumental behavior is based on second-order Pavlovian conditioning with the goal object as the US, and (2) such second-order CSs are often insensitive to changes in the US. Rescorla and Holland (1982) offer additional alternative explanations of certain aspects of these results.

One final type of post-conditioning change removes the availability of the old instrumental response but offers an opportunity for the subject to perform some functionally equivalent behavior. Rats trained to swim through a maze performed almost perfectly when the water was removed and they had to run to the goal (MacFarlane, 1930). In an experiment by Lashley and Ball (1929), rats that received cerebellar lesions after learning to run correctly through a maze staggered and stumbled through it without error even though they were physically able only to make small circling movements. These studies are variants of the experiments on place versus response learning discussed above, and the results consistently dispute the notion that animals acquire relatively fixed, stereotyped movements during spatial learning. Tolman stressed the flexibility of response in the face of changed circumstances that occurs in many such situations.

Thus the various techniques for assessing the content of instrumental learning and the nature of encoded stimulus, response, and reinforcer representations have yielded interesting but not conclusive overall results. A safe statement is that organisms are capable of forming representations of all these potential associative elements. Under different, as yet unspecified, circumstances they can associate each with any of the other two. The complexity and flexibility of the associative networks acquired during instrumental learning have probably not yet been fully recognized. Refinement of the techniques described above, as well as the development of new ones, should foster further analysis of these provocative possibilities.

### From Learning to Performance

In instrumental conditioning the experimenter supposedly selects some rather arbitrary response, follows it by reinforcement, and measures changes in its magnitude, latency, or probability. Is it useful to distinguish between learning and performance in such arrangements? Skinner commented that the learning-performance distinction might have been useful in early work on learning because performance changes were somewhat erratic; however, "improved techniques have revealed an orderly relation between performance and contingencies and have eliminated the need to appeal to a separate inner learning process" (1974, p. 66). For Skinner, learning merely involves changes in the subject's performance, as a result of reinforcement.

This optimistic view about the direct mapping of learning into performance is open to challenge, however. Years ago, Tolman (cited in Premack, 1965, p. 164) remarked that standard operant conditioning arrangements and procedures are unsuitable for studying general laws of learning because Skinner's barren situations make acquisition occur artificially fast. Further-

more, both preliminary magazine training and shaping of the target response are neglected by students of operant conditioning who do not stress them as explicit, important components of the basic conditions for learning. What happens after the first or second reinforced instance of the final target response, Tolman would argue, involves changes in performance. Skinnerians have emphasized the investigation of variables affecting steady-state performance, rather than transitions from one state to another—which would include those that occur during learning. Consequently, Skinnerians concentrate on studying such factors as reinforcement schedule, amount and delay of reinforcement, availability of other responses, and so on, and determine how they affect an already well-learned response like key pecking or lever pressing.

Regardless of this type of theoretical disagreement (e.g., Hull was closer to Tolman than to Skinner in his views on the learning-performance distinction), research indicates that the form, frequency, and stereotypy of instrumental behavior depend on various features of the conditioning procedure and situation. The same target response may display different molecular properties depending on aspects of the cue and reinforcer; and the occurrence of other (often ignored) behaviors is also affected by such factors. An adequate theory of instrumental learning must eventually explain why the imposition of a particular response-reinforcer relation produces certain specific changes in both the target response and other reactions.

Although lacking a broad theoretical base, a number of experiments have suggested some relevant variables to be considered in any global theory. (For a discussion of how contemporary perception-centered, cognitive approaches to instrumental learning might handle the learning-performance issue, see Mackintosh and Dickinson, 1979.) The topography and stereotypy of instrumental behavior are controlled by the type of prevailing motivational state, the presence of appropriate stimulus supports, and the kind of reinforcer anticipated in the situation. The form of operant keypecking in pigeons depends on whether subjects are thirsty and pecking for water reward or are hungry and pecking for food reward (Wolin, 1968; see also Hearst & Jenkins, 1974). Pearce, Colwill, and Hall (1978) obtained unusually high levels of instrumental scratching in rats that had to wear a tight collar. The use of appetitive versus aversive reinforcers affects the conditionability and topography of lever-pressing behavior in rats, presumably because of complex interactions with active or passive responses evoked by the US or displayed in anticipation of it (Bolles, 1970). Breland and Breland's descriptions of misbehavior (above, p. 80) provide analogous instances.

Therefore, prior knowledge of the effects produced on various baseline behavioral patterns by mere presentations of USs—in the absence of any instrumental contingency—is of value in predicting the performance changes that characterize any case of instrumental learning. Fortunately, such detailed observational-ethological analysis has become more frequent in recent years, as species-specific reactions and biological aspects of learning increasingly engage the concern of students of conditioning (see Marler & Terrace, 1984). This type of research has the added advantage of paving the way for an integration of the phenomena obtained in studies of habituation, sensitization, and Pavlovian conditioning with the phenomena of instrumental learning—a goal toward which this chapter has been organized.

Based on the kinds of facts and principles summarized here, as well as the new knowledge that is constantly being acquired now or will be gained in coming years, future research and theory on the psychology of conditioning and learning should progress in closer alliance with work performed by biologists, cognitive scientists, and psychologists in other fields. As noted in the introduction to this chapter, animal learning mechanisms are not so simple after all, and insularity, overspecialization, and a focus on relatively abstract problems and paradigms will not enable us to meet the challenges presented by the complexities. Today one can detect a growing rapprochement and exchange among workers inside and outside our particular field—a promising signal for important advances.

# REFERENCES

Adams, C. & Dickinson, A. (1981). Actions and habits: Variations in associative representations during instrumental learning. In N.E. Spear & R.R. Miller (Eds.), *Information processing in animals: Memory mechanisms* (pp. 143–165). Hillsdale, NJ: Erlbaum.

Allison, J. (1979). Demand economics and experimental psychology. *Behavioral Science, 24,* 403–415.

Allison, J. (1981). Economics and operant conditioning. In P. Harzem & M.D. Zeiler (Eds.), *Advances in analysis of behavior: Vol. 2. Predictability, correlation, and contiguity* (pp. 321–353). New York: Wiley.

Allison, J. (1983). *Behavioral economics.* New York: Praeger.

Amsel, A. (1967). Partial reinforcement effects on vigor and persistence: Advances in frustration theory derived from a variety of within-subjects experiments. In K.W. Spence & J.T. Spence (Eds.), *The psychology of learning and motivation: Vol. 1.* (pp. 1–65). New York: Academic Press.

Amsel, A. (1972a). Behavioral habituation, counter-conditioning, and a general theory of persistence. In A.H. Black & W.F. Prokasy (Eds.), *Classical conditioning II: Current research and theory* (pp. 409–426). New York: Appleton-Century-Crofts.

Amsel, A. (1972b). Inhibition and mediation in classical, Pavlovian and instrumental conditioning. In R.A. Boakes & M.S. Halliday (Eds.), *Inhibition and learning* (pp. 275–299). New York: Academic Press.

Amsel, A., Hug, J.J., & Surridge, T. (1969). Subject-to-subject trial sequence, odor trails, and patterning at 24-h ITI. *Psychonomic Science, 15,* 119–120.

Amsel, A. & Stanton, M. (1980). Ontogeny and phylogeny of paradoxical reward effects. In J.S. Rosenblatt, R.A. Hinde, C. Beer, & M.C. Busnel (Eds.), *Advances in the study of behavior: Vol. 11* (pp. 227–274). New York: Academic Press.

Anderson, J.R. & Bower, G.H. (1973). *Human associative memory.* New York: Wiley/Winston.

Anrep, G.V. (1920). Pitch discrimination in the dog. *Journal of Physiology, 53,* 367–385.

Azrin, N.H. & Holz, W.C. (1966). Punishment. In W.K. Honig (Ed.), *Operant behavior: Areas of research and application* (pp. 380–447). New York: Appleton-Century-Crofts.

Baer, D.M. (1962). Laboratory control of thumbsucking by withdrawal and re-presentation of reinforcement. *Journal of the Experimental Analysis of Behavior, 5,* 525–528.

Baker, A.G. & Mackintosh, N.J. (1979). Preexposure to the CS alone, US alone, or CS and US uncorrelated: Latent inhibition, blocking by context, or learned irrelevance? *Learning and Motivation, 10,* 278–294.

Baker, T.W. (1968). Properties of compound conditioned stimuli and their components. *Psychological Bulletin, 70,* 611–625.

Balsam, P.D. & Tomie, A. (Eds.). (1985). *Context and learning.* Hillsdale, NJ: Erlbaum.

Bandura, A. (1977). *Social learning theory*. Englewood Cliffs, NJ: Prentice-Hall.

Barber, L. (1980). *The heyday of natural history*. New York: Doubleday.

Barker, L.M. (1976). CS duration, amount, and concentration effects in conditioning taste aversions. *Learning and Motivation, 7*, 265–273.

Barker, L.M., Best, M.R., & Domjan, M. (Eds.). (1977). *Learning mechanisms in food selection*. Waco, TX: Baylor University Press.

Bauer, R.H. (1972). The effects of CS and US intensity on shuttlebox avoidance. *Psychonomic Science, 27*, 266–268.

Berlyne, D.E. (1960). *Conflict, arousal, and curiosity*. New York: McGraw-Hill.

Berlyne, D.E. (1967). Arousal and reinforcement. In D. Levine (Ed.), *Nebraska Symposium on Motivation: Vol. 15* (pp. 1–110). Lincoln: University of Nebraska Press.

Bernard, C. (1957). *An introduction to the study of experimental medicine*. New York: Dover. (Original work published 1865.)

Bindra, D. (1976). *A theory of intelligent behavior*. New York: Wiley.

Bindra, D. (1978). How adaptive behavior is produced: A perceptual-motivational alternative to response-reinforcement. *Behavioral and Brain Sciences, 1*, 41–91.

Bitterman, M.E. (1975). The comparative analysis of learning: Are the laws of learning the same in all animals? *Science, 188*, 699–709.

Bitterman, M.E. (1979). Historical introduction. In M.E. Bitterman, V.M. LoLordo, J.B. Overmier, & M.E. Rashotte, *Animal learning: Survey and analysis* (pp. 1–23). New York: Plenum Press.

Bitterman, M.E., LoLordo, V.M., Overmier, J.B., & Rashotte, M.E. (1979). *Animal learning: Survey and analysis*. New York: Plenum Press.

Black, A.H. & Prokasy, W.F. (Eds.). (1972). *Classical conditioning II: Current research and theory*. New York: Appleton-Century-Crofts.

Black, R.W. (1968). Shifts in magnitude of reward and contrast effects in instrumental and selective learning: A reinterpretation. *Psychological Review, 75*, 114–126.

Black, R.W. (1976). Reward variables in instrumental conditioning: A theory. In G.H. Bower (Ed.), *The psychology of learning and motivation: Vol. 10* (pp. 199–244). New York: Academic Press.

Blackman, D. (1977). Conditioned suppression and the effects of classical conditioning on operant behavior. In W.K. Honig & J.E.R. Staddon (Eds.), *Handbook of operant behavior* (pp. 340–363). Englewood Cliffs, NJ: Prentice-Hall.

Blough, D.S. (1975). Steady-state data and a quantitative model of operant generalization and discrimination. *Journal of Experimental Psychology: Animal Behavior Processes, 1*, 3–21.

Boakes, R.A. (1973). Response decrements produced by extinction and by response-independent reinforcement. *Journal of the Experimental Analysis of Behavior, 19*, 293–302.

Boakes, R.A. (1984). *From Darwin to behaviorism: Psychology and the minds of animals*. Cambridge: Cambridge University Press.

Boakes, R.A. & Halliday, M.S. (Eds.). (1972). *Inhibition and learning*. New York: Academic Press.

Boice, R. & Denny, M.R. (1965). The conditioned licking response in rats as a function of the CS-UCS interval. *Psychonomic Science, 3*, 93–94.

Bolles, R.C. (1970). Species-specific defense reactions and avoidance learning. *Psychological Review, 77*, 32–48.

Bolles, R.C. (1975). Learning, motivation, and cognition. In W.K. Estes (Ed.), *Handbook of learning and cognitive processes: Vol. 1. Introduction to concepts and issues* (pp. 249–280). Hillsdale, NJ: Erlbaum.

Bottjer, S.W. (1982). Conditioned approach and withdrawal behavior in pigeons: Effects of a novel extraneous stimulus during acquisition and extinction. *Learning and Motivation, 13*, 44–67.

Bower, G.H. & Hilgard, E.R. (1981). *Theories of learning* (5th ed.). Englewood Cliffs, NJ: Prentice-Hall.

Breland, K. & Breland, M. (1961). The misbehavior of organisms. *American Psychologist, 16*, 681–684.

Breland, K. & Breland, M. (1966). *Animal behavior*. New York: Macmillan.

Brimer, C.J. (1972). Disinhibition of an operant response. In R.A. Boakes & M.S. Halliday (Eds.). *Inhibition and learning* (pp. 205–227). New York: Academic Press.

Brogden, W.J. (1939). Sensory pre-conditioning. *Journal of Experimental Psychology, 25*, 323–332.

Brogden, W.J. (1951). Animal studies of learning. In S.S. Stevens (Ed.), *Handbook of experimental psychology* (pp. 568–612). New York: Wiley.

Brogden, W.J. (1962). Contiguous conditioning. *Journal of Experimental Psychology, 64*, 172–176.

Brown, J.S. & Cunningham, C.L. (1981). The paradox of persisting self-punitive behavior. *Neuroscience and Biobehavioral Reviews, 5*, 343–354.

Brown, P.L. & Jenkins, H.M. (1968). Auto-shaping of the pigeon's key-peck. *Journal of the Experimental Analysis of Behavior, 11*, 1–8.

Brush, F.R. (Ed.). (1971). *Aversive conditioning and learning*. New York: Academic Press.

Burstein, K.R. (1973). On the distinction between conditioning and pseudoconditioning. *Psychophysiology, 10*, 61–66.

Butler, R.A. (1957). The effect of deprivation of visual incentives on visual exploration motivation in monkeys. *Journal of Comparative and Physiological Psychology, 50,* 177–179.

Bykov, K.M. (1959). *The cerebral cortex and the internal organs.* Moscow: Foreign Languages Publishing House.

Camp, D.S., Raymond, G.A., & Church, R.M. (1967). Temporal relationship between response and punishment. *Journal of Experimental Psychology, 74,* 114–123.

Campbell, B.A. & Church, R.M. (Eds.). (1969). *Punishment and aversive behavior.* New York: Appleton-Century-Crofts.

Cannon, D.S., Berman, R.F., Baker, T.B., & Atkinson, C.A. (1975). Effect of preconditioning unconditioned stimulus experience on learned taste aversions. *Journal of Experimental Psychology: Animal Behavior Processes, 1,* 270–284.

Capaldi, E.D. & Hovancik, J.R. (1973). Effects of previous body weight level on rats' straight-alley performance. *Journal of Experimental Psychology, 97,* 93–97.

Capaldi, E.J. (1966). Partial reinforcement: A hypothesis of sequential effects. *Psychological Review, 73,* 459–477.

Capaldi, E.J. (1967). A sequential hypothesis of instrumental learning. In K.W. Spence & J.T. Spence (Eds.), *The psychology of learning and motivation: Vol. 1* (pp. 67–156). New York: Academic Press.

Capaldi, E.J. (1971). Memory and learning: A sequential viewpoint. In W.K. Honig & P.H.R. James (Eds.), *Animal memory* (pp. 111–154). New York: Academic Press.

Capaldi, E.J. (1978). Effects of schedule and delay of reinforcement on acquisition speed. *Animal Learning and Behavior, 6,* 330–334.

Carlton, P.L. (1963). Cholinergic mechanisms in the control of behavior by the brain. *Psychological Review, 70,* 19–39.

Carlton, P.L. (1969). Brain-acetylcholine and inhibition. In J.T. Tapp (Ed.), *Reinforcement and behavior* (pp. 286–327). New York: Academic Press.

Castellucci, V. & Kandel, E.R. (1976). An invertebrate system for the cellular study of habituation and sensitization. In T. Tighe & R.N. Leaton (Eds.), *Habituation: Perspectives from child development, animal behavior, and neurophysiology* (pp. 1–47). Hillsdale, NJ: Erlbaum.

Catania, A.C. (1979). *Learning.* Englewood Cliffs, NJ: Prentice-Hall.

Catania, A.C. & Keller, K.J. (1981). Contingency, contiguity, correlation, and the concept of causation. In P. Harzem & M.D. Zeiler (Eds.), *Advances in analysis of behavior: Vol. 2. Predictability, corre-lation, and contiguity* (pp. 125–167). New York: Wiley.

Catania, A.C. & Reynolds, G.S. (1968). A quantitative analysis of the responding maintained by interval schedules of reinforcement. *Journal of the Experimental Analysis of Behavior, 11,* 327–383.

Champion, R.A. (1962). Stimulus-intensity effects in response evocation. *Psychological Review, 69,* 428–449.

Chance, P. (1979). *Learning and behavior.* Belmont, CA: Wadsworth.

Channell, S. & Hall, G. (1981). Facilitation and retardation of discrimination learning after exposure to the stimuli. *Journal of Experimental Psychology: Animal Behavior Processes, 7,* 437–446.

Chen, J. & Amsel, A. (1980). Recall (versus recognition) of taste and immunization against aversive taste anticipations based on illness. *Science, 209,* 831–833.

Church, R.M. (1964). Systematic effect of random error in the yoked control design. *Psychological Bulletin, 62,* 122–131.

Cofer, C.N. (1979). Human learning and memory. In E. Hearst (Ed.), *The first century of experimental psychology* (pp. 323–369). Hillsdale, NJ: Erlbaum.

Cofer, C.N. & Appley, M.H. (1964). *Motivation: Theory and research.* New York: Wiley.

Cohen, J. (1969). *Operant behavior and operant conditioning.* Chicago: Rand McNally.

Corning, W.C., Dyal, J.A., & Willows, A.O.D. (Eds.). (1973a). *Invertebrate learning: Vol. 1. Protozoans through annelids.* New York: Plenum Press.

Corning, W.C., Dyal, J.A., & Willows, A.O.D. (Eds.). (1973b). *Invertebrate learning: Vol. 2. Arthropods and gastropod mollusks.* New York: Plenum Press.

Corning, W.C., Dyal, J.A., & Willows, A.O.D. (Eds.). (1975). *Invertebrate learning: Vol. 3. Cephalopods and echinoderms.* New York: Plenum Press.

Cowey, A. (1968). Discrimination. In L. Weiskrantz (Ed.), *Analysis of behavioral change* (pp. 189–238). New York: Harper & Row.

Crowell, C.R. & Anderson, D.C. (1972). Variations in intensity, interstimulus interval, and interval between preconditioning CS exposures and conditioning with rats. *Journal of Comparative and Physiological Psychology, 79,* 291–298.

Daly, H.B. (1974). Reinforcing properties of escape from frustration aroused in various learning situations. In G.H. Bower (Ed.), *The psychology of learning and motivation: Vol. 8* (pp. 187–231). New York: Academic Press.

Daly, H.B. & Daly, J.T. (1982). A mathematical model of reward and aversive nonreward: Its application in over 30 appetitive learning situations. *Journal of Experimental Psychology: General, 111,* 441–480.

D'Amato, M.R. (1969). Instrumental conditioning. In M.H. Marx (Ed.), *Learning: Processes* (pp. 35–118). New York: Macmillan.

D'Amato, M.R., Safarjan, W.R., & Salmon, D. (1981). Long-delay conditioning and instrumental learning: Some new findings. In N.E. Spear & R.R. Miller (Eds.), *Information processing in animals: Memory mechanisms* (pp. 113–142). Hillsdale, NJ: Erlbaum.

Darwin, C. (1871). *The descent of man*. London: John Murray.

Davenport, J.W. (1956). *Choice behavior as a function of drive strength and rate of learning*. Unpublished doctoral dissertation, State University of Iowa.

Davey, G. (1981). *Animal learning and conditioning*. Baltimore: University Park Press.

Davis, H. (1968). Conditioned suppression: A survey of the literature. *Psychonomic Monograph Supplements, 2*, (14, Whole No. 30), 283–291.

Davis, M. (1970). Effects of interstimulus interval length and variability on startle-response habituation in the rat. *Journal of Comparative and Physiological Psychology, 72*, 177–192.

Davis, M. (1972). Differential retention of sensitization and habituation of the startle response in the rat. *Journal of Comparative and Physiological Psychology, 78*, 260–267.

Davis, M. (1974). Sensitization of the rat startle response by noise. *Journal of Comparative and Physiological Psychology, 87*, 571–581.

Davis, M. & Wagner, A.R. (1968). Startle responsiveness after habituation to different intensities of tone. *Psychonomic Science, 12*, 337–338.

de Villiers, P. (1977). Choice in concurrent schedules and a quantitative formulation of the law of effect. In W.K. Honig & J.E.R. Staddon (Eds.), *Handbook of operant behavior* (pp. 233–287). Englewood Cliffs, NJ: Prentice-Hall.

Diamond, S. (Ed.). (1974). *The roots of psychology: A source book in the history of ideas*. New York: Basic Books.

Dickinson, A. (1980a). The US-omission effect and static-cue conditioning: A comment on Kremer, Specht, and Allen. *Animal Learning and Behavior, 8*, 686–688.

Dickinson, A. (1980b). *Contemporary animal learning theory*. Cambridge: Cambridge University Press.

Dickinson, A. & Boakes, R.A. (Eds.). (1979). *Mechanisms of learning and motivation: A memorial volume to Jerzy Konorski*. Hillsdale, NJ: Erlbaum.

Dickinson, A. & Dearing, M.F. (1979). Appetitive-aversive interactions and inhibitory processes. In A. Dickinson & R.A. Boakes (Eds.), *Mechanisms of learning and motivation: A memorial volume to Jerzy Konorski* (pp. 203–231). Hillsdale, NJ: Erlbaum.

Dickinson, A., Hall, G., & Mackintosh, N.J. (1976). Surprise and the attentuation of blocking. *Journal of Experimental Psychology: Animal Behavior Processes, 2*, 313–322.

Dickinson, A. & Mackintosh, N.J. (1978). Classical conditioning in animals. *Annual Review of Psychology, 29*, 587–612.

Dinsmoor, J.A. (1954). Punishment: I. The avoidance hypothesis. *Psychological Review, 61*, 34–46.

Dinsmoor, J.A. (1960). Studies of abnormal behavior in animals. In R.H. Waters, D.A. Rethlingshafer, & W.E. Caldwell (Eds.), *Principles of comparative psychology* (pp. 289–324). New York: McGraw-Hill.

Dinsmoor, J.A. (1977). Escape, avoidance, punishment: Where do we stand? *Journal of the Experimental Analysis of Behavior, 28*, 83–95.

Dinsmoor, J.A. & Sears, G.W. (1973). Control of avoidance by a response-produced stimulus. *Learning and Motivation, 4*, 284–293.

Dodwell, P.C. & Bessant, D.E. (1960). Learning without swimming in a water maze. *Journal of Comparative and Physiological Psychology, 53*, 422–425.

Domjan, M. (1980). Ingestional aversion learning: Unique and general processes. In J.S. Rosenblatt, R.A. Hinde, C. Beer, & M.C. Busnel (Eds.), *Advances in the study of behavior: Vol. 11* (pp. 275–336). New York: Academic Press.

Domjan, M. (1983). Biological constraints on instrumental and classical conditioning: Implications for general process theory. In G.H. Bower (Ed.), *The psychology of learning and motivation: Vol. 17* (pp. 215–277). New York: Academic Press.

Domjan, M. & Galef, B.G. (1983). Biological constraints on instrumental and classical conditioning: Retrospect and prospect. *Animal Learning and Behavior, 11*, 151–161.

Donegan, N.H. (1981). Priming-produced facilitation or diminution of responding to a Pavlovian unconditioned stimulus. *Journal of Experimental Psychology: Animal Behavior Processes, 7*, 295–312.

Dunham, P.J. (1968). Contrasted conditions of reinforcement: A selective critique. *Psychological Bulletin, 69*, 295–315.

Dunham, P.J. (1977). The nature of reinforcing stimuli. In W.K. Honig & J.E.R. Staddon (Eds.), *Handbook of operant behavior* (pp. 98–124). Englewood Cliffs, NJ: Prentice-Hall.

Durlach, P.J. & Rescorla, R.A. (1980). Potentiation rather than overshadowing in flavor-aversion learning: An analysis in terms of within-compound associations. *Journal of Experimental Psychology: Animal Behavior Processes, 6*, 175–187.

Eikelboom, R. & Stewart, J. (1982). Conditioning of drug-induced physiological responses. *Psychological Review, 89*, 507–528.

Estes, W.K. (1956). The problem of inference from curves based on group data. *Psychological Bulletin, 53,* 134–140.

Estes, W.K. & Skinner, B.F. (1941). Some quantitative properties of anxiety. *Journal of Experimental Psychology, 29,* 390–400.

Evans, J.G.M. & Hammond, G.R. (1983). Differential generalization of habituation across contexts as a function of stimulus significance. *Animal Learning and Behavior, 11,* 431–434.

Falk, J.L. (1971). The nature and determinants of adjunctive behavior. *Physiology and Behavior, 6,* 577–588.

Falk, J.L. (1977). The origin and functions of adjunctive behavior. *Animal Learning and Behavior, 5,* 325–335.

Fantino, E. (1977). Conditioned reinforcement: Choice and information. In W.K. Honig & J.E.R. Staddon (Eds.), *Handbook of operant behavior* (pp. 313–339). Englewood Cliffs, NJ: Prentice-Hall.

Fantino, E. & Logan, C.A. (1979). *The experimental analysis of behavior: A biological perspective.* San Francisco: Freeman.

Fearing, F. (1964). *Reflex action.* New York: Hafner. (Original work published 1930. Baltimore: Williams & Wilkins.)

Ferster, C.B. & Skinner, B.F. (1957). *Schedules of reinforcement.* New York: Appleton-Century-Crofts.

Flaherty, C.F. (1982). Incentive contrast: A review of behavioral changes following shifts in reward. *Animal Learning and Behavior, 10,* 409–440.

Fowler, H. (1965). *Curiosity and exploratory behavior.* New York: Macmillan.

Fowler, H. & Miller, N.E. (1963). Facilitation and inhibition of runway performance by hind- and forepaw shock of various intensities. *Journal of Comparative and Physiological Psychology, 56,* 801–805.

Fowler, H. & Trapold, M.A. (1962). Escape performance as a function of delay of reinforcement. *Journal of Experimental Psychology, 63,* 464–467.

Fudim, O.K. (1978). Sensory preconditioning of flavors with a formalin-produced sodium need. *Journal of Experimental Psychology: Animal Behavior Processes, 4,* 276–285.

Galef, B.G. & Dalrymple, A.J. (1981). Toxicosis-based aversions to visual cues in rats: A test of the Testa and Ternes hypothesis. *Animal Learning and Behavior, 9,* 332–334.

Garcia, J. & Ervin, F.R. (1968). Gustatory-visceral and teleleceptor-cutaneous conditioning: Adaptation in internal and external milieus. *Communications in Behavioral Biology, 1,* 389–415.

Garcia, J., Ervin, F.R., & Koelling, R.A. (1966). Learning with prolonged delay of reinforcement. *Psychonomic Science, 5,* 121–122.

Garcia, J. & Koelling, R.A. (1966). The relation of cue to consequence in avoidance learning. *Psychonomic Science, 4,* 123–124.

Garcia, J. & Rusiniak, K.W. (1980). What the nose learns from the mouth. In D. Müller-Schwarze & R.M. Silverstein (Eds.), *Chemical signals* (pp. 141–156). New York: Plenum Press.

Garner, W.R., Hake, H.W., & Eriksen, C.W. (1956). Operationism and the concept of perception. *Psychological Review, 63,* 149–159.

Gibbon, J. (1981). The contingency problem in autoshaping. In C.M. Locurto, H.S. Terrace, & J. Gibbon (Eds.), *Autoshaping and conditioning theory* (pp. 285–308). New York: Academic Press.

Gibbon, J. & Balsam, P. (1981). Spreading association in time. In C.M. Locurto, H.S. Terrace, & J. Gibbon (Eds.), *Autoshaping and conditioning theory* (pp. 219–253). New York: Academic Press.

Gibson, E.J. (1969). *Principles of perceptual learning and development.* New York: Appleton-Century-Crofts.

Glanzer, M. (1953). The role of stimulus satiation in response alternation. *Journal of Experimental Psychology, 45,* 387–393.

Gleitman, H. (1955). Place learning without prior performance. *Journal of Comparative and Physiological Psychology, 48,* 77–79.

Glickman, S.E. & Schiff, B.B. (1967). A biological theory of reinforcement. *Psychological Review, 74,* 81–109.

Gollub, L. (1977). Conditioned reinforcement: Schedule effects. In W.K. Honig & J.E.R. Staddon (Eds.), *Handbook of operant behavior* (pp. 288–312). Englewood Cliffs, NJ: Prentice-Hall.

Gormezano, I. (1965). Yoked comparisons of classical and instrumental conditioning of the eyelid response; and an addendum on "voluntary responders." In W.F. Prokasy (Ed.), *Classical conditioning: A symposium* (pp. 48–70). New York: Appleton-Century-Crofts.

Gormezano, I. & Kehoe, E.J. (1975). Classical conditioning: Some methodological-conceptual issues. In W.K. Estes (Ed.), *Handbook of learning and cognitive processes: Vol. 2. Conditioning and behavior theory* (pp. 143–179). Hillsdale, NJ: Erlbaum.

Gormezano, I. & Kehoe, E.J. (1981). Classical conditioning and the law of contiguity. In P. Harzem & M.D. Zeiler (Eds.), *Advances in analysis of behavior: Vol. 2. Predictability, correlation, and contiguity* (pp. 1–45). New York: Wiley.

Gormezano, I. & Moore, J.W. (1969). Classical conditioning. In M.H. Marx (Ed.), *Learning: Processes* (pp. 121–203). London: Macmillan.

Gormezano, I. & Tait, R.W. (1976). The Pavlovian analysis of instrumental conditioning. *Pavlovian Journal of Biological Sciences, 11,* 37–55.

Gottlieb, G. (1979). Comparative psychology and ethology. In E. Hearst (Ed.), *The first century of experimental psychology* (pp. 147–173). Hillsdale, NJ: Erlbaum.

Grant, D.A., Hunter, H.G., & Patel, A.S. (1958). Spontaneous recovery of the conditioned eyelid response. *Journal of General Psychology, 59,* 135–141.

Grastyán, E. & Vereczkei, L. (1974). Effects of spatial separation of the conditioned signal from the reinforcement: A demonstration of the conditioned character of the orienting response or the orientational character of conditioning. *Behavioral Biology, 10,* 121–146.

Gray, J.A. (1965). Stimulus intensity dynamism. *Psychological Bulletin, 63,* 180–196.

Gray, J.A. (1975). *Elements of a two-process theory of learning.* New York: Academic Press.

Gray, J.A. (1980). *Ivan Pavlov.* Middlesex, England: Penguin.

Greenough, W.T. (1976). Enduring brain effects of differential experience and training. In M.R. Rosenzweig & E.L. Bennett (Eds.), *Neural mechanisms of learning and memory* (pp. 255–278). Cambridge, MA: MIT Press.

Grice, G.R. (1948). The relation of secondary reinforcement to delayed reward in visual discrimination learning. *Journal of Experimental Psychology, 38,* 1–16.

Grice, G.R. & Hunter, J.J. (1964). Stimulus intensity effects depend upon the type of experimental design. *Psychological Review, 71,* 247–256.

Groves, P.M. & Thompson, R.F. (1970). Habituation: A dual-process theory. *Psychological Review, 77,* 419–450.

Guthrie, E.R. (1935). *The psychology of learning.* New York: Harper.

Guthrie, E.R. (1952). *The psychology of learning* (rev. ed.). New York: Harper.

Guthrie, E.R. & Horton, G.P. (1946). *Cats in a puzzle box.* New York: Rinehart.

Haddad, N.F., Walkenbach, J., Preston, M., & Strong, R. (1981). Stimulus control in a simple instrumental task: The role of internal and external stimuli. *Learning and Motivation, 12,* 509–520.

Haggbloom, S.J. (1981). Blocking in successive differential conditioning: Prior acquisition of control by internal cues blocks the acquisition of control by brightness. *Learning and Motivation, 12,* 485–508.

Halgren, C.R. (1974). Latent inhibition in rats: Associative or nonassociative? *Journal of Comparative and Physiological Psychology, 86,* 74–78.

Hall, G. (1980). Exposure learning in animals. *Psychological Bulletin, 88,* 535–550.

Hall, J.F. (1976). *Classical conditioning and instrumental learning: A contemporary approach.* New York: Lippincott.

Hammond, L.J. (1980). The effect of contingency upon the appetitive conditioning of free-operant behavior. *Journal of the Experimental Analysis of Behavior, 34,* 297–304.

Harris, J.D. (1943a). Studies on nonassociative factors inherent in conditioning. *Comparative Psychology Monographs, 18* (1, Whole No. 93).

Harris, J.D. (1943b). Habituatory response decrement in the intact organism. *Psychological Bulletin, 40,* 385–422.

Hartshorne, C. (1956). The monotony-threshold in singing birds. *Auk, 73,* 176–192.

Harzem, P. & Harzem, A.L. (1981). Discrimination, inhibition, and simultaneous association of stimulus properties: A theoretical analysis of reinforcement. In P. Harzem & M.D. Zeiler (Eds.), *Advances in analysis of behavior: Vol. 2. Predictability, correlation, and contiguity* (pp. 81–124). New York: Wiley.

Harzem, P. & Zeiler, M.D. (Eds.). (1981). *Advances in analysis of behavior: Vol. 2. Predictability, correlation, and contiguity.* New York: Wiley.

Hearst, E. (1972). Some persistent problems in the analysis of conditioned inhibition. In R.A. Boakes & M.S. Halliday (Eds.), *Inhibition and learning* (pp. 5–39). New York: Academic Press.

Hearst, E. (1975a). The classical-instrumental distinction: Reflexes, voluntary behavior, and categories of associative learning. In W.K. Estes (Ed.), *Handbook of learning and cognitive processes: Vol. 2. Conditioning and behavior theory* (pp. 181–223). Hillsdale, NJ: Erlbaum.

Hearst, E. (1975b). Pavlovian conditioning and directed movements. In G.H. Bower (Ed.), *The psychology of learning and motivation: Vol. 9* (pp. 215–262). New York: Academic Press.

Hearst, E. (1979). Classical conditioning as the formation of interstimulus associations: Stimulus substitution, parasitic reinforcement, and auto-shaping. In A. Dickinson & R.A. Boakes (Eds.), *Mechanisms of learning and motivation: A memorial volume to Jerzy Konorski* (pp. 19–52). Hillsdale, NJ: Erlbaum.

Hearst, E., Besley, S., & Farthing, G.W. (1970). Inhibition and the stimulus control of operant behavior. *Journal of the Experimental Analysis of Behavior, 14,* 373–409.

Hearst, E., Bottjer, S.W., & Walker, E. (1980). Conditioned approach-withdrawal behavior and some signal-food relations in pigeons: Performance and positive versus negative "associative strength." *Bulletin of the Psychonomic Society, 16,* 183–186.

Hearst, E., Franklin, S., & Mueller, C.G. (1974). The "disinhibition" of extinguished operant behavior in pigeons: Trial-tempo shifts and novel-stimulus effects. *Animal Learning and Behavior, 2,* 229–237.

Hearst, E. & Jenkins, H.M. (1974). *Sign-tracking: The stimulus-reinforcer relation and directed action.* Austin, TX: Psychonomic Society.

Hearst, E. & Koresko, M.B. (1968). Stimulus generalization and the amount of prior training on variable-interval reinforcement. *Journal of Comparative and Physiological Psychology, 66,* 133–138.

Hebb, D.O. (1955). Drives and C. N. S. (conceptual nervous system). *Psychological Review, 62,* 243–255.

Hendry, D.P. (Ed.). (1969). *Conditioned reinforcement.* Homewood, IL: Dorsey Press.

Heth, C.D. & Rescorla, R.A. ((1973). Simultaneous and backward fear conditioning in the rat. *Journal of Comparative and Physiological Psychology, 82,* 434–443.

Hilgard, E.R. (1951). Methods and procedures in the study of learning. In S.S. Stevens (Ed.), *Handbook of experimental psychology* (pp. 517–567). New York: Wiley.

Hilgard, E.R. & Marquis, D.G. (1940). *Conditioning and learning.* New York: D. Appleton-Century.

Hill, W.F. (1978). Effects of mere exposure on preferences in nonhuman mammals. *Psychological Bulletin, 85,* 1177–1198.

Hinde, R.A. (1954). Factors governing the changes in strength of a partially inborn response, as shown by the mobbing behaviour of the chaffinch (*Fringilla coelebs*): II. The waning of the response. *Proceedings of the Royal Society* (Lond.), *B142,* 331–358.

Hinde, R.A. (1966). *Animal behavior: A synthesis of ethology and comparative psychology.* New York: McGraw-Hill.

Hinde, R.A. (1970). Behavioural habituation. In G. Horn & R.A. Hinde (Eds.), *Short-term changes in neural activity and behavior* (pp. 3–40). Cambridge: Cambridge University Press.

Hinde, R.A. & Stevenson-Hinde, J. (Eds.). (1973). *Constraints on learning.* London: Academic Press.

Hinson, R.E. (1982). Effects of UCS preexposure on excitatory and inhibitory rabbit eyelid conditioning: An associative effect of conditioned contextual stimuli. *Journal of Experimental Psychology: Animal Behavior Processes, 8,* 49–61.

Hoffman, H.S. & Ratner, A.M. (1973). A reinforcement model of imprinting: Implications for socialization in monkeys and men. *Psychological Review, 80,* 527–544.

Holland, P.C. (1977). Conditioned stimulus as a determinant of the form of the Pavlovian conditioned response. *Journal of Experimental Psychology: Animal Behavior Processes, 3,* 77–104.

Holland, P.C. (1980a). Influence of visual conditioned stimulus characteristics on the form of Pavlovian appetitive conditioned responding in rats. *Journal of Experimental Psychology: Animal Behavior Processes, 6,* 81–97.

Holland, P.C. (1980b). CS-US interval as a determinant of the form of Pavlovian appetitive conditioned responses. *Journal of Experimental Psychology: Animal Behavior Processes, 6,* 155–174.

Holland, P.C. & Forbes, D.T. (1980). Effects of compound or element preexposure on compound flavor aversion conditioning. *Animal Learning and Behavior, 8,* 199–203.

Holland, P.C. & Ross, R.T. (1981). Within-compound associations in serial compound conditioning. *Journal of Experimental Psychology: Animal Behavior Processes, 7,* 228–241.

Hollis, K.L. (1982). Pavlovian conditioning of signal-centered action patterns and autonomic behavior: A biological analysis of function. In J.S. Rosenblatt, R.A. Hinde, C. Beer, & M.C. Busnel (Eds.), *Advances in the study of behavior: Vol. 12* (pp. 1–64). New York: Academic Press.

Holman, E.W. (1980). Irrelevant-incentive learning with flavors in rats. *Journal of Experimental Psychology: Animal Behavior Processes, 6,* 126–136.

Honig, W.K. (Ed.). (1966). *Operant behavior: Areas of research and application.* New York: Appleton-Century-Crofts.

Honig, W.K. & Staddon, J.E.R. (Eds.). (1977). *Handbook of operant behavior.* Englewood Cliffs, NJ: Prentice-Hall.

Horn, G. & Hill, R.M. (1966). Responsiveness to sensory stimulation of units in the superior colliculus and subjacent tectotegmental regions of the rabbit. *Experimental Neurology, 14,* 199–223.

Horn, G. & Hinde, R.A. (Eds.). (1970). *Short-term changes in neural activity and behavior.* Cambridge: Cambridge University Press.

Hull, C.L. (1943). *Principles of behavior.* New York: D. Appleton-Century.

Hull, C.L. (1952). *A behavior system: An introduction to behavior theory concerning the individual organism.* New Haven: Yale University Press.

Hulse, S.H., Fowler, H., & Honig, W.K. (Eds.). (1978). *Cognitive processes in animal behavior.* Hillsdale, NJ: Erlbaum.

Humphrey, G. (1933). *The nature of learning in its relation to the living system.* London: Kegan, Paul.

Humphreys, L.G. (1939). The effect of random alternation of reinforcement on the acquisition and extinction of conditioned eyelid reactions. *Journal of Experimental Psychology, 25,* 141–158.

Hursh, S.R. (1980). Economic concepts for the analysis

of behavior. *Journal of the Experimental Analysis of Behavior, 34*, 219–238.

Hutt, P.J. (1954). Rate of bar pressing as a function of quality and quantity of food reward. *Journal of Comparative and Physiological Psychology, 47*, 235–239.

Jenkins, H.M. (1970). Sequential organization in schedules of reinforcement. In W.N. Schoenfeld (Ed.), *The theory of reinforcement schedules* (pp. 63–109). New York: Appleton-Century-Crofts.

Jenkins, H.M. (1977). Sensitivity of different response systems to stimulus-reinforcer and response-reinforcer relations. In H. Davis & H.M.B. Hurwitz (Eds.), *Operant-Pavlovian interactions* (pp. 47–66). Hillsdale, NJ: Erlbaum.

Jenkins, H.M. (1979). Animal learning and behavior theory. In E. Hearst (Ed.), *The first century of experimental psychology* (pp. 177–228). Hillsdale, NJ: Erlbaum.

Jenkins, H.M., Barnes, R.A., & Barrera, F.J. (1981). Why autoshaping depends on trial spacing. In C.M. Locurto, H.S. Terrace, & J. Gibbon (Eds.), *Autoshaping and conditioning theory* (pp. 255–284). New York: Academic Press.

Jenkins, H.M., Barrera, F.J., Ireland, C., & Woodside, B. (1978). Signal-centered action patterns of dogs in appetitive classical conditioning. *Learning and Motivation, 9*, 272–296.

Jenkins, H.M. & Moore, B.R. (1973). The form of the auto-shaped response with food or water reinforcers. *Journal of the Experimental Analysis of Behavior, 20*, 163–181.

Jobe, J.B., Mellgren, R.L., Feinberg, R.A., Littlejohn, R.L., & Rigby, R.L. (1977). Patterning, partial reinforcement, and N-length effects at spaced trials as a function of reinstatement of retrieval cues. *Learning and Motivation, 8*, 77–97.

Johnston, T.D. (1981). Contrasting approaches to a theory of learning. *Behavioral and Brain Sciences, 4*, 125–173.

Kalat, J.W. (1977). Biological significance of food aversion learning. In N.W. Milgram, L. Krames, & T.M. Alloway (Eds.), *Food aversion learning* (pp. 73–103). New York: Plenum Press.

Kalish, H.I. (1969). Stimulus generalization. In M.H. Marx (Ed.), *Learning: Processes* (pp. 207–297). New York: Macmillan.

Kamin, L.J. (1957). The effects of termination of the CS and avoidance of the US on avoidance learning: An extension. *Canadian Journal of Psychology, 11*, 48–56.

Kamin, L.J. (1961). Trace conditioning of the conditioned emotional response. *Journal of Comparative and Physiological Psychology, 54*, 149–153.

Kamin, L.J. (1965). Temporal and intensity charac-

teristics of the conditioned stimulus. In W.F. Prokasy (Ed.), *Classical conditioning: A symposium* (pp. 118–147). New York: Appleton-Century-Crofts.

Kamin, L.J. (1969). Predictability, surprise, attention, and conditioning. In B.A. Campbell & R.M. Church (Eds.), *Punishment and aversive behavior* (pp. 279–296). New York: Appleton-Century-Crofts.

Kandel, E.R. (1976). *The cellular basis of behavior.* San Francisco: Freeman.

Kandel, E.R. & Schwartz, J.H. (1982). Molecular biology of learning: Modulation of transmitter release. *Science, 218*, 433–443.

Kaplan, P.S. (1984). Importance of relative temporal parameters in trace autoshaping: From excitation to inhibition. *Journal of Experimental Psychology: Animal Behavior Processes, 10*, 113–126.

Kaplan, P.S. & Hearst, E. (1982). Bridging temporal gaps between CS and US in autoshaping: Insertion of other stimuli before, during, and after CS. *Journal of Experimental Psychology: Animal Behavior Processes, 8*, 187–203.

Karpicke, J., Christoph, G., Peterson, G., & Hearst, E. (1977). Signal location and positive versus negative conditioned suppression in the rat. *Journal of Experimental Psychology: Animal Behavior Processes, 3*, 105–118.

Keehn, J.D. (Ed.). (1979). *Psychopathology in animals: Research and clinical implications.* New York: Academic Press.

Kehoe, E.J. & Gormezano, I. (1980). Configuration and combination laws in conditioning with compound stimuli. *Psychological Bulletin, 87*, 351–378.

Kelleher, R.T. & Gollub, L.R. (1962). A review of positive conditioned reinforcement. *Journal of the Experimental Analysis of Behavior, 5*, 543–597.

Keller, F.S. (1973). *The definition of psychology* (2nd ed.). New York: Appleton-Century-Crofts.

Kessen, W. (1953). Response strength and conditioned stimulus intensity. *Journal of Experimental Psychology, 45*, 82–86.

Kimble, D.P. & Ray, R.S. (1965). Reflex habituation and potentiation in *Rana pipiens. Animal Behavior, 13*, 530–533.

Kimble, G.A. (1961). *Hilgard and Marquis' conditioning and learning.* New York: Appleton-Century-Crofts.

Kimble, G.A. (Ed.). (1967). *Foundations of conditioning and learning.* New York: Appleton-Century-Crofts.

Kimmel, H.D. (1966). Inhibition of the unconditioned response in classical conditioning. *Psychological Review, 73*, 232–240.

Kimmel, H.D. & Burns, R.A. (1975). Adaptational aspects of conditioning. In W.K. Estes (Ed.), *Handbook of learning and cognitive processes: Vol. 2.*

*Conditioning and behavior theory* (pp. 99–142). Hillsdale, NJ: Erlbaum.

Klein, B. (1969). Counterconditioning and fear reduction in the rat. *Psychonomic Science, 17,* 150–151.

Kling, J.W. & Stevenson, J.G. (1970). Habituation and extinction. In G. Horn & R.A. Hinde (Eds.), *Short-term changes in neural activity and behavior* (pp. 41–61). Cambridge: Cambridge University Press.

Köhler, W. (1925). *The mentality of apes.* London: Routledge and Kegan Paul.

Köhler, W. (1947). *Gestalt psychology.* New York: Liveright.

Konarski, E.A. (1979). The necessary and sufficient conditions for increasing instrumental responding in the classroom: Response deprivation vs. probability differential (Doctoral dissertation, University of Notre Dame).

Konarski, E.A., Johnson, M.R., Crowell, C., & Whitman, T.L. (1980). Response deprivation, reinforcement, and instrumental academic performance in an EMR classroom. Paper presented at the thirteenth annual Gatlinburg Conference on Research in Mental Retardation and Developmental Disabilities, Gatlinburg, Tenn.

Konorski, J. (1948). *Conditioned reflexes and neuron organization.* Cambridge: Cambridge University Press.

Konorski, J. (1967). *Integrative activity of the brain.* Chicago: University of Chicago Press.

Konorski, J. (1972). Some ideas concerning physiological mechanisms of so-called internal inhibition. In R.A. Boakes & M.S. Halliday (Eds.), *Inhibition and learning* (pp. 341–357). London: Academic Press.

Kraeling, D. (1961). Analysis of amount of reward as a variable in learning. *Journal of Comparative and Physiological Psychology, 54,* 560–565.

Kramer, T.J. & Rilling, M. (1970). Differential reinforcement of low rates: A selective critique. *Psychological Bulletin, 74,* 225–254.

Krane, R.V. (1980). Toxiphobia conditioning with exteroceptive cues. *Animal Learning and Behavior, 8,* 513–523.

Krane, R.V. & Wagner, A.R. (1975). Taste aversion learning with a delayed shock US: Implications for the "generality of the laws of learning." *Journal of Comparative and Physiological Psychology, 88,* 882–889.

Kremer, E.F. (1978). The Rescorla–Wagner model: Losses in associative strength in compound conditioned stimuli. *Journal of Experimental Psychology: Animal Behavior Processes, 4,* 22–36.

LaBerge, D. (1975). Acquisition of automatic processing in perceptual and associative learning. In P.M.A. Rabbit & S. Dornic (Eds.), *Attention and*

*performance: Vol. 5* (pp. 50–64). New York: Academic Press.

Lantz, A. (1973). Effect of number of trials, interstimulus interval, and dishabituation during CS habituation on subsequent conditioning in a CER paradigm. *Animal Learning and Behavior, 1,* 273–277.

Lashley, K.S. (1942). An examination of the "continuity theory" as applied to discriminative learning. *Journal of General Psychology, 26,* 241–265.

Lashley, K.S. & Ball, J. (1929). Spinal conduction and kinesthetic sensitivity in the maze habit. *Journal of Comparative Psychology, 9,* 71–105.

Lea, S.E.G. (1978). The psychology and economics of demand. *Psychological Bulletin, 85,* 441–466.

Leaton, R.N. & Tighe, T.J. (1976). Comparisons between habituation research at the developmental and animal-neurophysiological levels. In T.J. Tighe & R.N. Leaton (Eds.), *Habituation: Perspectives from child development, animal behavior, and neurophysiology* (pp. 321–340). Hillsdale, NJ: Erlbaum.

LeClerc, R. & Reberg, D. (1980). Sign-tracking in aversive conditioning. *Learning and Motivation, 11,* 302–317.

Leibrecht, B.C. (1972). Habituation, 1940–1970: Bibliography and key word index. *Psychonomic Monograph Supplements, 4,* 189–217.

Leibrecht, B.C. (1974). Habituation: Supplemental bibliography. *Physiological Psychology, 2* (Whole Number 3B), 1–19.

Leibrecht, B.C. & Kemmerer, W.S. (1974). Varieties of habituation in the chinchilla (*Chinchilla lanigera*). *Journal of Comparative and Physiological Psychology, 86,* 124–132.

Lett, B.T. (1975). Long delay learning in the T-maze. *Learning and Motivation, 6,* 80–90.

Lett, B.T. (1979). Long-delay learning: Implications for learning and memory theory. In N.S. Sutherland (Ed.), *Tutorial essays in psychology: A guide to recent advances: Vol. 2.* (pp. 1–38). Hillsdale, NJ: Erlbaum.

Lett, B.T. (1980). Taste potentiates color-sickness association in pigeons and quails. *Animal Learning and Behavior, 8,* 193–198.

Levis, D.J. (1971). Short- and long-term auditory history and stimulus control in the rat. *Journal of Comparative and Physiological Psychology, 74,* 298–314.

Lindblom, L.L. & Jenkins, H.M. (1981). Responses eliminated by noncontingent or negatively contingent reinforcement recover in extinction. *Journal of Experimental Psychology: Animal Behavior Processes, 7,* 175–190.

Lipsitt, L.P. & Kaye, H. (1964). Conditioned sucking in the human newborn. *Psychonomic Science, 1,* 29–30.

Locurto, C.M., Terrace, H.S., & Gibbon, J. (Eds.). (1981). *Autoshaping and conditioning theory.* New York: Academic Press.

Logan, F.A. (1954). A note on stimulus intensity dynamism, V. *Psychological Review, 61,* 77–80.

Logan, F.A. (1960). *Incentive.* New Haven: Yale University Press.

Logan, F.A. & Gordon, W.C. (1981). *Fundamentals of learning and motivation* (3rd ed.). Dubuque, IA: William C. Brown.

Logue, A.W. (1979). Taste aversion and the generality of the laws of learning. *Psychological Bulletin, 86,* 276–296.

LoLordo, V.M. (1969). Positive conditioned reinforcement from aversive situations. *Psychological Bulletin, 72,* 193–203.

LoLordo, V.M. (1979a). Classical conditioning. The Pavlovian perspective. In M.E. Bitterman, V.M. LoLordo, J.B. Overmier, & M.E. Rashotte, *Animal learning: Survey and analysis* (pp. 25–59). New York: Plenum Press.

LoLordo, V.M. (1979b). Classical conditioning: Contingency and contiguity. In M.E. Bitterman et al., *Animal learning.* Ref. as above. (pp. 61–97).

LoLordo, V.M. (1979c). Classical conditioning: Compound CSs and the Rescorla–Wagner model. In M.E. Bitterman et al., *Animal learning.* Ref. as above. (pp. 99–126).

LoLordo, V.M. (1979d). Selective associations. In A. Dickinson & R.A. Boakes (Eds.), *Mechanisms of learning and motivation: A memorial volume to Jerzy Konorski* (pp. 367–398). Hillsdale, NJ: Erlbaum.

Lubow, R.E. (1973). Latent inhibition. *Psychological Bulletin, 79,* 398–407.

Lubow, R.E., Rifkin, B., & Alek, M. (1976). The context effect: The relationship between stimulus preexposure and environmental preexposure determines subsequent learning. *Journal of Experimental Psychology: Animal Behavior Processes, 2,* 38–47.

Lubow, R.E., Weiner, I., & Schnur, P. (1981). Conditioned attention theory. In G.H. Bower (Ed.), *The psychology of learning and motivation: Vol. 15* (pp. 1–49). New York: Academic Press.

Lyon, D.O. (1968). Conditioned suppression: Operant variables and aversive control. *Psychological Record, 18,* 317–338.

MacCorquodale, K. & Meehl, P.E. (1954). Edward C. Tolman. In W.K. Estes, S. Koch, K. MacCorquodale, P.E. Meehl, C.G. Mueller, W.N. Schoenfeld, & W.S. Verplanck, *Modern learning theory* (pp. 177–266). New York: Appleton-Century-Crofts.

MacFarlane, D.A. (1930). The role of kinesthesis in maze learning. *University of California Publications in Psychology, 4,* 277–305.

Mackintosh, N.J. (1974). *The psychology of animal learning.* London: Academic Press.

Mackintosh, N.J. (1975). A theory of attention: Variations in the associability of stimuli with reinforcement. *Psychological Review, 82,* 276–298.

Mackintosh, N.J. (1978). Cognitive or associative theories of conditioning: Implications of an analysis of blocking. In S.H. Hulse, H. Fowler, & W.K. Honig (Eds.), *Cognitive processes in animal behavior* (pp. 155–175). Hillsdale, NJ: Erlbaum.

Mackintosh, N.J. & Dickinson, A. (1979). Instrumental (Type II) conditioning. In A. Dickinson & R.A. Boakes (Eds.), *Mechanisms of learning and motivation: A memorial volume to Jerzy Konorski* (pp. 143–169). Hillsdale, NJ: Erlbaum.

Maher, B.A. & Maher, W.B. (1979). Psychopathology. In E. Hearst (Ed.), *The first century of experimental psychology* (pp. 561–621). Hillsdale, NJ: Erlbaum.

Mahoney, W.J. & Ayres, J.J.B. (1976). One-trial simultaneous and backward fear conditioning as reflected in conditioned suppression of licking in rats. *Animal Learning and Behavior, 4,* 357–362.

Maier, S.F. & Jackson, R.L. (1979). Learned helplessness: All of us were right (and wrong): Inescapable shock has multiple effects. In G.H. Bower (Ed.), *The psychology of learning and motivation: Vol. 13* (pp. 155–218). New York: Academic Press.

Maier, S.F. & Seligman, M.E.P. (1976). Learned helplessness: Theory and evidence. *Journal of Experimental Psychology: General, 105,* 3–46.

Malmo, R.B. (1959). Activation: A neuropsychological dimension. *Psychological Review, 66,* 367–386.

Marler, P. (1970). A comparative approach to vocal learning: Song development in white-crowned sparrows. *Journal of Comparative Psychology Monograph, 71*(2), 1–25.

Marler, P. & Peters, S. (1981). Sparrows learn adult song and more from memory. *Science, 213,* 780–782.

Marler, P. & Terrace, H.S. (Eds.). (1984). *The biology of learning.* (Dahlem Konferenzen). Berlin: Springer-Verlag.

Marlin, N.A. & Miller, R.R. (1981). Associations to contextual stimuli as a determinant of long-term habituation. *Journal of Experimental Psychology: Animal Behavior Processes, 7,* 313–333.

Marshall, B.S., Gokey, D.S., Green, P.L., & Rashotte, M.E. (1979). Spatial location of first- and second-order visual conditioned stimuli in second-order conditioning of the pigeon's keypeck. *Bulletin of the Psychonomic Society, 13,* 133–136.

Maser, J.D. & Seligman, M.E.P. (Eds.). (1977). *Psychopathology: Experimental models.* San Francisco: Freeman.

Mason, W.A. & Lott, D.F. (1976). Ethology and comparative psychology. *Annual Review of Psychology, 27,* 129–154.

Masters, W.H. & Johnson, V.E. (1966). *Human sexual response.* Boston: Little, Brown.

McAllister, W.R. & McAllister, D.E. (1971). Behavioral measurement of conditioned fear. In F.R. Brush (Ed.), *Aversive conditioning and learning* (pp. 105–179). New York: Academic Press.

McNamara, H.J., Long, J.B., & Wike, E.L. (1956). Learning without response under two conditions of external cues. *Journal of Comparative and Physiological Psychology, 49,* 477–480.

McSweeney, F.K., Ettinger, R.H., & Norman, W.D. (1981). Three versions of the additive theories of behavioral contrast. *Journal of the Experimental Analysis of Behavior, 36,* 285–297.

Meehl, P.E. (1950). On the circularity of the law of effect. *Psychological Bulletin, 47,* 52–75.

Mellitz, M., Hineline, P.N., Whitehouse, W.G., & Laurence, M.T. (1983). Duration-reduction of avoidance sessions as negative reinforcement. *Journal of the Experimental Analysis of Behavior, 40,* 57–67.

Menzel, E.W. (1978). Cognitive mapping in chimpanzees. In S.H. Hulse, H. Fowler, & W.K. Honig (Eds.), *Cognitive processes in animal behavior* (pp. 375–422). Hillsdale, NJ: Erlbaum.

Milgram, N.W., Krames, L., & Alloway, T.M. (Eds.). (1977). *Food aversion learning.* New York: Plenum Press.

Millenson, J.R. & Leslie, J.C. (1979). *Principles of behavioral analysis.* New York: Macmillan.

Miller, N.E. (1944). Experimental studies of conflict. In J. McV. Hunt (Ed.), *Personality and the behavior disorders* (pp. 431–465). New York: Ronald Press.

Miller, N.E. (1951). Learnable drives and rewards. In S.S. Stevens (Ed.), *Handbook of experimental psychology* (pp. 435–472). New York: Wiley.

Miller, N.E. (1959). Liberalization of basic S-R concepts: Extensions to conflict behavior, motivation, and social learning. In S. Koch (Ed.), *Psychology: A study of a science: Vol. 2* (pp. 196–292). New York: McGraw-Hill.

Miller, N.E. (1963). Some reflections on the law of effect produce a new alternative to drive reduction. In M.R. Jones (Ed.), *Nebraska Symposium on Motivation: Vol. 11* (pp. 65–112). Lincoln: University of Nebraska Press.

Miller, N.E. (1969). Learning of visceral and glandular responses. *Science, 163,* 434–445.

Miller, R.E. & Murphy, J.V. (1964). Influence of the spatial relationships between the cue, reward, and response in discrimination learning. *Journal of Experimental Psychology, 67,* 120–123.

Miller, R.R. & Balaz, M.A. (1981). Differences in adaptiveness between classically conditioned responses and instrumentally acquired responses. In N.E. Spear & R.R. Miller (Eds.), *Information processing in animals: Memory mechanisms* (pp. 49–80). Hillsdale, NJ: Erlbaum.

Miller, S. & Konorski, J. (1969). On a particular form of conditioned reflex. (B.F. Skinner, trans.). *Journal of the Experimental Analysis of Behavior, 12,* 187–189. (Original publication in *Compte Rendu Hebdomadaire des Séances et Mémoires de la Société de Biologie,* 1928, *99,* 1155–1157).

Mis, F.W., Gormezano, I., & Harvey, J.A. (1979). Stimulation of abducens nucleus supports classical conditioning of the nictitating membrane response. *Science, 206,* 473–475.

Moffit, A.R. (1971). Consonant cue perception by twenty- to twenty-four-week-old infants. *Child Development, 42,* 717–731.

Moore, B.R. (1973). The role of directed Pavlovian reactions in simple instrumental learning in the pigeon. In R.A. Hinde & J. Stevenson-Hinde (Eds.), *Constraints on learning* (pp. 159–188). London: Academic Press.

Moore, B.R. & Stuttard, S. (1979). Dr. Guthrie and *Felis domesticus* or: Tripping over the cat. *Science, 205,* 1031–1033.

Moore, J.W. & Gormezano, I. (1977). Classical conditioning. In M.H. Marx & M.E. Bunch (Eds.), *Fundamentals and applications of learning* (pp. 87–120). New York: Macmillan.

Moore, J.W. & Stickney, K.J. (1980). Formation of attentional-associative networks in real time: Role of the hippocampus and implications for conditioning. *Physiological Psychology, 8,* 207–217.

Moruzzi, G. & Magoun, H.W. (1949). Brainstem reticular formation and activation of the EEG. *Electroencephalography and Clinical Neurophysiology, 1,* 455–473.

Mowrer, O.H. (1947). On the dual nature of learning—A reinterpretation of "conditioning" and "problem-solving." *Harvard Educational Review, 17,* 102–148.

Nevin, J.A. (1973a). Conditioned reinforcement. In J.A. Nevin (Ed.), *The study of behavior: Learning, motivation, emotion, and instinct* (pp. 155–198). Glenview, IL: Scott, Foresman.

Nevin, J.A. (1973b). The maintenance of behavior. In J.A. Nevin (Ed.), *The study of behavior: Learning, motivation, emotion, and instinct* (pp. 201–236). Glenview, IL: Scott, Foresman.

Nevin, J.A. (1979). Reinforcement schedules and response strength. In M.D. Zeiler & P. Harzem (Eds.), *Advances in analysis of behavior: Vol. 1. Reinforcement and the organization of behavior* (pp. 117–158). New York: Wiley.

Notterman, J.M. & Mintz, D.E. (1965). *Dynamics of response*. New York: Wiley.

O'Connell, J.M. & Rashotte, M.E. (1982). Reinforcement magnitude effects in first- and second-order conditioning of directed action. *Learning and Motivation, 13*, 1–25.

Olson, G.M. (1976). An information-processing analysis of visual memory and habituation in infants. In T.J. Tighe & R.N. Leaton (Eds.), *Habituation: Perspectives from child development, animal behavior, and neurophysiology* (pp. 239–277). Hillsdale, NJ: Erlbaum.

Olton, D.S. (1979). Mazes, maps, and memory. *American Psychologist, 34*, 583–596.

Overmier, J.B. (1979a). Punishment. In M.E. Bitterman, V.M. LoLordo, J.B. Overmier, & M.E. Rashotte, *Animal learning: Survey and analysis* (pp. 279–311). New York: Plenum Press.

Overmier, J.B. (1979b). Avoidance learning. In M.E. Bitterman et al., *Animal learning*. Ref. as above. (pp. 313–348).

Overmier, J.B. (1979c). Theories of instrumental learning. In M.E. Bitterman et al., *Animal learning*. Ref. as above. (pp. 349–384).

Pavlov, I.P. (1927). *Conditioned reflexes* (G.V. Anrep, Trans.). London: Oxford University Press.

Pavlov, I.P. (1928). *Lectures on conditioned reflexes*. New York: International Publishers.

Pearce, J.M., Colwill, R.M., & Hall, G. (1978). Instrumental conditioning of scratching in the laboratory rat. *Learning and Motivation, 9*, 255–271.

Pearce, J.M. & Hall, G. (1980). A model for Pavlovian learning: Variations in the effectiveness of conditioned but not of unconditioned stimuli. *Psychological Review, 87*, 532–552.

Peckham, G.W. & Peckham, E.G. (1887). Some observations on the mental powers of spiders. *Journal of Morphology, 1*, 383–419.

Peden, B., Browne, M.P., & Hearst, E. (1977). Persistent approaches to a signal for food despite food omission for approaching. *Journal of Experimental Psychology: Animal Behavor Processes, 3*, 377–399.

Peeke, H.V.S. & Herz, M.J. (Eds.). (1973). *Habituation* (2 vols.). New York: Academic Press.

Perkins, C.C. (1947). The relation of secondary reward to gradients of reinforcement. *Journal of Experimental Psychology, 37*, 377–392.

Perkins, C.C. (1953). The relation between conditioned stimulus intensity and response strength. *Journal of Experimental Psychology, 46*, 225–231.

Perkins, C.C. (1968). An analysis of the concept of reinforcement. *Psychological Review, 75*, 155–172.

Pinel, J.P.J., Treit, D., & Wilkie, D.M. (1980). Stimulus control of defensive burying in the rat. *Learning and Motivation, 11*, 150–163.

Platt, J. (1964). Strong inference. *Science, 146*, 347–353.

Platt, J.R. (1973). Percentile reinforcement: Paradigms for experimental analysis of response shaping. In G.H. Bower (Ed.), *The psychology of learning and motivation: Vol. 7* (pp. 271–311). New York: Academic Press.

Platt, J.R. & Scott, G.K. (1981). Analysis of the superiority of discrete-trials over free-operant procedures in temporal response differentiation. *Journal of Experimental Psychology: Animal Behavior Processes, 7*, 269–277.

Premack, D. (1959). Toward empirical behavior laws: I. Positive reinforcement. *Psychological Review, 66*, 219–234.

Premack, D. (1965). Reinforcement theory. In D. Levine (Ed.), *Nebraska Symposium on Motivation: Vol. 13* (pp. 123–180). Lincoln: University of Nebraska Press.

Premack, D. (1971). Catching up with common sense or two sides of a generalization: Reinforcement and punishment. In R. Glaser (Ed.), *The nature of reinforcement* (pp. 121–150). New York: Academic Press.

Prokasy, W.F. (Ed.). (1965a). *Classical conditioning: A symposium*. New York: Appleton-Century-Crofts.

Prokasy, W.F. (1965b). Classical eyelid conditioning: Experimenter operations, task demands, and response shaping. In W.F. Prokasy (Ed.), *Classical conditioning: A symposium* (pp. 208–225). New York: Appleton-Century-Crofts.

Rachlin, H., Battalio, R., Kagel, J., & Green, L. (1981). Maximization theory in behavioral psychology. *Behavioral and Brain Sciences, 4*, 371–417.

Randich, A. & LoLordo, V.M. (1979). Associative and nonassociative theories of the UCS preexposure phenomenon: Implications for Pavlovian conditioning. *Psychological Bulletin, 86*, 523–548.

Rashotte, M.E. (1979a). Reward training: Methods and data. In M.E. Bitterman, V.M. LoLordo, J.B. Overmier, & M.E. Rashotte, *Animal learning: Survey and analysis* (pp. 127–166). New York: Plenum Press.

Rashotte, M.E. (1979b). Reward training: Latent learning. In M.E. Bitterman et al., *Animal learning*. Ref. as above. (pp. 167–193).

Rashotte, M.E. (1979c). Reward training: Contrast effects. In M.E. Bitterman et al., *Animal learning*. Ref. as above. (pp. 195–239).

Rashotte, M.E. (1979d). Reward training: Extinction. In M.E. Bitterman et al., *Animal learning*. Ref. as above. (pp. 241–278).

Rashotte, M.E. (1981). Second-order autoshaping: Contributions to the research and theory of Pavlovian reinforcement by conditioned stimuli. In C.M. Locurto, H.S. Terrace, & J. Gibbon (Eds.),

*Autoshaping and conditioning theory* (pp. 139–180). New York: Academic Press.

Ratner, S.C. (1970). Habituation: Research and theory. In J.H. Reynierse (Ed.), *Current issues in animal learning: A colloquium* (pp. 55–84). Lincoln: University of Nebraska Press.

Razran, G. (1971). *Mind in evolution: An East–West synthesis of learned behavior and cognition.* New York: Houghton Mifflin.

Reiss, S. & Wagner, A.R. (1972). CS habituation produces a "latent inhibition effect" but no active "conditioned inhibition." *Learning and Motivation, 3,* 237–245.

Renner, K.E. (1964). Delay of reinforcement: An historical review. *Psychological Bulletin, 61,* 341–361.

Rescorla, R.A. (1967). Pavlovian conditioning and its proper control procedures. *Psychological Review, 74,* 71–80.

Rescorla, R.A. (1968). Probability of shock in the presence and absence of CS in fear conditioning. *Journal of Comparative and Physiological Psychology, 66,* 1–5.

Rescorla, R.A. (1969). Pavlovian conditioned inhibition. *Psychological Bulletin, 72,* 77–94.

Rescorla, R.A. (1971a). Summation and retardation tests of latent inhibition. *Journal of Comparative and Physiological Psychology, 75,* 77–81.

Rescorla, R.A. (1971b). Variation in the effectiveness of reinforcement and nonreinforcement following prior inhibitory conditioning. *Learning and Motivation, 2,* 113–123.

Rescorla, R.A. (1972). Informational variables in Pavlovian conditioning. In G.H. Bower (Ed.), *The psychology of learning and motivation: Vol. 6* (pp. 1–46). New York: Academic Press.

Rescorla, R.A. (1976). Stimulus generalization: Some predictions from a model of Pavlovian conditioning. *Journal of Experimental Psychology: Animal Behavior Processes, 2,* 88–96.

Rescorla, R.A. (1977). Pavlovian second-order conditioning: Some implications for instrumental behavior. In H. Davis & H.M.B. Hurwitz (Eds.), *Operant–Pavlovian interactions* (pp. 133–164). Hillsdale, NJ: Erlbaum.

Rescorla, R.A. (1979). Conditioned inhibition and extinction. In A. Dickinson & R.A. Boakes (Eds.), *Mechanisms of learning and motivation: A memorial volume to Jerzy Konorski* (pp. 83–110). Hillsdale, NJ: Erlbaum.

Rescorla, R.A. (1980). *Pavlovian second-order conditioning: Studies in associative learning.* Hillsdale, NJ: Erlbaum.

Rescorla, R.A. (1982). Effect of a stimulus intervening between CS and US in autoshaping. *Journal of Experimental Psychology: Animal Behavior Processes, 8,* 131–141.

Rescorla, R.A. & Cunningham, C.L. (1979). Spatial contiguity facilitates Pavlovian second-order conditioning. *Journal of Experimental Psychology: Animal Behavior Processes, 5,* 152–161.

Rescorla, R.A. & Furrow, D.R. (1977). Stimulus similarity as a determinant of Pavlovian conditioning: *Journal of Experimental Psychology: Animal Behavior Processes, 3,* 203–215.

Rescorla, R.A. & Holland, P.C. (1976). Some behavioral approaches to the study of learning. In M.R. Rosenzweig & E.L. Bennett (Eds.), *Neural mechanisms of learning and memory* (pp. 165–192). Cambridge, MA: MIT Press.

Rescorla, R.A. & Holland, P.C. (1982). Behavioral studies of associative learning in animals. *Annual Review of Psychology, 33,* 265–308.

Rescorla, R.A. & Skucy, J.C. (1969). Effect of response-independent reinforcers during extinction. *Journal of Comparative and Physiological Psychology, 67,* 381–389.

Rescorla, R.A. & Solomon, R.L. (1967). Two-process learning theory: Relationships between Pavlovian conditioning and instrumental learning. *Psychological Review, 74,* 151–182.

Rescorla, R.A. & Wagner, A.R. (1972). A theory of Pavlovian conditioning: Variations in the effectiveness of reinforcement and nonreinforcement. In A.H. Black & W.F. Prokasy (Eds.), *Classical conditioning. II: Current research and theory* (pp. 64–99). New York: Appleton-Century-Crofts.

Restle, F. (1957). Discrimination of cues in mazes: A resolution of the "place-vs.-response" question. *Psychological Review, 64,* 217–228.

Revusky, S. (1971). The role of interference in association over a delay. In W.K. Honig & P.H.R. James (Eds.), *Animal memory* (pp. 155–213). New York: Academic Press.

Revusky, S. (1977a). Interference with progress by the scientific establishment: Examples from flavor aversion learning (Appendix to Chapter 1). In N.W. Milgram, L. Krames, & T.M. Alloway (Eds.), *Food aversion learning* (pp. 53–71). New York: Plenum Press.

Revusky, S. (1977b). Learning as a general process with an emphasis on data from feeding experiments. In N.W. Milgram, L. Krames, & T.M. Alloway (Eds.), *Food aversion learning* (pp. 1–51). New York: Plenum Press.

Revusky, S. & Garcia, J. (1970). Learned associations over long delays. In G.H. Bower (Ed.), *The psychology of learning and motivation: Vol. 4* (pp. 1–84). New York: Academic Press.

Reynolds, G.S. & McLeod, A. (1970). On the theory of interresponse-time reinforcement. In G.H. Bower (Ed.), *The psychology of learning and motivation: Vol. 4* (pp. 85–107). New York: Academic Press.

Richter, C.P. (1942–1943). Total self-regulatory functions in animals and human beings. *Harvey Lectures, 38,* 63–103.

Riess, D. & Farrar, C.H. (1972). Shock intensity, shock duration, Sidman avoidance acquisition, and the "all or nothing" principle in rats. *Journal of Comparative and Physiological Psychology, 81,* 347–355.

Riess, D. & Farrar, C.H. (1973). UCS duration and conditioned suppression: Acquisition and extinction between-groups and terminal performance within-subjects. *Learning and Motivation, 4,* 366–373.

Roper, T.J. (1981). What is meant by the term "schedule-induced," and how general is schedule induction? *Animal Learning and Behavior, 9,* 433–440.

Rosenzweig, M.R. (1971). Effects of environment on development of brain and of behavior. In E. Tobach, L.R. Aronson, & E. Shaw (Eds.), *The biopsychology of development* (pp. 303–342). New York: Academic Press.

Rosenzweig, M.R. & Bennett, E.L. (Eds.). (1976). *Neural mechanisms of learning and memory.* Cambridge, MA: MIT Press.

Rozeboom, W.W. (1958). "What is learned?"—An empirical enigma. *Psychological Review, 65,* 22–33.

Rubel, E.W. & Rosenthal, M.H. (1975). The ontogeny of auditory frequency generalization in the chicken. *Journal of Experimental Psychology: Animal Behavior Processes, 1,* 287–297.

Rudy, J.W. (1974). Stimulus selection in animal conditioning and paired-associate learning: Variation in associative processing. *Journal of Verbal Learning and Verbal Behavior, 13,* 282–296.

Rudy, J.W., Rosenberg, L., & Sandell, J.H. (1977). Disruption of a taste familiarity effect by novel exteroceptive stimulation. *Journal of Experimental Psychology: Animal Behavior Processes, 3,* 26–36.

St. Claire-Smith, R. (1979). The overshadowing and blocking of punishment. *Quarterly Journal of Experimental Psychology, 31,* 51–61.

St. Claire-Smith, R. & MacLaren, D. (1983). Response preconditioning effects. *Journal of Experimental Psychology: Animal Behavior Processes, 9,* 41–48.

Schlosberg, H. (1937). The relationship between success and the laws of conditioning. *Psychological Review, 44,* 379–392.

Schnaitter, R. (1978). Circularity, trans-situationality, and the law of effect. *The Psychological Record, 28,* 353–362.

Schneider, W. & Shiffrin, R.M. (1977). Controlled and automatic human information processing: I. Detection, search, and attention. *Psychological Review, 84,* 1–66.

Schneiderman, N. & Gormezano, I. (1964). Conditioning of the nictitating membrane of the rabbit as a function of CS-US interval. *Journal of Comparative and Physiological Psychology, 57,* 188–195.

Schnur, P. & Lubow, R.E. (1976). Latent inhibition: The effects of ITI and CS intensity during preexposure. *Learning and Motivation, 7,* 540–550.

Schoenfeld, W.N. (Ed.). (1970). *The theory of reinforcement schedules.* New York: Appleton-Century-Crofts.

Schwartz, B. (1974). On going back to nature: A review of Seligman and Hager's biological boundaries of learning. *Journal of the Experimental Analysis of Behavior, 21,* 183–198.

Schwartz, B. & Gamzu, E. (1977). Pavlovian control of operant behavior. In W.K. Honig & J.E.R. Staddon (Eds.), *Handbook of operant behavior* (pp. 53–97). Englewood Cliffs, NJ: Prentice-Hall.

Seligman, M.E.P. (1970). On the generality of the laws of learning. *Psychological Review, 77,* 406–418.

Seligman, M.E.P. (1975). *Helplessness: On depression, development, and death.* San Francisco: Freeman.

Seligman, M.E.P. & Hager, J.L. (1972). *Biological boundaries of learning.* New York: Appleton-Century-Crofts.

Shalter, M.D. (1975). Lack of spatial generalization in habituation tests of fowl. *Journal of Comparative and Physiological Psychology, 89,* 258–262.

Sheffield, F.D. (1965). Relation between classical conditioning and instrumental learning. In W.F. Prokasy (Ed.), *Classical conditioning: A symposium* (pp. 302–322). New York: Appleton-Century-Crofts.

Sheffield, F.D. (1966). A drive-induction theory of reinforcement. In R.N. Haber (Ed.), *Current research in motivation* (pp. 98–122). New York: Holt.

Sheffield, F.D., Wulff, J.J., & Backer, R. (1951). Reward value of copulation without sex drive reduction. *Journal of Comparative and Physiological Psychology, 44,* 3–8.

Sheffield, V.F. (1949). Extinction as a function of partial reinforcement and distribution of practice. *Journal of Experimental Psychology, 39,* 511–526.

Sherrington, C.S. (1906). *The integrative action of the nervous system.* New Haven: Yale University Press.

Shettleworth, S.J. (1972). Constraints on learning. In D.S. Lehrman, R.A. Hinde, & E. Shaw (Eds.), *Advances in the study of behavior: Vol. 4* (pp. 1–68). New York: Academic Press.

Shettleworth, S.J. (1975). Reinforcement and the organization of behavior in golden hamsters. *Journal of Experimental Psychology: Animal Behavior Processes, 104,* 56–87.

Shettleworth, S.J. (1979). Constraints on conditioning in the writings of Konorski. In A. Dickinson & R.A. Boakes (Eds.), *Mechanisms of learning and motivation: A memorial volume to Jerzy Konorski* (pp. 399–416). Hillsdale, NJ: Erlbaum.

Shiffrin, R.M. & Schneider, W. (1977). Controlled and

automatic human information processing: II. Perceptual learning, automatic attending, and a general theory. *Psychological Review, 84,* 127–190.

Shimp, C.P. (1981). The local organization of behavior: Discrimination of and memory for simple behavioral patterns. *Journal of the Experimental Analysis of Behavior, 36,* 303–315.

Sidman, M. (1952). A note on functional relations obtained from group data. *Psychological Bulletin, 49,* 263–269.

Sidman, M. (1953). Two temporal parameters of the maintenance of avoidance behavior by the white rat. *Journal of Comparative and Physiological Psychology, 46,* 253–261.

Sidman, M. (1960). *Tactics of scientific research.* New York: Basic Books.

Sidman, M. (1966). Avoidance behavior. In W.K. Honig (Ed.), *Operant behavior: Areas of research and application* (pp. 448–498). New York: Appleton-Century-Crofts.

Siegel, S. (1972). Latent inhibition and eyelid conditioning. In A.H. Black & W.F. Prokasy (Eds.), *Classical conditioning II: Current research and theory* (pp. 231–247). New York: Appleton-Century-Crofts.

Siegel, S. (1979). The role of conditioning in drug tolerance and addiction. In J.D. Keehn (Ed.), *Psychopathology in animals: Research and clinical implications* (pp. 143–168). New York: Academic Press.

Siegel, S., Hearst, E., George, N., & O'Neal, E. (1968). Generalization gradients obtained from individual subjects following classical conditioning. *Journal of Experimental Psychology, 78,* 171–174.

Singer, B. (1981). History of the study of animal behavior. In D. McFarland (Ed.), *The Oxford companion to animal behavior* (pp. 255–272). Oxford: Oxford University Press.

Skinner, B.F. (1938). *The behavior of organisms: An experimental analysis.* New York: Appleton-Century-Crofts.

Skinner, B.F. (1948). "Superstition" in the pigeon. *Journal of Experimental Psychology, 38,* 168–172.

Skinner, B.F. (1953). *Science and human behavior.* New York: Macmillan.

Skinner, B.F. (1966). Operant behavior. In W.K. Honig (Ed.), *Operant behavior: Areas of research and application* (pp. 12–32). New York: Appleton-Century-Crofts.

Skinner, B.F. (1974). *About behaviorism.* New York: Knopf.

Skinner, B.F. (1981). Selection by consequences. *Science, 213,* 501–504.

Smith, J.C. & Roll, D.L. (1967). Trace conditioning with X-rays as an aversive stimulus. *Psychonomic Science, 9,* 11–12.

Smith, M.C., Coleman, S.R., & Gormezano, I. (1969). Classical conditioning of the rabbit's nictitating membrane response at backward, simultaneous, and forward CS-US intervals. *Journal of Comparative and Physiological Psychology, 69,* 226–231.

Sokolov, Y.N. (1963). *Perception and the conditioned reflex.* Oxford: Pergamon Press.

Sokolov, Y.N. (1976). Learning and memory: Habituation as negative learning. In M.R. Rosenzweig & E.L. Bennett (Eds.), *Neural mechanisms of learning and memory* (pp. 475–479). Cambridge, MA: MIT Press.

Solomon, R.L. (1980). The opponent-process theory of acquired motivation: The costs of pleasure and the benefits of pain. *American Psychologist, 35,* 691–712.

Solomon, R.L. & Corbit, J.D. (1974). An opponent-process theory of motivation: I. Temporal dynamics of affect. *Psychological Review, 81,* 119–145.

Spear, N.E. & Campbell, B.A. (Eds.). (1979). *Ontogeny of learning and memory.* Hillsdale, NJ: Erlbaum.

Spence, K.W. (1950). Cognitive versus stimulus-response theories of learning. *Psychological Review, 57,* 159–172.

Spence, K.W. (1951). Theoretical interpretations of learning. In S.S. Stevens (Ed.), *Handbook of experimental psychology* (pp. 690–729). New York: Wiley.

Spence, K.W. (1956). *Behavior theory and conditioning.* New Haven: Yale University Press.

Spetch, M.L., Wilkie, D.M., & Pinel, J.P.J. (1981). Backward conditioning: A reevaluation of the empirical evidence. *Psychological Bulletin, 89,* 163–175.

Staddon, J.E.R. (1977). Schedule-induced behavior. In W.K. Honig & J.E.R. Staddon (Eds.), *Handbook of operant behavior* (pp. 125–152). Englewood Cliffs, NJ: Prentice-Hall.

Staddon, J.E.R. (Ed.). (1980). *Limits to action: The allocation of individual behavior.* New York: Academic Press.

Staddon, J.E.R. & Simmelhag, V.L. (1971). The "superstition" experiment: A re-examination of its implications for the principles of adaptive behavior. *Psychological Review, 78,* 3–43.

Stein, L. (1966). Habituation and stimulus novelty: A model based on classical conditioning. *Psychological Review, 73,* 352–356.

Stickrod, G., Kimble, D.P., & Smotherman, W.P. (1982). In utero taste/odor aversion conditioning in the rat. *Physiology and Behavior, 28,* 5–7.

Sutherland, N.S. & Mackintosh, N.J. (1971). *Mechanisms of animal discrimination learning.* New York: Academic Press.

Tarpy, R.M. & Sawabini, F.L. (1974). Reinforcement delay: A selective review of the last decade. *Psychological Bulletin, 81,* 984–997.

Terrace, H.S. (1973). Classical conditioning. In J.A. Nevin (Ed.), *The study of behavior: Learning, motivation, emotion, and instinct* (pp. 71–112). Glenview, IL: Scott, Foresman.

Testa, T.J. (1974). Causal relationships and the acquisition of avoidance responses. *Psychological Review, 81*, 491–505.

Testa, T.J. (1975). Effects of similarity of location and temporal intensity pattern of conditioned and unconditioned stimuli on the acquisition of conditioned suppression in rats. *Journal of Experimental Psychology: Animal Behavior Processes, 4*, 114–121.

Testa, T.J. & Ternes, J.W. (1977). Specificity of conditioning mechanisms in the modification of food preferences. In L.M. Barker, M.R. Best, & M. Domjan (Eds.), *Learning mechanisms in food selection* (pp. 229–253). Waco, TX: Baylor University Press.

Thompson, R.F. (1972). Sensory preconditioning. In R.F. Thompson & J.F. Voss (Eds.), *Topics in learning and performance* (pp. 105–129). New York: Academic Press.

Thompson, R.F., Groves, P.M., Teyler, T.J., & Roemer, R.A. (1973). A dual-process theory of habituation: Theory and behavior. In H.V.S. Peeke & M.J. Herz (Eds.), *Habituation: Vol. 1. Behavioral studies* (pp. 239–269). New York: Academic Press.

Thompson, R.F. & Spencer, W.A. (1966). Habituation: A model phenomenon for the study of neuronal substrates of behavior. *Psychological Review, 73*, 16–43.

Thorndike, E.L. (1913). *Educational psychology: The psychology of learning: Vol. II.* New York: Teachers College.

Thorpe, W.H. (1963). *Learning and instinct in animals* (2nd ed.). London: Methuen.

Thorpe, W.H. (1979). *The origins and rise of ethology: The science of the natural behavior of animals.* New York: Praeger.

Tighe, T.J. & Leaton, R.N. (Eds.). (1976). *Habituation: Perspectives from child development, animal behavior, and neurophysiology.* Hillsdale, NJ: Erlbaum.

Timberlake, W. (1979). Licking one saccharin solution for access to another in rats: Contingent and noncontingent effects in instrumental performance. *Animal Learning and Behavior, 7*, 277–288.

Timberlake, W. (1980). A molar equilibrium theory of learned performance. In G.H. Bower (Ed.), *The psychology of learning and motivation: Vol. 14* (pp. 1–58). New York: Academic Press.

Timberlake, W. (1983a). The functional organization of appetitive behavior: Behavior systems and learning. In M.D. Zeiler & P. Harzem (Eds.), *Advances in analysis of behavior: Vol. 3. Biological factors in learning* (pp. 177–221). Chichester, England: Wiley.

Timberlake, W. (1983b). Appetitive structure and straight alley running. In R. Mellgren (Ed.), *Animal cognition and behavior* (pp. 165–222). Amsterdam: North-Holland.

Timberlake, W. & Allison, J. (1974). Response deprivation: An empirical approach to instrumental performance. *Psychological Review, 81*, 146–164.

Timberlake, W. & Grant, D.L. (1975). Autoshaping in rats to the presentation of another rat predicting food. *Science, 190*, 690–692.

Tinklepaugh, O.L. (1928). An experimental study of representative factors in monkeys. *Journal of Comparative Psychology, 8*, 197–236.

Tolman, E.C. (1932). *Purposive behavior in animals and men.* New York: Century.

Tolman, E.C. & Brunswik, E. (1935). The organism and the causal texture of the environment. *Psychological Review, 42*, 43–77.

Tolman, E.C., Ritchie, B.F., & Kalish, D. (1946). Studies in spatial learning: II. Place learning versus response learning. *Journal of Experimental Psychology, 36*, 221–229.

Tolman, E.C., Ritchie, B.F., & Kalish, D. (1947). Studies in spatial learning: V. Response learning versus place learning by the non-correction method. *Journal of Experimental Psychology, 37*, 285–292.

Tomie, A. (1981). Effect of unpredictable food on the subsequent acquisition of autoshaping: Analysis of the context-blocking hypothesis. In C.M. Locurto, H.S. Terrace, & J. Gibbon (Eds.), *Autoshaping and conditioning theory* (pp. 181–215). New York: Academic Press.

Trabasso, T. & Bower, G.H. (1968). *Attention in learning: Theory and research.* New York: Wiley.

Trapold, M.A. & Fowler, H. (1960). Instrumental escape performance as a function of the intensity of noxious stimulation. *Journal of Experimental Psychology, 60*, 323–326.

Trapold, M.A. & Overmier, J.B. (1972). The second learning process in instrumental learning. In A.H. Black & W.F. Prokasy (Eds.), *Classical conditioning II: Current research and theory* (pp. 427–452). New York: Appleton-Century-Crofts.

Tryon, W.W. (1976). Models of behavior disorder: A formal analysis based on Woods's taxonomy of instrumental conditioning. *American Psychologist, 31*, 509–518.

Vandercar, D.H. & Schneiderman, N. (1967). Interstimulus interval functions in different response systems during classical discrimination conditioning of rabbits. *Psychonomic Science, 9*, 9–10.

Wagner, A.R. (1969). Stimulus validity and stimulus selection in associative learning. In N.J. Mackintosh & W.K. Honig (Eds.), *Fundamental issues in associative learning* (pp. 90–122). Halifax, Canada: Dalhousie University Press.

Wagner, A.R. (1976). Priming in STM: An information-processing mechanism for self-generated or retrieval-generated depression in performance. In T.J. Tighe & R.N. Leaton (Eds.), *Habituation: Perspectives from child development, animal behavior, and neurophysiology* (pp. 95–128). Hillsdale, NJ: Erlbaum.

Wagner, A.R. (1978). Expectancies and the priming of STM. In S.H. Hulse, H. Fowler, & W.K. Honig (Eds.), *Cognitive processes in animal behavior* (pp. 177–209). Hillsdale, NJ: Erlbaum.

Wagner, A.R. (1979). Habituation and memory. In A. Dickinson & R.A. Boakes (Eds.), *Mechanisms of learning and motivation: A memorial volume to Jerzy Konorski* (pp. 53–82). Hillsdale, NJ: Erlbaum.

Wagner, A.R. (1981). SOP: A model of automatic memory processing in animal behavior. In N.E. Spear & R.R. Miller (Eds.), *Information processing in animals: Memory mechanisms* (pp. 5–47). Hillsdale, NJ: Erlbaum.

Wagner, A.R. & Pfautz, P.L. (1978). A bowed serial-position function in habituation of sequential stimuli. *Animal Learning and Behavior, 6,* 395–400.

Wagner, A.R. & Rescorla, R.A. (1972). Inhibition in Pavlovian conditioning: Application of a theory. In R.A. Boakes & M.S. Halliday (Eds.), *Inhibition and learning* (pp. 301–336). New York: Academic Press.

Walters, G.C. & Grusec, J.E. (1977). *Punishment.* San Francisco: Freeman.

Wasserman, E.A. (1972). Auto-shaping: The selection and direction of behavior by predictive stimuli (Doctoral dissertation, Indiana University).

Wasserman, E.A. (1973). The effect of redundant contextual stimuli on autoshaping the pigeon's key-peck. *Animal Learning and Behavior, 1,* 198–206.

Wasserman, E.A., Franklin, S., & Hearst, E. (1974). Pavlovian appetitive contingencies and approach versus withdrawal to conditioned stimuli in pigeons. *Journal of Comparative and Physiological Psychology, 86,* 616–627.

Watson, J.B. (1913). Psychology as the behaviorist views it. *Psychological Review, 20,* 158–177.

Watson, J.B. (1914). *Behavior: An introduction to comparative psychology.* New York: Holt.

Watson, J.B. (1924). *Behaviorism.* Chicago: University of Chicago Press.

Watts, F.N. (1979). Habituation model of systematic desensitization. *Psychological Bulletin, 86,* 627–637.

Whitlow, J.W. (1975). Short-term memory in habituation and dishabituation. *Journal of Experimental Psychology: Animal Behavior Processes, 1,* 189–206.

Wickens, D.D. (1973). Classical conditioning, as it contributes to the analyses of some basic psycho-logical processes. In F.J. McGuigan & D.B. Lumsden (Eds.), *Contemporary approaches to conditioning and learning* (pp. 213–243). Washington, DC: V.H. Winston.

Wickens, D.D. & Wickens, C.D. (1942). Some factors related to pseudoconditioning. *Journal of Experimental Psychology, 31,* 518–526.

Wike, E.L. (1966). *Secondary reinforcement: Selected experiments.* New York: Harper & Row.

Willner, J.A. (1978). Blocking of a taste aversion by prior pairings of exteroceptive stimuli with illness. *Learning and Motivation, 9,* 125–140.

Wilson, G.T. & Davison, G.C. (1971). Processes of fear reduction in systematic desensitization: Animal studies. *Psychological Bulletin, 76,* 1–14.

Winnick, W.A. & Hunt, J.McV. (1951). The effect of an extra stimulus upon strength of response during acquisition and extinction. *Journal of Experimental Psychology, 41,* 205–215.

Wolfe, J.B. (1934). The effect of delayed reward upon learning in the white rat. *Journal of Comparative Psychology, 17,* 1–21.

Wolin, B.R. (1968). Difference in manner of pecking a key between pigeons reinforced with food and with water. Paper read at the Conference on the Experimental Analysis of Behavior, 1948. Reprinted in A.C. Catania (Ed.), *Contemporary research in operant behavior.* Glenview, IL: Scott, Foresman.

Wolpe, J. & Lazarus, A.A. (1966). *Behavior therapy techniques.* Oxford: Pergamon Press.

Woods, P.J. (1974). A taxonomy of instrumental conditioning. *American Psychologist, 29,* 584–597.

Woodworth, R.S. (1947). Reinforcement of perception. *American Journal of Psychology, 60,* 119–124.

Woodworth, R.S. (1958). *Dynamics of behavior.* New York: Holt.

Zahorik, D.M. (1977). Associative and non-associative factors in learned food preferences. In L.M. Barker, M.R. Best, & M. Domjan (Eds.), *Learning mechanisms in food selection* (pp. 181–199). Waco, TX: Baylor University Press.

Zeaman, D. (1976). The ubiquity of novelty-familiarity (habituation?) effects. In T.J. Tighe & R.N. Leaton (Eds.), *Habituation: Perspectives from child development, animal behavior, and neurophysiology* (pp. 297–320). Hillsdale, NJ: Erlbaum.

Zeiler, M. (1977). Schedules of reinforcement: The controlling variables. In W.K. Honig & J.E.R. Staddon (Eds.), *Handbook of operant behavior* (pp. 201–232). Englewood Cliffs, NJ: Prentice-Hall.

Zimmer-Hart, C.L. & Rescorla, R.A. (1974). Extinction of Pavlovian conditioned inhibition. *Journal of Comparative and Physiological Psychology, 86,* 837–845.

# Chapter 2

# SELECTION, REPRESENTATION, AND EQUIVALENCE OF CONTROLLING STIMULI

**Peter D. Balsam,** *Barnard College of Columbia University*

## INTRODUCTION

All areas of psychology seek to specify the relations between antecedent input and behavioral output. Behavior, from the simplest variations in speed of random movements in a sow bug to complex human social, perceptual, and cognitive judgments, has been analyzed in terms of specifying the nature of antecedent stimuli and the functions that relate these stimuli to behavior (Fraenkel & Gunn, 1940, 1966; Kahneman & Tversky, 1984; Latane & Darley, 1970; Shepard, 1984; Stevens, 1951). The focus of this chapter is on how a controlling relation between antecedent stimuli and behavior is established through experience.

This chapter is dedicated to the memory of Aaron J. Brownstein, mentor, colleague, and friend. I thank W.P. Fifer, R.J. Herrnstein, E. Segal, and H.S. Terrace for comments and discussions of earlier versions of this chapter. I am especially grateful to J.G. Gibbon and the New York State Psychiatric Institute for providing the stimulating environment in which I worked on this project.

Behavioral regulation mechanisms that involve control by antecedent stimuli have been studied in a wide range of species. Some of these mechanisms are closed, in the sense that experience cannot modify connections between a stimulus input and particular response output. At least for the adults of a given species, taxes, kineses, modal action patterns, and unconditioned reflexes are closed with respect to both the range of antecedents which will evoke behavior and the form of the behavior which is evoked. Experience may only influence the dynamic properties of control (e.g., speed or intensity) in these systems. Other behavioral regulation mechanisms allow for modification of the antecedent stimuli that will evoke a response but are relatively fixed in the form of the response that will be evoked. Behaviors acquired through imprinting and Pavlovian conditioning are of this type. In imprinting, exposure to certain objects during infancy determines the range of antecedent stimuli that will release adult sexual behavior (Hess & Petrovitch, 1977). Similarly, in Pavlovian conditioning, the pairing of two stimuli results in a new stimulus coming to evoke responses that were previously controlled by other stimuli (see Hearst, Chapter 1). Other behavior regulation mechanisms allow for experience to modify both the antecedent stimuli that control a response and the particular response that occurs. In operant (instrumental) conditioning, for example, both the antecedent stimuli and the particular response that comes to be controlled by those stimuli can be modified through experience (see Hearst, Chapter 1). Hence, the study of how antecedent stimuli acquire control over behavior is to be found in the study of learning mechanisms.

In fact, one could characterize the psychology of learning as consisting mainly of studies of how stimuli that previously did not evoke a response come to do so. The framing of the problem in these terms owes largely to a strong historical influence of reflexology and is reflected in most theories of learning. The global theories of learning proposed during the first half of this century were variants of stimulus-response (S-R) theories (Guthrie, 1935; Hull, 1943; Thorndike, 1898, 1911). The debates were about the necessary conditions for establishing S-R connections, not about whether this was an appropriate model for learning. Even in cases where the possibility of stimulus-stimulus (S-S) learning was acknowledged (Pavlov, 1927; Tolman, 1948), the problem at an empirical level remained as one of analyzing how a new antecedent for a response was established.

This tradition led to contemporary analyses of learning in which each response is viewed as being caused by an antecedent stimulus. This framework implies that there are two aspects to an account of why a particular response occurs. The antecedent stimuli must be identified and the mechanisms by which it comes to control a response must be understood. These two aspects of how stimuli control behavior are the subject matter of this chapter. First, the conditions that give rise to stimulus control are reviewed, and the mechanisms that underlie the acquisition and expression of stimulus control are discussed. Second, the problem and methods of specifying the nature of antecedent stimuli are discussed, and the roles of cognitive processes in stimulus control are considered.

## Definition and Measurement of Stimulus Control

The control of learned behavior by antecedent stimuli has been studied under the rubrics of *discrimination* and *generalization*. These terms have been used in several different ways (J.S. Brown, 1965). At an empirical level, generalization and discrimination refer to the relation between responding in the presence of different stimuli. When responding is similar in the presence of different stimuli, stimulus generalization is said to occur, when responding differs in the presence of different stimuli, discrimination is said to occur. Generalization and discrimination have also been used to refer to processes which underlie the level of responding observed in the presence of different stimuli. In this chapter, these terms will be used to refer to procedures and processes, and they will be explicitly designated as such. The term *stimulus control* will be used to refer to the empirical relationship between antecedent stimuli and behavior (cf. Terrace, 1966).

Stimulus control refers to the covariation between antecedent stimuli and responses (Skinner, 1938; Terrace, 1966). Stimulus control is demonstrated to the extent that variations in stimuli result in changes in responding. There are two aspects to the control exerted by antecedent stimuli. First, absolute differences in response strength in the presence and absence of a stimulus is taken as a reflection of the *strength* of stimulus control. The greater the difference in response strength in the presence and absence of a stimulus, the stronger is the controlling relation. The second aspect of stimulus control is derived from analyzing changes in the strength of control when stimuli are varied systematically along a single dimension. The slope of the generalization gradient obtained in this fashion is an index of the *sharpness* of stimulus control. The strength and sharpness of stimulus control characterize the influence of antecedent stimuli on behavior in both Pavlovian and instrumental conditioning.

In the prototypical operant discrimination procedure, discriminative learning is inferred to the extent that there is a difference in response strength in the presence and absence of the discriminative stimulus ($S^+$). For example, Guttman and Kalish (1956) intermittently reinforced

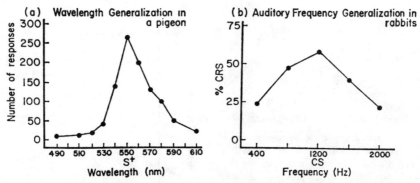

**Figure 2.1.** The left panel shows the mean generalization gradient obtained from a group of pigeons whose keypecking was reinforced in the presence of the 550 nm stimulus. From "Discriminability and Stimulus Generalization" by N. Guttman and H.J. Kalish, 1956, *Journal of Experimental Psychology, 51,* p. 81. Copyright 1956 by the American Psychological Association. Reprinted by permission of the publisher and author. The right panel shows the mean generalization gradient obtained from a group of rabbits that had a 1200 Hz tone paired with shock. From "Stimulus Control: Studies of Auditory Generalization in Rabbits" by J.W. Moore, 1972, in Abraham H. Black, William F. Prokasy (eds.), *Classical Conditioning II: Current Research and Theory,* (c) 1972, p. 214. Reprinted by permission of Prentice-Hall, Inc., Englewood Cliffs, NJ.

pigeons for pecking a disk illuminated with monochromatic light. The key and chamber were darkened between trials. After the pigeons had been reinforced for pecking the keylight for a number of sessions, a generalization test was conducted. The generalization test consisted of illuminating the response key with light of varying wavelength and recording the number of responses made in the presence of the different colors. During test trials subjects were not reinforced. As Figure 2.1a shows, pigeons pecked the key more in the presence of the reinforced stimulus than in the presence of any of the test stimuli.

In the standard Pavlovian conditioning experiment, learning is inferred only to the extent that stimulus control is demonstrated. Learning is demonstrated when a conditioned response (CR) occurs in the presence of a conditioned stimulus (CS) but not in its absence. The measurement of both strength and sharpness of stimulus control is illustrated in Moore's (1972) study of nictitating membrane response (NMR) conditioning. Rabbits were trained by pairing an auditory CS with brief electric shock to the eye. Shock elicits a closure of the nictitating membrane over the eye. After a number of pairings, the NMR was exhibited much more in the presence of the CS than in its absence. Subjects were then exposed to test stimuli that differed in frequency from the original training CS. The generalization gradient shown in Figure 2.1b illustrates that

response strength is greater in the presence of the CS than in the presence of any of the other test stimuli.

Some manipulations may affect both the strength of responding and the sharpness of control. Generalization gradients based on relative response rates can be computed to allow comparison of the sharpness of control across conditions that generate different absolute levels of responding. Rates may be computed relative to either the total response output or relative to the rate of responding to the training $S^+$. Figure 2.2 illustrates the value of using a relative measure of performance as the index of stimulus control. In this experiment (Hearst & Koreski, 1968), generalization gradients along the orientation dimension were obtained after 2 or 14 prior sessions in which pigeons had been reinforced on a variable interval (VI) schedule for responding in the presence of a vertical line. It appears from the absolute gradients presented in Figure 2.2 that sharpness of control increases with increased exposure to the schedule. However, Figure 2.2 shows that when the response rates in the presence of each stimulus are replotted as proportions of total responding, sharpness of stimulus control does not change as a function of the amount of training. There do not appear to be any *a priori* reasons for choosing between an absolute and relative analysis of the sharpness of control. The analyses that maximize

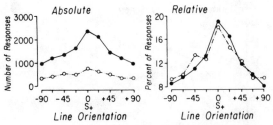

**Figure 2.2.** Generalization gradients for pigeons exposed to either 2 or 14 prior training sessions in which a vertical line served as S⁺. The left panel shows the absolute rates of responding in the presence of each stimulus. The right panel shows the relative rate of responding in the presence of each stimulus. From "Stimulus Generalization and Amount of Prior Training on Variable Interval Reinforcement" by E. Hearst and M.B. Koresko, 1968, *Journal of Comparative and Physiological Psychology*, *66*, pp. 135–136. Copyright 1968 by the American Psychological Association. Reprinted by permission of the publisher and author.

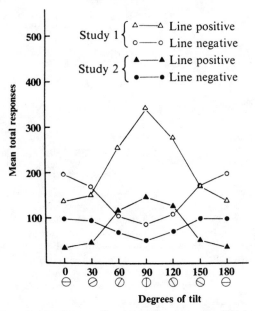

**Figure 2.3.** Two replications of a generalization test after subjects were trained with vertical lines as either positive (S⁺) or negative (S⁻) stimuli. From "Positive and Negative Generalization Gradients Obtained After Equivalent Training Conditions" by W.K. Honig, C.A. Boneau, K.R. Burstein, and H.S. Pennypacker, 1963, *Journal of Comparative and Physiological Psychology*, *56*, p. 112. Copyright 1963 by the American Psychological Association, Reprinted by permission of the publisher and author.

theoretical and empirical consistency will dominate (Nevin, 1973). In this chapter, generalization test data are most frequently portrayed in absolute rather than relative gradients to allow for comparisons of both the strength and sharpness of stimulus control. Discrepancies between absolute and relative measures will be discussed as needed.

The preceding examples illustrate excitatory stimulus control, in that response strength was greater in the presence of the training stimulus than in its absence. Some stimuli may affect behavior in an opposite way by inhibiting ongoing behavior. These stimuli exert inhibitory stimulus control in that response strength is less in the presence of these stimuli than in their absence (see Hearst, Chapter 1). The definitions and procedures for studying inhibitory stimulus control are parallel to those aspects of the study of excitatory control. The strength of inhibitory control refers to the difference in response strength in the presence and absence of the inhibitory stimulus. Hence, there must be a non-zero level of responding in the absence of the test stimulus (an excitatory background) in order to detect inhibition. The greater the suppression in the presence of the inhibitory stimulus, the *stronger* the inhibitory control. Similarly, the *sharpness* of inhibitory control refers to the slope of a gradient obtained by systematically varying the inhibitory stimulus along a single dimension.

The similarity in procedures for studying excitatory and inhibitory control is illustrated in a study by Honig, Boneau, Burstein, and Pennypacker (1963). For one group of pigeons keypecking was reinforced in the presence of a vertical line (90°) projected onto a response key (S⁺) and not reinforced when the key was blank (S⁻). In a second group, keypecking was reinforced in the presence of the blank key (S⁺) and extinguished in the presence of the vertical line (S⁻). Figure 2.3 shows two separate replications of the experiment in which generalization gradients were obtained along the line-tilt dimension. When the vertical line served as the S⁻, inhibitory control was demonstrated. Subjects emitted fewest responses in the presence of the S⁻ and responded at progressively greater rates as the similarity to the training value decreased. Typical excitatory gradients were obtained from the subjects whose Keypecks were reinforced in the presence of the vertical line. Thus, comparable

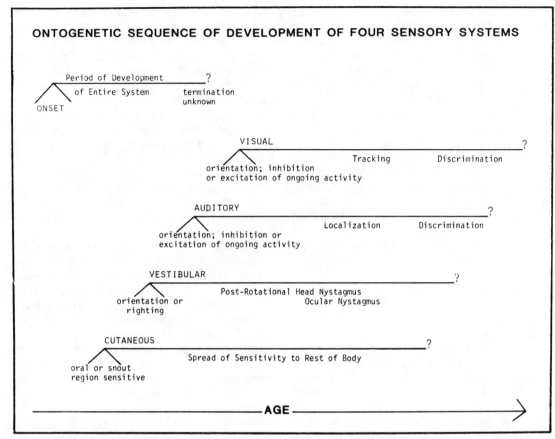

ONTOGENETIC SEQUENCE OF DEVELOPMENT OF FOUR SENSORY SYSTEMS

**Figure 2.4.** The sequence of development of different sensory systems. Changes in the sensory control of behavior may parallel the ontogeny of sensory systems. From "Ontogenesis of Sensory Function in Birds and Mammals" by G. Gottlieb in *The Biopsychology of Development* (p. 69), E. Tobach, L.R. Aronson, and E. Shaw (Eds.), 1971. New York: Academic Press. Copyright 1971 by Academic Press. Reprinted by permission.

methods may be used to study excitatory and inhibitory control.

A full review of inhibitory stimulus control is beyond the scope of this chapter and may be found elsewhere (Hearst, Besley, & Farthing, 1970; LoLordo & Fairless, 1985; Rilling, 1977). However, inhibitory processes are central to the understanding of stimulus control. In particular, the interaction of excitatory and inhibitory control is crucial in the analysis of discrimination training. Hence, some aspects of inhibitory control are considered in detail, although the emphasis throughout the chapter is on excitatory control. Factors that affect the acquisition of excitatory stimulus control are considered next.

## ACQUISITION OF STIMULUS CONTROL

### Ontogeny of Stimulus Control

One characteristic of development in all species is that as an organism grows older the sensory modalities that regulate behavior change. Gottlieb (1971) has suggested that the transitions in sensory control of behavior follow the pattern shown in Figure 2.4. For example, the begging response of young gulls is initially evoked by tactile stimuli. During development the begging response comes under the control of auditory and then visual stimuli (Tinbegen & Perdeck, 1950). Similarly, transitions in controlling stimuli have been described for feeding (Graf, Balsam, & Silver, 1985; Hall & Williams, 1983), home orientation (Rosenblatt, 1979), and huddling (Alberts, 1978; Alberts & Brunjes, 1979). Although the developmentalist emphasizes the role of sensory maturation in producing these changes (Gottlieb, 1983; Rosenblatt, 1979), learning processes may heavily contribute to these transitions as well (Galef, 1976, 1977; Graf, Balsam, & Silver, 1985; Hogan, 1973, 1984; Holt, 1931). The ontogeny of stimulus control will, therefore, involve not only maturation of sensory and motor systems, but will also depend on the development of learning abilities (Amsel, 1979; Cheatle & Rudy, 1979; Hyson & Rudy, 1984; Rudy & Hyson, 1984; Spear & Campbell, 1979; Spear & Kucharski, 1984; Vogt & Rudy, 1984) and the specific experiences of the young organism.

## Experiences That Affect Stimulus Control

The role of experience in the acquisition of stimulus control has received much recent attention from both developmental (Gottlieb, 1983; Hinde, 1983; Immelmann, Barlow, Petrinovitch, & Main, 1981; Lewis & Starr, 1979) and learning perspectives (Balsam & Tomie, 1985; Gilbert & Sutherland, 1969; Mostofsky, 1965; Roitblat, Bever, & Terrace, 1984). In the developmental tradition, experience tends to be defined as exposure to a single event over days, weeks, or months, whereas the learning tradition has emphasized experiences that involve repeated exposure to events that occur for seconds, minutes, or hours. Not surprisingly, researchers in the two traditions have analyzed and emphasized different paradigms and processes in the acquisition of stimulus control.

### Exposure

Exposure to stimuli at specific times in development can result in profound changes in controlling stimuli. For example, shortly after hatching and for a relatively brief period of time, referred to as the sensitive period, newly hatched ducks or geese will imprint on moving stimuli (Hess & Petrovitch, 1977). The immediate consequence of this exposure is the acquisition of control over the following response by the imprinted stimulus. When the birds reach maturity, the nature of the stimuli that will be effective in evoking sexual behavior is influenced by quali-

ties of the imprinting stimulus. Similarly, early experience with conspecifics determines the stimuli that will be effective in evoking later adult sexual and social behavior in many species (Harlow & Harlow, 1962; Hinde, 1983; Leiderman, 1981). Likewise, early exposure to particular foods affects adult eating preferences (Capretta, 1977), and in humans, prenatal exposure to the mother's voice may affect postnatal reactions to the mother's speech (DeCasper & Fifer, 1980).

In adults, exposure to offspring also seems to play an important role in determining the nature of the offspring's control of parental behavior (Rosenblatt, 1979). Exposure to offspring shortly after birth is necessary for the offspring to control parental behavior in some species. Without exposure to the young shortly after birth, goats will not take care of their young, whereas exposure to the young results in parental behavior under the control of the offspring (Klopfer, Adams, & Klopfer, 1964). While these examples of changes in stimulus control have been described as resulting from exposure to a single stimulus, the actual events and contingencies involved in these experiences may be quite complex, since they may include interactions of behavior and environment.

The effects of exposure to a single event on stimulus control have also been studied within the learning tradition. Typically, subjects in these studies are repeatedly exposed to brief duration stimuli. As in the preceding examples, exposure to a single stimulus affects both the control exerted by the repetitively presented stimulus as well as that exerted by other stimuli.

Repeated presentations of a stimulus sometimes result in a decrease in the strength of stimulus control and sometimes result in enhanced stimulus control. Figure 2.5 shows the effect of repeated presentations of either a rubber nipple or a rubber tube on the sucking response of human infants (Lipsitt & Kaye, 1965). Repeated presentations of the nipple resulted in an increase in the effectiveness of the nipple in evoking sucking, whereas repeated presentations of the tube resulted in a decrease of control by the stimulus. In equivalent procedures, except for the nature of the stimuli, the repeated presentation of some stimuli results in enhanced control, while repeated presentation of other stimuli results in diminished control (Davis, 1974; Groves & Thompson, 1970).

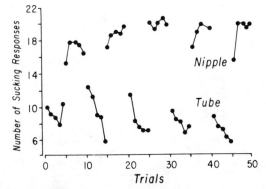

**Figure 2.5.** The effects of repeated exposure to either a nipple or rubber tube on the sucking response of human infants. From "Changes in Neonatal Response to Optimizing and Non-Optimizing Suckling Stimulation" by L.P. Lipsitt and H. Kaye, 1965, *Psychonomic Science, 2,* p. 221. Copyright 1965 by the Psychonomic Society. Reprinted by permission.

The decrease in strength of control as a result of repeated stimulus presentations is referred to as *habituation.* Responding declines as a function of the number of stimulus presentations, recovers after rest periods, and the decrement generalizes to other stimuli as a function of their similarity to the training stimulus (Balderrama & Moldonado, 1971; Groves & Thompson, 1970; Hawkins & Kandel, 1984). Habituation is faster and greater when stimuli are presented frequently (massed) than when they are widely spaced. However, if tested under common spacing conditions, subjects originally trained with more widely spaced trials evidence more of a response decrement than do subjects originally exposed to massed stimulus presentations (Davis, 1970). The decline in response strength in habituation is very much like the extinction of a learned response in procedure and outcome (see Hearst, Chapter 1). In fact, there is enough functional similarity between extinction and habituation to argue that a common process underlies the decrease of responding (Groves & Thompson, 1970; Hawkins & Kandel, 1984).

In procedures that are formally identical to ones in which habituation is obtained, repeated exposure to a stimulus sometimes results in enhanced stimulus control. As Figure 2.5 shows, repeated presentations of the nipple resulted in an increase in ability of that stimulus to evoke sucking. This result is referred to as *sensitization.* Sensitization may occur so that the control

by the initially presented stimulus is enhanced or the repeated presentation of one stimulus may facilitate responding in the presence of different stimuli. For example, a few presentations of a noxious stimulus (e.g. electric shock) may result in sensitization, in that subsequent presentations of a previously ineffective stimulus (e.g., light or tone) will evoke a defensive action (Hawkins & Kandel, 1984; Razran, 1971).

Repeated exposure to a stimulus sometimes resulted in enhanced stimulus control and sometimes in decreased control. Groves and Thompson (1970) suggested that two independent processes are initiated by stimulus presentation. One process changes the connection between a stimulus and a response (S-R connection), and a second process changes the organismic state so as to affect the readiness to respond in particular ways. They suggested that habituation worked directly on the S-R link, whereas sensitization occurs through the action of the state change. This state change makes many S-R links more effective. A dual process account has also been offered by Kandel and his colleagues (see Kandel & Hawkins, 1984) in their analysis of the cellular mechanisms of habituation and sensitization in *Aplysia.*

In sum, one effect of episodic exposure to stimuli is the modification of existing stimulus-response connections. When exposure results in diminished stimulus control, habituation is said to occur. Enhanced stimulus control as a result of exposure to a stimulus is called sensitization. Prolonged exposure to stimuli can also affect stimulus control.

Pavlov (1927), Hull (1939, 1943) and Spence (1936, 1937) had conceptually similar hypotheses about the mechanisms which determined which stimuli in addition to the training stimulus would evoke a learned response. In their views, generalization gradients reflected an innate neural process whereby habit strength (excitation) was spread to non-reinforced stimuli as a function of their similarity to the training stimulus. In contrast, Lashley and Wade (1946) viewed generalization as a result of an organism's failure to discriminate between training and test stimuli and argued that discrimination was a function of prior experience. The controversy over the role of experience in generalization gave rise to much research on the conditions that are necessary for stimulus control to develop.

Early rearing experience was manipulated as

one means of testing these hypotheses. If Hull, Spence, and Pavlov were correct, then rearing conditions would have little impact on the sharpness of stimulus control. On the other hand, if Lashley and Wade were correct, prior experience with a stimulus dimension should be crucial for obtaining control by that dimension. Experiments were conducted in which generalization gradients obtained from subjects given restricted exposure to a particular stimulus dimension were compared to gradients obtained from subjects not given such restricted experience. For example, N. Peterson (1962) reared ducklings in monochromatic light and found flat generalization gradients after reinforcing pecking at a key illuminated with the same wavelength of light. Subjects reared in white-light (all wavelengths) showed steep gradients under these conditions. These initial findings, however, turned out to be complicated by color preferences that affected the level of pecking to different wavelengths (Tracy, 1970).

Like most versions of the nature-nurture controversy, there is evidence to support both an innate as well as an experiential influence on stimulus control. For example, Ganz and Riesen (1962) demonstrated that during initial testing, monkeys reared in darkness showed some evidence of control by the wavelength of a visual stimulus that had been present when responses were reinforced. Performance of normally reared subjects showed much sharper control by the wavelength dimension. Similarly, in a carefully designed set of experiments, Rudolph, Honig, and Gerry (1969) examined wavelength generalization gradients in quail and chicks reared either in normal or monochromatic light. Figure 2.6 shows gradients obtained from two groups of quail after this differential rearing experience. One group of birds was reared in white light, while the experimental group was reared in monochromatic green light (530 nm). All subjects were trained to peck at a response key illuminated with the green light. Subsequently, the quail were given a wavelength generalization test. The wavelength gradient for monochromatically reared subjects is less steep than the gradient obtained from subjects reared in white light. Nevertheless, the generalization gradient of the monochromatically reared subjects is not flat. In general, it has been found that experience with a particular stimulus dimension sharpens control by that dimension but is not necessary

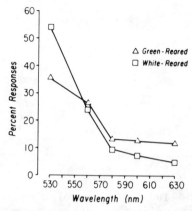

**Figure 2.6.** Wavelength generalization gradients from two groups of quail trained to respond in the presence of the 530 nm stimulus. The groups differed with respect to the wavelengths of light they had experienced prior to testing. From "Effects of Monochromatic Rearing on the Acquisition of Stimulus Control" by R.L. Rudolph, W.K. Honig, and J.E. Gerry, 1969, *Journal of Comparative and Physiological Psychology, 67*, p. 51. Copyright 1969 by the American Psychological Association. Reprinted by permission of the publisher and author.

for some degree of control to develop (Kerr, Ostapoff, & Rubel, 1979; Mountjoy & Malott, 1968; Riley & Leuin, 1971; Tracy, 1970).

### Differential Reinforcement

Prior exposure to a stimulus dimension may sharpen control by that dimension, but it does not guarantee control by that stimulus property. In their now classic experiment, Jenkins and Harrison (1960) reinforced key pecking in normally reared pigeons while a 1000 cps tone was presented continuously. When the tone frequency was varied in a generalization test, flat gradients were obtained. Because the pigeons had prior exposure to many different auditory stimuli, the flat gradients indicate that prior exposure to a stimulus dimension and its presence during learning is not a sufficient condition for the development of stimulus control. On the other hand, subjects whose responding was reinforced in the presence of the tone and extinguished in its absence showed steep gradients. This suggested that differential reinforcement in the presence of a stimulus was a sufficient, and perhaps necessary, condition (Terrace, 1966) for the development of stimulus control. However, there are other examples in which a stimulus that is not obviously part of a differential reinforcement contingency gains control over responding. Terrace (1966) argued that this occurs when implicit differential reinforcement contingencies are present. Indeed, there are *always* differential reinforcement contingencies present in Pavlovian and operant conditioning experiments.

In a typical Pavlovian-conditioning experiment, a single CS is paired with an unconditioned stimulus (US). After such training, sloping generalization gradients are reliably obtained (B.L. Brown, 1970; Hoffman, 1965; Moore, 1972). This procedure does provide for a differential reinforcement contingency. Subjects are reinforced in the presence of the CS but not reinforced in the presence of the contextual cues when they are presented alone during the intertrial interval (ITI). Similarly, operant experiments such as those of Guttman and Kalish (1956), in which responding is reinforced in the presence of a single stimulus, often employ ITIs during which subjects are not reinforced. Thus, any procedure that employs an ITI also provides for a differential reinforcement contingency.

Nonreinforced exposure to ITI stimuli is not necessary for stimulus control to develop. Thomas and his colleagues (Thomas, 1985; Thomas, Ernst, & Andry, 1971; Thomas, Svinicki, & Svinicki, 1970) have reported a number of experiments in which a cue continuously presented throughout an experimental session gains control over responding. In these procedures, pigeons were reinforced for pecking at a key light continuously illuminated with a vertical line (Thomas, Svinicki, & Svinicki, 1970), and fairly steep generalization gradients were obtained when control by the angle of the line was tested. Here, too, there are potential sources of differential reinforcement. One source of differential reinforcement in these studies might arise from the use of localizable cues and manipulanda. In the Thomas et al. experiments, for example, the stimuli that subjects were exposed to when their keypecks were reinforced were, in all likelihood, quite different from the stimuli that the subjects were exposed to when they were not key pecking and not reinforced. This is one possible source of differential reinforcement. In a very clever experiment directed at this account of how a continuously present cue could gain control over responding, Heinemann and Rudolf (1963) reinforced pigeons in the presence of a continuously illuminated stimulus which surrounded a

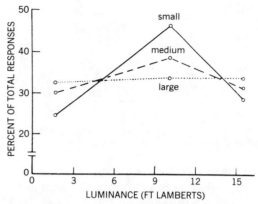

**Figure 2.7.** Generalization gradients for three groups of pigeons trained to peck in the presence of stimuli of different sizes. The S⁺ ranged in size from a small circle around the response key to almost a whole wall of an experimental chamber. From "The Effect of Discriminative Training on the Gradient of Stimulus Generalization" by E.G. Heinemann and R.L. Rudolph, 1963, *American Journal of Psychology, 76*, p. 656. Copyright 1963 by the University of Illinois Press. Reprinted by permission.

response key. In different experimental groups, the size of this stimulus ranged from almost an entire wall of the chamber to a small ring immediately surrounding the response key. Subjects were tested for control by the luminance of the stimulus. Figure 2.7 shows that the steepness of control was inversely related to the size of the stimulus surrounding the keylight. Hence, differential reinforcement in the presence and absence of stimuli on and off the manipulanda may play a role in the acquisition of stimulus control.

Even where cues are continuously present throughout an experimental session and not localizable, they may gain control over responding (Hearst, 1962; Thomas, 1985). In these circumstances, it is still possible to argue that stimuli are different when subjects are making responses (and reinforced) from those that are perceived when they are not responding (and not reinforced). It is always possible to assert that implicit differential reinforcement contingencies are necessary for the acquisition of stimulus control. Even without relying on post-hoc assumptions about stimulus properties, there is a sense in which all cues present in an experimental session are differentially reinforced.

Figure 2.8 shows a schematic representation of a discriminative conditioning procedure in

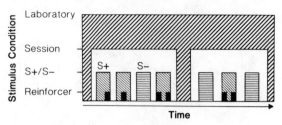

**Figure 2.8.** Schematic representation of a discriminative conditioning experiment.

which subjects are placed in experimental sessions across days and reinforced in the presence of one stimulus ($S^+$) and not reinforced either in the presence of a second stimulus ($S^-$) or during the interval between stimuli. There are three sources of differential reinforcement depicted here. The $S^+$ is differentially reinforced with respect to the $S^-$, with respect to the intra-experimental contextual (ITI) cues, and with respect to the extra-experimental cues. Notice that when there is no explicit $S^-$, two sources of differential reinforcement remain. Even if the only cues present are those which are continuous throughout a session, the continuous contextual cues are still differentially reinforced with respect to extra-session cues. Contextual cues of this sort can, in fact, act as conditioned stimuli (Balsam, 1982, 1984, 1985; Rescorla, Durlach, & Grau, 1984) and do exert a strong influence on the control exerted by other stimuli presented within the experimental session (Balsam, 1982, 1985; Mackintosh, 1977; Thomas, 1985).

In summary, it may be impossible to account for all sources of differential reinforcement. Therefore, it may not be possible to determine if differential reinforcement is a necessary condition for the acquisition of stimulus control. However, it is possible to investigate whether differential reinforcement is a sufficient condition for the development of stimulus control by explicitly manipulating contingencies within experimental sessions.

### Discrimination Training
Procedures which arrange for differential reinforcement in the presence of different stimuli are referred to as *discrimination training procedures*. Responses are reinforced in the presence of the $S^+$ ($S^D$, $CS^+$) and not reinforced in the presence of at least one other stimulus $S^-$ ($S^\Delta$, $CS^-$). In a typical discrimination learning experiment, the $S^+$ comes to control a high rate of

responding and little, if any, responding occurs in the presence of the $S^-$. The stimuli in a discrimination learning procedure may be presented successively, or subjects may choose between a simultaneously presented $S^+$ and $S^-$. In the typical operant discrimination procedure, stimuli associated with different schedules of reinforcement or extinction are presented successively. More complete treatments of the acquisition of discriminative responding are found in reviews by Mackintosh (1974) and Terrace (1966).

Honig (1969) points out that there are three components to the experimental study of the effects of differential reinforcement on stimulus control. First, there must be discrimination training between two stimuli. Second, there must be acquisition of responding in the presence of a stimulus value on the dimension of generalization. (This is usually, but not always, implicit in the discrimination training.) Lastly, there must be a generalization test. The relationship between the stimuli employed in discrimination training and the stimuli employed during testing may be varied (Switalski, Lyons, & Thomas, 1966). When the stimuli employed in discrimination training differ along the dimension that is varied in the generalization test, the procedure is refered to as *intradimensional training*. For example, the $S^+$ and $S^-$ might be lights of two different colors, and wavelength might be varied during the generalization test. Alternatively, when only one of the stimuli used in discrimination training (usually the $S^+$) lies on the dimension of the generalization test, the procedure is referred to as *interdimensional training*. For example, prior to generalization testing along the wavelength dimension, subjects might be trained with a colored light as $S^+$ and an auditory stimulus as $S^-$. Finally, when neither the $S^+$ nor $S^-$ lie on the dimension of generalization testing, the procedure is referred to as *extradimensional training*. The effects of each of these differential reinforcement procedures is described below.

### INTRADIMENSIONAL TRAINING
Probably the most frequently studied form of discrimination learning involves procedures in which both the $S^+$ and $S^-$ differ along the dimension which is varied in generalization testing. Hanson (1959), for example, trained separate groups of pigeons with an $S^+$ of 550 nm. The groups differed according to the wavelength of

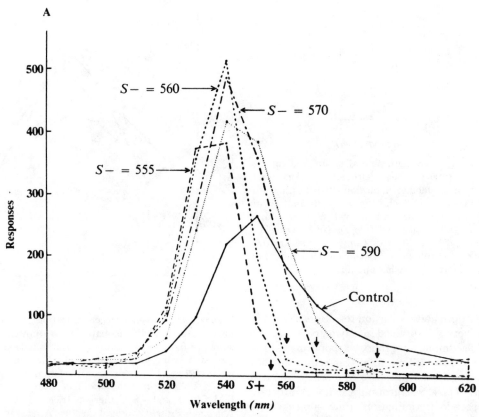

**Figure 2.9.** Wavelength generalization gradients for groups of pigeons trained with a 550 nm stimulus. The groups differed according to the wavelength of light that served as the S⁻. The control group received no negative stimulus. From "Effects of Discrimination Training on Stimulus Generalization" by H.M. Hanson, 1959, *Journal of Experimental Psychology, 58*, p. 324. Copyright 1959 by the American Psychological Association. Reprinted by permission of the publisher and author.

light which served as the S⁻. Figure 2.9 shows the generalization gradients for the experimental groups, as well as for a control group that was not given explicit discrimination training. Control by the wavelength dimension is much sharper in all of the experimental groups as compared to the control group. Secondly, the peak response rates in the experimental groups are higher than that of the control group. The increase in response rate as a result of differential reinforcement is referred to as *behavioral contrast* (see Williams, Chapter 3). Lastly, in the group not given discrimination training, the wavelength that controls the maximal response rate is the S⁺ value, whereas in the differentially trained groups the peak rate occurs in the presence of a stimulus other than the S⁺. The shift in the control of maximal response rate from the S⁺ to a stimulus

in the direction opposite the S⁻ is called *peak shift*. The closer S⁺ and S⁻ are to one another, the greater the shift will be (Blough, 1975). In summary, the three major effects of intradimensional descrimination training are (1) stimulus control sharpens along the dimensions in which the S⁺ and S⁻ differ; (2) behavioral contrast is induced; and (3) peak shift occurs.

INTERDIMENSIONAL TRAINING

The S⁺ and S⁻ in an interdimensional discrimination training procedure differ along independent dimensions. For example, the S⁺ and S⁻ might consist of a light and tone. The effects of this type of discrimination training are detailed in an experiment by Switalski, Lyons, and Thomas (1966). Pigeons were reinforced in the presence of a continuously present 555 nm light and given

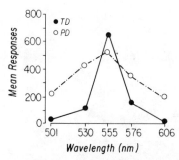

**Figure 2.10.** Wavelength generalization gradients for groups of pigeons exposed to either a true discrimination (TD) or pseudodiscrimination (PD) training procedure. From "The Effects of Interdimensional Training on Stimulus Generalization" by R.W. Switalski, J. Lyons, and D.R. Thomas, 1966, *Journal of Experimental Psychology, 72,* pp. 663–664. Copyright 1966 by the American Psychological Association. Reprinted by permission of the publisher and author.

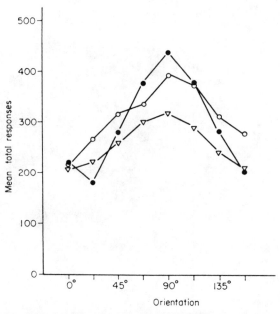

**Figure 2.11.** Wavelength generalization gradients following either true discrimination (closed circle), single-stimulus (triangles), or pseudodiscrimination (open circles) training. From "Attentional Factors Governing the Slope of the Generalization Gradient" by W.K. Honig in *Animal Discrimination Learning* (p. 40), R.M. Gilbert and N.S. Sutherland (Eds.), 1969. London: Academic Press. Copyright 1969 by Academic Press. Reprinted by permission.

a wavelength generalization test. Subsequently, the subjects were divided into two groups. In the true discrimination group, responding in the presence of the 555 nm light was reinforced but responding in the presence of a white vertical line on a black background was not reinforced. In the pseudodiscrimination group, subjects were exposed to the stimuli and reinforced equally often in the presence of both cues. Figure 2.10 shows the results of generalization testing. Control is sharper in the discrimination group than in the pseudodiscrimination group. Furthermore, the gradient obtained after discrimination training is steeper than the gradient obtained after the initial single stimulus training. Hence, interdimensional training results in an increase in the sharpness of stimulus control. Additionally, the peak rate of responding is greatest for the discrimination group. Hence, behavioral contrast may occur both when $S^+$ and $S^-$ come from the same dimension and when they lie along independent dimensions. While $S^+$ and $S^{-}$ need not be drawn from the same dimension for some contrast to occur, the similarity of $S^+$ and $S^-$ is a factor in the amount of contrast obtained. Hearst (1969) found that both intradimensional and interdimensional training produce contrast, but the intradimensional procedure generated more contrast when $S^+$ and $S^-$ were more similar. Interdimensional discrimination training therefore (1) sharpens stimulus control and (2) produces behavioral contrast.

## EXTRADIMENSIONAL TRAINING

Extradimensional training also sharpens stimulus control. Honig (1969) exposed three groups of pigeons to either true discrimination, pseudo-discrimination, or single stimulus ($S^+$) training in which white and pink keylights served as stimuli. This phase was followed by single stimulus training in which all subjects were reinforced for responding in the presence of a key illuminated with white light and three vertical lines. The results of subsequent generalization tests along the angularity dimension are shown in Figure 2.11. Steeper gradients were obtained from subjects pretrained in the true discrimination procedure than were obtained from subjects not exposed to a differential reinforcement contingency. Similarly, Thomas, Freeman, Svinicki, Burr, and Lyons (1970) trained subjects to discriminate between wavelengths and then reinforced keypecking in the presence of a continuously present vertical white line superimposed on the previous $S^+$. Sharper generalization gradients along the angularity dimension were obtained from the differentially trained subjects than from a comparable pseudodiscrimination group. Hence, extradimensional discrimination training increases the sharpness of stimulus control. The effects of extradimensional training on absolute response rates have not been the object of much scrutiny. Most experiments on extradimensional training result in peak response rates to the $S^+$ value that are equal to or greater than the peak response rates in comparable single stimulus or pseudodiscrimination control groups (Honig, 1969; Thomas et al., 1970).

In summary, subjects exposed to either single stimulus training or pseudodiscrimination training often show generalization gradients of nonzero slope. Thus, for stimuli to gain some control over responding, it is not necessary for reinforcement conditions *within* an experimental session to be differentially correlated with stimuli changes *within* the actual session. However, discrimination training does sharpen stimulus control. This is true for intradimensional, interdimensional, and extradimensional training procedures. Additionally, behavioral contrast has been reliably demonstrated with both intradimensional and interdimensional training procedures, and peak shift has been obtained with intradimensional training procedures in which both positive and negative stimuli are drawn from the same dimension.

### Differential Reinforcement in Operant and Pavlovian Conditioning

The data from operant conditioning experiments reviewed in the preceding section make it clear that differential reinforcement within an experimental session is not a necessary condition for the acquisition of stimulus control. On the other hand, discussions of Pavlovian conditioning frequently argue that a differential correlation between stimuli and reinforcement is a *necessary* condition for the development of stimulus control (Rescorla, 1967). Hearst (Chapter 1) reviews the evidence that supports this position. Briefly, excitatory CRs emerge in Pavlovian procedures when the probability of the US in the presence of the CS is greater than the probability of the US in the absence of the CS. Inhibitory control develops when the probability of reinforcement in the presence of the CS is less than the probability of reinforcement in the absence of the CS. When the probability of the US in the presence and absence of the CS is equal, no CR is evoked by the CS. Hence, it is possible that differential reinforcement is necessary for the emergence of stimulus control in Pavlovian procedures but not in operant procedures. However, the procedures used to study nondifferential reinforcement are generally quite different in instrumental and Pavlovian experiments, as are the responses used to assess stimulus control.

The typical operant and Pavlovian procedure differ drastically in the percentage of time that the stimuli are present. Pavlovian procedures usually have long ITI periods without any $CS^+$ or $CS^-$ presentations. Conversely, typical operant discrimination procedures have most of a session filled with $S^+$ and $S^-$ presentations—that is, there is usually little or no ITI. When the nominal stimuli in a Pavlovian experiment are on for a large proportion of the session, as they are in a typical operant experiment, excitatory control has been observed after exposure to nondifferential reinforcement procedures (Benedict & Ayres, 1972; Brandon, 1981; Kremer & Kamin, 1971). Furthermore, the Pavlovian equivalent of single stimulus training does result in control by that stimulus, although there is not within-session differential reinforcement (Balsam, 1982, 1984, 1985; Durlach, 1982; Rescorla, Durlach, & Grau, 1985; Tomie, 1985). Balsam (1985) presented food to hungry doves in the presence of continuous contextual cues. General activity levels rapidly increased. Control of activity by contextual cues was tested by exposing subjects to contexts that were either the same as or different from the training context in visual, auditory, and tactile cues. Figure 2.12 shows the results of one experiment in which the test consisted of five sesions of nonreinforced exposure to the test context. Only those subjects tested in the presence of the context previously associated with food show much activity. The activity extinguishes across days and shows spontaneous recovery from the end of one session to the beginning of the next. Thus, continuously presented cues in Pavlovian procedures may gain control over conditioned responses even though there is no explicit differential reinforcement.

These experiments show that the form of the response that is controlled by contextual cues may be very different from the response that would have been controlled by a discrete CS. If

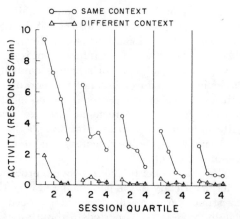

**Figure 2.12.** General activity levels during extinction for two groups of doves. The extinction context was the same as or different from the training context. From "The Functions of Context in Learning and Performance" by P.D. Balsam in *Context and Learning* (p. 8), P. Balsam and A. Tomie (Eds.), 1985. Hillsdale, NJ: Erlbaum. Copyright 1985 by Lawrence Erlbaum Associates Inc. Reprinted by permission.

the food had been signaled by a change in the illumination of a keylight, the keylight would have come to control a keypeck response (Brown & Jenkins, 1968), a response form that is very different from the locomotor activity controlled by contextual cues. While keylights and contextual cues differ in many ways, two salient differences are their duration and the frequency of reinforcement in their presence. Both of these factors may influence the form of the Pavlovian CR (Holland, 1980a; Innis, Simmelhag-Grant, & Staddon, 1983). Since these variables may influence response form as well as response strength, it is possible that differential, single stimulus, and nondifferential procedures may result in topographically different CRs. In the comparable operant experiment, the response form is selected by the contingencies. Hence, instrumental response forms will be identical in nondifferential, single stimulus, and differential procedures. The apparent difference in the conditions that give rise to stimulus control in operant and Pavlovian procedures may, therefore, result from procedural and measurement differences in the two paradigms. It is premature to attribute differences in the effects of nondifferential reinforcement in operant and Pavlovian procedures to differences in underlying processes.

## STIMULUS SELECTION

While differential reinforcement of stimuli within an experimental session may not be necessary, it is a sufficient condition for bringing behavior under the control of stimuli correlated with different reinforcement conditions. However, stimuli are not unidimensional. All stimuli are multidimensional, in that they lie on more than one sensory continuum. A visual stimulus, for example, will have wavelength, intensity, goemetric, spatial, and temporal properties. All stimuli are also multidimensional in the sense that they are always presented as part of a stimulus compound composed of the nominal stimulus and the experimental context (see Figure 2.8). Hence, an account of stimulus control must include an explication of which aspects of a stimulus gain control over responding.

In order to explore this question experimentally, stimuli must be chosen which allow for the manipulation of qualities along at least two independent dimensions. The independence of dimensions is desirable so that control by a particular dimension can be established. For example, changes in the frequency of an auditory stimulus affect perceived loudness as well as pitch. Hence, behavior change correlated with variation in frequency may be under the control of pitch and/or loudness. Although such effects make for some difficulty in specifying the controlling stimulus, in practice, the dimension that is varied by the experimenter is referred to as the controlling dimension. One way in which such interactions are thought to be minimized is by studying stimulus compounds whose elements can be added, subtracted, and presented separately. The capacity of each separate element to act as a controlling stimulus when presented *alone* suggests that its controlling power does not depend on the modulation of the controlling power of other elements with which it was originally compounded. The assumption is that these discrete elements are analogous to the dimensions of what we consider in everyday experience as a unitary stimulus (see Riley, 1984, for a discussion of different types of compound stimuli).

For example, Reynolds (1961) reinforced pigeons' keypecks when a keylight was illuminated with a red triangle (S$^+$). When the keylight was illuminated with a green circle, no keypecks were reinforced (S$^-$). The left side of Figure 2.13 shows the performance of two

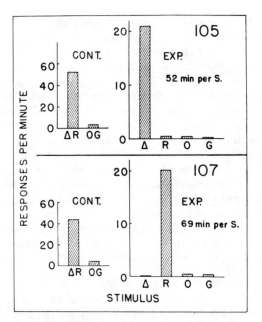

**Figure 2.13.** The left panels show the response rate of two subjects in the presence of red triangle (S⁺) and green circle (S⁻). The right panels show the response rate in the presence of each separately presented element. From "Attention in the Pigeon" by G.S. Reynolds, 1961, *Journal of the Experimental Analysis of Behavior, 4*, p. 204. Copyright 1961 by the Society for the Experimental Analysis of Behavior, Inc. Reprinted by permission.

subjects in the presence of the S⁺ and S⁻. Both subjects respond more in the presence of the red triangle than in the presence of the green circle. The shapes and colors were also separately presented during test trials. The right side of Figure 2.13 shows that one subject's behavior was under the control of the shape projected on the key, whereas the other subject's behavior was under the control of the keylight color. Differential reinforcement insures that some, but not necessarily all, aspects of a stimulus will control responding.

## Factors Affecting Stimulus Selection

As Reynolds' (1961) study illustrates, not all aspects of stimuli in whose presence a response is reinforced gain control over responding. Which particular element gains control is influenced by many factors, including properties of stimuli, training contingencies, the past history of the subject, and the species under study.

### Salience

The intensity or *salience* of a stimulus element affects the strength of control that the element will gain over responding when it is part of a compound stimulus. Kamin (1969a, 1969b) examined the disruption of an ongoing food-reinforced operant by the elements of an audio-visual compound that had been paired with shock. When the compound consisted of a light and soft noise, there was very little suppression to the noise alone. When the light was compounded with a loud noise during training, there was more suppression to the auditory stimulus but still less suppression than if the noise alone had been paired with shock. The light overshadowed the noise, in that the presence of the light in compound with the noise interfered with the strength of control acquired by the noise. The amount of overshadowing of the noise by the light was inversely related to the intensity of the noise. In general, as the salience of a cue increases, the level of control acquired by that cue, as opposed to other concurrently presented cues, increases (Mackintosh, 1975; Rescorla & Wagner, 1972).

### Cue-Consequence Specificity

The aspects of a stimulus that gain control over responding are also influenced by the particular combination of conditioned and unconditioned stimuli (Domjan, 1980, 1983). The taste aversion studies of Garcia and his colleagues (Garcia & Koelling, 1966; Garcia, McGowen, & Green, 1972) have often been used to make this point. In these studies, rats were either shocked or made ill with a toxin after consuming saccharin solution in the presence of a light and clicker. Subsequently, subjects were tested for an aversion in the presence of each of the elements of the compound. Figure 2.14 summarizes the results of the test and shows that when the US caused illness, the gustatory stimuli overshadowed the audio-visual cues. On the other hand, when shock was used as the US, the audio-visual cues overshadowed the gustatory stimuli. Cue-consequence specificity has also been shown to vary with the species under study. For example, many birds, unlike the rat, learn to reject food that has been associated with illness on the basis of visual cues rather than gustatory ones (Braverman, 1977; Wilcoxin, Dragoin, & Kral, 1971). Cue-consequence specificity has also been demonstrated with food and shock USs. When trained

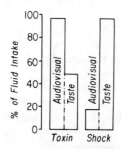

**Figure 2.14.** Summary of experimental results in which gustatory-audio-visual compounds served as CSs. Different USs result in different elements gaining control over the aversion. From "Biological Constraints on Conditioning" in Abraham H. Black, William F. Prokasy (Eds.), *Classical Conditioning II: Current Research and Theory*, (c) 1972, p. 8. Reprinted by permission of Prentice-Hall, Inc., Englewood Cliffs, NJ.

with audio-visual compounds, both chicks (Shettleworth, 1972) and pigeons (Foree & LoLordo, 1973) show strongest control by the visual component when the US is ingestional but strongest control by the auditory component when the US is shock.

Cue-consequence specificity is sometimes offered as an example of a species-specific adaptation, implying that the specific selectivity in a given species is genetically determined (Foree & LoLordo, 1973; Garcia, McGowen, & Green, 1972; LoLordo, 1979; Rozin & Kalat, 1971). However, studies of cue-consequence specificity are generally done with adult animals. There is, therefore, much opportunity for past experience to exert an influence on cue selectivity.

### Response Quality

Another interesting, though little studied, determinant of stimulus selection is the nature of the response. Harrison (1983) has demonstrated that the relationship between the spatial location of discriminative stimuli and the spatial location of response manipulanda has an influence on the acquisition of stimulus control. When antecedent stimuli and response manipulanda are in close spatial proximity, there is substantial facilitation of the acquisition of discriminative performance. Along these lines, Dobrzecka, Szwejkowska, and Konorski (1966) trained two groups of dogs to discriminate between a metronome positioned in front of the dog and a buzzer located behind the dog. One group of subjects was trained to lift one foreleg in response to one of the stim-

uli and to lift the other foreleg to the other stimulus. The second group was trained in a go/no-go discrimination, in which they were required to lift one foreleg in the presence of one stimulus and to refrain from responding in the presence of the alternative stimulus. After discriminative performance had been established in both groups, subjects were tested with the spatial location of the metronome and buzzer reversed. Subjects previously trained to raise one or the other foreleg responded on the basis of the location of the auditory stimulus. Subjects trained on the go/no-go procedure responded on the basis of the quality of the stimulus and not on its location. Hence, the nature of the required response, can affect which aspects of a stimulus gain control over responding.

### Stimulus Discriminability

Another factor related to the salience of the stimuli is how discriminable elements of the $S^+$ are from elements of the $S^-$. Miles and Jenkins (1973) studied the effects of stimulus discriminability on the acquisition of stimulus control in pigeons. Subjects were reinforced in the presence of an audio-visual compound and not reinforced in the presence of a visual $S^-$ that only differed from the visual component of the $S^+$ in intensity. In different groups of subjects the difference between the intensity of the visual stimulus on $S^+$ and $S^-$ trials was varied. Figure 2.15 shows that the control by the light and tone were inversely related to one another. When the visual discrimination was easy, the light overshadowed the tone; when the visual discrimination was difficult, the tone overshadowed the light. In the extreme case, when the light was identical on $S^+$ and $S^-$ trials, the tone exerted maximal control over responding.

### Predictive Validity

The importance of the predictiveness or validity of a cue as a determinant of stimulus control was suggested by Spence (1936) and Hull (1939) in their analyses of discrimination learning. They acknowledged that in any discrimination learning situation there are many simultaneously presented cues which could gain control over responding. They assumed that, on any reinforced trial, the control exerted by *all* stimuli present at the time of reinforcement would increase. This included the elements of background or context present at the time of

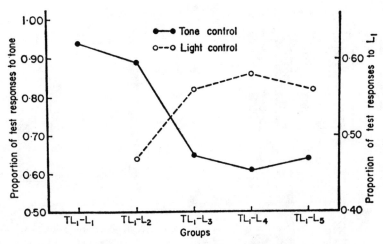

**Figure 2.15.** Control by light and tone elements of a compound, shown as a function of the discriminability of the light element that appeared on positive and negative trials. The light stimuli are ordered with respect to their difference from L1. From *The Psychology of Animal Learning* (p. 581) by N.J. Mackintosh, 1974. London: Academic Press. Copyright 1974 by Academic Press. Reprinted by permission.

reinforcement, as well as the elements of the $S^+$. Similarly, nonreinforced trials decreased the associative strength of *all* nonreinforced cues. The degree of control exerted by a stimulus was assumed to be a function of increments to excitatory strength on reinforced trials and decrements to excitatory strength on nonreinforced trials. In this view, the net excitatory strength that accrues to elements of a compound will depend on how often a particular element appears in reinforced and nonreinforced trials. The predictive validity of a cue will, therefore, affect its control over responding. Notice that this analysis implies that cues that are common to reinforced and nonreinforced trials (common or incidental cues) will have some associative value, albeit less than the explicit $S^+$.

Hearst (Chapter 1) has indicated that cues compete with one another for control over behavior in Pavlovian conditioning. This can be framed in terms of competition for associative value (Rescorla & Wagner, 1972), attention (Mackintosh, 1975; Pearce & Hall, 1980; Thomas, 1970), or processing resources (Wagner, 1978, 1981). Differences in these theories aside, they all agree that the extent to which a cue gains control over behavior is inversely related to the control of other concurrently presented cues. This assumption regarding the role of cues that are part of the reinforced compound is quite different from the one proposed by Hull (1939)

and Spence (1936). Wagner (1969a) illustrated this difference by analyzing the control acquired by a stimulus element that is presented on both $S^+$ and $S^-$ trials. In this example, the common element, $S_c$, is reinforced when it is compounded with one stimulus ($S_1 S_c^+$) and not reinforced when in compound with a second stimulus ($S_2 S_c^-$). According to Hull-Spence theory, the value of $S_c$ will only depend on how frequently it is reinforced or extinguished, whereas according to competition theories, the value of $S_c$ will depend on how reliable a predictor $S_1$ and $S_2$ are.

Wagner, Logan, Haberlandt, and Price (1968) investigated these differing predictions by reinforcing rats for bar pressing in the presence of compound stimuli. Two kinds of compounds were presented. On all trials a light was presented ($S_c$). On half of the trials the light was compounded with one auditory stimulus ($S_1$) and on the remaining trials the light was compounded with a second auditory stimulus ($S_2$). For one group of subjects, half of each kind of trial was followed by reinforcement. For a second group of subjects, every $S_1 S_c$ trial was reinforced and no $S_2 S_c$ trial was reinforced. Hence, in both groups the light ($S_c$) was reinforced on 50% of its presentations. Control by the compound and each of the elements was assayed separately. If stimulus control depends only on the number of reinforced and nonreinforced trials, the light should gain equal control over responding in

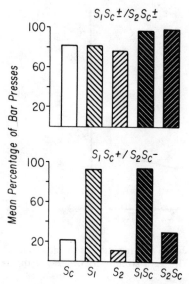

**Figure 2.16.** Control of responding by elements and compounds when S1 and S2 were better correlated with reinforcement conditions (lower panel) than Sc or uncorrelated with reward conditions (top panel). From "Stimulus Selection in Animal Discrimination Learning" by A.R. Wagner, F.A. Logan, K. Haberlandt, and R. Price, 1968, *Journal of Experimental Psychology, 76*, p. 173. Copyright 1968 by the American Psychological Association. Reprinted by permission of the publisher and author.

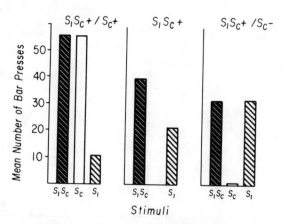

**Figure 2.17.** Control by elements of compounds after reinforced compound trials were intermixed with either reinforced or extinguished presentations of one of the elements by itself. From "Stimulus Validity and Stimulus Selection in Associative Learning" by A.R. Wagner, in *Fundamental Issues in Associative Learning* (p. 97), N.J. Mackintosh and W.K. Honig (Eds.). Halifax: Dalhousie University Press. Reprinted by permission.

both groups. If the relative validity of the cue is the determinant of stimulus control, the light should have less control over responding in the group in which the tone was perfectly correlated with reinforcer presentations than in the group in which the tone and light were equally predictive of reinforcement. Figure 2.16 shows the level of control exerted by the elements of the compounds in both groups. When the tones were perfectly correlated with the reinforcement condition (lower panel), the light ($S_c$) acquired little control over responding. However, the light acquired considerable control over responding in the uncorrelated condition (upper panel), when it was as predictive of reinforcement as the tones.

The role of the relative predictiveness of a cue in acquisition of stimulus control is also illustrated in the analysis of feature discriminations, in which the presence of one element distinguishes between $S^+$ and $S^-$ trials. Wagner (1969b) reports a number of studies in which the strength of control exerted by $S_1$ and $S_c$ were

evaluated after either $S_1S_c^+/S_c^+$ training or after $S_1S_c^+/S_c^-$ training. The results of one experiment in which $S_1$ was a tone and $S_c$ was a light and rats' bar pressing was reinforced are shown in Figure 2.17. In all groups, $S_1$ was reinforced an equal number of times while in compound with $S_c$. Therefore any differences between groups in the control exerted by $S_1$ must be due to differences in the relative validity of the common cue. When $S_c$ was reinforced separately, $S_1$ gained little control over responding. When $S_c$ was presented separately and not reinforced, $S_1$ exerted strong control over responding. Hence, the control exerted by $S_1$ and that exerted by $S_c$ were inversely related to each other and determined by the predictiveness of each cue relative to other concurrently presented cue. Numerous other Pavlovian and operant conditioning experiments (Hearst, Chapter 1; Mackintosh, 1974, 1983) have established that the relative validity of a cue is an important determinant of the strength of stimulus control. Furthermore, the relative validity of a cue also affects the sharpness of stimulus control.

Gray and Mackintosh (1973) exposed groups of pigeons to either a true discrimination (TD) or pseudodiscrimination (PD) procedure in a design that was similar to the Wagner et al. (1968) experiment. In this case, pigeons given

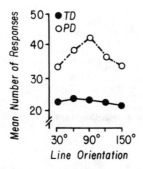

**Figure 2.18.** Generalization gradients following either pseudodiscrimination (PD) or true discrimination (TD) training in which a vertical line served as an element common to both trial types. From "Control by an Irrelevant Stimulus in Discrete-Trial Discrimination Learning by Pigeons" by V.A. Gray and N.J. Mackintosh, 1973, *Bulletin of the Psychonomic Society*, *1*, p. 194. Copyright 1973 by the Psychonomic Society. Reprinted by permission.

differential training (TD) were reinforced in the presence of a tone $S_1$ and vertical line $S_c (S_1 S_c^+)$ and extinguished in the presence of a white noise and vertical line $(S_2 S_c^-)$. Pigeons given nondifferential training (PD) were reinforced equally often in the presence of both stimuli. Postdiscrimination generalization gradients for the line orientation dimension $(S_c)$ are shown in Figure 2.18. The generalization gradients show that $S_c$ controls lower response rates when it was the common cue in a differential procedure, replicating the Wagner et al. (1968) results. The slopes of the gradients show that control was sharper when $S_c$ was a more valid predictor of reinforcement than when $S_c$ was a poor predictor of reward relative to other cues. Hence, the predictive validity of a cue is directly related to both the strength and sharpness of control exerted by that cue (but see Thomas, Burr, & Eck, 1970).

In all discriminative conditioning procedures, contextual cues are common to both reinforced and nonreinforced trials. Consequently, the context may play a role comparable to that of an explicit $S_c$. In the usual conditioning procedure, reinforcers are presented in the presence of one stimulus $(S_1)$ in compound with the contextual cues, and contextual cues are presented alone and extinguished during the ITI. Contextual cues are, therefore, common to reinforced and nonreinforced trials. In the mixture of $S_1 S_c^+$ and $S_c^-$ trials, $S_1$ is a good predictor of reinforcement relative to $S_c$. Hence, the procedure results in

strong control by the $S^+$. If reinforcers were presented during the ITI as well as during the $S^+$ $(S_1 S_c^+$ and $S_c^+)$, then the increase in the predictive validity of contextural cues should result in increased control by the context and decreased control by $S_1$. Random control procedures (Hearst, Chapter 1; Rescorla, 1967) arrange for an equal likelihood of reinforcement in the presence and absence of a CS. Under these conditions, there is little control acquired by the CS, but context conditioning is strong (Tomie, 1981, 1985).

The effects of various temporal manipulations may also be understood in terms of the relative predictiveness of cues and contexts. In this case, the relative temporal predictiveness of the cue and context will influence the level of control acquired by each (Gibbon, 1977). Cues that signal brief delays to reinforcement, relative to the delays signaled by the context, will gain strong control over behavior. Cues that do not signal briefer delays to reinforcement than the context gain relatively little control over responding.

At least in Pavlovian procedures, as the delay to reinforcement in the presence of a signal (T) relative to the delay of reinforcement in the context (C) decreases, the probability of a CR increases (Balsam, 1984; Gibbon, Baldock, Locurto, Gold, & Terrace, 1977; Gibbon & Balsam, 1981; Gormezano & Kehoe, 1981). Figure 2.19 shows the number of trials it took pigeons to acquire a CR when a keylight was paired with grain in a number of different experiments. Acquisition speed is shown as a function of the ratio of the total time between reinforcer presentations (C) to CS duration (T). It is clear that the acquisition of control by the CS is a function of the ratio of these two variables. As CS duration increases relative to the time between reinforcer presentations, control by the CS decreases. According to the foregoing analysis, along with the decline in CS control, there should be a concomitant increase in control by the context. One fear-conditioning study (Odling-Smee, 1975) analyzed context conditioning as a function of CS duration and concluded that control by contextual cues increased with increases in CS duration,

In summary, the predictive validity of a cue relative to that of other concurrently presented cues strongly influences the strength and sharpness of control exerted by those cues.

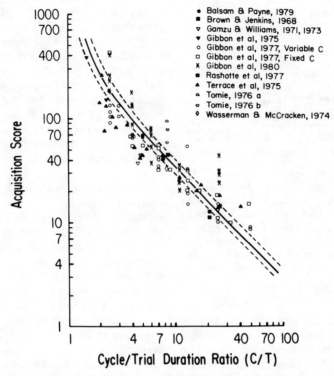

**Figure 2.19.** Acquisition speed shown as a function of the ratio of the average overall delay of reinforcement in the context (C) to the average delay of reinforcement in the CS (T). From "The Spread of Association in Time" by J.G. Gibbon and P.D. Balsam in *Autoshaping and Conditioning Theory* (p. 245), C.M. Locurto, H.S. Terrace, and J.G. Gibbon (Eds.), 1981. New York: Academic Press. Copyright 1981 by Academic Press. Reprinted by permission.

### Prior Conditioning

Not only does the relative validity of cues influence which aspects of a stimulus acquire control over behavior, but so does the prior reinforcement history of the various aspects of a stimulus. As Hearst (Chapter 1) points out, if one stimulus is paired with a reinforcer and subsequently compounded with a novel stimulus, the novel stimulus will acquire less control over responding than it would have if it had been conditioned without a pretrained element present. The pretrained element is said to block the acquisition of control by the novel element (Kamin, 1969a, 1969b). Both the strength and sharpness of stimulus control can be blocked in this fashion (Hall & Honig, 1974; Johnson, 1970; Miles, 1970; Vom Saal & Jenkins, 1970; Welker, Tomie, Davitt, & Thomas, 1974).

A study conducted by Mackintosh and Honig (1970) illustrates both aspects of blocking. Subjects were trained on a line orientation discrimination during the first phase of this experiment.

The second phase of the experiment consisted of further discrimination training, in which the $S^+$ and $S^-$ were compounded with different colored backgrounds. Control by the wavelength dimension was assessed in this group, as well as in a group of subjects that had only been trained on the compound stimuli. Figure 2.20 shows that pretraining on the orientation dimension decreased both the strength and sharpness of control exerted by the wavelength dimension.

In summary, there is an inverse relation between the control exerted by one element or aspect of a stimulus and the control exerted by other concurrently present aspects of that stimulus. More salient, relevant, or predictive cues gain more control over responding than do less salient, or predictive stimuli. However, operations that appear procedurally identical to ones that interfere with the acquisition of stimulus control sometimes result in enhanced, rather than diminished, control by elements of a compound.

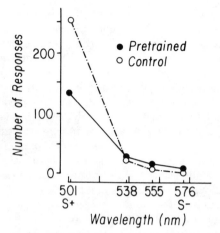

**Figure 2.20.** Control by the wavelength dimension for groups of subjects trained with a colored light compounded with a vertical line as an $S^+$. One group of subjects had been pretrained on a line orientation discrimination, whereas the control group had not. From "Blocking and Attentional Enhancement of Stimulus Control in Pigeons" by N.J. Mackintosh and W.K. Honig, 1970, *Journal of Comparative and Physiological Psychology, 73,* p. 80. Copyright 1970 by the American Psychological Association. Reprinted by permission of the publisher and author.

## Potentiation

Sometimes stronger control is exerted by a stimulus when it has been trained as one element of a compound than if that stimulus had been given an equivalent amount of training by itself. For example, when ingestion of a substance with novel visual and gustatory properties is followed by a toxin, the resulting visually controlled aversion is stronger than when the visual cue by itself is followed by poisoning (Clark, Westbrook, & Irwin, 1979; Galef & Osborne, 1978; Lett, 1980). Potentiation of control by one element when it is trained as part of a compound has also been observed in several other types of compounds (Durlach & Rescorla, 1980; Lett, 1982; Mackintosh & Honig, 1970; Rusniak, Hankins, Garcia, & Brett, 1979; Thomas, Freeman, Svinicki, Burr, & Lyons, 1970).

On the one hand, there is an extensive literature (reviewed in the preceding section) that demonstrates competition between elements of a compound for control over responding. On the other hand, potentiation demonstrates that sometimes greater control over responding is achieved in compound conditioning than by single element training. The source of this apparent contradiction has been analyzed by Durlach and Rescorla (1980).

Durlach and Rescorla (1980) point out that during compound conditioning subjects may, in addition to learning about the relationship between stimuli and reinforcers, acquire associations between the elements of compounds themselves. Hence, performance controlled by one element of a compound may be a reflection of its own direct control over behavior, as well as control over behavior via its association with other elements of a compound. Durlach and Rescorla reasoned that if interelement associations mediate the potentiation effect, nonreinforced presentation of one element of a compound should extinguish interelement associations and eliminate potentiation. In the actual experiment, they first established that an aversion to an odor was greater when it had been trained as part of an odor-taste compound than if it had been trained as the sole cue prior to toxin presentation. In order to investigate the role of the odor-taste association in producing this potentiation, they poisoned rats after exposure to two odor-taste compounds and after exposure to a third odor presented alone. Following aversion conditioning to all three substances, one of the tastes was presented and not reinforced. Figure 2.21 shows the result of tests in which subjects were given a choice between the singly trained odor (O1) and one of the two odors trained in compound with a taste. The left panel shows potentiation, in that subjects consumed less in the presence of the odor when it had been trained as part of the taste-odor compound (O2) than when it had been trained by itself (O1). The right panel shows that there was no difference between the amount consumed of the singly trained odor (O1) and the compound trained odor if subjects had experienced nonreinforced exposure to the taste element between training and testing (O3). Reduced control by the odor cue implies that its control over the aversion was mediated by the within-compound association. Nonreinforced exposure to the taste element could have reduced the associative value of the taste and/or weakened the associative connection between the taste and the odor. Other manipulations which reduce within-compound associations (separate presentation of elements; serial as opposed to simultaneous presentation of elements) also reduce potentiation (Durlach & Rescorla,

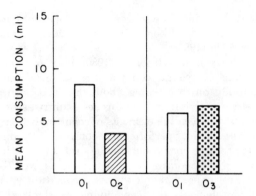

**Figure 2.21.** Amount of fluid consumed as a function of whether odor had been trained singly (O1), in compound with a flavor (O2), or in compound with the flavor but had the flavor extinguished prior to testing (O3). From "Potentiation Rather Than Overshadowing in Flavor-Aversion Learning" by P. Durlach and R.A. Rescorla, 1980, *Journal of Experimental Psychology: Animal Behavior Processes, 6*, p. 184. Copyright 1980 by the American Psychological Association. Reprinted by permission of the publisher and author.

1980; Rescorla, 1981a, 1981b; Rescorla & Colwill, 1984). Other manipulations which increase interelement associations (prior exposure to compounds (Rescorla, 1981a; Rescorla & Colwill, 1984; pairings of elements (Rescorla, 1980)) result in the transfer of control from one element to another. This is true for both Pavlovian conditioned stimuli (Rescorla, 1980), as well as for transfer of control from one discriminative stimulus to another (Terrace, 1966; Trapold & Overmier, 1972). Hence, potentiation appears to result from accrual of control by a particular cue through its association with other cues— cues which are themselves valid signals for reinforcers.

The net control exerted by a particular stimulus element results from the simultaneous operation of both competition and potentiation between aspects of stimuli. The elements of a stimulus simultaneously compete with one another for stimulus control and enhance the control exerted by an element through their mutual association. If a compound stimulus, $S_1 S_2$, is a valid cue for reinforcement, $S_1$ and $S_2$ will compete with each other for control over performance. Since they are presented simultaneously, $S_1$ and $S_2$ are also likely to become associated with one another. The control exerted by $S_1$ will reflect the combined effect of its competi-

tion with $S_2$ for direct control over responding as well as the indirect control over responding mediated by associations with $S_2$. As has already been pointed out, the strength of these processes is modulated by separate experiences with elements of the compound, the temporal and spatial structure of the compound, and the physical similarity of elements (Rescorla, 1980). Standard assays of blocking or overshadowing may therefore underestimate the degree of competition between stimuli, whereas studies of potentiation may underestimate the enhanced control mediated by interelement associations.

In summary, the net strength and sharpness of stimulus control appears to result from the simultaneous action of two processes that describe the interaction of stimulus elements. One process is competition between elements for direct control over behavior. The second source of stimulus control is via the associations between elements of compound stimuli. All stimuli are multidimensional and presented in an environmental context. The level of control acquired by a particular aspect of a stimulus is the result of the interactions of that stimulus with all the other aspects of that stimulus and its context. Hence, in even the simplest sort of discrimination experiment, such as that depicted in Figure 2.8, the control exerted by the $S^+$ will be a function of both the relative validity of $S^+$ and the strength of mediated control that is acquired through the associations between the $S^+$, the context, the $S^-$, and the reinforcer (Rescorla, 1984).

## Mechanisms of Stimulus Selection

Generally the control acquired by a particular cue is inversely related to the control acquired by concurrently presented cues. This has been termed the *inverse hypothesis* by Thomas (1970), and a number of mechanisms have been suggested to account for the apparent competition between stimuli for control over responding.

There are two general ways to interpret the decrease in control by some cues that is concomitant to an increase in control by other cues. One interpretation is that the stimuli actually compete with each other in some process that affects the acquisition of stimulus control (Blough, 1975, 1983; Mackintosh, 1975; Rescorla, 1976; Rescorla & Wagner, 1972; Thomas, 1970; Wagner, 1969a, 1969b). Competition may occur for some limited resource, such as attention

(Lovejoy, 1968; Sutherland & Mackintosh, 1971), memory (Mazur & Wagner, 1982; Wagner, 1978, 1981), or associative strength (Blough, 1975; Rescorla, 1976; Rescorla & Wagner, 1972). To the extent that a stimulus commands these resources, the strength of control over behavior is enhanced and, because the resource is limited, control by other stimuli is decreased.

Alternatively, manipulations which result in increases in stimulus control may do so through performance mechanisms. An increase in control may occur as a result of "neutralizing" the control exerted by other concurrently presented cues (Mackintosh, 1977; Thomas, 1985). The neutralization of these stimuli may allow control by other cues to be expressed. The degree of stimulus control exerted by a cue may, therefore, be the result of changes in the control exerted by that stimulus and/or changes in the ability of other stimuli to mask control by that cue.

Both masking and overshadowing are illustrated in a study conducted by Farthing (1972). Two groups of pigeons were trained on a discrimination in which a vertical line on a red background served as the S+. For one group (line-color compound) the S− consisted of a green keylight; for the second group (line only) the keylight color was the same on positive and negative trials. Figure 2.22 shows the results of a generalization test for control by the orientation dimension, both in the presence and in the absence of the red background. Control is stronger and sharper during the test in the absence of the red background than in its presence. This difference illustrates a masking effect. Even when tested in the absence of the colored background, however, the group trained with orientation as the only relevant cue shows stronger and sharper control than do subjects trained with both color and orientation as relevant dimensions. This residual difference reflects a difference in the strength of stimulus control acquired during original training (Farthing, 1972; Mackintosh, 1977, 1983; Thomas, 1985). Hence, different aspects of a cue may interfere with each other at both a learning and performance level. Concurrently presented stimuli may compete with one another, affecting the level of stimulus control that is acquired during training. They may also interfere with the expression of stimulus control at the performance level by masking existing levels of control.

The masking of control by concurrently pres-

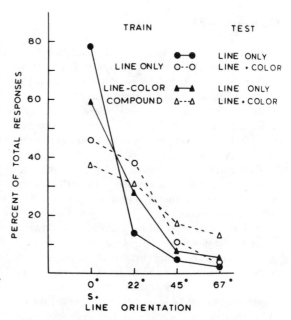

**Figure 2.22.** Generalization gradients along the orientation dimension for groups of subjects that were either trained with a line-color compound or line alone as the S+. Testing took place either in the presence or absence of the color. From "Overshadowing in the Discrimination of Successive Compound Stimuli" by G.W. Farthing, 1972, *Psychonomic Science, 28*, p. 31. Copyright 1972 by the Psychonomic Society. Reprinted by permission.

ented stimuli may reflect a very general process. Gibbon and colleagues (Gibbon, 1977, 1979; Gibbon & Balsam, 1981; Gibbon & Church, 1984) have suggested that the strength of performance of learned behavior is inversely related to the value of the reinforcement context in which the performance is tested. The strength of performance controlled by a particular stimulus depends on the ratio of the reinforcement value of a signal to the reinforcement value of the context. This formulation is quite similar to conceptualizations of choice which are framed in terms of the reinforcement context in which choices are made (see Williams, Chapter 3). Similar proposals have been offered for the analysis of inhibitory control (Balsam, 1984; Kaplan & Hearst, 1985; Miller & Schachtman, 1985).

In summary, both the degree to which a stimulus comes to control a response and the strength with which that control is expressed are inversely related to the control acquired by other concurrently presented cues.

## Contents of Learning

Thus far it has not been necessary to distinguish between stimulus control in operant and Pavlovian conditioning. The relative validity of a cue seems to be a basic determinant of control in both paradigms, and, at a procedural level, variables that affect stimulus selection do so comparably in both paradigms. However, in the instrumental case the nature of the response that leads to reinforcement must be learned, whereas no such requirement is imposed in the Pavlovian case. Thus, the contents of learning might differ in the two procedures.

A Pavlovian procedure consists of arranging a contingency between two stimuli, and an instrumental procedure arranges contingencies between two stimuli and at least one response. The associations that are acquired through these experiences may be structured in several ways. When a response occurs in the presence of a stimulus and is followed by reinforcer presentation, three binary forward associations are possible. Antecedent stimuli may become associated with responses (S-R), antecedent stimuli may become associated with reinforcers (S-S), and responses may become associated with reinforcers (R-S). Additionally, a hierarchical associative network might result in which one element signals relations between other elements. For example, a discriminative stimulus signals the status of a response-reinforcer relation (Skinner, 1938). Its function, therefore, might be to gate a response-reinforcer association. There has been surprisingly little work done on the contents of association, and this work is almost exclusively in the Pavlovian domain.

The most commonly used technique for studying the contents of Pavlovian associations is attributed to Rozeboom (1958). The basic strategy is to alter the stimulus properties of one of the potentially associated elements and to assay the impact of that manipulation on the control exerted by other elements. For example, the nature of aassociations in second-order conditioning has been studied fairly extensively by pairing S2 with S1 (which has been paired with a US). After conditioned responding has been established to S2, S1 is extinguished. Presumably behavior which is derived from S-S associations will be altered. By default, it is assumed that S-R associations are not affected by postconditioning alterations in reinforcer value. Evidence for both S-S and S-R learning has been obtained in this way. Some experiments find little effect of S1 value on behavior controlled by S2 (Amiro & Bitterman, 1980; Cheatle & Rudy, 1978; Holland & Rescorla, 1975; Nairne & Rescorla, 1981; Rizley & Rescorla, 1972), while other experiments have found considerable impact of S1 value on S2 controlled performance (Durlach & Rescorla, 1980; Rashotte, Griffin, & Sisk, 1977; Rescorla, 1980; Rescorla & Colwill, 1983). It appears that these differences between experiments may be attributed to differences in factors that promote either S-S or S-R learning. For example, stimulus similarity and simultaneity encourage S-S rather than S-R learning (Nairne & Rescorla, 1981; Rescorla, 1980). These types of learning are not mutually exclusive.

In first-order conditioning, evidence for both S-S and S-R associations has also been obtained. Postconditioning US devaluation via satiation, habituation, or counterconditioning has been shown to produce changes in the strength of the CR evoked by the CS (Holland & Rescorla, 1975; Holland & Straub, 1979), but in at least one study (Riley, Jacobs, & LoLordo, 1976), attempts to change US properties have failed to affect CR strength. Furthermore, Holland and Straub (1979) found that US manipulations may affect some responses controlled by the CS, while leaving other CR forms unaffected by the manipulation. Hence, both S-S and S-R connections have been shown to underlie the control over behavior exerted by Pavlovian CSs, and both kinds of connections can and do exist simultaneously.

In early theories of instrumental conditioning, S-R connections were thought to underlie the acquisition of stimulus control (Guthrie, 1935; Hull, 1943; Thorndike, 1911; Watson, 1919). In contrast to these views, Tolman (1932) suggested that instrumental learning also involved learning about the goal object, the reinforcer. Later analyses of instrumental learning allowed for the learning of both S-S associations and S-R associations (Mowrer, 1947; Spence, 1956). In these and related views (Rescorla & Solomon, 1967), the role of the S-S association was important in the performance of the response, but the instrumental response itself was thought to be learned through S-R associations. Modifications of these theories allowed for the association of the stimulus feedback from responses to be associated with reinforcers (Miller, 1963; Mowrer, 1960).

More recent theoretical analyses have included R-S associations as a basis of instrumental learning (Bolles, 1972; Dickinson, 1980; Mackintosh, 1974, 1983; Mackintosh & Dickinson, 1979) and allowed for interactions between S-S, R-S, and/ or S-R associations to determine performance (Bolles, 1972; Dickinson, 1980; Mackintosh, 1983; Overmier & Lawry, 1979; Trapold & Overmier, 1972). Finally, the possibility of an associative structure in which a $S^+$ acts as a higher order control element for other associations has also been suggested (Estes, 1972, 1976, 1979). In this role, the $S^+$ enables or gates the effectiveness of an R-S connection. In other words, the antecedent stimulus exerts control over a whole R-S unit. Perhaps because of the explicit way in which reinforcement depends on the subject's behavior in the instrumental procedure, S-(R-S) control has been suggested as a mechanism of control in instrumental learning (Colwill & Rescorla, 1983, 1985; Jenkins, 1977; Mackintosh, 1983; Skinner, 1938).

With so many possible associations for the reinforcer to enter into, the effects of postconditioning change in reinforcer value are of considerable interest. St. Claire-Smith and MacLaren (1983) did an experiment in which rats' bar presses were followed by a light or a tone. Subsequently, the lights or tones were paired with either food or electric shock. Responses that had previously produced the stimulus that was subsequently paired with food increased in frequency, whereas responses that had produced the stimulus subsequently paired with shock decreased in frequency. Along similar lines, Colwill and Rescorla (1985) trained rats to make two different responses for two distinct reinforcers. Subsequently, the value of one of the reinforcers was changed via counterconditioning or satiation, and the strength of both responses was tested. The results showed that postconditioning devaluation of the reinforcer decreased the strength of the response that had led to that reinforcer during training, but the strength of the response that had led to the alternative reinforcer was unaffected by the manipulation. Thus an association between a specific response and specific reinforcer (R-S) is acquired through operant conditioning.

A similar conclusion has been reached by Peterson (1984) but with very different methodology (Trapold, 1970). In these studies, the role of US expectancy in discrimination learning was investigated in two-choice discriminative conditioning procedures, in which the different choices were sometimes associated with unique outcomes. In the differential outcome condition, one cue (S1) signaled that one response (R1) would be followed with a particular reinforcer (O1; e.g., a food pellet). The second response alternative (R2) was never reinforced in the presence of S1. When a second cue (S2) was presented, R1 was no longer reinforced but R2 was followed by a different unique outcome (O2; e.g., water). Subjects learned this discrimination much faster than either a discrimination in which outcomes of the two responses are randomly mixed (O1 and O2) or a discrimination in which both responses lead to the same outcome (O1 or O2) (Carlson & Wielkiewicz, 1972; Peterson & Trapold, 1980, 1982; Peterson, Wheeler, & Armstrong, 1978; Peterson, Wheeler, & Trapold, 1980). Hence, information about which particular response leads to which particular reinforcer is part of what may be learned in instrumental conditioning.

While unique response-outcome correlations facilitate the acquisition of the two-choice discrimination, they are not necessary for accurate discriminative performance to develop. Subjects in the common and mixed outcome conditions do eventually solve the discrimination problem. The successful performance of subjects in the mixed and common cue conditions demonstrates that subjects are capable of more than R-S and S-S associations in instrumental learning. If the only associations possible in instrumental procedures were S-S or R-S, the discrimination would not be solvable, since both stimuli and responses are associated with identical outcomes. Furthermore, one can eliminate differential S-S contingencies and maintain discriminative performance. If reinforcers are presented in the absence of the $S^+$ at the same rate at which they can be earned in the presence of the $S^+$, the stimulus-reinforcer relationship is degraded, yet subjects will confine their responding, albeit at lower rates, to the presence of the $S^+$ (Jenkins, 1977; Weiss, 1971). Some linkage between S and R (S-R and/or S-[R-S]) must also be acquired.

The analysis of associative structure in Pavlovian and instrumental learning suggests the possibility that the learning that underlies stimulus control in both procedures might be identical or share common features. If this is the case, we should expect to find that a Pavlovian $CS^+$ and an instrumental $S^+$ to be functionally interchangeable. Indeed, there is much evidence that Pavlovian training facilitates the acquisition of instrumental discriminations when the relation between stimuli and reinforcers is preserved in the two procedures (Mellgren & Ost, 1969; Trapold & Overmier, 1972). However, there is also evidence that $CS^+$ and $S^+$ may not serve identical functions.

Holman and Mackintosh (1981) investigated the interchangeability of $CS^+$ and $S^+$ in blocking paradigms. As described above, a pretrained $CS^+$ or $S^+$ will block the acquisition of control by stimulus elements that are redundant with the pretrained cue. If the underlying basis for control was identical in Pavlovian and instrumental paradigms, then an $S^+$ should be able to block acquisition of control by a $CS^+$ and vice versa. Holman and Mackintosh found that a stimulus trained as a discriminative stimulus could block the acquisition of control by other stimuli in instrumental procedures but was ineffective in blocking control by other stimuli in Pavlovian procedures. Similarly, a Pavlovian $CS^+$ was found to be an effective blocker in Pavlovian procedures but not effective in instrumental paradigms. This result suggests that at least some of the content of the learning that underlies the acquisition of stimulus control differs in instrumental and Pavlovian procedures.

One possible difference in instrumental and Pavlovian learning is that a hierarchical associative network may be generated in the instrumental case, but hierarchical associations may not be acquired through exposure to simple Pavlovian procedures. In the instrumental case, the $S^+$ may set the occasion (Skinner, 1938, 1953) on which a R-S association is effective. In the Pavlovian case, control of response strength may reflect direct S-S associations. The occasion-setting function of a stimulus in the Pavlovian case (Holland, 1983) corresponds to the role of a conditional cue that signals the presence or absence of a S-S relation. The difference between direct and conditional control has been documented in studies of Pavlovian feature-positive and feature-negative discrimination learning.

In these procedures a distinctive cue is presented as a signal for either positive or negative trials. Positive and negative trials are composed of presentations of $S_1 S_c$ and $S_c$. When $S_1 S_c$ is reinforced and $S_c$ trials are not reinforced, the procedure is referred to as feature positive.

When the roles of the stimuli are reversed, the procedure is called feature negative. The feature-negative procedure (in which the subject is reinforced in the presence of the common cue, $S_c$, except in the presence of the unique feature, $S_1$) is the paradigm for establishing a stimulus as a conditioned inhibitor. Conditioned inhibitors are thought to act in the conditional mode of control, in that they are thought to affect existing associations rather than acting directly on behavior (Holland, 1985; Rescorla, 1985; but see Kaplan, 1984; Kaplan & Hearst, 1985; Wasserman, Franklin, & Hearst, 1974). The inhibitor acts as a gate to suppress a US representation and/or to suppress an association between CS and US (Holland, 1985). The feature-positive discrimination, however, appears to be solved in several different ways.

In the feature-positive procedure, the compound $S_c S_1$ is reinforced and all other stimuli are not. It is, therefore, possible that unique configural features of the compound gain direct control over responding. S-S or S-R associations between the configural cue and the stimulus or response features of the US may be acquired (Holland & Block, 1983; Saavedra, 1975). Alternatively, the elements of stimuli may be separately learned (Wagner, 1969a, 1969b). In this case, $S_1$ is a more valid predictor of reinforcement than any other cue. Hence, it is possible for $S_1$ to gain more direct control over responding than any other cue. Finally, subjects may learn the conditionality of the relation between $S_c$ and the US. In the latter view, the elements of the compound stimulus perform different functions (Heinemann & Chase, 1970). In our example, $S_1$ might instruct (Honig, 1978) or set the occasion on which $S_c$ will be paired with the US (Holland, 1983; Ross & Holland, 1981). The conditional cue, $S_1$, acts as a control element to gate the $S_c$-US association.

It appears that subjects do not solve feature-positive type discrimination through the use of configural cues unless they are forced to do so by the contingencies. For example, if the compound is reinforced and each of the elements are presented separately and not reinforced, a configural cue may come to control responding (Holland, 1983; Holland & Block, 1983; Saavedra, 1975). Under the usual procedure, in which there are no separate nonreinforced presentations of the positive feature, the amount of responding evoked by the positive feature alone ($S_1$) is generally equal to that evoked by the compound $(S_1S_c)$ of which it is a part (Hearst, 1978; Holland, 1983; Jenkins & Sainsbury, 1969). Hence, a configural cue cannot be the controlling stimulus. The virtually complete control acquired by the positive feature alone also shows that $S_1$ does not perform an occasion-setting function in the procedures described above. However, when the positive feature is presented prior to, rather than at the same time as, the common cue, occasion setting appears to be the dominant mode of control that develops.

The separation of direct and conditional control over responding is illustrated in experiments by Holland and Ross (1981). These experiments take advantage of the fact that qualitatively different CS paired with food come to control topographically different CRs in rats (Holland, 1980a, 1980b, 1984). For example, when a flashing houselight served as the CS, rats' CR topographies included rearing (standing with front paws off the floor) and magazine tending (head in the feeder aperture). When a tone was used as the CS, it came to evoke startle responses at its onset and head jerking (brief abrupt movements of the head) during the CS presentation. Direct control over responding as a result of CS-US pairings is manifest in different topographies, depending on the nature of the conditioned stimulus. Consequently, when stimulus compounds are reinforced, the nature of the underlying control can be inferred from the response topography controlled by the compound.

In one experiment, Ross and Holland (1981) trained subjects on a feature-positive procedure in which a simultaneous light-tone compound was reinforced. One group of subjects received additional nonreinforced tone presentations $(LT^+/T^-)$. A second group of subjects received additional nonreinforced presentations of the light $(LT^+/L^-)$, and a third group of subjects only received reinforced compound trials $(LT^+)$. The results of testing the compound as well as each of the elements is shown in Figure 2.23. Notice that the behavior observed in compound testing is a reflection of the behavior controlled by the separate elements. In group $LT^+$, subjects show a mixture of head jerking and rearing. In group $LT^+/T^-$, subjects showed rearing but no head jerking during compound trials, indicating almost complete overshadowing of the tone by the light, which was confirmed by the single element tests. Similarly, subjects in group $LT^+/L^-$

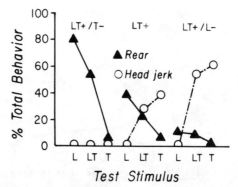

**Figure 2.23.** Control of rearing and head-jerking by light, tone, and compound for three groups of rats. From "Conditioning of Simultaneous and Serial Feature-Positive Discriminations" by R.T. Ross and P.C. Holland, 1981, *Animal Learning and Behavior, 9,* p. 296. Copyright 1981 by the Psychonomic Society. Reprinted by permission.

showed head jerking and little rearing during compound trials, indicating overshadowing of the light by the tone. Hence, the topographies controlled by a compound stimulus can be used to infer the strength of control exerted by the elements of the compound.

When the elements of a feature-positive discrimination are presented serially rather than simultaneously, behavior may come to be evoked by the common cue (Looney & Griffin, 1978; Ross & Holland, 1981). Ross and Holland investigated the difference between serial and simultaneous feature discriminations by varying the interval from the onset of $S_1$ (a light) to the onset of $S_c$ (a tone). As Figure 2.24 shows, at all delays considerable direct control over rearing accrued to the light, and the control over magazine behavior by the light declined as the interelement interval was increased. The light's modulation of control by the tone, however, was evident in all of the serial compound groups. Subjects in all group responded little to the tone on noncompound trials. On trials in which the tone was preceded by the light, the tone evoked substantial head jerking. The light's control over the behavior during the tone, which is appropriate to a tone-US association, suggests that the function of the light is to act as a modulator of direct control over behavior by the tone. The control over rearing and magazine behavior exerted by the light is

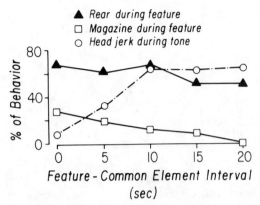

**Figure 2.24.** Strength of rearing and magazine behavior conditioned to a light and head-jerk to the tone when the light and tone served as the feature and common cue in a feature-positive discrimination. Performance is shown as a function of the interval between the feature and common element. From "Conditioning of Simultaneous and Serial Feature-Positive Discriminations" by R.T. Ross and P.C. Holland, 1981, *Animal Learning and Behavior, 9,* pp. 299–300. Copyright 1981 by the Psychonomic Society. Reprinted by permission.

evidence that a stimulus may exert several functions simultaneously. It may exert direct control over responding while simultaneously serving an occasion-setting function.

The direct and conditional control functions of stimuli appear to be relatively independent of each other. Nonreinforced presentations of the common feature reduce the direct control exerted by the common cue (e.g., the light controls less rearing) but have little effect on the occasion-setting function of the light (e.g., substantial head jerking occurs on tone trials preceded by the light; Holland & Ross, 1981). Along similar lines, Rescorla and colleagues (Rescorla, 1985; Rescorla, Durlach, & Grau, 1985) have shown that posttraining inflation or deflation of the associative value of a positive feature exerts little effect on its ability to act as an occasion setter for the common cue. Similarly, Ross (1983) demonstrated that pretraining of one of the elements of a subsequently reinforced feature-positive compound can block the acquisition of direct control by the non-pretrained element but that the pretraining in and subsequent compound presentation of that cue with the positive feature did not affect the acquisition of the occasion-setting function.

Therefore, it appears that there are least

three independent mechanisms whereby stimuli exert control over behavior. Antecedent stimuli may control behavior via their direct association with stimuli, via their direct association with responses, and by playing an occasion-setting or instructional function in which they gate subordinate associations. The discriminative stimulus acts to gate a R-S and/or S-R association, while a Pavlovian occasion setter acts to gate a S-S and/or S-R association. This view might help explain the noninterchangeability of the instrumental $S^+$ and Pavlovian CS, as these two kinds of stimuli perform different functions. In this view, a Pavlovian occasion setter is analogous to an instrumental $S^+$, and, therefore, these two types of stimuli might be interchangeable with one another. Indeed, Ross and LoLordo (1986, 1987) have shown that although a Pavlovian $CS^+$ does not block the acquisition of occasion-setting, an instrumental $S^+$ is effective in blocking the occasion-setting function. Similarly, the response in the instrumental paradigm bears the same relation to the reinforcer as the CS does to the US in the Pavlovian paradigm. Hence, responses and CSs might be interchangeable in their functional roles. The latter suggestion is supported by reports that Pavlovian CSs may compete with instrumental responses for association with the reinforcer (Hall, 1982; Hall, Channell, & Pearce, 1981; Pearce & Hall, 1978; Williams, 1975, 1978, 1982; but see Roberts, Tarpy, & Lea, 1984).

## REPRESENTATIONS

The preceding section reviewed the factors that influence which aspects of the external environment gain control over behavior. If behavior could be completely predicted on the basis of current external inputs, it would suffice to describe the exteroceptive stimulus as the antecedent cause of a response. However, behavior may be controlled by stimuli that are no longer physically present, and the nature of controlling stimuli cannot be analyzed solely on the basis of their exteroceptive characteristics. To mediate the gap between external input and behavioral output, antecedents for behavior may be conceived of in terms of a representational system. Three sorts of observations motivate the conception that representations act as antecedents for behavior.

First, as the preceding section on stimulus selection points out, not all aspects of a physically defined stimulus will gain control over responding. Although many aspects of an object stimulate sensory receptors, only certain aspects of that stimulation are effective controlling stimuli. One explanation of this selectivity relies on differential encoding of stimuli to account for the selective nature of stimulus control. Lawrence (1949, 1950, 1963) proposed that subjects acquired a mediating response that altered the perceptual representation of stimuli. The perceptual response mediated the acquired distinctiveness of cues correlated with reward. The "stimulus-as-coded" (Lawrence, 1963) was the effective controlling stimulus.

A second observation that is used to argue for a representational view of stimulus control is that stimuli may influence behavior when they are no longer present. Psychologists, perhaps because of strong roots in reflexology, seem uncomfortable with the idea of a stimulus acting over a temporal distance. Theories are generally formulated so that the cause of a behavior precedes the behavior closely in time. For example, if you request that a friend bring you a book from home, it is assumed that something must mediate the delay between your request and the actions of your friend many hours later. The request is assumed to be represented in way that allows for it to be effective over long periods of time. The nature of the representation of stimuli over delays was first discussed by Hunter (1913). In Hunter's delayed reaction experiments, subjects (sometimes rats, dogs, or children) would be shown a stimulus indicating which of several choices was correct for that trial. A delay was interposed between observation of the stimulus and the test. Hunter noticed that the rats and dogs performed better on this task if they learned to adopt a body orientation toward the correct alternative during the delay period. He speculated that, even when he did not observe such a response, some "intra-organic factor" came to "stand for" the stimulus. He further speculated that these holding cues might be verbal in humans. Since Hunter's work, additional evidence has shown that responses may mediate delays in many species (Blough, 1959; Eckerman, 1970; Spiker, 1956). It should be noted that not all behavioral scientists find it necessary to postulate cognitive processes between stimulus inputs and temporally remote behavioral output (Branch, 1977; Rachlin, 1978; Skinner, 1953).

A third and most compelling argument that the bases of stimulus control may not correspond to the physical dimensions of a stimulus input stems from the observation that stimuli may be treated as similar even though they are physically very dissimilar. For example, if people are asked to learn a list of visually presented consonants, errors tend to consist of confusions with letters that sound like the letters on the list, rather than with letters that look like letters on the learned list (Conrad, 1964). From this result it may be inferred that the representation of visually presented letters is similar (if not identical) to the code generated by acoustic presentation of stimuli rather than a code of visual information. There is, of course, no way to predict this solely from the physical properties of the stimuli used in the experiment. An understanding of stimulus control requires a specification of representation of stimuli.

The role of representation in guiding behavior is specified through the analysis of the content, code, dynamics, and processing components of a representation (Roitblat, 1982). The content of a representation refers to the features of the world that are preserved by a representation. The previous section on stimulus selection is primarily concerned with specifying the determinants of which features of the world are represented. The code of a representation consists of the rules for mapping features of the world into the representation. For example, in the previously described experiment in which subjects memorized a list of consonants, the stimuli were encoded acoustically. Visual stimuli were represented with a code similar to the one that is employed for acoustically presented material. The changes in a representation over time are the dynamic properties of representation. How a representation is formed and what aspects of it change with time are of particular importance to an understanding of control by antecedent stimuli over temporal delays. Lastly, the rules which specify how the component features of a representation interact are the processing aspects of a representational system. The prior discussion of the processes that underlie multidimensional interactions in the acquisition of stimulus control provide an example of this aspect of a representational system.

A full understanding of how stimuli control

behavior requires an analysis of the underlying representational system. Two examples of this type of analysis are considered here, and more detailed discussions of representations in animal memory can be found in several recent reviews and books (Bever, 1984; Church & Meck, 1983; Dickinson, 1980; Honig, 1984; Hulse, 1978; Hulse, Fowler, & Honig, 1978; Mackintosh, 1983; Olton, 1979; Roitblat, 1982; Terrace, 1984). The representation of spatial relations by the rat and the control of behavior by serial order information are the examples described here. In the next section on stimulus equivalence, the analysis of control by conceptual categories serves as a third example.

## Representations of Spatial Relations

The spatial memory of rats has been extensively studied in variants of radial arm mazes. As shown in Figure 2.25, the arms of a radial arm maze stretch out from a central platform like the spokes of a wheel. Each of the arms is baited with a single piece of food, which is not visible to the subjects while they are on the central platform. The rats are allowed to roam through the maze until all of the food is obtained. Rats very quickly learn to visit each arm once during a given trial. In an eight-arm maze, rats usually take fewer than 20 trials before they enter 8 different alleys on the first 8 choices in a trial (Olton & Samuelson, 1976). Four-arm problems are solved in about 5 trials (Walker & Olton, 1979), and even in a 17-arm maze, after about 50 training trials, rats will visit about 15 different arms

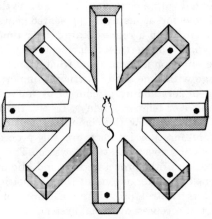

**Figure 2.25.** Radial arm maze.

in the first 17 choices (Olton, Collison, & Werz, 1977). What are the controlling stimuli for this remarkably efficient performance?

In order to solve the maze problem so efficiently, rats' choices must be under the control of cues correlated with the presence or absence of food in each alley. For example, rats might choose alleys on the basis of whether or not they can smell food at the end of an alley, or they might leave an odor trail in those alleys that they already visited. After reaching asymptotic performance in the standard procedure, rats can be tested in several ways to evaluate these possibilities. When alleys are rebaited after initial choices, animals still choose the alleys that have not been entered on that trial (Olton & Samuelson, 1976; Roberts, 1979). Hence, choices are not based on the presence or absence of food itself. In other experiments, the arms of the maze are rotated with respect to the surrounding room after the rat has made three choices (Olton & Samuelson, 1976). Choices after rotation are guided by the spatial location of the arm with respect to the surrounding room, not on the basis of whether or not there is food at the end of the arm or whether the arm has been previously visited (Cheng & Gallistel, 1984; Olton, 1978; Olton & Samuelson, 1976; Suzuki, Augerinos, & Black, 1980). Therefore, accurate performance does not depend on the presence of intramaze cues correlated with the presence of food in an alley.

Efficient performance in the radial arm maze could be based on both a response rule and the rat's sensitivity to its own past behavior. For example, the rat's behavior might be generated by an algorithm such as choosing one arm to the right of the arm last chosen. This too could result in efficient performance. Although it is possible for rats to learn this sort of solution to the radial arm maze under some conditions (Roberts & Dale, 1981), performance in the maze is not usually described by such a simple response rule. Olton and Samuelson (1976) found that neither the pattern of choices or errors was regular enough to account for the performance of their subjects. Furthermore, a trial can be interrupted in a number of ways that make it unlikely that subjects are returned to their previous spatial location, yet subjects still respond differentially to visited and unvisited arms. Neither removal from the experimental room, change in ambient cues, feeding, exposure to another maze, or even a four-hour delay between the first four and last four choices in an eight-arm maze results in a substantial decrement in performance during the last four trials (Beatty & Shavalia, 1980; Maki, Brokofsky, & Berg, 1979; Roberts, 1981). The high accuracy of performance after these interruptions makes it very unlikely that choices are based on cues specifically generated by a particular sequence of choices.

It appears that the stimuli controlling choices in the radial arm maze contain both information about each arm's spatial location and whether or not it has been visited. Two analogies have been suggested to describe the nature of the underlying spatial representation. One suggestion is that the representation is analogous to the representation of spatial relations in a map (Cheng & Gallistel, 1984; Menzel, 1978; O'Keefe & Nadel, 1978; Olton, 1978; Roberts, 1984; Suzuki et al., 1980; Tolman, 1948). In addition to a cognitive map of the maze, accurate performance on the task requires that information about which arms still contain food be represented during each trial and information about the orientation of the map relative to the external environment must also be retained. If information about which arms still contained food was represented as a spatial analogue, then one would expect errors to reflect spatial confusion. Subjects should be more likely to make errors near unvisited arms than near already visited arms. These types of errors occur no more often than would be expected by chance (Olton & Samuelson, 1976). Hence, the aspects of the representation that preserve information about the locations that do and do not contain food are not wholly analogous to a map. The errors that do occur in the spatial maze tend to be returns to arms that were visited early in the sequence of choices. As Olton (1978) points out, if information were encoded solely in terms of which arms still contain food, then errors should be randomly distributed with respect to serial position (information about which arms were visited earlier or later should be unavailable). On the basis of the failure to find spatial confusions and on the presence of a serial position effect, Olton suggested that the performance in the radial arm maze is guided by a representation that is analogous to a list of points in space that have been visited.

The characterization of spatial representations as a list of independently represented spatial locations is incomplete. There is considerable evidence that the relations between points in space are also represented, as one would expect from the map analogy (but not from the list analogy). First, arms are chosen on the basis of their relation to extra-maze cues, rather than on the basis of a particular configuration of cues at the end of an arm. Suzuki et al. (1980) did an experiment with an eight-arm maze in a room that eliminated any extramaze spatial cues. The maze was surrounded by a black curtain, and the ceiling and floor were also a uniform black color. At the end of each arm a salient cue was hung on the surrounding curtain. Rats quickly learned to visit each arm once, as they do in the standard radial maze procedure. Subjects were allowed to run down three of the arms and were then confined to the central platform while the cues were moved. In one condition the cues were rotated 360°, so that nothing was altered. In a second condition the cues were rotated 180°, and in a third condition the cues were rearranged in a random fashion. If subjects were responding to the unique cues at the end of each arm, after the delay, subjects in all three conditions should go to arms that they had not previously visited on that trial. If the controlling stimuli involve the spatial relations between cues, then performance in the random condition should be poor, because the relative spatial location of cues is changed in this condition. The manipulation in the rotation and control conditions preserves the relative spatial location of cues. The results of the experiment showed that subjects in the control and rotation conditions chose new arms after the delay, but subjects in the random condition performed significantly more poorly. However, the performance in the random group was more accurate than would be expected by chance. Thus is it possible that arms were identified both in terms of their relative spatial location and in terms of the unique stimuli associated with each location. Subsequent work by Cheng and Gallistel (1984) has confirmed that rats do use the relative spatial position between landmarks to orient themselves in space. Mazmanian and Roberts (1983) have shown that rats have difficulty learning a spatial maze unless information about the relative location of arms is available.

A second line of evidence that encourages the use of a map metaphor for describing the representation of spatial relations comes from studies that demonstrate that after learning about spatial locations from one point in space, subjects perform correctly from other points in space. For example, Tolman, Ritchie, and Kalish (1946) trained rats to run to a goal box via an indirect route. When given the opportunity to traverse a runway that went directly to the goal they did so, even though they had never been previously been rewarded for following that path. Therefore, their behavior was not under the control of the specific cues that had previously been correlated with the reinforced performance. Rather, the approach to the goal was under the control of a representation of spatial locations. In general, if rats are rewarded for reaching a goal from one particular location, they have little trouble approaching the goal from locations that they had not previously experienced (Morris, 1981; Olton, 1979; Tolman et al., 1946; Walker & Olton, 1979).

In summary, the rat's solution to a radial arm maze appears to involve the representation of spatial relations between objects. Subjects do not learn only to approach particular stimuli. This forces an account of performance in terms of the relative spatial locations of stimuli. The nature of this controlling stimulus is likened to a map, as many of the relations that are preserved by a map appear to be important in the control of spatial behavior, including the preservation of angles and distances and the capacity to arrive at any point on the map from any other point without having actually traversed that path in the past.

## Representations of Serial Order

Behavior can come under the control of the serial position in which a cue is presented. In these circumstances it is not the presence or absence of a cue but its temporal relation to other cues that determines its relevance. A number of studies have investigated the discrimination of stimulus order. For example, subjects might be reinforced only after a light followed by tone but not after two lights, two tones, or a tone followed by light. Animals readily learn such discriminations (Wasserman, Nelson, & Larew, 1980; Weisman & von Konigslow, 1984; Weisman, Wasserman, Dodd, & Larew, 1980). Longer and more complex serial orders can be discriminated, as evidenced by the ease with which animals learn to anticipate monotonic sequences of changing reward magnitude (Capaldi, 1967; Capaldi, Nawrocki, &

Verry, 1983; Fountain & Annau, 1984; Fountain, Henne, & Hulse, 1984; Hulse, 1978; Hulse & Dorsky, 1977, 1979) or sequences of auditory stimuli (Hulse, Cynx, & Humpal, 1984, 1985).

Serial order problems do not necessarily require that information about serial order be encoded. For example, in a sequence discrimination each stimulus might evoke a response which is modified by each stimulus in the sequence. Thus, the animal might be guided by its immediately preceding performance or experience and the current input. The representation that guides a subject's behavior need not contain information about the whole sequence. For example, in learning a sequence of increasing reward magnitudes, the subject's behavior might be guided by a rule (Fountain & Annau, 1984; Fountain et al., 1984; Hulse, 1978; Hulse & Dorsky, 1977, 1979). Alternatively, each reward magnitude (Capaldi et al., 1983) or a response to each component in the sequence (Roitblat, 1982) might serve as a cue for the next step in the sequence. In any of these cases, the serial order of individual items need not be directly represented. In the case of reward magnitude, the evidence seems to favor a rule-learning interpretation (Fountain & Annau, 1984; Fountain et al., 1984; Hulse, 1980; but see Capaldi et al., 1983). In the case of discrimination of simple sequences, subjects appear to be under the control of the current input and a representation of the preceding input, not under the control of a representation of a whole sequence (Weisman & von Konigslow, 1984). However, in other serial learning problems, representations of serial order do control performance.

Terrace and his colleagues (Straub, Seidenberg, Bever, & Terrace, 1979; Straub & Terrace, 1981; Terrace, 1983, 1984; Terrace, Straub, Bever, & Seidenberg, 1977) have investigated how pigeons learn to peck a sequence of response keys. In their experiments, a pigeon is presented with four response keys that are illuminated with different colors (A, B, C, D). On any given trial the different colors appear in different positions, but the pigeon must always peck the keys in the same order to obtain reward (A-B-C-D). Pigeons were able to learn to do this task and responded correctly to novel spatial arrangements of the four colors. Additionally, performance on subsets of the whole array was quite accurate. When presented only with colors A and C or colors B and D, subjects first pecked the color whose serial position occurred earlier in the training sequence. Successful transfer to the subsets indicates that the subject's performance was not under the control of the immediately preceding response or stimulus. Further evidence for a representation of the sequence was obtained in transfer tests in which subjects learned new sequences. Terrace (1983) trained pigeons to produce a three element sequence, A-B-C. Following successful acquisition of this sequence, subjects were given a new sequence to learn, in which two of the elements were novel (X, Y) and the third element was the middle color from the original list (B). One group learned a sequence with B in its original ordinal position (X-B-Y), while two other groups of subjects learned new sequences with B in novel positions (X-Y-B, B-X-Y). The group that was trained on the novel sequence with B in the original position learned the sequence much faster than either of the other two groups. Additionally, subjects in the former group learned the novel sequence faster than the original A-B-C sequence, whereas subjects in the latter two groups learned the novel sequence more slowly than the original A-B-C sequence. All of these experiments taken together indicate that a representation of a whole sequence of events can come to control responding.

As these examples illustrate, it is often not possible to specify the nature of controlling stimuli solely in physical terms. Only certain features of physical stimuli influence behavior and only in accord with active transformations of those inputs based on the subject's past history. How a stimulus representation guides behavior is considered in the next section.

# STIMULUS EQUIVALENCE

Any account of stimulus control must address the question of generalization. What makes one stimulus be treated like another one? This is an enduring question and a central problem in many areas of psychology (Gibson, 1966; Stevens, 1951). Hull (1939) put it this way:

"The problem of stimulus equivalence is essentially this: How can we account for the fact that a stimulus will sometimes evoke a reaction to which it has never been conditioned. . . ? For example, it is evident that a given physical object sensed by the eye, say, probably never

presents the same physical pattern of light energy to the retina on any two occasions. On the other hand, we have the equally well recognized fact that within limits mammalian organisms will react to such an object or situation in substantially the same way. . . on the different occasions of its presentation."

Indeed, all behavior is governed not by any one stimulus but by a whole class of stimuli (Skinner, 1935). The complexity and methodology of defining stimulus classes is illustrated by the previously described experiments on spatial learning, in which rats accurately approached a goal from positions which they had never previously experienced (Morris, 1981; Tolman et al., 1946). As this example illustrates, specifying the structure of these stimulus classes involves training one stimulus and testing subjects with stimuli that differ from the training stimulus. This is, of course, a generalization test. Hence, an understanding of the determinants of the shape of generalization gradients is the domain in which this problem has been studied. Indeed, a considerable effort has been made to understand the performance mechanisms involved in the control by antecedent stimuli. These processes include underlying sensitivity to different stimulus dimensions, mechanisms that modulate which aspects of a stimulus are attended to, stimulus encoding processes, retrieval of information about the past history of similar stimuli, and rules for deciding what response to make.

## Strength Models

For Hull and Spence, the strength of control exerted by an antecedent stimulus reflected the net excitatory and inhibitory tendencies evoked by that stimulus. Excitatory strength accrued to a stimulus as a result of conditioning and through generalization as a result of conditioning to similar stimuli. The excitation summed with conditioned and generalized inhibitory effects to yield the net excitatory strength of stimulus. Figure 2.26 illustrates Spence's (1937) account of the effects of intradimensional discrimination training ($S^+$ and $S^-$ are from the same dimension) on response strength. Separate gradients of excitation (solid gradient) and inhibition (dashed gradient) were thought to develop around the $S^+$ and $S^-$ as a result of reinforcement and extinction. Response strength was hypothesized

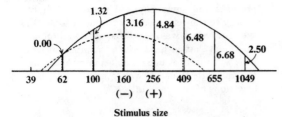

**Stimulus size**

**Figure 2.26.** Theoretical gradients of excitation and inhibition following intradimensional training. Numbers under gradient represent difference between excitation and inhibition. From "The Differential Response in Animals to Stimuli Within a Single Dimension" by K.W. Spence, 1937, *Psychological Review*, *44*, p. 433. Copyright 1937 by the American Psychological Association. Reprinted by permission to the publisher.

to be a function of the difference between these two opposing tendencies. Notice that the maximum difference between the gradients is shifted away from the $S^+$ in a direction opposite the $S^-$. Hence, the peak shift that is often obtained after intradimensional training is predicted by this strength model. This account of response strength was used to explain transpositional control. If subjects were trained with the 256 sq cm object as the $S^+$ and the 160 sq cm object as the $S^-$, did they learn to respond to the absolute value of the $S^+$ or did they learn to respond to the larger of two objects? When tested with the former $S^+$ and a larger test stimulus, subjects chose the larger test stimulus. Subjects can respond to the relations between stimuli, but Spence's analysis of the transposition problem illustrates that what appears to be relational responding may sometimes be controlled by absolute features of a stimulus.

According to the Hull-Spence account of stimulus control, the shape of the empirical gradient will depend on the shape of the underlying gradients of excitation and inhibition. Hearst (1969) tested this aspect of the model by predicting the form of an intradimensional gradient from separately obtained gradients of excitation and inhibition. The separate gradients of excitation and inhibition were obtained from subjects given interdimensional training. For example, control after intradimensional training on the wavelength dimension was predicted by combining the excitatory gradient obtained from subjects trained with a visual $S^+$ and auditory $S^-$ with the inhibitory gradient obtained from subjects

trained with an auditory $S^+$ and visual $S^-$. The gradients obtained from subjects trained with the visual $S^+$ and visual $S^-$ were remarkably similar to the shape of the gradients predicted by summating the excitatory and inhibitory gradients obtained from the interdimensional groups. Hence, at least one aspect of response production rules involves a combination of excitatory and inhibitory tendencies.

This sort of account of performance is incomplete, in that the direct effects of discrimination training on the strength of control (e.g., contrast effects) are not readily captured by these processes alone. Accounts of generalization gradients in terms of the interaction of static excitatory and inhibitory gradients do account for certain aspects of the shape of a generalization gradient, but they do not help illuminate the process(es) that produce contrast (Blough, 1975, 1983). An interesting alternative that can account for some contrast effects is Blough's (1975) incremental model.

The incremental model's account of contrast is illustrated by Blough's (1975) analysis of an experiment in which responses were reinforced in the presence of many stimuli that varied along a single dimension until a uniform response rate was obtained in the presence of each stimulus. In the next phase of the experiment, responses were no longer reinforced in the presence of one of the stimuli. Response rate decreased in the presence of the nonreinforced stimulus, but increased in the presence of adjacent stimulus values. Blough's model accounts for the contrast by assuming that strength of control accrues to individual stimuli via a learning process very similar to the one described by Rescorla and Wagner (1972) (see Hearst, Chapter 1). The increment in learning on a given trial depends on the discrepancy between the strength of control already exerted by the stimuli present at the time of reinforcement and the asymptotic amount of learning that is supported by the particular reinforcer. Blough adds to this model the assumption that, as a function of the similarity of stimuli to the training stimulus, generalized excitatory and inhibitory strength will accrue to nontraining stimuli. Furthermore, in order to be consistent with a variety of data (Blough, 1975; Rescorla & Wagner, 1972), the model assumes that the incremental learning rate is greater than the decremental one. Figure 2.27 shows how contrast in the above experiment could be produced by this

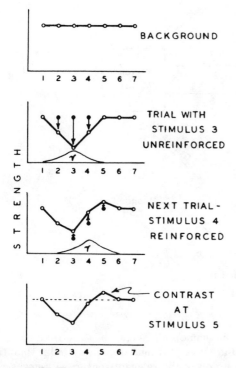

**Figure 2.27.** Theoretical analysis of changes in response strength after nonreinforcement of stimulus 3 followed by reinforcement in the presence of stimulus 4. Theoretical spread of excitation and inhibition is shown below the appropriate stimulus. Because the generalized increment to stimulus 5 when stimulus 4 is reinforced is greater than the net effect of the generalized decrement to 4 when 3 is not reinforced and the direct effect of reinforcing stimulus 4, both peak shift and contrast are obtained. From "Alternative Accounts of Dimensional Stimulus Control" by D.S. Blough, 1984, p. 63. Reprinted with permission from Commons, Herrnstein, and Wagner's *Quantitative Analysis of Behavior*, Volume IV, Copyright 1984, Ballinger Publishing Company.

process. The generalized decrement to stimulus 4 produced by the nonreinforcement of stimulus 3 (row 2) may result in a large enough discrepancy between the value of stimulus 4 and asymptote to produce a generalized increment to stimulus 5 when stimulus 4 is reinforced (row 3) large enough to result in contrast (row 4). Thus a model based on accrual of net excitatory and inhibitory tendency at the time of learning may successfully account for variations in peak height as a function of stimulus similarity and reincement contingencies.

## Information-Processing Models

The strength models do a good job in capturing processes that modulate the strength of control but provide only limited principles for understanding sharpness of control. The dimensional basis of equivalence is not considered in a strength account but is the focus of many information-processing models of generalization. Figure 2.28 illustrates a decision-making model of stimulus control. In this model, a distinction is made between working and reference memory (Honig, 1978; Miller, Galanter, & Pribram, 1960; Olton, 1978; Roitblat, 1982). Working memory is thought to contain information relevant only to the current trial or episode, while reference memory contains information that is useful and relevant across trials. Sensory inputs are represented in working memory. These sensory representations must be compared to representations of past sensory inputs and, on the basis of this comparison, a response is made.

This general class of models is referred to as signal-recognition models because the stimulus input (signal) is processed and identified. Tendencies to respond or not respond in the presence of a particular stimulus are conceived to be the result of applying a decision criterion to a representation of sensory input (Gibbon & Church, 1984: Heinemann, 1983; Heinemann, Avin, Sullivan, & Chase, 1969; Heinemann & Chase, 1975; Wright & Sands, 1981). Figure 2.29 illustrates Blough's (1983) characterization of the signal-recognition model. A physical stimulus is presumed to generate an internal effect that varies over time. Stimuli that differ generate different distributions of internal effects. The top part of Figure 2.29 shows the distribution of effects for two stimuli of differing wavelength. Criteria for responding are set through conditioning so that a response is generated when the sensory effect of a stimulus falls within acceptable limits. Response frequency to a given stimulus is proportional to the area under the curve that falls within the response criteria (dotted area for the 590 nm stimulus; hatched area for the 586 nm signal). Variations in response probability are, therefore, related to the probability that the current input matches a representation of inputs that have been reinforced in the past. The greater the discrepancy between training and test stimuli, the less likely it will be that the sensory representation of the test stimulus will

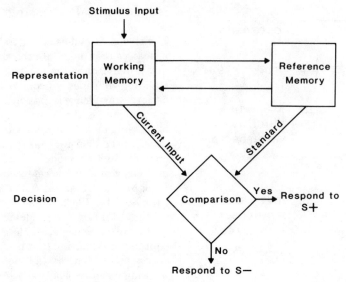

**Figure 2.28.** Generalized decision model of stimulus control.

fall within criterion. Hence, according to this type of model sensitivity, memory, and decision processes are all involved in generating the performance controlled by antecedent stimuli.

At one time Lashley and Wade (1946) proposed that all stimulus equivalences were the result of an inability to detect the difference between stimuli. However, generalization functions frequently do not correspond to an organism's ability to detect stimulus differences (see Kimble, 1961; Terrace, 1966). As the information processing models suggest stimuli may be treated equivalently for several reasons. First, stimuli may be functionally equivalent because of their physical similarity. To the extent that stimuli

share common elements, they are reacted to in similar ways. If stimuli are more similar than the resolution of the relevant sensory systems, stimuli will be reacted to as equivalent (identical). Second, physically different stimuli may be encoded in similar ways. Lastly, even though stimuli may be represented differently, they may enter into decision rules so as to produce identical output. Hence, stimulus equivalence may be obtained via all of the processes that govern discriminative performance.

## Memory

Current conceptualizations of memory distinguish between long term storage of information and information that is retained for a limited period of time (Honig, 1978; Tulving, 1983). The enduring memory is referred to as long-term, semantic, or reference memory. Reference memory contains information that is retained after long periods of time, and it is thought to be of unlimited capacity. Reference memory contains information about the meaning of an event or about the procedural rules that apply to a given episode. In a given situation, stimulus inputs act as retrieval cues for information about reinforcement contingencies and what response to make. In this way, long-term memory influences performance in a given episode. Though active processing of information is required to store

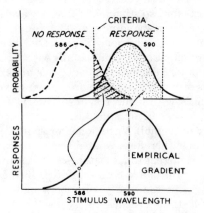

**Figure 2.29.** Signal-recognition model.

information in reference memory, no active process have been identified for the maintenance of information in the long-term store.

Working memory, on the other hand, refers to a process that only retains information for a limited period of time (Miller et al., 1960). Sometimes referred to as short-term or episodic memory, working memory only retains information while that information is being actively processed. Information from stimulus inputs and information retrieved from reference memory are processed in working memory. Working memory is thought to have a limited capacity, but its limits have not been specified (Grant, 1984; Maki, 1984; Olton, 1978; Roberts, 1979; Sands, Urcuioli, Wright, & Santiago, 1984; Thompson & Herman, 1977; Wagner, 1981). Sometimes a distinction is made between types of working memory (Atkinson & Shiffrin, 1968; Bower, 1975; Honig, 1984; Maki, 1984; Wagner, 1981; Wicklegren, 1973), but no such distinction is made here, as our primary interest is with the contents of memory, not with the memory process, *per se*.

Stimulus representations in working memory, therefore, contain information about the current inputs and about the past associations of the inputs. Since the decision process is based on a comparison between a representation of a current input and a representation of past experience, an understanding of discriminative control requires a specification of how that stimulus is represented in memory.

### Representations

In the earlier section on representation, it was suggested that when stimuli act over temporal delays or in ways only understandable in terms of past learning, it is useful to think of behavior as under the control of a representation of a stimulus. In this view, stimuli may be functionally equivalent because of an equivalence of representation. This is most clearly illustrated by examples of functional equivalence of physically distinct stimuli, as is the case in some examples of semantic generalization (Osgood, 1953). If a response is conditioned to a picture of a tulip, other flowers, such as a daisy, may evoke the conditioned reaction even though they do not look very much like a tulip. Similarly if a CR was established under the control of an actual tulip, the written word "tulip" and the written word "daisy" would also be likely to evoke the CR, even though the test stimuli share few phys-ical properties with the training stimulus and are easily discriminable. It is assumed that exteroceptive stimuli that lack physical equivalence but that are behaviorally equivalent must be represented identically. The basis for generalization is presumed to be some response that equates the stimuli for meaning (Osgood, 1953).

Because stimulus equivalence cannot always be predicted from physical properties of stimuli, it is assumed that equivalence may be the result of equivalence of code and content of representation. In general terms, equivalence that is not based on physical similarity has been described as mediated by the evocation of a common response (Hull, 1939; Miller, 1948) or mediated by common stimulus associations (Sidman, 1971; Trapold, 1970). In the case of semantic generalization, presentation of the tulip might evoke the verbal response "flower." The feedback from the mediating response might become associated with the US. When the stimulus word "daisy" is presented, it, too, might evoke the mediating response "flower" and, therefore, lead to the CR. Stimulus equivalence based on mediating responses and associations has been documented and analyzed in a number of paradigms.

Equivalence of stimuli that is based on evocation of a common response has been experimentally investigated by Grice (1965; Grice & Davis, 1958, 1960). The basic paradigm employed in these experiments was a differential conditioning procedure with three stimuli. One of the stimuli was always paired with the US, the other two stimuli were never paired with the US. The subjects also made two manual or verbal responses to the stimuli. One of the responses was trained to be made to both the $S^+$ and one of the $S^-$ stimuli. The second response was trained to occur in the presence of the second $S^-$. It was found that greater generalization of the CR occurred to the $S^-$ whose response was identical to the $S^+$ response than to the alternate $S^-$ whose response differed from the $S^+$ response. Similarly, when humans are taught to name stimulus objects and later conditioned to one of the objects, generalization tends to be greater between stimuli given the same name than between the same stimuli given different names (Eisman, 1955; Jeffrey, 1953; Spiker, 1956). Some of the most interesting cases of mediated generalization are found in examples of metaphor and simile. Many metaphors are probably the result of response mediated generalization (Skinner, 1957). When Romeo says "'tis the east and Juliet is the sun," he is probably not classifying Juliet and the sun in the same category, on the basis of physical similarity. Chances are that the similarity of warm feelings produced by the sight of Juliet and warm feelings produced by the sun at dawn mediated the generalization. Similarly, loud noises and loud clothing share little in the way of common elements, but do evoke similar startle responses.

In addition to mediated generalization occurring on the basis of evoked behavior, physically dissimilar stimuli may evoke similar behavior by virtue of associations with common elements. In the experiments described earlier, Trapold (1970) and, more recently, Peterson (1984) exposed rats to two-choice conditional discriminations. Presentation of stimulus 1 signaled that response 1 would be reinforced but that response 2 would not. Presentation of stimulus 2 signaled that response 2 would be reinforced but response 1 would not. In one group of subjects, the differential outcome group, each alternative produced a different reinforcer (food pellets or sucrose). For a second group of subjects, the common outcome group, both alternatives produced one of the two outcomes. Subjects in the differential outcome groups learned the discrimination much faster than subjects in the common outcome group, presumably because of the generalization mediated by the common association in the latter group. The superior discriminability of stimuli associated with differential outcomes to stimuli associated with nondistinct outcomes has been replicated with both qualitative (Brodigan & Peterson, 1976; Peterson & Trapold, 1980; Peterson, Wheeler & Armstrong, 1978; Peterson, Wheeler, & Trapold, 1980) and quantitative (Carlson & Wielkiewicz, 1972; DeLong & Wasserman, 1981) differences in rewards associated with different alternatives. Peterson (1984) provided additional evidence that stimulus-outcome associations could mediate generalization. In this experiment, it was found that after training in a differential outcome procedure, control over responding generalized to stimuli that had not undergone explicit discrimination training but which have been paired with the different rewards. The generalization was outcome specific. The stimulus that gained control over a particular response was the stimulus that had been paired with the outcome previously associated with that alternative. Hence, associations of two different stimuli with the same outcome may produce substantial generalization between the stimuli.

Stimulus equivalence may be explicitly trained by establishing mediated associations. Sidman and colleagues (Sidman, 1971, 1985; Sidman & Cresson, 1973; Sidman et al., 1982; Sidman & Tailby, 1982) have shown that with humans it is possible to establish multiple element equivalence classes of stimuli via mediated associations. In their experiments, an equivalence relation is established between stimulus A and stimulus B by training subjects to choose stimulus B when stimulus A is presented. Equivalence between stimulus B and stimulus C is also explicitly trained. Without explicit training, stimulus A and stimulus C will be equivalent. At least with humans, if a new stimulus is trained to be equivalent to any of the elements of the class, then equivalence is established between the new element and all members of the class. It should be noted that procedures that give rise to mediated equivalence in human children do not give rise to equivalence classes in monkeys (Sidman et al., 1982).

### Decision Rules

The decision phase of the model presented in Figure 2.28 involves a comparison between a representation of current input and a representation of stimuli experienced in the past. Stimulus equivalence may, therefore, result from how inputs enter into decision rules. For example, according to the stimulus-recognition model depicted in Figure 2.29, all stimuli that fall within the criterion boundaries will be treated equivalently. Hence, functional equivalence between stimuli may be obtained because different inputs result in identical output from the response production process. An analysis of this stage of the performance process requires specification of both the elements that enter into comparison and the rules of comparison themselves.

Two general alternatives have been suggested for the nature of the representation against which current inputs are compared. One alternative is that current inputs are compared to a prototype of the positive stimulus (Posner & Keele, 1968). A prototype is thought to be the central tendency of an $S^+$, the average reinforced stimulus. Alternatively, subjects might store individual exemplars of categories, and judgments might be based on retrieval of one or more stored exemplars. A thorough evaluation of these alternatives is beyond the scope of this chapter. However, much evidence favors the view that individual exemplars enter into the comparison process. In human classification learning (Medin & Schaffer, 1978; Medin & Smith, 1981), pigeon's discrimination learning (Chase, 1983; Heinemann, 1983), and rat's time discriminations (Gibbon & Church, 1984), there is evidence that favors the view that judgments are based on a comparison of current input to a representation of individual exemplars.

Two general sorts of comparison rules have been suggested for the comparison of current input to the representation of past experience. The classification may depend on the difference between current input and past experience or on the ratio of the two. In both cases, the result of the comparator process must fall within some criterion for a response to $S^+$ to occur. There have been few tests of the relative adequacy of ratio and difference rules in animal discrimination learning (but see Church & Meck, 1983; Gibbon & Church, 1984).

The specific comparison rules themselves may be quite complex, as they will typically involve comparing an input to a criterion representation along many dimensions. Shepard (1965) has characterized the problem as identifying the underlying combination rule that specifies how various stimulus dimensions combine to produce psychological similarity. Many combination rules are possible, and different sets of stimuli and differential experience with them may influence the form of the combination rule that applies (Cross, 1965). For the purposes of discussion, we will restrict the possible combination rules to either additive or multiplicative models of attribute interactions. For a given example, the total similarity (S) of stimulus A and B might be expressed as a linear combination of independent similarities along n dimensions ($S = s1 + s2 + s3 + \ldots + sn$) or as a function of the product of similarities ($S = s1 \times s2 \times s3 \times \ldots \times sn$). In a more general case, the different dimensions of comparison may be differentially weighted.

Butter (1963) trained pigeons to respond in the presence of a colored line. In generalization tests, the color and/or the orientation of the stimuli were varied. An additive model did not provide a very good description of the data, because decrements to test stimuli that differed along both dimensions were greater than the sum of the decrements to those stimuli when testing occurred separately on a single dimension. A multiplicative model of the interaction between dimensions yielded a good approximation to the data. Subsequent work on multidimensional control (Johnson, 1970) confirmed that a multiplicative combination rule best characterized the interaction of stimulus dimensions.

In summary, an adequate account of performances controlled by antecedent stimuli requires both a detection-recognition system and processes that determine strength of control. Detection-recognition models appear to be well suited for describing the processes that determine the range of stimuli that will be effective in evoking a response (sharpness of control), while interactions of response tendencies are required to account for strength of control. Stimulus equivalence may be obtained at all levels of the discrimination process. Physical similarity, representational similarity, and similarity in the response production process may all contribute to stimulus equivalence.

The next section presents an example of the steps involved in analyzing the basis of stimulus equivalence. Each of components involved in stimulus equivalence have been examined in experiments on classification of stimuli into abstract categories.

## Conceptual Classification

One of the most provocative areas of research with animals in recent years has been in the area of concept learning and categorization. Herrnstein and Loveland (1964) showed that pigeons could distinguish sets of slides that contained images of people from slides that did not. The individuals depicted differed from slide to slide, as did the background setting and whether a whole person or part of a person was displayed. Yet pigeons were able to learn the discrimination rapidly and to respond appropriately to novel exemplars the first time they were presented. Similarly accurate and rapid discriminations have been demonstrated for categories such as fish (Herrnstein & De Villiers, 1980), trees (Herrnstein, 1979), people (Herrnstein & Loveland, 1964; Malott & Siddal, 1972), pigeons (Poole & Lander, 1971), human-made objects (Lubow, 1974), particular individuals (Herrnstein, Loveland, & Cable, 1976), water (Herrnstein et al., 1976), the

**Figure 2.30.** Some stimuli used in discrimination of oak leaves from non-oak leaves. From "Visual Classes and Natural Categories in the Pigeon" by J. Cerella, 1979, *Journal of Experimental Psychology: Human Perception and Performance, 5* p. 70. Copyright 1979 by the American Psychological Association. Reprinted by permission of the publisher and author.

cartoon character Charlie Brown (Cerella, 1980, 1982), and oak leaves (Cerella, 1979).

The learning of the oak leaf category in Cerella's (1979) experiment illustrates that categorical classification is well within the capacities of a pigeon. Figure 2.30 shows some of the representative leaves used in this experiment. White oak leaves, shown in the top row of the figure, differ in many dimensions, as do the leaves of sycamore, sassafrass, and elm trees, shown in the bottom row. Pigeons learned quickly to discriminate between a set of 40 oak leaves from a set of 40 non-oak leaves. When tested with novel instances of oak leaves, the pigeons responded to the novel slides as members of the positive class. Additionally, novel exemplars of the negative class were not responded to. Hence, the pigeons were learning something which allowed the proper classification of novel negative, as well as novel positive, instances. When trained with only a single instance of oak leaf as a positive stimulus (the one in the center of the figure), the pigeons responded positively to novel examples of oak leaves. Even a single instance may induce a category that exerts control over behavior.

Successful classification depends on treating stimuli of certain qualities as equivalent. An understanding of the classification process, therefore, requires an understanding of all of the ways in which stimuli may be equivalent. The physical controlling stimuli must be identified, the nature of the controlling representations must be described, and the decision pro-

cesses involved in the classification must be analyzed. Hence, the analysis of classification may be conceived as the problem of identifying the controlling stimuli for the appropriate classification response.

Consider again the categories of fish, oak leaves, or people. These are not concepts which can be defined by a set of features that are individually necessary or, as a group, sufficient for classification. Rather, individual exemplars may vary in the number and specific features that they possess. Some instances are better examples of a category than others. Whales, for example, are not as good an example of the concept of "mammal" as are dogs. Instances of these categories are not arbitrarily associated with categories nor strictly linked by defining features. Since conceptual categorization is not based on a set of necessary and sufficient features, they are referred to as polymorphous categories (Morgan, Fitch, Holman, & Lea, 1976). The current view is that categorization judgments are based on some combination of features (Herrnstein, 1984; Herrnstein et al., 1976; Lea & Ryan, 1983). There are two aspects to understanding how a polymorphous concept can control performance. The nature of the controlling features must be identified, and the combination rules for the response production process must be specified.

*Features*

In several experiments pigeons have been taught to discriminate letters from other letters or numbers (Blough, 1982; Lea & Ryan, 1983; Morgan et al., 1976), and no set of features has been shown to be necessary and sufficient for the proper identification. Interestingly, the pattern of confusions in pigeons is quite similar to human confusion patterns (Blough, 1982), suggesting that there may be some very general aspects to the way in which organisms encode visual stimuli. One method for identifying features is illustrated in an experiment reported by Lea and Ryan (1983) in which pigeons were trained to discriminate the letter *A* from the other letters of the alphabet in several typefaces. After training, subjects were tested on the letter discrimination in five different typefaces. The results of this test are depicted in Figure 2.31. In all typefaces, subjects showed good discrimination of the letter *A*. Fourteen features, such as the number of feet, number of closed areas, and the

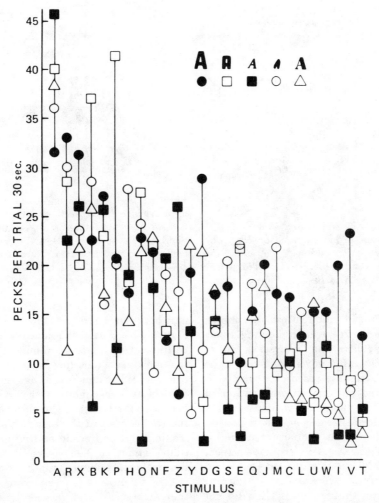

**Figure 2.31.** Response rates to letters in different typefaces. Letters are arranged in order of response rates controlled by each. From "Feature Analysis of Pigeons' Acquisition of Discrimination Between Letters" by S.E.G. Lea and C.M.E. Ryan, 1984, p. 243. Reprinted with permission from Commons, Herrnstein, and Wagner's *Quantitative Analysis of Behavior*, Volume IV, Copyright 1984, Ballinger Publishing Company.

area of letter relative to the area of the letter *A*, were identified and used as independent variables in a regression analysis to predict response rates. The weightings of the various features were then used to predict the response rates to the same letter in different typefaces, with moderate success. Hence, it is possible to identify the nature of the controlling stimuli and to specify at least their relative weightings in the decision process.

Blough (1982) used multidimensional scaling procedures (Shepard, 1980) to identify the underlying dimensions of control. One of these scaling

procedures groups together letters that have similar patterns of confusion. The clusters of letters produced by this procedure are illustrated in Figure 2.32. From these clusters one can infer controlling features. For example, the left-most branch suggests that small closed loop was an important feature, and the other clusters suggest that letter curvature, large closed loop, number of vertices, crossing lines, number of horizontal lines, and presence or absence of a vertical line might serve as the features used in a letter discrimination task.

As in the case of simple stimuli, we are unable

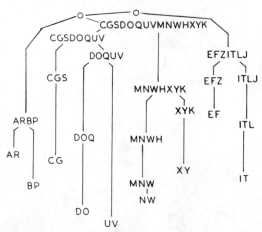

**Figure 2.32.** Clusters of letters based on confusion errors. From "Pigeon Perception of Letters of the Alphabet" by D.S. Blough, 1982, *Science, 218*, p. 398. Copyright 1982 by the AAAS. Reprinted by permission.

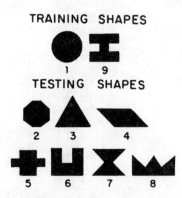

**Figure 2.33.** Training and test stimuli from an experiment in which the compactness of the stimulus acquired control over behavior. From "Judgments of Shape Similarity in the Barbary Dove (Streptopelia risoria)" by O. Hrycenko and D.W. Harwood, 1980, *Animal Behavior, 28*, p. 587. Copyright 1980 by Bailliere Tindall. Reprinted by permission.

to specify in advance which features of complex stimuli will gain control over responding. Species differences in controlling features, as well as experience-induced differences, are likely to be discovered as this area of research grows. Cerella (1980) studied pigeons' discrimination of line drawings that humans perceive as three dimensional. Performance during generalization testing in which stimuli were rotated and/or only portions of the stimuli were shown (e.g., obstructed views of the stimuli) led Cerella to conclude that pigeons were under the control of local features of these stimuli. They did not respond to them as three-dimensional objects, as humans would. As Herrnstein (1984) points out, it would be premature to claim that pigeons represent all visual information in two dimensions (Cerella, 1980), but it is clear that, due to either experience or species capacity, humans and pigeons respond to different features in line drawings.

As in the case of simple stimuli, one determinant of which aspect of a stimulus gains control over responding is the correlation of that aspect of the stimulus with reinforcement. Cues with the greatest predictive validity gain the greatest control over behavior. The multidimensional analogue of this principle is that those features that maximize the difference between positive and negative instances become controlling features. For example, Hrycenko and Harwood (1980) trained barbary doves to discrimi-

nate between the shapes shown in the top row of Figure 2.33. The test stimuli varied from the training stimuli along a number of possible controlling dimensions (e.g., area, shape of upper edge, etc.). The dimension that exerted the most control over responding was a measure of compactness: the length of the perimeter divided by the square root of the area. This measure was maximal for the circle and minimal for the I-shaped stimulus. Dimensions, like area, in which the circle and I-shaped stimulus do not differ did not gain control over responding. The features that maximize the difference between positive and negative instances of a given problem may be selected by reinforcement contingencies.

### Representation
What are the ways in which a pigeon might represent the information needed to successfully solve the conceptual categorization problem? First, no concept may guide performance. It is possible that the pigeons memorize all of the individual slides as positive or negative. Such a solution is possible, as pigeons are capable of remembering large numbers of visually presented stimuli over long periods of time (Greene, 1983; Vaughan & Greene, 1983, 1984; Wright, Santiago, Sands, & Urcuioli, 1984). For example Vaughan & Green (1983) found that the same slides that were used in teaching pigeons the concept of fish in the Herrnstein and de Villiers (1980) study could be randomly assigned to

positive and negative categories, and pigeons had little difficulty learning the discrimination. The capacity to learn large numbers of exemplars makes it possible that conceptual behavior is the result of memorizing individual instances. In this view, generalization to novel instances must be based on the similarity of the novel exemplar to already experienced stimuli. Alternatively, concept formation may involve the development of a prototype that is representative of the abstraction, not individual instances. The prototype might correspond to the average exemplar, that is, the mean value on all relevant dimensions. A test of whether classification is based on a comparison to individual exemplars or to a prototype is possible. Imagine that a subject had previously experienced only two different examples of a category. Prototype theory would predict that categorization would be easiest for a probe stimulus that was intermediate to the two training exemplars. The alternative hypothesis predicts that probes closer to previously experienced stimuli would be easier to classify than would probes that were midway between the training exemplars. Medin and colleagues (Medin & Reynolds, 1985; Medin & Schaffer, 1978; Medin & Smith, 1981) have done several experiments conceptually identical to the one described here and found that similarity to individual exemplars is a better predictor of ease of classification than is similarity to the category mean. Hence, the data relevant to this issue suggest that representations of individual exemplars of categories serves as the basis for comparison in the decision process.

### Decision Rules

An account of categorization of multidimensional stimuli requires a statement of the rules for combining dimensions. One way of categorizing stimuli would be to sum the evidence of categorical membership and to compare it to some criterion. This is explicitly employed by Lea and his colleagues in the letter identification experiments. Categories that are partitioned on the basis of additive combinations of component information are called linearly separable.

In human classification learning, Medin and his colleagues (Medin, Altom, Edelson, & Freko, 1982; Medin & Reynolds, 1985, Medin & Schaffer, 1978; Medin & Schwanenflugel, 1981) have devoted attention to examining the role of linear separ-

ability in concept formation. They have found that tasks involving linearly separable categories are not easier to learn than are categories that are not linearly separable (Medin & Schwanenflugel, 1981). Furthermore, because correlated attributes provide only redundant information, they will not contribute to categorizations that are based on weighted linear combinations of features. However, Medin et al. (1982) found that correlated attributes do, in fact, play an important role in the classification process. There is little evidence to support the hypothesis that component information combines additively in categorical judgments. What evidence there is seems to favor models based on a multiplicative combination of component information in a wide range of both animal and human discrimination data (Butter, 1963; Johnson, 1970; Medin & Reynolds, 1985).

It seems likely that reinforcement contingencies will play a role in the acquisition of combination rules that apply to a given problem. In the same way that features which maximize the difference between positive and negative exemplars come to control behavior, it is possible that attribute combination rules which maximize the difference between positive and negative instances come to be used. The role of past history and reinforcement contingencies in the acquisition of combination rules is definitely in need of study.

In summary, there are three aspects to understanding the range of antecedent stimuli which will act as effective controlling stimuli in cases where the particular stimuli might not have received explicit training. As the study of conceptual categorization illustrates, the physical features of the external environment, their representation in memory, and the decision process that leads to behavior must all be specified. Functional equivalence between stimuli arises at all three levels of analysis. Stimuli might be equivalent because of common physical properties, common representation, or common function in the response production process.

## GENERAL DISCUSSION

This chapter started with the assumption that all behavior has antecedent causes. The processes that underlie the influence of antecedent stimuli on behavior are revealed in the study of stimulus control. Three general topics emerged as central to understanding how antecedent conditions affect behavior.

First, the conditions that give rise to the acquisition of stimulus control were discussed. Implicit in this analysis was the assumption that the external world can be divided into a set of features (Tversky, 1977). Stimuli are assumed to exist in the environment. Hence, the acquisition of stimulus control refers to stimulus *selection* processes. Stimuli with certain properties or relationships to other stimuli are selected to control behavior. Alternatively, stimuli might be *created* by experiences. In the same way that reinforcement can shape new responses, perhaps new stimuli are shaped by stimulus contingencies (Gibson, 1960; Herrnstein, 1984). It is a fact that the dimensions which come to control a behavior are those along which positive and negative stimuli are most different. Perhaps controlling dimensions are, at least some of the time, created by this experience rather than selected from existing dimensions. This alternative certainly deserves more consideration than it has received. It has the merit of forcing us to grapple with the difficult questions of specifying the structure of stimuli and whether stimuli should be specified in the environment, at the receptor, or at some later stage of processing (cf. Gibson, 1960).

Next, the role of stimulus representations as antecedents for behavior was developed as means of discussing the nature of antecedents that are not specifiable in terms of exteroceptive properties. The fact that we cannot specify these events in physical terms may, of course, be a limitation of our knowledge. Skinner (1953) and Gibson (1960, 1966) advocated the description of control in terms of the physical properties of antecedent stimuli. Gibson, in particular, pointed out that stimuli may be quite complex and that our failures to predict behavior from exteroceptively defined antecedents may reflect the limitations of our physical descriptions, rather than transformations of physical input by the organism.

The third issue raised in this chapter relates to the problem of stimulus equivalence: What determines the range of novel stimuli that act as effective antecedents for behavior? Three aspects of stimulus equivalence were identified. Equivalence could be attributed to physical similarity, representational similarity, or similarity in the response production process. What we take for evidence of equivalence not based on physical similarity may also be a product of our inability to provide the relevant physical description of the stimulus. When we see variance in stimulus input and invariance in behavioral output, we look to sources of equivalence that are outside the stimulus (inside the organism). Perhaps more complete descriptions of stimulus properties will provide the stimulus invariance necessary to account for invariance in behavior (Gibson, 1966).

In conclusion, much progress has been made in understanding stimulus control. General principles are emerging in the study of how antecedent stimuli control behavior which may be very useful in many sub-areas of psychology. The prospects for immediate application of these principles seem most exciting in the areas of development, neurophysiology, and artificial intelligence.

There has been relatively little crossover between the study of learning and the study of development. Yet, behavioral regulation mechanisms that involve control by antecedent stimuli are an important aspect of developmental change (Gottlieb, 1971; Lewis & Starr, 1979; Rosenblatt, 1979). Studies of stimulus control, therefore, provide a powerful conceptual framework and set of principles for the ontogenetic analysis.

In the neurophysiological area, several groups are currently exploring the neural mechanisms that underlie learning (see Thompson et al., Chapter 4) and cognitive processing (see Goodglass & Butters, Chapter 13). The rules for learning and performance at the behavioral level set the problem at the physiological level. Hence, models of stimulus control provide the psychobiologist with the functional characteristics of the neural system that underlies the behavior.

Lastly, in the area of artificial intelligence, there is considerable interest in developing machines that can adapt their behavior to changes in environmental conditions. Therefore, models of stimulus control may serve as the basis for developing detection-recognition-action systems. Certainly any system which must mimic the operating characteristics of a living organism (e.g., humans) must conform to these principles.

The above three areas were singled out only because there seems to be much current interest and activity in them. The methods and principles of stimulus control described in this chapter are relevant to all areas of psychology. As

Stevens (1951) said,

"In a sense there is only one problem of psycho-physics, namely, the definition of the stimulus. In this same sense there is only one problem in all of psychology—and it is the same problem . . . . The reason for equating psychology to the problem of defining stimuli can be stated thus: the complete definition of the stimulus to a given response involves the specification of all the transformations of the environment, both internal and external that leave the response invariant. The specification of the conditions of invariance would entail, of course, a complete understanding of the factors that produce and that alter responses."

# REFERENCES

Alberts, J.R. (1978). Huddling by rat pups: Multisensory control of contact behavior. *Journal of Comparative and Physiological Psychology, 92*, 220–230.

Alberts, J.R. & Brunjes, P.C. (1979). Ontogeny of olfactory and thermal determinants of huddling in the rat. *Journal of Comparative and Physiological Psychology, 92*, 897–906.

Amiro, T.W. & Bitterman, M.E. (1980). Second-order appetitive conditioning in goldfish. *Journal of Experimental Psychology: Animal Behavior Processes, 6*, 41–48.

Amsel, A. (1979). The ontogeny of appetitive learning and persistence in the rat. In N.E. Spear & B.A. Campbell (Eds.), *Ontogeny of learning and memory* (pp. 189–224). Hillsdale, NJ: Erlbaum.

Atkinson, R.C. & Shiffrin, R.M. (1968). Human memory: A proposed system and control process. In K.W. Spence & J.T. Spence (Eds.), *The psychology of learning and motivation* (pp. 90–197). New York: Academic Press.

Balderrama, N. & Maldonado, H. (1971). Habituation of the deimatic response in the mantid (*Stagmatoptera biocellata*). *Journal of Comparative and Physiological Psychology, 75*, 98–106.

Balsam, P.D. (1982). Bringing the background to the foreground: The role of contextual cues in autoshaping. In M. Commons, R. Herrnstein, & A.R. Wagner (Eds.), *Quantitative analyses of behavior: Acquisition*, (Vol. 3, pp. 145–171). Cambridge: Ballinger.

Balsam, P.D. (1984). Relative time in trace conditioning. In J. Gibbon & L. Allan (Eds.), *Timing and time perception* (pp. 211–227). New York: New York Academy of Sciences.

Balsam, P.D. (1985). The functions of context in learning and performance. In P. Balsam & A. Tomie

(Eds.), *Context and learning* (pp. 1–21). Hillsdale, NJ: Erlbaum.

Balsam, P.D. & Tomie, A. (1985). *Context and learning*. Hillsdale, NJ: Erlbaum.

Beatty, W. & Shavalia, D. (1980). Rat spatial memory: Resistance to retroactive interference at long retention intervals. *Animal Learning and Behavior, 8*, 550–552.

Benedict, J.O. & Ayres, J.B. (1972). Factors affecting conditioning in the truly random control procedure in the rat. *Journal of Comparative and Physiological Psychology, 78*, 323–330.

Bever, T.G. (1984). The road from behaviorism to rationalism. In H. Roitblat, T. Bever, & H. Terrace (Eds.), *Animal cognition* (pp. 61–75). Hillsdale, NJ: Erlbaum.

Blough, D.S. (1959). Delayed matching in the pigeon. *Journal of the Experimental Analysis of Behavior, 2*, 151–160.

Blough, D.S. (1975). Steady state data and a quantitative model of operant generalization and discrimination. *Journal of Experimental Psychology: Animal Behavior Processes, 1*, 3–21.

Blough, D.S. (1982). Pigeon perception of letters of the alphabet. *Science, 218*, 397–398.

Blough, D.S. (1983). Alternative accounts of dimensional stimulus control. In M. Commons, R. Herrnstein, & A.R. Wagner (Eds.), *Quantitative analyses of behavior: Discrimination processes* (Vol. 4, pp. 59–72). Cambridge, MA: Ballinger.

Bolles, R.C. (1972). Reinforcement, expectancy, and learning. *Psychological Review, 79*, 394–409.

Bower, G.H. (1975). Cognitive psychology: An introduction. In W.K. Estes (Ed.), *Handbook of learning and cognitive processes* (pp. 25–80). Hillsdale, NJ: Erlbaum.

Branch, M.N. (1977). On the role of "memory" in the analysis of behavior. *Journal of the Experimental Analysis of Behavior, 28*, 171–179.

Brandon, S.E. (1981). Key-light-specific associations and factors determining key pecking in noncontingent schedules. *Journal of Experimental Psychology: Animal Behavior Processes, 7*, 348–361.

Braverman, N.S. (1977). Visually guided food avoidance of poisonous foods in mammals. In L.M. Barker, M.R. Best, & M. Domjan (Eds.), *Learning mechanisms in food selection* (pp. 455–473). Waco, TX: Baylor University Press.

Brodigan, D.L. & Peterson, G.B. (1976). Two-choice conditional discrimination performance of pigeons as a function of reward expectancy, prechoice delay, and domesticity. *Animal Learning and Behavior, 4*, 121–124.

Brown, B.L. (1970). Stimulus generalization in salivary conditioning. *Journal of Comparative and Physiological Psychology, 71*, 467–477.

Brown, J.S. (1965). Generalization and discrimination. In D. Mostofsky (Ed.), *Stimulus generalization* (pp. 7–23). Stanford: Stanford University Press.

Brown, P.L. & Jenkins, H.M. (1968). Auto-shaping of the pigeon's key-peck. *Journal of the Experimental Analysis of Behavior, 11*, 1–8.

Butter, C.M. (1963). Stimulus generalization along one and two dimensions in pigeons. *Journal of Experimental Psychology, 65*, 339–346.

Capaldi, E.J. (1967). A sequential hypothesis of instrumental learning. In K.W. Spence & J.T. Spence (Eds.), *The psychology of learning and motivation* (pp. 67–157). New York: Academic Press.

Capaldi, E.J., Nawrocki, T.M., & Verry, D.R. (1983). Difficult serial anticipation learning in the rat: Rule encoding vs. memory. *Animal Learning and Behavior, 10*, 167–170.

Capretta, P.J. (1977). Establishment of food preferences by exposure to ingestive stimuli early in life. In L.M. Barker, M.R. Best, & M. Domjan (Eds.), *Learning mechanisms in food selection* (pp. 99–121). Waco, TX: Baylor University Press.

Carlson, J.G. & Wielkiewicz, R.M. (1972). Delay of reinforcement in instrumental discrimination learning of rats. *Journal of Comparative and Physiological Psychology, 81*, 365–370.

Cerella, J. (1979). Visual classes and natural categories in the pigeon. *Journal of Experimental Psychology: Human Perception and Performance, 5*, 68–77.

Cerella, J. (1980). The pigeon's analysis of pictures. *Pattern Recognition, 12*, 1–6.

Cerella, J. (1982). Mechanisms of concept formation in the pigeon. In D. Ingle, M. Goodale, & R. Mansfield (Eds.), *Analysis of visual behavior* (pp. 241–260). Cambridge, MA: MIT Press.

Chase, S. (1983). Pigeons and the magical number seven. In M.L. Commons, R.J. Herrnstein, & A.R. Wagner (Eds.), *Quantitative analyses of behavior*, Vol. 4 (pp. 37–57). Cambridge, MA: Ballinger.

Cheatle, M.D. & Rudy, J.W. (1978). Analysis of second-order odor-aversion conditioning in neonatal rats: Implications for Kamin's blocking effect. *Journal of Experimental Psychology: Animal Behavior Processes, 4*, 237–249.

Cheatle, M.D. & Rudy, J.W. (1979). Ontogeny of second order odor-aversion conditioning in neonatal rats. *Journal of Experimental Pschology: Animal Behavior Processes, 5*, 237–249.

Cheng, K. & Gallistel, C.R. (1984). Testing the geometric power of an animal's spatial representation. In H. Roitblat, T. Bever, & H. Terrace (Eds.), *Animal cognition* (pp. 409–424). Hillsdale, NJ: Erlbaum.

Church, R.M. & Meck, W.H. (1983). Acquisition and cross-model transfer of classification rules for temporal intervals. In M.L. Commons, R.J. Herrnstein,

& A.R. Wagner (Eds.), *Quantitative analyses of behavior*, Vol. 4 (pp. 75–97). Cambridge, MA: Ballinger.

Clark, J.C., Westbrook, R.F., & Irwin, J. (1979). Potentiation instead of overshadowing in the pigeon. *Behavioral and Neural Biology, 25*, 18–29.

Colwill, R.M. & Rescorla, R.A. (1985). Postconditioning devaluation of a reinforcer affects instrumental responding. *Journal of Experimental Psychology: Animal Behavior Processes, 11*, 120–132.

Conrad, R. (1964). Acoustic confusions in immediate memory. *British Journal of Psychology, 55*, 78–84.

Cross, D.V. (1965). Metric properties of multidimensional stimulus generalization. In D.I. Mostofsky (Ed.), *Stimulus generalization* (pp. 72–93). Stanford, CA: Stanford University Press.

Davis, M. (1970). Effects of interstimulus interval length and variability on startle-response habituation in the rat. *Journal of Comparative and Physiological Psychology, 72*, 177–192.

Davis, M. (1974). Sensitization of the rat startle response by noise. *Journal of Comparative and Physiological Psychology, 87*, 571–581.

DeCasper, A.J. & Fifer, W.P. (1980). Of human bonding: Newborns prefer their mother's voices. *Science, 208*, 1174–1176.

DeLong, R.E. & Wasserman, E.A. (1981). Effects of differential reinforcement expectancies on successive matching-to-sample performance in pigeons. *Journal of Experimental Psychology: Animal Behavior Processes, 7*, 394–412.

Dickinson, A. (1980). *Contemporary animal learning theory*. Cambridge: Cambridge University Press.

Dobrzecka, C., Szwejkowska, G., & Konorski, J. (1966). Qualitative versus directional cues in two forms of differentiation. *Science, 153*, 87–89.

Domjan, M. (1980). Ingestional aversion learning: Unique and general processes. In J.S. Rosenblatt, R.A. Hinde, C. Beer, & M.C. Busnel (Eds.), *Advances in the study of behavior*, Vol. 2 (pp. 275–336). New York: Academic Press.

Domjan, M. (1983). Biological constraints on instrumental and classical conditioning: Implications for general process theory. In G.H. Bower (Ed.), *The psychology of learning and motivation*, Vol. 17 (pp. 216–277). New York: Academic Press.

Durlach, P. (1982). Pavlovian learning and performance when CS and US are uncorrelated. In M. Commons, R. Herrnstein, & A. Wagner (Eds.), *Quantitative analyses of behavior: acquisition*, Vol. 3 (pp. 173–193). Cambridge, MA: Ballinger.

Durlach, P. & Rescorla, R.A. (1980). Potentiation rather than overshadowing in flavor-aversion learning. *Journal of Experimental Psychology: Animal Behavior Processes, 6*, 175–187.

Eckerman, D.A. (1970). Generalization and response mediation of a conditional discrimination. *Journal of the Experimental Analysis of Behavior, 13*, 301–316.

Eisman, B.S. (1955). Attitude formation: The development of a color-preference response through mediated generalization. *Journal of Abnormal and Social Psychology, 50*, 321–326.

Estes, W.K. (1972). An associative basis for coding and organization in memory. In A.W. Melton & E. Martin, (Eds.), *Coding processes in human memory* (pp. 161–190). Washington, DC: V.H. Winston.

Estes, W.K. (1976). Structural aspects of associative models for memory. In C.N. Cofer (Ed.), *The structure of human memory* (pp. 31–54). New York: W.H. Freeman.

Estes, W.K. (1979). Cognitive processes in conditioning. In A. Dickinson and R.A. Boakes (Eds.), *Mechanisms of learning and motivation* (pp. 417–441). Hillsdale, NJ: Erlbaum.

Farthing, G.W. (1972). Overshadowing in the discrimination of successive compound stimuli. *Psychonomic Science, 28*, 29–32.

Foree, D.D. & LoLordo, V.M. (1973a). Attention in the pigeon: The differential effects of food-getting vs. shock-avoidance procedures. *Journal of Comparative and Physiological Psychology, 85*, 551–558.

Foree, D.D. & LoLordo, V.M. (1973b). Relation of cue to consequence in avoidance learning. *Psychonomic Science, 4*, 123–124.

Fountain, S.B. & Annau, Z. (1984). Chunking, sorting, and rule-learning from serial patterns of brain-stimulation reward by rats. *Animal Learning and Behavior, 12*, 265–274.

Fountain, S.B., Henne, D.R., & Hulse, S.H. (1984). Phrasing cues and hierarchical organization in serial pattern learning by rats. *Journal of Experimental Psychology: Animal Behavior Processes, 10*, 30–45.

Fraenkel, G.S. & Gunn, D.L. (1949). *The orientation of animals: Kineses, taxes and compass reactions.* Oxford: Clarendon Press.

Galef, B.G., Jr. (1976). Social transmission of acquired behavior: A discussion of tradition and social learning in vertebrates. In J.S. Rosenblatt, R.A. Hinde, E. Shaw, & C. Beer (Eds.), *Advances in the study of behavior*, Vol. 6 (pp. 77–100). New York: Academic Press.

Galef, B.G., Jr. (1977). Mechanisms for the social transmission of acquired food preferences from adult to weanling rats. In: L.M. Barker, M.R. Best & M. Domjan (Eds.), *Learning mechanisms in food selection* (pp. 123–148). Waco, TX: Baylor University Press.

Galef, B.G., Jr. & Osborne, B. (1978). Novel taste facilitation of the association of visual cues with toxicosis in rats. *Journal of Comparative and Physiological Psychology, 92*, 907–916.

Ganz, L. & Riesen, A.H. (1962). Stimulus generalization to hue in the dark-reared macaque. *Journal of Comparative and Physiological Psychology, 55*, 92–99.

Garcia, J. & Koelling, R.A. (1966). Relation to cue to consequence in avoidance learning. *Psychonomic Science, 4*, 123–124.

Garcia, J., McGowan, B.K., & Green, K.F. (1972). Biological constraints on conditioning. In A. Black & W. Prokasy (Eds.), *Classical conditioning II: current theory and research* (pp. 3–27). New York: Appleton-Century-Crofts.

Gibbon, J. (1977). Scalar expectancy theory and Weber's law in animal timing. *Psychological Review, 84*, 279–325.

Gibbon, J. (1979). Timing the stimulus and the response in aversive control. In M.D. Zeiler & P. Harzem (Eds.), *Reinforcement and the organization of behavior* (pp. 299–340). New York: Wiley & Sons.

Gibbon, J., Baldock, M.D., Locurto, C., Gold, L., & Terrace, H.S. (1977). Trial and intertrial durations in autoshaping. *Journal of Experimental Psychology: Animal Behavior Processes, 3*, 264–284.

Gibbon, J.G. & Balsam, P.D. (1981). The spread of association in time. In: C.M. Locurto, H.S. Terrace, & J.G. Gibbon (Eds.), *Autoshaping and conditioning theory* (pp. 219–253). New York: Academic Press.

Gibbon, J.G. & Church, R.M. (1984). Sources of variance in an information theory of timing. In H.L. Roitblat, T.G. Bever, & H.S. Terrace (Eds), *Animal cognition* (pp. 465–488). Hillsdale, NJ: Erlbaum.

Gibson, J.J. (1960). The concept of the stimulus in psychology. *American Psychologist, 15*, 694–703.

Gibson, J.J. (1966). *The senses considered as perceptual systems.* Boston: Houghton Mifflin Co.

Gilbert, R.M. & Sutherland, N.S. (1969). *Animal discrimination learning.* London: Academic Press.

Gormezano, I. & Kehoe, E.J. (1981). Classical conditioning and the law of contiguity. In P. Harzem & M.H. Zeiler (Eds.), *Predictability, correlation and contiguity* (pp. 1–45). London: Wiley.

Gottlieb, G. (1971). Ontogenesis of sensory functions in birds and mammals. In E. Tobach, L.R. Aronson, & E. Shaw (Eds.), *The biopsychology of development* (pp. 67–128). New York: Academic Press.

Gottlieb, G. (1983). The psychobiological approach to developmental issues. In P.H. Mussen (Ed.), *Handbook of child psychology*, Vol. 2 (pp. 1–26). New York: John Wiley & Sons.

Graf, J.S., Balsam, P.D., & Silver, R. (1985). Associative factors and the development of pecking in ring doves. *Developmental Psychobiology, 18*, 447–460.

Grant, D.S. (1984). Rehearsal in pigeon short-term memory. In H. Roitblat, T. Bever, & H. Terrace (Eds.), *Animal cognition* (pp. 99–116). Hillsdale, NJ: Erlbaum.

Gray, V.A. & Mackintosh, N.J. (1973). Control by an irrelevant stimulus in discrete-trial discrimination learning by pigeons. *Bulletin of the Psychonomic Society, 1*, 193–195.

Greene, S.L. (1983). Feature memorization in pigeon concept formation. In M.L. Commons, R.J. Herrnstein, & A.R. Wagner (Eds.), *Quantitative analyses of behavior: Discrimination Processes*, Vol. 4 (pp. 209–229). Cambridge, MA: Ballinger.

Grice, G.R. (1965). Investigations of response-mediated generalization. In D.I. Mostofsky (Ed.), *Stimulus generalization* (pp. 373–382). Stanford, CA: Stanford University Press.

Grice, G.R. & Davis, J.D. (1958). Mediated stimulus equivalence and distinctiveness in human conditioning. *Journal of Experimental Psychology, 35*, 565–571.

Grice, G.R. & Davis, J.D. (1960). Effect of concurrent responses on the evocation and generalization of the conditioned eyeblink. *Journal of Experimental Psychology, 59*, 391–395.

Groves, P.M. & Thompson, R.F. (1970). Habituation: A dual-process theory. *Psychological Review, 77*, 419–450.

Guthrie, E.R. (1935). *The psychology of learning.* New York: Harper & Row.

Guttman, N. & Kalish, H.J. (1956). Discriminability and stimulus generalization. *Journal of Experimental Psychology, 51*, 79–88.

Hall, G. (1982). Effects of a brief stimulus accompanying reinforcement on instrumental responding in pigeons. *Learning and Motivation, 13*, 26–43.

Hall, G., Channell, S., & Pearce, J.M. (1981). The effects of a signal for free or earned reward: Implications for the role of response-reinforcer associations in instrumental performance. *Quarterly Journal of Experimental Psychology, 33*, 95–107.

Hall, G. & Honig, W.K. (1974). Stimulus control after extra-dimensional training in pigeons: A comparison of response contingent and noncontingent training procedures. *Journal of Comparative and Physiological Psychology, 87*, 945–952.

Hall, W.G. & Williams, C.L. (1983). Suckling isn't feeding, or is it? A search for developmental continuities. In J.S. Rosenblatt, R.A. Hinde, C. Beer, & M. Busnel (Eds.), *Advances in the study of behavior*, Vol. 13 (pp. 219–254). New York: Academic Press.

Hanson, H.M. (1959). Effects of discrimination training on stimulus generalization. *Journal of Experimental Psychology, 58*, 321–334.

Harlow, H.F. & Harlow, M.K. (1962). Social deprivation in monkeys. *Scientific American, 207*, 137–146.

Harrison, J.M. (1983). Naturalistic considerations in the study of discrimination. In M.L. Commons, R.J. Herrnstein, & A.R. Wagner (Eds.), *Quantitative analyses of behavior*, Vol. 4 (pp. 319–335). Cambridge, MA: Ballinger.

Hawkins, R.D. & Kandel, E.R. (1984). Is there a cell-biological alphabet for simple forms of learning? *Psychological Review, 91*, 375–391.

Hearst, E. (1969). Excitation, inhibition and discrimination learning. In N.J. Mackintosh & W.K. Honig (Eds.), *Fundamental issues in associative learning* (pp. 1–41). Halifax: Dalhousie University Press.

Hearst, E. (1978). Stimulus relationships and feature selection in learning and behavior. In S.H. Hulse, H. Fowler, & W.K. Honig (Eds.), *Cognitive processes in animal behavior* (pp. 51–88). Hillsdale, NJ: Erlbaum.

Hearst, E., Besley, S., & Farthing, G.W. (1970). Inhibition and the stimulus control of operant behavior. *Journal of Experimental Psychology: Animal Behavior Processes, 14*, 373–409.

Hearst, E. & Koresko, M.B. (1968). Stimulus generalization and amount of prior training on variable interval reinforcement. *Journal of Comparative and Physiological Psychology, 66*, 133–138.

Heinemann, E.G. (1983). A memory model for decision processes in pigeons. In M.L. Commons, R.J. Herrnstein, & A.R. Wagner (Eds.), *Quantitative analyses of behavior: Discrimination processes*, Vol. 4 (pp. 3–19). Cambridge, MA: Ballinger.

Heinemann, E.G., Avin, E., Sullivan, M.A., & Chase, S. (1969). Analysis of stimulus generalization with a psychophysical method. *Journal of Experimental Psychology: Animal Behavior Processes, 80*, 215–224.

Heinemann, E.G. & Chase, S. (1970). Conditional stimulus control. *Journal of Experimental Psychology, 84*, 187–197.

Heinemann, E.G. & Chase, S. (1975). Stimulus generalization. In W.K. Estes (Ed.), *Handbook of learning a cognitive processes*, Vol. 2 (pp. 305–350). Hillsdale, NJ: Erlbaum.

Heinemann, E.G. & Rudolph, R.L. (1963). The effect of discriminative training on the gradient of stimulus generalization. *American Journal of Psychology, 76*, 653–658.

Herrnstein, R.J. (1979). Acquisition generalization and discrimination reversal of a natural concept. *Journal of Experimental Psychology: Animal Behavior Processes, 5*, 116–129.

Herrnstein, R.J. (1984). Objects, categories, and discriminative stimuli. In H. Roitblat, T. Bever, & H. Terrace (Eds.), *Animal cognition* (pp. 233–261). Hillsdale, NJ: Erlbaum.

Herrnstein, R.J. & DeVilliers, P.A. (1980). Fish as a natural category for people and pigeons. In G.H.

Bower (Ed.), *The psychology of learning and motivation*, Vol. 14. New York: Academic Press.

Herrnstein, R.J. & Loveland, D.H. (1964). Complex visual concept in the pigeon. *Science, 146*, 549–551.

Herrnstein, R.J., Loveland, D.H., & Cable, C. (1976). Natural concepts in pigeons. *Journal of Experimental Psychology: Animal Behavior Processes, 2*, 285–302.

Hess, E.H. & Petrovich, S.B. (1977). Imprinting. Stroudsburg, Pa: Dowden, Hutchinson, & Ross, Inc.

Hinde, R.A. (1983). Ethology and child development. In Paul H. Mussen (Ed.), *Handbook of child psychology*, Vol. 2 (pp. 27–94). M.M. Haith & J.J. Campos (Vol. Eds), *Infancy and developmental psychobiology*. New York: John Wiley & Sons.

Hoffman, H.S. (1965). The stimulus generalization of conditioned suppression. In D.I. Mostofsky (Ed.), *Stimulus generalization* (pp. 356–372). Stanford, CA: Stanford University Press.

Hogan, J.A. (1973). How young chicks learn to recognize food. In R.A. Hinde & J. Stevenson-Hinde (Eds.), *Constraints on learning* (pp. 119–139). London: Academic Press.

Hogan, J.A. (1984). Pecking and feeding in chicks. *Learning and Motivation, 15*, 360–376.

Holland, P.C. (1980a). CS-US interval as a determinant of the form of Pavlovian appetitive conditioned responses. *Journal of Experimental Psychology: Animal Behavior Processes, 6*, 155–174.

Holland, P.C. (1980b). Influence of visual conditioned stimulus characteristics on the form of Pavlovian appetitive conditioned responding in rats. *Journal of Experimental Psychology: Animal Behavior Processes, 6*, 81–97.

Holland, P.C. (1983). "Occasion-setting" in Pavlovian feature-positive discriminations. In M. Commons, R. Herrnstein, & A.R. Wagner (Eds.), *Quantitative analyses of behavior: Discrimination processes*, Vol. 4 (pp. 183–206). Cambridge, MA: Ballinger.

Holland, P.C. (1984). Origins of behavior in Pavlovian conditioning. In G.H. Bower (Ed.), *The psychology of learning and motivation* Vol. 18 (pp. 129–174). New York: Academic Press.

Holland, P.C. (1985). The nature of conditioned inhibition in serial and simultaneous feature negative discriminations. In R.R. Miller & N.E. Spear (Eds.), *Information processing in animals: Inhibition and contingencies* (pp. 267–297). Hillsdale: NJ: Erlbaum.

Holland, P.C. & Block, H. (1983). Evidence for a unique cue in positive patterning. *Bulletin of the Psychonomic Society, 21*, 297–300.

Holland, P.C. & Rescorla, R.A. (1975). The effect of two ways of devaluing the unconditioned stimulus after first- and second-order appetitive conditioning. *Journal of Experimental Psychology: Animal Behavior Processes, 1*, 355–363.

Holland, P.C. & Ross, R.T. (1981). Within-compound associations in serial compound conditioning. *Journal of Experimental Psychology: Animal Behavior Processes, 7*, 228–241.

Holland, P.C. & Straub, J.J. (1979). Differential effects of two ways of devaluing the unconditioned stimulus after Pavlovian appetitive conditioning. *Journal of Experimental Psychology: Animal Behavior Processes, 5*, 65–78.

Holman, J.G. & Mackintosh, N.J. (1981). The control of appetitive instrumental responding does not depend on classical conditioning to the discriminative stimulus. *Journal of Experimental Psychology: Animal Behavior Processes, 33B*, 21–31.

Holt, E.B. (1931). *Animal drive and the learning process*. New York: Henry Holt & Co.

Honig, W.K. (1969). Attentional factors governing the slope of the generalization gradient. In R.M. Gilbert & N.S. Sutherland (Eds.), *Animal discrimination learning* (pp. 35–62). London: Academic Press.

Honig, W.K. (1978). Studies of working memory in the pigeon. In S.H. Hulse, H. Fowler, & W.K. Honig (Eds.), *Cognitive processes in animal behavior* (pp. 211–248). Hillsdale, NJ: Erlbaum.

Honig, W.K. (1984). Contributions of animal memory to the interpretation of animal learning. In H.L. Roitblat, T.G. Bever, & H.S. Terrace (Eds.), *Animal cognition* (pp. 29–44). Hillsdale, NJ: Erlbaum.

Honig, W.K., Boneau, C.A., Burstein, K.R., & Pennypacker, H.S. (1963). Positive and negative generalization gradients obtained after equivalent training conditions. *Journal of Comparative and Physiological Psychology, 56*, 111–116.

Hrycenko, O. & Harwood, D.W. (1980). Judgments of shape similarity in the Barbary dove (*Streptopelia risoria*). *Animal Behavior, 28*, 586–592.

Hull, C.L. (1939). The problem of stimulus equivalence in behavior theory. *Psychological Review, 46*, 9–30.

Hull, C.L. (1943). *Principles of behavior*. New York: Appleton-Century-Crofts.

Hulse, S.H. (1978). Cognitive structure and serial pattern learning by animals. In S.H. Hulse, H. Fowler, & W.K. Honig (Eds.), *Cognitive processes in animal behavior* (pp. 311–340). Hillsdale, NJ: Erlbaum.

Hulse, S.H. (1980). The case of the missing rule: Memory for reward vs. formal structure in serial-pattern learning by rats. *Animal Learning and Behavior, 8*, 689–690.

Hulse, S.H., Cynx, J., & Humpal, J. (1984). Cognitive processing of pitch and rhythm structures. In H.L. Roitblat, T.G. Bever, & H.S. Terrace (Eds.), *Animal cognition* (pp. 183–198). Hillsdale, NJ: Erlbaum.

Hulse, S.H., Cynx, J., & Humpal, J. (1985). Pitch context and pitch discrimination by birds. In P. Balsam and A. Tomie (Eds.), *Context and learning* (pp. 273–293). Hillsdale, NJ: Erlbaum.

Hulse, S.H. & Dorsky, N.P. (1977). Structural complexity as a determinant of serial pattern learning. *Learning and Motivation, 8,* 488–506.

Hulse, S.H. & Dorsky, N.P. (1979). Serial pattern learning by rats: Transfer of a formally defined stimulus relationship and the significance of nonreinforcement. *Animal Learning and Behavior, 7,* 211–220.

Hulse, S.H., Fowler, H., & Honig, W.K. (1978). *Cognitive processes in animal behavior.* Hillsdale, NJ: Erlbaum.

Hunter, W.S. (1913). The delayed reaction in animals and children. *Behavior Monographs, 2,* 1 (Serial No. 6).

Hyson, R.L. & Rudy, J.W (1984). Ontogenesis of learning: II. Variation in the rat's reflexive and learned responses to acoustic stimulation. *Developmental Psychobiology, 17,* 263–283.

Immelmann, K., Barlow, G.W., Petrinovich, L., & Main, M. (1981). *Behavioral development.* Cambridge: Cambridge University Press.

Innis, N.K., Simmelhag-Grant, V.L., & Staddon, J.E.R. (1983). Behavior induced by periodic food delivery: The effects of interfood interval. *Journal of the Experimental Analysis of Behavior, 39,* 309–322.

Jeffrey, W.E. (1953). The effects of verbal and nonverbal responses in mediating an instrumental act. *Journal of Experimental Psychology, 45,* 327–333.

Jenkins, H.M. (1977). Sensitivity of different response systems to stimulus-reinforcer and response-reinforcer relations. In H. Davis & H.M.B. Hurwitz (Eds.), *Operant-Pavlovian interactions* (pp. 47–66). Hillsdale, NJ: Erlbaum.

Jenkins, H.M. & Harrison, R.H. (1960). Effects of discrimination training on auditory generalization. *Journal of Experimental Psychology, 59,* 246–253.

Jenkins, H.M. & Sainsbury, R.S. (1969). The development of stimulus control through differential reinforcement. In N.J. Mackintosh & W.K. Honig (Eds.), *Fundamental issues in associative learning* (pp. 123–161). Halifax: Dalhousie University Press.

Johnson, D.F. (1970). Determiners of selective stimulus control in the pigeon. *Journal of Comparative and Physiological Psychology, 70,* 298–307.

Kahneman, D. & Tversky, A. (1984). Choices, values, and frames. *American Psychologist, 39,* 341–351.

Kamin, L.J. (1969a). Selective association and conditioning. In N.J. Mackintosh and W.K. Honig (Eds.), *Fundamental issues in associative learning* (pp. 42–64). Halifax: Dalhousie University Press.

Kamin, L.J. (1969b). Predictability, surprise, attention, and conditioning. In B. Campbell & R. Church (Eds.), *Punishment and aversive behavior* (pp. 279–296). Englewood Cliffs, NJ: Prentice-Hall, Inc.

Kaplan, P. (1984). Importance of relative temporal parameters in trace autoshaping: From excitation to inhibition. *Journal of Experimental Psychology: Animal Behavior Processes, 10,* 113–126.

Kaplan, P. & Hearst, E. (1985). Contextual control and excitatory vs. inhibitory learning: Studies of extinction, reinstatement, and interference. In P. Balsam and A. Tomie (Eds.), *Context and learning* (pp. 195–224). Hillsdale, NJ: Erlbaum.

Kerr, L.M., Ostapoff, E.M., & Rubel, E.W. (1979). Influence of acoustic experience on the ontogeny of frequency generalization gradients in the chicken. *Journal of Experimental Psychology: Animal Behavior Processes, 5,* 97–115.

Kimble, G.A. (1961). *Hilgard & Marquis' conditioning and learning.* New York: Appleton-Century-Crofts.

Klopfer, P.H., Adams, D.K., & Klopfer, M.S. (1964). Maternal "imprinting" in goats. *The National Academy of Science Proceedings, 52,* 911–914.

Kremer, E.F. & Kamin, L.J. (1971). The truly random procedure: Associative or nonassociative effects in rats. *Journal of Comparative and Physiological Psychology, 74,* 203–210.

Lashley, K.S. & Wade, M. (1946). The Pavlovian theory of generalization. *Psychological Review, 53,* 72–87.

Latane, B. & Darley, J.M. (1970). *The unresponsive bystander: Why doesn't he help?* New York: Appleton-Century-Crofts.

Lawrence, D.H. (1949). Acquired distinctiveness of cues: I. Transfer between discriminations on the basis of familiarity with the stimulus. *Journal of Experimental Psychology, 39,* 770–784.

Lawrence, D.H. (1950). Acquired distinctiveness of cues: II. Selective association in a constant stimulus situation. *Journal of Experimental Psychology, 40,* 175–188.

Lawrence, D.H. (1963). The nature of a stimulus: Some relationships between learning and perception. In S. Koch (Ed.), *Psychology: A study of a science,* Vol. 5 (pp. 179–212). New York: McGraw-Hill.

Lea, S.E.G. & Ryan, C.M.E. (1983). Feature analysis of pigeons' acquisition of discrimination between letters. In M.L. Commons, R.J. Herrnstein, & A.R. Wagner (Eds.), *Quantitative analyses of behavior: Discrimination processes,* Vol. 4 (pp. 239–253). Cambridge, MA: Ballinger.

Leiderman, P.H. (1981). Human mother-infant social bonding: Is there a sensitive phase? In K. Immelmann, G.W. Barlow, L. Petrinovich, & M. Main (Eds.), *Behavioral development* (pp. 454–468). Cambridge: Cambridge University Press.

Lett, B.T. (1980). Taste potentiates color-sickness associates in pigeons and quail. *Animal Learning and Behavior, 8,* 193–198.

Lett, B.T. (1982). Taste potentiation in poison-avoidance learning. In M.L. Commons, R.J. Herrnstein,

& A.R. Wagner (Eds.), *Quantitative analyses of behavior: Acquisition*, Vol. 3 (pp. 273–293). Cambridge, MA: Ballinger.

Lewis, M. & Starr, M.D. (1979). Developmental continuity. In S. Osofsky (Ed.), *Handbook of infant development* (pp. 653–670). New York: Wiley.

Lipsitt, L.P. & Kaye, H. (1965). Changes in neonatal response to optimizing and non-optimizing suckling stimulation. *Psychonomic Science, 2,* 221–222.

LoLordo, V.M. (1979). Selective associations. In A. Dickinson & R.A. Boakes (Eds.), *Mechanisms of learning and motivation* (pp. 367–398). Hillsdale, NJ: Erlbaum.

LoLordo, V. & Fairless, J.L. (1985). Pavlovian conditioned inhibition: The literature since 1969. In R.R. Miller & N.E. Spear (Eds.), *Information processing in animals: Inhibition and contingencies* (pp. 1–49). Hillsdale, NJ: Erlbaum.

Looney, T.S. & Griffin, R. (1978). A sequential feature-positive effect using tone as the distinguishing feature in an autoshaping procedure. *Animal Learning and Behavior, 6,* 401–405.

Lovejoy, E. (1968). *Attention in discrimination learning.* San Francisco: Holden-Day.

Lubow, R.E. (1974). High-order concept formation in the pigeon. *Journal of the Experimental Analysis of Behavior, 21,* 475–483.

Mackintosh, N.J. (1974). *The psychology of animal learning.* London: Academic Press.

Mackintosh, N.J. (1975). A theory of attention: Variations in the associability of stimuli with reinforcement. *Psychological Review, 82,* 276–298.

Mackintosh, N.J. (1977). Stimulus control: Attentional factors. In W.K. Honig & J.E.R. Staddon (Eds.), *Handbook of operant behavior* (pp. 481–513). Englewood Cliffs, NJ: Prentice-Hall.

Mackintosh, N.J. (1983). *Conditioning and associative learning.* Oxford: Oxford University Press.

Mackintosh, N.J. & Dickinson, A. (1979). Instrumental (Type II) conditioning. In A. Dickinson & R.A. Boakes (Eds.), *Mechanisms of learning and motivation* (pp. 143–169). Hillsdale, NJ: Erlbaum.

Mackintosh, N.J. & Honig, W.K. (1970). Blocking and enhancement of stimulus control in pigeons. *Journal of Comparative and Physiological Psychology, 73,* 78–85.

Maki, W.S. (1984). Some problems for a theory of working memory. In H.L. Roitblat, T.G. Bever, & H.S. Terrace (Eds.), *Animal cognition* (pp. 117–134). Hillsdale, NJ: Erlbaum.

Maki, W.S., Brokofsky, S., & Berg, B. (1979). Spatial memory in rats: Resistance to retroactive interference. *Animal Learning and Behavior, 7,* 25–30.

Malott, R.W. & Siddall, J.W. (1972). Acquisition of the people concept in pigeons. *Psychological Reports, 31,* 3–13.

Mazmanian, D.S. & Roberts, W.A. (1983). Spatial memory in rats under restricted viewing conditions. *Learning and Motivation, 12,* 261–281.

Mazur, J.E. & Wagner, A.R. (1982). An episodic model of associative learning. In M.L. Commons, R.J. Herrnstein, & A.R. Wagner (Eds.), *Quantitative analyses of behavior: Acquisition*, Vol. 3 (pp. 3–39). Cambridge, MA: Ballinger.

Medin, D., Altom, M., Edelson, S., & Freko, D. (1982). Correlated symptoms and simulated medical classification. *Journal of Experimental Psychology: Learning, Memory, and Cognition, 8,* 37–50.

Medin, D. & Reynolds, T. (1985). Cue-context interactions in discrimination, categorization, and memory. In P. Balsam and A. Tomie (Eds.), *Context and learning* (pp. 323–356). Hillsdale, NJ: Erlbaum.

Medin, D. & Schaffer, M. (1978). Context theory of classification learning. *Psychological Review, 85,* 207–238.

Medin, D. & Schwanenflugel, P. (1981). Linear separability in classification learning. *Journal of Experimental Psychology: Human Learning and Memory, 7,* 355–368.

Medin, D. & Smith, E.E. (1981). Strategies and classification learning. *Journal of Experimental Psychology: Human Learning and Memory, 7,* 241–253.

Mellgren, R.L. & Ost, J.W.P. (1969). Transfer of Pavlovian differential conditioning to an operant discrimination. *Journal of Comparative and Physiological Psychology, 67,* 390–394.

Menzel, E.W. (1978). Cognitive mapping in chimpanzees. In S.H. Hulse, H. Fowler, & W.K. Honig (Eds.), *Cognitive processes in animal behavior* (pp. 375–422). Hillsdale, NJ: Erlbaum.

Miles, C.G. (1970). Blocking the acquisition of control by an auditory stimulus with pretraining on brightness. *Psychonomic Science, 19,* 133–134.

Miles, C.G. & Jenkins, H.M. (1973). Overshadowing in operant conditioning as a function of discriminability. *Learning and Motivation, 4,* 11–27.

Miller, G.A., Galanter, E., & Pribram, K.H. (1960). *Plans and the structure of behavior.* New York: Holt, Rinehart and Winston.

Miller, N.E. (1948). Theory and experiment relating psychoanalytic displacement to stimulus response generalization. *Journal of Abnormal and Social Psychology, 43,* 155–178.

Miller, N.E. (1963). Some reflections on the law of effect produce a new alternative to drive reduction. In M.R. Jones (Ed.), *Nebraska symposium on learning and motivation*, Vol. 11 (pp. 65–112). Lincoln: University of Nebraska Press.

Miller, R. & Schachtman, T. (1985). The several roles of context at the time of retrieval. In P. Balsam & A. Tomie (Eds.), *Context and Learning* (pp. 167–194). Hillsdale, NJ: Erlbaum.

Moore, J.W. (1972). Stimulus control: Studies of auditory generalization in rabbits. In A.H. Black & W.F. Prokasy (Eds.), *Classical conditioning, Vol. 2: Current research and theory* (pp. 206–230). Englewood Cliffs, NJ: Prentice-Hall, Inc.

Morgan, M.J., Fitch, M.D., Holman, J.G., & Lea, S.E.G. (1976). Pigeons learn the concept of an "A". *Perception, 5,* 57–66.

Morris, R.G.M. (1981). Spatial localization does not require the presence of local cues. *Learning and Motivation, 12,* 239–260.

Mostofsky, D. (1965). *Stimulus generalization.* Stanford: Stanford University Press.

Mountjoy, P.P. & Malott, M.K. (1968). Wavelength generalization curves for chickens reared in restricted portions of the spectrum. *Psychological Record, 18,* 575–583.

Mowrer, O.H. (1947). On the dual nature of learning—a reinterpretation of conditioning and problem solving. *Harvard Educational Review, 17,* 102–148.

Mowrer, O.H. (1960). *Learning theory and behavior.* New York: Wiley.

Nairne, J.S. & Rescorla, R.A. (1981). Second-order conditioning with diffuse auditory reinforcers in the pigeon. *Learning and Motivation, 12,* 65–91.

Nevin, J.A. (1973). Stimulus control. In J.A. Nevin (Ed.), *The Study of Behavior* (pp. 115–152). Glenview, IL: Scott, Forsman & Company.

Odling-Smee, F.J. (1975). Background stimuli and the interstimulus interval during Pavlovian conditioning. *Quarterly Journal of Experimental Psychology, 27,* 387–392.

O'Keefe, J. & Nadel, L. (1978). *The hippocampus as a cognitive map.* Oxford: Clarendon Press.

Olton, D.S. (1978). Characteristics of spatial memory. In S.H. Hulse, H. Fowler, & W.K. Honig (Ed.), *Cognitive processes in animal behavior* (pp. 341–374). Hillsdale, NJ: Erlbaum.

Olton, D.S. (1979). Mazes, maps, and memory. *American Psychologist, 34,* 583–596.

Olton, D.S., Collison, C., & Wertz, W.A. (1977). Spatial memory and radial arm maze performance by rats. *Learning and Motivation, 8,* 289–314.

Olton, D. & Samuelson, R.J. (1976). Remembrance of places passed: Spatial memory in rats. *Journal of Experimental Psychology: Animal Behavior Processes, 2,* 97–116.

Osgood, E. (1953). *Method and theory in experimental psychology.* New York: Oxford.

Overmier, J.B. & Lawry, J.A. (1979). Pavlovian conditioning and the mediation of behavior. In G.H. Bower (Ed.), *The psychology of learning and motivation,* Vol. 13 (pp. 1–56). New York: Academic Press.

Pavlov, I.P. (1927). *Conditioned reflexes.* Oxford: Oxford University Press.

Pearce, J.M. & Hall, G. (1978). Overshadowing the instrumental conditioning of a lever press response by a more valid predictor of reinforcement. *Journal of Experimental Psychology: Animal Behavior Processes, 4,* 356–367.

Pearce, J.M. & Hall, G. (1980). A model for Pavlovian learning: Variations in the effectiveness of conditioned but not of unconditioned stimuli. *Psychological Review, 87,* 532–552.

Peterson, G.B. (1984). How expectancies guide behavior. In H.L. Roitblat, T.G. Bever, & H.S. Terrace (Eds.), *Animal cognition* (pp. 135–148). Hillsdale, NJ: Erlbaum.

Peterson, G.B. & Trapold, M.A. (1980). Effects of altering outcome expectancies in pigeons' delayed conditional discrimination performance. *Learning and Motivation, 11,* 267–288.

Peterson, G.B. & Trapold, M.A. (1982). Expectancy mediation of concurrent conditional discriminations. *American Journal of Psychology, 95,* 571–580.

Peterson, G.B., Wheeler, R.L., & Armstrong, G.D. (1978). Expectancies as mediators in the differential-reward conditional discrimination performance of pigeons. *Animal Learning and Behavior, 6,* 279–285.

Peterson, G.B., Wheeler, R.L., & Trapold, M.A. (1980). Enhancement of pigeons' conditional discrimination performance by expectancies of reinforcement and nonreinforcement. *Animal Learning and Behavior, 8,* 22–30.

Peterson, N. (1962). Effect of monochromatic rearing on the control of responding by wavelength. *Science, 116,* 554–555.

Poole, J. & Lander, D.G. (1971). The pigeon's concept of pigeon. *Psychonomic Science, 25,* 157–158.

Posner, M.I. & Keele, S.W. (1968). On the genesis of abstract ideas. *Journal of Experimental Psychology, 77,* 353–363.

Rachlin, H. (1978). A molar theory of reinforcement schedules. *Journal of the Experimental Analysis of Behavior, 30,* 345–360.

Rashotte, M.E., Griffin, R.W., & Sisk, C.L. (1977). Second-order conditioning of the pigeon's keypeck. *Animal Learning and Behavior, 5,* 25–38.

Razran, G. (1971). *Mind in evolution: An east/west synthesis of learned behavior and cognition.* Boston: Houghton Mifflin.

Rescorla, R.A. (1967). Pavlovian conditioning and its proper control procedures. *Psychological Review, 74,* 71–80.

Rescorla, R.A. (1976). Stimulus generalization: Some predictions from a model of Pavlovian conditioning. *Journal of Experimental Psychology: Animal Behavior Processes, 2,* 88–96.

Rescorla, R.A. (1980). *Pavlovian second-order conditioning.* Hillsdale, NJ: Erlbaum.

Rescorla, R.A. (1981a). Simultaneous associations. In P. Harzem & M. Zeiler (Eds.), *Predictability, Correlation and Contiguity* (pp. 46–59). London: Wiley.

Rescorla, R.A. (1981b). Within-signal learning in autoshaping. *Animal Learning and Behavior, 9,* 245–252.

Rescorla, R.A. (1984). Associations between Pavlovian CSs and context. *Journal of Experimental Psychology: Animal Behavior Processes, 10,* 195–204.

Rescorla, R.A. (1985). Conditioned inhibition and facilitation. In R.R. Miller & N.E. Spear (Eds.), *Information processing in animals: Inhibition and contingencies* (pp. 299–326). Hillsdale, NJ: Erlbaum.

Rescorla, R.A. & Colwill, R.M. (1983). Within-compound associations in unblocking. *Journal of Experimental Psychology: Animal Behavior Processes, 9,* 390–400.

Rescorla, R., Durlach, P., & Grau, J. (1985). Contextual learning in Pavlovian conditioning. In P. Balsam and A. Tomie (Eds.), *Context and Learning* (pp. 23–56). Hillsdale, NJ: Erlbaum.

Rescorla, R.A. & Solomon, R.L. (1967). Two-process learning theory: Relationships between Pavlovian conditioning and instrumental learning. *Psychological Review, 74,* 151–182.

Rescorla, R.A. & Wagner, A.R. (1972). A theory of Pavlovian conditioning: Variations in the effectiveness of reinforcement and non-reinforcement. In A.H. Black and W.F. Prokasy (Eds.), *Classical conditioning II: Current theory and research* (pp. 64–99). New York: Appleton-Century-Crofts.

Reynolds, G.S. (1961). Attention in the pigeon. *Journal of the Experimental Analysis of Behavior, 4,* 203–208.

Riley, A.L., Jacobs, W.J., & LoLordo, V.M. (1976). Drug exposure and the acquisition and retention of a conditioned taste aversion. *Journal of Comparative and Physiological Psychology, 90,* 799–807.

Riley, D.A. (1984). Do pigeons decompose stimulus compounds? In H.L. Roitblat, T.G. Bever, & H.S. Terrace (Eds.), *Animal cognition* (pp. 333–350). Hillsdale, NJ: Erlbaum.

Riley, D.A. & Leuin, T.C. (1971). Stimulus-generalization gradients in chicks reared in monochromatic light and tested with a single wavelength. *Journal of Comparative and Physiological Psychology, 75,* 399–402.

Rilling, M. (1977). Stimulus control and inhibitory processes. In W.K. Honig & J.E.R. Staddon (Eds.), *Handbook of operant behavior* (pp. 432–480). Englewood Cliffs, NJ: Prentice-Hall, Inc.

Rizley, R.C. & Rescorla, R.A. (1972). Associations in second-order conditioning and sensory preconditioning. *Journal of Comparative and Physiological Psychology, 81,* 1–11.

Roberts, J.E., Tarpy, R.M., & Lea, S.E.G. (1984). Stimulus-response overshadowing: Effects of signaled reward on instrumental responding as measured by response rate resistance to change. *Journal of Experimental Psychology: Animal Behavior Processes, 10,* 244–255.

Roberts, W.A. (1979). Spatial memory in the rat in a hierarchical maze. *Learning and Motivation, 10,* 117–140.

Roberts, W.A. (1981). Retroactive inhibition in rat spatial memory. *Animal Learning and Behavior, 9,* 566–574.

Roberts, W.A. (1984). Some issues in animal spatial memory. In H.L. Roitblat, T.G. Bever, & H.S. Terrace (Eds.), *Animal cognition* (pp. 425–443). Hillsdale, NJ: Erlbaum.

Roberts, W.A. & Dale, R.H.I. (1981). Remembrance of places lasts: Proactive inhibition and patterns of choice in rat spatial memory. *Learning and Motivation, 12,* 261–281.

Roitblat, H. (1982). The meaning of representation in animal memory. *The Behavioral and Brain Sciences, 5,* 353–406.

Roitblat, H.L., Bever, T.G., & Terrace, H.S. (1984). *Animal cognition.* Hillsdale, NJ: Erlbaum.

Rosenblatt, J.S. (1979). The sensorimotor and motivational bases of early behavioral development of selected altricial mammals. In N.E. Spear & B.A. Campbell (Eds.), *Ontogeny of learning and memory* (pp. 1–38). Hillsdale, NJ: Erlbaum.

Ross, R.T. (1983). Relationships between the determinants of performance in serial feature-positive discriminations. *Journal of Experimental Psychology: Animal Behavior Processes, 9,* 349–373.

Ross, R.T. & Holland, P.C. (1981). Conditioning of simultaneous and serial feature-positive discriminations. *Animal Learning and Behavior, 9,* 293–303.

Ross, R.T. & LoLordo, V.M. (1986). Blocking during serial feature-positive discriminations: associative versus occasion-setting functions. *Journal of Experimental Psychology: Animal Behavior Processes, 12,* 315–324.

Ross, R.T. & LoLordo, V.M. (1987). Evaluation of the relation between Pavlovian occasion-setting and instrumental discriminative stimuli: a blocking analysis. *Journal of Experimental Psychology: Animal Behavior Processes, 13,* 3–16.

Rozeboom, W.W. (1958). What is learned? An empirical enigma. *Psychological Review, 78,* 22–33.

Rozin, P. & Kalat, J.W. (1971). Specific hungers and poisoning as adaptive specializations of learning. *Psychological Review, 78,* 459–486.

Rudolph, R.L., Honig, W.K., & Gerry, J.E. (1969). Effects of monochromatic rearing on the acquisition of stimulus control. *Journal of Comparative and Physiological Psychology, 67,* 50–58.

Rudy, J.W. & Hyson, R.L. (1984). Ontogenesis of learning: III. Variation in the rat's differential reflexive and learned responses to sound frequencies. *Developmental Psychobiology, 17*, 285–300.

Rusiniak, K.W., Hankins, W.G., Garcia, J., & Brett, L.P. (1979). Flavor-illness aversions: Potentiation of odor by taste in rats. *Behavioral and Neural Biology, 25*, 1–17.

Sands, S.F., Urcuioli, P.J., Wright, A.A., & Santiago, H.C. (1984). Serial position effects and rehearsal in primate visual memory. In H.L. Roitblat, T.G. Bever, & H.S. Terrace (Eds.), *Animal cognition* (pp. 375–388). Hillsdale, NJ: Erlbaum.

Saavedra, M.A. (1975). Pavlovian compound conditioning in the rabbit. *Learning and Motivation, 6*, 314–326.

Shepard, R.N. (1965). Approximation to uniform gradients of generalization by monotone transformations scale. In D.I. Mostofsky (Ed.), *Stimulus generalization* (pp. 94–110). Stanford, CA: Stanford University Press.

Shepard, R.N. (1980). Multidimensional scaling, tree-fitting and clustering. *Science, 24*, 390–398.

Shepard, R.N. (1984). Ecological constraints on internal representation: Resonant kinematics of perceiving, imagining, thinking, and dreaming. *Psychological Review, 91*, 417–447.

Shettleworth, S.J. (1972). Stimulus relevance in the control of drinking and conditioned fear responses in domestic chicks (*Gallus gallus*). *Journal of Comparative and Physiological Psychology, 80*, 175–198.

Sidman, M. (1971). Reading and auditory-visual equivalences. *Journal of Speech and Hearing Research, 14*, 5–13.

Sidman, M. (1985). Functional analysis of emergent verbal classes. In T. Thompson, & M.D. Zeiler (Eds.), *Units of analysis and integration of behavior* (pp. 213–245). Hillsdale, NJ: Erlbaum.

Sidman, M. & Cresson, O. (1973). Reading and transfer of crossmodal stimulus equivalences in severe retardation. *American Journal of Mental Deficiency, 77*, 515–523.

Sidman, M., Rauzin, R., Lazar, R., Cunningham, S., Tailby, W., & Carrigan, P. (1982). A search for symmetry in the conditional discrimination of rhesus monkeys, baboons, and children. *Journal of the Experimental Analysis of Behavior, 37*, 23–44.

Sidman, M. & Tailby, W. (1982). Conditional discrimination vs. matching to sample: An expansion of the testing paradigm. *Journal of the Experimental Analysis of Behavior, 37*, 5–22.

Skinner, B.F. (1935). The generic nature of the concepts of stimulus and response. *Journal of General Psychology, 12*, 40–65.

Skinner, B.F. (1938). *The behavior of organisms: An experimental analysis.* Englewood, NJ: Prentice-Hall.

Skinner, B.F. (1953). *Science and human behavior.* New York: Free Press.

Skinner, B.F. (1957). *Verbal behavior.* New York: Appleton-Century-Crofts.

Spear, N.E. & Campbell, B.A. (1979). *Ontogeny of learning and memory.* Hillsdale, NJ: Erlbaum.

Spear, N.E. & Kucharski, D. (1984). Ontogenetic differences in the processing of multi-element stimuli. In H.L. Roitblat, T.G. Bever, & H.S. Terrace (Eds.), *Animal cognition* (pp. 545–567). Hillsdale, NJ: Erlbaum.

Spence, K.W. (1936). The nature of discrimination learning in animals. *Psychological Review, 43*, 427–449.

Spence, K.W. (1937). The differential response in animals to stimuli varying within a single dimension. *Psychological Review, 44*, 430–444.

Spence, K.W. (1956). *Behavior theory and conditioning.* New Haven: Yale University Press.

Spiker, C.C. (1956). Experiments with children on the hypotheses of acquired distinctiveness and equivalence of cues. *Child Development, 27*, 253–263.

St. Claire-Smith, R. & MacLaren, D. (1983). Response preconditioning effects. *Journal of Experimental Psychology: Animal Behavior Processes, 9*, 41–48.

Stevens, S.S. (1951). Mathematics, measurement and psychophysics. In S.S. Stevens (Ed.), *Handbook of experimental psychology* (pp. 1–49). New York: Wiley.

Straub, R.O., Seidenberg, M.S., Bever, T.G., & Terrace, H.S. (1979). Serial learning in the pigeon. *Journal of Experimental Analysis of Behavior, 32*, 137–148.

Straub, R.O. & Terrace, H.S. (1981). Generalization of serial learning in the pigeon. *Animal Learning and Behavior, 9*, 454–468.

Sutherland, N.S. & Mackintosh, N.J. (1971). *Mechanisms of animal discrimination learning.* New York: Academic Press.

Suzuki, S., Augerinos, G., & Black, A.H. (1980). Stimulus control of spatial behavior on the eight-arm maze in rats. *Learning and Motivation, 11*, 1–18.

Switalski, R.W., Lyons, J., & Thomas, D.R. (1966). The effects of interdimensional training on stimulus generalization. *Journal of Experimental Psychology, 72*, 661–666.

Terrace, H.S. (1966). Stimulus Control. In W.K. Honig (Ed.), *Operant behavior: Areas of research and application* (pp. 271–344). New York: Appleton-Century-Crofts.

Terrace, H.S. (1983). Simultaneous chaining: The problem it poses for traditional chaining theory. In M. Commons, R. Herrnstein, & A. Wagner (Eds.),

*Quantitative Analysis of Behavior: Discrimination Processes* (pp. 115–137). Cambridge: Ballinger.

Terrace, H.S. (1984). Animal cognition. In H.L. Roitblat, T.G. Bever, & H.S. Terrace (Eds.), *Animal cognition* (pp. 7–28). Hillsdale, NJ: Erlbaum.

Terrace, H.S., Straub, R.O., Bever, T.G., & Seidenberg, M.S. (1977). Representation of a sequence by a pigeon. *Bulletin of the Psychonomic Society, 10*, 269.

Thomas, D.R. (1970). Stimulus selection, attention, and related matters. In J.H. Reynierse (Ed.), *Current issues in animal learning* (pp. 311–356). Lincoln: University of Nebraska Press.

Thomas, D.R. (1985). Contextual stimulus control of operant responding in pigeons. In P. Balsam & A. Tomie (Eds.), *Context and learning* (pp. 295–321). Hillsdale, NJ: Erlbaum.

Thomas, D.R., Burr, D.E.S., & Eck, K.O. (1979). Stimulus selection in animal discrimination learning. An alternative interpretation. *Journal of Experimental Psychology, 86*, 53–62.

Thomas, D.R., Ernst, A.J., & Andry, D.K. (1971). More on masking of stimulus control during generalization testing. *Psychonomic Science, 23*, 85–86.

Thomas, D.R., Freeman, F., Svinicki, J.G., Burr, D.E.S., & Lyons, J. (1970). Effects of extradimensional training on stimulus generalization. *Journal of Experimental Psychology Monograph, 83* (1, Pt. 2).

Thomas, D.R., Svinicki, M.K., & Svinicki, J.G. (1970). Masking of stimulus control during generalization testing. *Journal of Experimental Psychology, 84*, 479–482.

Thompson, R.K.R. & Herman, L.M. (1977). Memory for lists of sounds by the bottle-nosed dolphin: Convergence of memory processes with humans? *Science, 153*, 501–503.

Thorndike, E.L. (1898). Animal intelligence: An experimental study of the associative processes in animals. *Psychological Review, Monograph Supplement, 2*, 8.

Thorndike, E.L. (1911). *Animal intelligence*. New York: Macmillan.

Tinbergen, N. & Perdeck, A.C. (1950). On the stimulus situation releasing the begging response in the newly hatched herring gull chick (*Larus argentatus argentatus* Pont.). *Behavior, 3*, 1–39.

Tolman, E.C. (1932). *Purposive behavior in animals and men*. New York: Appleton-Century-Crofts.

Tolman, E.C. (1948). Cognitive maps in rats and men. *Psychological Review, 55*, 189–208.

Tolman, E.C., Ritchie, B.F., & Kalish, D. (1946). Studies in spatial learning. I. Orientation and ths short-cut. *Journal of Experimental Psychology, 36*, 13–24.

Tomie, A. (1981). Effects of unpredictable food upon the subsequent acquisition of autoshaping: Analysis of the context blocking hypothesis. In C.M.

Locurto, H.S. Terrace, & J. Gibbon (Eds.), *Autoshaping and conditioning theory* (pp. 181–215). New York: Academic Press.

Tomie, A. (1985). Effects of test context on the acquisition of autoshaping to a formerly random keylight or a formerly contextual keylight. In P. Balsam & A. Tomie (Eds.) *Context and Learning* (pp. 57–72). Hillsdale, NJ: Erlbaum.

Tracy, W.K. (1970). Wavelength generalization and preference in monochromatically reared ducklings. *Journal of the Experimental Analysis of Behavior, 13*, 163–178.

Trapold, M.A. (1970). Are expectancies based upon different positive reinforcing events discriminably different? *Learning and Motivation, 1*, 129–140.

Trapold, M.A. & Overmier, J.B. (1972). The second learning process in instrumental learning. In A.A. Black & W.F. Prokasy (Eds.), *Classical conditioning: II. Current research and theory* (pp. 427–452). New York: Appleton-Century-Crofts.

Tulving, E. (1983). *Elements and episodic memory*. Oxford: Oxford University Press.

Tversky, A. (1977). Features of similarity. *Psychological Review, 84*, 327–352.

Vaughan, W., Jr. & Greene, S.L. (1983). Acquisition of absolute discriminations in pigeons. In M.L. Commons, R.J. Herrnstein, & A.R. Wagner (Eds.), *Quantitative analyses of behavior acquisition*, Vol. 4 (pp. 231–238). Cambridge, MA: Ballinger.

Vaughan, W., Jr. & Greene, S.L. (1984). Pigeon visual memory capacity. *Journal of Experimental Psychology: Animal Behavior Processes, 10*, 256–271.

Vogt, M.B. & Rudy, J.L. (1984). Ontogenesis of learning: I. Variation in the rat's reflexive and learned responses to gustatory stimulation. *Developmental Psychobiology, 17*, 11–33.

Vom Saal, W. & Jenkins, H.M. (1970). Blocking the development of stimulus control. *Learning and Motivation, 1*, 52–64.

Wagner, A.R. (1969a). Incidental stimuli and discrimination learning. In R.M. Gilbert & N.S. Sutherland (Eds.), *Animal discrimination learning* (pp. 83–111). London: Academic Press.

Wagner, A.R. (1969b). Stimulus validity and stimulus selection in associative learning. In N.J. Mackintosh & W.K. Honig (Eds.), *Fundamental issues in associative learning* (pp. 90–122). Halifax: Dalhousie University Press.

Wagner, A.R. (1978). Expectancies and the priming of STM. In S.H. Hulse, H. Fowler, & W.K. Honig (Eds.), *Cognitive mechanisms in animal behavior* (pp. 177–210). Hillsdale, NJ: Erlbaum.

Wagner, A.R. (1981). SOP: A model for automatic memory processing in animal behavior. In N.E. Spear & R.R. Miller (Eds.), *Information processing in animals: Memory mechanisms* (pp. 5–48). Hillsdale, NJ: Erlbaum.

Wagner, A.R., Logan, F.A., Haberlandt, K., & Price, T. (1968). Stimulus selection in animal discrimination learning. *Journal of Experimental Psychology, 76,* 171–180.

Walker, J.A. & Olton, D.S. (1979). The role of response and reward in spatial memory. *Learning and Motivation, 10,* 73–84.

Wasserman, E.A., Franklin, S.R., & Hearst, E. (1974). Pavlovian appetitive contingencies and approach versus withdrawal to conditioned stimuli in pigeons. *Journal of Comparative and Physiological Psychology, 86,* 616–627.

Wasserman, E.A., Nelson, K.R., & Larew, M.B. (1980). Memory of sequences of stimuli and responses. *Journal of the Experimental Analysis of Behavior, 34,* 49–59.

Watson, J.B. (1919). *Psychology from the standpoint of a behaviorist.* Philadelphia: Lippincott.

Weisman, R.G. & von Konigslow, R. (1984). Order competencies in animals: Models for the delayed sequence discrimination task. In H.L. Roitblat, T.G. Bever, & H.S. Terrace (Eds.), *Animal cognition* (pp. 199–214). Hillsdale, NJ: Erlbaum.

Weisman, R.G., Wasserman, E.A., Dodd, P.W.D., & Larew, M.B. (1980). Representation and retention of two-event sequences in pigeons. *Journal of Experimental Psychology: Animal Behavior Processes, 6,* 312–325.

Weiss, J.M. (1971). Effects of coping behavior in different warning signal conditions on stress pathology in rats. *Journal of Comparative and Physiological Psychology, 77,* 1–13.

Welker, R.L., Tomie, A., Davitt, G.A., & Thomas, D.R. (1974). Contextual stimulus control over operant responding in pigeons. *Journal of Comparative and Physiological Psychology, 86,* 549–562.

Wicklegren, W.A. (1973). The long and the short of memory. *Psychological Bulletin, 80,* 425–438.

Wilcoxon, H.C., Dragoin, W.B., & Kral, P.A. (1971). Illness-induced aversions in rats and quail: Relative salience of visual and gustatory cues. *Science, 171,* 826–828.

Williams, B.A. (1975). The blocking of reinforcement control. *Journal of the Experimental Analysis of Behaviour, 24,* 215–227.

Williams, B.A. (1978). Information effects on the response-reinforcer association. *Animal Learning and Behavior, 6,* 371–379.

Williams, B.A. (1982). Blocking the response-reinforcer association. In M.L. Commons, R.J. Herrnstein, & A.R. Wagner (Eds.), *Quantitative analyses of behavior: Acquisition,* Vol. 3 (pp. 427–447). Cambridge, MA: Ballinger.

Wright, A.A. & Sands, S.F. (1981). A model of detection and decision processes during matching to sample by pigeons: Performance with 88 different wavelengths in delayed and simultaneous matching tasks. *Journal of Experimental Psychology: Animal Behavior Processes, 7,* 191–216.

Wright, A.A., Santiago, H.C., Sands, S.F., & Urcuioli, P.J. (1984). Pigeon and monkey serial probe recognition: Acquisitions, strategies and serial position effects. In H.L. Roitblat, T.G. Bever, & H.S. Terrace (Eds.), *Animal cognition* (pp. 353–374). Hillsdale, NJ: Erlbaum.

Chapter **3**

# REINFORCEMENT, CHOICE, AND RESPONSE STRENGTH

**Ben A. Williams,** *University of California, San Diego*

## INTRODUCTION

### Origins of the Law of Effect

This chapter is concerned with how reward and punishment determine behavior. The notion that organisms seek pleasure and avoid pain is as old as antiquity. From Aristotle, through the English Utilitarians, to William James, considerable discussion has focused on the psychological underpinnings of the pleasure-pain principle, ranging from hypotheses about the nature of instincts to the determinants of conscious experience. The modern chapter of this history begins with Thorndike (1898), who subsumed

The author thanks David Case, Helen Daly, John A. Nevin, and William Vaughan for their helpful comments on earlier drafts on this chapter. Special thanks is due Richard Herrnstein, whose many insightful and judicious criticisms greatly improved the quality of this chapter and made its writing a much easier task. Preparation of the chapter was supported by NIMH grant RO1-MH 35572-02 and NSF grant BNS 84-08878.

hedonism within the study of conditioning in the form of the Law of Effect. According to Thorndike, responses that led to "satisfaction" were "stamped-in," while responses that led to "discomfort" were "stamped-out." Thus, the strength of behavior was determined by the value of the behavioral consequences associated with past instances of that behavior. The task for a sizable fraction of psychology since Thorndike has been to flesh out that simple statement, by specifying the rules that govern response strength.

Although the general notion that behavior is a function of its consequences is now virtually unquestioned, its adoption by psychology initially encountered considerable resistance. Thorndike's contemporaries in the early 1900s were enamored with the concept of the reflex, which suggested the possibility of reducing all behavior to the mechanistic actions of a collection of stimulus-response units. In order to understand the strength of behavior, therefore, one needed only to know which stimuli elicited a particular response, and whether that stimulus was in the animal's environment. As shown by Pavlov (1927), new reflex units could be formed in the animal's lifetime, but the strength of behavior at any moment was a function of its eliciting stimuli, not the value of the activities to which the behavior led. A notable example of such reflexology was Watson's (1914) early formulation of behaviorism in his general survey of comparative psychology. In it Watson explicitly rejected the Law of Effect, because its rewards and punishers smacked of subjective experience, which Watson viewed as the handmaiden of the introspective psychology he sought to displace. For Watson, and others of his generation, the only principle of conditioning needed to explain adaptive behavior was the law of contiguity, which operated to form new reflex units whenever responses occurred in new stimulus situations.

Although the history of contiguity theories of behavior is of genuine interest, its consideration would take us far afield. In spite of virtuoso efforts to sustain a purely reflexological behaviorism (e.g., Guthrie, 1935), the importance of the consequences of behavior was widely accepted by at least the 1930s and remains so today. This is not to say that Thorndike's original formulation has survived intact. Instead, two broad (but not necessarily independent) classes of behavior are now recognized: respondents, which obey the law of contiguity as championed by Watson, and operants, which are determined by their consequences. Thorndike's position has been eroded further by the "learning-performance" distinction, which implies that learning may occur even when reward and punishment are not obviously involved. Whereas Thorndike regarded the pleasure-pain principle to be necessary for the formation of the associative connections between stimulus and response, modern theories are either agnostic about how response consequences affect learning or explicitly argue that they are independent of learning (e.g., Mackintosh, 1974).

The topic for the present chapter is not learning, but the determinants of response strength. The rewards and punishers that follow behavior may be administered in a variety of ways, so the task is to determine how changes in behavior result from parametric variations. Among the variables that have been studied are the frequency, quality, and magnitude of the response

consequence, as well as its delay, and the degree of deprivation corresponding to the reward that is employed. The goal of such investigation has been to provide quantitative characterizations of each separate functional relation, so that the total response strength can be predicted from the particular combinations of parameters. Such specification is necessary if the Law of Effect or its modern equivalent, the principle of reinforcement, is to transcend the intuitive notion that animals behave adaptively. By providing precise rules by which contingencies of reinforcement determine behavior, it is possible to obviate the many historical discussions of the internal processes mediating such adaptation, and proceed on to the science of behavior itself. As will be seen later in this chapter, substantial progress toward such quantitative treatments has been achieved, especially during the past two decades.

## Measures and Methodologies

Early research on the parameters of reinforcement was dominated by Hullian (1943, 1951, 1952) behavior theory, which proposed particular mathematical functions for how the various parameters combined to determine response strength. Much of that research was focused on the learning-performance distinction, as some variables (e.g., drive) were viewed as affecting only the vigor of performance, while others (e.g., frequency of reinforcement) were thought to affect the underlying habit strength. Still others (amount, delay) initially were regarded as learning variables but were changed to the performance category in later treatments, although such changes remained a subject of disagreement (e.g., Spence, 1956). Crucial to this distinction was the notion that effects on learning were long lasting and highly resistant to change, while performance effects were more dynamic. Thus, for example, a major transformation occurred in Hullian behavior theory when reductions in the amount of reward were found to produce immediate reductions in the vigor of behavior (Crespi, 1944), causing that variable to no longer be considered of the learning variety. The distinction between learning and performance is orthogonal to most of the discussion that will follow, because the research to be considered is concerned primarily with the laws governing steady-state behavior, not the dynamics of transition. The effects on performance that are observed are thus assumed to reflect the value of the response consequences, rather than incomplete learning about the response-reinforcer contingency.

By far the most frequent procedure used in early research on the parameters of reinforcement involved a straight alley, with the dependent variable being the running speed measured from the start to the goal box. One difficulty with this method is that running speed often is not homogeneous throughout the entire alley. For example, when only 50 percent of the trials terminate in reward, speed early in the alley is often greater than when 100 percent reward is used, but then slower than the 100 percent condition when the animal approaches the goal box (Wagner, 1961). While such differences have provided the impetus for important theoretical developments (Amsel, 1967), they also imply that the measurement of response strength will yield different outcomes depending upon the particular details of the measurement procedure (e.g., the length of the alley).

A second limitation on procedures like the straight alley is that the opportunity to respond is presented only during discrete trial periods; the animal must be removed from the apparatus during the interim. Because of the disadvantages of a procedure that has such built-in sources of variability, the great majority of recent research has come from *free-operant procedures* in which the animal remains in an unchanging environment throughout an experimental session, usually free to respond at any time. The free-operant method was introduced by Skinner in the 1930s (Skinner, 1938), first with rats pressing levers, but now more commonly with pigeons pecking small illuminated disks. The practical advantages of the method, confirmed by the often remarkably orderly data it produces, have resulted in its ubiquitous adoption, even by investigators who have remained unimpressed, if not unaffected, by the Skinnerian intellectual heritage.

The increasing dominance of free-operant procedures is noteworthy not only because of methodological concerns, but because it has been accompanied by a change in the most frequently studied dependent variable. Because the subject remains in a constant conditioning environment for fixed periods of time, rate of responding seems the natural and obvious variable for describing behavioral changes. Moreover, the absence of obvious stimulus changes that are correlated with the occurrence or nonoccurrence of responding offers little encouragement for the notion that responses are elicited by just-preceding stimuli. Consequently, Skinner characterized operant behavior as emitted, with different rates of emission corresponding to different strengths. Accordingly, the function of the stimulus situation was not to elicit the response directly, but rather to serve as a discriminative cue for the presence of a prevailing contingency of reinforcement, which was itself the primary determinant of the degree of strength. Skinner thus abandoned the reflexological tradition, and strength became an attribute of behavior, per se.

Accompanying the notion that operant behavior is emitted has been increasing emphasis on the importance of the schedule by which reinforcement is delivered. Whereas discrete-trial procedures typically provided reward or punishment on every trial, the continuous availability of the response in the free-operant case and the high rates of responding that result provide the opportunity for wide variation in both the percentage and pattern of behavior that is reinforced. For example, several thousand responses may occur in a typical experimental session, while only a small fraction of them (e.g., 1 in 50) may be followed by reward.

Because the type of schedule used to reward behavior will play an important role in understanding many of the effects to be discussed, they will be introduced now. The simplest schedule is the fixed ratio (FR), in which every $n$th response is followed by reinforcement. A variation of this is the variable ratio (VR), in which the number of responses required for reinforcement changes irregularly after each reinforcement, but with the average response requirement kept at some constant value. A second class of schedules, based on time rather than the amount of behavior, specifies the interval since the last reinforcement before the next response will be reinforced. A fixed-interval (FI) schedule imposes a constant minimum period between reinforcement, while with a variable interval (VI), the length of time without reinforcement varies irregularly, with the average interval held at some constant value.

The characteristic behavior patterns produced by these different schedules are shown in

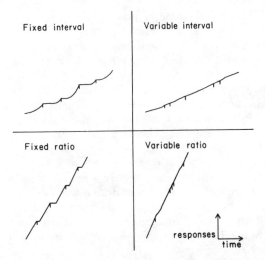

**Figure 3.1.** Each quadrant shows typical behavior for each of the four most common simple schedules of reinforcement. Plotted on the ordinate are the cumulative number of responses; plotted on the abscissa is time. The slope of the function thus corresponds to the rate of responding (i.e., flat functions correspond to zero response rates). The diagonal slashes correspond to deliveries of the reinforcer.

Figure 3.1 in the form of cumulative records. Variable schedules (VR and VI) produce relatively steady response rates, while fixed schedules (FR and FI) usually result in pauses after reinforcement before responding is resumed. Also, the response rates maintained by ratio schedules usually are one and one-half to three times greater than the rates maintained by interval schedules that deliver equivalent rates of reinforcement.

These four basic schedules may be combined to produce more complex varieties, as when two different response alternatives are simultaneously available and each is associated with its own independent schedule (concurrent schedules) or when different schedules are correlated with distinctive stimuli that are successfully presented (multiple schedules). Similarly, the reinforcement contingency for one schedule may be access to a second schedule rather than to the primary reinforcer itself (chain schedules). Later sections will discuss such variations more extensively, as they provide important tools for assessing the laws of response strength.

## Alternative Conceptions of Response Strength

Consideration of the various methods is important, partly because they have fostered different notions about how behavioral strength should be conceptualized. With free-operant procedures, for example, the regular variation of response rate as a function of reinforcement contingency has suggested a graded measure of behavior that is presumably mapped in some meaningful fashion on an underlying continuum of response strength. Various conceptions of the nature of that continuum have been offered, ranging from the gradual increase of habit strength (Hull, 1943), the increase in the reflex reserve (Skinner, 1938), and the increase in the percentage of stimulus elements associated with the response (Estes, 1959). Despite their differences, all of these learning theorists have agreed that changes in the frequency of observed behavior correspond to changes in the scale value of some underlying unitary dimension.

A quite different view of response strength arises from the notion that reinforcement affects behavior by response selection, rather than by strengthening per se. Such a notion is inspired by the phenomenon of *shaping*, by which a particular response form is selected out of a hodgepodge of unspecified behavior by differential reinforcement of increasingly close approximations to the response that has been targeted. Such changes are not easily interpretable in terms of some type of continuous strengthening, but instead appear to be described more appropriately as a series of transitions across response forms of overlapping topographies and increasing efficiency in earning reinforcement. To the extent that such changes are typical of all conditioning, it is possible that changes in strength seen in conventional procedures, such as increases in speed in a straight alley or increases in response rates in a free-operant procedure, also correspond to the selection of increasingly efficient response forms.

An illustration of the differences between these two conceptions is provided by a learning curve obtained in one of Thorndike's (1898) puzzle boxes, as shown in Figure 3.2. In Thorndike's experiments (initially done with chicks, but later with cats, dogs, fish, and monkeys), animals could escape from a box by tripping a

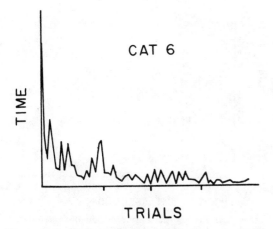

CAT 6

**Figure 3.2.** Time to escape across successive trials for a cat trained in Thorndike's puzzle box.

latch or operating some other simple mechanism. Thorndike measured the time to escape on successive trials, which, as Figure 3.2 shows, gradually decreased to some asymptotic level. According to Thorndike's description, the animal reacted instinctively to the situation on the early trials by attempting various maneuvers such as clawing the bars, biting the walls, and so forth. Then by accident the correct response was hit upon and because of its success, its connection to the stimulus situation was strengthened. On successive trials the correct response became increasingly more probable, until finally the animal performed that response immediately upon being placed in the apparatus. The gradual nature of the conditioning was regarded by Thorndike as critical, since for him it represented definitive proof that the improvement was due to the stamping-in of the response rather than to reasoning, inference, or some other higher mental process.

But a very different interpretation was offered by Guthrie and Horton (1946), who repeated the basic features of Thorndike's procedure while photographing the actual behavior that occurred on successive trials. Rather than a particular response being gradually strengthened, their results showed a successive shift in the topography of the response that released the escape mechanism. Early forms of the response alternated between several different topographies and were often inefficient, but then, through response selection, the most efficient response form emerged.

Comparable differences in interpretation

have been proposed even when the measure of response strength has been the frequency of a seemingly well-defined response unit. With free-operant procedures, for example, an interpretation of changes in response rate as a continuous dimension has been challenged by a variety of schedule effects. The fact that ratio schedules routinely produce response rates significantly higher than interval schedules with equivalent rates of reinforcement is perhaps the most notable, as this difference has been interpreted by some investigators as the result of different response topographies being selected by different types of schedules (Peele, Casey, & Silberberg, 1984). Thus, the higher rates of responding seen with ratio schedules should not be taken as certain evidence that ratio schedules produce greater response strengths.

Similarly, variation in the parameters of reinforcement for a given type of schedule may be interpreted as affecting either the strength or topography of behavior. The most notable such example is the effect of different reinforcement rates on response rates maintained by VI schedules; this will be considered in some detail because it has important implications for many of the parametric investigations of reinforcement that will be considered later in this chapter.

Shown in Figure 3.3 are results from Catania and Reynolds (1968), in which individual pigeons were presented different VI schedules across experimental conditions, with training on each condition continuing until stable performance was achieved. Plotted are the asymptotic response rates generated by each reinforcement rate. As can be seen, response rate rises rapidly as reinforcement rate is increased from zero, but very quickly approaches its asymptotic level. To the extent that response rate reflects response strength, such results show that asymptotic strength is achieved with relatively low rates of reinforcement, which implies that the strength of behavior generated by, for example, a VI 30-second schedule (corresponding to 120 reinforcements per hour) is virtually indistinguishable from that generated by a VI 60-second schedule (corresponding to 60 reinforcers per hour).

But an alternative interpretation of Figure 3.3 is suggested by the fact that animals are quite sensitive to the temporal properties of their own behavior, in particular the time between successive responses (known as the interresponse

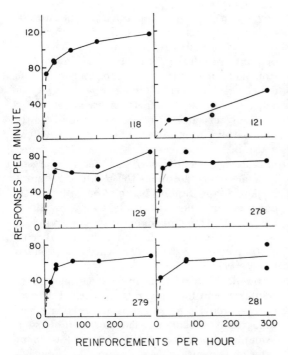

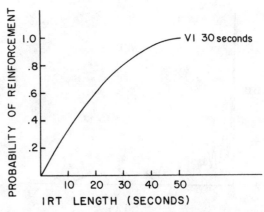

**Figure 3.4.** Probability of reinforcement for a peck as a function of the time since the preceding peck, for behavior maintained on a VI 30-second schedule.

**Figure 3.3.** Rates of key-pecking as a function of rate of reinforcement for six pigeons, taken from Catania & Reynolds (1968). Key-pecking was maintained by VI schedules with different conditions having different mean intervals. Each point represents the average response rates over the last five sessions of a given schedule. From "A Quantitative Analysis of the Responding Maintained by Interval Schedules of Reinforcement" by A.C. Catania and G.S. Reynolds, 1968, *Journal of the Experimental Analysis of Behavior, 11*, p. 331. Copyright 1968 by the Society for the Experimental Analysis of Behavior, Inc. Reprinted by permission.

time, or IRT). For example, pigeons that are reinforced only when their responses are separated from the preceding response by an interval greater than some criterion (known as differential reinforcement of low rates, or a DRL schedule) will respond at a slow rate, whereas those that are reinforced only for responses that follow the preceding response by less than the criterion (known as differential reinforcement of high rates, or a DRH schedule) will respond rapidly. The ability of reinforcement schedules to select low or high response rates depending upon the IRT contingency thus suggests that pecks with different IRTs may be qualitatively different response units. This possibility assumes considerable importance for behavior main-

tained by VI schedules, since such schedules entail different probabilities of reinforcement for responses with different IRTs. Because VI schedules make reinforcers available after the required interval has elapsed and then hold their availability until the next response occurs, the interreinforcement interval becomes more likely to terminate the longer the time since the last response. Figure 3.4 shows this relation, in terms of the probability of reinforcement on a VI 30-second schedule as a function of the time since the last response.

Given that VI schedules impose higher reinforcement probabilities for longer IRTs and that animals can be trained to emit responses with different IRTs, the question is whether such differential selection is a critical component of the relation between response rate and reinforcement rate seen in Figure 3.3. If so, different rates of responding should not be regarded as indices of different response strengths, but instead as different collections of various response units. The further implication is that the effects of different parameters of reinforcement cannot be understood simply in terms of average response rate, but must include changes in the entire distribution of interresponse times. Such a possibility would, of course, greatly complicate any quantitative analysis of the effects of reinforcement.

None of the analyses of VI performance in terms of the differential selection of IRTs (Anger, 1956; Reynolds & McLeod, 1970; Shimp, 1974) has as yet been fully convincing to most investigators, in part because they have not accounted for the properties of the functions seen in Figure 3.3. But there now seems no doubt that some degree of response selection is involved, based on recent evidence that isolates the effects of the IRT contingency (Platt, 1979). With his procedure, the differential probability of reinforcement for different IRTs intrinsic to VI schedules was simulated by explicitly programming different probabilities of reinforcement for different IRTs, with the probabilities proportional to the duration of the IRT, as in Figure 3.4. Rate of reinforcement was varied independently of these differential contingencies by multiplying all of the different probabilities by some constant. Platt then compared the relation between response rate and reinforcement rate from such a procedure with that from a related procedure in which different IRTs were not differentially reinforced. This was accomplished by again scheduling different probabilities for different IRTs, but with the probability corresponding to a particular response determined by the value of the fifth IRT preceding that response. Thus, the probability of reinforcement for any particular response was independent of its own duration. The comparison of the two procedures revealed that response rates were uniformly higher for the second procedure, in which differential reinforcement did not occur. However, both procedures generated functions similar to those seen in Figure 3.3, with the two functions differing by an approximately constant difference at all of the various reinforcement rates.

Platt's results demonstrate that the differential IRT contingencies embedded in a VI schedule do affect response rates, but also that such an effect does not account for the more molar aspects of the relation between reinforcement frequency and rate of responding. Reinforcement thus appears to change behavior in two separate ways: by selecting the response unit and by determining the strength of that unit. Similar conclusions about the dual effects of reinforcement were reached by Morse (1966) and Nevin (1982) after reviewing a variety of different schedule situations. The obvious difficulty, however, is determining which type of reinforcement effect is involved, since the correct interpretation of various changes in behavior often depends critically on their dissociation. As will be seen, this issue has not been totally resolved, as the distinction between response strengthening versus response selection will reemerge as alternative interpretations of a variety of phenomena currently at question.

## Behavioral Regulation: An Alternative to the Concept of Response Strength

The response-strengthening and response-selection views of reinforcement effects both assume that reinforcers can be identified independently of the behavior that they affect and that changes in behavior can be accounted for by the history of response-reinforcer pairings. An alternative approach assumes that the operant behavior and the activities constituting the reinforcer must be viewed as a single package, the value of which is optimized by the animal. The subject is thus assumed to have some preference structure for particular distributions of the activities available in the situation, which may be revealed empirically by allowing the animal free access to those activities. The effect of a contingency of reinforcement is then to prevent the animal from obtaining the most desired distribution, with the result that the animal adjusts its behavior to come as close as possible to the optimum (Timberlake, 1984).

As an example of how regulatory analyses are applied, consider a situation in which only two activities, running and eating, are available. Given free access to both, the animal will engage in those behaviors at some rates, as assessed over some specified time frame. This distribution of running and eating, which is assumed to reflect the optimal allocation of the animal's activities, is depicted in Figure 3.5a as a single point labeled as $R_0$, $E_0$. Now suppose that a ratio schedule is imposed that specifies that two running responses are required for each eating response. This schedule constraint is depicted by the solid schedule line. The subject is thus required to locate its behavioral distribution at some point on the schedule line, with the cardinal assumption being that the actual behavior will be that point which is closest to the original optimal distribution.

Although several different metrics for describing the deviations from the optimal level have been proposed, the most accepted has been simply the distance in Euclidean space. Thus, the cost ($C$) of any possible behavioral outcome is given by equation 1, which provides a formula for calculating Euclidean distance between the point of optimal distribution $(R_0, E_0)$ and any point on the schedule line $(R_x, E_x)$.

$$C_{(R_x, E_x)} = [(R_0 - R_x)^2 + (E_0 - E_x)^2]^{0.5} \quad (1)$$

For the subject to behave optimally, it then chooses that point on the schedule line that minimizes the cost function. This is shown graphically in Figure 3.5a by that point on the schedule line which intersects with a perpendicular line connecting the point of optimal distribution.

To show how the minimum distance model predicts how behavior will be affected by changes in the schedule requirement, Figure 3.5b shows several different schedules lines, corresponding to different ratio requirements. The points on each line that are nearest the free behavior point are connected, demonstrating that the effects of increasing the ratio requirement (moving counterclockwise through the schedule lines) is first to increase the rate of running and then eventually to decrease it. Whether the empirical effects of changing schedule requirements actually conform to this nonmonotonic function is a matter of some disagreement and will be considered later.

The preceding discussion has assumed that the cost of deviations from the optimal distribution of activity is scaled in the units of measurement shown on the abscissa and ordinate. However, some types of deviations might be more important than others. For example, with eating and running as the activities, small deviations from the optimal amount of eating might be more costly than large deviations from the optimal amount of running. To incorporate such effects, it is necessary to modify equation 1 to include weights for the relative costs of the two types of deviation. The simplest method to do this is shown as equation 2, with the terms $a$ and $b$ being the weighted costs of deviations from the optimal levels of running and eating, respectively. Note that the 0.5 exponent has been omitted, since the minimum of the power of any function is the same as that of the function itself.

$$C_{(R_x, E_x)} = a (R_0 - R_x)^2 + b (E_0 - E_x)^2 \quad (2)$$

Similar regulatory accounts have been elaborated by several different investigators for more complex cases involving three or more responses (Allison, Miller, & Wozny, 1979; Rachlin & Burkhard, 1978; Staddon, 1979). Such accounts postulate a multi-dimensional space with each dimension corresponding to a separate response and

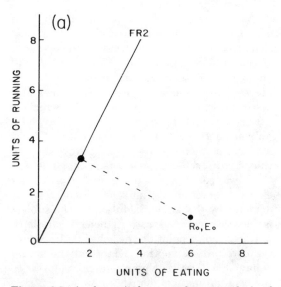
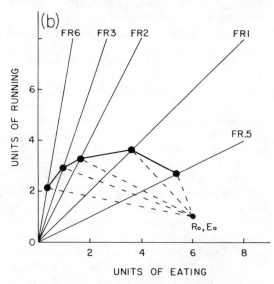

**Figure 3.5.** A schematic for a regulatory analysis of a situation involving only eating and drinking. The left portion shows the point of optimal distribution of the two activities $(R_0, E_0)$ and the line depicting the constraint on behavior produced by a schedule requiring two running responses for each eating response. The right portion shows additional schedule lines and the points of minimum distance from the optimal distribution. The heavy solid line connecting the various points predicts the effects on rate of running of changes in the schedule requirement.

each point in the space representing a particular distribution of activities for the time available. Despite the increase in complexity, such models are conceptually similar to that depicted in Figure 3.5, with the major modification being that an additional term corresponding to each additional activity is required for the cost function given by equation 2.

Regulatory models have been influential partly because they have sponsored accounts of behavior in terms of economic concepts such as elasticity and substitutability (see Rachlin, Battalio, Kagel, & Green, 1981; Hursh, 1980, for representative examples). Regulatory models also have made contact with related ecological accounts that assume that operant responding must be considered as only part of larger strategies of adaptation (e.g., Collier, 1982). Despite their influence, however, these conceptions will not be considered in detail in the present chapter, because the bulk of research supporting them have differed from that to be discussed in a fundamentally important way. Namely, such research has studied behavior in situations in which the motivational level of the animal has been free to vary within experimental sessions. For example, much of the research involves animals living continuously in the experimental chamber or animals which feed to satiation within experimental sessions. Thus, at least from this perspective, much of this interesting research seems more relevant to a deeper understanding of the concept of drive than to the study of reinforcement in its usual sense. While it may be possible to integrate the two types of research (see Staddon, 1983, for a noteworthy effort), such an enterprise will not be attempted here.

# CHOICE AND THE MATCHING LAW

## The Matching Law

### Initial Development

Figure 3.3 discussed in the preceding section, shows that asymptotic response rate is sensitive to rate of reinforcement only over a small range when reinforcement is delivered according to a VI schedule. This could mean that rate of responding is a poor reflection of response strength or that the maximum amount of conditioning is achieved with relatively low rates of reinforcement. The proper interpretation of the data

shown in Figure 3.3 is still in question and will be discussed in a later section. For the present discussion, our attention shifts to a more complex class of procedures—those in which the animal chooses between two (or more) alternatives. The reason for considering choice procedures first is that, paradoxically, in view of the added complexity they appear to entail, such procedures yield orderly relations between measures of reinforcer value and behavior. As a result, the study of choice has become a major focus of interest over the past twenty years and has led to several quantitative theories of reinforcement.

The choice procedure that has been studied most commonly is known as a concurrent schedule, in which two independent responses are available simultaneously, each maintained by its own independent schedule of reinforcement. Thus, in addition to the absolute response rates to each alternative, the proportion of the total behavior to each response may also be assessed. As will be seen, it is this relative measure that is extremely sensitive to the parameters of reinforcement.

Two methods of programming concurrent schedules have been used. In one of these, referred to as the two-key procedure, the two response alternatives are spatially separate response keys or levers, so that the subject changes from side to side in switching between the response alternatives. With the second, known as the changeover (CO) key procedure, the two alternatives are correlated with two different stimuli alternately presented on the same key, and the subject switches between alternatives by responding on a second changeover key, which changes the schedule in effect on the first, operant key. An illustration of the differences between the two procedures is shown in Figure 3.6. In general, their results are interchangeable, with the major difference between them being that the CO-key procedure is usually preferred whenever measures of time allocation are an important feature of the results.

An additional procedural feature of most studies of concurrent schedules is some method of ensuring that responses to the two alternatives are independent. Simply because the two responses are recorded separately and are reinforced according to independent schedules does not mean that the subject regards them as independent behaviors, especially since the first

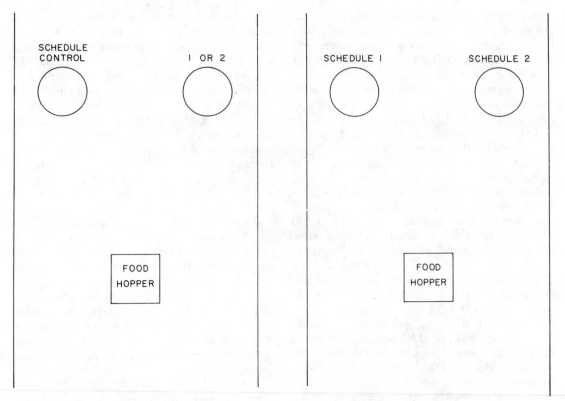

**Figure 3.6.** Representation of two methods of programming concurrent schedules. The left panel represents a changeover-key concurrent schedule, the right panel a two-key concurrent schedule.

response after a changeover usually has the highest probability of reinforcement (for reasons that will be considered later). The result is that alternation between the keys can become the dominant response pattern, which obviates any use of the concurrent response procedure as a measure of preference between two reinforcement schedules (Catania & Cutts, 1963). Consequently, it has become customary to impose some type of contingency which prevents reinforcement for alternation behavior. The most common such procedure involves a changeover delay (COD), such that some minimum time interval must elapse between a changeover between alternatives and the next reinforced response. Typically, to insure that the response alternatives are treated as independent behaviors, the delay values need range only from one to five seconds.

Interest in concurrent schedules was principally inspired by a finding that has come to be known as the matching law (Herrnstein, 1961). In the first demonstration of this finding, pigeons were presented with two simultaneously available response keys, each reinforced according to independent VI schedules. The sum of reinforcement rates for the two schedules was held constant at 40 per hour, while the number allocated to one key or the other was systematically varied across experimental conditions. The results, shown in Figure 3.7, revealed a remarkably orderly relation between the choice measure and the reinforcement rates. That is, the proportion of the total behavior to either key was approximately equal to the proportion of the total reinforcement allocated to that key. The matching relation is captured algebraically by equation 3, in which $B_1$ and $B_2$ represent the response rates for the two behaviors, and $R_1$ and $R_2$ represent the corresponding reinforcement rates.

$$\frac{B_1}{B_1 + B_2} = \frac{R_1}{R_1 + R_2} \qquad (3)$$

To appreciate the significance of this finding, it is important to recognize that the matching

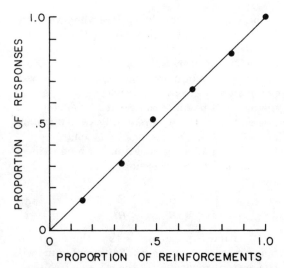

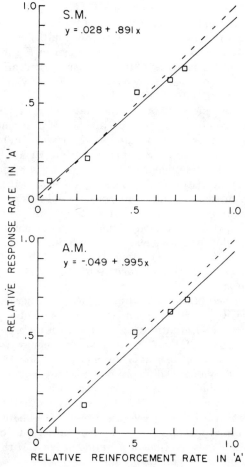

**Figure 3.7.** The relative frequency of responding to one alternative in a two-choice procedure as a function of the relative frequency of reinforcement. Independent VI schedules governed reinforcements for each alternative. The diagonal line shows matching between the relative frequencies. From "On the Law of Effect" by R.J. Herrnstein, 1970, *Journal of the Experimental Analysis of Behavior, 13*, p. 253. Copyright 1970 by the Society for the Experimental Analysis of Behavior, Inc. Reprinted by permission.

relation is not generally constrained by the reinforcement schedules, per se. A significant constraint would occur if there were relatively few responses per reinforcer or if the number of responses per reinforcer were required to be some fixed value. In fact, however, the VI schedules used by Herrnstein (1961) permitted many different response patterns that would have produced the same pattern of obtained reinforcement. Thus, the finding that only one particular distribution occurred out of all of those possible constitutes a significant, and perhaps surprising, discovery.

### Generality of the Matching Law
Given that the matching relation was first established with food-deprived pigeons as subjects, it is noteworthy that it seems to apply equally well to humans who are rewarded with points that later can be exchanged for money. In a study by Bradshaw, Szabadi, and Bevan (1976), one response alternative was rewarded according to five independent VI schedules, ranging from VI 17-sec to VI 720-sec, each of which was correlated with a different stimulus light. Each

**Figure 3.8.** The relative frequency of responding to one component of a concurrent schedule as a function of its relative reinforcement frequency. The dashed lines show perfect matching. The solid lines are the best-fitting empirical functions which also are shown in algebraic form below the subjects' initials. From "Behavior of Humans in Variable-Interval Schedules of Reinforcement" by C.M. Bradshaw, E. Szabadi, and P. Bevan, 1976, *Journal of the Experimental Analysis of Behavior, 26*, p. 139. Copyright 1976 by the Society for the Experimental Analysis of Behavior, Inc., Reprinted by permission.

separate schedule was presented alternately for periods of ten minutes, separated by five-minute rest periods. Concurrently available with each of the five schedules was a second response alternative, which was always rewarded according to a VI 51-sec schedule. For both alternatives, the response was a button press, and rewards were points that could be exchanged for money after the experiment was completed.

The issue of interest is how the choice between the two alternatives varied as a function of the proportion of reinforcement. The results for the two subjects in the study are shown in Figure 3.8, and it is evident that they are essentially similar to those shown in Figure 3.7 which Herrnstein (1961) obtained with pigeons.

The generality of the matching relation has been confirmed by a large number of different experiments. Such studies have shown matching, at least to a first approximation, with different species (pigeons, humans, monkeys, rats), different responses (keypecking, lever pressing, eye movements, verbal responses), and different reinforcers (food, brain stimulation, money, cocaine, verbal approval). Apparently, the matching relation is a general law of choice.

### Matching with Reinforcers of Different Value

If we accept the generality of the matching relation, we can analyze choice situations involving response alternatives associated with different types of reinforcers. In other words, we may use the matching law as a method of scaling the relative values of different rewards. For example, if the subject chooses a response rewarded with chocolate candies (M&Ms) twice as often as one rewarded with peanuts, other things being equal, we would conclude that the value of M&Ms is twice that of peanuts, at least at the given rate of consumption.

A more sophisticated version of such hedonic scaling is exemplified by Miller (1976). On a concurrent schedule with two response alternatives, his pigeons chose between buckwheat and hemp (seed), while the relative frequency of the two types of reward varied over a wide range. Next, the choice was between wheat and buckwheat, again with a range of relative reinforcement frequencies. Finally, the pigeons chose between hemp and wheat, to determine whether the relative values of the three types of reward established in the first two phases of the experiment would allow quantitative predictions for the degree of preference in the third phase.

To appreciate the method used by Miller (1976), it is helpful to rewrite the matching relation in terms of response ratios, as shown in equation 4:

$$\frac{B_1}{B_2} = \frac{R_1}{R_2} \qquad (4)$$

Equation 4 describes choice data whenever both response and reinforcement frequencies involve commensurate units. However, if the values of the two reinforcers differ or if the responses are of different topography, the response ratios will not match the reinforcement frequencies, but instead will be biased in favor of the response associated with the more highly valued reward or the less effortful response. One characterization of such a bias is equation 5, which reduces to equation 4 whenever no bias is present ($b = 1.0$).

$$\frac{B_1}{B_2} = b\,\frac{R_1}{R_2} \qquad (5)$$

Equation 5 presupposes that the degree of bias generated by rewards of different value will be constant regardless of the relative frequency of the different rewards. Although not inherent in the matching law, this assumption simplifies its use as a tool for scaling value. The results of any of the three phases of Miller's study provide a test of this assumption, since equation 5 should provide an accurate description of the preference with the different relative frequencies of reinforcement only if bias was indeed constant. In fact, his choice results were quite accurately described by equation 5, as over 98 percent of the variance in choice was accounted for in each of the three comparisons. But the more stringent test of equation 5 is provided by the relation between the biases in the three phases of his study. If the constant $b$ corresponds to the relative values of the different rewards, it should be possible to predict the value of $b$ in the third phase on the basis of the values obtained in phases one and two. His result for the hemp/buckwheat comparison was a $b$ value of 0.91, indicating a small bias in favor of buckwheat. The value of $b$ for the wheat/buckwheat comparison was 1.40, indicating a substantial bias in favor of wheat. The bias for the hemp/wheat comparison in phase three should be predicted by the value of $b$ in phase one divided by that in phase two, which yields a value of 0.65. The obtained value was 0.70, which, while not perfectly in accord with the predicted value, is well within the range of experimental error. The use of equation 5 thus allows transsituational predictions about the relative values of different types of rewards.

One limitation on the hedonic scaling procedure used by Miller (1976) is that the different reinforcers being scaled must be motivationally independent. Such a limitation is often violated, since the delivery of one type of reinforcer may alter the value of the alternative reinforcer. For example, if subjects are both food deprived and water deprived, the delivery of food increases the value of water, since the hunger and thirst systems apparently interact (Hursh, 1978). The result is that the choice between different frequencies of food and water is not described by equation 5. While such a finding does set limits on the generality of this simple extension of the matching law, it also suggests that matching can be a valuable tool for studying motivational systems. Where equation 5 does not apply, the matching principle can be used to unearth motivational interactions, such that new, non-obvious relationships between motivational systems may be revealed (Rachlin & Krasnoff, 1983).

A second limitation on the generality of equation 5 is when two different reinforcers satiate at different rates. For example, if the value of one type of reinforcer decreases within an experimental session, while that of a competing reinforcer remains constant, choice, summed over the entire session, will not be described by the simplest forms of the matching relation. This restriction, like that noted above, results because of an assumption implicit in equation 5—that the relative value of each reward alternative is independent both of its own consumption rate and the consumption rates of the alternatives. If such independence does not apply, the value of $b$ would vary with the relative reinforcement rates, and so equation 5 does not apply. Alternative formulations which incorporate interactions between the value of the different rewards have been proposed (Rachlin, Kagel, & Battalio, 1980), but the mathematical expressions associated with such treatments are too complex to be considered here.

## Matching of Time Allocation

The discussion of equations 3 through 5 has made no distinction between response rate and response frequency. The two measures are interchangeable as long as the rate of responding for each alternative is calculated with respect to the same time base, for example, the entire duration of the experimental session. But such overall rates of responding can be distinguished from the local rate, which is calculated with respect to the time actually spent working on a particular response alternative. This distinction is especially clear with the CO-key procedure, in which only one response alternative is present at any given time; the other alternative can only be reached via an explicit changeover response. As a result, it is easy to measure the amount of time either alternative is available and, thus, to calculate the local rate of responding with respect to each one, rather than to overall session time. The matching law as such does not apply to the local rates of responding. Instead, the local rates for the two alternatives are approximately equal, independent of the overall frequency of responding to the two alternatives across the entire session (Stubbs & Pliskoff, 1969).

The matching relation with respect to overall response rates taken together with equal local response rates implies that relative time allocation also matches relative reinforcement rate. If $B_1$ and $B_2$ are the response frequencies for the two alternatives, and $T_1$ and $T_2$ are the times each alternative is available, equal local response rates mean that

$$\frac{B_1}{T_1} = \frac{B_2}{T_2} \qquad (6)$$

Rearranging terms, and assuming equation 4, the result is equation 7, which represents the matching of time allocation to rate of reinforcement:

$$\frac{T_1}{T_2} = \frac{R_1}{R_2} \qquad (7)$$

Matching with respect to time allocation has been explicitly demonstrated by Brownstein and Pliskoff (1968). They presented pigeons a CO-key procedure in which pecks to the CO key alternated components of the concurrent schedule, as usual, but no further responses were required for reinforcement. That is, the reinforcers scheduled by the two independent VI schedules were delivered independently of responding, as long as the subject was in the component associated with the particular reinforcer. The pigeons matched the proportion of the session time spent in the presence of the two components to the proportion of reinforcements associated with the different components.

Given that relative response rate (calculated with respect to the entire session) and relative time allocation both match relative reinforcement rate, considerable attention has been given to which measure of choice is more fundamental. The usual strategy for making this distinction has been to accept the matching law as given and then ask which measure of choice yields the closest approximation to matching. On the basis of an extensive review of existing studies Baum (1979) concluded that time-allocation provided the closer approximation, but other writers (Wearden & Burgess, 1982; Mullins, Agunwamba, & Donohoe, 1982) have argued that the two measures are equivalent. Explicit attempts to separate the two measures experimentally have also led to inconclusive results (Baum, 1976).

## The Generalized Matching Law

The preceding discussion has disregarded deviations from the matching relation. Perfect matching obviously is an idealization to which the results for individual subjects are unlikely to conform. As a typical example, consider subject S.M. from the study by Bradshaw et al. (1976), shown in Figure 3.8. Whereas matching of relative response rates to relative reinforcement rates implies a best-fitting line with a slope of 1.0, the obtained result was a best-fitting line with a slope less than 1.0. Such a finding has come to be called undermatching. The issue is whether it, and other deviations from matching, are to be ascribed to experimental error or whether they represent significant alternatives to matching.

Before considering undermatching in detail, it is helpful to have some quantitative method of expressing the degree of deviation from the matching relation. Equation 8 provides such a method and has come to be known as the *generalized matching law* (Baum, 1974; Lander & Irwin, 1968; Staddon, 1968).

$$\frac{B_1}{B_2} = b \left( \frac{R_1}{R_2} \right)^a \qquad (8)$$

Equation 8 differs from equation 5 only in the addition of the exponent, $a$, which captures the sensitivity of the response ratio to the reinforcement ratio. Strict matching implies that $a$ equals 1.0; undermatching implies $a$ is less than 1.0. When $a$ is less than 1.0, preference for an alternative is less extreme than simple matching would imply. As will be seen, there are also some cases in which $a$ is greater than 1.0, and this is referred to as overmatching, meaning that

preference is more extreme than matching. Equation 8 has the advantage of separating two classes of deviation from the matching relation: a bias effect due presumably to differences in reward value or different units of measurement for the two responses, captured by the value of $b$, and sensitivity of the choice measure to the reinforcement ratios, as captured by the value of $a$. This distinction is often quite valuable, especially when applying the matching law to responses maintained by different types of reinforcement schedules (e.g., ratio vs. interval schedules).

Valuable as it has been, equation 8 is only one way, out of an indefinitely large number, to express deviations from matching. Among other things, even for varying response typographies and types of reward, it assumes that the ratio of the alternative behaviors is a power function of the ratio of rewards and that two parameters are sufficient to accommodate any systematic departures from matching. In effect, departures are either cases of bias ($b \neq 1.0$), undermatching ($a < 1.0$), or overmatching ($a > 1.0$). We would not argue that the assumptions implicit in equation 8 have been substantiated in general, only that they have served reasonably well for most of the range of data available at this writing. In all likelihood, subsequent findings will dictate still more complex expressions to describe choice.

### UNDERMATCHING

In several reviews of the literature, equation 8 has been fitted to the data for individual subjects (Baum, 1979; Myers & Myers, 1977; Wearden & Burges, 1982). Undermatching has been the most frequent finding; the median value of the exponent $a$ has fallen between 0.8 and 0.9, depending upon the set of studies encompassed. According to some accounts (Baum, 1979), the degree of undermatching is substantially less when time allocation rather than response rate is used as the measure of preference. However, other reviews of the literature (Wearden & Burgess, 1982) suggest that the degree of undermatching is similar for the two measures.

The prevalence of undermatching has led some writers to question the generality of the matching law and to propose alternative formulations that do not assume strict matching as the normative result (e.g., Davison, 1982). Before adopting such an approach, however, it is worthwhile to consider the various reasons for why undermatching may occur even if matching is the underlying principle of choice. It is possible that undermatching can be avoided if proper procedures are employed.

The most commonly cited procedural feature is the COD. As noted above, early studies of concurrent schedules (e.g., Catania & Cutts, 1963) demonstrated the importance of withholding reinforcement immediately after a change-over between responses, in order to prevent alternation from becoming the dominant response pattern. Alternation, in fact, is strongly encouraged by the contingencies imposed by concurrent interval schedules, because the highest probability of reinforcement for either response alternative is for the first response after a changeover (since reinforcers are set up by one schedule while the subject is working on the other response alternative). Undermatching is a direct result, since frequent alternation tends to equalize responding to the two alternatives.

Although the rationale for using a COD is clear, it is hard to say how much of a factor excessive response alternation has been in the observed undermatching. The problem is knowing what duration of COD is necessary to ensure adequate differentiation of the response alternatives as independent behaviors. Several studies (e.g., Shull & Pliskoff, 1967) have shown that increasing the COD may substantially increase the approximation to perfect matching and also that there may be considerable variance across subjects in the value of delay that is needed (e.g., Brownstein & Pliskoff, 1968). It is possible, therefore, that the values used (e.g., one to three seconds for pigeons) are less than optimal, either in general or for some subjects because of individual differences in sensitivity to the delay contingency.

Alternative explanations for undermatching have also been proposed. The results of Keller and Gollub (1977) suggest the involvement of some type of interference between successive experimental conditions, since they obtained near-perfect matching when a single value of relative reinforcement rate was presented to each subject but substantial undermatching when each subject received various different relative rates of reinforcement. Todorov, Castro, Hanna, Bittencourt de Sa and Barreto (1983) investigated this effect systematically and dem-

onstrated that the estimate of $a$ in equation 8 decreased regularly as the number of successive conditions presented to the same subjects was increased from five to nine. They also demonstrated that the value of $a$ was increased by using a larger number of training sessions per condition, with the increasing trend continuing for over 60 sessions, which is substantially more than the number used in typical studies of concurrent schedules. The number of sessions per condition also appears to account for a substantial portion of the undermatching reported previously: Studies reviewed by Todorov et al. (1983) that used 20 or more training sessions produced a median value of $a$ very close to 1.0, while those which used fewer sessions produced values of $a$ significantly below 1.0.

Still another source of undermatching appears to be the method of constructing the variable-interval schedules. Some studies have used arithmetic distributions in which the various intervals are symmetrically distributed on either side of the mean interval. Thus, the longest interval will be no longer than twice that of the mean schedule value. A second method involves exponential distributions, such that the distribution of intervals is skewed toward longer durations. Exponential distributions (sometimes known as random-interval schedules) have the advantage of keeping constant the probability of reinforcement independent of the time since the last reinforcer.

Although it is not obvious why the two types of distributions should have differential effects in a choice procedure, the degree of undermatching is evidently greater when arithmetic schedules are involved. Taylor and Davison (1983) subdivided the existing literature according to which type of schedule was used and found that the mean sensitivity of relative response rates to the reinforcement ratios (exponent $a$ in equation 8) was 0.96 when exponential schedules were used, but only 0.79 when arithmetic schedules were used. A similar, but smaller, difference was obtained with time allocation as the measure, as the corresponding numbers were 0.96 and 0.89. The implication is that matching, not undermatching, is the normative result whenever the reinforcers are randomly distributed in time.

OVERMATCHING

Matching and undermatching are only two of

the possible outcomes of a choice experiment. A third possibility is overmatching, which means that the measures of preference are more extreme than the relative reinforcement rate. In terms of equation 8, overmatching entails values of the exponent $a$ greater than 1.0. Unlike the case for undermatching, for which a variety of explanations rapidly come to mind, overmatching has no obvious conceptual rationale. Various kinds of errors and indiscriminabilities may cause an animal to underestimate the difference between reinforcements from two sources, hence to undermatch, but systematic overestimations should be rarer, as apparently they are.

Reviews of previous studies (Baum, 1979) with the usual concurrent VI procedure with CODs separating the response alternatives report sufficiently few cases of $a$ greater than 1.0 as to be ascribable to sampling errors. Recently, however, it has become clear that a variation in the method of programming changeover responses can produce substantial overmatching. Instead of some minimum time being required before reinforcement after a changeover response (the COD procedure), the subject is required to peck the CO key on a ratio schedule, with no minimum delay required for reinforcement after the ratio requirement has been fulfilled. Studies using such a procedure (Dunn, 1982; Pliskoff, Cicerone, & Nelson, 1978; Pliskoff & Fetterman, 1981) have shown that the value of the ratio requirement affects how well matching is approximated. Whereas undermatching typically occurs with an FR-1 schedule, overmatching has been obtained with ratio requirements in the range of FR 4 to 10. The degree of overmatching has often been quite substantial, with values of $a$ in the range of 1.2 to 2.0.

Overmatching also has been reported by Baum (1982) with a different type of changeover requirement. Instead of a CO-key procedure, a physical barrier was placed between the two response keys. Baum then manipulated the changeover requirement by varying the length of the barrier and whether or not it contained a hurdle. The results were similar to those obtained with the FR requirements on a CO key, as increases in the travel requirement increased the preference for the higher-valued response alternative. With the largest travel requirement used, severe overmatching was obtained, with values of the exponent $a$ in the range of 1.5 to 2.5.

In these examples, it may be the case that the subject overmatches because the separation (temporal or spatial) between alternatives causes an overvaluation of whichever alternative is being attended at a given moment. If so, it can be shown that preferences would seem to be more extreme than simple matching implies, even if the subject was in fact matching to its own weighting of the competing rewards. We may not, however, need to postulate anything so involved. One important difference between all of the above experiments and other studies of concurrent schedules was the method by which response rates were calculated. With the usual procedure involving a COD, pecks during the COD are included in the measure of response rate. But in the experiments involving FR requirements on the CO key, pecks to the CO key itself have been excluded. Since the changeover rates were often quite high, this meant that a substantial percentage of the total behavior during the experimental session was not included in the measure of preference. If, however, pecks to the CO key are included in the calculation of response rates (by taking the total amount of CO-key behavior and dividing it equally between the two alternatives), the overmatching effect disappears. For example, as calculated by Taylor and Davison (1983), values of $a$ for the study of Pliskoff et al. (1978) fell in the range of 1.16 to 1.96 without CO pecks, but were reduced to 0.58 to 0.98 when CO-key behavior was included. Thus, what appears to be overmatching is eliminated if all of the behavior in the session is included in the measure of preference.

Baum (1982) has questioned such inclusion, on the grounds that changeover behavior is clearly discriminated from responding to the choice alternatives themselves, not only when the CO requirement is distinctly different (as with his travel requirement), but also with the more conventional procedures involving CODs. However, matching has been obtained by several studies without a COD requirement (Baum, 1974; Bradshaw et al. 1976; Heyman, 1979; Stubbs & Pliskoff, 1969) and in discrete-trial procedures (e.g., Nevin, 1969) in which a single response is emitted each trial, so that again no COD is involved. The implication is that matching is not an incidental result of particular methods of scheduling changeovers. Given that matching is obtained whenever the measure of preference included the total behavior in the session, regardless of the proportion of that behavior devoted to changeovers, the further implication is that studies that exclude CO responses probably do not provide an accurate reflection of how relative response rates are determined by the relative values of the reinforcement schedules.

Given the present state of knowledge, we may conclude that the matching law should be considered the normative finding for concurrent VI VI schedules that vary relative frequency of reinforcement. Undermatching and overmatching both occur under some circumstances, but plausible arguments can be given for why matching is not obtained. Still to be determined is the generality of matching for other schedule comparisons and parameters of reinforcement.

## Extension to Other Parameters of Reinforcement

### Amount of Reinforcement

As noted in the introduction, frequency and amount of reinforcement historically have been regarded as having quite different effects on behavior. For example, in the final version of Hull's (1952) system, frequency of reinforcement was regarded as a learning variable, while magnitude was viewed as having only incentive effects (i.e., no direct effect on habit strength). Although the two variables may not be equivalent in all respects, frequency and amount both contribute to the relative value of a reinforcement schedule, so that matching may apply to relative amount, just as it does to relative frequency (Rachlin & Baum, 1969). Equation 9 describes this relation, as it depicts the generalized matching law with amount instead of frequency.

$$\frac{B_1}{B_2} = b \left( \frac{A_1}{A_2} \right)^a \qquad (9)$$

Before considering the evidence bearing on equation 9, different methods of scheduling different amounts should be distinguished. The most frequent has been to vary the duration of reinforcement, for example, to vary the duration of the subject's access to a tray of food. The second method has involved variations in the hedonic quality of the reinforcer, for example, the percentage of sucrose in a given amount of liquid. One important difference between the two methods is the temporal relation between the choice responses and the different amounts

of reinforcement. With the latter method the initial instant of reinforcer delivery allows the subject to detect which reinforcer amount has occurred, but with the former the difference is apparent only after the duration of the shorter reinforcer has elapsed. One might expect, therefore, that the sensitivity of preference to amount of reinforcement would be greater when reinforcer quality, rather than duration, is varied. A third possible method seems to be intermediate between the two. Amount can obviously also be varied in food pellets or scoops of fluid of differing sizes. The subject may then discover at the instant of reinforcement which of the differing sizes it has at hand, but there would still be an interaction between amount of reinforcement and time taken to consume it. A larger pellet or scoop is unavoidably diluted over a longer time of consumption.

Results from concurrent schedules involving differential amounts are difficult to interpret because they have been quite variable. Close approximations to matching have been reported for both relative duration (Brownstein, 1971; Catania, 1963a) and relative concentration of the reinforcer (Iglauer & Woods, 1974), but substantial undermatching has also occurred (Schneider, 1973; Todorov, 1973; Todorov, Hanna, & Bittencourt de Sa, 1984; Walker, Schnelle, & Hurwitz, 1970). Dunn (1982) has also reported substantial overmatching to relative duration, although this probably was due to the use of an FR changeover requirement (see discussion of overmatching in the preceding section). There is also some evidence that the sensitivity of responding to relative amount varies with the absolute values of the different durations, although the evidence is conflicting. Davison & Hogsden (1984) have reported that greater sensitivity to relative duration occurred when longer feeding times were involved, while Logue and Chavarro (1987) reported greater sensitivity with shorter feeding times.

Perhaps the most informative results are those from studies in which variation in relative amount is compared with concurrent variation in relative frequency. Equation 10 provides a formal method for such a comparison, as fits of the parameters $a$ and $c$ (using multiple regression techniques) allow a quantitative assessment of the effects of the two types of reinforcement variation. If matching occurs to the total amount of food associated with each alternative, both exponents should approximate 1.0. If the subject is more sensitive to variations in frequency or amount, the two exponents should differ from each other accordingly.

$$\frac{B_1}{B_2} = b\left(\frac{R_1}{R_2}\right)^a \cdot \left(\frac{A_1}{A_2}\right)^c \qquad (10)$$

Several studies have varied both reinforcement parameters over a wide range, but again with conflicting results. Schneider (1973) (using different numbers of food pellets), Todorov (1973), and Todorov et al. (1984) (using different durations of food availability) have all reported substantially greater values of $a$ than for $c$, indicating greater sensitivity to reinforcement frequency. However, Keller and Gollub (1977), also using different durations of food availability, reported no consistent differences between the two variables, while Hamblin and Miller (1977), using different concentrations of the reinforcer (sucrose), reported significantly greater sensitivity to amount ($a < c$). The inconsistencies across experiments preclude any strong conclusions.

A possible reason for undermatching to relative amount is suggested by the results of Keller and Gollub (1977), who found undermatching to both relative amount and relative frequency when several different values of each were presented successively to the same subject, but not when a single condition was presented to each subject. That is to say, only their between-subject design produced matching with respect to the total amount of feeding time (frequency × amount). This finding suggests that the not infrequent failures to find matching to relative amount may be due, to some extent, to the subjects' inability to discriminate the amounts reliably.

But discrimination factors probably are not the only source of the inconsistent data. Another possibility is that different amounts may not correspond exactly to different values. For example, human psychophysical data suggest that the ratio of two different concentrations of sucrose may not precisely equal the ratio of their hedonic values, if sweetness is the measure of hedonic values. Similarly, given two different durations of food, the value of the first morsels may not necessarily be equivalent to the last morsels. They are, at any rate, separated from the response by different delays. To actually test the matching law with respect to amount of reward, therefore, it is necessary first to determine how the amount variable is scaled in value units.

Miller's (1976) use of the matching law to establish relative values for different types of grain, described previously, is a model of how amount of reinforcement itself could be scaled, but no such work has been reported as yet. However, if matching can be extended to choices between qualitatively different reinforcers, as Miller's work suggests, it seems likely that it can also be extended to varying amounts of a single reinforcer, once proper allowance is made for psychophysical characteristics or other biases.

### Delay of Reinforcement

Chung and Herrnstein (1967) presented pigeons with a concurrent schedule in which the two responses were rewarded according to equal VI schedules, but with the reinforcers delayed for varying times. One alternative had a constant delay (either 8 or 16 seconds), while the other had both shorter and longer delays in successive experimental conditions. During all delays, lights in the chamber were off. Choice between the two alternatives approximately matched the relative immediacy (the inverse of delay) of the two reinforcers. That is, with $D_1$ the delay for response one and $D_2$ the delay for response two,

$$\frac{B_1}{B_2} = \frac{\dfrac{1}{D_1}}{\dfrac{1}{D_2}} \qquad (11)$$

The matching relation with respect to relative immediacy has been interpreted as evidence for delay of reinforcement as a determinant of reinforcement value, in the same sense as the other parameters of frequency and amount. Thus, the most general form of the matching relation collapses the effect of the three parameters into a single intervening variable, *value*, as in equation 12:

$$\frac{B_1}{B_2} = \frac{R_1}{R_2} \times \frac{A_1}{A_2} \times \frac{\dfrac{1}{D_1}}{\dfrac{1}{D_2}} = \frac{V_1}{V_2} \qquad (12)$$

Equation 12 depends upon the premise that matching occurs with respect to each parameter when considered separately and that their effects are interchangeable.

Although the generalization of the matching law given by equation 12 is attractive on the grounds of conceptual simplicity, its validity has been questioned by the failure of equation 11 to describe accurately the outcomes of delayed reinforcement procedures. When the separate delays contingent on the two choice alternatives are signaled by different stimuli (a procedure known as concurrent chains, which will be discussed more extensively in the section on conditioned reinforcement), matching to relative immediacy is not obtained, as the degree of preference depends upon the absolute value of the delay intervals, not simply their ratio. For example, MacEwen (1972) had pigeons choose between FI schedules that differed by a constant ratio (e.g., FI 5 seconds versus FI 10 seconds, FI 15 seconds versus FI 30 seconds). Contrary to the constant preference predicted by the matching formulation, preference for the shorter schedule increased with longer absolute values.

The major difference between such procedures and that of Chung and Herrnstein (1967) is whether the different delays contingent on the two choice responses were signaled by the same or different stimuli. To determine if this was indeed the cause of the conflicting results, Williams and Fantino (1978) investigated the effects of different delay values under two conditions: one in which the same stimuli were used to signal the different delay values contingent on the two choice responses and one in which a different stimulus was correlated with each delay. For both procedures, the ratio of the delay values was held constant while their absolute duration was varied across successive experimental conditions. Although the overall degree of preference was reduced when the same cue was used, the pattern of results was similar in both cases. Preference for the shorter delay was greater the longer the absolute delay values. Williams and Fantino then reanalyzed the original results of Chung and Herrnstein and found that a similar pattern had been obtained there, as shown in Figure 3.9. The mean results of their four subjects trained with a constant 8-second delay are plotted in terms of the logarithmic form of the generalized matching law (equation 8). Thus, the slope of the function corresponds to the value of the exponent, $a$, and reflects the sensitivity of the choice proportions to the relative delay values. The separate functions are for conditions with variable delays longer than

eight seconds and for variable delays shorter than eight seconds. Whereas equation 11 implies that the sensitivity should be the same for both sets of delay values, Figure 3.9 shows that the sensitivity to delay was greater when longer delay values were involved.

A possible reason for the deviation from matching shown in Figure 3.9 has been suggested by Herrnstein (1981). He noted that the matching formulation assumes that the choice alternatives are rewarded according to mutually independent schedules. With delay-of-reinforcement procedures, on the other hand, the consequences of the two responses are not independent, because the schedules for both responses stop operating during the delay interval. Thus, each response produces not only its own associated delay of reinforcement but also a time-out from the alternative reinforcement schedule. The severity of the time-out contingency then increases as the length of the delay interval is increased relative to the average interreinforcement interval. Thus, given a constant ratio

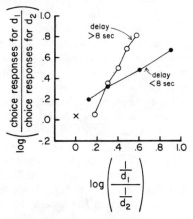

**Figure 3.9.** The results shown are the average choice ratios for four subjects in the 8-sec constant-delay conditions of Chung & Herrnstein (1967). The results are plotted in terms of the logs of the choice ratios versus the logs of the delay ratios, with $D_1$ always corresponding to the shorter delay. The separate functions are for the variable delays longer, or shorter, than the 8-sec constant delay. The unconnected point ($x$) depicts the data when the variable delay was 8 sec. From "Effects on Choice of Reinforcement Delay and Conditioned Reinforcement" by B.A. Williams and E. Fantino, 1978, *Journal of the Experimental Analysis of Behavior, 29*, p. 85. Copyright 1978 by the Society for the Experimental Analysis of Behavior, Inc. Reprinted by permission.

between the two delays contingent on the choice alternatives, increases in the absolute delay values will increase the role of the time-out contingency relative to the pure effects of the ratio of the delay-of-reinforcement intervals. Given that the duration of the time-out contingency is greater for the longer delay interval, this implies that the response associated with the shorter delay should be preferred increasingly the longer the absolute delay values, which is the pattern shown in Figure 3.9. This interpretation becomes questionable, however, in light of a subsequent study (Snyderman, 1983b), in which a time-out was added to the shorter delay in order to equate the total amount of time-out contingent on the two choice responses. Despite this modification, Snyderman found that preference for the shorter delay nevertheless increased with the absolute delay values, in the same manner as previous studies in which the time-out values were not equated.

An alternative approach to preserving the notion of matching to relative immediacy is to reconsider the assumption, implicit in equation 11, that psychological delay is mapped in a 1:1 fashion onto absolute time. Just as it may be necessary to determine the value units corresponding to different durations of food access (see preceding section), a similar rescaling may be necessary with respect to time before the matching notion may be properly tested. Unfortunately, no attempts to scale relative delay in terms of relative value, in a manner analogous to that used by Miller (1976), have been reported.

At some level there must be a function specifying the response strength associated with different delays, although it need not be simply inversely proportional to delay. However, this does not mean that this function will describe performance in conventional delay-of-reinforcement procedures, because it is uncertain whether delay is the sole determinant of performance. The problem, recognized at least since Spence (1947), is that the onset of the delay interval has stimulus properties, which may acquire value in their own right as conditioned reinforcers. Thus, performance will be a joint function of the delay to primary reinforcement and the strength of the immediate conditioned reinforcer. The latter variable is presumably also correlated with the delay to primary reinforcement, since that delay determines the rate of reinforcement associated with that stimulus. This joint deter-

mination may apply even when the same stimulus is associated with the different delays contingent on the two choice responses (e.g., the blackout during all delays as used by Chung & Herrnstein, 1967), although in that case the conditioned reinforcement values contingent on the two choice response are equal, so that any differential behavior will be due to the different delays to primary reinforcement.

The status of conditioned reinforcement in delay-of-reinforcement procedures is currently a matter of disagreement, as some models explicitly differentiate it as a separate source of response strength (Killeen, 1982b), while others ignore it altogether (Ainslie & Herrnstein, 1981). At present, therefore, the validity of equation 11 (and equation 12) is also in question, since any independent role for conditioned reinforcement would imply such simple formulations cannot adequately describe the obtained behavior. This issue will be discussed further in later sections of this chapter, both in conjunction with the explicit treatment of conditioned reinforcement and in the investigation of self-control procedures in which delay and amount of reinforcement are varied conjointly.

### Untested assumptions

The effect of absolute delay on control by relative delay, seen in Figure 3.9, highlights the possibility that the most general form of the matching law, equation 12, depends critically on several assumptions that have not been stringently tested. The effects of each separate parameter are assumed to be independent of either the relative or absolute values of the others, so that delay effects are assumed to be independent of the amounts and rates of reinforcement involved, and vice-versa. Each separate effect is also assumed to be governed solely by the ratio of the values contingent on the different choice alternatives independent of their own absolute values. The fact that the matching law describes the outcomes of a large number of studies in which reinforcement parameters have varied widely provides prima facie evidence that these assumptions are generally valid. Nevertheless, recent evidence suggests that important violations may occur. Logue and Chavarro (1987) examined the sensitivity exponent for each of the parameters discussed above and reported that sensitivity varied systematically with the absolute values of all three parameters. In addition to more extreme preference with longer absolute delays, as noted above, they also reported that preference was less extreme with larger reinforcer amounts, and that preference was more extreme with higher reinforcer frequencies. Such effects clearly pose an important challenge to the matching law as a general principle of choice.

A second potentially serious violation is provided by the results of Silberberg, Warren-Boulton and Asano (1987), who demonstrated that preference for one of two different types of food varied as a function of the overall availability of food. Monkeys chose between a large bitter pellet and a small regular pellet either with short or long intertrial intervals between successive choices. When the interval between trials was short, corresponding to a high overall availability of food, the monkeys chose more of the smaller pellet. But when the interval was long, they chose more of the larger bitter pellet. There is nothing in the matching law as described above that incorporates such effects, because the effects of reinforcer amount (or quality) and reinforcer frequency are assumed to be independent, an assumption which is supported by several previous studies (Hamblin & Miller, 1977; Miller, 1976; Rodriguez & Logue, 1986). As yet it is unclear to what extent such effects have generality, so that any assessment of their theoretical importance must await further research.

## Extension to Other Schedule Comparisons

### Fixed versus Variable

All of the research discussed heretofore has involved VI schedules of reinforcement. Such schedules are used most often because they make the probability of reinforcement more or less independent of the time since the last reinforcer, which produces a generally steady rate of responding. But obviously not all schedules produce constant local rates of responding. When studied in isolation, both FR and FI schedules produce substantial pauses after a reinforcer, so that the local rates of responding are nonhomogeneous. It is of some interest, therefore, to determine whether matching applies to situations in which either FI or FR are involved as one of the components.

Nevin (1971) had pigeons choose between VI

and FI schedules, while varying the relative reinforcement rate from the two schedules, and reported that the generalized matching law (equation 8) did accurately describe the data, but with substantial undermatching. Whereas the value of the exponent $a$ typically is in the range of 0.8 to 1.0 for concurrent VI VI schedules, his best fitting value was approximately 0.5. Similar results were obtained by Trevett, Davison, and Williams (1972), who obtained an average $a$ value of 0.62 for response rate data and 0.66 for time-allocation data. In addition, Trevett et al. reported a substantial bias in favor of the VI schedules (represented in terms of equation 8 by the value of $b$ deviating from 1.0). Rider (1981) reported somewhat higher $a$ values with a concurrent FI VR schedule, using rats as subjects, with the average $a$ value of 0.85 for the response rate measure and 0.71 for the time allocation measure. He also reported a substantial bias in favor of the variable schedule.

An explanation for both the undermatching and bias has been offered by Baum (1979). The basis of his analysis was the investigation of simple FI schedules by Schneider (1969), who argued FI behavior could be described as two discrete states: periods of little or no responding (which were variable from interval to interval) and periods of high constant response rates until the reinforcer was obtained. Baum argued that such a pattern made a concurrent VI FI schedule functionally equivalent to a multiple schedule in which the two alternating components were a concurrent VI EXT and a concurrent VI VI. The result is that matching could apply to both components of the multiple independently, but then not apply to the total behavior in the situation. As an example, consider a concurrent VI 60-sec FI 60-sec schedule and assume that the breakpoint at which responding is initiated averages out at the midpoint of the FI interval. Since the FI then becomes a multiple EXT, VI 30-sec schedule, the procedure as a whole becomes alternating components of concurrent VI 60-sec, EXT and concurrent VI 60-sec, VI 30-sec. Assume further that the sum of the local response rates for the two alternatives during each component is constant (e.g., at 50 responses/min) and that matching occurs for both components of the multiple schedule. This implies that during the concurrent VI 60-sec, EXT, 50 responses would be allotted to the VI component and none to the EXT component. Then, with the concurrent VI 60-sec, VI 30-sec component, the corresponding numbers would be 17 and 33. Thus, the total behavior to the VI response alternative would be 67 while that to the FI would be 33, which implies a bias toward the VI. The degree of bias depends upon the relative size of the VI, with the smaller biases occurring when the VI yields high rates of reinforcement. In a parametric study of several different VI FI pairs, the estimated bias would be the average of that produced by the various schedule pairs, and the averaging process would result in under-matching.

In support of Baum's argument are White and Davison's (1973) results for concurrent FI FI schedules. When both schedules produced simi-lar patterns, whether an increasing or steady rate of responding throughout the interval, matching was approximated. But with different patterns, the result was undermatching, with bias toward the most VI-like alternative. We may conclude that the undermatching and bias seen in concurrent procedures involving discri-minated periods of nonreinforcement are not fundamental departures from matching but are the result of adding together nonhomogeneous rates of responding.

### Ratio versus Interval Schedules

Variable interval and variable ratio schedules in isolation both produce relatively constant local response rates, but with the VR rate typi-cally 1.5 to 3 times higher given equal frequen-cies of reinforcement. We noted earlier that on concurrent VI VI schedules, for which local rates of responding are equal, both response fre-quency and time allocation conform to match-ing. Given that local response rates for VI and VR differ, the implication is that simple match-ing should not occur with concurrent VI VR with both time and response measures of behav-ior. Several studies of concurrent VI VR (Herrn-stein, 1971; Herrnstein & Heyman, 1979; Herrn-stein & Loveland, unpublished but plotted by de Villiers, 1977, Figure 5) have found close approximations to matching with bias. That is to say, when the results from several subjects were pooled, the parameter $a$ in equation 8 fell quite near 1.0 (ranging from 1.01 to 1.06) for both the time and response measures. In addition, the time measure indicated a bias toward the VI schedule, while the response measure was biased toward the VR (i.e., the parameter $b$ of

equation 8 as above or below 1.0, depending on which measure was employed). For example, when receiving half of their reinforcements from each schedule, the subjects allocated more than half of their time to the interval schedule, but emitted more than half of their responses to the ratio schedule. Corresponding biases occurred for other distributions of reinforcement as well.

Herrnstein and Heyman (1979) also calculated the local response rates maintained by the two schedules and found that the VI rate was an approximately constant fraction (mean of 0.59) of the VR rate for all of the relative reinforce-ment values that were studied. They suggested that this was the result of the two schedules maintaining different responses topographies, as behavior maintained by interval schedules may involve more time in which the bird is not in contact with the response key. Such differen-ces would easily explain bias toward the VR schedule with respect to the response measure, but their implications for the opposite bias with respect to time allocation are less clear. One explanation of the latter effect is that the time-allocation measure does not truly reflect the time actually spent responding. That is to say, some amount of off-key time might belong to some other response class (e.g., leisure), and because more off-key time occurs with VI than VR responding, more of this leisure time would be artifactually assigned to the VI alternative, producing the bias toward the VI. A second, related explanation is that the different res-ponse topographies differ with respect to their effort or aversiveness, so that the more leisurely response rate maintained by the VI increased the value of its reinforcers relative to those of the VR, which again would account for the observed time bias toward the VI.

We will discuss concurrent VI VR in greater detail in conjunction with the issue of rein-forcement maximization (see section on opti-malization). For the moment, therefore, we will summarize by noting that matching applies to concurrent VI VR schedules, albeit with a bias that depends on whether time or individual responses are taken as the measure of behavior. Such applicability is perhaps surprising, since interval and ratio schedules differ profoundly in the nature of the reinforcement contingency. On ratio schedules, reinforcement rate is propor-tional to response rate; on interval schedules there is no such proportionality. That matching nevertheless applies is further evidence of its generality and robustness.

# DYNAMIC MODELS OF MATCHING

## Overview

As discussed in the preceding section, the matching law states a direct proportionality between relative reinforcement rate and molar measures of behavioral allocation. While the law appears to be quite general, it says nothing about the individual responses constituting the molar measures. If behavior obeys the matching law in the aggregate, what is controlling the individual pecks or lever presses? As will be seen, matching has been derived from several different fundamental assumptions about the nature of response strength.

The most frequent approach has been to assume that the best estimates of the local response probabilities are their molar probabilities. Matching is then the automatic result of each alternative response occurring in proportion to its own strength, without further specification of each response occurrence (e.g., Catania, 1973; Herrnstein, 1970; Killeen, 1982a; Myerson & Miezin, 1980). In other words, matching is what we observe when some underlying law of response strength is iterated across a set of response alternatives.

A second approach assumes that dynamic processes occur at the level of individual responses, or small numbers of responses, which, if identified, would allow a specification of which response is to be chosen at any moment. Matching is then the result of adjustments to changing contingencies, and it is these adjustments, not matching itself, which reveal the fundamental principles of behavior (e.g., Herrnstein & Vaughan, 1980; Hinson & Staddon, 1983a; Shimp, 1966). The several examples of this view that we outline below mainly differ with respect to which local contingencies are taken to be crucial.

A third approach also pictures matching as a byproduct of more fundamental processes, but the processes operate on the same aggregations of behavior that show matching (e.g., Rachlin, et al., 1981; Staddon & Motheral, 1978). Here, as illustrated below, we usually find some version of optimality theory. Thus, to the extent that matching occurs, it does so presumably only because it is correlated with a pattern of behavior that earns the best returns in reward.

## Momentary Matching

If matching is just the iteration of a law of response strength across alternatives, it should apply to both large and small aggregations of behavior; it should not depend on the level of analysis. Unfortunately, it is hard to know whether matching occurs at a local level, for the estimate of local reinforcement rates often depends upon the time interval over which the estimate is obtained. A subject may be obeying the matching law with every single response, given his estimate of the momentary rates of reinforcement, but his estimate may differ from ours. Some specification of how the subject calculates local reinforcement is thus necessary before it can be said that the distribution of responding is not obeying matching. Although several method of calculating local reinforcement rates have been suggested (e.g., Killeen, 1981), none has been meaningfully tested within the matching framework.

Another method has instead been explored in several studies. If matching in a typical concurrent schedule is the result of the separate strengths of each response, then responses that are first stabilized separately might be expected to conform to the matching law the first time they occur together. Herrnstein and Loveland (1976) tested this implication by training pigeons with four different VI reinforcement schedules, each associated with a separate response key. Initial training consisted of a series of sessions broken into separate presentations of four of the six possible pairs for eight-minute periods, with each of the four keys involved in two of the training pairs. The training produced approximate matching to each individual pair, although there was considerable variation, perhaps because of variations in obtained reinforcement rates. The remaining two pairs were then presented during 30-sec test periods in which no reinforcement was available. Given that each member of the new pairs was familiar, did responding to the new pairs obey matching? The answer is no. Instead of matching, there was a strong tendency for the response key associated with the higher-valued schedule to be preferred exclusively. Similar results were obtained by Edmon, Lucki, and Gresham (1980), who tested pigeons with new concurrent schedules after each component had first been trained as members of a multiple schedule.

Such results imply that matching depends on the subject having direct experience with the response alternatives within the context of a particular concurrent schedule, since it does not occur if the alternatives are established in a different concurrent schedule or in a multiple schedule. This result obviously fails to support the first approach to matching, but it does not refute it either. Shifting contexts, as these experiments do, may interfere with responding or otherwise introduce factors affecting performance. There are, in fact, good reasons for supposing that context is a significant variable in its own right. Thus, the apparently simple motion of momentary matching has proven to be quite difficult to test; not surprisingly, then, the other approaches have stimulated more research.

## Momentary Maximizing

### Response-sequence Models

The second approach assumes that a moment-by-moment analysis would reveal local dynamics that yield matching in the aggregate. Before discussing such accounts it may be helpful to consider the changes in local probability of reinforcement that are inherent in concurrent VI VI schedules, since this is the procedure most often used to demonstrate simple matching. Since each VI schedule runs continuously, a reinforcer may become available for one response key while the animal is working on the alternative key. Such reinforcers are then held until the subject returns to the response key, with the result that the first response after a changeover usually has the highest probability of reinforcement. The percent of the total reinforcers that occurs just after a changeover is, in fact, the complement of the percent of the total time the animal spends on that key (Dreyfus, Dorman, Fetterman, & Stubbs, 1982), assuming the usual pattern of switching from key to key. For example, if 25 percent of the animal's time is allocated to a response alternative, approximately 75 percent of the total reinforcers for that alternative will occur just after the changeover. But the most important feature of concurrent contingencies is that the probability of reinforcement grows continuously the more the elapsed time without a response to that sched-

ule, so at some point the local probability of reinforcement for the schedule with the lower average value will equal or exceed the local probability of reinforcement for the higher-valued schedule. It can be shown analytically (Staddon, Hinson, & Kram, 1981) that a momentary maximizing strategy implies a particular response sequence. For example, if the schedule for the right key is VI 1 minute, while that for the left key is VI 3 minutes, the sequence that follows the maximizing strategy is RRRLRRRL, assuming constant and equal interresponse times.

Shimp (1966, 1969) was the first to propose that the molar matching relation was the result of subjects following a momentary maximizing strategy. He noted that animals do learn such strategies when explicitly reinforced for them in situations not involving concurrent schedules (but see Williams, 1972, 1983b, for exceptions), and demonstrated by computer simulation that adherence to a maximizing strategy within a concurrent VI VI schedule generates an overall distribution of behavior approximately consistent with the molar matching law. He then tested whether a maximizing strategy did in fact occur by analyzing the response sequences from a discrete-trial choice procedure in which the probabilities of reinforcement for each alternative grew with time since the last response to that alternative, as is the case with the typical concurrent VI VI. The result was that the obtained response sequences were correlated with those predicted by momentary maximizing. Silberberg, Hamilton, Ziriax, and Casey (1978) subsequently replicated Shimp's results, although again the adherence to the maximizing strategy was imperfect.

On the basis of their results, Shimp and Silberberg et al. argued that the matching law was the artifactual result of pooling response sequences, each of which was determined by the local probability of reinforcement. But their conclusions have been questioned because the deviations from the maximizing strategy were often substantial and were regarded by them as errors. However, in order for molar matching to be derived from their analysis, the distribution of errors themselves had to be assumed to be consistent with molar matching. Thus, it becomes unclear whether momentary maximizing or molar matching is the more fundamental principle.

But even more important evidence against

the maximizing explanation is that matching has been obtained in situations where the analysis of response sequences contain no evidence of momentary maximizing. Nevin's results (1969, 1979) are perhaps the most cited example. He trained pigeons on a discrete-trial procedure in which one response was reinforced according to a VI 1-minute schedule while the second response was reinforced according to a VI 3-minute schedule. A single peck was allowed for each trial, with trials separated by six-second intertrial intervals. The independent VI schedules ran continuously during the intertrial intervals, so that the changeover contingencies were essentially like those of conventional concurrent schedules in which the two response keys are continuously present.

The critical feature of momentary maximizing accounts is that the choice probabilities should correspond to changes in the local probability of reinforcement. In Nevin's procedure the probability of reinforcement for one alternative increased the larger the number of preceding responses to the other alternative. Thus, the probability of a changeover response should also increase the longer the run of consecutive responses to the same key. Contrary to this prediction, Nevin reported that the probability of a changeover slightly decreased as a function of run length, as shown in Figure 3.10. Also

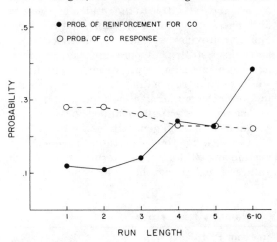

**Figure 3.10.** The probability of a changeover response, and the reinforcement for a changeover response, as a function of the number of preceding responses to the same response key. Data shown are the averages of three subjects from Experiment 1 of Nevin (1969). Data points from each subject were estimated from his Figure 4.

shown are the actually obtained probabilities of reinforcement for a changeover, and it is clear that the two functions change in opposite directions. Very similar results have been obtained by Herrnstein (unpublished data, plotted as Figure 4 in de Villiers, 1977) and by Williams (1985). Such data provide no evidence of adherence to a maximizing strategy, despite the occurrence of overall matching.

Similar evidence against maximizing has been provided by Heyman (1979), who recorded changeovers as a function of run length in several conventional concurrent VI VI schedules. His primary finding was that the probability of changeovers was essentially independent of the number of preceding responses and could be modeled successfully by a Markov process that assumes each changeover response to be statistically independent. There were some deviations from the model, but these apparently were due to the effects of response topography (e.g., the occurrence of double pecks) and were usually inconsistent with the maximizing strategy.

Although the role of response sequences in concurrent schedules remains a subject of controversy (Silberberg & Ziriax, 1982; Nevin, 1982), the lack of correspondence between reinforcement probability and response probability provides prima facie evidence against momentary maximizing as a general explanation. It is true that molar matching is sometimes accompanied by response sequences consistent with maximizing, but it is also true that molar matching occurs regardless of the particular response sequence. Thus, any attempt to reduce molar matching to the pooling of different response sequences seems unpromising.

### Time-based Models

A somewhat simpler approach to momentary maximizing has been provided by Staddon et al. (1981). They noted that the probability of reinforcement governed by a VI schedule involving an exponential distribution of intervals is independent of the time since the last reinforcement and depends only on the time since the last response and the overall scheduled rate of reinforcement. Thus, such probabilities can be described by equation 13, in which $t$ is the time since the last response and $\lambda$ is the average rate of reinforcement.

$$P_i = 1 - e^{-\lambda_i t_i} \qquad (13)$$

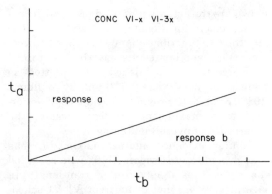

**Figure 3.11.** An example of the "clock-space" used by Hinson & Staddon (1983) in their analysis of momentary maximizing. The ordinate plots time since the last response to the first alternative; the abscissa plots the time since the last response to the second alternative. The line represents the relation between the two time values that provides equal probabilities of reinforcement for each response alternative. Choices located in the space below the line occur when the higher probability of reinforcement is for response $b$; choices located above the line occur when the higher probability of reinforcement is for response $a$.

Since a momentary maximizing strategy is simply to choose the response ($a$ or $b$) associated with the higher momentary probability of reinforcement, this can be determined by solving equation 13 for both response alternatives, thus determining which has the higher probability of reinforcement at that moment in time. As noted by Staddon et al., a convenient method of assessment is to define an indifference contour by determining the values of $t_a$ and $t_b$ that equate the reinforcement probabilities for the two responses. Equation 14, which results from setting the value of $P_a$ (from equation 13) equal to $P_b$ defines such a contour.

$$t_b = \frac{\lambda_a t_a}{\lambda_b} \qquad (14)$$

The graphical representation of equation 14 is referred to by Staddon et al. (1981) as a *clock-space*, and an example with the reinforcement rate for response $a$ three times that of response $b$ is shown in Figure 3.11. If momentary maximizing is adhered to perfectly, all of the responses to alternative $a$ should lie to the left and above the indifference contour, while all responses to alternative $b$ should lie to the right and below the line.

Hinson and Staddon (1983a, 1983b) assessed the occurrence of maximizing by analyzing the distribution of responses in clockspaces corresponding to various concurrent VI VI schedules. In order to define a quantitative test, they defined the metric, $m$, which was calculated by determining the reinforcement probabilities for each separate response, as defined by equation 13. They then subtracted the reinforcement probability of the response not chosen from the reinforcement probability for the response that was chosen. The difference is positive for correct responses and negative for incorrect responses, with the magnitude of the error corresponding to the magnitude of reinforcement-probability differences. The metric $m$ was then calculated by placing the absolute value of the probability difference in a 2 by 2 matrix, as shown in Table 3.1. By then computing the proportion of probability difference associated with correct responses (cells a and d) relative to the total of probability differences (the sum of all cells), the resulting quantity provides an index of adherence to the maximizing strategy. Accordingly, perfect adherence to maximizing implies that $m$ equals 1.0, while random responding with respect to the indifference contour implies a value of 0.5.

The $m$ values actually obtained by Hinson and Staddon (1983a) fell generally in the range from 0.7 to 0.9, indicating a partial adherence to a maximizing strategy. The interpretation of such values is ambiguous, however, since response

**Table 3.1. Procedure for Obtaining the Momentary Maximizing Estimate $m$.**

| | | Reinforcement Probability | |
|---|---|---|---|
| | | $p(R/t_1) > p(R/t_2)$ | $p(R/t_1) < p(R/t_2)$ |
| Response | 1. | $\Sigma\,(p_1 - p_2) = a$ | $\Sigma\,(p_2 - p_1) = b$ |
| | 2. | $\Sigma\,(p_1 - p_2) = c$ | $\Sigma\,(p_2 - p_1) = d$ |
| | | $m = (a + d)/(a + b + c + d)$ | |

patterns only partially correlated with maximizing (simple alternation) would produce values of $m$ greater than 0.5. To further support maximizing, Hinson and Staddon determined the hypothetical schedule values that would produce the highest value of $m$, given the particular response distributions that occurred. The result was that the hypothetical values were usually quite close to the actual schedule values, thus demonstrating that the deviations of $m$ below 1.0 were not systematic in nature. Hinson and Staddon concluded that choice behavior was governed by a maximizing strategy, although subjects often made errors in assessing which response had the higher reinforcement probability.

Although Hinson and Staddon (1983a, 1983b) make a strong case that momentary maximizing may occur in concurrent schedules, the relation between maximizing and molar matching remains unclear. In order to demonstrate that maximizing is the fundamental process underlying matching, it is essential that both occur in the same situation. In fact, however, Hinson and Staddon (1983b) reported substantial undermatching, as the average value of the exponent $a$ (from equation 8) for their six subjects was 0.71. Hinson and Staddon did not employ a COD, which suggests that an important source of such undermatching was frequent alternation between the response alternatives. This is noteworthy because adherence to a maximizing strategy depends critically on frequent alternation. Thus, it is plausible that the use of a COD would weaken the evidence for maximizing by reducing the number of changeovers, while at the same time increasing the approximation to matching. The implication would be that maximizing does not underlie molar matching, but instead is a competing response pattern that occurs when frequent changeovers can be reinforced.

The generality of the analysis of Hinson and Staddon is also challenged by the failure of other investigations to find a correspondence between changeover probability and the number of preceding responses to the same alternative (cf. Heyman, 1979). Hinson and Staddon argue that such evidence is not critical because there is no necessary relation between reinforcement probability for a changeover and run length, since interresponse times may be quite variable and reinforcement probability is determined by time, not the number of responses. While their argument is correct with respect to free-operant procedures, it cannot be applied to situations in which run length and interresponse time are strongly correlated, as with Nevin's (1969) discrete-trial procedure in which a single response was allowed every six seconds. Thus, the results shown in Figure 3.10 provide evidence against both response-sequence and time-based models.

## Optimization (Molar Maximizing)

### Derivations of Optimization

The maximizing accounts just discussed assume that the controlling variable is the momentary probability of reinforcement for each of the responses that are available. A second form of maximizing, usually known as optimality theory, assumes that the controlling variable is more molar in nature, being the total return in reinforcement (reward minus cost) aggregated over an extended time period (usually an entire experimental session). Such an approach makes no attempt to deal with the molecular processes generating such molar maximizing, but instead provides a normative description of the optimal pattern of behavior, given some set of values for the various commodities/activities available in the environment. Its underlying assumption is that behavior is fundamentally adaptive, so that control of behavior by its consequences has evolved to produce maximum benefit (value) for the organism. For at least some of the treatments we will consider, this assumption is itself axiomatic, so that the task of the experimenter is to discover the value structure of the subject that corresponds to optimization, given the particular distributions of responding that are observed.

The first step of optimality analyses of choice procedures is to specify for each response alternative the schedule feedback function, which describes the rate of reinforcement produced by any given rate of responding. For a VI schedule, the average time to reinforcement is given by the average scheduled interreinforcement interval, plus the time required to obtain the reinforcer after it has been scheduled. Thus, the feedback function is given by equation 15, in which $R$ represents the obtained rate of reinforcement, $t$ the average programmed interreinforcement interval, and $E$ the average time between the setting up of the reinforcement and its procurement by the next response:

$$R_{\text{VI}} = \frac{1}{t + E} \qquad (15)$$

For VR schedules the rate of reinforcement is given simply by the rate of behavior ($B$) divided by the ratio requirement. Letting $n$ equal the ratio requirement, the schedule feedback rule is given by equation 16:

$$R_{\text{VR}} = \frac{B}{n} \qquad (16)$$

Given the schedule feedback functions for the response alternatives that are available, the task for the subject is to distribute its behavior in such a way as to maximize the total reinforcement from all sources. For situations in which a single response alternative is available, the maximum rate of reinforcement can, of course, be obtained only by responding with infinitely fast rates. However, such effects are offset by an additional response cost function, so that the actually obtained rates are predicted by net returns of reinforcement minus cost. The effects of response cost will be ignored in the present analysis, since the purpose is to predict relative response rates, not absolute rates, and it is plausible that the response costs are equal for the two response alternatives.

To apply optimality analysis to a concurrent VI VI schedule, equation 15 is rewritten for each alternative to provide the expression for the total reinforcement in the situation:

$$R_{\text{VI}_1} + R_{\text{VI}_2} = \frac{1}{t_1 + E_1} + \frac{1}{t_2 + E_2}$$

However, such as expression is not predictively useful without some more explicit specification of the values of $E$. In fact, the correct specification is a matter of controversy, with the different expressions that have been proposed leading to somewhat different outcomes (cf. Heyman, 1983a; Heyman & Luce, 1979; Houston & McNamara, 1981). For the purpose of illustration we will consider perhaps the simplest assumption, offered by Baum (1981) and Staddon and Motheral (1978), who argued that the time to obtain a reinforcement after it was scheduled was proportional to the simple inverse of the response rate. Thus, the expression for the total rates of reinforcement for a concurrent VI is

given by equation 17, in which $B_1$ and $B_2$ correspond to the rates of behavior to the two response alternatives:

$$R_{\text{VI}_1} + R_{\text{VI}_2} = \frac{1}{t_1 + \dfrac{1}{B_1}} + \frac{1}{t_2 + \dfrac{1}{B_2}} \qquad (17)$$

Several additional assumptions are also necessary before the distribution of behavior producing the maximum rate of reinforcement can be determined. Thus, Baum (1981) assumed that the response rates to the two alternatives represented the total behavior possible. $B_1$ and $B_2$ then become simple proportions of that total (i.e., $B_1 = pB$; $B_2 = [1 - p]B$). The result is equation 18:

$$R_{\text{VI}_1} + R_{\text{VI}_2} = \frac{1}{t_1 + \dfrac{1}{pB}} + \frac{1}{t_2 + \dfrac{1}{(1 - p)B}} \qquad (18)$$

The maximum rate of reinforcement is then given by setting to zero the partial derivative of equation 18 with respect to $p$. Accordingly,

$$\partial \frac{R_1 + R_2}{\partial p} = \frac{R_1^2}{p^2 B} - \frac{R_2^2}{(1 - p)^2 B} \qquad (19)$$

so

$$\frac{R_1^2}{p^2 B} = \frac{R_2^2}{(1 - p)^2 B}$$

and

$$\frac{p}{1 - p} = \frac{R_1}{R_2}$$

And given the definition of $p$, the result is the matching law:

$$\frac{B_1}{B_2} = \frac{R_1}{R_2}$$

Baum's (1981) analysis thus demonstrates that matching is the distribution of behavior that produces the maximum total reinforcement rate, given his assumptions about the nature of schedule feedback functions. As noted earlier, however, different assumptions about the characterization of $E$ lead to somewhat different outcomes, although even such alternative treatments lead to predictions quite close to matching and thus are very difficult to distinguish empirically (cf. Heyman, 1983a).

Although matching in concurrent VI VI schedules can be derived analytically from optimality theory, molar maximizing as the principle underlying such matching becomes dubious when it is recognized that the total reinforcement provided by distributions of behavior other than matching are extremely similar. That is to say, the total amount of reinforcement produced by concurrent VI VI schedules is virtually constant regardless of the distribution of behavior, as long as the subject occasionally samples both response alternatives. For example, with a concurrent VI 1-minute VI 3-minute schedule, the subject can deviate from matching by plus or minus 20 percent with the loss of no more than a single reinforcer per hour. In order for the subject's actual behavior to converge on matching, therefore, it must be extremely sensitive to small differences in obtained reinforcement rate. Such sensitivity seems implausible, especially considering that the random variations in obtained reinforcement (e.g., due to variations in the sampling of which intervals are included within an experimental session) are usually considerably greater than the variation caused by different response patterns.

Baum (1981) also applied optimality analysis to concurrent VI VR, which others (Herrnstein & Heyman, 1979) have argued provides a strong violation of optimality theory. The outcome of that analysis (which will not be considered in detail because it is directly analogous to that used for concurrent VI VI) is equation 20, in which $n$ is once again the ratio requirement:

$$\frac{B_{VR}}{B_{VI}} = \sqrt{n}\left(\frac{R_{VR}}{R_{VI}}\right) \tag{20}$$

Equation 20 implies that optimizing predicts a different outcome depending on how relative reinforcement rate is varied. With variation due to changes in the VI component, the result is a form of biased matching, since $n$ remains constant as long as the ratio component is unchanged. Thus, $n$ is then analogous to the bias term, $b$, of equation 5. This prediction does not apply, however, when the relative reinforcement rate is varied by changes in the VR requirement. The value of $n$ then changes across experimental conditions, which implies that the degree of bias will covary with the rates of reinforcement produced by the ratio component. The naure of such changes can be seen more clearly by rearranging terms in equation 20 after setting $n$ equal to $B_{VR}/R_{VR}$. The result is

equation 21, which implies that undermatching should be the result, since the ratio of response rates is proportional to the square root of the reinforcement rates.

$$\frac{B_{VR}}{B_{VI}} = \left(\frac{B_{VR}}{R_{VI}}\right)^{0.5} \cdot \left(\frac{R_{VR}}{R_{VI}}\right)^{0.5} \tag{21}$$

Baum's (1981) analysis of concurrent VR VI makes several unambiguous predictions that can be tested against the empirical findings. First, when relative rate of reinforcement is varied via changes in the VI schedule, the generalized matching law should apply with an exponent near 1.0 and a bias toward the VR component. At first glance his prediction appears to be confirmed by the findings of Herrnstein and Heyman (1979), who did indeed find matching with a bias toward the VR component. However, a closer analysis reveals several difficulties. As noted by Baum, the degree of bias (approximately 1.4 on the average) was considerably less than that predicted by equation 20, since their ratio requirement ranged from VR 30 to VR 60, which implies a bias between 5.5 and 7.7. Moreover, the bias obtained by Herrnstein and Heyman with respect to time allocation favored the VI alternative, which is directly contrary to Baum's (1981) analysis. This is noteworthy because it is the time-allocation measure, not response rate, which is consistent with the simplifying assumptions underlying Baum's derivation.

A second critical prediction from equations 20 and 21 is that the sensitivity of relative response rate to relative reinforcement rate should be substantially less when relative reinforcement rate is varied by changes in the VR, rather than the VI. As noted by Baum (1981), the data of Herrnstein and Heyman (1979) do not provide a strong test of this prediction because VI and VR reinforcement rate were not varied independently. However, more recent data from Davison (1982) provide a direct test, as Davison explicitly compared the effects of independent variation of interval and ratio schedules. And contrary to optimality theory, Davison reported a closer approximation to matching when the ratio requirement, rather than the VI value, was varied. Similar results were obtained by Williams (1985) using rats trained on a discrete-trial concurrent schedule.

Although results from concurrent VI VR schedules appear to provide strong evidence against optimality theory, proponents of alternative versions (e.g., Rachlin et al., 1981) have argued that such problems can be surmounted if the concept of leisure is incorporated into the analysis. Thus, rather than the total value in the situation being given by the sum of the reinforcement rates from the two sources, value is also determined by the time spent not responding, because presumably it has value in its own right (e.g., pigeons may preen when not pecking). Thus, the choice between VI and VR alternatives is actually a choice between different packages of food and leisure. Because ratio schedules maintain higher local response rates than do interval schedules, this implies that the choice of the interval schedule will be rewarded by a greater amount of leisure, thus offsetting the bias toward the VR component that is expected on the basis of the above analysis that includes only the obtained rates of food.

The method by which leisure is incorporated into optimality theory is complex and will not be elaborated here. However, it is important to note that such an analysis depends critically on the assumption that leisure has different values depending on whether it is associated with the interval versus the ratio component. That is, not responding must be worth more when it is considered part of the ratio package than when it is part of the interval package (see Prelec, 1982, for a development of why this must be so). Such an assumption seems questionable, since it requires that the animal recognize different types of leisure, depending on the types of behavior immediately surrounding it.

The role of leisure in choice between VR and VI alternatives can be assessed directly by concurrent shcedules in which the response requirement is eliminated, as investigated by DeCarlo (1985) and Heyman and Herrnstein (1986). A change-over key procedure was used such that reinforcers were delivered freely whenever the subject was in the presence of the discriminative stimulus correlated with the appropriate schedule. The "VI-like" alternative was like that normally used: The schedule continued to operate while the subject was in the presence of the alternative cue, so that reinforcers that were set up during that time could be obtained upon return to the VI alternative. For the "VR-like" alternative, the schedule only operated while the animal was in the presence of its stimulus. A moment's reflection reveals that the optimal strategy would be for the subject to

spend most of its time in the presence of the "VR-like" alternative while only occasionally visiting the "VI-like" alternative to pick up any reinforcers that had been scheduled. That is, just as with conventional concurrent VI VR schedule, optimality theory predicts a substantial bias toward the "VR-like" alternative. The results of both studies were quite similar and strongly opposed to the optimality prediction: Time allocated to one or the other schedule closely matched the relative rate of reinforcement obtained in the presence of the correlated stimuli, which necessitated that the subjects obtained many fewer than the maximum number of reinforcers. A similar outcome was obtained by Williams (1985) using a discrete-trial procedure in which a single response was possible for each choice. Such findings cannot be salvaged by appeals to differential roles for leisure in the presence of the two schedules, since the response requirement was the same for both alternatives. Apparently, therefore, the predictions of optimality theory are strongly contradicted by choice results with concurrent VI VR schedules (but see Green, Hanson, & Rachlin, 1983, for conflicting findings).

### Can Optimality Theory be Tested?

Although several different tests of optimality theory have been reported, we will consider the results of Mazur (1981) as a single example. The reason for limiting our scope is that evaluations of optimality theory appear to have less to do with particular empirical outcomes than with the assumptions available to optimality theorists to preserve their account. As will be seen, apparently strong negative evidence can be reconciled with optimality theory if appropriate assumptions are made regarding the relative values of the different activities available in the situation.

Mazur (1981) trained pigeons on a concurrent VI VI schedule in which pecks to both keys were rewarded by 3-second periods of darkness, some of which included food deliveries. The critical feature of his procedure was that a single VI tape governed the reinforcers scheduled for both response alternatives, with 50% of the blackouts assigned randomly to each response alternative after they were scheduled. Once a reinforcer was assigned, the VI tape then stopped until the reinforcer was obtained by the next peck to the appropriate key. The independent variable in the experiment was the percentage of the total blackout periods that included food. For example, in one condition, 100% of the blackouts contingent on one response included food, whereas only 10% of the blackouts contingent on the second response included food.

The rationale of Mazur's study can be seen by comparing the predictions of optimality theory versus simple matching. Optimality theory predicts that each response should be sampled frequently and equally, because each key is equally likely to be primed to deliver a blackout and the schedule only progressed as the assignments were collected by pecks to the appropriate key. For matching, on the other hand, preference should simply track the obtained relative rates of reinforcement from the two keys. The results were unambiguously in favor of matching, as preference closely followed relative reinforcement rates, although slight undermatching rather than matching was obtained (*a* of equation 8 was 0.85). Moreover, control by relative reinforcement rate was correlated with substantial losses in obtained rates of reinforcement, indicating that the overall rate of reinforcement was not the controlling variable.

Mazur's results are typical of a number of others showing that animals will sacrifice a reduction in total reinforcements to respond in accordance with the matching law. Proponents of optimality theory have answered such results by arguing that subjects cannot be expected to maximize unless they can discriminate which rates of reinforcement result from which behavioral distributions, and such discrimination is impeded whenever long delays separate responding from its consequences. Thus, in Mazur's study the pigeons had to discriminate that certain sequences of responses produced higher rates of reinforcement than other sequences, so it is possible that the first members of the sequences were too far removed from the delivery of the reinforcers to allow the correct sequence to be learned.

The possibility of inadequate discrimination of remote contingencies is only one example of a more general issue for optimality theory—how temporal variables are to be included. For example, when animals chose between small, immediate rewards and large, delayed rewards (known as self-control procedures), the usual preference for the former can be explained by optimality theory only by assuming that the values

of the different rewards are determined by their temporal distance from the point at which the choice is made. As argued by Prelec (1982), however, such inclusion undermines a fundamental aspect of optimality theory. Any role for temporal discounting implies that the subject reevaluates the value of different packages of commodities at each moment in time. The result is that the molar value of the package, aggregated over some large time frame, will be indeterminant, because it will depend on the particular temporal distributions of choices that are included in the aggregate. Such indeterminancy poses a serious problem, one that has not been adequately addressed by proponents of optimality theory, since its major objective has been to account for the molar value structure of the commodities continuously available in the environment.

Despite the above criticisms, it still may be premature to make a final assessment of the virtues of optimality analyses. As noted by Rachlin et al. (1981), there must be biological constraints modifying an animal's ability to make an optimal choice, and it remains to be determined how such constraints are to be incorporated. It should be recognized, however, that attempts to test the theory directly have produced generally negative results, so that any final form of the theory will need to predict behavior that is substantially different from the normative patterns that produce the maximum rate of the normal reinforcement. It remains to be seen whether such an account will have any predictive utility.

## Melioration

### Control by Local Reinforcement Rates
The last example of attempts to reduce matching to more fundamental processes is known generally as *melioration* (Herrnstein & Vaughan, 1980; also see Rachlin, 1973, for a related formulation). Its level of analysis lies intermediate between the molecular account of momentary maximizing and the molar level of optimality theory. Like momentary maximizing, it assumes that choice responses are determined by local reinforcement contingencies that change continuously during a session. But unlike that theory, such local control does not necessarily entail that each choice response is controlled by its own individual reinforcement probability prevailing at that moment.

The foundation of melioration comes from the observation that matching to both response frequency and time allocation entails equal local rates of reinforcement, and equal rates of responding, for each alternative. That is,

$$\frac{B_1}{B_2} = \frac{R_1}{R_2}$$

and

$$\frac{T_1}{T_2} = \frac{R_1}{R_2}$$

so

$$\frac{R_1}{T_1} = \frac{R_2}{T_2} \text{ and } \frac{B_1}{T_1} = \frac{B_2}{T_2}$$

This suggests that matching is obtained because the subject shifts its behavior to whichever alternative is associated with the higher local rate of reinforcement, with this adjustment continuing until equal local rates of reinforcement are obtained.

To see how such a process works, consider a concurrent VI 1-minute VI 3-minute schedule with behavior equally distributed to each alternative at the start of training. Assuming that all of the scheduled reinforcers are obtained, the initial local rate of reinforcement for the VI 1-minute alternative would be 120 reinforcers per hour, while that for the VI 3-minute schedule would be 40 reinforcers per hour. Behavior should thus shift to the VI 1-minute alternative. Now consider the same schedule but with 90% of the responding initially allocated to the VI 1-minute alternative. The local rate of reinforcement for the VI 1-minute alternative would be 66.7 reinforcers per hour, while that for the VI 3-minute alternative would be 200 reinforcers per hour. Behavior would then shift toward the VI 3-minute alternative. Equilibrium between the two types of shifts occurs only when the local rates of reinforcement are equal, which is uniquely defined by the point at which matching occurs.

Impressive evidence favoring melioration as the mechanism underlying molar matching has been provided by Vaughan (1981). He presented pigeons a modified concurrent VI VI schedule which differed from conventional schedules in two respects. First, the schedule values changed continuously as a function of the subject's behavior, as will be described later. Second, the

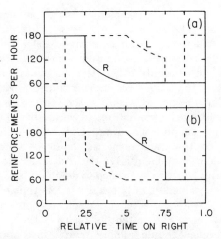

**Figure 3.12.** Programmed local rates of reinforcement on left (L) and right (R) alternatives as a function of the proportion of the total time working on the right. The two conditions, a and b, shown in the two panels, differed only over the range from 0.25 to 0.75. From "Melioration, Matching, and Maximization" by W. Vaughan, 1981, *Journal of the Experimental Analysis of Behavior, 36,* p. 143. Copyright 1981 by the Society for the Experimental Analysis of Behavior, Inc. Reprinted by permission.

two schedules advanced only when the subject was working on them, so that reinforcement for one alternative did not grow in probability with time spent on the other alternative. In addition, neither schedule advanced when the subject was not working, as defined by any period greater than two seconds without a response.

The critical feature of Vaughan's experiment was that the overall reinforcement rates were determined by the choice allocation. With relative time on the right key between 0 and 0.125, reinforcement was 180 reinforcers per hour for the right key and 60 reinforcers per hour for the left key. With relative time between 0.125 and 0.250, reinforcement rate for the two keys was equal, at 180 reinforcers per hour. For relative time allocation to the right key between 0.750 and 0.875, the two reinforcement rates were again equal, but at 60 reinforcers per hour, while from 0.875 to 1.0, reinforcement rate was 60 reinforcers per hour for the right key and 180 reinforcers per hour for the left key. The rates of reinforcement associated with the various time allocations are diagrammed in Figure 3.12.

All of the reinforcement rates just described were held constant for the two conditions of Vaughan's experiment. The two conditions

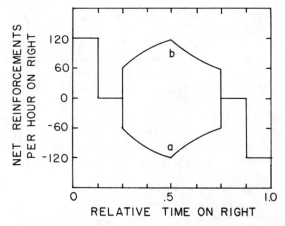

**Figure 3.13.** Local rate of reinforcement on the right minus local rate of reinforcement on the left as a function of relative time on the right alternative. Conditions $a$ and $b$ differ only in the range from 0.25 to 0.75. From "Melioration, Matching, and Maximization" by W. Vaughan, 1981, *Journal of the Experimental Analysis of Behavior, 36*, p. 147. Copyright 1981 by the Society for the Experimental Analysis of Behavior, Inc. Reprinted by permission.

differed with respect to the contingencies associated with time allocation between 0.25 and 0.75, illustrated in the mid-portion of Figure 3.12. For condition $a$, the left key paid off at a higher rate than the right key over that range, while for condition $b$, the reinforcement rates for the two keys were simply reversed.

The rationale of the experiment with respect to the concept of melioration is shown diagrammatically in Figure 3.13. Plotted there is the difference between the local reinforcement rates on the right key and the local reinforcement rates on the left key, as captured by equation 22:

$$R_D = \frac{R_R}{T_R} - \frac{R_L}{T_L} \qquad (22)$$

According to melioration, responding should shift toward the right key whenever $R_D$ is positive and toward the left key whenever it is negative, with equilibrium reached only when $R_D = 0$. Such equilibrium could thus occur only when the choice proportions fell in the range of either 0.125 to 0.250 or 0.750 to 0.875.

For condition $a$, all three subjects stabilized in the 0.125 to 0.250 range, which was also where the highest overall rate of reinforcement occurred. The critical test of melioration was then the effects of shifting to condition $b$. Given that the subjects were approximately matching at the

end of condition $a$ and that the highest possible rate of reinforcement during condition $b$ was still in the 0.125 to 0.250 range, there is no clear rationale for a shift in preference unless behavior was under the control of differences in local reinforcement probability. That is, if subjects sampled the range of 0.25 to 0.75, this produced a value of $R_D$ which was positive, so preferences should be shifted toward the right key. Such a shift would then continue until the value of $R_D$ again reached zero, which occurs in the new range of 0.75 to 0.875. It should be noted that the overall rate of reinforcement for that range was only 60 reinforcers per hour, which implies that control by local reinforcement rates could occur only at the expense of a substantial loss of reinforcement. In fact, all subjects did shift to the new range, indicating control by local reinforcement rates. Such control provides strong evidence against accounts based on molar optimization.

In general, predictions based on the concept of melioration are isomorphic with those based on matching, because matching must occur whenever the melioration process reaches equilibrium ($R_D = 0$). However, control by the local reinforcement rates may occur in conjunction with strong momentary deviations from matching. In Vaughan's (1981) procedure, for example, conditions $a$ and $b$ both produced equilibrium results consistent with matching, but the transition between the two conditions required the subject to leave a behavioral distribution consistent with matching (the 0.125 to 0.250 range) and pass through a range (0.25 to 0.75) with strong deviations from matching before a new equilibrium could be achieved. Vaughan's results are thus consistent with those discussed earlier (e.g., Herrnstein & Loveland, 1976) in showing that momentary matching is not the fundamental process underlying the molar matching phenomenon.

It is also important to recognize the relation between melioration and momentary maximizing. Both assume that the subject always chooses the response alternative with the higher local rate of reinforcement. The critical difference between them is not the decision rule that determines which response is chosen, but rather the method by which local reinforcement contingencies exert their effect. Whereas momentary maximizing assumes that the subject is sensitive to the local reinforcement probabilities updated at each moment in time, melioration relaxes the demands on the animal's cognitive abilities by assuming only that the reinforcement estimates involve some local, but unspecified, time frame. The two approaches are not incompatible, since melioration reduces to maximizing if the subject is sufficiently flexible in its response categories. That is, if the subject can learn any arbitrary response unit (e.g., a left peck after three right pecks, instead of just left pecks versus right pecks), the predictions of melioration and maximizing converge.

### Empirical Challenges to Melioration

Perhaps the most fundamental problem faced by melioration is the specification of the method by which local reinforcement rates are calculated. The controlling variable is assumed to be the difference in local reinforcement rates, as given by equation 22. Implicit in that expression is the assumption that all reinforcers contribute equally toward the determination of the local reinforcement rates, so reinforcers just after a changeover have no special status. In fact, however, there is strong evidence that such reinforcers have a disproportionate influence. For example, Shull, Spear, and Bryson (1981) presented pigeons a modified concurrent schedule in which one component was a VI schedule and the other was an FI. The modification was that the choice of the FI alternative resulted in a fixed-duration exposure to that component during which a fixed number of reinforcers were delivered. The rationale of the study was to hold constant the rate of reinforcement during the FI component while varying delay of reinforcement, as measured from the changeover response. The result was that preference for the FI component was strongly determined by the location of the reinforcers within the FI component, with the degree of preference predicted by the sum of the reciprocals of the delay intervals associated with each separate reinforcer. Thus, rather than the choice of the FI component being determined by its average rate of reinforcement, the controlling variable was instead the composite effects of the individual delays of reinforcement contingent on the changeover response.

Additional evidence of the importance of changeover contingencies is provided by the results of Pliskoff (1971), who presented pigeons a concurrent VI 3-min VI 3-min schedule with different COD values contingent on the two types of changeover responses. For example,

switching from schedule one to schedule two entailed a COD of three seconds, whereas a switch from schedule two to schedule one entailed a COD of nine seconds. The result was that the component followed by a long COD was preferred substantially more than was predicted by its relative rate of reinforcement. Presumably, this occurred because changeover responses leaving that component were reinforced only after a long delay, whereas changeovers going to that component were reinforced after a substantially shorter delay.

On the surface, at least, the above results appear to conflict with the concept of melioration. Whereas that notion relies on reinforcement rates calculated per unit of time the subject works on a schedule alternative, the effects of changeover contingencies suggest that such rates are actually an amalgam of individual effects of delayed reinforcers. This conflict may be only superficial, however, since there has been no attempt to relate the melioration process to the molecular structure of changeover behavior. One potential approach is to dissociate melioration into separate components, such that four different estimates of local reinforcement rate are entailed. Instead of simple comparison between the local reinforcement rates for component one versus component two, two separate comparisons would be required, one between the local rate of reinforcement for continuing to work on component one versus the rate for a changeover response (the inverse of delay) and the second between the local rate for continuing to work on component two versus the range for a changeover response to component one. As yet, however, such an approach has not been explored.

A different type of challenge to melioration comes from experiments that suggest that interactions in concurrent schedules do not depend upon competition for time allocation. According to melioration, responding shifts between schedules whenever the local reinforcement rate is higher for the alternative response, with the critical determinant of local reinforcement rates being the actual time allocated to each alternative. However, response rates in concurrent schedules may change independently of the time-allocation contingencies. One example of such effects is seen when a variable time (VT) schedule of free reinforcement is added concurrent with a simple VI. The result is that

VI-maintained responding decreases regularly as a function of the frequency of VT reinforcement, in much the same way as when frequency of reinforcement is varied by a second VI in a typical concurrent VI VI. Such effects pose a problem for melioration because there is no obvious reason why free reinforcement should decrease the time allocation to the VI alternative. No behavior is required for delivery of the free reinforcement, and, in fact, it often occurs when the subject is engaged in VI behavior (Rachlin & Baum, 1972). Moreover, the effects of free reinforcement occur regardless of whether the VI alternative is available at the time of VT reinforcement, as when VT reinforcers are presented during blackouts separating opportunities for VI responding (Nevin, 1974). Thus, there appears to be some general decremental effect of adding alternative reinforcement that has little to do with the behavior actually maintained by that alternative reinforcement.

One interpretation of such results is that they represent a different type of schedule interaction, and thus lie outside the explanatory domain of the melioration process. Such effects, in fact, occur in a variety of different procedures (e.g., multiple schedules) which melioration was not designed to explain, so that some independent effect of context of reinforcement seems plausible. The major difficulty with such a task is that the effects of context of reinforcement have been claimed to be similar regardless of the response contingency (cf. Catania, 1963b, 1966; Rachlin & Baum, 1969, 1972), so that they may also pertain to conventional concurrent procedures, which melioration was designed to explain. That is, even with the usual concurrent procedure, generalized effects of context of reinforcement may account for changes in response rate independent of the local reinforcement rates governing the time-allocation contingencies.

Evidence in favor of two separate effects of alternative reinforcement comes from a study by Duncan and Silberberg (1982), who trained pigeons on a constant VI 4-minute schedule with either a VI 1-minute, signaled VI 1-minute, VT 1-minute, or no alternative reinforcement presented concurrently. If the effects were due entirely to competition for time allocation, response rates to the VI 4-minute schedule should be lowest with the VI 1-minute as the alternative and similar in the latter three, since none of the other conditions maintained any significant

behavior that would provide competition for time allocation. On the other hand, if the effects were due entirely to the context of reinforcement, the response rate to the VI 4-minute schedule should be equal for the first three conditions and much higher in the case when the VI 4-minute schedule was presented alone. The result was an intermediate pattern of responding, as the lowest response rate did occur with the concurrent VI 4-minute VI 1-minute, but with a still sizable decrement for the other schedules of alternative reinforcement as well. The average response rate was about 35 responses per minute when the VI 4-minute schedule was presented alone, 14 responses per minute when the alternative schedule was VI 1-minute, and 18 and 21 responses per minute when the alternative schedule was signaled VI 1-minute and VT 1-minute, respectively. Thus, there was both a strong effect of alternative reinforcement independent of the response contingency and an additional decrement when the alternative reinforcement maintained substantial amounts of behavior.

The preceding discussion demonstrates that melioration, like the three other process theories previously discussed, still faces serious empirical obstacles. However, the data contrary to melioration show only that the theory is incomplete, not that it is violated in any fundamental way. For the alternative three accounts, on the other hand, there now exist data that seem to contradict their most basic assumptions. Moreover, melioration has the additional support of predicting matching as a necessary feature of choice procedures, whereas momentary maximizing and optimization imply that it is merely an incidental by-product. It may be that the form of melioration theory will change substantially as a function of meeting the empirical challenges that have been discussed, but at present it provides an account of the dynamic processes underlying matching that is most consistent with the available data.

## RESPONSE STRENGTH IN SIMPLE SCHEDULES

### Response Rate is a Hyperbolic Function of Reinforcement

Whatever the underlying dynamics, the matching law remains a robust empirical phenomenon showing that behavioral measures can be extremely sensitive to parameters of reinforcement. The issue for the present section is how such sensitivity is to be reconciled with the generally weak relation between reinforcement rate and absolute measures of response rate, as discussed earlier (see Figure 3.3). Does the difference in sensitivity reflect an intrinsic difference between relative versus absolute measures of behavior, or does the matching law provide some fundamental insight into the nature of the functions involving absolute measures of responding? To foreshadow the discussion, a strong case can be made that absolute response rates themselves should be viewed as the products of choice, in that the organism always is faced with a choice between the behavior measured by the experimenter and some other alternative.

Before the matching law can be applied to absolute response rates, it is necessary first to specify the relationship between absolute rates and parameters of reinforcement. Empirical functions relating response rate maintained by VI schedules to reinforcement frequency were shown earlier in Figure 3.3 and are characterized as monotonically increasing functions that approach asymptote at relatively low rates of reinforcement. Herrnstein (1970) demonstrated that the data shown in Figure 3.3 were described well by a hyperbolic function, as given by equation 23, in which $B$ refers to the rate of behavior, $R$ to rate of reinforcement, and $k$ and $R_e$ to empirically determined constants (the reasons for the particular designations will be discussed later):

$$B = k\,\frac{R}{R + R_e} \qquad (23)$$

Subsequently, de Villiers and Herrnstein (1976) demonstrated that the function accurately described a large variety of studies that determined the relation between absolute measures of response strength and various parameters of reinforcement. Included were studies using response rate, response latency, and running speed as dependent variables, and frequency, amount, and delay of reinforcement as the independent variables. Also included were different types of reinforcers, as well as different responses and species as subjects. In most cases more than 90 percent of the variance was accounted for, indi-

cating that equation 23 has wide generality as a description of asymptotic response strength.

An apparent exception to equation 23 are the results from simple ratio schedules. It is well known that responding ceases abruptly whenever the ratio requirement exceeds some critical value. Yet equation 23 describes a continuous function for rates of reinforcement down to zero. However, as shown by Pear (1975), abrupt cessation of responding is predicted by equation 23, when it is appreciated that reinforcement rates from ratio schedules are determined by the response rates. That is, the value of $R$ in equation 23 is the result of the response rate ($B$) divided by the ratio requirement ($n$). Substituting $B/n$ for $R$ in equation 23, the result is equation 24, which implies that nonzero response rates will occur only when the value of $k$ is greater than the product of the ratio requirement and the parameter $R_e$.

$$B = k - nR_e \qquad (24)$$

Since these two parameters are both constants, equation 24 entails that an increase in ratio requirement should produce a point at which responding halts.

A second problem presented by the results from simple ratio schedules, depicted in Figure 3.14, is that response rate decreases at very high rates of reinforcement (i.e., very small ratio values). In contrast, equation 23 entails that response rate continually increases until the asymptotic level. The significance of this empirical violation of equation 23 is difficult to determine, however, for several reasons. First, the range over which the inverse relation holds involves extremely high rates of reinforcement, so short-term satiation effects may play an important role. Such effects would obviate the application of equation 23, since it assumes that the value of the individual reinforcers is independent of reinforcement frequency. A related problem is that the topography of responding, which determines the asymptotic response rate and, thus, the value of $k$, may change systematically as a function of the high reinforcement rates involved. Since responding is frequently interrupted by access to the reinforcer (which typically is spatially separated from the response location), the result is that responding to the manipulation is interspersed with frequent approaches to the feeder site. This may include the nominal response into a response chain that

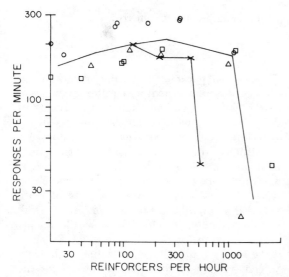

**Figure 3.14.** Performance on variable-ratio schedules as a function of obtained reinforcement rates. Unconnected points show individual subject data from Brandauer (1958), the line without symbols shows the average across subjects. Points marked $x$ show average data from Lieberman (1972). From "Optimization and the Matching Law as Accounts of Instrumental Behavior" by W.M. Baum, 1981, *Journal of the Experimental Analysis of Behavior, 36,* p. 396. Copyright 1981 by the Society for the Experimental Analysis of Behavior, Inc. Reprinted by permission.

acts as a functional unit. The frequency of the measured response would then be reduced because of the topographical change.

A third problem in interpretation is that responding maintained by ratio schedules always involves some amount of postreinforcement pausing (which typically increases the higher the value of the reinforcer because of discriminative effects), and it is unclear whether the time spent pausing should be included in the time base used to calculate the response rates. As noted by Priddle-Higson, Lowe, and Harzem (1976), when pause time is excluded, a monotonic relation between response rate and reinforcement frequency is obtained (but see Timberlake, 1977).

Thus, to the extent that ratio-maintained behavior does violate equation 23, a plausible case can be made that such violations result from artifacts of measurement rather than being fundamental. On the basis of present evidence, therefore, equation 23 appears to be a general description of behavior obtained in single-response procedures.

## Relation between the Hyperbolic Function and the Matching Law

But how is the hyperbolic function given by equation 23 to be interpreted? Herrnstein (1970, 1974) argued that the function follows directly from the matching law, given the plausible assumption that the subject has sources of reinforcement other than that programmed by the experimenter. The result is that the subject is confronted with a continuous choice between engaging in the specified response and whatever other behavior will produce the alternative reinforcement. Given that assumption, the matching law should apply, so that equation 1 can be written as

$$\frac{B_1}{B_1 + B_e} = \frac{R_1}{R_1 + R_e}$$

where $B_e$ refers to behavior other than that measured by the experimenter, and $R_e$ to the reinforcement obtained from that behavior. If the additional assumption is made that $B_1$ and $B_e$ exhaust the behaviors available and thus are a constant, the result is

$$\frac{B_1}{k} = \frac{R_1}{R_1 + R_e}$$

Rearranging terms then produces equation 23. The interpretation of its empirically determined constants is that $k$ refers to the total amount of behavior the subject can emit, and $R_e$ to the rate of reinforcement available from other sources.

The interpretation of equation 23 just given has profound implications for the concept of response strength. It assumes that the strength of an individual response can never be assessed in isolation, because any empirical assessment always reflects relative strength and is therefore dependent on the reinforcement available for alternative activities. It further assumes that the total amount of operant behavior is a constant and independent of the reinforcement frequency in the situation. (This is not to say that the value of $k$ will always be the same, since it will vary with the units of measurement.) Thus, the traditional concept of response strength (which has been assumed to be a property of an individual piece of behavior) is mistaken, since the effect of reinforcement is only to select, not to strengthen in its usual sense.

## Effects of Amount, Delay, and Drive

Although equation 23 deals only with the relation between response rate and reinforcement frequency, it can be extended to other parameters with relatively simple additions. For variations of reward magnitude, the expression becomes equation 25, in which the frequency of reinforcement is modified by a simple scale factor analogous to the bias term used in equation 5:

$$B = k \frac{aR}{aR + R_e} \qquad (25)$$

Dividing both the numerator and denominator by $a$ yields:

$$B = k \frac{R}{R + \dfrac{R_e}{a}}$$

which is equivalent to:

$$B = k \frac{R}{R + R'_e} \quad \text{where } R'_e = R_e/a$$

Thus, given two separate experiments in which frequency of reinforcement is similarly varied among several values, with the two experiments differing only in the amount of reinforcement delivered at each frequency, the difference between the two sets of results will be in terms of the value of $R_e$, despite the rate of reinforcement for alternative behavior presumably being equivalent for both experiments. The larger reward yields a smaller value of $R_e$ because $R_e$ is scaled in the units of the actually delivered reinforcement, and those units are larger with larger reward magnitudes.

An analogous variation of equation 23 allows the inclusion of delay of reinforcement, as given by equation 26, which assumes that the value of the contingent reinforcement is inversely related to its delay. Note that equation 26 assumes that there still is some minimum delay even when $D$ is nominally zero.

$$B = k \frac{\dfrac{R}{D}}{\dfrac{R}{D} + R_e} \quad (D > 0) \qquad (26)$$

Multiplying both the numerator and denominator by $D$, the result is

$$B = k \frac{R}{R + DR_e}$$

which is again equivalent to:

$$B = k \frac{R}{R + R'_e} \quad \text{with } R'_e = R_e D$$

Thus, given parametric manipulations of frequency of reinforcement with different delays of reward as independent factors, the effects of delay will also be captured by changes in $R_e$, with larger delays producing larger values.

Although the conceptualization of the effects of amount and delay in terms of changes in $R_e$ is a straightforward extension of the matching law, it is less clear how the effects of motivational manipulations (e.g., deprivation level) should be included. One effect should almost certainly be in terms of the value of $R_e$, since drive level should affect the value of the contingent reward relative to the reward for the unmeasured behavior. But whether such effects can be captured entirely by changes in $R_e$ is challenged by traditional treatments of motivation, which have almost always viewed drive level as a multiplier of the underlying associative strength. Drive level should then affect the asymptotic rate of behavior, which is defined by equation 23 in terms of $k$. Thus, increases in hunger level, or some analogous motivational manipulation, might be expected to increase the level of $k$ but decrease $R_e$.

Despite the historical tradition of considering drive as a general energizer. Herrnstein (1974) has argued that its effects must be contained only in terms of changes in $R_e$, because the constancy of $k$ is a necessary derivative of the matching law. That is, matching can be derived from the equations for absolute response rates only if $k$ for a given response is independent of both the incentive conditions associated with itself and of the incentive conditions associated with other responses in the situation. This can be seen by considering the most general form of the absolute rate equation, given by equation 27:

$$B_1 = k \frac{R_1}{\Sigma R} \qquad (27)$$

Or as applied to the absolute response rates in a two-alternative concurrent schedule:

$$B_1 = k \frac{R_1}{R_1 + R_2 + R_e} \qquad (28)$$

Given equation 28, the matching law can be derived only if the value of $k$ is constant for both response alternatives. That is, relative response rate is given by the relation between the expressions for the absolute response rates for each alternative. Thus,

$$\frac{B_1}{B_1 + B_2}$$

$$= \frac{k_1 \dfrac{R_1}{R_1 + R_2 + R_e}}{k_1 \dfrac{R_1}{R_1 + R_2 + R_e} + k_2 \dfrac{R_2}{R_1 + R_2 + R_e}}$$

which produces the matching law only if the $k$ values for the different responses cancel. Such constancy would not occur if $k$ were a function of the denominator of equation 28. And since that value presumably does change as a function of the different motivational levels (since drive level would affect the relative value of the contingent reinforcer versus competing activities), the implication is that $k$ itself should not change as a function of drive. Thus, if the relation between the absolute rate equation and the matching law is to be retained, motivational effects cannot be conceptualized in terms of a general energization.

## Tests of the Matching-Law Interpretation

A critical feature of Herrnstein's (1974) analysis is that $k$ must be independent of incentive variables. Thus, the only determinant of its value is the nature of the response requirements, which determines the units in which behavior is measured. Because the total behavior is, in principle, always constant, different values of $k$ simply reflect whether large or small response units are being counted. The determinants of the response unit may be complex, including not only the nature of the response manipulandum, but the schedule contingencies as well. For example, ratio schedules clearly produce higher values of $k$ than do interval schedules. Similarly, as discussed in the introduction, the differential reinforcement of longer IRTs inherent in interval schedules produces response units of longer duration than occur when the IRT contingency is removed (Platt, 1979). But regardless of such complexities, the critical implication is that, for a given situation, $k$ must be independent of incentive variables.

This implication can be tested by experiments that vary frequency (or some comparable parameter) of reinforcement under two or more values of some other incentive parameter. Equation 23 can then be fitted to each separate variation of frequency, and the values of $k$ and $R_e$ can be compared for each value of the orthogonal incentive parameter. Table 3.2 summarizes the existing studies in the literature with such variations that were described well by equation 23. The values of $k$ and $R_e$ that are shown were taken from the fits of equation 23 reported by deVilliers and Herrnstein (1976), with the exceptions of the studies by Bradshaw, Ruddle, and Szabadi (1981); Bradshaw, Szabadi, and Bevan (1978); Bradshaw, Szabadi, Ruddle, and Pears (1973); McDowell and Wood (1984); and Snyderman (1983a), who fit equation 23 to their own data. Studies above the dashed line varied either magnitude or quality of the reinforcer; those below it varied motivational level. If the matching law interpretation is correct, both manipulations should be reflected only in terms of changes in $R_e$, with $k$ remaining constant. Thus, higher values of the incentive, and higher drive levels, should produce smaller values of $R_e$.

Four studies shown in Table 3.2 varied drive level, with conflicting results. Three produced appropriate changes in the value of $R_e$, while $k$ remained approximately constant. However, the remaining study (Snyderman, 1983) produced a significantly higher value of $k$ with greater food deprivation, with little change in $R_e$. The reason for the discrepancy is uncertain, although Snyderman did use a different response type (nose-pressing).

A similar pattern of variability occurred for the studies that varied quality or magnitude. Four of the nine studies produced an approximately constant value of $k$ with decreases in $R_e$ with higher incentive values. But for five studies the value of $k$ did not remain constant, but increased along with the value of the reinforcer. And for the most systematic of these studies (Bradshaw et al., 1978; McDowell & Wood, 1984), such increases were highly significant statistically. Thus, under at least some circumstance, the value of $k$ does not appear to be independent of incentive variation.

The interpretation of the results shown in Table 3.2 relies heavily on the statistical properties of the curve-fitting procedures used to

**Table 3.2. Least-square Fits of Equation 23 for Various Studies Involving Manipulations of Two Different Incentive Variables. (Notes at bottom provide details of study.)**

| *Gutman (1954)*[a] | $k$ | $R_e$ | *Keesey (1964)*[f] | $k$ | $R_e$ |
|---|---|---|---|---|---|
| Glucose | 16.1 | 11.0 | 1.5 ma | 14.9 | .10 |
| Sucrose | 15.6 | 7.1 | 3.0 ma | 21.0 | .15 |
| *Kraeling (1961)*[b] | | | *Keesey (1962)*[g] | | |
| 5 cc | 89.4 | 2.4 | Duration | 15.1 | * |
| 25 cc | 87.9 | 2.2 | Intensity | 20.4 | * |
| 125 cc | 88.7 | 1.4 | Frequency | 25.0 | * |
| *Schrier (1965)*[c] | | | *Keesey & Kling (1961)*[h] | | |
| .33 cc | 88.0 | 16.1 | Peas | 118.6 | * |
| .83 cc | 67.2 | 6.3 | Hemp | 67.0 | * |
| *Bradshaw, Szabadi, & Bevan (1978)*[d] | | | *McDowell & Wood (1984)*[i] Group 1 | | |
| .00 M | 11.2 | 31.6 | .25 ¢ | 35.0 | * |
| .05 M | 18.6 | 17.9 | 1 ¢ | 49.0 | * |
| .32 M | 23.0 | 8.1 | 35 ¢ | 78.3 | * |
| *Bradshaw, Ruddle, & Szabadi (1981)*[e] | | | Group 2 | | |
| .02 cc | 127.6 | 310.6 | 1 ¢ | 96.4 | * |
| .05 cc | 132.2 | 136.6 | 4 ¢ | 100.3 | * |
| .10 cc | 103.7 | 70.6 | 12 ¢ | 108.4 | * |
| *Logan (1960-Expt. 55D)*[j] | | | *Conrad & Sidman (1956)*[k] | | |
| Low Drive | 64.9 | .075 | 48 hrs. deprived | 16.3 | 3.7 |
| High Drive | 64.9 | .016 | 72 hrs. | 17.6 | 1.7 |
| *Snyderman (1983)*[l] | | | *Bradshaw, Szabadi, Ruddle, & Pears (1983)*[m] | | |
| 90% weight | 45.7 | .53 | 90% weight | 93.5 | 50.5 |
| 70% weight | 64.7 | .52 | 80% weight | 96.5 | 50.5 |

[a] Rats were trained to lever press on a VI 1-min schedule for seven different concentrations of sucrose and glucose. Results are the means of eight subjects, each exposed to each value of both reinforcers.

[b] Rats were trained to run in a straight alley for different concentrations of sucrose, with each concentration run at three different magnitudes. Independent groups of rats were trained for each concentration and magnitude.

[c] Monkeys were trained to lever press for five different concentrations of sucrose, with each concentration run with two different magnitudes. Results are the means of six subjects, each exposed to each value of both magnitudes.

[d] Rats were trained to lever press on different VI schedules, with each VI value run on each of three concentrations of sucrose (.00 = water). Results are the means of three subjects, each exposed to each value of all three concentrations.

[e] Rats were trained to lever press on six different VI schedules, with sucrose as the reinforcer. Each VI value was run with three different magnitudes. Results are the means of three subjects, each exposed to all reinforcement conditions.

[f] Rats were trained to lever press on a VI schedule for different durations of brain stimulation at two different intensities. Results are means of 10 subjects, each exposed to all values of each parameter.

[g] Rats were trained to lever press on a VI schedule for six different durations, six different intensities, and six different pulse frequencies. Results are the means of 10 subjects, each exposed to all values of both parameters. Note that $R_e$ is not included because it would necessarily be in different units, which prevents comparison across the three different types of stimulation.

[h] Pigeons were trained to keypeck on a VI schedule for different numbers of peas (1–4) and different numbers of hemp seed (2–8). Different groups of subjects were trained with peas and hemp, with each group receiving each of the different numbers. Note that $R_e$ is not included because it would be in different units for peas versus hemp, thus preventing their comparison.

[i] Humans were trained to lever press on different VI schedules for money, with reward levels ranging from 0.25 to 35 ¢. Results are means of the fitted values for two separate groups of subjects ($N$ = 4 and 3, respectively) who received different ranges of reward magnitude. Some reward values are omitted because they were not used with all subjects in a group. Values of $R_e$ were not reported.

[j] Rats were trained in a straight alley on five different delays of reinforcement. Different groups of rats were run at each delay value, with each group run at both high and low drive levels.

[k] Monkeys were trained to lever press on a VI schedule for five different concentrations of sucrose at two drive levels. Results are the means of four subjects, each exposed to all concentrations at both drive levels.

[l] Rats were trained to nose press on six different VI values to obtain food pellets, under two different percentages of their free-feeding body weights. Results are the fits to the aggregates of five subjects, each exposed to all values of each parameter.

[m] Rats were trained to lever press to obtain a sucrose solution under two different percentages of free-feeding body weight. Results are in terms of the mean parameter values of three subjects, each exposed to all values of each parameter.

obtain the parameter estimates. In addition, the nature of extensive parametric investigations requires long periods of training, which may introduce the passage of time as an experimental variable in its own right. For example, the efficiency of responding (and hence the value of $k$) may vary simply because of age changes. Because of such vagaries, more direct tests of the interpretation of the parameters of equation 23 are highly desirable.

A direct test of the interpretation of $R_e$ has been provided by Bradshaw (1977). Rats were trained on a series of different VI values, first with no other response available, and then with the same series of VI values in the presence of a second schedule that was held constant at VI 3 minutes. The rationale of the design was that the description of the two situations in terms of equation 23 should differ only with respect to the total reinforcement in the situation (the denominator of equation 27). Thus, the value of $k$ should remain constant, while the two estimates of $R_e$ should differ by 20 reinforcers per hour (the rate of reinforcement delivered by the VI 3-minute schedule). As predicted, the value of $k$ was approximately constant, with a mean value of 49.9 in the presence of the second schedule and 46.6 in its absence. However, the difference in the value of $R_e$ was substantially larger than predicted, as the mean value was 33.1 without the second response available, but 118.3 when it was added. Thus, changes in the value of $R_e$ seem to reflect more than simply the amount of alternative reinforcement that was added to the situation.

Direct tests of the interpretation of $k$ are more difficult, because it is not clear how one can measure the total amount of behavior without a prior determination of the units of measurement. One approach is to assess the total amount of general activity, although even here it is not clear whether greater activity corresponds to greater amounts of behavior. For example, given that reinforcement is contingent on such behavior, standing quietly may reflect just as much response strength as high levels of wing flapping. In fact, however, the total amount of general activity does appear to be strongly related to the rate of reinforcement. Killeen (1975) and Killeen, Hanson, and Osborne (1978) presented pigeons different frequencies of response-independent food, while measuring the number of displacements of the floor panel, which was broken into a large number of different sections. The result was that activity level grew rapidly as a function of reinforcement rate, and Killeen et al. (1978) argued convincingly that the hypothetical construct, arousal, was a linear function of reinforcement frequency. Moreover, the effects of reinforcement rate on the degree of arousal was similar even when the reinforcement was contingent on keypecking. Thus, reinforcement seems to affect not only the behavior on which it is contingent, but also the total quantity of behavior in the situation. The implication is that the total amount of behavior is not independent of reinforcement frequency and, thus, is not constant.

A variety of other data suggest that the estimated value of $k$ is not independent of incentive variables. For example, fits of equation 23 to response rates generated by different FI schedules (Schneider, 1969) produce $k$ values 1.5 to 2 times higher than those usually obtained with VI schedules. A similar, and probably related, effect occurs with multiple schedules (to be discussed in the next section) in which VI schedules are alternated with periods of extinction; the asymptotic response rates obtained with VI schedules in isolation are substantially lower than when the same schedule is alternated with periods of extinction. The apparent implication is that the value of $k$ in the former case cannot be taken to represent the total behavior that is possible. Such effects may perhaps be ascribed to changes in the response unit (see discussion of Platt, 1979, in the introduction), but given that interval schedules are used in both cases, such an alternative interpretation seems implausible.

## Alternative Derivations of the Hyperbolic Function

Partly because of the evidence contrary to the matching-law interpretation. several other conceptual rationales for the hyperbolic relation between response rate and reinforcement rate have been proposed. One of the earliest alternatives was provided by Catania (1973), who argued that responding maintained by simple VI schedules was controlled by two separate effects: an excitatory effect, described by equation 29, by which response strength is directly proportional to the rate of reinforcement.

$$B_E = kR \qquad (29)$$

and an inhibitory effect, described by equation 30, whereby all behavior in the situation is suppressed in a degree monotonically related to the delivered rate of reinforcement.

$$b_I = \frac{1}{1 + \dfrac{R}{C}} \qquad (30)$$

Note that $k$ of equation 28 is simply a scale parameter, whereas $C$ in equation 30 is a constant of inhibition. Catania then assumed that the two effects interacted multiplicatively to determine the actual response rate, with equation 31 as the result.

$$B = kC \frac{R}{R + C} \qquad (31)$$

Note that the only difference between equations 23 and 31 is that $k$ of equation 23 is replaced by $kC$ in equation 31. Since $k$ and $C$ are both constants, it is possible to replace their product by a new constant, $k'$, which makes the two expressions identical. It should be noted, however, that Catania's derivation of equation 23 implies that the estimates of $k$ and $R_e$ should be correlated, whereas the derivation in terms of the matching law entails that they are independent.

The critical assumption underlying Catania's analysis is that reinforcement produces a generalized inhibition of responding, which applied both to the behavior upon which the reinforcement is contingent and all other behavior in the situation. In support of this assumption is the finding, discussed earlier in the section on melioration, that VI response rates are regularly decreased by additional reinforcement in the situation, even when that additional reinforcement is delivered freely or according to a signaled VI. Assuming that significant amounts of behavior are not maintained by that reinforcement, and thus competition for time allocation is not a significant factor, the implication is that such effects may be characterized as a generalized inhibition. But it also should be noted that Catania's derivation of equation 23 depends critically upon the particular function chosen for the growth of inhibition (equation 30), and there is no independent evidence for that function. Nor is it clear whether the inhibition-by-reinforcement effect is to be considered a primordial process, or whether it can be reduced to some more fundamental basis.

A theoretically simpler derivation of the hyperbolic function has been advanced by Staddon (1977). Like Catania (1973), he assumed that response strength is directly proportional to reinforcement rate (equation 29). However, given that responding requires time, the measured response rate will be reduced because of the limitations on time allocation. Thus, the actual time available for responding ($t_{av}$) is the total time minus the number of responses multiplied by the average response duration ($d$). The expression for available time is thus given by equation 32, which assumes that the time measures have been normalized with respect to the total session time, which is taken to be of unit length.

$$t_{av} = 1 - dB \qquad (32)$$

And since the total number of responses emitted in that unit time will be the strength of behavior (equation 29) multiplied by the time available for responding to occur (equation 32), equation 33 is derived by multiplying the right side of equation 29 by the right side of equation 32.

$$B = \frac{\left(\dfrac{1}{d}\right) R}{R + \left(\dfrac{1}{dk}\right)} \qquad (33)$$

The expressions, $1/d$ and $1/(dk)$ are both constants, so equation 33 is formally equivalent to equation 23. Thus, with the simplest possible assumptions about the function for response strength and the limitations on time allocation for translating that strength into behavioral measures, the hyperbolic function is the result.

Still another derivation of equation 23, based on a linear systems analysis, has been developed by McDowell and Kessel (1979) and elaborated by McDowell (1980) and McDowell, Bass, and Kessel (1983). They argued that organisms can be regarded as simple linear filters of the input reinforcement schedules and employed the Laplace method to generate a transfer function that predicts output. The input function was the discrete distribution of reinforcers through time with the parameters of reinforcer value and duration, while the output function was the distribution of responses in time constrained by the parameters of response duration and intensity. The mathematics underlying the development of the transfer function is too advanced to be considered here, but the result is a relation between response rate and reinforcement that is formally equivalent to equation 23. As with the alternative derivations of the equation just described, their derivation does not depend upon choice between operant and competing behavior as the underlying process, with the result that the parameters of the hyperbolic function have different (and complex) interpretations.

Although there are still other derivations of equation 23 (see Killeen, 1982a; Staddon, 1977), the alternatives that have been considered suffice to show that several different approaches to the underlying basis of response strength are compatible with the empirically determined function. The issue, therefore, is whether there is any empirical basis for separating the alternatives. One approach is whether the various interpretations of the $k$ and $R_e$ parameters implied by the various derivations of equation 23 are supported by the manner in which their estimates change due to experimental manipulations. As noted above, the matching interpretation implies that $k$ should be independent of variations in incentive, while the value of $R_e$ should be decreased by larger amounts of reward and increased by longer delays. Although most of the alternative derivations have not addressed this issue, both Killeen (1982a) and McDowell (1980) have defined several predictions that differentiate their derivations from the matching interpretation. For example, McDowell has noted that the $k$ parameter should be increased by larger amounts of reinforcement, rather than unchanged, and this prediction is supported by several studies (see Table 3.2, especially Bradshaw et al. 1978, and McDowell & Wood, 1984). It is thus possible that further evidence will uniquely support one of the various derivations over the others.

The only conclusion permitted by the available evidence is that equation 23, while providing an excellent description of various measures of response strength in single-response situations, is susceptible to several different interpretations, the merits of which have not yet been distinguished empirically. Resolution of this issue is perhaps the most important of all of those that we have considered, since the alternative approaches have fundamentally different implications for the most basic conceptions of conditioning. Whereas all of the alternative interpretations of equation 23 are based on the traditional assumption that the strength of individual responses can be specified independently of other possible behaviors, the matching law interpretation assumes that all behavior involves choice, so that the assessment of the strength of a single response in isolation is illusory. Thus, response rates, latencies, and so forth, only reflect the value of the reinforcement contingent on the particular response *relative* to the value of the alternative activities. Given the equivocal outcome of the empirical tests that have been discussed, it is now uncertain whether this bold assertion can be sustained. At present, however, it provides an organizational framework that encompasses a large variety of different findings and several clear directions by which the general framework can be tested. The outcome of such tests will determine our most basic issue—how response strength should be conceptualized.

## MULTIPLE SCHEDULES

### Relative Rate of Reinforcement as the Controlling Variable

Intermediate between simple schedules involving a single response and concurrent schedules, with the simultaneous availability of two or more responses, are multiple schedules, in which two different responses are available successively. For example, a pigeon is presented three-minute periods with a red key correlated with a VI 3-min schedule alternated with three-minute periods with a green key correlated with a VI 1-min schedule. A large amount of research with such schedules has shown that relative rate of reinforcement is a major influence on response rate (Williams, 1983a). That is, rate of responding maintained by a constant reinforcement schedule during one component varies inversely with the rate of reinforcement available in the alternative component. Although some investigators (cf. Schwartz & Gamzu, 1977) have suggested that these effects are due to biological factors independent of the processes of operant conditioning (e.g., because contrast occurs more readily with pigeons than with rats), more recent evidence (Williams, 1983a) supports the view that relative rate of reinforce-

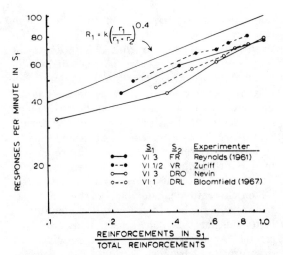

**Figure 3.15.** Results from several contrast experiments in which the schedule in the altered component was different. The response rates shown are from the constant VI components. The relative frequency of reinforcement varied as a consequence of variations in the schedule value in the alternated component. The results were taken from Zuriff (1970), Bloomfield (1967), Reynolds (1961), and Nevin (1968). Note that both the abscissa and ordinate are in logarithmic units. From "Another Look at Contrast in Multiple Schedules" by B.A. Williams, 1983, *Journal of the Experimental Analysis of Behavior, 39*, pp. 347, 373. Copyright 1983 by the Society for the Experimental Analysis of Behavior, Inc. Reprinted by permission.

ment is a fundamental variable regardless of the particular experimental preparations. Thus, the interactions seen in multiple schedules (usually referred to as behavioral contrast) are similar to those in concurrent schedules, despite the two response alternatives never being simultaneously available.

An important feature of contrast effects is that they do not depend upon the schedule with which the alternative reinforcement is presented. Shown in Figure 3.15 are results from several studies in which a constant VI schedule (which differed across studies) was alternated with a variety of other schedules in which the rate of reinforcement was varied. As can be seen, the response rate maintained by the constant schedule increased as its reinforcement constituted a greater percentage of the total reinforcement in the situation. Moreover, the function governing that increase was similar regardless of whether the alternative component involved high rates of responding (FR and VR) or very low rates (DRL and DRO).

A major determinant of interactions in multiple schedules is the period with which the components of the multiple schedule alternate. With very long component durations, the effect of reinforcement rate in the alternative component is minimal and then progressively increases as component duration is shortened. With very short periods of alternation (5 to 10 seconds), the relative rates of responding in the two components may match their relative rates of reinforcement (Shimp & Wheatley, 1971). This suggests that interactions in short-component multiple schedules are functionally similar to those already described for concurrent schedules.

## Multiple Schedules and the Matching Law

### Interactions at a Distance

One method of relating multiple and concurrent schedules was proposed by Herrnstein (1970), who adapted the function for absolute response rates in concurrent schedules (equation 28) to multiple schedules. Arguing that the major difference between multiple and concurrent schedules is that the alternative reinforcement has less impact in a multiple schedule because it is temporally removed, he suggested that equation 28 could be modified by providing a simple weighting factor for the alternative reinforcement, as shown in equation 34.

$$B_1 = k \frac{R_1}{R_1 + mR_2 + R_e} \qquad (34)$$

The parameter $m$ allows the response-rate function to be like that for simple schedules when the effects of the alternative reinforcement are minimal, and like a concurrent schedule when maximally strong ($m = 1.0$). Thus, those variables that increase the size of contrast effects (e.g., component duration) exert their influence by increasing the value of $m$, or in other words, the contribution of the alternative schedule to the total context of reinforcement.

Relative response rates can be derived from equation 34 by writing a corresponding expression for both components of the multiple schedule. Thus,

$$\frac{B_1}{B_2} = \frac{\dfrac{kR_1}{R_1 + mR_2 + R_e}}{\dfrac{kR_2}{R_2 + mR_1 + R_e}} \qquad (35)$$

Equation 35 makes explicit that the approximation of matching of relative response rates to relative reinforcement rates $(R_1/R_2)$ in a multiple schedule is a direct function of the similarity between the context of reinforcement for the two components. The approximation to matching will be increased when either $m$ increases or the value of $R_e$ is large relative to $R_1$ and $R_2$. Support for the first of these predictions has already been noted with respect to the effects of component duration. Support for the second prediction comes from several studies (McLean & White, 1983; Nevin, 1974) in which the rate of additional reinforcement was varied while keeping constant the reinforcement rates during the components of the multiple schedules themselves (e.g., by presenting the extra reinforcement during blackouts separating the components). Similar support comes from studies of food deprivation (Herrnstein & Loveland, 1974) in which the approximation to matching increases the less the degree of hunger, presumably because the values of $R_1$ and $R_2$ are decreased relative to $R_e$.

Despite the intuitive appeal of Herrnstein's (1970) analysis and the substantial evidence in its favor, there are now strong empirical reasons for doubting its validity. The most fundamental is that equation 34 predicts that absolute response rates in a multiple schedule never can be higher than those in a simple VI schedule with the same rate of reinforcement. This is true because equation 34 becomes identical to the expression for absolute rates in a simple schedule (equation 23) when the value of $R_2$ goes to zero. In fact, however, response rates in a multiple VI EXT schedule are regularly higher than in a simple VI schedule, as such a comparison is commonly used to demonstrate behavioral contrast. A related problem is that equation 34 predicts that absolute response rates should decrease with shorter components (since $m$ increases) for both components of the schedule, whereas, in fact, the response rate in the component with the higher reinforcement rate typically increases (cf. de Villiers, 1977; Williams, 1980). Thus, while Herrnstein's analysis provides an excellent account of the changes in relative response rates in a multiple schedule, changes in absolute response rates seem to require a different explanation.

### Behavioral Competion Theory

An alternative approach to behavioral contrast,

based directly on matching in concurrent schedules, has been proposed by Staddon (1982) and McLean and White (1983). They argue that behavior during either component of a multiple schedule can be understood in terms of the matching law and that the measured response, $B_1$, and the alternative behavior that is unmeasured, $B_e$, constitute the total behavior. Thus, equation 23, rewritten here for convenience, applies to multiple schedules as well.

$$B_1 = k \frac{R_1}{R_1 + R_e}$$

For reinforcement in the alternative component to have an effect, therefore, it must be mediated by changes in the value of the alternative reinforcement, $R_e$. A mechanism for such mediation has been suggested by Staddon (1982) in terms of transitory satiation and deprivation effects with respect to the activities generating $R_e$. Figure 3.16 depicts how such changes may occur for a two-component multiple schedule in which a component with a high reinforcement rate alternates with one that supplies a lower rate of reinforcement. During the rich component, the high value of the scheduled reinforcement

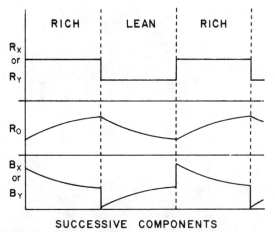

**Figure 3.16.** Depiction of the hypothetical values of the operant reinforcement (top) and reinforcement for "other" behavior (middle) and the hypothetical levels of operant behavior (bottom) that result from their competition. The operant schedules are assumed to be constant in value within a component but differ between components. The value of the other behavior is a function of the amount of momentary satiation/deprivation, which is a function of the competition from the operant response. Time is represented along the abscissa. Adapted from Staddon (1982).

causes its behavior to occur at the expense of $B_e$, producing a gradual deprivation of $R_e$ and, thus, an increase in its value (shown in the middle panel). As a result, the value of $R_e$ is at its maximum at the beginning of the lean component, so $B_e$ provides maximal competition with the operant response at that time. Because of the higher frequency of $B_e$ during the lean component (since $R_2$ provides weaker competition because of its lower reinforcement rate); its value gradually diminishes due to temporary satiation. The value of $R_e$, and the response competition it engenders, is at its minimum at the start, once again, of the rich component. And since the actually measured response rate in the two components reflects the outcome of the competition between $B_e$ and the operant response, the pattern of response shown

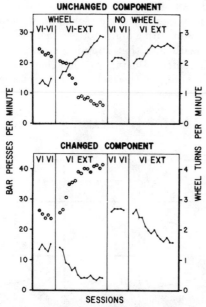

**Figure 3.17.** Response rates from the contrast experiment of Hinson & Staddon (1978). The top portion shows both lever pressing (the operant response) and wheel turning (unfilled circles) in the unchanged VI component. The bottom portion shows the corresponding results during the component that was changed from VI to EXT. The left side of each panel shows the results when the running wheel was available; the right portion shows the results when the wheel was removed. From "Behavioral Competition: A Mechanism for Schedule Interactions" by J. Hinson and J.E.R. Staddon, 1978, *Science, 202*, p. 433. Copyright 1978 by the AAAS. Reprinted by permission.

in the bottom of Figure 3.16 is the predicted outcome.

Evidence in favor of the behavioral competition hypothesis has been provided by Hinson and Staddon (1978), who studied the occurrence of contrast with rats as subjects as a function of the availability of a running wheel in the experimental chamber (see Henton & Iversen, 1978, for a similar experiment). Their assumption was that the opportunity to run entailed a high value of $R_e$, so that contrast should be more likely when the running wheel was available. One group of rats was trained to lever press on a multiple VI schedule and then shifted to a multiple VI EXT with the wheel continuously present; a second group received the same sequence of training but with the wheel locked. As shown in Figure 3.17, the major result was that rats with the running wheel exhibited large, reliable contrast effects, while those without the running wheel showed smaller, unreliable effects. Most importantly, the occurrence of contrast in the former group was paralleled by a shift in the location of the running behavior. During the multiple VI VI, equal amounts of running occurred in both components of the schedule, but after the shift to multiple VI EXT, virtually all of the running shifted to the EXT component. Within the unchanged VI, lever pressing was no longer reduced by competition from running, so that the rate increase that is seen can be viewed as due to an increase in time allocation to the operant behavior. However, this conclusion must be tempered by the fact that wheel availability also substantially increased the degree of discrimination. Poor discrimination is a frequent source of the failure to find contrast, so the differences in discrimination seen in Figure 3.17 may account for the differences in contrast independent of any affect of response competition, per se.

Despite the evidence shown in Figure 3.17 behavioral competition models of contrast are challenged by a fundamental problem. The notion of behavioral competition pits the nominal response against $B_e$, hence contrast should depend upon the frequency of responding in the altered component, not the frequency of reinforcement. But as shown earlier in Figure 3.15, the actual behavior in the altered component seems largely irrelevant, as the controlling variable is the relative rate of reinforcement. This is exemplified best when a multiple VI VT schedule, or a multiple VI signaled VI schedule, is changed to multiple VI EXT. Since there is minimal operant behavior required either by the VT or the signaled VI schedule, this means there should be little competition from $B_e$ during the baseline. The change to EXT should, therefore, cause little change in the frequency of $B_e$ during the altered component, and little change should occur in the unaltered component as well. Much smaller contrast effects would be expected. To the contrary, however, interactions with such schedules appear basically similar to those seen when multiple VI VI is changed to multiple VI EXT (Halliday & Boakes, 1974; Williams, 1980). The degree of contrast does not vary with manipulations that should affect the degree of response competition. The implication is that choice, conceptualized as behavioral competition, cannot explain the interactions seen in multiple schedules; hence, the relation between such interactions and matching in concurrent schedules remains uncertain.

## General Effects of the Context of Reinforcement

If the matching framework cannot account for contrast effects in multiple schedules, what are the alternative explanations? One simple notion that may help is the supposition that response rate is inversely related to the *context of reinforcement* in which it occurs. Recall from the discussion of concurrent schedules, that the rate of responding maintained by a constant VI schedule is inversely related to the frequency (or amount) of alternative reinforcement in the same situation, independent of whether the additional reinforcement generates any operant behavior of its own. Response rate is decreased either when additional reinforcement is delivered independently of responding or on a signaled VI schedule (cf. Duncan & Silberberg, 1982; Rachlin & Baum, 1969, 1972). Such procedures differ from multiple schedules only in that the alternative reinforcement comes while the operant response is immediately available; on multiple schedules the alternative reinforcement comes at a different time and in the presence of a different stimulus. This distinction between procedures lies on a continuum, however, as the effects of alternative reinforcement in a multiple schedule increase with smaller temporal separations (i.e., contrast is larger with

short component durations). The issue becomes, therefore, how to capture this continuum.

Equation 34, proposed by Herrnstein (1970), provides one method by which context of reinforcement can be conceptualized, but, as already discussed, it is contradicted by several empirical results. However, a simple change in that expression, such that the denominator represents the weighted average rate of reinforcement in the situation rather than the sum of such rates, takes account of most of the contrary findings. Equation 36 provides such a modification:

$$B_1 = k \frac{R_1}{\dfrac{R_1 + mR_2}{1 + m} + R_e} \tag{36}$$

To see how equation 36 captures the average rate of reinforcement, it is helpful to consider the effects of different values of $m$. If $m$ equals 1.0, reinforcement in both components is weighted equally in determining the average, so that the first term of the denominator simply represents the average rate of reinforcement in a session. But all reinforcement cannot be weighted equally, given the decreasing magnitude of contrast effects when component duration is increased. With longer component durations $m$ must be less than 1.0, so the rate of reinforcement in the alternative component has a diminishing role in determining the average.

To see the advantages of this modification, consider the two criticisms of equation 34 noted above. For the case in which a simple VI is changed to multiple VI EXT, equation 36 predicts contrast because the denominator of the expression decreases when the EXT component is added. For the case of decreasing component duration, when $m$ is increased, the prediction is more complicated because it depends on the relative value of the two components. Whereas equation 34 implies that response rate should always decrease when $m$ increases, equation 36 predicts an increase in rate when $R_1$ is greater than $R_2$ and a decrease in rate when $R_1$ is less than $R_2$. Both predictions are confirmed by existing data (de Villiers, 1977).

A major obstacle faced by equation 36 is that the context of reinforcement cannot be captured simply in terms of the average rate of reinforcement in the situation. The reason is that context of reinforcement, at least in multiple schedules, is temporally asymmetric in its effects. At least

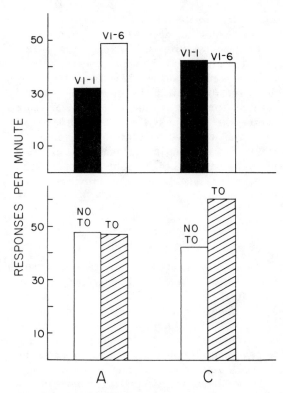

**Figure 3.18.** Results of a three-component multiple schedule in which the three components recycled continuously (Williams, 1981, Experiment 2). The top portion shows the response rates during components A and C, which were held constant at VI 3-min, when the reinforcement schedule in component B was changed from VI 1 min to VI 6 min. The bottom portion shows the response rates during Components A and C when a TO was added after the completion of each complete cycle (after component C) while holding all other schedules constant.

when the stimuli associated with the components of the multiple schedule are highly dissimilar, the alternative reinforcement that precedes some target component produces relatively small contrast effects, whereas alternative reinforcement that occurs subsequent to the target behavior produces strong contrast. Such effects are exemplified in Figure 3.18, which depicts the mean results of four subjects trained on a continuously recycling three-component schedule (ABCABC, etc.) in which components A and C were always associated with identical VI 3-minute schedules (Williams, 1981). The top pair of comparisons shows the results when the schedule for the middle com-

ponent (B) was changed from VI 1 minute to VI 6 minutes. The expected increase in response rate in the constant components (contrast) then occurred only during component A, as response rates during component C remained largely unaffected. The bottom pair of comparisons shows the results when a Time-Out (TO) period was added to each completed cycle (ABC, TO, ABC, TO) while holding all of the schedules constant. There the increase in response rate occurred only during component C, while responding during component A remained approximately constant. In both cases the major effect of changing the relative rate of reinforcement was due to variations in the *following* schedule. Comparable results have been obtained in several other studies (Farley, 1980a; Williams, 1976, 1979).

Given the asymmetry seen in Figure 3.18, some modification of equation 36 is clearly needed. Equation 37 provides one possibility, as it allows the effective context of reinforcement to be a weighted average of the prevailing component ($n$), the following component ($n + 1$), and the preceding component ($n - 1$), with different weights possible for all three sources of reinforcement:

$$B_n = k \frac{R_n}{\dfrac{R_n + pR_{n-1} + fR_{n+1}}{1 + p + f} + R_e} \quad (37)$$

In the case when the preceding and following schedules are the same (when two-component schedules are used), the effects of $p$ and $f$ are presumably additive and the expression becomes equivalent to equation 36. Equation 37 was tested by Williams and Wixted (1986), who varied reinforcement rates in each component of a three-component multiple schedule. The results were that equation 37 accounted for 90–95% of the variance in response rates and that the value of $f$ was substantially larger than the value of $p$, consistent with previous findings that schedule interactions are temporally assymetric.

The asymmetrical effects of the context of reinforcement suggest the possibility of a more molecular account, but previous attempts to discover it have been unsuccessful (Williams, 1979, Experiments 2 through 4). Whatever the outcome of future investigations, it is noteworthy that context effects with multiple schedules are similar to those reported with other, quite different conditioning procedures. For example, a recent account of autoshaping (Gibbon, 1981; Gibbon & Balsam, 1981) assumes that the rate of conditioning to a CS is controlled by the reinforcement rate during the CS relative to the average rate in the situation. Similarly, Fantino's delay-reduction theory of conditioned reinforcement (cf. Fantino, 1977; see discussion in section on conditioned reinforcement) assumes that the effectiveness of a stimulus as a conditioned reinforcer is a function of its average time to reinforcement, compared to the average interreinforcement time (the inverse of rate) in the situation as a whole. The implication is that reinforcement is inherently relativistic in its effects, so that any account of the determinants of response strength must include the context of reinforcement as a major component.

## AVERSIVE CONTROL

### Negative Reinforcement: Functional Relations

All of the discussion heretofore has concerned conditioning situations in which hedonically positive events have been used to reward behavior. We turn now to situations using aversive events, events which animals typically respond vigorously to reduce, eliminate, or avoid. The reason for separate consideration is that aversive conditioning has been viewed, at least historically, as requiring different explanatory principles. Whereas the study of positive reinforcement has seemed a relatively straightforward task of relating the parameters of the response-reinforcer relation to some measure of behavioral strength, accounts of aversive control have appealed to internal states (i.e., fear, anxiety, etc.), which have been assumed in order to provide motivational impetus for the behavior. Such assumptions are too intermeshed with the historical development of behaviorism to be considered in detail here (see Herrnstein, 1969), but, in general, they were advanced to account for avoidance conditioning in which the reinforcement seemed, paradoxically, to be a future aversive event that failed to materialize. The internal motivational machinery was designed to circumvent the paradox. Instead of being reinforced by an undelivered electric shock, an avoiding subject was presumably reinforced by escaping from its ongoing fear or anxiety. We will have little to say about such accounts, partly because they were justifed by polemical defenses of behaviorism that are no longer strongly felt, and partly because advances in the empirical analysis of aversive reinforcement contingencies make such theories unnecessary.

The thesis we will defend is that negative reinforcement (the strengthening of behavior that eliminates or avoids aversive stimuli) obeys the same laws of response strength as positive reinforcement. To foreshadow the discussion, essentially all of the functional relations that have been considered for positive reinforcement in this chapter also have been demonstrated with negative reinforcement. Parsimony thus dictates that positive and negative reinforcement are simply two sides of the same coin, as a single set of reinforcement principles is sufficient, regardless of the qualitative nature of the contingent events that maintain behavior.

### Matching of Relative Response Rates

Baum (1973b) was the first to report matching for negative reinforcement. Pigeons were presented brief electric shocks at 1-second intervals in the absence of responding, and responses were reinforced by 2-minute time-out periods during which no shock was presented. Time-outs were determined by a concurrent VI VI schedule, with each independent VI associated with standing on one or the other side of the experimental chamber. When either VI scheduled the availability of a time-out, it was presented if the pigeon was standing on the appropriate side; otherwise, it was held until the pigeon returned to that side. The values of the different VI components were then varied over several different experimental conditions. Individual results were more variable than normally obtained with positive reinforcement, which Baum ascribed to technical difficulties in administering the shock. Even so, when the ratio of time allocation was plotted against the ratio of reinforcement frequencies for the aggregate of all four subjects, the result was a fit of equation 8 (the generalized matching law) with an exponent of 1.01.

Subsequent studies of matching with negative reinforcement have generally confirmed Baum's analysis, but with somewhat greater variability in the exponent of equation 8. Poling (1978), using rats as subjects in a similar procedure, obtained exponents for individual subjects ranging from 0.99 to 0.92, with much less variability in the individual data. Hutton, Gardner, and Lewis (1978) used pigeons as subjects but with keypecking as the response instead of different locations of standing; equation 8 accounted for over 95 percent of the variance for all individual subjects, but with exponents from 0.60 to 0.85. A possible reason for the undermatching was that no COD was used, an omission known to produce undermatching with concurrent schedules of positive reinforcement. In general, therefore, choice between different frequencies of negative reinforcement seems to obey the matching law in much the same way as does positive reinforcement.

### Hyperbolic Functions for Response Strength

The generality of the hyperbolic rate function, equation 23, for negative reinforcement was demonstrated by de Villiers (1974), who trained rats to lever press to avoid randomly presented brief shocks. All scheduled shocks were presented if no lever press occurred, while the effect of a response was to cancel the next scheduled shock. Additional responses occur-

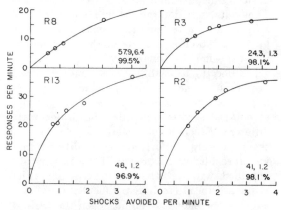

**Figure 3.19.** Response rates for rats trained on a shock-avoidance schedule. The least-squares fit of equation 23 is plotted for each rat. The $k$ and $R_e$ values and the percentage of the variance accounted for are shown for each individual subject. Original results are from de Villiers (1974) as re-analyzed by de Villiers and Herrnstein (1976). From "Toward a Law of Response Strength" by P. de Villiers and R.J. Hernstein, 1976, *Psychological Bulletin, 83*, p. 1144. Copyright 1976 by the American Psychological Association. Reprinted by permission.

ring before a scheduled but already canceled shock had no additional effect. All shocks could be avoided if the rat responded at least once within each intershock interval, but the duration of those intervals varied unpredictably. Across conditions, the average intershock interval spanned four values from VI 15 seconds to VI 75 seconds. The rate of lever pressing was related to the frequency of shocks avoided according to a hyperbolic function, as shown in Figure 3.19. For four subjects, the percent variance accounted for by equation 23 ranged from 96.9 to 99.1 percent.

Additional support for the extension of equation 23 to negative reinforcement comes from various discrete-trial procedures (typically involving a rat in a straight alley) in which the reinforcement is a reduction in voltage level of a continuously presented shock. Seven such studies were analyzed by de Villiers and Herrnstein (1976): The relation between speed of responding and the magnitude of voltage reduction was described well by equation 23, with over 90 percent of the variance accounted for in most cases.

### Effects of Reinforcement Context

Although much less research has evaluated context-of-reinforcement effects with negative reinforcement, what little there is supports their generality. Hutton and Lewis (1979) trained pigeons to keypeck to terminate a shock schedule in which brief shocks were presented every three seconds. On a VI 45-second schedule, pecks occasionally produced two-minute shock-free time-out periods. As noted above, such schedules generate steady, substantial rates of behavior. After establishing the behavior with the shock termination schedule, the experimenters added extra shock-free periods, independent of responding, with the frequency of such periods varied over a wide range. The rate of pecking maintained by the constant VI shock-termination schedule varied inversely with the frequency of response-independent shock-free periods, in a manner similar to the effects of response-independent positive reinforcement (cf. Duncan & Silberberg, 1982).

### Contrast in Multiple Schedules

Wertheim (1965) published the first report of behavioral contrast in a multiple shock-avoidance, shock-avoidance schedule. By using a lever press, rats could shut off a continuous shock and delay its onset by various time periods (8 to 20 seconds). As long as the inter-response time was less than the response-shock (R-S) interval, no shocks were delivered. Different response levers, correlated with different stimulus lights, were associated with the two successively presented components of the multiple schedule; the value of the R-S interval was varied systematically in each component separately. Decreasing the R-S interval in one component increased the response rate in that component but also decreased the response rate in the alternative component for which the R-S interval was held constant. Conversely, increasing the R-S interval decreased the associated response rate but increased the response rate in the constant alternative. The inverse relation between the density of the shock schedule and the response rate in the alternative component was similar to contrast interactions seen with positive reinforcement schedules. Similar contrast effects with shock-avoidance schedules have been reported by de Villiers (1972).

Although contrast occurs in multiple schedules composed of avoidance schedules with varying contingencies of shock-rate reduction, the generality of such effects for other, related manipulations remains uncertain. For example, in two studies (Bushnell & Weiss, 1980; Klein & Rilling, 1974) pigeons started on a multiple schedule in which avoidance contingencies were initially present in both components; they then were shifted to a schedule in which one of the components was a shock-free period, while the other component was unchanged. For no subject in either study were clear contrast effects evident, as response rates in the unchanged component remained generally unaffected. Similarly, Bersh and Lambert (1975) shifted rats from a simple shock-avoidance schedule to a multiple schedule to which one component retained the same avoidance contingency while the other component presented random non-avoidable shocks. Once again, no contrast effects were evident, although the data were generally variable.

One difficulty in interpreting such results is the ambiguity in the conditions that produce contrast. One alternative says that response rate will be determined by the relative value of the two components; a second says that response rate is determined by the relative rate of rein-forcement for responding. Whereas these two statements are usually equivalent when food schedules are used, negative reinforcement schedules dissociate them. For example, when a multiple shock-avoidance, shock-avoidance schedule is changed to multiple shock-avoidance, shock-free time-out, the elimination of shocks in the second component removes the opportunity for negative reinforcement—by removing not only the response contingency but the aversive events themselves, thus increasing the value of that component. The analogue for food schedules would be to remove not only the food reinforcement, but also the hunger. The former effect suggests that response rate in the unchanged component should increase (positive contrast); the latter suggests that response rate should decrease (negative contrast). Thus, the prediction depends critically on the manner in which the procedural change is conceptualized.

## The Nature of Reinforcement in Avoidance Learning

Traditional accounts of avoidance learning (Mowrer & Lamoreaux, 1946; Rescorla & Solomon, 1967) postulated two separate components, hence the name *two-factor theory*. First, the animal is classically conditioned to fear the stimulus situation prior to the avoidance response, then the avoidance response itself is maintained by the negative reinforcement of removing the conditioned aversive stimulus. An alternative account (Herrnstein, 1969; Herrnstein & Hineline, 1966) argued that an appeal to fear reduction was unnecessary, because the reinforcer for avoidance behavior was simply the reduction in shock frequency contingent on the response. Although the two accounts are essentially equivalent with respect to most qualitative predictions (cf. Dinsmoor, 1977), the demonstration of quantitative relations governing avoidance behavior does allow them to be differentiated. No basis for such predictions is offered by two-factor theory, because it requires the operation of two separate conditioning processes (the fear conditioning itself and then the instrumental conditioning due to negative reinforcement, which is determined, in turn, by the amount of fear conditioning), neither of which has known quantitative properties. The notion of shock-frequency reduction, on the other hand, provides a clear framework for quantitative predictions, since the parameters of reinforcement are given by the observable characteristics of the stimulus presentations (i.e., the number and intensity of the shocks that are avoided). To the extent that clear quantitative functions are obtained, the simpler formulation would receive strong support.

As shown in Figure 3.19, de Villiers (1974, experiment 1) demonstrated that the hyperbolic rate function (equation 23) described response rates maintained by avoidance contingencies just as well as those maintained by positive reinforcement. Most importantly, his fit of equation 23 used the number of shocks actually avoided (the number scheduled minus the number received) as the independent variable. Equation 23 was also fitted to the data using the number of shocks actually received as the independent variable, on the assumption that shocks received should be the best correlate of the amount of fear conditioning. To the extent lever pressing was maintained by fear reduction, therefore, response strength should be best predicted by shocks received as the independent variable. As compared to the shocks-avoided measure, however, the fit of equation 23 using the number of shocks received was substantially worse.

Other strong support for shock-frequency reduction as the reinforcer was obtained by de Villiers (1974) in his second experiment involving a multiple schedule. Noting that research with food schedules had shown that relative response rates in a multiple schedule increasingly approximate the relative reinforcement rates as component duration is shortened (Shimp & Wheatley, 1971), he varied component duration from 13 seconds to six minutes in a series of multiple schedules with avoidance contingencies in both components. At issue was which correlate of negative reinforcement, number of shocks avoided or number of shocks received, would yield a functional relation like that obtained with appetitive schedules. Shocks avoided gave a better approximation to matching with shorter components; with the duration producing the maximal interaction (40 seconds), the average absolute deviation from matching was only 0.03. With number of shocks received as the measure, there was no systematic effect of component duration, and the absolute deviations from matching were substantially larger.

Additional support for shock-frequency reduction comes from Logue and de Villiers

(1978), who trained rats on a choice procedure with avoidance schedules operating during both components of a concurrent schedule. Fitting their data with the generalized matching law (equation 8) resulted in values of $a$ for the shocks-avoided measure of 0.82 and 0.92 for their two subjects, while the corresponding values for shocks received were 0.50 and 0.48. Moreover, the variance accounted for by the generalized matching laws was over 90 percent for the shocks-avoided measure but less than 50 percent for the number of shocks received. Shock-frequency reduction thus appears to be the proper measure of negative reinforcement, assuming that positive and negative reinforcement obey the same laws.

Although quantitative analyses of avoidance behavior support shock-frequency reduction as the controlling variable, its effects clearly require further specification. A critical issue is the temporal interval over which shock frequency is calculated. For example, does the animal consider only that period immediately following a response, or are frequencies of shocks integrated over a longer time frame? Gardner and Lewis (1976) demonstrated that the delay interval between responding and shock presentation was an important variable (also see Lambert, Bersh, Hineline, & Smith, 1973), in that avoidance responding was maintained in rats despite having the effect of increasing the total number of shocks in the situation. During one stimulus condition, shocks were presented randomly with an average rate of two per minute. A response activated a three-minute alternate stimulus condition during which the rats received a series of 12 shocks that began 158 seconds after the response. Thus, the overall shock rate during the stimulus condition produced by the response was higher than during the stimulus preceding the response. Responding was nevertheless maintained for all subjects. However, when the number of delayed shocks was increased from four per minute to six per minute, only one of three subjects maintained responding. Subsequent work (Lewis, Gardner, & Hutton, 1976) indicated that delays to each separate shock contributed to the overall aversiveness of the stimulus situation, with the controlling variable being the integrated delay to shock following a response compared to the integrated delay of shock in the absence of a response. Avoidance contingencies may thus be characterized as procedures in which a response produces a transition to a situation of less aversiveness than that prior to the response, with the degree of aversiveness determined jointly by the rate and delay of shock presentations.

The preceding discussion has argued that avoidance behavior can be accounted for without recourse to internal states such as conditioned fear, relief and so forth. This is not to claim, however, that conditioned aversiveness to stimuli in the environment (or to interoceptive stimuli) may not play an important role, at least in some situations. Just as initially neutral stimuli may acquire conditioned reinforcement properties via their association with primary reward (see next section), they may also acquire conditioned aversiveness through association with primary aversive stimuli. Involvement of conditioned aversive stimuli may be an important component of a variety of situations, especially those regarded as analogues to human psychopathology (see Levis & Boyd, 1979, for an important example). However, the issue is whether avoidance behavior *requires* an explanation in terms of escape from conditioned aversive stimuli. The evidence that has been described argues strongly that such an explanation is unnecessary, as avoidance behavior appears best accounted for by the change in the objective pattern of aversive stimulation produced by the avoidance response.

## Effects of Punishment

Influential early investigators argued either that punishment was ineffective (Thorndike, 1932) or that its effects were temporary and did not depend upon the response-punisher contingency (Estes, 1944; Skinner, 1938). Even after research (Azrin & Holz, 1966) showed that punishment was like reinforcement in its effects (but opposite in sign), some theories of punishment continued to deny that its response decrements reflected a decrease in the strength of the punished response itself. Instead, the decrements were said to occur indirectly, via the strengthening of other responses (cf. Dinsmoor, 1977). (The analogous view for reinforcement—that its increments were due to the weakening of other responses—was not seriously advanced.) Proprioceptive or contextual stimuli associated with the punished response are assumed to become conditioned aversive stimuli, and the

behavior that terminates those stimuli (any response other than the punished response) is negatively reinforced. Consequently, the strength of the punished response itself is not changed, but the frequency of that response decreases because of increased response competition.

It should be apparent that the traditional theory of punishmnt is similar to the two-factor theory of avoidance; both assume that behavior is strengthened by removing conditioned aversive stimuli. The major difference between them is that, for avoidance learning, the primary effect is on the measured response itself, while, for punishment, it is on other (usually unspecified) behaviors that supposedly compete with the measured response. Given that the two-factor theory is neither a parsimonious nor accurate account of avoidance learning, the implication is that the two-factor theory of punishment should be questioned as well.

One method for dissociating the different accounts of punishment is the study of combinations of food and shock in a choice procedure. Farley (1980b) and de Villiers (1980) both studied concurrent schedules in which independent schedules of food and shock were contingent on each of two separate responses. At issue was how the addition of shock should be conceptualized in terms of the matching law. If two-factor theory were correct, the effect of shock from both schedules should be to increase the aversiveness of response-related stimuli, and thus increase the strength of behavior incompatible with the operant responses. In terms of the equation for response strength (equation 23), the effect should be to increase $R_e$, the value of competing activities. But since $R_e$ cancels when the matching law itself is considered (see discussion of equation 28), the prediction for concurrent schedules is that the addition of shock should have no effect on the preference determined by the independent food schedules.

A second alternative, also based on the notion that punishment strengthens competing behavior, is that each response is, to some extent, negatively reinforced by being an escape from the conditioned aversive stimuli associated with the alternative response. That is, the shock schedule for one response produces negative reinforcement for the other response and vice versa (cf. DeLuty, 1976). Just how much of the total negative reinforcement will be associated with the two operant responses, as opposed to activities associated with $R_e$, cannot be determined beforehand, but presumably it should depend on the probability of operant responding determined by the food schedules. This notion is captured by equation 38, which simply adds the two sources of reinforcement, one positive and the other negative, for each operant response (the parameter $c$ serves as a scale parameter relating the two sources of reinforcement).

$$\frac{B_1}{B_2} = \frac{R_1 + cP_2}{R_2 + cP_1} \tag{38}$$

Still a third alternative is based on the notion that shock can be conceptualized in terms of negative food units, with each shock having an equivalent, but opposite, effect to some amount of food. Accordingly, the new reward value for each response alternative is its food schedule minus its shock schedule, as given by equation 39.

$$\frac{B_1}{B_2} = \frac{R_1 - cP_1}{R_2 - cP_2} \tag{39}$$

To distinguish among these formalizations, de Villiers (1980) presented pigeons unequal frequencies of food contingent on two choice alternatives, but with each alternative also receiving equal frequencies of shock. He found that preference for the more lucrative food schedule was increased as the shock intensity was raised (presumably increasing the value of $c$), which supports equation 39. In contrast, the notion that shock affects only $R_e$ predicts no effect on preference, while equation 38 predicts that equal frequencies of shock should shift preference for the two food schedules toward indifference. Similar results supporting equation 39 were obtained by Farley (1980b), who studied several different food plus shock combinations.

Although the purely subtractive version of negative reinforcement accounts well for preference between different combinations of shock plus food, it has greater difficulty accounting for absolute rates of responding taken from the same experiments. De Villiers (1982) analyzed the absolute rate data from Farley's (1980b) experiments in which both food and shock were varied over a substantial range. Instead of equation 23, which applies to absolute rates for situations in which only food rates are varied, he used equation 40, which includes the subtractive effects of punishment.

$$B_1 = k \frac{R_1 - cP_1}{R_1 - cP_1 + R_e} \tag{40}$$

The question was whether the addition of shock could be captured solely in terms of the values of $P_1$, or whether it also affected the values of $k$ and $R_e$. If either of the latter possibilities obtained, the simple subtractive model would require modification. The result of de Villiers' analysis was that $k$ was not systematically affected by variation in the shock values, but that $R_e$ was generally increased as the shock intensity or frequency was increased. This implies that the value of activities other than the operant response was increased by the addition of shock, which is the result predicted by accounts of punishment that rely upon negative reinforcement of competing behavior. As de Villiers noted, however, the increase in value of competing activities does not necessarily imply any role for negative reinforcement, since such increases might occur because of responses elicited by shock. For example, it is known that aggressive behavior is elicited by brief shock, and that animals will work to emit such behavior just after shock but not otherwise (Azrin, Hutchinson, & McLaughlin, 1965). Thus, the addition of shock may evoke transitory motivational states that provide new sources of reinforcement in the situation, even without any role for negative reinforcement due to the elimination of conditioned aversive stimuli.

Regardless of the interpretation given to changes in $R_e$, it is clear from the preference data that the major effect of punishment is to reduce the value of the response on which it is contingent. The absolute rate data do suggest that other effects occur as well and that a complete account of punishment may require an amalgam of several different processes. Nevertheless, the quantitative analysis of punishment provides strong support for a negative law of effect by which aversive stimuli weaken the strength of the responses on which they are contingent.

## CONDITIONED REINFORCEMENT

All of the preceding discussion has concerned behavior maintained by primary reinforcement, either positive or negative. In fact, the immediate consequences of much behavior are stimulus changes that themselves have no biological significance. Such stimuli traditionally have been labeled as conditioned reinforcers, on the assumption that they acquire value in their own right as a function of their relation to the primary reinforcers. The concept of conditioned reinforcement has played an important role in the history of behavior theory, as it allows behavior to be maintained in situations in which the primary reinforcers are available only after substantial delays (e.g., Spence, 1947).

The processes underlying the effect of stimuli intervening in delay-of-reinforcement intervals are now a matter of dispute. Despite clear demonstrations that delayed reinforcers in the absence of such stimuli maintain behavior poorly (Williams, 1976) and that animals will work to obtain such stimuli at the expense of delayed primary reinforcers (e.g., Cronin, 1980), several writers have argued that they do not have value in their own right, but instead serve to bridge the temporal gap between response and delayed reinforcer (e.g., Baum, 1973a; also see Rescorla, 1982, for a related interpretation of analogous effects in classical conditioning). Rather than consider this issue directly, the present approach will be to assess the value of conditioned reinforcers as a function of their associated reinforcement contingencies. That is, by assuming that the matching law applies to the relative value of conditioned reinforcers, we then can determine the functional relations between relative value (measured as preference) and the contingencies associated with the various stimuli serving a conditioned reinforcement function. By considering the nature of those functional relations, it may be possible to arrive at a clearer conception of the status of conditioned reinforcement as a psychological construct.

## Concurrent-Chains Schedules

A concurrent schedule that has conditioned reinforcers as the immediate consequences of choice is known generally as a *concurrent-chains schedule* and is diagramed in Figure 3.20. The subject initially works on two concurrently available alternatives, each associated with its own reinforcement schedule (typically equal-valued VIs). Whenever either of these initial-link schedules is completed, a new stimulus appears, along with the terminal link of the

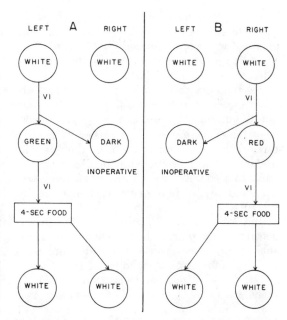

**Figure 3.20.** The concurrent-chains procedure. Panel A indicates the sequence of events when responses on the left key are reinforced; panel B presents the analogous sequence on the right key. Responses in the presence of the colored lights (the stimuli of the terminal links) are reinforced with food according to some schedule. The measure of choice is the relative rate of responding in the presence of the concurrently available white lights.

chain. During either terminal link, the other key becomes dark and inoperative. Responses in the presence of the terminal-link stimuli earn primary reinforcement (usually food) on some schedule. In most experiments, a single primary reinforcement reinstates the initial link, and the entire procedure recycles. The assumption underlying the procedure is that choice during the initial links reflects the relative value of the two terminal-link stimuli.

## Determinants of the Value of Conditioned Reinforcers

Early research (Autor, 1960; Herrnstein, 1964) suggested a very simple relation between the measure of preference and the value of the terminal-link stimuli. That is, the ratio of response rates in the initial link of the schedule approximately matched the ratio of reinforcement rates during the two terminal-link stimuli. Herrnstein (1964) demonstrated that this relation held independent of the schedules used in the different terminal links, as matching was obtained when one terminal-link schedule was VI while the other was VR, despite the response rates in the terminal links themselves being much higher with the VR. Thus, the reinforcing value of the terminal-link stimulus was not determined by probability of reinforcement for each response, but rather by rate of reinforcement per unit time the stimulus was present. Such a relationship implies that the value of a conditioned reinforcer is simply proportional to the reinforcement density in its presence.

But limitations of a simple reinforcement-density notion quickly became apparent. First, subjects are also sensitive to the absolute number of reinforcers, independent of the rate, as shown by Fantino and Herrnstein (1968). In their procedure pigeons chose between two terminal-link stimuli, both associated with VI 15-sec schedules of reinforcement. During one stimulus the terminal link ended after a single reinforcer was delivered, while during the other the number of reinforcers was varied from 1 to 10 across conditions. The result was that preference for the multiple-reinforcer terminal link increased with larger number of reinforcers, although the increase in preference was not proportional to the number. That is, each additional reinforcer contributed less and less to the preference.

A related finding is that the value of any particular reinforcer in the presence of a terminal-link stimulus apparently depends upon its temporal distance from the onset of the stimulus. For example, Killeen (1968) presented an FI schedule during one terminal link and a VI schedule with the same average reinforcement rate during the second terminal link. Despite the same rate of reinforcement in the presence of the two stimuli, preference was strongly in favor of the VI stimulus, with the degree of preference primarily determined by the shortest interreinforcement interval in the VI distribution. Killeen then suggested that the proper measure of the reinforcement rate was not the arithmetic mean of the interreinforcement intervals, but rather the harmonic mean. Thus the average interreinforcement interval is given by the inverse of the mean of the reciprocals of each interreinforcement interval, as given in equation 41:

$$R_{\bar{x}} = \frac{n}{\dfrac{1}{r_1} + \dfrac{1}{r_2} + \cdots \dfrac{1}{r_n}} \qquad (41)$$

where $r_1$, $r_2$, and so forth, refer to the individual interreinforcement intervals. With this method of averaging, the mean reinforcement rate is determined primarily by the values of the shortest interreinforcement intervals. As noted by Killeen, matching to the harmonic mean of the interreinforcement intervals is equivalent to the matching of relative immediacy of reinforcement, as reported by Chung and Herrnstein (1967), as long as only one reinforcer is presented during each terminal-link presentation. Accordingly, studies of choice between delays of reinforcement and studies of choice between different reinforcement schedules may be functionally equivalent.

Although the use of the harmonic mean as a method of determining reinforcement rate provides an adequate description for the results of a number of studies, it clearly is inadequate for a variety of others, which implicate determinants of the value of the terminal-link stimuli other than the response-reinforcer intervals that they signal. One example comes from studies in which one terminal-link is composed of a chained schedule, such that two different stimuli are interposed between the onset of the terminal link and the delivery of the reinforcer. For example, Duncan and Fantino (1972) had pigeons choose between a simple FI schedule in one terminal link and a chain FI FI in the second terminal link, with the total length of the chain equal to the value of the simple FI. The result was a clear preference for the simple FI, indicating that the interreinforcement interval, per se, was not a sufficient predictor of the results.

A second example comes from comparisons of multiple versus mixed schedules in the different terminal links. In such studies, choice responses are followed sometimes by periods of reinforcement and sometimes by periods of extinction. Typically, half of the terminal-link entries would be periods in which a VI was in effect, and the other half of the entries would be periods of equal duration in which extinction occurred. The distribution of such periods is then held constant for both terminal links. The independent variable is whether the periods of reinforcement and extinction are signaled by different stimuli (a multiple schedule) or by the same stimulus (a mixed schedule). Such comparisons have consistently shown a strong preference for the terminal link associated with the multiple schedule (Green, 1980; Hursh & Fantino, 1974). Since the interreinforcement intervals associated with the two choice alternatives are equivalent in such situations, the implication is that some other determinant of the value of the terminal-link stimuli must be involved.

Still a third complication is that the values of the terminal-link stimuli are not determined solely by the terminal-link schedules themselves. Instead, there is an interaction between the reinforcement rates during the terminal links and the absolute value of the initial-link schedules. Fantino (1969) first demonstrated this effect by presenting a VI 120-second schedule in one terminal link and a VI 30-second schedule in the other, while the initial-link schedules were either equal VI 40-seconds, equal VI 90-seconds, or equal VI 600-seconds. If choice in the initial link were determined solely by the relative value of the two terminal-link stimuli, and if these in turn were determined solely by their associated schedules, the degree of preference should have been constant across all of the initial-link values. Instead, preference was greatest with the shortest (VI 40-sec) initial-link schedule and near indifference with the longest (VI 600-sec) schedule. More extensive variation of the initial-link and terminal-link schedule (Fantino & Davison, 1983; Squires & Fantino, 1971), have revealed a similar pattern of results: The degree of preference depends upon the relative duration of the initial-link and terminal-link reinforcement intervals.

## Theories of Conditioned Reinforcement

### Delay Reduction
Largely because of the interaction between the durations of the initial and terminal links, Fantino (1969, 1977, 1981) has propounded the *delay reduction hypothesis* of conditioned reinforcement, which states that the strength of a stimulus as a conditioned reinforcer is a function of the reduction in time to reinforcement correlated with the onset of that stimulus. Thus, the value of a stimulus is not determined simply by the rate of reinforcement presented in its

presence, but by that rate relative to the context of reinforcement in which it occurs. For example, a stimulus associated with a FI 30-second schedule would be a stronger conditioned reinforcer if preceded by a 60-second period of extinction than if preceded by a 10-second period. In the first case, the onset of the 30-second interval is correlated with a two-thirds reduction in time to food (since, of the total waiting time of 90 seconds, only 30 seconds remain once the FI stimulus appears), while in the second case, with only a one-fourth reduction in time to food.

As applied to concurrent-chains schedule with equal initial-link schedules, delay reduction is captured by equation 42, in which $T$ represents the average delay to primary reinforcement from the onset of either initial-link stimulus (i.e., the average interreinforcement interval in the situation), and $t_{2L}$ and $t_{2R}$ represent the average duration of the terminal links associated with the left and right choice alternatives.

$$\frac{B_L}{B_L + B_R} = \frac{T - t_{2L}}{(T - t_{2L}) + (T - t_{2R})}$$
$$(t_{2L} < T, t_{2R} < T) \qquad (42)$$

In addition, exclusive preference is assumed for cases in which the terminal-link duration for one alternative is equal to or greater than the value of $T$.

Not only does equation 42 provide an account of the effects of the absolute value of the initial-link schedules, it makes corresponding predictions about the values of the terminal-link schedules. Recall from the discussion of delayed reinforcement effects on choice, that preference for the shorter delay increases with longer absolute delay values. For example, MacEwen (1972) presented pigeons a choice between FI 10-second and FI 20-second and then between FI 20-second and FI 40-second, with equal VI 60-second schedules in the initial links in both cases. The result was a greater preference for the shorter terminal-link schedules with the FI 20/40 comparison. How delay reduction accounts for this effect can be seen by noting that the value of $T$ is 45 seconds in the 10/20 comparison but 60 seconds in the 20/40 comparison. Thus, the percent delay reduction for the FI 10-second stimulus is 78 percent and for the FI 20-second stimulus, 56 percent, while the corresponding values for the FI 20-second and FI 40-second schedules are 67 percent and 33 percent, respectively. Thus, the ratio between the two values of delay reduction is considerably greater with the longer delay values.

An important implication of delay-reduction theory is that the degree of preference between a given pair of alternatives that are held constant will vary as a function of which additional alternatives are also present, because the additional alternatives may change the overall rate of reinforcement in the situation (the value of $T$). Fantino and Dunn (1983) tested this prediction by first presenting pigeons a two-alternative concurrent-chain schedule, in which both initial-link schedules were VI 60-seconds, with one terminal link being a VI 20-second and the other VI 60-second. They then added a third alternative that also had a VI 60-second initial-link schedule, but a VI-9-second terminal link. As predicted by delay-reduction theory, preference for the VI 20-second schedule relative to the VI 60-second terminal link was substantially increased by the addition of the higher-valued alternative. It should be noted that this prediction is quite different from what would be expected in a simple concurrent schedule. That is, if a simple concurrent VI 20-second VI 60-second schedule were changed to a concurrent VI 20-second, VI 60-second, VI 9-second schedule, the ratio of responding for the VI 20/VI 60 comparison would be unaffected by the presence of the third alternative (Davison & Hunter, 1976).

Some insight into the reason for context of reinforcement playing an important role perhaps can be gained by considering similar effects that occur in classical conditioning. Historically, classical conditioning has been regarded as the process underlying conditioned reinforcement, so it should be expected that any role of context of reinforcement should be similar in both cases. In fact, a theory of classical conditioning essentially similar to delay reduction theory, but developed independently of it, has been proposed by Gibbon (1981) and Gibbon and Balsam (1981). According to their formulation, the primary determinant of the rate of acquisition is the ratio of reinforcement during the CS, relative to the average interreinforcement interval in the situation independent of the CS. Such context effects appear similar to those discussed earlier with respect to multiple and concurrent schedules.

Although delay-reduction theory does account

well for the effects of context of reinforcement, it cannot explain a variety of other data. For example, it does not account for the differences as a function of one versus two stimuli in the terminal links (Duncan & Fantino, 1972) and it fails to explain the differences obtained with multiple versus mixed schedules. Moreover, as represented by equation 42, it does not account for concurrent-chains schedules in which unequal initial-link schedules are presented. To incorporate such effects, equation 42 has been modified (Fantino & Davison 1983; Squires & Fantino, 1971) to include the overall reinforcement rates associated with each choice alternative (summed over the initial and terminal links). While the modification does extend the domain of application for the account, it also adds a role for primary reinforcement as a determinant of choice. Delay reduction theory thus ceases to be an account purely in terms of conditioned reinforcement.

### Killeen's Incentive Theory

A second account that assumes a combined influence of primary and conditioned reinforcement has been offered by Killeen (1982b), derived from his earlier work on how reinforcement rate affects generalized arousal (Killeen, 1975; Killeen et al., 1978). Its fundamental assumption is that the reinforcement rate associated with a particular response alternative determines the degree of arousal, while the amount of combined primary and conditioned reinforcement contingent on keypecking serves to direct that arousal into the form of pecking the response key. Thus, his account assumes that three separate factors determine choice:

1. Arousal, as determined by the rate of reinforcement ($R$) summed over the initial and terminal links for a particular response key, which is thus inversely proportional to the sum of the durations of the initial ($I$) and terminal ($T$) links, as given by equation 43:

$$R = 1/(I + T) \qquad (43)$$

2. The delayed primary reinforcement ($P$), which is assumed to follow an exponential decay function, with the amount of decay determined by the time between the choice response and the primary reinforcer, which usually is the duration of the terminal

link. Thus, the value of $P$ is given by equation 44:

$$P = e^{-qT} \qquad (44)$$

3. The immediate conditioned reinforcement ($C$), the value of which is proportional to the rate of reinforcement in the presence of the particular terminal-link stimulus, and thus inversely proportional to the average duration of the terminal link, as given by equation 45:

$$C = 1/T \qquad (45)$$

The effects of primary and conditioned reinforcement are assumed to be additive, and their sum is combined multiplicatively with the degree of arousal to determine the response strength ($B$), as given by equation 46:

$$B_1 = R_1(P_1 + C_1) \qquad (46)$$

Substituting the separate terms into equation 46 yields a more explicit description, as given by equation 47:

$$B_1 = \frac{1}{I_1 - T_1}\left(e^{-qT_1} + \frac{1}{T_1}\right) \qquad (47)$$

Choice in the initial link of a concurrent-chains schedule is then assumed to reflect the ratio of the response strengths associated with the two keys (i.e., $B_1/B_2$).

Equation 47 was tested by Killeen (1982b) by applying it to a variety of previously published concurrent-chains experiments, including preference between FI versus FI, FI versus VI, and VI versus VI. The results are shown in Figure 3.21 which was plotted with only the value of $q$ as a free parameter (which was held constant for all of the various studies). The excellent description of the results shown in Figure 3.21 provides strong support for the validity of equation 47, especially since alternative accounts have been unsuccessful in accounting for the range of studies that are included.

Killeen (1982b) also extended his model to preference for a simple FI versus a chain FI FI (Duncan & Fantino. 1972) and to multiple versus mixed schedules (Green, 1980) and demonstrated that his model generated predictions that were at least qualitively correct.

Although Killeen's model has the major advantage of being derived from conceptually simple first principles, it faces difficulties on at least two counts. First, its conception of arousal

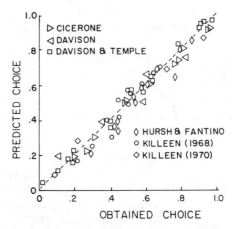

**Figure 3.21.** Predicted versus obtained relative rates of responding in the initial links of several different concurrent-chains studies. Predictions are from equation 47 with $q$ set at 0.125 for all studies. From Killeen (1982b). The studies from which results were taken are listed next to the corresponding symbols. From "Incentive Theory: II. Models for Choice" by P.R. Killeen, 1982, *Journal of the Experimental Analysis of Behavior, 38,* p. 220. Copyright 1982 by the Society for the Experimental Analysis of Behavior, Inc. Reprinted by permission.

($R$) is notably different from that supported by earlier investigations (Killeen, 1975), which provided strong evidence that a general activation effect occurred independent of the response on which the reinforcement was contingent. That is to say, all behavior in the situation was aroused, not just that which the reinforcer followed. Yet the discussion of equation 43 implies that different degrees of arousal may occur for the different choice alternatives, depending upon the overall reinforcement rates associated with each response key. As yet, no rationale has been offered for why arousal should be response independent in some situations and response dependent in others. Second, other investigators (Fantino & Davison, 1983; Vaughan, 1985) have argued that the fits provided by equation 47 are notably inferior to those provided by other models (e.g., delay reduction theory) for major subsets of data. In particular, the model does poorly with respect to variation in the duration of the initial link of a concurrent chain, which produces decreases in preference as the duration of the initial-link schedules are increased (Fantino, 1969). Killeen's model can incorporate such effects only in terms of the value of $R$, with the result that his model does not predict effects of initial-link durations that are nearly as large as those actually observed. The importance of such criticisms is difficult to evaluate, since minor modifications may allow the model to handle the criticisms without difficulty.

### Conditioned Value as a Hyperbolic Function of Reinforcement Rate

The last account that will be considered is perhaps the simplest, since it assumes that preference can be explained solely in terms of the relative values of the conditioned reinforcers contingent on the two choice responses and that these values are determined entirely by the value of the stimuli to which they lead (usually food) and of the rate of transition to those following stimuli. Vaughan (1985) has argued that such assumptions are sufficient to explain a wide variety of the empirical findings that were discussed earlier, as long as the function relating the growth of value to the rate of transition is of the general shape of a hyperbola. Equation 48 is one such function (Vaughan notes that other related functions might serve equally well), with $V_1$ representing the eventual value of the conditioned reinforcer, $V_1'$ its value before training, $V_2$ the value of the stimulus to which it leads, $r$ the rate of transition between the conditioned reinforcer and the following stimulus, and $a$ an empirically determined constant:

$$V_1 = \frac{r(V_2 - V_1')}{r + a} + V_1' \qquad (48)$$

Accordingly, the value of the conditioned reinforcer is assumed to increase in a negatively accelerated manner as a function of the rate of transition, and will asymptote at $V_2$ when the rate of transition is extremely high.

Vaughan's account can be exemplified by its explanation of how preference is changed by the absolute value of the terminal-link schedules. As noted above, several studies (e.g., MacEwen, 1972; Williams & Fantino, 1978) have demonstrated that the degree of preference between schedule alternatives that differ by a constant ratio increases the larger the absolute value of the shorter schedule. For example, preference is greater for a comparison of FI 6 seconds versus FI 12 seconds than for a comparison of FI 3 seconds versus FI 6 seconds. Such an effect is explained by equation 48 as shown in Figure

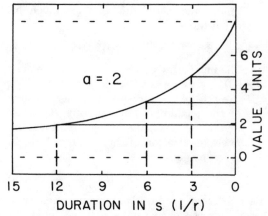

**Figure 3.22.** A plot of equation 48 with $a$ set at 0.2. Note that shorter delays to reinforcement correspond to higher rates of transition. The vertical dashed lines intersect the function at the delays of 3, 6, and 12 seconds. The solid horizontal lines indicate the value of the function at those points. Value plotted on the abscissa is in arbitrary units. Adapted from Vaughan, 1985.

3.22, which plots the values of the various terminal-link stimuli as a function of their associated delays to reinforcement. Note that delay to transition is simply the inverse of the rate of transition, so, for example, a delay of 20 seconds corresponds to a rate of transition of 180 per hour. For purposes of the demonstration, the value of $V_1'$ is assumed to be zero, so that numerical units may be assigned to conditioned reinforcers associated with the different FI schedules. As noted by the vertical dashed lines, the values corresponding to delays of 3, 6 and 12 seconds are (approximately) 4.7, 3.3, and 2.1, respectively. Since the matching law implies that the degree of preference should be given by the ratios of the respective values, the result is that the ratio for the comparison between the shorter delays (4.7/3.3 = 1.42) is smaller than the comparison between the longer delays (3.3/2.1 = 1.57). Thus, the degree of preference should be greater in the latter case.

A second example of Vaughan's account is its explanation of preference for a terminal link consisting of a single schedule (e.g., FI 8 seconds) versus one consisting of a chain schedule of the same total duration (chain FI 4 second FI 4 second). Equation 48 predicts such a preference because separate values must be calculated for each component of the chain.

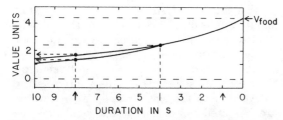

**Figure 3.23.** Plot of equation 48 with *a* again set at 0.2. The continuous function that begins at zero delay is for a simple FI schedule, with the dashed vertical lines indicating its value at 4 and 8 seconds. The lower-limb function is also a plot of equation 48, but with a value of $V_2$ set equal to the value of upper function at the 4-sec delay. The functions correspond to the comparison between a simple FI 8-second versus a chain FI 4-sec FI 4-sec. Adapted from Vaughan, 1985.

Figure 3.23 plots equation 48 (again in terms of $1/r$, the delay to transition) with the values for an FI 4-second food schedule designated by the dashed lines. The value of the second FI 4-second schedule (the first stimulus of the chain) is then given by calculating equation 48 with a value of $V_2$ equal to the value of the FI 4-second food schedule. The lower limb of the function shown in Figure 3.23 plots the results of that calculation. Thus, the value of the second FI 4-second component is less than the value of the simple FI 8-second schedule, so the simple schedule should be preferred in a choice test.

Vaughan's analysis provides an explanation of a variety of other findings as well, although at least some well-documented phenomena (the preference for a multiple schedule over a mixed schedule, e.g., Green, 1980) appear to lie outside its domain. But it is also challenged seriously by problems posed by its conceptualization of rate of transition. That notion seems to imply that the value of a conditioned reinforcer should be determined by the rate of food presentation in its presence, whereas, as noted above, rate, per se, is not the controlling variable. For example, when several reinforcers are presented during one terminal-link presentation (e.g., Fantino & Herrnstein, 1968), each reinforcer is not weighted equally, but instead the increment in value is determined by the temporal distance between each reinforcer and the entry into the terminal link. A related difficulty is the preference for a VI schedule relative to an FI of corresponding duration (cf. Killeen, 1968), since the rate of

transition for the two schedules is nominally the same. While it is possible to account for such findings by additional assumptions about changes in the functionally effective stimulus (i.e., each reinforcer delivery changes the stimulus, with each new stimulus assuming a different conditioned reinforcement value; the temporal differentiation allowed by an FI schedule makes it functionally similar to a chain schedule), at present such assumptions seem arbitrary. Further empirical work may, of course, make the case in their favor more compelling.

### Conclusion

Perhaps more than any other area that has been discussed, choice between conditioned reinforcers has generated a variety of competing explanations. At present, however, the available evidence does not allow a differentiation among the alternatives, as all are challenged by at least some findings. Moreover, the various accounts differ in the number of variables they invoke, as some are couched purely in terms of conditioned reinforcement (Vaughan, 1985), while others argue that conditioned reinforcement is necessarily combined with several other factors (Killeen, 1982b); It is possible, and perhaps likely, that the value of a conditioned reinforcer is multiply determined, so that no simple formulation will suffice to encompass all of the empirical relations that have been described. Despite such complexities, conditioned reinforcement remains among the most important theoretical constructs in the analysis of behavior, and comprehensive theories of choice should continue to play an important role in resolving its status.

## EXTENSIONS AND APPLICATIONS

The research considered in the preceding sections has concerned traditional problems in the study of reinforcement. The matching law has served as an integrative theme for much of that research, as it provides a common metric by which the relative value of different response consequences can be assessed in different situations. The research now to be described also has the matching law as a major focus, but extends it to domains usually regarded outside the scope of reinforcement theory. As will be seen, a variety of such extensions are possible, as the matching law has important ramifications for several diverse areas of psychological research.

## Self-Control

Individuals are regarded as impulsive or as exhibiting self-control, depending upon whether their behavior is controlled by its immediate consequences or by longer-term consequences that ultimately are of greater importance. For example, impulsive behavior is said to occur when we enjoy the immediate pleasures of smoking cigarettes at the expense of a substantial increase in future health hazards. Self-control is simply the converse.

Discussion of the determinants of self-control has occurred in a variety of arenas, including developmental psychology, sociology, economics, and personality theory. Much of that discussion has focused on the personal characteristics of individuals who are regarded as impulsive (i.e., correlational research), but there also have been experimental investigations of the situational determinants as well (e.g., Mischel & Ebbesen, 1970). The present treatment will by-pass the multifarious discussion of the issue, but will instead provide a general conceptual framework in which the problem can be analyzed. Its underlying assumption is that self-control and impulsiveness are simply alternative behaviors for any given situation, so that general theories of choice should apply.

Viewed in terms of behavioral processes, whether impulsiveness or self-control will occur has little to do with the self, but depends instead on the outcome of the competition between different reinforcement contingencies. That is, the consequences of impulsiveness versus self-control as alternative behaviors usually differ in two dimensions—the delay and amount of reinforcement. Impulsiveness occurs when the more immediate, but smaller, reinforcer determines the choice; self-control is exhibited when the choice is controlled by the more delayed, but larger, reinforcer. Given such a characterization, the matching law should provide insight into the circumstances under which self-control will or will not occur, since the problem reduces to how the different parameters combine to determine total reinforcement value for the competing alternatives.

The major empirical phenomenon in the experimental analysis of self-control is that impulsiveness decreases the longer the delay to the less delayed but smaller reward. In other words, impulsiveness is likely to occur when the smaller reward is immediately contingent on behavior, but self-control may emerge as the delays to both the smaller and larger rewards are increased. For example, an alcoholic may be unable to resist the temptations of alcohol when his favorite liquor is immediately available, but given the choice between drinking and abstinence when the opportunity to drink is some time away, he may choose abstinence. Such a choice would then commit him to a course of action that would preclude the opportunity to drink when alcohol later became available (e.g., by taking Antabuse in the morning).

Figure 3.24 illustrates how this phenomenon of preference reversal is understood in terms of the matching law. Shown is the reward effectiveness for two different reinforcers, which are assumed to differ in value by some factor ($a$) that is represented by the relative heights of the heavy bars. For both reinforcers, reward effectiveness declines as the time between the response and reward is increased. The rate of this decrease is given by equation 26, which is derived from the interpretation of delay-of-reinforcement effects in terms of the matching law (see section on response strength). The only difference between the functions for the two choice alternatives is that the larger reward is $a$

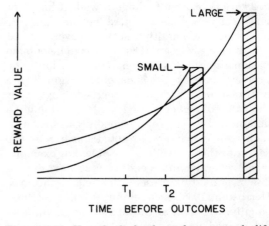

**Figure 3.24.** Hypothetical values of two rewards differing in amount and delay as a function of the time before their outcome. The ratio of the two reward magnitudes is arbitrarily defined as a factor $a$ (see text).

times more valuable than the smaller, which is represented in equation 26 by multiplying the reinforcement rate, $R$, by $a$. Thus equation 26 for the larger reward becomes

$$B_L = k \frac{\dfrac{aR}{D}}{\dfrac{aR}{D} + R_e}$$

while for the smaller reward it is simply

$$B_S = k \frac{\dfrac{R}{D}}{\dfrac{R}{D} + R_e}$$

The critical feature of Figure 3.24 is that the two reward alternatives are located at different points in time. At $T_2$ on the abscissa, the delay to the smaller reward is very short, while the delay to the larger reward is relatively much greater. Thus, the height of the reward gradient is greater for the smaller reward and it should be preferred. As the delay to both alternatives is then increased by equal amounts of time, the delay functions eventually cross, and the reward effectiveness becomes greater for the larger reward ($T_1$). Preference reversal thus can be understood as the direct result of the nature of the delay-of-reinforcement gradients, with their hyperbolic shapes derived from the matching-law interpretation.

Preference reversal also can be understood in terms of the algebraic expression of the matching law, as applied to the combination of amount and delay of reinforcement. The most general form of the matching law, equation 12, is rewritten here for convenience, with the terms for the rates of reinforcement removed since they are assumed to be equal for the two alternatives and thus cancel from the expression.

$$\frac{B_1}{B_2} = \frac{A_1}{A_2} \cdot \frac{\dfrac{1}{D_1}}{\dfrac{1}{D_2}}$$

Given some constant ratio between the two amounts, preference for the smaller reward will occur whenever the ratio between the two delays exceeds the ratio between the amounts in the opposite direction. As equal delays are then added to both alternatives, the ratio between the delays moves toward 1.0, so that the ratio of

the amounts will eventually dominate the expression, and self-control should occur. As an example, consider a situation in which the reward amounts differ by a factor of $2:1$, and the delays initially are 2 seconds and 10 seconds, for the smaller and larger rewards, respectively. Since the delay ratio is greater than the amount ratio, the smaller reward would be preferred. But if 10 seconds were then added to each delay value, the ratio between the delays drops below that for the amounts, and the larger reward would be chosen.

An important feature of experimental studies of self-control is that the point of preference reversal is often highly variable across subjects. Such individual differences have been a major concern of traditional accounts of self-control, since they are correlated with a host of variables, including social class, IQ, and age of the subject. Moreover, even with animal subjects, the degree of self-control has been shown to vary systematically with the training history of the subject (e.g., Mazur & Logue, 1978). Because equation 26, rewritten above, provides no account for such variability, Herrnstein (1981) modified it in the form of equation 49, which adds an additional parameter, $I$, for individual differences in the degree of impulsiveness. Equation 49 also differs from equation 26 in terms of $R_e$ being divided by $D$.

$$B = \frac{k \dfrac{R}{D}}{\dfrac{R}{D} + \dfrac{R_e}{D} + I} = k \frac{R}{R + R_e + DI} \qquad (49)$$

The role of the $I$ parameter is to provide a scale factor for delay, as subjects that discount time sharply (those more sensitive to delay) have high values of $I$, resulting in a steep decline in reward effectiveness as delay is increased. Such subjects would appear impulsive, while those with lower values of $I$ would be more likely to exhibit self-control. Training procedures used to increase the degree of self-control can also be captured in terms of $I$, since their primary effect is to decrease the steepness of the delay-of-reinforcement gradient (cf. Mazur & Logue, 1978). As suggested by Herrnstein (1981), $I$ should also vary systematically with other procedural variables, such as the degree of motivation corresponding to the contingent reinforcer (with higher motivational levels producing greater impulsiveness).

The preceding analysis demonstrates that the matching law provides a simple framework for incorporating several of the major results of self-control experiments. However, as noted earlier the analysis of delay-of-reinforcement experiments in terms of the matching law has remained a subject of controversy, since the simple matching to relative immediacy (equation 12) does not appear to be an accurate description of the actual results. In particular, matching is violated by the effect of absolute delay value even when the ratio between the different delays is held constant (Williams & Fantino, 1978). Similar effects have also occurred in the self-control literature, as preference for the smaller versus larger reward is systematically affected by the absolute delay values independent of their ratio (Navarick & Fantino, 1976).

An example of the effect of absolute value on the delay intervals is shown in Figure 3.25 taken from Snyderman (1983b). He presented pigeons a concurrent-chains procedure in which the reward magnitudes for the two alternatives

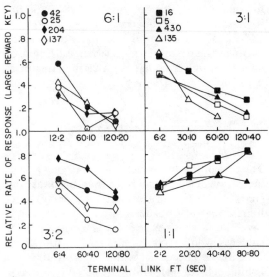

**Figure 3.25.** Relative rate of responding for the larger reward alternative as a function of the terminal fixed-delay schedules for each subject. Different quadrants correspond to the different delay ratios. The individual delay values involved in each choice comparison are shown along the abscissa for each condition. From "Delay and Amount of Reward in a Concurrent Chain" by M. Snyderman, 1983, *Journal of the Experimental Analysis of Behavior, 39*, p. 443. Copyright 1983 by the Society for the Experimental Analysis of Behavior, Inc. Reprinted by permission.

were held constant in a ratio of $3:1$. Different conditions were then defined by the ratio of the delays associated with the different amounts, with the shorter delay always associated with the smaller amount. The different delay ratios, shown in separate quadrants of Figure 3.25, were $6:1$, $3:1$, $3:2$, and $1:1$. For each separate ratio, three separate delay durations were studied, with the absolute values ranging from 2 to 120 seconds.

Figure 3.25 demonstrates that preference for the shorter delays (and thus the smaller reward) increased the longer the absolute delay durations. Thus, a simple multiplicative rule, such as that given by equation 26, cannot adequately describe the interaction between delay and amount. As noted by Snyderman (1983), such results also pose difficulties for other accounts of choice in concurrent-chains schedules, including those discussed earlier in the section on conditioned reinforcement (Fantino, 1977; Killeen, 1982b).

The results seen in Figure 3.25 imply that any account of the effects of relative delay on choice must be more complex than the simple matching of relative immediacy. A possible alternative is offered by equation 49. If the response strength of each delay-amount combination is assumed to follow equation 49, with the amount of reinforcement contingent on the two responses differing by a factor of $a$, preference between the two is given by equation 50:

$$\frac{B_L}{B_S} = \frac{k\dfrac{aR}{aR + R_e + D_L I}}{k\dfrac{R}{R + R_e + D_S I}} \tag{50a}$$

To see how it applies to Figure 3.25, consider the fourth quadrant in which the delays for the two alternatives were equal. The increased preference for the larger reward with increasing delay is the finding that poses the most serious difficulty for previous accounts. In fact, however, it is predicted by equation 50, as can be seen by its rearrangement (note that $D_L = D_S$):

$$\frac{B_L}{B_S} = \frac{a(R + R_e + DI)}{aR + R_e + DI} \tag{50b}$$

Equation 50b makes clear that an increase in the absolute value of $D$ will produce a larger change in the numerator of the right-hand side of the equation. Thus, increases in delay should increase the preference for the larger reward alternative, which is the result shown in Figure 3.25. A similar analysis (cf. Herrnstein, 1981) also explains the results seen in the other quadrants of Figure 3.25. It should be noted, however, that equation 50 omits the reinforcement for the alternative response as part of the context of reinforcement, which is not done for simple concurrent schedules (see discussion of equation 28). Whether such an omission is justifiable for concurrent-chains schedules remains unclear, although it does allow an explanation of the results seen in Figure 3.25 that has not been forthcoming from alternative explanations.

As indicated by the above discussion, the matching-law account has had major success in explaining the central features of self-control experiments. Some uncertainty remains about the trade-off between delay and amount of reinforcement, primarily because of uncertainty about the effects of delay of reinforcement in isolation. However, the cardinal assumption of the matching-law account—that delay and amount of reinforcement are commensurate methods of changing the value of response consequences—remains unchallenged. Given the validity of that assumption, self-control may be viewed as simply one variant of choice behavior and thus should be understandable as the outcome of the general processes of reinforcement.

## Signal-Detection Theory

A different type of application of the matching law is to signal-detection theory, which is widely used in studies of psychophysics and decision making to differentiate effects of sensory sensitivity from motivational or demand characteristics of the experimental situations. The standard signal-detection procedure arranges two stimulus conditions, signal plus noise versus noise alone, which are presented successively across trials. On any given trial, the subject emits either a "yes" response or "no" response, indicating his judgment about whether the signal occurred. Thus, two different responses are possible for either stimulus condition, as shown in Table 3.3. Responses in cells 1 and 4 represent accurate discrimination, while those in 2 and 3 represent errors.

The number of entries in each cell of Table 3.3

**Table 3.3. Schematic Outline of the Yes–No Signal Detection Procedure**

| Stimuli | *Responses* | |
|---|---|---|
| | $R_1$ (Yes) | $R_2$ (No) |
| Signal + Noise | Correct detection (Hit) | Miss |
| Noise Alone | False Report | Correct Rejection |

obviously depends on factors other than sensory confusion between the two stimuli. For example, if the pay-off for hits is substantially higher than the pay-off for correct rejections, one might expect an increase in both the number of hits and the number of false reports. Differential pay-offs are one of several ways of creating response bias independent of the sensory characteristics of the stimuli, which necessitates some method of isolating the sensory effects alone.

The conventional model of signal-detection performance (Green & Swets, 1966) represent the sensory effects of the stimuli, signal versus noise, by overlapping normal distributions on some unidimensional observational axis, as shown in Figure 3.26. The distance between the midpoints of the two distributions is designated as $d'$, which indicates the degree of separation between the two stimuli in standard deviation units. Because of the overlap between the distributions, there is some probability of the subject perceiving the noise when the signal is presented and vice versa, with the probability of such sensory errors given by the overlap of the two distributions. However, the degree of overlap interacts with the subject's judgment processes, which determine a response criterion, as represented

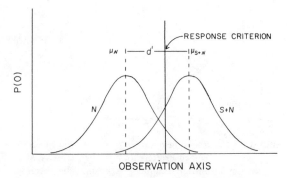

**Figure 3.26.** A schematic of the theory of signal detection. See text for explanation.

by the vertical line. Thus, all points to the right of the line will evoke a signal response, while those to the left will evoke a judgment of noise. The probability of hits versus false alarms is then given by the relative areas of the two distributions to the right of the line, while the probabilities of misses versus correct rejections is given by their relative areas to the left of the line. As the criterion is shifted farther to the left (i.e., a more lax criterion is adopted), the overall ratio of "yes" to "no" responses will increase, producing an increase in hits but also an increase in false alarms. The criterion itself is assumed to change according to the relative values of hits versus correct detections or, more typically, as a function of the overall probability of signal presentation.

The isolation of sensory sensitivity effects (the value of $d'$) from the effect of the response criterion typically is accomplished by generating a receiver-operator curve (ROC), which results when the sensory characteristics of the signal are held constant while either the response pay-off or signal probability is varied over some range. Shown in Figure 3.27 are several such curves, which show the relation between the probability of a yes response given the signal and the probability of a yes response given the noise. Increasingly little overlap between the two distributions shown in Figure 3.26 corresponds to curves of increasing distance from the major diagonal, with the amount of distance

corresponding to $d'$. To the extent that no discrimination is possible (i.e., the signal and noise distributions completely overlap) all of the points would lie along the diagonal itself. The functions shown in Figure 3.27 are known as isosensitivity curves.

The possibility that the matching law may provide some insight into signal-detection performance is suggested by the similarity between the procedure shown in Table 3.3 and a concurrent schedule. That is, with the signal present, the subject chooses between two responses, yes and no, with their relative frequency being a joint function of the sensory confusion between the signal and noise and the relative pay-offs for hits versus correct rejections. Similarly, when the noise is present, the same two response alternatives are available and the same determining variables apply. Thus, a signal-detection procedure may be conceptualized as a multiple schedule in which each component is a concurrent schedule with one response associated with reinforcement while the alternative is associated with extinction. However, the response associated with EXT is also associated with reinforcement in the alternative component, so it should be expected to receive some degree of generalized strength from the alternative component.

Nevin (1981) has advanced an account of signal-detection performance on the preceding conceptualization. Given the presence of the signal, the ratio of yes versus no responses should match the ratio of the reinforcement for yes responses in the signal component to reinforcement for the no responses during the noise weighted by some generalization factor. Equation 51 formalizes this notion, with the term $g$, which ranges from 0 to 1.0, corresponding to the degree of generalization.

$$\frac{B_{\text{yes}/S}}{B_{\text{no}/S}} = \frac{R_{\text{yes}/S}}{gR_{\text{no}/N}} \qquad (51a)$$

When there is no confusion between the signal and noise, the degree of generalization would be zero, and thus all responding would be to the yes alternative. Conversely, complete confusion would produce responding that strictly matched the overall reinforcement rates for the yes and no responses independent of which stimulus was present.

A corresponding expression can be written for the choice of the yes/no response during the

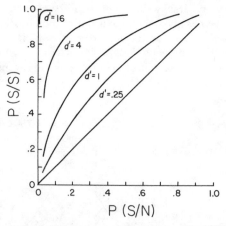

**Figure 3.27.** Receiver-operating curves for different values of $d'$. The ordinate plots the probability of a signal response when a signal was present; the abscissa plots the probability of a signal response in the absence of the signal.

noise component, as given by equation 51b:

$$\frac{B_{\text{yes}/N}}{B_{\text{no}/N}} = \frac{g R_{\text{yes}/S}}{R_{\text{no}/N}} \qquad (51b)$$

The parameter $g$ corresponds to the similarity between the signal and noise, so that its inverse, $(1/g)$ analogous to the concept of $d'$ derived from conventional signal-detection theory. Isolation of $g$ from the reinforcement contingencies is given by simply dividing equation 51a by equation 51b, with the resulting expression (equation 52) providing an index of stimulus similarity based entirely on the obtained behavioral allocations in the presence of the two stimuli.

$$\frac{B_{\text{yes}/S}}{B_{\text{no}/S}} \cdot \frac{B_{\text{no}/N}}{B_{\text{yes}/N}} = \left(\frac{1}{g}\right)^2 \qquad (52)$$

If changes in $g$ are functionally similar to $d'$, changes in the overall occurrence of yes/no responses resulting from variation in the incentive/demand characteristics of the situation should leave its value unaffected. As reviewed by Nevin (1971), signal-detection experiments with animals do indeed produce approximately constant values of $g$ when the reinforcement schedules contingent on correct yes and no responses are varied. Moreover, the relation between hits and false alarms produced in such experiments are similar to those seen in Figure 3.27, with the different curves shown there corresponding to different values of $g$. Thus, $g$ performs like $d'$ as a measure of sensory confusion. Unlike signal-detection theory, however, Nevin's analysis has the advantages of being based totally on observed behavioral processes.

A second model of signal-detection behavior based on the matching law, but based on somewhat different assumptions, has been proposed by Davison and Tustin (1978). Rather than use the strict matching law as their starting point, they assumed only the generalized matching law (equation 8), which is rewritten here with respect to behavior in a signal-detection experiment.

$$\frac{B_{\text{yes}}}{B_{\text{no}}} = b \left(\frac{R_{\text{yes}}}{R_{\text{no}}}\right)^a$$

Equation 8 would apply if the signal and noise were indistinguishable. To incorporate the effects of stimulus discriminability, Davison and Tustin argued that the effects of the particular stimulus could be regarded as a form of bias,

with the presence of the signal biasing the choice toward the yes response and the presence of the noise biasing it toward the no response. In terms of equation 8, this implies that the term for bias becomes the product of the usual sources of bias (e.g., different response requirements) and the effects of stimulus discriminability, represented by $d$. Accordingly, equation 53a describes such effects for the yes/no behavior during the signal, while equation 53b describes the behavior during the noise, when the discriminability bias is assumed to be in the opposite direction.

$$\frac{B_{\text{yes}/S}}{B_{\text{no}/S}} = b \cdot d \left(\frac{R_{\text{yes}}}{R_{\text{no}}}\right)^a \qquad (53a)$$

$$\frac{B_{\text{yes}/N}}{B_{\text{no}/N}} = b \cdot \frac{1}{d} \cdot \left(\frac{R_{\text{yes}}}{R_{\text{no}}}\right)^a \qquad (53b)$$

For the purpose of isolating the value of $d$ independent of the reinforcement frequencies, it is helpful to convert both expressions into their logarithmic forms, so that equation 53a becomes:

$$\log \frac{B_{\text{yes}/S}}{B_{\text{no}/S}} = \log b + \log d + a \log \frac{R_{\text{yes}}}{R_{\text{no}}}$$

and equation 53b becomes

$$\log \frac{B_{\text{yes}/S}}{B_{\text{no}/N}} = \log b - \log d + a \log \frac{R_{\text{yes}}}{R_{\text{no}}}$$

The bias effects due to stimulus discriminability is then given by subtracting the logarithmic form of equation 53b from that of equation 53a, which yields equation 54. Note that equation 54 is identical to equation 52 except for the change in notation.

$$\log \frac{B_{\text{yes}/S}}{B_{\text{no}/S}} - \log \frac{B_{\text{yes}/N}}{B_{\text{no}/N}} = 2 \log d \qquad (54)$$

The terms for the reinforcement ratios are thus removed, leaving $d$ as a measure of stimulus discriminability derived solely from the relation between the behavior ratios during the signal and noise stimuli. The validity of its interpretation as a pure measure of stimulus discriminability is supported by empirical results that have established that $d$ varies inversely with the degree of stimulus similarity and is unaffected by the relative reinforcement rates associated with the two types of correct responses (McCarthy & Davison, 1980).

The derivations of both equations 52 and 54 assumed that the judgment criterion invoked by signal detection theory (the location of the vertical line in Figure 3.26) is the direct result of the relative reinforcement frequencies for the two choice alternatives, yes versus no. However, the usual method for generating ROC functions like those seen in Figure 3.27 is to vary the probability of signal presentation, not the relative pay-off for hits versus correct rejections. Thus, to establish the applicability of the matching-law analysis, it must be shown that the effect of the probability of signal presentation can be interpreted in terms of relative reinforcement rates. Variation in the probability of signal presentation does, in fact, covary with the obtained frequency of reinforcement, because of the usual method of programming response feedback. That is, both hits and correct rejections are reinforced on a ratio schedule (usually positive feedback for each correct response), so that the obtained reinforcements of yes versus no, summed over an entire session, are determined by the probability of signal presentation.

To separate the effects of obtained reinforcement frequencies from signal probability, per se, McCarthy and Davison (1979) compared the results of three similar signal-detection experiments with pigeons, which differed in the schedule by which response were reinforced. In all three experiments the discriminative stimuli were two different light intensities projected on the center key of a three-key pigeon chamber. Following presentation of either intensity, the two side keys were illuminated, with correct responses then defined as a left-key peck after the brighter light and a right-key peck following the dimmer light. In the first experiment, the probability of signal presentation was varied, while reinforcing both correct responses on the same variable-ratio schedule. Such a procedure is similar to that generally used in signal-detection experiments, which has the result that the obtained reinforcement frequencies are a function of the behavioral allocation. A second experiment used the same stimulus conditions, but the reinforcement for the correct responses was controlled by nonindependent concurrent VI VI schedule in which a single VI tape determined the availability of the reinforcer, and a probability generator assigned that reinforcer to one response or the other (cf. Stubbs & Pliskoff, 1969). The VI schedule then resumed only after the assigned reinforcer was obtained

by the next correct response to the designated alternative. Such a procedure fixes the relative frequencies of reinforcement for the two response alternatives, independent of the actual frequencies of those responses. Finally, in the third experiment, the probability of signal presentation was held constant, but the ratio of reinforcement obtained for the choice responses was varied by changing the dependent concurrent VI VI schedules.

The primary issue in the three experiments was whether the response bias effects observed in signal-detection experiments were due solely to the obtained relative reinforcement rates. Their results were that typical ROC functions were obtained in the first experiment in which signal probability and obtained reinforcement rate co-varied, but that such functions were not obtained in the second experiment, as the response bias remained approximately constant regardless of the probability of signal presentation. Typical ROC functions were then obtained again in the third experiment, in which the probability of signal presentation was held constant while relative reinforcement frequencies varied independently, indicating that obtained relative reinforcement rate was indeed the controlling variable. Such a finding has important implications for human signal-detection experiments, since it suggests that reliable estimates of response bias can be obtained only if the relation between procedural variations (such as probability of signal presentation) and obtained reinforcement frequencies are properly understood.

The preceding discussion demonstrates that the matching law generates models of signal-detection behavior that are formally similar to classical signal-detection theory. Unlike the classical theory, however, the basic processes underlying the matching models are empirically observable and common to many other behavioral phenomena. Given that signal-detection theory has had wide applicability to human decision processes in many situations, the implication is that the matching law has a similar generality, with implications for many phenomena far beyond its original domain.

### Other Applications
Space does not permit a detailed description of the variety of applications of the matching law to other behavioral phenomena. Among those that could be considered are the interpretation

of adjunctive behaviors such as polydipsia (Heyman & Bouzas, 1980), the interpretation of various types of drug effects (Heyman, 1983b), the determinants of various clinical behaviors such as self-mutilation (McDowell, 1982), and the prediction of behavior in foraging situations, as studied in biology (Lea, 1981). Some of these extensions may, of course, prove to be cul-de-sacs. At present, however, the quantitative analysis of reinforcement contingencies has proven to be a rich explanatory framework with ramifications for a sizable fraction of experimental psychology.

## CONCLUSIONS

This chapter has reviewed the functional relations that describe how behavior is determined by its consequences. The validity of these functional relations is an empirical issue, to be determined by whether measures of behavior conform closely to the pattern predicted by the various equations. At that level the research of the past twenty years has been remarkably successful, as various quantitative formulations have been shown to describe behavior with considerable accuracy. But the nature of those functional relations also has a deeper theoretical significance, because they constrain how the notion of behavioral strength should be conceptualized. The particular conception sponsored by the empirical functions that have been considered is that the dimension of response strength corresponds to the *relative value* of the response consequences. Value is thus a hypothetical construct, which emerges because of the interchangeability of the effects of different types of reinforcement contingencies. Evidence supporting such interchangeability was reviewed in the section on choice and the matching law.

Conceptualization of response strength in terms of the dimension of value differs significantly from traditional approaches to behavior theory, which generally have viewed response strength to be determined by probability of reinforcement. The most common such treatment has been in terms of stochastic learning models, which entail that each individual reinforcement or nonreinforcement changes the existing level of response strength to some new value. Such an approach assumes, at least implicitly, that the effect of a reinforcement contingency is to

generate particular levels of response strength for each individual behavior, so that choice between alternatives reduces simply to the response with the highest probability of reinforcement being emitted. A major problem faced by such approaches (and for related approaches such as contingency theory (e.g., Gibbon, Berryman, & Thompson, 1974) is that different parameters are regarded as qualitatively different in their mode of action. For example, in the final version of Hull's system (1952), amount of reinforcement was regarded as an incentive variable with a growth function quite different from that for frequency of reinforcement, which was regarded as a learning variable. Such accounts are challenged by the evidence reviewed here, which makes a strong case that amount and frequency are totally interchangeable in their effects, often in extraordinarily simple ways (e.g., Miller, 1976). Such interchangeability demands a common denominator for the two separate attributes of reinforcement, which is provided by the value concept.

A corollary of the concept of value is an emphasis on rate, rather than probability of reinforcement, as the critical determinant of conditioning. That is, the value of a consequence is determined by the pay-off per unit time the animal is engaged in the particular behavior, with the pay-off determined by the combined influence of the various reinforcement parameters that are operative. Conceptions of response strength based on probability of reinforcement have had little role for time variables, because they deal only with the occurrence/nonoccurrence of reinforcement given the behavior, independent of the time frame required for that behavior. While such approaches may be applicable to discrete-trial situations in which the occurrence of behavior can be predicted from immediate stimulus changes, they have much greater difficulty with free-operant procedures in which behavior is emitted in an unchanging environment. Application of the concept of probability of reinforcement to such situations requires a definition not only of the particular instances of responding, but also of the occurrence of nonreinforcement. Both are problematic, as seen in the earlier discussion of VI versus VR reinforcement schedules, where the simple occurrence/ nonoccurrence of the behavior provides a poor index of the true response strength, at least as assessed by a choice test. Perhaps because of such difficulties, analyses of free-operant behavior in terms of reinforcement probability are generally regarded as having failed (cf. Morse, 1966).

A second corollary of the conceptualization of response strength in terms of relative value is that the strength of an individual response never can be specified in isolation. Behavior never occurs in a vacuum, so that any measure of strength can be viewed as the result of the organism's choice between reinforcement contingencies. Thus, even simple rates of responding, when only a single response is measured, reflect the relative value of the response consequences. Perhaps more than any other issue in the study of operant behavior, this implication of the concept of value has remained the most controversial. As discussed in the section on response strength, the conceptual framework it implies allows the theoretical integration of a large variety of different research areas. But as also discussed, its empirical status remains in question, as several types of conflicting data have been reported. Whether the conflicting findings can be accounted for by plausible additional assumptions, or whether they reflect a fundamental violation of the concept of relative value as the basis of response strength, remains to be determined. Whatever the eventual outcome, the extension of the concept of relative value to the single response situation has proven to be provocative, with implications for the very foundations of behavior theory.

# REFERENCES

Ainslie, G. & Herrnstein, R.J. (1981). Preference reversal and delayed reinforcement. *Animal Learning & Behavior, 9,* 476–482.

Allison, J., Miller, M., & Wozny, M. (1979). Conservation in behavior. *Journal of Experimental Psychology: General, 108,* 4–34.

Amsel, A. (1967). Partial reinforcement effects on vigor and persistence. In K.W. Spence & J.T. Spence (Eds.), *The psychology of learning and motivation.* (Vol. 1, pp. 1–65). New York: Academic Press.

Anger, D. (1956). The dependence of interresponse times upon the relative reinforcement of different interresponse times. *Journal of Experimental Psychology, 52,* 145–161.

Autor, S.M. (1960). The strength of conditioned reinforcers as a function of frequency and probability of reinforcement. Unpublished doctoral dissertation, Harvard University.

Azrin, N.H. & Holz, W.C. (1966). Punishment. In W.K. Honig (Ed.), *Operant behavior: Areas of research and application* (pp. 380–447). Englewood Cliffs, NJ: Prentice-Hall.

Azrin, N.H., Hutchinson, R.R., & McLaughlin, R. (1965). The opportunity for aggression as an operant reinforcer during aversive stimulation. *Journal of the Experimental Analysis of Behavior, 8,* 171–180.

Baum, W.M. (1973a). The correlation-based law of effect. *Journal of the Experimental Analysis of Behavior, 20,* 137–153.

Baum, W.M. (1973b). Time allocation and negative reinforcement. *Journal of the Experimental Analysis of Behavior, 20,* 313–322.

Baum, W.M. (1974). On two types of deviation from the matching law: Bias and undermatching. *Journal of the Experimental Analysis of Behavior, 22,* 231–242.

Baum, W.M. (1976). Time-based and count-based measurement of preference. *Journal of the Experimental Analysis of Behavior, 26,* 27–35.

Baum, W.M. (1979). Matching, undermatching, and overmatching in studies of choice. *Journal of the Experimental Analysis of Behavior, 32,* 269–281.

Baum, W.M. (1981). Optimization and the matching law as accounts of instrumental behavior. *Journal of the Experimental Analysis of Behavior, 36,* 387–403.

Baum, W.M. (1982). Choice, changeover, and travel. *Journal of the Experimental Analysis of Behavior, 38,* 35–49.

Bersh, P.J. & Lambert, J.V. (1975). The discriminative control of free-operant avoidance despite exposure to shock during the stimulus correlated with nonreinforcement. *Journal of the Experimental Analysis of Behavior, 23,* 111–120.

Bloomfield, T.M. (1967). Behavioral contrast and relative reinforcement frequency in two multiple schedules. *Journal of the Experimental Analysis of Behavior, 10,* 151–158.

Bradshaw, C.M. (1977). Suppression of response rates in variable-interval schedules by a concurrent schedule of reinforcement. *British Journal of Psychology, 68,* 437–480.

Bradshaw, C.M., Ruddle, H.V., & Szabadi, E. (1981). Relationship between response rate and reinforcement frequency in variable-interval schedules: II. Effects of the volume of sucrose reinforcement. *Journal of the Experimental Analysis of Behavior, 35,* 263–269.

Bradshaw, C.M., Szabadi, E., & Bevan, P. (1976). Behavior of humans in variable-interval schedules of reinforcement. *Journal of the Experimental Analysis of Behavior, 26,* 135–141.

Bradshaw, C.M., Szabadi, E., & Bevan, P. (1978). Relationship between response rate and reinforcement frequency in variable-interval schedules: The effect of the concentration of sucrose reinforcement. *Journal of the Experimental Analysis of Behavior, 29,* 447–452.

Bradshaw, C.M., Szabadi, E., Ruddle, H.V., & Pears, E. (1983). Herrnstein's equation: Effect of deprivation level on performance in variable-interval schedules. *Behavior Analysis Letters, 3,* 267–273.

Brandauer, C.M. (1958). The effects of uniform probabilities of reinforcement upon the response rate of the pigeon. Doctoral dissertation, Columbia University.

Brownstein, A.J. (1971). Concurrent schedules of response-independent reinforcement: Duration of the reinforcing stimulus. *Journal of Experimental Analysis of Behavior, 15,* 211–214.

Brownstein, A.J. & Pliskoff, S.S. (1968). Some effects of relative reinforcement rate and changeover delay in response-independent concurrent schedules of reinforcement. *Journal of the Experimental Analysis of Behavior, 11,* 683–688.

Bushnell, M.C. & Weiss, S.J. (1980). An investigation of peak shift and behavioral contrast for autoshaped and operant behavior. *Journal of the Experimental Analysis of Behavior, 33,* 101–118.

Catania, A.C. (1963a). Concurrent performances: A baseline for the study of reinforcement magnitude. *Journal of the Experimental Analysis of Behavior, 6,* 299–300.

Catania, A.C. (1963b). Concurrent performances: Reinforcement interaction and response independence. *Journal of the Experimental Analysis of Behavior, 6,* 253–263.

Catania, A.C. (1966). Concurrent operants. In W.K. Honig (Ed.), *Operant behavior: Areas of research and application* (pp. 213–270). Englewood Cliffs, NJ: Prentice-Hall.

Catania, A.C. (1973). Self-inhibiting effects of reinforcement. *Journal of the Experimental Analysis of Behavior, 19,* 517–526.

Catania, A.C. & Cutts, D. (1963). Experimental control of superstitious responding in humans. *Journal of the Experimental Analysis of Behavior, 6,* 203–208.

Catania, A.C. & Reynolds, G.S. (1968). A quantitative analysis of the responding maintained by interval schedules of reinforcement. *Journal of the Experimental Analysis of Behavior, 11,* 327–383.

Chung, S.H. & Herrnstein, R.J. (1967). Choice and delay of reinforcement. *Journal of the Experimental Analysis of Behavior, 10,* 67–74.

Collier, G.H. (1982). Determinants of choice. In D.J. Bernstein (Ed.), *Nebraska Symposium on Motivation (1981): Response structure and organization* (pp. 69–127). Lincoln: University of Nebraska Press.

Conrad, D.G. & Sidman, M. (1956). Sucrose concentration as reinforcement for lever pressing by monkeys. *Psychological Reports, 2,* 381–384.

Crespi, L.P. (1944). Amount of reinforcement and level of performance. *Psychological Review, 51,* 341–357.

Cronin, P.B. (1980). Reinstatement of postresponse stimuli prior to reward in delayed-reward discrimination learning by pigeons. *Animal Learning & Behavior, 8,* 352–358.

Davison, M.C. (1982). Preference in concurrent variable-interval fixed-ratio schedules. *Journal of the Experimental Analysis of Behavior, 37,* 81–96.

Davison, M. & Hogsden, I. (1984). Concurrent variable-interval schedule performance: Fixed versus mixed reinforcer durations. *Journal of the Experimental Analysis of Behavior, 41,* 169–182.

Davison, M.C. & Hunter, I.W. (1976). Performance on variable-interval schedules arranged singly and concurrently. *Journal of the Experimental Analysis of Behavior, 25,* 335–345.

Davison, M.C. & Tustin, R.D. (1978). The relation between the generalized matching law and signal-detection theory. *Journal of the Experimental Analysis of Behavior, 29,* 331–336.

DeCarlo, L.T. (1985). Matching and maximizing with variable-time schedules. *Journal of the Experimental Analysis of Behavior, 43,* 75–81.

DeLuty, M.Z. (1976). Choice and the rate of punishment in concurrent schedules. *Journal of the Experimental Analysis of Behavior, 25,* 75–80.

de Villiers, P.A. (1972). Reinforcement and response rate interaction in multiple random-interval avoidance schedules. *Journal of the Experimental Analysis of Behavior, 18,* 499–507.

de Villiers, P.A. (1974). The law of effect and avoidance: A quantitative relationship between response rate and shock-frequency reduction. *Journal of the Experimental Analysis of Behavior, 21,* 223–235.

de Villiers, P.A. (1977). Choice in concurrent schedules and a quantitative formulation of the law of effect. In W.K. Honig, & J.E.R. Staddon (Eds.), *Handbook of operant behavior* (pp. 233–287). Englewood Cliffs, NJ: Prentice-Hall.

de Villiers, P.A. (1980). Toward a quantitative theory of punishment. *Journal of the Experimental Analysis of Behavior, 33,* 15–25.

de Villiers, P.A. (1982). Toward a quantitative theory of punishment. In M.L. Commons, R.J. Herrnstein, & H. Rachlin (Eds.), *Quantitative analyses of behavior: Vol. 2. Matching and maximizing accounts* (pp. 327–344). Cambridge, MA: Ballinger.

de Villiers, P.A. & Herrnstein, R.J. (1976). Toward a law of response strength. *Psychological Bulletin*, *83*, 1131–1153.

Dinsmoor, J.A. (1977). Escape, avoidance, punishment: Where do we stand? *Journal of the Experimental Analysis of Behavior*, *28*, 83–95.

Dreyfus, L.R., Dorman, L.G., Fetterman, J.G., & Stubbs, D.A. (1982). An invariant relation between changing over and reinforcement. *Journal of the Experimental Analysis of Behavior*, *38*, 327–338.

Duncan, B. & Fantino, E. (1972). The psychological distance to reward. *Journal of the Experimental Analysis of Behavior*, *18*, 23–34.

Duncan, H.J. & Silberberg, A. (1982). The effects of concurrent responding and reinforcement on behavioral output. *Journal of the Experimental Analysis of Behavior*, *38*, 125–132.

Dunn, R.M. (1982). Choice, relative reinforcer duration, and the changeover ratio. *Journal of the Experimental Analysis of Behavior*, *38*, 313–319.

Edmon, E.L., Lucki, I., & Gresham, M. (1980). Choice responding following multiple schedule training. *Animal Learning & Behavior*, *8*, 287–292.

Estes, W.K. (1944). An experimental study of punishment. *Psychological Monographs*, *57* (Whole No. 263).

Estes, W.K. (1959). The statistical approach to learning. In S. Koch (Eds.), *Psychology: A study of a science* (Vol. 2, pp. 380–491). New York: McGraw-Hill.

Fantino, E. (1969). Choice and rate of reinforcement. *Journal of the Experimental Analysis of Behavior*, *12*, 723–730.

Fantino, E. (1977). Conditioned reinforcement: Choice and information. In W.K. Honig, & J.E.R. Staddon (Eds.), *Handbook of operant behavior* (pp. 313–339). Englewood Cliffs, NJ: Prentice-Hall.

Fantino, E. (1981). Contiguity, response strength, and the delay-reduction hypothesis. In P. Harzem & M.D. Zeiler (Eds.), *Advances in analysis of behavior: Vol. 2. Predictability, correlation, and contiguity* (pp. 169–201). New York, Wiley.

Fantino, E. & Davison, M. (1983). Choice: Some quantitative relations. *Journal of the Experimental Analysis of Behavior*, *40*, 1–13.

Fantino, E. & Dunn, R. (1983). The delay-reduction hypothesis: Extension to three-alternative choice. *Journal of Experimental Psychology: Animal Behavior Processes*, *9*, 132–146.

Fantino, E. & Herrnstein, R.J. (1968). Secondary reinforcement and number of primary reinforcements. *Journal of the Experimental Analysis of Behavior*, *11*, 9–14.

Farley, J. (1980a). Automaintenance, contrast, and contingencies: Effects of local vs. overall and prior vs. impending reinforcement context. *Learning and Motivation*, *11*, 19–48.

Farley, J. (1980b). Reinforcement and punishment effects in concurrent schedules: A test of two models. *Journal of the Experimental Analysis of Behavior*, *33*, 311–326.

Gardner, E.T. & Lewis, P. (1976). Negative reinforcement with shock-frequency increase. *Journal of the Experimental Analysis of Behavior*, *25*, 3–14.

Gibbon, J. (1981). The contingency problem in autoshaping. In C.M. Locurto, H.S. Terrace, & J. Gibbon, (eds.), *Autoshaping and conditioning theory* (pp. 285–308). New York: Academic Press.

Gibbon, J. & Balsam, P. (1981). Spreading association in time. In C.M. Locurto, H.S. Terrace, & J. Gibbon (Eds.), *Autoshaping and conditioning theory* (pp. 219–253). New York: Academic Press.

Gibbon, J., Berryman, R., & Thompson, R. (1974). Contingency spaces and measures in classical and instrumental conditioning. *Journal of the Experimental Analysis of Behavior*, *21*, 585–605.

Green, D.M. & Swets, J.A. (1966). *Signal detection theory and psychophysics*. New York: Wiley.

Green, L. (1980). Preference as a function of the correlation between stimuli and reinforcement outcomes. *Learning and Motivation*, *11*, 238–255.

Green, L., Rachlin, H., & Hanson, J. (1983). Matching and maximizing with concurrent ratio-interval schedules. *Journal of the Experimental Analysis of Behavior*, *40*, 217–224.

Guthrie, E.R. (1935). *The psychology of learning*. New York: Harper.

Guthrie, E.R. & Horton, G.P. (1946). *Cats in a puzzle box*. New York: Rinehart Press.

Gutman, N. (1954). Equal-reinforcement values for sucrose and glucose solutions compared with equal sweetness values. *Journal of Comparative and Physiological Psychology*, *47*, 358–361.

Halliday, M.S. & Boakes, R.A. (1974). Behavioral contrast without response-rate reduction. *Journal of the Experimental Analysis of Behavior*, *22*, 453–462.

Hamblin, R.L. & Miller, H.L. (1977). Matching as a multivariate power law: Frequency of behavior versus frequency and magnitude of reinforcement. *Learning and Motivation*, *8*, 113–125.

Henton, W.W. & Iversen, I.H. (1978). *Classical conditioning and operant conditioning: A response pattern analysis*. New York: Springer-Verlag.

Herrnstein, R.J. (1961). Relative and absolute strength of response as a function of frequency of reinforcement. *Journal of the Experimental Analysis of Behavior*, *4*, 267–272.

Herrnstein, R.J. (1964). Secondary reinforcement and rate of primary reinforcement. *Journal of the*

*Experimental Analysis of Behavior, 7,* 27–36.

Herrnstein, R.J. (1969). Method and theory in the study of avoidance. *Psychological Review, 76,* 49–69.

Herrnstein, R.J. (1970). On the law of effect. *Journal of the Experimental Analysis of Behavior, 13,* 243–266.

Herrnstein, R.J. (1971). Quantitative hedonism. *Journal of Psychiatric Research, 8,* 399–412.

Herrnstein, R.J. (1974). Formal properties of the matching law. *Journal of the Experimental Analysis of Behavior, 21,* 159–164.

Herrnstein, R.J. (1981). Self control as response strength. In C.M. Bradshaw, E. Szabadi, & C.F. Lowe (Eds.), *Quantification of steady-state operant behavior* (pp. 3–20). New York: Elsevier.

Herrnstein, R.J. & Heyman, G.M. (1979). Is matching compatible with reinforcement maximization on concurrent variable interval, variable ratio? *Journal of the Experimental Analysis of Behavior, 31,* 209–223.

Herrnstein, R.J. & Hineline, P.N. (1966). Negative reinforcement as shock-frequency reduction. *Journal of the Experimental Analysis of Behavior, 9,* 421–430.

Herrnstein, R.J. & Loveland, D.H. (1974). Hunger and contrast in a multiple schedule. *Journal of the Experimental Analysis of Behavior, 21,* 511–517.

Herrnstein, R.J. & Loveland, D.H. (1976). Matching in a network. *Journal of the Experimental Analysis of Behavior, 26,* 143–153.

Herrnstein, R.J. & Vaughan, W. (1980). Melioration and behavioral allocation. In J.E.R. Staddon (Ed.), *Limits to action* (pp. 143–176). New York: Academic Press.

Heyman, G.M. (1979). A Markov model description of changeover probabilities on concurrent variable-interval schedules. *Journal of the Experimental Analysis of Behavior, 31,* 41–51.

Heyman, G.M. (1983a). Optimization theory: Close but no cigar. *Behavior Analysis Letters, 3,* 17–26.

Heyman, G.M. (1983b). A parametric evaluation of the hedonic and motoric effects of drugs: Pimozide and amphetamine. *Journal of the Experimental Analysis of Behavior, 40,* 113–122.

Heyman, G.M. & Bouzas, A. (1980). Context dependent changes in the reinforcing strength of schedule-induced drinking. *Journal of the Experimental Analysis of Behavior, 33,* 327–335.

Heyman, G.M. & Herrnstein, R.J. (1986). More on concurrent interval-ratio schedules: A replication and review. *Journal of the Experimental Analysis of Behavior, 46,* 331–351.

Heyman, G.M. & Luce, R.D. (1979). Operant matching is not a logical consequence of maximizing reinforcement rate. *Animal Learning & Behavior, 7,*

133–140.

Hinson, J.M. & Staddon, J.E.R. (1978). Behavioral competition: A mechanism for schedule interactions. *Science, 202,* 432–434.

Hinson, J.M. & Staddon, J.E.R. (1983a). Hill-climbing by pigeons. *Journal of the Experimental Analysis of Behavior, 39,* 25–47.

Hinson, J.M. & Staddon, J.E.R. (1983b). Matching, maximizing, and hill-climbing. *Journal of the Experimental Analysis of Behavior, 40,* 321–331.

Houston, A.I. & McNamara, J. (1981). How to maximize reward on two variable-interval schedules. *Journal of the Experimental Analysis of Behavior, 35,* 367–396.

Hull, C.L. (1943). *Principles of behavior.* New York: Appleton-Century-Crofts.

Hull, C.L. (1951). *Essentials of behavior.* New Haven: Yale University Press.

Hull, C.L. (1952). *A behavior system: An introduction to behavior theory concerning the individual organism.* New Haven: Yale University Press.

Hursh, S.R. (1978). The economics of daily consumption controlling food- and water-reinforced responding. *Journal of the Experimental Analysis of Behavior, 29,* 475–491.

Hursh, S.R. (1980). Economic concepts for the analysis of behavior. *Journal of the Experimental Analysis of Behavior, 34,* 219–238.

Hursh, S.R. & Fantino, E. (1974). An appraisal of preference for multiple versus mixed schedules. *Journal of the Experimental Analysis of Behavior, 22,* 31–38.

Hutton, L., Gardner, E.T., & Lewis, P. (1978). Matching with a key-peck response in concurrent negative reinforcement schedules. *Journal of the Experimental Analysis of Behavior, 30,* 225–230.

Hitton, L. & Lewis, P. (1979). Effects of response-independent negative reinforcers on negatively reinforced keypecking. *Journal of the Experimental Analysis of Behavior, 32,* 93–100.

Iglauer, C. & Woods, J.H. (1974). Concurrent performances: Reinforcement by different doses of intravenous cocaine in rhesus monkeys. *Journal of the Experimental Analysis of Behavior, 22,* 179–196.

Keesey, R.E. (1962). The relation between pulse frequency, intensity, and duration and the rate of responding for intracranial stimulation. *Journal of Comparative and Physiological Psychology, 55,* 671–678.

Keesey, R.E. (1964). Duration of stimulation and the reward properties of hypothalamic stimulation. *Journal of Comparative and Physiological Psychology, 58,* 201–207.

Keesey, R.E. & Kling, J.W. (1961). Amount of reinforcement and free-operant responding. *Journal of* the *Experimental Analysis of Behavior, 4,* 125–132.

Keller, J.V. & Gollub, L.R. (1977). Duration and rate of responding as determinants of concurrent responding. *Journal of the Experimental Analysis of Behavior, 22,* 179–196.

Killeen, P. (1968). On the measure of reinforcement frequency in the study of preference. *Journal of the Experimental Analysis of Behavior, 11,* 263–269.

Killeen, P. (1970). Preference for fixed-interval schedules of reinforcement. *Journal of the Experimental Analysis of Behavior, 14,* 127–131.

Killeen, P. (1975). On the temporal control of behavior. *Psychological Review, 82,* 89–115.

Killeen, P.R. (1981). Averaging theory. In C.M. Bradshaw, E. Szabadi, & C.F. Low (Eds.), *Quantification of steady-state operant behavior* (pp. 21–34). New York: Elsevier.

Killeen, P.R. (1982a). Incentive theory. In D.J. Berrnstein (Ed.), *Nebraska symposium on motivation 1981: Vol. 29. Response structure and organization* (pp. 169–216). Lincoln: University of Nebraska Press.

Killeen, P.R. (1982b). Incentive theory: II. Models for choice. *Journal of the Experimental Analysis of Behavior, 38,* 217–232.

Killeen, P.R., Hanson, S.J., & Osborne, S.R. (1978). Arousal: Its genesis and manifestation as response rate. *Psychological Review, 85,* 571–581.

Klein, M. & Rilling, M. (1974). Generalization of free-operant avoidance behavior in pigeons. *Journal of the Experimental Analysis of Behavior, 21,* 75–88.

Kraeling, D. (1961). Analysis of amount of reward as a variable in learning. *Journal of Comparative and Physiological Psychology, 54,* 560–565.

Lambert, J.V., Bersh, P.J., Hineline, P.N., & Smith, G.D. (1973). Avoidance conditioning with shock contingent upon the avoidance response. *Journal of the Experimental Analysis of Behavior, 19,* 361–367.

Lander, D.G. & Irwin, R.J. (1968). Multiple schedules: Effects of the distribution of reinforcement between components on the distribution of responses between components. *Journal of the Experimental Analysis of Behavior, 11,* 517–524.

Lea, S.E.G. (1981). Correlation and contiguity in foraging behaviour. In P. Harzem & M.D. Zeiler (Eds.), *Advances in analysis of behavior: Vol. 2. Predictability, correlation, and contiguity* (pp. 344–406). New York: Wiley.

Levis, D.J. & Boyd, T.L. (1979). Symptom maintenance: An infrahuman analysis and extension of the conservation of anxiety principle. *Journal of Abnormal Psychology, 88,* 107–120.

Lewis, P., Gardner, E.T., & Hutton, L. (1976). Integrated delays to shock as negative reinforcement. *Journal of the Experimental Analysis of Behavior, 26,* 379–386.

Lieberman, D.A. (1972). Secondary reinforcement and information as determinants of observing behavior in monkeys (*Macaca mulatta*). *Learning and Motivation, 3,* 341–358.

Logan, R.A. (1960). *Incentive.* New Havan: Yale University Press.

Logue, A.W. & Chavarro, A. (1987). Effect on choice of absolute and relative values of reinforcer delay, amount, and frequency. *Journal of Experimental Psychology: Animal Behavior Processes, 13,* 280–291.

Logue, A.W. & de Villiers, P.A. (1978). Matching in concurrent variable-interval avoidance schedules. *Journal of the Experimental Analysis of Behavior, 29,* 61–66.

MacEwen, D. (1972). The effects of terminal-link fixed-interval and variable-interval schedules on responding under concurrent chained schedules. *Journal of the Experimental Analysis of Behavior, 18,* 253–261.

Mackintosh, N.J. (1974). *The psychology of animal learning.* New York: Academic Press.

Mazur, J.E. (1981). Optimization theory fails to predict performance of pigeons in a two-response situation. *Science, 214,* 823–825.

Mazur, J.E. & Logue, A.W. (1978). Choice in a "self-control" paradigm: Effects of a "fading" procedure. *Journal of the Experimental Analysis of Behavior, 30,* 1–17.

McCarthy, D. & Davison, M. (1979). Signal probability, reinforcement and signal detection. *Journal of the Experimental Analysis of Behavior, 32,* 373–386.

McCarthy, D. & Davison, M. (1980). Independence of sensitivity to relative reinforcement rate and discriminability in signal detection. *Journal of the Experimental Analysis of Behavior, 34,* 273–284.

McDowell, J.J. (1980). An analytic comparison of Herrnstein's equations and a multivariate rate equation. *Journal of the Experimental Analysis of Behavior, 33,* 397–408.

McDowell, J.J. (1982). The importance of Herrnstein's mathematical statement of the law of effect for behavior therapy. *American Psychologist, 37,* 771–779.

McDowell, J.J., Bass, R., & Kessel, R. (1983). Variable-interval rate equations and reinforcement and response distributions. *Psychological Review, 90,* 364–375.

McDowell, J.J. & Kessel, R. (1979). A multivariate rate equation for variable-interval performance. *Journal of the Experimental Analysis of Behavior, 31,* 267–283.

McDowell, J.J. & Wood, H.M. (1984). Confirmation of linear system theory prediction: Changes in Herrnstein's $k$ as a function of changes in reinforcer magnitude. *Journal of the Experimental Analysis of Behavior, 14,* 183–192.

McLean, A.P. & White, K.G. (1983). Temporal constraint on choice: Sensitivity and bias in multiple schedules. *Journal of the Experimental Analysis of Behavior, 39,* 405–426.

Mischel, W. & Ebbesen, E.B. (1970). Attention in delay of gratification. *Journal of Personality and Social Psychology, 16,* 329–337.

Miller, H.L. (1976). Matching-based hedonic scaling in the pigeon. *Journal of the Experimental Analysis of Behavior, 26,* 335–347.

Morse, W.H. (1966). Intermittent reinforcement. In W.K. Honig (Ed.), *Operant behavior: Areas of research and application* (pp. 52–108). New York: Appleton-Century-Crofts.

Mowrer, O.H. & Lamoreaux, R.R. (1946). Fear as an intervening variable in avoidance conditioning. *Journal of Comparative Psychology, 39,* 29–50.

Mullins, E., Agunwamba, C.C., & Donahoe, A.J. (1982). On the analysis of studies of choice. *Journal of the Experimental Analysis of Behavior, 37,* 323–327.

Myers, D.L. & Myers, L.E. (1977). Undermatching: A re-appraisal of performance on concurrent variable-interval schedules of reinforcement. *Journal of the Experimental Analysis of Behavior, 27,* 203–214.

Myerson, J. & Miezin, F.M. (1980). The kinetics of choice: An operant systems analysis. *Psychological Review, 87,* 160–174.

Navarick, D.J. & Fantino, E. (1976). Self-control and general models of choice. *Journal of Experimental Pschology: Animal Behavior Processes, 2,* 75–87.

Nevin, J.A. (1968). Differential reinforcement and stimulus control of not responding. *Journal of the Experimental Analysis of Behavior, 11,* 715–726.

Nevin, J.A. (1969). Interval reinforcement of choice behavior in discrete trials. *Journal of the Experimental Analysis of Behavior, 12,* 875–885.

Nevin, J.A. (1971). Rates and patterns of responding with concurrent fixed-interval and variable-interval reinforcement. *Journal of the Experimental Analysis of Behavior, 16,* 241–247.

Nevin, J.A. (1973). The maintenance of behavior. In J.A. Nevin & G.S. Reynolds (Eds.), *The study of behavior: Learning, motivation, emotion, and instinct* (pp. 200–236). Glenview, IL: Scott, Foresman.

Nevin, J.A. (1974). Response strength in multiple schedules. *Journal of the Experimental Analysis of Behavior, 21,* 389–408.

Nevin, J.A. (1979). Overall matching versus momentary maximizing: Nevin (1969) revisted. *Journal of Experimental Psychology: Animal Behavior Processes, 5,* 300–306.

Nevin, J.A. (1981). Psychophysics and reinforcement schedules: An integration. In M.L. Commons & J.A. Nevin (Eds.), *Quantitative analyses of behavior: Vol. 1. Discriminative properties of reinforcement schedules* (pp. 3–27). Cambridge, MA: Ballinger.

Nevin, J.A. (1982). Some persistent issues in the study of matching and maximizing. In M.L. Commons, R.J. Herrnstein, & H. Rachlin (Eds.), *Quantitative analyses of behavior: Vol. 2. Matching and maximizing accounts* (pp. 153–165). Cambridge, MA: Ballinger.

Pavlov, I.P. (1927). *Conditioned reflexes.* Oxford: Oxford University Press.

Pear, J.J. (1975). Implications of the matching law for ratio responding. *Journal of the Experimental Analysis or Behavior, 23,* 139–140.

Peele, D.B., Casey, J., & Silberberg, A. (1984). Primacy of interresponse-time reinforcement in accounting for rate difference under variable-ratio and variable-interval schedules. *Journal of Experimental Psychology: Animal Behavior Processes, 10,* 149–167.

Platt, J.R. (1979). Interresponse-time shaping by variable-interval-like interresponse-time reinforcement contingencies. *Journal of the Experimental Analysis of Behavior, 31,* 3–14.

Pliskoff, S.S. (1971). Effects of symmetrical and asymmetrical changeover delays on concurrent performances. *Journal of the Experimental Analysis of Behavior, 16,* 249–256.

Pliskoff, S.S., Cicerone, R., & Nelson, T.D. (1978). Local response-rate constants in concurrent variable-interval schedule of reinforcement. *Journal of the Experimental Analysis of Behavior, 29,* 431–446.

Pliskoff, S.S. & Fetterman, J.G. (1981). Undermatching and overmatching: The fixed-ratio changeover requirement. *Journal of the Experimental Analysis of Behavior, 36,* 21–27.

Poling, A. (1978). Performance of rats under concurrent variable-interval schedules of negative reinforcement. *Journal of the Experimental Analysis of Behavior, 30,* 31–36.

Prelec, D. (1982). Matching, maximizing, and the hyperbolic feedback function. *Psychological Review, 89,* 189–230.

Priddle-Higson, P.J., Lowe, C.F., & Harzem, P. (1976). After-effects of reinforcement on variable-ratio schedules. *Journal of the Experimental Analysis of Behavior, 25,* 347–354.

Rachlin, H. (1973). Contrast and matching. *Psychological Review, 80,* 217–234.

Rachlin, H., Battalio, R., Kagel, J., & Green, L.

(1981). Maximization theory in behavioral psychology. *The Behavioral and Brain Sciences, 4,* 371–388.

Rachlin, H. & Baum, W.M. (1969). Response rate as a function of amount of reinforcement from a signalled concurrent response. *Journal of the Experimental Analysis of Behavior, 12,* 11–16.

Rachlin, H. & Baum, W.M. (1972). Effects of alternative reinforcement: Does the source matter? *Journal of the Experimental Analysis of Behavior, 18,* 231–241.

Rachlin, H.C. & Burkhard, B. (1978). The temporal triangle: Response substitution in instrumental conditioning. *Psychological Review, 85,* 22–47.

Rachlin, H., Kagel, J.H., & Battalio, R.C. (1980). Substitutability in time allocation. *Psychological Review, 87,* 355–374.

Rachlin, H. & Krasnoff, J. (1983). Eating and drinking: An economic analysis. *Journal of the Experimental Analysis of Behavior, 39,* 385–404.

Rescorla, R.A. (1982). Effect of a stimulus intervening between CS and US in autoshaping. *Journal of Experimental Psychology: Animal Behavior Processes, 8,* 131–141.

Rescorla, R.A. & Solomon, R.L. (1967). Two-process learning theory: Relationships between Pavlovian conditioning and instrumental learning. *Psychological Review, 74,* 151–182.

Reynolds, G.S. (1961). Relativity of response rate and reinforcement frequency in a multiple schedule. *Journal of the Experimental Analysis of Behavior, 4,* 179–184.

Reynolds, G.S. & McLeod, A. (1970). On the theory of interresponse-time reinforcement. In G.H. Bower (Ed.), *The psychology of learning and motivation* (Vol. 4, pp. 85–107). New York: Academic Press.

Rider, D.P. (1981). Concurrent fixed-interval variable-ratio schedules and the matching relation. *Journal of the Experimental Analysis of Behavior, 36,* 317–328.

Rodriguez, M.L. & Logue, A.W. (1986). Independence of the amount and delay ratios in the generalized matching law. *Animal Learning & Behavior, 14,* 29–37.

Schneider, B.A. (1969). A two-state analysis of fixed-interval responding in the pigeon. *Journal of the Experimental Analysis of Behavior, 12,* 667–687.

Schneider, J.W. (1973). Reinforcer effectiveness as a function of reinforcer rate and magnitude: A comparison of concurrent performances. *Journal of the Experimental Analysis of Behavior, 20,* 461–471.

Schrier, A.M. (1965). Response rates of monkeys under varying conditions of sucrose reinforcement. *Journal of Comparative and Physiological Psychology, 59,* 378–384.

Schwartz, B. & Gamzu, E. (1977). Pavlovian control of operant behavior. An analysis of autoshaping and its implications for operant conditioning. In W.K. Honig & J.E.R. Staddon (Eds.), *Handbook of operant behavior* (pp. 53–97). Englewood Cliffs, NJ: Prentice-Hall.

Shimp, C.P. (1966). Probabilistically reinforced choice behavior in pigeons. *Journal of the Experimental Analysis of Behavior, 9,* 433–455.

Shimp, C.P. (1969). Optimum behavior in free-operant experiments. *Psychological Review, 76,* 97–112.

Shimp, C.P. (1974). Time allocation and response rate. *Journal of the Experimental Analysis of Behavior, 21,* 491–499.

Shimp, C.P. & Wheatley, W.L. (1971). Matching to relative reinforcement frequency in multiple schedules with short component durations. *Journal of the Experimental Analysis of Behavior, 15,* 205–210.

Shull, R.L. & Pliskoff, S.S. (1967). Changeover delay and concurrent schedules: Some effects on relative performance measures. *Journal of the Experimental Analysis of Behavior, 10,* 517–527.

Shull, R.L., Spear, D.J., & Bryson, A.E. (1981). Delay or rate of food delivery as a determiner of response rate. *Journal of the Experimental Analysis of Behavior, 35,* 129–143.

Silberberg, A., Hamilton, B., Ziriax, J.M., & Casey, J. (1978). The structure of choice. *Journal of Experimental Psychology: Animal Behavior Processes, 4,* 368–398.

Silberberg, A., Warren-Boulton, F.R., & Asano, T. (1987). Inferior-good and Giffen-good effects in monkey choice behavior. *Journal of Experimental Psychology: Animal Behavior Processes, 13,* 292–301.

Silberberg, A. & Ziriax, J.M. (1982). The interchange-over time as a molecular dependent variable in concurrent schedules. In M.L. Commons, R.J. Herrnstein, & H. Rachlin (Eds.), *Quantitative analyses of behavior: Vol. 2. Matching and maximizing accounts* (pp. 131–151). Cambridge, MA: Ballinger.

Skinner, B.F. (1938). *The behavior of organisms.* New York: Appleton-Century-Crofts.

Snyderman, M. (1983a). Body weight and response strength. *Behavior Analysis Letters, 3,* 255–265.

Snyderman, M. (1983b). Delay and amount of reward in a concurrent chain. *Journal of the Experimental Analysis of Behavior, 39,* 437–447.

Spence, K.W. (1947). The role of secondary reinforcement in delayed reward learning. *Psychological Review, 54,* 1–8.

Spence, K.W. (1956). *Behavior theory and conditioning.* New Haven: Yale University Press.

Squires, N. & Fantino, E. (1971). A model for choice in simple concurrent and concurrent-chains schedules. *Journal of the Experimental Analysis of Behavior, 15,* 27–38.

Staddon, J.E.R. (1968). Spaced responding and choice: A preliminary analysis. *Journal of the Experimental Analysis of Behavior, 11,* 669–682.

Staddon, J.E.R. (1977). On Herrnstein's equation and related forms. *Journal of the Experimental Analysis of Behavior, 28,* 163–170.

Staddon, J.E.R. (1979) Operant behavior as adaptation to constraint. *Journal of Experimental Psychology: General, 108,* 48–67.

Staddon, J.E.R. (1982). Behavioral competition, contrast, and matching. In M.L. Commons, R.J. Herrnstein, & H. Rachlin (Eds.), *Quantitative analyses of behavior: Vol. 2. Matching and maximizing accounts* (pp. 243–261). Cambridge, MA: Ballinger.

Staddon, J.E.R. (1983). *Adaptive behavior and learning.* New York: Cambridge University Press.

Staddon, J.E.R., Hinson, J.M., & Kram, R. (1981). Optimal choice. *Journal of the Experimental Analysis of Behavior, 35,* 397–412.

Staddon, J.E.R. & Motheral, S. (1978). On matching and maximizing in operant choice experiments. *Psychological Review, 85,* 436–444.

Stubbs, D.A. & Pliskoff, S.S. (1969). Concurrent responding with fixed relative rate of reinforcement. *Journal of the Experimental Analysis of Behavior, 12,* 887–895.

Taylor, R. & Davison, M. (1983). Sensitivity to reinforcement in concurrent arithmetic and exponential schedules. *Journal of the Experimental Analysis of Behavior, 39,* 191–198.

Thorndike, E.L. (1898). Animal intelligence: An experimental study of the associative processes in animals. *Psychological Review Monographs Supplement, 2* (No. 8).

Thorndike, E.L. (1932). Reward and punishment in animal learning. *Comparative Psychology Monographs, 8* (No. 39).

Timberlake, W. (1977). The application of the matching law to simple ratio schedules. *Journal of the Experimental Analysis of Behavior, 25,* 215–217.

Timberlake, W. (1984). Behavior regulation and learned performance: Some misapprehensions and disagreements. *Journal of the Experimental Analysis of Behavior, 41,* 355–375.

Todorov, J.C. (1973). Interaction of frequency and magnitude of reinforcement on concurrent performance. *Journal of the Experimental Analysis of Behavior, 19,* 451–458.

Todorov, J.C., Castro, J.M.O., Hanna, E.S., Bittencourt de Sa, M.C.N., & Barreto, M.Q. (1983). Choice, experience, and the generalized matching law. *Journal of the Experimental Analysis of Behavior, 40,* 99–111.

Todorov, J.C., Hanna, E.S., Bittencourt de Sa, M.C.N. (1984). Frequency versus magnitude of reinforcement: New data with a different procedure. *Journal of the Experimental Analysis of Behavior, 41,* 157–167.

Trevett, A.J., Davison, M.C., & Williams, R.J. (1972). Performance in concurrent interval schedules. *Journal of the Experimental Analysis of Behavior, 17,* 369–374.

Vaughan, W. (1981). Melioration, matching, and maximization. *Journal of the Experimental Analysis of Behavior, 36,* 141–149.

Vaughan, W. (1985). Choice: A local analysis. *Journal of the Experimental Analysis of Behavior, 43,* 383–405.

Wagner, A.R. (1961). Effects of amount and percentage of reinforcement and number of acquisition trials on conditioning and extinction. *Journal of Experimental Psychology, 62,* 234–242.

Walker, S.F., Schnelle, J.F., & Hurwitz, H.M.B. (1970). Rates of concurrent responses and reinforcement duration. *Psychonomic Science, 21,* 173–175.

Watson, J.B. (1914). *Behavior: An introduction to comparative psychology.* New York: Holt.

Wearden, J.H. & Burgess, I.S. (1982). Matching since Baum (1979). *Journal of the Experimental Analysis of Behavior, 38,* 339–348.

Wertheim, G.A. (1965). Behavioral contrast during multiple avoidance schedules. *Journal of the Experimental Analysis of Behavior, 8,* 269–278.

White, A.J. & Davison, M.C. (1973). Performance in concurrent fixed-interval schedules. *Journal of the Experimental Analysis of Behavior, 19,* 147–153.

Williams, B.A. (1972). Probability learning as a function of momentary probability of reinforcement. *Journal of the Experimental Analysis of Behavior, 17,* 363–368.

Williams, B.A. (1976). The effects of unsignalled delayed reinforcement. *Journal of the Experimental Analysis of Behavior, 26,* 441–449.

Williams, B.A. (1979). Contrast, component duration, and the following schedule of reinforcement. *Journal of Experimental Psychology: Animal Behavior Processes, 5,* 379–396.

Williams, B.A. (1980). Contrast, signaled reinforcement, and the relative law of effect. *American Journal of Psychology, 93,* 617–629.

Williams, B.A. (1981). The following schedule of reinforcement as a fundamental determinant of steady-state contrast in multiple schedules. *Journal of the Experimental Analysis of Behavior, 35,* 293–310.

Williams, B.A. (1983a). Another look at contrast in

multiple schedules. *Journal of the Experimental Analysis of Behavior, 39,* 345–384.

Williams, B.A. (1983b). Effects of intertrial interval on momentary maximizing. *Behaviour Analysis Letters, 3,* 35–42.

Williams, B.A. (1985). Choice behavior in a discrete-trial concurrent VI-VR: A test of maximizing theories of matching. *Learning and Motivation, 16,* 423–443.

Williams, B.A. & Fantino, E. (1978). Effects on choice of reinforcement delay and conditioned reinforcement. *Journal of the Experimental Analysis of Behavior, 29,* 77–86.

Williams, B.A. & Wixted, J.T. (1986). An equation for behavioral contrast. *Journal of the Experimental Analysis of Behavior, 45,* 47–62.

Zuriff, G.E. (1970). A comparison of variable-ratio and variable-interval schedules of reinforcement. *Journal of the Experimental Analysis of Behavior, 13,* 369–374.

# Chapter 4

# THE PSYCHOBIOLOGY OF LEARNING AND MEMORY[1]

**Richard F. Thompson, Nelson H. Donegan** *and* **David G. Lavond,**
*Stanford University*

## INTRODUCTION

Perhaps the greatest scientific challenge of our time is to understand the functioning of nervous systems and how their operation governs the behavior of organisms. Of particular interest are the ways that nervous systems acquire, store, integrate, and utilize information about experienced events and the ways such information interacts with more genetically determined behavioral capacities and tendencies to determine the exhibited behaviors of organisms. In this chapter we focus on the mechanisms of acquisition and storage—The neural bases of learning and memory.[1]

The belief that learning results from changes in the structural and functional properties of neurons and their interconnections is based in the work of Cajal, who first demonstrated that nervous systems are made up of discrete units, such as neurons (Cajal, 1911). Given the framework of the neuron doctrine, early neuroscientists such as Lugaro (1899), Tanzi (1893), and Cajal (1911) proposed that learning might be due to changes in cell to cell interactions via changes in synaptic functioning. Since then the growth in knowledge about the architecture, neurophysiology, and neurohumoral properties of nervous systems has been staggering, especially in the past twenty-five years with the emergence of the discipline of neuroscience. Yet in spite of this deluge of facts, our understanding of the mechanisms of learning and memory remains rudimentary. The advances of the past quarter of a century have brought the field to the point where we can now *begin* to identify neural mechanisms responsible for learning and memory. Given such a complex problem, the most striking progress has been made in the analysis of simpler forms of learning in vertebrates and in organisms having relatively simple nervous systems—invertebrates.

This chapter considers the requirements of

[1]Supported in part by Grants from the National Science Foundation (BNS8117115), the Office of Naval Research (N00014-83-K-0238), the Sloan Foundation and the McKnight Foundation.

We thank the following colleagues for helpful suggestions: Tom Carew, Greg Clark, Michael Davis, Richard Herrnstein, Mark Konishi, James McGaugh, Donald Meyer, Larry Squire, and Garth Thomas.

an explanation of learning, some of the difficulties of developing psychobiological explanations, and the advantages of the model systems approach. It then addresses vertebrate and invertebrate literatures on the psychobiology of learning and memory. Material presented within each section is organized, for expository purposes, around three basic procedures used in behavioral analyses of animal learning: Habituation/sensitization, classical conditioning, and instrumental conditioning. Instructive examples from the literature demonstrate the progress in identifying the neural substrates responsible for the development and expression of learned behavior under consideration. Deviations from this format will be made at appropriate times to discuss findings that do not fall neatly within this organizational framework. Note that the objective of this chapter is not to provide a review of the literature, but rather to emphasize conceptual issues and to present examples that illustrate the progress that has been made in developing biological explanations of learning. (A survey just published by Byrne (1987) is highly recommended.) The variety of mechanisms by which nervous systems have been shown or hypothesized to exhibit plasticity and their implications for understanding learned changes in behavior will also be discussed.

## DEVELOPING PSYCHOBIOLOGICAL ACCOUNTS OF LEARNING

### Demonstration and Explanations of Learning

Learning is traditionally defined as a change in behavior produced by prior experience. Accordingly, in all investigations of learning, subjects are allowed to experience a set of events at time $t_1$ and their behavior is later assessed at time $t_2$. The basis for inferring learning is demonstrating that the behavior observed at $t_2$ is dependent upon the events occurring at $t_1$. Procedures used in experimental analyses of learning are distinguished by the relationships arranged between the events occurring at $t_1$ (see below, and Hearst, chapter 4).

Once one has observed changes in behavior that are categorized as products of learning, the question becomes, what are the requirements for developing an explanation of these observa-

tions? The first requirement is to determine the conditions under which the learned behavior is and is not exhibited; to identify the stimuli that control the expression of the learned behavior.[2] The second requirement is a specification of the conditions of training that are necessary for the development of the learned behavior (i.e., a specification of the observed regularities (lawful relationships) between conditions of training and changes in behavior). A third requirement is the identification of the neural mechanisms necessary for the development and expression of the learned behavior. The fourth requirement is to specify how the organism's genetic endowment determines the structural and functional properties of its nervous system that in turn determine the lawful relationships between experience and learning.

Behavioral analyses of learning have focused on the first two requirements. Learning theorists have sought to explain the "laws of learning" in terms of models that exhibit the same input–output relationships that the animal exhibits during training. In order to predict the ways in which an organism's prior experience will influence its subsequent behavior under particular conditions of stimulation, the model must be able to (1) represent the state of the organism in terms of a constellation of theoretical constructs (2) specify the relationships between conditions of stimulation and the state of the organism (i.e., what gets encoded), (3) describe how the state of the organism (as described by the theory's constructs) is modified by experience, i.e., specify the learning rules of the model, and (4) specify the relationship between

---

[2]The expression "the learned behavior" should always be treated as a euphemism for "the particular response chosen by the experimenter to index learning". Since even relatively simple experiences produce changes in a variety of behaviors, measuring changes in a single behavior merely documents one of the products of learning induced by the previous experience. Whether the many instances of learning reflect a diversity of mechanisms for behavioral change or whether a few processes are responsible for the varied array of learned behavior an organism exhibits is an empirical question yet to be answered. Currently, there is no agreement on how many kinds of learning exist. At the neural level this issue can be addressed experimentally, but with the potential for great confusion. The diversity of neural processes responsible for producing learned changes in behavior will depend upon the level of analysis at which neural plasticity is assessed, for example, changes in the logic of complex neural circuits to changes in intracellular biochemical events regulating membrane permeability for a particular species of ion (e.g., $K^+$).

the state of the organism and measures of behavior (the response generation rules). For purposes of predicting the behavioral consequences of particular histories of experience, there are few constraints on the nature of the constructs that the theorist adopts. For example, the constructs can be drawn from the concepts of computer science and automata theory as in the case of information processing theories (e.g., Bower, 1975; Simon, 1979). The utility of the model depends on (1) its ability to deduce the "laws of learning" and organize the data upon which such laws are based and (2) the degree to which it can be used for the prediction and control of behavior, as in the development and use of behavior modification procedures.

## Psychobiological Explanations of Learning

What distinguishes a psychobiological theory of learning from behavioral theories is that its constructs, and the properties they are allowed to exhibit, must be drawn from the facts of biology. Thus, psychobiological theories are constrained by biology and the behavioral laws they seek to explain. The learning rules must specify how experience modifies the functioning of the nervous system, and the response generation rules must specify the relationships between states of the nervous system and behavior. The task is one of identifying the neural circuitry and cellular mechanisms responsible for the learned behavior—specifying the mechanisms of information acquisition, storage, and retrieval—and determining how that circuitry becomes functional as a result of experience.

### The Problem of Localization
The problem of localizing the neuronal substrates of learning and memory, first explored in depth by Lashley (1929) and later by Hebb (1949), has been the greatest barrier to progress and remains fundamental to all work on the biological basis of learning and memory. In considering this issue, it seems useful to distinguish between the neural circuitry essential for the development and expression of a particular form of learning—the memory trace circuit—and the subset of neural elements that exhibit the training induced plasticity necessary for the development of such behavior. We will term the latter subset of elements the *memory trace*. Assuming

that in many learned behaviors the sites of plasticity are more central than the principal sensory systems or the motor neurons, we will use the term *sensory-motor circuit* to designate the part of the memory trace circuit that does not include the memory trace.

The premise that memory traces are localized does not necessarily imply that a particular trace has a single anatomical location. Rather, the memory trace circuit might involve a number of loci, parallel circuits, and feedback loops. It may be said that for a given form of learning, there is a discrete set of loci whose neuronal elements exhibit the essential neuronal plasticity defining the memory trace. Evidence detailed below strongly supports this view. However, not all workers agree; some argue that the memory trace is distributed, either widely (John, 1967) or somewhat less widely (Pribram, 1971).

For simpler forms of learning, it seems evident that at least some components of the sensory-motor circuit and the memory trace must be localized. An animal trained to a particular conditioned stimulus will not respond to a very different conditioned stimulus and must be given additional training to do so. The existence of a stimulus generalization gradient argues strongly that sensory-specific information is to some degree preserved in the elements of the memory trace. In addition, a well-trained animal usually exhibits a precise, stereotyped learned response. The fact that activation of motor neurons can be highly selective implies that the motor portion of the memory-trace circuit must itself show specificity. Both the sensory- and motor-specific aspects of learning suggest localization of the memory trace circuit.

### Methods of Localization
The most widely used methods for localizing the memory trace circuit have been lesions (including reversible lesions as with disruptive electrical stimulation) and electrophysiological recording. Pharmacological and anatomical methods have been used only recently to address the issue of localization.

In a typical lesion experiment, animals are trained on some task, a candidate brain structure is destroyed, and the animal is allowed to recover. Subsequently, subjects are tested on the previously learned task and their post-lesion performance is compared to their prelesion performance. Outcomes range from abolition of the learned behavior with no recovery over time, to varying degrees of deficits with or without recovery, to no effect on performance. The problem, as with all other localization techniques, is how to interpret the results. If the lesion abolishes the learned behavior, the effect is selective (i.e., the animal is still capable of generating the behavior used to index learning), and nonspecific factors such as generalized depression of activity or motivational deficits can be ruled out, then two interpretations are indicated. The first is that the lesioned structure is part of the circuitry involved in generating the learned response. (This does not mean, however, that the lesioned structure contains the neural elements exhibiting the plasticity necessary for the development of the learned behavior.) The second possibility is that the lesioned structure exerts a modulatory influence on the learned-response circuit. If, however, the lesion has no effect on performance of the learned behavior, one cannot conclude that the region in question plays no role in learning; parallel circuits may exist.

Another tool often used for localization of the memory trace is disruptive electrical stimulation (see Berman & Kesner, 1981, for a review). During the course of acquisition, abnormal activity in a candidate brain structure is induced by electrical stimulation. The consequences are determined by comparing rates of acquisition of the learned response with groups not receiving stimulation or, alternatively, receiving stimulation of other structures. The major limitation of this procedure is that the effective site of action of the disruptive stimulus is not necessarily at the electrode tip; it can be far removed. (Pharmacologically induced seizure activity faces similar problems for localization, as in cortical spreading depression.) Recent findings indicate that electrical stimulation of certain brain structures is much more likely to produce impairment of learning and memory than stimulation of other structures, even though the stimulated structures are not necessary for learning to occur. For example, disruptive electrical stimulation or induced seizures of the hippocampus prevent or severely impair simple conditioned-response learning (Thompson et al., 1980). Yet the same conditioned response can be learned perfectly well by animals with prior bilateral removal of the hippocampus (Solomon

& Moore, 1975). In this case, the simplest inference is that abnormal activation of the hippocampus interferes with development of the memory trace elsewhere in the brain (Isaacson, 1982).

Electrophysiological recording of neural activity has also been a widely used technique for identifying the circuitry involved in generating learned behavior. The first step is to identify brain structures that show changes in activity that correlate with changes in the learned behavior. However, as Thompson, Patterson, and Teyler (1972) and Tsukahara (1981) have noted, demonstration of a learning-induced change in neuronal activity in a given brain structure is not in itself sufficient to conclude that the neurons being monitored have changed. Rather, such changes in unit activity indicate only that the structure is either a part of the normal memory trace circuit or is influenced by it. Various criteria for identifying sites of plasticity electrophysiologically have been suggested, including sites showing learning-induced changes that appear with the shortest latency within a trial (Olds, Disterhoft, Segal, Hornblith, & Hirsch, 1972) and those showing the earliest appearance of changed activity over trials (Thompson et al., 1976). However, the former could be secondary to tonic changes elsewhere and the latter by itself is not sufficient.

To determine whether or not a learning-induced change in activity in a given brain structure develops there, or is simply relayed from elsewhere, one can compare activity of the target structure with activity in sites afferent to the target structure. Specifically, the activity of output neurons within a nucleus, as defined by antidromic and collision criteria (Fuller & Schlag, 1976), can be compared with the activity of nuclei providing afferent projections to the target nucleus. If the output of the target nucleus shows changes over training, but the activity of afferent nuclei does not, then one has evidence of training-induced neural plasticity within the target region. Even so, such observations cannot speak to the issue of whether or not the changes in neural activity play a role in the generation of the learned behavior. Only if lesions of the same target nucleus selectively abolish the learned response can one reasonably conclude that the structure exhibits training-induced plasticity essential for the development and expression of the learned behavior. But, as mentioned earlier, if destruction of the structure does not impair responding, it does not mean that the structure plays no role in learning. For example, Cohen (1982) found that two visual thalamic regions in the pigeon exhibit learning induced changes during heart-rate conditioning. Lesioning either region alone had no effect but lesioning both abolished conditioned heart-rate responses. Thus, either of the two thalamic regions can support heart-rate conditioning in the pigeon.

A variety of other techniques may also be used within this context. Localized neurochemical and neuroanatomical changes induced by learning also can provide evidence for localization of the memory trace and suggestions about putative mechanisms. Localized intracranial injections of drugs that block or activate neuronal systems permit one to selectively study the role of particular neurotransmitter–receptor systems. Newer techniques such as 2-deoxyglucose, receptor binding, and in-vitro autoradiography, are promising but have not yet been much applied to the study of neural substrates of learning and memory. Note that in order to be informative, such structural and biochemical changes or effects must be shown to be specific to the changes in learned behaviors and must be shown to have differential regional distributions in the brain.

It is sometimes argued that one technique revels causal relationships between neural functioning and behavior more readily than another. Actually, all techniques for identifying brain–behavior relations are equally correlational—one simply starts with relationships between experimental manipulations and their consequences (e.g., the relations between locus and extent of a lesion and the effect on behavior, between the type and amount of drug given and the effect on behavior, between training-induced changes in behavior and the level of a neurotransmitter in the brain, etc). However, different approaches have particular advantages: Electrophysiological recording is at present the most convenient, relatively noninvasive method for identifying structures in the brain showing learning-produced changes in activity. Lesions can provide evidence about localization of essential circuitry, and drug and neurotransmitter studies and microanatomical approaches provide evidence regarding localization and putative mechanisms.

Determining the neural bases of learning will require the intelligent use of many of the techniques mentioned above. Appropriate selection and combinations of techniques should allow one to rule out alternative interpretations concerning the role that various brain structures play and to converge upon a precise characterization of their function in the development and generation of the learned behavior. Of course, the selection of techniques is also guided by the level of analysis at which the properties of the critical circuitry are to be characterized; for example, localizing the neural elements of the memory trace circuit, identifying elements of the circuit that exhibit plasticity, determining the nature of the plasticity (e.g., changes in width of action potentials or changes in receptor properties), or determining the biochemical processes that alter structural properties of the neuron that in turn alter its functioning.

### The Model Systems Approach

In our view, the most promising research strategy for investigating the neural basis of behavior is the model systems approach (e.g., see Hoyle, 1980, Kandel, 1976; Krasne, 1969; Thompson et al., 1976). The strategy of this approach is to select an organism capable of exhibiting a range of behavioral phenomena that one wishes to explain and whose nervous system possesses properties that make neuroanatomical, neuropharmacological, and neurophysiological experimentation tractable. The goal is to work out in detail (to a cellular level) how a nervous system controls some type of behavior. This description then is taken to be a model of how the same and related behavioral phenomena are produced in other species.[3] The typical tradeoff is that the more complex the behavior one wishes to explain, the less tractable are the nervous systems of organisms capable of exhibiting such behavior. The chief advantage of model systems is that the facts gained from anatomical, physiological,

---

[3]The belief that the pursuit of a comparative approach to understanding behavior and its neural basis is not only feasible but profitable originates from the proposals of Darwin that one can observe continuities in behavior as well as morphology across species and that knowledge of the structure and function of one species provides a fertile source of hypotheses regarding the structure and functioning of related species (Darwin, 1860).

and behavioral investigations for a particular preparation are cumulative and tend to have synergistic effects on theory development and research.

Each approach and model preparation has particular advantages. The unique value of invertebrate preparations as model systems results from the fact that certain behavioral functions are controlled by ganglia containing relatively small numbers of large, identifiable cells—cells which can be consistently identified across individuals of the species (Alkon, 1980a; Davis & Gillette, 1978; Hoyle, 1980; Kandel, 1976; Krasne, 1969). As a result of knowing the architecture of the system, one can begin to determine systematically which neurons of the system are responsible for the behavior under investigation. Upon defining such neural circuits, one can then evaluate how the functioning of the neurons in the circuit are affected by training procedures. Once the neurons exhibiting plasticity are known, it is possible to identify changes in their structure and function that are responsible for the observed changes in behavior.

With vertebrate model systems, these goals are considerably more difficult to attain. Vertebrates are used for the simple reason that, in order to understand vertebrate nervous systems, they must at some point be studied. In addition, if the behavior is complex, it might be observed only in vertebrates. It is clear that higher vertebrates have developed increasing capacities for learning and have made use of these capacities in the development of adaptive behavior. It would seem that the evolution of the mammalian brain has resulted in systems especially well adapted for information processing, learning, and memory.

## LEARNING PHENOMENA AND THEIR NEURAL CORRELATES— VERTEBRATE PREPARATIONS

This section is organized around vertebrate preparations and is divided into subsections on habituation/sensitization, Pavlovian conditioning, and instrumental conditioning. Within each of these subsections, the training procedures are defined, characteristic behavioral findings are briefly discussed, and research commenting on neural mechanisms involved is presented.

## Habituation and Sensitization

The most ubiquitous form of behavioral plasticity is *habituation*; a decreased responsiveness to repeated presentations of a single stimulus that cannot be attributed to factors such as sensory adaptation or effector fatigue. Habituation can be observed in organisms ranging from the hydra (e.g., Rushforth, 1965) to man (e.g., Sokolov, 1969) and from simple responses like defensive reflexes to tactile stimuli to complex orienting responses to complex stimuli. Furthermore, a wide range of responses in a variety of preparations exhibit similar properties of habituation (Thompson & Spencer, 1966). One of the core properties of habituation is stimulus specificity. This means that the response decrement is to some degree specific to the exposed stimulus and altering the features of the habituated stimulus increases the response (e.g., Thompson & Spencer, 1966; Westenberg & Weinberger, 1976a, 1976b). Over the course of repeated stimulus presentations, there is in general less of a response decrement from initial levels with intense stimuli than with weak stimuli (Thompson & Spencer, 1966). However, when the conditions of testing and stimulus exposure are arranged to be independent of one another, for example, by presenting different groups with high, medium, or low intensity stimuli and subsequently testing each group's responsivity to all three stimulus intensities; the more intense the training stimulus, the greater is the amount of habituation observed in testing (Davis & Wagner, 1968). These generalizations are further complicated by the possibility of interactions of stimulus intensity with inter-stimulus-intervals (see Davis, 1970; Whitlow & Wagner, 1984). Furthermore, in some preparations (e.g., startle in the intact animal) stimulus presentation results in both a short-term, refractatory-like decrement in responding and a longer-term decrement, the former being more apparent when stimulus presentation is massed and the latter when stimulus presentation is spaced (Davis, 1970). Such observations suggest that more than one underlying process may be responsible for the range of observations classified under the heading of habituation. (For detailed accounts of the results and implications of behavioral analyses of habituation, see Groves & Thompson, 1970; Hearst, this volume; Horn & Hinde, 1970; Peeke & Herz, 1973; Sokolov,

1963; Thompson & Spencer, 1966; Wagner, 1979; Whitlow & Wagner, 1984.)

A second common form of behavioral plasticity is *sensitization*, a process by which presentation of a stimulus can increase responsiveness to subsequent stimulus presentation. A sensitizing stimulus typically has the property of being novel, noxious, or appetitive. Its effects are often not specific to a particular stimulus dimension or response system and are often thought to reflect a general state change, such as an increase in arousal. For example, a noxious shock tends to potentiate defensive reflexes (e.g., Thompson & Spencer, 1966) and a small amount of food given to a hungry animal tends to potentiate consumatory behaviors (e.g., Kupferman, 1974). Thus, a characteristic feature of sensitization is that it affects a class of response systems (e.g., defensive reflexes) elicited by a variety of stimuli.

The fact that both habituation and sensitization can result from the presentation of a single stimulus indicates that the behavioral consequences of repeated stimulus presentation can be complex and depend upon the parameters of stimulation. For example, an intense stimulus may initially produce an increased responsiveness followed by a decreased responsiveness to the stimulus. Thompson and Spencer (1966) have provided evidence that such outcomes can be viewed as the summation of sensitization and habituation processes produced by the stimulus. They further argue that *dishabituation*, the restoration of a habituated response by interpolated presentation of a potent stimulus, in many preparations simply reflects the summation of sensitization produced by the dishabituator and the habituation process, rather than a removal of habituation. However, Whitlow (1975) illustrated that not all instances of dishabituation involve sensitization. He used the vasomotor response in the rabbit to show that a dishabituator could restore response to an habituated stimulus without increasing the level of response to stimuli capable of eliciting the same response. More recently, Rankin and Carew (in press) have been able to dissociate the phenomena of dishabituation and sensitization in *Aplysia* at different stages of development.

## Neural Mechanisms of Habituation and Sensitization

The hindlimb flexion reflex in the chronic and acute spinal cat has proved to be a useful model system for studying the neural basis of short-term habituation and sensitization (e.g., Groves, Glanzman, Patterson, & Thompson, 1970; Groves, DeMarco, & Thompson, 1969; Groves and Thompson, 1970; Spencer, Thompson, & Neilson, 1966a, 1966b, 1966c; Thompson & Spencer, 1966). In this preparation, Thompson and Spencer showed that habituation and sensitization were both central, that short-term habituation and sensitization were separate processes at both behavioral and neuronal levels (motor neurons show no change in excitability during habituation but increased excitability during sensitization), and developed evidence that habituation was due to synaptic depression (Spencer et al., 1966a, 1966b, 1966c). Depending upon stimulation parameters, repetitive presentation of a cutaneous shock stimulus results in a diminished reflex amplitude over the stimulus series or, alternatively, an initial increase in responsivity followed by a larger diminution of response amplitude. From single unit extracellular recordings of neurons in the lumbro-sacral region of the cord, Groves, DeMarco, and Thompson (1969) and Groves, Glanzman, Patterson, and Thompson (1970) were able to observe neurons whose rates of discharge to the shock stimulus paralleled the course of response potentiation (termed type $S$ neurons) or response diminution (termed type $H$ neurons). In addition, type $H$ neurons showed response latencies short enough to be involved in the generation of the flexion reflex to a paw shock, whereas type $S$ neurons did not. From these and related observations, Groves and Thompson (1970) developed a dual process theory of habituation. They showed that by making the simple assumptions that habituation was due to synaptic depression in the stimulus–response or mediating pathway and that sensitization was a tonically acting superimposed process, many more complex behavioral phenomena of habituation and sensitization in intact vertebrates could be accounted for. Subsequent work using a monosynaptic system in the frog spinal cord extended the observations of the previous work, showing that habituation in this preparation was a result of homosynaptic depression (Farel, Glanzman, & Thompson, 1973; Glanzman, 1976).

The most complete analysis to date of the circuitry responsible for habituation and sensitization in the vertebrate brain is to be found in the work of Davis and colleagues (see Davis, Gendelman, Tischler, & Gendelman, 1982). They have focused on the circuitry involved in the generation and habituation of the short-latency acoustic startle response in the rat. Through a series of experiments using discrete lesioning and stimulation techniques, Davis et al. (1982) were able to define the auditory pathways and motor pathways that appear to be essential for the acoustically generated startle. From the ventral cochlear nucleus, the putative circuit projects to the ventral and dorsal nuclei of the lateral lemniscus (via the acoustic stria), then through the pons in the region of the nucleus reticularis pontis caudalis (NRPC), and finally to motor neurons in the spinal cord (see Figure 14.1) Lesioning the ventral cochlear nucleus or structures connecting it to the pontine nuclei abolished the startle response to a punctate acoustic stimulus. Conversely, brief pulses of electrical stimulation applied to any of these structures resulted in the elicitation of the startle response. The latency of response elicitation decreased as stimulation was shifted from afferent to more efferent segments of the circuit.

Using stimulation elicited startle, Davis and colleagues were able to localize regions of plasticity within this system. Repetitive electrical stimulation of the first afferent element, the ventral cochlear nucleus, resulted in habituation of the startle response, showing all of the properties of habituation produced by presentation of an acoustic stimulus. In contrast, repeated electrical stimulation of a more efferent element, the NRPC, did not produce habituation of the startle response (Davis, Parisi, Gendelman, Tischler, & Kehne, 1982). Interestingly, the response to electrical stimulation of the NRPC

was potentiated by prolonged exposure (e.g., 30 min.) to a white noise, which also produced sensitization of the acoustically-elicited startle response. On the basis of these and the above findings, Davis, Parisi, Gendelman, Tischler, and Kehne (1982b) proposed that sensitization processes can exert their influence either at the NRPC or the neurons in the spinal cord, but that habituation processes occur in more afferent elements of the circuit.

The acoustic startle reflex can also be potentiated by associative processes responsible for conditioned emotional states (e.g., fear). Preceding a startle eliciting tone by a visual (light), conditioned stimulus (CS) previously paired with shock results in an enhancement of the startle response (e.g., Brown, Kalish, and Farber, 1951; Davis and Astrachan, 1978). The mediation of this form of response enhancement by a conditioned fear state is suggested by the fact that anxiolytics (drugs that reduce anxiety) selectively abolish the ability of the fear CS to potentiate the response (Davis, 1979a, 1979b) while drugs that elevate anxiety further enhance potentiation (Davis, Redmond, & Baraban, 1979). Davis and colleagues propose that the associative effects of the light act through the dorsal lateral geniculate → visual cortex → insular cortex → central nucleus of the amygdala pathway which impinges upon the startle circuit at the region of the lateral lemniscus (Davis, in press; Hitchock & Davis, 1986; Tischler & Davis, 1983).

The above observations on enhancement of acoustic startle are especially important in showing that all instances of response enhancement are not reflections of a unitary phenomenon. The data provide evidence for two qualita-

---

**Figure 4.1.** Schematic diagram of a primary acoustic startle circuit. The abbreviations used are: AC = aqueduct; CNIC = central nucleus of the inferior colliculus; CU = cuneate nucleus; DCN = dorsal cochlear nucleus; DLL = dorsal nucleus of the lateral lemniscus; DP = decussation of pyramids; DR = dorsal raphe nucleus; ENIC = external nucleus of the inferior colliculus; IO = inferior olive; LL = lateral lemniscus; LM = medial meniscus; LV = lateral vestibular nucleus; MLF = medial longitudinal fasciculus; MTB = medial nucleus of the trapezoid body; MV = medial vestibular nucleus; nVII = nucleus of the seventh nerve; P = pyramids; RGI = nucleus reticularis gigantocellularis; RPC = nucleus reticularis pontis caudalis; RPO = nucleus reticularis pontis oralis; RST = reticulospinal tract; SO = superior olive; TSV = spinal tract of the fifth nerve; VAS = ventral acoustic stria; VCN = ventral cochlear nucleus; VII = seventh nerve; VLL = ventral nucleus of the lateral lemniscus. From "A Primary Acoustic Startle Circuit: Lesion and Stimulation Studies" by M. Davis, D.S. Gendelman, M.D. Tischler, and P.M. Gendelman, 1982, *The Journal of Neuroscience, 2*, p. 794. Copyright 1982 by the Society for Neuroscience. Reprinted by permission.

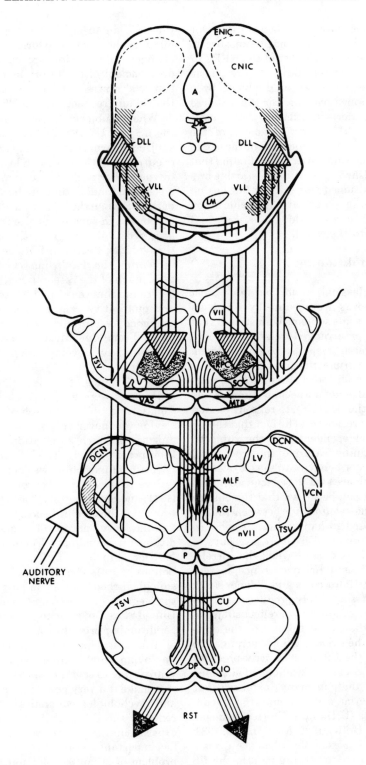

tively different mechanisms of facilitation. One is engaged by relatively extended exposure to white noise and exerts its effect at the NRPC or the cord. The second results in a more phasic form of response potentiation produced by a punctate conditioned fear elicitor (light paired with shock) that exerts its effect on the acoustic startle circuit at the ventral nucleus of the lateral lemniscus. The distinctness of these two processes is further indicated by the finding that morphine abolished potentiated startle produced by a conditioned fear elicitor but has no effect on response potentiation produced by exposure to white noise (M. Davis, personal communication to Donegan).

## Pavlovian Conditioning

*Pavlovian* (or classical) *conditioning* is most generally defined as a procedure by which an experimenter presents subjects with stimuli that occur in some prearranged relationship and measures changes in response to one of them. Typically, the experimenter arranges for one of the stimuli, the conditioned stimulus (CS), to be relatively neutral, and for a second stimulus, the unconditioned stimulus (US), to reliably elicit a readily measured response. (The fact that the CS and US occur independently of the subjects' behavior is a defining feature of the procedure.) Changes in subjects' behavior to the CS over the course of training are said to reflect associative learning when it can be shown that the change is due only to the *relationship* between the CS and US as opposed to habituation or sensitization processes produced by mere exposure to the two events, for example, when the correlation between CS and US occurrence is zero (e.g., Rescorla, 1967; Rescorla and Wagner, 1972; Wagner, 1969). Associatively produced changes in subjects' behavior are said to reflect subjects' learning about the causal texture of the environment. When the CS and US are arranged to occur such that the CS onset shortly precedes US onset, the CS comes to elicit conditioned responses (CRs) that, in many instances (but probably not the majority), mimic the unconditioned response (UR) to the US (see Donegan & Wagner, 1987; Hollis, 1982; Mackintosh, 1983; Williams, 1981). For example, when the CS is a tone and the US is food in the mouth, the CS comes to elicit salivation (Pavlov, 1927); when

the US is an air-puff to the eye, the CS comes to elicit eyelid closure (Gormezano, 1972). Such changes in behavior are said to reflect the development of excitatory association between subjects' representations of the CS and US or the CS and response to the US.

When subjects receive presentations of the CS and US that are negatively correlated, subjects learn that the CS predicts the non-occurrence of the US. Such learning is revealed by the ability of the CS to diminish response to a second stimulus that predicts the occurrence of the US when the two CSs are presented simultaneously. In such cases, the CS is said to have acquired inhibitory properties (see Hearst, 1972, this volume; Rescorla, 1975).

Within the Pavlovian conditioning literature, much of the research has been designed to determine the ways in which temporal, logical, and qualitative relationships between stimuli influence conditioning (see Hearst, this volume). From this diverse data base, learning theorists have developed models of associative learning.

In the hands of Pavlov, these conditioning procedures were used as tools to elucidate the functioning of the cerebral cortex. Oddly, Pavlov was never very specific about the mechanisms by which associations were formed or their precise nature. The influence of his theory of cortical functioning was minimized due to his failure to accept the neuron doctrine of Cajal (1911) and Sherrington (1906) and by demonstrations that the cerebral cortex was not necessary for the development of some forms of conditioned responding (Bromiley, 1948; Girden, Mettler, Finch & Culler, 1936; Poltyrew & Zeliony, 1930). The dismissal of Pavlov's physiological theories was, in part, responsible for the neglect of Pavlovian conditioning in the United States, relative to the use of instrumental conditioning procedures.

The considerable resurgence of interest in Pavlovian conditioning over the past twenty years is due to several features of the procedure that make it a very powerful tool for behavioral and psychobiological analysis. First, the occurrence of the CS and US is determined by the experimenter, not by the subjects' behavior. This has important consequences for the study of the problem of stimulus selection as subjects' histories of experience with the CS and US can be precisely manipulated (see Hearst, this volume). Of particular importance to the psychobiologist is the fact that conditioned response is time-locked to the CS. Therefore, neural events can be analyzed relative to known temporal referents. This feature is a great advantage when trying to detect correlations between changes in neural events, say through electrophysiological recording, and changes in behavior.

Second, and perhaps the greatest advantage to psychobiologists, is that the effects of experimental manipulations on learning rather than performance can be more easily evaluated than in instrumental procedures. This problem of learning versus performance has plagued the study of brain substrates of learning from the beginning. For example, does a brain lesion or the administration of a pharmacological agent impair a learned behavior because it damages the memory trace or because it alters the animal's ability or motivation to respond? By using Pavlovian procedures in preparations in which the CR mimics the UR, one can estimate the relative effects of such manipulations on learning and performance by comparing the subject's ability to generate the CR and UR before and after making a lesion or administering a drug. If the CR is affected and the UR is unaffected, one can reasonably assume that sensory or memory processes are being affected rather than motor processes responsible for generating the behavior.

Third, Pavlovian conditioning procedures permit more adequate controls for nonspecific effects of training on biological processes than do instrumental procedures. The same kind and density of stimulation and unconditioned responses can be produced in both experimental and control conditions. With instrumental training procedures, the nature and density of stimulation will differ (except in the yoked control—which can even be confounded by nonassociative factors; Church, 1964) as will the behavioral responses. For example, suppose the brain levels of a protein are measured in animals trained to run in an alley to avoid shock. Typically, a control group would receive shocks that could not be avoided. In such cases, subjects' behavior (the amount of running activity) may differ markedly. In this example, it is impossible to determine if differences in brain chemistry between groups is due to the experimental group

learning to avoid shock, to the difference in amount of running activity, to the degree of stress in the situation, etc.

Fourth, Pavlovian conditioning can be demonstrated in a wide range of organisms. The ability of a variety of invertebrates to show Pavlovian conditioning has made it possible to investigate associative learning processes at a cellular level (see below). The finding that many of the phenomena of Pavlovian conditioning can be found in both vertebrates and invertebrates (Carew, Hawkins, & Kandel, 1983; Hawkins, Carew, & Kandel, 1983; Hawkins & Kandel, 1984; Sahley, Rudy, & Gelperin, 1981; Walters, Carew, & Kandel, 1979) supports the view that the neural mechanisms of conditioning may be similar across species.

It should be noted that two classes of responses to the CS used to index excitatory conditioning have been distinguished (Hull, 1934). In *alpha conditioning*, the response to be conditioned is initially elicited by the CS and typically has a short latency. As a result of paired training, this response increases in amplitude and/or duration compared to unpaired stimulus presentations. In *beta conditioning*, the response to be conditioned is not initially elicited by the CS, is said to have a longer latency than the alpha response, develops over training so that its peak occurs near the time of onset of the US, and its onset latency moves forward in time within the trial. There may be problems with these definitions; for example, the latency of the alpha and beta responses can be quite similar. Whether the CS elicits the response to be conditioned may be partly due to the extent to which motor neuron threshold is exceeded prior to training (Patterson, Cegavske, & Thompson, 1973). For these reasons, and because alpha conditioning may have acquired surplus meaning, we suggest type A and type B. The key distinctions follow. In type B, the CR amplitude reaches a maximum at the approximate time of the US onset over the range of CS–US onset intervals in which conditioning occurs. In type A, the latency of the maximum amplitude CR remains relatively fixed (CR duration often increases). In type B, the onset latency of the CR begins at about the time of US onset and moves forward in time within the CS–US interval over the course of training. The type A CR onset latency does not alter appreciably with training. Note that a classification of response types in this way does not necessarily comment on the similarity or dissimilarity of the neural mechanisms responsible for associatively produced changes in responding to the CS (see below).

Most conditioning studies of brain substrates of learning have utilized an aversive US. Aversive learning in both Pavlovian and instrumental procedures is commonly characterized as occurring in two processes or phases, an initial associative process of conditioned fear or *conditioned emotional response* (CER) and a later process that involves learning of discrete, adaptive skeletal muscle responses (see Konorski, 1967; Mowrer, 1947; Prokasy, 1972; Rescorla & Solomon, 1967; the details in these accounts vary considerably). Weinberger (1982a) surveyed the literature on classical conditioning with aversive USs in infrahuman animals in terms of the rate of learning and noted two clearly distinct categories. Nonspecific responses, indices of conditioned fear, are acquired in 5 to 15 trials but specific skeletal muscle responses require many more trials, from 50 to several hundred, depending upon the parameters of training. Nonspecific responses are mostly autonomic—heart rate, blood pressure, pupil diameter, galvanic skin response—but include nonspecific skeletal motor activity as well. Under normal conditions both kinds of responses are learned. Thus, in rabbits having a CS paired with a periorbital shock US, conditioned heart-rate deceleration develops in a few trials (Schneiderman, Smith, Smith, & Gormezeno, 1966). As training continues, the animal begins to show the adaptive conditioned eyelid closure/nictitating membrane extension response. As this develops, the conditioned heart-rate deceleration fades away (Powell, Lipkin, & Milligan 1974). Evidence to date suggests that the neuronal substrates for these two types or aspects of aversive learning differ to a substantial degree (see below) and that the nonspecific CER system can modulate the generation of CRs and URs by the discrete, adaptive skeletal muscle response system (Thompson, Donegan, Clark, Lavond, Lincoln, Madden, Mamounas, Mauk & McCormick, 1986).

### Neural Mechanisms of Pavlovian Conditioning

#### SPINAL CORD
*Spinal conditioning*—classical conditioning of

hindlimb flexor reflexes in the acute spinal mammal—had a very controversial early histroy (see Fitzgerald & Thompson, 1967; Morgan, 1951; Patterson, 1980; Thompson et al., 1972). The occurrence of spinal conditioning is now well established. The paradigm now in use involves weak stimulation of skin or cutaneous nerve as a CS and stronger stimulation of skin as a US. The CS typically elicits a weak reflex response, measured as a flexor muscle response or a motor nerve volley. With pairing under appropriate conditions, the amplitude of the CS reflex response increases significantly. No such increase occurs in unpaired control animals (Patterson et al., 1973).

In an extensive series of studies, Patterson and associates have characterized the parametric features of spinal conditioning (Beggs, Steinmetz, Romano, & Patterson, 1983; Patterson, 1975, 1976; Patterson, Steinretz, Beggs, & Romano, 1982). First, the conditioned response is an increase in the amplitude of the CS elicited reflex response with no change in latency. It is an alpha or type A conditioned response. Forward pairing with a CS–US onset interval of 250 msec is optimal. No conditioning develops with simultaneous or backward pairing and little develops with forward intervals of 2 sec or more. A 45 sec intertrial interval is optimal. These are similar to the conditions that yield optimal conditioning of discrete behavioral responses in aversive classical conditioning in intact animals.

In analytic studies to date essential participation of the gamma system has been ruled out (use of flaxedil in Patterson's studies), as have changes in excitability of the CS afferent fiber terminals (unpublished observations). Durkovic (1975) showed that to be effective, the US must activate higher threshold afferents in the group III range (i.e., must be nociceptive or aversive). Spinal conditioning is thus a most promising model system for analysis of the cellular processes that underlie an elementary or basic form of associative conditioning in the vertebrate nervous system.

Spinal conditioning is the extreme example in vertebrates of a reduced preparation showing associative learning. Several points in this chapter note that decorticate mammals can learn a wide range of classical and instrumental tasks and that decerebrate mammals can learn (e.g., the classically conditioned eyelid response).

Some caution is necessary in drawing strong conclusions from reduced preparations. Conditioning of the hindlimb flexor response can be established in the acute spinal cat. This does not necessarily mean that such neuronal plasticity is normally induced at the spinal level when an intact animal is so trained. To show this, it would seem to be necessary to train the animals before spinal section and test for retention after section.

## MOTOR NEURONS AND REFLEX PATHWAYS IN INTACT ANIMALS

It seems unlikely on *a priori* grounds that an essential component of the memory trace is localized to motor neurons or nuclei. If this were the case then the remainder of the brain would seem not to be necessary for learning and memory. There are several reports that electrical stimulation in the vicinity of motor nuclei, or antidromic activation of motor nerves, can serve as a US to support conditioning (e.g., Black-Cleworth, Woody, & Niemann, 1975; Martin, Land, & Thompson 1980; Mis, Gormezono, Rosewall-Hervey, 1978). However, activation of afferents cannot be ruled out in the former. While this may or may not occur in the latter, *reafferent activity*—sensory information from the UR itself—does and will provide information to other regions of the brain.

There is growing evidence against the possibility that the motor neurons or reflex pathways contain an essential component of the memory trace in the mammalian brain. In particular, if lesions, drugs, or other treatments selectively abolish a learned response but have no effect at all on the reflex response, then it seems unlikely that the reflex pathways, including the motor neurons, play an essential role in the memory trace. Such data now exist for several learning paradigms. Ablation of the motor cortex prevents learning of the conditioned alpha eyelid response but does not affect the reflex response to glabellar tap in cat (Woody, Yarowskey, Owens, Black-Cleworth, & Crow, 1974). Lesions of the hypothalamus or amygdala selectively abolish the conditioned heart-rate response but have no effect on reflex cardiovascular responses in baboon, rabbit, and pigeon (Cohen, 1980; Kapp, Frysinger, Gallagher, & Haselton, 1979; Smith, Astley, DeVit, Stein, & Walsh, 1980). Ipsilateral lesions at several loci in the cerebellum and pontine brain stem selectively

abolish the conditioned eyelid/nictitating membrane (NM) response in rabbit but have no effect at all on the reflex response to corneal airpuff or periorbital shock (Desmond and Moore, 1982; Lavond, McCormick, Clark, Holmes, & Thompson, 1981; McCormick, Lavond, Clark, Kettner, Rising, & Thompson, 1981; McCormick, Clark, Lavond, & Thompson, 1982). Systemic injection of morphine similarly abolishes the conditioned eyelid/NM response but has no effect on the reflex response (Mauk, Madden, Barchas, & Thompson, 1982).

Another kind of evidence argues against an essential component of the memory trace being localized to motor nuclei as well as motor neurons. In most classical conditioning situations, the learned response involves several components and muscle groups, even though only one might be measured. These responses are not necessarily tightly coupled at the reflex level. For example, in conditioning of the rabbit eyelid/NM response, eyeball retraction (Accessory 6th and 6th nuclei), eyelid closure, and contraction of facial musculature (5th and 7th nuclei) occur on the side of the face of the eye being trained and to a much lesser and more variable degree on the other side of the face (McCormick, Lavond, & Thompson, 1982). The left NM and the right eyelid responses are not closely coupled reflexes (either can be obtained singly by using appropriate stimulation). Yet the increase in these two responses (in animals where the eyelid response of the contralateral eye occurs) has a positive correlation of .98 over the course of learning. Such a high correlation would not be expected if the memory trace developed separately in each of the several motor nuclei involved.

Another possible locus of the memory trace is in the alpha response pathway—the pathway from CS to motor nuclei that elicits the short latency behavioral alpha response. The startle response to a sudden acoustic-stimulus is an example. For the eyelid, the alpha response to an acoustic stimulus is about 20 msec (Woody and Brozek, 1969). There must be relatively direct connections from auditory nuclei to motor nuclei. Excluding the conditioned alpha response (see below), the standard adaptive conditioned eyelid response has a minimum onset latency of about 80 msec in a range of species, and instrumental and autonomic responses typically have longer latencies. Relatively direct connections from CS pathways to motor nuclei, as in the alpha or startle response pathways, would have latencies that are much too short to account for learned response latencies. Furthermore, at least in the conditioned alpha-eyelid response, ablation of motor cortex prevents learning of the CR (see below).

CONDITIONED STIMULUS PATHWAYS

The data here are more complex. Lesions of the CS pathways are of little help since it is not possible to distinguish between damage to sensory-specific pathways necessary for the learned response and damage to the memory trace. Selective abolition of learned responses by lesions of higher brain structures certainly raises doubts that the entire memory trace is in the sensory pathways. If it is, why would a particular structure like the amygdala or cerebellum be necessary? There are many alternative routes from sensory pathways to motor neurons. On *a priori* grounds it would not seem particularly adaptive to have all learning occur in sensory pathways—the appearance of the world would continuously change. On the other hand, the existence of the CS generalization gradient argues that some aspects of sensory-specific information exist in the memory-trace system.

Electrophysiological data at least provide direct information about whether neuronal unit responses in sensory pathways change over learning. Results are mixed. Most such studies have used an acoustic CS. Changes in unit activity in auditory pathways concomitant with training in a variety of paradigms have been reported for virtually all levels of the auditory system in at least some studies: ventral cochlear nucleus (Oleson, Ashe, & Weinberger, 1975), inferior colliculus (Disterhoft & Stuart, 1976), medial geniculate body (Buchwald, Hala, & Schramm, 1966; Disterhoft & Stuart, 1977; Gabriel, Sattwich, & Miller, 1975; Olds et al., 1972; Ryugo & Weinberger, 1978), auditory cortex (Buchwald et al., 1966; Disterhoft & Stuart, 1976; Kitzes, Farley, & Starr, 1978; Olds et al., 1972), and association cortex (Disterhoft et al., 1982; Woody, Knispel, Crow, & Black-Cleworth, 1976). Negative results were also reported in several of these studies for certain areas, including the inferior colliculus, medial geniculate body and auditory cortex. Other studies have reported purely negative results for cochlear

nucleus, inferior colliculus and medial geniculate body (Lonsbury-Martin, Martin, Schwartz, & Thompson, 1976; Kettner, Shannon, Nguyen, & Thompson, 1980).

Further data have clarified these seeming contradictions. In an important series of studies using classical conditioning of pupillary response to shock in paralyzed cats (a preparation particularly well suited to the study of the auditory system), clear training-induced changes in the medial but not the ventral division of the medial geniculate body were found (Ryugo & Weinberger, 1976, 1978; Weinberger, 1980, 1982a, 1982b). Gabriel et al. (1975) reported such changes more medially than ventrally in the medial geniculate body of the rabbit in instrumental avoidance learning. Birt and Olds (1982), using a hybrid classical-instrumental procedure with food reward in rats, similarly find no learning-related changes in unit activity in the ventral nucleus of the inferior colliculus or in the ventral nucleus of the medial geniculate body, but they do report changes in structures that are not auditory specific (e.g., intermediate and deep layers of superior colliculus). Another category of neurons showed changes early in training that later disappeared. These include the anterior portion of the cuneiform nucleus, external nucleus of the inferior colliculus, and the medial division of the medial geniculate body.

The observation that tone-CS evoked activity of units in an auditory relay nucleus shows or does not show an increase as a result of training, is simply a statement of a correlation, with its attendant problems of interpretation. Use of a signal detection paradigm, where equal probability of occurrence and failure of occurrence of the learned response to the same acoustic stimulus can be established (absolute auditory threshold), permits the presence of the learned response to be used as the independent variable (Kettner et al., 1980; Kenner & Thompson, 1982, 1985). Under these conditions, there are no learning-related changes in responses of units in the anteroventral cochlear nucleus, central nucleus of the inferior collicular, or ventral division of the medial geniculate body in eyelid/NM conditioning.

In sum, there is a consensus that the mainline auditory relay nuclei do not show training-induced changes in neuronal activity. When such changes are observed, they occur in the surround nuclei and regions that are not auditory-specific.

Since these regions are anatomically distinct from the main line auditory relay nuclei, selective lesions could be made. These studies have not yet been done.

Cohen has reported learning-related changes in unit activity in the visual pathways during heart-rate conditioning to a visual stimulus in the pigeon. The visual pathways necessary for learning are themselves of interest in this preparation. There are three parallel pathways, any one of which could support conditioning. Ganglion cell activity recorded from optic nerve fibers shows no training-induced modification. However, the phasic but not tonic components of the responses of neurons in two central thalamic optic relays—the principal optic nucleus and the nucleus rotundus—are differentially modified by associative training (Cohen, 1982; Gibbs & Cohen, 1980; Wall, Wild, Broyles, Gibbs, & Cohen, 1980). (See Figure 14.2A.)

The occurrence of training-related changes in CS-evoked neuronal activity in higher sensory structures, e.g., thalamus and cortex, illustrates that electrophysiological and lesion data can be discordant. A wide range of conditioned responses can be learned in the absence of the cerebral cortex. The older view that the cortex was necessary for instrumental but not classical conditioning is no longer tenable. Yet cortical neurons show training-related changes. In terms of our earlier distinctions, training-induced neuronal plasticity is a part of the memory trace system, or at least reflects the influences of the memory-trace circuit, even if not an essential part for a given form of learning. Typically, such regions as the cerebral cortex and hippocampus play increasingly important roles in more complex aspects of behavior and are essential for certain forms and aspects of learning and/or complex behavior. Yet neurons in these regions become engaged in even the simplest forms of learning. Although this may be unsatisfactory from an analytic point of view, it seems to be the way nature designed the system.

## Hypothalamus and Amygdala

A relatively consistent picture is emerging from studies on cardiovascular conditioning in three different species: baboon, rabbit, and pigeon. The paradigm is classical conditioning in which a several second auditory or visual CS terminates with an electric shock US, delivered variously to feet, abdomen, chest, ear, or in the vicinity of the eye. As noted above, the conditioned heart-rate response is viewed by most workers as a component or reflection of the more general process of fear conditioning, the conditioned emotional response (CER) (e.g., Schneiderman, 1972). Important paradigmatic contributions have been made by Smith et al. (1980) in their work on the baboon. They include a behavioral measure of the CER, lever-press response suppression in the cardiac conditioning regime, along with a measure of effects of exercise. Small, discrete bilateral lesions of the perifornical region of the hypothalamus in the baboon abolish the entire learned cardiovascular response complex—heart rate increase, blood pressure increases, changes in renal flow, terminal aortic flow and oxygen consumption —completely, permanently and selectively. The lesion has no effect on the behavioral measure of CER—conditioned suppression of lever pressing—or on cardiovascular changes associated with exercise. Electrical stimulation in this same region in intact animals elicits the cardiovascular response complex. In sum, this hypothalamic region is not necessary for reflex and exercise-induced cardiovascular regulation —for unlearned cardiovascular changes—only for the learned response. It seems to be on the efferent or motor-specific side of the learned-response circuit since the behavioral signs of conditioned fear are still present. This result is perhaps the clearest lesion demonstration to date of a selective action on a motor-specific substrate of a learned response. In some sense, it is surprising that a structure as ancient as the hypothalamus exhibits such a highly selective action for a *learned* response, as opposed to reflex and general regulation.

The rabbit is the only other mammalian species in which brain substrates of learned cardiovascular responses have been studied in depth. In rabbit, the learned response is a decrease in heart rate (without accompanying blood pressure changes) as opposed to the pressor response in baboon and is likely mediated by the vagus nerve. This may reflect the behavioral propensity of the rabbit to freeze when threatened. The unconditioned response to shock in the rabbit, incidentially, is heart rate and blood pressure increase (Schneiderman et al., 1969; Yehle, Dauth, & Schneiderman 1967). Electrical stimulation of a number of brain regions can elicit either decreased or

## CS–CR PATHWAY FOR HEART RATE CONDITIONING

### CONDITIONED STIMULUS PATH

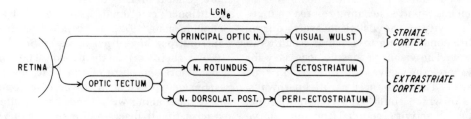

### INTRATELENCEPHALIC PATH

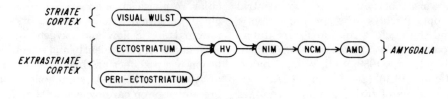

### DESCENDING (CONDITIONED RESPONSE) PATH

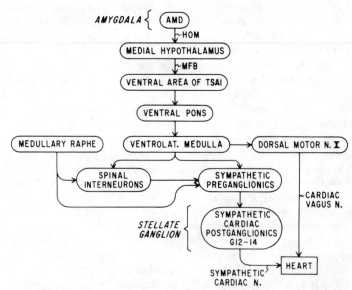

**Figure 4.2.** Schematic illustration of the CS–CR pathways and their coupling for heart-rate conditioning in pigeon. *CS path.* Three ascending visual pathways each transmit effective CS information. The thalamofugal pathway involves a retinal projection to the principal optic nucleus of the thalamus, which is equivalent to the mammalian dorsal lateral geniculate nucleus and is designated LGNe. LGNe then projects to the visual Wulst, the analogue of striate cortex. The other two pathways are tectofugal pathways. One relays through the nucleus rotundus of the thalamus and then to the ectostriatum. The other relays through the nucleus dorsolateralis posterior of the thalamus (N. DORSOLAT. POST.) and then to a periectostriatal region. The ectostriatal and periectostriatal terminal regions are considered analogous to mammalian extrastriate cortex. *Intratelencephalic path.* The most rostral component of the descending (CR) path is the avian amygdalar homologue, and the relevant telencephalic visual areas access the amygdala through intratelencephalic (equivalent to intracortical) circuitry. HV, hyperstriatum ventrale; NIM, neostriatum intermediale, pars mediale; NCM, neostriatum

increased heart rate in rabbit and other mammals. Schneiderman and associates have utilized hypothalamic stimulation as the US and conditioned the bradycardia response in rabbit. Interestingly, brain stimulation that itself was rewarding (lateral hypothalamus) or aversive (medial hypothalamus) could serve as an effective US, so long as the brain stimulus elicited bradycardia.

To our knowledge, no one has yet examined effects of appropriate hypothalamic lesions on the conditioned heart-rate slowing response in the rabbit. Far lateral hypothalamic lesions have little effect (Francis, Hernandez, & Powell, 1981). In a series of papers, Kapp, Gallager and associates have shown that the amygdala plays an important role (see Kapp, Gallagher, Applegate, & Frysitger, 1982). Lesions of the central nucleus markedly attenuate conditioned heart-rate slowing in the rabbit but have no effect on the reflex responses or on the initial orienting response to the CS, which itself is a slowing. The amygdala is of particular interest because it has been implicated in both unlearned and learned aspects of the expression of fear and in aversive learning in a large number of studies (see below, and Blanchard & Blanchard, 1972; Goddard, 1964; Werka, Skar, & Ursih, 1978). Injection of beta-adrenergic blockers in the central nucleus (Gallagher, Kapp, Frysitger, & Rapp, 1980) partially attenuates the CR, as does injection of the opiate peptide levorphanol. Interestingly, injection of naloxone enhances the CR (Kapp et al., 1982). Administration in the fourth ventricle of tiny amounts of opiate analogues having selective action on the mu opiate receptor also selectively and reversibly abolishes the conditioned heart-rate response in the rabbit (Lavond, Mauk, Madden, Barchas, & Thompson, 1983). Electri-cal stimulation of the central nucleus elicits bradycardia in both anesthetized and awake rabbits, which can be blocked by atropine. It appears that a direct pathway exists from central nucleus of amygdala to the vagal preganglionic cardioinhibitory neurons in the dorsal motor nucleus of the vagus (Kapp et al., 1982). In awake rabbits, the stimulus also produces arrest of ongoing movement. Stimulation of the central nucleus of the amygdala in awake rats elicits a wide range of somatic and autonomic signs of fear (Grossman, Grossman, & Walsh, 1975; McIntyre & Stein, 1973). To date, simultaneous measurement of conditioned bradycardia and behavioral measures of fear conditioning have not been made in the rabbit. Finally, unit recordings in the central nucleus indicate that at least some neurons show increases during the development of conditional bradycardia (12/34) and a few show significant correlations with the magnitude of the CR (3/24) (Kapp et al., 1982).

Lesions of other brain structures can also influence conditioned bradycardia in the rabbit. Both hippocampal lesions and lateral septal lesions enhance the heart-rate CR (Powell & Buchanan; 1980). Lesions of the anterior cingulate region of the cerebral cortex produce a substantial impairment of the conditioned bradycardiac response (Buchanan & Powell, 1982). Although it is difficult to compare across laboratories, this cingulate lesion impairment does not appear to be as great as the amygdala lesion impairment found by Kapp and associates.

In sum, a region of the hypothalamus is clearly essential for the expression of the learned cardiovascular responses believed to index conditioned fear. This same region of the hypothalamus is not essential for reflex and regulatory

---

activities of the cardiovascular system. In this sense it is a learning-specific brain region but on the motor-specific side. The central nucleus of the amygdala also appears important, at least for conditioned bradycardia in the rabbit. On the other hand, it is not essential for the retention of at least certain behavioral aspects of fear conditioning and avoidance learning, although it clearly plays a role in the expression of both autonomic and skeletal signs of fear and fear conditioning. In this sense it appears to be more on the motor side of the learned-response circuit. However, there is no decisive evidence yet to argue against the possibility that the central nucleus of the amygdala may contain at least a part of the memory trace for the cardiovascular components of fear conditioning. Anatomical connections from amygdala to hypothalamus and to medullary cardiovascular centers are either direct or almost direct in the mammal (Kapp et al., 1982; Smith et al., 1980). The possible relation of the cingulate cortex to this system is unclear. There are likely other brain structures involved that have yet to be characterized.

Cohen and associates have completed the most extensive and detailed analysis of both the efferent and afferent limbs of the learned response circuit for heart-rate conditioning in their work on the pigeon (e.g., Cohen, 1969, 1974, 1975, 1980, 1982). (See Figure 4.2) Like the baboon, the pigeon shows a conditioned increase in heart rate. Both the vagi and the sympathetic nerves participate, but the predominant influence is from the right sympathetic cardiac nerve. The preganglionic projections to these neurons are located in the column of Terni in the spinal cord. The brain stem was mapped with electrical stimulation, together with electrophysiological recording, anatomical and lesion-behavior studies and the efferent pathway defined (see Cohen, 1980). In brief, there is a system from the avian homologue of the amygdala to the hypothalamus, which then projects down to the neurons of the final common path via a ventral brainstem pathway (Cohen, 1980). The CR is largely or completely prevented by lesions of the amygdala, of the terminal field of the amygdala fibers in the hypothalamus, and of the brain stem course of fibers from this region of the hypothalamus, for example, the ventral area of Tsai (Cohen, 1975; Cohen, 1980; Cohen & MacDonald, 1976). Large brain stem lesions that

do not include this system have no effect, nor do lesions of other cardioactive regions of the brain like the septum. As in the mammal, these lesion effects are selective in that they abolish only the conditioned response not the reflex cardiovascular responses. Other aspects of fear conditioning, such as skeletal muscle responses or instrumental behavior, have yet to be explored in this preparation. This pathway from amygdala to motor neurons is clearly critical for expression of the conditioned heart-rate response in the pigeon, as in the mammal. It is not yet known whether some part of the memory-trace circuit may be included in the amygdala. Recent evidence from Cohen's laboratory suggests involvement of the afferent components of the learned-response circuit in the associative process, as noted above.

Kapp et al. (1982) interpret the role of the amygdala in aversive conditioning to be motoric (i.e., on the motor-specific side of the learned-response circuit), at least insofar as conditioned bradycardia is concerned in the rabbit. The more general role of the amygdala in fear conditioning is not clear. There is no question that it is somehow involved (see Kaada, 1972; Kesner & Wilbrun, 1974, for reviews). In a recent study from McGaugh's laboratory (Liang et al., 1982), the impairment of retention of aversive learning (one-trial inhibitory avoidance in rats) produced by amygdalar lesions was found to depend strongly on the time of lesion. If the lesion is made 10 days after training, it produces no deficit in retention. They interpret this result to mean that the amygdala plays a modulatory role in aversive learning (i.e., that it acts on a memory-trace system established elsewhere in the brain).

It appears that the amygdala plays a critical role in taste and odor aversion learning. Large lesions of the basolateral amygdala significantly disrupt a previously learned taste aversion in rats (Nachman & Ashe, 1974), as do lesions of the gustatory neocortex (Quellet, Kower, & Braun, 1975). In recent work, Garcia, Rusiniak, Kieler, and Bermudez-Rattoni (1982) have examined lesion effects on learned odor aversion, taste aversion and taste potentiation of odor aversion. Lesions of the necortical taste area disrupt taste aversion conditioning but not odor aversion, taste potentiation, or odor aversion learning (i.e., the cortical deficit may be in taste discrimination; see also Lasiter & Glanzman,

1982). In marked contrast, reversible (procaine) lesions of the amygdala disrupt learned odor aversion and taste potentiation of odor aversion induced by pairing with an illness stimulus (lithium chloride), but do not disrupt conditioned response suppression with an odor stimulus conditioned to a footshock US. Garcia's experimental differentiation between the associative and sensory-discriminative aspects of odor-taste aversion learning appears to provide a most useful paradigm for further analysis of neuronal substrates of this important form of learning.

Finally, it should be noted that the amygdala is also implicated in appetitive learning. Spiegler and Mishkin (1981) showed that lesions of the amygdala markedly impair one-trial learning of object reward associations in the monkey. The same lesions do not impair one-trial object recognition learning (Mishkin & Oubre, 1977).

## Motor Cortex

Woody and associates have made significant progress in analyzing cellular mechanisms of a form of learning (Brons & Woody, 1980; Woody, 1970; Woody, 1982a, b, c; Woody & Black-Cleworth, 1973; Woody & Brozek, 1969; Woody, Vassilevsky, & Engel, 1970; Woody, Yarowsky, Owens, Black-Cleworth, & Crow, 1974). It is unique in several ways. First, it is an alpha or type A response. The CR, a short-latency eyeblink to click in the cat, also is elicited by the click at the beginning of training. This response habituates rapidly with repeated stimulus presentations. The click is paired with glabellar tap with a 400 msec interstimulus interval (ISI). Animals given paired conditioning show a gradual increase in eyeblink to CS compared to unpaired control animals. Asymptotic learning requires 600 to 900 trials. The learned response has a latency of 20 msec. Ablation of the motor areas of the cerebral cortex prevents development of the learned response. This short-latency type A conditioned response thus differs from conventional or type B adaptive eyelid or NM conditioning in six ways: it is elicited by the CS at the beginning of training, it has a very short latency, the latency does not shift over training, it is not adaptive in the sense that the CR is not present at the time of the UR, it requires a much longer time for learning, and the motor cortex is essential for development of the conditioned response. The fact that the

motor cortex is essential is perhaps surprising, particularly given the short latency of the response.

The development of the conditioned type A response is selective. If the CS is paired with glabellar tap, the eyelid response becomes conditioned; if paired with stimulation of the nose, a nose twitch develops. Extracellular microstimulation of the motor cortex indicates that threshold activation level of those neurons eliciting the CR is reduced following conditioning—they are more excitable. This effect is specific, as in eyelid versus nose twitch training. In a technical tour-de-force, Brons and Woody (1980) recorded intracellularly from 290 neurons in motor cortex in the absence of peripheral stimulation and measured threshold currents in already trained animals. The paradigm was complex. Results indicated that cells in animals given CS-alone training had the highest threshold to current injection and cells in the US-only group showed some decrease in threshold. Cells in a delay US group (where a delay of several days intervened between US presentations and recording) did not show decreases. Cells in three groups given paired CS–US training—immediate or delayed—showed the largest decreases. In short, the US-only condition produced a decreased threshold, but it did not persist over days, and all paired groups showed decreases that did persist. This decrease persisted in an extinction group (US–CS) over the course of extinction training. In other work, the increased excitability of motor cortex neurons was not accompanied by increases in spontaneous discharge activity or by detectable changes in resting membrane potential (Woody and Black-Cleworth, 1973). Similar effects could be produced by extracellular application of acetylcholine or cyclic GMP. Woody (1982) suggests that these results could be due to long-lasting changes in the post-synaptic neurons, for example, an increase in dendritic resistance.

In sum, increased excitability of motor cortex cells occurred in both paired and US alone conditions, but the paired effect was greater than persisted longer. At least one aspect of the behavioral learned response, extinction, apparently cannot be accounted for by this cellular process. Woody's work suggests that the motor cortex is a part of the essential memory trace circuit for the conditioned alpha eyelid response and that there is cellular plasticity involving increased excitability of neurons there, probably due to persisting post-synaptic changes in the neurons studied. However, it is not yet certain whether the motor cortex is the site of the memory trace or simply a part of the essential circuit. As noted above, most conditioned responses, both classical and instrumental, do not require the motor cortex. It would be interesting if Woody's results were found to hold for all instances of type A conditioning, at least for skeletal muscle responses. If so, it would suggest a fundamental difference in neuronal substrates between type A and type B conditioning.

Voronin (1971, 1980) has used simple analogues of classical conditioning in studies of cellular plasticity in the motor cortex. Direct electrical stimulation of the motor cortex in rabbit was the US and the CS was a more remote cortical stimulus. The measured response was intracellular recording from neurons close to the US electrode. Although short duration facilitation (30 sec) could be obtained, it did not persist except in a few instances. Further, unpaired stimulus presentations could also yield facilitation. A more consistent and prolonged facilitation could be obtained when the US was a compound including stimulation of the lateral hypothalamus. Finally, Voronin developed a paradigm somewhat analogous to Woody's in that a click was used as the CS. The US was again motor cortex stimulation plus hypothalamic stimulation, and the behavioral CR was electromyelogram (EMG) activity in the contralateral forepaw. Intracellular recordings were made from cortical neurons. The latency of the behavioral responses was the same to a loud startling click and for the CR that developed to a weaker, initially neutral click and to a neutral click under chloralose, and very short, 12 to 17 msec. In general, cortical neurons showed increased excitability over the course of pairings. Some neurons showed initial responses to the neutral click, and virtually all responded to the loud click with the same latency distribution as the neutral click after paired training. Voronin notes that these cortical and EMG responses to loud clicks are components of the startle response (perhaps analogous to a type A response). The conditioning regime increases the excitability of the startle circuit.

O'Brien and associates have developed an interesting analogue of differential classical conditioning for cells of origin of pyramidal tract fibers in the motor cortex of the paralyzed cat (O'Brien, Wilder, & Stevens, 1977; O'Brien and Quinn, 1982). Left and right hindpaw shocks were used as the CS + and CS −, and the CS + was paired with antidromic stimulation of the pyramidal tract as the US. Activity of neurons so identified in motor cortex were recorded. A significantly greater increase in response developed for the CS +. When electrical stimulation of ventrolateral (VL) or ventroposterolateral (VPL) regions of the thalamus were used as CS + and CS −, no differential conditioning developed, an interesting result because the peripheral hindpaw stimuli are activating some portions of VPL and VL. As O'Brien notes, these data cannot be explained by a simple pairing theory of conditioning in which any two pathways to a neuron can be used as the CS and US. Voronin (1980) emphasized the same point in noting that paired motor cortex and lateral hypothalamic stimulation was a more effective US than motor cortex stimulation alone. Woody (1982) finds that pairing of hypothalamic stimulation with the globellar tap US in his paradigm leads to much more rapid learning.

## CEREBELLUM

A number of studies have shown that highly localized circuitry in the cerebellum is a part of the essential memory-trace circuit and appears likely to be the actual locus of the memory traces, the conditioned eyelid response, and other discrete, adaptive behavioral responses learned to deal with aversive USs. Classical conditioning of the eyelid and/or nictitating membrane (NM) response (beta or type B conditioning) has become a widely used behavioral paradigm for the study of the neuronal basis of associative learning, usually in the rabbit but also in other species (Thompson et al., 1976). The conditioned eyelid response was first studied in infrahuman animals by Hilgard and Marquis (1934, 1936) who were also first to use it as a model preparation for the study of neural substrates of learning and memory (Marquis & Hilgard, 1936, 1937). Gormezano introduced measurement of the nictitating membrane response (Gormezano, Schneiderman, Deaux, & Fuentes, 1962). However, the conditioned eyelid and NM responses behave essentially identically and are almost perfectly correlated over the course of learning (Deaux & Gormezano, 1963; Gormezano et al., 1962; McCormick, Lavond,

& Thompson, 1982; Schneiderman, Fuentes, & Gormezano, 1962). The conditioned eyelid response in the rabbit also has been used to good effect in analysis of theoretical issues in learning (Donegan & Wagner, 1983; Gormezano, 1972; Wagner, 1981). The NM/eyelid response has a number of advantages, including the fact that there is a very large body of behavioral literature on eyelid conditioning in a number of species, particularly humans. It exhibits the basic properties of Pavlovian or classical conditioning. A CS (usually tone or light) is paired with corneal airpuff or periorbital shock US, with CS–US intervals ranging from 100 msec to 2 sec. Under most conditions, there is no alpha or type A response. The CR begins to develop in 30 to 100 trials, depending upon conditions, and first occurs at the time of the US onset and gradually moves forward in time with training. The response is adaptive in that the peak amplitude of the CR always tends to occur at the time of onset of the US over the range of CS–US onset intervals effective for learning.

Decorticate and thalamic rabbits can learn the conditioned response, as can decerebrate cats (Norman, Buchwald, & Villablance, 1977; Oakley & Russell, 1972). Importantly, the learned eyelid response is retained following chronic decortication (Oakley & Russell, 1977) and acute decerebration (Mauk and Thompson, 1987) thus indicating that the essential memory-trace circuit is below the level of the thalamus.

Neuronal unit recordings from the lateral interpositus nucleus and localized regions of cerebellar cortex ipsilateral to the trained eye show the development of a temporal neuronal model (a pattern of increased frequency of unit discharges that models the amplitude—time course of the behavioral response) of the learned response but not the unlearned reflex response. This neuronal temporal model of the learned response develops over the course of training in very close association with the development of the learned behavior (eyelid response) and precedes it in time within a trial (McCormick, Clark, Lavond, & Thompson, 1982b; McCormick et al., 1981; Kettner and Thompson, 1982).

Unilateral lesions of several types in the cerebellum—large ablations of the lateral portion of the hemisphere; localized electrolytic lesions of the lateral interpositus nucleus, small, discrete lesions of the superior cerebellar peduncle—all produce selective and permanent abolition of the ipsilateral learned response with no effect on the reflex response (Clark, McCormick, Lavond, & Thompson, 1984; McCormick, Clark, Lavond, & Thompson, 1982; McCormick, Guyer, & Thompson, 1982; McCormick et al., 1981). The contralateral eye is able to learn and retain, thus controlling for nonspecific lesion effects. The localized electrolytic lesion of the dentate/interpositus nuclei result has been replicated by Yeo, Hardiman, and Glickstein (1985), using light as well as tone CSs and a periorbital shock US, thus extending the generality of the effect. If training is given before unilateral cerebellar lesion, the ipsilateral eye cannot learn, but the contralateral eye subsequently learns normally (Lincoln, McCormick, & Thompson, 1982). If training is given before unilateral cerebellar lesion, the learned response is abolished in the ipsilateral eye but the contralateral eye learns rapidly (McCormick, Clark, Lavond, & Thompson, 1982; McCormick et al., 1981; McCormick, Lavond, & Thompson, 1982). Kainic acid lesions of no more than about a cubic millimeter of cellular tissue in the lateral interpositus nucleus produce the same selective and permanent abolition of the CR (Lavond, Hembree, & Thompson, 1985). Since kainic acid is believed not to destroy fibers of passage or axon terminals of projection systems, the critical region does appear to be the lateral interpositus, and the lesion effect cannot be interpreted in terms of subsequent degeneration of afferent projections. Unilateral lesions of the lateral cerebellum/dentate-interpositus nuclear region abolish or severely impair the conditioned hindlimb flexion response in the rabbit when the US (paw shock) is given to the ipsilateral hindpaw. Both hindlimbs develop the CR. The critical region of the interpositus is more medial than that essential for the learned eyelid response (Donegan, Lowry, & Thompson, 1983). To date, it has not been possible to permanently abolish the CR by removal of any one or two lobes or cerebellar cortex (McCormick & Thompson, 1984a, b; but see Yeo, Hardiman & Glickstein, 1984). But this does not rule out the possibility of a multiple cortical cerebellar trace. Localized microinfusions of GABA antagonists (e.g., bicuculline) only into the critical region in the interpositus and also in localized regions of overlying cerebellar cortex, selectively and reversibly abolishes the CR (Mamouns, Madden, Barchas, & Thompson 1983), suggesting an important involvement of GABA inhibitory neurons (see, e.g., Roberts, 1976).

In this context, there is an earlier Soviet literature indicating that in dogs well trained in leg-flexion conditioning, complete removal of the cerebellum permanently abolishes the ability of the animal to make the learned discrete leg-flexion response but not to show conditioned generalized motor activity (Karamian, Fanaralijian, & Kosareva, 1969). The interpositus lesion effective in abolishing the conditioned eyelid response in the rabbit also abolishes the conditioned eyelid response in the cat and the eyelid response learned as an instrumental avoidance response in the rabbit (Patterson, 1984). Thus, the critical lesion effect holds across conditioned stimulus modalities, response systems, response contingencies, and species.

Lesions in several locations in the midbrain and brainstem can also selectively abolish the learned response (Desmond & Moore, 1982; Haley, Lavond, & Thompson, 1983; Lavond et al., 1981; Madden, Haley, Barchas, & Thompson, 1983; Thompson et al., 1982). Effective sites track the course of the superior cerebellar pedecule, the major efferent system from the cerebellum, the magnocellular division of the red nucleus (contralateral), and the descending rubral pathways. These studies appear to have defined the efferent portion of the essential memory-trace circuit: interpositus nucleus → superior cerebellar peduncle → red nucleus → rubral pathway → motor nuclei. This efferent circuit is consistant with the well-described anatomy of the system (Broadal, 1981). (See Figure 4.3.)

Recent studies appear to have identified the climbing fiber system from a portion of the inferior olive as the essential US or teaching input. In brief, lesions of the rostromedial portion of the dorsal accessory olive contralateral to the trained eye result in behavioral extinction of the CR with continued paired training which is indistinguishable from extinction produced by omission of the US in normal animals (McCormick, Steinmetz, & Thompson, 1985). Lesions of all other regions of the inferior olive have no effect. Electrical microstimulation of the dorsal accessory olive (DAO) evokes integrated behavioral responses, the nature of the response determined by the exact location of the stimulating microelectrode. If this is used as the US, the exact behavioral response elicited by DAO stimulation becomes conditioned to the CS (e.g., tone) in what appears to be a completely normal manner (Mauk & Thompson, 1984). This result is comparable to the pioneering study by Brogden and Gantt (1942) where electrical stimulation of cerebellar cortex or white matter was found to be an effective US and provides a possible explanation for it; for example, they were stimulating climbing fibers. In animals where the DAO stimulus evoked an eyelid response that was trained to tone, lesions of the interpositus nucleus abolished both the CR and the behavioral response evoked by the DAO stimulus. The electrical DAO-US was effective for conditioning even when at just threshold for eliciting a behavioral response, arguing against feedback from the UR as an important component of the US. In contrast to aversive peripheral USs, electrical stimulation of the DAO does not appear to be aversive. In sum, the DAO climbing fiber system appears to serve a teaching function for the learning of discrete adaptive behavioral CRs —it is both the necessary and sufficient teaching input. (See Figure 4.3.)

The cerebellum has been suggested by several authors as the locus for the coding of learned motor responses (e.g., Albus, 1971; Brindley, 1964; Eccles, 1977; Ito, 1970; Marr, 1969). All these theories proposed that the inferior olive-climbing fiber system is the teaching input. The results described just above represent the first clear empirical support for this notion in the context of associative learning. Ito has developed analogous findings in the context of plasticity of the vestibulo-ocular reflex and Llinas, Watton, Hillman, & Sotelo (1975) report a similar role for the inferior olive-climbing fiber system in recovery from posterial abnormalities following vestibular damage. Cerebellar lesions impair a variety of skilled movements in animals and humans (Brooks, 1979; Brooks, Kozlovskaya, Atkin, Horvatz, & Uno, 1973) and can produce learning and memory defects in humans (Gilman, Bloedel, & Lechtenberg, 1981). Neuronal recordings from Purkinje cells of cerebellar cortex have implicated this structure in the plasticity of various responses (Dufosse, Ito, Jastrehoff, & Miyashita, 1978; Gilbert & Thach, 1977; Ito, 1982).

Cerebellar learning theories propose that the mossy fiber-granule cell-parallel fiber system is the learning input. Lesion and microstimulation

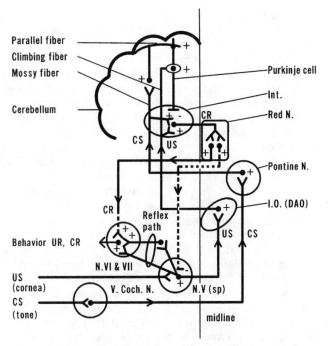

**Figure 4.3.** Simplified schematic of hypothetical memory-tract circuit for discrete behavioral responses learned as adaptations to aversive events in mammals. The US (corneal airpuff) pathway seems to consist of somatosensory projections to the dorsal accessory portion of the inferior olive (DAO) and its climbing fiber projections to the cerebellum. The tone CS pathway seems to consist of auditory projections to pontine nuclei (Pontine N) and their mossy fiber projections to the cerebellum. The efferent (eyelid closure) CR pathway projects from the interpositus nucleus (Int) of the cerebellum to the red nucleus (Red N) and via the descending rubral pathway to act ultimately on motor neurons. The red nucleus may also exert inhibitory control over the transmission of somatic sensory information about the US to the inferior olive (IO), so that when a CR occurs (eyelid closes), the red nucleus dampens US activation of climbing fibers. Evidence to date is most consistent with storage of the memory traces in localized regions of the cerebellar cortex and possibly interpositus nucleus as well. Pluses indicate excitatory and minuses inhibitory synaptic action. Additional abbreviations: N V (sp), spinal fifth cranial nucleus; N VI, sixth cranial nucleus; N VII, seventh cranial nucleus; V Coch N, ventral cochlear nucleus. From "The Neurobiology of Learning and Memory" by R.F. Thompson, 1986, *Science, 233,* p. 941. Copyright 1986 by the AAAS. Reprinted by permission.

data suggest that the essential conditioned stimulus (CS) pathway includes mossy fiber projections to the cerebellum via the pontine nuclei (see Figure 14.3). Thus, sufficiently large lesions of the middle cerebellar peduncle prevent acquisition and immediately abolish retention of the eyelid CR to all modalities of CS (Solomon et al., 1986), whereas lesions in the pontine region can selectively abolish the eyelid CR to an acoustic CS (Steinmetz et al., 1987). Consistent with this result is current anatomical evidence for a direct contralateral projection from the ventral cochlear nucleus to this same region of the pons (Thompson, Lavond, & Thompson, 1986) and electrophysiological evidence of the "primary-like" auditory relay

nucleus in this pontine region (Logan, Steinmetz, & Thompson, 1986). Finally, electrical microstimulation of the mossy fiber system serves as a very effective CS, producing rapid learning, on average more rapid than with peripheral CSs, when paired with, e.g., a corneal airpuff US (Steinmetz et al., 1985b).

There is an extensive literature showing that electrical stimulation of many brain regions, particularly cerebral cortex, can serve as an effective CS (see Doty, Rutledge, & Larsen, 1956; Doty & Rutledge, 1959). In their studies, animals were typically trained to make discrete responses with an aversive US. With hindsight, it seems very likely that the cerebellar circuit formed the essential memory-trace circuit in these studies and that the cerebral cortical CS accessed the memory-trace circuit via the pontine nuclei (see Figure 4.3.)

Finally, conditioned responses that are normal in every regard (except for more rapid extinction) are learned with electrical stimulation of mossy fibers as the CS and climbing fibers as the US (Steinmetz et al., 1985). All of these results taken together build a strong case for localization of the essential memory traces to the cerebellum, either in the interpositus nucleus, or in multiple cerebellar cortical sites, or both (see Thompson, 1986).

Eyelid/NM conditioning is an instance of aversive learning. Two-phase models (e.g., Miller, 1948; Mowrer, 1947; Rescorla & Solomon, 1967; Prokasy, 1972) suggest an initial CER (as in cardiovascular conditioning) and later development of the discrete, adaptive and precisely timed skeletal muscle response (e.g., eyelid/NM), as noted earlier. In this context, the cerebellar system seems a very good candidate for the second phase of learning for associative conditioned responses that involve discrete, adaptive, striated muscle responses. Indeed, the fact that the DAO–climbing fiber system appears to be the necessary and sufficient (and non-aversive) teaching component of the US argues that the first phase, involving aversive, motivational aspects of learning, is not necessary for development of the discrete learned response; they seem to be parallel processes with different time courses. Systemic injection of morphine or local application of opioids to the floor of the 4th ventrical selectively abolishes the learned eyelid/NM response when it has just been learned (Mauk, Madden, Borchas, & Thompson, 1982; Mauk, Warren, & Thompson, 1982). Overtraining tends to protect against the effects of morphine but not against the effects of ipsilateral cerebellar lesions. The two processes in behavioral theories of aversive learning may be represented in the brain by two systems, one concerned with the CER and the other, involving the cerebellar system, concerned with the learning of specific, adaptive skeletal muscle responses (Thompson et al., 1986).

Ito has developed a most interesting experimental model of induced neuronal plasticity using the vestibulo-oscular reflex (VOR) and applied the general Marr–Albus cerebellar model of motor learning (e.g., Ito, 1970, 1982,

1984). Plasticity of the VOR was reviewed in depth by Miles and Lisberger (1981) and by Ito (1982). In brief, gain control can be altered by using lenses or by moving the visual field and head. The VOR shows a long-lasting adaptation to changed gain. This adaptation appears to be neuronal and not due simply to a learned strategy (Miles & Lisberger, 1981). Ablation of the flocculus (Ito, 1974) or of the vestibular cerebellum including the flocculus (Robinson, 1976) abolished VOR adaptation. Miles and Lisberger (1981) developed a case against VOR plasticity occurring in the cerebellum in the primate, based primarily on the properties of neuronal unit responses in the flocculus, and suggested instead that it occurs in the brain stem. They interpreted the flocculus lesion effect as afferent or modulatory (i.e., the flocculus is important in the induction of VOR plasticity in brain stem neurons).

Evidence from Ito's laboratory supports his view that at least an analogous plasticity can in fact be established in the flocculus in the rabbit (Ito, 1984). In brief, using the high decerebrate rabbit, responses of identified Purkinje cells were recorded in response to single pulse stimulation of vestibular nerve (2/sec). They showed a short-latency excitatory response. Similar excitation was shown by putative basket cells. Conjunctive stimulation of vestibular nerve (20/sec) and inferior olive (4/sec) for 25 sec, and *only* conjunctive stimulation, depressed the subsequent excitatory Purkinje cell response to single pulse stimulation of vestibular nerve for periods as long as an hour. Similarly, iontophoretic application of glutamate (the putative parallel fiber neurotransmitter—see Sandavol & Cotman, 1978) in conjunction with 4/sec olivary stimulation depressed the subsequent glutamate sensitivity on the Purkinje cells for a period of an hour. Similar results have been obtained with conjoint stimulation of parallel and climbing fibers in the cerebellar explant ("slice"). Regardless of the final outcome of localization of VOR plasticity, Ito would seem to have developed an analogous simplified model of the process where cellular plasticity does appear to be developed in the cerebellar cortex. He suggests two possible cellular mechanisms, both of which involve decreased sensitivity of chemical (glutamate?) receptors on Purkinje cells (Ito, 1984).

RED NUCLEUS

A major efferent target of the cerebellar hemisphere, via the superior cerebellar peduncle, is the contralateral red nucleus. It is also a major ipsilateral target of descending fibers from the motor cortex (corticorubral fibers). In turn, it gives rise to decending fibers to the brain stem and spinal cord (rubrospinal path) which cross and descend contralateral to the cells of origin in the red nucleus. In a most interesting study, Smith (1970) reported that large unilateral lesions in the red nucleus and vicinity markedly impaired a classically conditioned flexion response of the forelimb contralateral to, but not ipsilateral to, the lesion in cats. (He did not report what effect the lesion had on the reflex response). Tsukahara (1981, 1982) has recently developed an ingenious simplified preparation based on this paradigm. A stimulating electrode serving as the CS is implanted in the cerebral peduncle and the peduncle lesioned caudal to the corticorubral fibers. The unconditioned stimulus is shock to the contralateral forepaw. The CS pulse train is adjusted to produce a weak flexion response of the forelimb, and then, the CS and US are paired in training. Animals learn the leg flexion response to peduncle stimulation in several days of training. The shortest latency forelimb EMG response to peduncle stimulation is 8 msec, and the latency range is 8 to 34 msec. Excitability and threshold of the system are measured in terms of the behavioral limb flexion to peduncle stimulation. Over the course of training, this excitability measure (termed performance) increases markedly, but excitability of the behavioral response to interpositus stimulation does not. Tsukahara argues that since the two pathways are presumably the same from red nucleus to forelimb, the excitability increase is at the synaptic junctions of peduncle fibers on the red nucleus. Recordings from red nucleus neurons show that their probability of response to the CS increases significantly after training. Tsukahara and associates have also shown that lesion-induced sprouting of corticorubral synapses occurs in both neonatal and adult animals and that the newly formed synapses are physiologically effective (see Tsukahara, 1981; Tsukahara, 1982; Tsukahara, Oda, & Notsu 1981). The corticorubral system is capable of considerable plasticity. However, in the case of learning of discrete, adaptive CRs with periph-

eral stimuli in the normal intact mammal, the red nucleus appears to be efferent from the memory trace, as noted previously.

An earlier literature indicates that carnivores can learn a discrete leg-flexion response following complete neodecortication (e.g., Bromily, 1948; Poltrew and Zeliony, 1930). Consequently, although the corticorubral tract may normally be involved in leg-flexion conditioning in the intact animal, it is not essential. Cerebellar lesions, on the other hand, do permanently abolish the discrete leg-flexion conditioned response (see above). The effects of cerebellar lesions have not yet been examined in Tsukahara's simplified preparation.

LIMBIC SYSTEM AND CEREBRAL CORTEX

There is an extensive literature involving lesion, stimulation, and recording studies of higher brain regions in learning and memory. Much of this work has been done with instrumental and complex tasks and will be treated in that context later (motor cortex was treated above). Many early classical conditioning studies involved CS–US pairing or CS–brain stimulation pairings (see above) and measurement of brain activity but no measurement of behavior. Cells in cerebral cortex and limbic system often showed changes under such conditions, but the relations of such changes to behavioral aspects of learning and memory are unknown (Thompson et al., 1972).

Neuronal activity in such structures as the hippocampus becomes massively engaged in simple classical and instrumental learning tasks, often selectively under conditions where learning occurs, even though the hippocampus is not essential for the learning of these tasks. The common conclusion, that the hippocampus therefore plays no role in learning in these tasks, is not correct; it does by definition have a role insofar as neuronal activity is concerned. Indeed, the hippocampus can become important when more complex demands are placed on the animal, even in classical conditioning.

Olds and co-workers began a pioneering and extensive analysis of cellular responses during a conditioned food-retrieval task that involved both classical and instrumental learning (Olds et al., 1972; Segal & Olds, 1972). The behavioral response was movement, detected by a floating wire in the head plug that was very sensitive to any gross bodily movements. Animals first received unpaired CS1, CS2 (tones of 1 kHz or 10 kHz) and stored food-pellet dispenser-click-plus-food. The intertrial interval was about one minute. Then in the next session either CS1 or CS2 become CS+ (paired with click-food) and the other CS−. In some studies, the animal was required to be motionless for a period of one second to receive a CS+ or CS−. This latter requirement adds an instrument component but the basic paradigm was differential classical appetitive conditioning. The noisy cable response was required to be 5 times the amplitude of that in the control phase to the CS+ for the animal to have reached behavioral learned response criterion.

The activity of neurons was usually multiple unit, recorded during paired and unpaired presentations of conditioned stimuli. Localization of primary sites of neural change was a central issue in these studies, and Olds et al. (1972) reasoned that, during paired conditioning, cells responding with the shortest latencies after CS onset represent such sites. Cells responding at the shortest latency could not be reflecting phasic responses of other afferent cells. However, Olds et al. (1972) recognized the possibility that short latency sites might still be reflecting changes in tonic activity from afferent projections. In a wide sample of brain areas, Olds et al. (1972) showed that the hippocampus, specifically the CA3 field, exhibited among the shortest latency responses after CS presentation. Segal and Olds (1972) continued analysis of the hippocampal system and reported that in terms of changes in cell activity across trials, the dentate gyrus was the first component of the hippocampus to reveal significant increases above spontaneous firing rates. Later in training, CA3 and then CA1 cell regions exhibited discriminative responding, in accordance with the principle circuit of the hippocampus.

The effect of hippocampal ablation was not specifically tested on the paradigm used by Olds, but all other evidence suggests that an intact hippocampus is not required for learning such a task (see Douglas, 1967; Hirsh, 1974; Kimble, 1968; O'Keefe and Nadel, 1978). Discrimination reversal is one type of learning which is consistently impaired by damage to the hippocampal system (see Hirsh, 1974; Berger & Orr, 1982). Disterhoft and Segal (1978) examined the activity of hippocampal pyramidal and granule cells

during two-tone discrimination and reversal of food retrieval behavior. They showed that hippocampal cells exhibited differentially enhanced discharges to the CS+ after differential behavioral responding had stabilized. Interestingly, within subsequent reversal sessions, hippocampal neurons maintained elevated rates of responding to the previous CS+ (the new CS−) and changed (increased) response rates only to the new CS+ (the previous CS−). Thus, hippocampal activity was more closely related to changing behavioral responsiveness to the positively reinforced stimulus, and did not correlate well with changing behavioral responsiveness to the nonreinforced CS.

Segal (1977a, 1977b) has since applied a different strategy to the localization of cellular changes during learning. He was used chronically implanted stimulation electrodes to test the synaptic efficacy of afferents to the hippocampus during associative conditioning in rat. Results have shown that averaged potential responses evoked by commissural stimulation are augmented by conditioning and that this enhancement is probably mediated by changes in the activity of catecholaminergic afferents of the hippocampus. Weisz, Clark, and Thompson (1982) have used a similar procedure with classical conditioning in the NM response and demonstrated a gradually enhanced efficacy of entorhinal-dentate synapses during behavioral classical conditioning.

Berger and Thompson (1978a, 1978b, 1978c) used classical conditioning of the rabbit NM/eyelid response to study the activity of the hippocampus and other limbic system neurons during classical conditioning of the NM/eyelid in the rabbit (see also Berger, Berry, & Thompson, 1986; Berry & Thompson, 1978). Initial studies showed that neurons recorded from the pyramidal cell region of the hippocampus increased frequency of discharge very early during the course of training and preceeded onset of conditioned behavioral responding by a considerable number of trials. Extinction of the behavioral response is associated with a decrease in the frequency of firing of hippocampal neurons. Within conditioning trials, hippocampal cells exhibit a distinctive pattern of firing that correlates highly with amplitude of the conditioned behavioral response (Berger, Clark, & Thompson, 1980). In this sense, the firing of hippocampal neurons produces a temporal model of the learned behavior (Thompson et al., 1980). Berry and associates (Berry & Oliver, 1982) used an appetitive classical conditioning task, conditioned jaw movements to sweetened water in water-deprived rabbits, and showed that unit activity in the CA1 pyramidal region shows contingency-dependent responses that develop in the first 5 to 10 trials and form a predictive temporal model of the behavioral conditioned response, which is a rhythmic 7 to 9 Hz jaw movement, thus extending the hippocampal temporal model phenomenon to appetitive learning.

Single unit analyses of physiologically identified cell groups in eyelid conditioning have shown that pyramidal neurons are the hippocampal cell type modified during conditioning and that other cell types exhibit different response patterns (Berger, Rinaldi, Weisz, & Thompson, 1983; Berger & Thompson, 1978c). Additional studies have demonstrated that hippocampal cellular plasticity with these characteristics also occurs in other species besides the rabbit (Patterson, Berger, & Thompson, 1979), with the use of at least two different sensory modalities as the CS, and when other response systems than the nictitating membrane are conditioned (Thompson, Berger, Berry, Hoehler, Kettner, & Weisz, 1980). Analysis of hippocampal activity during a variety of control conditions has shown that these cellular changes only occur during associative learning and are not due to nonassociative aspects of the conditioning process (Berger & Thompson, 1978a, b, c; Hoehler & Thompson, 1980). The lateral cerebellar deep nuclei are essential for the component of the hippocampal neuronal response in the CS period (Clark et al., 1984). However several lines of evidence (Weisz, Clark, & Thompson, 1984; Mamounas, Thompson, Lynch, & Baudry, 1984) suggest that neuronal plasticity coding this hippocampal "memory trace" develops in significant part within the hippocampus.

Many of the above studies have been conducted using a delay conditioning paradigm. While lesions of the hippocampus do not disrupt learning under delay conditions (Schmaltz & Theois, 1972; Solomon & Moore, 1975), more recent analyses have shown that hippocampal lesions do affect NM/eyelid conditioning in other paradigms, and that changes in hippocampal cellular activity similar to those described above occur during learning in those paradigms (e.g., Berger & Orr, 1982).

## Instrumental Conditioning

In a typical instrumental conditioning procedure, the experimenter arranges for some designated response to produce an appetitive or aversive stimulus. Learning is indexed by changes in some measure of the response (e.g., latency, frequency, or amplitude) and is said to be associative when the changes can be demonstrated to result from the response-outcome contingency (see Hearst, this volume).

In interpreting the effects of a manipulation on subjects' behavior in a learning task, one is always confronted with the learning versus performance distinction: The problem lies in determining whether the experimental manipulation affects learning processes or the subjects' ability to perform the behavior used to index learning. This problem can be difficult—which class of effects a manipulation influences is rarely transparent and developing comparison conditions for factoring out learning and performance effects can require much ingenuity.

Several strategies used to rule out performance effects in instrumental learning tasks include using response measures that are less affected by general state changes (e.g., choice measures rather than response latency or amplitude measures). Another strategy is to assess treatment effects in two tasks for which the response measures are opposites, e.g., passive and active avoidance conditioning. A third strategy is to develop two orthogonal learning tasks that both involve the same general response components (e.g., different maze learning tasks or different discrimination and discrimination reversal tasks). The effects of a treatment on retention of a previously learned task and on learning of the second also has the potential of allowing one to factor out learning effects from performance effects. For example, D.M. Thompson & Moerschbaecker (1979) have developed a promising paradigm in which drug effects on learning of new response sequences by pigeons can be compared with performance on other well learned sequences. Another approach would be to look at the effect of a physiological manipulation in conjunction with training treatments known to primarily affect performance, rather than learning, in some learning task and to see if the effects of the physiological manipulation and the training treatment covary or are orthogonal. Along these lines, Heyman

(1983) has made use of Herrnstein's matching law (Herrnstein, 1970; Herrnstein & Heyman, 1979) to distinguish between motoric, motivational, and associational aspects of drug actions in appetetitive operant learning. It should be recognized that any one strategy has advantages and disadvantages peculiar to the form of learning and the physiological treatments used. The optimal approach is to take advantage of as many ways of distinguishing between learning and performance effects as one can arrange.

A second problem in the study of the neural basis of instrumental conditioning (or Pavlovian conditioning) is showing that the changes in behavior one observes result from the instrumental contingencies the experimenter has arranged, rather than from Pavlovian contingencies embedded in the events the animal experiences during training (and/or habituation/sensitization; see Mackintosh, 1983, ch. 2; Rescorla & Holland, 1976; Williams, 1981). Many studies of the neural basis of instrumental and Pavlovian conditioning are studies of the effects of physiological manipulations on the behavioral change produced by *the training procedure that the experimenter has arranged*, rather than being studies of the effects of physiological manipulations on a behavioral change demonstrated to be under the control of a particular instrumental (or Pavlovian) contingency.

The effects of Pavlovian contingencies embedded within instrumental training procedures can be seen in passive and active instrumental avoidance tasks, which are among the most popular paradigms for examining the effects on memory of interventions such as electroconvulsive shock (ECS), lesions, and drugs. The interpretative problems that each of these tasks poses have been pointed out by several authors (Bolles, 1978; Gash & Thomas, 1983; Heise, 1981; Weisz & Thompson, 1983). Rats tend to freeze when frightened. Such freezing behavior may come under the control of the context stimuli as a result of a Pavlovian pairing of the context with the shock that is to be avoided (Bolles, 1978) or an aversive experimental manupulation (e.g., ECS). Thus, in passive avoidance learning, the suppression of the punished response may be due to a Pavlovianly conditioned freezing response rather than the inhibition of responding due to the response → shock contingency. In active avoidance learning, the development

of such freezing responses should interfere with performance. The problem here is to determine if a physiological manipulation that affects performance on an active avoidance task does so by affecting the behavior under the control of the instrumental contingency or the Pavlovian contingency. For example, Naloxone, an opiate antagonist, enhances fear-freezing in shock situations (Fanselow & Bolles, 1979). Consequently, at least under certain circumstances, naloxone ought to impair learned active avoidance and to enhance learned passive avoidance, and indeed it does (Koob & Bloom, 1982; Weisz & Thompson, 1983). On the assumption that naloxone exerts this effect on behavior by blocking endogenous opioid actions in the brain, it would be predicted that opioids would enhance active avoidance and impair passive avoidance as a secondary consequence of their actions on freezing behavior. Indeed, just such effects have been reported for endogenous opioids on passive and active avoidance (Martinez et al., 1982; Weisz & Thompson, 1983). Freezing behavior is but one example of species-specific defensive responses. As Bolles (1970, 1978) notes, these innate defensive reflexes are elicited by aversive stimulation and pose serious problems for analysis of avoidance learning at the behavioral level, not to mention the biological level (but also see Deluty, 1982; de Villiers, 1982).

A different kind of problem exists for biological analysis in more complex learning situations, such as maze learning, where the number of cues that can gain discriminative control over the subject's behavior are often numerous, and the stimulus dimension controlling behavior can change during the course of training as a result of manipulations such as lesions. This problem makes interpretation of the experimental manipulation very difficult, as witnessed by Lashley's dilemma (Hunter, 1929).

## Neural Mechanisms of Instrumental Conditioning

### The Consolidation Hypothesis

A large proportion of work on putative brain substrates of instrumental learning and memory in vertebrates (usually the rat) has been done in the context of the *consolidation hypothesis*. Simply put, this hypothesis states that there are two phases in memory formation, an initial phase where memories can be altered by treatments and a subsequent phase where they are relatively impervious to treatment. Muller and Pilzecker (1900) are credited with the initial statement of the hypothesis and McDougall (1901) quickly pointed out that this view could account for retrograde amnesia in humans following head injury.

DISRUPTIVE ELECTRICAL STIMULATION. Electroconvulsive shock (ECS) was introduced as a clinical treatment for mental illness in 1938 (Cerletti & Bini), and several studies in the early 1940s reported that ECS treatment produced retrograde amnesia in humans. In 1949, Hebb and Gerard independently proposed a dual-trace hypothesis of memory storage—an initial consolidation phase involving reverberating activity through wide-spread neural circuits and a subsequent storage phase that involved permanent structural–physical changes in the brain. In this year, Duncan published the classic report that began the experimental study of consolidation. He trained rats in an active avoidance task—one trial a day followed by ECS—and varied the time between training and ECS in different groups. The result was a clear gradient of amnesia, with maximal impairment at a 20 sec training–ECS interval and no impairment at or beyond a one hour interval.

In the years since Duncan's classic study, there have been literally thousands of animal studies on the effects of ECS, brain stimulation, and drugs on memory performance. Virtually all of these studies have used some form of instrumental learning paradigm, usually avoidance learning. Favored tasks have been those where learning occurs in one or a few trials, simple tasks like active and passive avoidance with a strongly aversive shock US. However, both impairment and facilitation of retention performance have also been reported with appetitive instrumental tasks (McGaugh & Herz, 1972). There is no question that a wide range of treatments can impair or facilitate subsequent retention performance. However, we still have no idea whether these treatments are acting directly on memory processes in the brain, let alone which brain regions are involved. For the most part, the memory versus performance problem has not yet been solved in the context of memory consolidation. In a careful study of strychnine facilitation of learning and extinction of the classically conditioned rabbit nictitating membrane response (Cholewiak, Hammond, Seigler, & Papsdorf, 1968), strychnine appeared to be acting on performance variables rather than on memory processes, *per se*.

There have been several ongoing controversies in the consolidation literature. A major issue concerns the exact time course of the *consolidation gradient*—the relationship between the degree of treatment effect and the time of treatment after training. Many different gradients were found, ranging from a few seconds to many hours or even days (see, e.g., Squire & Barondes, 1974; Zornetzer, Abraham, & Appleton, 1978). The gradient depends upon species, tasks, conditions of training and stimuli, treatment parameters, and even laboratory. An intriguing study by Robbins and Meyer (1970) shows that under some circumstances ECS can selectively impair the older of two previously learned habits. In brief, rats were trained in a series of three tasks under one of two motivational conditions, food approach or shock avoidance, and a single ECS given immediately after learning the third task. Subsequent retention of the earlier learned task was impaired only for the task learned under the same motivational conditions as the one learned just before ECS, regardless of which was learned first.

In studies of ECS effects on retention in humans, memories are in general found to be impaired for a substantial period of time, up to two years or so prior to ECS treatment (which typically involves a series of ECS treatments) (Square & Cohen, 1979, see also chapter by Goodglass & Butters in this volume). Squire and Spanis (1984) trained mice in a single trial step through passive avoidance task, then gave a series of four ECS treatments at hour intervals at 1 to 70 days after training and then tested retention 2 weeks after ECS. Retention was impaired if ECS was given up to 21 days following the training trial, a result more consistent with ECS effects in humans.

From all these data it would seem difficult to argue that there is a single consolidation gradient, particularly with a single ECS treatment, and even whether there are one, two or several stages to memory formation (see reviews by Gold & McGaugh, 1975; Lewis, 1979; McGaugh & Hertz, 1972; Meyer & Meyer, 1982).

In early studies, ECS was delivered via the external ears. Not surprisingly, animals found this aversive, which led to the conditioned fear hypotheses. Thus, Coons and Miller (1960) showed that ECS given soon after training caused increased signs of fear (e.g., urination and defecation). Further, they showed that if animals were first trained to avoid one side of a grid and then shocked for entering the safe side, the closer in time it was to the training trial, the more ECS impaired learning of the new inhibitory response. These results led them to a conditioned fear hypothesis of ECS effects on retention performance. In subsequent studies from several laboratories, it was found that behavioral signs of fear (avoidance) generally develop with multiple ECS treatments but are more variable following a single ECS (McGaugh & Herz, 1972).

Conditioned fear cannot be the whole explanation. This was made clear by studies using disruptive electrical brain stimulation, which in many instances does not appear to be aversive, in place of ECS (Kesner, Gibson, & le Clair, 1970, see below). Other alternatives to the consolidation hypothesis include the conditioning of competing responses by ECS (Lewis & Maher, 1965) and the incubation of conditioned emotional responses (Chorover & Schiller, 1966).

In general, most studies of amnesia induced by disruptive electrical brain stimulation report concomitant seizure activity, and the thresholds for both are similar (McGaugh & Herz, 1972). It is difficult to prove that brain stimulation-induced amnesia can be obtained in the absence of brain seizure activity—to do so would require measurement of all neuronal activity in the brain. A case in point is a study by Kesner and Doty (1968). Amnesia was produced by either hippocampal or amygdaloid stimulation, with amygdala thresholds being lower. To be disruptive, hippocampal stimulation had to induce afterdischarge in the amygdala, but it was not necessary to induce measureable seizures in the hippocampus itself. The converse, brain seizures without amnesia, has been reported (Zornetzer & McGaugh, 1971).

Stimulation of a number of brain structures can induce amnesia, including the cerebral cortex, basal ganglia, limbic system, and brain stem tegmentum. Several laboratories have explored amnesia thresholds. The anterior cortex has lower thresholds than the posterior cortex but the structures having the lowest thresholds are the hippocampus and the amygdala, which also have the lowest thresholds for stimulation-induced seizures (McGaugh & Herz, 1972). It was ini-

tially hoped that this approach would serve to localize sites of memory storage, but that has not been possible. As noted earlier, induced seizure activity in the hippocampus can block acquisition of a conditioned response, yet animals with prior bilateral ablation of the hippocampus can learn the same conditioned response normally. Hippocampal stimulation/seizures would seem to be exerting disruptive actions elsewhere.

There is an extraordinary result in work with patients at UCLA (Babb, 1982) that deserves special comment here. These patients, who have normal recent memory, have unilateral hippocampal abnormalities. Up to 40 electrodes are implanted in the contralateral hippocampus, presumed to function normally, and surrounding structures. Weak electrical stimulation that induces afterdischarge in the normal hippocampus selectively abolishes recent memory—for the duration of afterdischarge the patients become temporary HMs. (HM is the classic amnestic patient with bilateral, temporal lobectomy; Milner, 1966).

The amygdala has the lowest stimulation-induced amnesia thresholds in the brain. It is also involved in autonomic activity, fear, aversive behavior, aversively motivated learning, and appetitive learning (see above and Goddard, 1964; Kaada, 1972; Kesner & Wilbrun, 1974; Spiegler & Mishkin, 1981). Impairment of retention of aversively motivated instrumental learning by bilateral ablation of the amygdala has been reported in some studies (Kesner & Wilbrun, 1974) and not in others (Kleiner, Meyer, & Meyer, 1967). As noted earlier, Liang et al. (1982) found that if the amygdalar lesions were made ten days after training (one trial passive avoidance in rat) they produced no deficit in retention, although these same lesions produced a massive deficit if made immediately after training. While the amygdala would seem to play a role in relation to aversive learning and immediate post-training events, it cannot be the locus of the memory trace, at least for this type of aversive instrumental learning.

A variety of drugs and treatments other than ECS and brain stimulation can also serve as amnestic agents (protein synthesis inhibitors are treated below). Some of these, pentylenetetrazol (PTZ), strychnine (at certain doses), flurothyl, diethyldithiocarbamate (DDS), and certain protein inhibitors, induce seizures. Still other amnestic agents include L-protine (in chick—Cherkin & von Herreveld, 1978) and amino acid uptake inhibitors (Gibbs, Robertson, & Hambly, 1977). Finally, more generalized insults such as deep anethesia, $CO_2$ inhalation, and anoxia induce amnesia (see Dunn, 1980; McGaugh & Herz, 1972).

PROTEIN SYNTHESIS INHIBITION. A seemingly consistent picture has developed from the use of protein synthesis inhibitors to impair memory. Pioneering studies by Flexner, Flexner, and Stellar (1983) and Flexner, Flexner, Stellar, de la Haba, and Roberts (1962), Barondes and associates (Barondes & Cohen, 1968a, b; Barondes & Jarvik, 1964; Cohen & Barondes, 1966) and Agranoff and associates (Agranoff, 1980; Agranoff, Davis, & Brink, 1966) reported that intracerebral injections of protein synthesis inhibitors impaired permanent memory performance. To take Agranoff's well-controlled studies on the goldfish as an example, intracerebral injection of puromycin immediately following training (instrumental shock avoidance to a light CS in a two compartment shuttle tank) prevented long term retention. If the drug was administered a few hours later it had no effect. Giving the drug before training had no effect on initial acquisition and short term retention but prevented long term retention. These general findings hold for fish, birds, and mammals and for three classes of drugs that block protein synthesis in different ways (Dunn, 1980). All such drugs prevent long term retention performance of learned habits if they inhibit cerebral protein synthesis by 85 percent or more. The effect occurs with intracerebral injection and with peripheral injection, but the latter must be with much higher doses, arguing for a central action (Agranoff, Burrell, Dokas, & Springer, 1978; Dunn, 1980).

It seems very reasonable to suppose that permanent memory storage processes, whatever their mechanisms (growth and change in synaptic structures is a commonly suggested possibility), will require protein synthesis. Such may seem the most parsimonious hypothesis to account for amnesia induced by protein synthesis inhibition, but there are serious problems. First of all, there are alternatives. Most obvious is that memory storage does not require protein synthesis directly but rather depends on other processes that do (e.g., altered neurotransmitter/receptor activities). More generally, memory storage may require normally functioning brain tissue, which would not be present after inhibition of protein synthesis. Furthermore, substances that inhibit protein synthesis make animals very sick.

Another alternative is that protein synthesis inhibitors have other actions which, as aside effect, may impair permanent memory. Many of the protein synthesis inhibitors apparently induce seizures or abnormal brain activity (Dunn, 1980). A case in point is the observation by Flexner and Flexner (1967): Injection of puromycin into the hippocampus in mice prevented long-term memory for an avoidance task. If saline were then injected into the same brain locus 60 days later, it reversed the puromycin block, and the memory that (supposedly) had not been formed then appeared. The simplest explanation for this is that the puromycin caused a local abnormality, perhaps hippocampal seizures, which interfered with retrieval/performance processes. The saline administration may then have, to some extent, reversed this abnormality.

Still another side effect hypothesis is that protein synthesis inhibitors impair catecholamine metabolism, particularly norepinephrine/epinephrine. Catecholamine involvement in learning and memory has been one of the major neurotransmitter theories (e.g., Kety 1970—see below). Remarkably, adrenergic agonists reverse antibiotic induced amnesia (Barondes & Cohen, 1968b). Several protein synthesis inhibitors inhibit tyrosine hydroxylase activity *in vitro* (Flexner, Serota, & Goodman, 1973). However, careful analysis of effects of antibiotics and adrenergic agonists (e.g., amphetamine) on tyrosine, norepinephrine, and dopamine systems in animals yield results that cannot be interpreted simply (Bloom, Quinton, & Carr, 1977; Goodman, Flexner, & Flexner, 1975).

Quartermain, McEwen, and Azmitia (1970) reported a dramatic instance of reversal of cycloheximide-induced amnesia by the simple process of giving a reminder US prior to the retention test. In their studies, protein synthesis was inhibited over 90 percent and amnesia was profound, yet it was reversed by a reminder stimulus (see Quartermain, 1976). The fact that several procedures can reverse amnesia that has been induced by protein synthesis inhibition would seem to raise serious problems for any theory that assumes that protein synthesis inhibitors are preventing the initial formation of long-term memory. The memory traces are, in fact, there, but are much more difficult to access, at least in studies where they can be accessed at all. But it is always possible to argue that protein synthesis must be completely blocked to completely prevent the formation of long-term memory. Davis and Squire (1984) reviewed the protein synthesis and memory literature in great detail and tend to favor the view that protein synthesis is an essential step in the formation of long-term memory. It does seem reasonable that long-term memory must have a structural basis in the nervous system, and indeed, there is much evidence that early experience can cause structural alterations in neurons (see below). Such structural changes require protein synthesis. But the relationship between the synthesis of proteins and the formation of memory, to the extent that the former can be shown to be essential for the latter, remains unknown.

DRUG FACILITATION OF LEARNING AND MEMORY. Drug treatments can facilitate subsequent memory performance. Lashley (1917) first reported that low doses of strychnine given to rats before daily training increased the rate of maze learning. McGaugh and Petrinovich (1959) replicated and extended Lashley's early observations and interpreted them in the context of memory consolidation. To counter the objection that the drug was acting on performance, McGaugh, Thompson, Westbrook, and Hudspeth (1982) first showed that post-trial injection facilitated retention performance the next day, after the drug effect had dissipated. The possibility that posttrial strychnine injection was rewarding was countered by Westbrook and McGaugh (1964) by use of a latent learning paradigm. Meyer, Horel, and Meyer (1963) showed that amphetamine can recover habits that had been abolished by cortical lesions (see also Meyer, 1972a).

To summarize a large literature in a few words, the following is a partial list of substances that have been reported to facilitate memory performance: strychnine, picrotoxin, and other convulsants; amphetamine, caffine, and other stimulants; epinephrine, norepinephrine, and adrenergic agonists; dopamine; acetylcholine and cholinergic drugs; a number of peptide hormones; opioids and other peptides; certain hallucinogens; certain pituitary hormones (Dunn, 1980; Heise, 1981; McGaugh & Herz, 1972; Squire & Davis, 1981). We will consider several of these separately below. Our concern here is more in the context of consolidation theory. Most of these facilitating drug effects have been on retention with the drug typically given shortly after training and well before (i.e., 24 hours) retention testing. It cannot necessarily be assumed that direct actions of the drug have completely dissipated. A single anesthetic dose of a barbiturate has obvious anesthetic/sedative effects for a few hours but significant effects on behavior that persist for days. Indeed, facilitating effects of many of these drugs are also found on retrieval, where the drugs are given just before retention testing. Dose-response curves for both retention and retrieval are typically the inverted U characteristic of the relation between emotion or arousal and behavioral performance (Lindsley, 1951).

Electrical stimulation of the brain has also been reported to enhance learning. Although facilitation has been reported with reticular stimulation (e.g., Bloch, Denti, & Schmaltz, 1966; Denti, McGaugh, Landfield, & Shinkman, 1970) most work has been on the hippocampal system. Learning of a variety of both instrumental and classical tasks can be facilitated by electrical stimulation of the hippocampus (e.g., Erickson & Patel, 1969; Prokasy, Kesner, & Calder, 1983; Stein & Chorover, 1968). In recording studies, high correlations have been found between parameters of hippocampal theta activity and subsequent rate of classical conditioning (Berry & Thompson, 1978) and resistance to amnestic treatment in instrumental learning (Landfield, McGaugh, & Tusa, 1972). Driving of hippocampal theta by repetitive electrical stimulation of the septal area can facilitate instrumental learning, and blocking of theta (e.g., by higher frquency stimulation) can impede learning (see section on Septal area below).

CONSOLIDATION: MEMORY FORMATION OR RETRIEVAL PERFORMANCE? The fundamental problem in interpretation of the consolidation literature is that of learning versus performance and it is compounded in most instances by our inability to assess the initial process of memory formation. Thus, under certain circumstances the consolidation time can be less than 0.5 seconds (Lewis, Miller, & Misanin, 1969). So we can only assess memory storage by measurement of subsequent retention performance. The behavioral measure is two steps removed from the hypothetical memory storage process. The most debated issue in the field has been memory storage versus retention (retrieval) processes. Evidence favoring interference with retention processes comes from several sources, including the absence of a consistent gradient of amnesia and the fact that, under some circumstances, ECS can interfere with the older of two memories. Perhaps the reminder studies are most significant (Lewis, Miller, & Misanin, 1968; Miller and Springer, 1974). If animals are given a reminder noncontingent US (e.g., footshock) just prior to the retention test, the amnestic effect of the prior ECS treatment (or protein synthesis inhibitors) is ameliorated. Gold, Haycock, Macri, and McGaugh (1973) argued that such stimuli can themselves become conditioned to context cues and hence influence test performance, but this cannot explain ECS impairment of the older two habits. Although it is not possible to draw a strong conclusion, it would seem that retention performance is easier to manipulate than the initial formation of memory.

CONSOLIDATION: MECHANISM OR MODULATION?
The many difficulties noted above for the simple consolidation hypothesis gradually led to a conceptual shift toward the notion of modulation: Treatments that alter retention performance may function more in the nature of modulatory influences. The focus of work shifted from analysis of the nature and time course of memory formation to analysis of the conditions under which retention performance can be altered (see Gold & McGaugh, 1975; Gold & Zornetzer, 1983; Lewis, 1979; McGaugh, 1977; Meyer, 1972a; Meyer & Meyer, 1982; Zurnetzer, 1978). Thus, for a long time it was assumed that manipulations that altered memory performance were acting on memory processes, or at the very least acting directly on the brain, as seemed evident in the case of interfering electrical brain stimulation. However, a number of puzzling observations accumulated. Posttraining peripheral injection of epinephrine has very potent facilitating effects on subsequent retention performance (passive avoidance). However, epinephrine does not cross the blood-brain barrier to any appreciable degree. Peripheral injection of d-amphetamine, an adrenergic agonist, also markedly facilitates retention, and it does cross the blood brain barrier freely. However, central administration of the drug has no effect on retention (McGaugh, 1983a, 1983b). Peripheral doses of beta endorphin and Met- and Leu-enkephalin too low to have any detectable central effects can attenuate amnesia in rats (Koob & Bloom, 1982).

In 1970, Flexner and Flexner made the extraordinary observation that the amnesia produced by central administration of puromycin was prevented by prior removal of the adrenal gland. The effect could be due to either the adrenal cortex or medulla or both; subsequent work implicated the medulla. Serota, Roberts, and Flexner (1972) blocked protein synthesis inhibitor amnesia by giving metaraminal, a peripherally acting adrenergic receptor agonist. Peripheral administration of alpha and beta adrenergic antagonists block the amnestic effects of disruptive electrical stimulation of the frontal cortex and amygdala and of pentylenetetrazol, cyclohexamide and DDC (see Gold & Sterberg, 1980; McGaugh, 1983). However, central administration of these same adrenergic antagonists does not block the amnestic effects of frontal cortex stimulation, suggesting peripheral actions. In a series of studies, McGaugh, Martinez, Richter, and associates have found that prior removal of the adrenal medulla prevents facilitation by amphetamine, effects of opioids, and impairment by electrical stimulation of the amygdala (Martinez, Jensen, Messing, Righter, & McGaugh, 1981; McGaugh, 1983a, 1983b). Section of the stria terminalis, an efferent from the amygdala, also abolished amygdala stimulation-induced amnesia.

In sum, the types of manipulations that exert the most powerful effects on retention performance—drug facilitation, amnesia by protein synthesis inhibitors, and disruptive brain stimulation—can all be blocked by prior removal of the adrenal medulla. Replacement therapy by administration of epinephrine at appropriate times can to some degree reinstate these effects (McGaugh et al., 1983a, 1983b). Of course, demedullation has not been tried for all effective manipulations. Nonetheless, results to date suggest that many manipulations that alter retention performance are not acting directly on the mechanisms of memory storage and retrieval in the brain and in fact are not acting directly on the brain at all but rather on the adrenal medulla. The critical links between the peripheral actions of treatments that alter retention performance via the adrenal medulla and any presumed central actions on mechanisms that relate to brain processes of learning and memory remain largely unknown. It has, however, been known for a very long time that emotional state can have a profound effect on how well experiences are remembered. It may be that consolidation of memory reflects this fact. Release of epinephrine and/or norepinephrine (and other substances?) by the adrenal medulla is a normal concomitant of emotions, as in fear and stress. Ample evidence exists that appetitive as well as aversive learning tasks can activate the pituitary–adrenal axis in laboratory animals.

NEUROCHEMISTRY AND MEMORY—
NEUROTRANSMITTER SYSTEMS

Chemical approaches to memory constitute a larger literature than all other aspects of the psychobiology of learning and memory combined. The only conclusion that can be drawn at present from this vast literature with any degree of confidence is that chemical processes seem somehow to be involved in learning and memory.

Some workers who administer substances are fond of distinguishing between what they term interventive and correlational approaches, sometimes with the implication that the former are somehow more causal than the latter. In fact, administering a drug and observing effects on behavior and administering a training and observing effects on brain chemistry are epistemologically equivalent. We reviewed two explicitly interventive chemical approaches above, effects of protein synthesis inhibitors and facilitating agents, and concluded that no clear conclusion is possible.

It would be astonishing if the major chemical neurotransmitters in the brain were not involved in learning and memory. To argue that they are not is tantamount to saying that the brain is uninvolved. However, problems seem to have arisen, in part by confusion between the messenger and the message. For example, acetylcholine (ACh) is the neurotransmitter at vertebrate skeletal neuromuscular junctions. It is essential for all skeletal muscle activity. But the ACh molecule does not somehow code movement. It happens to be the transmitter at the critical junctions in a neuronal system that functions to produce movements because of its anatomical organization. Dopamine, for example, appears to be involved in both Parkinson's disease and schizophrenia. These two quite different presumed roles are thought to be due to the fact that dopamine appears to be a neurotransmitter in two different pathways in the brain.

CATECHOLAMINES. Kety (1970) proposed involvement of the catecholamines, particularly the diffuse norepinephrine projection system from locus coeruleus via the dorsal bundle to higher brain regions, in learning and memory. Aspects of this literature were reviewed above in the context of consolidation. Adrenergic drugs are among the most effective treatments for altering learning and retention in certain tasks, as noted. Many of the pharmacological studies have used drugs that alter both norepinephrine and dopamine (e.g., tyrosine hydroxylase inhibitors). In general, substances that interfere with catecholamine synthesis and metabolism interfere with learning and memory, whereas agonists improve them, but opposite effects have also been reported (Dunn, 1980; Squire & Davis, 1981).

There are correlations between brain norepinephrine (NE) levels and retention, but they are not simple. A decrease in forebrain NE of 10 to 30 percent after passive avoidance training correlated with good retention and even facilitation, but greater decreases correlated with impairment of retention (Gold & Van Buskirk, 1978a, 1978b). Destruction of the locus coerulus or of the dorsal bundle with subsequent marked depletion of brain norepinephrine seems to have no effect on learning in a variety of tasks (Mason, 1979; Squire & Davis, 1981). Such lesions may or may not have effects on retention (Mason & Iverson, 1979; Roberts, Price, & Fibiger, 1976; Zornetzer & Gold, 1976). Impairments in learning have been reported with combined lesion of the brain NE system (dorsal bundle) and removal of the entire adrenal gland (e.g., Ogren & Fuxe, 1974; Roberts & Fibiger, 1977). However, there are also negative reports of effects of such joint ablations (McGaugh, 1983a, 1983b).

The literature on catecholamine and memory is vast, contradictory, and confusing. Recent observations of the role of the adrenal medulla may eventually bring more order to this chaos. We quote from two comprehensive reviews:

"Catecholamines clearly modulate memory in important ways, but their action is not essential for the formation of memory." (Dunn, 1980, p. 377)

". . . brain NE seems not to play an essential role in the formation of memory." (Squire & Davis, 1981, p. 342).

ACETYLCHOLINE (ACh). Although ACh has a long-known role as a neurotransmitter at neuromuscular and autonomic synapses, ACh pathways in the brain have only been identified in the past few years (Fibiger, 1982). So far as is known, there is only one major region of ACh containing neurons in the forebrain, a band of cells extending from the nucleus basalis to the medial septum in the basal forebrain. These ACh neurons project widely and diffusely to the cerebral cortex and hippocampus. Since this system has only recently been characterized, little experimental work has been done on it.

In an early and careful series of studies, Deutsch (1973a, b) reported complex effects of intracerebrally administered cholinergic drugs on learning and memory in the rat. Drugs such as physostigmine that block the breakdown enzyme cholinesterase, that were given prior to retention testing resulted in impaired performance, or facilitated performance, or no effect depending on the time of testing after training. Anticholinergic drugs (scopalamine) tended to have opposite effects. The nature of the effects also depends upon the degree of initial learning (see also Stanes, Brown, & Singer, 1976). In normal humans, infusions of arecoline or physostigmine facilitated verbal learning, as did oral choline. The effects are significant but small (Drachman, 1977; Davis et al., 1981; Siteram, Weingartner, & Gillin 1978). Scopolamine produces marked impairment in memory and cognitive functions in humans and monkeys (Bartus, 1979).

Recent interest in the role of the brain ACh system in learning and memory stems from the discoveries that critical levels of ACh are markedly reduced in Alzheimer's disease and that the ACh neurons in the nucleus basalis are mostly degenerated (Coyle, Price, & DeLong, 1983). Treatment with physiostigmine and cholinergic agonists or precursors (e.g., arecoline, choline) have been reported to improve learning and memory performance in aged mice and monkeys (Bartus, 1981) and even to be of some help in Alzheimer's disease (Thal & Fuld, 1983; Thal, Rosen, Sharpless, & Crystal, 1981), but the

effects are small. To add confusion, naloxone, the opiate antagonist, has been reported to produce similar beneficial results with Alzheimer's patients (Reisberg, 1983). There is at present no direct evidence implicating the brain ACh system(s) in learning and memory. The cholinergic drug studies in humans and monkeys involve peripheral administration, so effects could be peripheral and/or central. The large number of studies showing alterations in learning and memory performance with septal manipulations may map into this system (see below). In any event, the recent characterization of the brain ACh system and its degeneration in Alzheimer's disease will undoubtedly lead to a much larger literature.

ENDOCRINE SYSTEM. The endocrine system, particularly the pituitary–adrenal axis, is engaged during training and testing procedures in animals. Indeed, there are substantial and systematic increases in release of ACTH and cortisol (from adrenal cortex) in aversive learning and even in appetitive learning and in as seemingly mild events as exploring a new environment (Levine, 1968, 1971). These increases are not, of course, specific substrates of memory storage and retrieval but rather more generalized state and situational dependent effects.

Administration of ACTH or $ACTH_{4-10}$ produces several effects, most prominently an increased resistance to habituation and to extinction in aversive and appetitive tasks (Levine, 1971; deWied, 1969; deWied, 1974). If given just before a retention test, it is reported to attenuate a previously induced retrograde amnesia (Flood, Jarvik, Bennett, & Orme, 1976; Rigter, Elbertse, & Van Riezen, 1975). It may or may not have effects on initial learning (Gold and McGaugh, 1977). It has generally been assumed that these ACTH effects are secondary to its normal peripheral hormonal actions (i.e., release of cortisol). Some studies report similar effects on memory with the $ACTH_{4-10}$ fragment, which apparently has no hormonal action on the adrenal cortex, but other studies report no memory effects (Dunn, 1980). Perhaps the most reasonable conclusion at present is that the putative effects of ACTH and $ACTH_{4-10}$ are secondary to peripheral endocrine and/or more generalized state actions (Squire & Davis, 1981; Dunn, 1980).

Vasopressin, the antidiuretic peptide hormone, requires separate treatment because of recent reports of putative actions on memory.

Vasopressin is a nanopeptide synthesized by neurons in the paraventricular nucleus of the hypothalamus and released from their terminals in the neurohypophesis. It has well known peripheral actions in regulating fluid and electrolyte balance and can have significant pressor action (increases blood pressure).

Initial observations on apparent memory actions of vasopressin came from DeWied's laboratory. They found that extinction of shuttle box avoidance in rats was prolonged following neurohypophesectomy but that subcutaneous injections of vasopressin analogues reversed this effect (deWied, 1971). DeWied and other groups reported that peripheral or central administration of vasopressin improved retention of passive avoidance responding (prolonged extinction) (Bohus, Kovacs, & deWied, 1978; Gold and Van Buskirk, 1976). Effective doses for central administration were less than 1/1000th the effective peripheral dose, arguing strongly for a central action. Unfortunately, some other laboratories have not been able to reproduce these effects, at least with peripheral administration (e.g., Hostetter, Jubb, & Kozlowski, 1980).

Critical evidence came from the Brattleboro rat homozygous for diabetes insipidus (HO–DI). These animals have a virtual absense of vasopressin in the blood, pituitary, and brain. DeWied and associates reported that HO–DI rats tested for passive avoidance show a severe memory inpairment which is reversed by vasopressin treatment (deWied, 1980; deWied, Bohus, Van Winersma Greidanus, 1975). However, an extensive and careful replication found no evidence of memory deficits in either passive or active avoidance in the HO–DI rats (Carey & Miller, 1982), and another laboratory found the HO–DI rats to be superior to normals in passive avoidance memory (Bailey & Weiss, 1979).

In a study by LeMoal et al. (1981) that did find a positive effect of intracerebrally administered vasopressin on active avoidance memory, it was suggested that vasopressin influences avoidance behavior through its peripheral actions, particularly by causing increased blood pressure. Direct anatomical pathways that can mediate such blood pressure effects exist from the vasopressin (and oxytocin) neurons in the paraventricular nucleus of the hypothalamus to cell groups of both the sympathetic and parasympathetic divisions of the autonomic nervous system (Swanson & Sawchenko, 1983). Intracranial administration of vasopressin in doses over the range that yield memory effects causes substantial increases in peripheral blood pressure in both Sprague–Dawley and HO–DI rats (Gash & Thomas, 1983). A recent review states that:

> "In summary, it seems that while the thesis that vasopressin directly modulates memory processes is becoming increasingly untenable, evidence is mounting that vasopressin has direct visceral (autonomic) effects which may indirectly influence other behaviors, perhaps by modulating emotional–motivational (arousal) and temperamental factors subserving the specific responses from which higher cognitive functions (like "memory") are inferred." (Gash and Thomas, 1983, p. 198.)

Nonetheless, vasopressin does have very powerful effects on retention performance.

In a comprehensive series of studies, Chambers and associates have demonstrated a powerful effect of the steroid hormone testosterone on memory (see Chambers, 1985, for review). The rate of extinction of a learned taste aversion varies inversely with blood level of testosterone in rats. Normal females extinguish much faster than normal males, but manipulation of blood level of testosterone produces the same effects on rate of extinction in both sexes. Furthermore, blood level of testosterone at the time the taste aversion is learned has no effect on rate of extinction; only the blood level at the time of extinction training is critical—one of the many lines of evidence arguing that extinction ("forgetting") is not simply the fading away of whatever storage processes occurred during acquisition.

OPIOID PEPTIDES. What kind of opioid peptide effect on learning or memory would the reader prefer? Almost any can be provided from a large and inconsistent literature (Koob & Bloom, 1982; Martinez et al., 1981; Squire & Davis, 1981). The original opiate, morphine (an alkaloid, not a peptide) has relatively consistent effects, attenuating both aversive and appetitive learning and memory behaviors. In classical conditioning of the NM/eyelid response to tone, morphine and opiate analogues abolish the just learned response (but not an overlearned response). The effect is central, not peripheral and the primary site of action is in the vicinity of the fourth ventricle. The effect can be obtained by selective action on the presumed mu receptor, is not due to attenuation of information in the primary auditory relay nuclei, and can be reversed with the opiate antagonist naloxone (Mauk et al., 1982). As noted above, central morphine and certain other opiates also abolish the classically conditioned heart-rate response. At least in aversive learning, this opiate action has often been interpreted in the context of fear and conditioned fear.

Naloxone alone increases retention behavior in active and passive avoidance tasks (Koob & Bloom, 1982), implying a contrary action by endogenous opioid peptides. Peripherally administered endorphine and Leu- and Met-enkephalin attenuate amnesia effects in rats (Rigter, 1978). Met-enkephalin and alpha and beta endorphin delay extinction of a pole-jumping task (deWied, Bohus, Van Ree, Kovacs, & Greven, 1978). Gamma endorphin, only one amino acid larger than alpha, produces an opposite effect (deWied et al., 1980). Low peripheral doses of Met-enkephalin and analogues facilitate performance in an appetitive maze learning task (Kasin, Scollan, King, Schally, & Coy, 1976). In appetitive operant behavior, alpha endorphin delayed extinction and gamma endorphin facilitated extinction. In approach to a water reward, however, both alpha and gamma endorphin delayed extinction (Koob et al., 1981; LeMoal et al., 1981). Most of these inconsistent, peripherally administered effects occur at doses that are believed to be too low to have any central action (Koob & Bloom, 1982). Several of these effects are abolished by prior removal of the adrenal medulla, as noted above.

## CHEMICAL CORRELATES OF MEMORY IN THE BRAIN

"We are . . . confronted with an enormous haystack that we believe contains a needle of undetermined size, probably miniscule . . . . At present, the approach has an element of 'Catch 22'—if a change in labelling pattern is detected in a whole brain extract as a result of training, it can probably safely be ruled out as being a part of an informational process, i.e., related to the learning of a specific new task. Observed changes can more reasonably be attributed to grosser and less specific concomitants of learning related to brain states, such as stress, attentiveness, etc." (Agranoff et al., 1978, p. 628).

The fundamental problem again is localization. Analysis of putative neurochemical changes involved in the coding and storage of memory can only be done when the specific storage sites in the brain have been localized. Otherwise, the signal-to-noise problem is overwhelming, as Agranoff notes above. Indeed, significant progress has been made or appears possible only in those cases where the learned-response circuit has to some degree been identified and localized.

In virtually every study that has looked for biochemical changes in the brain as a result of learning, changes of some sort have been reported. How these changes may relate to processes of memory storage in the brain remains unknown. In some instances, the changes may not even be specific to brain. Rees et al. (1974) found that avoidance training in the rat increased the incorporation of $[^3H]$ lysine into protein in brain and liver. This change was also produced by several other behavioral manipulations, decreased with repeated treatments, and produced by injection of ACTH (Rees & Dunn, 1977). Unfortunately, many studies of biochemical changes in brain with learning have not been so carefully done and have not used liver or other control tissues.

Biochemical studies of learning and memory have been reviewed at length (e.g., Agranoff et al., 1978; Dunn, 1980; Rainbow, 1979; Squire & Davis, 1981). See particularly, the comprehensive and critical review by Dunn (1980), where problems of a chemical nature, as well as more general issues of controls and interpretations, are treated in detail.

Early work focused on changes, usually increases and/or alterations, in brain RNA. For example, Hyden and Lange (1968) reported a significant increase in the RNA content of hippocampal CA3 neurons contralateral to the trained paw in a reversal of handedness task in rats, comparable to similar asymmetrical changes in RNA content of cortical neurons (Hyden & Egyhazi, 1964). However, Cupello and Hyden (1976) found no differences between left and right hippocampal neurons in a replication.

In a number of studies over the years, Hyden and associates have reported changes in RNA content and/or composition as a result of various learning tasks. Hyden is to be credited for use of cellular dissection. In his studies, at least, it is neuron RNA that is analyzed rather than whole brain RNA. Glassman's group has also focused on RNA; for example, they reported increased RNA synthesis in brain but not kidney and liver in mice trained in a shock-avoidance (jump to platform) task but have been cautious in their interpretations (Zemp, Wilson, Schlesinger, Boggan, & Glassman, 1966). Work on brain RNA and learning in general has decreased markedly over the past years. According to Dunn (1980):

"problems with the interpretation of the biochemical data [in these and other studies of brain RNA] and other aspects of this work have encouraged most groups to direct their efforts to the study of proteins or other chemicals." (p. 345).

The overriding problem of localization remains. Until the locus of a given memory trace in the brain is known, one can never be sure that the biochemical changes observed have anything to do with the memory, as opposed to nonspecific changes in activity, hormonal actions, etc.

Analysis of changes in brain protein with learning may be more satisfactory from a chemical point of view (Dunn, 1980; Agranoff et al., 1978), but the very same problems of localization specificity, and controls remain. Many studies have used instrumental avoidance learning in rodents, where satisfactory controls are difficult to achieve (see above). We treated effects of protein synthesis inhibition above in the context of the consolidation theory. As noted there, initial memory formation is too rapid to be coded by protein synthesis. Long-term memory formation may or may not require protein synthesis. The focus here is on putative protein synthesis that results from training procedures. Following are a few examples of brain protein changes that have been reported. Most of these involve the incorporation of radioactively labeled precursor amino acids into proteins. Hyden and associates have reported inconsistent changes in hippocampal pyramidal neuron protein following handedness and maze tasks (e.g., Hyden & Lange, 1970). Matthies's group (e.g., Pohle & Matthies, 1976) reported changes in hippocampal protein in a shock-motivated brightness discrimination task in rats. Routtenberg, George, and Davis (1974) reported changes in labeling of glycoproteins in a rat active avoidance task in two bands from caudate and one from temporal cortex. Dunn (1980) notes that

this study involved 3 behavioral situations, 4 brain regions, 4 time points, and 28 gel bands. He wonders about the number of statistically significant effects that can arise by chance alone.

A protein termed S-100 (found only in brain) has been a factor in many studies. It was initially thought to be contained in neurons but is now believed to be glial and not neuronal. Hyden and Lange (1970) reported S-100 to increase in the hippocampus following training in reverse-handedness food pellet retrieval in the rat. Zomzely-Neurath et al. (1976) reported that S-100 increased following T-maze learning. Intraventricular administration of antisera against S-100 produced amnesia in rats (Hyden & Lange, 1970; Rapport & Karpiak, 1976). Hyden (1979) proposed that S-100 itself may serve as a calcium-dependent mechanism for synaptic modulation—it can be phosphorylated by brain nuclear protein kinases and therefore may affect gene expression. As will be seen below, these observations on S-100 may relate to one class of suggested mechanisms of memory (e.g., Lynch & Baudry, 1984). Shashoua (1982) reports that S-100 is highly concentrated in brain extracellular fluid of several species. The reader may consult the above noted reviews for many other examples of this literature.

Two non-mammalian vertebrate preparations are of interest in this context: postural adjustment learning in the goldfish (see Shashoua, 1982) and imprinting in the chick (see below; Rose, 1980). In Shashoua's work on the goldfish, a float is attached to the ventral surface of the fish, and it must learn to remain upright. Shashoua reports formation of new proteins in the brain following training. (Control problems here are formidable.) More recently his group has reported synthesis of the similar new proteins (i.e., bands that migrated on SDS-gels at similar molecular weights) in thirsty mice trained to find water in a T-maze. Antisera to these proteins impaired retention of the float-balancing skill in goldfish. As it happens, these proteins are major constitutents of the cerebrospinal fluid in fish and are also present in rat CSF and appear to be secreted by ependymal cells and not neurons. Shashoua has suggested that they may act as a modulatory factor in some aspect of learning, reminiscent of current views of hormone and drug effects on learning and memory performance (see above).

Imprinting in the chick is of interest in part because it is one of the rare cases where an essential part of the memory-trace circuit has been localized to a part of the forebrain roof—the medial hyperstriatum ventrale. This interesting model of learning will be discussed later. Here we note only that both RNA and protein changes were found which were localized to this region of neuronal tissue (Bateson, Horn, & Rose, 1975; Horn, 1981; Rose, 1980).

## Brain Substrates of Instrumental Learning

With the possible exception of certain visual learning tasks, the learned-response circuits essential for the vast array of instrumental and complex learning tasks studied in infrahuman animals have not been identified or localized, except that, in most instances, the cerebral neocortex does not appear to be essential. In general, brain lesions of higher regions produce partial and/or recoverable deficits. Lower brain systems that may be essential have not yet been defined. In spite of a very large literature, there has been relatively little systematic work defining the neuronal circuits essential for any instrumental task or even the circuits essential for learning-induced changes in neuronal activity in a given brain region.

Lower brain systems. We noted earlier that a variety of classically conditioned responses can be learned and/or retained following complete removal of the cerebral neocortex. The same has been shown for a variety of instrumental tasks (Bromiley, 1948; Meyer, 1972a; Oakley, 1979).

One investigator, Robert Thompson, has approached the localization of subcortical brain systems involved in complex instrumental learning tasks by using multiple lesions. In various studies, he has examined effects of literally hundreds of different lesions, many of them multiple, on both acquisition and retention of a number of instrumental tasks. The results of this approach have led Thompson (1983) to propose a number of functionally related neural complexes. Perhaps the most interesting is that labeled the "basal ganglia-reticular formation-limbic midbrain complex." Multiple lesions placed in this complex result in severe global amnesia that encompasses a wide variety of learned behaviors. Many of the lesion effects in Thompson's studies are partial, often small, and

generally recoverable. Lesioned animals learn or relearn statistically more slowly than controls, but they do learn and relearn. Except for the global amnesia effect, the lesion deficits are, in general, not great. Because complex instrumental tasks are used, it is not clear why lesioned animals show deficits. Thus, large bilateral lesions of the lateral hypothalamus-nigrostriatal bundle produce the syndrome of sensory neglect with its attendant aphagia and unresponsiveness to stimuli (Marshall, Richardson, & Teitelbaum, 1974). Such animals perform poorly in many instrumental learning tasks, but the deficit may not be due to interference with learning and memory processes in the brain, *per se.*

The septal area. Brady and Nauta (1953) reported that septal lesions weakened conditioned emotional responses but had no effect on the acquisition of new emotional responses. Many subsequent studies showing impairments in avoidance conditioning were interpreted in terms of an emotional deficit in animals with septal and limbic cortex lesions. McCleary (1961) showed that such a unifactor explanation is unlikely. Using cats with cingulate or septal lesions and two different shock-motivated avoidance tasks, he found a double dissociation between the lesions and the tasks. Cingulate lesions produced a deficit on active avoidance (animal required to perform a response) but not passive avoidance (animal required to inhibit a response); septal lesions interfered with passive but not active avoidance. In general, septal lesions tend to facilitate active avoidance learning but produce deficits in retention (Kenyan & Krieckhaus, 1965; Moore, 1964), whereas, lesions of the amygdala retard acquisition and impair or have no effect upon relearning of avoidance habits (see above; Horvath, 1963; Weiskrantz, 1956).

Recent interest in the role of the septum in learning and memory has focused on the close interrelations of the septum and hippocampus. The medial septum projects to the hippocampus via a putative ACh pathway thought to be the hippocampal theta pacemaker (see below) and the hippocampus projects to the lateral septal areas.

Effects of septal lesions that share behavioral similarities with hippocampal lesions include lack of effect on reward behavior, escape behavior, and simultaneous discrimination tasks;

no change in threshold for detecting shock, increased-response rate on intermittent operant schedules; improvements in both two-way active avoidance and non-spatial avoidance tasks; impaired acquisition of Pavlovian conditioning (or no effect, depending on size of lesion); impaired passive avoidance, DRL performance, reversal learning, and successive discrimination performance; reduced spontaneous alternation; increased resistance to extinction, but decreased resistance to extinction after partial reinforcement (PRF) training, impairment of working memory, impairment of spatial memory.

By comparison, effects of septal lesions which are dissimilar to those seen following hippocampal lesions include increased responding on operant CRF (continuous reinforcement) schedules, decreased fear responses in open field activity, increased probability of shock-induced aggression (i.e. septal hyper-reactivity), and impaired one-way active avoidance (though this effect may also occur with hippocampal lesions). In some of these cases the effect of the lesion is temporary [e.g., septal hyperreactivity (Yutzey, Meyer, & Meyer, 1964)]; in other cases it may be related to extra-septo-hippocampal connections (Albert, Brayley, & Milner, 1978). A striking difference is a marked increase in social cohesiveness in septal rats (Meyer, Ruth, & Lavond, 1978). It is perhaps of interest that wherever the effects of the two kinds of lesions are similar, they resemble those produced by anti-anxiety drugs. This observation provides some support for the idea that anti-anxiety drugs act by somehow impairing septo-hippocampal function (Gray, 1970, 1982).

Recent septal lesion studies have focused on two current theories of hippocampal function, spatial or *cognitive map theory* (O'Keefe & Nadel, 1978) and *working memory theory* (Olton, Becker, & Naudelman, 1979, 1980). (See discussion of hippocampus below.) In fact, septal lesions impair spatial memory and working memory performance (e.g., in elevated mazes with spatial cues and in the radial arm maze). Thomas and associates have attempted to dissect these possibilities (Thomas et al., 1982). Thus, using a plus shaped elevated maze and spatial memory tasks that involved reference memory and an alternation task that required working memory (see Olton et al., 1979 for an extended discussion of these terms), they examined effects of small medial septal lesions

(Thomas, Brito, Stein, & Berko, 1982). In their studies, lesions markedly impaired working memory alteration performance but not reference spatial memory performance. In this context it may be noted that so far as the anatomy of hippocampal projections in concerned, spatial information is much more likely to be conveyed to the hippocampus from the entorhinal cortex, which receive extensive inputs from the cerebral cortex, than from the septal nuclei (see Swanson et al., 1982).

An intriguing aspect of septo-hippocampal relations is the hippocampal theta rhythm. Cells in the medial septal nucleus and nucleus of the diagonal band fire in bursts which are steadily in phase with theta recorded simultaneously in the hippocampus (Petsche & Gogolak, 1962). Furthermore, interference with these cells, either acutely (e.g., by local anesthetic injection or high-frequency electrical stimulation) or chronically (e.g., by surgical destruction of the medial septal tissue) disrupts the hippocampal theta rhythm. Conversely, stimulation of the medial septal pacemaker cells using frequencies which lie normally within the theta band can artificially induce (drive) a theta-like rhythm in the hippocampus: Each pulse to the septum produces a corresponding wave in the hippocampal EEG; the resultant hippocampal rhythm is identical in frequency to the septal stimulus within the theta range.

Berry and Thompson (1979) found that small lesions limited to the medial septum that abolished hippocampal theta significantly impaired rate of acquisition of the classically conditioned NM/eyelid response in the rabbit, even though large septal lesions have no effect (Solomon 1979). Again, it appears that, like hippocampus, a malfunctioning septo-hippocampal system is worse than no septum at all, implying that learning is impaired by actions on other brain structures. Evidence suggests strongly that the pathway from medial septum to hippocampus is cholinergic. Systemic administration of scopolamine impairs acquisition of the NM/eyelid response (Solomon & Moore, 1979). However, if the hippocampus is first removed bilaterally, scopolamine does not impair acquisition, implying that it is exerting its direct action in the intact animal on the cholinergic septum-to-hippocampus pathways, which in turn causes disruption elsewhere (Solomon, Solomon, Vauderschaaf & Perry, 1983).

Many experiments have used both high- and low-frequency electrical stimulation of the septum to produce behavioral effects in learning paradigms. High-frequency (60 Hz) medial septal stimulation increases the acquisition rate of a two-way shuttlebox avoidance task, produces no effect on either brightness or position simultaneous discrimination but reversal is impaired in both cases (Donovick & Schwartzbaum, 1966). In contrast, septal stimulation in the theta range tends to facilitate learning and memory performance activity (Landfield, 1977).

Other experiments examined effects on the extinction of rewarded behavior: Low frequency produced effects opposite to those seen after either septal or hippocampal lesion or anti-anxiety drug administration (Gray, 1972); high-frequency acted in the same manner as lesions and anti-anxiety drugs (Gray, Araujo-Silva, & Quintao, 1972). Recently, it has become apparent that septal stimulation can have long-lasting behavioral effects which are unrelated to the behavior which may accompany the septal induction procedure. Thus, low-frequency theta-driving septal stimulation has been shown to facilitate proactively the acquisition of T-maze performance (Deupree, Coppock, & Willer, 1982) as well as lever-pressing performance on both fixed ratio (Holt & Gray, 1983) and random-interval (Holt, 1982) schedules. Conversely, high-frequency theta-blocking septal stimulation proactively produced exactly the opposite behavioral effects: delayed acquisition of fixed ratio lever-pressing and decreased resistance to extinction (Holt & Gray, 1983).

To state some oversimplified conclusions, there is no convincing evidence that the septal area is directly involved in processes of memory storage and retrieval. In studies where efforts have been made to dissect effects of septal lesions on performance versus learning, effects seem to be on performance (Kleiner et al., 1967). On the other hand, the septal area is much involved in behavioral signs of immobility, anxiety, and social cohesiveness. Influences that manipulations of the septal area exert on learned behaviors may be mediated in part by its actions on the hippocampus and appear to be modulatory in nature.

HIPPOCAMPUS. Modern views of hippocampal function date from the experiments of Kluver and Bucy (1937) and from a theoretical paper published by Papez in the same year. The two kinds

of deficits that characterize the Kluver–Bucy syndrome are related to emotional–motivational aspects of behavior and to visual discrimination learning. Most of the former are now attributed to amygdala damage and much of the latter to temporal neocortical damage. The first seemingly clear demonstration of learning and memory functions associated with the hippocampus came from the studies by B. Milner, W. Penfield, and W.B. Scoville on HM, a patient with bilateral hippocampal lesions, and similar patients (B. Milner et al., 1966). The basic syndrome associated with HM was an apparent inability to store new verbal-experiential information in long-term memory. This syndrome has often been attributed to the surgical removal of parts of the hippocampus on both sides of the brain, but it is important to note that adjacent parts of the temporal lobes (including the amygdala) were involved as well (see Squire, 1982).

The syndrome of HM proved very difficult to replicate in animals. Indeed, it was only in 1978 that Mishkin showed that a similar deficit in memory function (recent visual memory—delayed nonmatching to sample) can be produced in monkeys subjected to bilateral ablation of both the hippocampus and the amygdala. The deficit that follows bilateral ablation of either structure alone is much less pronounced. But Squire and Zola-Morgan (1983) have recently shown that lesions of the hippocampus alone can also yield this deficit, so the role of the amygdala is not clear. Now, several hundred studies after HM, it is clear that hippocampal lesions are followed by various deficits in learning and memory in animals, although not necessarily of the type shown by HM. Indeed, the problem is that too many deficits are known, not that they have been difficult to find. Many of the deficits involved altered behavioral response tendencies (e.g., response perseveration), and may therefore be acting more on performance than on processes of learning and memory.

Hippocampal lesions produce the following behavioral effects in animals, some of which resemble the septal lesion effects noted above (see Isaacson, 1982, Isaacson & Pribram, 1975; O'Keefe & Nadel, 1978; Olten et al., 1980; Solomon & Moore, 1975; Swanson et al., 1982): greater willingness to undertake new behavioral acts; decreased tendency to become inactive under stress; hyperactivity in open field; lowered distractability; decreased spontaneous alternation; deficit in one-way active avoidance; deficit in passive avoidance; deficit in successive discrimination learning; deficit in simultaneous discrimination learning; deficit in discrimination reversal; increased resistance to extinction of learned responses; severe deficit in DRL performance in operant learning; classical conditioning—disruption of latent inhibition; disruption of blocking, impairment in discrimination reversal, impairment of ability to learn the trace CR; deficit in spatial-maze learning and performance, and deficit in working memory in radial-arm maze.

As Isaacson (1974) has emphasized, an abnormal hippocampus is worse than no hippocampus at all. For example, massive deficits in the acquisition or retention of simple (one-trial) learning situations are found after disruptive electrical stimulation of the hippocampus, induced hippocampal seizure activity prevents conditioned response learning, and induced hippocampal afterdischarge in humans produces a reversible HM syndrome (see above). However, prior ablation of hippocampus in infrahuman animals does not produce such deficits. There are several possible interpretations of these devastating effects of abnormal hippocampal activity on learning and memory. Perhaps the most likely is that abnormal activity is relayed to other structures, impairing their normal functions.

Deadwyler, West, and Lynch (1979) and Deadwyler (1979) have shown that two-tone CS-evoked dentate field potentials of differing waveform and latency develop differentially over training, discrimination, and reversal in an appetitive instrumental task in rat. Both the shorter latency response and the differential behavioral responding are impaired by damage to entorhinal cortex.

A number of studies have reported altered neuronal activity (field potential EEG, multiple-unit activity, unidentified single unit responses) in a variety of instrumental learning situations (see O'Keefe & Nadel, 1978; Thompson et al., 1972; Thompson, Berger, & Madden, 1983). At this point, perhaps the only general conclusion to be drawn is that neuronal activity in the hippocampus becomes markedly engaged in almost any learning situation. Because of the generalized nature of the neuronal responses (at least 80 per cent of pyramidal neurons in CA1 to CA3 appear to become engaged in the same

manner and exhibit the same pattern of response in eyelid conditioning—see above), it seems unlikely that specific informational content regarding the particular stimuli of the learning situation is present in the hippocampus. The hippocampus appears to become engaged in any situation that is of biological/behavioral significance for the animal. We remind the reader of the curious fact that the highest concentration of corticosterone (an adrenal cortical stress hormone) receptors in the brain is in the hippocampus (McEwen, 1982).

Lesions of the hippocampus (and septal nuclei) have also been shown to impair severely learning of spatial tasks in the rat (see O'Keefe & Nadel 1978) but so have frontal cortical lesions (Kolb, Sutherland, & Wishow, 1982). Consistent with the hippocampal lesion effect are electrophysiological data demonstrating strong correlations between increased firing of certain hippocampal neurons and location of an animal in space (Miller & Best, 1980; O'Keefe, 1976; O'Keefe & Conway 1978; Olton, Branch, & Best 1978). This evidence has been interpreted within the framework of spatial memory (O'Keefe & Nadel, 1978), but Olton et al. (1979, 1980) have developed an alternative interpretation in terms of working memory. It is not clear that the spatial correlates of hippocampal neurons develop as a result of learning. In fact, available evidence indicates that spatial correlates of hippocampal cells are present at an animal's first exposure to a new environment and are not modified by time or experience in that environment (Hill, 1978; Kubie & Ranck, 1982). Furthermore, the same unit will respond in a particular place in a maze and in half of a lever press box (Kubie & Ranck, 1982). Thus, although demonstrations of spatially related unit correlates are quite striking, their relation to specific sensory information and to associative learning is uncertain.

To state some oversimplified conclusions, the hippocampus appears to play some kind of role in the storage and/or retrieval of memories but is not itself the site of memory storage. In many cases, the role the hippocampus plays is modulatory in nature. Manipulations of it can influence performance in learning and memory tasks, but it is not itself an essential part of the memory-trace circuits. Possible exceptions to this last generalization are the important role the hippocampus appears to play in certain spatial memory tasks in the rat and in recent visual memory performance in the monkey, not to mention its apparently critical role in one aspect of human memory (see below).

THE CEREBRAL CORTEX. Studies of the sensory cerebral neocortices continue to provide a wealth of information. Hubel and Wiesel, in particular, have well characterized the location, connections, and interactions of neurons in the visual cortices (e.g., 1959, 1962, 1965b, 1968, 1974; Hubel, Wiesel, & Stryker, 1977), including anatomical and physiological characterization of visual orientation columns (e.g., Hubel & Wiesel, 1968, 1974), X and Y geniculocortical afferents (e.g., Stone & Dreher, 1973, but see Movshon, 1975), ocular-dominance columns (Wiesel, Hubel, & Lam, 1974), and binocular disparity (Blakemore, 1970; Hubel and Wiesel, 1970b). The organization of the auditory cortex is not as well understood (e.g., Imig & Morel, 1983; Neff, 1960; Whitfield & Evans, 1965). Neff, Diamond, and Casseday (1975) summarize a large literature suggesting that auditory cortex is important for sound localization, temporal pattern discrimination, sound duration, and complex spectra discriminations. Tone frequency appears to be represented spatially to some degree in the auditory cortex (Evans, Ross, & Whitfield, 1965; Evans & Whitfield, 1964; Goldstein, Abeles, Daly, and McIntosh, 1970; Hind, Rose, Davies, Wodsey, Benjamin, Welker, & Thompson, 1960; Imig & Morel, 1983). It has been suggested that a columnar organization within the auditory cortex may be found to be related to changes in frequency rather than to frequency itself (Bindman & Lippold, 1981).

The somatosensory cortices have well developed maps of the body surface (Woolsey, 1958; Woolsey, Settlage, Meyer, Spencer, Pinto-Hamuy, & Travis, 1950; see Werner & Whitsel, 1968) and columnar organization (Mountcastle, 1957). It appears that lesions of somatosensory cortices impair the ability to learn and relearn tactile discriminations (Riddley & Ettlinger, 1976). Cells within somatosensory cortex display stimulus direction sensitivity (Whitsel, Roppolo, Werner, 1972), responses to joint position and subcutaneous and cutaneous stimulation (Mountcastle, 1957), vibration (Mountcastle, Talbot, Darian-Smith, & Kornhuber, 1967), and temperature (Cragg & Downer, 1967). There is a vast gulf between what is known at this physiological/behavioral level and what our own experiences

tell us. The mind-body problem (Boring, 1950; Sperry, 1952) remains the superstructure of attempts to understand the functioning of the cerebral cortex.

The discovery of the columnar organization of the neocortex (Mountcastle, 1957; Hubel & Wiesel, 1968) can be taken as supporting evidence for the serial processing model of cerebral functioning (Flechsig, 1898; Pavlov, 1927). The general notion here is that sensory information is initially analyzed in primary sensory cortex, analyzed into finer features in successive secondary sensory-association areas, integrated with other sensory modalities in the association cortex, judged by the frontal cortex and acted upon by the motor cortex to cause the appropriate action. On the other hand, studies in which the transcortical association fibers have been severed (e.g., Lashley; 1926, 1944; Sperry, 1947a; Sperry, Miner, & Myers, 1955) or in which primary visual receptive areas have been removed without affecting pattern perception (see Diamond & Hall, 1969) support a parallel processing model. Pribram (1954, 1971) noted that lesions of different parts of the posterior association cortex resulted in sensory-specific perceptual deficits in vision (Blum, Chow, & Pribram, 1950; Chow, 1952; Mishkin & Pribram, 1954), in somesthesis (Pribram & Barry, 1956; Wilson, 1957), in audition (Mishkin & Weiskrantz, 1958), and in gustation (Bagshaw & Pribram, 1953) but in which simple discriminations still were possible. In parallel processing models neocortical regions act independently through subcortical structures (e.g., Penfield, 1958). There is no reason to think that, under normal conditions, serial and parallel processings are mutually exclusive.

Fritsch and Hitzig (1870) developed the first map of the primary motor cortex, and it is now clear that there are several secondary motor representations (Woolsey et al., 1950). The origins of the pyramidal tract include postcentral and parietal cortices as well as the precentral cortex (Coulter, Ewing, & Carter, 1976; Jones & Wise, 1977). The motor cortex appears to be essential for a variety of skilled movements, particularly those involving the extremities in primates (Brooks, 1979; Evarts, 1973). There are also multiple sensory areas (see Merzenich & Kass, 1980). The secondary visual projections are particularly striking in that as many as 15 maps of the visual field in the neocortex have been described (Van Essen & Maunsell, 1983).

Sensory areas and certain association areas of the cerebral cortex are thus essential for a variety of learned discriminations and motor areas for certain types of skilled (i.e., learned) movements. However, it is not possible at present to distinguish between these as essential sensory-motor components of memory-trace circuits or as loci of memory traces. Results of studies on frontal and temporal association areas of the primate cerebral cortex are more suggestive of memorial function.

FRONTAL LOBES. The most prominent, consistent and general behavioral deficit following frontal lobe lesions is seen in the delayed-response problem (French & Harlow, 1962; Jacobsen, 1936; Lawicka & Konorski, 1959; Milner, 1972; Pribram, Krugger, Robinson, & Berman, 1955; Pribram, Mishkin, Rosvold, & Kaplan, 1952; Teuber, 1964) as an inability to remember, even for very short durations, under which cup a reward is placed if a screen is lowered during the delay. The first demonstration of double dissociation (a criterion proposed by Teuber, 1955) was made between the functions of the frontal and temporal cortices (Harlow, Davis, Settlage, & Meyer, 1952). Lesions of the frontal cortex resulted in a deficit on delayed response but not visual discrimination tasks, whereas lesions of the temporal lobe had the opposite results. The effective frontal locus for delayed response is a few millimeters in the middle of the principle sulcus (Butters & Pandya, 1969; Butters, Pandya, Sanders, & Dye, 1971).

The deficit can be seen as memorial or attentional (or both); these interpretations are given full consideration in an excellent review by Fuster (1980). Distractions interfere with memory storage and such effects may account in part for the delayed response deficit (Bartus & LeVere, 1977). Animals with frontal lesions can have very good memories if not distracted (Blake, Meyer, & Meyer, 1966; Harlow et al., 1952; Malmo, 1942; Meyer, 1972b; Meyer & Settlage, 1958). The delay in delayed response testing (e.g., Jacobsen, 1936) and in delayed alternation testing (Rosvold & Delgado, 1956; Rosvold, Mishkin, & Szwarcbart, 1958; Stamm, 1964) may cause performance deficits in part through distractions and massed testing, which enhance perseverative tendencies (Meyer et al., 1976; Pribram & Tubbs, 1967). The deficits caused by

frontal lobe lesions on conditioned inhibition (Brutkowski 1964; Konorski, 1961; Lawicka & Konorski, 1959) and on discrimination reversal (see Warren, 1964) may share a similar problem of interpretation.

Pribram (1971) has argued that the frontal cortex be considered the highest level of the limbic system. Lesions of the frontal cortex, besides increasing distractability, also have effects on emotion. These effects, unlike the delayed response deficit, are dependent upon the species, and one might suggest that they represent a release of a prepotent behavior (McCleary, 1966). Lesions of the orbitofrontal cortex in monkeys (Butter & Snyder, 1972) result in emotionally aggressive animals. Humans with lesions of the frontal cortex more often show no change (Teuber, 1964) (possibly because the lesions are not similar) or a lack of affect (Barber, 1959; although persons with frontal lobotomies can still feel pain they appear to be less bothered by it). Cats, dogs, New World monkeys, and humans (Brody & Rosvold, 1952; Lashley, 1948; Miles & Blomquist, 1960; Spaet & Harlow, 1943; Teuber, 1964) are not hyperreactive to stimuli, but other animals are (Ferrier, 1886; French, 1959; Gross, 1963; Isacc & Devito, 1958).

Recent studies have added significantly to our understanding of the frontal lobes. Modern anatomical studies demonstrate afferent (Goldman-Rakic & Schwartz, 1982) and efferent connections (Schwartz & Goldman-Rakic, 1984) between the frontal and parietal cortices, as well as columnar organization within the frontal cortex (Goldman & Nauta, 1977). Similarly, functional differences between the orbital (e.g., object discrimination) and dorsolateral (e.g., delayed response) prefrontal cortices have been described (Akert, Orth, Harlow, & Schiltz, 1960; Goldman, 1971, 1972; Goldman, Rosvold, & Mishkin, 1970a, 1970b; Harlow, Blomquist, Thompson, Schiltz, & Harlow, 1968; Miller, Goldman, & Rosvold, 1973; Mishkin, 1964; Tucker & Kling, 1967, 1969).

The dopamine projection to the frontal cortex (Berger, Thierry, Tassin, & Moyne, 1976; Hokfelt, Ljungdahl, Fuxe, & Johansson, 1974; Lindvall, Bjorklund, & Divac, 1978; Thierry, Blanc, Sobel, Stinus, & Glowinski, 1983) may be important in the symptoms seen in monkeys with frontal cortical lesions. Thus, hyperreactivity, perseveration, and hypoemotionality are some of the permanent characteristics shown by rats with lesions of the ventral tegmental area (Le Moal, Stinus & Galey, 1976; Stinus, Gaffori, Simon & Le Moal, 1978). Deficits in delayed alternation have also been observed after prefrontal dopamine depletion (Brozovski, Brown, Rosvold, & Goldman, 1979; Simon, Scatton, & Le Moal, 1980). Interestingly, aged monkeys that show deficits in delayed response (Arnsten & Goldman-Rakic, 1984; Bartus, Fleming, & Johnson, 1978) have been shown to have neurotransmitter depletions in frontal cortex and brainstem (Goldman-Rakic & Brown, 1981; Sladek & Blanchard, 1981).

Unit activity in the frontal cortex has been measured extensively in behaving animals since it was first described for monkeys trained on delayed response (Fuster & Alexander, 1971) or delayed alternation (Kubota & Niki, 1971). Several basic firing patterns have been described (Fuster, 1973). Most cells react to stimulus presentation. Many cells react to the stimulus if it has meaning due to previous experience (i.e., learning, context?). Some cells react to the rewarding stimulus. Some cells display sustained cell discharge during the delay period that appears to be related to performance of the task and may be involved in temporal integration. A particularly interesting type of cell seems to be related to sensory-motor integration (Kubota, Iwamoto, & Suzuki, 1974). It appears, then, that the types of cell activities found in the frontal cortex support the notion that the frontal cortex is involved in determining situational context and appropriate goal-directed behaviors and, perhaps, in the retention process itself.

TEMPORAL LOBES. Lesions of the medial temporal lobes can result in one of the more striking behavioral alterations. In monkeys with medial temporal lobe lesions (i.e., including inferotemporal cortex plus amygdala and hippocampus) Kluver and Bucy (1937) described a number of resultant emotional deficits (e.g., absence of fear, abnormal sexual behavior) and deficits in visual perception—such as psychic blindness, in which the animal cannot visually discriminate edible and nonedible objects without first tasting them (Blum, Chow, & Pribram, 1950; Mishkin, 1951; Riopelle & Ades, 1951; Riopelle, Alper, Strong, & Ades, 1953). Horel and Keating (1972) demonstrated the inferotemporal cortically lesioned monkeys can be trained to discriminate between edible versus

nonedible pairs but that the deficit reoccurs if a novel item is introduced. Indeed, inferotemporal monkeys cannot learn a new learning set (Riopelle et al., 1953) but can relearn a learning set that was established before the lesion was made (Akert, Gruesen, Woolsey, & Meyer, 1961). Thus, it appears that the inferotemporal lobe may be involved in concept formation.

In general, bilateral lesions of the inferotemporal area do not abolish the ability of monkeys to discriminate between real objects but do abolish their ability to discriminate visual forms (i.e., two-dimensional pictures of forms; Mishkin, 1970). The essential circuit for this latter discrimination includes the striate, peritriate and inferotemporal areas (Mishkin, 1966). Monkeys were trained to discriminate between pictures of a cross and a square. Serial lesions were performed to make lesions of the unilateral inferotemporal cortex and the contralateral occipital cortex. Relearning between operations and re-relearning after the two surgeries yielded good retention. However, when the splenium of the corpus callosum was subsequently cut, thus preventing visual processing between the intact striate-peristriate cortex on one side with the contralateral peristriate-inferotemporal cortex, the animals lost the ability to discriminate the visual patterns. This result supports the idea that cortical processing is serial.

Mishkin (1982) has recently demonstrated an interaction between inferotemporal cortex and the amygdala-hippocampus in an analogous crossed lesion experiment for recent visual memory. The test used was delayed nonmatching to sample with increasing delays and increasing lists of stimuli. Monkeys with crossed inferotemporal cortex and amygdala-hippocampal lesions and with resection of the anterior commissure performed nearly as poorly on visual recognition as did monkeys given bilateral amygdala-hippocampal lesions (Mishkin, Spiegler, Saunders, & Malamut, 1982). Mishkin (1982) proposes that short-term visual memories may be stored within the inferotemporal cortex by actions of the amygdala-hippocampus complex, but the actual locus of storage is, of course, not yet known (see Hippocampus above).

Horel (1978) suggested that the amnesias seen after lesions of the medial temporal lobe were due to destruction of the underlying fibers (the temporal stem) connecting the temporal area with the cerebral cortex rather than due to damage to the hippocampus. Lesions of the temporal stem result in visual discrimination impairment (Horel & Misatone, 1976). However, in a demonstration of double dissociation, Zola-Morgan, Squire, & Mishkin (1981) showed that temporal stem lesions impair visual form discrimination and lesions of the amygdala-hippocampus impair delayed nonmatching to sample but not vice versa. Thus, lesions of the temporal stem have the same effect on perceptual processes as do inferotemporal cortical lesions (possibly by disconnecting the inferotemporal area from the striate-peristriate region), but they do not cause the sort of impairment seen in human amnesics (Squire & Zola-Morgan, 1983).

In humans, a severe global anterograde amnesia for some tasks results from bilateral medial temporal lobe damage (see above and reviews by Butters, 1979; Mishkin & Petri, 1984; Squire, 1982; and the chapter by Goodglass & Butters, this volume). A wide variety of other tasks, however, can be learned and retained (Brooks & Baddeley, 1976; Cohen & Squire, 1980; Milner, 1962; Sidman, Stoddard, & Mohr, 1968; Warrington & Weiskrantz, 1968; Weiskrantz & Warrington, 1970, 1979; Winocur & Weiskrantz, 1976). Two memory systems have been postulated to explain this apparent discrepancy (Cohen & Squire, 1980; Cormier, 1981; Cutting, 1978; Gaffan, 1972; Graf, Mandler, & Haden, 1982; Hirsh, 1974, 1980; Hirsh & Krajden, 1982; Huppert & Piercy, 1976; Kinsbourne & Wood, 1975; O'Keefe & Nadel, 1978; Mishkin, Malamut, & Bachevalier, 1984; Olton et al., 1979; Stern, 1981; Warrington & Weiskrantz, 1982; Wickelgren, 1979). But the difficulty in categorizing the dichotomy itself is best reflected by the variety of adjective pairs used: pure versus habit memory (Bergson, 1910), memory with or without record (Bruner, 1969), elaborative versus integrative processing (Graf et al., 1982), episodic versus semantic memory (Kinsbourne & Wood, 1975), semantic versus operational memory (Kolers, 1975), memory versus habit system (Mishkin et al., 1984), reference versus working memory (Olton et al., 1979), vertical versus horizontal associative memory (Wickelgren, 1979), declarative versus procedural memory (Cohen & Squire, 1980; Winograd, 1975). It is the first type of memory in each of the above pairs for which there is global amnesia in humans. Huppert and Piercy (1978, 1979) suggest that the

former type of memory is associated with lesions of the medial temporal cortices while the latter type of memory is associated with diencephalic midline lesions.

Until recently, animal models of human global amnesia have not been especially successful in mimicking amnesia, in part because of difficulty in making the extents of the lesions similar and certainly because the behavioral tests have not been comparable (Douglas, 1967; Horel, 1978; Iversen, 1976; O'Keefe & Nadel, 1978; Rozin, 1976; Weiskrantz, 1971). In a recent review of the literature, Squire and Zola-Morgan (1983) recommend (with some caution) conjoint damage of hippocampus and amygdala, and testing on visual discrimination, concurrent tasks, delay matching and nonmatching to sample tasks, and spatial tasks, in order to see deficits in monkeys that are similar to those seen in human amnesic cases (see Zola-Morgan, Squire, & Mishkin, 1981). The behavioral impairments following lesions of the inferotemporal cortex in animal studies may also relate to concept formation (e.g., learning sets, delayed nonmatching to sample), discontinuities of stimulus and response (e.g., stimulus-response contiguity, see Kluver, 1941; and also Meyer, 1972b; Meyer, Treichler, & Meyer, 1965), and inattentiveness (Butter and Hirtzel, 1970).

RECOVERY OF FUNCTION
There is an increasingly large body of research using animal models concerned with recovery of functioning following injury to the central nervous system, particularly the cerebral cortex (cf. Bach-y-Rita, 1980; Cotman, 1978; Finger, 1978; Isaacson & Spear, 1982; Miller, Sandman, & Kastin, 1977; Stein, Rosen, & Butters, 1974; Walsh & Greenough, 1976). The field itself grew out of the results of lesion studies designed to determine the functioning of components of the brain, particularly with respect to the mechanisms of learning and memory, but also with respect to reflexes, feeding and species-specific motor patterns (cf. Berntson & Micco, 1976). The work of Lashley (1929, 1935) on the locus of learning and memory can serve as an example of the fundamental observation. In one series of experiments (1935), he trained rats to discriminate between two visual brightness cues. He then removed portions of the cerebral neocortex and retested the animals. If he removed anterior neocortex then Lashley observed that the rats

retained fairly well. On the other hand, if the visual areas were injured, then Lashley observed upon retesting that the rats showed no signs of retention. The rats could, however, relearn the problem in as many trials as it took to learn the task in the first place. Removal of the remaining neocortex did not prevent retention. These results have been replicated more recently (Horel, Bettinger, Royce, & Meyer, 1966; Jonason, Lauber, Robbins, Meyer, & Meyer, 1970). Lashley's result demonstrated that none of the neocortex is essential for brightness discrimination and that none of the neocortex is essential for storage of the memory of the task—it is not very well appreciated today that there is little evidence for the neocortex as a storage place for this and many other types of memories. Lashley (Lashley, 1931; Lashley & Frank, 1932) subsequently found that visual discriminations of patterns were absent following removal of the visual neocortex, a finding which has been supported by other behavior/lesion studies (Dalby, Meyer, & Meyer, 1970; Doty, 1971; Horel et al., 1966; Jonason et al., 1970; Lavond & Dewberry, 1980; Lavond et al., 1978; Ritchie, Meyer, & Meyer, 1976; Sprague, Levy, DiBerardino, & Berlucchi, 1965) and by implication from physiological studies of visual cortical functioning (Hubel & Wiesel, 1959, 1962, 1965b; DeValois, 1965). The difference between recovery of a brightness discrimination and nonrecovery of a pattern discrimination illustrates Hunter's (1930) criticism of mass action and equipotentiality.

Lashley's pessimistic conclusion that "in reviewing the evidence on the localization of the memory trace . . . the necessary conclusion is that learning just is not possible" (1950, p. 478) perhaps overshadowed his many real contributions. Lashley popularized the model system approach to studying the functions of the neocortex, developed an efficient method for behavioral testing of visual functions, introduced "large Ns" as an appropriate estimator of the effects of lesions, standardized surgical ablations and histological reconstructions, legitimized the use of retrograde degeneration (some histologists at the time considered the neural responses to be signs of low-grade infections), and left a wealth of data that forms a standard for comparison.

His influence today can be seen in standardized studies using footshock avoidance in learning of brightness discriminations (the apparatus is strikingly similar to Lashley's jumping stand without the jump). Robert Thompson (1960) trained rats to approach and push down a white door leading to a safe shock-free area instead of a locked black door. He then removed their posterior visual neocortex unilaterally, retrained them on the discrimination, and removed the remaining posterior visual neocortex: They showed savings on final re-retraining. Similarly lesioned rats who do not have interoperative retraining, however, take as many trials to relearn without any posterior visual cortex as required to originally learn the problem, and are thus like Lashley's rats (1935) who had their posterior neocortices removed all at once. (See also Horel et al., 1966; Glendenning, 1972; Kircher, Braun, Meyer, & Meyer, 1970.) The "serial lesion effect" itself was not new but the study provided the opportunity for studying the quantitative relations of the effects of ablation of the neocortices. (See also the review by R. Thompson, 1983, of his work.)

A striking illustration of the quantitative, model systems approach to behavioral recovery of function following brain injury is the work of D.R. and P.M. Meyer (see their 1977 review) which they have called "the pseudomathematics of the cortex" (1984). If the neocortex is divided into anterior versus posterior and right versus left neocortices, then a general rule states that an injury to any quadrant of the neocortex costs 8 to 9 spaced retraining trials. Thus, a group of rats that take 25 trials to learn a simple black–white discrimination will require 8 to 9 retraining trials if any quadrant of the neocortex has subsequently been injured (they have perfect retention otherwise). Rats trained and then lesioned in two quadrants (one anterior and one posterior quadrant, or both anterior quadrants) will take twice as many trials as a single quadrant, or 17 retraining trials. These numbers are in fact observations and the conjecture of the rule is an inference made upon such instances. The major exception to this mass action is when both posterior neocortices are injured and it takes 25 trials to relearn rather than 17 trials. A recent study (Cloud, Meyer, & Meyer, 1982) shows that the extra 8 trials are accounted for by a sensory-specific (visual) impairment that is independent of distributed functions of the neocortex. That mass action and specificity of function are not mutually exclusive was recognized by Flourens (1824 and 1825, cited by Boring, 1950).

Recovery of functioning can be improved under some circumstances with drug therapies (cf. Brailowsky, 1980); with interoperative retraining provided there is an intervening procedure (e.g., Meyer, Isaac, & Maher, 1958; Petrinovich & Carew, 1969; Thompson, 1960); with extensive retraining (e.g., Diamond & Hall, 1969; Spear & Barbas, 1975) or training on similar problems (Chow, 1952); with maturation of the nervous system (e.g., Benjamin & Thompson, 1959; Goldman, 1974; Johnson, 1972; Kennard, 1942); with physical therapy (Dru, Walker, & Walker, 1975a, 1975b; Travis & Woolsey, 1956); and with substitution of behaviors (cf. Murray and Goldberger, 1974; Sperry, 1947b); substitution of strategies (cf. Morgan, 1951), or substitution of discriminations (cf. Lavond & Dewberry, 1980; Lavond et al., 1978); or by preventing substitution of new behaviors and forcing recall of memories (Davis & LeVere, 1979). A number of theories about the biological mechanisms of recovery have been proposed, including vicariation (Fritsch & Hitzig, 1870; Munk, 1881; Scheff & Wright, 1977; Scheff, Wright, Morgan, & Bowers, 1977; but see Gray & LeVere, 1980) in which recovery is explained as a part of the nervous system taking over the functions of the injured area; recovery from diaschisis (von Monakow, 1914; Meyer, 1972a; compare T. Woolsey, 1978; with Wall, 1980), in which recovery is explained as a dissipation of neural trauma/shock (see also Buchtel, Camarda, Rizzolatti, & Scandolara, 1979; Sherman, 1977; Kirvel, 1975; Kirvel, Greenfield, & Meyer, 1974; Sprague, 1966); neural reorganization (for a competing view, see LeVere, 1980) in which surviving tissue compensates for the injury, which might include sprouting that helps recovery (e.g., Goldberger & Murray, 1978; Goodman & Horel, 1966; Liu and Chambers, 1958; Raisman, 1969; Steward, Cotman, & Lynch, 1976) or hinders recovery (McCouch, Austin, Liu, & Liu, 1958; Schneider, 1973; Schneider & Jhaveri, 1974), growth of neuronal spines and dendrites through environmental/sensory stimulation that is specifically related to the deficient behavior (e.g., Greenough, Fass, & DeVoogd, 1976; Rosensweig, 1980; but see Davis & LeVere, 1982; and Gray & Meyer, 1981), unmasking of latent connectivity (Wall, 1980), or supersensitivity (Cannon & Rosenblueth, 1949). Perhaps the most surprising (and hopeful) result of all this work is the tenacity of learned behaviors and memories to survive neocortical injury, so much so that true instances of non-recoverability in infrahuman animals (e.g., problem set learning and delayed-response deficits) provide important insights into the functioning of the cerebral neocortex.

ENVIRONMENTAL STIMULATION AND PLASTICITY

Two basic, complimentary approaches have established the importance of environmental stimulation in physiological and anatomical plasticity of the nervous system. Both ways involve manipulation of the sensory environment: One to enhance stimulation, one to detract, and then to observe the effect upon cells and behavior. The most commonly studied paradigm involves some sort of visual deprivation or alteration (e.g., see the reviews by Barlow, 1975; Ganz, 1975; and by Layton, Corrick, & Toga, 1978; Riesen, 1975). The techniques include dark-rearing, lid-suture, black or translucent contact lenses, selective deprivation (e.g., to particular orientations), and alterations (e.g., by strabismus). The deprivation or alteration can be monocular or binocular and can be made at varying ages. The greatest deprivation effects are seen when young animals are monocularly deprived and tested for binocular competence (Chow & Stewart, 1972; Hubel & Wiesel, 1970a). Physiological recordings demonstrate significantly fewer binocular cells; behaviorally the deprived cats cannot make brightness, form, or depth discriminations (Ganz & Fitch, 1968). Contour deprivation results in reduced physiological orientation preference (Blakemore & Cooper, 1970; Hirsch & Spinelli, 1970, 1971) although its behavioral consequence is less deleterious. The evidence for structural changes following deprivation procedures seems to indicate that the most sensitive elements of neurons are their soma size, dendrites, and dendritic spines (Blakemore, Garey, Henderson, Swindale, & Vital-Durand, 1980; Borges & Berry, 1976; Coleman & Riesen, 1968; Cragg, 1967; Fifkova, 1968, 1969, 1970; Garey & Pettigrew, 1974; Globus, 1975; Gyllensten, Malmfors, & Norrlin, 1965; Hubel, Wiesel, & LeVay, 1977; LeVay, Wiesel, & Hubel, 1980; Muller, Pattiselanno, & Vrensen, 1981; Valverde, 1967, 1968, 1971; Vrensen & DeGroot, 1975; Wiesel, Hubel, & Lam, 1974), the same elements that appear most sensitive to enhancement studies (see below). This agrees with the physiological data that the number of cells seems to remain constant and that no silent areas result from alternating monocular deprivation (Hubel & Wiesel, 1965a)—monocular deprivation studies seem to indicate complementary widening and shrinking of cortical terminal fields due to sprouting (Blakemore, Garey, Henderson, Swindale, & Vital-Durand, 1980; Hubel, Wiesel, & LeVay, 1977).

There is clearly a period of time when deprivation has its greatest effects (Dews & Wiesel, 1970; Hubel & Wiesel, 1970a), but it is less certain that the period is critical rather than susceptible to disruption (Cynader, Timney, & Mitchell, 1980). What is most interesting is that adults continue to be affected by deprivation. For example, Creutzfeld and Heggelund (1975) deprived normal adult cats of all but vertical stripes. Upon immediate testing, they found a predominance of cortical cells oriented horizontally. The permanence of the effect was not examined. In the converse experiments, deprived kittens were allowed to experience vertical stripes (Blakemore & Mitchell, 1973) or normal environments (Peck & Blakemore, 1975) on the 28th or 29th day and were found to have dramatically altered cortical physiology (more normal in the former, more dominant in the latter). The changes in the latter experiment were more marked when a period of two days intervened before testing, a finding that might suggest a consolidation-like process (Layton, Corrick, & Toga, 1978). Others have also documented the plasticity of the adult visual system (Brown & Salinger, 1975; Maffei & Fiorentini, 1976) while still others have not found plasticity (Berman, Murphey, & Salinger, 1979). The fact that adults can demonstrate anatomical and physiological plasticity is a critical feature for a putative mechanism of learning and memory; in fact, adults would seem to be better models for questions about the physical basis of learning and memory, in that developmental effects are less overpowering.

The type of sensory environment that rats are raised in can dramatically affect brain morphology. Animals given enriched environments have much greater amounts of dendritic branching, processes, spines and spine densities (and by implication, more synapses—see Turner & Greenough, 1985) than rats given deprived environments (e.g., Altman & Das, 1964; Diamond, Johnson, Ingham, Rosenzwieg, & Bennett, 1975; Diamond et al., 1966; Globus, Rosenzweig, Bennett, & Diamond, 1973; Greenough, West, &

DeVoogd, 1978; Mollgaard, Diamond, Bennet, Rosenzweig, & Lindner, 1971; Rosenzweig & Bennett, 1976; Schapiro & Vukovich, 1970; Volkmar & Greenough, 1972; West & Greenough, 1972). These morphological changes also can be seen when older animals are given enriched environments (Connor, Melone, Yuen, & Diamond, 1981; Green, Schlumpf, & Greenough, 1981; Riege, 1971; Rosenzweig & Bennett, 1976; Uylings, Kuypers, Diamond, & Veltman, 1978) and appear to be relatively long-lasting (Cummins, Walsh, Budtz-Olsen, Konstantinos, & Horsfall, 1973). That cellular morphology changes as a result of environmental stimulation, that the change is in the direction one would expect from our understanding of cellular functioning, that animals of all ages are capable of showing these changes, and that the changes are relatively long-lasting, are consistent with the hypothesis that this is at least a possible mechanism for long-term memory storage.

Furthermore, there are behavioral differences between animals raised in enriched versus impoverished environments. Environmentally enriched rats are unquestionably superior in learning maze habits (e.g., Bernstein, 1973; Bingham & Griffiths, 1952; Brown, 1968; Forgays & Read, 1962; Forgus, 1955; Hymovitch, 1952; Nyman, 1967; Schwartz, 1964; Walk, 1958; Walsh and Greenough, 1976; see also Rosenzweig, 1980) and are superior on appetitive operant tasks (Morgan, 1973) as well as on avoidance tasks (Greenough, Fulcher, Yuwiler, & Geller, 1970). Interestingly, posteriorly decorticated rats that are raised in enriched environments show increases in dendritic growth, gross weight measurements, and RNA/DNA content of the surviving anterior neocortex that are associated with improved performance on maze problems (Will & Rosenzweig, 1976; Will, Rosenzweig, & Bennett, 1976; Will, Rosenzweig, Bennett, Hebert, & Morimoto, 1977). Importantly, the recovery of the ability to perform maze problems following cortical injuries is associated with the similarity between the enriched environment and the maze problem. However, none of these studies have shown a specific change in morphology in a specific part of the brain to a specific regimen of training.

Such evidence has been provided in a number of recent studies that have compared the effects of training, rather than nonspecific environmental stimulation, on brain morphology. In the experiment by Cummins and colleagues (Cummins, Walsh, Budtz-Olsen, Konstantinos, & Horsfall, 1973), for example, it was found that adult rats that had been raised in an impoverished environment and then were given maze training had increased forebrain weight. In a more specific training task, forepaw handedness reversal, Larson and Greenough (1981) reported greater branching of the distal portions of the apical dendrites of layer V cells in the contralateral motor cortex corresponding to the forelimb than in the ipsilateral motor cortex. This study is important because the animals were adult, the increase of dendritic branching occurred in a specifically related brain structure, and because of the nature of the task the animal served as its own control. Analogous findings have been reported for the neocortex, with maze learning (Chang & Greenough, 1982; Greenough, Jaraska, & Volkmar, 1979), when classical conditioning with neocortical stimulation was used as the CS for a foreleg shock UCS (Rutledge, Wright, & Duncan, 1974) (but see discussion of classical conditioning, above), for hippocampal CA1 pyramidal cells when using a brightness discrimination (Wenzel, Kammerer, Kirsch, Matthies, & Wenzel, 1980), for molecular cells of the hippocampal dentate gyrus when using a conditioned appetitive response (Fifkova, Van Der Wede, & Van Harreveld, 1978; Fifkova & Van Harreveld, 1978), for the visual cortex when using operant pattern discrimination (Vrensen & Cardozo, 1981), and for the somatosensory cortex after operant avoidance training (Spinelli & Jensen, 1979; Spinelli, Jensen, & DiPrisco, 1980). Interestingly, Spinelli and Jensen (1979) reported greater polymodal responsiveness of the somatosensory cells to the orientation of the stripes used as a cue for the avoidance response, as well as greater dendritic branching (Spinelli, Jensen, & DiPrisco, 1980).

While the results of recent studies on the relationship between specific brain locations, morphology, physiology and specific behavioral performance are provocative, there remained a number of unresolved questions. As yet there is no compelling proof that the structural or physiological changes represent the memory trace. Indeed, it is critically important to address the issues of whether the alterations are cause or effect, and whether the alterations are related to performance or to learning. The majority of research on the effects of environmental

enhancement or deprivation study these effects on the morphology and physiology of the cells in cortex (neocortex or hippocampus), and for most of the tasks used, learning and memory occur without such tissue (see Recovery of Function in this chapter). This is not to deny, however, a role of these tissues in normal functioning, but it is clear they they are not necessary and sufficient for learning and memory of the tasks involved. To this extent, it may be difficult to establish the functional significance or causality of the plasticity. This literature shares a number of the same problems of interpretation with much of the lesion literature (Chow, 1967; Gregory, 1961; Isaacson, 1976; John, 1972; Lynch, 1976; Shoenfeld & Hamilton, 1977; Webster, 1973). Effects often can be shown readily, but their specific roles in learning and memory are difficult to determine.

## Imprinting and Bird Song Learning

Two learning phenomena that are receiving increased attention in experimental psychology and do not fall within the framework of the foregoing procedures are imprinting and bird song learning. The growing interest of experimental psychologists in these forms of learning reflects a broadening in the scope of inquiry within the field of animal learning and the merging interests of experimental psychologists and ethologists. Bird song learning and imprinting have also proved to be promising preparations for investigating the neural bases of behavioral plasticity, and, in fact, research in these areas has resulted in findings that may significantly change our thinking about the way in which vertebrate nervous systems can function (e.g., Nottebohm, 1984; Paton & Nottebohm, 1984).

### Imprinting

Imprinting is the development of a social attachment to visually conspicuous objects as a result of repeated exposure to such stimuli very early in life. Most of what is known about imprinting comes from work done with hatchling chickens, ducks, and geese (for review see Bateson, 1966; Hess, 1973; Hoffman & Ratner, 1973; Rajecki, 1973; Sluckin, 1972). From such work, two forms of imprinting have been distinguished: filial and sexual. Filial imprinting is manifest as a strong preference to be near objects repeatedly experienced soon after hatching compared to objects not experienced during that period. For example, ducklings repeatedly exposed to a moving object will engage in a wide range of behaviors in order to remain in the presence of the imprinting stimulus and will show signs of distress if the object is removed (Bateson, 1966; Eiserer & Hoffman, 1973; Hoffman, Searle, Toffey, & Kazma, 1966; Starr, 1978). The development of this stimulus control is believed to be the product of several processes: An initial tendency to avidly approach visually conspicuous objects, familiarization with these objects through repeated exposure, and a later tendency to avoid novel objects—this having the effect of narrowing the range of objects the bird will approach to those made familiar in the initial phase (Bateson, 1979; Hoffman & Segal, 1983). In addition, stimuli initially not effective in eliciting approach behavior can acquire the ability to do so by being paired with a stimulus that is effective in eliciting approach (Hoffman, Barrett, Ratner, & Singer, 1972).

Filial behavior towards an imprinting stimulus becomes attenuated as the bird reaches adulthood. At this point, the effects of early experience become manifest in mate selection. The work of Vidal (1980) suggests that filial and sexual imprinting may be the products of distinct processes that occur at different stages of development (i.e., different stimuli can come to control filial behavior and mate selection).

### Neural Mechanisms of Imprinting

The most systematic work on the neural basis of imprinting has been done on filial imprinting in chicks by Bateson, Horn, Rose, and colleagues. In addressing the problem of localizing critical brain areas, the authors reasoned that the learning induced by exposure to the imprinting stimulus involves some form of growth process in CNS sites of neuronal plasticity (e.g., changes in size or number of synaptic junctions) that may be associated with increased protein synthesis. Given this reasoning, sites of plasticity should show greater levels of incorporation of radioactive amino acids into proteins in birds that have been imprinted than in birds that have not. Bateson et al. (1969, 1972) found that chicks exposed to an imprinting stimulus (flashing light) showed a greater uptake of [$^3$H] uracil into dorsal forebrain structures compared with other brain structures, whereas control chicks did not show differential uptake. A diverse series of experiments designed to distinguish among a variety of interpretations of these results (e.g., learning related to impringing vs. nonspecific effects such as differential amounts of visual evoked activity, locomotor activity, and general arousal) suggest that the increased uptake of [$^3$H] uracil in the dorsal forebrain is due to changes specific to imprinting (see Horn, 1981, for review). In one experiment, chicks had their optic commisures cut (thereby restricting visual input to the ipsilateral forebrain) and were trained with one eye occluded. When presented with the imprinting stimulus and a novel stimulus, they showed a preference for the imprinted stimulus when tested on the trained eye, but no preference when tested on the untrained eye. In addition, the dorsal forebrain showed a differential incorporation of [$^3$H] uracil on the side ipsilateral to the nonoccluded eye (Horn, Horn, Bateson, & Rose, 1971; Horn, Rose, & Bateson, 1973). These observations indicate that the greater uptake of [$^3$H] uracil in the dorsal forebrain following imprinting is not due to general increases in arousal and locomotion that might accompany imprinting.

Additional experiments revealed that the greatest density of [$^3$H] uracil was localized in the medial portion of the hyperstriatum ventrale $HV_m$; a dorsal forebrain nucleus that receives visual input (Bateson, Rose, & Horn, 1973). The fact that other visual projection areas of the forebrain did not show differential labeling is consistent with the proposal that $HV_m$ is involved in processes critical to imprinting, as are the observations that imprinting produces an increased uptake of [$^{14}$C] 2-deoxyglucose in regions of $HV_m$ (Kohsaka, Takometso, Aoki, & Tsukada, 1979).

Another means of evaluating the role of a structure in the development and expression of a particular behavior is to identify the afferents of the structure and the major targets of its output. One can then assess the likelihood that the circuitry allows for the input of necessary sensory information, its integration, and the generation of the range of behavior observed. In the chick, direct afferents to $HV_m$ include (1) visual Wulst and optic tectum, (2) neostriatum (which may relay auditory and somatosensory input), (3) hippocampus, and (4) the septal nuclei of the hypothalamus. The efferent structures include (1) paleostriatum augmentatum (pa), which has been compared to the caudate-putamen complex, (2) the intermediodorsal part of the archistriatum (which projects to the brain stem and spinal cord—a pathway that may be comparable to the pyramidal tract of primates) and (3) the posterior archistriatum (which projects to the medial and lateral hypothalamus), making this nucleus comparable to the amygdala of mammals (Bradley & Horn, 1978; Bradley, Davies, & Horn, 1981; Davies & Bradley, 1981). These observations support the proposal that $HV_m$ is involved in imprinting in that they show that $HV_m$ receives input from the appropriate sensory modalities and is associated with structures capable of generating affective and motor responses exhibited in imprinting.

Studies designed to assess the fine structure of the $HV_m$ and changes induced by imprinting by use of electron microscopy reveal hemispheric asymmetries in the average length of synaptic apposition zones in chicks having been briefly exposed to an imprinting stimulus; the average length of apposition zones being greater on the right than on the left (Bradley, Horn, & Bateson, 1981). Increasing the amount of exposure to the imprinting stimulus results in a lengthening of synaptic apposition zones in the left $HV_m$, eliminating the asymmetry. Thus, exposure to the imprinting stimulus produces changes in the connectivity of neurons within the $HV_m$.

The effects of lesioning $HV_m$ on filial imprinting in chicks are complicated. They suggest that $HV_m$ is critical for acquisition, but not retention, and that additional structures are involved in storage and retrieval. Bilateral destruction of the $HV_m$ prior to exposure to the imprinting stimulus results in a failure of the chick to develop a preference for the exposed stimulus (McCabe, Horn, & Bateson, 1981). When bilateral lesions of $HV_m$ are made three hours after training, retention of the preference for the training stimulus is impaired but not abolished. However, bilateral lesions of $HV_m$ made 26 hours post training do not significantly impair retention (Cipolla-Neto et al., 1981; Horn, Cipolla-Neto, & McCabe, 1980). From additional experiments on the effects of serial lesions, the authors suggest that, in addition to $HV_m$, other structures are involved in the storage of information necessary for the retention of preferences for trained stimuli, that they consolidate such information more slowly than $HV_m$, and that the right $HV_m$ is critical for such consolidation.

The evidence from the foregoing experiments strongly implicates the $HV_m$ as having a critical role in the development of filial imprinting in the chick. It remains for future research to determine the nature of its role and the cellular mechanism involved.

### Bird Song Acquisition

In the course of normal song development, male passarine birds learn to produce the song of male conspecifics heard during a critical period early in their development (e.g., Immelmann, 1965, 1966; Marler, 1970; Marler & Tamura, 1962, 1964; Poulsen, 1951; Thorpe, 1958; Wasser & Marler, 1977). The onset of singing in juveniles is characterized by crude and variable vocalizations (subsong) which progress to more lengthy and less variable songs approximating those of conspecifics heard during the critical period. By the start of the breeding season, the songs have become quite invariant (crystallized) and can be characterized in terms of a number of features (e.g., number of songs in the repertoir, duration of song, number of segments, note structure). Singing, in many species, is seasonal, occurring almost exclusively during breeding season, and is under the control of testosterone (e.g., Nottebohm, 1980a).

Experiments evaluating the consequences of isolation and/or deafening during infancy reveal that, in many species, the development of certain features of normal song (e.g., timing and note structure) depend upon auditory experience —hearing the song of a male conspecific during the critical period and the bird hearing its own vocalizations during song development. The importance of hearing a model song during the critical period is illustrated by the finding that male white crowned sparrows raised in isolation develop a more simple song than do birds exposed to the song of adult males (yet they still contained elements common in normal songs (Marler & Tamura, 1964)). That early experience with a model song influences later song development is also shown by the finding that exposing some species of passarine birds (e.g., meadowlarks, linnet, bullfinch, zebra finch) to the song of another species, results in the development of songs that approximate the model heard when juveniles rather than the songs characteristic of their wild conspecifics (Immelmann, 1969; Lanyon, 1957; Nicolai, 1959; Poulsen, 1954).

The role of auditory feedback—the bird hearing himself sing—in song development has been adventageously explored in species for whom the critical period and the onset of subsong occur at different times (e.g., white crowned sparrow; Marler, 1970; Marler & Tamura, 1964). In many species, birds exposed to the song of conspecifics but deafened prior to the onset of subsong develop highly abnormal songs (especially in the fine structure of notes and syllables) that show even fewer features of normal song than do birds raised in isolation (Konishi, 1965b; Nottebohm, 1966, 1967, 1968). But, although highly abnormal, the songs of some species of birds deafened in infancy still contain species specific features (e.g., Guettinger, 1981; Konishi, 1965a; Marler & Sherman, 1983). In other species of birds, deafening in infancy has much less of an effect as they are able to develop nearly normal songs or normal calls, suggesting that the development of such vocalizations are much less dependent on learning guided by auditory feedback and may have more to do with the development of innate central song generators (Konishi, 1963, 1964, 1965a, 1965b; Nottebohm and Nottebohm, 1971). Once a bird's song has crystallized (its motor program established), auditory feedback is no longer necessary for normal song production and maintenance—birds deafened at this point show no degradation in the fidelity of the song (Konishi, 1965b; Nottebohm, 1966, 1967, 1968; Price, 1979).

The results reviewed above suggest that the development of the various complex features of bird song are under the control of several layered processes. The operation of central song generators that develop independently of learning through auditory feedback have been postulated to account for the presence of some normal song patterns in the songs of birds deafened in infancy (e.g., in canaries, Marler & Wasser, 1977; in song sparrows, Marler & Sherman, 1983). *Innate templates* are thought to shape the development of song through a learning process that involves comparing auditory feedback from vocalization with the template. An isolate is said to develop a motor program for song by comparing its vocal productions against its innate, albeit crude, template and modifying its vocalizations so as to form an acceptable approximation to the model. Such a mechanism is responsible for the more normal songs of isolates compared to birds deafened in infancy (Marler, 1970; Marler & Tamura, 1964). The modification or acquisition of a model template

as a consequence of auditory experience during the critical period is a third process by which song development can be guided. This form of plasticity allows the bird to develop songs having a great deal of fidelity to the particular songs heard during infancy. The conditions under which an innate template can be modified may set constraints on the particular auditory features that will induce changes in the template/model, and thereby determine the degree of selectivity in song learning a species exhibits (Marler & Peters, 1977, 1980, 1982).

NEURAL MECHANISMS OF BIRD SONG

The results of studies using electrophysiological recording, lesion, and anatomical tracing techniques have defined a set of nuclei and their interconnections that control song production in birds (Kelley & Nottebohm, 1979; Nottebohm, Stokes, & Leonard, 1976; Nottebohm, Kelley, & Paton, 1982; McCasland & Konishi, 1981; McCasland, 1983). The principle circuit includes three forebrain nuclei: the Nucleus interface (NIF), nucleus hyperstriatum ventrale, pars caudale ($HV_c$), and nucleus robustus archistriatalis (RA); NIF → $HV_c$ → RA. The RA projects directly and indirectly (through the dorsomedial nucleus (DM) of the midbrain) to the nucleus hypoglossus, pars tracheosyringealis (XIIts) which innervates the musculature controlling the vocal organ, the syrinx. This circuit is represented bilaterally, with each circuit controlling the ipsilateral syringeal musculature. Lesioning $HV_c$, RA, or XIIts nuclei results in a marked deterioration in the songs of adult birds (Nottebohm et al., 1976).

Patterns of neural activity and inactivity that correspond to periods of sound and silence in singing birds have been observed in NIF, $HV_c$, and RA (McCasland, 1983; McCasland & Konishi, 1981). Latencies between increased neural activity and sound production are greatest in the NIF, intermediate in the $HV_c$, and shortest in the RA, suggesting a flow of control from NIF → $HV_c$ → RA, which is consistent with the connectivity of these nuclei revealed by anatomical studies. Recordings form the sole input to the NIF; the nucleus uva (UVA) show no song related changes in activity, and lesioning this structure has no effect on song production, suggesting that the motor program for the song may reside in NIF (Konishi, 1985). Single unit recordings in the $HV_c$ of mockingbirds have revealed several classes of neurons that show different levels of specificity for sound production. Some neurons show an increased activity prior to song onset, others show stereotyped patterns of activity for a few syllable types, and other neurons fire for one particular syllable but not for other similar syllables—these being designated as motor-specific neurons (McCasland, 1983; McCasland & Konishi, 1981). The $HV_c$ also contains neurons that respond to auditory input with elements of the bird's own song (phrases or parts of phrases) being the most effective stimulus (Margoliash, 1983; McCasland & Konishi, 1981).

The proposal that the NIF → $HV_c$ → RA → XIIts pathway controls song production received additional support from a variety of studies in which differences in structure and function of these nuclei (particularly $HV_c$ and RA) within and across species are compared to differences in song production. Differences in structure and function can occur naturally, for example, as a result of species differences, sex differences, and/or due to seasonal variations in circulating hormones (e.g., testosterone) or can be experimentally induced by lesions (see above) or administering drugs.

A number of cross-species comparisons indicate that the forebrain nuclei $HV_c$, RA, and perhaps NIF occur only in birds capable of vocal imitation. In addition, species in which individuals raised in isolation show abnormal song development have these nuclei, but species that show normal vocal development in isolation do not (Kroodsma, 1984; Nottebohm, 1980a). Similarly, birds that show abnormal vocal development when deafened as infants possess these structures while birds that develop normal vocalizations in spite of deafening do not (Konishi, 1963; Nottenbohm & Nottebohm, 1971).

Comparing individuals within a species, one can observe a positive correlation between song complexity/repertory size and the volume of forebrain nuclei involved in singing. In the long-billed march wrens (*Cistohorus palustris*), Western populations with large song repertories have larger $HV_c$s than do Eastern populations with small repertories (Canady, Kroodsma, & Nottebohm, 1984). Canaries having larger numbers of syllables in their songs tend to have larger $HV_c$s and RAs than those having smaller numbers of syllables (a statistically weak corre-

lation; Nottebohm, Kasparian, & Pendazis, 1981).

Additional support for the role of $HV_c$ and RA in song development and production comes from canaries, who, unlike most passarine birds, develop new song repertories each year "by adding, dropping, or modifying components" of the old song (Nottebohm & Nottebohm, 1978). These additions and deletions can be taken as indices of song learning as canaries deafened after the first season of singing are unable to maintain or increase their syllable repertoire in following seasons (Nottebohm, 1980a; Nottebohm et al., 1976). Male canaries show seasonal variation in singing and song repertoire, size of $HV_c$ and RA, and levels of circulating testosterone. Comparing male canaries in the spring (during full song) and the fall (when little or no singing occurs), the volumes of $HV_c$ and RA nuclei decrease dramatically in the fall, as do levels of circulating testosterone and size of the testes (Nottebohm, 1981). Related observations indicate that testosterone can stimulate young males, females, and castrated males to song and increases the volume of $HV_c$ and RA nuclei (Nottebohm, 1980b; DeVoogd & Nottebohm, 1981a).

Comparing female canaries (which do not normally sing) with males, there do not appear to be any differences in the connectivity between the song control nuclei, but there are differences in the microanatomy of the $HV_c$ and RA nuclei; the volume and density of dendrites are smaller in females (DeVoogd & Nottebohm, 1981b; Nottebohm & Arnold, 1976; Nottebohm, Kelley, & Paton, 1982). Ovariectomized females given testosterone develop songs, although more simple ones than males, and show large increases in RA volume with the dendritic branches of neurons in this nucleus being considerably longer and more complex, compared to females not treated with testosterone (DeVoogd & Nottebohm, 1981b; Nottebohm, 1980b).

Structural changes in the avian forebrain and hippocampus can also result from neurogenesis in the adult bird (Nottebohm & Kasparian, 1983; Paton & Nottebohm, 1984). Neurogenesis in the forebrain has been observed in male and female canaries, zebra finches, doves, and male parakeets (Nottebohm, 1984). As the maximal weight of the brain does not increase after the first year, new neurons are presumably replacing old neurons. Paton and Nottebohm (1984) observed that in the canary $HV_c$, new neurons identified by incorporation of labeled amino acids were functional, showing normal properties by electrophysiological criteria. These new neurons branch and terminate within the $HV_c$, presumably functioning as local circuit interneurons. Neurogenesis appears to be going on continuously, and there is no evidence that it is under hormonal control. Goldman and Nottebohm (1983) observed that female canaries treated with testosterone showed equivalent labeling for new neurons in $HV_c$ to females treated with cholesterol, even though testosterone treated females developed song and cholesterol treated birds did not. No evidence of new neurons in RA was observed in either group. At this point, there is no clear evidence that neurogenesis per se is responsible for hormonally modulated changes in the volume of the $HV_c$ and RA nuclei or in learning of any kind (see Nottebohm, 1984 for discussion).

On the basis of a number of findings reviewed above, Nottebohm and colleagues have proposed that the $HV_c$ and RA provide a substrate for plasticity required for song development, i.e., the learning of motor programs responsible for song production. Nottebohm (1981) has pointed to a positive correlation between song and development in canaries during the first year and the growth of $HV_c$ and RA, the atrophy of $HV_c$ and RA and the forgetting of songs/motor programs in canaries, and the development of more complex dendritic trees and the learning of new songs in the second season (DeVoogd & Nottebohm, 1981a) as support for his interpretation. These increases in dendritic mass and presumably connectivity in $HV_c$ and RA during the spring are said to facilitate learning of new songs by (1) allowing for new interneuronal relations and (2) bringing into existence synapses not yet altered by previous patterns of use (Nottebohm, 1981). Following this reasoning, Nottebohm has pointed out that if the variation in the size of RA and $HV_c$ in the canary allows the bird to shed old motor programs and provide the basis for new motor programs for song, then one might expect that species of birds whose song is invariant across seasons would not show seasonal variation in the size of $HV_c$ and RA. This is the case in the zebra finch, whose song remains stable throughout the bird's life (Immel-mann, 1969). Even though seasonal onset of song is testosterone dependent (Arnold, 1975), the $HV_c$ and RA of the zebra finch show no changes in volume.

A different interpretation of the relationship between the changes in $HV_c$ and RA and variation in canary song repertoire across seasons has been suggested by Konishi (1985, p. 155). He has pointed out that changes in the volume and structure of the $HV_c$ and RA nuclei may be involved in the development of new motor programs in canaries, but that such changes do not necessarily reflect changes due to learning. The changes in these nuclei may give rise to changes in song content through a reorganization of a central pattern generator for song, a reorganization that is independent of auditory feedback from vocal productions. Consequently, the "distinction between the anatomical and physiological changes associated with feedback-controlled modification of song on one hand and those related to central reorganization and use–disuse phenomena on the other will be important" (Konishi, 1985, p. 155).

It should be noted that even if learning processes shape song development in canaries during the second season, the increases in neuron number and dendritic field size cannot be taken for the mechanisms of plasticity responsible for the learning of songs. Rather, these structural changes provide the neural *substrate* necessary for song learning to occur. The cellular mechanisms that are responsible for the development of specific motor programs for song are yet to be determined. The research to date has principally solved the problem of localization of structures where changes in motor programs take place. Important issues to be addressed include specification of the nature of the innate template, how it is modified by experience, and how the template interacts with motor-program circuitry to shape song development.

Given the rich variability across species in the degree to which birds are able to learn songs that vary from those of conspecifics (the ability to mimic songs heard in their critical period) and the variability in the importance of auditory feedback from their own vocalizations (Konishi & Nottebohm, 1969; Marler & Sherman, 1983), bird song learning offers a very fruitful area of research for a comparative approach to developing psychobiological theories of learning and memory. (More detailed discussions of song learning and its neural control can be found in Kroodsma and Miller (1982) and Konishi (1985).)

# INVERTEBRATE PREPARATIONS

## Neural Mechanisms of Habituation

The most extensive work on the cellular basis of short- and long-term habituation has been done with the sea slug *Aplysia californica* (e.g., Bruner & Tauc, 1966; Bruner & Kehoe, 1970; Kandel, 1976; Pinsker et al., 1970). The best studied behaviors are the defensive gill and siphon withdrawal reflexes which are elicited by application of tactile stimuli to the skin covering and surrounding these areas (e.g., Pinsker et al., 1970). Neuroanatomical and electrophysiological experiments have shown that siphon and gill withdrawal reflexes are predominantly under the control of motor neurons located in the abdominal ganglia and in the periphery. (Peripheral neurons also can contribute to gill and siphon withdrawal responses and may be involved in the habituation of these responses (e.g., Peretz, Jacklet, & Lukowiak, 1976)). Gill and siphon motor neurons in the abdominal ganglion react primarily to direct (monosynaptic) and indirect excitatory input from sensory neurons in the skin that respond to touch and pressure (the majority of the input comes from the sensory neurons).

Having identified neural circuits controlling gill and siphon withdrawal, Kandel and colleagues were then able to investigate the cellular basis of short-term habituation of these responses produced by repetitive tactile stimulation. They were able to eliminate sensory adaptation and response fatigue as mechanisms responsible for the reduced responding observed over the course of habituation training by showing that the responsivity of sensory neurons did not change with repeated application of the tactile stimulus at frequencies used for habituation (Byrne, Castellucci, & Kandel, 1974a, b; Kupferman, Carew, & Kendel, 1970) and that electrical stimulation of individual motor neurons at similar frequencies did not result in a diminution in the contraction of the gill musculature that it innervates (Carews, Pinsker, Rubinson, & Kandel, 1974; Kupferman et al.,

1970). Thus, the site of neural plasticity responsible for habituation must be more central. While recording from gill motor neurons in the abdominal ganglion, Kuppferman et al. (1970) observed a progressive decrease in discharge during habituation that paralleled the decrease in the gill withdrawal response. When the motor neuron was hyperpolarized so as to prevent the occurrence of action potentials, repetitive stimulation of sensory neurons resulted in diminished complex EPSPs in the motor neuron (Castellucci, Pinsker, Kupferman, & Kandel, 1970). To determine whether the decreased EPSPs in motor neurons was due to presynaptic or postsynaptic mechanisms, reduced preparations involving the critical neural elements of the reflex circuit were used in conjunction with quantal analysis and other procedures. The evidence indicated that the decrement in the motor neuron EPSPs was due to a decrease in the amount of transmitter being released at the synapses of the sensory neurons. Thus, short-term habituation in this preparation appears to be a consequence of homosynaptic depression produced by presynaptic changes (Castellucci & Kandel, 1974; Kandel, Brunelli, Byrne, & Castellucci, 1976).

The mechanism of short-term habituation of defensive reflexes in other invertebrates, e.g., the crayfish tail-flip response, appears to be the same as in *Aplysia*. Namely, homosynaptic depression resulting from changes in the presynaptic terminals of sensory neurons (e.g., Krasne, 1969; Krasne & Woodsmall, 1969; Wine, Krasne, & Chen, 1975; Zucker, 1972a, 1972b).

One biophysical basis of this presynaptic form of homosynaptic depression appears to be a reduced availability of $Ca^{++}$ to participate in the release of the transmitter. One of the putative roles intracellular $Ca^{++}$ plays is to facilitate the binding of synaptic vesicles containing the transmitter substance to the release sites and the release of transmitter into the synaptic cleft. Repetitive stimulation of the sensory neuron, and consequent invasion of the terminal areas by the action potentials, is thought to result in a reduced level of free intracellular $Ca^{++}$ due to (1) uptake of free $Ca^{++}$ within the cell by mitochondria or (2) a reduced permeability to $Ca^{++}$ leading to a reduced influx of extracellular $Ca^{++}$ during each action potential (Kandel, 1976; Klein, Shapiro, & Kandel, 1980). A second, and probably more important mechanism, is depletion of transmitter from stores at the release site (Gingrich & Byrne, 1985).

In *Aplysia*, as in other organisms, presentation of a salient and/or aversive stimulus (e.g., shock) can produce a restoration of an habituated gill or siphon withdrawal response, i.e., the habituated response can be dishabituated (Carew, Castellucci, & Kandel, 1971). After presentation of the sensitizing stimulus (shock to the head or tail) stimulation of the sensory neurons results in an increased EPSP in the motor neurons, and consequently, a greater amplitude behavioral response. The basis of the increased behavioral responsivity to stimulation after sensitization is in part due to an increase in the duration of action potentials in the sensory neurons. This broadening of the action potential results in an increased influx of $Ca^{++}$ into the neuron which, in turn, facilitates the binding of vesicles to release sites in the presynaptic terminals, resulting in more transmitter being released, larger EPSPs in motor neurons, and an increased motor response (Castellucci & Kandel, 1976). In addition, a dishabituating stimulus may restore an habituated response by promoting mobilization of transmitter vesicles from storage sites to depleted release sites (Gingrich & Byrne, 1985). (Also see Rankin & Carew, in press.)

The mechanism by which a sensitizing stimulus produces a broadening of the action potential in sensory neurons is the activation of a facilitator interneuron that acts presynaptically upon the terminals of the sensory neuron (Baily, Hawkins, Chen, & Kandel, 1981; Hawkins, Castellucci, & Kandel, 1981). Activation of facilitator interneurons results in the release of serotonin or neuropeptides onto the sensory neuron terminals (Abrams, Castellucci, Camardo, Kandel, & Lloyd, 1984; Baily et al., 1981; Brunelli, Castelluci, & Kandel, 1976). Stimulation of the facilitator neuron, or application of serotonin to sensory neurons, increases the levels of intracellular cAMP in the sensory neurons which, through a cascade of intracellular reactions not fully understood, causes a particular class of potassium ($K^+$) channels in the sensory neuron to close, thereby reducing the overall efflux of $K^+$ at the time of depolarization by the action potential. Because the repolarization of the neuron is due to an efflux of $K^+$, a decreased outward movement of $K^+$ ions

results in a longer period of depolarization produced by each action potential, which in turn, results in an increased influx of extracellular $Ca^{++}$ and transmitter release (see Kandel & Schwartz, 1982, for an overview). (More recently, post-synaptic changes have been observed (Frost, Castellucci, Hawkins & Kandel, 1985).)

The fact that habituation and sensitization can persist for several days, weeks, or even months (e.g., Carew, Pinsker & Kandel, 1972; Leaton, 1976; Pinsker, Henning, Carnew, & Kandel, 1973) indicates that long lasting changes in neural functioning have been produced, presumably by stable structural changes. In their investigations of the long-term basis of habituation and sensitization of the gill-withdrawal reflex in *Aplysia*, Baily and Chen (1983) have observed structural changes in sensory neuron terminals (varicosities) that might mediate the long-term changes in behavior. After giving repeated presentations of an habituating stimulus or a sensitizing stimulus, Baily and Chen (1983) compared the number of active zones (regions within varicosities where transmitter release occurs) to the total number of varicosities (note: not all varicosities contain active zones). The ratio of active zones to varicosities was 12 percent in subjects receiving habituation training, 41 percent in nontrained subjects, and 65 percent in subjects receiving the sensitizing stimulus. In addition, the size of active zones and the number of vesicles associated with each zone was decreased by habituation training and increased by sensitization training. These results suggest that sensitization and habituation training might produce long-term changes in synaptic efficacy, and thus behavior, by altering the size and number of active zones and the loading of vesicles within each. These findings of structural changes in sensory neuron terminals, and the $Ca^{++}$ dependent changes in transmitter release from these neurons mentioned above, suggest that long- and short-term habituation and sensitization have common loci within this preparation.

## Neural Mechanisms of Pavlovian Conditioning

Associative learning in invertebrates has been demonstrated in a number of species using a variety of Pavlovian conditioning preparations.

The greatest progress in the analyses of the cellular mechanisms of associative learning comes from studies using gastropod molluscs, e.g., work with *Aplysia* by Kandel and colleagues (e.g., Clark & Kandel, 1984; Hawkins, Abrams, Carew, & Kandel, 1983) and *Hemissenda* by Alkon and colleagues (e.g., Alkon, 1984b).

Conditioning of the defensive siphon-withdrawal reflex in the sea slug *Aplysia californica* has been demonstrated by Carew et al. (1983). In one experiment, weak tactile stimulation of the upper portion of the animal's siphon served as $CS_1$ while stimulation of the lower siphon area served as $CS_2$. At the outset, both CSs produced a low amplitude siphon withdrawal response. Discrimination training involved presenting both CSs but following only one of the CSs with electric shock to the tail (e.g., $CS_1 \rightarrow US$; $CS_2 \rightarrow NoUS$). Over the course of discrimination training, both CSs came to elicit more prolonged siphon withdrawal responses (sensitization was observed); more importantly, however, the withdrawal response to the CS paired with shock US was significantly longer than to the CS not paired with shock. That is, the authors were able to demonstrate an enhancement of responding that was specific to the CS paired with the shock US. In this instance, associative learning is evidenced as a pairing-specific enhancement of a previously existing response to the CS (i.e., is a form of type A, or alpha, conditioning).

Hawkins et al. (1983) were able to demonstrate differential conditioning in a reduced preparation, allowing them to identify cellular mechanisms involved in the associative learning observed in *Aplysia*. The CSs were produced by intracellular stimulation of each of two siphon sensory neurons (call them $SN_1$ and $SN_2$) that projected onto a common interneuron, and the US was tail shock (see Figure 4.4A). During training, each sensory neuron was stimulated once every five minutes. Stimulation of one of the sensory neurons was immediately followed by tail shock, while stimulation of the other neuron was specifically unpaired with the shock (i.e., $SN_1 \rightarrow US$; $SN_2 \rightarrow NoUS$). At the outset, stimulating $SN_1$ and $SN_2$ resulted in equivalent EPSPs in the common motor neuron. As training progressed, EPSPs elicited by both $SN_1$ and $SN_2$ activation increased (sensitization was observed). However, activation of $SN_1$ resulted in greater amplitude EPSPs than $SN_2$ activa-

tion, thereby demonstrating a pairing-specific, and thus associative, facilitation of responding. In other words, activating a sensory neuron just prior to US onset resulted in an enhancement of its ability to generate EPSPs.

Additional observations (Hawkins et al., 1983; also see Kandel & Schwartz, 1982) suggest that the effect of the US (both sensitization and associative enhancement of EPSPs) is produced by the activation of facilitatory neurons that terminate presynaptically on the sensory neurons. As was noted in the previous discussion of sensitization, activation of the facilitator neuron initiates a sequence of intracellular biochemical events (e.g., increased cAMP) which inactivates a select population of $K^+$ channels which in turn results in a broadening of the action potential. The broadened action potential results in an increased influx of extracellular $Ca^{++}$ which facilitates release of neurotransmitter, resulting in larger EPSPs. (The relationship between the broadening of the action potential in the sensory neuron, and consequent increases in EPSPs, and the prolonged conditioned siphon withdrawal response (Carew et al., 1983) is not yet known). Findings of Abrams, Carew, Hawkins, and Kandel (1983) suggest that the activity-dependent amplification of presynaptic facilitation results from $Ca^{++}$ influx accompanying the activation of sensory neurons. The influx of $Ca^{++}$ is thought to transiently modulate the cyclase system through which the facilitator neurons exert their action, and thereby produce the temporal specificity observed in this and possibly other preparations (i.e., the observation that the level of conditioning is strongly influenced by the length of the interval between presentation of the CS and the US).

Having observed that conditioning results in a pairing specific increase in the sensory neuron's ability to produce EPSPs in neurons innervating siphon withdrawal, Clark and Kandel (1984) asked if the change is cell-wide (i.e., occurring at all terminals of the sensory neuron), or whether it is specific to terminals on the branches of the sensory neuron that receive input from the facilitator interneuron. If the latter is the case, then a sensory neuron having branches that project to different motor neurons could show response specificity—a training produced change in the sensory neuron's ability to elicit one class of responses but not others.

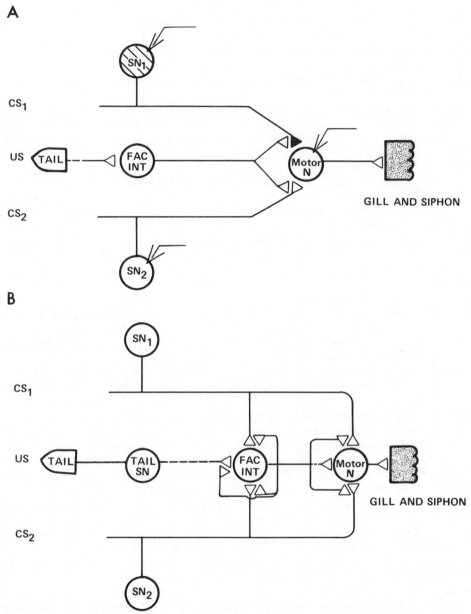

**Figure 4.4.** A. Essential neuronal circuit in the reduced preparation in *Aplysia* for demonstrating differential conditioning of the gill and siphon withdrawal reflex. Two siphon sensory neurons (SN) and a siphon motor neuron (MN) were simultaneously impaled with electrodes. Stimulation of the SNs produced monosynaptic EPSPs in the MN. (See text for further explanation.) From "A Cellular Mechanism of Classical Conditioning in *Aplysia*: Activity-Dependent Amplification of Presynaptic Facilitation" by R.D. Hawkins, T.W. Abrams, T.J. Carew, and E.R. Kandel, 1983, *Science, 219,* p. 401. Copyright 1983 by the AAAS. Reprinted by permission.

B. A more complete neuronal circuit involved in the gill and siphon withdrawal reflex. Projections from SNs to the facilitator interneuron (Fac.) and projections from Fac. to SN terminals suggest that such a circuit may be capable of producing blocking and second-order conditioning, as measured in training-produced changes in the efficacy of SN → MN synapses. (See text for details.) From "Is There a Cell-Biological Alphabet for Simpler Forms of Learning?" by R.D. Hawkins and E.R. Kandel, 1984, *Psychological Review, 91,* p. 383. Copyright 1984 by the American Psychological Association. Reprinted by permission of the author.

Such specificity would occur to the degree that facilitator neurons for different USs synapse selectively upon subsets of sensory neuron branches that drive different motor neurons. Alternatively, if facilitation is cell-wide, then conditioning would produce changes in the amplitude/probability of all responses receiving input from the sensory neuron. Clark and Kandel (1984) have shown that facilitation in siphon sensory neurons that project to central and peripheral motor neurons is branch specific. Pairing sensory neuron activation with a local application of serotonin to one of the branches (or stimulation of a facilitatory interneuron that projects to the central branch, but not the peripheral) resulted in pairing specific increases in EPSPs in motor neurons receiving input from the trained branch of the sensory neuron but not in motor neurons receiving input from the untrained branch.

Hawkins and Kandel (1984) have developed a model of associative learning based on the circuitry and cellular mechanisms involved in habituation, sensitization, and conditioning of the siphon withdrawal response in *Aplysia*. They demonstrate how, using these facts of biology, one might deduce a variety of associative learning phenomena, e.g., extinction, spontaneous recovery, blocking, retardation of acquisition with interpolated US-alone trials, and second order conditioning. Response decrements observed during extinction are said to result from habituation developing within the S–R pathway (*homosynaptic depression*) as a result of repeated activation of the sensory neuron. Spontaneous recovery of the conditioned response with rest results from the dissipation of this short term form of habituation. Although recovery from extinction training appears to be complete within their model (see Figure 4 in Hawkins & Kandel, 1984), one could presumably get long lasting decrements in responding as a result of long-term habituation because of lasting structural changes in terminals (Bailey & Chen, 1983; see above). In both cases, extinction results from a loss of association rather than the development of inhibitory processes. In the model, habituation is produced by simple activation of the sensory neuron; thus, increments in habituation accrue both on reinforced and nonreinforced trials. The challenge to such a model is to specify how behavior can be maintained at some asymptotic level with

very extended training, yet be extinguished when the CS is no longer followed by the US. That is, specify what prevents habituation from increasing during prolonged training to levels sufficient to prevent elicitation of the CR. If habituation is said to asymptote at some level that allows continued elicitation of CRs in training, then one faces the problem of how to get further increments in habituation during subsequent extinction training in order to get a decrease in response. To the degree that habituation and sensitization/facilitation processes are said to be independent and additive (e.g., Groves & Thompson, 1970), this can be a difficult problem, much the same one that Hull (1943) faced with his assumptions regarding the development of conditioned inhibition. Some assumption that sensitization processes interact with and impair the development of habituation appears to be required. Or, one could explore the possibility that in addition to habituation, sensory neuron activation causes $K^+$ channels closed by training to become functional (but at a lower rate than they are closed by reinforcement).

As noted above, nonreinforcement of a CS during extinction does not result in the development of inhibitory processes that modulate the activity in the S–R pathway. Similarly, the model does not currently allow inhibition to accrue to a neutral CS nonreinforced in compound with a previously trained $CS^+$—conditioned inhibition falls outside of the scope of the model in its current form. (It may turn out that conditioned inhibition cannot be obtained in *Aplysia*, making the model consistent with the data from conditioning experiments with *Aplysia*, but inconsistent with the data from experiments demonstrating conditioned inhibition in vertebrates.)

The observation that sensory neurons send projections to the facilitator interneuron, as well as to motor neurons, allows the model to account for the blocking effect (see Figure 4.4B). As a result of conditioning, it is proposed that a sensory neuron is able to activate the facilitator interneuron and cause it to become refractory, resulting in a subsequent US presentation promoting less US processing and thus less conditioning to a neutral CS when it appears in compound with a previously trained CS. This account of blocking in terms of signal produced variation in US effectiveness is in the spirit of

Wagner's priming model (1976, 1979). (See Donegan, Gluck, and Thompson (in press) and Wagner and Donegan (in press) for a more detailed discussion). The ability of the sensory neuron to activate the facilitatory interneuron as a result of conditioning also endows it with some reinforcing potential (i.e., an ability to produce second order conditioning). Activation of a sensory neuron ($SN_2$) not previously conditioned followed by the conditioned sensory neuron ($SN_1$) results in the development of second order conditioning of an S–R form (a strengthening of the input of $SN_2$ onto motor neurons) as opposed to an S–S form through $SN_2 \rightarrow SN_1$ associations.

The model of Hawkins and Kandel (1984) is impressive in its attempt to derive a number of higher-order aspects of associative learning that have been influential in the development of molar behavioral theories of associative learning. By providing new ways of thinking about associative learning processes, the model will certainly be provocative to anyone interested in theories of learning.

Another invertebrate preparation that has yielded a great amount of information about the cellular mechanisms of a simple form of associative learning is the conditioned reduction of a positive phototactic response in the nudibranch mollusk *Hermissenda Crassicornis* (Alkon, 1980a, b, 1983, 1984a, 1984b). The tendency for *Hermissenda* to approach a light source is reduced by pairing the presentation of a light with bodily rotation (which stimulates the animal's primitive vestibular system; Alkon, 1974; Crow & Alkon, 1978). In addition, pairings of light and rotation result in the light coming to elicit a contraction of the animal's caudal foot, a response elicited by rotation, but not detectable by the light, prior to training (Lederhendler, Gart, & Alkon, 1983). Exposure to the light or rotation alone, or to both in a random or unpaired relationship, produces no detectable effect on the latency of subjects' response to the light, indicating that the increase in response latency in subjects having the two stimuli paired is the product of associative learning processes. Simultaneous presentation of the light and rotational stimulus results in greater levels of conditioning than do forward or backward pairings of the CS and US (Farley & Alkon, 1982a; Grover & Farley, 1983). Interpolating light alone or rotation alone trials

between paired trials retards acquisition (Farley & Kern, cited in Alkon, 1984b). Conditioning, which can last for many weeks, can be extinguished by repeated light alone presentations (Richards, Farley, & Alkon, 1983).

Intracellular recordings from photoreceptors and motor neurons in intact animals and in reduced preparations indicate that the learning induced changes in phototaxis result from a change in the excitability of photoreceptors within the eye (e.g., Alkon, 1984a, 1984b). Each of a *Hermissenda's* eyes are made up of two types of photoreceptors, A and B. Activation of the medial type A cell excites, via identified interneurons, motor neurons that cause turning of the animal's foot in the direction of the light source (Goh & Alkon, 1984). Activation of the medial B cell inhibits the medial type A cell, thereby reducing the phototatic response. Pairing of the light with rotation results in an increased excitability of B cells (e.g., light presentation causes a greater potential change and a greater number of action potentials to be triggered, Crow & Alkon, 1980, Farley & Alkon, 1982b) and a decreased excitability of the medial type A cell (Richards, Farley, & Alkon, 1983). Both of these effects, but principally the increased excitability of the inhibitory B cell, reduce the ability of the medial type A cell to activate motor neurons responsible for producing movement towards the light source. Electrical stimulation of the B cell in intact subjects with microelectrodes in a way that mimics activation during normal training results in animals showing a decreased positive phototaxis when tested the next day (Farley, Richards, Ling, Llimen, & Alkon, 1983). Thus Alkon and colleagues have succeeded in identifying neurons showing training induced changes in activity, characterizing the nature of the cellular changes (see below), and directly relating these cellular changes to the changes in behavior produced by conditioning.

The learning induced changes in excitability of the B photoreceptor result from membrane changes that reduce two of the several ion currents the cell exhibits, an early, voltage-gated outward $K^+$ current and a calcium dependent outward $K^+$ current (Alkon, Lederhendler, & Shoukinas, 1982; Farley, Sakakibara, & Alkon, 1984; Foreman, Alkon, Sokakibara, Harrigan, Lederhendler, & Ferby, 1984). These changes in $K^+$ ion conductances result from a cumulative membrane depolarization of the type B cell and prolonged elevation of intracellular calcium induced by pairings of light and rotational stimuli (Alkon, 1980b; Alkon, Shoukimas, & Heldman, 1982; Connor & Alkon, 1984). Current evidence suggests that the reduction of outward $K^+$ currents results from a calcium dependent phosphorylation of proteins that cause two species of $K^+$ channels to close (Neary, 1984; Acosta-Urquidi, Alkon, & Neary, 1984). Thus, membrane changes in $K^+$ currents in *Hermissenda* photoreceptors depend upon membrane depolarization and consequent increases in intracellular calcium, but do not require the presence of a synaptic transmitter substance (as in the case of *Aplysia* sensory neurons, see above) or circulating neurohormones, although such substances may influence the amount of change (Alkon, 1984a; McElearney & Farley, 1983; Sakakibara, Alkon, Lederhendler, & Heldman, 1984). A different account of conditioned decreases in phototaxis in *Hermissenda* has been proposed by Cvow (1983, 1985). He proposes that activation of B photoreceptors elicit an approach to light (as do A receptors) and that training reduces the excitability of B receptors to long duration lights.

Comparing the mechanisms of Pavlovian conditioning in *Aplysia* and *Hermissenda*, one can describe the mechanisms as being very similar or different, *depending upon the level of analysis*. Both forms of conditioning result in changes in the output of sensory neurons as a result of changes in ion conductances induced by sensory neuron activation and converging input from neurons in the US pathway. Changes in sensory neuron function in both species result from reduced outward $K^+$ currents. In each case, the associatively produced changes in $K^+$ conductance depends upon the level of intracellular $Ca^{++}$. However, the cellular mechanisms of conditioning differ in that different species of $K^+$ channels/currents are responsible for the observed changes in sensory neurons: broadened action potentials in *Aplysia* sensory neurons versus a cumulative depolarization of the B photoreceptor in *Hermissenda*. In addition, the sequences of biochemical reactions evoked by CS–US pairings leading to the membrane changes also differ; in *Aplysia*, elevated levels of intracellular $Ca^{++}$ augment cAMP elevation induced by transmitter release from the facilitator interneuron, in *Hermissenda*,

increased levels of intracellular $Ca^{++}$ are sufficient.

Another molluscan model system developed to study the neural basis of associative learning is the conditioned odor and taste aversion preparation in the terrestrial mollusc *Limax Maximus* (Gelperin, Wieland, & Bary, 1984). *Limax* readily develops conditioned odor aversions after receiving pairings of the juice of a preferred food (e.g., carrot), with a very bitter solution of quinidine sulfate (Sahley, Gelperin, & Rudy, 1981). Other Pavlovian phenomena, e.g., higher-order conditioning and blocking of odor aversions, have also been demonstrated in *Limax* (Sahley, Rudy, & Gelperin, 1981).

The feeding motor pattern of the *Limax* is generated in the buccal ganglion and is activated by stimulation of chemoreceptors on the lip via interneurons in the cerebral ganglion (Gelperin et al., 1984). Reduced preparations containing the lip, cerebral and buccal ganglia, and their connectives are capable of displaying one-trial discriminative taste aversion learning. For example, a pairing specific reduction in the ability of a food flavor to elicit activity in feeding motor neurons in the buccal ganglion is observed after a prior pairing of the flavor with quinidine (Chang & Gelperin, 1980; Culligan & Gelperin, 1983). Cerebral neurons that project to the buccal ganglion have been shown to contain catecholamines (Osborne & Cottrell, 1971; Wieland & Gelperin, 1983). High concentrations of exogenous dopamine flowing over a reduced preparation results in a triggering of the feeding motor pattern in a dose-dependent fashion (Copeland & Gelperin, 1983). The possible involvement of this system in odor aversion learning in *Limax* is suggested by the observation that feeding subjects a choline enriched diet facilitates retention of a learned odor aversion (Sahley, Feinstein, & Gelperin, 1981).

The exact nature of the circuitry responsible for odor and taste aversion learning in *Limax*, and consequently the neurons showing learning induced plasticity, have not yet been identified. This is, in part, due to the fact that the neurons in the relevant ganglia are quite small, especially in comparison to other invertebrate preparations. On the basis of what is currently known of the circuitry responsible for taste and odor aversion learning in *Limax*, Gelperin and colleagues have developed a model of associative learning to deduce the range of associative learning phenomena that have been observed (Gelperin, Hopfield, & Tank, 1985).

A variety of associative learning phenomena have been demonstrated in bees using Pavlovian and instrumental conditioning procedures as well as hybrids of the two (Bitterman, Menzel, Fietz, & Schater, 1983; Couvillion & Bitterman, 1980, 1982; Erber, 1975a, 1975b; Menzel & Erber, 1972, 1978). One form of behavioral plasticity that has been used to characterize the neural mechanisms of learning in the bee is the conditioned proboscis extension reflex (Erber, 1980, 1981). The procedure involves exposing the bee to an odor and then applying sugar water to one antenna, to which the bee responds by extending its proboscis, whereupon it is allowed to drink a drop of the sugar water. Pairings of an odor and sugar water in this way result in a marked increase in the ability of the odor to elicit proboscis extension, even after a single training trial.

Olfactory information is processed in the antennal lobes, mushroom bodies, and central region of the bee brain. Cooling the antennal lobes or mushroom bodies within a few minutes of the first training trail results in disruption of learning (Erber, Masuhr, & Menzel, 1980; Menzel, 1984). Electrophysiological recording of first-order interneurons that project from antennal lobes to the calyx of the mushroom bodies have not shown learning related changes in activity (Homberg, 1981), nor have such changes been observed in neurons within the mushroom bodies (Erber, 1984). However, learning related changes have been observed in higher-order olfactory interneurons in the central part of the bee brain. Neurons in this region receive inputs from several sensory modalities. Single-unit recordings from these cells indicate that learning related changes in activity are only seen in neurons that respond to both odor and sugar water (Erber, 1978, 1980, 1981). However, these cells respond to a variety of odors, and the learning produced changes in responding are not specific to the conditioned odor.

Application of sugar water to a bee's antenna and the proboscis also results in a sensitization of one form of the reflex, the upward antennal response to a downward moving visual stimulus. Single-unit recordings from the lobula have identified cells that respond to moving visual stimuli and are sensitive to the direction of movement (Hertel, 1980; Erber & Gronenberg, 1981). Over 75 percent of the movement-sensitive neurons recorded from in the lobula responded to other sensory modalities as well, many responding to the application of sugar water applied to the antennae of proboscis. Erber (1980, 1981) has shown that the direction-specific responses to visual stimulation of these multimodal neurons show marked changes when the bee is stimulated with sugar water. Furthermore, the changes in neural activity correlate with changes in the visually evoked upward movement of the antennae. Erber proposes that the sensitization of the antennae response produced by sugar water occurs as a result of plastic changes occurring in the visual interneurons of the lobula. That such changes do not occur in structures afferent to the lobula interneurons is suggested by the finding that neurons in the structure afferent to the lobula (the medulla) that are responsive to visual stimuli do not show directional specificity and show little responsivity to stimuli from other sensory modalities. Erber (1984) has also proposed that the data from recordings of single neurons in odor conditioning experiments and sensitization of antennal responses to visual stimuli suggest a general rule: " . . . that only those cells that receive input from the two sensory modalities that are involved in learning show response changes." This generalization is consistent with the findings from the analyses of conditioning produced changes in neuronal functioning observed in *Aplysia* and *Hermassinda*. The findings from Kandel and Alkon's labs show that the cells receiving converging input from the CS and US are the ones that show changes in membrane properties (ion conductances) as a result of CS–US pairings.

Conditioned odor aversions and preferences have been described in the fruit fly, *Drosophila*, by Quinn and colleagues (Aceves-Pina & Quinn, 1979; Dudia, Jan, Byers, Quinn, & Benzer, 1976; Quinn, Harris, & Benzer, 1974; Tempel, Bonini, Dawson, & Quinn, 1983). Flies given pairings of Odor-1 and shock and nonreinforced presentations of Odor-2 show a reduced tendency to approach the odor paired with shock in a two odor choice test. Presentation of shock alone or unpaired presentations of Odor-1 and shock do not produce such shifts in the choice of odors. Conversely, pairing Odor-1 with sucrose and nonreinforcing Odor-2 results in flies preferring Odor-1 to Odor-2 (Tempel et al., 1983). Both conditioned odor aversions and preferences are extinguished by nonreinforced presentations of the conditioned odor. Interestingly, a conditioned aversion to an odor extinguishes more rapidly than a conditioned preference for an odor (Tempel et al., 1983). The two forms of conditioning also differ in the time course over which learning can be disrupted by post-conditioning cooling—aversive conditioning having a shorter time course of disruptability (30 to 40 min) than appetitive conditioning (90 to 120 min). These observations suggest that the two forms of conditioning are served by different mechanisms (see Tempel et al., 1983, for further discussion).

Additional evidence that second messengers (e.g., cAMP) play important roles in learning (see the discussion of conditioning in *Aplysia* and *Hermissenda* above) comes from learning deficits in several mutant strains of *Drosophila*. The *dunce* mutant shows impairment in habituation, sensitization, and the development and/or retention of conditioned odor aversions or preferences (Dudai, 1979; Duerr & Quinn, 1982; Tempel et al., 1983). It turns out that *dunce* mutants lack an isozyme form of the enzyme cAMP phosphodiasterase (Byers, Davis, & Kiger, 1981). The mutant *rutabaga* shows deficits in conditioning of odor aversions and retention of conditioned odor preferences (Tempel et al., 1983). *Rutabaga* mutants have been shown to have reduced levels of of adenylate cyclase enzyme activity (Livingston, Sziber, & Quinn, 1982).

## Neural Mechanisms of Instrumental Conditioning

Instrumental conditioning has been studied in numerous species of invertebrates (see Bullock & Horrige, 1965; Eisenstein, 1967; Maier & Schenerla, 1935, for reviews), including earthworms (Clark, 1965; Datta, 1962; Yerkes, 1912), planaria (Best, 1965), cockroaches and locusts (Eisenstein & Cohen, 1965; Horrige, 1962, 1965; Hoyle, 1965, 1980, 1982), honeybees (Couvillion & Bitterman, 1980, 1982; Menzel & Erber, 1972, 1978), and octopi (Mackintosh, 1962; Young, 1962; Mackintosh & Holgate, 1965).

The neural basis of taste aversion learning in the gastropod mollusc *Pleurobrancheae califir-*

*nica* has been studied by W.J. Davis and colleagues. Training involves squirting a jet of liquefied food substance (e.g., squid homogenate) on the oral veil, which in hungry animals typically elicits proboscis extension or a bite/strike response. When the subject emits a feeding response, it immediately receives an electric shock applied to the head and oral veil, which elicits a convulsive contraction of the body and movement of the head away from the source of the shocks (e.g., Mpitsos & Collins, 1975). Feeding responses to the food become suppressed within a few trials. The acquired aversion is the product of associative processes and lasts for several weeks (Davis et al., 1980; Mpitsos & Collins, 1975; Mpitsos et al., 1978). Although the procedure is an instrumental one, the contingency producing the change in feeding response is probably Pavlovian—the food → shock pairing, rather than the responses → shock pairing—being responsible for the conditioned aversion to the food stimulus.

Davis and colleagues have succeeded in identifying much of the central circuitry that regulates feeding behavior (rythmic proboscis extension and retraction) in *Pleurobranchaea* (Davis, Gillete, Kovac, Goll, & Matera, 1983; Kovac et al., 1983a, 1983b). Feeding is initiated by activating command interneurons making up the paracerebral feeding command system, which project to motor neurons in the buccal ganglion that generate feeding behavior. The paracerebral command system receives peripheral input from chemical and tactile sensory pathways and central input from excitatory and inhibitory interneurons.

Studies of conditioning produced changes in neuronal activity have focused on one of the four types of feeding command interneurons, the phasic paracerebral feeding command interneuron ($PC_p$, Davis et al., 1983). Prior to conditioning, presentation of food to a hungry animal causes a phasic activation of the $PC_p$s and the onset of feeding movements. The phasic nature of the activation is produced by recurrent inhibition for a network of central inhibitory neurons. After conditioning, presentation of food or tactile stimulation to the oral veil or rhinophores (which contain chemoreceptors) results in inhibition of $PC_p$s—a suppression of spontaneous activity and "a tonic barrage of hyperpolarizing potentials that typically persists for several seconds" (Davis et al., 1983).

Note that the food stimulus is actually a compound stimulus—liquid squid plus tactile stimulation produced by squirting the liquid onto the oral veil. In some cases, the tactile component gains more control over the behavior than the food component. In contrast, animals that received unpaired presentations of food and shock responded similarly to naive animals: Presentation of food strongly excites $PC_p$s while tactile stimuli have weak excitatory effects. Interestingly, sating a naive animal has much the same effects as the aversive conditioning procedure, in both cases applying the liquified squid produces inhibition in $PC_p$s.

Davis et al. (1983) propose that the conditioned suppression of feeding responses to the food stimulus results from a change in the bias of chemosensory and tactile input pathways. In the naive animal these pathways are said to provide strong excitatory input to neurons in the paracerebral command system and weak excitatory input to neurons in the central inhibitory network (which provide inhibitory inputs to the neurons in the paracerebral command system that strongly drive the feeding motor output, $PC_p$s, PSEs, and $ET_{II}$s; Davis et al., 1983; Kovac et al., 1983a). Training is said to strengthen the input of the sensory pathways to the central inhibitory network, resulting in conditioned food and tactile stimuli strongly driving the inhibitory network which in turn produces a net inhibitory effect upon the paracerebral command system. The neuronal elements that are responsible for the training induced changes in feeding behavior (i.e., the neurons showing plasticity), are presumed to be afferent to the paracerebral command system.

Progress in elucidating the cellular basis of a form of instrumental behavior comes from the work on conditioning of leg-position in locusts and cockroaches. In training, an intact subject can be positioned so that movement of the tibia or tarsal portion of only a single leg is permitted and various leg positions are arbitrarily defined as criterion responses. These responses allow the subject to avoid negative events (e.g., aversive sounds or aversive heat) or gain access to positive events (rewarding heat or fresh grass). Under such conditions the insects can learn the criterion response (Forman & Hoyle, 1978; Hoyle, 1979). Using a reduced preparation to investigate the mechanisms of leg-lift learning to avoid shock, Hoyle (1965)

found that, in most instances, a single tonic postural muscle (the anterior adductor of the coxa) generated the learned behavior and that this muscle was innervated by a single excitatory neuron. The tonic rate at which this motor neuron fired could be increased by punishing a slowing of the firing rate or decreased by punishing an increase in firing rate. Experiments by Woollacott and Hoyle (1977) suggest that the training procedure modified leg position by altering the pacemaker rates of the motor neuron. Hoyle (1979) reports that training-induced changes in pacemaker rates are related to changes in membrane potential. Training that produces an increased rate of firing lowers the membrane potential, while training that produces a decreased rate of firing increases the membrane potential. It is proposed that such changes are produced as a result of long-lasting changes in $K^+$ conductance. Hoyle (1979) assumes that the number of active $K^+$ channels fluctuates around some mean value and that the direction of fluctuation can be altered by the training procedure, thereby altering the mean number of active $K^+$ channels. Decreasing the number of active $K^+$ channels produces an increase in firing rate and increasing the number of active $K^+$ channels decreases the firing rate. The mechanisms responsible for such regulation of active $K^+$ channels are unknown.

These results indicate that long-lasting changes in neural activity and behavior can be produced by nonsynaptic changes and that elements as far down in the circuit as the final efferent element can show plasticity. Although the latter well accounts for learned leg positioning in locusts, such a finding cannot be true of most forms of motor learning. If learning is stored in the final common pathway, how does the motor neuron/muscle differentially participate in a variety of unrelated, learned behaviors? With regard to general mechanisms of behavioral plasticity, perhaps the most important finding of this research is that long-term changes in behavior can be produced by changes in the tonic/pacemaker activity of neurons through nonsynaptic processes such as changes in ion conductances. If such elements were to be located in more central portions of circuitry controlling motor behavior, one could imagine that certain behavioral activities could be initiated by gating such elements into the circuit and that the vigor and duration of the behavior could be determined in part by the rate of pacemaker activity. Training-produced changes in pacemaker activity could then act to change the vigor and duration of some classes of behaviors.

## NEURAL-MECHANISMS OF LEARNING

The list of *candidate* mechanisms of neural plasticity responsible for the forms of behavioral plasticity attributed to learning includes all biophysical changes known to affect the functional properties of neurons. The list is very large (e.g., see Bullock, 1980; Bullock, Orkland, & Grinell, 1977). We focus here only on putative mechanisms for which some empirical evidence exists. To become a member of the class of mechanisms involved in learning, the biophysical change under consideration must be induced by the sequence of stimulus events that normally produce the learned behavior. In addition, the biophysical change must be shown to play a role in the development and/or expression of the learned behavior. In considering mechanisms of neural plasticity that may be involved in learning, we will distinguish between several levels at which changes in neural structure can produce organizational and functional changes in neural networks.

### Gross Morphological or Organizational Changes

Pavlov (1927, pp. 25–26) proposed that learning (the development of conditioned reflexes) results from the development of new pathways between CS and US centers (representations) in the cerebral cortex (also see Morgan, 1904, pp. 181–182). The formation of new projections between CS and US centers was said to be induced by the joint activation of the two centers by the presentation of the CS closely followed by the US. Our current knowledge of the functioning of the adult CNS indicates that such changes do not occur. Even in the unusual instance of song nuclei in the avian brain, when new neurons are formed in the adult canary (which may or may not relate directly to song learning), they are local circuit interneurons and not principle neurons projecting to other regions.

### Local Organizational Changes

Konorski (1948, pp. 87–94, 138), in his effort to account for the variety of associative learning phenomena in the Pavlovian conditioning literature in terms of current principles of neurobiology, rejected Pavlov's idea that learning involved the development of new projections. Instead he proposed, as had Cajal, that learning results from changes in preexisting neural circuits through the formation of new synapses.

> Obviously, it is hardly to be believed that, as a result of repetitive application of one or another combination of stimuli, new, previously nonexistent, *nerve paths* could arise in the cerebral cortex. There is clear morphological evidence against this assumption, and moreover, the very fact of the sometimes extraordinarily rapid formation of the conditioned reflex (even after one association of adequate stimuli) points to its extreme improbability. Thus we have to assume that the formation of new intercentral connexions must be regarded as a *synaptic process*, . . . In other words, we have to assume that before a conditioned reflex is established, there exist *potential* interneuronic connexions, directed from the centre of the stimulus to be conditioned to the centre of the reinforcing stimulus, and that as the result of repetitive associations of these stimuli these potential connexions are transformed into actual connexions. (Konorski 1948, p. 87; all italics in the original.)

Observations that provide support for the proposal that learning involves the formation of new synapses include those of sprouting in response to neural damage (e.g., Liu & Chambers, 1958; Raisman, 1969; Steward, Cottman, & Lynch, 1976; Tsukahara, 1981) and that sprouting plays a role in the recovery of behavioral function (e.g., Goldberger & Murray, 1978; Goodman & Horel, 1966). The extensive literature reviewed above concerning effects of early environment and stimulation on brain development indicates that several structural features of neurons in the cerebral cortex can be markedly influenced, including the formation of new synapses (e.g., dendritic spines). There is some evidence that synaptogenesis can occur as a result of training in adult animals (see above). Recent evidence indicates that new synapses may be formed in the hippocampus in as short a time as 10 minutes following induction of long-term-potentiation (LTP)—(see below and Lee, Schottler, Oliver, & Lynch, 1980, 1981; Chang and Greenough, 1984). As early as 1893 both Cajal and Tanzi proposed that the structural plasticity seen in development extended into adulthood and could form the basis of learning. But at present we can only assert that certain forms of experience are apparently accompanied by synaptogenesis and other structural alterations in neurons. Whether such processes are in fact the substrate of memory traces remains to be determined. But as noted above in Memory Consolidation, initial formation of long-term memories resistant to disruption can apparently occur in less than 1 second.

## Changes in the Strength of Already Existing Synapses

The idea that learning involves the strengthening of preexisting connections between sensory and motor systems was used by Cason (1922) to explain the conditioning of the eyeblink response in humans and was proposed by Watson (1924) as a possible explanation of conditioning in general. Watson (1924, pp. 168–169) states that the problem that the psychologist leaves the physiologist is:

> Stimulus X will not now call out reaction R, stimulus Y will call out reaction R (unconditioned reflex); but when stimulus X is presented first and then Y (which does call out R) shortly thereafter, X will thereafter call out R. In other words, stimulus X becomes ever thereafter substitutable for Y. (original italicized)

> The physiologist may come back at once with some such explanation as this: "You are wrong in your assumption about X not stimulating the organism. X does stimulate the whole organism and consequently does faintly arouse reaction R, *only not strongly enough to appear as an overt response.* (Italics added) Y does call out R overtly because the organism is biologically built to respond overtly with R when stimulated by Y (unconditioned responses). But after Y has called out R, resistance or inertia in this whole sensory motor segment is lessened to such an extent that X, which only faintly called out R, will now call out R overtly.

The most influential modern version of this view is the *Hebb synapse* (Hebb, 1949). In essence, Hebb proposed that a synaptic connection on a neuron would be strengthened if the synapse (i.e., terminal from the CS channel) was active at the time the neuron was fired by the US pathway, or at least activated synaptically (a less restrictive current formulation). The requirements for inducing associative changes specified by the Hebb synapse do not appear to be operative in classical conditioning of the *Aplysia* gill withdrawal reflex (Carew, Hawkins, Abrams, & Candel, 1984), which provides the only direct test to date: The associative changes in the sensory neuron occur as a result of sensory neuron activation followed by input to terminals of the sensory neuron—firing of the post synaptic neuron is not required for plastic changes to occur.

The work reviewed in previous sections suggests that the strength of a preexisting synapse can be modified in several ways. Among the simplest is a change in transmitter release from presynaptic terminals. The work of Kandel and colleagues has shown that in Aplysia short-term habituation results from a decreased transmitter release by the sensory neuron due to a reduction in intracellular $CA^{++}$ and depletion, and that long-term habituation results in part from a decreased loading of synaptic vesicles (Bailey & Chen, 1983). Similarly, in vertebrate spinal cord, habituation appears due to a process of synaptic depression (Thompson & Spencer, 1966) due in turn to decreased presynaptic transmitter release (Farel & Thompson, 1976; Glanzman & Thompson, 1980). In *Aplysia*, both sensitization and a conditioned facilitation of responding result from an augmented transmitter release. The mechanism of sensitization is in part synaptic (an increased loading of synaptic vesicles; Bailey & Chen, 1983). Both sensitization- and conditioning-produced increases in transmitter release have been shown to result from nonsynaptic changes: A broadening of the action potential resulting from training produced changes in one form of an outward $K^+$ current (see section on invertebrate preparations). Similary, the training produced increase in the output of the type B photoreceptor in *Hermissenda* is due to a training induced decrease in polarization resulting from a reduction in outward $K^+$ currents (e.g., Alkon, 1984a, 1984b; see discussion in the section of invertebrates above). In both *Hermissenda* and *Aplysia*, conditioning produced changes occur in sensory neurons, which receive convergent input from US pathways, as opposed to the post synaptic neuron e.g., as in a Hebbian synapse.

There is some evidence in *Aplysia* that long-term habituation and sensitization involve structural changes in presynaptic terminals. Thus, Bailey and Chen (1983) provide evidence that a reduction in the area of active zones in the sensory neuron of *Aplysia* may mediate long-term habituation and that increases in the area of active zones in the same neurons may mediate long-term sensitization.

In the vertebrate brain, most work on structural alterations of synapses has focussed on postsynaptic elements, for example, dendritic spines. In addition to reports of new spine synapse formation (see above), several works have reported alterations in spine morphology, particularly as a result of induction of long-term-potentiation (LTP) in the hippocampus (Fifkova & von Harreveld, 1977; Lee et al., 1980). More generally, LTP has become popular as a putative mechanism of memory (see Swanson et al., 1982 for a detailed review). In brief, a short tetanus (e.g., a few seconds at 100 Hz) to certain pathways induces an increased synaptic excitability that can persist for days or weeks (Bliss & Gardner-Medwin, 1973; Bliss & Lømo, 1970; Lømo, 1966). It was first found in the perforant path to granule cells in the dentate gyrus and for some time was thought to be unique to the hippocampus, but it has now been reported in other brain regions as well (Swanson et al., 1982). Long-term potentiation resembles post-tetanic potentiation (PTP), a phenomena early proposed as a mechanism of memory (Eccles, 1964), except that LTP has a much longer duration.

The mechanisms underlying LTP are not yet known—it is not even clear whether they are presynaptic, postsynaptic or both, or whether interneurons are critically involved (Swanson et al., 1982). The fact that LTP, *per se*, does not involve activation of convergent inputs (i.e., from CS and US) remained a problem until it was shown that a form of associative LTP could be established in the hippocampus by appropriate convergent stimulation of two input pathways (Buenonuevo & Brown, 1983; Levy & Steward, 1979, 1983).

The most detailed hypothesis relating LTP to memory is that of Lynch and Baudry (1984), who propose a biochemical mechanism for LTP that could serve as an intermediate step in memory formation. In brief, calcium is hypothesized to increase rapidly and irreversibly the number of receptors for glutamate (a probable neurotransmitter) in forebrain synaptic membranes by activating a proteinase that degrades a specific protein, which in turn could produce long-lasting changes in synaptic chemistry and ultra-structure. There is considerable evidence that LTP is accompanied by increased glutamate receptor binding in the hippocampus (see Lynch & Baudry, 1984) and even some evidence of increased glutamate receptor binding in hippocampal membranes as a result of associative learning in the intact mammal (Mamounas et al., 1984).

It should be recognized that the analysis of mechanisms of neural plasticity involved in learning is but one step in the development of psychobiological theories of learning. Characterizing mechanisms of plasticity entails identifying the circuitry responsible for the development and expression of a form of learning to be explained, determining the sites of plasticity within the circuit, and then elucidating the cellular mechanisms by which training-induced changes in cellular functioning occur. However, after completing this reductionistic odyssey, one is still left with the task of developing an explanation of the learned behavior. Groves and Thompson (1970) and Hawkins and Kandel (1984) provide examples of how findings from the cellular analysis of learning in simplified preparations might be generalized to account for a variety of learning phenomena observed in both invertebrates and vertebrates.

Characterizations of neural sytems involved in learning and memory have, almost exclusively, relied on circuit analysis—a specification of the neural elements involved and their interconnections, i.e., providing a *diagram* of the neural network thought to produce the behavior to be accounted for. The problem of the circuit analysis approach to the development of explanations having some fidelity to the learned behavior is that these two-dimensional, static diagrams of the nervous system fail to capture the complexity of the actual neural machinery and its environment. Our diagrams fail to represent a tremendous number of the relevant cellular and extracellular events as well as the temporal relationships and interactions between these events (see Bullock, 1981, pp. 278–283; 1983, pp. 407–408 for a critique of circuit analysis).

The full task confronting the development of psychobiological theories of learning and memory is to develop simulations that capture the true complexity of the neural *systems* being modeled and show that the model of the system is capable of demonstrating the forms of learning to be explained according to two criteria: (1) that the neural elements of the model function and change in ways consistent with the function and changes observed in the corresponding elements in the nervous system and (2) that the behavioral products of the model are consistent with the behavioral products of training (Gluck and Thompson, 1987).

# REFERENCES

Abrams, T.W., Carew, T.J., Hawkins, R.D., & Kandel, E.R. (1983). Aspects of the cellular mechanism of temporal specificity in conditioning in *Aplysia*: Preliminary evidence for $Ca^{2+}$ influx as a signal of activity. *Society for Neuroscience Abstracts, 9,* 168.

Abrams, T.W., Castellucci, V.F., Camardo, J.S., Kandel, E.R., & Lloyd, P.E. (1984). Two endogenous neuropeptides modulate the gill and siphon withdrawal reflex in *Aplysia* by presynaptic facilitation involving cAMP-dependent closure of a serotonin sensitive potassium channel. *Proceedings of the National Academy of Science, USA, 81,* 7956–7960.

Aceves-Pina, E.O., & Quinn, W.G. (1979). Learning in normal and mutant *Drosophila* larvae. *Science, 206,* 93–96.

Acosta-Urquidi, J., Alkon, D.L., & Neary, J.T. (1984). $Ca^{2+}$-dependent protein kinase injection in photoreceptor mimics biophysical effects in associative learning. *Science, 224,* 1254–1257.

Agranoff, B.W. (1980). Biochemical events mediating the formation of short-term and long-term memory. In Y. Tsukada and B.W. Agranoff (Eds.), *Neurobiological basis of learning and memory.* New York: Wiley.

Agranoff, B.W., Burrell, H.R., Dokas, L.A., & Springer, A.D. (1978). Progress in biochemical approaches to learning and memory. In M.A. Lipton, A. DiMascio, & K.F. Killam, (Eds.), *Psychopharmacology: A generation of progress,* pp. 623–635. New York: Raven Press.

Agranoff, B.W., Davis, R.E., & Brink, J.J. (1965). Memory fixation in the goldfish. *Proceedings National Academy of Sciences, 54,* 788–793.

Agranoff, B.W., Davis, R.E., & Brink, J.J. (1966). Chemical studies on memory fixation in goldfish. *Brain Research, 1,* 303–309.

Akert, K., Gruesen, R.A., Woolsey, C.N., & Meyer, D.R. (1961). Kluver–Bucy syndrome in monkeys with neocortical ablations of the temporal lobes. *Brain, 84,* 480–497.

Akert, K., Orth, O.S., Harlow, H.F., & Schiltz, K.A. (1960). Learned behavior of rhesus monkeys following neonatal bilateral prefrontal lobotomy. *Science, 132,* 1944–1945.

Albert, D.J., Brayley, K.N., & Milner, J.A. (1978). Connections from the lateral septum modulating reactivity in the rat. *Physiology & Behavior, 21,* 761–767.

Albus, J.S. (1971). A theory of cerebellar function. *Mathematical Bioscience, 10,* 25–61.

Alkon, D.L. (1974). Associative training of *Hermissenda. Journal of General Physiology, 64,* 70–84.

Alkon, D.L. (1980a). Cellular analysis of a gastropod (*Hermissenda Crassicornis*) model of associative learning. *The Biological Bulletin, 159,* 505–560.

Alkon, D.L. (1980b). Membrane depolarization accumulates during acquisition of an associative behavioral change. *Science, 210,* 1375–1376.

Alkon, D.L. (1983). Learning in a marine snail. *Scientific American, 249,* 70–85.

Alkon, D.L. (1984a). Calcium-mediated reduction of ionic currents: A biophysical memory trace. *Science, 226,* 1037–1045.

Alkon, D.L. (1984b). Persistent calcium-mediated changes of identified membrane currents as a cause of associative learning. In D.L. Alkon & J. Farley (Eds.), *Primary neural substrates of learning and behavioral change.* Cambridge MA: Cambridge University Press.

Alkon, D.L., Lederhendler, I., & Shoukimas, J.J. (1982). Primary changes of membrane currents during retention of associative learning. *Science, 215,* 693–695.

Alkon, D.L., Shoukimas, J., & Heldman, E. (1982). Calcium-mediated decrease of a voltage-dependent potassium current. *Biophysics, 40,* 245–250.

Altman, J., & Das, G.D. (1964). Autoradiographic examination of the effects of enriched environment on the rate of glial multiplication in the adult rat brain. *Nature, 204,* 1161–1163.

Arnold, A.P. (1975). The effects of castration and androgen replacement on song, courtship, and aggression in zebra finches (*Poephila guttata*). *Journal of Experimental Zoology, 191,* 309–326.

Arnstein, A.F.T., & Goldman-Rakic, P.S. (1984). Catecholamines and cognition in aged monkeys: Improvement in delayed response performance by the alpha-2 agonist, clonidine. *Neuroscience Abstracts, 10,* 774.

Babb, T.L. (1982). Short-term and long-term modification of neurons and evoked potentials in the human hippocampal formation. *Neurosciences Research Progress Bulletin 20*(5), 729–739.

Bach-y-Rita, P. (Ed.) (1980). *Recovery of function: Theoretical considerations for brain injury rehabilitation.* Balitmore, Maryland: University Park Press.

Bagshaw, M.H., & Pribram, K.H. (1953). Cortical organization in gustation (*Macaca mulatta*). *Journal of Neurophysiology, 16*, 499–508.

Bailey, C.H., & Chen, M. (1983). Morphological basis of long-term habituation and sensitization in *Aplysia. Science, 220*, 91–93.

Bailey, C.H., Hawkins, R.D., Chen, M.C., & Kandel, E.R. (1981). Interneurons involved in mediation and modulation of gill-withdrawal reflex in *Aplysia*: IV. Morphological basis of presynaptic facilitation. *Journal of Neurophysiology, 45*, 340–360.

Bailey, W.H., & Weiss, J.M. (1979). Evaluation of a memory deficit in vasopressin-deficient rats. *Brain Research, 162*, 174–178.

Barber, T.X. (1959). Toward a theory of pain: Relief of chronic pain by prefrontal leucotomy, opiates, placebos, and hypnosis. *Psychological Bulletin, 56*, 430–460.

Barlow, H.B. (1975). Visual experience and cortical development. *Nature, 258*, 199–204.

Barondes, S.H., & Cohen, H.D. (1968a). Arousal and the conversion of short-term to long-term memory. *Proceedings of the National Academy of Science of the United States of America, 61*, 923–929.

Barondes, S., & Cohen, H.D. (1968b). Memory impairment after subcutaneous injection of acetoxycycloheximide. *Science, 160*, 556–557.

Barondes, S.H., & Jarvik, M.E. (1964). The influence of actinomycin-D on brain RNA synthesis and on memory. *Journal of Neurochemistry, 1*, 187–195.

Barrionuevo, G. & Brown, T.H. (1983). Associative long-term potentiation in hippocampal slices. *Proceedings of the National Academy of Science, USA, 80*, 7247–7351.

Bartus, R.T. (1979). Aging in the rhesus monkey: Specific behavioral impairments and effects of pharmacological intervention. In H. Orimo, K. Shimado, M. Iriki, & D. Maeda (Eds.), Recent Advances in Gerontology, (pp. 225–227). *Proceedings of the XI International Congress Gerontology* Amsterdam: Excerpta Medicus.

Bartus, R.T., Fleming, D., & Johnson, H.R. (1978). Aging in the rhesus monkey: debilitating effects on short-term memory. *Journal of Gerontology, 33*, 858–871.

Bartus, R.T., & LeVere, T.E. (1977). Frontal decortication in rhesus monkeys: A test of the interference hypothesis. *Brain Research, 119*, 233–248.

Bateson, P.P.G. (1966). The characteristics and context of imprinting. *Biological Reviews, 41*, 117–220.

Bateson, P.P.G. (1979). How do sensitive periods arise and what are they for? *Animal Behavior, 27*, 470–486.

Bateson, P.P.G., Horn, G., & Rose, S.P.R. (1969). Effects of an imprinting procedure on regional incorporation of tritiated lysine into protein of chick brain. *Nature, 223*, 534–535.

Bateson, P.P.G., Horn, G., & Rose, S.P.R. (1972). Effects of early experience on regional incorporation of precursors into RNA and protein in the chick brain. *Brain Research, 39*, 449–465.

Bateson, P.P.G., Horn, G., & Rose, S.P.R. (1975). Imprinting: Correlations between behavior and incorporation of [$^{14}$C] uracil into chick brain. *Brain Research, 84*, 207–220.

Bateson, P.P.G., Rose, S.P.R., & Horn, G. (1973). Imprinting: Lasting effects on uracil incorporation into chick brain. *Science, 181*, 576–578.

Beggs, A.L., Steinmetz, J.E., Romano, A.G., & Patterson, M.M. (1983). Extinction and retention of a classically conditioned flexor nerve response in acute spinal cat. *Behavioral Neuroscience, 97*, 530–540.

Benjamin, R.M., & Thompson, R.F. (1959). Differential effects of cortical lesions in infant and adult cats on roughness discrimination. *Experimental Neurology, 1*, 305–321.

Berger, B., Thierry, A.M., Tassin, J.P., & Moyne, M.A. (1976). Dopaminergic innervation of the rat prefrontal cortex: a fluorescence histochemical study. *Brain Research, 106*, 133–145.

Berger, T.W., Berry, S.D., & Thompson, R.F. (1986). Role of the hippocampus in classical conditioning of the aversive and appetitive behavior. In R.L. Isaacson and K.H. Pribram (Eds.), *The Hippocampus*, Vol. II and IV. New York: Plenum Press, in press.

Berger, T.W., Clark, G.A., & Thompson, R.F. (1980). Learning-dependent neuronal responses recorded from limbic system brain structures during classical conditioning. *Physiological Psychology, 8*(2), 155–167.

Berger, T.W., & Orr, W.B. (1982). In C.D. Woody (Ed.). *Conditioning: Representation of involved neural functions* (pp. 1–12). New York: Plenum.

Berger, T.W., Rinaldi, P., Weisz, D.J., & Thompson, R.F. (1983). Single unit analysis of different hippocampal cell types during classical conditioning of the rabbit nictitating membrane response. *Journal of Neurophysiology, 50*(5), 1197–1219.

Berger, T.W., & Thompson, R.F. (1978a). Identification of pyramidal cells as the critical elements in hippocampal neuronal plasticity during learning.

*Proceedings of the National Academy of Sciences (Washington) 75,* 1572–1576.

Berger, T.W., & Thompson, R.F. (1978b). Neuronal plasticity in the limbic system during classical conditioning of the rabbit nictitating membrane response. I. The hippocampus. *Brain Research, 145,* 323–346.

Berger, T.W., & Thompson, R.F. (1978c). Neuronal plasticity in the limbic system during classical conditioning of the rabbit nictitating membrane response: II. Septum and mammillary bodies. *Brain Research, 156,* 293–314.

Bergson, H.L. (1910). *Matter and memory.* (N.M. Paul & W.S. Palmer, Trans.). London: George Allen. (Original work published.)

Berman, N., Murphey, E.H., & Salinger, W.L. (1979). Monocular paralysis in the adult cat does not change cortical ocular dominance. *Brain Research, 164,* 290–293.

Berman, R.F., & Kesner, R.P. (1981). Electrical stimulation as a tool in memory research, In M.M. Patterson & R.P. Kesner (Eds.), *Electrical stimulation research techniques,* (pp. 173–218). New York: Academic Press.

Bernstein, L. (1973). A study of some enriching variables in a free-environment for rats. *Journal of Psychosomatic Research, 17,* 85–88.

Berntson, G.G., & Micco, D.J. (1976). Organization of brain stem behavioral systems. *Brain Research Bulletin, 1,* 471–483.

Berry, S.D., & Thompson, R.F. (1978). Prediction of learning rate from the hippocampal EEG. *Science, 200,* 1298–1300.

Berry, S.D., & Thompson, R.F. (1979). Medial septal lesions retard classical conditioning of the nictitating membrane response in rabbits. *Science, 205,* 209–211.

Best, J.B. (1965). Behavior of planaria in instrumental learning paradigms. *Animal Behavior, Supplement 1, 13,* 69–75.

Bindman, L., & Lippold, O. (1981). *The Neurophysiology of the cerebral cortex.* London: Edward Arnold.

Bingham, W.E., & Griffiths, W.J., Jr. (1952). The effect of different environments during infancy on adult behavior in the rat. *Journal of Comparative & Physiological Psychology, 45,* 307–312.

Birt, D., & Olds, M.E. (1982). Auditory response enhancement during differential conditioning in behaving rats. See Woody 1982. In press.

Bitterman, M.E.., Menzel, R., Fietz, A., & Schafer, S. (1983). Classical conditioning of proboscis-extension in honeybees. *Journal of Comparative & Physiological Psychology, 97,* 107–119.

Black-Cleworth, P., Woody, C.D., & Niemann, J. (1975). A conditioned eye blink obtained by using

electrical stimulation of the facial nerve as the unconditioned stimulus. *Brain Research, 90,* 45–56.

Blake, M.O., Meyer, D.R., & Meyer, P.M. (1966). Enforced observation in delayed response learning by frontal monkeys. *Journal of Comparative & Physiological Psychology, 61,* 374–379.

Blakemore, C. (1970). The representation of three-dimensional visual space in the cat's striate cortex. *Journal of Physiology, 209,* 155–178.

Blakemore, C., & Cooper, G.F. (1970). Development of the brain depends on the visual environment. *Nature, 228,* 477–478.

Blakemore, C., Garey, L.J., Henderson, Z.B., Swindale, N.V., & Vital-Durand, F. (1980). Visual experience can promote rapid axonal reinnervation in monkey visual cortex. *Journal of Physiology, 307,* 25P–26P.

Blakemore, C., & Mitchell, D.E. (1973). Environmental modification of the visual cortex and the neural basis of learning and memory. *Nature, 241,* 467–468.

Blanchard, D.C., & Blanchard, R.J. (1972). Innate and conditioned reactions to threat in rats with amygdaloid lesions. *Journal of Comparative & Physiological Psychology, 81,* 281.

Bliss, T.V.P., & Lomo, T. (1970). Plasticity in a monosynaptic cortical pathway. *Journal of Physiology (London), 207,* p. 61.

Bloch, V., Denti, A., & Schmaltz, G. (1966). Effets de la stimulation reticulaire sur la phase de consolidation de la trace amnesique. *Journal of Physiology, 58,* 469–470.

Bloom, A.S., Quinton, E.E., & Carr, L.A. (1977). Effects of cycloheximide, diethyldithiocarbamate and D-amphetamine on protein and catecholamine biosynthesis in mouse brain. *Neuropharmacology, 16,* 411–418.

Blum, J.S., Chow, K.L., & Pribram, K.H. (1950). A behavioral analysis of the organization of the parieto-temporo-occipital cortex. *Journal of Comparative Neurology, 93,* 53–100.

Bohus, B., Kovacs, G., & de Wied, D. (1978). Oxytocin, vasopressin and memory: Opposite effects on consolidation and retrieval processes. *Brain Research, 157,* 414–417.

Bolles, R.C. (1970). Species-specific defense reactions and avoidance learning. *Psychological Review, 71,* 32–48.

Bolles, R.C. (1978). The role of stimulus learning in defensive behavior. In S.H. Hulse, H. Fowler, & W.K. Honig (Eds.), *Cognitive processes in animal behavior.* Hilsldale, NJ: Erlbaum.

Borges, S., & Berry, M. (1976). Preferential orientation of stellate cell dendrites in the visual cortex of the dark-reared rat. *Brain Research, 112,* 141–147.

Boring, E.G. (1950). *A history of experimental psychology*. New York: Appleton-Century-Crofts.

Bouton, M.E., & Bolles, R.C. (1979). Role of conditioned contextual stimuli in reinstatement of extinguished fear. *Journal of Experimental Psychology: Animal Behavior Processes, 5*, 368–378.

Bower, G.A. (1975). Cognitive Psychology: An Introduction. In W.K. Estes (Ed.), *Handbook of learning and cognitive processes: Vol. 1. Introduction to concepts and issues*. Hillsdale, NJ: Erlbaum.

Bradley, P., Davies, D.C., & Horn, G. (1981). A neuroanatomical study of the connections of the chick hyperstriatum. *Neuroscience Letters, Supplement 7*, S406.

Bradley, P., Horn, G., & Bateson, P. (1981). Imprinting: an electron microscopic study of chick hyperstriatum ventrale. *Experimental Brain Research, 41*, 115–120.

Brady, J.V., & Nauta, W.J. (1953). Subcortical mechanisms in emotional behavior: Affective changes following septal forebrain lesions in the albino rat. *Journal of Comparative & Physiological Psychology, 46*, 339–346.

Brailowsky, S. (1980). Neuropharmacological aspects of brain plasticity. In P. Bach-y-Rita (Ed.), *Recovery of function: Theoretical considerations for brain injury rehabilitation*. Baltimore, MD: University Park Press.

Brindley, G.A. (1964). The use made by the cerebellum of the information that it receives from sense organs. *Int. Brain Res. Org. Bull., 3*, 80.

Brodal, A. (1981). *Neurological anatomy in relation to clinical medicine*. New York: Oxford University Press.

Brody, E.B., & Rosvold, H.E. (1952). Influence of prefrontal lobotomy on social interaction in a monkey group. *Psychosomatic Medicine, 14*, 406–415.

Brogden, W.J., & Gantt, W.H. (1942). Interneural conditioning: Cerebellar conditioned reflexes. *Archives of Neurology & Psychiatry, 48*, 437–455.

Bromily, R.B. (1948b). The development of conditioned responses in cats after unilateral decortication. *Journal of Comparative & Physiological Psychology, 41*, 155–164.

Bromiley, R.B. (1948a). Conditioned responses in a dog after removal of neocortex *Journal of Comparative & Physiological Psychology, 41*, 102–110.

Brons, J.F., & Woody, C.D. (1980). Long-term changes in excitability of cortical neurons after Pavlovian conditioning and extinction. *Journal of Neurophysiology, 44*, 605.

Brooks, D.N., & Baddeley, A. (1976). What can amnesic patients learn? *Neuropsychologia, 14*, 111–122.

Brooks, V.B. (1979). Control of the intended limb movements by the lateral and intermediate cerebellum. In H. Asanuma & V.J. Wilson (Eds.). *Integration in the nervous system* (pp. 321–356). New York: Igaku-Shoin.

Brooks, V.B., Kozlovskaya, I.B., Atkin, A., Horvath, F.E., & Uno, M. (1973). Effects of cooling dentate nucleus on tracking-task performance in monkeys. *Journal of Neurophysiology, 36*, 974–995.

Brown, J.S., Kalish, H.I., & Farber, I.E. (1951). Conditioned fear as revealed by magnitude of startle response to an auditory stimulus. *Journal of Experimental Psychology, 41*, 317–328.

Brown, R.T. (1968). Early experience and problem-solving ability. *Journal of Comparative & Physiological Psychology, 65*, 433–440.

Brown, R.T., & Salinger, W.L. (1975). Loss of x-cells in lateral geniculate neurons with monocular paralysis: neural plasticity in the adult cat. *Science, 189*, 1011–1012.

Brozovski, T.J., Brown, R.M., Rosvold, H.E., & Goldman, P.S. (1979). Cognitive deficit caused by regional depletion of dopamine in prefrontal cortex of rhesus monkey. *Science, 205*, 929–932.

Brunelli, M., Castellucci, V., & Kandel, E.R. (1976). Synaptic facilitation and behavioral sensitization in *Aplysia*: Possible role of serotonin and cAMP. *Science, 194*, 1178–1181.

Bruner, J.S. (1969). Modalities of memory. In G.A. Talland & N.C. Waugh (Eds.), *The Pathology of Memory* (pp. 253–259). New York: Academic Press.

Bruner, J., & Kehoe, J. (1970). Long-term decrements in the efficacy of synaptic transmission in molluscs and crustaceans. In G. Horn & R.A. Hinde (Eds.), *Short-term changes in neural activity and behavior* (pp. 323–359). Cambrdge, England: Cambridge University Press.

Bruner, J., & Tauc, L. (1966). Long-lasting phenomena in the molluscan nervous system. *Symposium of Society of Experimental Biology, 20*, 457–475.

Brutkowski, S. (1964). Prefrontal cortex and drive inhibition. In J.M. Warren & K. Akert (Eds.), *The frontal granular cortex and behavior*. New York: McGraw-Hill.

Buchanan, S.L., & Powell, D.A. (1982). Cingulate cortex: Its role in Pavlovian conditioning. *Journal of Comparative & Physiological Psychology*.

Buchtel, H.A., Camarda, R., Rizzolatti, G., & Scandolara, C. (1979). The effect of hemidecortication on the inhibitory interactions in the superior colliculus of the cat. *Journal of Comparative Neurology, 184*, 795–810.

Buchwald, J.S., Halas, E.S., & Schramm, S. (1966). Changes in cortical and subcortical unit activity during behavioral conditioning. *Physiology & Behavior, 1*, 11–22.

Bull, T. (1980). Reassessment of neural connectivity and its specification. In H.M. Pinsker & W.D. Willis (Eds.), *Information processing in the nervous system*. New York: Raven Press.

Bullock, T.H. (1981). Spikeless neurons: Where do we go from here? In A. Roberts & B.M. Bush (Eds.), *Neurons without impulses*. Cambridge: Cambridge University Press.

Bullock, T.H. (1983). Epilogue: Neurobiological roots and neuroethological sprouts. In F. Huber & H. Markl (Eds.), *Neuroethology and behavioral physiology*. Berlin: Springer-Verlag.

Bullock, T.H., & Horridge, G.A. (1965). *Structure and function in the nervous systems of invertebrates: Vols. 1 & 2*. San Francisco: W.H. Freeman.

Bullock, T.H., Orkland, R., & Grinnell, A. (1977). *Introduction to nervous systems*. San Francisco: W.H. Freeman Co.

Butter, C.M., & Hirtzel, M. (1970). Impairment in sampling visual stimuli in monkeys with inferotemporal lesions. *Physiology & Behavior, 5,* 369–370.

Butter, C.M., & Snyder, D.R. (1972). Alterations in adversive and aggressive behaviors following orbital frontal lesions in monkeys. *Acta Neurobiologiae Experimentalis, 32,* 535–565.

Butters, N. (1979). Amnesic disorders. In K. Heilman & E. Valenstein (Eds.), *Clinical Neuropsychology*. New York: Oxford University Press.

Butters, N., & Pandya, D. (1969). Retention of delayed-alternation: effect of selective lesions of sulcus principalis. *Science, 165,* 1271–1273.

Butters, N., Pandya, D., Sanders, K., & Dye, P. (1971). Behavioral deficits in monkeys after selective lesions within the middle third of sulcus principalis. *Journal of Comparative & Physiological Psychology, 76,* 8–14.

Byers, D., Davis, R.L., & Kiger, J.A. (1981). Defect in cyclic AMP phosphodiasterase due to the *dunce* mutation of learning in *Drosophila. Nature (London), 289,* 79–81.

Byrne, J.H. (1987). Cellular analysis of associative learning. *Physiological Reviews, 57,* 329–439.

Byrne, J., Castellucci, V., & Kandel, E.R. (1974a). Quantitative aspects of the sensory component of the gill-withdrawal reflex in *Aplysia. Program and Abstract of the Society for Neurological Sciences,* Fourth Annual Meeting, 160.

Byrne, J., Castelucci, V.R., & Kandel, E.R. (1974b). Receptive fields and response properties of mechanoreceptor neurons innervating siphon skin and mantle shelf in *Aplysia. Journal of Neurophysiology, 37,* 1041–1064.

Canady, R.A., Kroodsma, D.E., & Nottebohm, F. (1984). Population differences in complexity of a learned skill are correlated with brain space involved. *Proceedings of the National Academy of Sciences, 81,* 6232–6234.

Cannon, W.F., & Rosenblueth, A. (1949). *The supersensitivity of denervated structures*. New York: Macmillan.

Carew, T.J., Castellucci, V.F., & Kandel, E.R. (1971). An analysis of dishabituation and sensitization of the gill-withdrawal reflex in *Aplysia. International Journal of Neuroscience, 2,* 79–98.

Carew, T.J., Hawkins, R.D., Abrams, T.W., & Kandel, E.R. (1984). A test of Hebb's postulate at identified synapses which mediate classical conditioning in *Aplysia. Journal of Neuroscience, 4,* 1217–1224.

Carew, T.J., Hawkins, R.D., Kandel, E.R. (1983). Differential classical conditioning of a defensive withdrawal reflex in *Aplysia californica. Science, 219,* 397–400.

Carew, T.J., Pinsker, H.M., & Kandel, E.R. (1972). Long-term habituation of a defensive withdrawal reflex in *Aplysia, Science, 175,* 451–454.

Carew, T.J., Pinsker, H., Rubinson, K., & Kandel, E.R. (1974). Physiological and biochemical properties of neuromuscular transmission between identified motoneurons and gill muscle in *Aplysia. Journal of Neurophysiology, 37,* 1020–1040.

Carey, R.J., & Miller, M. (1982). Absence of learning and memory deficits in the vasopressin-deficient rats (Battleboro strain). *Behavioral Brain Research, 6,* 1–13.

Cason, H. (1922). The conditioned eyelid reaction. *Journal of Experimental Psychology, 5,* 153–196.

Castellucci, V., & Kandel, E.R. (1974). A quantal analysis of the synaptic depression underlying habituation of the gill-withdrawal reflex in *Aplysia. Proceedings of the National Academy of Sciences USA, 71,* 5004–5008.

Castellucci, V., & Kandel, E.R. (1976). An invertebrate system for the cellular study of habituation and sensitization. In T. Tighe & R.N. Leaton (Eds.), *Habituation: Perspectives from child development, animal behavior, and neurophysiology*. Hillsdale, NJ: Erlbaum.

Castellucci, V., Pinsker, H., Kupferman, I., & Kandel, E.R. (1970). Neuronal mechanisms of habituation and dishabituation of the gill-withdrawal reflex in *Aplysia. Science, 167,* 1745–1748.

Cerletti, U., & Bini, L. (1938). Electric shock treatment. *Boll. Acad. Med. Roma, 64,* 36.

Chambers, K.C. (1985). Sexual dimorphisms as an index of hormonal influences on conditioned food aversions. In N. Broveman and P. Bronson (Eds.) *Experimental Assessments and Clinical*

*Applications of Conditioned Food Aversions.* (Vol. 443, pp. 110–125). New York: Annals of the New York Academy of Sciences.

Chang, J.J., & Gelperin, A. (1980). Rapid taste-aversion learning by an isolated molluscan central nervous system. *Proceedings of the National Academy of Sciences, 77,* 6204–6206.

Chang, F.L.F., & Greenough, W.T. (1982). Lateralized effects of monocular training on dendritic branching in adult split-brain rats. *Brain Research, 232,* 283–292.

Chang, F.L.F., & Greenough, W.T. (1984). Transient and enduring morphological correlates of synaptic activity and efficacy changes in the rat hippocampal slice. *Brain Research, 309,* 35–46.

Cherkin, A., & Van Herreveld, A. (1978). L-Proline and related compounds: correlation of structure, amnesic potency and antispreading depression potency. *Brain Research, 156,* 265–273.

Cholewiak, R.W., Hammond, R., Seigler, I.C., & Papsdorf, J.D. (1968). The effects of strychnine sulphate on the classically conditioned nictitating membrane response of the rabbit. *Journal of Comparative & Physiological Psychology, 66,* 77–81.

Chorover, S.L., & Schillar, P.H. (1966). Reexamination of prolonged retrograde amnesia in one-trail learning. *Journal of Comparative Physiological Psychology, 61,* 34–41.

Chow, K.L. (1952). Conditions influencing the recovery of visual discriminative habits in monkeys following temporal neocortical ablations. *Journal of Comparative & Physiological Psychology, 45,* 430–437.

Chow, K.L. (1967). Effects of ablation. In G.C. Quarton, T. Melnechuk, & F.O. Schmitt (Eds.), *The Neurosciences* (pp. 705–713). New York: Rockefeller University Press.

Chow, K.L., & Stewart, D.L. (1972). Reversal of structural and functional effects of long-term visual deprivation in cats. *Experimental Neurology, 34,* 409–433.

Church, R.M. (1964). Systematic effect of random error in the yoked control design. *Psychological Bulletin, 62,* 122–131.

Cipolla-Neto, J., Horn, G., & McCabe, B.J. (1982). Hemispheric asymmetry and imprinting: The effect of sequential lesions to the hyperstriatum ventrale. *Experimental Brain Research, 48,* 22–27.

Clark, G.A., & Kandel, E.R. (1984). Branch-specific heterosynaptic facilitation in *Aplysia* siphon sensory cells. *Proceedings of the National Academy of Sciences USA, 81,* 2577–2581.

Clark, G.A., McCormich, D.A., Lavond, D.G., & Thompson, R.F. (1984). Effects of lesions of cerebellar nuclei on conditioned behavioral and hippocampal neuronal responses. *Brain Research, 291,* 125–136.

Clark, R.B. (1965). The learning abilities of nereid polychaetes and the roles of the supra-cesophagenal ganglion. *Animal Behavior, Supplement 1, 13,* 89–100.

Cloud, M.D., Meyer, D.R., & Meyer, P.M. (1982). Inductions of recoveries from injuries to the cortex: dissociation of equipotential and regionally specific mechanisms. *Physiological Psychology, 10,* 66–73.

Cohen, D.H. (1969). Development of a vertebrate experimental model for cellular neurophysiologic studies of learning. *Conditioned Reflexes, 4,* 61–80.

Cohen, D.H. (1974). The neural pathways and informational flow mediating a conditioned autonomic response. In L.V. DiCara (Ed.), *Limbic and autonomic nervous system research.* New York: Plenum.

Cohen, D.H. (1975). Involvement of the avian amygdalar homologue (archistriatum posterior and mediale) in defensively conditioned heart rate change. *Journal of Comparative & Physiological Psychology, 160,* 13–36.

Cohen, D.H. (1980). The functional neuroanatomy of a conditioned response. In *Neural mechanisms of goal-directed behavior and learning,* R.F. Thompson, L.H. Hicks, Shvyrkov, V.B. (Eds.) New York: Academic Press.

Cohen, D.H. (1982). Central processing time for a conditioned response in a vertebrate model system. See Woody, 1982a.

Cohen, D.H., & Barondes, S.H. (1966). Further studies of learning and memory after intracerebral actinomycin-D. *Journal of Neurochemistry, 13,* 207–211.

Cohen, D.H., & Macdonald, R.L. (1976). Involvement of the avian hypothalamus in defensively conditioned heart rate change. *Journal of Comparative Neurology, 167,* 465–480.

Cohen, N.J., & Squire, L.R. (1980). Preserved learning and retention of pattern-analyzing skill in amnesia: dissociation of knowing how and knowing that. *Science, 210,* 207–210.

Coleman, P.D., & Riesen, A.H. (1968). Environmental effects on cortical dendritic fields I. Rearing in the dark. *Journal of Anatomy, 102,* 363–374.

Connor, J.A., & Alkon, D.L. (1984). Light-induced changes of intracellular $Ca^{++}$ in *Hermissenda. Journal of Neurophysiology, 51,* 745–752.

Connor, J.R., Melone, J.H., Yuen, A.R., & Diamond, M.C. (1981). Dendritic length in aged rats' optical cortex: An environmentally induced response. *Experimental Neurology, 73,* 827–830.

Coons, E.E., & Miller, N.E. (1960). Conflict vs. consolidation of memory traces to explain "retrograde amnesia" produced by ECS. *Journal of*

*Comparative & Physiological Psychology*, *53*, 524–531.

Copeland, J., & Gelperin, A. (1983). Feeding and a serotonergic interneuron activate an identified autoactive salivary neuron in *Limax maximus*. *Comparative Biochemistry Physiology*, *76A*, 21–30.

Cormier, S.M. (1981). A match-mismatch theory of limbic system function. *Physiological Psychology*, *19*, 3–36.

Cotman, C.W. (Ed.) (1978). *Neuronal plasticity*. New York: Raven Press.

Coulter, J.D., Ewing, L., & Carter, C. (1976). Origin of primary sensorimotor cortical projections to lumbar spinal cord of cat and monkeys. *Brain Research*, *103*, 366–372.

Couvillion, P.A., & Bitterman, M.E. (1980). Some phenomena of associative learning in honeybees. *Journal of Comparative & Physiological Psychology*, *94*, 878–885.

Couvillion, P.A., & Bitterman, M.E. (1982). Compound conditioning in honeybees. *Journal of Comparative & Physiological Psychology*, *96*, 192–199.

Coyle, J.T., Price, D.L., & DeLong, M.R. (1983). Alzheimer's disease: A disorder of central cholinergic innervation. *Science*, *219*, 1184–1190.

Cragg, B.G. (1967). Changes in visual cortex on first exposure of rats to light: Effect on synaptic dimensions. *Nature*, *215*, 251–253.

Cragg, B.G., & Downer, J. deC. (1967). Behavioural evidence for cortical involvement in manual temperature discrimination in the monkey. *Experimental Neurology*, *19*, 433–442.

Creutzfeld, O.D., & Heggelund, P. (1975). Neural plasticity in visual cortex of adult cats after exposure to visual patterns. *Science*, *188*, 1025–1027.

Crow, T. (1983) Conditioned modification of locomotion of sensory adaptation in *Hermissenda crassicornis*: analysis of time dependent associative and nonassociative components. *Journal of Neuroscience*, *3*, 2621–2628.

Crow, T. (1985). Conditioned modification of phototatic behavior in *Hermissenda*. II. Differential light adaptation of B-photoreceptors. *Journal of Neuroscience*, *5*, 215–223.

Crow, T.J., & Alkon, D.L. (1978). Retention of an associative behavioral change in *Hermissenda*. *Science*, *201*, 1239–1241.

Crow, T.J., & Alkon, D.L. (1980). Associative behavioral modification in *Hermissenda*: cellular correlates. *Science*, *209*, 412–414.

Culligan, N., & Gelperin, A. (1983). One-trial associative learning by an isolated molluscan CNS: Use of different chemoreceptors for training and testing. *Brain Research*, *266*, 319–327.

Cummins, R.A., Walsh, R.N., Budtz-Olsen, O.E., Kostantinos, T., & Horsfall, C.R. (1973). Environmentally induced changes in the brains of old rats. *Nature*, *243*, 516–517.

Cupello, A., & Hyden, A. (1976). Alterations of the pattern of hippocampal nerve cell RNA labelling during training in rats. *Brain Research*, *114*, 453–460.

Cutting, J. (1978). A cognitive approach to Korsakoff's syndrome. *Cortex*, *14*, 485–495.

Cynader, M., Timney, B.N., & Mitchell, D.E. (1980). Period of susceptibility of kitten cortex to the effects of monocular deprivation extends beyond six months of age. *Brain Research*, *191*, 545–550.

Dalby, D.A., Meyer, D.R., & Meyer, P.M. (1970). Effects of occipital neocortical lesions upon visual discriminations in the cat. *Physiology & Behavior*, *5*, 727–734.

Datta, L.G. (1962). Learning in the earthworm, *Lumbricus terrestris*. *American Journal of Psychology*, *75*, 531–553.

Davies, D.C., & Bradley, P.M. (1981). The connexions of hyperstriatum ventrale in the chick brain: A retrograde fluorescence labelling study. *Journal Anatomy, London*, *133*, 126.

Davis, H.P., & Squire, L.R. (1984). Protein synthesis and memory: A review. *Psychological Bulletin*, *96*, 518–559.

Davis, K.L., Mohs, R.C., Tinklenberg, J.R., Pfefferbaum, A., Kopell, B.S. & Hollister, L.E. (1978). Physostigmine-improvement of long-term memory processes in normal humans. *Science*, *201*, 272–274.

Davis, M. (1970). Effects of inter stimulus interval length and variability on startle habituation in the rat. *Journal of Comparative & Physiological Psychology*, *72*, 177–192.

Davis, M. (1979a). Diazepam and Flurazapam: Effects on conditioned fear as measured with the potentiated startle paradigm. *Psychopharmacology*, *62*, 1–7.

Davis, M. (1979b). Morphone and naloxone: Effects on conditioned fear as measured with the potentiated startle paradigm. *European Journal of Pharmacology*, *54*, 341–347.

Davis, M. (in press). Anxiety and the amygdala: Pharmacological and anatomical analysis of the fear-potentiated startle paradigm. In G.H. Bower (Ed.) *The psychology of learning and motivation*. New York: Academic Press.

Davis, M., Gendelman, D.S., Tischler, M.D., & Gendelman, P.M. (1982). A primary acoustic startle circuit: Lesion and stimulation studies. *Journal of Neuroscience*, *2*, 791–805.

Davis, M., Parisi, T., Gendelman, D.S., Tischler, M., & Kehne, J.H. (1982). Habituation and sensitization of startle reflexes elicited electrically from the brain stem. *Science, 218,* 688–690.

Davis, M., Redmond, D.E., & Baraban, J.M. (1979). Noradrenergic agonists and antagonists: Effects on conditioned fear as measured by the potentiated startle paradigm. *Psychopharmacology, 65,* 111–118.

Davis, M., & Wagner, A.R. (1968). Startle responsiveness following habituation of different intensities of tone. *Psychonomic Science, 12,* 337–338.

Davis, N., & LeVere, T.E. (1979). Recovery of function after brain damage: Different processes and facilitation of one. *Physiological Psychology, 7,* 233–240.

Davis, N., & LeVere, T.E. (1982). Recovery of function after brain damage: The question of individual behaviors or functionality. *Experimental Neurology, 75,* 68–78.

Davis, W.J., & Gillette, R. (1978). Neural correlates of behavioral plasticity in command neurons of *Pleurobranchaea. Science, 199,* 801–804.

Davis, W.J., Gillette, R., Kovac, M.P., Croll, R.P., & Matera, E.M. (1983). Organization of synaptic imputs to paracerebral feeding command interneurons of *Pleurobranchea californica:* III. Modifications induced by experience. *Journal of Neurophysiology, 49,* 1557–1572.

Davis, W.J., Villet, J., Lee, D., Rigler, M., Gillette, R., & Prince, E. (1980). Selective and differential avoidance learning in the feeding and withdrawal behaviors of *Pleurobranchea. Journal of Comparative Physiology, 138,* 157–165.

Deadwyler, S.A., West, M., & Lynch, G. (1979a). Activity of dentate granule cells during learning: Differentiation of perforant path input. *Brain Research, 169,* 29–43.

Deaux, E.G., & Gormezano, I. (1963). Eyeball retraction: Classical conditioning and extinction in the albino rabbit. *Science, 141,* 630–631.

Deluty, M.Z. (1982). Maximizing, minimizing, and matching between reinforcement and punishment situations. In M. Commons, R.J. Herrnstein, & H. Rachlin (Eds.), *Quantitative Analyses of Behavior: Vol. II.* Cambridge, MA: Ballinger.

Denti, A., McGaugh, J.L., Landfield, P., & Shinkman, P. (1970). Facilitation of learning with posttrial stimulation of the reticular formation. *Physiology & Behavior, 5,* 659–662.

Desmond, J.E., & Moore, J.W. (1982). A brain stem region essential for classically conditioned but not unconditioned nictitating membrane response. *Physiology & Behavior, 28,* 1029–1033.

Deupree, D., Coppock, W., & Willer, H. (1982). Pretraining septal driving of hippocampal rhythmic slow activity facilitates acquisition of visual

discrimination. *Journal of Comparative & Physiological Psychology, 96,* 557–563.

Deutsch, J.A. (1973a). The cholinergic synapse and the site of memory. In J.A. Duetsch (Ed.), *The physiological basis of memory* (pp. 59–76). New York: Academic Press.

Deutsch, J.A. (1973b). Electroconvulsive shock and memory. In J.A. Duetsch (Ed.), *The physiological basis of memory* (pp. 113–124). New York: Academic Press.

De Valois, R.L. (1965). Behavioral and electrophysiological studies of primate vision. In W.D. Neff (Ed.), *Contributions to sensory physiology:* Vol. 1. New York: Academic Press.

De Villers, P.A. (1982). Toward a quantitative theory of punishment. In M. Commons, R.J. Herrnstein, & H. Rachlin (Eds.), *Quantitative analyses of behavior; Vol. II.* Cambridge, MA: Ballinger.

DeVoogd, T., & Nottebohm, F. (1981a). Gonadal hormones induce dendritic growth in the adult avian brain. *Science, 214,* 202–204.

DeVoogd, T., & Nottebohm, F. (1981b). Sex differences in dendritic morphology of a song control nucleus in the canary: A quantitative Golgi study. *Journal of Comparative Neurology, 196,* 309–316.

DeWied, D. (1969). Effects of peptide hormones on behavior. In W.F. Ganong and J.L. Martini (Eds.), *Frontiers in neuroendocrinology.* New York: Oxford University Press.

DeWied, D. (1971). Long term effect of vasopressin on the maintenance of a conditioned avoidance response in rats. *Nature, 232,* 58–60.

DeWied, D. (1974). Pituitary-adrenal system hormones and behavior. In F.O. Schmitt & F.G. Worden (Eds.), *The neurosciences, third study program* (pp. 653–666). Cambridge, MA: MIT Press.

DeWied, D. (1980). *Proceedings Royal Society of London, Serial, B, 210,* 183–195.

DeWied, D., Bohus, B., Van Ree, J.M., Kovac, G.L., & Greven, H.M. (1978). Neuroleptic-like activity of [des-try]-gamma-endorphin in rats. *Lancet, 1,* 1046.

DeWied, D., Bohus, B., & van Wimersma Greidanus, Tj.B. (1975). Memory deficit in rats with hereditary diabetis-insipidus. *Brain Research, 85,* 152–156.

DeWied, D., Van Ree, J.M., & Greven, H.M. (1980). Neuroleptic-like activity of peptides related to [Des-tyr gamma]-gamma-endorphin: Structure activity studies. *Life Science, 26,* 1575–1579.

Dews, P.B., & Wiesel, T.M. (1970). Consequence of monocular deprivation on visual behavior in kittens. *Journal of Physiology, 206,* 437–455.

Diamond, I.T., & Hall, W.C. (1969). Evolution of neocortex. *Science, 164,* 251–262.

Diamond, M.C., Johnson R.E., Ingram, C., Rosenzweig, M.E., & Bennett, E.L. (1975). Effects of differential experience on neuronal nuclear and perikarya dimensions in the rat cerebral cortex. *Behavioral Biology, 15,* 107–111.

Diamond, M.C., Law, F., Rhodes, H., Lindner, B., Rosenzweig, M.R., Krech, D., & Bennett, E.L. (1966). Increases in cortical depth and glial numbers in rats subjected to enriched environments. *Journal of Comparative Neurology, 128,* 117–126.

Disterhoft, J.F., & Segal, M. (1978). Neuron activity in rat hippocampus and motor cortex during discrimination reversal. *Brain Research Bulletin, 3,* 583–588.

Disterhoft, J.F., & Stuart, D.K. (1976). The trial sequence of changed unit activity in auditory system of alert rat during conditioned response acquisition and extinction. *Journal of Neurophysiology, 39,* 266–281.

Disterhoft, J.F., & Stuart, D.K. (1977). Differentiated short latency response increases after conditioning in inferior colliculus neurons of alert rat. *Brain Research, 130,* 315–333.

Donegan, N.H., Gluck, M.A., & Thompson, R.F. (in press). Integrating behavioral and biological models of classical conditioning. In R.D. Hawkins & G.H. Bower (Eds.), *The psychology of learning and motivation.* New York: Academic Press.

Donegan, N.H., Lowry, R.W., & Thompson, R.F. (1983). Effects of lesioning cerebellar nuclei on conditioned leg-flexion responses. *Neuroscience Abstracts, 91,* 331 (No. 100.7).

Donegan, N.H., & Wagner, A.R. (1987). Conditioned diminution and facilitation of the UCR: A sometimes-apparent-process interpretation. In I. Gormezano, W.F. Prokasy, & R.F. Thompson (Eds.), *Classical conditioning: III. Behavioral, neurophysiological and neurochemical studies in the rabbit.* Hillsdale, NJ: Erlbaum.

Donovick, P.J., & Schwartzbaum, J.S. (1966). Effects of low-level stimulation of the septal area on two types of discrimination reversal in the rat. *Psychonomic Science, 6,* 3–4.

Doty, R.W. (1971). Survival of pattern vision after removal of striate cortex in the cat. *Journal of Comparative Neurology, 143,* 341–369.

Doty, R.W., & Rutledge, L.T. (1959). Generalization between cortically and peripherally applied stimuli eliciting conditioned reflexes. *Journal of Neurophysiology, 22,* 428–435.

Doty, R.W., Rutledge, L.T., Jr., & Larsen, R.M. (1956). Conditioned reflexes established to electrical stimulation of cat cerebral cortex. *Journal of Neurophysiology, 19,* 401–415.

Douglas, R.J. (1967). The hippocampus and behavior. *Psychological Bulletin, 67,* 416–442.

Drachman, D.A. (1977). Memory and cognitive function in man: Does the cholinergic system have a specific role? *Neurology, 27,* 783–790.

Dru, D., Walker, J.P., & Walker, J.B. (1975a). Recovery of pattern vision following serial lesions of striate cortex. *Brain Research, 88,* 353–356.

Dru, D., Walker, J.P., & Walker, J.B. (1975b). Self-produced locomotion restores visual capacity after striate lesions. *Science, 187,* 265–266.

Dudai, Y. (1979). Behavioral plasticity in a *Drosophila* mutant, *dunce* DB276. *Journal of Comparative Physiology, 130,* 217–275.

Dudai, Y., Jan, Y.N., Byers, D., Quinn, W.G., & Benzer, S. (1976). *Dunce,* a mutant of *Drosophila* deficient in learning. *Proceedings of the National Academy of Sciences USA, 73,* 1684–1688.

Duerr, J.S., & Quinn, W.G. (1982). Three *Drosophila* mutations that block associative learning also affect habituation and sensitization. *Proceedings of the National Academy of Sciences USA, 79,* 3646–3650.

Dufosse, M., Ito, M., Jastrehoff, P.J., & Miyashita, Y. (1978). Diminution and reversal of eye movements induced by local stimulation of rabbit cerebellar flocculus after partial destruction of the inferior olive. *Experimental Brain Research, 33,* 139–141.

Duncan, C.P. (1949). The retroactive effect of electroshock on learning. *Journal of Comparative Physiological Psychology, 42,* 32–44.

Dunn, A.J. (1980). Neurochemistry of learning and memory: An evaluation of recent data. *Annual Review of Psychology, 31,* 343–390.

Durkovic, R.G. (1975). Classical conditioning, sensitization, and habituation of the flexion reflex of the spinal cat. *Physiology & Behavior, 14,* 297–304.

Eccles, J.C. (1964). *The physiology of synapses.* New York: Academic Press.

Eccles, J.C. (1977). An instruction-selection theory of learning in the cerebellar cortex. *Brain Research, 127,* 327–352.

Eisenstein, E.M. (1967). The use of invertebrate systems for studies on the basis of learning and memory. In G.C. Quarton, T. Melnechuk, and F.O. Schmitt (Eds.), *The Neurosciences: A study program.* New York: Rockefellar University Press.

Eisenstein, E.M., & Cohen, M.J. (1965). Learning in an isolated prothoracic insect ganglion. *Animal Behavior, 13,* 104–108.

Eiserer, L.A., & Hoffman, H.S. (1973). Priming of duckling's responses by presenting an imprinted stimulus. *Journal of Comparative & Physiological Psychology, 82,* 345–359.

Erber, J. (1975a). The dynamics of learning in the honeybee (*Apis mellifica carnica*): I. The time dependence of the choice reaction. *Journal of Comparative Physiology, 99,* 231–242.

Erber, J. (1975b). The dynamics of learning in the honeybee (*Apis mellifica carnica*): II. Principles of information processing. *Journal of Comparative Physiology*, *99*, 243–255.

Erber, J. (1978). Response characteristics and after effects of multimodal neurons in the mushroom body area of the honey bee. *Physiological Entomology*, *3*, 77–89.

Erber, J. (1980). Neural correlates of non-associative and associative learning in the honey bee. *Verhandlugen der Deutschen Zoologischen Gesellshaft* (Gottingen), *73*, 250–261.

Erber, J. (1981). Neural correlates of learning in the honey bee. *Trends in Neuroscience*, *4*, 270–273.

Erber, J. (1984). Response changes of single neurons during learning in the honeybee. In D.L. Alkon & J. Farley (Eds.), *Primary neural substrates of learning and behavioral change*. Cambridge: Cambridge University Press.

Erber, J., & Gronenberg, W. (1981). Multimodality and plasticity of visual interneurons in the bee. *Verhandlugen der Deutschen Zoologischen Gesellshaft* (Gottingen) (Abstract), *74*, 177.

Erber, J., Masuhr, Th., & Menzel, R. (1980). Localization of short-term memory in the brain of the bee, *Apis mellifera*. *Physiological Entomology*, *5*, 343–358.

Erickson, C.K., & Patel, J.B. (1969). Facilitation of avoidance learning by posttrial hippocampal electrical stimulation. *Journal of Comparative & Physiological Psychology*, *68*, 400–406.

Evans, E.F., Ross, H.F., & Whitfield, I.C. (1965). The spatial distribution of unit characteristic frequency in the primary auditory cortex of the cat. *Journal of Physiology*, *179*, 238–247.

Evans, E.F., & Whitfield, I.C. (1964). Classification of unit responses in the auditory cortex of the unanesthetized and unrestrained cat. *Journal of Physiology*, *171*, 476–493.

Evarts, E.V. (1973). Motor cortex reflexes associated with learned movement. *Science*, *179*, 501.

Fanselow, M.S., & Bolles, R.C. (1979). Naloxone and shock-elicited freezing in the rat. *Journal of Comparative & Physiological Psychology*, *93*, 736–744.

Farel, P.B., Glanzman, D.L., & Thompson, R.F. (1973). Habituation of a monosynaptic response in the vertebrate central nervous system: Lateral column-motoneuron pathway in isolated frog spinal cord. *Journal of Neurophysiology*, *36*, 1117–1130.

Farel, P.B., & Thompson, R.F. (1976). Habituation of a monosynaptic response in frog spinal cord: Evidence for presynaptic mechanism. *Journal of Neurophysiology*, *39*, 661–666.

Farley, J., & Alkon, D.L. (1982a). Associative neural and behavioral change in *Hermissenda*: Consequences nervous system orientation for light- and pairing-specificity. *Journal of Neurophysiology*, *48*, 785–808.

Farley, J., & Alkon, D.L. (1982b). Cumulative cellular depolarization and short-term associative conditioning in *Hermissenda*. *Society for Neuroscience Absracts*, *8*, 825.

Farley, J., Richards, W.G., Ling, L.J., Lliman, E., & Alkon, D.L. (1983). Membrane changes in a single photoreceptor cause associative learning in *Hermissenda*. *Science*, *221*, 1201–1203.

Farley, J., Sakakibara, M., & Alkon, D.L. (1984). Associative-training correlated changes in $I_{Ca-K}$ in *Hermissenda* type B photoreceptors. *Society for Neuroscience Abstracts*, *10*, 270.

Ferrier, D. (1886). *The functions of the brain*. London: Smith & Elder.

Fibiger, H.C. (1982). The organization and some projections of cholinergic neurons of the mammalian forebrain. *Brain Research Review*, *4*, 327–388.

Fifkova, E. (1968). Changes in the visual cortex of rats after unilateral deprivation. *Nature*, *220*, 379–381.

Fifkova, E. (1969). The effect of monocular deprivation on the synaptic contacts of the visual cortex. *Journal of Neurobiology*, *1*, 285–294.

Fifkova, E. (1970). The effect of unilateral deprivation on visual centers in rats. *Journal of Neurobiology*, *1*, 285–294.

Fifkova, E., Van Der Wede, B., & Van Harreveld, A. (1978). Ultrastructural changes in dentate molecular layer during conditioning. *Anatomical Record*, *190*, 394.

Fifkova, E., & Van Harreveld, A. (1977). Long-lasting morphological changes in dendritic spines of dentate granular cells following stimulation of the entorhinal area. *Journal of Neurocytology*, *6*, 211–230.

Fifkova, E., & Van Harreveld, A. (1978). Changes in dendritic spines of the dentate molecular layer during conditioning. *Neuroscience Abstracts*, *4*, 257.

Finger, S. (Ed.). (1978). *Recovery from brain damage*. New York: Plenum Press.

Fitzgerald, L.A., & Thompson, R.F. (1967). Classical conditioning of the hindlimb flexion reflex in the acute spinal cat. *Psychonomic Science*, *9*, 511–512.

Flechsig, P.E. (1898). Neue Untersuchungen uber die Markbildung in den menschlichen Grosshirnlappen. *Neurol. Abl.*, *17*, 977–996.

Flexner, J.B. & Flexner, L.B. (1967). Restoration of expression of memory lost after treatment with puromycin. *Proceedings of the National Academy of Sciences. USA*, *57*, 1651–1654.

Flexner, J.B., & Flexner, L.B. (1970). Adrenalectomy

and the suppression of memory by puromycin. *Proceedings of the National Academy of Sciences USA, 66,* 46–52.

Flexner, J.B., Flexner, L.B., & Stellar, E. (1963). Memory in mice as affected by intracerebral puromycin. *Science, 141,* 57–59.

Flexner, J.B., Flexner, L.B., Stellar, E., de la Haba, G., & Roberts, R.B. (1962). Inhibition of protein synthesis in brain and learning and memory following puromycin. *Journal of Neurochemistry, 9,* 595–605.

Flexner, L.B., Serota, R.G., & Goodman, R.H. (1973). Cycloheximide and acetoxycycloheximide: inhibition of tyrosine hydroxylase activity and amnestic effects. *Proceedings of the National Academy of Sciences USA, 70,* 354–356.

Flood, J.F., Jarvik, M.E., Bennett, E.L., & Orme, A.E. (1976). Effects of ACTH peptide fragments on memory formation. *Pharmacology Biochemistry Behavior, 5,* 41–51.

Foreman, R., Alkon, D.L., Sakakibara, M., Harrigan, J., Lederhendler, I., & Farley, J. (1984). Changes in $I_A$ and $I_C$ but not $I_{Na}$ accompant retention of conditioned behavior in *hermissenda. Society for Neuroscience Abstracts, 10,* 121.

Forgays, D.G., & Read, J.M. (1962). Crucial periods for free-environmental experience in the rat. *Journal of Comparative & Physiological Psychology, 55,* 816–818.

Forgus, R.H. (1955). Early visual and motor experience as determiners of complex maze learning ability under rich and reduced stimulation. *Journal of Comparative & Physiological Psychology, 9,* 207–214.

Forman, R., & Hoyle, G. (1978). Position learning in behaviorally appropriate situation. *Eighth Annual Meeting Neurosciences Society,* abstract #591.

Francis, J., Hernandez, L.L., & Powell, D.A. (1981). Lateral hypothalamic lesions: Effects on Pavlovian conditioning of eyeblink and heart rate responses in the rabbit. *Brain Research Bulletin, 6,* 155–163.

French, G.M. (1959). Locomotor effects of regional ablation of frontal cortex in rhesus monkeys. *Journal of Comparative & Physiological Psychology, 52,* 18–24.

French, G.M., & Harlow, H.F. (1962). Variability of delayed-reaction performance in normal and brain-damaged rhesus monkeys. *Journal of Neurophysiology, 25,* 585–599.

Fritsch, G.T., & Hitzig, E. (1870). Uber die elektrische Erregbarkeit des Grosshirns. *Arch. Anat. Physiol. wiss Med., 37,* 300–332.

Frost, W.N., Castellucci, V.F., Hawkins, R.D., & Kandel, E.R. (1985) Monosynaptic connections made by the sensory neurons of the gill- and siphon-withdrawal reflex in *Aplysia* participate in the storage of long-term memory for sensitization. *Proceedings of the National Academy of Science, USA, 82,* 8266–8269.

Fuller, H.H., & Schlag, J.D. (1976). Determination of antidromic excitation by the collision test: Problems of interpretation. *Brain Research, 112,* 283–298.

Fuster, J.M. (1973). Unit activity in prefrontal cortex during delayed-response performance: neuronal correlates of transient memory. *Journal of Neurophysiology, 36,* 61–78.

Fuster, J.M. (1980). *The prefrontal cortex: Anatomy, physiology and neuropsychology of the frontal lobes.* New York: Raven.

Fuster, J.M., & Alexander, G.E. (1971). Neuronal activity related to short-term memory. *Science, 173,* 652–654.

Gabriel, M., Saltwich, S.L., & Miller, J.D. (1975). Conditioning and reversal of short-latency multiple-unit response in the rabbit medial geniculate nucleus. *Science, 189,* 1108–1109.

Gaffan, D. (1972). Loss of recognition memory in rats with lesion of the fornix. *Neuropsychologia, 10,* 327–341.

Gallagher, M., Kapp, B.S., Frysinger, R.C., & Rapp, P.R. (1980). Beta-adrenergic manipulation in amygdala central nucleus alters rabbit heart rate conditioning. *Pharmacology, Biochemistry & Behavior, 12,* 419.

Ganz, L. (1975). Orientation in visual space by neonates and its modification by visual deprivation. In A.H. Riesen (Ed.), *The development neuropsychology of sensory deprivation.* New York: Academic Press.

Ganz, L., & Fitch, M. (1968). The effect of visual deprivation on perceptual behavior. *Experimental Neurology, 22,* 638–660.

Garcia, J., Rusiniak, K.W., Kiefer, S.W., & Bermudez-Rattoni, F. (1982). The neural integration of feeding and drinking habits. See Woody 1982. In press.

Garey, L.J., & Pettigrew, J.D. (1974). Ultrastructural changes in kitten visual cortex after environmental modification. *Brain Research, 66,* 165–172.

Gash, D.M., & Thomas, G.J. (1983). What is the importance of vasopressin in memory processes? *Trends in Neurosciences, 6*(6), 197–198.

Gelperin, A., Hopfield, J.J., & Tank, D.W. (1985). The logic of *Limax* learning. In A.I. Selverston (Ed.) *Model Neural Networks and Behavior.* New York: Plenum Press.

Gelperin, A., Wieland, S.J., & Barry, S.R. (1984). A strategy for cellular analysis of associative learning in a terrestrial mollusk. In D.L. Alkon &

J. Farley (Eds.), *Primary neural substrates of learning and behavioral change.* Cambridge MA: Cambridge University Press.

Gerard, R.W. (1949). Physiology and psychiatry. *American Journal of Psychiatry, 106,* 161–173.

Gibbs, C.M., & Cohen, D.H. (1980). Plasticity of the thalamofugal pathway during visual conditioning. *Neuroscience Abstracts, 6,* 424.

Gibbs, M.E., Robertson, S., & Hambly, J. (1977). Amino acid uptake required for long-term memory formation. *Neuroscience Letters, 4,* 293–297.

Gilbert, P.F.C., & Thack, W.T. (1977). Purkinje cell activity during motor learning. *Brain Research, 128,* 309–328.

Gilman, S., Bloedel, J.R., Lechtenberg, R. (1981). In *Disorders of the cerebellum.* Philadelphia, PA: F.A. Davis Company.

Gingrich, K.J. & Byrne, J.H. (1985). Simulation of synaptic depression, posttetanic potentiation, and presynaptic facilitation of synaptic potentials from sensory neurons mediating gill-withdrawal reflex in *Aplysia. Journal of Neurophysiology, 53,* 652–669.

Girden, E., Mettler, F.A., Finch, G., & Culler, E. (1936). Conditioned responses in a decorticate dog to acoustic, thermal, and tactile stimulation. *Journal of Comparative Psychology. 21,* 376–385.

Glanzman, D.L. (1976). Synaptic mechanisms of habituation. Dissertation submitted to University of California at Irvine.

Glanzman, D.L., & Thompson, R.F. (1980). Alterations in spontaneous miniature potential activity during habituation of a vertebrate monosynaptic pathway. *Brain Research, 189,* 377–390.

Glendenning, R.L. (1972). Effects of training between two unilateral lesions of visual cortex upon ultimate retention of black–white habits by rats. *Journal of Comparative & Physiological Psychology, 80,* 216–229.

Globus, A. (1975). Brain morphology as a function of presynaptic morphology and activity. In A.H. Riesen (Ed.), *The developmental neuropsychology of sensory deprivation* (pp. 9–92). New York: Academic Press.

Globus, D., Rosenzweig, M.R., Bennett, E.L., & Diamond, M.C. (1973). Effects of differential experience on dendritic spine counts in rat cerebral cortex. *Journal of Comparative & Physiological Psychology, 82,* 175–181.

Gluck, M.A., & Thompson, R.F. (1987). Modeling the neural substrates of associative learning and memory: A computational approach. *Psychological Review, 94,* 176–191.

Goddard, G. (1964). Functions of the amygdala. *Psychological Bulletin, 62,* 89–109.

Goh, Y., & Alkon, D.L. (1984). Sensory, interneuronal, and motor interactions within *Hermissenda* visual pathway. *Journal of Neurophysiology, 52,* 156–169.

Gold, P.E., Haycock, J.W., Macri, J., McGaugh, J.L. (1973). Retrograde amnesia and the "reminder effect": An alternative interpretation. *Science, 180,* 1199–1201.

Gold, P.E., & McGaugh, J.L. (1975). A single-trace, two process view of memory storage processes. In D. Deutsch & J.A. Deutsch (Eds.), *Short-term memory* (pp. 355–378). New York: Academic Press.

Gold, P.E., & McGaugh, J.L. (1977). Hormones and memory. In L.H. Miller, C.A. Sandman, & A.J. Kastin (Eds.), *Neuropeptide influences on the brain and behavior* (pp. 127–143). New York: Raven.

Gold, P.E. & Sternberg, D.B. (1980). Neurobiology of amnesia. *Science, 209,* 836–837.

Gold, P.E., & van Buskirk, R. (1976). Effects of posttrial hormone injections on memory processes. *Hormones & Behavior, 7,* 509–517.

Gold, P.E., & van Buskirk, R. (1978a). Post-training brain norepinephrine concentrations: Correlation with retention performance of avoidance training and with peripheral epinephrine modulation of memory processing. *Behavioral Biology, 23,* 509–520.

Gold, P.E., & van Buskirk, R. (1978b). Effects of alpha and beta-adrenergic receptor antagonists on posttrial epinephrine modulation of memory: Relationship to post-training brain norepinephrine concentrations. *Behavioral Biology, 24,* 168–184.

Gold, P.E., & Zornetzer, S.F. (1983). The mnemon and its juices: Neuromodulation of memory processes. *Behavioral & Neural Biology, 38,* 151–189.

Goldberger, M.E., & Murray, M. (1978). Recovery of movement and axonal sprouting may obey some of the same laws. In C.W. Cotman (Ed.), *Neuronal plasticity.* New York: Raven Press.

Goldman, P.S. (1971). Functional development of the prefrontal cortex in early life and the problem of neuronal plasticity. *Experimental Neurology, 32,* 366–387.

Goldman, P.S. (1972). Developmental determinants of cortical plasticity. *Acta Neurobiologiae Experimentalis, 32,* 495–511.

Goldman, P.S. (1974). An alternative to developmental plasticity: heterology of CNS structures in infants and adults. In D.G. Stein, J.J. Rosen, & N. Butters (Eds.), *Plasticity and recovery of function in the central nervous system* (pp. 149–174). New York: Academic Press.

Goldman, P.S., & Nauta, W.J.H. (1977). Columnar distribution of cortico-cortical fibers in the frontal association, motor, and limbic cortex of the developing rhesus monkey. *Brain Research, 122,* 393–413.

Goldman, P.S., Rosvold, H.E., & Mishkin, M. (1970a). Evidence for behavioral impairment following prefrontal lobectomy in the infant monkey. *Journal of Comparative & Physiological Psychology, 70,* 454–463.

Goldman, P.S., Rosvold, H.E., & Mishkin, M. (1970b). Selective sparing of function following prefrontal lobectomy in infant monkeys. *Experimental Neurology, 29,* 221–226.

Goldman, S.A., & Nottebohm, F. (1983). Neuronal production, migration and differentiation in a vocal control nucleus of the adult female canary brain. *Proceedings of the National Academy of Sciences, 80,* 2390–2394.

Goldman-Rakic, P.S., & Brown, R.M. (1981). Regional changes of monamines in cerebral cortex and subcortical structures of aging rhesus monkeys. *Neuroscience, 6,* 177–187.

Goldman-Rakic, P.S., & Schwartz, M.L. (1982). Interdigitation of contralateral and ipsilateral columnar projections to frontal association cortex in primates. *Science, 216,* 755–757.

Goldstein, M.H., Jr., Abeles, M., Daly, R.L., & McIntosh, J. (1970). Functional architecture in cat primary auditory cortex: Tonotopic organization. *Journal of Neurophysiology, 33,* 188–197.

Goodman, D.C., & Horel, J.A. (1966). Sprouting of optic tract projections in the brain stem of the rat. *Journal of Comparative Neurology, 127,* 71–88.

Goodman, R.H., Flexner, J.B., & Flexner, L.B. (1975). The effect of acetoxycycloheximide on rate of accumulation of cerebral catecholamines from circulating tyrosine as related to its effect on memory. *Proceedings of the National Academy of Sciences USA, 72,* 479–482.

Gormezano, I. (1972). Investigations of defense and reward conditioning in the rabbit. In A.H. Black and W.F. Prokasy (Eds.), *Classical conditioning: II. Current research and theory* (pp. 151–181). New York: Appleton-Century-Crofts.

Gormezano, I., Schneiderman, N., Deaux, E., & Fuentes, I. (1962). Nictitating membrane: Classical conditioning and extinction in the albino rabbit. *Science, 138,* 33–34.

Graf, P., Mandler, G., & Haden, P.E. (1982). Simulating amnesic symptoms in normal subjects. *Science, 218,* 1243–1244.

Gray, J.A. (1970). Sodium amobarbital, the hippocampal theta rhythm and the partial reinforcement extinction effect. *Psychological Review, 77,* 465–480.

Gray, J.A. (1982). *The Neuropsychology of Anxiety.* Oxford: Oxford University Press.

Gray, J.A., Araujo-Silva, M.T. & Quintao, L. (1972). Resistance to extinction after partial reinforcement training with blocking of the hippocampal theta rhythm by septal stimulation. *Physiol. Behav., 8,* 497–502.

Gray, T.S., & LeVere, T.E. (1980). Infant posterior neocortical lesions do not induce visual responses in spared anterior neocortex. *Physiological Psychology, 8,* 487–492.

Gray, T.S., & Meyer, D.R. (1981). Effects of mixed training and overtraining on recoveries from amnesias in rats with visual cortical ablations. *Physiological Psychology, 9,* 54–62.

Green, E.J., Schlumpf, B.E., & Greenough, W.T. (1981). The effects of complex or isolated environments on cortical dendrites of middle-aged rats. *Neuroscience Abstracts, 7,* 65.

Greenough, W.T., Fass, B., & DeVoogd, T.J. (1976). The influence of experience on recovery following brain damage in rodents: Hypotheses based on development research. In R.N. Walsh & W.T. Greenough (Ed.), *Environments as therapy for brain dysfunction.* New York: Plenum Press.

Greenough, W.T., Fulcher, J.K., Yuwiler, A., & Geller, E. (1970). Enriched rearing and chronic electroshock: Effects on brain and behavior in mice. *Physiology & Behavior, 5,* 371–373.

Greenough, W.T., Juraska, J.M., & Volkmar, F.R. (1979). Maze training on dendritic branching in occipital cortex of adult rats. *Behavioral & Neural Biology, 26,* 287–297.

Greenough, W.T., West, R.W., & DeVoogd, T.J. (1978). Subsynaptic plate perforations: Changes with age and experience in the rat. *Science, 202,* 1096–1098.

Gregory, R.L. (1961). The brain as an engineering problem. In W.H. Thorpe & O.L. Zangwill (Eds.). *Current problems in animal behavior.* Cambridge, MA: Cambridge University Press.

Gross, C.G. (1963). Locomotor activity under various stimulus conditions following partial lateral frontal cortical lesions in monkeys. *Journal of Comparative & Physiological Psychology, 56,* 232–236.

Grossman, S.P., Grossman, L., & Walsh, L. (1975). Functional organization of the rat amygdala with respect to avoidance behavior. *Journal of Comparative & Physiological Psychology, 88,* 829.

Grover, L., & Farley, J. (1983). Temporal order sensitivity of associative learning in *Hermissenda. Society for Neuroscience Abstracts, 9,* 915.

Groves, P.M., DeMarco, R., & Thompson, R.F. (1969). Habituation and sensitization of spinal interneuron activity in acute spinal cat. *Brain Research, 14,* 521–525.

Groves, P.M., Glanzman, D.L., Patterson, M.M., & Thompson, R.F. (1970). Excitability of cutaneous afferent terminals during habituation and sensitization in acute spinal cat. *Brain Research, 18,* 388–392.

Groves, P.M., & Thompson, R.F. (1970). Habituation: A dual-process theory. *Psychological Review, 77,* 419–450.

Guettinger, H.R. (1981). Self-differentiation of song organization rules by deaf canaries. *Zeitschrift fur Tierpsychologie, 56,* 323–340.

Gyllensten, L., Malmfors, T., & Norrlin, M. (1965). Effect of visual deprivation on the optic centers of growing and adult mice. *Journal of Comparative Neurology, 124,* 149–160.

Haley, D.A., Lavond, D.G., & Thompson, R.F. (1983). Effects of contralateral red nuclear lesions on retention of the classically conditioned nictitating membrane/eyelid response. *Neuroscience Abstracts, 9,* 643 (No. 190.8).

Harlow, H.F., Blomquist, A.J., Thompson, C.I., Schiltz, K.A., & Harlow, M.K. (1968). In R. Isaacson (Ed.), *The Neuropsychology of development* (pp. 79–120). New York: Wiley.

Harlow, H.F., Davis, R.T., Settlage, P.H., & Meyer, D.R. (1952). Analysis of frontal and posterior association syndromes in brain-damaged monkeys. *Journal of Comparative & Physiological Psychology, 45,* 419–429.

Hawkins, R.D., Abrams, T.W., Carews, T.J., & Kandel, E.R. (1983). A cellular mechanism of classical conditioning in *Aplysia*: Activity-dependent amplification of presynaptic facilitation. *Science, 219,* 400–405.

Hawkins, R.D., Carew, T.J., & Kandel, E.R. (1983). Effects of interstimulus interval and contingency on classical conditioning in *Aplysia. Society for Neurophysiology Abstracts, 9,* 168.

Hawkins, R.D., Castellucci, V.F., & Kandel, E.R. (1981). Interneurons involved in mediation and modulation of gill-withdrawal reflex in *Aplysia:* II. Identified neurons produce heterosynaptic facilitation contributing to behavioral sensitization. *Journal of Neurophysiology, 45,* 315–326.

Hawkins, R.D., & Kandel, E.R. (1984). Is there a cell-biological alphabet for simple forms of learning? *Psychological Review, 91,* 375–391.

Hearst, E. (1972). Some persistent problems in the analysis of conditioned inhibition. In R.A. Boakes, & M.S. Halliday (Eds.), *Inhibition and learning.* (pp. 5–39). New York: Academic Press.

Hebb, D.O. (1949). *The organization of behavior.* New York: Wiley.

Heise, G.A. (1981). Learning and memory facilitators: Experimental definition and current status. *Trends in Pharmacological Science, June,* 158–160.

Herrnstein, R.J. (1970). On the law of effect. *Journal of the Experimental Analysis of Behavior, 13,* 243–266.

Herrnstein, R.J., & Heyman, G.M. (1979). Is matching compatible with reinforcement maximization on concurrent variable interval, variable ratio? *Journal of the Experimental Analysis of Behavior, 31,* 209–223.

Hertel, H. (1980). Chromatic properties of identified interneurons in the optic lobes of the bee. *Journal of Comparative Physiology, 137,* 215–231.

Hess, E.H. (1973). *Imprinting.* New York: Van Nostrand Reinhold.

Heyman, G.M. (1983). A parametric evaluation of the hedonic and motoric effects of drugs: Pimozide and amphetamine. *Journal of the Experimental Analysis of Behavior, 40,* 113–122.

Hilgard, E.R., & Marquis, D.G. (1935). Acquisition, extinction, and retention of conditioned lid responses to light in dogs. *Journal of Comparative Psychology, 19,* 29–58.

Hilgard, E.R., & Marquis, D.G. (1936). Conditioned eyelid responses in monkeys, with a comparison of dog, monkey, and man. *Psychological Monographs, 47*(212), 186–198.

Hilgard, E.R., & Marquis, D.G. (1940). *Conditioning and learning.* New York: Appleton, Century, Crofts.

Hill, A.J. (1978). First occurrence of hippocampal spatial firing in a new environment. *Experimental Neurology, 62,* 282–297.

Hind, J.E., Rose, J.E., Davies, P.W., Woolsey, C.N., Benjamin, R.M., Welker, W.I., & Thompson, R.F. (1960). Unit activity in the auditory cortex. In G.L. Rasmussen & W.F. Windle (Eds.) *Neural Mechanisms of the Auditory and Vestibular Systems.* Springfield, Illinois: Thomas.

Hirsh, H.V.B., & Spinelli, D.N. (1970). Visual experience modifies distribution of horizontally and vertically oriented receptive fields in cats. *Science, 168,* 869–871.

Hirsch, H.V.B., & Spinelli, D.N. (1971). Modification of the distribution of receptive field orientation in cats by selective visual exposure during development. *Experimental Brain Research, 13,* 509–527.

Hirsch, R. (1974). The hippocampus and contextual retrieval of information from memory: A theory. *Behavioral Biology, 12,* 421–444.

Hirsch, R. (1980). The hippocampus, conditional operations, and cognition. *Physiological Psychology, 8,* 175–182.

Hirsch, R., & Krajden, J. (1982). The hippocampus and the expression of knowledge. In R.L. Isaacson & N.E. Spear (Eds.), *The expression of knowledge.* New York: Plenum.

Hitchcock, J., & Davis, M. (1986). Lesions of the amygdala but not the cerebellum or red nucleus, blocked conditioned fear as measured with the potentiated startle paradigm. *Behavioral Neuroscience, 100*, 11–22.

Hoehler, F.K., & Thompson, R.F. (1980). Effect of the interstimulus (CS-UCS) interval on hippocampal unit activity during classical conditioning of the nictitating membrane response of the rabbit, *Oryctrolagus cuniculus. Journal of Comparative & Physiological Psychology, 94*, 201–215.

Hoffman, H.S., Barrett, J., Ratner, A., & Singer, D. (1972). Conditioned suppression of distress calls in imprinted ducklings. *Journal of Comparative & Physiological Psychology, 80*, 357–364.

Hoffman, H.S., & Ratner, A.M. (1973). A reinforcement model of imprinting: Implications for socialization in monkeys and men. *Psychological Review, 80*, 527–544.

Hoffman, H.S., & Segal, M. (1983). Biological factors in social attachments: A new view of a basic phenomenon. In M.D. Zeiler & P. Harzem (Eds.), *Advances in the analysis of behavior; Vol. 3.* New York: John Wiley & Sons.

Hoffman, H.S., Searle, J.L., Toffey, S., & Kozma, F., Jr. (1966). Behavioral control by an imprinted stimulus. *Journal of the Experimental Analysis of Behavior, 9*, 177–189.

Hokfelt, T., Ljungdahl, A., Fuxe, K., & Johansson, O. (1974). Dopamine nerve terminals in the rat limbic cortex: Aspects of the dopamine hypothesis of schizophrenia. *Science, 184*, 177–179.

Hollis, K.L. (1982). Pavlovian conditioning of signal-centered action patterns and automatic behavior: A biological analysis of function. In J.S. Rosenblatt, R.A. Hinde, C. Beer, & M.C. Busnel (Eds.), *Advances in the study of behavior; Vol. 12.* New York: Academic Press.

Holt, L., & Gray, J.A. (1983). Septal driving of the hippocampal theta rhythm produces a long-term, proactive and non-associative increase in resistance to extinction. *Quarterly Journal of Experimental Psychology, 358*, 97–118.

Homberg, U. (1981). Recordings and Lucifer yellow stainings of neurons from the tractus olfactoglobularis in the bee brain. *Verh. Deut. Zool. Gesell.* (Abstract), *74*, 176.

Horel, J.A. (1978). The neuroanatomy of amnesia: A critique of the hippocampal memory hypothesis. *Brain, 101*, 403–445.

Horel, J.A., Bettinger, L.A., Royce, G.J., & Meyer, D.R. (1966). Role of neocortex in the learning and relearning of two visual habits by the rat. *Journal of Comparative & Physiological Psychology, 61*, 66–78.

Horel, J.A., & Keating, E.G. (1972). Recovery from a partial Kluver–Bucy syndrome in the monkey produced by disconnection. *Journal of Comparative & Physiological Psychology, 79*, 105–114.

Horel, J.A., & Misatone, L.J. (1976). Visual discrimination impaired by cutting temporal lobe connections. *Science, 193*, 336–338.

Horn, G. (1971). Neural mechanisms of learning: An anlysis of imprinting in the domestic chick. *Proceeding of the Royal Society of London Ser. B. 213*, 101–137.

Horn, G. (1981). Neural mechanisms of learning: An analysis of imprinting in the domestic chick. *Proceedings of the Royal Society of London Ser. V, 213*, 101–137.

Horn, G., Cipolla-Neto, J., & McCabe, B.J. (1980). Imprinting: Effects of sequential lesions to medial hyperstriatum ventrale (MHV). *Proc. XXVIII int. Cong. Physiol. Sci., 14*, 478. Budapest: Hungarian Physiological Society.

Horn, G., & Hinde, R.A. (Eds.) (1970). *Short-term changes in neural activity and behavior.* Cambridge MA: Cambridge University Press.

Horn, G., Horn, A.L.D., Bateson, P.P.G., & Rose, S.P.R. (1971). Effects of imprinting on uracil incorporation into brain RNA in the "split-brain" chick. *Nature, 229*, 131–132.

Horn, G., Rose, S.P.R., & Bateson, P.P.G. (1973). Monocular imprinting and regional incorporation of tritiated uracil into the brains of intact and "split-brain" chicks. *Brain Research, 56*, 227–237.

Horridge, G.A. (1962). Learning of leg position by the ventral nerve cord in headless insects. *Proceedings of the Royal Society (London), Ser. B, 157*, 33–52.

Horridge, G.A. (1965). The electrophysiological approach to learning in isolatable ganglia. *Animal Behavior, Supplement 1, 13*, 163–182.

Horvath, F.E. (1963). Effects of basolateral amygdalectomy on three types of avoidance behavior in cats. *Journal of Comparative & Physiological Psychology, 56*, 380–389.

Hostetter, G., Jubb, S.L., & Kozlowski, G.P. (1980). *Neuroendocrinology, 30*, 174–177.

Hoyle, G. (1965). Neurophysiological studies on "learning" in headless insects. In J.E. Treherne & J.W.L. Beament (Eds.), *The physiology of the insect central nervous system.* New York: Academic Press.

Hoyle, G. (1979). mechanisms of simple motor learning. *Trends in Neuroscience, 2*, 153–159.

Hoyle, G. (1980). Learning, using natural reinforcements, in insect preparations that permit cellular neuronal analysis. *Journal of Neurobiology, 11*, 323–354.

Hoyle, G. (1982). Cellular basis of operant-conditioning

of leg position. In C.E. Woody (Ed.), *Conditioning*. New York: Plenum.

Hubel, D.H., & Wiesel, T.N. (1959). Receptive fields of single neurones in the cat's striate cortex. *Journal of Physiology, 148*, 574–591.

Hubel, D.H., & Wiesel, T.N. (1962). Receptive fields, binocular interaction and functional architecture in the cat's visual cortex. *Journal of Physiology, 160*, 106–154.

Hubel, D.H., & Wiesel, T.N. (1965a). Binocular interaction in striate cortex of kittens reared with artificial squint. *Journal of Neurophysiology, 28*, 1041–1059.

Hubel, D.H., & Wiesel, T.N. (1965b). Receptive fields and functional architecture in two nonstriate visual areas (18 and 19) of the cat. *Journal of Neurophysiology, 28*, 229–289.

Hubel, D.H., & Wiesel, T.N. (1968). Receptive fields and functional architecture of monkey striate cortex. *Journal of Physiology, 195*, 215–243.

Hubel, D.H., & Wiesel, T.N. (1970a). Stereoscopic vision in macaque monkey. Cells sensitive to binocular depth in area 18 of macaque monkey cortex. *Nature, 225*, 41–42.

Hubel, D.H., & Wiesel, T.N. (1970b). The period of susceptibility to the physiological effects of unilateral eye closure in kittens. *Journal of Physiology, 206*, 419–436.

Hubel, D.H., & Wiesel, T.N. (1974). Sequence regularity and geometry of orientation in the monkey striate cortex. *Journal of Comparative Neurology, 158*, 267–293.

Hubel, D.H., Wiesel, T.N., & LeVay, S. (1977). Plasticity of ocular dominance columns in monkey striate cortex. *Philosophical Transactions of the Royal Society of London, B., 278*, 377–409.

Hubel, D.H., Wiesel, T.N., & Stryker, M.P. (1977). Orientation columns in macaque monkey visual cortex demonstrated by the 2-deoxyglucose autoradiographic technique. *Nature, 269*, 328–330.

Hull, C.L. (1934). Learning II: The factor of the conditioned reflex. In C. Murchison (Ed.), *Handbook of general experimental psychology*. Worcester, MA: Clark University Press.

Hull, C.L. (1943). *Principles of Behavior*. New York: Appleton-Century-Crofts.

Hunter, W.S. (1). The sensory control of the maze habit in the white rat. *Journal of Genetic Psychology, 36*, 505–537.

Hunter, W.S. (1930). A consideration of Lashley's theory of the equipotentiality of cerebral action. *Journal of Genetic Psychology, 3*, 455–468.

Hunter, W.S. (1934). Learning: IV. Experimental studies of learning. In C. Murchison (Ed.), *Hand-book of general experimental psychology*. Worcester, MA: Clark University Press.

Huppert, F.A., & Piercy, M. (1976). Recognition memory in amnesic patients: effect of temporal context and familiarity of material. *Cortex, 12*, 3–20.

Huppert, F.A., & Piercy, M. (1978). Dissociation between learning and remembering in organic amnesia. *Nature, 275*, 317–318.

Huppert, F.A., & Piercy, M. (1979). Normal and abnormal forgetting in organic amnesia: effects of locus of lesion. *Cortex, 15*, 385–390.

Hyden, H. (1979). A calcium-dependent mechanism for synapse and nerve cell membrance modulation. *Proceedings of the National Academy of Sciences USA, 71*, 2965–2968.

Hyden, H., & Egyhazi, E. (1964). Changes in RNA content and base composition in cortical neurons of rats in a learning experiment involving transfer of handedness. *Proceedings of the National Academy of Sciences USA, 52*, 1030–1035.

Hyden, H., & Lange, P.W. (1968). Protein synthesis in the hippocampal pyramidal cells of rats during a behavioral test. *Science, 159*, 1370–1373.

Hyden, H., & Lange, P.W. (1970). The effects of antiserum to S100 protein on behavior and amount of S100 in brain cells. *Journal of Neurobiology, 12*(3), 201–210.

Hyden, H., & Lange, P.W. (1975). Brain proteins in undernourished rats during learning. *Neurobiology, 5*, 84–100.

Hymovitch, B. (1952). The effects of experimental variables on problem solving in the rat. *Journal of Comparative & Physiological Psychology, 45*, 313–321.

Imig, T.J., & Morel, A. (1983), Organization of the thalamocortical auditory system in the cat. *Annual Review of Neuroscience, 6*, 95–120.

Immelmann, K. (1965). Pragungerscheinugen in der Gesangsentwicklung junger Zebrafinken. *Naturwiss., 52*, 169–170.

Immelmann, K. (1966). Zur ontogenetischen Gesangsentwicklung bei Prachtfinken. *Verhandlungen der Deutschen Zoologischen Gesellschaft (Gottingen)*, supplement 320–332.

Immelmann, K. (1969). Song development in the zebra finch and other estrildid finches. In R.A. Hinde (Ed.) *Bird vocalizations* (pp. 61–77). Cambridge, MA: Cambridge University Press.

Isaac, W., & DeVito, J.L. (1958). Effect of sensory stimulation on the activity of normal and prefrontal lobectomized monkeys. *Journal of Comparative & Physiological Psychology, 51*, 172–174.

Isaacson, R.L. (1976). Experimental brain lesions and memory. In M.R. Rosenzweig & E.L. Bennett

(Eds.), *Neural mechanisms of learning and memory* (pp. 521–543). Cambridge, MA: MIT Press.

Isaacson, R.L. (1982). *The limbic system* (2nd ed.). New York: Plenum Press.

Isaacson, R.L., & Pribram, K.H. (1975). *The hippocampus: Vols. 1, 2.* New York: Plenum.

Isaacson, R.L., & Spear, N.E. (Eds.) (1982). *The expression of knowledge.* New York: Plenum Press.

Ito, M. (1970). Neurophysiological aspects of the cerebellar motor control system. *International Journal of Neurology, 7,* 162–176.

Ito, M. (1974). The control mechanisms of cerebellar motor system. In F.O. Schmitt, & R.G. Worden (Eds.), *The neurosciences, third study program.* Boston: MIT Press.

Ito, M. (1982). Cerebellar control of the vestibulo-ocular reflex: Around the flocculus hypothesis. *Annual Review of Neuroscience, 5,* 275–296.

Ito, M. (1984). In *The cerebellum and neural control.* New York: Raven Press.

Iverson, S.D. (1976). Do hippocampal lesions produce amnesia in animals? *International Review of Neurobiology, 19,* 1–49.

Jacobsen, C.F. (1936). Studies of cerebral functions in primates: I. The functions of the frontal association areas in monkeys. *Comparative Psychology Monographs, 23,* 101–112.

John, E.R. (1967). *Mechanisms of memory.* New York: Academic Press.

John, E.R. (1972). Switchboard versus statistical theories of learning and memory. *Science, 177,* 850–864.

Johnson, D.A. (1972). Development aspects of recovery of function following septal lesions in the infant rat. *Journal of Comparative & Physiological Psychology, 78,* 331–348.

Jonason, K.R., Lauber, S., Robbins, M.J., Meyer, P.M., & Meyer, D.R. (1970). The effects of dl-amphetamine upon discrimination behaviors in rats with cortical lesions. *Journal of Comparative & Physiological Psychology, 73,* 47–55.

Jones, E.G., & Wise, S.P. (1977). Size, laminar and columnar distribution of efferent cells in the sensory-motor cortex of monkeys. *Journal of Comparative Neurology, 175,* 391–438.

Kaada, B.R. (1972). Stimulation and regional ablation of the amygdaloid complex with reference to functional representations. In B.E. Elftheriou (Ed.), *The neurobiology of the amygdala* (pp. 205–281). New York: Plenum.

Kandel, E.R. (1976). *Cellular basis of behavior.* San Francisco: W.H. Freeman and Co.

Kandel, E.R., Brunelli, M., Byrne, J., & Castellucci, V. (1976). A common presynaptic locus for the synaptic changes underlying short-term habituation and sensitization of the gill-withdrawal reflex in *Aplysia. Cold Spring Harbor Laboratory Symposium on Quantitative Biology LX: The Synapse,* 465–482.

Kandel, E.R., & Schwartz, J.H. (1982). Molecular biology of learning: Modulation of transmitter release. *Science, 218,* 433–443.

Kapp, S., Frysinger, R.C., Gallagher, M. & Haselton, J. (1979). Amygdala central nucleus lesions: Effects on heart rate conditioning in the rabbit. *Physiology & Behavior, 23,* 1109.

Kapp, B.S., Gallagher, M., Applegate, C.D., & Frysinger, R.C. (1982). The amygdala central nucleus: Contributions to conditioned cardiovascular responding during aversive Pavlovian conditioning in the rabbit. In C.D. Woody (Ed.), *Conditioning: Representation of involved neural functions* (pp. 581–599). New York: Plenum Press.

Karamian, A.I., Fanaralijian, V.V., & Kosareva, A.A. (1969). The functional and morphological evolution of the cerebellum and its role in behavior. In R. Llinas (Ed.), *Neurobiology of cerebellar evolution and development, first international symposium.* Chicago: American Medical Association

Kastin, A.J., Scollan, E.L., King, M.G., Schally, A.V., & Coy, D.H. (1976). Enkephalin and a potent analog facilitate maze performance after intraperitoneal administration in rats. *Pharmacology, Biochemistry & Behavior, 5,* 691–695.

Kelley, D.E., & Nottebohm, F. (1979). Projections of a telencephalic auditory nucleus—field L—in the canary. *Journal of Comparative Neurology, 183,* 455–470.

Kennard, M. (1942). Cortical reorganization of motor function: Studies on series of monkeys of various ages from infancy to maturity. *Archives of Neurology & Psychiatry, 47,* 227–240.

Kenyon, J., & Krieckhaus, E.E. (1965). Enhanced avoidance behavior following septal lesions in the rat as a function of lesion size and spontaneous activity. *Journal of Comparative & Physiological Psychology, 59,* 466–468.

Kesner, R.P., & Doty, R.W. (1968). Amnesia produced in cats by local seizure activity initiated from the amygdala. *Experimental Neurology, 21,* 58–68.

Kesner, R.P., Gibson, W.E., & LeClair, M.J. (1970). ECS as a punishing stimulus: Dependency on route of administration. *Physiology & Behavior, 5,* 683–686.

Kesner, R.P., & Wilbrun, M.W. (1974). A review of electrical stimulation of the brain in context of learning and retention. *Behavioral Biology, 10,* 259–293.

Kettner, R.E., Shannon, R.V., Nguyen, T.M., &

Thompson, R.F. (1980). Simultaneous behavioral and neural (Cochlear Nucleus) measurement during signal detection in the rabbit. *Perception & Psychophysics, 28*(6), 504–513.

Kettner, R.E., & Thompson, R.F. (1982). Auditory signal detection and decision processes in the nervous system. *Journal of Comparative & Physiological Psychology, 96*, 328–331.

Kettner, R.E., & Thompson, R.F. (1985). Cochlear nucleus, inferior colliculus and medial geniculate responses during auditory signal detection behavior in the rabbit. *Journal of the Acoustic Society of America.*

Kety, S.S. (1970). The biogenic amines in the central nervous system: Their possible roles in arousal, emotion, and learning. In F.O. Schmitt (Ed.), *The neurosciences, second study program* (pp. 324–336). New York: Rockefeller University Press.

Kimble, D.P. (1963). Hippocampus and internal inhibition. *Psychological Bulletin, 70*, 285–295.

Kinsbourne, M., & Wood, F. (1975). Short-term memory processes and the amnesic syndrome. In D. Deutsch & J.A. Deutsch (Eds.), *Short-term memory.* New York: Academic Press.

Kircher, K.A., Braun, J.J., Meyer, P.M., & Meyer, D.F. (1970). Equivalence of simultaneous and successive neocortical ablations in production of impairments of retention of black–white habbits. *Journal of Comparative & Physiological Psychology, 71*, 420–425.

Kirvel, R.D. (1975). Sensorimotor responsiveness in rats with unilateral superior collicular and amygdaloid lesions. *Journal of Comparative & Physiological Psychology, 89*, 882–891.

Kirvel, R.D., Greenfield, R.A., & Meyer, D.R. (1974). Multimodal sensory neglect in rats with radical unilateral posterior ablations. *Journal of Comparative & Physiological Psychology, 87*, 156–162.

Kitzes, L.M., Farley, G.R., & Starr, A. (1978). Modulation of auditory cortex unit activity during the performance of a conditioned response. *Experimental Neurology, 62*, 678–697.

Kleiner, F.B., Meyer, P.M., & Meyer, D.R. (1967). Effects of simultaneous septal and amygdaloid lesions upon emotionality and retention of a black–white discrimination. *Brain Research, 5*, 459–468.

Klein, M., Shapiro, E., & Kandel, E.R. (1980). Synaptic plasticity and the modulation of the $Ca^{2+}$ current. *Journal of Experimental Biology, 89*, 117–157.

Kluver, H. (1941). Visual functions after removal of the occipital lobes. *Journal of Psychology, 11*, 23–45.

Kluver, H., & Bucy, P.C. (1937). "Psychic blindness"

and other symptoms following bilateral temporal lobectomy in rhesus monkeys. *American Journal of Physiology, 119*, 352–353.

Kohsaka, S., Takamatsu, K., Aoki, E., & Tsukada, Y. (1979). Metabolic mapping of chick brain after imprinting using $[^{14}C]^2$-deoxyglucose technique. *Brain Research, 172*, 539–544.

Kolb, B., Sutherland, R.J., & Whishaw, I.Q. (1982). A comparison of the contributions of the frontal and parietal association cortex to spatial localization in rats. *Journal of Comparative Physiological Psychology*, in press.

Kolers, P.A. (1975). Specificity of operations in sentence recognition. *Cognitive Psychology, 7*, 289–306.

Konishi, M. (1963). The role of auditory feedback in the vocal behavior of the domestic foul. *Zeitschrift fur Tierpsychologie, 20*, 349–367.

Konishi, M. (1964). Song variation in a population of Oregon juncos. *Condor, 66*, 423–436.

Konishi, M. (1965a). Effects of deafening on song development in American robins and black-headed grosbeaks. *Zeitschrift fur Tierpsychologie, 22*, 584–599.

Konishi, M. (1965b). The role of auditory feedback in the control of vocalization in the white-crowned sparrow. *Zeitschrift fur Tierpsychologie, 22*, 770–783.

Konishi, M. (1985). Birdsong: From behavior to neuron. *Annual Review of Neuroscience, 8*, 125–170.

Konishi, M., & Nottebohm, F. (1969). Experimental studies in the ontogeny of avian vocalizations. In R.A. Hinde (Ed.), *Bird vocalizations* (pp. 29–48). Cambridge MA: Cambridge University Press.

Konorski, J. (1948). *Conditioned reflexes and neuron organization.* New York: Hafner Publishing Company.

Konorski, J. (1961). The physiological approach to the problem of recent memory. In J.F. Delafresnaye (Ed.), *Brain mechanisms and learning.* Oxford: Blackwell.

Konorski, J. (1967) *Integrative activity of the brain: An interdisiplinary approach.* Chicago: University of Chacago Press.

Koob, G.E., & Bloom, F.E. (1982). Behavioral effects of neuropeptides: Endorphins and vasopressin. *Annual Review of Physiology, 44*, 571–582.

Koob, G.F., Le Moal, M., Gaffori, O., Manning, M., Sawyer, W.H., Rivier, J., & Bloom, F.E. (1981). Arginine vasopressin and a vasopressin antagonist peptide: Opposite effects on extinctin of active avoidance in rats. *Regul. Peptides., 2*, 153–164.

Kovac, M.P., Davis, W.J., Matera, E.M., & Croll, R.P. (1983a). Organization of synaptic inputs to paracerebral feeding command interneurons of

*Pleurobranchaea californica:* I. Excitatory inputs. *Journal of Neurophysiology, 49,* 1517–1538.

Kovac, M.P., Davis, W.J., Matera, E.M., & Croll, R.P. (1983b). Organization of synaptic inputs to paracerebral feeding command interneurons of *Pleurobranchaea californica:* II. Inhibitory inputs. *Journal of Neurophysiology, 49,* 1539–1556.

Krasne, F.B. (1969). Excitation and habituation of the crayfish escape reflex: The depolarizing response in lateral giant fibres of the isolated abdomen. *Journal of Experimental Biology, 50,* 29–46.

Krasne, F.B., & Woodsmall, K.S. (1969). Waning of the crayfish escape response as a result of repeated stimulation. *Animal Behavior, 17,* 416–424.

Kroodsma, D.E. (1984). Songs of the alder fly-catcher (*Empidonax alnorum*) and willow fly-catcher (*Empidonax traillii*) are innate. *Auk, 101,* 13–24.

Kroodsma, D.E., & Miller, E.H. (Eds). (1982). *Acoustic communication in birds: Vol. I & II.* New York: Academic Press.

Kuble, J.L., & Ranck, J.G. Jr. (1982). Tonic and phasic firing of rat hippo-campal complex-spike cells in three different situations: Context and place. In C.D. Woody (Ed.), *Conditioning: Representation of involved neural functions.* New York: Plenum.

Kubota, K., Iwamoto, T., & Suzuki, H. (1974). Visuo-kinetic activities of primate prefrontal neurons during delayed-response performance. *Journal of Neurophysiology, 37,* 1197–1212.

Kubota, K., & Niki, H. (1971). Prefrontal cortical unit activity and delayed alternation performance in monkeys. *Journal of Neurophysiology, 34,* 337–347.

Kupferman, I. (1974). Feeding behavior in the *Aplysia:* A simple system for the study of motivation. *Behavioral Biology, 10,* 1–26.

Kupferman, I., Carews, T.J., & Kandel, E.R. (1970). Neuronal correlates of habituation and dishabituation of the gill-withdrawal reflex in *Aplysia. Science, 167,* 1743–1745.

Landfield. P.W. (1977). Different effects of posttrial driving or blocking of the theta rhythm on avoidance learning in rats. *Physiology & Behavior, 18,* 439–445.

Landfield, P.W., McGaugh, J.L., & Tusa, R.J. (1972). Theta rhythm: A temporal correlate of memory storage processes in the rat. *Science, 175,* 87–89.

Lanyon, W.E. (1957). The comparative biology of the meadowlarks (*Sturnella*) in Wisconsin. *Publication of the Nuttal Ornithological Club: No. I* (pp. 1–67). Cambridge, MA.

Larson, J.R., & Greenough, W.T. (1981). Effects of handedness training on dendritic branching of neurons of forelimb area of rat motor cortex. *Neuroscience Abstracts, 7,* 65.

Lashley, K.S. (1917). The effects of strychnine and caffeine upon the rate of learning. *Psychobiology, 1,* 141–170.

Lashley, K.S. (1926). Studies of cerebral function in learning: VII. The relation between cerebral mass, learning and retention. *Journal of Comparative Neurology, 41,* 1–58.

Lashley, K.S. (1929). *Brain mechanisms and intelligence.* Chicago: University of Chicago.

Lashley, K.S. (1931). The mechanism of vision: IV. The cerebral areas necessary of pattern vision in the rat. *Journal of Comparative & Physiological Psychology, 53,* 419–478.

Lashley, K.S. (1935). The mechanism of vision: XII. Nervous structures concerned in the acquisition and retention of habits based on reactions to light. *Comparative Psychology Monographs, 11,* 43–79.

Lashley, K.S. (1944). Studies of cerebral function in learning: XIII. Apparent absence of transcortical association in maze learning. *Journal of Comparative Neurology, 80,* 257–281.

Lashley, K.S. (1948). The mechanism of vision: XVIII. Effects of destroying visual "associative areas" in monkeys. *Genetic Psychology Monographs, 37,* 107–166.

Lashley, K.S. (1950). In search of the engram. *Society of Experimental Biology, Symposium 4,* 454–482.

Lashley, K.S., & Frank, M. (1932). The mechanism of vision: VI. The lateral position of the area striata in the rat: A correction. *Journal of Comparative Neurology, 55,* 525–529.

Lasiter, P.S., & Glanzman, D.L. (1982). Cortical substrates of taste aversion learning: Dorsal prepiriform (Insular) lesions disrupt taste aversion learning. *Journal of Comparative & Physiological Psychology, 96,* 376–392.

Lavond, D.G., & Dewberry, R.G. (1980). Visual form perception is a function of the visual cortex: II. The rotated horizontal–vertical and oblique-stripes pattern problems. *Physiological Psychology, 8,* 1–8.

Lavond, D.G., Hata, M.G., Gray, T.S., Geckler, C.L., Meyer, P.M., & Meyer, D.R. (1978). Visual form perception is a function of the visual cortex. *Physiological Psychology, 6,* 471–477.

Lavond, D.G., Hembree, T.L., & Thompson, R.F. (1985). Effect of kainic acid lesions of the cerebellar interpositus nucleus on eyelid conditioning in the rabbit. *Brain Research, 326,* 179–182.

Lavond, D.G., Mauk, M.D., Madden, J. IV, Barchas, J.D., & Thompson, R.F. (1983). Abolition of conditioned heart-rate responses in rabbits following central administration of [N-Me-Ph$^3$, D-Pro$^4$] morphiceptin. *Pharmacology, Biochemistry & Behavior, 19,* 379–382.

Lavond, D.G., McCormick, D.A., Clark, G.A., Holmes, D.T., & Thompson, R.F. (1981). Effects of ipsilateral rostral pontine reticular lesions on retention of classically conditioned nictitating membrane and eyelid responses. *Physiological Psychology, 9,* 335–339.

Lawicka, W., & Konoroski, J. (1959). The physiological mechanism of delayed reactions: III. The effects of prefrontal ablations on delayed reactions in dogs. *Acta Biologiae Experimentalis, 19,* 221–231.

Layton, B.S., Corrick, G.E., & Toga, A.W. (1978). Sensory restriction and recovery of function. In S. Finger (Ed.), *Recovery from brain damage: Research and theory* (pp. 331–368). New York: Plenum Press.

Leaton, R.N. (1976). Long-term retention of the habituation of lick suppression and startle response produced by a single auditory stimulus. *Journal of Experimental Psychology: Animal Behavior Processes, 2,* 248–260.

Lederhendler, I., Gart, S., & Alkon, D.L. (1983). Associative learning in *Hermissenda crassicornis* (*Gastrapoda*): Evidence that light (the CS) takes on characteristics of rotation (the UCS). *Biol. Bull. Abstr.* (*Woods Hole, MA*), *165,* 528.

Lee, K.S., Oliver, M., Schottler, F., and Lynch, G. (1981). Electron microscopic studies of brain slices: The effects of high-frequency stimulation on dendritic ultrastructure. In G.A. Kerkut & H.V. Wheal (Eds.), *Electrophysiology of isolated mammalian CNS preparations* (pp. 189–212). New York: Academic Press.

Lee, K.S., Schottler, F., Oliver, M., & Lynch, G. (1980). Brief bursts of high-frequency stimulation produce two types of structural change in rat hippocampus. *Journal of Neurophysiology, 44,* 247–258.

LeMoal, M., Koob, G.F., Koda, L.Y., Bloom, F.E., Manning, M., Sawyer, W.H., & Rivier, J. (1981). Vasopressin antagonist peptide: Blockade of pressor receptor prevents behavioral action of vasopressin. *Nature, 291,* 491–493.

LeMoal, M., Stimus, L., & Galey, D. (1976). Radio-frequency lesion of the ventral mesencephalic tegmentum: Neurological and behavioral considerations. *Experimental Neurology, 50,* 521–535.

LeVay, S., Wiesel, T.N., & Hubel, D.H. (1980). The development of ocular dominance columns in normal and visually deprived monkeys. *Journal of Comparative Neurology, 191,* 1–51.

LeVere, T.E. (1980). Recovery of function after brain damage: A theory of the behavioral deficit. *Physiological Psychology, 8,* 297–308.

Levine, S. (1968). *Hormones and Conditioning. Nebraska Synp. Motivation* (pp. 85–101). Lincoln: University of Nebraska Press.

Levine, S. (1971). Stress and behavior. *Scientific American, 224,* 26–31.

Levy, W.B., & Steward, O. (1979). Synapses as associative memory elements in the hippocampal formation. *Brain Research, 179,* 233–245.

Levy, W.B., & Steward, O. (1983). Temporal contiguity requirements for long term associative potentiation/depression in the hippocampus. *Neuroscience, 8,* 799–808.

Lewis, D.J. (1979). Psychobiology of active and inactive memory. *Psychological Bulletin, 86,* 1054–1083.

Lewis, D.J., & Maher, B.A. (1965). Neural consolidation and electroconvulsive shock. *Psychological Review, 72,* 225–239.

Lewis, D.J., Miller, R.R., & Misanin, J.F. (1968). Control of retrograde amnesia. *Journal of Comparative & Physiological Psychology, 66,* 48–52.

Lewis, D.J., Miller, R.R., & Misanin, J.F. (1969). Selective amnesia in rats produced by electroconvulsive shock. *Journal of Comparative & Physiological Psychology, 69,* 136–140.

Liang, K.C., McGaugh, J.L., Martinez, J.L., Jr., Jensen, R.A., Vasquez, B.J., & Messing, R.B. (1982). Post training amygdaloid lesions impair retention of an inhibitory avoidance response. *Behavioral Brain Research, 4,* 237–250.

Lincoln, J.S., McCormick, D.A., & Thompson, R.F. (1982). Ipsilateral cerebellar lesions prevent learning of the classically conditioned nictitating membrane/eyelid response. *Brain Research, 242,* 190–193.

Lindsley, D.B. (1951). *Emotion.* In S.S. Stevens (Ed.), *Handbook of experimental psychology* (pp. 473–516). New York: John Wiley & Sons.

Lindvall, O., Bjorklund, A., & Divac, I. (1978). Organization of catecholamine neurons projecting to the frontal cortex in the rat. *Brain Research, 142,* 1–24.

Liu, C.N., & Chambers, W.W. (1958). Intraspinal sprouting of dorsal root axons. *Archives of Neurology & Psychiatry, 79,* 46–61.

Livingston, M.S., Sziber, P.P., & Quinn, W.G. (1982). Defective adenylate cyclase in the *Drosophila* learning mutant, *Rutabaga. Society for Neuroscience Abstracts, 8,* 384.

Llinas, R., Walton, K., Hillman, E.D., & Sotelo, C. (1975). Inferior olive: Its role in motor learning. *Science, 190,* 1230–1231.

Logan, D.G., Steinmetz, J.E., & Thompson, R.F. (1986). Acoustic related responses recorded from the region of the pontine nuclei. *Neuroscience Abstracts, 12,* 754.

Lomo, T. (1966). Frequency potentiation of excitatory synaptic activity in the dentate area of the hippocampal formation. *Exp. Physiol. Scand., 68* (Suppl. 277), 128.

Lonsbury-Martin, B.L., Martin, G.K., Schwartz, S.M., & Thompson, R.F. (1976). Neural correlates of auditory plasticity during classical conditioning in the rabbit, *Journal of the Acoustic Society of America, 60,* S82.

Lugaro, E. (1899). I recenti progressi dell' anatomia del sistema nervoso in reporto alla psicologia et alla psichiatria. *Riv. Patol. nerv. ment., t. IV,* fasc. 11–12. (Cited in Cajal, 1911).

Lynch, G. (1976). Some difficulties associated with the use of lesion techniques in the study of memory. In M.R. Rosenzweig, & E.L. Bennett (Eds.), *Neural mechanisms of learning and memory.* Cambridge, MA: MIT Press.

Lynch, G., & Baudry, M. (1984). The biochemistry of memory: A new and specific hypotheses. *Science, 224,* 1057–1063.

Mackintosh, N.J. (1962). An investigation of reversal learning in *Octopus Vulgaris* Lamark. *Quarterly Journal of Experimental Psychology, 14,* 15–22.

Mackintosh, N.J. (1983). *Conditioning and associative learning.* Oxford: Oxford University Press.

Mackintosh, N.J., & Holgate, V. (1965). Overtraining and extinction of a discrimination in *Octopus. Journal of Comparative & Physiological Psychology, 60,* 260–264.

Madden, J. IV, Haley, D.A., Barchas, J.D., & Thompson, R.F. (1983). Micro-infusion of picrotoxin into the caudal red nucleus selectively abolishes the classically conditioned nictitating membrane/eyelid response in the rabbit. *Neuroscience Abstracts, 9,* 830 (no. 240.9).

Maffei, L., & Fiorentini, A. (1976). Asymmetry of motility of the eyes and change of binocular properties of cortical cells in adult cats. *Brain Research, 105,* 73–78.

Maier, N.R.F., & Schneirla, T.C. (1935). *Principles of animal psychology.* New York: McGraw–Hill.

Malmo, R.B. (1942). Interference factors in delayed response in monkeys after removal of frontal lobes. *Journal of Neurophysiology, 5,* 295–308.

Mamounas, L.A., Madden, J. IV, Barchas, J.D., & Thompson, R.F. (1983). Microinfusion of GABA antagonists into the cerebellar deep nuclei selectively abolishes the classically conditioned eyelid response in the rabbit. *Neuroscience Abstracts, 9,* 830 (No. 240.8).

Mamounas, L.A., Thompson, R.F., Lynch, G., & Baudry, M. (1984). Classical conditioning of the rabbit eyelid response increases glutamate receptor binding in hippocampal synaptic membranes, *Proceedings of the National Academy of Sciences, 81*(8), 2548–2552.

Margoliash, D. (1983). Acoustic parameters underlying the responses of song-specific neurons in the white-crowned sparrow. *Journal of Neuroscience, 3,* 1039–1057.

Marler, P. (1970). A comparative approach to vocal learning: Song development in the white-crowned sparrows. *Journal of Comparative & Physiological Monographs, 71,* 1–25.

Marler, P., & Peters, S. (1977). Selective vocal learning in a sparrow. *Science, 198,* 519–521.

Marler, P., & Peters, S. (1980). Birdsong and speed: Evidence for special processing. In P. Eimas & J. Miller (Eds.)., *Perspectives on the study of speech.* Hillsdale, NJ: Lawrence Erlbaum Associates.

Marler, P., & Peters, S. (1982). Subsong and plastic song: Their role in the vocal learning process. In D.E. Kroodsma & E.H. Miller (Eds.), *Acoustic communication in birds: Vol. II.* New York: Academic Press.

Marler, P., & Sherman, V. (1983). Song structure without auditory feedback: Emendations of the auditory template hypothesis. *The Journal of Neuroscience, 3,* 517–531.

Marler, P., & Tamura, M. (1962). Song "dialects" in three populations of white-crowned sparrows. *Condor, 64,* 368–377.

Marler, P., & Tamura, M. (1964). Culturally transmitted patterns of vocal behavior in sparrows. *Science, 146,* 1483–1486.

Marler, P., & Wasser, M.S. (1977). The role of auditory feedback in canary song development. *Journal of Comparative & Physiological Psychology, 91,* 8–16.

Marquis, D.G., & Hilgard, E.R. (1936). Conditioned lid responses to light in dogs after removal of the visual cortex. *Journal of Comparative Psychology, 22,* 157–178.

Marquis, D.G., & Hilgard, E.F. (1937). Conditioned responses to light in monkeys after removal of the occipital lobes. *Brain, 60,* 1–12.

Marr, D. (1969). A theory of cerebellar cortex. *Journal of Physiology (London) 202*: 437–470.

Marshall, J.F., Richardson, J.S., & Teitelbaum, P. (1974). Nigrostriatal bundle damage and the lateral hypothalmic syndrome. *Journal of Comparative & Physiological Psychology, 87,* 800–830.

Martin, G.K., Land, T., & Thompson, R.F. (1980). Classical conditioning of the rabbit (*Oryctolagus cuniculus*) nictitating membrane response using electrical brain stimulation as the unconditioned stimulus. *Journal of Comparative & Physiological Psychology, 94,* 216–226.

Martinez, J.L. Jr., Jensen, R.A., Messing, R.B., Rigter, H., & McGaugh, J.L. (1981) (Eds.), *Endogenous peptides and learning and memory processes.* New York: Academic Press.

Mason, S.T. (1979). Noradrenaline: Reward or extinction? *Neuroscience & Biobehavioral Review, 3,* 1–10.

Mason, S.T., & Iverson, S.D. (1979). Theories of the

dorsal bundle extinction effect. *Brain Research Review, 1*, 107–137.

Mauk, M.D., Madden, J., IV, Barchas, J.D., & Thompson, R.F. (1982). Opiates and classical conditioning: Selective abolition of conditioned responses by activation of opiate receptors within the central nervous system. *Proceedings of the National Academy of Science, 79*, 7598–7602.

Mauk, M.D., & Thompson, R.F. (1984). Classical conditioning using stimulation of the inferior olive as the unconditioned stimulus. *Neuroscience Abstracts, 10*, 122 (No. 36.5).

Mauk, M.D., & Thompson, R.F. (1987). Retention of classically conditioned eyelid responses following acute decerebration. *Brain Research, 493*, 89–95.

Mauk, M.D., Warren, J.T., & Thompson, R.F. (1982). Selective, naloxone-reversible morphine depression of learned behavioral and hippocampal responses. *Science, 216*, 434–435.

McCabe, B.J., Horn, G., & Bateson, P.P.G. (1981). Effects of restricted lesions of the chick forebrains on the acquisition of filial preferences during imprinting. *Brain Research, 205*, 29–37.

McCasland, J.S. (1983). *Neuronal control of bird song production*, Ph.D. thesis, California Institute of Technology, Pasadena, CA.

McCasland, J.S., & Konishi, M. (1981). Interaction between auditory and motor activities in an avian song control nucleus. *Proceedings of the National Academy of Sciences USA, 78*, 7815–7819.

McCleary, R.A. (1961). Response specificity in the behavioral effects of limbic system lesions in the cat. *Journal of Comparative & Physiological Psychology, 54*, 605–613.

McCleary, R.A. (1966). Response-modulating functions of the limbic system. In E. Stellar & J.M. Sprague (Eds.), *Progress in Physiological Psychology* (pp. 209–272). New York: Academic Press.

McCormick, D.A., Clark, G.A., Lavond, D.G., & Thompson, R.F. (1982). Initial localization of the memory trace for a basic form of learning. *Proceedings of the National Academy of Sciences, 79* (8), 2731–2742.

McCormick, D.A., Guyer, P.E., & Thompson, R.F. (1982). Superior cerebellar peduncle selectively abolish the ipsilateral classically conditioned nictitating membrane/eyelid response of the rabbit. *Brain Research, 244*, 347–350.

McCormick, D.A., Lavond, D.G., Clark, G.A., Kettner, R.E., Rising, C.E., & Thompson, R.F. (1981). The engram found? Role of the cerebellum in classical conditioning of nictitating membrane and eyelid responses. *Bulletin of the Psychonomic Society, 18*(3), 103–105.

McCormick, D.A., Lavond, D.G., & Thompson, R.F. (1982). Concomitant classical conditioning of the rabbit nictitating membrane and eyelid responses: Correlations and implications. *Physiology & Behavior, 28*, 769–775.

McCormick, D.A., Steinmetz, J.E., & Thompson, R.F. (1985). Lesions of the inferior olivary complex cause extinction of the classically conditioned eyeblink response. *Brain Research, 359*, 120–130.

McCormick, D.A., & Thompson, R.F. (1984a) Cerebellum: Essential involvement in the classically conditioned eyelid response. *Science, 223*, 296–299.

McCormick, D.A., & Thompson, R.F. (1984b). Neuronal responses of the rabbit cerebellum during acquisition and performance of a classically conditioned nictitating membrane–eyelid response. *Journal of Neuroscience, 4*(11), 2811–2200.

McCouch, G.P., Austin, G.M., Liu, C.N., & Liu, C.Y. (1958). Sprouting as a cause of spasticity. *Journal of Neurophysiology, 21*, 205–223.

McDougall, W. (1901). Experimentalle Beitrage Zur Lehre vom Gedachtniss, by G.E. Muller and A. Pilzecker. *Mind, 10*, 388–394.

McElearney, A., & Farley, J. (1983). Persistent changes in *Hermissenda* B photoreceptor membrane properties with associative training: A role for pharmacological modulation. *Society for Neuroscience Abstracts, 9*, 915.

McEwen, B.S. (1982). Glucocorticoids and hippocampus: Receptors in search of a function. In D. Ganten, & D. Pfaff (Eds.). *Current topics in neuroendocrinology, Vol. 2, Adrenal actions on brain* (pp. 1–22). New York: Springer-Verlag.

McGaugh, J.L. (1973). Drug facilitation of learning and memory. *Annual Review of Pharmacology, 13*, 229–241.

McGaugh, J.L. (1983a). Hormonal influences on memory. *Annual Review of Psychology, 34*, 297–323.

McGaugh, J.L. (1983b). Hormonal influences on memory storage. *American Psychologist. 38*(2), 161–174.

McGaugh, J.L., & Herz, M.J. (1972). In *Memory consolidation*. San Francisco, CA: Albion Publishing Company.

McGaugh, J.L., & Patrinovich, L.F. (1959). The effect of strychnine sulphate on maze-learning. *American Journal of Psychology, 72*, 99–102.

McGaugh, J.L., Thomson, C.W., Westbrook, W.H., & Hudspeth, W.J. (1962). A further study of learning facilitation with strychnine sulphate. *Psychopharmacologia (Berlin), 3*, 352–360.

McIntyre, M., & Stein, D.G. (1973). Differential effects of one vs. two stage amygdaloid lesions on activity, exploratory and avoidance behavior in the albino rat. *Behavioral Biology, 9*, 451.

Menzel, R. (1984). Short-term memory in bees. In

D.L. Alkon & J. Farley (Eds.), *Primary neural substrates of learning and behavioral change.* Cambridge MA: Cambridge University Press.

Menzel, R., & Erber, J. (1972). Influence of the quantity of reward on the learning performance in honeybees. *Behavior, 41,* 27–42.

Menzel, R., & Erber, J. (1978). Learning and memory in bees. *Scientific American, 239,* 102–110.

Merzenich, M.M., & Kaas, J.H. (1980). Principles of organization of sensory-perceptual systems in mammals. In J.M. Sprague & A.N. Epstein (Eds.), *Progress in psychobiology and physiological psychology.* New York: Academic Press.

Messing, R.B., Jensen, R.A., Martinez, J.R., Jr., Spiehler, V.R., Vasquez, B.J., Soumireu-Mourat, B., Liang, D.C., & McGaugh, J.L. (1979). Naloxone enhancement of memory. *Behavioral & Neural Biology, 27,* 266–275.

Meyer, D.R. (1972a). Access to engrams. *American Psychologist, 27,* 124–133.

Meyer, D.R. (1972b). Some features of the dorsolateral frontal and inferotemporal syndromes in monkeys. *Acta Neurobiologia Experimentalis, 32,* 235–260.

Meyer, D.R., & Beattie, M.S. (1977). Some Properties of Substrates of Memory. In L.H. Miller, C.A. Sandman, & A.J. Kastin (Eds.), *Neuropeptide influences on the brain and behavior* (pp. 145–162). New York: Raven Press.

Meyer, D.R., Hughes, H.C., Bucholz, D.J., Dalhouse, A.D., Enlow, L.J., & Meyer, P.M. (1976). Effects of successive unilateral ablations of principalis cortex upon performances of delayed alternation and delayed response by monkeys. *Brain Research, 108,* 397–412.

Meyer, D.R., Isaac, W., & Maher, B. (1958). The role of stimulation in spontaneous reorganization of visual habbits. *Journal of Comparative & Physiological Psychology, 51,* 546–548.

Meyer, D.R., & Meyer, P.M. (1977). Dynamics and Bases of recoveries of functions after injuries to the cerebral cortex. *Physiological Psychology, 5,* 133–165.

Meyer, D.R., & Meyer, P.M. (1984). Bases of recoveries from perinatal injuries to the cerebral cortex. In S. Finger & C.R. Almli (Eds.), *The behavioral biology of early brain damage.* New York: Academic Press.

Meyer, D.R., Ruth, R.A., & Lavond, D.G. (1978). The septal social cohesiveness effect: Its robustness and main determinants. *Physiology & Behavior, 21,* 1027–1029.

Meyer, D.R., & Settlage, P.H. (1958). Analysis of simple searching behavior in the frontal monkey. *Journal of Comparative & Physiological Psychology, 51,* 408–410.

Meyer, D.R., Treichler, F.R., & Meyer, P.M. (1965). Discrete-trial training techniques and stimulus variables. In A.M. Schrier & H.F. Harlow (Eds.), *Behavior of non-human primates.* New York: Academic Press.

Meyer, P.M., Horel, J.A., & Meyer, D.R. (1963). Effects of dl-amphetamine upon placing responses in neodecorticate cats. *Journal of Comparative & Physiological Psychology, 56,* 402–404.

Meyer, P.M., Johnson, D.A., & Vaughn, D.W., (1970). The consequences of septal and neocortical ablations upon learning a two-way conditioned avoidance response. *Brain Research, 22,* 113–120.

Meyer, P.M., & Meyer, D.R. (1982). Memory, remembering and amnesia. In R.L. Isaacson & N.E. Spear (Eds.), *The expression of knowledge* (pp. 179–212). New York: Plenum.

Miles, F.A., & Lisberger, S.G. (1981). Plasticity in the vestibulo-orular reflex: A new hypothesis. *Annual Review of Neuroscience, 4,* 273–299.

Miles, R.C., & Blomquist, A.J. (1960). Frontal lesions and behavioral deficits in monkey. *Journal of Neurophysiology, 23,* 471–484.

Miller, E.A., Goldman, P.S., & Rosvold, H.E. (1973). Delayed recovery of function following orbital prefrontal lesions in infant monkeys. *Science, 182,* 304–306.

Miller, L.H., Sandman, C.A., & Kastin, A.J. (Eds.) (1977). *Neuropeptide Influences on Brain and Behavior.* New York: Raven Press.

Miller, N.E. (1948). Studies of fear as an acquirable drive: I. Fear as motivation and fear-reduction as reinforcement in learning of new responses. *Journal Experimental Psychology, 38,* 89–101.

Miller, R.R., & Springer, A.D. (1974). Implications of recovery from experimental amnesia. *Psychological Review, 80,* 69–79.

Miller, V.M., & Best, P.J. (1980). Spatial correlates of hippocampal unit activity are altered by lesions of the fornix and endorhinal cortex. *Brain Research, 194,* 311–323.

Milner, B. (1962). Les troubles de la memoire accompagnant des lesions hippocampiques bilaterales. In *Physiologie de l'hippocampe.* Parts: Centre National de la Rechesche Scientifique.

Milner, B. (1966). Amnesia following operation on the temporal lobes. In C.W.M. Whitty and O.L. Zangwill (Eds.), *Amnesia* (pp. 109–133). London: Butterworths.

Milner, B. (1972). Disorders of learning and memory after temporal lobe lesions in man. *Clinical Neurosurgery, 19,* 421–446.

Mis, F.W., Gormezano, I., Rosewall, D., & Harvey, J.A. (1978) Electrical stimulation of the abducens nucleus in classical conditioning of the rabbit's nictitating membrane response. *Neuroscience Abstracts, 4,* 261.

Mishkin, M. (1951). Effects of selective ablations of the temporal lobes on the visually guided behavior of monkeys and baboons. Unpublished doctor's thesis, McGill University.

Mishkin, M. (1964). Perseveration of central sets after frontal lesions in monkeys. In J.M. Warren & K. Akert (Eds.), *The frontal granular cortex and behavior* (pp. 219–237). New York: McGraw-Hill.

Mishkin, M. (1966). Visual mechanisms beyond the striate cortex. In R.W. Russell (Ed.), *Frontiers in Physiological Psychology* (pp. 93–119). New York: Academic Press.

Mishkin, M. (1970). Cortical visual areas and their interactions. In A.G. Karezmar (Ed.), *The brain and human behavior.* Berlin: Springer.

Mishkin, M. (1978). Memory in monkeys severely impaired by combined but not by separate removal of amygdala and hippocampus. *Nature, 273,* 297–298.

Mishkin, M. (1982). A memory system in the monkey. *Philosophical Transactions of the Royal Society of London B, 298,* 85–95.

Mishkin, M., Malamut, B., & Bachevalier, J. (1984). Memories and habits: Two neural systems. In G. Lynch, J.L. McGaugh, & N.M. Weinberger (Eds.). *Neurobiology of learning and memory.* New York: Guilford Press.

Mishkin, M., & Oubre, J.L. (1977). Dissociation of deficits on visual memory tasks after inferior temporal and amygdala lesions in monkeys. *Society for Neuroscience Abstracts, 2,* 1127.

Mishkin, M., & Petri, H.L. (1984). Memories and habits: Some implications for the analysis of learning and retention. In N. Butters & L. Squire (Eds.), *Neuropsychology of memory* (pp. 287–296). New York: Guilford Press.

Mishkin, M. & Pribram, K.H. (1954). Visual discrimination performance following partial ablations of the temporal lobe: I. Ventral vs. lateral. *Journal of Comparative & Physiological Psychology, 47,* 14–20.

Mishkin, M., Spiegler, B.J., Saunders, R.C., & Malmut, B.L. (1982). An animal model of global amnesia. In S. Corkin, K.L. Davis, J.H. Growde, E. Usdin, & R.J. Wurtman (Eds.), *Alzheimer's disease: A review of progress.* New York: Raven Press.

Mishkin, M., & Weiskrantz, L. (1958). Effects of delaying reward on visual-discrimination performance in monkeys with frontal lesions. *Journal of Comparative & Physiological Psychology, 51,* 276–281.

Mollgaard, K., Diamond, M.C., Bennett, E.L., Rosenzweig, M.R., & Lindner, B. (1971). Quantitative synaptic changes with differential experience in rat

brain. *International Journal of Neuroscience, 2,* 113–128.

Moore, R.Y. (1964). Effects of some rhinecephalic lesions on retention of conditioned avoidance behavior in cats. *Journal of Comparative & Physiological Psychology, 57,* 65–71.

Morgan, C.L. (1904). *An introduction to comparative psychology.* London: Walter Scott.

Morgan, C.T. (1951). Some structural factors in perception. In R.R. Blake & G.V. Ramsey (Eds.), *Perception: An approach to personality* (pp. 25–55). New York: Ronald Press.

Morgan, M.J. (1973). Effects of post-weaning environment on learning in the rat. *Animal Behavior, 21,* 25–55.

Mountcastle, V.B. (1957). Modality and topographic properties of single neurons of cat's somatic sensory cortex. *Journal of Neurophysiology, 20,* 408–434.

Mountcastle, V.B., Talbot, W.H., Darian-Smith, I., & Kornhuber, H.H. (1967). Neural basis of the sense of flutter vibration. *Science, 155,* 597–600.

Movshon, J.A. (1975). The velocity tuning of single units in cat striate cortex. *Journal of Physiology, 249,* 445–468.

Mowrer, O.H. (1947). On the dual nature of learning—a reinterpretation of "conditioning" and "problem-solving". *Harvard Educational Review, 17,* 102–148.

Mpitsos, G.J., & Collins, S.D. (1975). Learning: Rapid aversive conditioning in the gastropod mollusk *Pleurobranchaea. Science, 188,* 954–957.

Mpitsos, G.J., Collins, S.D., & McClellan, A.D. (1978). Learning: A model system for physiological studies. *Science, 199,* 497–506.

Muller, G.E., & Pilzecker, A. (1900). Experimentelle Beitrage zur Lehre vom Gedachtniss. *Z. Psychol, 1,* 1–288.

Muller, L., Pattiselanno, A., & Vrensen, G. (1981). The postnatal development of the presynaptic grid in the visual cortex. *Journal of Neurophysiology, 20,* 408–434.

Munk, H. (1881). *Uber die funktionen der groshirn-rinde.* Berline.

Murray, M., & Goldberger, M.E. (1974). Restitution of function and collateral sprouting in the cat spinal cord: The partially hemisected animal. *Journal of Comparative Neurology, 155,* 19–36.

Nachman, M., & Ashe, J.H. (1974). Effects of basolateral amygdala lesions on neophobia, learned taste aversions, and sodium appetite in rats. *Journal of Comparative & Physiological Psychology, 87,* 622–643.

Neary, J.T. (1984). Biochemical correlates of associative learning: Protein phosphorylation in

*Hermissenda crassicornis*, a nudibranch mollusk. In D.L. Alkon & J. Farley (Eds.), *Primary neural substrates of learning and behavioral change*. New York: Cambridge University Press.

Neff, W.D. (1960). Role of the auditory cortex in sound discrimination. In G.L. Rasmussen & W.F. Windle (Eds.), *Neural mechanisms of auditory and vestibular systems*. Springfield, IL: C.C. Thomas.

Neff, W.D., Diamond, I.T., & Casseday, J.H. (1975). Behavioral studies of auditory discrimination: Central nervous system. In W.D. Keidel & W.E. Neff (Eds.), *Handbook of sensory physiology:* Vol. V/2, 307–400.

Nicolai, J. (1959). Familientradition in der Gesangsentwicklung des Gimpels (*Pyrrhula pyrrhula L.*). *Journal fur Ornithologie, 100*, 39–46.

Norman, R.J., Buchwald, J.S., & Villablance, J.R. (1977). Classical conditioning with auditory discrimination of the eyeblink in decerebrate cats. *Science, 196*, 551–553.

Nottebohm, F. (1966). The role of sensory feedback in the development of avian vocalizations. PhD. dissertation, University of California, Berkeley, CA.

Nottebohm, F. (1967). The role of sensory feedback in the development of avian vocalizations. *Proceedings of the 14th International Ornithological Congress (1966)*, 265–280.

Nottebohm, F. (1968). Auditory experience and song development in the chaffinch (*Fringilla coelebs*): Ontogeny of a complex motor pattern. *Ibis, 110*, 549–568.

Nottebohm, F. (1969). The "critical period" for song learning in birds. *Ibis, 3*, 386–387.

Nottebohm, F. (1980a). Brain pathways for vocal learning in birds: A review of the first 10 years. *Progress in Psychobiological Psychology, 9*, 85–124.

Nottebohm, F. (1980b). Testosterone triggers growth of brain vocal control nuclei in adult female canaries. *Brain Research, 189*, 429–436.

Nottebohm, F. (1981). A brain for all seasons: Cyclical anatomical changes in song control nuclei of the canary brain. *Science, 214*, 1368–1370.

Nottebohm, F. (1984). Birdsong as a model in which to study brain processes related to learning. *The Condor, 86*, 227–236.

Nottebohm, F., & Arnold, A. (1976). Sexual dimorphism in vocal control areas of the songbird brain. *Science, 194*, 211–213.

Nottebohm, F., & Kasparian, S. (1983). Widespread labeling of avian forebrain neurons after systematic injections of $^3$H-thymidine in adulthood. *Society for Neuroscience Abstracts, 9*, 380.

Nottebohm, F., Kasparian, S., & Pandazis, C. (1981).

Brain space for a learned task. *Brain Research, 213*, 99–109.

Nottebohm, F., Kelley, D.B., & Paton, J.A. (1982). Connections of vocal control nuclei in the canary telencephalon. *Journal of Comparative Neurology, 207*, 344–357.

Nottebohm, F., & Nottebohm, M.E. (1971). Vocalizations and breeding behavior in surgically deafened ring doves, *Streptopelia resoria*. *Animal Behavior, 19*, 313–327.

Nottebohm, F., & Nottebohm, M.E. (1978). Relationship between song repertoire and age in the canary, *Serinus canarius*. *Zeitschrift fur Tierpsychologie, 46*, 298–305.

Nottebohm, F., Stokes, T.M., & Leonard, C.M. (1976). Central control of song in the canary, *Serinus canarius*. *Journal of Comparative Neurology, 165*, 457–486.

Nyman, A.J. (1967). Problem solving in rats as a function of experience at different ages. *The Journal of Genetic Psychology, 110*, 31–39.

Oakley, D.A. (1979). Cerebral cortex and adaptive behavior. In D.A. Oakley & H.C. Plotkin (Eds.), *Brain, behavior and evolution* (pp. 154–188). London: Methuen.

Oakley, D.A., & Russell, I.S. (1972). Neocortical lesions and classical conditioning. *Physiology & Behavior, 8*, 915–926.

Oakley, D.A., & Russell, I.S. (1977). Subcortical storage of Pavlovian conditioning in the rabbit. *Physiology & Behavior, 18*, 931–937.

O'Brien, J.H., & Quinn, K.J. (1982). Central mechanisms responsible for classically conditioned changes in neuronal activity. See Woody 1982. In press.

O'Brien, J.H., Wilder, M.B., & Stevens, C.D. (1977). Conditioning of cortical neurons in cats with antidromic activation as the unconditioned stimulus. *Journal of Comparative & Physiological Psychology, 91*, 918–929.

Ogren, S.O., & Fuxe, K. (1974). Learning, brain noradrenaline and the pituitary-adrenal axis. *Medical Biology* (Helsinki), *52*, 399–405.

O'Keefe, J. (1976). Place units in the hippocampus of the freely moving rat. *Experimental Neurology, 51*, 78–109.

O'Keefe, J., & Conway, D.H. (1978). Hippocampal place units in the freely moving rat: Why they fire where they fire. *Experimental Brain Research, 31*, 573–590.

O'Keefe, J., & Nadel, L. (1978). *The hippocampus as a cognitive map*. New York: Oxford University Press.

Olds, J., Disterhoft, J.F., Segal, M., Hornblith, C.L., & Hirsch, R. (1972). Learning centers of rat brain mapped by measuring latencies of conditioned unit responses. *Journal of Neurophysiology, 35*, 202–219.

Olds, S., Ninhuis, R., & Olds, M.E. (1978). Pattern of conditioning unit responses in the auditory system of rat. *Experimental Neurology, 59*, 209–228.

Oleson, T.D., Ashe, J.H., & Weinberger, N.M. (1975). Modification of auditory and somatosensory system activity during pupillary conditioning in the paralyzed cat. *Journal of Neurophysiology, 38*, 1114–1139.

Olton, D.S., Becker, J.T., & Handelmann, G.E. (1979). Hippocampus, space and memory. *Behavioral & Brain Science, 2*, 313–365.

Olton, D.S., Becker, J.T., & Handelmann, G.E. (1980). Hippocampal function: Working memory or cognitive mapping. *Physiological Psychology, 8*(2), 239–246.

Olton, D.S., Branch, M., & Best, P.J. (1978). Spatial correlates of hippocampal unit activity. *Experimental Neurology, 58*, 387–409.

Orr, W.B., & Berger, T.W. (1981). Hippocampal lesions disrupt discrimination reversal learning of the rabbit nictitating membrane response. *Neuroscience Abstracts, 7*, 648.

Osborne, N.N., & Cottrell, G.A. (1971). Distribution of biogenic amines in the slug *Limax maximus*. *Z. Aellforsch, 112*, 15–30.

Papez, J.W. (1937). A proposed mechanism of emotion. *Arch. neurol. Psychiat., 38*, 725–743.

Paton, J.A., & Nottebohm, F.N. (1984). Neurons generated in pre-adult brain are recruited into functional circuits. *Science, 225*, 1046–1048.

Patterson, M.M. (1980). Mechanisms of classical conditioning of spinal reflexes. See Thompson et al., 1980, pp. 263–272.

Patterson, M.M. (1975). Effects of forward and backward classical conditioning procedures on a spinal cat hindlimb flexor nerve response. *Physiological Psychology, 3*, 86–91.

Patterson, M.M. (1976). Mechanisms of classical conditioning and fixation in spinal mammals. In A.H. Riesen & R.F. Thompson (Eds.), *Advances in psychobiology*. New York: Wiley.

Patterosn, M.M., Berger, T.W., & Thompson, R.F. (1979). Neuronal plasticity recorded from cat hippocampus during classical conditioning. *Brain Research, 163*, 339–343.

Patterson, M.M., Cegavske, C.F., & Thompson, R.F. (1973). Effects of a classical conditioning paradigm on hindlimb flexor nerve response in immobilized spinal cat. *Journal of Comparative & Physiological Psychology, 84*, 88–97.

Patterson, M.M., Steinmetz, J.E., Beggs, A.L., & Romano, A.G. (1982). Associative processes in spinal reflexes. In C.D. Woody (Ed.), *Conditioning: Representation of involved neural functions*. New York: Plenum.

Pavlov, I.P. (1927). *Conditioned reflexes*. Oxford: Oxford University Press.

Peck, C.K., & Blakemore, C. (1975). Modification of single neurons in the kitten's visual cortex after brief periods of monocular visual experience. *Experimental Brain Research, 22*, 57–68.

Peeke, H.V., & Herz, M.J. (Eds.) (1973). *Habituation: Vol. 1. Behavioral studies*. New York: Academic Press.

Penfield, W. (1958). *The excitable cortex in conscious man*. Liverpool: Liverpool University Press.

Peretz, B., Jacklet, J., & Lukowiak, K. (1976). Habituation of reflexes in *Aplysia*: Contribution of the peripheral nervous system. *Science, 191*, 396–399.

Petrinovich, L., & Carew, T.J. (1969). Interaction of neocortical lesion size and interoperative experience in retention of a learned brightness discrimination. *Journal of Comparative & Physiological Psychology, 68*, 451–454.

Petsche, H., & Gogolak, G. (1962). The significance of the rabbit's septum as a relay station between the midbrain and the hippocampus: I. The control of hippocampus arousal activity by the septum cells. *Electroencephalography & Clinical Neurophysiology, 14*, 202–211.

Pinsker, H.M., Henning, W.A., Carews, T.J., & Kandel, E.R. (1973). Long-term sensitization of a defensive withdrawal reflex in *Aplysia*. *Science, 182*, 1039–1042.

Pinsker, H., Kupfermann, I., Castellucci, V., & Kandel, E.R. (1970). Habituation and dishabituation of the gill-withdrawal reflex in *Aplysia*. *Science, 167*, 1740–1742.

Pohle, W., & Matthies, H. (1976). Influence of uridine-5-monophosphate on $^3$H-leucine incorporation into hippocampal neurons during learning. *Pharmacology, Biochemistry & Behavior, 4*, 225–229.

Poltrew, S.S., & Zeliony, G.P. (1930). Grosshirnrinde und Assoziationsfunktion. *Z. Biol., 90*, 157–160.

Poulsen, H. (1951). Inheritance and learning in the song of the chaffinch, *Fringilla coelebs*. *Behavior, 3*, 216–228.

Poulsen, H. (1954). On the song of the linnet (*Carduelis cannabina* L.). *Dansk Ornithologisk Forenings Tidsskrift, 48*, 32–37.

Powell, D.A., & Buchanan, S. (1980). Autonomic-somatic relationships in the rabbit (*Oryctolagus cuniculus*): Effects of hippocampal lesions. *Physiological Psychology, 8*(4), 455–462.

Powell, D.A., Lipkin, M., & Milligan, W.L. (1974). Concomitant changes in classically conditioned heart rate and corneoretinal potential discrimination in the rabbit (*Oryctolagus cuniculus*). *Learning & Motivation, 5*, 532–547.

Pribram, H.B., & Barry, J. (1956). Further behavioral

analysis of the parieto-temporo preoccipital cortex. *Journal of Neurophysiology, 19,* 99–106.

Pribram, K.H. (1954). Toward a science of neuropsychology (method and data). In R.A. Patton (Ed.), *Current trends in psychology and the behavioral sciences,* (pp. 115–142). Pittsburgh, PA: University of Pittsburgh Press.

Pribram, K.H. (1971). *Languages of the brain: Experimental paradoxes and principles in neuropsychology.* Monterey, CA: Brooks/Cole Publishing Co.

Pribram, K.H., Krugger, L., Robinson, F., & Berman, A.J. (1955). The effects of precentral lesions on the behavior of monkeys. *Yale Journal of Biology and Medicine, 28,* 428–443.

Pribram, K.H., Mishkin, M., Rosvold, H.E., & Kaplan, S.J. (1952). Effects on delayed-response performance of lesions of dorsolateral and ventromedial cortex of baboons. *Journal of Comparative & Physiological Psychology, 45,* 567–575.

Pribram, K.H., & Tubbs, W.E. (1967). Short-term memory, parsing, and the primate frontal cortex. *Science, 156,* 1765–1767.

Price, P.H. (1979). Developmental determinants of structure in zebra finch song. *Journal of Comparative & Physiological Psychology, 93,* 260–277.

Prokasy, W.F. (1972). Developments with the two-phase model applied to human eyelid conditioning. In A.H. Black and W.F. Prokasy (Eds.), *Classical conditioning: II. Current research and theory* (pp. 119–147). New York: Appleton-Century-Crofts.

Prokasy, W.F., Kesner, R.P., & Calder, L.D. (1983). Posttrial electrical stimulation of the dorsal hippocampus facilitates acquisition of the nictitating mebrane response. *Behavioral Neuroscience, 97,* 890–896.

Quartermain, D. (1976). The influence of drugs on learning and memory. In M.R. Rosenzweig & E.L. Bennett (Eds.), *Neural mechanism of learning and memory.* Cambridge, MA: MIT Press.

Quartermain, D., McEwen, B.S., & Azmitia, E.C., Jr. (1970). Amnesia produced by electroconvulsive shock or cycloheximide: Conditions for recovery. *Science, 169,* 683–686.

Quellet, J.V., Kower, H.S., & Braun, J.J. (1975). Failure to retain a learned taste aversion after lesions of the gastatory neocortex. Presented at Annual Meeting Western Psychology Association, Sacramento, CA.

Quinn, W.G., Harris, W.A., & Benzer, S. (1974). Conditioned behavior in *Drosophila melanogaster. Proceedings of the National Academy of Sciences, USA, 71,* 708–712.

Rainbow, T.C. (1979). Role of RNA and protein synthesis in memory formation. *Neurochemical Research, 4,* 297–312.

Raisman, G. (1969). Neuronal plasticity in the septal nuclei of the adult rat. *Brain Research, 14,* 25–48.

Rajecki, D.W. (1973). Imprinting in precocial birds: Interpretation, evidence and evaluation. *Psychological Bulletin, 79,* 48–58.

Ramon y Cajal, S. (1893). Neue darstellung vom histologischen bau des central nervensystem. *Archiv fur Anatomie und Physiologie (Anatomie),* 319–428.

Ramon y Cajel, S. (1911). In *Histologie du systeme nerveux de l'homme et des vertebres;* vol. 2. (pp. 886–890). Paris: Maloine.

Rankin, C.H. & Carew, T.J. (in press). Dishabituation and sensitization emerge as separate processes during development in *Aplysia. Journal of Neuroscience.*

Rapport, M., & Karpiak, S.E. (1976). Discriminative effects of antisera to brain constituents on behavior and EEG activity in rats. *Res. Commun. Psychol. Psychiatr. Behav., 1,* 115–123.

Rees, H.D., Brogan, L.L., Entingh, D.J., Dunn, A.J., Shinkman, P.G., Damstra-Entingh, T., Wilson, J.E., & Gassman, E. (1974). Effect of sensory stimulation on the uptake and incorporation of radioactive lysine into protein of mouse brain and liver. *Brain Research, 68,* 143–156.

Rees, H.D., & Dunn, A.J. (1977). The role of pituitary-adrenal system in the foot-shock-induced increase of [$^3$H] lysine incorporation into mouse brain and liver proteins. *Brain Research, 120,* 317–325.

Rescorla, R.A. (1967). Pavlovian conditioning and its proper control procedures. *Psychological Review, 74,* 71–80.

Rescorla, R.A. & Holland, P.C. (1976). Some behavioral approaches to the study of learning. In M.R. Rosenzweig & E.L. Bennett (Eds.), *Neural mechanisms of learning and memory.* Cambridge, MA: MIT Press.

Rescorla, R.A., & Solomon, R.L. (1967). Two-process learning theory: Relationships between Pavlovian conditioning and instrumental learning. *Psychological Review, 74,* 151–182.

Recorla, R.A., & Wagner, A.R. (1972). A theory of Pavlovian conditioning: Variations in the effectiveness of reinforcement and nonreinforcement. In A.H. Black & W.A. Prokasy (Eds.), *Classical conditioning: II. Current theory and research.* New York: Appleton-Century-Crofts.

Richards, W., Farley, J., & Alkon, D.L. (1983). Extinction of associative learning in *Hermissenda:* Behavior and neural correlates. *Society for Neuroscience Abstracts, 9,* 916.

Riddley, R.M., & Ettlinger, G. (1976). Impaired tactile learning and retention after removals of the second somatic sensory projection cortex (SII) in the monkey. *Brain Research, 109,* 656–660.

Riege, W.H. (1971). Environmental influences on brain and behavior of year-old rats. *Developmental Psychology, 4,* 151–167.

Riesen, A.H. (Ed.) (1975). *The developmental neuropsychology of sensory deprivation.* New York: Academic Press.

Rigter, H. (1978). Attenuation of amnesia in rats by systemically administered enkephalin. *Science, 200,* 83–85.

Rigter, H., Elbertse, R., & Van Riezen, H. (1975). Time-dependent anti-amnesic effect of $ACTH_{4-10}$ and desglycinamide-lysine vasopressin. *Progress in Brain Research, 42,* 164–171.

Riopelle, A.J., & Ades, H.W. (1951). Discrimination following deep temporal lesions. *American Psychologist, 6,* 261–262.

Riopelle, A.J., Alper, R.G., Strong, P.N., & Ades, H.W. (1953). Multiple discrimination and patterned string performance of normal and temporal-lobectomized monkeys. *Journal of Comparative & Physiological Psychology, 46,* 145–149.

Ritchie, G.D., Meyer, P.M., & Meyer, D.R. (1976). Residual spatial vision of cats with lesions of the visual cortex. *Experimental Neurology, 53,* 227–253.

Roberts, D.C.S., & Fibiger, H.C. (1977). Evidence for interactions between central noradrenergic neurons and adrenal hormones in learning and memory. *Pharmacology, Biochemistry & Behavior, 7,* 191–194.

Roberts, D.C.S., Price, M.T.C., Fibiger, H.C. (1976). The dorsal tegmental noradrenergic projection: Analysis of its role in maze learning. *Journal of Comparative & Physiological Psychology, 90,* 363–372.

Roberts, E. (1976). Desinhibition as an organizing principle in the nervous system—the role of the GABA system. In E. Roberts, T.N. Chase, D.B. Tower (Eds.), *GABA in nervous system function* (pp. 515–539). New York: Raven Press.

Robbins, M.J., & Meyer, D.R. (1970). Motivational control of retrograde amnesia. *Journal of Experimental Psychology, 84,* 220–225.

Robinson, D.A. (1976). Adaptive gain control of vestibulo-ocular reflex by the cerebellum. *Journal of Neurophysiology, 39,* 954–969.

Rose, S.P.R. (1980). Neurochemical correlates of early learning on the chick. In Y. Tsukada & B.W. Agranoff (Eds.), *Neurobiological bases of learning and memory* (pp. 179–191). New York: Wiley.

Rosenzweig, M.R. (1980). Animal models for effects of brain lesions and for rehabilitation. In P. Bach-y-Rita (Ed.), *Recovery of function: Theoretical considerations for brain injury rehabilitation.* Baltimore, MD: University Park Press.

Rosenzweig, M.R., & Bennett, E.L. (1976). Enriched environments: facts, factors, and fantasies. In L. Petrinovich & J.L. McGaugh (Eds.), *Knowing, thinking, and believing* (pp. 179–212). New York: Plenum Press.

Rosvold, H.E., & Delgado, J.M.R. (1956). The effect of delayed alternation test performance of stimulating or destroying electrically structures within the frontal lobes of the monkey's brain. *Journal of Comparative & Physiological Psychology, 49,* 365–372.

Rosvold, H.E., Mishkin, M., & Szwarcbart, M.K. (1958). Effects of subcortical lesions in monkeys on visual-discrimination and single-alternation performance. *Journal of Comparative & Physiological Psychology, 51,* 437–444.

Routtenberg, A., George, D.R., & Davis, L.G. (1974). Memory consolidation and fucosylation of crude synaptosomal glycoproteins resolved by gel electrophoresis: A regional study. *Behavioral Biology, 12,* 461–475.

Rozin, P. (1976). The psychobiological approach to human memory. In M.R. Rosenzweig & E.L. Bennett (Eds.), *Neural mechanisms of learning and memory* (pp. 3–48). Cambridge, MA: MIT Press.

Rushforth, N.B. (1965). Behavioral studies of the coelenterate *Hydra pirardi. Animal Behavior Supplements, 1,* 30–42.

Rutledge, L.T., Wright, C., & Duncan, J. (1974). Morphological changes in pyramidal cells of mammalian neocortex associated with increased use. *Experimental Neurology, 44,* 209–228.

Ryugo, D.K., & Weinberger, N.M. (1976). Differential plasticity of morphologically distinct neuron populations in the medial geniculate body of the cat during classical conditioning. *Society for Neuroscience Abstracts, 2,* 435.

Ryugo, D.K., & Weinberger, N.M. (1978). Differential plasticity of morphologically distinct neuron populations in the medial geniculate body of the cat during classical conditioning. *Behavioral Biology, 22,* 275–301.

Sahley, C.L., Feinstein, S.R., & Gelperin, A. (1981). Dietary choline increases retention of an associative learning task in the terrestrial mollusc, *Limax maximus. Society for Neuroscience Abstracts, 7,* 353.

Sahley, C.L., Gelperin, A., & Rudy, J.W. (1981). One-trial associative learning in a terrestrial mollusc. *Proceedings of the National Academy of Sciences, 78,* 640–642.

Sahley, C.L., Rudy, J.W., & Gelperin, A. (1981). An analysis of associative learning in a terrestrial mollusc: I. Higher-order conditioning, blocking and a transient US pre-exposure effect. *Journal of Comparative Physiology, 144,* 1–8.

Sakakibara, M., Alkon, D.L., Lederhendler, I., &

Heldman, E. (1984). Alpha 2-receptor control of $Ca^{++}$-mediated reduction of voltage dependent $K^+$ currents. *Society for Neuroscience Abstracts, 10*, 950.

Sandoval, M.E., & Cotman, C.W. (1978). Evaluation of glutamate as a neurotransmitter of cerebellar parallel fibers. *Neuroscience, 3*, 199–206.

Schapiro, S., & Vukovich, K.R. (1970). Early experience effects upon cortical dendrites: A proposed model for development. *Science, 167*, 292–294.

Scheff, S.W., & Wright, D.C. (1977). Behavioral and electrophysiological evidence for cortical reorganization of function in rats with serial lesions of the visual cortex. *Physiological Psychology, 5*, 103–107.

Scheff, S.W., Wright, D.C., Morgan, W.K., & Bowers, R.P. (1977). The differential effects of additional cortical lesions in rats with single or multiple stage lesions of the visual cortex. *Physiological Psychology, 5*, 97–102.

Schmaltz, L.W., & Theios, J. (1972). Acquisition and extinction of a classically conditioned response in hippocampectomized rabbits (Orcytolagus cuniculus), *Journal of Comparative & Physiological Psychology, 79*, 328–333.

Schneider, G.E. (1973). Early lesions of superior colliculus: Factors affecting the formation of abnormal retinal projections. *Brain, Behavior & Evolution, 8*, 73–109.

Schneider, G.E., & Jhaveri, S.R. (1974). Neuroanatomical correlates of spared or altered function after brain lesions in the newborn hamster. In D.G. Stein, J.J. Rosen, & N. Butters (Eds.), *Plasticity and recovery of function in the central nervous system*. New York: Academic Press.

Schneiderman, N. (1972). Response system divergencies in aversive classical conditioning. See Prokasy 1972, pp. 341–378.

Schneiderman, N., Fuentes, I., & Gormezano, I. (1962). Acquisition and extinction of the classically conditioned eyelid response in the albino rabbit. *Science, 136*, 650–652.

Schneiderman, N., Smith, M.C., Smith, A.C., & Gormezano, I. (1966). Heart rate classical conditioning in rabbits. *Psychonomic Science, 6*, 241–242.

Schneiderman, N., VanDercar, D.H., Yehle, A.L., Manning, A.A., Golden, T., et al. (1969). Vagal compensatory adjustment: Relationship to heart rate classical conditioning in rabbits. *Journal of Comparative & Physiological Psychology, 68*, 175–183.

Schoenfeld, T.A., & Hamilton, L.W. (1977). Secondary brain changes following lesions: A new paradigm for lesion experimentation. *Physiology & Behavior, 18*, 951–967.

Schwartz, M.L., & Goldman-Rakic, P.S. (1984). Ipsi-lateral and contralateral connectivity of the prefrontal association cortex: Relation between intraparietal and principal sulcal cortex. *Journal of Comparative Neurology, 226*, 403–420.

Schwartz, S. (1964). Effect of neonatal cortical lesions and early environmental factors on adult rat behavior. *Journal of Comparative & Physiological Psychology, 55*, 429–437.

Segal, M. (1977a). Changes if interhemispheric hippocampal responses during conditioning in the rat. *Experimental Brain Research, 29*, 553–565.

Segal, M. (1977b). Excitability changes in rat hippocampus during conditioning. *Experimental Neurology, 55*, 67–73.

Segal, M., & Olds, J. (1972). The behavior of units in the hippocampal circuit of the rat during learning. *Journal of Neurophysiology, 35*, 680–690.

Serota, R.G., Roberts, R.B., & Flexner, L.B. (1972). Acetoxycycloheximide-induced transient amnesia: Protective effects of adrenergic stimulants. *Proceedings of the National Academy of Sciences USA, 69*, 340–342.

Shashoua, V.E. (1982). Molecular and cell biological aspects of learning: Toward a theory of memory. *Advances in Cellular Neurobiology, 3*, 97–141.

Sherman, S.M. (1977). The effect of superior colliculus lesions upon the visual fields of cats with cortical ablations. *Journal of Comparative Neurology, 172*, 211–230.

Sherrington, C.S. (1906). *The integrative action of the nervous system*. New Haven CT: Yale University Press.

Sidman, M., Stoddard, L.T., & Mohr, J.P. (1968). Some additional quantitative observations of immediate memory in a patient with bilateral hippocampal lesions. *Neuropsychologia, 6*, 245–254.

Simon, H.A. (1979). *Models of thought*. New Haven CT: Yale University Press.

Simon, H., Scatton, B., & LeMoal, M. (1980). Dopaminergic AlO neurones are involved in cognitive functions. *Nature (London), 286*, 150–151.

Sitaram, N., Weingartner, H., & Gillin, J. (1978). Human serial learning: Enhancement with arecoline and choline, and impairment with scopolamine. *Science, 201*, 274–276.

Sladeck, J.R., & Blanchard, B.C. (1981). Age-related declines in perikaryl monamine histofluorescence in the Fischer 344 rat. *Aging, 17*, 13–21.

Sluckin, W. (1972). *Imprinting and early learning (2nd ed.)*. London: Methuen.

Smith, A.M. (1970). The effects of rubral lesions and stimulation on conditioned forelimb flexion responses in the cat. *Physiology & Behavior, 5*, 1121–1126.

Smith, O.A., Astley, C.A., DeVit, J.L., Stein, J.M., &

Walsh, K.E. (1980). Functional analysis of hypothalamic control of the cardiovascular responses accompanying emotional behavior. *Federation Proceedings, 39*(8), 2487–2494.

Sokolov, E.N. (1963). *Perception and the conditioned reflex*. New York: Pergamon Press.

Sokolov, E.N. (1969). The modeling properties of the nervous system. In M. Cole & I. Maltzman (Eds.), *Handbook of contemporary Soviety psychology*. New York: Basic Books.

Solomon, P.R. (1979). Temporal vs. spatial information processing theories of hippocampal function. *Psychological Bulletin, 86*, 1272–1279.

Solomon, P.R., Lewis, J.L., LoTurco, J., Steinmetz, J.E., & Thompson, R.F. (1986). The role of the middle cerebellar peduncle in acquisition and retention of the rabbits classically conditioned nictitating membrane response. *Bulletin of the Psychonomic Society, 24*(1), 75–78.

Solomon, P.R., & Moore, J.W. (1975). Latent inhibition and stimulus generalization for the classically conditioned nictitating membrane response in rabbits (*Oryctolagus cuniculus*) following dorsal hippocampal ablation. *Journal of Comparative & Physiological Psychology 89*, 1192–1203.

Solomon, P.R., Solomon, S.D., Vander Schaaf, E., & Perry, H.E. (1983). Altered activity in the hippocampus is more detrimental to classical conditioning than removing the structure. *Science, 220*, 329–333.

Spaet, T., & Harlow, H.F. (1943). Problem solution by monkeys following bilateral removal of the prefrontal areas: II. Delayed reaction problems involving use of the matching-from-sample method. *Journal of Experimental Psychology, 32*, 424–434.

Spear, P.D., & Barbas, H. (1975). Recovery of pattern discrimination ability in rats receiving serial or one-stage visual cortex lesions. *Brain Research, 94*, 337–346.

Spencer, W.A., Thompson, R.F., & Neilson, D.R., Jr. (1966a). Alterations in responsiveness of ascending and reflex pathways activated by interated cutaneous afferent volleys. *Journal of Neurophysiology, 29*, 240–252.

Spencer, W.A., Thompson, R.F., & Neilson, D.R., Jr. (1966b). Decrement of ventral root electrotonus and intracellularly recorded post-synaptic potentials produced by iterated cutaneous afferent volleys. *Journal of Neurophysiology, 29*, 253–274.

Spencer, W.A., Thompson, R.F., & Neilson, D.R., Jr. (1966c). Response decrement of flexion reflex in acute spinal cat and transient restoration by strong stimuli. *Journal of Neurophysiology, 29*, 221–239.

Sperry, R.W. (1947a). Cerebral regulation of motor coordination following multiple transection of sensorimotor cortex. *Journal of Neurophysiology, 10*, 275–294.

Sperry, R.W. (1947b). Effect of crossing nerves to antagonistic limb muscles in the monkey. *Archives of Neurology & Psychiatry, 58*, 452–473.

Sperry, R.W. (1952). Neurology and the mind-brain problem. *American Scientist, 40*, 291–312.

Sperry, R.W., Miner, N., & Myers, R.E. (1955). Visual pattern perception following subpial slicing and tantalum wire implantations in the visual cortex. *Journal of Comparative & Physiological Psychology, 48*, 50–58.

Spiegler, B.J., & Mishkin, M. (1981). Evidence for the sequential participation of inferior temporal cortex and amygdala in the acquisition of stimulus-reward associations. *Behavioral Brain Research, 3*, 303–317.

Spinelli, D.N., & Jensen, F.E. (1979). Plasticity: The mirror of experience. *Science, 203*, 75–78.

Spinelli, D.N., Jensen, F.E., & DiPisco, G.V. (1980). Early experience effect on dendritic branching in normally reared kittens. *Experimental Neurology, 68*, 1–11.

Sprague, J.M. (1966). Interaction of cortex and superior colliculus in mediation of visually guided behavior in the cat. *Science, 153*, 1544–1547.

Sprague, J.M., Levy, J., DiBerardino, A., & Berlucchi, G. (1965). Visual cortical areas mediating visually guided behavior. *Experimental Neurology, 11*, 115–146.

Squire, L.R. (1982). The neurophysiology of human memory. *Annual Review of Neuroscience, 5*, 241–273.

Squire, L.R., & Barondes, S.H. (1974). Anisomycin, like other inhibitors of cerebral protein synthesis, impairs "long-term" memory of a discrimination task. *Brain Research, 66*, 301–308.

Squire, L.R., & Cohen, N. (1979). Memory and amnesia: Resistence to disruption develops for years after learning. *Behavioral & Neural Biology, 25*, 115–125.

Squire, L.R., & Davis, H.P. (1981). The pharmacology of memory: A neurobiological perspective. *Annual Review of Pharmacological Toxicology, 21*, 323–356.

Squire, L.R., & Spanis, C.W. (1984). Long gradient of retrograde amnesia in mice: Continuity with the findings in humans. *Behavioral Neuroscience, 98*, 345–348.

Squire, L.R., & Zola-Morgan, S. (1983). The neurology of memory: The case for correspondence between the findings for man and non-human primates. In J.A. Duetsch (Ed.), *The Physiological basis of memory* (2nd ed.). New York: Academic Press.

Stanes, M.D., Brown, C.P., Singer, G. (1976). Effects of physotigmine on Y-maze discrimination retention in the rat. *Psychopharmacologia, 46*, 269–276.

Starr, M.D. (1978). An opponent-process theory of motivation: I. Time and intensity variables in the development of separation-induced distress calling in ducklings. *Journal of Experimental Psychology: Animal Behavior Processes, 4,* 338–355.

Stein, D.G., & Chorover, S.L. (1968). Effects of post-trial stimulation of hippocampus and caudate nucleus on maze learning in the rat. *Physiology & Behavior, 3,* 787–791.

Steinmetz, J.E., Lavond, D.G., & Thompson, R.F. (1985). Classical conditioning of skeletal muscle responses with mossy fiber stimulation CS and climbing fiber stimulation US. *Neuroscience Abstracts, 11,* 982 (No. 290.6).

Steinmetz, J.E., Rosen, D.J., Chapman, P.F., Lavond, D.G., & Thompson, R.F. (1986). Classical conditioning of the rabbit eyelid response with a mossy fiber stimulation CS. I. Pontine nuclei and middle cerebellar peduncle stimulation. *Behavioral Neuroscience, 100,* 871–880.

Steinmetz, J.E., Logan, C.G., Rosen, D.J., Thompson, J.K., Lavond, D.G., & Thompson, R.F. (1987). Initial localization of the acoustic conditioned stimulus projection system to the cerebellum essential for classical eyelid conditioning. *Proceedings of the National Academy of Sciences, 84,* 3531–3535.

Stamm, J.S. (1964). Retardation and facilitation in learning by stimulation of frontal cortex in monkeys. In J.M. Warren & K. Akert (Eds.), *The frontal granular cortex and behavior* (pp. 102–125). New York: McGraw-Hill.

Stein, D.G., Rosen, J.J., & Butters, N. (Eds.) (1974). *Plasticity and recovery of function in the central nervous sytem.* New York: Academic Press.

Stern, L.D. (1981). A review of theories of human amnesia. *Memory & Cognition, 9,* 247–262.

Steward, O., Cotman, C.W., & Lynch, G.S. (1976). A quantitative autoradiographic and electrophysiological study of the reinnervation of the dentate gyrus by the contralateral entorhinal cortex following ipsilateral entorhinal lesions. *Brain Research, 114,* 181–200.

Stinus, L., Gaffori, O., Simon, H., & LeMoal, M. (1978). Disappearance of hoarding and disorganization of eating behavior after ventral mesencephalic tegmentum lesions in rats. *Journal of Comparative & Physiological Psychology, 92,* 288–296.

Stone, J., & Dreher, B. (1973). Projection of X- and Y-cells of the cat's lateral geniculate nucleus to areas 17 and 18 of visual cortex. *Journal of Neurophysiology, 36,* 551–567.

Swanson, L.W., & Sawchenko, P.E. (1983). *Annual Review of Neuroscience, 6,* 269–324.

Swanson, L.W., Teyler, T.J., & Thompson, R.F. (Eds.). (1982a). *Mechanisms and functional implications of hippocampal LTP.* Neurosciences Research Program, 20. Boston, MA: MIT Press.

Swanson, L.W., Teyler, T.J., & Thompson, R.F. (1982b). Hippocampal long-term potentiation: Mechanisms and implications for memory. *Neurosciences Research Program Bulletin, 20*(5).

Tanzi, E. (1893). I fatti e le induzioni nell'odierna istologia del sistema nervoso. *Rivista sperimentale di freniatria e medicina legale delle mentali alienazioni, 19,* 419–472.

Tempel, B.L., Bonini, N., Dawson, D.R., & Quinn, W.G. (1983). Reward learning in normal and mutant *Drosophila. Proceedings of the National Academy of Science USA., 80,* 1482–1486.

Teuber, H.L. (1955). Physiological psychology. *Annual Review of Psychology, 6,* 267–296.

Teuber, H.L. (1964). The riddle of frontal function in man. In J.M. Warren & K. Adert (Eds.), *The frontal granular cortex and behavior* (pp. 410–444). New York: McGraw-Hill.

Thal, L.J., Rosen, W., Sharpless, N.S., & Crystal, H. (1981). Choline chloride fails to improve cognition in Alzheimer's disease. *Neurology of Aging, 2,* 205–208.

Thal, L.J., & Fuld, P.A. (1983). Memory enhancement with oral physotigmine in Alzheimer's disease. *New England Journal of Medicine, 308*(12), 720–721.

Thierry, A.M., Blanc, G., Sobel, A., Stimus, L., & Glowinski, J. (1983). Dopaminergic terminals in the rat cortex. *Science, 182,* 499–501.

Thomas, G.J., Brito, G.N.O., Stein, D.P., & Berko, J.K. (1982). Memory and septo-hippocampal connections in rats. *Journal of Comparative & Physiological Psychology, 96,* 339–347.

Thompson, D.M., & Moerschbaecher, J.M. (1979). An experimental analysis of the effects of *d*-amphetamine and cocaine on the acquisition and performance of response chains in monkeys. *Journal of the Experimental Analysis of Behavior, 32,* 433–444.

Thompson, R. (1960). Retention of a brightness discrimination following neocortical damage in the rat. *Journal of Comparative & Physiological Psychology, 53,* 212–215.

Thompson, R. (1983). Brain systems and long-term memory. *Behavioral & Neural Biology, 37,* 1–45.

Thompson, R.F. (1986). The neurobiology of learning and memory. *Science, 233,* 941–947.

Thompson, R.F., Berger, T.W., Berry, S.D., Hoehler, F.K., Kettner, R.E., & Weisz, D.J. (1980). Hippocampal substrate of classical conditioning. *Physiological Psychology, 8*(2), 262–279.

Thompson, R.F., Berger, T.W., Cegavski, C.F., Patterson, M.M., Roemer, R.A., Teyler, T.J., & Young,

R.A. (1976). The search for the engram. *American Psychologist, 31,* 209–227.

Thompson, R.F., Berger T.W., & Madden, J., IV (1983). Cellular processes of learning and memory in the mammalian CNS. *Annual Review of Neuroscience, 6,* 447–491.

Thompson, R.F., Clark, G.A., Donegan, N.H., Lavond, D.G., Madden, J., IV, Mamounas, L.A., Mauk, M.D., & McCormick, D.A. (1984). Neuronal substrates of basic associative learning. In L. Squire & N. Butters, (Eds.), *Neuropsychology of memory,* pp. 424–442. New York: Guilford Press.

Thompson, R.F., Donegan, N.H., Clark, G.A., Lavond, D.G., Lincoln, J.S., Madden, J., IV, Mamounas, L.A., Mauk, M.D., & McCormick, D.A. (1987). Neuronal substrates of discrete, defensive conditioned reflexes, conditioned fear states, and their interactions in the rabbit. In I. Gormezano, W.F. Prokasy and R.F. Thompson (Eds.), *Classical conditioning: III. Behavioral, neurophysiological, and neurochemical studies in the rabbit.* Hillsdale, NJ: Erlbaum.

Thompson, R.F., Donegan, N.H., Clark, G.A., Lavond, D.G., Lincoln, J.S., Madden, J. IV, Mamounas, L.A., Mauk, M.D., & McCormick, D.A. (1987). Neuronal substrates of discrete, defensive conditioned reflexes, conditioned fear states, and their interactions in the rabbit. In I. Gormezano, W.F. Prokasy, & R.F. Thompson (Eds.), *Classical conditioning* (3rd ed.) (pp. 371–399). Hillsdale, NJ: Erlbaum.

Thompson, R.F., McCormick, D.A., & Lavond, D.G. (1984). Localization of the essential memory trace system for a basic form of associative learning in the mammalian brain. In S. Hulse (Ed.), *G. Stanley Hall centennial volume.* Baltimore MD: Johns Hopkins University Press.

Thompson, R.F., Patterson, M.M., & Teyer, T.J. (1972). The neurophysiology of learning. *Annual Review of Psychology, 23,* 73–104.

Thompson, R.F., & Spencer, W.A. (1966). Habituation: A model phenomenon for the study of neuronal substrates of behavior. *Psychological Review, 73,* 16–43.

Thorpe, W.H. (1958). The learning of song patterns by birds, with especial reference to the song of the chaffinch, *Fringilla coelebs. Ibis, 100,* 535–570.

Thorpe, W.H. (Ed.) (1973). Learning and associated phenomena in invertebrates. *Animal Behavior Supplement 1.* London: Bailliere, Tindall, & Cassell.

Tischler, M.D., & Davis, M. (1983). A visual pathway that mediates fear-conditioned enhancement of acoustic startle. *Brain Research, 276,* 55–71.

Travis, A.M., & Woolsey, C.N. (1956). Motor performance of monkeys after bilateral partial and total cerebral decortications. *American Journal of Physical Medicine, 35,* 273–310.

Tsukahara, N. (1981). Synaptic plasticity in the mammalian central nervous system. *Annual Review of Neuroscience, 4,* 351–379.

Tsukahara, N. (1982). Classical conditioning mediated by the red nucleus in the cat. See Woody 1982. In press.

Tsukahara, N., Oda, Y., & Notsu, T. (1981). Classical conditioning mediated by the red nucleus in the cat. *Journal of Neuroscience, 1,* 72–79.

Tucker, T.J., & Kling, A. (1967). Differential effects of early and late lesions of frontal granular cortex in the monkey. *Brain Research, 5,* 377–389.

Tucker, T.J., & Kling, A. (1969). Perseveration of delayed response following combined lesions of prefrontal and posterior association cortex in infant monkeys. *Experimental Neurology, 23,* 491–502.

Turner, A.M., & Greenough, W.T. (1985). Differential rearing effects on rat visual cortex synapses: I. Synaptic and neuronal density and synapses per neuron. *Brain Research, 329,* 195–203.

Uylings, H.B.M., Kuypers, K., Diamond, M.C., & Veltman, W.A.M. (1978). Effects of differential environments on plasticity of dendrites of cortical pyramidal neurons in adult rats. *Experimental Neurology, 62,* 658–677.

Valverde, F. (1967). Apical dendritic spines of the visual cortex and light deprivation in the mouse. *Experimental Brain Research, 3,* 337–352.

Valverde, F. (1968). Structural changes in the area striate of the mouse after enucleation. *Experimental Brain Research, 5,* 274–292.

Valverde, F. (1971). Rate and extent of recovery from dark rearing in the visual cortex of the mouse. *Experimental Brain Research, 33,* 1–12.

Van Essen, D.C., & Maunsell, J.H.R. (1983). Hierarchical organization and functional streams in the visual cortex. *Trends in Neuroscience, 6,* 370–375.

Vidal, J.M. (1980). The relations between filial and sexual imprinting in the domestic foul: Effects of age and social experience. *Animal Behavior, 28,* 880–891.

Volkmar, F.R., & Greenough, W.T. (1972). Rearing complexity affects branching of dendrites in visual cortex of the rat. *Science, 117,* 1445–1447.

von Monakow, C. (1914). *Die lokalisation im grosshirn und der abbau der funktion durch kortikale herde.* Wiesbaden: Bergmann.

Voronin, L.L. (1971). Microelectrode study of cellular analogs of conditioning. *Proc. 25th Intl. Congr. Physiol. Sci. Munich, 8,* 199–200.

Voronin, L.L. (1980). Microelectrode analysis of the

cellular mechanisms of conditioned reflex in rabbits. *Acta Neurobiol. Exp.*, *40*, 335–370.

Vrensen, G., & Cardozo, J.N. (1981). Changes in size and shape of synaptic connections after visual training: An ultrastructural approach of synaptic plasticity. *Brain Research, 219*, 79–97.

Vrensen, G., & De Groot, D. (1975). The effect of monocular deprivation on synaptic terminals in the visual cortex of rabbits. A quantitative electron microscopic study. *Brain Research, 93*, 15–24.

Wagner, A.R. (1969). Stimulus selection and a "modified continuity theory". In G.H. Bower & J.T. Spence (Eds.), *The psychology of learning and motivation: Vol. 3.* New York: Academic Press.

Wagner, A.R. (1976). Priming in STM: An information processing mechanism for self-generated or retrieval-generated depression in performance. In T.J. Tighe & R.M. Leaton (Eds.), *Perspectives from child development, animal behavior, and neurophysiology.* Hillsdale, NJ: Erlbaum.

Wagner, A.R. (1979). Habituation and memory. In A. Dickinson & R.A. Boakes (Eds.), *Mechanisms of learning and motivation.* Hillsdale, NJ: Erlabum.

Wagner, A.R. (1981). SPO: A model of automatic memory processing in animal behavior. In N.E. Spear and R.R. Miller (Eds.), *Information processing in animals: Memory mechanisms.* Hillsdale, NJ: Erlbaum.

Wagner, A.R., & Donegan, N.H. (in press). A neurobiological interpretation of SOP. In R.D. Hawkins & G.H. Bower (Eds.) *The psychology of learning and motivation.* New York: Academic Press.

Walk, R.D. (1958). Visual and visual-motor experience: a replication. *Journal of Comparative & Physiological Psychology, 51*, 785–787.

Wall, J., Wild, J.M., Broyles, J., Gibbs, C.M., Cohen, D.H. (1980). Plasticity of the tectofugal pathway during visual conditioning. *Neuroscience Abstracts, 6*, 424.

Wall, P.D. (1980). Mechanisms of plasticity of connection following damage in adult mammalian nervous systems. In P. Bach-y-Rita (Ed.), *Recovery of function: Theoretical considerations for brain injury rehabilitation.* Baltimore, MA: University Park Press.

Walsh, R.N., & Greenough, W.T. (1976). *Environments as therapy for brain dysfunction:* Vol. 17. New York: Plenum Press.

Walters, E.T., & Byrne, J.H. (1983). Associative conditioning of single sensory neurons suggests a cellular mechanism for learning. *Science, 219*, 405–408.

Walters, E.T., Carew, T.J., & Kandel, E.R. (1979). Classical conditioning in *Aplysia californica. Proceedings of the National Academy of Science USA, 76*, 6675–6679.

Warren, J.M. (1964). The behavior of carnivores and primates with lesions in the prefrontal cortex. In J.M. Warren & K. Akert (Eds.), *The frontal granular cortex and behavior.* New York: McGraw–Hill.

Warrington, E.K., & Weiskrantz, L. (1968). New method of testing long-term retention with special reference to amnesic patients. *Nature, 217*, 972–974.

Warrington, E.K., & Weiskrantz, L. (1982). Amnesia: A disconnection syndrome? *Neuropsychologia 20*, 233–248.

Wasser, M.S., & Marler, P. (1977). Song learning in canaries. *Journal of Comparative & Physiological Psychology, 91*, 1–7.

Watson, J.B. (1924). *Behaviorism.* New York: Peoples Institute Pub.

Webster, W.G. (1973). Assumptions, conceptualizations, and the search for the functions of the brain. *Physiological Psychology 1*, 346–350.

Weinberger, N.M. (1980). Neurophysiological studies of learning in association with the pupillary dilation conditioned reflex. See Thompson et al. 1980.

Weinberger, N.M. (1982a). Effects of conditioned arousal on the auditory system. In A.L. Beckman (Ed.), *The neural basis of behavior.* Jamaica, NY: Spectrum.

Weinberger, N.M. (1982b). Sensory plasticity and learning: The magnocellular medial geniculate nucleus of the auditory system. See Woody 1982.

Weiskrantz, L. (1956). Behavioral changes associated with ablation of the amygdaloid complex in monkeys. *Journal of Comparative & Physiological Psychology, 49*, 381–391.

Weiskrantz, L. (1971). Comparison of amnesic states in monkey and man. In L.E. Jarrard (Ed.), *Cognitive Processes of Non-human Primates* (pp. 25–46). New York: Academic Press.

Weiskrantz, L.R., & Warrington, E.K. (1970). Verbal learning and retention by amnesic patients using partial information. *Psychonomic Science, 20*, 210–211.

Weiskrantz, L.R., & Warrington, E.K. (1979). Conditioning in amnesic patients. *Neuropsychologia, 17*, 187–194.

Weisz, D.J., Clark, G.A., & Solomon, P.R. (1982). Activity of dentate gyrus during NM conditioning in rabbit. In C.D. Woody (Ed.), *Conditioning: Representation of involved neural functions* (pp. 131–145). New York: Plenum Press.

Weisz, D.J., Clark, G.A., & Thompson, R.F. (1984). Increased activity of dentate granule cells during nictitating membrane response conditioning in rabbits. *Behavioral Brain Research, 12*, 145–154.

Weisz, D.J., & Thompson, R.F. (1983). Endogenous opioids: Brain-behavior relations. In P.K. Levison, D.R. Gerstein, & D.R. Maloff (Eds.), *Commonalities in substance abuse and habitual behavior*, (pp. 297–322). Lexington, MA: DC Heath and Company.

Wenzel, S., Kammerer, E., Kirsche, W., Matthies, H., & Wenzel, M. (1980). Electron microscopic and morphometric studies on synaptic plasticity in the hippocampus of the rat following conditioning. *J. Hirnforsch.*, *21*, 647–654.

Werka, T., Skar, J., & Ursin, H. (1978). Exploration and avoidance in rats with lesions in amygdala and piriform cortex. *Journal of Comparative & Physiological Psychology*, *92*, 672.

Werner, G., & Whitsel, B.L. (1968). Topology of the body representation in somatosensory area I of primates. *Journal of Neurophysiology*, *31*, 856–869.

West, R.W., & Greenough, W.T. (1972). Effect of environmental complexity on cortical synapses of rats: Preliminary results. *Behavioral Biology*, *7*, 279–284.

Westbrook, W.H., & McGaugh, J.L. (1964). Drug facilitation of latent learning. *Psychopharmacologia (Berlin)* *5*, 440–446.

Westenberg, I.S., & Weinberger, N.M. (1976). Evoked potential decrements in auditory cortex: II. Critical test for habituation. *Electroencephalography and Clinical Neurophysiology*, *40*, 356–369.

Whitfield, I.C. (1967). *The auditory pathway*. London: Edward Arnold.

Whitfield, I.C., & Evans, E.F. (1965). Responses of auditory cortical neurons to stimuli of changing frequency. *Journal of Neurophysiology*, *28*, 655–672.

Whitlow, J.W. (1975). Short-term memory in habituation and dishabituation. *Journal of Experimental Psychology: Animal Behavior Processes*, *1*, 189–206.

Whitlow, J.W. Jr., & Wagner, A.R. (1984). Memory and habituation. In H.V.S. Peeke & L. Petrinovich (Eds.), *Habituation, Sensitization and Behavior*. New York: Academic Press.

Whitsel, B.L., Roppolo, J.R., & Werner, G. (1972). Cortical information processing of stimulus motion on primate skin. *Journal of Neurophysiology*, *35*, 691–717.

Wickelgren, W.A. (1979). Chunking and consolidation: A theoretical synthesis of semantic networks, configuring in conditioning, S–R versus cognitive learning, normal forgetting, the amnesic syndrome, and the hippocampal arousal system. *Psychological Review*, *86*, 44–60.

Wieland, S.J., & Gelperin, A. (1983). Dopamine elicits feeding motor program in *Limax maximus*. *Journal of Neuroscience*, *3*, 1735–1745.

Wiesel, T.N., Hubel, D.H., & Lam, D.M.K. (1974). Autoradiographic demonstration of ocular-dominance columns in the monkey striate cortex by means of transneuronal transport. *Brain Research*, *79*, 273–279.

Will, B.E., & Rosenzweig, M. (1976). Effets de L'environnement sur la recupeeration fonctionnelle apres lesions cerebrales chez des rats adultes. *Behavioral Biology*, *1*, 5–16.

Will, B.E., Rosenzweig, M.R., & Bennett, E.L. (1976). Effects of differential environments on recovery from neonatal brain lesions, measured by problem-solving scores and brain dimensions. *Physiology & Behavior*, *16*, 603–611.

Will, B.E., Rosenzweig, M.R., Bennett, E.L., Hebert, M., & Morimoto, H. (1977). Relatively brief environmental enrichment aids recovery of learning capacity and alters brain measures after postweaning brain lesions in rats. *Journal of Comparative & Physiological Psychology*, *91*, 33–50.

Williams, D.R. (1981). Biconditional behavior: Conditioning without constraint. In C.M. Lacurto, H.S. Terrace, & J. Gibbon (Eds.), *Autoshaping and conditioning theory*. New York: Academic Press.

Wilson, M. (1957). Effects of circumscribed cortical lesions upon somesthetic discrimination in the monkey. *Journal of Comparative & Physiological Psychology*, *50*, 630–635.

Wine, J.J., Krasne, F.B., & Chen, L. (1975). Habituation and inhibition of cray-fish lateral giant fiber escape responses. *Journal of Experimental Biology*, *63*, 433–450.

Winocur, G., & Weiskrantz, L. (1976). An investigation of paired associate learning in amnesic patients. *Neuropsychologia*, *14*, 97–110.

Winograd, T. (1975). Frame representations and the declarative-procedural controversy. In D.G. Bobrow & A.M. Collins (Eds.), *Representation and understanding studies in cognitive science*. New York: Academic Press.

Woody, C.D. (1970). Conditioned eye blink: Gross potential activity at coronal-precruciate cortex of the cat. *Journal of Neurophysiology*, *33*, 838–850.

Woody, C.D. (Ed.). (1982a). *Conditioning: Representation of involved neural functions*. New York: Plenum.

Woody, C.D. (1982b). Neurophysiologic correlates of latent facilitation. In C.D. Woody (Ed.), *Conditioning: Representation of involved neural functions* (pp. 233–248). New York: Plenum.

Woody, C.D. (1982c). *Memory, learning and higher function*. New York: Springer–Verlag.

Woody, C.D., & Black-Clewarth, P.A. (1973). Differences in the excitability of cortical neurons as a function of motor projection in conditioned cats. *Journal of Neurophysiology, 36,* 1104–1116.

Woody, C.D., & Brozek, G. (1969). Changes in evoked responses from facial nucleus of cat with conditioning and extinction of an eye blink. *Journal of Neurophysiology, 32,* 717–726.

Woody, C.D., Knispel, J.D., Crow, T.J., & Black-Cleworth, P.A. (1976). Activity and excitability to electrical current of cortical auditory receptive neurons of awake cats as affected by stimulus association. *Journal of Neurophysiology, 39*(5), 1045–1061.

Woody, C.D., Vassilevsky, N.N., & Engel, J., Jr. (1970). Conditioned eye blink: Unit activity at coronal-pericruciate cortex of the cat. *Journal of Neurophysiology, 33,* 851–864.

Woody, C.D., Yarowsky, P., Owens, J., Black-Cleworth, P., & Crow, T. (1974). Effect of lesions of coronal motor areas on acquisition of conditioned eye blink in the cat. *Journal of Neurophysiology, 37,* 385–394.

Woollacott, M., & Hoyle, G. (1977). Neural events underlying learning: Changes in pacemaker. *Proceedings of the Royal Society (London), Ser. B, 195,* 395–415.

Woolsey, C.N. (1958). Organization of somatic sensory and motor areas of the cerebral cortex. In H.F. Harlow & C.N. Woolsey (Eds.), *Biological and biochemical bases of behavior.* Madison, WI: University of Wisconsin Press.

Woolsey, C.N., Settlage, P.H., Meyer, D.R., Spencer, W., Pinto-Hamuy, T., & Travis, A.M. (1950). Patterns of localization in precentral and "supplementary" motor areas and their relation to the concept of a premotor area. In *Patterns of organization in the central nervous system* (pp. 238–264). Baltimore, MD: Williams & Wilkins.

Woolsey, T.A. (1978). Lesion experiments: Some anatomical considerations. In S. Finger (Ed.), *Recovery from brain damage.* New York: Plenum Press.

Yehle, A.L., Dauth, G., & Schneiderman, N. (1967). Correlates of heart-rate classical conditioning in curarized rabbits. *Journal of Comparative & Physiological Psychology, 64,* 93–104.

Yeo, C.H., Hardiman, M.J. & Glickstein, M. (1984). Discrete lesions of the cerebellar cortex abolish the classically conditioned nictitating membrane response of the rabbit. *Behavioral Brain Research, 13,* 261–266.

Yeo, C.H., Hardiman, M.J., & Glickstein, M. (1985).

Classical conditioning of the nictitating membrane response of the rabbit. I. Lesions of the cerebellar cortex. *Experimental Brain Research, 60,* 99–113.

Yerkes, R.M. (1912). The intelligence of earthworms. *Journal of Animal Behavior, 2,* 332–352.

Young, J.Z. (1962). Repeated reversal training in *Octupus. Quarterly Journal of Experimental Psychology, 14,* 206–222.

Yutzey, D.A., Myer, D.M., & Myer, D.A. (1964). Emotionality changes following septal and neocortical ablations in rats. *Journal of Comparative & Physiological Psychology, 58,* 463–467.

Zemp, J.W., Wilson, J.E., Schlesinger, K., Boggan, W.O., & Glassman, E. (1966). Brain function and macromolecules: I. Incorporation of uridine into RNA of mouse brain during short-term training experience. *Proceedings of the National Academy of Sciences, 55,* 1423–1431.

Zola-Morgan, S., Squire, L.R., & Mishkin, M. (1981). The anatomy of amnesia: Amygdala-hippocampus vs. temporal stem. *Neuroscience Abstracts, 7.*

Zola-Morgan, S., Squire, L.R., & Mishkin, M. (1982). The neuroanatomy of amnesia: Amygdala-hippocampus versus temporal stem. *Science, 218,* 1337–1339.

Zomzley-Neurath, C.P., Marangos, P.J., Hymonowitz, N., Perl, W., Ritter, A. (1976). Changes in brain-specific proteins during learning. *Trans. Am. Soc. Neurochem., 7,* 242.

Zornetzer, S.F. (1978). Neurotransmitter modulation and memory: A new neuro-pharmacological phrenology? In M.A. Lipton, A. DiMascio, & K.F. Killam (Eds.), *Psychopharmacology: A generation of progress* (pp. 637–649). New York: Raven Press.

Zornetzer, S.F., & Gold, M. (1976) The locus coerulus: Its possible role in memory consolidation. *Physiology & Behavior, 16,* 331–336.

Zornetzer, S.F., & McGaugh, J.L. (1971). Retrograde amnesia and brain seizures in mice. *Physiology & Behavior, 7,* 401–408.

Zornetzer, S.F., Abraham, W.C., & Appleton, R. (1978). The locus coeruleus and labile memory. *Pharmacology, Biochemistry & Behavior, 9,* 227–234.

Zucker, R.S. (1972a). Crayfish escape behavior and central synapses: I. Neural circuit exciting lateral giant fiber. *Journal of Neurophysiology, 35,* 599–620.

Zucker, R.S. (1972b). Crayfish escape behavior and central synapses: II. Physiological mechanisms underlying behavioral habituation. *Journal of Neurophysiology, 35,* 621–637.

# COGNITION

# Chapter 5

# HUMAN LEARNING AND MEMORY

**W.K. Estes,** *Harvard University*

Several strands of theory enter importantly into the organization of this chapter. One of these comprises ideas deriving from preexperimental psychology and philosophy that are robust enough to remain influential despite changes in fashion. The second strand comes from general learning theory, deriving largely from research on animal learning. The third principal theme is associated with contemporary cognitive psychology. Learning is just one aspect of the human information-processing system, and the products of learning can only be fruitfully interpreted in relation to concepts of representation in memory.

The history of research on human learning can be seen as a succession of attempts to solve three major problems: (a) How to bring the experimental method to bear on a complex subject matter; (b) how to relate the results of circumscribed lines of experimental research to general theoretical ideas; and (c) how to relate the results of experimental and theoretical analysis to practical problems.

Preparation of this chapter was supported in part by grant MH 33917 from the National Institute of Mental Health and grant BNS 80–26656 from the National Science Foundation.

When the study of human learning first began its transition from a branch of philosophy to a laboratory-based discipline, there was little in the way of general psychological theory, so the first of these problems had to be addressed before the second and third could be considered. The course the new discipline would follow over its first half century was largely set by the accomplishments of Ebbinghaus (1885/1913) and Thorndike (1913). These investigators analyzed learning in the laboratory with highly simplified materials amenable to controlled manipulation and to the generation of interpretable quantitative data. Concurrently, an increasingly energetic research effort was directed toward empirically oriented experiments bearing on the learning of materials of the kind studied in school, but on the whole these yielded little in the way of generalizable results.

Progress toward general theory was initiated after relatively formal and systematic learning and behavior theories began to appear in the 1940s and efforts ensued to bring human learning into the domain of general learning theory, though with the research instigated still being largely carried out in the simplified paradigms of the Ebbinghaus-Thorndike tradition (Atkinson, Bower, & Crothers, 1965; Estes, 1959; Gibson, 1940; Hull, Hovland, Ross, Hall, Perkins, & Fitch, 1940; Spence, 1956). A new wave of theoretical advances came with the beginning of the information-processing movement in cognitive psychology around 1960 (Feigenbaum, 1963; Hunt, 1962). The new theoretical approach was related in many respects to concurrent developments in artificial intelligence, as was the still more substantial continuing effort of Anderson and Bower (1973). Finally, within the last decade, the theoretical framework provided by the combination of learning and information-processing models and the associated quantitative and computer simulation methods enabled fruitful attacks on learning in tasks complex enough to relate meaningfully to extra-laboratory situations of practical interest (Anderson, 1976; Kintsch, 1974; Norman & Rumelhart, 1975; Smith & Medin, 1981).

## LEARNING AND INFORMATION PROCESSING

The theoretical framework appropriate to organize a review of research on human learning in the 1980's differs radically from the one that shaped Hovland's (1951) review some three decades ago. The difference turns in part on the sharp distinction between the character of normal human learning and that of learning in laboratory situations that was the basis for virtually all learning theory prior to about mid-century. The crux of the distinction is that, in normal human learning, memory is much less closely coupled to action.

In the learning of animals and of human subjects in restricted laboratory tasks, the information being acquired is closely related to current task demands. Consequently, it was entirely natural both in classical learning theories (Hilgard, 1956) and in the functional psychology of human learning (McGeoch, 1942) to formulate laws and principles in terms of relationships between conditions of learning and resulting changes in performance, usually improvement relative to some goal. But in normal human learning, information acquired in a given situation is more often relevant only to behavior that may be called for at much later times and in very different circumstances. An

appreciation of this aspect of the human learner leads us to understand that we can hope to comprehend human learning only within theories that explain how information becomes transformed and organized in memory and how it is retrieved (or why it fails to be retrieved) in tests and problem situations. This view epitomizes the currently highly influential information-processing approach to human learning and cognition.

The almost revolutionary shift in theoretical outlook over the last few decades poses a difficult problem of organization. How can we take adequate account of the body of experimental methods and facts accumulated by research in the earlier framework, while at the same time maintaining a coherent vocabulary and frame of reference for the interpretation of these plus the large volume of newer results? My approach will be first to outline the overall architecture of the information-processing framework[1], then to survey briefly the classic research findings that have brought this viewpoint to wide acceptance, and finally to review major lines of research on human learning, with earlier findings for the most part being interpreted in terms of modern ideas.

### The Flow of Information Processing

It has become a generally accepted tenet of learning theories that the stimulus terms in theories are not events as described in physical terms, but rather events as perceived and interpreted (encoded) by the learner (Lawrence, 1963; Sutherland & Mackintosh, 1971). The product of a learning experience resides in memory for relationships between encoded stimulus information and behavioral dispositions. In the information-processing approach, one probes more deeply into what the individual is doing while learning is taking place. The goal is to construct a theoretical representation of the sequence of events that occur while stimulus information is transformed by perceptual and cognitive operations into the encoded forms that are preserved in organized memory.

The first stage of information processing is assumed to begin when a pattern of sensory information is impressed on the receptor apparatus

---

[1] The summary given here follows in essentials the more extended presentations of Baddeley (1976), Lindsay and Norman (1977), and Shiffrin (1976).

and generates a corresponding patterned representation in what is termed *primary memory*, a term used by William James (1890) but first given quantitative specification by Waugh and Norman (1965). The pattern of information in primary memory can have several different fates. It is vulnerable to disruption by immediately succeeding inputs, and under conditions of high information input, individual patterns may be lost with no detectable trace. If registration of a pattern of information in primary memory is followed by an interval free of distraction, and in particular if the input has some motivational significance for the learner, then the memory may be consolidated in the form of an image that can provide the basis for later recognition if the situation recurs. During the short interval when an information pattern is in primary memory, attentional processes may select some constituent objects or events (normally on the basis of relevance to current task demands or long-term motivations) for further processing, and these items are then encoded in terms of sensory or abstract attributes. The resulting representations constitute the currently active subsytem of memory commonly termed *working memory*, or the *rehearsal buffer*. While items are in working memory, information about them can be retrieved for recognition or recall by search processes. Also, relationships among the items or their attributes may be encoded and enter into the associative structures that make up long-term memory.

Two subsystems of the long-term memory system are commonly distinguished: Representations of events, together with their temporal and situational contexts, are said to belong to *episodic memory*, which constitutes a chronological record of a learner's experiences. Categorizations or other representations of relations among objects or events that are independent of particular contexts constitute *semantic* or *categorical memory* (Tulving, 1983).

Once information is stored in episodic or semantic memory it is generally assumed to be permanent and available for retrieval when the system is probed by appropriate retrieval cues that characteristically take the form of elements of an original context for episodic memories and properties or attributes of remembered factual material in the case of semantic memory. However, even if the assumption is correct that the contents of long-term memory are permanent,

the system is by no means presumed to be static. Particular items or elements in memory vary constantly in availability for retrieval, availability being increased by the act of retrieval and declining during periods of disuse when other information is undergoing retrieval. Also, cognitive operations performed on elements retrieved from long-term memory may give rise to new knowledge structures, for example hypotheses or rules, that are of a different order of abstraction from the representations of the original learning experiences.

## Research on Information Processing

### Distinguishing Primary from Secondary Memory

The conception of stages of information processing sketched above leads us to expect that if a person has heard a series of items, for example the digits of a telephone number or the words of a sentence, recall a short time afterward will generally reflect a mixture of primary and secondary memory. Presumably the last items of the sequence will still be in primary memory if the test is given soon enough while earlier items may have been transferred to secondary memory.

A method for quantitatively assessing the two components of recall was first proposed by Waugh and Norman (1965). Their method was explicated in relation to a short-term, partial-recall experiment designed for the purpose. Subjects were presented with sequences of 16 digits at rates of either 1 per sec or 4 per sec. The last digit presented, termed the *probe*, had occurred earlier in the list exactly once, at some point between position 3 and position 14. The subject's task was to recall the digit that had followed the probe on its earlier occurrence. The observed recall function (Figure 5.1) followed an inverted S course from virtually 100 percent when only one digit intervened between the test digit and the point of recall to 50 percent at four to five intervening digits and to 10 percent at about ten intervening digits. Since there was only a small and statistically insignificant difference between the functions for the two input rates, it was concluded that number of intervening items rather than amount of elapsed time was the principal determinant of retention loss.

The model Waugh and Norman (1965) proposed for the purpose of assessing primary and secondary memory components was based on

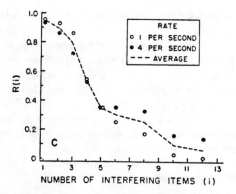

**Figure 5.1.** Relative frequency of digit recall as a function of number of items intervening between presentation of the digit and the cue for recall. From "Primary Memory" by N.C. Waugh and D.A. Norman, 1965, *Psychological Review, 72*, p. 91. Copyright 1965 by the American Psychological Association. Reprinted by permission of the authors.

the assumption that their contributions to recall combine probabilistically according to the function:

$$R_i = P_i + S_i - P_iS_i,$$

in which $R_i$ denotes relative frequency of recall following $i$ intervening item presentations and $P_i$ and $S_i$ the contributions of primary and secondary memory, respectively. In order to use this function to estimate the primary component, it is assumed that, for long lists, recall of all but the last few items must come entirely from secondary memory. Waugh and Norman tested their model on several sets of data from free recall of word lists, estimated $S_i$ from the observed percentage recall of items from the middle of the lists, then entered the estimates in Equation 1 together with observed values of $R_i$ and solved for $P_i$ at each value of $i$. The estimated functions for forgetting from primary memory so obtained from several experiments agreed very well with the observed functions obtained from the probe digit experiment, in which recall was presumed to depend solely on primary memory.

The fact that presentation rate had little effect in Waugh and Norman's probe digit experiment might suggest that the transition of an item from primary to secondary memory is relatively independent of its presentation time. However, that conclusion proves to be justified only for simple items such as individual digits or letters. An experiment by Potter and Levy (1969) addressed this issue with regard to memory

for complex visual scenes. They presented film strips of 16 unrelated naturalistic pictures at rates varying from 125 to 2000 msec per frame, then tested recognition immediately at the end of a sequence by showing the previously presented pictures together with an equal number of new pictures of similar kinds, the subject being instructed to indicate whether each test picture had or had not been present on the film strip. The proportion of correct recognitions of new pictures was virtually 100 percent independent of presentation rate, whereas correct recognition of old pictures varied as a virtually linear function of log presentation time from about 15 percent at 125 msec to about 95 percent at 2000 msec. The possibility that pictures might not have been perceived clearly at the fast rates was ruled out by a later study (Potter, 1976) in which it was found, for the same pictures, that when the task was changed from recognition to detection (reporting whether a picture shown or named in advance occurred anywhere within the sequence) accuracy was 75 to 95 percent even at the shortest exposure times. Thus, when each presented item contains a large amount of information, its consolidation into a secondary trace that can survive a number of subsequent presentations of different items is strongly related to the interval during which the given item is allowed to undergo undisturbed processing. For simple, easily verbalizable items like digits or words, this necessary encoding time can be extended by rehearsal (presumably almost entirely precluded in the Waugh and Norman experiment) but for complex displays such as naturalistic pictures, it can be achieved only by uninterrupted presentation.

An important property of primary memory is that its contents are subject to the mental operations that can select particular constituent items according to criteria set by task demands. Selective attention can be directed to items in primary memory just as it can to elements of a visual scene or an auditory message. This capability was demonstrated in particularly clear form in a study by Sperling (1960), utilizing tachistoscopic displays of letters and what came to be known as a *partial report* procedure. In a typical condition of Sperling's study, a trial included a 50 msec exposure of three rows of random letters, for example:

SDN

TZR
DRF

followed by a bright postexposure field to preclude after-images. In the normal, *full report*, condition, the subject simply attempted immediately following a display to report as many letters as possible; the resulting accuracy of about 50 percent might be taken to imply that about half the letters in the display could be perceived at a 50 msec exposure. Sperling's new procedure was to present immediately following a display a tone of a high, medium, or low frequency to indicate to the subject whether he or she was to report the top, middle, or bottom row of the display (the partial report procedure). When the cue was presented immediately at offset of the display, subjects proved able to report the cued row with 90 percent accuracy. Since the row was randomly selected and could not have been anticipated by the subject, this result implies that about 90 percent of the items in the display must have been perceived; the lower value for the full report procedure must signify that some perceived items are lost from primary memory during the time required to generate a report. When the auditory cue was delayed for various intervals following display offset, partial report declined to about 60 to 65 percent at a 1 sec delay, following a course much like Waugh and Norman's primary memory function.

For items presented in temporal sequence, subjects show similar capability of locating items according to postcues for temporal position (Anderson, 1960). Studies employing other types of postexposure cues have revealed some capability for assessing items in primary memory in response to cues relating to attributes of the items such as color or form, but this task is characteristically much more difficult than locating items by cues for spatial or temporal position, and the information necessary for cueing on the basis of perceptual attributes evidently fades very rapidly from primary memory (von Wright, 1968, 1972).

Patterns of information consolidated from primary memory can provide the basis for recognition after long intervals of time. For example, Shepard (1967) gave subjects single exposures of a few seconds apiece to as many as 600 pictures of natural scenes, then obtained correct recognition scores ranging from over 95 percent at an interval of 2 hr to 87 percent after a week and

nearly 60 percent even after 4 months. Shepard also obtained recognition scores of about 90 percent for immediate tests following administration of series of more than 500 words and more than 1200 meaningful sentences. In contrast, information registered in primary memory typically becomes inaccessible to recall after an interval of only a few seconds if rehearsal is precluded by interfering tasks (Peterson & Peterson, 1959). The critical factor in preparing material for later recall appears to be its selection from primary memory for passage into a much more limited capacity active short-term system commonly termed *working memory* (Baddeley, 1976).

### Active Short-term Memory (*Working Memory*)

This system differs from primary memory in several important respects: (a) It is strictly limited in capacity; (b) items of information are passively registered in primary memory but are actively selected for entry to the working-memory system either by a voluntary act on the part of the individual or by virtue of a well-learned strategy, as in reading or listening; and (c) items in working memory are subject to mental manipulations, for example, rehearsal, reordering, or comparison.

No satisfactory means has been found to quantify the number of items or bits of information that can be held in short-term memory, but the characteristic of limited capacity has been brought out by a number of indirect approaches. In one of these, subjects are engaged in tasks that are presumed to draw on working memory, for example, reasoning or comprehension, and it is found that performance on these tasks is impaired if the subjects are required concurrently to hold in mind sequences of random digits that would have to be kept active in working memory (Baddeley & Hitch, 1974). Similarly, learning in a free recall situation appears to draw on limited capacity working memory. Baddeley and Hitch (1977) gave subjects lists of words to be studied for free recall and, while the words were being presented, required the subjects to keep in mind varying numbers of random digits. Recall of the last few items of a word list was unaffected by the concurrent digit memory requirement, but recall of earlier items in the list was significantly impaired. The interpretation was that the last few items could be reported directly from primary memory but the earlier items could be reported only if they were maintained in active working memory, in which they had to compete for a limited capacity with the concurrently remembered digits.

Entry of items into working memory appears to be a necessary but not sufficient condition for learning, in the sense of preparation for later recall or reconstruction of the learned material. Maintenance of items in active working memory simply by what is termed *primary* or *maintenance* rehearsal, that is, rote repetition, serves to increase the probability of later recognition but within wide limits has no detectable effect on later recall (Craik & Watkins, 1973; Woodward, Bjork, & Jongeward, 1973). In contrast, rehearsal of the type termed *elaborative*, in which the individual actively attends to semantic properties of rehearsed items and relationships between them, or performs such mental operations as composing images or relating items in sentences, does effectively set the stage for later recall (Bower & Winzenz, 1969; Craik & Lockhart, 1972).

A principal function of elaborative rehearsal is to encode an item in terms of attributes that are relevant to later recall. The term *coding* is to be understood with reference to the conception that the representation of an item in memory takes the form, in effect, of a list of its values on various attributes that may range from simple sensory dimensions to abstract semantic properties (Bower, 1967; Smith, Shoben, & Rips, 1974). Thus, for example, if the word *jay* has been entered in memory with reference to a kind of bird, to the degree that the representation includes an auditory code, it might be recalled if the individual were asked to give the name of a bird that rhymes with *hay*, whereas to the degree that the representation is encoded semantically, it might be recalled if the individual were asked for the name of a bird that has blue feathers, a crest, and a raucous call.

Evidence that items are encoded in memory in terms of attributes comes from several types of data. One of these is the occurrence of confusion errors in recall. Conrad (1967) had subjects recall short lists of randomly ordered letters

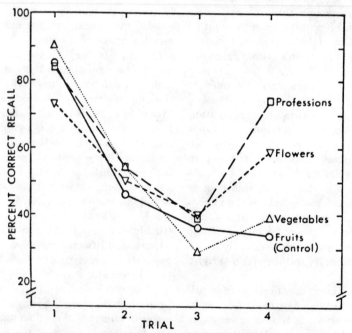

**Figure 5.2.** Release from proactive inhibition, indexed by the increased recall on Trial 4 when semantic category of the stimulus was shifted. All conditions had fruits on Trial 4, preceded by the indicated categories on Trials 1 through 3. From "Characteristics of Word Encoding" by D.D. Wickens in *Coding Processes in Human Memory* (p. 207), A.W. Melton and E. Martin (Eds.), 1972. Washington, DC: V.H. Winston & Sons, Inc. Copyright 1972 by Hemisphere Publishing Corp. Reprinted by permission.

that varied in degree of auditory confusability and demonstrated that errors in recall were significantly related to confusability of vowel sounds, a finding extended later by other investigators to other auditory attributes (Drewnowski & Murdock, 1980).

A quite different type of evidence comes from studies of a phenomenon termed "release from pro-active interference" (Wickens, 1970). The standard procedure in Wickens's paradigm is to present subjects with a series of short lists of items, usually words, with the items in a list sharing some property either auditory, such as a vowel sound, or semantic, such as a taxonomic category. At the end of each list the subject is tested for immediate recall. The characteristic finding, illustrated in Figure 5.2, is that over a series of lists all having a common property, the level of recall decreases uniformly and progressively, but if a list of items drawn from a different category is inserted after several lists have been presented and tested, the level of recall is restored to the original level (the phenomenon of release from proactive interference).

An interpretation in terms of encoding turns on the fact that the subject's task in the experiment is not learning the items, all of which are familiar, but remembering which particular subset of items in active memory occurred in the most recently presented list. Following the first list of a series, the common property (for example that all of the words rhymed with *hat* or that all denoted varieties of birds) is a helpful cue in differentiating the words to be recalled from other words that might be active in short-term memory. On a succession of lists in all of which the items share the same common attribute, the attribute becomes progressively less useful as a differentiating cue, but if at some point the common attribute is changed (for example, from birds to furniture) the newly introduced common attribute serves very effectively to differentiate the just presented list from earlier ones. Results with this technique have reliably revealed the release phenomenon when the common properties are auditory or semantic attributes but not when they are syntactic attributes. Thus it appears that the words an individual hears or reads are normally encoded in terms of auditory and meaningful properties but not in terms of grammatical class.

## Processing Symbolic Information into Long-term Memory

Much research on human memory, like much normal adult cognitive activity outside the laboratory, has to do with acquiring information from symbols, for example, numbers, letters, and words. Memory for the sequences of symbols encountered in reading or listening has two aspects. Rote memory for the specific items seen or heard, for example, verbatim memory for a sentence, requires little more in the way of information processing than described above for arbitrary items. When a sentence is heard or read, the auditory or visual stimulus patterns are registered in primary memory and a sequence of words is selected for temporary maintenance in working memory. If the task is rote memorization, the only cognitive operation that evidently needs to be performed on the items in working memory is to attend to transitions between successive words with the result that the relation of succession is encoded in long-term memory,[2] but if the task is to remember the message conveyed by a sentence, substantial additional processing is needed. In the extensive analysis given by Anderson and Bower (1973), it is assumed that the perceived words are recognized as instances of corresponding concepts and it is the representations of the concepts that are arranged mentally in network format reflecting the relationships among the principal constituents of the sentence (for example, the subject, verb phrase, object phrase).

The network representation is the basis for recognition. More importantly, this representation of the sentence in short-term memory may then be analyzed to determine what propositions it contains (Anderson, 1976; Kintsch, 1974). A proposition is, roughly speaking, an expression of a fact in a form that can be true or false and normally comprises a predicate together with arguments (the arguments being the terms related by the predicate). Suppose, for example, that a sentence being processed is "The plan for the tall building shows apartments above offices." The principal proposition expressed by the sentence has as its predicate the verb *shows*, which expresses a relation among the arguments *apartments*, *above*, and *offices*. There is also a subsidiary proposition whose predicate is the

---

[2]This analysis is essentially the one given by Thorndike (1931), though not in quite the same terminology.

(understood) verb *is* and expresses a relation between the arguments *building* and *tall*.

Several kinds of experiments have yielded evidence that propositions are significant units of information in long-term memory. In one type, Kintsch (1974) compared reading times for sentences all 15 to 17 words in length but varying from 4 to 9 in the number of included propositions, and found that the reading time varied as a virtually linear function of the number of propositions. In another experiment, Kintsch presented subjects sets of sentences that they were then asked to recall and found that the percentage of complete sentences recalled varied significantly as a function of the number of propositions included when the number of content words in a sentence was constant.

In a quite different approach, Ratcliff and McKoon (1978) studied priming in relation to propositional structure. Priming refers to the observation that an individual's reaction time to respond to a word is typically reduced if the word has been preceded within a short interval by another word that is semantically related to it or that occurred contiguously to it in a recently processed passage. In Ratcliff and McKoon's study subjects were given sets of sentences to read, followed by a series of words to each of which the subject had to respond as quickly as possible with "yes" (the word was included in the material just read) or "no" (the word was not so included). The test series was arranged so that some target words were preceded at specific intervals either by words that were expected to have priming effects or by control words. Reaction time data showed an advantage of the order of 100 msec for responses to primed over unprimed words. But of more interest, within the class of primed words, mean reaction times ranged from 25 to 90 msec faster for target words preceded by a prime that had been within the same proposition in the original text than for primes that had been in different propositions.

Although many of the details of the processing whereby sentences heard or read are converted into propositional representations in memory remain to be filled in, the work already accomplished has some cogent implications. Perhaps most important, we are beginning to see at a reasonably specific level how critically the learning of complex material depends on the products of past learning. Newly encountered verbal material can only be analyzed in terms of propositions if the individual recognizes the concepts that are represented, and this capability in turn typically depends on a long period of prior learning in which concepts are developed as a consequence of varied learning experiences (the subject of a later section of this chapter).

### Retrieval of Information from Memory

Locating items in memory presents problems similar to that of finding an object in the visual field and evidently can be accomplished by the same two types of mechanisms—search or direct access. If, for example, one is confronted by a chessboard and asked whether it contains a black queen, one searches the objects on the board visually until a black queen is or is not found. If, rather, the viewer is asked simply whether there is any black piece on the board, it seems possible to answer without locating any particular black piece. The idea that an attribute of feature, such as a color, can be detected by a mechanism that operates in parallel across the visual field, whereas finding an object that represents a conjunction of properties requires a search process, implies that time to accomplish the task should be a linear function of the number of objects present in the latter case but independent of the number of objects in the former, an implication confirmed by Treisman and Gelade (1980).

It appears that the same two types of mechanisms are available for locating information in short-term memory. The search process has been the more intensively investigated, beginning with a study by Sternberg (1966) that demonstrated a linear relation between recognition time for items and the number of items held in short-term memory. In Sternberg's experiment, the subject was presented sequentially with a short list of random digits, then, after a short interval, with a probe digit that might or might not have appeared in the just-presented *memory set*. The subject's task was to respond as quickly as possible to the probe by operating an appropriate response key to indicate whether the probe did or did not belong to the memory set. In Sternberg's data, functions relating reaction time to memory set size were linear, the slopes being positive and parallel for positive and negative trials (trials on which the probe was or was not a member of the memory set). A common slope of about 40 msec per item suggested that the decision is based on a rapid exhaustive search of the set of items held in memory.

The linear function for reaction time versus set size has been obtained with a variety of materials and appears highly replicable so long as the memory set does not exceed the number of items, about six or seven, that can be maintained in a highly active state in working memory. When lists are much longer, the set-size function changes in a way that seems at first paradoxical, manifesting a much smaller slope than that of the short-term function, with values sometimes as low as 1 or 2 msec per item (Murdock & Anderson, 1975). The most widely accepted interpretation is that, for longer lists, the basis of response to the probe item shifts from a search for the corresponding representation in the memory set to an immediate response on the basis of the judged familiarity of the probe. In a model developed by Atkinson and Juola (1973), it is assumed that items vary in an orderly manner with respect to a subjective attribute of familiarity as a function of recency of occurrence and that the subject has the option of responding in the recognition situation either on the basis of a search of the memory set or on the basis of the familiarity of the probe in relation to a mental criterion representing the level of familiarity characterizing items that have been presented in memory sets. Predictions generated from the model with regard to set-size functions have been confirmed for lists of varying length (Wescourt & Atkinson, 1976).

Direct access to items in short-term memory that belong to a common category is not limited to long lists with categorization on the basis of familiarity. Briggs and Johnsen (1973) and Shiffrin and Schneider (1977) showed that, when subjects were given repeated practice with short lists, set-size functions that initially increased linearly with slopes characteristic of the Sternberg paradigm progressively flattened until eventually subjects gave recognition judgments with reaction times that were independent of set size. Shiffrin and Schneider have shown that the necessary condition for this change in the nature of the retrieval process is that practice be done under what they term a *constant mapping* constraint. Constant mapping means that throughout practice with a collection of lists, some items occur only as targets (that is occur as members of memory sets that may be probed) whereas

others occur only as distractors (that is only as probes on negative trials). Reviewing the large body of work in this area, Ryan (1983) proposed that rather than being simply alternative mechanisms that may be used under different circumstances, search and direct access represent two processes that are normally initiated by the probe in any recognition experiment and run in parallel, with the one that completes its course first providing the basis for response. Ordinarily, with short lists of unrelated items, the search process is faster, but with longer lists or with items having some common categorical property the direct-access process is faster.

Retrieval of information from long-term memory appears to involve the same mechanisms as retrieval from short-term memory but combined in more elaborate ways, depending on characteristics of test situations (for a thorough review see Schiffrin, 1970). When an unambiguous retrieval cue for a to-be-retrieved item is presented, as in typical paired-associate situations, direct access to the stored item is evidently possible (Feigenbaum, 1963; Shiffrin, 1970). The principal evidence for direct access is the fact that, with extended practice, reaction time becomes independent of the number of alternative items that might be cued in a situation (Estes, 1980; Seibel, 1963). Access time, estimated from reaction time to the retrieval cue corrected for components unrelated to retrieval, is of the order of 200 msec for recently practiced items (Estes, 1980; Sabol & DeRosa, 1976).

When the task is to recall the events that occurred in some spatial-temporal context, for example, the items of a free recall list, the best developed current theory assumes a recursive search process, rather more complex in character than that demonstrated for short-term memory (Raaijmakers & Shiffrin, 1981). In this model it is assumed that the items or events that occur within a limited time interval in a specific context become associated with each other and with attributes of the context. Memory search may be initiated by reinstatement of the context or by presentation of some attributes of the context together with one or more of the list items. These cues activate associative paths that lead to recall of the most closely associated items, then this subset in turn provides the retrieval cues for the next stage of the search, which may lead to retrieval of additional items. The process continues until all of the items have been retrieved or a criterion for stopping the search is encountered. Combining these assumptions with a ratio rule for probability of retrieval of an item given activation of associated cues, Raaijmakers and Shiffrin have formulated a computer model that provides simulations of a number of the phenomena of free recall.

As in short-term memory, presentation of the label for a category or an attribute common to members of a category may provide direct access to the corresponding subset of items in long-term memory, bypassing the necessity for an extended search. Once the category is accessed, the members may be read out, or they may be searched for a particular to-be-recalled item. The assumption of direct access to categories and search within categories has received support from studies showing that recall from a categorized word list is increased when categories are cued, and that the probability of recalling a member of a cued category is independent of the total length of the list from which recall might occur but decreases with the number of items within each category (Cohen, 1966; Tulving & Pearlstone, 1966).

Retrieving factual information from memory in response to questions may seem a far more complex process than retrieving memories of individual items or events, but it is, nonetheless, conceived to proceed in the same way. Assuming that factual information has been encoded in memory in the form of a network of propositions, the key assumption with regard to retrieval is that a question is encoded in exactly the same form (Anderson & Bower, 1973). Suppose, for example, that an individual has at some time heard or read the sentence "Education prepares one for life," and has encoded the message in memory in the form of a propositional network relating the predicate *prepares* to the arguments *one* (*person*) and *life*. Upon encountering the question "Does education prepare a person for life?", the individual would be presumed to encode the question in a similar propositional format, then to search the accumulated stock of propositional representations in memory until a match was found between the encoded question and the stored representation. If a match was found, the individual would answer yes, otherwise no (Anderson, 1976; Anderson & Bower, 1973). Evidence for this formulation has come largely from studies of reaction time in relation to properties of sets of remembered propositions.

For example, it is predicted, and observed, that if a number of stored propositions have terms in common (for example, "Education prepares one for life" and "Education requires effort") then reaction time is an increasing function of the number of common elements. The reasoning is that during the process of searching memory for a match, less cognitive activity, and therefore less time, is required to reject a complete mismatch between the probe and a stored representation than to reject a partial match (Anderson, 1976).

An overall guiding presumption of the information-processing approach to cognition is that learning is not simply a matter of passively registering information, but rather one of encoding and organizing information in preparation for retrieval. Storage and retrieval may be distinguished conceptually but must be closely related in practice, for the way information is coded is a major determination of its retrievability under possible test conditions.

## MOTIVATION AND PERFORMANCE

Learning as a component of adaptation requires not only the storage and retrieval of information but some mechanism to relate retrieval information to performance. Investigators associated with the information-processing approach to cognition have typically assumed simply that people behave rationally whenever they have sufficient information to prescribe rational strategies (Newell, 1981; Newell & Simon, 1972). Experimental psychologists, in contrast, take rational behavior and departures from it as phenomena to be explained by models relating learning to performance (Bower, 1959, 1975; Estes, 1982; Hull, 1943; Spence, 1960). Current models, incorporating ideas from research on both motivation and information processing, can best be understood in historical perspective, beginning with consideration of earlier conceptions of simple and direct linkages between motivation, reward, and performance.

A central issue during most of the history of experimental research on human learning has been whether reward enters into human learning much as it does into animal learning, that is, in the manner characterized by a strong form of Thorndike's law of effect. According to Thorndike (1913, 1931) reward is a necessary condition for learning and produces its effects by direct and automatic strengthening of rewarded stimulus-response connections. Thorndike's vast energy together with the activity of his numerous followers produced a large body of research on simple trial-and-error learning that appeared to support both assumptions.

### From Spread of Effect of Task Schemata

In the standard experimental paradigm of the Thorndikian studies, the materials comprised a list of stimuli, typically words or nonsense syllables, together with a list of possible responses, commonly digits. The responses were initially known only to the experimenter, and the subject's task was to discover the correct response assigned to each stimulus. On the first cycle through the list, a subject would be shown the stimuli singly and would try to guess the appropriate responses. For some proportion of the items, the experimenter, following a prearranged plan, would say "right" following the subject's response, whatever it was, and for the remaining items would say "wrong." On the second cycle, the stimuli were presented again, and it could be determined whether the subject was more likely to repeat rewarded (right) than punished (wrong) responses. Generally, rewarded responses were repeated more often, and, more importantly, the strengthening effect of the reward of a given stimulus-response association was found to spread to neighboring items in the list. The *spread of effect* was taken to be the most important evidence for the automatic strengthening effect of rewards on associations.

The standard interpretation of the spread of effect was challenged on various technical grounds (for a review see Postman, 1962) but continued to be influential until evidence demanding a reinterpretation resulted from an innovation in method introduced by Nuttin (Nuttin, 1953; Nuttin & Greenwald, 1968). Nuttin carried out an experiment similar in design to those of Thorndike, but on a test cycle asked subjects, not to try to make the correct response, but simply to recall whether the outcome for the given item has been "right" or "wrong" on the previous learning trial. He found that a subject's tendency to recall an actually wrong item as right was inversely related to the distance of that item from one that had been right. In effect, the subject's memory for the location of an outcome could be described by an uncertainty

gradient around its actual position in the original list as in models of memory for temporal position (Estes, 1972a). Thus it appears that what was earlier interpreted as spread of reward on associations can be better viewed as fallibility of memory for the location of a rewarding event.

In related experiments, Nuttin produced cogent demonstrations that the apparent strengthening or weakening effects of rewards and punishments in human learning depend critically on the learner's schema for the task situation. The concept of *schema* refers to a conceptual framework for a given type of situation, a product of prior learning, that includes representation of the kinds of events likely to be encountered and their expected relationships (Norman & Rumelhart, 1975; Woodworth, 1938). If the learner's schema leads him or her to expect to be subjected later to tests in which he or she will be called on to respond correctly on the basis of a given learning experience, reinforcements generally produce appropriate strengthening or weakening effects on response tendencies; but if such an expectation is not called for by the nature of the task, the effects do not appear. Confirmation of Nuttin's results was reported by Estes (1972b) from experiments simulating naturalistic learning situations.

### Intentional versus Incidental Learning

If an individual is motivated to learn material by appropriate instructions or incentives, one speaks of *intentional* learning. The contribution of the motivational factor may then be assessed by comparison with learning occurring under conditions comparable except that the motivational instructions or incentives are not supplied and the learner is led by some subterfuge to attend to the materials in much the same way as the intentional learners. Under the latter condition, one speaks of *incidental* learning. An early instance of the incidental procedure was a study by Wallach and Henle (1941). For their incidental subjects, the task was disguised as a study of extra-sensory perception and the result, as in many subsequent comparisons of similar character, was an advantage for the intentional learners in amount recalled. The gist of a large literature (reviewed by Postman, 1976) is that variation in the orienting tasks assigned to the incidental learners produces results varying from a substantial disadvantage to an actual

advantage for the incidental condition, indicating that intent, and therefore presumably
motivation, to learn has no direct effect on
information storage.

The relevant variable is the degree to which
the activities assigned to the subjects in the
incidental and intentional groups lead them to
attend to material and encode it in a form to
make it available for later retrieval. In particular, orienting tasks that require the subjects
to manipulate representations of the to-be-learned
materials in short-term working memory are
conductive to learning. Thus, for example, Hyde
and Jenkins (1969, 1973) found that in a free-
recall situation, subjects recalled words much
better if at the time of study they had been
instructed to engage in semantic judgments
about the words than if they had been instructed
to make judgments based on details of orthog-
raphy (such as word length). In the former case
the subjects would have had to operate with
representations of the words in short-term memory, thus allowing the formation of associations
with the current background context, whereas
under the latter condition such activity would
not have been called for. Further, investigations
that have compared recognition with recall as
an index of learning have yielded evidence that
with the same materials for which recall shows
a substantial advantage for an intentional over
an incidental condition, a recognition measure
shows no difference (Estes & DaPolito, 1967;
Postman, Adams, & Philips, 1955). These results
indicate, again, that motivation and intent are
important mainly in influencing the degree to
which the remembered items are organized in a
manner that will facilitate later recall.

### Awareness

In the original law of effect it was assumed not
only that rewards influence the strength of associations directly but also that the effect is automatic in the sense that the learner need not be
aware of the relationship between response and
reward. Results that seemed favorable to this
assumption appeared in a number of studies
carried out in the 1950s with the purpose of
extending Skinner's operant conditioning principles to human verbal learning. In a typical
task the subject would be engaged in conversation with the experimenter or would be given a
simple verbal task such as supplying words to
fill in blanks in sentences printed on cards, and
the experimenter would attempt to reinforce
certain classes of utterances, for example plural
nouns, by saying "uh-huh" or "good" after each
response by the subject that belonged to the
given class. Plots of frequency of utterances of
the reinforced class versus time showed properties much like operant conditioning curves,
with frequency of occurrence of a class of utterances increasing during a period when reinforcement was given and decreasing when reinforcement was withheld (Greenspoon, 1955; Taffel,
1955). Querying of the subjects after these
experiments yielded no evidence that the subjects were aware of the contingencies of reward
on their responses and hence the results were
taken to support the idea that human "verbal
conditioning" might be basically quite similar to
operant conditioning in animals (Krasner, 1958).

An obviously critical methodological question
about these studies is whether the technique for
assessing awareness was sufficiently sensitive.
Investigators unsympathetic to the conditioning interpretation were skeptical, and subsequent studies employing more searching methods
of interrogating the subjects and breakdowns of
data in terms of subjects manifesting differing
degrees of awareness of contingencies indicated
that the earlier conclusions were premature.
Apparently the performance changes observed
in these experiments actually depend to a major
extent on the degree to which the subjects attend
to and are potentially able to report contingencies between responses and rewards (Dulaney,
1962; Spielberger, Bernstein, & Ratliff, 1966).

### Delay of Reinforcement

The promptness with which reinforcement follows
a correct response has classically been taken to
be one of the major determinants of the efficacy
of reinforcement in animal learning (McGeoch
& Irion, 1952). In human motor learning the
same relation sometimes holds, but under other
circumstances the delay of reinforcing feedback
may be quite inconsequential (Bilodeau & Bilodeau, 1958). In other forms of human learning,
delay is commonly found to be ineffective within
wide limits, especially if adequate measures are
taken to ensure that delay of feedback does not
interfere with the learner's ability to perceive
and encode the relevant aspects of both response
and reward (Kintsch & McCoy, 1964).

Analyses of the difference in effectiveness
of delay between animal and human learning

indicate that the crux of the difference lies in the differential importance of temporal contiguity as a means of conveying information to the learner concerning the relationship of contingency between response and reward. For animals there may generally be no means for the organism to recognize which of its responses a reinforcing event depends on except by attending to the temporal coupling of response and reward. But for human learners, at least for adults, information can be conveyed in quite different ways, so that conditions bearing on attentional and memory capacity may be more immediately relevant than delay of reinforcement per se. Thus Saltzman (1951) observed that the delay of rewarding feedback was ineffective in the simplest form of a task but became relevant as memory load increased. In more analytic studies, Buchwald (1967) showed that the delay of reward in a Thorndikian trial and error situation can actually be advantageous under some circumstances. Buchwald hypothesized that performance depends, not on simple strengthening or weakening of response tendencies, but on the learner's remembering the responses and outcomes of preceding trials, these relations being stored in memory independently, and then retrieving and utilizing this information at the time of the subsequent test. On these assumptions he predicted, and his results confirmed, that delaying information about the correctness of a response on a given trial until the same item is tested on a subsequent trial facilitates learning. Evidently the delay in this case helps ensure that the learner will have available in working memory both the response and the outcome of the preceding trial at the point when this information is needed to guide a new choice.

## Effects of Values of Incentives

Graded variation in the magnitude of reward (for example amount or quality of food, degree of shock reduction) is commonly found to exert substantial effects on animal learning (for example, Kimble, 1961) and this variable entered as one of the basic parameters in the quantification of behavior theory by Hull (1943). But as with delay, similar effects are not characteristic of human learning. Orderly variation in the speed of learning with the amount of reward is demonstrable in young children under some circumstances (Terrell & Kennedy, 1957; Witryol, Tyrrell, & Lowden, 1965); however the latter investi-

gators found that the variation of the value of incentives used as rewards influenced the point at which learning curves began to rise above chance values rather than the slopes of the curves. This result was taken to indicate that reward value operated indirectly by influencing the degree of selective attention of the children to the relevant aspects of the situation rather than by influencing the rate of formation of associations directly.

In studies with normal adults, variation in the amount of reward between independent groups generally shows no effects, but variation in the magnitude of reward associated with different responses for the same individual may yield graded effects (Harley, 1965). The basis for this difference appears to lie in the degree to which variation in reward value conveys differential information to the learner relative to the probable value of differential payoffs for future choices. In a study reported by Keller, Cole, Burke, and Estes (1965), subjects were cycled through a list of items each constituting an identifying stimulus together with a pair of reward values assigned by the experimenter but initially unknown to the subjects. On each trial, when the stimulus appeared, the subject made a choice between two available responses and then received information concerning the value of the associated outcome under either a full or partial information condition. The partial condition corresponded to that of the Thorndikian trial and error experiments in that the subject was shown only the reward value associated with the response chosen on the particular trial. In contrast, in the full information condition, the subject on each trial was shown both the reward value for the chosen response and the reward value that would have been obtained

**Table 5.1. Mean Errors, under Partial versus Full Information Conditions, for Choices between Alternatives with Values Indicated by Row and Column Labels.**

(*Data of Keller et al., 1965*)

| | Partial Information Reward Value | | | | Full Information Reward Value | | | |
|---|---|---|---|---|---|---|---|---|
| | 2 | 4 | 6 | 8 | 2 | 4 | 6 | 8 |
| 1 | 5.2 | 5.4 | 5.0 | 3.2 | 2.5 | 3.1 | 2.9 | 2.1 |
| 2 | | 6.8 | 3.3 | 3.3 | | 2.2 | 2.1 | 2.4 |
| 4 | | | 6.7 | 4.9 | | | 2.1 | 1.8 |
| 6 | | | | 5.2 | | | | 2.1 |

for the alternative response. The rewards were given in the form of displayed point values, the points being exchangeable for monetary reward at the end of the experiment.

A strong and direct relationship was observed between the reward value and the speed of learning of correct choices under the partial information condition but no relation whatever for the full information condition. In the partial condition, performance depends jointly on the difference in reward values for the two members of the pair and on the absolute value of the correct member (Table 5.1).

The pattern of results fits an informational interpretation precisely. Under the full information condition, the subject on each trial can observe which of the alternative responses carries the higher reward, and the specific magnitude adds no additional information relative to which should be chosen on future tests. Under the partial condition, only one outcome is displayed on a trial, and on a statistical basis, the greater the magnitude of the displayed reward, the higher on the average is the probability that choosing the same response on a future trial will be advantageous. Follow-ups of the study employing a variety of manipulations to separate the informational from the motivational effects of reward magnitude uniformly confirmed this interpretation (Estes, 1969).

It might be supposed that in the studies with adults, a subject simply learns relationships between responses and reward values in a paired-associate fashion and then recalls these learned relationships and employs them at the point of a test. However this assumption proves unjustified. Allen (1972) and Allen and Estes (1972) used an experimental arrangement similar to that of Keller et al. but added the procedure of introducing recall tests for reward values at various points during learning. They found that subjects often met a criterion of 100 percent correct choices of the higher paying alternatives before they were able to recall the associated reward values upon presentation of the stimuli. Continuing analyses yielded evidence that adult learners in these situations do not generally learn verbalizable relationships between choice alternatives and specific reward values (though they are capable of doing so), but, rather, develop memory structures akin to utility scales on which different alternatives are represented in relation to their relative average reward values

(Estes, 1976b). The learning process that generates this structure is not one of memorizing particular stimulus-outcome relationships. Rather it appears to be one of making judgments of the relative values of outcomes occurring for given alternatives that are simultaneously represented in short-term memory and encoding the results of these judgments in the long-term memory representation.

## THE SEARCH FOR BASIC UNITS

By analogy with other sciences, the history of the psychology of learning might be expected to exhibit sustained attention to the problem of identifying basic units and relations—basic in the sense of being undecomposable by the techniques of the discipline and of being combinable into larger structures as constituents of complex forms of learning.

The two main approaches to the issue of basic units that were identifiable in the earliest stages of experimental psychology persist down to the present despite changes in particular concepts. One of these approaches, termed *analytic* by Robinson (1932) was identified with association theory and the view that the products of learning can be decomposed into associations or connections between simple units. The units were simply ideas in the earlier literature (James, 1890; Mill, 1829), psychological "dispositions" or activities in the more critically developed theories of the 1920s (Robinson, 1932), and stimuli and responses in the more behaviorally oriented variants of associationism (this usage beginning perhaps with Carr, 1931, and characterizing the approach of Guthrie, 1935).

The other approach, associated with the concept of *redintegration*, was basic to Hollingworth's (1926) treatment of memory and later the trace concept of Gestalt psychology (for example, Koffka, 1935). In this conception, the result of a learning experience is not the linking together of unitary representations of objects or events, but rather the formation of a configured memory trace that may be reactivated on a later occasion when the individual has experience with some of the components of the situation that gave rise to the trace.

Usage of the terms *trace* and *association* seems to be governed more by intuition and custom than by reasoned theoretical arguments.

Recognition has customarily been interpreted in terms of a trace concept, the act of recognition resulting from the comparison of the pattern of mental activity aroused by a new experience with the trace left by a preceding experience. This conception characterizes most of the more formal models for recognition (for example, Anderson, 1973; Norman & Wickelgren, 1969; Wickelgren, 1970).

For paired-associate learning, in contrast, associative conceptions seem so appropriate as often to be used without much question. In an experimental situation the subject is seen to observe the stimulus and response members of an item as they are presented and subsequently to recall the second member on presentation of the first. What is more natural than to assume that representations of each exist in the subject's memory system and are linked by association so that activation runs, in a sense, from one to the other? The more formal models developed for the quantitative analysis of paired-associate learning have uniformly been of an associative character (for example, Bower, 1961; Estes, 1959; Feigenbaum, 1963; Gibson, 1940). Nonetheless the associative interpretation is not uncontested; recently, for example, Greeno, James, DaPolito, and Polson (1978) have presented strong arguments in favor of the idea that a paired-associate presentation results in the formation of a holistic memory trace.

### Redintegration of Multi-element Structures

Interest of experimenters in the problem of unitary trace versus independent associations began long before the popularity of the paired-associate paradigm. Müller and Pilzecker (1900) presented subjects with triads of nonsense syllables, then cued for recall with any member of the triad. Their results suggested that (in modern terms) perception of a cluster of items generates a unitary memory complex that has the property that any member, but especially the first, can serve as a retrieval cue to reinstate the whole. Meyer (1939) replicated and then rounded out and extended the earlier study, obtaining a very substantial body of data suitable for testing quantitative predictions about independence of associations. Meyer found 60 to 66 percent total recall of triplets of items with very little variation according to whether the first, second, or third presented was used as the cue (.66, .62, and .61, respectively). Meyer reported no formal

tests of independence, but did report sufficiently full data that a reader can do his or her own and see that recall of both remaining members of a triplet upon presentation of one as a cue was much higher than the hypothesis of independent associations would allow. Also, Meyer found that when two syllables of a triplet were recalled, they were given in the correct order more than 90 percent of the time with virtually no difference depending on whether they had been presented in adjacent or separated positions.

### Models for Redintegration and Association

More recent investigators have tried to increase the decisiveness of results from the multiple constituent paradigm by carrying out experiments within the framework of models based on either the associative or the trace conception. One of the most systematic efforts on the associative side was that of Anderson and Bower (1972) dealing with memory for sentences. In a previous study Anderson and Bower (1971) had found that following the presentation of a list of sentences, cueing for recall with components typically yielded recall of fragments of sentences, suggesting that the memory structure was composed of multiple associations between elements. They reasoned that complete independence of recall of two or more parts of a sentence given another part as a cue would support their associative model, whereas, at the other extreme, complete dependence would have to be taken as evidence that memory was based on a single trace.

In a task used by Anderson and Bower (1972) to test for configural properties of sentence memory, subjects studied pairs of sentences with different subjects and verbs but common objects, for example,

> The child hit the landlord
> The minister praised the landlord.

On subsequent tests subjects were presented with constituents of the sentences and asked for recall of a missing constituent. In the particular tests of interest for the problem of independent associations, the cues presented were a subject and a verb from the pair of study sentences and the task of the experimental subject was to recall the object. One prediction tested was that the probability of recalling the object given the subject and verb of one of the sentences cannot, on the hypothesis of independent associations, be greater than the probability of recall given the subject and verb separately, that is, the following relation should be satisfied

$$P(O/SV) \leqslant P(O/S) + P(O/V)$$
$$- P(O/S)P(O/V),$$

in which $O$, $S$, and $V$ denote the object, subject, and verb respectively and a quantity such as $P(O/SV)$ is to be read "the probability of recall of the object given the subject and verb as cues." On the hypothesis of a configured memory trace, however, one might expect the quantity at the left of the expression to be greater than the quantity on the right, since the optimal retrieval cue would be the configuration of subject and verb.

Anderson and Bower (1972) also tested a second, and rather counterintuitive, prediction that the probability of recalling the object should be greater if cueing is by the subject of one sentence and the verb of the other sentence of the pair (for example, by "The child praised—" in the example above) than if the subject were cued with the subject and verb of one of the sentences (for example, "The child hit—"). Two experiments conducted with sentences of differing degrees of meaningfulness confirmed both predictions and thus seemed to lend some support to the independent association model. However, in subsequent experiments conducted with similar material but an incidental learning procedure, Anderson and Bower found support for neither prediction, and the same is true of a study by Foss and Harwood (1975). In fact, under the incidental procedure, cueing with subject and verb from the same sentence yielded higher probability of recall of the object than the "cross-over" procedure of cueing with the subject of one sentence and the verb of the other sentence of the pair. Foss and Harwood argued that, rather than simply forming associations between elements of a sentence, the individual in the course of comprehension generates a higher order memory node or unit representing the conjunction of particular elements, so that, in the example above, comprehension of the first sentence of the pair would involve generation of a single element in memory representing a "child who hit."

Thus a line of research that at one point appeared to provide decisive support for a particular kind of model now seems again to present unanswered questions. Evidently some rather difficult problems of method need to be solved before further progress can be expected. Some of these have do with individual differences between subjects and items in this type of experiment and their effect on estimates of quantities based on conditional recall probabilities. To take one example, the matter of whether the estimate of probability of recall of an object given subject and verb, $P(O/SV)$, obtained from data pooled over subjects or items should be equal to or differ from the product of the separate probabilities depends not only on properties of the underlying memory structure but on the range and nature of individual differences across subjects and items with respect to effects of the subjects and verbs as cues. (For discussions of the issue see Flexser, 1981; Hintzman, 1980.)

A more formal counterpart of Foss and Harwood's (1975) suggestion concerning the formation of configured traces of linguistic elements under some circumstances is the "fragmentation hypothesis" of Jones (1976). This hypothesis was developed in conjunction with experiments in which subjects viewed displays of common objects that might vary with respect to such attributes as visual form, color, spatial location in a display, or temporal position in a sequence of displays. On a later test, subjects might be cued with one or a combination of those attributes and asked to recall the remainder. Jones postulated that the result of a single learning experience is a memory trace corresponding to some fragment of the perceived situation. The trace can then be reexcited by any one of its constituents presented as a recall cue; what distinguishes this hypothesis from other similar ones is the assumption that multiple cueing tends to produce higher overall recall solely because of the increased likelihood that at least one of the component cues will correspond to a constituent of the trace stored in memory. Jones (1976, 1978) showed that his model could account in some quantitative detail for recall of pictures in his experimental situation and also for the data of Anderson and Bower (1973).

The tests of the model may not have been very exacting, however, since a large number of degrees of freedom in the data were used to estimate the numerical values of parameters— the probabilities that fragments of various sizes were stored as memory traces. If, for example, the stimulus presented on a trial were a large red triangle, the probabilities that the memory trace would include only the attribute triangle or would include red triangles, and so on are not predicted by Jones's model but must be evaluated from the data before predictions can be made as to whether presentation of any one attribute as a cue would yield recall of others. Under these circumstances empirical tests are not very informative, except to the degree that they compare the given model with others.

This last step was taken by Ross and Bower (1981) who evaluated the fragmentation hypothesis within a larger class of models characterized by two major properties: (a) The constituent aspects or elements of an event generate corresponding constituents of a memory trace; and (b) retrieval routes, that is relations between cues and recall responses, correspond to connections or links (associations) between the constituents of the memory trace. Within this class Ross and Bower noted that three types of submodels need to be distinguished on the basis of specific assumptions about the nature of the associations. One class, which they termed *Horizontal*, is essentially traditional association theory, with the assumption that pairwise associations link the representations of events or constituents of them in memory. The second type is the *Fragmentation model*. The third, termed *Schema* by Ross and Bower, is based on the assumption that representations of individual events or their constituents are linked indirectly in memory by way of associations with a common "grouping node." Ross and Bower tested these models against each other in a series of experiments in which the subject saw on each trial a quadruplet of words (either related or unrelated thematically), and later was tested for recall of the quadruplet by presentation of one or more of the words as cues. Results obtained with differing materials were not entirely consistent, but on the whole the schema model was the best supported and the fragmentation model the least.

A problem remaining for all of these approaches is an apparently ubiquitous tendency, manifest in these and many other sets of data, for multiple cues to be less effective in leading to recall than would be predicted, on the hypothesis of independent associations, from information about the efficacy of individual cues. Neither the schema nor the fragmentation model accounts fully for this finding. Another problem is that the tests of these models to date have all involved comparisons of the efficacy of individual and multiple cues that are subject to sources of correlation (due, for example, to variation in attention or other control processes) beyond those that would arise from differences in characteristics of the memory trace. It appears that further progress may wait on new methods that may be less subject to these possible artifacts.

### Tentative Conclusions about Elementary Units

Although no methods have appeared that can decisively answer questions about the existence and nature of elementary units of memory, accumulating evidence from a variety of approaches suggests some tentative generalizations. It appears that constituent elements or aspects of a perceived situation may enter into a memory trace that is configured in the sense that its properties cannot be accounted for on the hypothesis of an assemblage of independent, pairwise associations between elements. In the terminology of logical networks, constituents of the trace act as OR gates, so that activation of any one element may lead to reactivation of the whole structure. In general not all constituents of a trace are equally effective retrieval cues in this sense, and effectiveness appears to vary with frequency of occurrence in the same background situation. No general rules can yet be set down as to just what aspects or components of a perceived situation will be embodied in an effective memory trace. Selective attention at the time of the learning experience is surely important, and the answer to the question of whether or not a configured trace will be formed in any given instance may depend in part on the degree to which the constituent elements are perceptually integral or separable (Garner, 1974). However, the specific relationships between selective attention and encoding processes remain to be specified.

### Unitization

It may be that there are no hard-wired cognitive units, but, rather, that functional units take form as a result of learning. Hebb (1949) proposed, on the basis of neurophysiological arguments together with a variety of empirical observations, that during childhood (or in the adult under such special circumstances as recovery from blindness) a long period of slow learning leads to the formation of perceptual units that serve to identify objects and enter into the rapid associative learning characteristic of the adult. This idea is not easy to test experimentally, but some relevant evidence has accrued from specific domains. In reading, for example, it appears that initially the visual patterns representing letters are discriminated on the basis of visual features or attributes, but that with extended experience, frequently recurring clusters of features that define letters take on unitary properties; still later the same occurs for spelling groups and words, so that at each level the reader can identify units without explicitly attending to their constituents (Gibson, 1969; LaBerge, 1981; Smith & Haviland, 1972).

At higher cognitive levels, it is less clear how units can be defined. Anderson (1981) has suggested several criteria: all-or-none encoding of elements into an associative structure, all-or-none retrieval into working memory, and the capability of evaluating the meaning of the unit without expanding it into its components. The first of these seems questionable, since it is known that perceptual units can be formed gradually and the same may well be true for higher units. On the basis of the second and third criteria, concepts would seem to qualify; it is difficult to conceive of a category label, for example, being retrieved only in part, and certainly one can mentally manipulate labels for categories or concepts without explicitly recalling all possible exemplars. More formal evidence comes from laboratory studies showing that manipulation of frequency of presentation can to some degree influence recall of categories and exemplars independently (Alba, Chromiak, Hasher, & Attig, 1980; Mathews & Tulving, 1973) and that category labels, or other superordinate units, may be retained in memory even when subordinates have been forgotten during a retention interval following a learning experience (Nelson, Fehling & Moore-Glascock, 1979).

Anderson (1981) has reviewed evidence bearing on the possible unitary character of still more complex memory representations, such as propositions and schemata (interpreted as stereotyped clusters of propositions). It appears that these entities characteristically meet the criterion of being susceptible to recall and manipulation in working memory without explicit attention

to their constituents, but that they often fail the criterion of all-or-none retrieval. Thus a tentative conclusion with some support is that propositional representations and schemata may, but need not, exhibit unitary properties. It is quite possible that the negative instances are simply the result of observations made at intermediate stages of the learning process leading to unitization. This notion is lent some credibility by the many sources of evidence suggesting that the human information-processing system is strongly biased toward the generation of progressively higher-order units in all domains.

## LEARNING ABOUT ATTRIBUTES OF EVENTS

The most widely accepted view of what is learned from observations of events, or communications about them, is that the resulting memory representations incorporate information about attributes of the events or event sequences (Bower, 1967; Smith et al., 1974; Spear, 1976; Underwood, 1969). In this section the focus will be on the attributes of frequency, temporal position, and order of events, which are basic to the broad category of adaptive learning that underlies our capabilities for predicting future events.

### Frequency and Probability

Three basic methods are responsible for much of what we know about the way people acquire and use information about event frequencies: (a) Giving subjects blocks of information trials, on which they observe events that occur with varying relative frequencies, followed by tests calling for frequency judgments, probability estimates, or predictions about future events of the same type; (b) giving subjects repeated opportunities to predict which of a set of alternative events will occur or which will yield some significant outcome, such as a monetary payoff; and (c) asking subjects to choose between verbally described situations involving uncertainty or risk, for example, bets or insurance offers. These methods give rise to performance that seems on the surface to be quite disparate in many instances. Thus any prospect of successfully attacking the basic question of whether the memory representations carrying information about frequency and probability take the same form in all cases requires close attention to differences in conditions of information transmittal and task demands.

### Observation-test Studies

In a common paradigm, the words of a list are presented successively to a subject with different words repeated different numbers of times. At the end of the list the subject either is asked to make estimates of the absolute frequencies of occurrence of test words or is presented with pairs of test words and asked to judge which member of the pair has occurred more frequently (Underwood & Freund, 1970; Underwood, Zimmerman, & Freund, 1971). Results typically show a direct relation between either type of frequency judgment and the actual frequencies of the words.

Relative frequency judgments are the more extensively studied, perhaps because they are less subject to systematic biases. The most salient finding is the tendency, illustrated in Figure 5.3, for ratios of relative frequency judgments for any two items or events to match the ratio of relative frequencies of occurrence (Hintzman, 1969; Radtke, Jacoby, & Goedel, 1971). Further, if subjects are given a series of training cycles through a list in which items are repeated differing numbers of times, then are shifted to a new series on the same list but with the relative frequencies changed, proportions of relative frequency judgments for pairs of items

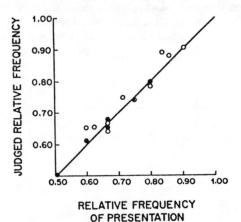

**RELATIVE FREQUENCY OF PRESENTATION**

**Figure 5.3.** Mean proportion of cases in which the higher-frequency member of a stimulus pair of given relative frequency was judged to be higher (data of Radtke, Jacoby, & Goedel, 1971, Table 1, p. 81 [closed circles] and Hintzman, 1969, Table 1, p. 141 [open circles]).

go to the new matching ratio at a rate very close to that of original learning (Whitlow & Estes, 1979). However, these simple relationships hold only for limited amounts of training in a situation, especially when subjects are fully instructed about the nature of the task. When subjects understand the task to be one of learning to make accurate frequency judgments, detailed analyses of individual data show that they ultimately begin to classify events into discrete categories (for example, common versus rare) and to make judgments on the basis of these categorizations (Altom, 1978).

The observation-test method has also been applied in studies in which the subjects' task is to predict future events rather than recall frequencies of past events. In a paradigm introduced by Reber and Millward (1968) and developed further by Estes (1976a, 1976b), information about event probabilities is conveyed solely on a sequence of observation trials and acquisition is tested on separate trials without feedback. For example, during an observation series, the subject might be shown initials of hypothetical election candidates, perhaps A and B on some trials and C and D on others, with an indication on each trial as to which member of the pair was the winner. Then on a test series, the subject would be presented with, for example, A versus B, C versus D (training pairs), or A versus C (a transfer pair), and would be asked to select the member of each pair more likely to be the winner. Over the observation series, constant win probabilities are assigned to the training pairs (e.g., .67 for A over B and .80 for C over D). Under these conditions, test performance mirrors quite directly what has been learned about probability, as indicated, for example, by sensitivity to very small differences in event probability and by similar performance on training and transfer pairs (Estes, 1976a, 1976b).

The idea that learning about frequencies and probabilities is a quite general and relatively automatic process is supported not only by special experiments on probability learning or memory for frequency, but also by demonstrations that probability matching tendencies (the analog of relative frequency matching) appear in tasks that do not explicitly call for judgments about probability or frequency. Examples occur in signal detection (Atkinson & Kinchla, 1964) and in the precriterion stage of concept formation (Mandler, Cowan, & Gold, 1964).

Most of the data on memory for frequency fit

the conception that the product of learning in these situations is a memory representation of a quantitatively graded attribute (Underwood, 1969; Underwood & Freund, 1970; Wells, 1974; Whitlow & Estes, 1979). However, there is one notably discordant finding, namely, that when the modality of presentation varies among words of a list, subjects show significant ability to remember the input modalities of individual occurrences of repeated words (Bray & Batchelder, 1972; Hintzman & Block, 1973; Hintzman, Block, & Summers, 1973). A possibility to be considered is that multiple representations are formed and that to some extent the individual has the option of referring to different representations in order to accomplish different tasks that depend on frequency information.

The results on presentation modality may be a special case of a general proclivity for storing information about categories of events. In many tasks individuals have occasion to categorize items in various ways, for example, the concept associated with a particular stimulus word, or the semantic category to which the word belongs, or, in the case of multilinguals, the language to which it belongs. There is considerable evidence that memory for relative frequency of experiences with concepts or categories accrues in much the same manner as memory for frequency of individual exemplars (Alba et al., 1980; Kolers, 1966; Kolers & Gonzales, 1980; Mathews & Tulving, 1973), and, further, that information concerning frequency of occurrence of categories to which an item or object belongs may be maintained at several levels concurrently (Whitlow & Skaar, 1979).

## Choice Studies

Research on the problem of how people or animals learn to anticipate uncertain events by utilizing informative feedback from their choices began to appear in the late 1930s. The multiple-choice method that became standard stemmed from the interest of Brunswik (1939) in generalizing simple T-maze learning situations in the direction of greater ecological validity, and from the work of Humphreys (1939), initiated with the idea of contriving a paradigm for research on human learning that might be analogous to conditioning under intermittent reinforcement.

In Humphreys's experimental situation, the prototype for much research that followed, a subject confronted a simple display panel on which a light might or might not appear following a start signal on each trial of a series. Actually, although the fact was initially unknown to the subject, the light simply occurred with some fixed probability. The subject's task on each trial was to indicate his expectation as to whether or not the light would occur. Humphreys looked only at the special cases of 0 percent, 50 percent, or 100 percent occurrence of the target light, but the paradigm was soon generalized by Grant, Hake, and Hornseth (1951) to other probability values, for example, 25 percent or 75 percent occurrences of the target light over a series. Subjects learned to improve their predictions in these experiments, though not rapidly, and there was a suggestion that the proportion of trials on which subjects would predict a target light might tend to approach the true probability,

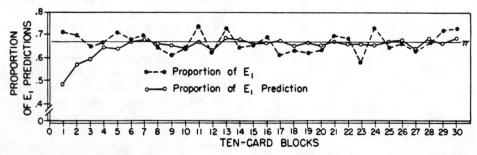

**Figure 5.4.** Proportion of predictions and proportion of occurrences of a random event ($E_1$) in successive 10-trial blocks. The predictions represent pooled data for 198 subjects; the events were sampled from a binomial distribution with probability .67. From "Comparison of Predictions and Estimates in a Probability Copyright 1959 by the American Psychological Association. Reprinted by permission of the authors.

a surmise borne out in more extensive experiments by Estes and Straughan (1954) and others, and generally known as the *probability matching* tendency. The fidelity with which probability matching obtains under some circumstances is illustrated in Figure 5.4 taken from a study by Neimark and Shuford (1959).

Research in this experimental paradigm has elucidated the conditions under which probability matching occurs or fails to occur, the more local tendencies for individuals to repeat or fail to repeat individual predictive responses depending on their success or failure, age trends, and the role of incentives (Estes, 1964b, 1972c; Myers, 1976). The fruit of this work is perhaps not as great as it might have been because many investigators were for a time preoccupied with what seems in hindsight to have been an extraneous issue of "matching" versus "maximizing." The former term refers to the tendency, just described, for individuals to adjust their predictions of uncertain events so as to reflect the true probabilities, whereas the latter term refers to a tendency to adopt the strategy, adaptive in some gambling situations, of discovering which of two alternatives is the more probable and then always predicting it in order to maximize the proportion of successes. An especially curious feature of the empirical results was that the maximizing strategy, which seemed more rational to economists and decision theorists, tended to be more prominent in the behavior of young children (Weir, 1964) and even animals (Meyer, 1960; Weinstock, North, Brody, & LoGuidice, 1965), but probability matching was more prominent in the behavior of relatively sophisticated adults (Friedman, Burke, Cole, Keller, Millward, & Estes, 1964; Myers, 1976).

Resolving the apparent contradictions depends on recognizing the important role of selective attention and the looseness of the coupling of learning and performance. It has been shown that instructions intended to bias adult subjects toward encoding or ignoring negative instances (failures of predicted events to occur) shift performance toward probability matching or maximizing, respectively (Estes, 1976b). Thus it is a plausible hypothesis that the proclivity for maximizing in young children may owe to their not yet having developed the habit of attending similarly to occurrences and nonoccurrences of predicted events. In adults, even if the advantages of maximizing are understood and information about relative frequencies has been acquired sufficiently to permit use of the strategy, there is no reason to adopt maximizing unless the sequence of events appears to be random. In several studies it has been found that performance tends to move from matching towards maximizing when instructions and task setting suggest that the events being predicted are random (Edwards, 1961; Morse & Runquist, 1960; Rubinstein, 1959). Rubinstein's study was the most definitive; it compared instructions indicating that events were or were not random and demonstrated a large and significant effect of this manipulation.

Studies of "multiple cue probability learning" have shed light on the considerable abilities of human subjects to utilize information in cue patterns even in complex diagnostic situations involving rather large numbers of cues (for example, Castellan & Edgell, 1973; Hammond, Hursch, & Todd, 1964; Peterson, Hammond, & Summers, 1965), but these results on performance need always be interpreted in light of the fact that learning on individual trials depends critically on the particular cues or relationships among cues that subjects attend to, encode, rehearse, and enter into the memory structures that ultimately guide performance.

### Verbal Information about Events and Probabilities

In a class of methods often employed by investigators interested more in economic behavior or gambling than memory processes, information that subjects have acquired about probabilities in everyday life is assessed by calling on the subjects to make choices between combinations of probabilities and values of uncertain events. The rationale, deriving from von Neumann and Morgenstern (1944), can be illustrated with a situation used by Mosteller and Nogee (1951). The subjects were offered opportunities to accept or reject gambles constructed with sets of poker dice for which the true probabilities of winning were supplied by the experimenter. The procedure was to fix the probability of winning and the value of one alternative (e.g., $-5$ for a loss) and vary the value of a win over successive trials until a value, $v$, was found for which the subject was indifferent between accepting and rejecting the gamble. Then the subject's utility (subjective value) for $v$ was computed from the equation

$$pu(v) = (1 - p)u(5)$$

in which $p$ is the probability of winning and $u(v)$ the subjective utility of $v$. Data were obtained for various combinations of probabilities and values. Now, if information about the subject's utility functions are available from independent preference studies, values of $u(v)$ can be entered in the equation, in order to solve for $p$, now interpreted as the subjective probability of a win (Greeno, 1968; Luce & Suppes, 1965). Generally, subjective probability is found to approximate true probability over the middle range but to overestimate slightly the true values at the low end and underestimate them at the high end. Since the same tendency is not observed with the other methods, there is a suggestion that supplying numerical odds may not activate a memory representation of the same form as that built up by actual experience with events varying in relative frequency.

Verbally presented problems have been used also by investigators interested in the informal inference rules, or *heuristics*, used by people in dealing with uncertainty. For example, Tversky and Kahneman (1973) selected a number of consonants—K, N, L, R, and V—that occur more often in the third than the first position of English words, and for each, asked student subjects whether the letter was more frequent in Position 1 or Position 3. The result was a $2:1$ bias for judging, contrary to fact, that these letters occur more often in Position 1. The interpretation offered by Tversky and Kahneman is that the subjects were misled by the differential *availability* in memory of words cued by letters in the first and third positions. Because it is easier to think of words that begin with K than words having K as their third letter, subjects judge the former to be the more frequent. Similar results were obtained when subjects were presented with lists of more or less famous men and women and queried as to which sex had more entries, that is, fame outweighed actual frequency. It appears that the memory attribute that is modified by event frequency is not best described as a representation of frequency, analogous, say, to a representation of color, but rather as the level of activation, or *availability*, of the representation of the event or category. When the conditions of a learning situation are such that availability actually varies directly with frequency, then the learner appropriately interprets variations in availability as reflecting variations in frequency. But when availability depends also on other factors that are not attended or whose relevance is not understood by the subject, variation in those factors may be the basis of judgments given in response to questions about frequency or probability.

## Theoretical Interpretations

Results emanating from the various approaches to frequency and probability learning present a number of salient findings that appear to call for interpretation in terms of an analog, or at least quantitatively graded, memory representation of relative frequency. One of these is the occurrence, under some circumstances, of probability and relative frequency matching. Another is the fineness of discrimination of small differences in event probabilities achieved by subjects in observation-test studies. Still another is the similarity of learning rates before and after shifts in event frequencies.

All of these properties fit an interpretation in terms of a model derived from stimulus-sampling theory (Atkinson & Estes, 1963; Estes, 1982, pp. 22–44, 79–106, 135–143). The basic assumptions are: (1) Learning always occurs in a background context comprising a population of aspects or cues that are randomly sampled from trial to trial; (b) the contextual elements sampled on a trial become associated with the event that occurs; and (c) the judged relative frequencies or probabilities of two events are in the ratio of the proportions of contextual elements associated with them in memory. The properties of frequency learning summarized above all flow from the model. Some apparently aberrant results, for example, instances of maximizing in choice situations, may be accounted for on the basis of the flexible mapping between memory representations and performance. If an individual understands an event sequence to be random and has formed an estimate of the event probabilities, he or she may, given knowledge of the appropriate strategy, choose always to predict the most frequent event.

A problem for the sampling theory is raised by the results of some detailed analyses of probability-learning data that provide sharp evidence for all-or-none learning (Atkinson & Estes, 1963; Friedman et al., 1964; Yellott, 1969). These results support what has been termed the *pattern model*, in which it is assumed that an event and its context are encoded in memory as an indivisible unit that enters into learning on an all-or-none basis.

It would be unsatisfactorily ad hoc to assume that episodes are sometimes encoded in memory as unitary patterns and sometimes as bundles of constituent associations if there were no principled basis for predicting the conditions under which each version occurs. However, a resolution is suggested by consideration of the relation between the two main types of experimental methods and the two kinds of results. One finds that the analyses pointing to a quantitatively graded memory representation of frequency have all come from studies employing the observation-test method, whereas all results pointing to all-or-none pattern learning have come from studies emloying the choice method.

The two methods entail different constraints on information processing that may be highly relevant to the differential findings. Namely, in the choice method, a subject can be presumed to have representations of the events of the preceding choice trial still in primary memory at the time when the response of the current trial is called for; but in the observation-test method, responses are all made during a block of test trials, when the events of observation trials would no longer be represented in primary memory. The suggestion emerges, then, that the formation of long-term memory representations proceeds in accord with the sampling model and that these representations are the basis for responses relating to event frequency or probability except under some special circumstances when learners have available a short-term representation of the preceding trial to enable use of a stategy such as "win-stay, lose-shift" (Levine, 1959).

## Memory for Temporal Positions of Events

Although learning the chronology of events must be important in people's management of their everyday affairs, it has not been a subject of intensive research. Exploratory studies indicate that people have considerable ability to estimate dates of past events, their memory for temporal separations between events depending on recency in a manner reminiscent of the Weber function. For example, in a study reported by Underwood (1977) subjects were asked to estimate the dates of events presumed to be familar by way of news-

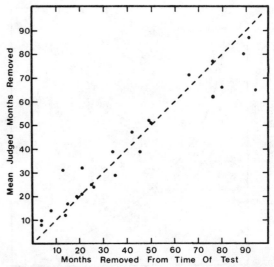

**Figure 5.5.** Mean judged months removed (from November, 1975) of 24 real-life events. The diagonal line represents perfect correspondence between judged and actual intervals. From *Temporal Codes for Memories: Issues and Problems* (p. 6) by B.J. Underwood, 1977. Hillsdale, NJ: Erlbaum. Copyright 1977 by Lawrence Erlbaum Associates, Inc. Reprinted by permission.

paper accounts and the like. The data showed a virtually linear relation between estimated and actual times since the occurrence of events (Figure 5.5); further, recall of the order of pairs of events was related to the temporal separations of the events according to a simple function, with higher discriminability for events well separated in time and poorer discriminability for events closer together (Figure 5.6).

Not much can be concluded from this kind of investigation since some of the events may have been associated with specific dates in people's memories and sequences of events may have been causally related in ways that would constrain their possible orders.

The few laboratory experiments designed to bear on this kind of memory have been conducted in list-learning situations similar to those used to study memory for frequency. The paradigm is highly simplified, but may represent a reasonable first approximation to the simulation of situations that arise in such matters as giving eye-witness testimony or recounting the chronology of symptoms in response to a physician's questions. Typically a list of words is presented sequentially to a subject, then the subject either is asked to estimate the temporal

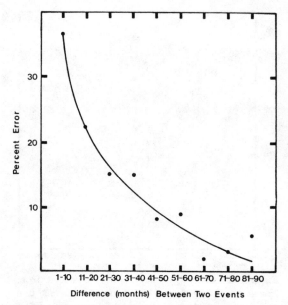

**Figure 5.6.** Errors in judged order of two real-life events as a function of their temporal separation. From *Temporal Codes for Memories: Issues and Problems* (p. 8) by B.J. Underwood, 1977. Hillsdale, NJ: Erlbaum. Copyright 1977 by Lawrence Associates, Inc. Reprinted by permission.

positions of various test words or is presented pairs of test words and asked to judge which occurred more recently.

A natural first attempt at theoretical interpretation of such experiments is to assume that, since the strength of memory traces typically declines regularly as a function of time and intervening events, the strength or availability of a test word in memory could be used by a subject as a basis for estimating its recency. Some of the earlier tests of this interpretation were encouraging. For example, Morton (1968) reasoned that since the strength of a memory trace must vary monotonically with both recency and number of repetitions, if some one item in a short sequence were repeated, then in a subsequent test it should exhibit an increased tendency to be judged more recent than items that had actually followed it in the sequence. This prediction was borne out in Morton's data. However, in the most extensive series of relevant experiments that has been reported, the strength interpretation did not fare well, most particularly because judgments of relative recency of pairs of words proved not to be related in any simple way to their actual separa-

tions (Underwood, 1977). Except for the cases of very short-term recall (as tested in the study of Morton, 1968), and very long-term recall (as in Underwood's study of real-life events) there is little evidence that individuals can make use of graded differences in memory trace strength as a basis for remembering chronology.

There is however a conspicuous advantage for the most recent event of a sequence, which has led Underwood (1977) to speak of a "recency principle," akin to the selector mechanism suggested earlier by Underwood and Schulz (1960). The idea here is that the most recently occurring member of any sequence of verbal units, whether the units be words in a list or lists in a series of lists, is in some manner tagged in memory so that it is actively remembered as the most recent event of its kind. This principle is presumed to be responsible not only for the accuracy of recency judgments but also for such phenomena as the perennially surprising paucity of intrusion errors from earlier lists in experiments concerned with proactive or retroactive inhibition.

Subjects' ability to judge relative recency of pairs of items prior to the last one of a series is assumed by Underwood to be mediated entirely by associative learning. Presumably the basic mechanism is the same as that responsible for ordinary paired-associate or list learning but with the special problem that in studies of memory for recency less is known concerning the elements that enter into the associations. However, as in the interpretation of memory for frequency, it may be assumed that each item presentation generates a memory trace including some attributes of the item and some attributes of the local context. Presumably many of the contextual cues available during presentations of successive items of a list would be quite homogeneous and provide little differential information on which to base recency judgments. When there are distinctive contexts associated with the end points of the list or any particularly conspicuous items (as occur in studies of the "Von Restorff effect," Woodworth, 1938), retrieval of these contextual cues would provide a basis for judging recency.

In an attempt to formalize ideas of this kind, Flexser and Bower (1974) proposed that these associations of items with local contexts serve as "time tags" that can be retrieved from memory at the time of a test. As a consequence of noise in the memory system, the temporal information carried by a time tag upon retrieval will, however, have associated with it an uncertainty distribution, closely akin to those that arise in some models for order and temporal position in short-term recall (Estes, 1972a; Lee & Estes, 1977). Flexser and Bower assumed these distributions to be normal in form and showed that on this assumption they could derive quantitative predictions about relationships between recency judgments and distance between presentations. Curiously, however, the model accounted quite well for results that arose when subjects were instructed on a test to choose the more recent of two stimuli, but not well for results occurring when subjects were asked to select the member of a pair that had occurred more remotely in time.

It is possible that the memory traces mediating the judgments are organized for retrieval in a hierarchical fashion, similar to that of the elements of semantic memory models, and that judgments of memory depend on retrieval of clusters of temporally contiguous events (Estes, 1980). If a test involves two events A and B, which occurred in that order, retrieval of a cluster of events including only one of these events plus a current anchor point (for example, the probe question), should lead the subject to judge that event as the more recent (correctly if it is B, incorrectly if it is A). However, in contrast with the case of semantic memory (see, e.g., Chase, 1978) there has as yet been very little experimental investigation of the temporal organization of episodic memory.

## Sequence Learning

Learning relative to sequences of events appears to be an essential constituent of the intellectual substrate for many forms of problem solving and decision making. Sequence learning may be considered in two principal categories: (a) learning of lists of elements, and (b) learning to anticipate successive members of indefinitely long sequences that are governed by some kind of order or pattern. Examples of the first type would be learning the sequence of signs or choice points on a route, the sequence of symbols in a telephone number or an address, the sequence of words in a message, or the sequence of notes in a musical passage. Examples of the latter would be learning to predict time series of events that

occur in business cycles or in forming inductive generalizations about rule-governed sequences (as, for example, mathematical series).

### Serial List Learning

The experimental psychology of human learning is generally held to have begun with studies by Ebbinghaus (1885/1913) on the learning of lists of meaningless items. By taking a firm stand on a major methodological issue, Ebbinghaus set the stage for the bifurcation of research strategies that has characterized the study of learning throughout its first century. One strategy is to design experiments so as to resemble in formal respects the situations of interest in ordinary environments but to use artificial materials so that the acquisition of new information can be studied uncontaminated by any effects of information the learner already possesses. The other strategy is deliberately to seek what is now termed "ecological validity," that is, to design experiments to simulate natural situations as closely as possible. For many decades following Ebbinghaus, most of the progress in the analysis of human learning was associated with the first strategy. In contrast, studies of the learning of sequences of meaningful materials, for example passages of poetry, led to little in the way of generalizable results, perhaps as a consequence of the fact that models that could guide significant analyses of such studies were far in the future.

Studies of the serial learning of lists of simple artificial units (in particular the consonant-vowel-consonant trigrams, termed CVCs or "nonsense syllables," introduced by Ebbinghaus) led quickly to quantitative descriptions of the course of acquisition and forgetting of lists susceptible first to mathematical accounts by the curve fitting of simple functions (Woodrow, 1942), and later by more elaboratory structured models (e.g., Hull et al., 1940).

A theoretical account of the learning of lists of unrelated items seems at first to require no more than the idea that mental associations or connections form between successive units. However, it was apparent even in the work of Ebbinghaus that this conception of simple mental connections between pairs of items must be augmented at least by an assumption of more remote associations. This elaboration enables an account of Ebbinghaus's observation that, following learning of a list of elements that

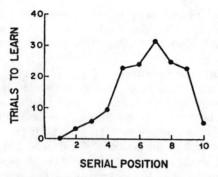

**Figure 5.7.** Serial position curve in terms of number of anticipation trials to learn words at each position of a 10-word list. (Data from Ebbinghaus, 1902, p. 626.)

might be denoted ABCDE, the learning of a new list is faster if some of the old elements remain in their original positions, for example AXCYE, than if the list is entirely new, and that savings decrease monotonically with the separation of the retained items.

Continuing analyses of list learning showed, however, that even direct plus remote associations were insufficient. It was quickly established that the relative difficulty of the items of a list follows a pattern described by a "bowed serial position curve," as illustrated in Figure 5.7, the end items being easiest to learn and the interior ones most difficult. This pattern in itself might be accounted for on the supposition that the end items of a list are more salient and on that account enter into associations more readily. This idea has found independent support: For example, Ebenholtz (1963) presented a list of items to subjects in a fixed sequence but with no demarcation between the end and the beginning of the list and with successive cycles starting at different points. Not only was the usual serial position pattern eliminated, but the learning of the list as a whole was much more difficult than that of comparable standard lists.

Augmentation of the hypothesis of simple interitem associations in terms of differential salience of items is insufficient to account for normal list learning, however, for the basic assumption has been undermined by relatively direct evidence. If a subject has learned a sequence, for example, ABCD . . . , primarily in terms of the formation of associations between adjacent items, then following such learning the individual should be able to perform almost perfectly on a paired-associate task made up of

pairs of adjacent items, that is A–B, C–D, and so forth. It has been found, however, that there is actually very little transfer from the serial to the paired-associate task (Young, 1961).

These various results have been taken to suggest an interpretation of serial learning in terms of a combination of processes considerably more complex than envisaged in early association theory. Associations may be formed between successive members of a list, but these are to an important extent conditional on context. For example, in the list ABCD, an association formed between items B and C would be conditional on the context of the B member, which would include the preceding item, A (Wickelgren, 1969). This context dependence can explain the well-known ability of people to learn different addresses or telephone numbers in which, for example, a digit 6 might be followed by an 8 in one address but by a 3 in another. However these associations may not be formed automatically, but may result from a process of rehearsal that is carried out only when task demands make it appropriate (Estes, 1972a).

In learning a list an individual typically forms a schema or mental representation of the structure of the task, including such elements as anchor points denoting the ends of the list. Then in the course of training, he or she associates items with their positions in this structure (the precision of these positional associations being greater for positions near than positions remote from anchor points).

Even the concepts of context-dependent associations and positional associations taken together do not suffice to account for some of the most interesting aspects of serial learning, for example, the points in particular lists that are unusually easy or unusually difficult for learners. One must recognize, in addition, that the units that enter into associations may not be the items identified by an experimenter but may be clusters or combinations of these that are viewed as unitary wholes by the learner.

Higher order units may, in some instances, be built up through a process of associative learning, but in others they appear to result from the direct perception of groupings in the sequence of events resulting from previous experience on the part of the learner. Consider, for example, a repeating sequence:

$$12\ 34\ 23\ 25\ 43$$

used in the study by Restle and Brown (1970a).

The serial position curve for learning of this sequence proves not to have the simple inverted U form of Figure 5.7 but rather a more complex one in which errors decrease uniformly over the first four positions, increase sharply on the fifth, decrease on the sixth, reach a maximum at position seven, and finally decrease over the last three positions. This pattern is precisely what Restle and Brown predicted on the assumption that the learner would perceive this sequence in terms of two kinds of higher order units, *runs* and *trills*. A run is a uniformly ascending or descending sequence of digits, like the first four digits 1234 in the example, whereas a trill, as in music, has the form illustrated by the sequence 232 that follows the initial run in the example. In another study Restle and Brown (1970b) obtained additional evidence for the function of these derived units by pretraining subjects to recognize runs in one condition and trills in another, then having the subjects of both groups learn an ambiguous test sequence. A segment of such a sequence might be

$$21\ 23\ 43$$

A group pretrained on runs would be expected to perceive the subsequence 1234 as a run and hence make a large number of errors on the next digit, 3. In contrast, a group pretrained on trills would be expected to perceive the 212 as a trill and the subsequent 34 as the beginning of another trill and hence to make relatively few errors on the sixth digit, 3. Again, Restle and Brown's results yielded the predicted difference.

### Induction

In a type of task related to but quite distinct from those just considered, the learner's objective is not to remember a sequence but to learn to anticipate successive members by abstracting the rule or rules that generate the sequence.

A start toward a characterization of learning processes that can cope with complex sequences has been reported by Bjork (1968) who studied the learning of unending sequences such as

$$0\ 4\ 2\ 1\ 5\ 3\ 2\ 6\ 4\ 3\ \ldots$$

The rules involved in generating the sequence are not immediately obvious, yet Bjork's subjects approached 100 percent correct anticipations of successive terms on the average after exposure to only about six to eight digits of the sequence. The general conception of the learning process that underlies Bjork's analysis is that the learner proceeds by first attending to and encoding events that are seen to recur then, in turn, encodes relations between these in the form of simple predictive rules. In the example, Bjork assumed that the first stage in learning is to notice that only three displacements between successive digits occur in the series—$+4$, $-2$, and $-1$—and once it has been noted that only these three local contexts occur, the problem becomes one of learning what response to associate with each. There is no simple rule to be found associating each of these displacements with particular digits, but it is the case that when one of these displacements has just occurred, the one that will occur next can always be predicted—that is, a displacement $-2$ is always followed by a $-1$, a $-1$ by a $+4$, and a $+4$ by a $-2$. By appropriate analyses, Bjork then showed that the learning of the correct predictive response for each of the local contexts proceeded in accord with the all-or-none model earlier found by Bower (1961) to describe learning in simple paired-associate and concept-identification experiments. That is, it was assumed that for each of the local contexts (a just preceding occurrence of $+4$, $-2$, or $-1$ displacement), performance in predicting the next item of the sequence would remain at a constant guessing level until learning occurred on an all-or-none basis on some trial; that there was some fixed probability that the learning would occur at each opportunity; and that, once learning occurred, the correct rule would be retained and thereafter be applied at each opportunity. Not only did the all-or-none model describe the learning of each of the three rules in relation to its local context separately, but when the three elementary learning processes were combined in a computer program, it proved possible to predict accurately the course of learning on the full sequence, as illustrated in Figure 5.8. A number of other sequences of varying degrees of complexity were handled equally well by this approach. It would not be realistic to expect the learning of all kinds of rule-governed sequences to yield to such a simple analysis, but nonetheless the results should be encouraging for attempts to analyze apparently complex learning into simpler subprocesses.

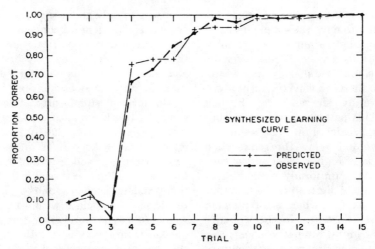

**Figure 5.8.** Curve for learning to anticipate members of a rule-governed sequence together with predictions from all-or-none Markov model. (Data from Bjork, 1968.)

## RETENTION AND FORGETTING

### Background

In normal adults the learning of simple associations is typically so rapid that tracing details of the process is difficult, but, in the absence of special measures, what is learned is nonetheless quickly forgotten. Similarly, school children typically learn a great deal of material and the practical probem often is not so much producing learning as ensuring that what is learned will be remembered when occasions for its use arise later outside the school.

At a very general level the most salient facts about forgetting are highly familiar, having been elucidated by preexperimental psychologists in the tradition of association theory and documented by everyday experience. One collection of these facts has to do with the salience of events and memory load. It is rarely difficult to remember and may be almost impossible to forget an unusual event that differs distinctively from all others in a person's experience, but it is very difficult to remember an event that is only one of a large number of similar instances. Studying and remembering a single word from a foreign language is trivial, but studying simultaneously a number of such words and remembering them for long may be beyond one's capability. A second set of facts has to do with recency and frequency of use. Other things being equal,

we find it easy to remember skills or items of information that have been frequently or recently practiced or rehearsed and difficult to reinstate or produce those that have been for some time dormant. A third set of facts has to do with variation in circumstances. People often have difficulty in remembering a speech except in the room in which it was rehearsed or in recalling the name of a newly introduced person when that individual is next met in a different context. Finally, it is well recognized that items tend to be easier to remember the more richly they are associated with others. A word may be very difficult to remember if one's sole experience with it is reading a dictionary definition, but it becomes easier to remember if used in a number of contexts and associated with a variety of other words or events. Each of these aspects of retention and forgetting has been the subject of extensive laboratory research and has been interpreted in a succession of different theoretical frameworks. This review is organized from the viewpoint of current cognitive psychology, the reader being referred to Hovland (1951), Postman and Underwood (1973), and Woodworth (1938) for historical perspectives.

### Information Processing and Retention

The concepts of retention and forgetting are foreign to general theories of information processing, but they become germane whenever attention is addressed specifically to information processing in living organisms, especially man. Whether information once processed into human long-term memory remains permanently in storage is a question that has been extensively discussed but that may never be answered. What is found experimentally is that measures of amount of information retained tend to decline over time following a learning experience. It is this decline that defines forgetting.

All tests for retention are, in effect, queries put to the learner, and these fall in two main classes depending on the way memory has to be addressed to yield an answer—by location of items or events in a chronological representation, or by content. The first type of query asks about the identity of the items that occurred at a particular time. Experimental examples occur in tests for free or ordered recall of the items that occurred during a particular list administration or for propositions abstracted from hearing or reading a particular passage of text. The second type of query asks what category an item belongs to or what its properties are, how two items are related, what a symbol means, or what action is appropriate whenever a given type of situation occurs. Experimental examples are tests for retention of semantic or categorical information or for maintenance of an acquired skill over time. The distinction between the two types of queries and the two modes of addressing memory needs to be taken into account in interpretation of both research and theory.

The strategy I shall follow in this survey of the extensive literature is to start by abstracting the most robust facts about forgetting, then relate these to the principal processes and mechanisms that seem relevant to their interpretation. The facts can conveniently be summarized in groups relating to classes of independent variables that are implicated in forgetting. The processes and mechanisms will be drawn mainly from the information-processing framework.

## Research on Determinants of Retention

### Conditions of Learning

Attempts to answer the question of whether forgetting depends on the degree of learning, dating from the early study of Luh (1922), have sometimes yielded superficially varying results, but the disparities seem to be resolved by clarification of the questions addressed and the methods of measurement (Slamecka & McElree, 1983). Forgetting can be presumed to refer to a decline in performance from an earlier to a later test, whether the same subjects or different groups are tested at the different times, but it is less apparent whether the decline should be measured in absolute or relative terms. There is no one answer, but in order to relate empirical results to models of forgetting (Anderson & Bower, 1973; Estes, 1955a; Wickelgren, 1972), it is necessary to distinguish the initial and terminal levels of performance and the slope of the curve of forgetting, that is, the rate at which performance moves from the initial to the terminal level. When analyses are not based on specific models, it is the usual practice to equate a difference in the rate of forgetting with a statistical interaction

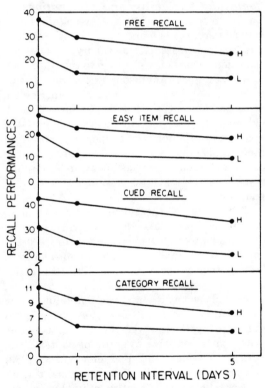

**Figure 5.9.** Recall at various retention intervals as a function of degree of learning (H = higher, L = lower). From "Normal Forgetting of Verbal Lists as a Function of Their Degree of Learning" by N.J. Slamecka and B. McElree, 1983, *Journal of Experimental Psychology: Learning, Memory, and Cognition, 9,* p. 388. Copyright 1983 by the American Psychological Association. Reprinted by permission of the authors.

in a set of retention functions and absence of a difference with no interaction, that is, with roughly parallel retention functions for the groups or conditions being compared. The data shown in Figure 5.9 exhibit the latter result for pairs of functions representing retention following different numbers of study trials and various measures of recall. Several experiments reported by Slamecka and McElree (1983) show the same pattern; as do a variety of earlier studies in which degree of learning was manipulated by instructions or meaningfulness of the material (reviewed by Underwood, 1964). Overall it can be concluded that the level of learning, however produced, is a powerful determinant of performance on an initial test of retention and of the final level after a long retention interval, but does not affect the rate of forgetting.

### Contextual Variability and Fluctuation

Variation in context has been recognized as a major determinant of forgetting since the earliest formulations of association theory, in some presentations even being elevated to the status of a Law of Context (Robinson, 1932). The characteristic observation is that if, say, an English word has been learned as a cue for a French synonym, the learner's likelihood of giving the appropriate French word upon encountering the English one depends importantly on the extent to which later tests occur under circumstances similar to those present at the time of learning.

The nature of the relevant circumstances, or contexts, may take the most varied forms. Changes between learning and test in the drug-controlled internal state of the subject (Eich, Weingartner, Stillman, & Gillin, 1975), the external environment (Smith, Glenberg, & Bjork, 1978), and semantic context of individual items (Gartman & Johnson, 1972) all have been found to impair recall. However, recognition is not as consistently sensitive to shifts of context. For example, Godden and Baddeley (1975, 1980) induced divers to undergo training and testing on word lists either in the normal open air environment or under water and found that recall, but not recognition, depended significantly on the similarity of the environments at the times of training and testing. The same distinction between recall and recognition was observed by Smith, Glenberg, and Bjork (1978) in a laboratory situation.

In human verbal learning another relevant type of context is provided by the learner's mental activity, as reflected in the associations evoked by words or phrases currently in active memory. Martin (1972) introduced the term *encoding variability* to denote the way in which an individual's encoding or interpretation of a verbal stimulus or event may change spontaneously from time to time with attendant variation in memory for earlier occasions. For example, if an individual on first learning the French equivalent of the English word "dog" had been thinking of a terrier as an exemplar, recall of the French word would be more likely on a later occasion if the individual happened again to have in mind a terrier as an instance of "dog" than if the instance were, say, a Great Dane. In several experiments, it has been found that, with adjectives used to set the semantic context for encoding meanings of nouns (e.g., *traffic jam* versus *sweet jam*), changes of context between learning and testing produce decrements in recognition similar in magnitude to those characteristic of recall with environmental changes (Light & Carter-Sobell, 1970).

The various results on effects of contextual shifts can be ordered in relation to the way context enters into the retrieval process in different test situations. In free recall, the task for memory search is to locate a set of items that have recently occurred in the experimental situation. Normally the items are familiar words that must have well-established long-term memory representations, as do all of the familiar words that did not occur in the experimental list. The only way the list words can be differentiated from the others is by means of episodic representations of the occurrence of these words in the background context of the list presentation. Thus, changes in background context between presentation and test eliminate cues that are essential to an effective memory search. These considerations imply the observed result that the largest and most uniform effects of contextual change are found in free recall.

When a memory representation takes the form of an associative structure, as in the learning of paired associates, ordered lists of items, or sentences, some element of the structure is ordinarily provided as a retrieval cue that can access the structure directly for recall. However, there is often ambiguity that can be resolved only by reference to context. If, for example, one has observed on a given occasion that object X is stored in location Y, as in a library or a computer program, then there may be ambiguity if one is later queried about the location of X, for X may have been stored in different locations on different occasions. If the query occurs in the same context as the original observation, then attention to aspects of the context will tend to yield recall of the appropriate episode; but if the query occurs in a different context, the same process may lead to recall of an inappropriate episode. Thus changes of context should be expected to be detrimental to associatively cued recall, although generally less than to free recall. In experiments providing direct comparisons of cued and free recall, Glenberg (1976, 1977) has demonstrated systematic effects of contextual change, controlled by variations in temporal spacing of events, in both cases, but stronger and more uniform effects for free recall.

When memory is tested by recognition, all of the elements of the to-be-remembered stimulus pattern are presented, and the subject's task is to search memory for a matching representation. If the elements have occurred together in the same pattern during only one learning experience, then the presence or absence of a match can be ascertained without reference to context. It seems likely that this stipulation has been met in the studies that have yielded no effect of context change on recognition. It should be possible, on this analysis, to produce a dependence of recognition on context by introducing ambiguity that can only be resolved by context, but this prediction seems not to have been tested experimentally.

Although research on the role of context has been largely limited to designs in which some experimentally induced change of context occurs between learning and testing, the results may extend to a much wider range of conditions both in the laboratory and in natural environments. It is universally accepted that the circumstances under which learning occurs never exactly repeat themselves and despite all efforts at control must be expected to vary randomly to some extent from one occasion to another. The numerous implications for the interpretation of memory that follow from this principle, together with the well-established fact that the effectiveness of any cue for recall depends on the intactness of earlier context, were developed quantitatively by Estes (1955a, 1955b, 1971) and, in

essentials, have been incorporated into treatments of recognition and recall by many investigators (Bower, 1967; Bowles & Glanzer, 1983; Martin, 1972; Murdock, 1974). Summaries of the theory that present the major implications with little mathematics have been provided by Bower (1967), Bower and Hilgard (1981), and Crowder (1976).

The flavor of some of the implications of contextual fluctuations can be conveyed in terms of a simple example. Suppose that the relation between a cue S and a response R has been learned on some occasion in the presence of a background context including elements a, b, c, and d. If the individual is tested immediately, before there is opportunity for the context to change, the probability of recall should be essentially unity. But if an interval of time passes, some of the contextual elements might become unavailable and be replaced by new ones, so that on the test the learner is confronted with, say, S plus contextual elements a, c, g, and h, in which case probability of recall would be expected to be lower than in the original context. On the supposition that these contextual changes occur randomly over time, probability of recall should be expected, on the average, to decline along the negatively accelerated course that characterizes classical forgetting curves.

Repeated learning experiences will be expected to increase probability of later recall, because with repetition there is opportunity for more of the contextual elements that might occur at recall to have been sampled on one or another of the learning trials. Thus within limits, sufficient repetition should cause the probability of recall to approach unity under all test conditions. Temporal spacing of learning trials is relevant, for if they are closely massed in time, there will be little opportunity for contextual variation from one trial to another and thus little gain in the number of additional contextual elements that accrue to support recall, whereas, contrariwise, wider temporal spacing permits more opportunities for contextual change and thus the accrual of more elements to support recall after a retention interval.

Further, the cross-over effect (Peterson, Hillner, & Saltzman, 1962) is predicted: Namely, retention curves following different degrees of spacing of learning trials show an interaction in that the curve for the more massed learning condition tends to be higher at the shortest retention intervals but the curves cross so that retention is better for the more spaced condition at longer retention intervals. A series of studies by Glenberg and his associates (Glenberg, 1977; Glenberg, Bradley, Kraus, & Renzaglia, 1983; Glenberg & Lehmann, 1980) with varying combinations of training and testing intervals (ranging from minutes to weeks) and various novel means of manipulating and analyzing relationships between training and test contexts provides a substantial illustration of the efficacy of these ideas and has led also to a collection of refinements and extensions that Glenberg terms the component-levels theory of spacing and retention. A particularly interesting outcome of Glenberg's studies, compatible with but going beyond what can be predicted from the basic fluctuation model, is a generalization to the effect that recall following long retention intervals tends to be directly proportional, but recall following short intervals inversely proportional, to the average duration of the intervals between trials during learning.

### Time and Disuse

Nothing is more obvious than that memories fade during periods when they are inactive. But nonetheless evidence bearing clearly on the possibility of an autonomous decay process is hard to obtain, for an interval of time is always filled with events that might be implicated in any forgetting that occurs.

Ebbinghaus (1885/1913) recognized this confounding but could see no way of obtaining experimental evidence to resolve it and was content to leave the issue in abeyance. However some other and even more influential psychologists were less demanding of positive evidence and in the early writings of Thorndike (1913) on learning, a Law of Disuse was elevated to the status of a general principle of forgetting, according to which learned connections weaken spontaneously during periods of inactivity. Perhaps because it is intuitively compelling to laymen as well as philosophers, this conception was widely held at the end of the first half century of the experimental psychology of memory, even though experimental investigations had revealed no positive evidence for spontaneous decay and in fact no methods that seemed in principle capable of doing so. This rather unsatisfying state of affairs led McGeoch (1942) in the first extensive review of the experimental study of

memory, to reject the decay theory entirely on the grounds not only that it lacked support but that evidence was rapidly accruing on the ways memories can be disturbed or rendered inaccessible by new learning that occurs between original learning and later tests.

Methods that might demonstrate autonomous retention loss became available only with the appearance of research on short-term memory beginning in the mid-1950s. Until that time, research on memory had typically used retention intervals ranging from minutes to days, and over such intervals it is impossible in practice to control the mental activities of human subjects closely enough to preclude learning or recall of material related in some way to the items that are to be tested at the end of the interval. The possibilities of adequate control were substantially increased, however, when Brown (1958) and Peterson and Peterson (1959) introduced a method for examining memory over much shorter time intervals. In their technique a small amount of material, typically a consonant trigram, was presented to a subject, following which the subject engaged in a presumably unrelated but still attention-demanding activity, for example counting backward, during a retention interval that might extend up to 15 to 20 sec and at the end of which recall was attempted. Under these conditions forgetting proved surprisingly rapid, retention of a trigram dropping by as much as 75 percent over a 15-sec interval with normal adult human subjects.

There remained the problem that the symbols being manipulated mentally by the subject during the retention interval might be a factor in the retention loss. In a further refinement, however, Reitman (1971) and Shiffrin (1973) replaced the backward counting task with one that required the subject simply to listen for a tonal signal during the retention interval, with instructions to avoid rehearsing and concentrate on the signal-detection task. Under these conditions, the initial results were an apparent total absence of forgetting during the period filled only with signal detection. However, subsequent more searching examination of the task with somewhat increased memory loads yielded evidence that subjects in these experiments were surreptitiously rehearsing the to-be-remembered items at some points during the retention intervals, and that when this rehearsal was apparently totally eliminated in particular cases, some retention loss appeared (Reitman, 1974).

Thus, although the issue is not closed, there now seems reason to believe that some spontaneous loss of availability of to-be-remembered items does occur during a retention interval regardless of the nature of intervening activities. Whether this process is best interpreted as one of decay of the memory trace is by no means sure, however. There is always some opportunity for fluctuations of context, both aspects internal to the learner and aspects of the external background, during an interval, and the fluctuation process may account for some or all of the forgetting that has been attributed to decay.

### Retroactive and Proactive Interference

For any combination of learning and test conditions, the principal determinant of forgetting of any item of information is to be found in other learning that has occurred before or after that of the given item. The overall generalization is that retention of information obtained from any episode is reduced by other learning that involves temporally proximal or categorically similar items or events. The classical interpretation is that the mechanism is one of interference. The learning that associates an item with a retrieval cue either simultaneously induces unlearning of any other item previously associated with the same cue or subsequently leads to competition between the new and old associations for access to response channels at the time of recall (Melton & Irwin, 1940). However, an analysis from an information-processing perspective suggests that the source of the effects may lie at least partly in capacity limitations. Cognitive activities such as rehearsal (termed control processes by Atkinson and Shiffrin, 1968) that are needed to maintain the availability of an item for recall can be applied to only one item at a time, so increasing the number of items associated with a given context reduces the processing each can receive. Thus I shall use interference only as a descriptive concept, assuming that its interpretation is to be found in processes of memory access, search, and retrieval that have some independent status.

Perhaps the most substantial body of research and theory yielded by the first 75-odd years of experimental study of human memory was addressed to the role of interference in retention.

A standard paradigm for studying interference was established by Müller and Pilzecker (1900) in the now familiar A–B, A–C paradigm. Subjects first receive paired-associate training trials on a list of stimulus items (for example, nonsense syllables), denoted A, paired with a list of responses (for example, adjectives), denoted B, then, after an interval receive training on either the same (A) or a similar (A′) list of stimuli paired with a new list of responses, denoted C. The classical finding, commonly denoted retroactive inhibition, is that on a later test for memory of the A–B list, recall is poorer for individuals receiving this sequence than for comparable individuals who receive the same training on A–B and are tested following the same interval but without the intervening training on A–C.

The counterpart to retroactive inhibition is the interfering effect of previously learned material on retention of newly learned items, denoted proactive inhibition. In terms of the A–B, A–C design, proactive inhibition is demonstrated by a reduction in the amount retained following a given degree of learning of A–C as a consequence of prior learning of A–B. Thus in the case of proactive inhibition, the controlled comparison defining the paradigm is a retention test for A–C associations at a given retention interval for individuals who have had the A–B, A–C sequence as compared to controls who have had training on A–C only.

In the earlier literature on interference there was less emphasis on proactive than retroactive effects, perhaps importantly as a consequence of a study by Melton and von Lackum (1941) that presented a controlled comparison of proactive and retroactive inhibition following equated amounts of learning on first and second lists and indicated that retroaction was the much more substantial effect.

The signficance of proactive interference as a robust phenomenon that must be given close attention in theoretical interpretations of forgetting was increased by a quantum jump upon the appearance of a major paper on interference and forgetting by Underwood (1957). Underwood began his new investigation from the observation that substantial forgetting is characteristically observed over periods of hours when college students subjects have learned lists of novel materials even though there is no obvious way in which there could be an appreciable amount of relevant new learning of interfering associations during the interval. On the other hand, in many such experiments the subjects have had previous experiences in learning similar materials, often distributed over considerable periods of time, and this prior learning could conceivably lead to the observed retention loss by a proactive effect. Underwood produced statistical support for this idea by an examination of retention losses as a function of the number of previous lists subjects had learned in the data of a large number of published experiments, and in addition carried out some specifically planned new studies in which subjects learned lists with controlled amounts of similarity on successive days, the results uniformly being substantial reduction in the retention of a list as a function of the number of lists previously learned (Greenberg & Underwood, 1950).

The salient facts that can be distilled from the very large literature on proactive and retroactive effects appear to be interpretable in terms of concepts of memory search and retrieval. If retroactive effects depended on unlearning of previously formed associations, then one would expect similar effects regardless of the mode of testing. However, it is observed that retroactive interference appears ubiquitously in recall but to a much smaller degree in recognition (Postman, 1976). If proactive interference involved some change in the storage of later-formed associations, one would expect the effects to be irreversible. However, it is observed that the effects can be eliminated by inserting a delay between the last of a series of items or lists that normally produce proaction and the item or list on which the effect is measured (Kincaid & Wickens, 1970). Further, both proactive and retroactive effects can be eliminated if the subject is supplied with distinct and unambiguous retrieval cues (Tulving & Psotka, 1971).

The study of Tulving and Psotka is particularly instructive. Independent groups of subjects were presented with differing numbers, from one to six, of 24-item word lists. Each list comprised six blocked subgroups of four words, each subgroup drawn from a common category and no category repeated across lists. A free recall test was given after each list, and following the last list, each group was given a test of free recall for all of the lists previously seen. At the end of the experiment, the subjects were given an additional total recall test on

**Table 5.2. Free and Cued Recall as a Function of Number of Preceding or Succeeding Lists.**
(*Data of Tulving & Psotka, 1971*)

| Group | Free Recall | | Cued Recall | |
|---|---|---|---|---|
| | First List | Last List | First List | Last List |
| 1 | 16.6 | 16.6 | 18.1 | 18.1 |
| 2 | 12.1 | 17.2 | 20.5 | 20.2 |
| 3 | 9.4 | 15.4 | 16.4 | 17.1 |
| 4 | 7.1 | 14.8 | 15.4 | 17.6 |
| 5 | 6.6 | 17.1 | 16.2 | 18.3 |
| 6 | 6.8 | 14.4 | 16.1 | 17.9 |

which category names were supplied as retrieval cues.

Interference effects can be assessed in the data for the total free recall test, summarized in the first two columns of Table 5.2. Strong retroactive interference is shown by the steep decline in recall of the first list of any group as a function of the number of succeeding lists (Column 1), but weak or absent proactive interference by the relative constancy of recall of the final list as a function of the number of preceding lists (Column 2). Since category names were not supplied in the free recall test, only the context could supply retrieval cues, and, on the assumption that context fluctuates over time, the similarity of the context for a given list to the context at the point of recall should decline with the number of intervening lists. Thus the retroactive effect would be predicted on the basis of varying availability of retrieval cues. This factor would not be expected to yield proactive interference in this situation, since similarity of list context to context at recall would not be affected by prior lists. When category names were supplied as retrieval cues in the final test, recall was increased somewhat and the retroactive effect was virtually eliminated (Column 3 of Table 5.2) with again no proactive effect. Further confirming the interpretation of the interference effects in terms of retrieval problems, the mean number of words recalled per recalled category was virtually constant over all lists in all recall tests.

Manipulations of time intervals between lists (reviewed by Postman, 1971) yield a pattern of results that fits an interpretation in terms of contextual variation. In the A–B, A–C design, a test for A–B recall given right after the second list comes when currently available contextual cues are associated with C, and therefore recall

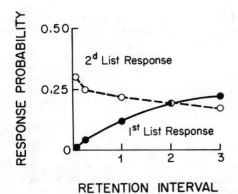

**Figure 5.10.** Illustrative functions computed from fluctuation model for recovery (increasing availability) of A–B associations during an interval following learning of A–B, A–C lists.

of B is minimal. If the test is delayed, some contextual cues that were associated with B during A–B learning but unavailable at the end of A–C learning will have fluctuated into the available state, leading to an increase in recall of B (termed "spontaneous recovery" by some investigators, by analogy with recovery from extinction in classical conditioning). The form of the recovery function predicted on the assumption of contextual fluctuation is illustrated in Figure 5.10, and may be compared with the orderly trends observed in a well-designed study by Briggs (1954), shown in Figure 5.11.

In a proactive design, learning of a list speeds the forgetting of a subsequently learned list if retrieval cues for the two lists are similar. Recall of the second list is maximal on an immediate test, when contextual cues that can

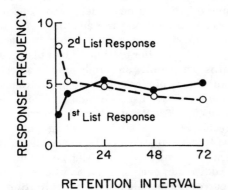

**Figure 5.11.** Mean frequency of first and second list responses during a retention interval (hours) following second list learning. Data from Briggs (1954).

resolve the ambiguity of the retrieval cues are associated with the response of the second list, but decreases on a delayed test when contextual cues associated with first-list responses have had an opportunity to fluctuate into the available state.

Similarity has been recognized as a pervasive factor in interference effects since the pioneering work of Poffenberger (1915), but, prior to about 1970, research was heavily concentrated in the paired-associate paradigm and oriented toward the formulation of a general empirical principle. This goal, as originally conceived, proved unrealistic as experimental analyses showed quite different effects of similarity at the level of relationships between list contexts and the level of commonalities between stimulus and response members of specific items. An important step toward clarifying the empirical issues was contributed by Osgood (1949) and the task was completed by Postman (1971).

In terms of information-processing concepts, the general principle emerging from a gradually expanding range of research is that similarity is detrimental to retention whenever it reduces the distinctiveness of retrieval cues for to-be-remembered items. In paired-associate learning, both proactive and retroactive interference are increased by similarity between stimuli that have different response assignments. The effects tend to be stronger in the proactive case, for responses of an earlier learned list are likely to be actively represented in memory during learning or retention of a given list only if activated by common or similar stimulus components. The commonalities need not be at the level of similarity on sensory dimensions, but may, rather, have to do with semantic attributes or categorical relationships. When the experimental task calls simply for free or ordered recall of items, similarity effects depend on retrieval demands. Similarity among items within a list is detrimental to retention of information about order or temporal position, as would be expected from the fact that similar items tend to be activated simultaneously by retrieval cues that are associated with their common aspects but do not distinguish their positions. At the same time, retention of item, as distinguished from order, information may be enhanced by similarity, which facilitates the rehearsal of clusters of related items (Lee & Estes, 1977; Murdock, 1974, 1976).

When the learner has had experience with two or more lists and recall of one of them is called for, similarity between items across lists would be expected to impair retention, since retrieval cues related to common aspects or categorical relationships would tend to activate items from uncued lists as well as from the cued list. The observed result is that, in general, both proactive and retroactive interference in all types of experiments depend on stimulus similarity across lists, both kinds of effects on recall of a given item or list increasing with increasing similarity of its retrieval cues to those of preceding or following items or lists (Osgood, 1949; Postman, 1971; Wickens, 1970).

When memory is tested by recognition, the retrieval cue for an item is the item itself, and performance on a recognition test depends on the degree to which elements or aspects of the item have become associated during learning with the context in which the test occurs. When these elements are unique to the given item, they contribute only to correct recognition, but when they are shared by distractors (items not presented during learning but included in the recognition test), they lead to errors. Proactive and retroactive effects on recognition of an item should be expected when the occurrence of similar items either before or after its presentation increases the number of its shared elements that are associated with the context. Bowles and Glanzer (1983) formalized this interpretation within the framework of a stimulus sampling model and showed that the model provides a quantitative account of proactive and retroactive effects on old/new recognition tests.

### Memory Load

There have been several quite different approaches to the question of why retention of a given item of information depends strongly on the body of material in which it is embedded. The earliest approach, beginning with the work of Ebbinghaus (1885/1913), addressed the effect of the number of items constituting the list or collection undergoing learning. Typical list-length data summarized in Table 5.3, from Woodworth (1938), exhibit a somewhat paradoxical result. Subjects learned lists of word pairs under a standard paired-associate, anticipation procedure. Immediate recall, measured in terms of percentage of correct responses on anticipation trials, decreased as a function of list length, but

**Table 5.3. Learning and Retention of Paired Associates in Relation to Number of Presentations and Length of List***

| Acquisition Data | List length (number of word pairs) | | | |
|---|---|---|---|---|
| | 5 | 10 | 20 | 30 |
| Number of preceding presentations | | | | |
| 1 | 68 | 60 | 50 | 35 |
| 2 | 94 | 80 | 71 | 55 |
| 3 | 100 | 91 | 84 | 71 |
| Retention Data | 4 | 16 | 36 | 34 |

*Data are percentages of correct recalls of response members of pairs (from Woodworth, 1938, p. 19).

on a retention test given two days later recall increased with list length. Woodworth interprets the latter finding as indicating that with longer lists the subjects have more incentive and more opportunity to rehearse in a way that will generate more associations between any given item and others in the list, thereby providing more support for retention. However, a confounding arises from the fact that the last few items of a list are still actively represented in short-term memory at the time of immediate recall, and thus are unlikely to receive the rehearsal that earlier items must have in order to be retrievable at the end of the list presentation. This subset of items that is likely to escape rehearsal, and thus be unrecallable after a long retention interval, constitutes a large proportion of a short list but only a small proportion of a long list.

More sharply controlled comparisons are available from studies in which a list is given a single presentation under conditions that restrict rehearsal and the amount of information retained in long-term memory is assessed only from the earlier portions of lists of different lengths. The results uniformly exhibit a decline in probability of recalling an item as a function of length of the list in which it is imbedded (Murdock, 1962; Raaijmakers & Shiffrin, 1981; Roberts, 1972). In studies dealing only with short-term recall, the picture is even clearer, the retention of an item being sharply reduced by the addition of even a single additional item to the current memory load (Reitman, 1974; Shiffrin, 1973; Shiffrin & Cook, 1978).

Considerable evidence points to the limited capacity of the rehearsal system in working memory as a major factor in memory load effects. One particularly cogent result comes from a study by Atkinson and Shiffrin (1971) in which subjects were presented for study either a 5-word or a 20-word list but then studied a second list of either 5 or 20 words before recall of one of the lists was called for. Probability of recalling a word was strongly related to the length of the list in which it occurred, with an advantage of approximately 2:1 for 5-word lists over 20-word lists, but was virtually unaffected by the length of the list that preceded or followed the one in which the given word occurred. This finding is understandable on the assumption that in order to be retrievable as a group at the time of the recall test, the items of a list have to be rehearsed together, allowing the formation of associations among them and between the items and a list tag or control element. Because of the limited capacity of the rehearsal buffer, a smaller proportion of items of a long list than of a short list will have the opportunity to enter into the necessary associations.

A quite different source of evidence for the role of rehearsal is provided by studies of "instructed forgetting" (Bjork, 1972). Bjork's studies started with the standard finding that if subjects are presented with two short lists of items successively and then probed for recall of the second, performance is much poorer than if only the second list is given, a variant of the memory load effect. Bjork's new procedure was to follow the first list under some circumstances with a symbol indicating to the subjects that they should forget the first list since it would never be tested, but that they might still expect a retention test for the second list. The result was recall of the second list on a par with a control condition in which only the second list was given, indicating that the normal, proactively interfering effects of the first list had been wiped out by the "forget" instruction.

It might be thought that this result simply demonstrates an ability of individuals to forget on command, but this interpretation was ruled out by a number of control measures. One of them was the giving of an unexpected recognition test for items from the first list, the results of which demonstrated that even though the first-list items were no longer producing proactive interference effects, they had not been lost from memory. A still more telling result was a demonstration that if the instruction to forget

the first list is given after the administration of the second list rather than after the administration of the first, it has no effect. When, a "forget" cue is given following a presentation of the first list, the subject evidently is able, by taking advantage of the list differentiating context, to discontinue rehearsing all of the items of the first list and thus to allot as much rehearsal to the second as though the first had never been presented.

## Cue Ambiguity and the Fan Effect

From evidence reviewed in preceding sections, it is clear that recall is most efficient when a unique retrieval cue is available to provide direct access to the to-be-recalled item in memory. This principle has been extended to the more general concept that the level of activation of any memory representation by an associated cue decreases as a function of the number of associative paths emanating from the cue (Anderson, 1976, 1983a; Hayes-Roth & Hayes-Roth, 1977; Watkins, 1979). This broader conception of cue ambiguity has been explicated by Anderson (1983a) in terms of the spread of activation in an associative network. In Anderson's model, each memory representation corresponds to a node in a network and can support recall or recognition to the degree that the node receives activation spreading along the internode paths from a retrieval cue. However, the node corresponding to the retrieval cue has only limited capacity to send activation into the network upon instigation by an incoming message, and the activation is divided equally among all paths emanating from it.

In Watkins's (1979) review of related literature, supporting qualitative evidence was drawn from the list-length effect (Murdock, 1960) and from the observation that in cued recall from categorized word lists, the probability of recall of any word declines as the number of words presented in its category increases (Watkins & Watkins, 1975). However, other factors may be implicated in these phenomena, as, for example, limitations on rehearsal capacity. Somewhat more direct demonstrations of the role of cue ambiguity come from studies of what is currently known as the *fan effect* in the literature on memory for complex materials (Anderson, 1974; Anderson & Bower, 1973; Smith, 1981).

The fan effect refers to the observation that under many circumstances, the more facts one learns about a concept, the slower and less accurate one is in recognizing any one factual relationship. Thus, in one kind of experiment extensively explored by Anderson (1976, 1981), a subject might be exposed to sentences of the form "The lawyer lives in Ohio," and after studying a number of such sentences would be tested for recognition, being presented (singly) either with some of the previously studied sentences or with distractor sentences and being required to respond yes or no in each case to the question, "Was the probe sentence in the studied set?" The general observation is that reaction time is shortest to a sentence such as "The lawyer lived in Ohio" if no other sentence about the lawyer occurred in the study set, but becomes progressively slower if the list has included also "The lawyer was wealthy," and so on.

In network models for such experiments, memory for one of the sentences, or for the proposition expressed by it, is interpreted in terms of a representation of the concept *lawyer*, corresponding to a node or point of intersection in an associative network, with associative pathways leading from that node to others representing the items of information to which lawyer was related in the study material—Ohio, court, wealth and so on (Anderson, 1976; Anderson & Bower, 1973). When the subject is probed for recognition by presentation of a test sentence, say "The lawyer spoke in court," the stimulus input from the probe is assumed to activate the nodes corresponding to "lawyer" and "court" in the network; then some form of activation is assumed to spread along the connections leading from each of these, and only if the activation from "lawyer" arrives at "court" and the activation from "court" arrives at "lawyer" does the individual being queried conclude that the probe does correspond to a memory representation and thus say yes to the test question. According to Anderson's model, this process is fastest if the pathways from "lawyer" to "court" and "court" to "lawyer" are the only ones emanating from these two nodes in the memory network and becomes progressively slower as the number of paths from these nodes increases (somewhat on the analogy of a voltage divider). The functional relationship operative seems closely analogous to that manifest in the other kinds of studies cited on cue ambiguity effects, that is, a retrieval cue becomes less and less efficient as a cue for a particular

**Table 5.4. Reaction Time in Seconds as a Function of Fan (Number of Associative Paths Emanating from a Retrieval Cue)**
*Data from Anderson (1983a, p. 116)*

| Fan | Recognition | Recall |
|-----|-------------|--------|
| 1   | 1.35        | 1.54   |
| 2   | 1.58        | 2.07   |
| 3   | 1.70        | 2.96   |

item in memory the more other items it is associated with.

A quantitative demonstration of parallel fan effects in recognition and recall from a study by Anderson (1983a) is summarized in Table 5.4. The subjects studied sentences cast in subject-verb-object format, then were cued for recall of the object of a sentence by presentation of the subject and verb or were presented with a full studied sentence (or an unstudied distractor sentence) on a recognition test. An excellent account of both the relation between reaction time and fan and the difference between recognition and recall was provided by simple formulas of the form

$$RT = a + b/(1 + 2/f)$$

for recognition and

$$RT = a + b/(2/f)$$

for recall, in which $f$ denotes the fan (1, 2, or 3).

Given that the cue ambiguity is an important factor in retrieval, why should it be implicated also in forgetting? The answer appears to be that other learning that either precedes or follows the learning of a given item can increase the ambiguity of its retrieval cues. For example, in a study by Anderson (1981), subjects received training on an A–B paired-associate list, the stimuli being nouns and the responses digits, then on a second list of the form A–Br (the same nouns repaired with different digits). At the end of this training, each stimulus item had been associated with two different digits, and thus had fan 2, whereas in a control condition with lists A–B and C–D, each stimulus item had fan 1. Thus, from the principle of cue ambiguity, better performance would be predicted for the control than the experimental condition on a final test. For a final test on the first list, we would speak descriptively of retroactive interference, and for a final test on the second list, we would speak of proactive interference. But in both cases the interpretation is the same, and, in fact, Anderson showed that the observed effects could be quantitatively described by an appropriate modification of the same model described above for sentence memory. Similar results were obtained from a parallel experiment conducted with recognition rather than recall tests. It appears that the principle of cue ambiguity, as embodied in the spreading activation model, and the concept of contextual fluctuation, taken together, account for much of what is known about interference effects in memory (Anderson, 1983b).

## Organization and Retention

Given the well-established conclusion that forgetting is mainly the result of failures to retrieve stored information, one expects that the keys to improving recall must lie primarily in the way information is organized in memory. Further, the role of organizational factors must depend on the type of memory access required by any given task.

### Recall from Episodic Memory

When a task calls for recall of a specific event or episode, access to the relevant memory representation must often, especially in relatively short term situations, be achieved by a search through a chronologically ordered sequence of memory traces. The strict limitations on our ability to accomplish retrieval from lengthy sequences of episodes, as evidenced, for example, in the list-length effect, indicates that the search process is quite fallible. One reason is surely related to the slowness of memory search and the consequent likelihood that a lengthy search will be interrupted by other cognitive activities. The problem is alleviated somewhat if the representation includes distinctive items or events that demark boundaries of lists, sublists, or other groupings of chronologically contiguous items. In general, interference effects are greater among items that fall between than items that are separated by such markers (Bower & Winzenz, 1969; Johnson, 1970).

An interpretation of the role of boundary markers has at least two aspects. (a) It is known that search is much faster when the target is a single feature or attribute than when it is a conjunction of features or attributes defining an item (Treisman & Gelade, 1980). Hence, if a property of a boundary marker for a segment of memory in which a target item is located is known to the individual in advance, then a rapid search can be conducted until the boundary marker is located, followed by a slow item by item search only within the segment (Anderson, 1960; Lee & Estes, 1981). (b) Items set off by list or sublist boundaries tend to be rehearsed together; thus associative links develop between the items and their common context, enabling retrieval of groups as higher order units.

Even in the absence of explicit boundary markers, sequences of episodic memories can often be segmented to some extent on the basis of the common contexts in which subsequences of events occurred. The context might be the locality in which the events occurred or a particular time interval (for example, "today" or "last Friday"). This kind of segmentation has been investigated experimentally under the concept of list differentiation, familiar in the verbal learning literature at least since its application to the retroactive inhibition paradigm by Underwood (1945). It refers in essentials to the fact that subjects who have learned two or more lists during an experimental session are able in some degree to remember which items occurred in which list, and thus to recall the particular list that is called for on a test.

The essentials of an organizational interpretation of list difference are as follows. During the learning of any list, learning occurs not only relative to the stimuli specifically presented by the experimenter but also with respect to background context that serves in the subject's mind to differentiate this learning episode from others. Thus, if in the learning of a particular list, a stimulus $S_1$ were paired with a response $R_1$ and a stimulus $S_2$ with a response $R_2$, the structure formed in the subject's memory would include, in effect, an association of $R_1$ with the compound of the list context together with $S_1$, an association of $R_2$ with the compound of the list context together with $S_2$, and so on. In an experimental situation, list context comprises aspects of the presentation of a list that enable the subject to remember it as a different episode than the presentation of another list. In the everyday life example of a person learning two languages, the counterpart of list context is any cue or aspect of a situation that signifies which language is appropriate. In general, recall of the response appropriate to any situation depends jointly on the availability of a specific retrieval cue and the reinstatement of elements of the context in which cue and response became associated. One important advantage of this form of organization over the simple pairwise associations of stimuli and responses assumed in classical association theories is that the memory representations of list contexts enable individuals to activate lists as units for such purposes as selective rehearsal.

Occurring in a common background context is only one way in which lists or other collections of items may take on some of the properties of higher order units in memory representations. Items having common sensory properties or having been perceived by common sensory channels tend to be organized so as to be accessible together, as do items having semantic or other abstract properties as a basis for categorization. For example, in a short-term situation, Darwin, Turvey, and Crowder (1972) showed that when subjects had been presented with tape-recorded stimuli from speakers in different locations, they could on a test report quite efficiently the items that came from any one of the speakers. Similarly, it has been found that if a list or sublist of items shares a common categorical property, then this property tends to be used by individuals to reduce the need for item by item search. In a study by Seamon (1973), for example, the subjects learned lists, ranging in length from 9 to 18 words, that were made up of several sublists of items belonging to particular semantic categories. Following the learning of a full list, the subject was probed by being presented with a category label together with an indication of a particular serial position within the categorized sublist, and asked to recall the indicated item. Analysis of reaction time in relation to the number and sizes of categories in the list supported the conclusion that access to an item is achieved by a relatively rapid memory search over the categorized sublists, followed by a slower search within the appropriate sublist. Evidence for a similar combination of global and local search processes has been reported by Oliver and Ericsson (1983) for the everyday life situation of recall of lines of a play by actors.

### Recall from Categorical/Semantic Memory

Recall of information about semantic or categorical relationships among items or events generally depends on direct access to the appropriate memory representations, since the learning responsible for storing the information has generally been distributed over many occasions and cannot be localized in any particular episodic memory. Evidently the capacity for access to semantic memory is almost unlimited if efficiency is not a criterion, as witness the very large number of vocabulary items that can be recognized or produced by an ordinary adult in unconstrained, everyday life situations. The very large capacity in the case of vocabulary presumably owes to the fact that both printed and spoken words provide unique retrieval cues for the corresponding memory representations. For other kinds of semantic memories, however, retrieval cues often are not as completely distinctive and hence the cue presented on a particular occasion may evoke recall of various distractors as well as the target item. Thus, if one is asked to recall the name of the President of the United States, the names of several presidents in addition to the current one are likely to be brought to mind, and reference to the current context is needed to eliminate the ambiguity. If one were, instead, asked to name all of the members of the current administration in Washington, one might well begin by recalling some who have been currently prominent in the news, but then, distracted by the associations aroused by these initial recalls, be unable to go on and complete the list. A basic difficulty is that the single retrieval cue "current administration in Washington" is associated with a large number of individual members and, in some cases, only weakly. The debilitating effect of this cue ambiguity might be alleviated, however, if one attempted to recall in an orderly manner by proceeding through major categories, for example, the members of the Cabinet, White House advisors, the heads of major agencies, and so on. In the latter strategy, each of the category labels would be associated with a relatively small number of individuals and hence would provide a more effective retrieval cue for their recall.

A large literature on free recall on word lists has demonstrated the advantages of categorization, with recall being facilitated especially if the categories are known in advance to the subjects and category cues are available at recall (see, for example, Bower, 1970; Mandler, 1967; Tulving, 1968). A particularly effective way of reducing cue ambiguity is to arrange items in a hierarchical arrangement of related categories and subcategories. In a study by Bower, Clark,

Lesgold, and Winzenz (1969), for example, particular to-be-recalled items such as gold, copper, steel, diamond, granite, could be arranged in a hierarchical scheme with *minerals* as the highest level category, *metals* and *stones* as subordinate categories, *rare* and *common* as subcategories under metals, and so on. Bower et al. found that when the hierarchical arrangement was made explicit to the subjects at the time of learning a word list, the speed of learning and the amount retained were very greatly increased in comparison to a control condition in which the same items were presented for the same amount of study time but in a random arrangement. Although it might be efficient for recall if long-term semantic memory were fully organized in a hierarchical fashion, there is little evidence that such is the case. However it does appear on the basis of work such as that of Bower et al. that individuals can organize and remember hierarchical retrieval schemes that provide efficient retrieval cues for limited bodies of semantic or factual material.

# COMPLEX LEARNING

## Concept Learning: Overview

In important respects concepts may be considered to be units of complex learning. In nearly all of the recent efforts to present broad models for the learning of factual information, the knowledge structure resulting from an individual's experience with a given type of material is assumed to take the form of an associative network in which concepts correspond to the nodes of the network and relationships between concepts to the pathways interconnecting them (Anderson, 1976; Anderson & Bower, 1973; Norman & Rumelhart, 1970). Within this framework, concept learning must be considered basic to all of the more elaborate forms of learning responsible for the acquisition of factual knowledge. However, although research on concept formation has a history of some 60 years, the work accomplished during at least the first half of the interval is largely irrelevant to what are now regarded as the significant theoretical issues concerning knowledge acquisition. Attention was largely confined to the way in which learners discover rules that enable them to classify exemplars of concepts, but with little systematic attention to

the nature of the memory representations that are the product of the learning.

Concept learning is easy to characterize in procedural terms. The test of a learner's attainment of a concept is the ability to classify items in the given domain according to some criterion—words into grammatical classes; philosophies into analytic and nonanalytic; animals into mammals, fish, birds, and so forth. However, what is learned, that is, the mental representation providing the basis for classifying, may vary from rote memorization of observed assignments of instances to full understanding of the basis of classification. Consequently, studies of concept learning need to be interpreted in relation to the information-processing requirements of the experimental tasks, or the natural situations being simulated. It is useful to distinguish several main types of tasks.

## Categorization of a Finite Set of Items with an Arbitrary Mapping Between Items and Classes

An extensively studied experimental paradigm falling in this category is "verbal discrimination learning," in which the subject simply learns to assign members of a list of items to two arbitrary categories (Eckert & Kanak, 1974; Ekstrand, Wallace, & Underwood, 1966). An everyday example of the kind of situation simulated would be a newspaper deliverer learning to categorize the homes along a street into those who have and have not ordered newspaper delivery. Although the problem for the learner may seem almost trivial, research on this task has yielded some instructive theoretical analyses. It has been found that when materials are chosen to minimize rehearsal, so that learning of the assignment of an item is confined to the trial on which it is presented, the course of learning can be fully characterized by an extremely simple mathematical process (Bower, 1961; Estes, 1964a).

In a model developed by Bower (1961), it is assumed that a subject's memory for the assignment of an item is at any time in either of two states—unlearned or fully learned—and that the learning occurs on any presentation with some probability $c$ that remains constant over the course of learning. Prior to learning, the subject guesses assignments randomly if required to respond. It is easily shown that in this model the predicted number of errors during learning is equal to $1/2c$. Bower evaluated $c$ for his subjects by setting this ratio equal to the observed mean number of errors and solving for $c$, the result being $c = .25$ (the data coming from an experiment in which Bower minimized rehearsal by using nonsense syllables as the items to be categorized). Given an estimate of $c$, it is possible to predict the values that should be observed for other statistics of the data.[3] For example, with the given estimate, the standard deviation of the distribution of errors during learning is predicted to be 1.98, which compares favorably with the observed value in Bower's study of 1.94. Again, the mean number of errors expected following any particular error during learning is predicted to be constant at a level of 1.49; the observed values in Bower's study following the first, second, third, fourth, or fifth error, respectively, were 1.52, 1.40, 1.56, 1.46, and 1.48 with an average of 1.48.

The elegant account of the learning data by means of this simple model has been replicated with variations on Bower's study (Atkinson, Bower, & Crothers, 1965), but the adequacy of the model is clearly limited to cases in which learning is confined to a trial to trial basis. Human subjects exhibit a ubiquitous tendency to seek common elements or aspects in the items to be categorized and may even generate such properties when they are absent in the material as presented. For example, studies of verbal discrimination learning in which the items to be categorized were words and nothing was done to interfere with rehearsal have yielded evidence that adult subjects characteristically adopt a strategy of selectively rehearsing the items that are assigned to one of the two categories and then on test trials assign items to one or the other category on the basis of their familiarity or remembered frequency (Ekstrand, Wallace, & Underwood, 1966; Medin, 1974). In effect, the subjects convert the task into the next type to be considered and solve it on a basis not intended by the experimenter.

### Multidimensional Items with a Rule for Categorization

In a paradigm much used in research with children, the stimuli are cards or blocks varying on such dimensions as color, size, or form; a typical task is to learn to sort all of the red stimuli into one category and all of the blue stimuli into

[3]These and other analyses are described in Estes (1964a).

another regardless of size or form. A simple everyday counterpart would be learning to classify substances as flammable or inflammable. In one major subclass of studies, a set of possible rules is known by the subjects prior to concept training, either on the basis of instructions or because they are obvious from the nature of the materials, and the task becomes one of formulating and testing hypotheses as to which rule is applicable until the correct one is selected. In the other major subclass, the appropriate rule has to be discovered or constructed by the subject, as in the case of a child learning to distinguish dogs from cats. Here the information-processing load is greater, for the learner must accumulate information about items and their relations to categories and then use the accumulated information to construct and test hypotheses or to assess probabilities of class membership for new items having various combinations of attributes.

### Categorization of Multidimensional Items into Classes Not Defined by Common Properties (Fuzzy Categories)

In natural environments categorization often involves collections of objects or events that are not delineated by the well-specified rules that are the norm in formal domains such as mathematics, logic, and some of the sciences. In one major subclass of this kind of situation, instances of a category are generated by variations on an underlying core pattern or prototype. An example is the task posed for a child learning to recognize people in photographs, even though the photographs of a given individual vary in the setting, clothes, facial expression, and so forth. In the other major subclass, categories are defined simply by the different degrees of family resemblance of exemplars within and between categories, as in such common examples as liberals versus conservatives or tools versus utensils. Since, in natural situations, learners generally do not know in advance whether they are dealing with rule-defined or fuzzy categories, a major problem for theory is to develop an account of how learning processes are organized so that is is possible for the learner, in effect, both to discover what class of information-processing task is represented in a particular case and then to bring into play the specific mechanisms or processes required to arrive at appropriate categorization.

Substantial bodies of research have been conducted on all of these varieties of categorization problems, each leading to an associated body of theory limited to the given type of task. Only recently have there been some efforts to construct a comprehensive theory that could handle all varieties as special cases. It will be convenient to review the research methods and results associated with the different information-processing tasks in roughly historical sequence, since the various distinctions among types of tasks have only emerged gradually in the course of continuing research.

## Concept Learning: Hypotheses and Decision Strategies

Progress toward analysis of the hypothesis-testing aspect of concept learning requires a characterization of the learner's conception of the universe of possibilities presented by the task. An analysis in terms of information theory by Hovland (1952) led directly to an experimental paradigm that has been the basis for a great part of the research on the learning of rule-defined concepts. In Hovland's paradigm, some of the unnecessary complications of earlier research are eliminated by constructing experimental materials so that all exemplars of the concepts being learned potentially convey the same amount of information. The items presented for categorization are characterized by their values on a limited set of stimulus dimensions, this schema either being known to the subject in advance of the experiment or being readily apparent so that the subject's concept of the universe of possible concepts corresponds to that of the experimenter.

In an influential realization of this paradigm, Shepard, Hovland, and Jenkins (1961) began with an analysis of all of the ways in which a set of exemplars generated by using two values on each of three dimensions can be categorized into two four-item categories. They showed that the 70 possible categorizations can be reduced to 6 basic types that differ in the number and kind of logical operations required to define the concepts and thus presumably also in the difficulty of learning. For example, their Type II requires a classification based on the conjunction of two dimensions. In a series of experiments these investigators showed that the relative difficulty of the different types of concepts was virtually independent of the particular kinds of stimulus

materials used. Further, they found that relative difficulty was virtually independent of stimulus overlap (that is, the number of properties common to exemplars of two different categories), although the degree of overlap was systematically related to identification of the same stimuli. On the other hand, the difficulty of categorization was related to the logical complexity of the problems, a finding that has been taken to suggest that the formulation and testing of hypotheses relative to logical operations on the dimensional values is an important phase of concept learning in that situation (Bourne, 1970).

Progress toward a theory of hypothesis testing in concept learning requires a characterization of hypotheses that makes them amenable to investigation and the accrual of relatively direct evidence concerning the strategies that guide their testing and selection. A start was made by Bruner, Goodnow, and Austin (1956) who analyzed concept learning in terms of the sequence of decisions that must be made by a learner in order to uncover the appropriate rule for correct performance. They distinguished two principal strategies—focusing and scanning. Following a focusing strategy, a subject formulates a hypothesis relating all features of the exemplar presented on the first trial of a concept learning experiment to its categorical assignment, continues to perform in accord with the initial hypothesis until a disconfirming instance appears, then combines the features common to the preceding hypothesis and the current instance to form the basis of a new hypothesis. This strategy, if followed without deviation, guarantees progress toward a solution of any soluble problem. Whether this strategy can be carried out without deviation depends on such matters as the memory capacity of the subject relative to demands of a given task. In a scanning strategy, the subject selects a hypothesis relating some features of a current instance to its category, then chooses in accord with the hypothesis until disconfirmation occurs, when the learner rejects the current hypothesis and takes into account as much remembered information from the preceding series as possible in formulating or choosing a new one.

Bruner et al. contrived an experimental situation in which the hypothesized decision process could be externalized. The tasks were multidimensional categorization problems much like those used by Shepard, Hovland, and Jenkins (1961). The subject was presented on each trial with a single exemplar of one of the alternative categories, followed by information as to the category assignment, then a request to verbalize his or her current hypothesis as to the rule for correct assignment. The subjects tended to follow the focusing strategy, but implemented it imperfectly. The degree to which their results could be taken to characterize the normal mode of hypothesis selection remains somewhat uncertain because the requirement of verbalizing hypotheses on each trial may have had important effects on the learning process.

Trabasso and Bower (1968) proposed a model for the process of hypothesis selection based on a conception of selective attention and all-or-none transitions between attentional states. In their model, the learner is conceived at any time to be in either a presolution or a solution state with regard to any specific problem. When in the presolution state the learner is attending to incorrect hypotheses and rejecting them as informative feedback on learning trials shows them to be irrelevant. Resampling occurs only on error trials, and the resampling is done in such a way that only hypotheses consistent with the information available on an error trial are brought into the "focus sample" to which the subject is attending. When, through the process of sampling hypotheses, rejecting incorrect ones, and resampling, the learner arrives at a hypothesis or subset of hypotheses that yields uniformly correct categorization, he or she is said to be in the solution state.

Trabasso and Bower obtained evidence for this view of the hypothesis-selection process in two quite independent ways. First, they realized their assumptions in a probabilistic model from which they could derive quantitative predictions concerning statistics of performance, as for example the frequency distribution of errors during learning, the expected trial of the last error, and the like, and found impressive correspondence between their predictions and the statistics of their data. Second, they carried out a series of experiments that confirmed some qualitative implications of the model, as, for example, that once a learner has arrived at a solution state, no further learning will occur even though the learner continues to be exposed to new exemplars and new features in the course of continuing experience with the situation.

An alternative approach to hypothesis selection that relates more closely to treatments of thinking and problem solving in the framework of cognitive science derives from Feigenbaum (1963), Hunt (1962), and Newell and Simon (1972). Hunt proposed that learning in general may be regarded as inductive problem solving, and that, in particular, the hypotheses that guide performance in classification tasks arise from a learning process that may be conceived as a form of induction from perceived relationships among positive and negative instances of a concept. The result of concept learning is the formation of a cognitive structure that takes the form of a decision tree in which the nodes represent tests that the learner may carry out on possible exemplars of concepts; the branches descending from these nodes terminate in categories of exemplars having particular combinations of features.

For an example of the formation of a decision tree, consider the problem represented in Table 5.5, an example of a Level II problem in the classification of Shepard, Hovland, and Jenkins (1961). As a first step toward concept formation the learner would have an opportunity to observe a number of positive and negative exemplars with feedback indicating the category in which each belonged. The attributes of these exemplars would have to be remembered well enough so that the learner could then perform a memory check and determine first of all whether positive and negative instances have any features in common. If so, the common features would be eliminated from further consideration. Next, the learner would determine which features, if any, occur with highest frequency in the positive category. In the example shown in Table 5.5 there are no common elements and all features of the set of positive exemplars occur equally often, so the learner would have to start the inductive process by selecting one feature at random and representing a test for that feature as the uppermost node in a decision tree, as illustrated in Figure 5.12. The answer to the

**Table 5.5.  A Type II Problem**

| Positive Instances | Negative Instances |
| --- | --- |
| Large, black circles | Large, black triangles |
| Large, white circles | Large, white triangles |
| Small, black triangles | Small, black circles |
| Small, white triangles | Small, white circles |

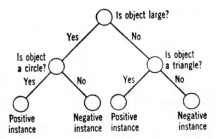

**Figure 5.12.** A possible decision tree for the concept problem of Table 2 in the model of Hunt (1962). From *Concept Learning: An Information Processing Problem* (p. 234) by E.B. Hunt, 1962. New York: Wiley. Copyright 1962 by John Wiley & Sons, Inc. Reprinted by permission of John Wiley & Sons, Inc.

## Concept Representations

The research related to hypothesis-selection models has provided useful characterizations of performance in problem solving situations in which task demands call for categorization; but in that tradition investigators have tended to lose sight of the idea of concept formation as a product of a learning process. Under the influence of more recent developments in cognitive psychology, interest has arisen anew in the problem of representation. The question is not only what is stored in memory during concept learning, but what is the format of the stored information and at what stages in an individual's processing of stimuli are the constituents of the representations generated.

In all classification tasks in which appropriate performance can potentially be generated by hypothesis testing and selection, categories are definable in terms of attributes or features, and it is possible that concept formation depends simply on recognition of these features and the learning of their relationship to categories. A representation of a concept would not, then, resemble instances of the concept in any ordinary sense but would simply constitute, in effect, a listing of features or dimension values together with their cue validities. The validity of an attribute value or feature relative to a category is commonly defined as the probability that a stimulus belongs to the category if it includes the given feature.

Another view of what is learned is that one's knowledge of a concept takes the form of an abstract or composite representation, somewhat akin to the schematic drawings used in dictionaries or encyclopedias to convey the essentials of the concept of atom, solar system, or the like. These abstract representations are termed prototypes (Posner & Keele, 1968) or schemata (Elio & Anderson, 1981). Still another possibility is that an individual's representation of a concept takes the form of a collection of memories of individual exemplars of the concepts that have occurred in the individual's past experience. These apparently quite divergent approaches differ in the degree to which they embody common a priori intuitions as to the nature of concepts, but all have received some empirical support and each has given rise to characteristic methods of studying concept learning.

question "is the object large" does not serve to categorize exemplars appropriately, so after the test is carried out and an answer obtained for a particular instance, a second test would have to be carried out to determine whether the object is, say, a circle or a triangle. The answer to this question, represented by the intermediate level of nodes in Figure 5.12, would suffice to complete the categorization process, leading to the assignment of all large circles and all small triangles to the positive category and all large triangles and small circles to the negative category, as represented by the lowermost row of nodes in Figure 5.12. In general, for any particular problem more than one decision tree might be formed that would suffice for correct categorization; the one actually formed by the given learner would depend to some degree on idiosyncrasies of the particular sequence of exemplars experienced during learning and to some degree on such factors as salience of cues or dimensions and biases or strategies of the learner arising from previous experience.

Hunt's model was realized in a computer program by Hunt, Marin, and Stone (1966), and the learning of human subjects on a set of classification problems involving consonant quadruplets as exemplars proved to be quite similar to the simulated learning of the program with regard to the relative difficulties of problems (simple disjunction, conjunction, inclusive or exclusive disjunction, biconditional). Not surprisingly, the simulations produced by the model were in best agreement with the performance of the older and more mathematically sophisticated subjects.

## Features and Cue Validities

The clearest evidence for the learning of cue validities has come from studies employing artificial stimuli and relatively large numbers of cues. In an experiment reported by Estes, Burke, Atkinson, and Frankmann (1957), the set of cues was an array of 12 signal lights. In order to pose a categorization task, the experimenters defined two different probability distributions over the set of 12 lights. Then, during learning, when feedback on the trial indicated to the learner that a test pattern should have been assigned to Category 1, the lights illuminated were selected from one probability distribution, and on trials when the correct assignment was Category 2, from the other probability distribution. Over about 100 training trials, learning curves approached an apparent asymptote of about 67 percent correct (when about 90 percent was the maximum possible) and remained virtually level for more than 400 additional trials. At the end of training, the subjects were given test trials on the individual signal lights, and probabilities of correct categorization of these corresponded closely enough to the actual sampling probabilities to provide substantial evidence that learning of the correct categorizations was primarily a process of acquiring information about the individual cue validities.

Although it seems clear that individuals can and under some circumstances do learn cue validities, this learning may provide the main basis for performance only under rather special circumstances. In studies of similar design to that of Estes et al. but employing smaller sets of cues, the frequencies of occurrence of particular errors during learning provide evidence that some information about individual cue validities is acquired. However, this learning tends to be masked or dominated by the learning of associations between higher-order compounds or patterns of cues and their category assignments. One source of evidence for the second-order process is found in levels of correct performance that are higher than could be achieved by using only information about individual cue validities. Another is the decline observed over the course of learning in the interference that initially occurs when successively presented patterns with different category assignments have cues in common (Friedman, Trabasso, & Mosberg, 1967; Johns, 1963).

In studies employing somewhat more natural-istic stimuli, for example, schematic faces, in which the individual cues or features are values on such attributes at the height of the forehead or the separation of the eyes, predictions from the assumption of independent cue learning have been less well supported (Reed, 1972, 1973). However, in the analysis of these experiments, it has been demonstrated that information about individual cues was not acquired, but only that predictions based solely on such information do not account fully for performance. It may be that the features defined by the experimenter and used as units of analysis do not always correspond to the features that are used by the learner in an experiment. Hayes-Roth and Hayes-Roth (1977) found that feature models predicted performance in a complex categorization task better than prototype or schema models when the conception of feature was expanded to include combinations of various orders. Their stimulus materials were verbal descriptions of hypothetical people. Elementary attributes such as the sex or occupation of an individual might be taken to be basic features or cues, but an adequate account of the data required the assumption that combinations of these functioned as features in the independent cue model.

## Prototypes

Although in some cases representations of concepts may take the form of feature lists or combinations, in other cases such a representation seems implausible. For example, one forms a stable conception of an object even though it is seen from time to time at different distances, from different perspectives, and under different illuminations, so that it could not reasonably be a single feature list. It is possible that in such cases a concept is based on a core representation, or prototype, whose attributes may vary to some limited extent and that an individual categorizes stimuli as instances of the concept of the extent that they resemble its prototype. In the more formal prototype models (Reed, 1973), it is conceived that both a prototype and exemplars can be represented in a multidimensional attribute space and that recognition depends on the distance in this space between an exemplar and a prototype.

In one of the first systematic investigations of prototype formation, Posner and Keele (1968) gave subjects the task of classifying stimulus patterns formed by entering dots in a 30 by 30 matrix. In order to generate stimuli they defined four prototypic patterns, a triangle, an M, an F, and a random dot pattern of similar dimensions. Then they produced exemplars of each of these "concepts" by small distortions in the positions of particular dots in these prototypic patterns. Three degrees of distortion were used, denoted by Levels 1, 5, and 7. These were so generated that Level 1 was least distorted and the exemplars of Level 7 were equally distant from Levels 1 and 5, both in terms of physical units and in terms of the results of a multidimensional scaling procedure. In the first of three experiments, college student subjects were given either no categorization training (control condition) or training with distortions of Level 1 or Level 5; then after the trained groups had met a criterion of perfect performance, all three groups were given training on a set of transfer distortions of Level 7. Mean errors during original learning and mean errors on the transfer task were as shown in Table 5.6. Learning was much slower for the group with distortions of Level 5, but, perhaps a bit surprisingly, transfer was significantly better than observed following training with lesser (Level 1) distortions. In a second experiment, conditions of learning were similar, but transfer was evaluated by a pattern recognition task. Over the whole set of transfer data a rank correlation of .97 was obtained between recognition and distance of a test pattern from its prototype. In a third experiment, Posner and Keele used only random prototypes, and defined three concepts by means of sets of four distortions of these prototypes. After learning to categorize a list of exemplars of the three concepts, subjects were tested on the prototypes (which had never occurred during learning), old exemplars, new exemplars produced by distortions of the prototype, and new exemplars that were random patterns unrelated to any of the concepts. No significant difference was observed with respect to errors on the prototypes versus the old exemplars and performance on both was superior to that on new exemplars. Reaction time measurements showed that old exemplars were classified faster than the prototypes, indicating that even though the subjects may have been accomplishing the transfer task primarily on the basis of similarity of test patterns to prototypes, they also may have retained and used some information stored in memory concerning the particular exemplars they had previously experienced.

The finding that subjects on test trials typically classified newly experienced prototypes as accurately as previously experienced distortions has been replicated several times (Homa & Chambliss, 1975; Posner & Keele, 1970). Further it has been found that retention of learned categorizations over an interval filled by other activity is greater when measured by categorization performance on previously unexperienced prototypes than by performance on non-prototypes that had been presented during learning (Homa & Vosburgh, 1976; Posner & Keele, 1970). Finally, Franks and Bransford (1971) found performance on transfer tests to be more accurately predicted by the similarity of transfer stimuli to prototypes of the categories than by the frequencies with which features of the transfer stimuli had been experienced during training.

These results suggest that mental representations of fuzzy categories include information about similarity relations among exemplars on salient attributes. However, they do not justify the conclusion that learners accomplish categorizations by computing similarities between exemplars and prototypes. One alternative that needs to be considered is that information stored in memory concerning experienced exemplars is retrieved and used directly rather than by way of the construction of a prototypic representation. Another is that similarities between exemplars and prototypes are confounded with probabilities of category memberships, and that it is information about probabilities that constitutes the basis for categorization performance. These possibilities have been investigated in connection with other types of models.

### Exemplar Models

Since experiments on the prototype approach have yielded some evidence that individuals retain information about specific exemplars of categories as well as information about more

**Table 5.6. Mean Scores during Learning and Transfer for Groups Given Concept Exemplars Distorted by Differing Degrees (1, 5, 7) from a Prototype.**

*Data of Posner and Keele, 1968; Table 1, p. 355*

| Group | Original Learning | Transfer |
|-------|-------------------|----------|
| 1 | 4.8 | 5.6 |
| 5 | 12.3 | 4.3 |
| 7 | – | 6.8 |

abstract characteristics, it is of interest to inquire whether memory for individual exemplars of categories might in itself provide an important mechanism for categorization. For many instances of learning in natural environments, especially on the part of children, the idea has considerable plausibility. For example, a child who has had only very limited experience with the assignment of a few family pets to the categories dog and cat and no opportunity to form useful prototypes or adequate feature lists, may nonetheless be able to categorize other newly encountered animals quite successfully on the basis of their differential similarity to the family dog or cat. Two types of experimental methods have been used to gain information on the way remembered exemplar information might enter into categorization, one approach being almost strictly empirical and the other based on a specific model.

The empirical approach is exemplified in a series of experiments by Brooks (1978). The strategy was to give subjects training intended to ensure memory for exemplars, then determine how this stored information would influence performance in an unexpected categorization task. In the first stage, subjects were given paired-associate training, the stimuli being letter strings generated by two different finite-state grammars and the responses being city or animal names. Each set of response members could be categorized into new-world or old-world items (for example *Chicago* versus *Cairo* for cities, *moose* versus *baboon* for animals) with these categories corresponding to the two grammars from which the stimulus strings were selected. Following the paired-associate training, the subjects were told about the old-world/new-world difference and then asked to sort new letter strings drawn from the two grammars into their appropriate categories. Their performance of 60 percent correct categorizations on the transfer task was significantly and substantially greater than chance (which would have been 33 percent). Further, Brooks compared performance of these subjects with that of subjects who in the first phase were not given the paired-associate training, but rather were trained specifically to sort letter strings according to which of two grammars had generated them. On a transfer task, performance of these subjects in sorting new strings was again significantly above chance, but only 47 percent as compared to

the 60 percent achieved by the paired-associate group. Brooks terms the two learning conditions *nonanalytic* verus *analytic*, since in the paired-associate task subjects would have had no reason to analyze the stimuli whereas in the other condition they would have reason to use any available strategies to analyze the strings into features or to form prototypes. The results were taken to support the conclusion that categorization performance is most effectively accomplished simply by storing representations of training stimuli in memory and classifying new instances on the basis of their similarity to remembered ones.

A model that would yield just such an interpretation has been proposed by Medin and Schaffer (1978). In their *exemplar model*, a learner is assumed to store in memory representations of specific exemplars experienced during learning in terms of their combinations of features on relevant dimensions. Then on tests with new exemplars of already learned categories, the learner is assumed to compute the overall similarity of a new stimulus to the stored representations of exemplars of each of the categories in memory and to be likely to assign the new stimulus to the category to which the computed similarity is greatest.

A number of properties of the exemplar model can be brought out conveniently in terms of an experiment reported by Medin and Schwanenflugel (1981). The stimuli to be categorized were pictures of faces of women taken from college yearbooks and so chosen that they could be characterized in terms of one or the other of two values on each of four relevant dimensions— hair color, shirt color, smile type, and hair length. The experimenters defined two categories, A and B, to which the pictures should be assigned and for two groups of subjects assigned three exemplars (pictures) to Category A and three to Category B. For one group (S) these assignments were made so that the two categories could be distinguished by a linear disciminant function over the dimension values, the condition necessary for achievement of perfect classification performance according to independent cue models (Reed, 1973). For the other group (N) this condition was not satisfied and thus according to independent cue models perfect performance should not be achievable. The structures of the two categories for each of the two groups, with values on the relevant

**Table 5.7.** Representation of Picture Classification Experiment in Terms of the Exemplar Model

| Exemplar | Dimension | | | | Category | |
|---|---|---|---|---|---|---|
| | 1 | 2 | 3 | 4 | A | B |
| *Separable Categories* | | | | | | |
| $A_1$ | 0 | 1 | 1 | 1 | $1 + d^2 + d^3$ | $d^4 + d^2 + d$ |
| $A_2$ | 1 | 1 | 1 | 0 | $d^2 + 1 + d^3$ | $d^2 + d^4 + d$ |
| $A_3$ | 1 | 0 | 0 | 1 | $d^3 + d^3 + 1$ | $d + d + d^4$ |
| $B_1$ | 1 | 0 | 0 | 0 | $d^4 + d^2 + d$ | $1 + d^2 + d^3$ |
| $B_2$ | 0 | 0 | 0 | 1 | $d^2 + d^4 + d$ | $d^2 + 1 + d^3$ |
| $B_3$ | 0 | 1 | 1 | 0 | $d + d + d^4$ | $d^3 + d^2 + 1$ |
| *Nonseparable Categories* | | | | | | |
| $A_1$ | 1 | 1 | 0 | 0 | $1 + d^4 + d^2$ | $d^2 + d^2 + d^2$ |
| $A_2$ | 0 | 0 | 1 | 1 | $d^4 + 1 + d^2$ | $d^2 + d^2 + d^2$ |
| $A_3$ | 1 | 1 | 1 | 1 | $d^2 + d^2 + 1$ | $d^4 + d^2 + d^2$ |
| $B_1$ | 0 | 0 | 0 | 0 | $d^2 + d^2 + d^4$ | $1 + d^2 + d^2$ |
| $B_2$ | 0 | 1 | 0 | 1 | $d^2 + d^2 + d^2$ | $d^2 + 1 + d^4$ |
| $B_3$ | 1 | 0 | 1 | 0 | $d^2 + d^2 + d^2$ | $d^2 + d^4 + 1$ |

dimensions being indicated simply by 1s and 0s, are given in Table 5.7. The right hand portion of the table gives the values of the assumed similarity of each exemplar to each of the two categories as computed according to Medin and Schaffer's model. This quantity is determined for a given exemplar relative to a given category by comparing the exemplar to each of the exemplars in that category and entering a value of 1 if the two are identical, a value of d if they differ on one dimension, a value of $d^2$ if they differ on two dimensions, and so on. Thus the entry for exemplar $A_1$ in the separable category condition under Category A is $1 + d^2 + d^3$ since $A_1$ differs from itself on no dimensions, from $A_2$ on two dimensions, and from $A_3$ on three dimensions. According to the model, the probability that a learner who has this memory structure will categorize $A_1$ into Category A is given by the entry under A, $(1 + d^2 + d^3)$ divided by the sum of the entries under both categories A and B, $(1 + d + 2d^2 + d^3 + d^4)$, and similarly for the other exemplars. In order to make predictions about the relative accuracy of categorization of different exemplars, it is necessary only to estimate the value of similarity parameter $d$ from some portion of the data and then use it to predict probabilities of correct categorization for all of the individual stimuli.

For Medin and Schwanenflugel's (1981) experiment, the model yields the prediction that performance for Group N should be superior to that for Group S regardless of the value of the similarity parameter. In a plot of errors versus blocks of three trials (Figure 5.13) Group N

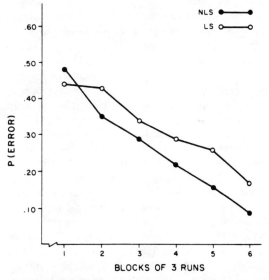

**Figure 5.13.** Concept learning in terms of errors per trial block in study of Medin and Schwanenflugel (1981). From "Linear Separability in Classification Learning" by D.L. Medin and P.J. Schwanenflugel, 1981, *Journal of Experimental Psychology: Human Learning and Memory*, 7, p. 369. Copyright 1981 by the American Psychological Association. Reprinted by permission of the authors.

shows a consistent advantage over Group S, the difference between groups being in the direction opposite to that predictable from independent cue models but in good agreement with prediction from the exemplar model.

In a series of experimental applications of the exemplar model, Medin and his associates have shown that it successfully predicts a number of phenomena that had seemed the special province of prototype models. Although in Medin's experiments, exemplars of categories are not chosen by producing variations on a prototype, one can nonetheless define prototypes for the categories used by choosing the modal values on each of the dimensions. For example, in Table 5.7 the modal prototype for Category A in the case of Group S would be 1111 and the modal prototype for Category B 0000. With this definition, learning of the modal prototypes has been found to be faster than that of other exemplars and the prototypes are better retained than other exemplars, these results being predictable from the exemplar model. Further, the exemplar model can be shown to predict, like prototype models, that a new test exemplar that is similar to the modal prototype of a category may be classified more accurately than previously experienced exemplars that are further from the prototype. The exemplar model also predicts correctly a result that does not follow from prototype models, namely that a new exemplar highly similar to one or more members of a given category and highly dissimilar to one or more members of the alternative category will be more readily classified correctly than an exemplar that is less extreme in both directions but falls closer to the prototype of its category. Finally, in recognition tasks given following categorization training, it has regularly been found that subjects are able to discriminate old from new exemplars of categories with considerable accuracy, a direct implication of the exemplar model but not of prototype models (Medin & Schaffer, 1978; Medin & Schwanenflugel, 1981). It seems clear that memory for specific exemplars can be a significant factor in categorization learning. Further, evidence that has seemed especially favorable to prototype models must be accepted with some reservation since most of the findings can also be accounted for on the basis of memory for exemplars plus similarity judgments.

Research conducted in connection with prototype and exemplar models, but more especially the latter, seems especially relevant to the interpretation of the way people learn to deal with natural categories in their ordinary environments. A series of articles by Rosch and her associates (Rosch, 1973, 1978; Rosch & Mervis, 1975) has assembled evidence from both anthropological and psychological studies to indicate that natural categories (for example, colors, tools, foods) cannot be satisfactorily defined in terms of limited lists of necessary and sufficient features but rather are only loosely definable in terms of the differences in degree of family resemblance, on both perceptual and functional attributes, within and between categories. Exemplars of such categories that are rated as most typical by subjects also proved to be classified most quickly and accurately and best recalled following categorization learning. When artificial categories are constructed to simulate natural ones, children have been found to learn to categorize more rapidly when their initial experiences are with good exemplars of the categories, goodness being defined in terms of the degree of family resemblance of a particular exemplar to other members of the category. These findings seem most simply interpretable in terms of the exemplar model, but this conclusion is a weak one for there have as yet been no systematic studies reported concerning the detailed course of learning of natural categories or simulations of them.

### Schema Abstraction

Some of the advantages of both exemplar and prototype models are combined in an extension of the ACT model of Anderson (1976) presented by Elio and Anderson (1981). It is assumed that on each presentation of an exemplar of a category, a representation is stored in memory, generally in the form of some subset of its features. But this storage process is augmented by one of generalization. When two different exemplars have occurred together with information that they both belong to the same category, a second-order representation is formed comprising the features common to the two stored representations, and it is this *generalization* that will be activated and determine categorization performance when in the future either of these exemplars or any other including the features of the generalization is presented. The model was applied by Elio and Anderson to experiments in which subjects were presented with brief descriptions of hypothetical people whom they were to categorize according to membership in one or the other of two clubs. Examples of these descriptions for a condition designed to be conductive to generalization are:

1. One member of the Dolphin Club is a Baptist, plays golf, works for the government, is college educated, and is single.
2. One member of the Dolphin Club is a Baptist, plays golf, works for a private firm, is college educated, and is married.

From these two exemplars subjects would be expected to form and store the generalization that an individual who is a Baptist, plays golf, and is college educated would belong to the Dolphin Club, and would so classify a new test item such as:

This person is a Baptist who plays golf, is unemployed, is college educated, and is divorced.

Although the person described in the test item possesses extraneous features, the three features belonging to the generalization are all present and would determine the categorization response. A series of experiments yielded several kinds of evidence supportive to the model: (a) Sets of items constructed to permit generalization were learned faster than sets of nongeneralization items even when the latter had greater interitem similarity; (b) learning was faster and transfer performance better when generalizable items were blocked in the series of training trials so as to facilitate the formation of generalizations. On the other hand, the data also showed clear effects of intermediate degrees of similarity of test to training exemplars on categorization performance, an effect not predictable from the schema abstraction model but quite in accord with the exemplar model.

A quite different approach to schema abstraction derives from the observation that the similarity of a test item to a prototype or a collection of remembered exemplars must ordinarily be confounded with the likelihood that the item belongs in the given category (Fried & Holyoak, 1984). In their model Fried and Holyoak assume that the goal of a learner is to construct a mental representation of the population distribution of exemplars of a category over their values on descriptive attributes or features. This construction is accomplished by a combination of top-down and bottom-up learning strategies. The top-down strategy, not always available, is to hypothesize the forms of the density distributions of exemplar feature values on the basis of the task instructions or other available information, and then to estimate the statistics (for example the mean and variance of a normal distribution) from cumulative observations. The bottom-up strategy is to store mental representations of observed exemplars is to store mental representations of observed exemplars and then to cluster these on the basis of their similarities on attribute values. This clustering strategy enables a learner proceeding in accord with the model to learn categorizations even without informative feedback during learning, a possibility evidently not considered by the developers of the various other types of categorization models. Once mental representations of the category distributions have been formed, the learner is assumed to make classification decisions on the basis of a relative likelihood decision rule, that is, assigning a test item to the category from which it is most likely to have been drawn on the basis of the accumulated information.

Fried and Holyoak (1984) carried out a number of experimental tests of the model, using an experimental paradigm similar to that of Posner and Keele (1970). The stimuli were dot patterns formed by imposing probabilistic distortions on a basic prototypic pattern for a category in such a way as to generate normal distributions of the exemplar patterns over the attributes defining the spatial positions of their elements. Learners were simply told that they would see a series of patterns that had been generated by two artists and should try to classify them. Slightly faster learning was observed for a group of subjects who received informative feedback on each trial, but a group receiving no feedback learned quite effectively, as predicted by the model. Their data confirmed the prediction following from both prototype and category density models that learning should be faster but transfer poorer the lower the variability of exemplars within a category. But, further, the transfer differences disappeared when the subjects were required to make forced choices between the two possible categories on each trial, a result predicted only by the category density model. In another test, intended to distinguish sharply between the two types of models, a high and a low variability category were paired; in this situation a distance-to-prototype model implies that equal proportions of test instances will be classified in each category but the density model predicts that more will be classified in the higher variability category (since a broader distribution will be learned). The latter prediction was supported, 61 percent of instances being assigned to the high variability category when 50 percent would have been chance expectation (the difference being significant at the 1 percent level).

The model of Fried and Holyoak is similar to that of Medin and Schaffer (1978) in that a bottom-up learning process begins with the storage of memory representations of individual category exemplars. The way in which these representations are assumed to be manipulated in memory differs between the two models in cases where exemplar distributions take on simple forms that can be estimated, but the differences largely disappear when categories are composed of unsystematically related exemplars.

## Multiple Processes in Categorization

In much of the theoretically oriented literature on categorization, the strategy has been to pit models of different types against each other in the effort to rule out one of the alternatives by suitably designed experiments—for example, exemplar versus prototype models (Reed, 1972), exemplar versus probabilistic feature models (Medin & Schaffer, 1978), and exemplar versus schema abstraction models (Elio & Anderson, 1981). This approach does not seem optimal, for none of the models proves fully adequate and the processes assumed in all of the principal alternatives appear to be implicated under some conditions. In particular, there seems clear evidence for the learning of feature probabilities, the storage and use of exemplar representations, and the abstraction of schemas or prototypes together with a generalization process. These constituent processes or strategies may combine in different ways for different tasks and for learners of different backgrounds, but little systematic information has yet been obtained on the boundary conditions.

## Acquisition of Knowledge

### Semantic Information

Research on the acquisition of word meanings and other semantic information has gone through several phases. During at least the first half of this century, relevant work was limited almost exclusively to statistical studies of the growth of vocabulary, but with little attention to the central questions of what psychological structures or processes enter into knowledge of the meaning of a word. Beginning in the early 1970s, investigators in the new tradition of cognitive psychology did begin to address these questions vigorously with the consequent emergence of network models (e.g., Collins & Quillan, 1972) and feature models (e.g., Smith, Shoben, & Rips, 1974). This work (reviewed in Chapter 8, this volume) was, however, largely cross-sectional in character, investigating the structure of associative networks and feature lists by means of reaction time studies.

The learning process dealing with the way these networks or feature lists grow and incorporate various kinds of stimulus information has scarcely begun to receive attention. This lag may have been due to the slow emergence of models capable of directing appropriate research on complex materials. The first model that might do so was introduced by Anderson (1976). This model, termed ACT, has the capability of providing computer simulations of the growth of semantic networks and the associated ensembles of *productions* that mediate performance. A production is, in effect, a conditional response rule that is executed upon activation of a certain subset of elements of the associative network (the condition of the production).

In a study that illustrates some of the methods available for testing hypotheses about the growth of semantic networks, Rosenberg and Simon (1977) presented subjects with sequences of displays constructed to convey information about specific ideas or events by means of either printed sentences or pictures, then gave tests that included items from the study list together with new items. The new items might represent either ideas or events that had not appeared in a study list or else ideas or events from the study list that had been translated from sentence to picture format or vice versa. On a test of verbatim recognition, subjects identified correct items with about 80 percent frequency, but also falsely recognized ideas translated into the alternative mode with substantial frequency and falsely recognized incorrect but semantically related items nearly as often (about 35 percent and 30 percent respectively). In another experiment, French–English bilingual subjects were presented with sentences in French or English. Results were rather similar, test sentences actually previously seen being accepted about 70 percent of the time, new but semantically related sentences 52 percent, and old sentences translated into the alternative language 33 percent. The results were described quite accurately by a computer simulation of a model similar in essentials to ACT. In the model it is assumed that learning constitutes, not the association of specific stimuli with responses as in earlier learning theories, nor even the storing of representations of these in memory, but rather the analysis of an input stimulus in terms of semantic themes or attributes, these being integrated into the network in a form independent of the original modality. Attributes of an input display having to do with modality may be incorporated in the network representation, but the learner is assumed to have a constant bias toward integrating thematically related sentences and pictures when possible, so modality specific information tends to be subordinate.

### Schemata and Knowledge Assembly

Just as in the recent approaches to concept learning, investigations of the acquisition of factual knowledge indicate that such learning is a more organized and internally directed process than the accumulation of associations between contiguously experienced items. A link between the earlier association theories and the kind of model that seems needed to deal with knowledge assembly has been presented by Hayes-Roth (1977). In her model it is assumed that when a learner is exposed to information of the kind that might be conveyed by a passage of text, the first stage of learning is the storage in memory of representations of lower order constituents, that is, words or the simple concepts denoted by them. These lower-order units are linked by associations that are strengthened by repetition until frequently recurring configurations take on the character of independent units that may be activated in an all-or-none fashion by associations with other similar units.

In an experiment designed to test this conception, subjects learned sets of novel propositions so constructed that any one shared concepts with from zero to five other propositions in the set. Each proposition could be represented in a simple subject-verb-object sentence, and the progress of learning was indexed, not by the subjects' ability to reproduce the sentences, but rather by their ability to judge test sentences as true or false on the basis of their experience during acquisition. It was predicted that, early in learning, verification time for a proposition should increase with the number of concepts that were shared with others in the set, since only the lower-order units, individual concepts, would be stored and these would tend to evoke competing yes and no reactions on the test trial. Late in learning, the configurations of concepts would have been unitized and the source of competition eliminated. Hayes-Roth's data showed a sharply increasing function during the first learning session that declined to virtually horizontal by the eleventh session.

Another interesting implication of Hayes-Roth's model has to do with transfer in the standard A–B, A–C paradigm. Early in A–B learning, subunits should be stored but not linked together, and if a shift to A–C occurred at that point the learner would have a head start, so to speak, on A–C learning, yielding positive transfer. With more learning on A–B, the subunits of the A and B terms would be linked, so that at the outset of A–C learning the A member would tend incorrectly to evoke recall of B, yielding negative transfer. But with still larger amounts of learning on A–B, the configurations would be unitized and then would yield no transfer either positive or negative to A–C. This complex pattern of transfer effects as a function of the degree of A–B learning was fully confirmed by Hayes-Roth's data, as illustrated in Figure 5.14.

Once constellations of subunits have taken on a unitary character, they should be expected not only to facilitate recall but also to provide schemata, or reference frames, to guide continued learning. In the first of two relevant studies, Hayes-Roth and Thorndyke (1979) analyzed conditions under which related facts that a learner encounters in the course of studying a passage of text become integrated into unitary schemata. Integration was facilitated both by temporal proximity of the lower-order units and by similarity of wording in the surface structure of the text. In the second study Thorndyke and Hayes-

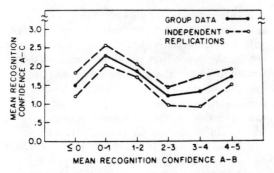

**Figure 5.14.** Transfer in A–B, A–C paradigm as a function of degree of A–B learning (measured by recognition confidence) in a study by Hayes-Roth (1977). From "Evolution of Cognitive Structures and Processes" by B. Hayes-Roth, 1977, *Psychological Review*, *84*, p. 274. Copyright 1977 by the American Psychological Association. Reprinted by permission of the author.

Roth (1979) demonstrated that the growth and use of a schema may entail both costs and benefits to the efficiency of learning new instances. Their subjects studied a sequence of facts about a conceptual category, such as constellations. It would be expected, on the basis of Hayes-Roth's model, that over the first few training passages a common schema would take form and its accessibility would increase with repetition, this factor by itself contributing to more effective learning and recall of successive passages. However, in the materials given to these learners, sentences in new passages sometimes changed principal components of sentences experienced earlier. For example, a new sentence to the effect that a certain constellation had been charted at Palomar Observatory would contain a common predicate but different arguments as compared to a sentence in an earlier passage that might have stated that a particular constellation had been charted at Mount Wilson Observatory. The activation of the common subunits at the time of presentation of the second of these sentences would yield a source of interference. As a consequence, it was predicted that recall of changed sentences would first increase and subsequently decrease as a function of the number of training passages, a pattern that was confirmed in their data.

One of the most salient and pervasive results of current research on complex human learning is the repeated demonstration of the important role of the products of prior learning in deter-

mining speed and robustness of new learning. This role of prior learning was appreciated intuitively much earlier, for example by Bartlett (1932) and Woodworth (1938), but further progress had to wait on the development of concepts and models that could guide analyses of the interaction between old and new learning. Schemata, or frames of reference, may develop in the course of the learning process itself, as indicated in the work of Hayes-Roth (1977), but in other cases may be established by prior learning in other situations or by instructions given to learners concerning the general characteristics of a task, as in the studies of Restle and Brown (1970a, 1970b). Until recently the learning that occurs on a single experience in a short-term memory experiment was generally conceived to be automatic in character, but here also manipulation of prior information and analyses within the framework of a model indicate a role for schemata (Lee & Estes, 1981).

A second specific role of prior learning is its function in establishing habits or strategies of selective attention that operate in a new learning situation, determining both what aspects of the situation are attended to and in what sequence. This mechanism was at the heart of the first influential computer simulation model for paired-associate learning (Feigenbaum, 1963). Rather than simply associating the stimulus and response members of the items to be learned, the learner was conceived to process a new item by analyzing the features or attributes of the item, and deciding as each new aspect is tested whether the information already processed sufficed to distinguish the item from others already in memory. Thus only enough need be learned—that is, stored in memory— concerning a new item to discriminate it from others, and in a test situation only relevant information in the test items need be processed.

If the function of prior learning is considered without adequate analysis, there appears to be a paradox. A large literature on proactive inhibition shows that in many situations prior learning of similar material leads to poor retention of newly learned material, whereas general educational experience together with the studies just cited show prior learning to be advantageous for new learning of related material. However, consideration of the model proposed by Rosenberg and Simon (1977) for the acquisition of semantic information suggests that a factor differentiating the two types of effects may be the use by learners of the strategy of noticing themes that are common to sets of related material or related learning situations, storing a list, in effect, of the themes that have occurred together with the situations they are related to, and utilizing these thematic "pointers" in new but thematically related situations.

Smith, Adams, and Schorr (1978) obtained evidence in a series of studies that facts that are thematically consistent do not suffer mutual interference provided that task demands require attention to these themes. Subsequent analyses within the framework of the ACT model by Anderson (1981) and Reder and Anderson (1980) indicate that, in fact, both interference and facilitation occur in these situations but with common themes tending to tip the balance toward facilitation. Interference occurs because, over successive learning situations involving related material, increasing numbers of factual items or concepts come to be associated with the same thematic or categorical tags, thus increasing the number of associates of these tags need to be scanned at the time of memory retrieval. The facilitation occurs primarily because the multiple associative paths established between specific items and thematic or categorical tags that provide alternative routes by which a learner in a test situation can retrieve information relevant to the judgments that need to be made about the test material.

In support of this analyses, Anderson found, for example, that in experiments in which subjects learned facts about hypothetical individuals, the learning was faster when the learners had prior information about the individuals, but retrieval of the information, as measured by reaction times, was slower. When common themes are lacking, as when one is trying to recall some one from a series of unrelated episodes or events, only interference is manifest. The larger the number of events associated with a common context the longer it will take to locate any one relevant association, but there is no compensating advantage since the given event cannot be brought to mind by inference from other information being recalled simultaneously.

## TRENDS IN RESEARCH ON HUMAN LEARNING

Most research on human learning today, as in the time of Ebbinghaus, is being carried on in simplified and tightly controlled laboratory situations. A recurring source of concern bears on the relevance of the accumulating body of work to practical problems of learning outside the laboratory. Ameliorating this concern without losing the advantages of rigorous experimental methods is not easy. Observations of learning in uncontrolled, naturalistic situations usually prove purely descriptive and difficult to generalize and rarely yield progress toward deeper understanding. In the experimental tradition, problems of relevance are being met at least in part by the continuing development of improved methodologies for theoretically guided research on increasingly complex forms of learning and laboratory simulations of natural situations. An important new influence is the development of "learning machines" in artificial intelligence—that is, programs for the acquisition of knowledge in various domains (Cohen & Feigenbaum, 1982, ch. 14). Progress in this line provides motivation and focus for related theoretical and experimental work from the psychological perspective.

Regarding trends in research methods and reports, it is interesting to note that some of the studies cited in this chapter from early years of the century could almost have come from current journals so far as the main experimental methods and data presentations are concerned. But superimposed on a relatively constant basic experimental methodology is a flourishing of models that influence the designs of studies and even more strongly structure the analyses of data. Mathematical and computer simulation models that allow the estimation of meaningful psychological parameters from experimental data are mainly responsible for our ability to do instructive research on increasingly complex forms of learning.

Another major trend, strongly influenced by developments in cognitive science and artificial intelligence, is an accelerating interest in analyzing both experimentally and theoretically the mental activities that go on during learning. The pattern of earlier research was simply to observe the relationships between conditions of learning and resulting changes in performance, the behavioral data being occasionally garnished by introspective comments from subjects about their learning strategies. The current style is, rather, to attempt detailed accounts of the steps of information processing that go into the storage, organization, and retrieval of information that constitute learning. Thus the study of human learning has become part and parcel of research on human information processing within the framework of cognitive science.

One by-product of this reorientation is a theoretical framework for the analysis of introspective reports from human learners. Introspection fell into disrepute in the early days of behaviorism because introspective reports were presented as privileged and basically unverifiable accounts of a learner's own mental processes. In the newer framework, introspection is simply a source of data that can be compared in detail with the protocols generated by computer simulation models of the learning process and subject to theoretical interpretation just as any form of behavioral data (Anzai & Simon, 1979; Ericsson & Simon, 1980).

Another by-product of the cognitive approach is the improved prospect of significant theoretical connections between research on human learning and related work in neural science. As progress is made in analyzing learning experiences into component cognitive processes, opportunities are materializing for relating these processes to effects of localized brain damage (Shallice, 1979) and to the neurophysiological data generated by new techniques of evoked potential recording (Hillyard & Kutas, 1983) and mappings of variations in cerebral blood flow during cognitive activities (Ingvar, 1979).

Overall, perhaps the most striking contrast between the review in this chapter and the one by Hovland (1951) in the previous edition of the *Handbook* is the vastly increased diversity of inputs from other disciplines. The consequence appears to be a commensurate injection of hybrid vigor into research on human learning and memory.

# REFERENCES

Alba, J.W., Chromiak, W., Hasher, L., & Attig, M.S. (1980). Automatic encoding of category size information. *Journal of Experimental Psychology: Human Learning and Memory, 6*, 370–378.

Allen, G.A. (1972). Memory probes during two-choice differential reward problems. *Journal of Experimental Psychology, 95*, 78–89.

Allen, G.A. & Estes, W.K. (1972). Acquisition of correct choices and value judgments in binary choice learning with differential rewards. *Psychonomic Science, 27*, 68–72.

Altom, M.W. (1978). Human memory for long-term frequency of events. Doctoral dissertation, Rockefeller University, New York, N.Y.

Anderson, J.A. (1973). A theory for the recognition of items from short memorized lists. *Psychological Review, 80*, 417–438.

Anderson, J.R. (1974). Retrieval of propositional information from long-term memory. *Cognitive Psychology, 6*, 451–474.

Anderson, J.R. (1976). *Language, memory and thought.* Hillsdale, NJ: Lawrence Erlbaum.

Anderson, J.R. (1981). Concepts, propositions, and schemata: What are the cognitive units? In J.H. Flowers (Ed.), *Nebraska Symposium on Motivation, 1980: Cognitive processes* (Vol. 28, pp. 121–162). Lincoln, NB: University of Nebraska Press.

Anderson, J.R. (1983a). *The architecture of cognition.* Cambridge, MA: Harvard University Press.

Anderson, J.R. (1983b). A spreading activation theory of memory. *Journal of Verbal Learning and Verbal Behavior, 22*, 261–295.

Anderson, J.R. & Bower, G.H. (1971). On an associative trace for sentence memory. *Journal of Verbal Learning and Verbal Behavior, 10*, 673–680.

Anderson, J.R. & Bower, G.H. (1972). Configural properties in sentence memory. *Journal of Verbal Learning and Verbal Behavior, 11*, 594–605.

Anderson, J.R. & Bower, G.H. (1973). *Human associative memory.* Washington, DC: Winston.

Anderson, N.H. (1960). Effect of first-order conditional probability in a two-choice situation. *Journal of Experimental Psychology, 59*, 73–93.

Anzai, Y. & Simon, H.A. (1979). The theory of learning by doing. *Psychological Review, 86*, 124–140.

Atkinson, R.C., Bower, G.W., & Crothers, E.J. (1965). *An introduction to mathematical learning theory.* New York: Wiley.

Atkinson, R.C. & Estes, W.K. (1963). Stimulus sampling theory. In R.D. Luce, R.R. Bush, & E. Galanter (Eds.), *Handbook of mathematical psychology* (Vol. 2, pp. 121–268). New York: Wiley.

Atkinson, R.C. & Juola, J.F. (1973). Factors influencing speed and accuracy of word recognition. In S. Kornblum (Ed.), *Attention and Performance IV* (pp. 583–612). New York: Academic Press.

Atkinson, R.C. & Kinchla, R.A. (1964). A learning model for forced-choice detection experiments. *British Journal of Mathematical and Statistical Psychology, 8*, 159–174.

Atkinson, R.C. & Shiffrin, R.M. (1968). Human memory: A proposed system and its control processes. In K.W. Spence & J.T. Spence (Eds.), *The psychology of learning and motivation: Advances in research and theory* (Vol. 2, pp. 89–195). New York: Academic Press.

Atkinson, R.C. & Shiffrin, R.M. (1971). The control of short-term memory. *Scientific American, 335*(2), 82–90.

Baddeley, A.D. (1976). *The psychology of memory.* New York: Basic Books.

Baddeley, A.D. & Hitch, G.J. (1974). Working memory. In G.H. Bower (Ed.), *The psychology of learning and motivation: Advances in research and theory* (Vol. 8, pp. 47–89). New York: Academic Press.

Baddeley, A.D. & Hitch, G.J. (1977). Recency reexamined. In S. Dornic (Ed.), *Attention and performance VI* (pp. 647–667). Hillsdale, NJ: Lawrence Erlbaum.

Bartlett, F.C. (1932). *Remembering: A study in experimental social psychology.* Cambridge, Eng.: Cambridge University Press.

Bilodeau, E.A. & Bilodeau, I. McD. (1958). Variable frequency of knowledge of results and the learning of a simple skill. *Journal of Experimental Psychology, 55*, 379–383.

Bjork, R.A. (1968). All-or-none subprocesses in the learning of complex sequences. *Journal of Mathematical Psychology, 5*, 182–195.

Bjork, R.A. (1972). Theoretical implications of directed forgetting. In A.W. Melton & E. Martin (Eds.), *Coding processes in human theory* (pp. 217–235). Washington, DC: Winston.

Bourne, L.E., Jr. (1970). Knowing and using concepts. *Psychological Review, 77*, 546–556.

Bower, G.H. (1959). Choice-point behavior. In R.R. Bush & W.K. Estes (Eds.), *Studies in mathematical learning theory* (pp. 109–124). Stanford, CA: Stanford University Press.

Bower, G.H. (1961). Application of a model to paired-associate learning. *Psychometrika, 26*, 255–280.

Bower, G.H. (1967). A multicomponent theory of the memory trace. In K.W. Spence & J.T. Spence (Eds.), *The psychology of learning and motivation: Advances in research and theory* (Vol. 1, pp. 229–325). New York: Academic Press.

Bower, G.H. (1970). Organizational factors in memory. *Cognitive Psychology, 1*, 18–46.

Bower, G.H. (1975). Cognitive psychology: An introduction. In W.K. Estes (Ed.), *Handbook of learning and cognitive processes: Introduction of concepts and issues* (Vol. 1, pp. 25–80). Hillsdale, NJ: Lawrence Erlbaum.

Bower, G.H., Clark, M.C., Lesgold, A.M., & Winzenz, D. (1969). Hierarchical retrieval schemes in recall of categorized word lists. *Journal of Verbal Learning and Verbal Behavior, 8*, 323–343.

Bower, G.H. & Hilgard, E.R. (1981). *Theories of learn-*

*ing* (5th Ed.). Englewood Cliffs, NJ: Prentice-Hall.

Bower, G.H. & Winzenz, D. (1969). Group structure, coding, and memory for digit series. *Journal of Experimental Psychology Monograph, 80* (2, Pt. 2).

Bowles, N.L. & Glanzer, M. (1983). An analysis of interference in recognition memory. *Memory and Cognition, 11*, 307–315.

Bray, N.W. & Batchelder, W.H. (1972). Effects of instructions and retention interval on memory of presentation mode. *Journal of Verbal Learning and Verbal Behavior, 11*, 367–374.

Briggs, G.E. (1954). Acquisition, extinction, and recovery functions in retroactive inhibition. *Journal of Experimental Psychology, 47*, 285–293.

Briggs, G.E. & Johnsen, A.M. (1973). On the nature of central process in choice reactions. *Memory and Cognition, 1*, 91–100.

Brooks, L. (1978). Nonanalytic concept formation and memory for instances. In E. Rosch & B.B. Lloyd (Eds.), *Cognition and categorization* (pp. 169–211). Hillsdale, NJ: Lawrence Erlbaum.

Brown, J. (1958). Some tests of the decay theory of immediate memory. *Quarterly Journal of Experimental Psychology, 10*, 12–21.

Bruner, J.S., Goodnow, J.J., & Austin, G.A. (1956). *A study of thinking.* New York: Wiley.

Brunswik, E. (1939). Probability as a determiner of rat behavior. *Journal of Experimental Psychology, 25*, 175–197.

Buchwald, A.M. (1967). Effects of immediate vs. delayed outcome in associative learning. *Journal of Verbal Learning and Verbal Behavior, 6*, 317–320.

Carr, H.A. (1931). The laws of association. *Psychological Review, 38*, 212–228.

Castellan, N.J., Jr. & Edgell, S.E. (1973). An hypothesis generation model for judgment in nonmetric multiple-cue probability learning. *Journal of Mathematical Psychology, 10*, 204–222.

Chase, W.G. (1978). Elementary information processes. In W.K. Estes (Ed.), *Handbook of learning and cognitive processes: Human information processing* (Vol. 5, pp. 19–90). Hillsdale, NJ: Lawrence Erlbaum.

Cohen, B.H. (1966). Some-or-none characteristics of coding behavior. *Journal of Verbal Learning and Verbal Behavior, 5*, 182–187.

Cohen, P.R. & Feigenbaum, E.A. (1982). *Handbook of artificial intelligence* (Vol. 3). Los Altos, CA: William Kaufmann.

Collins, A.M. & Quillian, M.R. (1972). How to make a language user. In E. Tulving & W. Donaldson (Eds.), *Organization of memory* (pp. 309–351). New York: Academic Press.

Conrad, R. (1967). Interference or decay over short retention intervals? *Journal of Verbal Learning and Verbal Behavior, 6,* 49–54.

Craik, F.I.M. & Lockhart, R.S. (1972). Levels of processing: A framework for memory research. *Journal of Verbal Learning and Verbal Behavior, 11,* 671–684.

Craik, F.I.M. & Watkins, M.J. (1973). The role of rehearsal in short-term memory. *Journal of Verbal Learning and Verbal Behavior, 12,* 599–607.

Crowder, R.G. (1976). *Principles of learning and memory.* Hillsdale, NJ: Lawrence Erlbaum.

Darwin, C.G., Turvey, M.T., & Crowder, R.G. (1972). An auditory analogue of the Sperling partial report procedure: Evidence for brief auditory storage. *Cognitive Psychology, 3,* 255–267.

Drewnowski, A. & Murdock, B.B., Jr. (1980). The role of auditory features in memory span for words. *Journal of Experimental Psychology: Human Learning and Memory, 6,* 319–332.

Dulaney, D.E., Jr. (1962). The place of hypotheses and intentions: An analysis of verbal control in verbal conditioning. In C.W. Eriksen (Ed.), *Behavior and awareness: A symposium of research and interpretation* (pp. 102–129). Durham, NC: Duke University Press.

Ebbinghaus, H. (1913). *Memory.* (H.A. Ruger & C.E. Bussenius, Trans.). New York: Teacher's College, Columbia University. (Original work published 1885)

Ebbinghaus, H. (1902). *Grundzüge der psychologie* [Foundations of Psychology] (Vol. 1). Leipzig: Verlag.

Ebenholtz, S.M. (1963). Serial learning: Position learning and sequential associations. *Journal of Experimental Psychology, 66,* 353–362.

Eckert, E. & Kanak, N.J. (1974). Verbal discrimination learning: A review of the acquisition, transfer, and retention literature through 1972. *Psychological Bulletin, 81,* 582–607.

Edwards, W. (1961). Probability learning in 1000 trials. *Journal of Experimental Psychology, 62,* 385–394.

Eich, J.E., Weingartner, H., Stillman, R.C., & Gillin, J.C. (1975). State-dependent accessibility of retrieval cues in the retention of a categorized list. *Journal of Verbal Learning and Verbal Behavior, 14,* 408–417.

Ekstrand, B.R., Wallace, W.P., & Underwood, B.J. (1966). A frequency theory of verbal-discrimination learning. *Psychological Review, 73,* 566–578.

Elio, R. & Anderson, J.R. (1981). The effects of category generalizations and instance similarity on schema abstraction. *Journal of Experimental Psychology: Human Learning and Memory, 7,* 397–417.

Ericsson, K.A. & Simon, H.A. (1980). Verbal reports as data. *Psychological Review, 87,* 215–251.

Estes, W.K. (1955a). Statistical theory of distributional phenomena in learning. *Psychological Review, 62,* 369–377.

Estes, W.K. (1955b). Statistical theory of spontaneous recovery and regression. *Psychological Review, 62,* 145–154.

Estes, W.K. (1959). The statistical approach to learning theory. In S. Koch (Ed.), *Psychology: A study of a science* (Vol. 2, pp. 380–491). New York: McGraw-Hill.

Estes, W.K. (1964a). All-or-none processes in learning and retention. *American Psychologist, 19,* 16–25.

Estes, W.K. (1964b). Probability learning. In A.W. Melton (Ed.), *Categories of human learning* (pp. 89–128). New York: Academic Press.

Estes, W.K. (1969). Reinforcement in human learning. In J. Tapp (Ed.), *Reinforcement and behavior* (pp. 63–94). New York: Academic Press.

Estes, W.K. (1971). Learning and memory. In E.G. Beckenback & C.B. Tompkins (Eds.), *Concepts of communication: Interpersonal, intrapersonal and mathematical* (pp. 282–300). New York: Wiley.

Estes, W.K. (1972a). An associative basis for coding and organization in memory. In A.W. Melton & E. Martin (Eds.), *Coding processes in human memory* (pp. 161–190). Washington, DC: Winston.

Estes, W.K. (1972b). Reinforcement in human behavior. *American Scientist, 60,* 723–729.

Estes, W.K. (1972c). Research and theory on the learning of probabilities. *Journal of the American Statistical Association, 67,* 81–102.

Estes, W.K. (1976a). The cognitive side of probability learning. *Psychological Review, 83,* 37–64.

Estes, W.K. (1976b). Some functions of memory in probability learning and choice behavior. In G.H. Bower (Ed.), *The psychology of learning and motivation: Advances in research and theory* (Vol. 10, pp. 1–45). New York: Academic Press.

Estes, W.K. (1980). Is human memory obsolete? *American Scientist, 68,* 62–69.

Estes, W.K. (1982). *Models of learning, memory and choice: Selected papers.* New York: Praeger.

Estes, W.K., Burke, C.J., Atkinson, R.C., & Frankmann, J.P. (1957). Probabilistic discrimination learning. *Journal of Experimental Psychology, 54,* 233–239.

Estes, W.K. & DaPolito, F. (1967). Independent variation in information storage and retrieval processes in paired-associate learning. *Journal of Experimental Psychology, 75,* 18–26.

Estes, W.K. & Straughan, J.H. (1954). Analysis of a verbal conditioning situation in terms of statistical learning theory. *Journal of Experimental Psychology, 47,* 225–234.

Feigenbaum, E.A. (1963). The simulation of verbal learning behavior. In E.A. Feigenbaum & J. Feldman

(Eds.), *Computers and thought* (pp. 297–309). New York: McGraw-Hill.

Flexser, A.J. (1981). Homogenizing the 2 × 2 contingency table: A method for removing dependencies due to subject and item differences. *Psychological Review, 88,* 327–339.

Flexser, A.J. & Bower, G.H. (1974). How frequency affects recency judgments: A model for recency discrimination. *Journal of Experimental Psychology, 104,* 706–716.

Foss, D.J. & Harwood, D.A. (1975). Memory for sentences: Implications for human associative memory. *Journal of Verbal Learning and Verbal Behavior, 14,* 1–16.

Franks, J.J. & Bransford, J.D. (1971). Abstraction of visual patterns. *Journal of Experimental Psychology, 90,* 65–74.

Fried, L.S. & Holyoak, K.J. (1984). Induction of category distributions: A framework for classification learning. *Journal of Experimental Psychology: Learning, Memory, and Cognition, 10,* 234–257.

Friedman, M.P., Burke, C.J., Cole, M., Keller, L., Millward, R.B., & Estes, W.K. (1964). Two-choice behavior under extended training with shifting probabilities of reinforcement. In R.C. Atkinson (Ed.), *Studies in mathematical psychology* (pp. 250–316). Stanford, CA: Stanford University Press.

Friedman, M.P., Trabasso, T., & Mosberg, L. (1967). Tests of a mixed model for paired-associates learning with overlapping stimuli. *Journal of Mathematical Psychology, 4,* 316–334.

Garner, W.R. (1974). *The processing of information and structure.* Potomac, MD: Lawrence Erlbaum.

Gartman, L.M. & Johnson, N.F. (1972). Massed versus distributed repetition of homographs: A test of the differential-encoding hypothesis. *Journal of Verbal Learning and Verbal Behavior, 11,* 801–808.

Gibson, E.J. (1940). A systematic application of the concepts of generalization and differentiation to verbal learning. *Psychological Review, 47,* 196–229.

Gibson, E.J. (1969). *Principles of perceptual learning and development.* New York: Appleton-Century-Crofts.

Glenberg, A.M. (1976). Monotonic and nonmonotonic lag effects in paired-associate and recognition memory paradigms. *Journal of Verbal Learning and Verbal Behavior, 15,* 1–16.

Glenberg, A.M. (1977). Influences of retrieval processes on the spacing effect in free recall. *Journal of Experimental Psychology: Human Learning and Memory, 3,* 282–294.

Glenberg, A.M., Bradley, M.M., Kraus, T.A., & Renzaglia, G.J. (1983). Studies of the long-term recency effect: Support for a contextually guided retrieval

hypothesis. *Journal of Experimental Psychology: Learning, Memory, and Cognition, 9,* 231–255.

Glenberg, A.M. & Lehmann, T.S. (1980). Spacing repetitions over one week. *Memory and Cognition, 8,* 528–538.

Godden, D.R. & Baddeley, A.D. (1975). Context-dependent memory in two natural environments: On land and underwater. *British Journal of Psychology, 66,* 325–331.

Godden, D.R. & Baddeley, A.D. (1980). When does context influence recognition memory? *British Journal of Psychology, 71,* 99–104.

Grant, D.A., Hake, H.W., & Hornseth, J.P. (1951). Acquisition and extinction of a verbal conditioned response with differing percentages of reinforcement. *Journal of Experimental Psychology, 42,* 1–5.

Greenberg, R. & Underwood, B.J. (1950). Retention as a function of stage of practice. *Journal of Experimental Psychology, 40,* 452–457.

Greeno, J.G. (1968). *Elementary theoretical psychology* Reading, MA: Addison-Wesley.

Greeno, J.G., James, C.T., DaPolito, F., & Polson, P.G. (1978). *Associative learning: A cognitive analysis.* Englewood Cliffs, NJ: Prentice-Hall.

Greenspoon, J. (1955). The reinforcing effect of two spoken sounds on the frequency of two responses. *American Journal of Psychology, 68,* 409–416.

Guthrie, E.R. (1935). *The psychology of learning.* New York: Harper.

Hammond, K.R., Hursch, C.J., & Todd, F.J. (1964). Analyzing the components of clinical inference. *Psychological Review, 71,* 438–456.

Harley, W.F., Jr. (1965). The effect of monetary incentive in paired-associate learning using a differential method. *Psychonomic Science, 2,* 377–378.

Hayes-Roth, B. (1977). Evolution of cognitive structures and processes. *Psychological Review, 84,* 260–278.

Hayes-Roth, B. & Hayes-Roth, F. (1977). Concept learning and the recognition and classification of exemplars. *Journal of Verbal Learning and Verbal Behavior, 16,* 321–338.

Hayes-Roth, B. & Thorndyke, P.W. (1979). Integration of knowledge from text. *Journal of Verbal Learning and Verbal Behavior, 18,* 91–108.

Hebb, D.O. (1949). *The organization of behavior: A Neurophysiological theory.* New York: Wiley.

Hilgard, E.R. (1956). *Theories of learning* (2nd ed.). New York: Appleton-Century-Crofts.

Hillyard, S.A. & Kutas, M. (1983). Electrophysiology of cognitive processing. *Annual Review of Psychology, 34,* 33–61.

Hintzman, D.L. (1969). Apparent frequency as a function of frequency and the spacing of repetitions. *Journal of Experimental Psychology, 80,* 139–145.

Hintzman, D.L. (1980). Simpon's paradox and the analysis of memory retrieval. *Psychological Review, 87,* 398–410.

Hintzman, D.L. & Block, R.A. (1973). Memory of spacing of repetitions. *Journal of Experimental Psychology, 99,* 70–74.

Hintzman, D.L., Block, R.A., & Summers, J.J. (1973). Modality tags and memory for repetitions: Locus of the spacing effect. *Journal of Verbal Learning and Verbal Behavior, 12,* 229–238.

Hollingworth, H.L. (1926). *The psychology of thought approached through studies of sleeping and dreaming.* New York: Appleton.

Homa, D. & Chambliss, D. (1975). The relative contribution of common and distinctive information on the abstraction from ill-defined categories. *Journal of Experimental Psychology: Human Learning and Memory, 1,* 351–359.

Homa, D. & Vosburgh, R. (1976). Category breadth and the abstraction of prototypical information. *Journal of Experimental Psychology: Human Learning and Memory, 2,* 322–330.

Hovland, C.I. (1951). Human learning and retention. In S.S. Stevens (Ed.), *Handbook of experimental psychology* (pp. 613–689) New York: Wiley.

Hovland, C.I. (1952). A "communication analysis" of concept learning. *Psychological Review, 59,* 461–472.

Hull, C.L. (1943). *Principles of behavior: An introduction to behavior theory.* New York: Appleton-Century.

Hull, C.L., Hovland, C.I., Ross, R.T., Hall, M., Perkins, D.T., & Fitch, F.B. (1940). *Mathematico-deductive theory of rote learning: A study of scientific methodology.* New Haven, CT: Yale University Press.

Humphreys, L.G. (1939). Acquisition and extinction of verbal expectations in situations analogous to conditioning. *Journal of Experimental Psychology, 25,* 294–301.

Hunt, E.B. (1962). *Concept learning: An informational processing problem.* New York: Wiley.

Hunt, E.B., Marin, J., & Stone, P.J. (1966). *Experiments in induction.* New York: Academic Press.

Hyde, T.S. & Jenkins, J.J. (1969). Differential effects of incidental tasks on the organization of recall of a list of highly associated words. *Journal of Experimental Psychology, 82,* 472–481.

Hyde, T.S. & Jenkins, J.J. (1973). Recall for words as a function of semantic, graphic, and syntactic orienting tasks. *Journal of Verbal Learning and Verbal Behavior, 12,* 471–480.

Ingvar, D.H. (1979). Patterns of activity in the central cortex related to memory function. In L-G. Nilsson (Ed.), *Perspectives on memory research: Essays in honor of Uppsala University's 500th anniversary* (pp. 247–255). Hillsdale, NJ: Lawrence Erlbaum.

James, W. (1890). *The principles of psychology.* New York: Holt.

Johns, M.D. (1963). Transfer of a pattern-vs-component discrimination in a probabilistic situation. *Dissertation Abstracts, 24*(1), 401–402.

Johnson, N.F. (1970). The role of chunking and organization in the process of recall. In G.H. Bower (Ed.), *Psychology of learning and motivation: Advances in research and theory* (Vol. 4, pp. 171–247). New York: Academic Press.

Jones, G.V. (1976). A fragmentation hypothesis of memory: Cued recall of pictures and sequential positions. *Journal of Experimental Psychology: General, 105,* 277–293.

Jones, G.V. (1978). Tests of a structural theory of the memory trace. *British Journal of Psychology, 69,* 351–367.

Keller, L., Cole, M., Burke, C.J., & Estes, W.K. (1965). Reward and information values of trial outcomes in paired-associate learning. *Psychological Monographs, 79* (12, Whole No. 605).

Kimble, G.A. (1961). *Hilgard and Marquis' conditioning and learning.* New York: Appleton-Century-Crofts.

Kincaid, J.P. & Wickens, D.D. (1970). Temporal gradient of release from proactive inhibition. *Journal of Experimental Psychology, 86,* 313–316.

Kintsch, W. (1974). *The representation of meaning in memory.* Hillsdale, NJ: Lawrence Erlbaum.

Kintsch, W. & McCoy, D.L. (1964). Delay of informative feedback in paired-associate learning. *Journal of Experimental Psychology, 68,* 372–375.

Koffka, K. (1935). *Principles of gestalt psychology.* New York: Harcourt Brace.

Kolers, P.A. (1966). Interlingual facilitation of short-term memory. *Journal of Verbal Learning and Verbal Behavior, 5,* 314–319.

Kolers, P.A. & Gonzales, E. (1980). Memory for words, synonyms, and translations. *Journal of Experimental Psychology: Human Learning and Memory, 6,* 53–65.

Krasner, L. (1958). Studies on the conditioning of verbal behavior. *Psychological Bulletin, 55,* 148–170.

LaBerge, D. (1981). Automatic information processing: A review. In J. Long & A. Baddeley (Eds.), *Attention and performance, IX* (pp. 173–186). Hillsdale, NJ: Lawrence Erlbaum.

Lawrence, D.H. (1963). The nature of a stimulus: Some relationships between learning and perception. In S. Koch (Ed.), *Psychology: A study of a science* (Vol. 5, pp. 179–212). New York: McGraw-Hill.

Lee, C.L. & Estes, W.K. (1977). Order and position in primary memory for letter strings. *Journal of Verbal Learning and Verbal Behavior, 16,* 395–418.

Lee, C.L. & Estes, W.K. (1981). Item and order information in short-term memory: Evidence for multi-level perturbation processes. *Journal of Experimental Psychology: Human Learning and Memory, 7,* 149–169.

Levine, M. (1959). A model of hypothesis behavior in discrimination learning set. *Psychological Review, 66,* 353–366.

Light, L.L. & Carter-Sobell, L. (1970). Effects of changed semantic context on recognition memory. *Journal of Verbal Learning and Verbal Behavior, 9,* 1–11.

Lindsay, P.H. & Norman, D.A. (1977). *Human information processing: An introduction to psychology* (2nd ed.). New York: Academic Press.

Luce, R.D. & Suppes, P. (1965). Preference, utility, and subjective probability. In R.D. Luce, R.R. Bush, & E. Galanter (Eds.), *Handbook of mathematical psychology* (Vol. 3, pp. 249–410). New York: Wiley.

Luh, C.W. (1922). The conditions of retention. *Psychological Monographs, 31* (3, Whole No. 142).

Mandler, G. (1967). Organization and memory. In K.W. Spence & J.T. Spence (Eds.), *The psychology of learning and motivation: Advances in research and theory* (Vol. 1, pp. 327–372). New York: Academic Press.

Mandler, G., Cowan, P.A., & Gold, C. (1964). Concept learning and probability matching. *Journal of Experimental Psychology, 67,* 514–522.

Martin, E. (1972). Stimulus encoding in learning and transfer. In A.W. Melton and E. Martin (Eds.), *Coding processes in human memory* (pp. 59–84). Washington, DC: Winston.

Mathews, R.C. & Tulving, E. (1973). Effects of three types of repetition on cued and uncued recall of words. *Journal of Verbal Learning and Verbal Behavior, 12,* 707–721.

McGeoch, J.A. (1942). *The psychology of human learning.* New York: Longmans, Green.

McGeoch, J.A. & Irion, A.L. (1952). *The psychology of human learning.* New York: Longmans, Green.

Medin, D.L. (1974). Frequency and coding responses in verbal discrimination learning. *Memory and Cognition, 2,* 11–13.

Medin, D.L. & Schaffer, M.M. (1978). Context theory of classification learning. *Psychological Review, 85,* 207–238.

Medin, D.L. & Schwanenflugel, P.J. (1981). Linear separability in classification learning. *Journal of Experimental Psychology: Human Learning and Memory, 7,* 355–368.

Melton, A.W. & Irwin, J.M. (1940). The influence of degree of interpolated learning on retroactive inhibition and the overt transfer of specific responses. *American Journal of Psychology, 53,* 173–203.

Melton, A.W. & von Lackum, W.J. (1941). Retroactive and proactive inhibition in retention: Evidence for a two-factor theory of retroactive inhibition. *American Journal of Psychology, 54,* 157–173.

Meyer, D.R. (1960). The effect of differential probabilities of reinforcement in discrimination learning by monkeys. *Journal of Comparative and Physiological Psychology, 53,* 173–175.

Meyer, G. (1939). Temporal organization and the initial reproductive tendency. *Journal of Psychology, 7,* 269–282.

Mill, J. (1829). *Analysis of the phenomena of the human mind.* London: Baldwin & Cradock.

Morse, E.B. & Runquist, W.H. (1960). Probability-matching with an unscheduled random sequence. *American Journal of Psychology, 73,* 603–607.

Morton, J. (1968). Selective interference in immediate recall. *Psychonomic Science, 12,* 75–76.

Mosteller, F. & Nogee, P. (1951). An experimental measurement of utility. *Journal of Political Economy, 59,* 371–404.

Müller, G.E. & Pilzecker, A. (1900). Experimentelle Beiträge zur Lehre vom Gedächtniss [Experimental Contributions to the Study of Memory]. *Zeitschrift für Psychologie der Sinnesorgane,* Ergänxungsband #1.

Murdock, B.B., Jr. (1960). The immediate retention of unrelated words. *Journal of Experimental Psychology, 60,* 222–234.

Murdock, B.B., Jr. (1962). The serial position effect in free recall. *Journal of Experimental Psychology, 64,* 482–488.

Murdock, B.B., Jr. (1974). *Human memory: Theory and data.* Hillsdale, NJ: Lawrence Erlbaum.

Murdock, B.B., Jr. (1976). Item and order information in short-term serial memory. *Journal of Experimental Psychology: General, 105,* 191–216.

Murdock, B.B., Jr. & Anderson, R.E. (1975). Encoding, storage, and retrieval of item information. In R.L. Solso (Ed.), *Information processing and cognition: The Loyola symposium* (pp. 145–194). Potomac, MD: Lawrence Erlbaum.

Myers, J.L. (1976). Probability learning and sequence learning. In W.K. Estes (Ed.), *Handbook of learning and cognitive processes: Approaches to human learning and motivation* (Vol. 3, pp. 171–205). Hillsdale, NJ: Lawrence Erlbaum.

Neimark, E.D. & Shuford, E.H. (1959). Comparison of predictions and estimates in a probability learning situation. *Journal of Experimental Psychology, 57,* 294–298.

Nelson, T.O., Fehling, M.R., & Moore-Glascock, J. (1979). The nature of semantic savings for items forgotten from long-term memory. *Journal of Experimental Psychology: General, 108,* 225–250.

Newell, A. (1981). Physical symbol systems. In D.A. Norman (Ed.), *Perspectives on cognitive science* (pp. 37–85). Hillsdale, NJ: Lawrence Erlbaum.

Newell, A. & Simon, H.A. (1972). *Human problem solving.* Englewood Cliffs, NJ: Prentice-Hall.

Norman, D.A. & Rumelhart, D.E. (1970). A system for perception and memory. In D.A. Norman (Ed.), *Models of human memory* (pp. 19–64). New York: Academic Press.

Norman, D.A. & Rumelhart, D.E. (1975). *Explorations in cognition.* San Francisco, CA: Freeman.

Norman, D.A. & Wickelgren, W.A. (1969). Strength theory of decision rules and latency in retrieval from short-term memory. *Journal of Mathematical Psychology, 6,* 192–208.

Nuttin, J.R. (1953). *Tâche, réussite, et échec: Théorie de la condite humaine* [Trial, Success, and Failure: Theory of the Human Condition]. Louvain, Belgium: Publications Universitaires de Louvain.

Nuttin, J.R. & Greenwald, A.G. (1968). *Reward and punishment in human learning.* New York: Academic Press.

Oliver, W.L. & Ericsson, K.A. (1983). Actors' memory for their parts. *Program of Psychonomic Society, 24th Annual Meeting* (p. 339). San Diego, CA.

Osgood, C.E. (1949). The similarity paradox in human learning. A resolution. *Psychological Review, 56,* 132–143.

Peterson, C.R., Hammond, K.R., & Summers, D.A. (1965). Optimal responding in multiple-cue probability learning. *Journal of Experimental Psychology, 70,* 270–276.

Peterson, L.R., Hillner, K., & Saltzman, D. (1962). Supplementary report: Time between pairings and short-term repetition. *Journal of Experimental Psychology, 64,* 550–551.

Peterson, L.R. & Peterson, M.J. (1959). Short-term retention of individual verbal items. *Journal of Experimental Psychology, 58,* 193–198.

Poffenberger, A.T. (1915). The influence of improvement in one mental process upon other related processes. *Journal of Educational Psychology, 6,* 459–474.

Posner, M.I. & Keele, S.W. (1968). On the genesis of abstract ideas. *Journal of Experimental Psychology, 77,* 353–363.

Posner, M.I. & Keele, S.W. (1970). Retention of abstract ideas. *Journal of Experimental Psychology, 83,* 304–308.

Postman, L. (1962). Reward and punishment in human learning. In L. Postman (Ed.), *Psychology in the making* (pp. 331–401). New York: Knopf.

Postman, L. (1971). Transfer, interference, and forgetting. In J.W. Kling & L.A. Riggs (Eds.), *Woodworth and Schlosberg's experimental psychology* (3rd ed., pp. 1019–1132). New York: Holt, Rinehart, & Winston.

Postman, L. (1976). Methodology of human learning. In W.K. Estes (Ed.), *Handbook of learning and cognitive processes: Approaches to human learning and motivation* (Vol. 3, pp. 11–69). Hillsdale, NJ: Lawrence Erlbaum.

Postman, L., Adams, P.A., & Philips, L.W. (1955). Studies in incidental learning: II. The effects of association value and of the method of testing. *Journal of Experimental Psychology, 49,* 1–10.

Postman, L. & Underwood, B.J. (1973). Critical issues in interference theory. *Memory and Cognition, 1,* 19–40.

Potter, M.C. (1976). Short-term conceptual memory for pictures. *Journal of Experimental Psychology: Human Learning and Memory, 2,* 509–522.

Potter, M.C. & Levy, E.I. (1969). Recognition memory for a rapid sequence of pictures. *Journal of Experimental Psychology, 81,* 10–15.

Raaijmakers, J.G.W. & Shiffrin, R.M. (1981). Search of associative memory. *Psychological Review, 88,* 93–134.

Radtke, R.C., Jacoby, L.L., & Goedel, G.D. (1971). Frequency discriminations as a function of frequency of repetition and trials. *Journal of Experimental Psychology, 89,* 78–84.

Ratcliff, R. & McKoon, G. (1978). Priming in item recognition: Evidence for the propositional structure of sentences. *Journal of Verbal Learning and Verbal Behavior, 17,* 403–417.

Reber, A.S. & Millward, R.B. (1968). Event observation in probability learning. *Journal of Experimental Psychology, 77,* 317–327.

Reder, L.M. & Anderson, J.R. (1980). A partial resolution of the paradox of interference: The role of integrating knowledge. *Cognitive Psychology, 12,* 447–472.

Reed, S.K. (1972). Pattern recognition and categorization. *Cognitive Psychology, 3,* 382–407.

Reed, S.K. (1973). *Psychological processes in pattern recognition.* New York: Academic Press.

Reitman, J.S. (1971). Mechanisms of forgetting in short-term memory. *Cognitive Psychology, 2,* 185–195.

Reitman, J.S. (1974). Without surreptitious rehearsal, information in short-term memory decays. *Journal of Verbal Learning and Verbal Behavior, 13,* 365–377.

Restle, F. & Brown, E.R. (1970a). Organization of serial pattern learning. In G.H. Bower (Ed.), *The psychology of learning and motivation: Advances in research and theory* (Vol. 4, pp. 249–331). New York: Academic Press.

Restle, F. & Brown, E.R. (1970b). Serial pattern learning. *Journal of Experimental Psychology, 83,* 120–125.

Roberts, W.A. (1972). Free recall of conditioned lists varying in length and rate of presentation: A test of total-time hypothesis. *Journal of Experimental Psychology, 92,* 365–372.

Robinson, E.S. (1932). *Association theory today: An essay in systematic psychology.* New York: Century.

Rosch, E. (1973). On the internal structure of perceptual and semantic categories. In T.E. Moore (Ed.), *Cognitive development and the acquisition of language* (pp. 111–144). New York: Academic Press.

Rosch, E. (1978). Principles of categorization. In E. Rosch & B.B. Lloyd (Eds.), *Cognition and categorization* (pp. 27–48). Hillsdale, NJ: Lawrence Erlbaum.

Rosch, E. & Mervis, C.B. (1975). Family resemblances: Studies in the internal structure of categories. *Cognitive Psychology, 7,* 573–605.

Rosenberg, S. & Simon, H.A. (1977). Modeling semantic memory: Effects of presenting semantic information in different modalities. *Cognitive Psychology, 9,* 293–325.

Ross, B.H. & Bower, G.H. (1981). Comparisons of models of associative recall. *Memory and Cognition, 9,* 1–16.

Rubinstein, I. (1959). Some factors in probability matching. *Journal of Experimental Psychology, 57,* 413–416.

Ryan, C. (1983). Reassessing the automaticity-control distinction. Item recognition as a paradigm case. *Psychological Review, 90,* 171–178.

Sabol, M.A. & DeRosa, D.V. (1976). Semantic encoding of isolated words. *Journal of Experimental Psychology: Human Learning and Memory, 2,* 58–68.

Saltzman, I.J. (1951). Delay of reward and human verbal learning. *Journal of Experimental Psychology, 41,* 437–439.

Seamon, J.G. (1973). Retrieval processes for organized long-term storage. *Journal of Experimental Psychology, 97,* 170–176.

Seibel, R. (1963). Discrimination reaction time for a 1,023-alternative task. *Journal of Experimental Psychology, 66,* 215–226.

Shallice, T. (1979). Neurophysiological research and the fractionation of memory systems. In L-G. Nilsson (Ed.), *Perspectives on memory research: Essays in honor of Uppsala University's 500th anniversary* (pp. 257–277). Hillsdale, NJ: Lawrence Erlbaum.

Shepard, R.N. (1967). Recognition memory for words, sentences, and pictures. *Journal of Verbal Learning and Verbal Behavior, 6,* 156–163.

Shepard, R.N., Hovland, C.I., & Jenkins, H.M. (1961). Learning and memorization of classifications. *Psychological Monographs, 75* (Whole No. 517).

Shiffrin, R.M. (1970). Memory search. In D.A. Norman (Ed.), *Models of human memory* (pp. 375–447). New York: Academic Press.

Shiffrin, R.M. (1973). Information persistence in short-term memory. *Journal of Experimental Psychology, 100,* 39–49.

Shiffrin, R.M. (1976). Capacity limitations in information processing, attention, and memory. In W.K. Estes (Ed.), *Handbook of learning and cognitive processes: Attention and memory* (Vol. 4, pp. 177–236). Hillsdale, NJ: Lawrence Erlbaum.

Shiffrin, R.M. & Cook, J.R. (1978). Short-term forgetting of item and order information. *Journal of Verbal Learning and Verbal Behavior, 17,* 189–218.

Shiffrin, R.M. & Schneider, W. (1977). Controlled and automatic human information processing: II. Perceptual learning, automatic attending, and a general theory. *Psychological Review, 84,* 127–190.

Slamecka, N.J. & McElree, B. (1983). Normal forgetting of verbal lists as a function of their degree of learning. *Journal of Experimental Psychology: Learning, Memory, and Cognition, 9,* 384–397.

Smith, E.E. (1981). Organization of factual knowledge. In J.H. Flowers (Ed.), *Nebraska Symposium on Motivation 1980: Cognitive processes* (pp. 163–209). Lincoln, NB: University of Nebraska Press.

Smith, E.E., Adams, N., & Schorr, D. (1978). Fact retrieval and the paradox of interferences. *Cognitive Psychology, 10,* 438–464.

Smith, E.E. & Haviland, S.E. (1972). Why words are perceived more accurately than nonwords: Inference versus unitization. *Journal of Experimental Psychology, 92,* 59–64.

Smith, E.E. & Medin, D.L. (1981). *Categories and concepts.* Cambridge, MA: Harvard University Press.

Smith, E.E., Shoben, E.J., & Rips, L.J. (1974). Structure and process in semantic memory: A featural model for semantic decisions. *Psychological Review, 81,* 214–241.

Smith, S.M., Glenberg, A.M., & Bjork, R.A. (1978). Environmental context and human memory. *Memory and Cognition, 6,* 342–353.

Spear, N.E. (1976). Retrieval of memories: A psychobiological approach. In W.K. Estes (Ed.), *Handbook of Learning and cognitive processes: Attention and memory* (Vol. 4, pp. 17–90). Hillsdale, NJ: Lawrence Erlbaum.

Spence, K.W. (1956). *Behavior theory and conditioning.* New Haven, CT: Yale University Press.

Spence, K.W. (1960). *Behavior theory and learning: Selected papers.* Englewood Cliffs, NJ: Prentice-Hall.

Sperling, G. (1960). The information available in brief visual presentations. *Psychological Monographs, 1960, 74* (11, Whole No. 498).

Spielberger, C.D., Bernstein, I.H., & Ratliff, R.G. (1966). Information and incentive value of the reinforcing stimulus in verbal conditioning. *Journal of Experimental Psychology, 71,* 26–31.

Sternberg, S. (1966). High-speed scanning in human memory. *Science, 153,* 652–654.

Sutherland, N.S. & Mackintosh, N.J. (1971). *Mechanisms of animal discrimination learning.* New York: Academic Press.

Taffel, C. (1955). Anxiety and the conditioning of verbal behavior. *Journal of Abnormal and Social Psychology, 51,* 496–501.

Terrell, G., Jr. & Kennedy, W.A. (1957). Discrimination learning and transposition in children as a function of the nature of the reward. *Journal of Experimental Psychology, 53,* 257–260.

Thorndike, E.L. (1913). *Educational psychology: Vol. II: The psychology of learning.* New York: Teacher's College, Columbia University.

Thorndike, E.L. (1931). *Human learning.* New York: Century.

Thorndyke, P.W. & Hayes-Roth, B. (1979). The use of schemata in the acquisition and transfer of knowledge. *Cognitive Psychology, 11,* 82–106.

Trabasso, T. & Bower, G.H. (1968). *Attention in learning: Theory and research.* New York: Wiley.

Treisman, A.M. & Gelade, G. (1980). A feature-integration theory of attention. *Cognitive Psychology, 12,* 97–130.

Tulving, E. (1968). Theoretical issues in free recall. In T.R. Dixon & D.L. Horton (Eds.), *Verbal behavior and general behavior theory* (pp. 2–36). Englewood Cliffs, NJ: Prentice-Hall.

Tulving, E. (1983). *Elements of episodic memory.* New York: Oxford University Press.

Tulving, E. & Pearlstone, Z. (1966). Availability versus accessibility of information in memory for words. *Journal of Verbal Learning and Verbal Behavior, 5,* 381–391.

Tulving, E. & Psotka, J. (1971). Retroactive inhibition in free recall: Inaccessibility of information available in the memory store. *Journal of Experimental Psychology, 87,* 1–8.

Tversky, A. & Kahneman, D. (1973). Availability: A heuristic for judging frequency and probability. *Cognitive Psychology, 5,* 207–232.

Underwood, B.J. (1945). The effect of successive interpolations on retroactive and proactive inhibition. *Psychological Monographs, 59* (3, Whole No. 273).

Underwood, B.J. (1957). Interference and forgetting. *Psychological Review, 64,* 49–60.

Underwood, B.J. (1964). Degree of learning and the measurement of forgetting. *Journal of Verbal Learning and Verbal Behavior, 3,* 112–129.

Underwood, B.J. (1969). Attributes of memory. *Psychological Review, 76,* 559–573.

Underwood, B.J. (1977). *Temporal codes for memories: Issues and problems.* Hillsdale, NJ: Lawrence Erlbaum.

Underwood, B.J. & Freund, J.S. (1970). Relative frequency judgments and verbal discrimination learning. *Journal of Experimental Psychology, 83,* 279–285.

Underwood, B.J. & Schulz, R.W. (1960). *Meaningfulness and verbal behavior.* Chicago, IL: Lippincott.

Underwood, B.J., Zimmerman, J., & Freund, J.S. (1971). Retention of frequency information with observations on recognition and recall. *Journal of Experimental Psychology, 87,* 149–162.

von Neumann, J. & Morgenstern, O. (1944). *Theory of games and economic behavior.* Princeton, NJ: Princeton University Press.

von Wright, J.M. (1968). Selection in visual immediate memory. *Quarterly Journal of Experimental Psychology, 20,* 62–68.

von Wright, J.M. (1972). On the problem of selection in iconic memory. *Scandanavian Journal of Psychology, 13,* 159–171.

Wallach, H. & Henle, M. (1941). An experimental analysis of the law of effect. *Journal of Experimental Psychology, 28,* 340–349.

Watkins, M.J. (1979). Engrams as cuegrams and forgetting as cue overload: A cueing approach to the structure of memory. In C.R. Puff (Ed.), *Memory organization and structure* (pp. 347–372). New York: Academic Press.

Watkins, M.J. & Watkins, O.C. (1975). A categorically postcategorical interpretation of the modality effect: A reply to Nilsson. *Journal of Experimental Psychology: Human Learning and Memory, 1,* 733–735.

Waugh, N.C. & Norman, D.A. (1965). Primary memory. *Psychological Review, 72,* 89–104.

Weinstock, S., North, A.J., Brody, A.L., & LoGuidice, J. (1965). Probability learning in the T maze with noncorrection. *Journal of Comparative and Physiological Psychology, 60,* 76–81.

Weir, M.W. (1964). Developmental changes in problem solving strategies. *Psychological Review, 71,* 473–490.

Wells, J.E. (1974). Strength theory and judgments of recency and frequency. *Journal of Verbal Learning and Verbal Behavior, 13,* 378–392.

Wescourt, K.T. & Atkinson, R.C. (1976). Fact retrieval processes in human memory. In W.K. Estes (Ed.), *Handbook of learning and cognitive processes: Attention and memory* (Vol. 4, pp. 363–413). Hillsdale, NJ: Lawrence Erlbaum.

Whitlow, J.W., Jr. & Estes, W.K. (1979). Judgments of relative frequency in relation to shifts of event frequencies: Evidence for a limited-capacity model. *Journal of Experimental Psychology: Human Learning and Memory, 5,* 395–408.

Whitlow, J.W., Jr. & Skaar, E. (1979). The role of numerosity in judgments of overall frequency. *Journal of Experimental Psychology: Human Learning and Memory, 5,* 409–421.

Wickelgren, W.A. (1969). Context-sensitive coding, associative memory, and serial order in (speech) behavior. *Psychological Review, 76,* 1–15.

Wickelgren, W.A. (1970). Multitrace strength theory. In D.A. Norman (Ed.), *Models of human memory* (pp. 65–102). New York: Academic Press.

Wickelgren, W.A. (1972). Trace resistance and the decay of long-term memory. *Journal of Mathematical Psychology, 9,* 418–455.

Wickens, D.D. (1970). Encoding categories of words: An empirical approach to meaning. *Psychological Review, 77,* 1–15.

Wickens, D.D. (1972). Characteristics of word encoding. In A.W. Melton & E. Martin (Eds.), *Coding processes in human memory* (pp. 191–216). Washington, DC: Winston.

Witryol, S.L., Tyrrell, D.J., & Lowden, L.M. (1965). Development of incentive values in childhood. *Genetic Psychology Monographs, 72,* 201–246.

Woodrow, H. (1942). The problem of general quantitative laws in psychology. *Psychological Bulletin, 39,* 1–27.

Woodward, A.E., Jr., Bjork, R.A., & Jongeward, R.N., Jr. (1973). Recall and recognition as a function of primary rehearsal. *Journal of Verbal Learning and Verbal Behavior, 12,* 608–617.

Woodworth, R.S. (1938). *Experimental psychology.* New York: Holt.

Yellott, J.I., Jr. (1969). Probability learning with noncontingent success. *Journal of Mathematical Psychology, 6,* 541–575.

Young, R.K. (1961). The stimulus in serial verbal learning. *American Journal of Psychology, 74,* 517–528.

# Chapter 6

# PSYCHOLINGUISTIC ASPECTS OF PRAGMATICS AND SEMANTICS

George A. Miller *and* Sam Glucksberg, *Princeton University*

The study of signs has three parts: syntax, semantics, and pragmatics. According to Morris (1938), syntax concerns relations between signs and signs, semantics concerns relations between signs and their designata, and pragmatics concerns relations between signs and the users of signs. For example, "is the subject of" is a syntactic relation between a noun phrase and a verb; "denotes" is a semantic relation between a word and what the word names; "asserts that" is a pragmatic relation between a speaker and a declarative sentence.

The study of signs takes on different appearances in different disciplines depending on which of these relationships is considered most fundamental. In linguistics, syntax has been the central issue; in philosophy, semantics; in psychology, pragmatics. This chapter examines two of these approaches, semantics and pragmatics, as they apply to experimental approaches to the psychology of language use.

Semantics pertains to the meanings of words and sentences. In philosophy, the central problem of semantics has been the definition of truth conditions for sentences of particular (often formal) languages, abstracted from the situations in which those sentences might be used for communication. Much discussion has been devoted to the claim that to know a sentence's meaning is to know the states of affairs in which it would be true (its truth conditions). To know the meaning of *Der Schnee ist weiss*, for example, is to know that *Der Schnee ist weiss* is true in all states of affairs (all possible worlds) in which snow is white. According to this view, in order to understand the sentence it is not necessary to know whether it is true or false, but merely to know under what conditions it would be true. In order to determine whether the sentence is true or false in the state of affairs we call the real world, for example, it would be necessary to locate some snow and look at it to see whether its color is what speakers of German call *weiss*. The actual evaluation involves processes (finding, seeing, judging) of considerable psychological interest, but it is sufficient for most philosophical purposes simply to know that such processes exist. Given the availability of such observational verification, the theory of semantics can be taken to be a theory of understanding.

This equivalence must be questioned, however.

Sentences expressing propositional attitudes, like *Karl glaubt, dass der Schnee schwartz ist* (Karl believes that snow is black), are particularly difficult to deal with solely in terms of truth conditions; the truth conditions for statements about what Carl believes are different from the truth conditions for his beliefs. Philosophers who doubt that understanding can be reduced to the appreciation of truth conditions are likely to emphasize the importance to understanding of such pragmatic factors as the speaker's intentions in using a particular sentence on a particular occasion. And psychologists who resist the identification of semantic theory with the theory of understanding are likely to point to differences in the kinds of information processing required to determine the truth values of different kinds of sentences.

We shall assume, therefore, that a theory of understanding must include pragmatic as well as syntactic and semantic components. For example, when utterances in a natural language (English, German, Turkish, etc.) are subjected to formal semantic analysis, the sentences that are actually spoken must be distinguished from the propositions that speakers intended to express by uttering them. Not only can different sentences express the same proposition, but the same sentence can express different propositions in different contexts of use. For example, *She is here* might be used on one occasion to express the proposition, *Mary Doe is on the northeast corner of Fifth Avenue and 59th Street in New York City at 10:25 A.M. on July 4, 1976*, and on another occasion to express a different proposition about someone else at another time and place. Formal semantics is concerned with the truth conditions of the proposition, not the sentence *per se*.

The sentence *She is here* is not meaningless, however, even though we cannot know its truth conditions without knowing the context in which it is used. A person who knows English knows how to interpret *She is here* within a context of use in order to obtain the proposition it expresses. Thus, two kinds of meaning can be distinguished, which Kaplan (1977) has called content and character. To know the content of *She is here* is to know the truth conditions of the proposition it expresses; to know the character of *She is here* is to know the rules for determining its content in any context of use. Contexts can be thought of as functions that map sentences

into propositions; propositions can be thought of as functions that map possible worlds into truth values.

While semantics explores the meanings of words and sentences, pragmatics examines their uses. As defined by Morris, pragmatics is an elusive and heterogeneous subject. It can be taken to include all that a speaker communicates over and above the propositional content of the utterance—information about a speaker's social class and education, for example. A narrower definition, however, limits pragmatics to the study of those aspects of the context that are necessary to determine propositional content. For example, it might be possible to determine from context, that the person who utters *She is here* is a man, but that information would have no bearing on the statement's propositional content, and so would be excluded under the narrow definition of pragmatics; the speaker's location at the time of utterance, however, must be known in order to determine the content, so the speaker's location in included under the narrow definition.

In this chapter we shall adopt the narrower definition of pragmatics. That is, our discussion of pragmatics will ignore aspects of the context of use that do not bear directly on the determination of the proposition that a speaker intends to express. We will also restrict our treatment to the semantics and pragmatics of single words and single sentences. Discussion of the semantics and pragmetics of discourse and text comprehension may be found in this volume.

Some theorists maintain that an utterance is not fully understood until the speaker's primary intention is known. Others feel that this goal is unattainable, and that determining the propositions a hearer could deduce as a result of processing an utterance is all that a theory of understanding can hope to accomplish. Since these goals for pragmatic theory differ, it is convenient to have different names for them. Let us call the first—the understanding that includes the speaker's intentions—*comprehension*. The second—determining the propositions expressible by an utterance, irrespective of intent—can be called *interpretation*. For example, a speaker's intention in uttering *It's raining* may be to get someone to shut a window. Therefore, comprehension of that utterance would include the recognition that the speaker was making a particular request. If the hearer concluded falsely that the speaker had used the sentence for some other purpose—to cancel a picnic, perhaps—the hearer would have interpreted the sentence, but without comprehending the speaker's intent. In general, the adequacy of a hearer's interpretations is far easier to determine than whether that hearer correctly comprehended the underlying intention of the speaker. Athough the distinction is not widespread among psycholinguists, we shall attempt to observe it in this chapter. When either comprehension or interpretation is appropriate, we shall speak of *understanding.*

To a psychologist, the distinction between sentences and propositions may suggest a multistage model of sentence comprehension: first, the intended proposition is determined from the sentence and its context; second, the truth conditions of the proposition are determined. Finally, but not necessarily, the truth of the proposition may be evaluated in the real world. In this form, the philosophical distinction is translated into a multi-stage, sequential, information-processing model, with pragmatic processing first and semantic processing second. As such, the model should be empirically testable.

A different and, in our opinion, more fruitful view is that pragmatics is not a separate device or component of the language understanding system. According to Sperber & Wilson (1981a), for example, pragmatics "is simply the domain in which linguistic abilities, logical abilities, and memory interact" (p. 285). In this view, pragmatics deals with a broad range of problems of interpretation, many of them beyond the scope of experimental methods. Much of pragmatics must, therefore, remain highly theoretical and speculative. Its value to psychology is in the perspective it provides on the nature and use of the various psychological mechanisms that contribute to language understanding.

No novel theories of pragmatics or semantics are attemped in these pages. The chapter is simply a didactic review of those aspects of pragmatics and semantics that we consider most relevant to an experimental psychology of language. Topics are introduced and discussed in proportion to the attention paid them in psycholinguistic publications through 1981. Consequently, some aspects of pragmatics and semantics important to philosophers or linguists are mentioned only in passing, if not ignored entirely.

# LANGUAGE USE

Students of language have generally assumed that the principal use of language is to communicate information. This assumption may derive from a preoccupation with scientific or scholarly texts. Under this assumption the truth of the information communicated by a text or discourse becomes of central importance. This attitude can be seen not only in those philosophical theories of semantics that are based on truth, but also in the many psychological studies of language comprehension that use some version of the sentence verification task: the time taken to decide whether a given sentence is true or false is frequently assumed to be a measure of the complexity of the mental processes involved in understanding it.

The narrowness of this view that language is used principally to communicate true information was recognized by Wittgenstein (1953), who emphasized the variety of uses to which language is put. Austin (1962) developed this aspect of Wittgenstein's thinking in his theory of performatives, which led to the theory of speech acts (Searle, 1969, 1979a).

## Performatives

Statements that describe states of affairs and which can be judged true or false—the kind of statements that had previously dominated philosophical discussions of language—Austin (1962) termed *constatives.* To this class he contrasted *performatives:* statements that accomplish something by virtue of being uttered. For Austin, to utter a performative is to do something; doing something is neither true nor false. *Close the window,* for example, can be used to perform the act of requesting; it may be effective or ineffective, but it is neither true nor false.

Having distinguished performatives from constatives, Austin argued that all utterances are performatives of one kind or another—effectively abolishing the distinction. To utter a constative, he held, is to perform the act of describing or asserting something.

Performatives can be either explicit or implicit. The statements *I'll bet you ten dollars it will rain tomorrow* and *I hereby declare you man and wife,* when uttered by a responsible person under the appropriate social circumstances, are examples of explicit performatives. By uttering them, the speaker performs an act (makes a wager, unites a couple in matrimony), and the speaker's intention to perform that act is explicit. A statement such as *It's awfully hot in here*, when intended as an indirect request for someone to open a window, also performs an act, but the speaker's intention to perform it is implicit and must be inferred by the hearer.

The description of a speech act can thus have four components:

1. The utterance act itself—the vocal behavior of generating the utterance
2. The locution of the utterance—the literal meaning of the utterance
3. The illocution of the utterance—the meaning intended by the speaker
4. The perlocution of the utterance—the effect of the utterance on the hearer

For example, speaking the words *It's hot in here* would be an utterance act. The locution has the form of a declarative sentence to the effect that the temperature in the place where the sentence is uttered is above some norm at the time of utterance. If the speaker's intention is to communicate information about the temperature there and then, the locution and the illocution of the utterance coincide. In certain contexts, however, a speaker might use this locution with the illocutionary force of a request: the speaker might intend the statement to be taken as a request for the hearer to turn on an air conditioner, perhaps. If the hearer then turned it on, the utterance would have had its intended perlocutionary effect, and illocution and perlocution would then agree.

In order to comprehend an utterance, therefore, it is not enough to know under what conditions it would be true or false. The speaker's intention in using the utterance must also be known. Although the attribution of some intention to a speaker is normally straightforward, the process is not infallible. Probably more communication failures result from mistaking a speaker's intentions than from any other source of error in linguistic interactions.

Various classifications of illocutions have been proposed. According to Searle (1979a), language is used in five general ways, so there are five general categories of illocutions: "We tell people how things are (assertives), we try to get them to do things (directives), we commit our-

selves to doing things (commissives), we express our feelings and attitudes (expressives), and we bring about changes in the world through our utterances (declarations)" (p. viii). Bach and Harnish (1979) proposed a different classification, as did Austin (1962). Lack of agreement in this matter poses serious difficulties for any linguist or psychologist who hopes to work with a definitive classification of language uses.

Theorists in this tradition generally agree that the central question for a theory of language use should be: How are speakers' intentions communicated to listeners? This question has two parts. First, how do speakers decide how to express a given intention? Second, how do listeners discover what a speaker's intention is?

## Speech Act Theory

A speaker who wants to request a hearer to close a window has several ways to do so. For example, the speaker can request it directly by saying *Please close the window*, or indirectly by saying *It's raining in*. Whatever the choice, however, the felicitous performance of this speech act presupposes certain conditions; for example, there must be an open window, and there must be a hearer who understands English and who is capable of closing windows. If the indirect way is chosen, the request will not be effective unless the hearer correctly infers the speaker's intention. How a hearer does this is not obvious: *It's raining in* could be interpreted as a statement of fact (an assertive), or as an expression of annoyance (an expressive), as well as an indirect request for action (a directive). Indeed, it is not even obvious how the hearer recognizes the speaker's intentions when the direct way is chosen, since *Please close that window* could be intended as a rebuke as well as a request for action—or could even be intended as a secret signal in some prearranged code.

Speech act theory is an attempt to state rules governing how a speaker chooses utterances to express particular intentions in particular contexts, rules that hearers also can use to attribute particular intentions to speakers in particular contexts. The rules should make explicit the conditions governing well-formed speech acts.

The simplest way to convey the nature of speech act theory is by example. Consider Searle's (1969) analysis of the conditions (often referred to as the *felicity* conditions) that must be satisfied in order for a speaker to make a promise (a commissive):

1. A speaker utters a sentence in the presence of a hearer.
2. A proposition is expressed in that utterance, which
3. can be taken to predicate a future action by the speaker.
4. The hearer would prefer that the speaker take this action rather than not, and the speaker believes that this is so. (Otherwise it might be a threat instead of a promise.)
5. Neither the speaker nor the hearer expect that the promised action would normally have been taken without this promise. (It is seldom appropriate to promise to continue breathing, for example.)
6. The speaker sincerely intends to perform the promised action.
7. By promising, the speaker takes on an obligation to carry out the promised action.
8. The speaker intends to inform the hearer that the speaker is taking on that obligation.

If these felicity conditions are met (as well as some others that need not concern us here), a well-formed promise is made.

It should be obvious that speech act theory assumes that far more than linguistic knowledge is required in order to use language successfully. Speakers and hearers must both know and be able to follow relatively complex rules governing social-verbal discourse, and they must be able to draw on conceptual and interpersonal knowledge to choose appropriate forms of utterance and to interpret indirect speech acts correctly. Those assumptions, if true, are of considerable importance for the psychology of language.

## The Cooperative Principle

A central insight of pragmatic analysis can be attributed to Grice (1975), who saw that linguistic competence and contextual knowledge are necessary but not sufficient for understanding language. Understanding also depends on a general communicative principle that is tacitly accepted by all participants.

A conversational exchange is not a random collection of unrelated sentences, nor must it follow some fixed sequence. Participants have considerable latitude in deciding what to say at any point, but there are constraints that must be respected. A conversation has a purpose or direction that organizes successive contributions, and participants implicitly agree to cooperate in achieving that purpose or advancing that direction—otherwise, they would not participate.

Grice proposed that participants in a conversation observe the "Cooperative Principle." This principle states that people will do what is required to further the purpose of their conversation: "Make your conversational contribution such as is required, at the stage at which it occurs, by the accepted purpose or direction of the talk exchange in which you are engaged (p. 67)." According to Grice, this is accomplished by following certain "conversational maxims":

1. Maxims of Quantity:
   Make your contribution as informative as is required (for the current purpose of the exchange).
   Do not make your contribution more informative than is required.
2. Maxims of Quality:
   Try to make your contribution one that is true.
   Do not say what you believe to be false.
   Do not say that for which you lack adequate evidence.
3. Maxim of Relation:
   Be relevant.
4. Maxims of Manner:
   Be perspicuous.
   Avoid obscurity of expression.
   Avoid ambiguity.
   Be brief (avoid unnecessary prolixity).
   Be orderly.

Grice's maxims are neither prescriptive nor descriptive of what actually happens in conversations. Rather, they express assumptions that a hearer can bring to bear, assumptions that any interpretation of a speaker's utterance should attempt to preserve. If someone seems to violate them during conversation, either the implicit conversational contract has been broken because the speaker wishes to withdraw, or the speaker expects the hearer to understand why the maxims were violated.

For example, Mary says to John, *I took the trash out last night*. If John already knows this, and knows that Mary knows he knows it, then Mary has violated the maxim to be informative. Since Mary does not seem to be breaking off the conversation, John concludes that she means something more than she said. The violation triggers a search for an additional interpretation, and John decides that Mary's hidden message is that she wants him to handle that chore tonight.

In this example, one might say that *I took the trash out last night* implies or suggests or means *You take the trash out tonight*. But "implies" has a logical sense that is too strong, "suggests" seems too weak, and "means" has too many other uses. Grice introduced the verb *implicate* and the noun *implicature* to cover this kind of relation. Grice's notion of conversational implicature provides a pragmatic solution for what had previously seemed to be a semantic problem.

By combining some notions from speech act theory with the cooperative principle, it is possible to outline the steps that might be involved in comprehending an utterance. Consider a case where student *A* says, *Let's go to a movie tonight*, and *B* replies, *I have an exam tomorrow morning*. How does *A* understand *B*'s answer? Krauss (1979), following Searle (1969), says that *A* must know or assume the following:

1. *B* is responding to a proposal with the statement *I have an exam tomorrow morning*.
2. *B* is cooperating, and therefore what *B* said is relevant.
3. A relevant response to a proposal is either an acceptance or a rejection.
4. The literal or conventional content of *B*'s statement is an assertion about a future event. Ordinarily it is neither an acceptance nor a rejection.
5. If assumptions 1, 2, 3, and 4 are correct, then the primary illocution (the speaker's meaning) is distinct from the locution (the sentence's meaning).
6. Examinations require studying.
7. Studying and going to the movies each take time.

8. Studying and going to the movies cannot be done simultaneously.
9. To accept a proposal assumes that one can act on that acceptance.
10. *B*'s statement implies that *B* could not sincerely accept *A*'s proposal.
11. Therefore, *B*'s reponse is rejection of *A*'s proposal.

In the course of this reasoning, *A* draws on knowledge of the world as well as on knowledge of English and of conversational conventions.

Note that this description assumes a sequential, multi-stage model of language comprehension. Whether or not people actually go through the successive steps implied by this account poses an important question for the experimental investigation of language understanding. As we shall see, this general question arises in several related problem areas, including indirect requests, idioms, metaphors, and irony. Indeed, the question arises for all language that is not literally intended. In general, the empirical evidence gathered to date argues against such sequential, multi-stage models, particularly when conventional usage is involved (see below). The case for nonconventional and complex literary usage has yet to be adequately studied.

## Indirect Speech Acts

The distinction between a sentence and the proposition it expresses may or may not entail successive stages of information processing, but it has generally been assumed that when a locution and its illocution are distinct, a multistage process is required for comprehension (Clark & Clark, 1977; Bach & Harnish, 1979). The direct sentence meaning (propositional content and direct illocutionary force) is constructed first. If that meaning cannot be accepted as the speaker's intended meaning, an alternative meaning is constructed in subsequent stages.

One version of an information processing model to interpret indirect speech acts was proposed by Clark and Lucy (1975):

First, the listener derives and represents the literal interpretation of the sentence. Second, he then tests this interpretation against the context to see whether it is plausible or not. If it seems appropriate to the context, then it is taken to be the intended meaning. If, however, it does not seem appropriate to the context, either because it contradicts some obvious fact or because it violates a rule of conversation, it is rejected as the intended interpretation. Third, in the case of such a rejection, the literal interpretation is combined with an appropriate rule of conversation and this leads, by deduction, to the appropriate intended meaning. (p. 58)

Clark and Lucy's analysis leads to the following predictions: (1) direct meanings are always and unconditionally constructed; (2) indirect meanings are optionally constructed—if the direct meaning makes sense, indirect meanings are not apprehended; (3) indirect meanings must always take longer to apprehend because they are constructed only after a direct meaning has been constructed and tested.

Clark and Lucy (1975) showed people a series of printed sentences, each sentence accompanied by a picture. Subjects were told that each sentence was to be taken as a request; they were to decide from the picture whether the request had been granted. For example, if *Please color the circle blue* is accompanied by a blue circle, the response should be "Yes," otherwise, "No."

The sentence *Must you color the circle blue?* was interpreted as a request not to color the circle blue: subjects responded "No" when that sentence appeared with a blue circle and "Yes" when it appeared with a red circle. In such cases, illocutionary force was said to be correctly inferred. Response latencies were consistent with this conclusion. Latencies for affirmative sentences, like *Color the circle blue*, were shorter when accompanied by a blue circle than when accompanied by a red circle; the reverse was true for negative sentences, like *Don't color the circle blue*. Sentences like *Must you color the circle blue*, whose direct meaning is affirmative but whose indirect meaning is negative, followed the same pattern of latencies as negative sentences. This result is consistent with the assumption that intended meaning, rather than literal meaning, is encoded and represented in memory.

As expected, indirect requests in Clark and Lucy's experiment took longer than direct requests, but that can be attributed to such factors as sentence length or the familiarity of the expressions used. The claim that direct meanings are always constructed first was not definitively tested.

Evidence that indirect requests need not take longer to understand comes from Gibbs (1979),

who also measured the time required to comprehend direct and indirect requests. However, Gibbs measured the latencies under two conditions: with and without a plausible context. Gibb's subjects read short passages, one sentence at a time. Sentence presentation was controlled by the subject, who pressed a key to see each new sentence. The time between presses was taken as an estimate of the time needed to comprehend each sentence. In a passage about opening a window, for example, some subjects might see a direct request, *Do not open the window*, others an indirect request, *Must you open the window*, after which a paraphrase of the request was presented to test understanding. When no supporting context was provided, Gibbs confirmed Clark and Lucy's observation that direct requests are understood more quickly. But when a plausible context was provided for indirect requests, they took no longer to understand than did the direct requests. Gibbs concluded that "people comprehend indirect requests directly without first analyzing the literal interpretation of the utterance" (p. 9).

If this conclusion is correct, literal interpretations of indirect requests would seem to be ignored in plausible contexts. Clark (1979) tested this possibility by analyzing responses to various forms of indirect request. Merchants were called by telephone and asked such questions as *Could you tell me what time you close tonight?* or *Would you mind telling me what time you close tonight?* Although the literal meanings of the two sentences are different, their indirect meanings are identical. If the literal meaning of such indirect requests is ignored, both should elicit the same replies. Clark found differences, however. Of 30 merchants asked *Could you tell me*, 29 responded with only the information about closing time. Only 21 of 30 merchants did this when asked *Would you mind telling me*; the others made some reply to the literal question, such as *Not at all*.

Clark concluded that, except for clichés and familiar idioms, people routinely construct both direct and indirect interpretations of requests, and both interpretations may be responded to explicitly. Several factors determine a hearer's estimate of how seriously the speaker intends the direct intepretation. When the direct meaning might be intended, the probability of a hearer responding to it is fairly high. One way to signal such an intention is by using a nonconventional form, as in *Are you able to tell me*. When this is done, hearers tend to take the direct meaning seriously, and there is a good chance that they will respond overtly to that interpretation by prefacing their reply with *Of course*.

Clark and Schunk (1980) obtained further evidence that both direct and indirect interpretations are constructed by asking subjects to rate the politeness of different types of responses to indirect requests. From their analysis of these ratings, Clark and Schunk concluded that the more attentive a listener is to all of the requester's meanings, the more polite the response is. Since people can deliberately vary the politeness of their responses, they must routinely construct both the literal and the indirect meanings of indirect requests.

These findings suggest a parallel rather than a serial model of speech comprehension. Available evidence on the comprehension of indirect speech acts supports the following tentative conclusions: (1) Indirect requests can be understood with minimal context; (2) Indirect requests can be understood as quickly as direct requests when set in a plausible context; (3) Both direct and indirect interpretations are registered, and each is responded to as a function of how important the hearer judges each to be.

## Figurative Language

Indirect requests are but one way to mean *q* while saying *p*. If both the literal and intended meanings of indirect requests are normally registered by hearers, perhaps both meanings are registered for other types of indirections as well. The most obvious example is figurative language.

### Irony

Irony illustrates the indirection of figurative language in an acute form. How does a hearer decide that a person means the opposite of what he or she has said? How can *p* implicate *not p*? Grice (1975) suggested that his notion of conversational implicatures could be extended to explain such cases.

A Gricean account might run as follows: When Mary, whom John knows to be a feminist, says *Politics are too complicated for women to understand*, John knows that she does not believe the literal interpretation of her assertion. Is Mary lying? No, Mary realizes that John knows she does not believe that, so she is not

trying to deceive him. She has deliberately flouted the conversational maxim to be truthful. John therefore infers that Mary is trying to communicate some proposition other than the one that is expressed by the sentence she uttered. It should be a related proposition; one obviously related proposition is the contradiction of what she actually said. Therefore, John substitutes this implicature for the proposition that Mary had actually expressed.

If this hypothetical reconstruction of the listener's thought processes is correct, he or she first registers the literal sense, finds it unsuitable, then constructs a figurative interpretation and substitutes it for the literal interpretation. This is, of course, directly analogous to the three-stage model for understanding indirect requests that was proposed by Clark and Lucy (1975). This model does not seem to hold for indirect requests, and is probably inadequate for irony as well. Unfortunately, empirical evidence on this particular issue is lacking, so this hypothesis cannot be unequivocally rejected. However, we can question the assumption that comprehension of irony can be explained solely on pragmatic grounds.

As Sperber and Wilson (1981b) pointed out, violation of the maxim to be truthful is neither necessary nor sufficient for an ironical interpretation; many false sentences are not ironic, and such examples as *It seems to be raining*, when uttered in a wry tone by someone caught in a heavy downpour, are ironic without being false. Sperber and Wilson suggest an alternative account for irony that draws on the important distinction between *use* and *mention*, rather than the distinction between literal and figurative uses of language.

For example, the sentence *Signal before turning left* can be used to instruct a novice in the rule of the road, but it is only mentioned in the statement *"Signal before turning left" is in the legal code of this State*. The distinction is of semantic importance because the truth value of a mentioned expression is irrelevant to the truth of the proposition that mentions it: *He said, "Snow is green"* could be true even though the mentioned sentence is clearly false.

Sperber and Wilson (1981b) suggest that irony should be regarded as an instance of echoic mention, rather than use. In the example above, Mary mentions the opinion, accepted as a norm by many men (and perhaps by John), that only men can understand politics; as she echoes this norm, she also expresses her own opinion in a way that would otherwise be difficult to capture in propositional form. Thus, John must recognize not that Mary's statement violates the maxim of truth, but that it is an instance of mention plus an expression of disdain. According to this account, there is no figurative proposition that a listener must substitute for the literal proposition. Rather, the listener is reminded echoically of some familiar proposition (whose truth value is irrelevant) and an attitude toward it is expressed. In Searle's terminology (1979a), irony is an expressive, not an assertive speech act.

Sperber and Wilson argue that their account of irony, which combines the semantic distinction between use and mention with the pragmatic notion of conventional implicature, has several advantages over an exclusively pragmatic explanation. Since nothing need be substituted for the proposition that is mentioned, the speaker's reason for uttering falsehoods is not so enigmatic as it seems under Grice's account. A wider range of ironic statements, including cases that are not literally false, can be explained. In addition, the similarities between irony and parody are more easily understood. The ironic tone of voice, for which Grice offers no explanation, can be seen as expressing the speaker's attitude toward the echoically mentioned proposition. Irony is asymmetrical (*How clever* can express *How stupid*, but not the other way round) because success is the conventional norm and, in an imperfect world, it is always possible to make ironic mention of a norm. Irony is often aimed at a particular victim, the natural target being the originators, real or imagined, of the utterance or opinion being echoed.

A theory of irony emphasizing the pragmatic distinction between literal and figurative uses of language makes different predictions from those of a theory emphasizing the semantic distinction between use and mention; but these differences have not been experimentally tested. Experimentation has focused instead on a less restricted aspect of the Gricean theory. As outlined, Grice's pragmatic account makes two psychological claims about the comprehension, not just of irony, but of figurative language generally: (1) both a literal and a figurative meaning are registered, and (2) the literal meaning is registered first. Experimental evidence

(still to be discussed) supports (1), but not (2). According to Sperber and Wilson, the interpretation of ironic utterances depends on a different double recognition: (1') that the utterance is a case of echoic mention, not use, and (2') that the speaker holds a particular attitude toward the proposition mentioned. Since no sequential order of these two processes is implied, the experimental evidence is generally consistent with Sperber and Wilson's theory. However, Sperber and Wilson (1981b) develop their theory for the special case of irony, whereas the experimental evidence comes from psycholinguistic studies of idioms and simple metaphors (Gibbs, 1980; Glucksberg, Gildea, & Bookin, 1982).

### Idioms

Idiomatic expressions are ambiguous. For example, *kick the bucket* has (1) a literal interpretation that can be constructed in the usual way from the conventional senses of "kick" and "bucket," and (2) an idiomatic interpretation, "die," that cannot be inferred from the meanings of the constituent words. How does a hearer decide which interpretation the speaker intended?

In one view, called the Idiom List Hypothesis (Swinney & Cutler, 1979), a literal analysis is always attempted on a word string before the idiom mode of processing is undertaken. Only when the result of literal analysis is absurd or otherwise unsuitable does the hearer consult a special list of idioms. This, again, is directly analogous to Clark and Lucy's (1975) model for understanding indirect requests. Bobrow and Bell (1973) found that by giving people different perceptual sets they could influence which meaning of an idiom was seen first. They concluded that there are two distinct processing modes, literal and idiomatic, which presumably draw on different stores of semantic information. Ordinarily the literal mode is tried before the idiomatic mode, but that order can change under special circumstances.

It is extremely unparsimonious, however, and therefore unlikely, that we have a special memory store for idioms. More likely, the meanings of idioms are not inferred but simply learned, much as the meanings of words are learned. If an idiom is an expression whose meaning is not a compositional function of its parts, then single words are the simplest examples of idioms (Fraser, 1970). Of course, all idioms must be ambiguous (or polysemous); single words need not be (but usually are).

If the meanings of *pass the buck, break the ice, beat around the bush*, and other idioms are learned as single words are learned, then they should be stored in lexical memory as single words are stored. For example, along with lexical information about the words *break, breakfast,* and *breakneck* would be lexical information about the idioms *break the ice, break bread,* and *break on the wheel*. According to this view, called the Lexical Representation Hypothesis (Swinney & Cutler, 1979), idiomatic and literal meanings are computed simultaneously, much as for lexical ambiguities (Foss & Jenkins, 1973; Lackner & Garrett, 1972).

Swinney and Cutler (1979) asked subjects whether particular three-word strings were acceptable English phrases. Idioms such as *on the wagon* and *cut it out* were judged acceptable more quickly than were comparable literal phrases such as *on the train* and *try it out*. Thus, a phrase with two meanings (literal and idiomatic) can be recognized as acceptable faster than a phrase that has only one. Since words with two meanings are also recognized as words more quickly than are words with one meaning (Rubenstein, Garfield, & Millikan, 1970; Rubenstein, Lewis, & Rubenstein, 1971), these results are consistent with the Lexical Representation Hypothesis.

Ortony, Schallert, Reynolds, and Antos (1978) had subjects read idiomatic expressions in two contexts, one consistent with the idiomatic meaning and the other consistent with the literal meaning; subjects pressed a key as soon as they comprehended the target phrase. Comprehension time was shorter when familiar idiomatic expressions were used idiomatically than when they were used literally. Gibbs (1980) confirmed this result, and showed that the time required to evaluate a paraphrase was also shorter when the target was used idiomatically than when it was used literally. Such results are incompatible with the Idiom List Hypothesis.

Available evidence thus indicates that familiar idioms behave much as do individual lexical items, at least with respect to how their several meanings are retrieved and with respect to the effects of context (Swinney, 1979). Therefore, a distinction between two kinds of meaning, lexical and idiomatic, seems unnecessary—as superfluous as a distinction between the kind of meaning in *breakfast* and the kind in *break* and *fast*.

## Metaphors

Metaphors pose a critical problem for psychological theories of semantic interpretation (Verbrugge & McCarrell, 1977). Like idioms, metaphors are ambiguous. Interpreted literally, they are false or nonsensical; interpreted figuratively, they express a resemblance or analogy. For example, a literal interpretation of the nominal metaphor *All men are children* yields a category error; the figurative interpretation is a simile, "All men are like children," i.e., male adults resemble children in some respects. A metaphor invites the listener or reader to compare the tenor or topic of the metaphor ("men," in this example) with the vehicle of the metaphor ("children"). This account is known as the Comparison Theory of metaphor.

Although traditional, the Comparison Theory is not universally accepted. Richards (1936), who proposed *tenor* and *vehicle* as the two terms of a metaphor, noted that interesting metaphors involve more than a comparison. In the predicative metaphor, *The rich must perform leisure*, for example, something more is involved than a comparison of wealthy leisure with the performance of duties. Richards spoke of a tension between the tenor and the vehicle that was resolved by a complex interaction of both meanings. This Interaction Theory of metaphor is elaborated by Black (1962, 1979), Wheelright (1962), and others.

Although nominal metaphors can usually be recast as similes by paraphrasing them with a copula of similitude (Miller, 1979), not all treatments of similitude are similes. *An escalator is like a stairway*, for instance, is a literal similitude, not a simile; deleting "like" does not yield a metaphor. Ortony (1979) has suggested tests to distinguish literal from figurative similitude. For example, the phrase "metaphorically speaking" is not felicitous before sentences expressing literal similitude—*Metaphorically speaking, an escalator is like a stairway* is odd; but the phrase is acceptable before true similes—*Metaphorically speaking, education is like a stairway*.

Moreover, literal similitudes are generally reversible—*North Korea is like China* and *China is like North Korea* are both acceptable, although the first is more natural (Tversky, 1977); but similes undergo radical changes in meaning when the order of terms is reversed—*Billboards are like warts* says something very different from *Warts are like billboards* (Ortony, 1979). Such examples have led to the speculation that it is the most salient or typical properties of the vehicle that are integrated with the meaning of the topic.

Thus, to say that a metaphor is an abbreviated simile simply moves the problem of defining metaphoricity from metaphors to similes. It does not explain the difference between literal and figurative similarity.

Some metaphors derive from statements of analogy. *The eagle is a lion among birds*, for example, can be understood as an abbreviated form of the analogy that eagles are to birds as lions are to mammals (Sternberg, Tourangeau, & Nigro, 1979; Touraneau & Steinberg, 1981). Analogic metaphors are intelligible to the extent that the implicit analogy holds, which in turn depends on the similarity relations among the terms of the analogy. Analogies involve two levels of similarity relations. In the example, the relations of eagles to other birds and of lions to

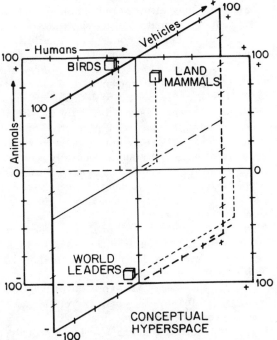

Figure 6.1. Within- and between-domain relations. From "Aptness in Metaphor" by R. Tourangeau and R.J. Sternberg, 1981, *Cognitive Psychology*, *13*, p. 32. Copyright 1981 by Academic Press. Reprinted by permission.

other mammals are intradomain similarities; the relation between these two domains, birds and mammals, is an interdomain factor. The general claim is that any concepts can be linked in an analogic metaphor, but the link will be comprehensible only if topics and vehicles occupy similar positions within their domains, and it will be interesting only if those domains are reasonably distant from one another.

Tourangeau and Sternberg obtained ratings of within-domain and between-domain distances, then correlated those ratings with judgments of metaphor goodness and aptness (See Figure 6.1). Intradomain correspondence was related to judged goodness (comprehensibility), but between-domain distance was not related to judged aptness (interest) in any simple way. This latter result is not surprising. After all, it is relatively easy to find examples of apt analogic metaphors that involve within-domain analogies, such as *Reagan may be the Hoover of the 1980's*; *The Citroen is the Cadillac of French cars*.

Similar results were obtained by Malgady and Johnson (1976), who based their argument on shared semantic features rather than semantic distances. When college undergraduates serve as judges, the goodness of a metaphor is positively correlated with the similarity of the topic and vehicle (Johnson & Malgady, 1979). It is surprising that goodness and similarity are linearly related; as Aristotle said in *The Poetics*, metaphors can be obscure or they can be dull; the terms must be related, but not too obviously or closely, lest the resemblance be banal. An adequate formalization of this observation would be an important advance.

How do listeners decide that an utterance is intended metaphorically? One view is that people first derive a literal meaning and, if it is "defective" (Searle, 1979b), an alternative, figurative interpretation is sought. This view—analogous to the already discussed views of indirect speech acts, idioms, and irony—has two major psychological implications. First, metaphors should require more time and cognitive effort to understand than should comparable literal sentences. Second, figurative meanings can be ignored when a literal interpretation is plausible in context.

With respect to the first hypothesis, Ortony, Schallert, Reynolds, and Antos (1978) found that metaphors do take longer to understand than do literal statements, but only when the context is minimal. When adequate textual context is available, metaphors and literal sentences are understood equally quickly, reminiscent of Gibbs' (1979) results for indirect requests.

With respect to the second hypothesis, Glucksberg, Gildea, and Bookin (1982) had people make rapid decisions about the literal truth of sentences of the form *Some X are Y*. When the sentence allowed a metaphorical interpretation, as in *Some jobs are jails*, it was correctly judged to be false, but the availability of a true metaphorical meaning produced interference that led to longer response latencies. So, with respect to this second hypothesis, people do not ignore figurative meanings, even in the impoverished context of a sentence verification experiment.

Poetic metaphors are often novel and striking, but many metaphorical expressions from everyday speech can be seen as variations on a stock of conventional vehicles (Lakoff & Johnson, 1980). In our culture, for example, argument is war (both are won or lost, involve strategy; weak points are attacked and defended); time is money (both are bought, spent, saved, borrowed, or wasted); happy is up (spirits are up, high, boosted, lifted vs. down, low, depressed, sunk), and so on. Lakoff and Johnson argue—somewhat speculatively, to be sure—that much of a person's conceptual system is organized by a limited number of such metaphors which are picked up uncritically in the process of acquiring the language. If such habits of thought are indeed deeply ingrained, it might explain why it is difficult to ignore the figurative meanings of metaphorical expressions.

Theories of metaphor interpretation have received far more attention than have theories of metaphor production. Why do people say one thing when they mean another? Indirect requests may serve important functions by providing options for both speaker and hearer that direct requests or imperatives do not. But metaphors do not seem to perform such interpersonal functions. Why, then, are they preferred when literal language might serve as well?

Two positions can be contrasted. At one extreme, metaphors are considered vague and misleading, to be avoided at all costs (Millar, 1976). At the other extreme, metaphors are said to be the only means available to express important, novel ideas (Black, 1979; Kuhn, 1970; Lackoff & Johnson, 1980). The first view is surely wrong; if a metaphor is an obscure way to say something that could be said clearly in a literal form, then it should be possible to find literal paraphrases for all metaphors. The general consensus, however, is that a literal paraphrase inevitably says too much, with the wrong emphasis: "it fails to be a translation because it fails to give the insight that the metaphor did" (Black, 1962, p. 46). The second view is more plausible, but fails to account for the frequent use of figurative language when literal language would have been perfectly adequate, at least for communicating simple propositional content.

Perhaps people use metaphor when more than simple propositional content is intended or required. Metaphor may be used when feelings or attributes about that content must be communicated, as in Gloria Steinem's remark that *A woman without a man is like a fish without a bicycle*. This simile surely expresses more than that women do not need men. It simultaneously expresses that idea *and* the speaker's attitude toward it.

Speakers may also use metaphor to pack a great deal of information into a short utterance, as when an unfamiliar concept is described in terms of a familiar concept. To say that *The atom is a miniature solar system* expresses an analogy between two concepts. A speaker or writer can use this method to describe complex relations if it can be assumed that the hearer or reader knows the essential properties of the vehicle (the solar system, in this case), and also knows that such expressions generally refer to relations among components, not to adventitious properties of the components themselves. In the atom-solar system analogy, it is the relation between a center and the various particles (planets) which orbit around that center that are important. The center of the atom need not be hot and bright as the sun for the analogy to be informative (Gentner, 1983).

Used in these ways—to express attitudes and feelings, or to express complex relations by analogy—metaphors can provide an efficient way to transmit multiple messages simultaneously. To express a metaphor's multiple messages in literal form might require far more time and effort than if the metaphor were to be used in the first place.

# DEIXIS

## Contexts of Use

An important part of pragmatic theory relates to terms that cannot be interpreted outside their contexts of use. As already noted, sentences such as *She is here* will express different propositions on different occasions of use, depending on who *she* is, and where and when the sentence is uttered. Such words are used to point to what the speaker is talking about, and they can point to different things on different occasions.

Terms that depend on contextual knowledge for their interpretation are called deictic, following Bühler (1934), or indexical, following Peirce (1932). Like variables in mathematical expressions, they can take different values in different applications. They are usually divided into three types:

1. Deixis of person: the interpretation of personal pronouns—*I, you, she, we*—depends on knowing who the speaker and listeners are, and that, in turn, depends on the context of use.
2. Deixis of place: the interpretation of demonstrative pronouns—*here, there, these, those*, often accompanied by an ostensive gesture —depends on knowing the speaker's location and orientation.
3. Deixis of time: tense markers and certain temporal adverbials—*how, then, soon, yesterday*—mark time relative to the moment of utterance. A listener must know the time of utterance, which is still another aspect of the context of use.

*She is here* involves all three: *she* (accompanied by a gesture) illustrates deixis of person; *here* illustrates deixis of place; the present tense of *is* illustrates deixis of time.

Contextual dependence in English is not restricted to these particular groups of terms, however. The verbs *come* and *go*, for example, incorporate deixis of place. Such spatial terms as *top, front, left* and *right* sometimes involve deixis of place and sometimes do not: the top of a table remains the top even when the table is upside down, whereas the particular side of a rock that is its top depends on the rock's orientation at the time of utterance. (English deixis has

been discussed by Miller & Johnson-Laird, 1976, and Lyons, 1977.)

When deictic expressions are quoted indirectly, they must be adjusted to fit the new context of use. For example, if John says *I am stupid* and Mary reports this remark to a third party, she will not say *He said I am stupid*.

Is some similar adjustment required in remembering deictic utterances? Or must all deictic expressions be replaced in memory by nondeictic propositions? Kaplan (1977) raises this question and considers the example of a woman kidnapped and locked in the trunk of a car; she has no way to know her spatial or temporal coordinates, hence no way to determine the correct nondeictic translation of such thoughts as *It's quiet here today*. Since the woman would presumably be able to remember her thoughts, her memory of them could hardly be propositional. On the other hand, studies of memory for gist (Fillenbaum, 1966; Sachs, 1967) make it seem unlikely that memory respects the exact linguistic form (with or without deictic adjustments). Miller (1982) argues from such examples that memories are neither linguistic nor propositional objects of thought, but rather are selectively incomplete mental presentations of the situation or event to which the deictic terms pointed.

The pragmatic phenomenon of deixis has interested students of cognitive development (Clark, 1973; Harris & Strommen, 1979), perhaps because ostensive reference is assumed to play such an important role in teaching children the names of concrete objects, but also because deictic terms are themselves interesting—they can hardly be learned in the same way as are words with fixed denotations.

Experimental psychologists have studied spatial and temporal aspects of experience (Howard & Templeton, 1966), but seldom with special attention to the language of space and time, either deictic or nondeictic. Thus, experimental studies of the psychology of deixis are still in an early stage. One line of research investigates the way speakers use deictic terms; another is concerned with the way listeners understand them.

## Production and Comprehension

A convenient way to obtain data about speakers' use of spatial deixis is to ask for directions to some location and to record and transcribe the answers. Such transcripts have been analyzed and found to be full of deictic devices (Klein, 1982; Wunderlich & Reinelt, 1982), although their analysis may shed more light on a speaker's knowledge of the environment than on any cognitive strategies that might determine deictic usage.

Alternatively, people can be asked to describe from memory some familiar scene or area. Linde and Labov (1975) asked apartment dwellers in New York City, *Could you tell me the layout of your apartment?* The order in which respondents named rooms was quite systematic. Subjects began at the outside entrance and moved room by room through the apartment. At branching points they selected one branch, described it, then jumped back to the last room with an unselected branch. In a real tour of an apartment, of course, one would reach the end of a complex branch, turn around, and move back to the branching point, in which case the deictic terms *left* and *right* would be reversed. In descriptions, this reversal of orientation never occurred. Linde and Labov also note that rooms were divided into major and minor: major rooms may be introduced with definite articles (*the dining room, the bedroom*), minor rooms are not (*a closet, a bathroom*); major rooms may be introduced as subject noun phrases, minor rooms only in complement phrases.

Ullmer-Ehrich (1982) asked people to describe their living rooms from memory, and found that they typically made a "gaze tour." In their imaginations they positioned themselves at the door and moved along the walls, describing pieces of furniture one by one, in order. It was not unusual for a subject to forget to mention furniture in the middle of the room.

These methods have the character of natural experiments; the data are objective, but respondents do not feel like subjects in a psycholinguistic experiment. Levelt (1982) sacrificed this naturalness in order to gain experimental control over the structures that speakers would describe. Levelt asked people to describe drawings of networks in which different colored nodes were connected by lines and the starting node was specified. The complexity of the networks varied, including linear strings of nodes, hierarchical arrangements, and networks containing loops. The subject was to devise a strategy for mapping a two-dimensional network into the unidimensional flow of speech, a linearization

task that was not easy with the hierarchical networks and was especially difficult for networks containing loops. Levelt's subjects fell into two groups. The majority consistently followed the strategy observed by Linde and Labov. They described a path to its end, then jumped back to a choice point and described another path, continuing in this manner until all paths originating at the choice point had been described. A substantial minority, however, would describe a path to its end, then move back along that same path to the choice point before describing a second path. Moving back over these network drawings did not require a left-right reversal. Here, as in more naturalistic situations, the deictic constructions that a speaker used depended on the linearization strategy that was chosen.

In general, a listener's understanding of deictic terms is easier to study experimentally than is a speaker's use of them, since the psycholinguist can control both the situation being described and the expression used to describe it. However, while there has been some interest in spatial and temporal language (e.g., Clark & Chase, 1972; Glushko & Cooper, 1978), little experimentation has focused on the interpretation of deictic terms by adults.

## DENOTATION AND SENSE

When words are used to indicate what a speaker is talking about, both words and speaker participate, but in different ways. In these cases we can say that speakers *refer* and words *denote*. Some authors use these terms interchangeably, but in this chapter *denotation* is the semantic relation between words and things, whereas *reference* is the speech act of using words to identify things. The distinction is part of the larger distinction between semantics and pragmatics.

The utility of a distinction between denotation and reference becomes apparent when a word is used to identify or refer to something that it does not name, that is, something outside its range of denotation. For example, given an appropriate context, a human being may be referred to as a ham sandwich, such as in a restaurant where the bartender asks a waiter, *What's the ham sandwich drinking?* (Nunberg, 1978). A person cannot, however, be named *the ham sandwich*. If no distinction were drawn between denotation and reference, the denotative range of every world would become both vast and uncertain—people who order sandwiches would have to be included in the denotation of *sandwich*—with disastrous consequences for any theory of meaning. Denotation depends on the language; reference is utterance-dependent.

## Word Meanings

Since words in isolation are neither true or false, one might claim that they have no semantics, and that since a speaker's intentions cannot be inferred from unspoken words, pragmatic analysis is also inappropriate. However, a long tradition of lexical semantics assumes that words in isolation do have meanings, that those meanings can be captured by definitions, and that the lexical concepts so defined are basic building blocks from which all larger meaningful expressions are built. We shall follow this tradition. We shall assume that words denote—that they have meanings even in isolation—and that knowing those denotations is an essential part of knowing the language.

What linguistic knowledge is required in order to use a word appropriately and to understand it when it is used by others? A minimal catalogue (Miller, 1978a) would include the following:

1. Pronunciation, including phonology and morphology
2. Syntactic category, including major category (noun, verb, preposition, etc.) and subcategorization (syntactic contexts)
3. Meaning, including definition (the concept expressed, relation to other concepts) and selectional restrictions (semantic contexts)
4. Pragmatic constraints, including situational as well as discourse contexts

Denotative properties and relations, which are included in (3), permit but do not fully determine the use of words in referring to objects, situations, actions, or events. How a language user's knowledge of these denotative properties and relations should be characterized is a central question for any psychological theory of language. We shall approach it by considering how

a speaker makes use of such knowledge for communicative purposes.

The choice of a word to refer to an object involves at least two kinds of classificatory decisions: one pertaining to category membership, the other to level of specificity. The former corresponds to the horizontal structure of categories, the latter to their vertical structure (Rosch, 1973).

### Shared Names

Some words are more specific than others. A table, for example, shares the word *thing* with books, shadows, and mountains; it shares *furniture* with chairs, lamps, and beds; it shares *table* only with tables. The smaller the variety of objects that share a name, the more specific that name is.

Given the availability of words at different levels of specificity, how does a speaker choose the one to use? The choice is made on pragmatic grounds. A speaker could, for example, refer to a table as a *thing, object,* or *piece of furniture*, or could be more specific: *kitchen table* or *coffee table*. All are appropriate labels for tables.

The word that a speaker chooses to use in any given context should be at a level of specificity sufficiently informative to determine the intended object in that context, but not so informative as to be redundant (cf. Grice's maxims). For example, if only one table is visible, a speaker can say *Put it on the table*. Given two or more tables, a more specific term or definite description may be needed to indicate the intended table, such as *coffee table, the table under the window,* or *that table* (accompanied by an appropriate gesture). The level of specificity that is most often used to designate a given class of objects is referred to by Brown (1958) as the *level of usual utility*, a notion related to Rosch's concept of basic-level terms. (See Table 6.1).

According to Rosch, Mervis, Gray, Johnson, and Boyes-Braem (1976), *table* would be a basic-level term in English. Of all the words in the furniture domain that might apply to tables, *table* is the most generic word for which there are distinctive perceptual features and patterns of behavior. Nouns superordinate to basic-level terms have few, if any, criterial features; subordinate nouns have relatively few criterial features over and above the criterial features of the basic-level term. Basic-level terms are among the first nouns learned by children, and

**Table 6.1.  Some examples of superordinate, basic-level and subordinate terms used by Rosch et al. (1976)**

| Superordinate | Basic Level | Subordinates | |
|---|---|---|---|
| Musical Instrument | Guitar | Folk guitar | Classical guitar |
| | Piano | Grand piano | Upright piano |
| | Drum | Kettle drum | Bass drum |
| Fruit | Apple | Delicious apple | Mackintosh apple |
| | Peach | Freestone peach | Cling peach |
| | Grapes | Concord grapes | Green seedless grapes |
| Tool | Hammer | Ball-peen hammer | Claw hammer |
| | Saw | Hacksaw | Cross-cutting handsaw |
| | Screwdriver | Phillips screwdriver | Regular screwdriver |
| Clothing | Pants | Levis | Doublt-knit pants |
| | Socks | Knee socks | Ankle socks |
| | Shirt | Dress shirt | Knit shirt |
| Furniture | Table | Kitchen table | Dining room table |
| | Lamp | Floor lamp | Desk lamp |
| | Chair | Kitchen chair | Living-room chair |
| Vehicle | Car | Sports car | Four-door sedan |
| | Bus | City bus | Cross-country bus |
| | Truck | Pickup truck | Tractor-trailer truck |

*Note*. From "Basic Objects in Natural Categories" by E. Rosch, C.B. Mervis, W.D. Gray, D.M. Johnson, and P. Boyes-Braem, 1976, *Cognitive Psychology, 8*, p. 388. Copyright 1976 by Academic Press. Reprinted by permission.

they are also the responses given spontaneously by adults performing naming tasks. People generally use basic-level terms unless there are situational reasons for using words at a different level of generality or specificity.

The organization of terms as a function of level of specificity is so common that the semantic relations involved have been given distinguishing names. In a taxonomic system, for example, the more specific term is said to be a hyponym of the more generic term; *oak* is a hyponym of *tree*. Moreover, *maple* is also a hyponym of *tree*, and a coordinate of *oak*. The statement *An oak is a tree* is true by virtue of its meaning. The statement *A tree has a trunk* entails the statement *An oak has a trunk* by virtue of its meaning. *A talkative oak* illustrates semantic anomaly, *an oaken maple* illustrates semantic contradiction, and *an oaken oak* illustrates semantic redundancy.

The choice of category membership—for example, whether a given tree should be called an oak or a maple—is more central to semantics. What information do people use to determine the denotative range of a word, to determine those entities that a word can appropriately

label? This question is, of course, the familiar one of concept or category identification.

### Extension and Intension

The denotative range of a word is its extension: all and only the particular instances that the word can name. The extension of *sandwich*, for example, is all sandwiches, past, present, and future, and only those. In contrast, a word's intension is the knowledge required to determine its extension. Intension can be thought of as a classificatory procedure; the extension or denotative range of a word is the set of entities that passes the classificatory test.

Note that words having no extension are not meaningless. For example, although the extension of *unicorn* is an empty class, *unicorn* is not a meaningless word, because we know its intension. We have sufficient knowledge from pictures and descriptions to recognize unicorns if they did exist. The definition called for in (3) in Miller's catalogue above is the word's intension, not its extension.

The distinction between intension and extension underlies Frege's (1892) well-known distinction between *Sinn* and *Bedeutung*, which are translated here as *sense* and *denotation*, respectively. Frege's distinction is required because two terms can be used to refer to the same thing, yet not have the same sense.

For example, to the ancients, *Hesperus* (the evening star) and *Lucifer* (the morning star) had different senses, even though (unbeknownst to them) both denoted the same object, which we now call *Venus*. Although the extension of *Hesperus* and *Lucifer* was the same, their intensions differed.

A word's sense—the lexical concept that the word can be used to express—cannot be identified with its intension, however. As Putnam (1975) pointed out, one can understand the meaning of *This is gold* without knowing the intension of *gold* that is, without being able to specify the metallurgical tests that would be required to determine whether the particular object is in the extension of the term *gold*. If one holds firm to the idea that intension determines extension, then one must give up the idea that knowing the meaning of a word is the same as knowing its intension.

### Multiple Meanings

The discussion of denotation is further complicated by words that have more than one sense. The word *line*, for example, has one sense as a noun, as in *She drew a line on the page*, and another sense as a verb, as in *She lined the coat with silk*. Moreover, as a noun it has several distinct senses: *line of poetry, line of kings, life line, an actor's line*, and so on (Kelly & Stone, 1975; Macnamara, 1971).

Apparently it is not possible to say exactly how many senses any particular word has; the bigger the dictionary, the more it will distinguish. Caramazza and Grober (1976) argue that large dictionaries greatly overestimate the number of distinct senses for any word, illustrating their argument with a demonstration of how subjective scaling clustered 26 senses of *line* into five more generic senses.

For any given dictionary, however, the most frequently used words have, on the average, the longest lists of alternative senses (Zipf, 1945). The speaker's apparent favoritism for words with multiple meanings would seem to place an extra interpretive burden on the hearer, and the fact that this burden is borne so lightly has been the subject of much psycholinguistic experimentation.

Words with more than one sense are said to be ambiguous, though that term can be misleading. The practice of organizing lexical data alphabetically has the effect of bringing different senses together, thus highlighting the fact that different concepts are sometimes expressed by the same phonological shapes. In actual contexts of use, however, words with several senses are seldom ambiguous. A more neutral term for such words is *polysemous* (see below).

### Similar Meanings

In addition to words with more than one meaning, there are meanings with more than one word—in short, *synonyms*. If synonyms are defined as words that can be interchanged in any context without a change of meaning, then there are no synonyms in natural languages. Words do share some senses, however, and so may be interchangeable in some contexts. But even when senses differ, some are more alike than others.

Rubenstein and Goodenough (1965) asked people to rate pairs of nouns on a five-point scale for their degree of synonymy. In their sample, *midday* and *noon* were most synonymous, *sage* and *wizard* less so, *hill* and *woodland* only slightly, and *cord* and *smile* not at all. The capacity to judge such degrees of similarity in meaning has been exploited in various attempts to explore the structure of the mental lexicon.

Could such a scale be continued beyond zero, into negative degrees of synonymy? *Up* and *down, good* and *bad, open* and *close, friend* and *enemy* are antonyms, words with senses that are directly opposed. Yet antonyms are similar to each other in many respects. For example, *sister* and *brother* both denote persons born of the same parents as someone else; their only difference is sex. Scales of semantic similarity and scales of the synonym-antonym contrast are not equivalent.

Discussions of the particular respects in which meanings are similar or different often assume that consistent aspects or dimensions of meaning can be identified. This assumption also underlies the construction of definitions. For example, *sister* and *female person having the same parent as another* are closely synonymous; the second can be taken as a definition of the first. The definition uses *female* and *person*, and therefore these concepts can be considered components of the concept expressed by *sister*. Such analysis is called *semantic decomposition*. How lexical meanings should be decomposed, if indeed they should be decomposed at all, has been a topic for extensive debate.

### Semantic Fields

Many linguists and psycholinguists share the belief that words are organized in semantic fields, although they differ on precisely how semantic fields should be defined (R.L. Miller, 1968).

Accoding to Trier (1934), different languages divide reality among their words in different ways. Moreover, each word's meaning depends on the meanings of other words in the language (the "field property"). Words are mapped into *conceptual fields*; words that are mapped into related concepts form a *lexical field*. Taken together, a lexical field and its corresponding conceptual field constitute a *semantic field*. A conceptual field can be inferred only from the corresponding lexical field; concepts identified in this manner can be called lexical concepts. This theory of semantic fields has led some linguists to undertake scrupulous intuitive analyses of the meaning relations among groups of conceptually related words (Weisgerber, 1962).

Hoermann (1979) has criticized such attempts to describe semantic fields intuitively, and called for more objective approaches. Fortunately, several objective approaches are available, partly as a consequence of psycholinguists' efforts to characterize the information people must have in their mental lexicons.

## Relations Among Concepts

In 1879, Galton introduced the technique of word association. Subsequently, a variety of ways to explore and describe relations among word meanings have been developed, particularly since 1960. These include associative relations among words (Deese, 1965; Szalay & Deese, 1978); associative-semantic networks (Anderson, 1976; Collins & Loftus, 1975; Norman & Rumelhart, 1975); semantic markers (Katz & Fodor, 1963); and spatial-geometric characterizations, usually involving multidimensional scaling (Fillenbaum & Rapaport, 1971) or factor-analytic techniques (Osgood, Succi, & Tannenbaum, 1957). Much of this work is better discussed under the broad heading of semantic memory. The discussion

here is limited to a brief catalogue of these approaches in the context of people's knowledge of relations among word meanings.

### Word Associations

The notion that ideas are associated in various ways has been central to both philosophical and psychological theories of the mind. Some aspects of associative structures can be inferred from the associations people give to words denoting various ideas (Cramer, 1968; Creelman, 1966; Deese, 1965).

In the simplest form of word-association procedure, subjects are instructed to respond to each word with the first word it makes them think of. Their responses can be used to support inferences about both the content and organization of lexical memory. Early applications of the technique were to clinical rather than to semantic issues: Jung (1918) used it to facilitate psychiatric diagnosis, and the first extensive and systematic word-association norms (Kent & Rosanoff, 1910) were collected specifically for psychiatric purposes.

The following are word-association phenomena that reflect some important aspects of the mental lexicon (Miller, 1978b). When familiar words are used as stimuli, different people tend to give the same response to a given probe word (Cattell & Bryant, 1889; Deese, 1965). People also tend to respond with words that are more frequently used in the language (Dauber, 1911; Palermo & Jenkins, 1964). These facts suggest that the content and organization of individual mental lexicons is fairly uniform among adults, and that word frequency is one determinant of word accessibility. Marbe's law—that common word associations tend to occur more quickly than uncommon ones—is one reflection of this important relation between frequency and accessibility (Thumb & Marbe, 1901).

For adults, responses usually come from the same semantic field as the probe word, and for commonly used words are often of the same grammatical form class as the probe: nouns tend to be given in response to noun probes, adjectives to adjectives, and, to a somewhat lesser extent, verbs to verbs (Deese, 1962; Fillenbaum & Jones, 1965; Palermo, 1963). Such responses are called paradigmatic. Young children, in contrast, generally show less commonality and fewer paradigmatic responses than do adults (Entwisle, Forsyth, & Muuss, 1964; Ervin, 1961). Such

Cohen, L.J. (1971). Some remarks on Grice's views about the logical particles in natural language. In Y. Bar-Hillel (Ed.), *Pragmatics of Natural Languages*. New York: Humanities Press.

Cole, R.A. & Perfetti, C.A. (1980). Listening for mispronunciations in a children's story: The use of context by children and adults. *Journal of Verbal Learning and Verbal Behavior, 19*, 297–315.

Collins, A.M. & Quillian, M.R. (1969). Retrieval time from semantic memory. *Journal of Verbal Learning and Verbal Behavior, 8*, 240–247.

Collins, A.M. & Loftus, E.F. (1975). A spreading-activation theory of semantic processing. *Psychological Review, 82*, 407–428.

Conrad, C.E.H. (1972). Cognitive economy in semantic memory. *Journal of Experimental Psychology, 92*, 149–154.

Conrad, C.E.H. (1974). Context effects in sentence comprehension: A study of the subjective lexicon. *Memory and Cognition, 2*, 130–138.

Craik, K. (1943). *The Nature of Explanation*. Cambridge: Cambridge University Press.

Cramer, P. (1968). *Word Associations*. New York: Academic Press.

Creelman, M.B. (1966). *The Experimental Investigation of Meaning: A Review of the Literature*. New York: Springer.

Cushing, S. (1982). *Quantifier Meanings: A Study in the Dimensions of Semantic Competence*. Amsterdam: North-Holland.

Dauber, J. (1971). Uber bevorzugte Assoziationen und verwandte Phanomene. [Concerning favored associations and related phenomena]. *Zeitschrift fur Psychologie, 59*, 176–222.

Deese, J. (1962). Form class and the determinants of association. *Journal of Verbal Learning and Verbal Behavior, 1*, 79–84.

Deese, J. (1965). *The Structure of Associations in Language and Thought*. Baltimore: Johns Hopkins Press.

DeValois, R.L. & Jacobs, G.H. (1968). Primate color vision. *Science, 162*, 533–540.

Entwisle, D.R. (1966). *Word Associations of Young Children*. Baltimore: The Johns Hopkins Press.

Entwisle, D.R., Forsyth, D.F., & Muuss, R. (1964). The syntagmatic-paradigmatic shift in children's word associations. *Journal of Verbal Learning and Verbal Behavior, 3*, 19–29.

Ervin, S.M. (1961). Changes with age in the verbal determinants of word associations. *American Journal of Psychology, 74*, 361–372.

Fahlman, S.E. (1979). *NETL: A System for Representing and Using Real-World Knowledge*. Cambridge, MA: MIT Press.

Fillenbaum, S. (1966). Memory for gist: Some relevant variables. *Language and Speech, 9*, 217–227.

Fillenbaum, S. (1971). On coping with ordered and unordered conjunctive sentences. *Journal of Experimental Psychology, 87*, 93–98.

Fillenbaum, S. (1974). *Or*, Some uses. *Journal of Experimental Psychology, 103*, 913–921.

Fillenbaum, S. (1975). *If*: Some uses. *Psychological Research, 37*, 245–260.

Fillenbaum, S. (1976). Inducements: On the phrasing and logic of conditional promises, threats, and warnings. *Psychological Research, 38*, 231–250.

Fillenbaum, S. (1977). Mind your *p*s and *q*s: The role of content and context in some uses of AND, OR, and IF. In G. Bower (Ed.), *The Psychology of Learning and Motivation, Vol. 11* (pp. 41–100). New York: Academic Press.

Fillenbaum, S. (1978). How to do some things with IF. In J.W. Cotton & R.L. Klatzky (Eds.), *Semantic Factors in Cognition* (pp. 169–174). Hillsdale: NJ: Erlbaum.

Fillenbaum, S. & Jones, L.V. (1965). Grammatical contingencies in word association. *Journal of Verbal Learning and Verbal Behavior, 4*, 248–255.

Fillenbaum, S. & Rapoport, A. (1971). *Structures in the Subjective Lexicon*. New York: Academic Press.

Forster, K.I. (1979). Levels of processing and the structure of the language processor. In W.E. Cooper & E.C.T. Walker (Eds.), *Sentence Processing* (pp. 27–85). Hillsdale, NJ: Erlbaum.

Foss, D.J. (1970). Some effects of ambiguity upon sentence comprehension. *Journal of Verbal Learning and Verbal Behavior, 9*, 699–706.

Foss, D.J., Cirilo, R.K., & Blank, M.A. (1979). Semantic facilitation and lexical access during sentence comprehension: An investigation of individual differences. *Memory and Cognition, 7*, 346–353.

Foss, D.J. & Jenkins, C. (1973). Some effects of context on the comprehension of ambiguous sentences. *Journal of Verbal Learning and Verbal Behavior, 12*, 577–589.

Fraser, B. (1970). Idioms within a transformational grammar. *Foundations of Language, 6*, 22–42.

Frege, G. (1949). On sense and nominatum. Translation in H. Feigel & W. Sellars (Eds.), *Readings in Philosophical Analysis* (pp. 85–102). New York: Appleton, Century, Crofts. (Original work published 1892.)

Galton, F. (1879–80). Psychometric experiments. *Brain, 2*, 149–162.

Gentner, D. (1983). Structure-mapping: A theoretical framework for analogy. *Cognitive Science, 7*, 155–170.

Gentzen, G. (1964). Investigations into logical deduction. *American Philosophical Quarterly, 1*, 288–306.

Gibbs, R.W. (1979). Contextual effects in understanding indirect requests. *Discourse Processes, 2*, 1–10.

Gibbs, R.W. (1980). Spilling the beans on understanding and memory for idioms in conversation. *Memory and Cognition, 8*, 149–156.

Glass, A.L. & Holyoak, K.J. (1974–75). Alternative conceptions of semantic memory. *Cognition, 3/4*, 313–339.

Glucksberg, S., Gildea, P., & Bookin, H.B. (1982). On understanding nonliteral speech: Can people ignore metaphors? *Journal of Verbal Learning and Verbal Behavior, 21*, 85–98.

Glucksberg, S., Kreuz, R.J., & Rho, S.H. (1986). Context can constrain lexical access: Implications for models of language comprehension. *Journal of Experimental Psychology: Learning, Memory and Cognition. 12*, 323–335.

Glucksberg, S., Trabasso, T., & Wald, J. (1973). Linguistic structure and mental operations. *Cognitive Psychology, 5*, 338–370.

Glushko, R.J. & Cooper, L.A. (1978). Spatial comprehension and comparison processes in verification tasks. *Cognitive Psychology, 10*, 391–421.

Gough, P.B. (1965). Grammatical transformations and speed of understanding. *Journal of Verbal Learning and Verbal Behavior, 4*, 107–111.

Gough, P.B. (1966). The verification of sentences: The effects of delay of evidence and sentence length. *Journal of Verbal Learning and Verbal Behavior, 5*, 492–496.

Grice, H.P. (1975). Logic and conversation. In D. Davidson & G. Harman (Eds.), *The Logic of Grammar* (pp. 64–75). Encino, CA: Dickenson.

Harris, L.J. & Strommen, E.A. (1979). The development of understanding of the spatial terms *front* and *back*. In H.W. Reese & L.P. Lipsitt (Eds.), *Advances in Child Development and Behavior, Vol. 14*. New York: Academic Press.

Hasher, L. & Zacks, R.T. (1979). Automatic and effortful processes in memory. *Journal of Experimental Psychology: General, 108*, 356–388.

Haviland, S.E. & Clark, H.H. (1974). What's new? Acquiring information as a process in comprehension. *Journal of Verbal Learning and Verbal Behavior, 13*, 512–521.

Heider, E.R. (1972). Universals in color naming and memory. *Journal of Experimental Psychology, 93*, 10–20.

Heider, E.R. & Olivier, D.C. (1972). The structure of the color space in naming and memory for two languages. *Cognitive Psychology, 3*, 337–354.

Henley, N.M. (1969). A psychological study of the semantics of animal terms. *Journal of Verbal Learning and Verbal Behavior, 8*, 176–184.

Hersh, H.M. & Caramazza, A. (1976). A fuzzy set approach to modifiers and vagueness in natural language. *Journal of Experimental Psychology: General, 105*, 254–276.

Hoermann, H. (1979). *Psycholinguistics: An Introduction to Research and Theory* (2nd ed.). Berlin: Springer-Verlag.

Hogaboam, T.W. & Perfetti, C.A. (1975). Lexical ambiguity and sentence comprehension. *Journal of Verbal Learning and Verbal Behavior, 14*, 265–274.

Hollan, J.D. (1975). Features and semantic memory: Set-theoretic or network model? *Psychological Review, 14*, 215–239.

Holmes, V.M., Arwas, R., & Garrett, M.F. (1977). Prior context and the perception of lexically ambiguous sentences. *Memory and Cognition, 5*, 103–110.

Hoosain, R. (1973). The processing of negation. *Journal of Verbal Learning and Verbal Behavior, 12*, 618–626.

Howard, I.P. & Templeton, W.B. (1966). *Human spatial orientation*. New York: Wiley.

Jameson, D. & Hurvich, L.M. (1959). Perceived color and its dependence on focal, surrounding, and preceding stimulus variables. *Journal of the Optical Society of America, 49*, 890–898.

Jastrzembski, J.E. (1981). Multiple meanings, number of related meanings, frequency of occurrence, and the lexicon. *Cognitive Psychology, 13*, 278–305.

Jastrzembski, J.E. & Stanners, R.F. (1975). Multiple word meanings and lexical search speed. *Journal of Verbal Learning and Verbal Behavior, 14*, 534–537.

Johnson, M.G. & Malgady, R.G. (1979). Some cognitive aspects of figurative language: Association and metaphor. *Journal of Psycholinguistic Research, 8*, 249–265.

Johnson, S.C. (1967). Hierarchical clustering schemes. *Psychometrika, 32*, 241–254.

Johnson-Laird, P.N. (1969a). On understanding logically complex sentences. *Quarterly Journal of Experimental Psychology, 21*, 1–13.

Johnson-Laird, P.N. (1969b). The interpretation of quantified sentences. In G.B. Flores D'Arcais & W.J.M. Levelt (Eds.), *Advances in Psycholinguistics* (pp. 347–372). Amsterdam: North-Holland.

Johnson-Laird, P.N. (1975). Models of deduction. In R.J. Falmagne (Ed.), *Reasoning: Representation and Process in Children and Adults* (pp. 7–54). Hillsdale, NJ: Erlbaum.

Johnson-Laird, P.N. (1983). *Mental Models: Towards a Cognitive Science of Language, Inference, and Consciousness*. Cambridge, MA: Harvard.

Johnson-Laird, P.N. & Tagart, J. (1969). How implication is understood. *American Journal of Psychology, 82*, 367–373.

Jung, C.G. (1918). *Studies in Word-Association*. London: Heinemann.

Just, M.A. (1974). Comprehending quantified sentences: The relation between sentence-picture and semantic memory verification. *Cognitive Psychology, 6,* 216–236.

Just, M.A. & Carpenter, P.A. (1971). Comprehension of negation with quantification. *Journal of Verbal Learning and Verbal Behavior, 10,* 244–253.

Kaplan, D. (1977, March). *Demonstratives: An essay on the semantics, logic, metaphysics, and epistemology of demonstratives and other indexicals.* Paper prepared for Symposium on Demonstratives at the meeting of the Pacific Division of the American Philosophical Association.

Katz, J.J. & Fodor, J.A. (1963). The structure of a semantic theory. *Language, 39,* 170–210.

Kelly, E. & Stone, P. (1975). *Computer Recognition of English Word Senses.* Amsterdam: North-Holland.

Kent, G.H. & Rosanoff, A.J. (1910). A study of association in insanity. *American Journal of Insanity, 67,* 37–96, 317–390.

Klein, W. (1982). Some aspects of route directions. In R. Jarvella & W. Klein (Eds.), *Speech, Place, and Action: Studies of Language in Context.* New York: Wiley.

Krauss, R.M. (1979). Communication models and communicative behavior. In R.L. Schiefelbusch & J.H. Hollis (Eds.), *Language Intervention from Ape to Child.* Baltimore: University Park Press.

Kruskal, J.B. (1964). Multidimensional scaling by optimizing goodness of fit to a nonmetric hypothesis. *Psychometrika, 29,* 1–27.

Kuhn, T.S. (1970). *The Structure of Scientific Revolutions* (2nd ed.). Chicago: University of Chicago Press.

Labov, W. (1973). The boundaries of words and their meanings. In C.-J.N. Bailey & R.W. Shuy (Eds.), *New Ways of Analyzing Variation in English, Vol. 1.* Washington: Georgetown University Press.

Lackner, J. & Garrett, M. (1972). Resolving ambiguity: Effect of biasing context on the unattended ear. *Cognition, 1,* 359–372.

Lakoff, G. & Johnson, M. (1980). *Metaphors We Live By.* Chicago: University of Chicago Press.

Lakoff, R. (1971). If's, and's, and but's about conjunction. In C.J. Fillmore & D.T. Langendoen (Eds.), *Studies in Linguistic Semantics* (pp. 114–149). New York: Holt, Rinehart & Winston.

Levelt, W.J.M. (1982). Linearization in describing spatial networks. In S. Peters & E. Saarinen (Eds.), *Processes, Beliefs, and Questions* (pp. 199–220). Dordrecht: D. Reidel.

Levelt, W. & Maasen, B. (1981). Lexical search and order of mention in sentence production. In W. Klein & W. Levelt (Eds.), *Crossing the Boundaries in Linguistics* (pp. 221–252). Dordrecht: D. Reidel.

Linde, C. & Labov, W. (1975). Spatial networks as a site for the study of language and thought. *Language, 51,* 924–939.

Lyons, J. (1977). *Semantics* (Vols 1–2). Cambridge, MA: Cambridge University Press.

MacKay, D.G. (1966). To end ambiguous sentences. *Perception and Psychophysics, 1,* 426–436.

Macnamara, J. (1971). Parsimony and the lexicon. *Language, 47,* 359–374.

Malgady, R.G. & Johnson, M.G. (1976). Modifiers in metaphors: Effects of constituent phrase similarity on the interpretation of figurative sentences. *Journal of Psycholinguistic Research, 5,* 43–52.

Marslen-Wilson, W.D. & Tyler, L.K. (1980). The temporal structure of spoken language understanding. *Cognition, 8,* 1–72.

Marslen-Wilson, W.D. & Welsh, A. (1978). Processing interactions and lexical access during word recognition in continuous speech. *Cognitive Psychology, 10,* 29–63.

McCloskey, M. & Glucksberg, S. (1979). Decision processes in verifying category membership statements: Implications for models of semantic memory. *Cognitive Psychology, 11,* 1–37.

McMahon, L.E. (1963). *Grammatical analysis as a part of understanding a sentence.* Unpublished doctoral dissertation, Harvard University, Cambridge, MA.

Mehler, J. (1963). Some effects of grammatical transformations on the recall of English sentences. *Journal of Verbal Learning and Verbal Behavior, 2,* 346–351.

Mehler, J. & Miller, G.A. (1964). Retroactive interference in the recall of simple sentences. *British Journal of Psychology, 55,* 295–301.

Mehler, J., Segui, J., & Carey, P. (1978). Tails of words: Monitoring ambiguity. *Journal of Verbal Learning and Verbal Behavior, 17,* 29–35.

Meyer, D.E. (1970). On the representation and retrieval of stored semantic information. *Cognitive Psychology, 1,* 242–300.

Meyer, D.E. & Schvaneveldt, R.W. (1971). Facilitation in recognizing pairs of words: Evidence of a dependence between retrieval operations. *Journal of Experimental Psychology, 90,* 227–234.

Millar, R.M. (1976). The dubious case for metaphors in educational writing. *Educational Theory, 26,* 174–181.

Miller, G.A. (1962). Some psychological studies of grammar. *American Psychologist, 17,* 748–762.

Miller, G.A. (1969). A psychological method to investigate verbal concepts. *Journal of Mathematical Psychology, 6,* 169–191.

Miller, G.A. (1978a). Semantic relations among words. In M. Halle, J. Bresnan, & G.A. Miller (Eds.), *Linguistic Theory and Psychological Reality* (pp. 60–118). Cambridge, MA: MIT Press.

Miller, G.A. (1978b). Lexical meaning. In J.F. Kavanagh & W. Strange (Eds.), *Speech and Language in the Laboratory, School and Clinic* (pp. 394–428). Cambridge, MA: MIT Press.

Miller, G.A. (1979). Images and models, similes and metaphors. In A. Ortony (Ed.), *Metaphor and Thought* (pp. 202–250). Cambridge, MA: Cambridge University Press.

Miller, G.A. (1982). Some problems in the theory of demonstrative reference. In R.J. Jarvella & W. Klein (Eds.), *Speech, Place, and Action: Studies of Language in Context* (pp. 61–72). New York: Wiley.

Miller, G.A. & Johnson-Laird, P.N. (1976). *Language and Perception*. Cambridge, MA: Harvard University Press.

Miller, R.L. (1968). *The Linguistic Relativity Principle and Humboldtian Ethnolinguistics*. The Hague: Mouton.

Morgan, J.L. (1975). Some interactions of syntax and pragmatics. In P. Cole & J.L. Morgan (Eds.), *Syntax and Semantics: Volume 3. Speech Acts* (pp. 289–303). New York: Academic Press.

Morris, C.W. (1938). *Foundations of the Theory of Signs*. Chicago: University of Chicago Press.

Newman, J.E. & Dell, G.S. (1978). The phonological nature of phoneme monitoring: A critique of some ambiguity studies. *Journal of Verbal Learning and Verbal Behavior, 17,* 359–374.

Norman, D.A. & Rumelhart, D.E. (1975). *Explorations in Cognition*. San Francisco: Freeman.

Nunberg, G.D. (1978). *The pragmatics of reference.* Doctoral dissertation, City University of New York. (Reproduced by the Indiana University Linguistics Club, 310 Lindley Hall, Bloomington, Indiana 47401, June 1978.)

Onifer, W. & Swinney, D.A. (1981). Accessing lexical ambiguities during sentence comprehension: Effects of frequency-of-meaning and contextual bias. *Memory and Cognition, 9,* 225–236.

Ortony, A. (1979). Beyond literal similarity. *Psychological Review, 86,* 161–180.

Ortony, A., Schallert, D.L., Reynolds, R.E., & Antos, S.J. (1978). Interpreting metaphors and idioms: Some effects of context upon comprehension. *Journal of Verbal Learning and Verbal Behavior, 17,* 465–477.

Osgood, C.E. (1980). *Lectures on Language Performance*. New York: Springer-Verlag.

Osgood, C.E. & Richards, M.M. (1973). From Yang and Yin to *and* or *but. Language, 49,* 380–412.

Osgood, C.E., Suci, J.G., & Tannenbaum, P.H. (1957). *The Measurement of Meaning*. Urbana, IL: University of Illinois Press.

Osherson, D.N. & Smith, E.E. (1981). On the adequacy of prototype theory as a theory of concepts. *Cognition, 9,* 35–58.

Palermo, D.S. (1963). Word associations and children's verbal behavior. In L.P. Lipsitt & C.C. Spiker (Eds.), *Advances in Child Development and Behavior, Vol. 1* (pp. 31–68). New York: Academic Press.

Palermo, D.S. & Jenkins, J.J. (1964). *Word Association Norms*. Minneapolis: University of Minnesota Press.

Peirce, C.S. (1932). *Collected Papers, Vol. 2.* Cambridge, MA: Harvard University Press.

Putnam, H. (1975). The meaning of 'meaning.' In K. Gunderson (Ed.), *Language, Mind, and Knowledge* (pp. 131–193). Minneapolis: University of Minnesota Press.

Quillian, M.R. (1967). Word concepts: A theory and simulation of some basic semantic capabilities. *Behavioral Science, 12,* 410–430.

Quillian, M.R. (1969). The teachable language comprehender. *Communications of the Association for Computing Machinery, 12,* 459–476.

Quine, W.V.O. (1941). *Elementary Logic*. Boston: Ginn.

Richards, I.A. (1936). *The Philosophy of Rhetoric.* Oxford: Oxford University Press.

Rips, L.J., Shoben, E.J., & Smith, E.E. (1973). Semantic distance and the verification of semantic relations. *Journal of Verbal Learning and Verbal Behavior, 12,* 1–20.

Rips, L.J., Smith, E.E., & Shoben, E.J. (1975). Set-theoretic and network models reconsidered: A comment on Hollan's "Features and semantic memory." *Psychological Review, 82,* 156–157.

Rips, L.J. & Stubbs, M.E. (1980). Genealogy and memory. *Journal of Verbal Learning and Verbal Behavior, 19,* 705–721.

Romney, A.K. & D'Andrade, R.G. (1964). Cognitive aspects of English kin terms. *American Anthropologist, 66* (no. 3, part 2), 146–170.

Rosch, E. (1973). On the internal structure of perceptual and semantic categories. In T.E. Moore (Ed.), *Cognitive Development and the Acquisition of Language* (pp. 111–144). New York: Academic Press.

Rosch, E. (1975). The nature of mental codes for color categories. *Journal of Experimental Psychology: Human Perception and Performance, 1,* 303–322.

Rosch, E. (1978). Principles of categorization. In E. Rosch & B.B. Lloyd (Eds.), *Cognition and Categorization* (pp. 27–48). Hillsdale, NJ: Erlbaum.

Rosch, E., Mervis, C.B., Gray, W.D., Johnson, D.M., & Boyes-Braem, P. (1978). Basic objects in natural categories. *Cognitive Psychology, 8,* 382–439.

Ross, J.R. (1967). *Constraints on variables in syntax.* Unpublished doctoral dissertation, Massachusetts Institute of Technology, Cambridge, MA.

Rubenstein, H., Garfield, L., & Millikan, J.A. (1970). Homographic entries in the internal lexicon. *Journal of Verbal Learning and Verbal Behavior, 9,* 487–494.

Rubenstein, H. & Goodenough, J.B. (1965). Contextual correlates of synonymy. *Communications of the ACM, 8,* 627–633.

Rubenstein, H., Lewis, S.S., & Rubenstein, M.A. (1971). Homographic entries in the internal lexicon: Effects of systematicity and relative frequency on meanings. *Journal of Verbal Learning and Verbal Behavior, 10,* 57–62.

Rumelhart, D.E. & Abrahamson, A.A. (1973). A model for analogical reasoning. *Cognitive Psychology, 5,* 1–28.

Sachs, J.S. (1967). Recognition memory for syntactic and semantic aspects of connected discourse. *Perception and Psychophysics, 2,* 437–442.

Sacks, H. (1972). On the analysability of stories by children. In J.J. Gumperz and D. Hymes (Eds.), *Directions in Sociolinguistics: The Ethnology of Communication* (pp. 329–345). New York: Holt, Rinehart & Winston.

Schmerling, S.F. (1975). Asymmetric conjunction and rules of conversation. In P. Cole & J.L. Morgan (Eds.), *Syntax and Semantics: Volume 3: Speech Acts* (pp. 211–231). New York: Academic Press.

Searle, J. (1969). *Speech Acts.* London: Cambridge University Press.

Searle, J. (1979a). *Expression and Meaning: Studies in the Theory of Speech Acts.* Cambridge, MA: Cambridge University Press.

Searle, J. (1979b). Metaphor. In A. Ortony (Ed.), *Metaphor and Thought* (pp. 92–125). Cambridge, MA: Cambridge University Press.

Seidenberg, M.S., Waters, G.S., Sanders, M., & Langer, P. (1984). Pre- and post-lexical loci of contextual effects on word recognition. *Memory and Cognition, 12,* 315–328.

Shepard, R.N. (1962). The analysis of proximities: Multidimensional scaling with an unknown distance function. *Psychometrika, 27,* 125–139, 219–246.

Sherman, M.A. (1976). Adjectival negation and the comprehension of multiply negated sentences. *Journal of Verbal Learning and Verbal Behavior, 15,* 143–157.

Simpson, G.B. (1981). Meaning dominance and semantic context in the processing of lexical ambiguity. *Journal of Verbal Learning and Verbal Behavior, 20,* 120–136.

Simpson, G.B. (1984). Lexical ambiguity and its role in models of word recognition. *Psychological Bulletin, 96,* 316–340.

Smith, E.E., Shoben, E.J., & Rips, L.J. (1974). Structure and process in semantic memory: A featural model for semantic decisions. *Psychological Review, 81,* 214–241.

Smith, E.E. (1978). Theories of semantic memory. In W.K. Estes (Ed.), *Handbook of Learning and Cognitive Processes, Vol. 6* (pp. 2–56). Hillsdale, NJ: Erlbaum.

Sperber, D. & Wilson, D. (1981a). Pragmatics. *Cognition, 10,* 281–286.

Sperber, D. & Wilson, D. (1981b). Irony and the use-mention distinction. In P. Cole (Ed.), *Radical Pragmatics* (pp. 295–318). New York: Academic Press.

Springston, F.J. & Clark, H.H. (1973). *And* and *or,* or the comprehension of pseudoimperatives. *Journal of Verbal Learning and Verbal Behavior, 12,* 258–272.

Sternberg, R.J., Tourangeau, R., & Nigro, G. (1979). Metaphor, induction, and social policy: The convergence of macroscopic and microscopic views. In A. Ortony (Ed.), *Metaphor and Thought* (pp. 325–353). Cambridge, MA: Cambridge University Press.

Sternheim, C.E. & Boynton, R.M. (1966). Uniqueness of perceived hues investigated with a continuous judgmental technique. *Journal of Experimental Psychology, 72,* 770–776.

Strawson, P.F. (1952). *Introduction to Logical Theory.* London: Methuen.

Swinney, D.A. (1979). Lexical access during sentence comprehension: (Re)consideration of context effects. *Journal of Verbal Learning and Verbal Behavior, 18,* 645–659.

Swinney, D.A. & Cutler, A. (1979) The access and processing of idiomatic expressions. *Journal of Verbal Learning and Verbal Behavior, 18,* 523–534.

Swinney, D.A. & Hakes, D. (1976). Effects of prior context upon lexical access during sentence comprehension. *Journal of Verbal Learning and Verbal Behavior, 15,* 681–689.

Swinney, D.A., Onifer, W., Prather, P., & Hirshkowitz, M. (1979). Semantic facilitation across sensory modalities in the processing of individual words and sentences. *Memory and Cognition, 7,* 159–165.

Szalay, L.B. & Deese, J. (1978). *Subjective Meaning and Culture: An Assessment Through Word Associations.* Hillsdale, NJ: Erlbaum.

Tannenhaus, M.K., Leiman, J.M., & Seidenberg, M.S. (1979). Evidence for multiple stages in the processing of ambiguous words in syntactic contexts. *Journal of Verbal Learning and Verbal Behavior, 18,* 427–440.

Taplin, J.E. Reasoning with conditional sentences. (1971). *Journal of Verbal Learning and Verbal Behavior, 10,* 219–225.

Thumb, A. & Marbe, K. (1901). *Experimentelle Untersuchingen uber die psychologischen Grundlagen der sprachlichen Analogiebildung.* Leipzig: Engelman.

Toglia, M.P. & Battig, W.F. (1978). *Handbook of Semantic Word Norms.* Hillsdale, NJ: Erlbaum.

Tourangeau, R. & Sternberg, R.J. (1981). Aptness in metaphor. *Cognitive Psychology, 13*, 27–55.

Trabasso, T., Rollins, H., & Shaughnessy, E. (1971). Storage and verification stages in processing concepts. *Cognitive Psychology, 2*, 239–289.

Trier, J. Das sprachliche Feld. (1934). *Neue Jahrbucher fur Wissenschaft und Jungenbilden, 10*, 428–449.

Tversky, A. (1977). Features of similarity. *Psychological Review, 84*, 327–352.

Ullmer-Ehrich, V. (1982). The structure of living space descriptions. In R.J. Jarvella & W. Klein (Eds.), *Speech, Place, and Action: Studies of Language in Context.* New York: Wiley.

Verbrugge, R.R. & McCarrell, N.S. (1977). Metaphoric comprehension: Studies in reminding and resembling. *Cognitive Psychology, 9*, 494–533.

Wallace, A.F.C. & Atkins, J. (1960). The meaning of kinship terms. *American Anthropologist, 62*, 58–79.

Wason, P.C. (1959). The processing of positive and negative information. *Quarterly Journal of Experimental Psychology, 11*, 92–107.

Wason, P.C. (1961). Response to negative and affirmative binary statements. *British Journal of Psychology, 52*, 133–142.

Wason, P.C. (1965). The contexts of plausible denial. *Journal of Verbal Learning and Verbal Behavior, 4*, 7–11.

Wason, P.C. & Johnson-Laird, P.N. (1972). *Psychology of Reasoning: Structure and Content.* London: Batsford.

Wason, P.C. & Jones, S. (1963). Negatives: Denotation and connotation. *British Journal of Psychology, 54*, 299–307.

Weisgerber, L. (1962). *Von den Kraften der deutschen Sprache, Vols 1–2.* Dusseldorf: Verlag Schwann.

Wexler, K.N. & Romney, A.K. (1972). Individual variations in cognitive structures. In A.K. Romney, R.N. Shepard, & S.B. Nerlove (Eds.), *Multidimensional Scaling, Vol. 2.* New York: Seminar Press.

Wheelwright, P.E. (1962). *Metaphor and Reality.* Bloomington: Indiana University Press.

Whorf, B.L. (1956). *Language, Thought, & Reality: Selected Writings of Benjamin Lee Whorf.* New York: Wiley.

Wilson, D. (1975). *Presuppositions and Non-truth-functional Semantics.* New York: Academic Press.

Wittgenstein, L. (1953). *Philosophical Investigations.* Oxford: Blackwell.

Wood, D. & Shotter, J. (1973). A preliminary study of distinctive features in problem solving. *Quarterly Journal of Experimental Psychology, 25*, 504–510.

Wunderlich, D. & Reinelt, R. (1982). Telling the way. In R.J. Jarvella & W. Klein (Eds.), *Speech, Place, and Action: Studies in Deixis and Related Topics* (pp. 183–201). New York: Wiley.

Zipf, G.K. (1945). The meaning-frequency relationship of words. *Journal of General Psychology, 33*, 251–256.

# Chapter 7

# HUMAN MOVEMENT CONTROL: COMPUTATION, REPRESENTATION, AND IMPLEMENTATION

**Richard W. Pew,** *Bolt Beranek and Newman Inc.*

**David A. Rosenbaum,** *University of Massachusetts*

## INTRODUCTION

The 1951 edition of *Steven's Handbook of Experimental Psychology* (1951) had four chapters devoted primarily or partially to the analysis of human movement control: T.C. Ruch's chapter on motor systems, G.A. Miller's chapter on

Preparation of this chapter began while the first author was on sabbatical leave from Bolt Beranek and Newman at Harvard University. BBN's financial support during the leave and the many kind services of Dr. David Green and Dr. Duncan Luce of Harvard's Department of Psychology and Social Relations are appreciated. The second author was supported by grants BNS-8408634 and BNS-8710933 from the National Science Foundation, by a Research Career Development Award from the National Institute of Neurological and Communicative Diseases and Stroke, and by the Massachusetts Institute of Technology Center for Cognitive Science under a grant from the A.P. Sloan Foundation's Particular Program in Cognitive Science during a sabbatical visit. The authors thank two anonymous reviewers for helpful comments, and Mrs. Mary Tiernan and Ms. Alysia Loberfeld for secretarial assistance.

speech and language, P.M. Fitts' chapter on engineering psychology and equipment design, and R.H. Seashore's chapter on work and motor performance. In reviewing these chapters nearly 35 years later, what most clearly distinguishes them from the chapter to be presented here was their emphasis on movement as *product* rather than on movement as *process*. Today, researchers concerned with movement control are more interested in understanding what goes on in the nervous system before, during, and after movements are performed than in classifying and measuring movement output and the variables that influence its success. The most fundamental question for modern investigators is what mechanisms and processes allow movements to be chosen and carried out. In the first edition of the *Handbook*, only Ruch's chapter, which was mainly concerned with motor physiology, provided a detailed discussion of the processes underlying movement control.

Movement scientists today are still concerned with the measurement issues that occupied workers of the previous era, but the advent of the computer has fostered a deeper appreciation of the computational foundations of behavior, as well as a greater conviction that the processes underlying behavior can be described in considerable detail. Indeed, a general approach to the study of behavior has emerged over the past two decades—the *information processing* approach—based on the general assumption that the workings of the nervous system can be meaningfully characterized in terms similar to those developed for computer programs. This perspective has had as much impact on movement science as on the other areas of experimental psychology.

For some people, the term information-processing psychology has come to be associated with a particular set of methodological and analytic tools identified with flowchart models and adherence to the notion that the nervous system is a digital, serial machine (see Lachman, Lachman, & Butterfield, 1979). But this view is really just a caricature of the information processing approach, more a description of the particular form that the approach has taken in some camps than a general description of the overarching thrust of the paradigm.

Marr (1982) offered a more sophisticated statement of the information processing view. He argued that analyzing an information processing system requires that its functions be understood at three explanatory levels. One, the *implementation* level, is concerned with the physical realization of the system, in this case, nerves, muscles, and joints. Another level is concerned with *representations* and *algorithms*. Representations are descriptions. They can be descriptions of perceptual events, remembered experiences, or intended actions. Algorithms are processes that create and transform such descriptions. Much of cognitive psychological research has been aimed at characterizing the representations underlying mental activity and the algorithms used in their formation and manipulation.

Marr's third level of explanation was still more abstract than the level of representations and algorithms. He called it the *computational* level. To illustrate this level of explanation, Marr mentioned an example relevant to this chapter—the analysis of bird flight. To understand how birds fly, Marr argued, one could begin by carefully studying feathers or delving into the neural structures underlying wing fluttering. But if these analyses were pursued without first considering aerodynamics, one would literally not know what to look for; one would not know what problem the bird's flight system had evolved to solve, and so the mechanisms used to solve the problem might remain forever out of reach. Thus the aim of description at the computational level is to articulate what problem is to be solved by an information processing system, and what the logic of the solution should be.

Marr applied his three-tiered approach to vision, but it can be applied, in principle, to any information processing activity, including movement. In this chapter we wish to keep Marr's framework in mind as we review recent developments in motor control research. By continually recalling the three levels of explanation that Marr emphasized, we hope to sort out some of the major areas of discussion within movement research today. As with most areas of research in which fundamental issues are still being explored, the area of movement control is currently experiencing a division arising from contrasting points of view. On the one hand, there are those who are comfortable with traditional cognitive accounts of movement control. They posit detailed plans for forthcoming movements, along with memory modules and retrieval operations for the plans' implementation (see Magill, 1983; Schmidt, 1982a; Stelmach, 1978). Another group can be identified by its "synergetic" approach (see Kelso, Tuller, & Harris, 1983; Turvey, 1977). For these researchers, it is essential to base as many behavioral phenomena as possible on known physical principles, even if the principles are stated in abstract terms.

Our aim in this chapter is not to legislate between the synergeticists and cognitivists, for we believe that their approaches are not mutually exclusive. Instead, the two groups appear to be seeking different levels of explanation in Marr's sense. The synergeticists seem to be seeking computational explanations of movement control, or at least explanations grounded in computational formulations. Cognitivists, or more specifically, cognitive psychologists studying motor control, appear to be more concerned with the second of Marr's explanatory levels, the representational and algorithmic level. The implementation level has consistently been the focus of physiologists, although cognitivists and synergeticists have also drawn upon data from this level of analysis to evaluate and elaborate their own models.

## The Problems

We will bring up Marr's explanatory framework from time to time in this chapter, but the chapter will mainly be organized around three central problems in the study of human movement control: (1) the *variable control* problem, (2) the *perceptual-motor integration* problem, and (3) the *skill acquisition* problem.

### The Variable Control Problem
Whenever a movement is performed, a large number of variables must be regulated. Understanding how this happens is the *variable control* problem. Historically, the variable control problem has been broken into two parts. One, the *serial order* problem (Lashley, 1951), is concerned with the way in which the parts of movement sequences are ordered and timed.

Another part of the variable control problem, the *degrees-of-freedom* problem (Bernstein, 1967), is concerned with the means by which one selects among the many possible means of achieving the same motoric end. For example, you can point to the tip of your nose through a huge number of trajectories, the actual number of which is constrained only by the total degrees of freedom of the series of joints connecting the shoulder to the finger. The degrees of freedom problem is to determine how these degrees of freedom are controlled so that a particular trajectory is performed. Much of the work on the degrees-of-freedom problem has been aimed at discovering ways of simplifying the problem for the motor control system, that is, reducing the degrees of freedom that enter into the choice. A related question is how the motor system can exploit its degrees of freedom so that movement control has generative power, allowing one to write for the first time with one's toes or teeth, or permitting one to open a car door with arms filled with packages.

### The Perceptual-Motor Integration Problem
It is more a matter of convenience than reality to assume that there is a movement control system separate and apart from the systems controlling other information-processing functions.

The need to recognize integration of function is nowhere more apparent than in considering the links between movement and perception. Our movements are normally made in response to some sort of perceptual input, often where the input specifies a discrepancy between an intended and an actual movement (i.e., feedback). Some theorists have suggested that the formation of plans for movement relies on anticipations (usually unconscious) of desired perceptual changes (Greenwald, 1970). Relatively little work has been done on the computational underpinnings of perceptual-motor integration, though this form of integration is vitally important for effective interaction with the environment (but see Arbib, 1981). Much more work has been done, however, on the representation and implementation of the connections between perception and movement, for example, in the work on stimulus-response compatibility. Furthermore, as in the discussion of movement control per se, there has been considerable debate between the cognitivists and the synergeticists about the sorts of linkages that should be posited. For the synergeticists, who largely come from a Gibsonian tradition, the favored position is that there are direct mappings from perception to action (and vice versa). Cognitivists, on the other hand, have argued that there are intermediate representations, as well as corresponding memory stores. Evidence for the latter position has been discussed since the time of Helmholtz (1866/1962) and has been considered in connection with the notion of *corollary discharge* (Sperry, 1950) or *efference copy* (von Holst & Mittelstaedt, 1950). The need for elaborate perceptual-motor integration schemes, including the suggestion that there are models of forthcoming perceptual changes (*feedforward*), have also been recognized in the engineering community (see Arbib, 1972).

### The Skill Acquisition Problem
Mentioning feedforward and feedback leads to the third major problem in the study of human movement control—the problem of skill acquisition. Skill acquisition in the present context is defined as the modifiability of motor behavior through the formation of new movement capabilities, usually through concerted practice. Learning to play the piano is a familiar example. Two important ideas that have emerged in this area are reliance on feedback to develop internal models of desired perceptual changes (Adams,

1971) and the notion that motor skill acquisition relies on the formation of abstract schemas (Pew, 1974; Schmidt, 1975). Recently, the synergeticists have also considered skill acquisition. They have focused on the physical problems that are confronted, and ultimately solved, during the refinement of motor skills (Fowler & Turvey, 1978).

## Scope and Goals of the Chapter

In a chapter of this kind we cannot provide an exhaustive review of the literature on human movement performance. We can only give a sense of the issues that workers in this area are concerned about and the tools they are using to address them. Since this book is a handbook of *experimental* psychology, we will review in some detail a few influential experiments in the field of human movement control. In so doing, we will give short shrift to several areas of study that bear on the analysis of movement control but that fall outside the purview of traditional experimental psychology. Thus, we will largely ignore work in neuropsychology, robotics, neurophysiology, and biomechanics, even though developments in these areas have deepened our understanding of movement control.

## THE DEGREES OF FREEDOM PROBLEM

We turn first to the problem of regulating the degrees of freedom of movement. Consider the simple act of a boxer extending his fist to a target. How many routes can be followed to reach the target? The question can be answered by considering the number of dimensions of movement that can be achieved by all the joints linking the shoulder to the hand. The number of such dimensions corresponds to the degrees of freedom of the arm. There are three degrees of freedom at the shoulder joint: The upper arm can move to the left or right, up or down, and about its own axis of rotation. There is one degree of freedom at the elbow, which can only vary its degree of flexion or extension. The elbow's associated joint, the radio-ulnar joint, allows for movement in one dimension, rotation about the axis of the forearm, and so has only one degree of freedom. The wrist permits movement in two dimensions: the horizontal and the vertical. Thus, there are seven degrees of freedom altogether, which means that, if the punch were planned in "joint space", that is, with respect to the motions of the individual joints, seven degrees of freedom would have to be explicitly specified. (If we were to consider tasks requiring articulation of the fingers, the total degrees of freedom would, of course, be even greater.)

How else might the plan be formulated? What alternatives are there to joint-space planning? We can consider planning systems that are either more abstract or less abstract than planning in joint space. If the plan were more abstract, it could be formulated in terms of "hand" space, that is, with respect to the trajectory of the hand, or a single point on the hand, connecting the starting and ending locations. If the plan were less abstract, the contractions and relaxations of individual muscle groups could be represented, which, for the arm, entails at least 26 degrees of freedom. If the plan were even less abstract, the planned units would be individual motor units (i.e., motor neurons and the sets of muscle fibers they innervate), which number at least 2600 for the shoulder-hand system (Turvey, Fitch, & Tuller, 1982). We see that the degrees of freedom to be controlled depends on the abstractness of the plan doing the controlling. In considering the sort of plan that might be used, it is desirable to minimize the degrees of freedom that must be explicitly specified, that is, to maximize the plan's abstractness.

How can we empirically determine what sort of plan is used? One approach is to record limb trajectories. Morasso (1981) recorded trajectories of the arm during the simple task of pointing to a target with one hand in the horizontal plane. He discovered that the trajectories usually followed straight paths, an observation that was later corroborated by Abend, Bizzi, and Morasso (1982) and Hollerbach and Flash (1982). The significance of this result can be appreciated by considering Figure 7.1, which depicts the outcomes that would be expected if arm movements were planned in hand space or in joint space. If a straight line were produced in hand space (panel B), the graph relating the joint angle of the shoulder ($\theta_1$) to the joint angle of the elbow ($\theta_2$) at each point in time would be curved. Conversely, if a straight line were produced in joint space (panel A), the hand trajectory would be curved. Since a curved path is (apparently) more complicated than a straight

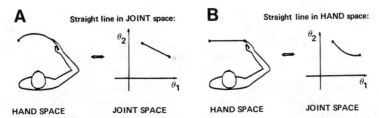

**Figure 7.1.** A: A diagram of a straight line movement in joint space and the corresponding path in hand space. B: A straight line movement in hand space and the corresponding path in joint space. ($\theta_1$ is the shoulder angle, and $\theta_2$ is the elbow angle.) From "Characterization of Joint-Interpolated Arm Movements" in *Experimental Brain Research Supplement* by J.M. Hollerbach and C.G. Atkinson, in press. New York: Springer-Verlag. Reprinted by permission.

path, the presence of a straight path in one space or the other can be taken to suggest which space is used for movement planning. Morasso concluded from the simplicity of the hand-space description and the complexity of the joint-space description that planning of hand movements is done in hand space.

An obvious difficulty with this claim is that people can draw curved lines. How can it be asserted that hand movements are planned in hand-space, when one of the main sources of evidence for this assertion—straight line paths in hand-space—is easily violated? The problem is compounded by the observation (Soechting & Lacquaniti, 1981) that there are lawful relationships between the elbow and shoulder joints during arm movements in a vertical plane. Based on the argument that simple relationships connote direct planning control, one could conclude from this observation that joint planning is also employed.

With respect to our ability to draw curved lines, Abend et al. (1982) observed that, when subjects are specifically asked to produce curved lines the lines they produce actually consist of straight-line segments, as defined by the velocity profiles. With respect to the findings concerning interrelationships between the joints, it should be noted that Soechting and Lacquaniti also found straight line trajectories of the hand; Hollerbach and Atkeson (1986) recently observed that the Soechting and Lacquaniti joint data (but not their straight-line hand data) can be shown to arise as simple consequences of kinematics. Thus, although the issue is still under discussion, it appears that planning of hand movements relies on hand space rather than joint space. From the point of view of minimizing

the degrees of freedom in the plan, this is clearly the preferable means of planning.

If the plan for an aimed hand movement used the coordinates of hand space, the problem still remains of how the plan is translated into movement. Ultimately, the joint angles needed to achieve the desired movement must be produced, the appropriate muscle groups must be activated, and within those muscle groups the necessary motor units must be turned on and off in the proper manner. Thus, having an abstract movement plan may minimize the complexity of the computations that enter into it, but without a clear understanding of how the abstract plan is physically realized, one may think that one has explained movement control while all that has actually been achieved is to demonstrate that physiologists have more work ahead of them than psychologists do.

There are two lines of research that have helped rescue motor psychologists from this dilemma. One is work on *synergies* and *coordinative structures*. The other is work pertaining to the *mass-spring* model of movement control. Each of these topics will now be discussed.

## Synergies and Coordinative Structures

One way of simplifying the degrees of freedom problem is to allow for dependencies between the components being controlled. For example, if two joints work interdependently, it may be possible to control the motion of both joints through instructions that specify fewer variables than would be required if each joint had to be controlled alone. Bernstein (1967) advocated this approach to the degrees of freedom problem, drawing attention to muscle *synergies* (see Lee, 1984, for review). More recently, Easton (1972) and Tuller, Turvey and Fitch (1982) focused on the closely related construct, the *coordinative structure*, which Tuller et al. defined as a "group of muscles often spanning several joints that is constrained to act as a single functional unit" (Tuller et al., 1982, p. 253).

Coordinative structures have been identified in a number of performance domains, ranging from breathing to catching baseballs. Initially, the main criterion for identifying coordinative structures was the observation of fairly consistent movement patterns, usually involving more than one limb or limb segment. Recently, workers in this area have adopted more stringent criteria, seeking evidence for task-dependent linkages between remote movement segments. For example, Kelso, Tuller, Vatikiotis-Bateson, and Fowler (1984) studied the control of speech for two simple utterances: "a /baeb/ again" and "a /baez/ again". Production of /b/ normally requires closure of the lips, while production

of /z/ normally requires bringing the tongue close to the palate or teeth. Kelso et al. asked what happens to production of the final /b/ in /baeb/ or the /z/ in /baez/ if the lower jaw is suddenly and unexpectedly tugged downward (with a torque motor) just prior to the initiation of lip or tongue closure. If speech production relies on coordinative structures, as would be expected given the large number of degrees of freedom to be controlled, the downward displacement of the lower lip caused by the perturbation should be immediately compensated for by lowering of the upper lip during the production of /b/. However, since such an outcome could merely reflect a simple physical linkage between the upper and lower jaws manifested at the lips, it would be important to demonstrate that upper lip compensation fails to occur during production of /z/ (i.e., where bilabial closure is not essential). The data supported this prediction (see Figure 7.2). Immediately after downward perturbation of the lower jaw and lip, the upper lip moved farther down than normal, but only

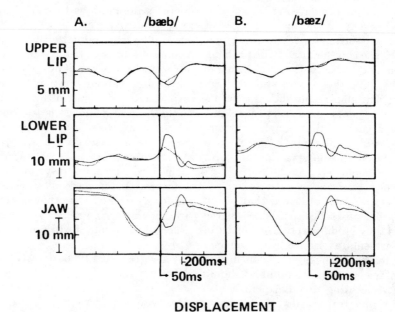

**DISPLACEMENT**

**Figure 7.2.** Upper lip, lower lip (with jaw movement contribution subtracted), and jaw displacement for the utterances /baeb/ and /baez/. (Each trace represents the average of 10 tokens for perturbed [solid line] and control [dotted line] conditions. The vertical line in each window marks the onset of torque to the jaw. In this case a torque of 5.88 N is applied for only 50 ms.) From "Functionally Specific Articulatory Cooperation Following Jaw Perturbations During Speech: Evidence for Coordinative Structures" by J.A.S. Kelso, B. Tuller, E. Vatikiotis-Bateson, and C.A. Fowler, 1984, *Journal of Experimental Psychology: Human Perception and Performance*, *10*, p. 822. Copyright 1984 by the American Psychological Association. Reprinted by permission of the author.

in the /b/ context. By contrast, when electromyographic (EMG) recordings were taken from the tongue, the EMG was amplified after perturbation but only in the /z/ context. These results provide support for task-dependent neuromotor linkages in the speech production system, as would be expected if there were coordinative structures for speech.

It is worth mentioning another example of a task-dependent alteration in performance evoked by an experimental perturbation. The example comes from a study of cat locomotion. Classical reflex theory suggests that a given stimulus will always produce a given response if mediated through a simple reflex arc. Forssberg, Grillner, and Rossignol (1975) tested this prediction by lightly touching the paw of the spinal cat (i.e., a cat whose brain and spinal cord were disconnected) at different phases of the gait cycle; the gait was driven with a treadmill over which the cat was suspended. Forssberg et al. found that the reaction to the stimulus depended on the phase during which the stimulus was applied. If the stimulus was applied during the flexion phase, as the cat removed its foot from the ground, the response was enhanced flexion, a reaction well suited to getting over obstacles. However, if the stimulus was applied during the stance phase, as the cat planted its foot on the ground, the reaction was enhanced extension, a response well suited to correcting a stumble; if the response had been added flexion at this point in the gait cycle the animal would normally fall over! This experiment shows that there are linkages within the cat spinal cord that promote adaptive responses to unexpected changes during locomotion. Since these contextually-based responses require the coordinated effort of large collections of muscles, the responses themselves can be taken to support the idea of coordinative structures.

Evidently, coordinative structures exist in systems as diverse as cat locomotion and human speech, which suggests that they constitute fundamentally important entities for motor control. The importance of coordinative structures presumably stems from the fact that they reduce the degrees of freedeom that the motor system must control.

## The Mass-Spring Model

While the coordinative structure approach to the solution of the degrees of freedom problem appeals to neural organization, the mass-spring model need not. The heart of the mass-spring model is related to the fact that muscles have properties similar to mechanical springs. Since there are well-known physical principles that apply to mechanical springs, these same principles may apply to muscles and may also simplify the way muscles are controlled. Before we turn to these principles, let us describe an experiment that seems to produce an impossible result. We will then show how the result can be explained by the spring-like properties of muscle.

Polit and Bizzi (1978) trained monkeys to point with one paw to any of several targets that could appear briefly in an otherwise dark room. The monkeys had no visual feedback about the position of the limb, nor did they have proprioceptive feedback, since the nerves providing such feedback were severed where they enter the back of the spinal cord. As seen in

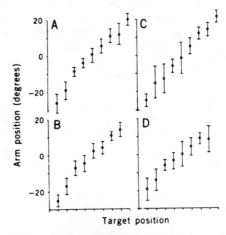

**Figure 7.3.** Means and standard deviations of final arm positions as a function of target position. Each point represents the average of 10 to 40 movements. Final arm positions recorded from (A) intact and (B) deafferented monkeys. (C and D) Final position reached by the arm in which initial position displaced in (C) intact and (D) deafferented animals. (Both movements toward and away from final position were computed.) The numbers on the ordinates represent arm position in degrees. The negative numbers represent flexion and the positive, extension with respect to a reference position (zero degree) that corresponds to an elbow angle of 90 degrees. Target positions are shown on the abscissa. Intertarget distance equals 5 degrees. From "Processes Controlling Arm Movements in Monkeys" by A. Polit and E. Bizzi, 1978, *Science, 201,* p. 1236. Copyright 1978 by AAAS. Reprinted by permission.

Figure 7.3 the monkeys were still able to point accurately to where the target appeared. In fact, they could also point to the target location when the limb was momentarily perturbed by a torque motor after the target light appeared but before the pointing movement began. Since the monkeys could not feel the perturbation, how could they compensate for it?

The answer lies in the mass-spring model of movement. Muscles contract and relax with measurable latencies, at limited rates, and produce limited forces. Limbs have mass and inertia and, as already suggested, the articulation of joints is restricted. It is possible to express quantitatively the contributions and interrelations among these elements using the language of biomechanics and kinematics. One can think of the neural commands of the muscles as a time-varying forcing function driving the movement of the limbs. According to the mass-spring model, instead of controlling the position of the hand or movement of joints per se, the neural commands provide the forcing function necessary to drive the muscles to a desired final state with respect to force balance and length.

Muscles have length-tension characteristics similar to springs. When a motor unit, the smallest element of a muscle that is independently innervated, is stimulated electrically, the unit produces a force tending to cause it to contract. If there is no load on the muscle, it will immediately contract, and the force will decrease to zero. If, on the other hand, both ends of the muscle are tied down, then the force will be maintained, at least until the energy supplied by the electrical signal is used up. The resting position of a pair of muscles occurs when the forces on them are in equilibrium. Thus, according to the mass-spring model, the tensions corresponding to a desired equilibrium point are set, and then these forces act over time until the new equilibrium point is reached. Any lags in the response are associated with inertia, damping, and friction resisting movement of the mass. Figure 7.4 shows the length-tension trade-off of a pair of agonist-antagonist muscles, illustrating this principle.

This behavior is analogous to that of a spring. If one pulls on a spring resting horizontally on a table with one end of the spring fixed, a force results that depends on how far the free end of the spring is displaced. If, on the other hand, there is a mass attached to the other end, an

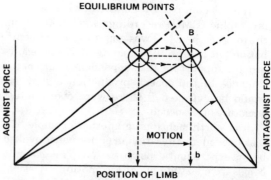

**Figure 7.4.** Graphical representation of the length-tension characteristics of an agonist-antagonist muscle pair. Suppose the two muscles are initially in equilibrium at point A. If the force on muscle 1 is increased or that on muscle 2 is decreased, then muscle 1 will stretch and muscle 2 will contract until the new equilibrium at point B is reached and movement from a to b is achieved. From "Feedback Control of Hand-Movement and Fitts' Law" by E.R.F.W. Crossman and P.J. Goodeve, 1983, *Quarterly Journal of Experimental Psychology, 35A,* p. 270. Copyright 1983 by the Experimental Psychology Society. Reprinted by permission.

initial force will be generated by the spring, but the force will return to zero over time as the mass moves in response to this force.

Now we are ready to use the mass-spring model to interpret the seemingly impossible result shown in Figure 7.3. Suppose the neural commands simply send signals to the muscles to tell them what tensions to set so that, when the dynamical result is played out through the limbs, the hand will end up in the correct final position. Under such a scheme, external forces applied to the limb would be irrelevant because the muscles are set to produce a final result regardless of what forces intervene, so long as those forces go away before the movement is completed. Proprioceptive feedback is unnecessary because the tension commands are programmed in advance of the actual movement.

There are, of course, problems with this model. Although it solves one degrees-of-freedom problem, that of describing the spatial trajectory of a movement and specifying which of a very large set will be followed, it creates a new degrees-of-freedom problem, namely, how does the system know what tensions to set for the infinite variety of possible movements that could be executed? It is clear that the concept of coordinative structures must operate here as well.

# THE SERIAL ORDER PROBLEM

Whereas discussion of the degrees-of-freedom problem has usually centered on "continuous" movements or single trajectories, the serial order problem has usually centered on series of discrete movements such as those involved in speech and keyboard performance. Two major theories have been discussed to explain how the elements of a movement sequence are ordered: *linear chain* theories and *hierarchical* theories. The distinction between these theories can be appreciated by considering two abstract types of elements: *movement* elements, whose activation leads directly to physical activity in the muscles, and *control* elements, whose activity can affect movement elements or other control elements (Rosenbaum, Kenny, & Derr, 1983). Linear chain theory holds that a given control element directly controls no more than one other control element. Hierarchical theory holds that a given control element can directly control more than one control element. (Both theories allow that a single control element can control more than one movement element to allow for coordinated activity in several muscles and to allow for simultaneous movements.)

Linear chain theory has usually been equated with the behavioristic notion of reflex chains. The idea is that sensory feedback from each element of a movement sequence defines and triggers the next element in the sequence. Given the abstract formulation of linear chain theory given above, however, it is unnecessary to restrict discussion of linear chain theory to this particular form of implementation. Indeed, as will be seen when we turn to the problem of timing, linear chain models have been discussed in a framework that makes no reference to peripheral feedback.

Evaluation of the reflex chain hypothesis has played an important role in the study of the serial order problem, and since this evidence bears indirectly on the status of linear chain theory, it is worth saying a little about it. A classic study in this area was done by Taub and Berman (1968), who studied the effect of unilateral cuts to the dorsal roots of the monkey spinal cord. The effect of these cuts was to eliminate sensory feedback from one arm; the question was whether the monkeys would be able to make skillful movements with the arm that could not be felt. The prediction of reflex chain theory was that skillful movements with the affected arm should cease, and, in fact, this is what Taub and Berman initially observed; the arm that could not be felt was hardly used at all. Taub and Berman then tried restraining the good arm. In a short period of time, they observed that the deafferented arm was used extensively, even when other sources of feedback, such as vision, were eliminated. Taub and Berman's results clearly demonstrate the importance of central control of movement in primates. The results also suggest that patients with unilateral neglect of one limb might be induced to revivify the neglected limb if the contralateral, working limb were restrained. Surprisingly, this simple idea has only recently, been applied in the clinic (Miller, 1985).

Scores of studies on feedback disruption have been performed on a wide range of animals, including man; extensive reviews of this work can be found in Evarts, Bizzi, Berke, DeLong, and Thach (1971) and Keele (1968). Although the exact effects of feedback depend on the species involved and the task being performed, it appears that, in the trained animal, feedback generally serves a tuning rather than a triggering function. That is, major movement elements generally do not seem to be turned on and off by the presence or absence of feedback, as classical reflex chain theory would predict. Instead, feedback permits fine adjustments in the shaping and timing of movement (see, for example, Grillner, 1985). There is an important exception to this general rule, however; if an organism is deprived of feedback during the early stages of motor skill learning, the skill may never develop properly.

## Evidence for Hierarchical Control

K.S. Lashley (1951) was one of the first to question whether serial chaining concepts were consistent with observed movement behavior. He introduced the phrase "the syntax of action," analogous to the syntax of language, to capture the sense in which he believed behavior is organized hierarchically. A recent experiment by Rosenbaum, Kenny, and Derr (1983) provided evidence for this type of organization. Subjects learned to produce simple sequences of finger taps such as IiIiMmMm, where I and i denote taps with the right and left index fingers, respectively, and M and m denote taps with the right and left middle fingers, respectively. The subject's

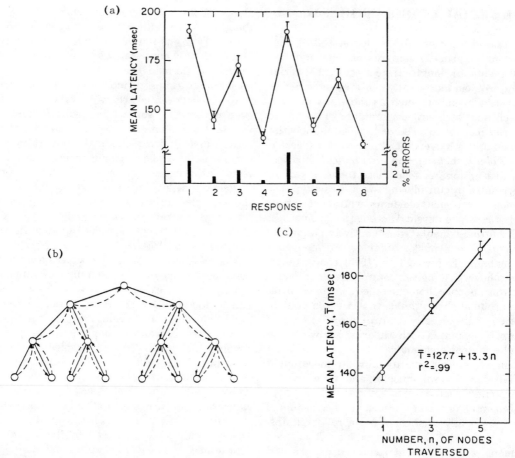

**Figure 7.5.** (a) Mean latencies of successive responses produced from memory in the experiment of Rosenbaum, Kenny, and Derr (1983); the mean latency of response 1 is the mean time to produce the first response after the eighth response. (b) Tree-traversal model. (c) Mean latency as a function of number of nodes to be traversed. From "Hierarchical Control of Rapid Movement Sequences" by D.A. Rosenbaum, S. Kenny, and M.A. Deer, 1983, *Journal of Experimental Psychology: Human Perception and Performance, 9*, pp. 88–100. Copyright 1983 by the American Psychological Association. Reprinted by permission.

task was to produce the learned sequence six times consecutively with the fingers resting on a button panel. Responses were to be produced as accurately and as quickly as possible, although simultaneous responses were prohibited (i.e., all interresponse times had to exceed 20 milliseconds). To free subjects from having to keep track of the number of completed renditions of the sequence, the computer that recorded the responses sounded a tone as soon as six renditions were done, and subjects were not penalized for making too may responses.

Sequences such as IiIiMmMm can be naturally organized in a hierarchical fashion, with two high-level groups (IiIi and MmMm), two

intermediate-level groups within each of those (Ii, Ii, Mm, and Mm), and, at the lowest level, two individual responses within each intermediate group. If hierarchical mechanisms are used to control serial order, sequences that are easily described in hierarchical terms should be controlled hierarchially. Indeed, as seen in Figure 7.5 the pattern of interresponse times was consistent with a hierarchical control hypothesis. Figure 7.5a shows that interresponse times depended on serial positions, such that responses 1 and 5 had the longest interresponse times, responses 3 and 7 had intermediate interresponse times, and responses 2, 4, 6, and 8 had the shortest interresponse times. These results are consistent with a hierarchical system, as seen in Figure 7.5b. Here it is assumed that each group of the hierarchy is fully decomposed into its constituents before any other groups are decomposed; the process can be depicted as a *tree-traversal* process. If it is assumed that a response is physically produced when its corresponding terminal node has been encountered and that each additional node traversal requires extra time, the time to produce response $i$ after response $i$-1 should increase with the number of nodes that must be traversed. In fact, as seen in Figure 7.5c, when the data of Figure 7.5a are replotted to evaluate this prediction, inter-response times are found to increase linearly with the number of nodes that must be traversed. Similar results have been obtained by Collard and Povel (1982), Povel (1982), and Schneider and Fisk (1983).

## Production of Response Bursts

Since the sequences used by Rosenbaum et al. (1983) were transparently hierarchical, the data from this study constitute relatively weak evidence for hierarchical control. Recently, it has been shown (Rosenbaum, 1985) that the tree-traversal model can also account for data

from an influential series of experiments by Sternberg, Monsell, Knoll, and Wright (1978). These investigators measured the timing of brief bursts of responses in typing and talking. In each trial, the subject memorized the responses to be produced (e.g., "one-two-three" in a talking experiment); then, after a series of warning signals, the subject was presented either with a "go" signal, which indicated that the responses were to be performed as quickly and as accurately as possible, or a "no-go" signal, which indicated that the responses were to be withheld. Of primary interest was the latency of the first response after the go signal, and the latencies of subsequent responses.

Figure 7.6 shows data from an experiment on talking. The latency of the first response increased linearly with the length of the sequence; the same result was obtained when subjects typed rather than talked, with number of forthcoming keystrokes being the main determinant of first response latency. Panel b of Figure 7.6 shows the second main result from these experiments. The time to complete the sequence, whether spoken or typed, increased quadratically with burst length, or, said differently, the mean time between responses increased with the length of the overall

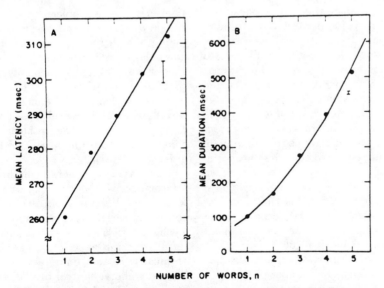

**Figure 7.6.** (a) Mean latency to say the first number in a list consisting of one to five numbers, with fitted linear function. (b) Mean duration of the entire list, with fitted quadratic function. From "The Latency and Duration of Rapid Movement Sequences: Comparisons of Speech and Typewriting" by S. Sternberg, S. Monsell, R.L. Knoll, and C.E. Wright, in *Information Processing in Motor Control and Learning* (p. 125), G.E. Stelmach (Ed.), 1978. New York: Academic Press. Copyright 1978 by Academic Press. Reprinted by permission.

sequence; Sternberg et al. (1978) found that the slope of the interresponse time function was often similar to the slope of the initial reaction time function. A third result, not shown in the figure, is that interresponse times were longer in the middle of the sequence than at the ends, although interresponse times increased with overall sequence length at all serial positions.

To account for these results, Sternberg et al. proposed that subjects prepare motor subprograms corresponding to the responses to be produced; but to produce a given response, its corresponding subprogram had to be retrieved from the prepared set. If the time to retrieve a subprogram grows with the number of subprograms in the prepared set, the time to produce a response should also increase with the number of possible responses. This model accounts for the fact that first response latencies and latencies of noninitial responses increased with sequence length. It does not uniquely predict the inverted U-shaped appearance of the serial position function, however.

The tree-traversal model described in the previous section can account for all of the three main results of Sternberg et al. (1978) (see Rosenbaum, 1985). Suppose that different hierarchical programs can be created for all the sequences of any given length. Suppose, in addition, that to produce the first response of a sequence with a given hierarchical program, control must pass from the top node of the hierarchy down to the leftmost terminal node; to produce the second response, control must pass to the next terminal node, and so on. If one considers all the binary hierarchies for sequences with two to six terminal nodes, and if one counts the number of nodes to be traversed to get from the top of the tree to the leftmost terminal node or each succeeding terminal node thereafter, the mean number of nodes for each response is as shown in Table 7.1. As the length of the sequence increases, the number of nodes that must be traversed to reach the leftmost terminal node (i.e., response 1) increases. Likewise, the mean number of nodes that must be traversed to produce noninitial responses (responses 2-$n$) also increases. Finally, the number of nodes to be traversed to reach terminal nodes at different serial positions increases as one shifts from the ends of the sequence toward the middle. Assuming that each extra node adds extra time, this model accounts for the additional finding

**Table 7.1. Mean number of steps predicted by the tree-traversal model for responses 1–6 in sequences of length 2–6\***

| Length | Response | | | | | | Mean (2–6) |
|--------|-----|-----|-----|-----|-----|-----|------------|
|        | 1   | 2   | 3   | 4   | 5   | 6   |            |
| 2      | 2.0 | 2.0 |     |     |     |     | 2.0        |
| 3      | 2.5 | 2.5 | 2.5 |     |     |     | 2.5        |
| 4      | 3.0 | 2.0 | 4.0 | 2.0 |     |     | 2.7        |
| 5      | 3.3 | 2.3 | 3.5 | 3.5 | 2.3 |     | 2.9        |
| 6      | 3.5 | 2.3 | 3.5 | 3.6 | 3.5 | 2.3 | 3.0        |

\*(Rosenbaum, 1985.)

from the Sternberg et al. studies that the number of higher-level units, notable stress groups in speech, rather than individual phonemes, predicts the rate at which response latencies depend on sequence length. The model's ability to account for all of these results suggests that the hierarchical processes and structures it assumes have considerable generality in movement control. Interestingly, the fact that hierarchical models have also been discussed in studies of recall of symbolic material (e.g., Johnson, 1970) suggests that similar mechanisms may be used for retrieving motoric and symbolic information.

## Control of Timing

The serial order problem, by definition, is concerned with ordinal information. The problem of timing, which revolves around the question of how delays of different length are placed between successive movement elements, is concerned with interval information. If a time interval between two movement elements is signed, the serial order of those elements is also given. Thus, a solution to the problem of timing may constitute a solution to the problem of serial order.

One way to determine whether serial order information is given by timing information is to ask whether the control of timing and the control of serial order are achieved by similar mechanisms. We saw in the last section that serial ordering appears to be controlled hierarchically. In the timing domain, the evidence for hierarchical control has been more elusive.

Wing and Kristofferson (1973) proposed an essentially linear model of timing control for tasks in which the subject tries to produce a sequence of equally-paced responses (i.e., tapping a key at a rate specified by a metronome). As

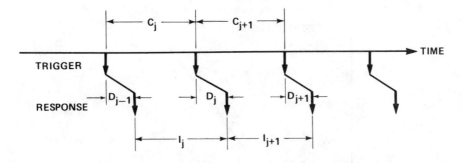

Key:

$C_j$  INTERVAL BETWEEN TIMEKEEPER TRIGGER PULSES

$D_j$  RESPONSE DELAY

$I_j$  INTERRESPONSE INTERVAL

**Figure 7.7.** Two-process model for the timing of repetitive discrete motor responses. From "Response Delays and the Timing of Discrete Motor Responses" by A.M. Wing and A.B. Kristofferson, 1973, *Perception and Psychophysics, 14*, p. 6. Copyright 1973 by the Psychonomic Society. Reprinted by permission.

shown in Figure 7.7 the Wing and Kristofferson model assumes a central time keeper that emits trigger pulses for predetermined responses, the production of those responses being subject to efferent delays. Wing and Kristofferson evaluated and elaborated this basic model with mathematical techniques that deserve careful study.

From Figure 7.7 it can be seen that a given interval $I_{j+1}$ between two observed responses $j$ and $j+1$ is

$$I_{j+1} = C_{j+1} + D_{j+1} - D_j,$$

from which it follows that, if by chance $D_j$ happens to lengthen, $I_j$ will lengthen, and $I_{j+1}$ will shorten. On the other hand, if $D_j$ happens to shorten, $I_j$ will shorten, and $I_{j+1}$ will lengthen. One therefore expects negative correlations between successive intervals, which is in fact what is observed, with the correlation usually occupying the range 0 to $-.5$.

Why does the negative correlation between successive intervals occupy this range? The answer can be found by allowing for the possibility that, just as efferent delays are subject to random variation, so too are intervals produced by the central timekeeper. Take the covariance of intervals $I_j$ and $I_{j-k}$,

$$cov(I_j, I_{j-k}) = cov((C_j + D_j - D_{j-1}),$$

$$(C_{j-k} + D_{j-k} - D_{j-k-1})),$$

and assume that successive timekeeper intervals and efferent delays are independent random variables. It can be shown that

$$cov(I_j, I_j) = var(I) = var(C) + 2var(D)$$

$$cov(I_j, I_{j-1}) = -var(D)$$

$$cov(I_j, I_{j-k}) = 0, \quad k > 1.$$

The correlation between intervals $I_j$ and $I_{j-1}$ can be rewritten

$$cor(I_j, I_{j-1}) = cov(I_j, I_{j-1})/var(I_j).$$

This follows from the fact that the covariance of $I_j$ and $I_{j-1}$ equals the correlation of $I_j$ and $I_{j-1}$ times the product of their standard deviations, which are assumed to be equal. Thus,

$$cor(I_j, I_{j-1}) = -1/(2 + var(C)/var(D)).$$

As var(C) gets larger and larger relative to var(D), $cor(I_j, I_{j-1})$ approaches zero, and as var(C) gets smaller and smaller relative to var(D), $cor(I_j, I_{j-1})$ approaches $-1/2$. Thus, the observed range of $cor(I_j, I_{j-1})$ is consistent with the assumptions of the model.

Other observations also support the model. For example, as seen above, nonconsecutive intervals (i.e., intervals that do not share a common response) are predicted to be uncorrelated, and they are. Further confirmation comes from the fact that, by rearranging terms, one can obtain expressions for the variance of the timekeeper delays and motor delays:

$$var(C) = var(I) + 2cov(I_j, I_{j-1}i)$$

$$var(D) = cov(I_j, I_{j-1}).$$

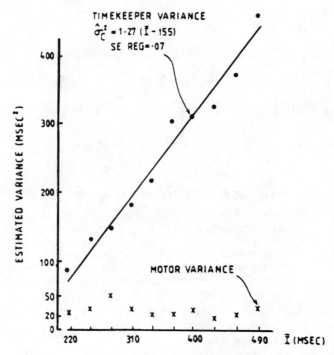

**Figure 7.8.** Estimated timekeeper and motor variance as a function of mean interresponse interval. From "The Long and Short of Timing in Response Sequences" by A. Wing in *Tutorials in Motor Behavior* p. 479), G.E. Stelmach, and J. Requin (Eds.), 1980. Amsterdam: North-Holland. Copyright 1980 by North-Holland Publishing Company. Reprinted by permission.

If lengthening the delay between two responses is achieved by letting the central timekeeper run longer, one would expect the estimate of var (C) to grow while the estimate of var (D) remains constant. As seen in Figure 7.8, this is exactly what happens. When subjects produce different mean interresponse intervals, var (D) remains roughly constant, but var (C) increases linearly, as would be expected if a central clock were ticking away, and the variance of the inter-tick intervals grew with the number of ticks that occurred (see Rosenbaum, 1983a, for further evidence). Finally, in a recent study aimed at evaluating the independence of timekeeper and motor delays, a patient with Parkinson's disease restricted almost entirely to one side of the brain was found to show considerably larger timekeeper variability for the affected hand than for the unaffected hand, while estimates of efferent delay variability were not much different for the two hands (Wing, Keele, & Margolin, 1984).

## Hierarchical Control of Timing

In view of the fact that the data just reviewed support the linear model of timing control proposed by Wing and Kristofferson (1973), the next question is whether evidence can be adduced for the hypothesis that timing is controlled hierarchically. Since the serial ordering of responses appears to be under hierarchical control, one might expect a similar style of control for timing.

In the studies of Wing and his colleagues, subjects were instructed to tap a key at a perfectly steady rate. This requirement may have led subjects to use a linear mode of timing control. Vorberg and Hambuch (1978) sought evidence for hierarchical control of timing by studying performance of grouped responses. As in the experiments of Wing and Kristofferson, subjects listened to a train of clicks and then produced responses in time with the clicks. In one condition, one response was to be performed for every click; in other conditions, two, three, or four successive responses were to be produced with each click. How might subjects control the timing of such groups of responses?

One possibility is that they use the linear timing system of Wing and Kristofferson, in which case correlations between consecutive intervals should always lie between 0 and $-.5$, correlations between nonconsecutive intervals should always be 0, and so on. Another possibility is that the subjects use a hierarchical timing system, where a control element that triggers a particular response, say the first response in a two-response group, also triggers two clocks—a clock that controls the delay until triggering of the first response of the next group, and a clock that controls the delay until triggering of the second response in the first group. One could imagine even more complicated timing systems for groups with more responses.

Determining whether a hierarchical timing system is used requires some fairly elaborate mathematical derivations that we shall avoid to save space. Suffice it to say that Vorberg and Hambuch (1978) did not obtain evidence for hierarchical timekeepers. To account for the appearance of higher-level groupings often found in studies of rhythmic performance, they proposed that timing and serial ordering rely on different mechanisms, the timing mechanism being linear and the serial ordering mechanism being hierarchical. According to Vorberg and Hambuch:

> Underlying rhythmic performance, there is a motor program by which appropriately ordered behavior is generated. The program contains both the information necessary to specify the identity of the individual movements and their succession as well as the relevant timing information. To account for the complexities of serial order, e.g., in music, the program's structure is likely to be hierarchic. However, when the program is executed, it ultimately has to be translated into a sequence of individual steps, the duration of which is controlled by the hypothetical timekeeper mechanisms after being supplied with the appropriate timing information. (1978, p. 553.)

More recently, Vorberg and Hambuch (1984) obtained evidence for hierarchical timekeeping when subjects performed sequences composed of unequal intervals (e.g., three quarter notes followed by a quarter rest). However, based on the fact that timing variability was considerably higher in these conditions than when subjects performed isochronous rhythms (sequences with equal intervals), Vorberg and Hambuch observed that serial timing structures have at least two advantages over hierarchical ones: (1) Hierarchically timed sequences are susceptible to scrambled response orders, which means that special control mechanisms must be called upon to minimize scrambling; (2) timing precision is compromised in hierarchical timing systems because of the long durations that must be controlled by high-level clocks.

The exact relation between timing and serial ordering is still under active discussion in the motor performance literature (e.g., Shaffer, 1976, 1982). An important development in this area has been the formulation of network models that posit activation and inhibition between movement elements, where the direction of activation and inhibition between elements dictates the order in which those elements are performed, and the laws governing which elements are mutually excitatory or inhibitory dictate which elements can be performed simultaneously (Meyer & Gordon, 1985; Rumelhart & Norman, 1982). How these sorts of models will be aligned with the models emerging from studies of rhythmic timing has yet to be determined.

## Timing of Well-Learned Movement Patterns

One area in which the relation between serial order and timing control has been studied in some detail is the timing of well-learned movement patterns. A seminal study in this area was performed by Armstrong (1970). He taught subjects to move a lever to the right and left so that the displacement and timing pattern matched a waveform presented periodically for memorization on a cathode ray tube. After subjects memorized the basic pattern, their performance exhibited an intriguing characteristic. When the duration of the entire pattern they produced was too short or too long, the intervals between each of the components of the pattern was also either too short or too long. It was as if the pattern that subjects generated could be stretched or shrunk on an elastic sheet.

Since Armstrong's initial observation of such time scaling effects, similar observations

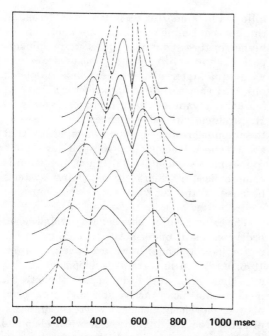

0    200    400    600    800    1000 msec

**Figure 7.9.** Tangential velocity profiles of the pen during handwriting. The subject was instructed to produce the same letter repeatedly at constant size while systematically changing the writing speed. The vertical lines show the temporal correspondence of common features even though the overall time scale changes from pattern to pattern. From "Space-Time Invariance in Learned Motor Skills' by P. Viviani and C. Terzuolo in *Tutorials in Motor Behavior* (p. 529), G.E. Stelmach and J. Requin (Eds.), 1980. Amsterdam: North-Holland. Copyright 1980 by North-Holland Publishing Company. Reprinted by permission.

have been made for other arm positioning tasks (Shapiro, 1977), series of button presses (Summers, 1975), piano playing (Michon, 1974, cited in Schmidt, 1982), and typing and handwriting (Viviani & Terzuolo, 1980). Figure 7.9 shows handwriting data from Viviani and Terzuolo (1980).

Recently, Gentner (1982) has challenged the view that time scaling actually applies to typewriting. His arguments revolve around the statistical procedures used by Viviani and Terzuolo (1980) to conclude that time scaling exists. In our opinion, the generality of time-scaling effects across a wide range of performance domains seems to vitiate the detailed criticisms that Gentner has advanced. Whether Gentner will ultimately be deemed right on this issue depends on how successfully he brings

his criticisms to bear on other performance domains.

If we allow, for the moment, that time scaling is a real rather than artifactual phenomenon, what does the phenomenon tell us about human movement control? It seems to suggest the operation of a system like that proposed by Vorberg and Hambuch (1978) in which there is a motor program that specifies the identities, order, and relative timing of movement elements but whose execution requires the pairing of those elements with distinct pulses of a clock that may run at different speeds during execution. According to this view, timing is represented abstractly in the program, for example, in the form of time *tags* that are associated with symbolic response identifiers. Thus, a motor program is like a schedule of planned events, in which the events actually occur when their associated clock pulses occur, and the rate at which the events are produced depends on how quickly the clock runs (see Rosenbaum, 1985, for a more detailed statement of this *scheduling* theory of motor programs).

## Construction of Programs for Movement Sequences

Thus far, our discussion of serial order and timing has focused on performance of constrained tasks in which the subject is certain about what is supposed to be done. Recent studies have also investigated performance when the subject does not know what response sequence will have to be performed until a signal is presented. These studies have addressed the question of how motor programs are constructed prior to their execution.

In an experiment that used choice reaction times for this purpose (Rosenbaum, Inhoff, & Gordon, 1984), subjects chose between mirror-image finger sequences (e.g., index-index-middle of the left versus the right hand) or, in other conditions, between nonmirror-image finger sequences (e.g., index-index-middle of the left hand versus index-middle-middle of the right hand). The time for the first response after the choice signal was significantly longer in the nonmirror-image choice condition than in the mirror-image choice condition. An intuitively satisfying explanation of this result is that, in the mirror-image condition, the choice simply entailed a decision about which hand to use, whereas in the nonmirror-image condition, additional decisions were required (e.g., what type of finger to use in the second position of the sequence). In the mirror-image condition, therefore, choice of hand served to specify an abstract programming parameter that could be applied in a distributive fashion to an ordered set of subprograms corresponding to the finger types required in serial positions 1, 2, and 3 (i.e., index, index, and middle). Further support for this idea can be found in Inhoff, Rosenbaum, Gordon, and Campbell (1984), who studied choices between other finger sequences, and Heuer (1984), who studied choices between oscillatory movements of the two hands.

What are the broader functional implications of positing abstract parameters for motor programming? The most important is that motor programs are schematic; they take arguments that allow for the generation of richly differentiated patterns of movement. Identifying these parameters is an important topic of current research (see Marteniuk & MacKenzie, 1980, and Rosenbaum, 1983b, for review). The complementary problem of identifying the programs to which the parameters are supplied is another important topic of study. A prevailing view is that programs not only take parameters as arguments but also call up other programs or subroutines (MacKay, 1982; Marteniuk & Romanow, 1983; Norman, 1981). We shall return to this point when we discuss the acquisition of motor skills.

## THE PERCEPTUAL-MOTOR INTEGRATION PROBLEM

Our discussion so far has largely ignored the role of perception in movement control. This separation cannot go on for long, however. One could not reach for or direct one's eyes toward external objects if the locations and characteristics of the objects were not registered through the senses. Likewise, one could not reach effectively for a part of one's own body if the relative positions of the body parts were unknown. Effective movement therefore depends on accurate perception.

The converse is also true: Movement is vital for perception. A dramatic demonstration of this fact is the well-known experiment on retinal stabilization, where an object projected onto a fixed part of the retina through a special contact lens disappears in a few seconds (Pritchard, 1961). In this experiment, the normal jitter of the retinal image caused by eye tremor is perfectly compensated for by the contact lens device. The fading of the image shows that the visual and oculomotor systems evolved in close harmony.

There is another critical way in which movement is vital for perception. Whenever a movement is made, sensory receptors are transported from one location to another, and new sensory information is acquired as a result. What is important about this new information is that it can be anticipated, albeit unconsciously and to only a certain level of detail, because it arises directly from the actions of the motor system. The perceptual consequences of such active control can be dramatic. If people have the opportunity to feel objects through active palpation, they can identify the objects more accurately than if their tactile exposure is passive (Gordon, 1978). Similarly, people can better reproduce arm positions if they actively select the positions than if the positions are communicated via passive manipulation (Paillard & Brouchon, 1968). In the domain of perceptual-motor learning, active movement in a perceptual environment leads to better coordination than does passive movement (Held, 1965).

These examples show that movement can benefit perception. It is also important for the perceptual system not to be confused by the perceptual changes that movements bring. Considering eye movements again, the image of the environment shifts quickly across the retina during a saccade (i.e., the rapid movement of the eye from one target to another), which raises the question of how the visual system knows that the eye has moved but the visual world has not. Similarly, during an eyeblink, how is it that the world does not seem to dim when the lids cover the pupil?

### Visual Suppression During Blinks and Saccades

To address these questions, several groups of investigators have measured changes in visual thresholds when saccades or eyeblinks occur. An experiment by Volkmann, Riggs, and Moore (1980) provides an example of this approach, as well as a model of experimental ingenuity. Volkmann and co-workers considered the question of why we do not experience momentary dimming of the visual world when we blink. Since eyeblinks last for 200 ms or more and people can detect dimming of light that lasts less than 100 ms, the possibility that blink-related dimming is simply too brief to be detected could be ruled out. A natural way to address the question of why we do not notice the dimming of the visual world during eyeblink is to present visual stimuli to subjects while they blink and find out how intense the stimuli must be to ensure detection. The problem with this approach is that if one finds that stimuli must be made more intense than usual to be seen during eyeblinks, this could result from the fact that the lids reduce the amount of light entering the eye. Volkmann et al. (1980) therefore bypassed the lids by delivering light through an optic fiber pressed against the roof of the mouth; light delivered in this way could still reach the retina.

Figure 7.10 shows how sensitivity to the light delivered through the roof of the mouth changed during electronically monitored eyeblinks. Since transmission of the light to the retina could not have been affected by the physical action of the lids themselves, the results suggest that central changes in the nervous system accompany blinking. Carrying out an eyeblink therefore results in centrally reduced sensitivity to incoming light that, in turn, makes us less sensitive to the optical changes that normally occur when we blink.

The central changes that accompany saccades are similar to those that accompany

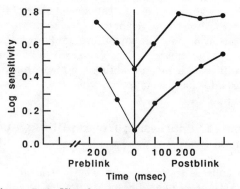

**Figure 7.10.** Visual suppression during eyeblinks. The two curves are for two different subjects, each at a different stimulus duration. From "Eyeblinks and Visual Suppression" by F.C. Volkman, L.A. Riggs, and R.K. Moore, 1980, *Science, 207*, p. 901. Copyright 1980 by the AAAS. Reprinted by permission.

blinks. Just as experimental stimuli must be intensified to ensure detection during blinks, they must also be intensified during saccades, including the period just before saccades are performed (Matin, 1972). *Saccadic suppression* is the term that has been given to this phenomenon. It is now fairly well established that saccadic suppression has central rather than peripheral origins. Having saccadic suppression achieves the same effect as having blink-related suppression. By being less sensitive to visual changes when a saccade is made, one is less likely to notice the visual effects of the saccade itself. Saccadic suppression explains why one cannot observe one's own saccades in a mirror, and it may explain why we have visual iconic memory.

## Corollary Discharge and Efference Copy

Visual suppression during saccades and blinks allows for perceptual attenuation of the retinal consequences of these two kinds of oculomotor activity. A more subtle problem must also be solved by the visual system when eye movements occur. The problem is to distinguish retinal displacements caused by the eyes moving across a stationary scene and a moving scene passing before stationary eyes.

Helmholtz (1866/1962) offered a computational theory to solve this problem. He suggested that the visual system subtracts the eye movement component from the retinal displacement vector. Note that this proposal ignores the possibility that there is enough information in the optical input to the eye to fully specify how retinal displacements arise, a point to which we shall return later.

Helmholtz wondered how the subtraction process was actually implemented. In particular, he wondered what sort of extraretinal information specifies eye movement. A simple observation led him to an intriguing suggestion. If one nudges one's eye with one's finger the external environment appears to move. This led Helmholtz to suggest that the main source of extraretinal information is not feedback arising from the eyes after eye movements have occurred but rather the set of central commands that are sent to the eyes before eye movements occur. Consider his argument: The stretch receptors in the extraocular muscles (i.e., the muscles that move the eyeball) are activated when the eyeball is pushed by the finger. These same stretch receptors are presumably also activated when the eye is moved in the normal way. If feedback from the stretch receptors provided the extraretinal information needed for subtraction, the world would appear stationary whenever such feedback is produced, that is, whether the feedback was produced through oculomotor commands or manual commands. The fact that the world appears to move only when normal oculomotor commands are missing suggests that oculomotor commands, or some concomitant of oculomotor commands, comprise the essential extraretinal information needed for the subtraction process. This signal has come to be called *corollary discharge* (Sperry, 1950) or *efference copy* (von Holst & Mittelstaedt, 1950).

Many studies have been performed to evaluate Helmholtz's claim, and we shall review some of them in a moment. It is interesting to mention parenthetically that Helmholtz's observation has recently been cited as evidence for the view that cognitive functions are organized in separate modules (Fodor, 1983). A general property of information processing that supports the modularity position is the appearance of encapsulated informational systems, that is, systems that, when triggered, function autonomously of other systems. The illusory motion of the visual world when the eyeball is nudged by the finger is an example of encapsulation, because whether the eyeball is moved by one's extraocular muscles or by one's finger the same volitional agent (i.e., the same person) is ultimately responsible for directing the action. The fact that the visual world does not appear to move when the extraocular muscles rotate the eye but does appear to move when the finger rotates the eye suggests that visual perception has access to normal oculomotor signals but does not have access to manual command signals. The oculomotor and visual systems therefore exhibit the property of encapsulation that modularity theory demands.

Let us now return to the studies that have been done to evaluate Helmholtz's original claim. A prediction arising from Helmholtz's theory is that paralysis of the extraocular muscles should lead to illusory displacements of the visual world when saccades are attempted. The reason is that, since the eye muscles cannot work when they are paralyzed, stretch receptors in the eye muscles cannot be activated. If the world appears to move when oculomotor commands are issued but have no effect on the eye muscles or their associated stretch receptors, illusory displacements of the visual environment must be attributed to a mismatch between corollary discharge (or efference copy) and the pattern of displacement (or nondisplacement) occurring on the retina. In fact, several studies have documented that patients and subjects with temporary or permanent paresis (partial paralysis) of the extraocular muscles see the visual world jump during attempted saccades (Jeanerrod, 1983). It must be observed, however, that Brindley, Goodwin, Kulikowski, and Leighton (1976) reported that when eye muscles are completely paralyzed rather than only partially paralyzed, illusory movements of the visual world do not occur. This report goes against the hypothesis that central commands rather than feedback signals give rise to illusory motion effects and leaves open the possibility that mismatches between retinal information and inflow from the periphery actually account for such illusions, including Helmholtz's passive eye movement phenomenon.

At this time, the main source of extraretinal information—peripheral feedback or central commands—is still unclear (Matin, Stevens, & Picoult, 1983). Given that the extraocular muscles are more richly endowed with stretch receptors than any other muscles, one wonders why signals from these receptors would not be used. Moreover, stationary stimuli are commonly seen to move during normal saccades when the stimuli are small and located in an otherwise dark room (Bridgeman, 1983). If a simple subtraction process allowed for space constancy during saccades, as Helmholtz proposed, one might not expect characteristics of the visual field to affect the success of the subtraction process.

## Perceptual Localization

Regardless of whether inflow, outflow, or visual information alone is used to maintain position constancy during eye movements, any process that incorporates these sources of information must not only determine whether external objects are moving but also where the objects are in space. Several studies have investigated this issue.

Matin (1972) presented two spots of light

successively and at different times relative to the start of saccades. The subject's task was to indicate whether the first spot appeared to the right or left of the second spot. By varying the spatial separation between the spots, Matin could measure the subject's localization ability prior to, during, and after saccades. He found that performance declined to fairly low levels during and shortly before saccades were performed.

Based on this result, it would be natural to conclude that saccades interfere greatly with the perception of direction. However, a study by Hallett and Lightstone (1976) leads to a different conclusion. Subjects in this study fixated a spot of light at location A and then redirected their gaze to another spot of light suddenly presented at location B. Just before execution of the saccade to B, a stimulus appeared at a third location C for a very brief time (i.e., it was off by the time the eyes reached B). Remarkably, after subjects moved their eyes to B, they could accurately saccade to the location where C had appeared. This result implies that the spatial location of C could be determined even while the eyes were being prepared to saccade to B. If, as Matin's (1972) study suggests, localization had been greatly impaired, subjects would have been unable to reach target C successfully. Moreover, if the location of C had merely been coded with respect to its retinal distance from B, accurate attainment of C would have been impossible.

The Hallet and Lightstone (1976) results have been replicated (Prablanc, Massé, & Echallier, 1978) and extended in an even more striking demonstration. Mays and Sparks (1980) trained monkeys to fixate a spot of light and then direct the eyes to another spot of light presented in a random location for a brief time in an otherwise dark room. Just before the eyes began to move to the new target, electrical stimulation was applied to the monkey's superior colliculus (a brain structure involved in the control of saccades) to trigger an eye movement to another location. After the eyes moved to this location, they moved immediately to the location where the original target had appeared. This observation is consistent with Hallet and Lightstone's study in showing that spatial locations of saccadic targets are accurately encoded and successfully define where saccades will be directed. If saccades were not programmed with respect to spatial location but instead were programmed with respect to retinally defined distances,

monkeys in the Mays and Spark experiment would have been unable to direct their eyes to the original target location after electrical stimulation deflected their eyes somewhere else.

How can the latter results be reconciled with Matin's (1972) results suggesting that perceptual localization is severely impaired during the initiation of saccades? The answer can be found in the nature of the response. Matin's subjects gave verbal, psychophysical judgments, whereas Hallet and Lightstone's and Mays and Spark's subjects made motor responses. That the response difference accounts for the disparity in performance levels in indicated by the fact that, when the same subjects are asked to give both types of responses within the same experiment, verbal responses indicate poor perception while motor responses indicate good perception. Skavenski and Hansen (1978) offered dramatic evidence for this kind of dissociation when they asked people to strike with a hammer at a briefly presented spot of light in an otherwise dark room. The test light was presented during saccades, and, although subjects verbally protested that they could not localize the target accurately, they in fact struck it accurately. Several other studies have shown that verbal responses about stimulus locations are inferior to direct motor responses, such as pointing or looking (see Jeannerod, 1983, for review). Hence, when perceptual-motor integration is studied, it is important to keep in mind that the response modality being used may dramatically affect the sorts of conclusions that are reached.

## Large-Scale Integration

Our discussion of perceptual-motor integration has been restricted so far to saccadic eye movements and blinks. We turn now to integration on a large scale: How is movement of the entire body through the environment perceptually controlled? There are two facets to this question. One is how perception aids movement, so that one can discern where it is safe to tread, determine whether one's reach has fallen short of a desired target, and so on. The other relates to the question of how one's movements are taken into account in relying on perceptual information. Since a treatment of the first of these issues would require a discourse on perception, we shall focus on the second issue and only mention a few findings from studies aimed at clarifying the first.

Let us turn to the visual input of a seeing animal as it moves through the environment. Classical perceptual theory would ask how the animal can evaluate the contributions of its own movement to the motion it perceives in the visual environment. Drawing on our discussion of eye movements, the animal could rely on corollary discharge (i.e., information about the commands issued to its own muscles), on proprioceptive input, or both. But is it really necessary to call upon these additional sources of information to aid in the interpretation of visual input? The question can be answered by considering the fact that an automobile passenger has no trouble interpreting the visual changes associated with transport of the car in which he or she is riding, although his or her efferent commands or proprioception bears little or no correspondence to the maneuvers of the car itself. That the passenger's motor activities are of little consequence is further demonstrated by the familiar experience of induced motion of self, in which one perceives one's car to be moving when it is actually at a standstill beside another moving vehicle. Observations like these led perceptionists, following J.J. Gibson (1966), to consider the possibility that vision alone provides all the information needed to specify motion through the environment.

A study by Lee and Aronson (1974) provides a dramatic example of this approach. They had toddlers stand in a special room with a stable floor but walls that were part of a large inverted box hanging from the laboratory ceiling. By having someone push the box from outside, the walls seen by the toddler could be made to approach or recede. The effect of such room movement was extraordinary. If the wall approached the toddler, the child tended to fall backward and, if the wall receded, he or she tended to fall forward. That the toddler fell at all attests to what Lee and Thomson (1982) call the *exproprioceptive* role of vision. Vision, like receptors in the muscles, joints, tendons, skin, and vestibular organs, provides direct information about the position of the seeing animal with respect to its surroundings. That the toddler tended to fall forward or backward depending on the direction of movement of the wall attests to the informational quality of the visual input received. The visual stimulation produced by an approaching wall is roughly equivalent to the stimulation that would be produced if the toddler fell forward, in which case motoric compensation in the backward direction would be the adaptive reaction. Similarly, the visual stimulation produced by a receding wall is roughly equivalent to the stimulation that would be produced if the toddler fell backward, in which case motoric compensation in the forward direction would be the adaptive reaction. Thus, falling forward when the wall recedes and backward when it approaches supports the view that visual information provides powerful input to the proprioceptive system, which implies further that the interpretation of visual information may not depend on efferent or proprioceptive signals.

Lee and Lishman (1975) showed that the exproprioceptive role of vision is not limited to young children. Adults standing on a balance beam in the moving room exhibit marked sway, the relation between the direction of sway and direction of wall movement being the same as for the toddlers. Interestingly, the more unstable the adult's stance (e.g., as induced by having him or her stand on one foot or adopt other awkward postures), the more likely or pronounced the induced sway becomes. Walking, automobile driving, and other activities have also been analyzed from the point of view of the visual information that specifies how the actor is proceeding through the visual world (Lee & Thomson, 1982).

## Expectancies for Movement-Produced Visual Change

Although the visual changes that signal displacement of the organism through the environment may greatly reduce the amount of computation needed to distinguish self-induced and externally induced motion, this is not to say that expectancies are not formed for such visual changes. Forming expectancies for visual changes that are likely to accompany movements is clearly desirable for deciding ahead of time which visual changes should or should not be experienced, that is, which motion path should or should not be pursued. The discovery that there are regular correspondences between movement through the world and its visual consequences suggests that the correspondences may be used in forming expectancies for movement-produced visual changes.

Thomson (1983) reported experiments that support this conjecture. He had subjects look at a specified location on the ground and then walk to that location with their eyes closed. The error in the final stopping point grew as the distance from the start to the target location increased, with the rate of growth of the error function increasing dramatically for distances exceeding nine meters. In another experiment, when subjects looked at the target location, closed their eyes, and waited until the experimenter's instruction to walk to the location, the error in reaching the target increased with the length of the wait (especially for waits longer than eight seconds), indicating that time was a critical determinant of the strength of the memory for location. Thomson next had subjects walk without visual guidance toward a target location, but in the course of walking, they were told to stop and throw a bean bag to the target. They could throw the bean bag to the target almost as accurately as in normal sighted conditions, which led Lee and Thomson (1982) to conclude that these subjects were apparently "visually guiding themselves with their eyes closed" (p. 428); in other words, subjects were continually updating their representation of the space in which they were walking. Presumably, this is an ability that is drawn upon whenever locomotory or other voluntary activities are performed.

## Evidence From Speech and Other Modalities

All of the material on sensorimotor integration that we have reviewed so far comes from the visual domain. Other modalities show similar effects, however. For example, visual suppression effects associated with saccades and blinking have analogues in touch and hearing. Thus, proprioceptive sensitivity is reduced during and just before ballistic movements (Demairé, Honoré, & Coquery, 1984), and auditory sensitivity diminishes during chewing (Rosenzweig & Leiman, 1982, p. 321). In addition, expectancy effects have been demonstrated for speech (Meyer & Gordon, 1983). At the beginning of each trial of the Meyer and Gordon (1983) experiment, a printed syllable was presented to the subject, and then, on half the trials, a response signal (a high-pitched tone) was presented after a series of warning tones; the subject was then supposed to say the syllable as

quickly as possible. On the other half of the trials, an auditory syllable was presented, and the subject was required to press one of several fingers to indicate which syllable was heard; at the beginning of the experiment the subject learned the associations between syllables and fingers. The variable of greatest interest was the phonetic relation between the second auditory syllable and the syllable being held in articulatory readiness. If preparing to say a syllable has auditory correlates, then one would expect the time to identify a heard syllable to depend on its relation to the syllable being readied for production. Indeed, Meyer and Gordon obtained evidence consistent with this hypothesis. They found that when the primary and secondary syllables shared the same voicing feature (e.g., *buh* and *duh*) the manual response time was significantly longer than when the two syllables did not share voicing (*buh* and *tuh*). Sharing place of articulation (*duh* and *tuh*) did not have a significant effect on manual response time. Why the effects were restricted to voicing and took the form of longer rather than shorter response times when voicing was shared need not concern us here. The main point is that these results are consistent with the view that perception and production of speech rely on shared mechanisms (see Gordon & Meyer, 1984, for more details) and can be taken to support the view that an expectancy for the auditory consequence of a forthcoming utterance accompanies preparation of the utterance.

## Movement Control Tasks Emphasizing Sensory Feedback

We have presented several critical issues concerning the interpretation of relationships between perceptual and motor activity. Further elaboration of these relationships is provided by a discussion of sensory feedback. Sensory feedback provides information that supports the acquisition and control of effective movement. To illustrate, we will describe a variety of motor control tasks for which sensory feedback is essential to performance.

### Single Motor Unit Control
Perhaps the simplest movement that one can execute is the firing of a single motor unit. The motor unit is the smallest element of a muscle that is innervated separately by a single nerve

fiber. It is therefore the smallest element that can be independently controlled.

Basmajian (1978) discovered that if an experimenter places a wire electrode subcutaneously in the abductor pollici brevis muscle of the subject's thumb (frequently, for this experiment, the experimenter and the subject are the same individual), and if the electrode is connected to a loudspeaker, then, with about one-half hour of practice, the subject can learn to produce a single click in the loudspeaker. This corresponds to delivering a command to a single motor unit. When accomplished successfully, the thumb produces only the most minute movement. With further practice it is possible to produce exactly two or three such responses, to produce repetitive rhythms, or to achieve independent control of up to five or six separate units.

The key to this amazing performance is the availability of sensory information, in this case auditory, concerning success or failure with respect to the goal. The feedback accomplishes two functions, (1) making it possible to eliminate behavior that is unsuccessful, and (2) providing a calibration of the commands that produce the desired result. If the loudspeaker is removed after the behavior is learned, the response quickly drifts, producing only occasional successes by chance, implying the importance of explicit feedback for the maintenance of the response. Feedback often serves this tuning function, providing a reference against which the subject can compare performance.

### Continuous Tracking Control

Figure 7.11 shows a block diagram of the tracking paradigm. If the tracking task is visually guided, the subject views a target on a visual display. The target can be a moving pointer on a meter or a moving symbol on a CRT. Displays are usually visual, but auditory or tactile displays have also been studied (see Poulton, 1974), for a review.

In all tracking tasks, the subject manipulates a control device so as to minimize the difference between the input signal and the output that is produced. This difference is called the system error. Control sticks, steering wheels, pencil-like styli, even discrete switches have been used to control the movement of a cursor in tracking tasks. Some devices are rigidly mounted and transduce force into output, while others move freely and sense position or displacement. Since the kinematics of each of these devices are different, each has a different effect on tracking performance (Poulton, 1974).

In Figure 7.11, the control device has been represented separately from the external process that is being controlled. In practical settings, the external process may be an automobile, an aircraft, a ship, or even a chemical process. Because the control device has dynamic effects of its own, it is important to distinguish the impact of the control device dynamics from that of the external process.

To understand these effects, consider how to produce a lateral displacement of a cursor across the screen with a simple joystick. It involves simply moving the stick a corresponding distance. Then consider accomplishing the same task with a steering wheel controlling an automobile. To produce a lateral displacement on the road requires rotating the steering wheel in one direction, holding it there for a period of time, and then returning the steering wheel to its original position. The limb movements required are quite different, but can be predicted if one knows the equations governing the motion of the external system.

A tracking task requires continuous sensory-motor integration because the position of the target is always changing. Review of the major phenomena of tracking performance that emerge from the extensive literature can be summarized with a few simple concepts, highlighting several ways in which sensory information is used to produce integrated performance.

### Sensory-Motor Delay

In the absence of signal predictability, there is always an intrinsic time delay between what

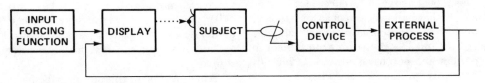

**Figure 7.11.** Block diagram of closed-loop tracking system.

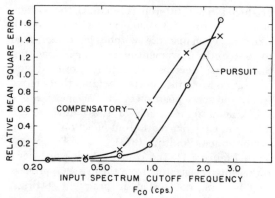

**Figure 7.12.** Effect of input signal frequency on tracking performance. The abscissa is the cutoff frequency that limits the bandwidth of the signal to be tracked. The ordinate is an index of the ratio of mean-square error to mean-square input signal. From "Characteristics of the Human Operator in Simple Manual Control Systems" by J.I. Elkind and C.D. Forgie, 1959, *IRE Transactions on Automatic Control, AC–4*, p. 50. Copyright (c) 1959 by the IRE (now IEEE). Reprinted by permission.

the subject senses and the production of the response. The faster the signal to be followed is changing (i.e., the higher the frequency content of the input signal), the greater the impact of this delay, and the more it degrades performance. Figure 7.12 illustrates this point. It shows the relative mean-square error—the ratio of the mean-square tracking error to the mean-square input signal—when the subjects were required to track randomly varying signals having a particular maximum frequency, $f_{co}$ (Elkind and Forgie, 1959). One can gain a feeling for the scale by noting that when the relative mean-square error exceeded one, the subjects would have been better off to stop responding because the mean square error was greater than the mean square of the input signal alone. Figure 7.12 also shows the difference in performance with the use of pursuit and compensatory displays. A pursuit display is one in which the subject views both the input and the output as cursors or pointers on the same display, and error is displayed as the difference between the two. On the other hand, a compensatory display presents a single pointer or cursor that indicates error directly and does not permit the subject to observe input and output separately. A pursuit display usually produces somewhat superior performance, as indicated, because it allows the

subject a greater opportunity to anticipate on the basis of the statistical patterns in the input signal. Practice tends to reduce the difference in performance with these two kinds of displays.

### Anticipation

In addition to the direct sensory information given by the cursor in a tracking display, the subject uses sensory feedback to predict, from the coherence in the input signal, the cursor's future movement trend in order to reduce the impact of sensory-motor delay. When the input is a predictable sine wave, the oscillation frequency at which satisfactory tracking can be maintained on the basis of anticipation is substantially higher than the 0.5 Hz cited above, because the path of the sine wave is completely predictable. With complete predictability, satisfactory tracking performance can be achieved with an oscillation frequency of 2.0 Hz (Pew, Duffendack, & Fensch, 1967). Anticipation also makes it possible to produce excellent performance at low frequencies as seen in Figure 7.12. The signal changes so slowly that it is predictable on the basis of its continuity. The subject integrates over the available sensory information to infer that its path is not going to change drastically during the next small time increment.

### Dynamic Filtering

Sometimes the sensory feedback provided to the subject is confounded by dynamic filtering effects that are intrinsic to the systems being studied. Display systems, control devices, and external physical systems have dynamic properties that attenuate high frequencies and introduce sluggishness in the response. These properties transform the signals being tracked in ways that inhibit effective human performance. For example, in a moving pointer display, damping and inertia are introduced that may prevent the meter needle from responding promptly to changes in the input signal. An aircraft or ship has sluggish dynamic properties that must be anticipated if their effects are to be minimized. Thus feedback also provides the basis for the subjects to compensate for delaying and distorting transformations that are embedded in the systems they attempt to control.

Tracking tasks, therefore, embody many of the principles that make sensory feedback such an important element in the accomplishment of effective sensory-motor integration.

## Movements of Controlled Accuracy

Whereas tracking movements are stimulus-bound in the sense that an error signal continuously informs the subject of the correct action, simple positional movements to a target of specified area provide an end point constraint but no path constraint. Such movements clearly require sensory-motor integration and, as pointed out in the discussion of degrees of freedom, have implications for the mechanisms of motor control. Can such movements be described by simple models from feedback control, or is the mass-spring model a better representation?

Woodworth (1899) first studied such movements and argued that they are carried out in two phases: an initial impulse phase and a current control phase. The initial impulse refers to the acceleration phase during which a pulse of force produces the maximum velocity that will initiate the movement. Current control refers to the deceleration phase, during which corrections are introduced and the movement gradually slows down and ends at the target position. The study of movements of constrained accuracy was further stimulated by Fitts (1954) in an era when information theory was popular. He showed that movement time was a linear function of an *Index of Difficulty* that he formulated in terms of the information metric:

$$ID = \log_2 (2A/W).$$

The A and W are the amplitude (distance from the starting point to the center of the target) and target width, respectively. The base-two logarithm allows the ID to be expressed in bits. The linear relationship between movement time and ID implies that the movement time increases logarithmically with increased distance and decreases logarithmically with increased accuracy tolerance. This relationship is frequently referred to as Fitts' Law. It is extremely robust, producing correlations above 0.90 between movement time and the ID. It works for arm movements (Fitts & Peterson, 1964), foot movements (Drury, 1975), and head movements (Soede, Stassen, van Lunteren, & Luitse, 1973). It even works for movements of underwater divers (Kerr, 1973) and for very small movements viewed

under a microscope (Langolf, Chaffin, & Foulke, 1976).

Fitts introduced his data in an information theoretic framework and argued that it reflected the limiting channel capacity of the human motor system. In 1963 Crossman and Goodeve (1983) first pointed out a number of other models that could predict the same basic relation between speed and accuracy demonstrated by Fitts. One particularly simple model assumes that when a subject responds with a speeded movement to a fixed target, first a limb velocity proportional to initial error is generated, and then the velocity is reduced systematically as the error gets smaller. That is, as the stylus or finger gets closer to the target, the subject slows down in order to gain accuracy. If one assumes that the movement terminates when the edge of the target is reached, then the Fitts' Law prediction can be derived by elementary control theory. Crossman and Goodeve (1983) and, subsequently, Keele (1968) developed a discrete correction version of the same model. Both of these models suggest that the dominant factor in control is sensory feedback with respect to target position. Langolf, Chaffin, and Foulke, (1976) provided additional ways to derive the relationship based on feedback principles.

The mass-spring model provides an alternative explanation of Fitts' Law. Consider first a study by Schmidt, Zelaznik, Hawkins, Frank, and Quinn (1979) who examined movements constrained to a given duration (less than 200 milliseconds) and used accuracy as the dependent variable. They found a linear rather than a logarithmic relationship between movement speed and the ratio of accuracy to distance. With such short durations, Schmidt et al. (1979) suggested that the movements were preprogrammed, and visual feedback was not used; the subject simply set the desired length-tension characteristics and initiated the impulse. The linear relationship was then predicted on the basis of the variability of the timing and magnitude of the resultant force impulses.

While not questioning the data of Schmidt and his colleagues, Meyer, Smith, and Wright (1982) provided an improved derivation of the predictions of Schmidt et al. (1979) and supported their basic assertion that movement accuracy for simple, rapid movements was limited by the preprogrammed force impulse magnitude and timing variability (see also rebuttal by

Schmidt, Sherwood, Zelaznik, and Leikind, 1984). Meyer et al. (1982) further showed how the same impulse variability model could predict the Fitts' Law relationship for longer movements by hypothesizing a sequence of overlapping force impulses.

Subsequently Meyer, Abrams, Kornblum, Wright, and Smith (in press) conducted a further experiment using the Fitts' paradigm with wrist movements, but including a very interesting condition designed to further test the role of feedback in accounting for Fitts' Law. They used a range of amplitudes and target widths, and on half the trials visual feedback was eliminated by blanking the screen on which the target was displayed as soon as the movement was initiated. While they found that movement accuracy was severely reduced by blanking the screen, the movement time versus ID function remained logarithmic with essentially the same slope and intercept.

This and other results of their experiment that were consistent with their impulse variability model (a variant of that of Meyer et al., 1982), while not denying the importance of visual feedback for producing accurate movements, provide an interesting contrast between the feedback and impulse variability approaches. The models derived from feedback considerations suggest that it is the current control portion of the movement that produces the Fitts' Law relationship, while the impulse variability model attributes the relationship to the variability in the initial impulse phase of the movement. The comparison serves therefore to further illuminate the various roles for feedback in the production of skilled movements.

## THE SKILL ACQUISITION PROBLEM

Improved performance results from practice on a motor task by a motivated subject when knowledge of results is available. Many researchers plot performance as a function of trials of practice; when the percentage change per additional trial is small, with respect to overall improvement, then the experimenter interested in studying skilled performance concludes that learning is sufficiently complete to terminate practice. This conclusion is predicated on the assumption that skill learning fits an exponentially decreasing curve which has an asymptote that is parallel to

the horizontal axis. On the contrary, there is good evidence that performance continues to improve for very long periods of practice. With motor skills, improvement is measured in weeks and months, perhaps years. Figure 7.13 from Fitts (1964) shows a few illustrative sets of data. When plotted on log-log coordinates they approximate a straight line. The only exception is shown in Figure 7.13c. It is the classic data set of De Jong (reported in Crossman, 1959) showing that an individual cigar roller's daily production tally finally levelled off after approximately three years and three million cigars, when performance finally became limited by the cycle time of the cigar rolling machine with which he had to work. None of these graphs is compatible with an exponential learning curve. Neither are the 40 or so sets of data examined by Mazur and Hastie (1978). With only minor exceptions they found that a hyperbola fit each set of data better than an exponential curve. These authors found that an extra parameter had to be added to the equation to take account for the effects of differential previous learning before each experiment began.

## Theories of Acquisition

Having established the typical pattern of improvement and acknowledging that the pattern is stochastic, that is, subject to statistical variation, we may now ask on what basis may one postulate that selective learning takes place? There are at least three hypotheses one may consider to answer this question—statistical selectivity, linear chaining, and hierarchical organization. We will discuss each and, where possible, show how they make contact with similar theories mentioned earlier in the context of the problem of serial and temporal organization.

### Statistical Selectivity

Crossman (1959) suggested that when subjects perform a speeded task, they have available a distribution of methods for accomplishing it that vary in speed and efficiency. Each time they attempt the task, they select a method at random from the distribution. Some are fast and efficient, and some are not. As a function of practice, methods that are tried and found efficient have an increased probability of being sampled again, while those that are found inefficient have reduced probability. In Crossman's model, the

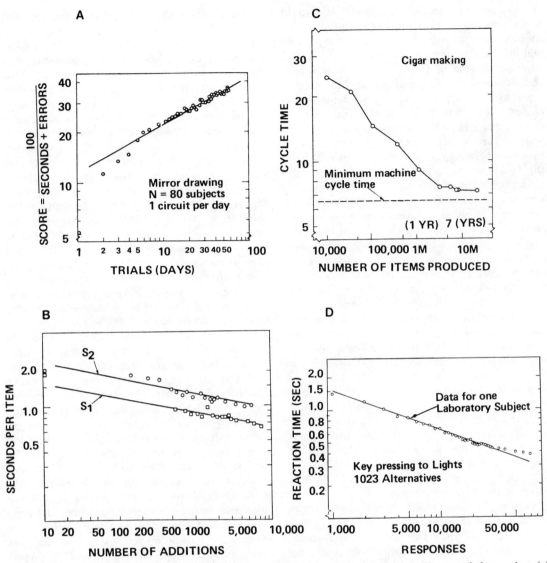

**Figure 7.13.** Data illustrating continued improvement in skilled performance with extended practice. (a) Mirror drawing. (b) Mental arithmetic. (c) Cigar rolling. (d) Key pressing. From "Perceptual-motor Skill Learning" by P.M. Fitts in *Categories of Human Learning* (pp. 266–267), A.W. Melton (Ed.), 1964. New York: Academic Press. Copyright 1964 by Academic Press. Reprinted by permission.

amount by which the selection probability is increased or decreased is a function of how much better or worse the performance is using the sampled method than the average performance prior to picking it. Thus, as average performance improves and shifts towards the upper tail of the distribution, the rate of gain in probability for better methods slows down. According to this hypothesis, then, as learning progresses it takes successively longer periods of practice to produce smaller increments in performance. A simulation of the behavior of this model produced a functional relation between performance and practice that approximated a power function.

### Linear Chaining
The linear chaining hypothesis suggests that each of the elements of a series is triggered by the completion of the last previous element.

With respect to learning, this hypothesis would predict that the early elements in the sequence should be improved earlier, more completely, and be retained longer because the success of subsequent elements depends on satisfactory completion of the earlier elements; they receive more successful practice. Any student of psychology who has observed the introductory demonstration in which a trained rat jumps into a pan, is carried up to an open doll house window by a counterweight, removes a small doll from the (burning) window, and climbs down the ladder with the doll in tow, will acknowledge both the serial chaining nature of the skill (if one stimulus object is missing the rat ends the sequence) and the obvious consequence that the first elements must be learned before the later ones. Any movement sequence in which the ability to perform a given element at all depends on satisfactory completion of the previous element will have this property; however, many skilled movements do not. In a tracking task, the subject continues to perform no matter how poor the performance on early elements, and improvement proceeds uniformly (Pew, 1974). In the movement pattern task of Marteniuk and Romanow (1983), in which performance from memory of an irregular five second pattern was required, they found that variability decreased with practice relatively uniformly throughout the pattern rather than systematically from the beginning to the end.

### Hierarchical Organization

According to the hierarchical organization model, subordinate elements of a skill are learned first or are brought to the task already learned. These elements are then organized and integrated into higher-level units, and performance focuses on these successively higher levels. Evidence for hierarchical models of performance was presented in the section on serial order.

A two-level version of the hierarchical model, specifically concerned with skill acquisition, has been proposed by MacKay (1982) in the context of the acquisition and performance of speech. He postulates that one level is associated with the muscle movement system, and the other is associated with the mental or cognitive system. The elements or nodes in the muscle movement system represent specific patterns of movement. In the case of speech, these nodes involve the tongue, lips, velum, and so on. The mental system nodes represent the cognitive elements controlling the muscle movement system. Again, for speech these components are phonemes, syllables, words, and so forth. They are organized by the phrase structure of the speech utterance.

In an impressive demonstration of the applicability of this theory, MacKay and Bowman (1969) conducted a learning and transfer of training study with English-German bilinguals. Each subject spoke speech sequences twelve times and spoke normal sentences, scrambled sentences, and nonsense strings. Time to produce each sequence was measured. After practice in their first language (half English, half German), there was a critical transfer condition. In the critical condition, the sentence to be produced was a word-for-word translation of the original sentence into the other language. The results are shown in Table 7.2. For the translation from normal sentences, transfer performance was identical to that on the final practice trials. For sentences that were not a word-for-word translation or were scrambled or nonsense strings, performance was no better than starting over. MacKay argues that even though the muscle movement system elements were very different in the second language, these elements were already highly practiced. On the other hand, the cognitive structures were identical, and it was the cognitive structures for which practice led to improved performance.

Table 7.2. Production time (in seconds per sentence) during practice, and transfer trials for normal sentences, scrambled sentences, and nonsense strings (MacKay, 1982)

| Material | Practice trials | | Transfer trials | | |
|---|---|---|---|---|---|
| | First four | Last four | Nontranslation | Translation | Facilitation (%) |
| Normal sentences | 2.33 | 2.03 | 2.44 | 2.03 | 17 |
| Scrambled sentences | 2.90 | 2.38 | 2.79 | 2.83 | −1 |
| Nonsense strings | 4.33 | 3.20 | 4.33 | 4.33 | 0 |

Although this theory is well suited to the speech domain, it has analogues in other motor performance domains. Trucks and sports cars have very different steering ratios and vehicle dynamics, requiring very different muscle movements to accomplish the same goals. We have no difficulty transferring from one vehicle to another so long as we are fluent in both types of vehicle at the muscle movement level.

Which of these theories about the acquisition of skill should we accept – statistical selectivity, linear chaining, or hierarchical organization? In each case there is a domain of skilled behavior for which they are relevant and applicable, but the sophisticated researcher can also find domains for which each theory would be rejected. At this stage in our understanding, it is not as important that any one theory be singled out for adoption as whether each is useful. The theories may be useful for building a foundation of understanding, for practical decision making in everyday life, or for answering important design questions. By these criteria we cannot eliminate any of the three theories.

## Form of Representation

In order for learning to be demonstrated, there must be evidence of retention, the buildup of a representation of performance that carries over from trial to trial or day to day. Movement researchers, just like those in other fields of learning, are interested in the possible forms of representation. In this connection we will discuss schemata, control laws, perceptual images, and coordinative structures.

## Motor Representation of Schemata

The idea that a schema is what is encoded with practice and retrieved from memory at the time of action has been popular among motor performance researchers (Pew, 1974; Schmidt, 1975; Rumelhart and Norman, 1982).

The concept of schemata can be traced at least to Head (1920); as used here, it is well defined by the experiments of Posner and Keele (1968, 1970). They created several sets of dot patterns by defining a set of standards, each having a randomly determined array of dots. Then, for each standard they created a set of distortions by moving a given dot a radial distance from its origin according to a proba-

bility distribution. The movement of dots was done systematically to control the uncertainty associated with each set of distortions (see Posner, Goldsmith, & Welton, 1967, for a description of the method by which the distortions were created). The subjects were trained to classify the collection of distortions into sets based on the standard from which they were derived. After achieving reliable classification, they were shown, (1) new random distortions they had not seen before, and (2) the standard patterns (also previously unseen). The subjects were able to classify the standards reliably better than the new distortions, and, in a separate experiment, after a one week delay, there was an increase in classification errors for the distortions that had been previously learned but no increase in errors for the classification of the standard patterns.

In the case of movements, then, a schema is a generalization or representation of a class of movements in memory. Presumably it is built up and refined by practice. Refinement is reflected both in terms of the level of generality at which it is represented and in terms of the constants and variables that characterize it. It is likely that we have schemata for handwriting, for speech, even for the various aspects of driving a car. In fact, in some unpublished research, Pew, Miller, and Dietrich (1982) found that quantitative spatio-temporal analysis of the patterns involved in shifting an automatic transmission revealed very regular patterns of movement. These patterns for shifting from one given gear shift position to another, such as drive to reverse, were remarkably repeatable within a subject from trial to trial but were often very different from subject to subject. Each subject had a unique signature, just as in handwriting.

How are schemata acquired? If one takes Posner and Keele (1968) as the defining experiment, then practice under conditions in which irrelevant parameters are varied while relevant ones are fixed should lead to robust schemata. Moxley (1979) showed that this procedure also works for motor skills, by training children to throw shuttle cocks at targets from one fixed or from four varying locations. She found that variable practice improved throwing accuracy from a new, unpracticed location better than did fixed practice.

One of the difficulties with the concept of schemata is that it is not clear where one

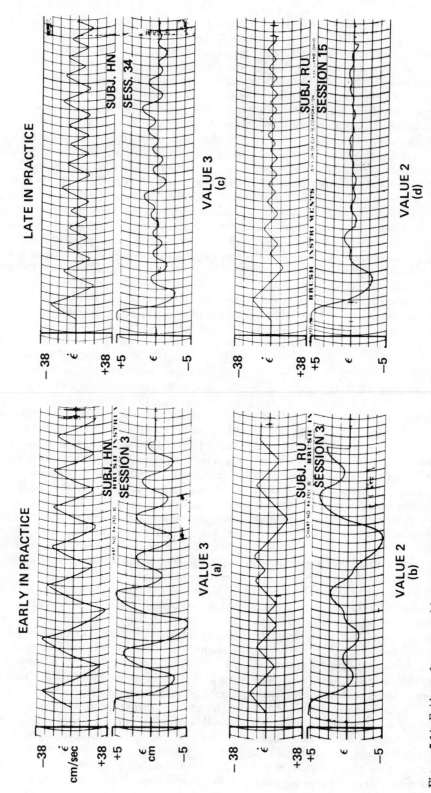

**Figure 7.14.** Evidence for a control law representation of movement control: (a) and (b) illustrate behavior of two different subjects early in practice; (c) illustrates use of response bursts with pauses for correction; (d) illustrates smooth modulation of response timing. From "Acquisition of Hierarchical Control Over the Temporal Organization of a Skill" by R.W. Pew, 1966, *Journal of Experimental Psychology, 71*, p. 768. Copyright 1966 by the American Psychological Association. Reprinted by permission.

schema ends and another begins, or whether two separate activities, like bicycle riding and carpentry, can share common schema elements, such as squeezing hand brakes and squeezing a pair of pliars. It is therefore difficult to be any more specific about how they are built up.

## Motor Representation as a Control Law

It is clear that there are many circumstances in which what must be learned in order to achieve good performance is a set of rules to be followed to produce success in an uncertain environment. Pew (1966) studied a task in which the subject controlled the position of a cursor by alternating responses between two keys. The left key caused the cursor to accelerate to the left, and the right key produced rightward acceleration. There was no off position, and, if the subject failed to respond, the cursor accelerated off the screen. Good performance involved keeping the target as close to the center of the screen as possible and this was accomplished by rapidly alternating between keys. However, fast responding with small differences in timing caused the cursor to drift to the left or right, and early in practice the subject would pause after each response, execute a correction, and resume rapid responding. This pattern is shown in Figure 7.14a and b and is indicative of a closed loop mode of control in which the subject monitors the accuracy and then introduces discrete corrections when necessary.

However, later in practice, the subjects acquired one of two strategies for improving their overall performance. Some, as shown in Figure 7.14c simply responded more rapidly, and when the drift became critical they paused, introduced a correction, and executed another response burst. Some subjects, on the other hand, adopted a much more sophisticated strategy, as shown in Figure 7.14d. While maintaining rapid alternating responses, they systematically adjusted the relative timing between adjacent pairs of responses to control the amount of drift without slowing down. Essentially, they modulated the duration of the response intervals systematically to achieve this higher level of control, and produced superior performance. These modes are indicative of the sense in which movement representation can be thought of not only in terms of producing a specific response

pattern, but also as strategies for ongoing control. Control theorists refer to this concept as a *control law*. That is, what is formulated is a set of rules and parameter settings for how a response will be produced, contingent on incoming sensory information, rather than a specific movement pattern. Flying an airplane is another example where control laws provide a better description of what is learned than specific movement patterns.

## Perceptual Images in Movement Representation

When a skill is acquired, in addition to the purposeful representation reflected in schemata or control laws, there is also acquisition of internal perceptual cues that are associated with successful performance. Adams (1971, 1976) gave the concept of a perceptual trace a central role in his description of skilled performance. He argued that a reference trace is needed with which to compare feedback from subsequent performance. In other contexts it is referred to as an image of the expected sensory consequences of a movement. Adams argued that the perceptual trace is built up with practice by aggregating the feedback from previous experiences. All sensory modes, including proprioception, are included, and Adams viewed the trace as a multi-sensory image. The skilled gymnast or diver who can report on the success of an individual performance on the basis of how it felt provides one source of anecdotal evidence for the concept of a perceptual image. The ability of a subject who has been trained through biofeedback to learn to change heart rate or muscle tension at will has learned to substitute internal cues for those originally provided explicitly by the biofeedback.

In the automobile automatic shifting behavior described earlier as an example of a movement schema, there were some subjects who shifted from park to drive by systematically counting the detents, that is, the feel of moving over each lever position and providing exactly three pulses of force to move from park-to-reverse-to-neutral-to-drive. The total movement time was less than one-half second. There were no pauses long enough to process feedback and react, but there were distinct hesitations in the movement before each new pulse was introduced. This phenomenon is illustrated in Figure 7.15. It

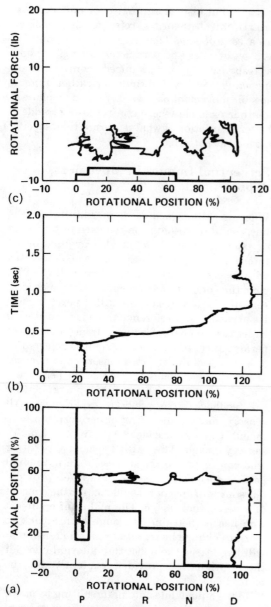

(c)

(b)

(a)

P    R    N    D

**Figure 7.15.** Characteristics of automobile automatic shifting behavior. Data are for one subject executing a single shift from park to drive: (a) rotational position versus axial position, illustrating that the subject lifts the shift lever out of the park stop and moves it approximately horizontally to drive, with some back tracking, and then releases it; (b) rotational position versus time, illustrating that the horizontal movement takes less than 0.5 seconds and shows three very brief hesitations along the way; (c) rotational force versus rotational position, illustrating the distinctive force patterns associated with moving across the intermediate positions.

shows an interesting example where internal sensory cues appear to have provided the basis for effective movement control.

## Coordinative Structures as Movement Representation

The concept of coordinative structures was introduced in the discussion of solutions to the degrees-of-freedom problem. It is clear that as a skill is learned and refined one aspect of what is learned is to use multiple muscle groups effectively to articulate particular kinds of movements. Turvey, Fitch, and Tuller (1982) studied precision sharpshooters. They showed that, to achieve the required stability, the skilled shooters learned to have one muscle group compensate for another. We say the movements of a production worker are skilled if they are smooth, eliminate wasted motion, and are assembled into a coherent whole. Smooth movements may be brought about through the more effective utilization of the elements of a coordinative structure.

As was discussed in the section on theories of organization, no single form of representation can be singled out for adoption. Rather, each form is useful, and different skills and different aspects of the same skill will have different forms of representation.

## CONCLUSIONS

Let us end in the spirit in which we began. What has changed about our knowledge and perspectives on motor performance since publication of the first edition of this handbook? First, it should be clear that the study of movement control has emerged as a topic of substantive interest to psychologists—or perhaps we should say reemerged—since it enjoyed considerable popularity in the late nineteenth and early twentieth centuries.

Second, as in other areas of psychology, the work has been revolutionized by the impact of developments in the information and control sciences. Since 1950 it has become possible to think of information as a concrete entity, and that machines can be controlled by the explicit manipulation of information. Movement research has been in a position to take particular advantage of these developments in representation because it requires explanations in informational terms, on the one hand, and in terms of the control of physical effectors on the other.

Consistent with Marr's (1982) broad view of information processing, there have been developments at all three levels, computation, representation, and implementation. Regrettably, because it has not been our focus, we have deemphasized the truly remarkable breakthroughs that have been achieved both in quantitative instrumentation and in substantive results at the physiological implementation level.

With respect to computation, a key contribution has been to determine what needs to be explained by movement theories. The efficacy of the mass-spring model provides the most insightful illustration. Consider the experiment of Polit and Bizzi (1978) in which monkeys made arm movements that were interfered with by perturbing the movement with a brief pulse from a torque motor. Prior to the introduction of this model, there would have been considerable discussion of the time constants, associated with response to the introduction of the torque motor pulse while the movement was in progress, that made it possible for the monkey to achieve the correct final position. Did the response involve central correction? Was it accomplished with a spinal level feedback path? If one believes in the mass-spring model, the result has a physical explanation at the computational level in terms of the dynamical system response of the limb, and needs no higher level explanation.

With respect to the representational level, the shackles of stimulus-response representations have been unlocked. As a result, there has been an explosion of cognitive models and of experiments to test them that has expanded our understanding of how movement behavior is organized and represented. While we still may know very little for sure, the concept of a motor program has been sharpened, and some very specific models, such as those postulating hierarchical organization, have been supported by data. The idea that programs can be responsive to environmental data and even can be formulated as a set of rules instead of literal repeatable movement patterns is a considerable step forward.

In the domain of sensory-motor integration, improved instrumentation and experimental control have led to major advances in our understanding of the interactions between perception and movement, particularly with respect to eye movements.

Finally, the area of skill acquisition has not received the same level of attention from cognitively-oriented movement researchers as the other topics we have discussed. Perhaps that is because the programming metaphor has less to contribute in this domain. Understanding the representation of skills as they are acquired requires a methodology for capturing dynamically changing knowledge representation, a topic for which computer scientists are just beginning to develop adequate tools.

# REFERENCES

Adams, J.A. (1971). A closed-loop theory of motor learning. *Journal of Motor Behavior, 3,* 111–149.

Adams, J.A. (1976). Issues for a closed-loop theory of motor learning. In G.E. Stelmach (Ed.), *Motor control: Issues and trends* (pp. 87–107). New York: Academic Press.

Abend, W., Bizzi, E., & Morasso, P. (1982). Human arm trajectory formation. *Brain, 105,* 331–348.

Arbib, M.A. (1972). *The metaphorical brain.* New York: Wiley.

Arbib, M.A. (1981). Perceptual structures and distributed motor control. In V.B. Brooks (Ed.), *Handbook of physiology—The nervous system II.* Bethesda, MD: American Physiological Society.

Armstrong, T.R. (1970). *Training for the production of memorized movement patterns* (Tech. Rep. No. 26). Ann Arbor: University of Michigan, Human Performance Center.

Basmajian, J.V. (1978). *Muscles alive: Their functions revealed through electromyography* (4th ed.). Baltimore: Williams & Wilkins.

Bernstein, N. (1967). *The coordination and regulation of movements.* London: Pergamon.

Brady, M., Hollerbach, J.M., Johnson, T.L., Lozano-Perez, T., & Mason, M.T. (Eds.). (1982). *Robot motion: Planning and control.* Cambridge, MA: MIT Press.

Bridgeman, B. (1983). Mechanisms of space constancy. In A. Hein & M. Jeannerod (Eds.), *Spatially oriented behavior* (pp. 263–279). New York: Springer-Verlag.

Brindley, G.S., Goodwin, G.M., Kulikowski, J.J., & Leighton, D. (1976). Stability of vision with a paralyzed eye. *Journal of Physiology, 258,* 65–66.

Collard, R. & Povel, D.-J. (1982). Theory of serial pattern production. *Psychological Review, 85,* 693–707.

Crossman, E.R.F.W. (1959). A theory of the acquisition of speed-skill. *Ergonomics*, *2*, 153–166.

Crossman, E.R.F.W. & Goodeve, P.J. (1983). Feedback control of hand-movement and Fitts' Law. Paper presented in 1963 at the meeting of the Experimental Psychology Society, Oxford, July. Published in *Quarterly Journal of Experimental Psychology*, *35A*, 251–278.

Demaire, C., Honoré, J., & Coquery, J.M. (1984). Effects of ballistic and tracking movements on spinal proprioceptive and cutaneous pathways in man. In S. Kornblum & J. Requin (Eds.), *Preparatory states and processes* (pp. 201–216). Hillsdale, NJ: Erlbaum.

Drury, C.G. (1975). Application of Fitts' Law to foot-pedal design. *Human Factors*, *17*, 368–373.

Easton, T.A. (1972). On the normal use of reflexes. *American Scientist*, *60*, 591–599.

Elkind, J.I. & Forgie, C.D. (1959). Characteristics of the human operator in simple manual control systems. *IRE Transactions on Automatic Control*, *AC-4*, 44–55.

Evarts, E.V., Bizzi, E., Burke, R.E., DeLong, M., & Thach, W.T., Jr. (1971). Central control of movement. *Neuroscience Research Program Bulletin*, *9* (1).

Fitts, P.M. (1954). The information capacity of the human motor system in controlling the amplitude of movement. *Journal of Experimental Psychology*, *47*, 381–391.

Fitts, P.M. (1964). Perceptual-motor skill learning. In A.W. Melton (Ed.), *Categories of human learning* (pp. 243–285). New York: Academic Press.

Fitts, P.M. & Peterson, J.R. (1964). Information capacity of discrete motor responses. *Journal of Experimental Psychology*, *67*, 103–112.

Fodor, J.A. (1983). *The modularity of mind*. Cambridge, MA: MIT Press.

Forssberg, H., Grillner, S., & Rossignol, S. (1975). Phase dependent reflex reversal during walking in chronic spinal cats. *Brain Research*, *55*, 247–304.

Fowler, C.A. & Turvey, M.T. (1978). Skill acquisition: An event approach for the optimum of a function of several variables. In G.E. Stelmach (Ed.), *Information processing in motor control and learning* (pp. 1–40). New York: Academic Press.

Gentner, D.R. (1982). Evidence against a central control model of timing in typing. *Journal of Experimental Psychology: Human Perception and Performance*, *8*, 793–810.

Gibson, J.J. (1966). *The senses considered as perceptual systems*. Boston: Houghton-Mifflin.

Gordon, G., Ed. (1978). *Active touch*. Oxford: Pergamon.

Gordon, P.C. & Meyer, D.E. (1984). Perceptual-motor processing of phonetic features in speech. *Journal of Experimental Psychology: Human Perception and Performance*, *10*, 153–178.

Greenwald, A.G. (1970). Sensory feedback mechanisms in performance control: With special reference to the ideo-motor mechanism. *Psychological Review*, *77*, 73–99.

Grillner, S. (1985). Neurobiological bases of rhythmic motor acts in vertebrates. *Science*, *228*, 143–149.

Hallet, P.E. & Lightstone, A.D. (1976). Saccadic eye movement towards stimuli triggered by prior saccades. *Vision Research*, *16*, 99–106.

Head, H. (1920). *Studies in neurology* (Vol. 2). London: Oxford University Press.

Heilman, K.M. & Valenstein, E. (Eds.). (1985). *Clinical neuropsychology (2nd ed.)*. New York: Oxford University Press.

Held, R. (1965). Plasticity in sensory-motor systems. *Scientific American*, *213*, 26–32.

Helmholtz, H. (1962). *Handbook of physiological optics*. New York: Dover. (Original work published in 1866.)

Heuer, H. (1984). Binary choice reaction time as a function of the relationship between durations and forms of responses. *Journal of Motor Behavior*, *16*, 392–404.

Hinton, G. (1984). Parallel computations for controlling an arm. *Journal of Motor Behavior*, *16*, 171–194.

Hollerbach, J.M. & Atkeson, C.G. (1986). Characterization of joint-interpolated arm movements. In H. Heuer & C. Fromm (Eds.), *Generation and modulation of action patterns* (pp. 41–54). Berlin: Springer-Verlag.

Hollerbach, J.M. & Flash, T. (1982). Dynamic interactions between limb segments during planar arm movements. *Biological Cybernetics*, *44*, 67–77.

Holst, E. von & Mittelstaedt, H. (1950). Das Reafferenzprinzip. Wechselwirkungen zwischen Zentralnervensystem und Peripherie. *Naturwissenschaften*, *37*, 464–476. (English translation in *The behavioral physiology of animals and man*. London: Methuen, 1973, pp. 139–173.)

Inhoff, A.W., Rosenbaum, D.A., Gordon, A.M., & Campbell, J.A. (1984). Stimulus-response compatibility and the motor programming of manual response sequences. *Journal of Experimental Psychology: Human Perception and Performance*, *10*, 724–733.

Jeannerod, M. (1983). How do we direct our actions in space? In A. Hein & M. Jeannerod (Eds.), *Spatially oriented behavior* (pp. 1–13). New York: Springer-Verlag.

Johnson, N.F. (1970). The role of chunking and organization in the process of recall. In G.H. Bower (Ed.), *Psychology of learning and motivation*, Vol. 4. New York: Academic Press.

Keele, S.W. (1968). Movement control in skilled motor performance. *Psychological Bulletin, 70,* 387–403.

Kelso, J.A.S., Tuller, B., & Harris, K.S. (1983). A "dynamic pattern" perspective on the control and coordination of movement. In P.F. MacNeilage (Ed.), *The production of speech* (pp. 137–173). New York: Springer-Verlag.

Kelso, J.A.S., Tuller, B., Vatikiotis-Bateson, E., & Fowler, C.A. (1984). Functionally specific articulatory cooperation following jaw perturbations during speech: Evidence for coordinative structures. *Journal of Experimental Psychology: Human Perception and Performance, 10,* 812–832.

Kerr, R. (1973). Movement time in an underwater environment. *Journal of Motor Behavior, 5,* 175–178.

Lachman, R., Lachman, J.L., & Butterfield, E.C. (1979). *Cognitive psychology and information processing: An introduction.* Hillsdale, NJ: Erlbaum.

Langolf, G.D., Chaffin, D.B., & Foulke, J.A. (1976). An investigation of Fitts' Law using a wide range of movement amplitudes. *Journal of Motor Behavior, 8,* 113–128.

Lashley, K.S. (1951). The problem of serial order in behavior. In L.A. Jeffress (Ed.), *Cerebral mechanisms in behavior.* New York: Wiley.

Lee, D.N. & Aronson, E. (1974). Visual proprioceptive control of standing in human infants. *Perception & Psychophysics, 15,* 529–532.

Lee, D.N. & Lishman, J.R. (1975). Vision—The most efficient source of proprioceptive information for balance control. *Aggressologie, 18A,* 83–94.

Lee, D.N. & Thomson, J.A. (1982). Vision in action: The control of locomotion. In D.J. Ingle, M.A. Goodale, & R.J.W. Mansfield (Eds.), *Analysis of visual behavior* (pp. 411–433). Cambridge, MA: MIT Press.

Lee, W.A. (1984). Neuromotor synergies as a basis for coordinated intentional action. *Journal of Motor Behavior, 16,* 135–170.

MacKay, D.G. (1982). The problems of flexibility, fluency, and speed-accuracy tradeoff in skilled behavior. *Psychological Review, 89,* 483–506.

MacKay, D.G. & Bowman, R.W. (1969). On producing the meaning in sentences. *American Journal of Psychology, 82,* 23–39.

Magill, R.A. (Ed.). (1983). *Memory and control of action.* Amsterdam: North-Holland.

Marr, D. (1982). *Vision.* San Francisco: W.H. Freeman.

Marteniuk, R.G. & MacKenzie, C.L. (1980). Information processing in movement organization and execution. In R.S. Nickerson (Ed.), *Attention and performance VIII* (pp. 29–57). Hillsdale, NJ: Erlbaum.

Marteniuk, R.G. & Romanow, S.K.E. (1983). Human movement organization and learning as revealed by variability of movement, use of kinematic

information, and Fourier analysis. In R.A. Magill (Ed.), *Memory and control of action* (pp. 167–197). Amsterdam: North-Holland.

Matin, L. (1972). Eye movements and perceived visual direction. In D. Jameson & L. Hurvich (Eds.), *Handbook of sensory physiology,* Vol. 7 (pp. 331–380). Berlin: Springer.

Matin, L., Stevens, J.K., & Picoult, E. (1983). Perceptual consequences of experimental extraocular muscle paralysis. In A. Hein & M. Jeannerod (Eds.), *Spatially oriented behavior* (pp. 243–262). New York: Springer-Verlag.

Mays, L.E. & Sparks, D.L. (1980). Saccades are spatially, not retinocentrically, coded. *Science, 208,* 1163–1165.

Mazur, J.E. & Hastie, R. (1978). Learning as accumulation: A reexamination of the learning curve. *Psychological Bulletin, 85,* 1256–1274.

Meyer, D.E., Abrams, R.A., Kornblum, S., Wright, C.E., & Smith, J.E.K. (In Press). Optimality in human motor performance: Ideal control of rapid aimed movements. *Psychological Review,* in press.

Meyer, D.E. & Gordon, P.G. (1983, November). *Shared mechanisms for perceiving and producing phonetic features in speech.* Paper presented at the Twenty-fourth Annual Meeting of the Psychonomic Society, San Diego, CA.

Meyer, D.E. & Gordon, P.G. (1985). Speech production: Motor programming of phonetic features. *Journal of Memory and Language, 24,* 3–26.

Meyer, D.E., Smith, J.E.K., & Wright, C.E. (1982). Models for the speed and accuracy of aimed limb movements. *Psychological Review, 89,* 449–482.

Miller, N.E. (1985). Rx: Biofeedback. *Psychology Today, 19*(2), 54–59.

Morasso, P. (1981). Spatial control of arm movements. *Experimental Brain Research, 42,* 223–227.

Moxley, S.E. (1979). Schema: The variability of practice hypothesis. *Journal of Motor Behavior, 11,* 65–70.

Norman, D.A. (1981). Categorization of action slips. *Psychological Review, 88,* 1–15.

Paillard, J. & Brouchon, M. (1968). Active and passive movements in the calibration of position sense. In S.J. Freedman (Ed.), *The neuropsychology of spatially oriented behavior* (pp. 37–55). Homewood, IL: Dorsey.

Pew, R.W. (1966). Acquisition of hierarchical control over the temporal organization of a skill. *Journal of Experimental Psychology, 71,* 764–771.

Pew, R.W. (1974). Human perceptual-motor performance. In B.H. Kantowitz (Ed.), *Human information processing: Tutorials in performance and cognition* (pp. 1–39). New York: Wiley.

Pew, R.W., Duffendack, J.C., & Fensch, L.K. (1967). Sine-wave tracking revisited. *IEEE Transactions* on *Human Factors in Electronics*, *HFE-8*, 130–134.

Polit, A. & Bizzi, E. (1978). Processes controlling arm movements in monkeys. *Science*, *201*, 1235–1237.

Posner, M.I., Goldsmith, R., & Welton, K.E. (1967). Perceived distance and the classification of distorted patterns. *Journal of Experimental Psychology*, *73*, 28–38.

Posner, M.I. & Keele, S.W. (1968). On the genesis of abstract ideas. *Journal of Experimental Psychology*, *77*, 353–363.

Posner, M.I. & Keele, S.W. (1970). Retention of abstract ideas. *Journal of Experimental Psychology*, *83*, 304–308.

Poulton, E.C. (1974). *Tracking skill and manual control.* New York: Academic Press.

Povel, D.-J. (1982). Structural factors in patterned finger tapping. *Acta Psychologica*, *52*, 107–124.

Prablanc, C., Massé, D., & Echallier, F. (1978). Corrective mechanisms in visually goal-directed large saccades. *Vision Research*, *18*, 557–560.

Pritchard, R.M. (1961). Stabilized images on the retina. *Scientific American*, *204*, 72–78.

Rosenbaum, D.A. (1983a). Central control of movement timing. *The Bell System Technical Journal: Special Issue on Human Factors and Behavioral Science*, *62*(6), 1647–1657.

Rosenbaum, D.A. (1983b). The movement precuing technique: Assumptions, applications, and extensions. In R.A. Magill (Ed.), *Memory and control of action* (pp. 231–274). Amsterdam: North-Holland.

Rosenbaum, D.A. (1985). Motor programming: A review and scheduling theory. In H. Heuer, U. Kleinbeck, and K.-M. Schmidt (Eds.), *Motor behavior: Programming, control, and acquisition* (pp. 1–33). Berlin: Springer-Verlag.

Rosenbaum, D.A., Inhoff, A.W., & Gordon, A.M. (1984). Choosing between movement sequences: A hierarchical editor model. *Journal of Experimental Psychology: General*, *113*, 372–393.

Rosenbaum, D.A., Kenny, S., & Derr, M.A. (1983). Hierarchical control of rapid movement sequences. *Journal of Experimental Psychology: Human Perception and Performance*, *9*, 86–102.

Rosenzweig, M.R. & Leiman, A.L. (1982). *Physiological psychology.* Lexington, MA: D.C. Heath.

Rumelhart, D.E. & Norman, D.A. (1982). Simulating a skilled typist: A study of skilled cognitive-motor performance. *Cognitive Science*, *6*, 1–36.

Schmidt, R.A. (1975). A schema theory of discrete motor skill learning. *Psychological Review*, *82*, 225–260.

Schmidt, R.A. (1982a). *Motor control and learning.* Champaign, IL: Human Kinetics.

Schmidt, R.A. (1982b). The schema concept. In J.A.S.

Kelso (Ed.), *Human motor behavior* (pp. 219–235). Hillsdale, NJ: Erlbaum.

Schmidt, R.A., Sherwood, D.E., Zelaznik, H., & Leikind, B.J. (1984). "Speed accuracy trade-offs in motor behavior: Theories of impulse variability". In U. Kleinbeck, H. Heuer, & K.-H. Schmidt (Eds.), *The psychology of motor behavior.* Berlin: Springer-Verlag.

Schmidt, R.A., Zelaznik, H., Hawkins, B., Frank, J.S., & Quinn, J.T., Jr. (1979). Motor output variability: A theory for the accuracy of rapid motor acts. *Psychological Review*, *86*, 415–451.

Schneider, W. & Fisk, A.D. (1983). Attention theory and mechanisms for skilled performance. In R.A. Magill (Ed.), *Memory and control of action* (pp. 119–143). Amsterdam: North-Holland.

Shaffer, L.H. (1976). Intention and performance. *Psychological Review*, *83*, 375–393.

Shaffer, L.H. (1982). Rhythm and timing in skill. *Psychological Review*, *89*, 109–122.

Shapiro, D.C. (1977). A preliminary attempt to determine the duration of a motor program. In D.M. Landers & R.W. Christina (Eds.), *Psychology of motor behavior and sport III.* Champaign, IL: Human Kinetics.

Soechting, J.F. & Lacquaniti, F. (1981). Invariant characteristics of a pointing movement in man. *Journal of Neuroscience*, *1*, 710–720.

Soede, M., Stassen, H.G., Lunteren, A. van & Luitse, W.J. (1973). A lightspot operated typewriter for physically handicapped patients. *Ergonomics*, *16*, 829–844.

Skavenski, A.A. & Hansen, R.M. (1978). Role of eye position information in visual space perception. In J. Senders, D. Fisher, & R. Monty (Eds.), *Eye movements and the higher psychological functions* (pp. 15–34). Hillsdale, NJ: Erlbaum.

Sperry, R.W. (1950). Neural basis of the spontaneous optokinetic response produced by visual inversion. *Journal of Comparative and Physiological Psychology*, *43*, 482–489.

Stelmach, G.E. (Ed.). (1978). *Information processing in motor control and learning.* New York: Academic Press.

Sternberg, S., Monsell, S., Knoll, R.L., & Wright, C.E. (1978). The latency and duration of rapid movement sequences: Comparisons of speech and typewriting. In G.E. Stelmach (Ed.), *Information processing in motor control and learning* (pp. 117–152). New York: Academic Press.

Stevens, S.S. (Ed.). (1951). *Handbook of Experimental Psychology.* New York: Wiley.

Summers, J.J. (1975). The role of timing in motor program representation. *Journal of Motor Behavior*, *7*, 229–242.

Taub, E. & Berman, A.J. (1968). Movement and learning in the absence of sensory feedback. In S.J. Freeman (Ed.), *The neuropsychology of spatially oriented behavior* (pp. 173–192). Homewood, IL: Dorsey.

Thomson, J.A. (1983). Is continuous visual monitoring necessary in visually guided locomotion? *Journal of Experimental Psychology, 9,* 427–443.

Tuller, B., Turvey, M.T., & Fitch, H.L. (1982). The Bernstein perspective: II. The concept of muscle linkage or coordinative structure. In J.A.S. Kelso (Ed.), *Human motor behavior* (pp. 253–270). Hillsdale, NJ: Erlbaum.

Turvey, M.T. (1977). Preliminaries to a theory of action with reference to vision. In R. Shaw & J. Bransford (Eds.), *Perceiving, acting, and knowing.* Hillsdale, NJ: Erlbaum.

Turvey, M.T., Fitch, H.L., & Tuller, B. (1982). The Berstein perspective: I. The problems of degrees of freedom and context-conditioned variability. In J.A.S. Kelso (Ed.), *Human motor behavior* (pp. 239–252). Hillsdale, NJ: Erlbaum.

Viviani, P. & Terzuolo, C. (1980). Space-time invariance in learned motor skills. In G.E. Stelmach & J. Requin (Eds.), *Tutorials in motor behavior* (pp. 525–533). Amsterdam: North-Holland.

Volkmann, F.C., Riggs, L.A., & Moore, R.K. (1980). Eyeblinks and visual suppression. *Science, 207,* 900–902.

Vorberg, D. & Hambuch, R. (1978). On the temporal control of rhythmic performance. In J. Requin (Ed.), *Attention and performance VII.* Hillsdale, NJ: Erlbaum.

Vorberg, D. & Hambuch, R. (1984). Timing of two-handed rhythmic performance. In J. Gibbon & L. Allan (Eds.), *Timing and time perception. Annals of the New York Academy of Science, 423,* 390–406.

Wing, A. (1980). The long and short of timing in response sequences. In G.E. Stelmach & J. Requin (Eds.), *Tutorials in motor behavior* (pp. 469–486). Amsterdam: North-Holland.

Wing, A.M., Keele, S.W., & Margolin, D.I. (1984). Motor disorder and the timing of repetitive movements. In J. Gibbon & L. Allan (Eds.), *Timing and time perception. Annals of the New York Academy of Sciences, 423,* 183–192.

Wing, A.M. & Kristofferson, A.B. (1973). Response delays and the timing of discrete motor responses. *Perception & Psychophysics, 14,* 5–12.

Woodworth, R.S. (1899). The accuracy of voluntary movement. *Psychological Review Monograph Supplements, 3*(No. 3).

# Chapter 8

# REPRESENTATION IN MEMORY

**David E. Rumelhart** *Stanford University*

**Donald A. Norman** *University of California, San Diego*

## REPRESENTATION IN MEMORY

Problems of representations are central issues in the study of memory and of cognition as a whole. Questions of how knowledge is stored and used are involved in nearly all aspects of cognition. In spite of its centrality (perhaps because of it) issues surrounding the nature of representation have become some of the most controversial aspects of the study of cognition. At the same time, representation has become one of its most muddled concepts. For most cognitive scientists, it is impossible even to imagine a cognitive system in which some system of representation does not play a central role. But even among those for whom the concept of representation is central, there are still tremendous debates concerning the precise nature of representation:

Preparation of this chapter was partially supported by Contract N00014-79-C-0323, NR 667-437 with the Personnel and Training Research Programs of the Office of Naval Research and by a grant from the System Development Foundation.

- What is a representation, anyway?
- Is it analogical or propositional?
- Is it procedural or declarative?
- Is there only one kind of representation or are there several?
- What does memorial information look like?
- Is the information stored in memory organized so that related information is stored together, or is it stored in packets or records, each independent of the other packets?
- Is knowledge stored as a collection of separate units, or are individual memory traces intertwined over large regions of memory?

### Representations: What Are They?

Much of the research in cognitive science has been concerned with the representation of knowledge and, more particularly, the representation of meaning. The rationale goes something like

511

this. Meaning is an important part of understanding, remembering, and cognition. If we want to make a process model of understanding or remembering or cognition, there must be something in our model corresponding to meaning. But what should meaning look like? It is natural to turn to the logicians for ideas on how to represent it. The major language of the logicians is the predicate calculus. Thus, most of the early ideas as to how we should represent meaning were formulas of the predicate calculus, and so our story starts there.

Suppose that Fido were a *DOG*, and that Fido were also a *PET*. We can represent these two statements by letting *PET* and *DOG* take Fido as a particular instance for their arguments:

$$A: \quad DOG(Fido)$$

$$B: \quad PET(Fido)$$

Now, let $x$ be any particular instance of a *PET*. If all possible instances of *PET* were also *ANIMALS*, we would express this as

$$\forall x(PET(x) \rightarrow ANIMAL(x))$$

where the symbol "$\forall$" is the "universal quantifier" and is to be read, "for all." The formula then reads, for all $x$, if $x$ is a *PET*, then $x$ is an *ANIMAL*. Note that if some person $p$ owns a rock and insists that it is a pet, then the formula is false, because for $x = rock$, $PET(x)$ but not $ANIMAL(x)$. To express the fact that there is at least one $x$ that is a *PET* and not an *ANIMAL* (namely the case where $x = p$'s rock), we would say

$$\exists x(PET(x) \; AND \; FALSE(ANIMAL(x)))$$

where the symbol "$\exists$" is the "existential quantifier" and is to be read, "there exists." This formula reads, there exists an $x$ such that $x$ is a *PET* and it is FALSE that $x$ is an *ANIMAL*.

In the early days of computer models of language understanding and semantic memory, this was a common representational format. When the predicate calculus representations were employed, the rules for operating on representations were based upon logical rules of inference. This led to the development of a number of artificial intelligence systems which, as a natural consequence of choosing the logician's method of representation, employed programs that made inferences by proving general theorems.

To many people, the very power of logical representation was its difficulty. The predicate calculus solves problems that people find difficult, and although this is virtuous in mathematics, it is not appropriate for a model of human thought. After all, a model of human representation should find easy what people find easy, difficult what people find difficult. However, in making this complaint, it is important not to confuse the tool with the product. The predicate calculus is a tool with considerable explanatory and mathematical power. It is a useful means for encoding our beliefs about human representation. With it, we can model the strengths and weaknesses of human thought. Just as we can model a bouncing ball with differential equations without believing that the ball itself understands or solves these equations, we can model human processes with various formalisms without believing that the human knows about, understands, or uses those formalisms. These tools are descriptive, not explanatory. Nonetheless, in general, models of human representational processes have tended to avoid using the full power of the predicate calculus.

We can illustrate another kind of problem people sometimes have with these systems by relating some of the problems encountered many years ago in trying to teach some of these systems to undergraduates. The problems came up with the representational scheme used in early studies of psycholinguistics by Clark and Chase (1972), but the point is much more general than their work. Clark and Chase presented their subjects simple pictures which sometimes had a star above a plus, sometimes a plus above a star. Then, their subjects were shown printed sentences of the form

"The plus is not below the star."

and asked to respond TRUE or FALSE depending on whether the information in the sentence matched that in the picture. The details are unimportant for this illustration. The important point is that Clark and Chase assumed that subjects looked at the picture and represented it in the form

$$(ABOVE(STAR, PLUS))$$

and then represented the sentence in something like the form

$$(NOT(BELOW(PLUS, STAR))).$$

The judgment was thought to be made on the basis of a comparison and transformation of these two representations. In spite of the impressive fit of their model to the data, our undergraduates could not be convinced that this theory was at all reasonable.

Our students said, "We certainly wouldn't do it that way." "Why not?" we asked. "Well," they replied, "the representation is too sparse, it lacks information of how much one object is above the other, and of the exact sizes and shapes of the plus and the star." In short, our students felt that regardless of the impressive fit of the theory to the data, the theory was wrong because the representations did not match the richness of their personal impressions of their own representations.

What is going on? Were Clark and Chase so caught up in their narrow view of things that they missed something so obvious that any sophomore could see it? Or were the undergraduates just too naive to understand the implications of their theories and the irrelevance of their intuitions. The real problem lies in our lack of clarity about what a representation is and about what properties a representation should have.

## Representation as Mappings

Let us now try to be clear about what kind of a thing a representation really is and use that to see why our students had so many problems. To begin, a representation is something that stands for something else. In other words, it is a kind of a model of the thing it represents. We have to distinguish between a *representing world* and a *represented world*. The representing world must somehow mirror some aspects of the represented world. Palmer (1978) has listed five features that must be specified for any representational system:

1. What the represented world is,
2. What the representing world is,
3. What aspects of the represented world are being modeled,
4. What aspects of the representing world are doing the modeling,
5. What the correspondences are between the two worlds.

These features are illustrated in Figure 8.1. In this example the represented world consists of

| | | I | II | III | IV |
|---|---|---|---|---|---|
| Objects: | (figure A) | A | \| | 15 | 7 |
| | (figure B) | B | l | 13 | 9 |
| Properties: | height | not directly represented | line length | numeric value | numeric value |
| Relations: | A taller than B | TALLERTHAN(A,B) | LONGERTHAN | GREATERTHAN | LESSTHAN |

REPRESENTED WORLD — REPRESENTING WORLD

**Figure 8.1.** The relationship between the represented world and the representing world showing four different ways the representing world might choose to model the physical relation of *TALLERTHAN* that holds between the two figures in the represented world. I shows a propositional representation: *TALLERTHAN(A, B)*. II shows a representation by means of line length. III shows a representation by means of numerical value. And IV shows that the relationship can be arbitrary, as when smaller numbers in the representing world represent larger figures in the represented world.

two stick figures, one taller than the other. We can imagine that each has the property of having some height and that the relationship *TALLERTHAN* holds between the first and second figure. We have illustrated four different possible representing worlds. In the first (I), we have the symbol *A* representing the taller figure and the symbol *B* representing the shorter. We represent the relationship between the height of the two by the formula *TALLERTHAN(A, B)*. There is no direct representation of height in this system. In the second example (II), the figures are represented by lines, and height is directly represented by line length. The *TALLERTHAN* relation is implicitly represented by the physical relation *LONGERTHAN* between the line segments. In the third example (III), numbers are used to represent the figures and the magnitudes of the numbers represent their heights. The *TALLERTHAN* relation is represented by the arithmetic relation of *GREATERTHAN* ( > ). Note that the representational format is quite arbitrary. Thus, example IV shows an alternative format for using the magnitudes of numbers to represent heights—in this case, with the taller figures represented by smaller numbers. The *TALLERTHAN* relation is represented by the arithmetic relation of *LESSTHAN* ( < ). If our only goal were to represent height, then the representational systems of III and IV would be functionally equivalent. These four examples illustrate how the same characteristic in the represented world can be represented very differently in different representing worlds.

We can express these ideas more precisely. In general, a world consists of a set of objects and a set of relations among those objects. So, for example, one world, the represented world, might consist of a set of objects *A*, and a set of relations *R*. In the formal language of relational theory this can be denoted by the two-tuple $\langle A, R \rangle$. Not all aspects of the represented world are modeled in the representing world, however, so we let *A'* and *R'* stand for those objects and relations, respectively, that are to be represented. This subset of the to-be-represented world can be designated $\langle A', R' \rangle$. In the representing world, there is a corresponding set of objects *B'*, and a function *f* such that for every object *a'* in *A'*, there is an object *b'* in *B'*, such that $f(a') = b'$. There is also a corresponding set of relations *S'* in the representing world such

that if $a'_1$ is related to $a'_2$ by relation $R'_{12}$ then $f(a'_1)$ is related to $f(a'_2)$ by relation $S'_{12}$. In other words, in a representational system, there are three relevant ordered pairs, one $\langle A, R \rangle$ for the represented world, one $\langle A', R' \rangle$ for those aspects of the represented world that are being modeled, and one $\langle B', S' \rangle$ for what is within the representing world. There are two relevant mappings: one between objects—*A'* and *B'*—and another between relations—*R'* and *S'*.

### Representation IN versus Representation OF the Mind

The most important point of a representation is that it allows us to reach conclusions about the thing being represented by looking only at the representing world. When considering how knowledge is represented in the human there are four kinds of things we need to keep in mind:

1. An environment in which there are objects and events;

2. A brain that attains certain states dependent on its current state and on the sensory information that impinges on it;

3. Our phenomenal experience, which is assumed to be a function of our brain state;

4. A model or theory of the environment, the brain states, and the experience.

In trying to understand representational systems, it is important to understand that there are several pairs of representing and represented worlds. These various worlds are shown in Figure 8.2. There is a physical environment that is, in some fashion, represented by physical states of the brain. The environment is the represented world, and the brain states are the representing world. Our phenomenal experience reflects brain states and so can be considered a representing world. When people think of representation, they often think of the relationship between phenomenal experiences and the environment. In fact, most representational issues are not about how the environment is represented in our phenomenal experience, nor about how the environment is represented by brain states. Instead, they concern the representational system in which our theories are the representing world, and the environment, brain states, and our phenomenal experience are the

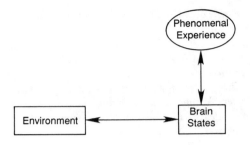

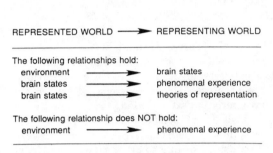

**Figure 8.2.** The relationships among the represented world, the brain, and the environment.

world to be represented. Thus although the representational issues are often phrased in terms of how the world is represented in our experience, most work on representation focuses on the question of how our experience (and our brain states) should be represented in our theories. As we shall see in this chapter, the questions often revolve around the representational power and efficacy of a particular representational system and the degree to which such a representational system allows us to formulate adequate theories of human cognition.

Presumably, our students had access to their own phenomenal experience, and when they compared it with the world represented by Clark and Chase, they found their experiences richer and more complete. However, Clark and Chase only claimed to represent $A'$ and $R'$, small, limited subsets of $A$ and $R$, not the full environment. Moreover, our students were comparing their phenomenal world with a limited representing world; there is no wonder that they were unhappy. Consider the sense in which our phenomenal experience represents the external world. There are objects in the world, and there are objects of experience. The objects of our experience are not the same as the objects of the

world, but they seem to reflect much of the structure of the world. In this way, it probably does make sense to speak of our experiential representation of the world.

## Overview of Representational Systems

The focus of research on representational systems fall into four basic categories. These are:

1. The propositionally based systems in which knowledge is assumed to be represented as a set of discrete symbols or propositions, so that concepts in the world are represented by formal statements.

2. Analogical representational systems in which the correspondence between the represented world and the representing world is as direct as possible, traditionally using continuous variables to represent concepts that are continuous in the real world. Examples are the use of electrical voltages in an analog computer to represent fluid flow or shaft rotation, or maps that are analogical representations of some geographical features of the world, or pictures in which three-dimensional space is represented by marks on a two-dimensional medium.

3. Procedural representational systems in which knowledge is assumed to be represented in terms of an active process or procedure. Moreover, the representation is in a form directly interpretable by an action system. Consider how to pronounce the word "serendipitous." The movement made by the vocal apparatus is clearly procedural in that it is tied up in the actual performance of the skill and usually is not available apart from the ability to do the task, even though one normally does have conscious control and accessibility to many of the components of the task. Thus, to describe the tongue movements made in pronouncing the word, most of us have to perform the task—that is, to say the word "serendipitous"—and then describe aloud the actions performed.

4. Distributed knowledge representational systems, in which knowledge in memory is not represented at any discrete place in memory, but instead is distributed over a

large set of representing units—each unit representing a piece of a large amount of knowledge.

Most actual representational systems are hybrids that fall into more than one of these four categories. Nevertheless, these categories form a useful framework within which to describe the various systems that have been proposed.

### Representational Systems Include both Representation and Process

We have introduced several categories of representational systems. There is, however, one more important aspect of a representation system that must be considered: the processes that operate upon the representations. Consider the four different representational formats illustrated in Figure 8.1. The point of this figure is to demonstrate some of the properties of the four formats. But note that the representations within the representing world do not carry their meaning without the assistance of some process that can make use of and interpret the representational structures. Thus, if height is to be represented by line length, there must exist some process capable of comparing line lengths. If height is to be represented by numbers, then there must be some processes that can operate upon those numbers according to the appropriate rules of mathematics and the rules established by the choice of representation (e.g., whether it is type III or IV in Figure 8.1). Similarly, the representational system established by the use of formulas from the predicate calculus requires interpretation and evaluation. In all these cases, the processes that evaluate and interpret the representations are as important as the representations themselves.

In general, a Representational System ($RS$) involves a relational pair:

$$RS \equiv \langle R, P \rangle,$$

where $RS$ is the entire system, $R$ is the representing world (which itself requires the several ordered pairs discussed earlier), and $P$ is the set of processes that operate upon and interpret $R$. In general, there are many forms of processes. Moreover, there is a tradeoff between $R$ and $P$, so that information that some systems chose to include within $R$ can be included within $P$ by others. In some systems, the distinction between

the representation ($R$) and the processes that operate upon them ($P$) is clear and distinct; in others, the $R$ and $P$ are so tightly intertwined that clear distinctions are impossible. In all cases, however, it is necessary to always recognize that a representational system is incomplete unless both the representations and the processes that operate upon them have been explicitly considered.[1]

## PROPOSITIONALLY BASED REPRESENTATIONAL SYSTEMS

Most of the representational systems that have been developed and evaluated to date fall into the category of propositional representations. These representational systems all share the characteristic that knowledge is represented as a collection of symbols. According to some views, these symbols are structured into trees or networks. According to other views, knowledge merely consists of lists of such symbols. According to still other views, knowledge is thought of as highly structured configurations of such symbols with associated procedures for interpreting the symbols.

In philosophy, a proposition is a statement that has a truth value, determined by conditions in the world. A predicate is a general statement; propositions are predicates with particular values substituted for the general variables of a predicate. Thus, $DOG(x)$ is a predicate and is often interpreted as the set of dogs. $DOG(Sam)$ is a propostion asserting that *Sam is a dog*; it is either true or false depending on the nature of *Sam*. The technical aspects of propositions and predicates have been relaxed considerably in the development of theories of representation in psychology and in artificial intelligence, most especially the requirements that a proposition have a truth value. In this section, we illustrate the use of propositional representation as it has been used in psychology, proceeding from the simplest to the most complex of propositional systems. In each case, we describe the basic issues addressed by the proponents of these systems.

---

[1]In general, the $R$ part of $RS$ is called the declarative part of the system and the $P$ part is called the procedural part. We return to this distinction later.

## Semantic Features or Attributes

Perhaps the simplest of the propositional representation systems is the assumption that concepts are properly represented as a set of semantic features or attributes. This means of representation is a very natural application of the language of set theory to the problem of characterizing the nature of concepts. Variations on this view have been popular in the study of semantic memory, and they have been widely used as assumptions for describing the representation of knowledge. According to these views, concepts are represented by a weighted set of features. Thus, concepts can stand in the familiar set relationships: two concepts can be disjoint (have no attributes in common), overlap (have some but not all attributes in common), be nested (all of the attributes of one concept are included in another), or be identical (be specified by exactly the same set of features). The features can have weights associated with them that represent their varying saliency and importance for the concepts in question.

Rather than review all of the applications of these ideas here, we choose to describe two well developed variations on this general theme: the feature comparison model proposed by Smith, Shoben, and Rips (1974), and the feature matching model of Tversky (1977; Tversky & Gati, 1978). The proposals of Smith et al. were made in the context of a series of studies that began with Collins and Quillian (1969) and Meyer (1970) on simple semantic verification tasks. The general procedure followed in these studies was to present a statement that asked whether a member of one semantic category could also be a member of another. Thus, typical sentences would be: *A robin is a bird*, *A vegetable is an artichoke*, or perhaps, *A rock is a furniture*. Subjects were asked to respond TRUE or FALSE to the sentences as quickly as possible. The basic representational assumption was that the words that represent the two categories to be considered can themselves be represented by a set of semantic features that vary in their relationship to the formal definition of the category. In particular, features could be divided into those that were defining (they must hold if an item is a member of the category) and those that were characteristic (they usually apply, but are not necessary for the definition). Thus, *has feathers* is a definitional feature for the concept bird, whereas *can*

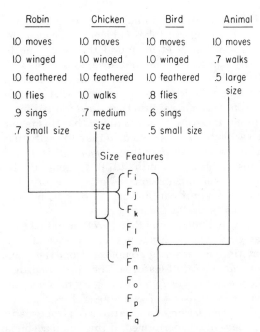

**Figure 8.3.** An illustrative set of features and weights for the concepts *robin, chicken, bird,* and *animal.* From *Categories and Concepts* (p. 63) by E.E. Smith and D.L. Medin, 1981. Cambridge, MA: Harvard University Press. Copyright 1981 by Harvard University Press. Reprinted by permission.

*fly* is a characteristic feature; birds characteristically can fly, but flying is not essential to a thing being a bird. In addition, the concept bird might have features specifying that it has a particular size, shape, and so on, things that might have features specifying that is a particular size, shape, and so on, things that might be true of only the most typical instances of birds. Figure 8.3 (from Smith & Medin, 1981) shows an illustrative set of features and weights for the concepts of *robin, chicken, bird,* and *animal.*

In formulating their proposal, Smith et al. had a number of empirical results in mind. Collins and Quillian (1969) found that subjects took less time to verify statements of the form *A canary is yellow,* than statements of the form *A canary has feathers,* which in turn took less than the time to verify *A canary eats food.* From this they deduced that the information is stored hierarchically; properties specific to canaries are stored with the concept canary, properties specific to birds in general are stored with bird, and properties specific to animals are stored with animal. Thus, the further up the hierarchy one has to search to find the relevant information, the longer it takes subjects to answer the question. Smith et al. found that the time to verify a statement does not always conform with the predictions from a hierarchical model. Thus, it might take longer to confirm that *A cat is a mammal* than to confirm that *A cat is an animal*. More interestingly, it was found that it is faster to verify that *A robin is a bird* than to verify that *A chicken is a bird* or that *A penguin is a bird* (Rips, Shoben, & Smith, 1973). In general, the more typical an instance is of a category, the more quickly it can be verified that it, in fact, belongs to that category.

Smith, Shoben, and Rips (1974) proposed that category membership is not a prestored characteristic but rather is computed from the comparison of a set of features. They proposed that the process of verifying a category membership statement consists of two stages. First, a very quick comparison of all features (characteristic and defining) is performed. If this comparison is sufficiently good, the question is answered in the affirmative. If the comparison is sufficiently poor, the question is answered in the negative. If the comparison leads to an intermediate result, a slower comparison of the defining features is initiated. This model accounts for the basic experimental results: true statements involving highly typical items (e.g., *A robin is a bird*) are affirmed very quickly; false statements involving very distinct items (e.g., *A door is a bird*) are rejected very quickly; statements involving less typical examples of a category (e.g., *A penguin is a bird*) are affirmed relatively slowly; and statements involving things similar to, but not members of, the category (e.g., *A bit is a bird*) are rejected relatively slowly.

A number of different kinds of verification proposals have been made, all somewhat different from one another, but all consistent with the spirit of this general approach. Thus, McCloskey and Glucksberg (1978) employ similar assumptions about representation of concepts, but their model only requires a single stage comparison process. The newer models, of course, usually account for the data better than do the earlier models. The important point, however, is that all of these models assume that conceptual knowledge is represented by a set of features and that these features include necessary and sufficient attributes to the concept as well as attributes that are only characteristic of it.

Because the category contains features that are typical of its instances, but that are not necessarily shared by its instances, these models are referred to as prototype theories of representation.

### Similarity and Featural Representations

Judgments of the similarity of two concepts pose a particularly interesting problem. The most obvious way to approach the problem is to state that two concepts are similar inasmuch as their underlying features are similar or overlapping. If each concept is represented by a set of $N$ features, then one can think of the features as representing an $N$-dimensional space, with each of the concepts being a point in the space. In models of this type, similarity is often assumed to be a monotonically decreasing function of the distance between points in the multidimensional space. Any geometric representation of this form must satisfy two major conditions: symmetry and the triangle inequality. The symmetry condition states that because similarity is a function of the distance between points, the similarity of A to B must be the same as the similarity of B to A. The second condition, the triangle inequality condition, states that for any three points, the distance between any two must be less than or equal to the sum of the distances between the other two. Because similarity is inversely related to the distance between points, the triangle inequality translates into the condition that the similarity of two concepts A and C must be greater than or equal to the sum of the similarity of A to B and of B to C. Both these basic properties may be violated (Tversky, 1977; Tversky & Gati, 1978).

Tversky points out that in certain cases similarity appears to be an asymmetric relation. For example, people generally judge the similarity of North Korea to mainland China to be greater than the similarity of China to North Korea, thus violating the symmetric property. The triangle inequality can also be violated. Thus, although Jamaica is very similar to Cuba (due to its geographical characteristics) and Cuba is similar to Russia (politically), Jamaica is not at all similar to Russia.

Tversky suggests that these violations can be readily accounted for by means of a simple model defined on a semantic feature representation. Tversky's major representational assumptions are essentially identical to those of Smith,

Shoben, and Rips (1974). Figure 8.4 shows the relationships between the representations of two overlapping concepts *a* and *b*. Note, there are seven sets of features distinguished in this relationship. These are:

1. The features of concept *a*: the set *A*,
2. The features of concept *b*: the set *B*,
3. The features common between *a* and *b*: the set $A \cap B$,
4. The total set of features either in *A* or in *B*: the set $A \cup B$,
5. The features that are in *a* but not in *b*: the set $A - B$,
6. The features that are in *b* but not in *a*: the set $B - A$, and
7. The features that are neither in *A* nor in *B*: the set $-(A \cup B)$.

Tversky proposes that the similarity of *a* to *b*, *S*(*a*, *b*), be given by the equation

$$S(a, b) = f(A \cap B) - \alpha f(A - B)$$
$$- \beta f(B - A)$$

where $f(X)$ is a numerical measure of the salience of the features in set *X*, and $\alpha$ and $\beta$ are constants. Tversky's account of similarity suggests that different aspects of the representation are treated differently depending upon the question being asked. Thus, if $\alpha > \beta$, then *a* is more similar to *b* than is *b* to *a*: $S(a, b) > S(b, a)$ (as in the China–Korea example). If in the course of the question, the weights associated with the different dimensions change, then such properties as the triangular inequality can be violated (as in the Jamaica–Cuba–Russia example).

### Similarity and Metaphor
Ortony (1979) has applied Tversky's model to the similarity of metaphorical statements such as:

*Lectures are like sleeping pills.*
*Sleeping pills are like lectures.*
*Lectures are like sermons.*

Like Tversky, Ortony noted an extreme asymmetry in the meaning of these statements. The first seems to be an altogether reasonable (albeit metaphorical) assertion, whereas the second seems to be nearly nonsensical. On the other hand, the third seems to be a straightforward

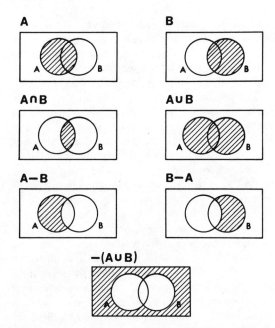

**Figure 8.4.** The seven different relationships that can apply among members of two overlapping sets (*A* and *B*). They may be members of one set (*A*) or of the other (*B*). They may be in common between the two sets ($A \cap B$). They may be in either *A* or *B* ($A \cup B$). They may be in *A* but not in *B* ($A - B$) or they may be in *B* but not in *A* ($B - A$), and finally, they might be in neither *A* nor *B* ($-(A \cup B)$ or $(-A) \cap (-B)$).

statement of literal similarity. Following Tversky, Ortony suggests that the meaning of the concepts lectures and sleeping pills are represented by sets of features, each with an importance or salience value. The meaning of these statements can be determined by matching the features of the predicate term with those of the subject term. In a normal, declarative sentence, highly salient features of the predicate term are also highly salient features of the subject term, as in the third example. A sentence contains a metaphor or a simile if highly salient predicate features are relatively less salient subject features. Finally, sentences of this form are nonsensical if the subject and predicate either have no features in common or if only features that are low in salience on the predicate term are held in common.

In spite of their relative simplicity, semantic feature models offer remarkably good accounts of a rather wide body of data. (A good review of these issues is presented in Smith and Medin,

1981.) Such theories do, however, have their limitations. In particular, almost all of the work has been with simple nominal concepts. It is much less clear how these models would be applied in the case of predicate concepts. Similarly, it is not clear how such models would represent simple facts (e.g., *typewriters are used for typing*) or simple events (e.g., *John went to the store*). The semantic feature model does not handle distinctions among the statements that a robin is a bird, a sparrow is a bird, and a sparrow is not a robin; if category membership were determined solely by defining characteristics, one might very well determine that a sparrow was a robin, or perhaps that a bird was a robin. In similar fashion, these models cannot account for problems of quantification, as represented in the contrast in meaning between the sentences *Everyone kissed someone* and *Someone was kissed by everyone*. In fairness to semantic feature models, they were not intended to solve all the problems of representation, but rather primarily those of similarity and of definition. In this, they do well. In interpreting the role of this class of models, it is useful to note Tversky's comments on the matter (which are also relevant to the dilemma faced by our poor undergraduates who felt that these representations were lacking in substance):

> Our total data base concerning a particular object (e.g., a person, a country, or a piece of furniture) is generally rich in content and complex in form. It includes appearance, function, relation to other objects, and any other property of the object that can be deduced from our general knowledge of the world. When faced with a particular task (e.g., identification or similarity assessment) we extract and compile from our data base a limited list of relevant features on the basis of which we perform the required task. Thus, the representation of an object as a collection of features is viewed as a product of a prior process of extraction and compilation (Tversky, 1977, p. 329).

In other words, Tversky actually makes no commitment to a feature set as one mechanism for the representation of knowledge in general, but rather merely contends that the feature representation is produced for the purpose of carrying out particular tasks. Tversky is not pretending to offer a proposal for the representation of knowledge in general. Rather, he provides a

nice account of how a feature based representation could solve the knotty problem of similarity.

## Symbolic Logic and the Predicate Calculus

The semantic feature representations are directed at the representations of word meanings. To represent knowledge in general we must be able to represent the meaning of arbitrary statements as well as the meaning of single words. When psychologists, linguists, and computer scientists began to concern themselves with this more general task, it was natural to look to the formalisms already developed for this purpose by mathematicians and logicians—namely, symbolic logic. In particular, a number of workers have been drawn to the predicate calculus (developed first by Frege, 1892) as an appropriate representational format for meaning in general. On this view the representational system consists of five kinds of entities:

*Constants* (designated $a, b, c, \ldots$), expressions that stand for individual objects. Examples: proper names, such as Fido or John.

*Variables* (designated $x, y, z, \ldots$), expressions that stand for some one of a set of constants, as in, for some $x$, such that $x$ is a person.

*Predicates* (designated $P(x, y, \ldots)$), expressions that stand for particular properties or relations among objects. $P$ stands for some particular property, and $x$ and $y$ for variables. Example: $ATE(x, y)$: some object $x$ ate some object $y$.

*Propositions* (designated $P(a, b, \ldots)$). Propositions are predicates in which particular constants have been substituted for the variables. When this occurs, we say that the predicate has been instantiated. Propositions have truth values: the statement encoded by the proposition is either true or false. Example: The predicate $ATE(x, y)$, which, when instantiated by Elaine and sandwich, forms the proposition $ATE(Elaine, sandwich)$—Elaine ate a sandwich—which is either true or false.

*Functions* (designated $f(x, y, \ldots)$), expressions containing variables that, when instantiated, form complex constants.

Example: *TEACH(agent, recipient, locative, time)*, which, when instantiated by appropriate constants, might become *TEACH (Don, graduate students, conference room, Monday noon)*, representing the sentence "Don teaches the graduate students in the conference room, Monday at noon."

*Quantifiers*, including the existential quantifier, ∃ (there exists an *x*) and the universal quantifier, ∀ (for all *x*).

*Logical connectives* consisting of negation (−), conjunction (∩), disjunction (∪), and implication (→). These connectives can combine predicates and propositions to produce more complex predicates and propositional expressions.

Consider how we might represent a few simple statements in the predicate calculus. First, consider the statement *John loves Mary*. In the predicate calculus formalism this becomes

$$LOVES(John, Mary)$$

Now consider the representation of *Someone loves Mary*. This would be represented as ∃*x(LOVES(x, Mary))*. In words, this formula says there exists an *x* such that *x* loves Mary. The *x* in the quantifier is said to be bound to the *x* in the predicate. Consider the statement *Everyone loves himself*. This would be represented ∀*x(LOVES(x, x))*. In words it reads, for all *x*, *x* loves *x*. Finally consider the statements *Everyone loves someone* and *Someone is loved by everyone*. In the predicate calculus formalism, these two would be represented by

$$∀(x)∃y(LOVES(x, y)) \text{ and } ∃y∀(x)(LOVES(x, y)).$$

Note that, in the first form, a different *y* can be chosen for each *x*. The existential quantifier is said to be within the scope of the universal quantifier. In the other, the universal quantifier is within the scope of the existential quantifier. Thus the difference in meaning between these two sentences is a matter of scope. Finally, consider the predicate calculus translation of a sentence of the form *All men are mortal*. This is translated to be

$$∀(x)(MAN(x) → MORTAL(x)).$$

The great advantage of the predicate calculus is the large body of logical, philosophical, and mathematical work that it calls upon. Many issues of representation, especially those involving quantification and logical connectives, have already been answered. The predicate calculus and versions of it have been extremely popular as a representational device in philosophical and linguistic treatments of meaning, in attempts to represent and reason with semantic information in artificial intelligence, and in psychological attempts to represent knowledge. Thus textbooks of methods in artificial intelligence sometimes suggest the use of the predicate calculus as a basic tool for the field (Nilsson, 1980).

### The Use of the Predicate Calculus in Psychology

One example of the use of the predicate calculus formalism in psychology is given by the work of Kintsch and his colleagues. It should be noted that Kintsch explicitly disavows the general version of the predicate calculus. Kintsch (1972) argues that:

> The formalism that appears to be best suited for the task is some kinds of low-order propositional calculus. I say low-order calculus because the attempt to translate language expressions into something like a fully quantified predicate calculus is surely misguided. Formal logic was developed precisely because language is so sloppy that it is insufficient for certain purposes (such as formal reasoning). To propose formal logic as a model for language only means forcing language into an intolerable straight-jacket . . . . What we need is a greatly less powerful and elegant formalism that permits the operation of lexical inference rules as well as the semantic-syntactic rules that are necessary to produce sentences, but that does not impose more order than there is.[2]

Kintsch and his colleagues have looked at the representation of an interrelated set of sentences treating text as a "connected, partially ordered list of propositions." The predicates are concepts named by English verbs, and the constants are other concepts, named either by English nouns or by other propositions. The variables of the predicates have associated labels indicating the role that the argument plays in the whole

---

[2]From "Notes on the Structure of Semantic Memory" by W. Kintsch in *Organization and Memory* (p. 252), E. Tulving and W. Donaldson (Eds.), 1972. New York: Academic Press. Copyright 1972 by Academic Press. Reprinted by permission.

Fragment of an Episode from a Short Story and the Corresponding Text Base [a]

| Text | Text base |
|---|---|
| This Landolfo, then, having made the sort of preliminary calculations merchants normally make, purchased a very large ship, loaded it with a mixed cargo of goods paid for out of his own pocket, and sailed with them to Cyprus. (The episode continues with a description of how this endeavor finally resulted in Landolfo's ruin.) | 1(PURCHASE,agent:L,object:SHIP)<br>2(LARGE,SHIP)<br>3(VERY,2)<br>4(AFTER,1,5)<br>5(CALCULATE,agent:L)<br>6(PRELIMINARY,5)<br>7(LIKE,5,8)<br>8(CALCULATE,agent:MERCHANT)<br>9(NORMAL,8)<br>10(LOAD,agent:L,goal:SHIP,object:CARGO)<br>11(MIXED,CARGO)<br>12(CONSIST OF,object:CARGO,source:GOODS)<br>13(PAY,agent:L,object:GOODS,instrument:MONEY)<br>14(OWN,agent:L,object:MONEY)<br>15(SAIL,agent:L,object:GOODS,goal:CYPRUS) |

[a]Modified from Kintsch (1976).

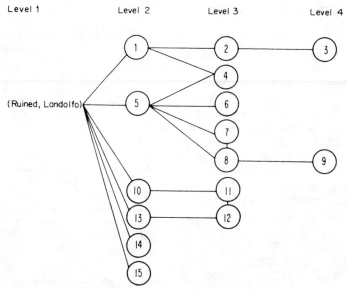

**Figure 8.5.** The text base hierarchy for the fragment of text shown at the top of the figure. Propositions are indicated only by their number; shared arguments among them are shown as connecting lines. From "Comprehension and Memory of Text" by W. Kintsch in *Handbook of Learning and Cognitive Processes, Vol. 6* (p. 60), W.K. Estes (Ed.), 1978. Hillsdale, NJ: Erlbaum. Copyright 1978 by Lawrence Erlbaum Associates, Inc. Reprinted by permission.

proposition. These role names are, by and large, drawn from the case grammar of Fillmore (1968) and include names such as agent, object, recipient, instrument, source, goal, and so on (see Figure 8.5). In Figure 8.5, the individual propositions are numbered, and when a given proposition serves as an argument for another, the number of the embedded proposition is given. The roles, when named, are indicated prior to the argument in each proposition. Note that the same argument appears in several propositions. Kintsch argues that the interconnection of propositions through shared arguments is a necessary condition for coherence of a text.

Although the predicate calculus approach to representation has the strong advantage of providing a consistent and powerful representational structure with a well worked out inferential component, it is nevertheless not the universal choice. The two most important reasons for this involve, first, the debate on the organization of knowledge in memory and, second, the notion that the logical processes of theorem proving, so natural to the predicate calculus formalism, do not seem to capture the ways people actually reason. Alternative representational systems may prove more useful when one wishes to define processes other than the ones most obvious for the predicate calculus. Thus, many authors have chosen representational systems in which the knowledge pieces are connected to each other to form an associative network of interrelated pieces of knowledge. In this way, the organization of information in memory is more perspicuously represented. Moreover, there has been a push to develop systems for representing knowledge in which heuristic reasoning processes more like those we see in our subjects are more easily definable.

Although the predicate calculus led the way, probably the most important work on representation has emphasized other aspects of knowledge than the formal issues of statements and quantification that the calculus addresses. Psychologists and workers in artificial intelligence have to a large extent explored representations that emphasize what can be thought of as the most salient psychological aspects of knowledge:

- The associative nature of knowledge;
- The notion of knowledge units or packages, so that knowledge about a single concept or event is organized together in one functional unit;
- The detailed structure of knowledge about any single concept or event;
- The consideration different levels of knowledge, each level playing a different organizational role, and with higher order units adding structure to lower order ones;
- The everyday reasoning of people, in which default values seem to be substituted for

information that is not known explicitly, in which information known for one concept is applied to other concepts, and in which inconsistent knowledge can exist.

These beliefs have guided studies of representation towards structures called semantic networks, schemata, frames, and scripts. These concepts are actually closely related to the formalisms of the predicate calculus, and in some cases are simply notational variations on the calculus. The difference in emphasis, however, is critical, because the emphasis puts the focus on functional aspects of representation, including just how a real, working system might be able to use the information. Historically, these approaches to the study of representation started with semantic networks, so let us start there as well.

## Semantic Networks and Their Properties

An important step in the representation of the associations within long term memory was Quillian's (1968) development of the semantic network. The basic notion is that knowledge can be represented by a kind of directed, labeled graph structure in which the basic structural element is a set of interconnected nodes by relations. Nodes represent concepts in memory. A relation is an association among sets of nodes. Relations are labeled and directed. In this view the meaning of a concept (represented by a node) is given by the pattern of relationships among which it participates. It is important to note that not all nodes in a semantic memory system have names corresponding to words in natural language. Some nodes represent concepts that have no natural language equivalent, and others represent instances (or tokens) of the concepts represented by other nodes. Thus, Figure 8.6 shows one form of network that evolved from the work of Quillian: his representation of the concept "plant" in its various meaning senses.

### Inheritance Properties and Default Values
One of the attractive features of the semantic network formalism is the convenience with which the property of *inheritance* is formulated. Figure 8.7 illustrates a common semantic

PLANT    1. Living structure which is not an animal, frequently with leaves, getting its food from air, water, earth.
         2. Apparatus used for any process in industry.
         3. Put (seed, plant, etc.) in earth for growth.

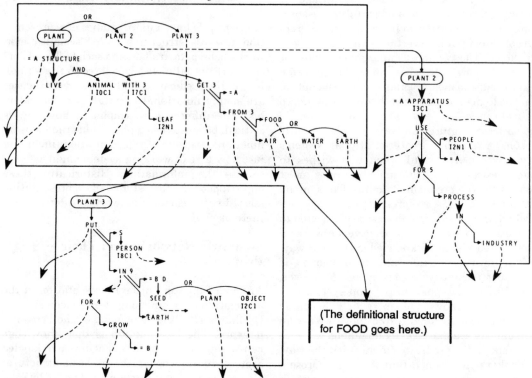

**Figure 8.6.** Quillian's (1968) semantic network representation for three meanings of the concept "plant." From "Semantic Memory" by M.R. Quillian in *Semantic Information Processing* (p. 236), M. Minsky (Ed.), 1968. Cambridge, MA: MIT Press. Copyright 1968 by the MIT Press. Reprinted by permission.

network representational format for information about animals. The basic structure of a network is illustrated in the figure. Nodes (the dots and angle brackets) stand for concepts: relations (the lines with arrows) stand for the relationship that applies between the nodes. The arrows are important for specifying the direction of the relation. Any given relationship between nodes can be represented by a triple consisting of the two nodes (let them be $a$ and $b$) and the relation (let it be $R$). In the network, the relationship is shown graphically as $a$–$R \rightarrow b$. It can also be stated in a formula, either in infix notation as $aRb$ or in the more standard predicate calculus prefix notation as $R(a, b)$. We will use all three notations, for all are equivalent, but are useful at different times. Note that at any node $a$ there may be a number of relations to other nodes;

indeed, this is how the network figures get constructed.[3]

[3]The semantic network, as drawn in Figure 8.7, is attractive in suggesting the kinds of interrelations that occur within the entire set of concepts in memory and in suggesting processing strategies. However, the notation becomes clumsy and unwieldy as the network structures become large and complex. Today, it is more usual to list each unit separately, putting it into what amounts to an outline form. Thus, the information in Figure 8.7 can be depicted in this way:

| animal | | person | |
|---|---|---|---|
| eats | food | subset | animal |
| breathes | air | has-as-part | legs |
| has | mass | has-as-part | arms |
| has-as-part | limbs | | |

The relation-node pairs (e.g., eats food) are called slots and fillers.

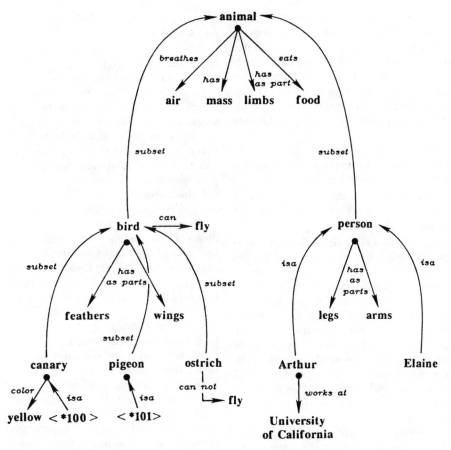

**Figure 8.7.** A simple semantic network, chosen so as to illustrate the use of inheritance.

There must exist a basic set of nodes and relations, the fundamental structures that are necessary for the semantic network to work properly. An important class of relations is that of type, which indicates that one node is an instance of the class pointed to by the relation. The two most important kinds of type relations are *isa* (where *a isa b* means that the concept represented by node *a* is an instance of the concept represented by node *b*) and *subset* (where *a subset b* means that the concept represented by node *a* is a subset of the concept represented by node *b*).

Suppose we wish to represent information about animals, as shown in Figure 8.7. We know that animals breathe, have mass, and eat food. This information is represented by relations from the node named animal. We know that people are animals, that Arthur and Elaine are instances of people, that birds are animals, and

that canaries, pigeons, and ostriches are kinds of birds. We also have seen particular birds, indicated by nodes ⟨*100⟩ and ⟨*101⟩ (indicated by angle brackets and arbitrary names). Note that the fact that Arthur eats food is derivable from the triples (Arthur isa person), (person subset animal), and (animal eats food). This derivation illustrates the property of inheritance: instances and subsets inherit the properties of their types. The general rule is that

*If (a type b) and (b R c), then (a R c)*

(both *isa* and *superset* are relations of class *type*). Note also that because the node for bird indicates that birds have feathers and fly, then by inheritance, we know that these properties apply to all birds, including all of the ones in Figure 8.7 (canaries, pigeons, ostriches, ⟨*100⟩, and ⟨*101⟩). When information is applied in this way, it is called a default value. That is, in the absence of other knowledge, we assume (deduce) that all birds have feathers and fly. In this case, the default for birds is wrong: ostriches don't fly. The solution is to add to the node for ostrich that it doesn't fly (as is done in the figure). But now we have inconsistent data in the data base. In semantic networks, the issue presents no difficulty if the appropriate processing rules are followed:

1. In determining properties of concepts, look first at the node for the concept.
2. If the information is not found, go up one node along the type relation and apply the property of inheritance.
3. Repeat 2 until either there is success or there are no more nodes.

This processing rule will always find the lowest (most specific) level relationship that applies to a given concept and will never even notice inconsistencies of the sort illustrated in the figure. The basic principle is that if two pieces of conflicting information appear to apply to a concept, accept the one that is most specific to that concept. This basic rule turns up frequently in the application of knowledge representation to applied problems.

Semantic networks provide a convenient and powerful formalism for representing knowledge, allowing for both inferential mechanisms and processing considerations. The nice thing about the network structure is that it matches many of our intuitions for the representation of a large domain of our knowledge.[4]

### The Representation of n-ary Relations in Semantic Networks

We have shown how the semantic network representation builds upon the node-relation-node triple ($aRb$). Because any node can have an indefinite number of relations from it to other nodes, it is also possible to view the representation as an $n$-place predicate that applies to the concept specified by the node. In particular, if the node specifies an $n$-place predicate (a predicate with $n$

arguments), then the node name can be identified with the predicate name. Each of the nodes pointed to by the relations leaving the node can be considered to be the arguments of the predicate. The relations specify the interpretation of each argument. This conceptualization makes it easy to represent complex verbs within the network, and was the scheme adopted by the LNR research group (Norman & Rumelhart, 1975). In this case, then, the basic representational unit, like that of the predicate calculus, consists of a predicate and its associated arguments. Figure 8.8 illustrates the basic scheme for representing an $n$-place predicate. The central node in Figure 8.8A represents an instance or token of the predicate $P$, the labels on the relations represent the roles played by the various arguments of the predicate, and the relation labeled *type* shows that this central node is a token of type $P$. Often, this structure is abbreviated as in Figure 8.8B.

### Types and Tokens

In a semantic network it is essential to distinguish between types and tokens of the concepts being represented. Figure 8.9A illustrates the kinds of confusion that arises from failure to make the distinction. This figure is intended to represent the facts "Cynthia threw the ball" and "Albert threw the book." Notice that because there is only one node for "threw," we are unable to determine who threw the ball and who threw the book. Figure 8.9B correctly represents the distinction between the events of Cynthia's throwing and Albert's throwing by introducing token nodes, illustrated by the ovals in the figure. These token nodes are instances of the type node for "threw," allowing us to distinguish the various incidents from one another.

A similar situation occurs with concepts, such as "ball." Thus, as shown in Figure 8.9C, when both Cynthia and Albert start throwing balls, we cannot tell from the representation whether or not they are throwing the same ball. We need to be able to represent that Cynthia threw a particular ball and that Albert threw some other particular ball. To do so, we use the type relation *isa* to point from a node that represents a token instance of a concept to the node that represents its more general, type concept. (The relation *isa* can be read as "is an instance of.") Figure 8.9D illustrates how this is done, using angle brackets to represent tokens of concepts. (In most actual drawings, the type or *isa*

---

[4]Note, however, that semantic networks fail to capture our intuitions of the phenomenology of mental structures. In particular, their information structures do not seem to be sufficiently dense to represent the rich, perceptual and motoric component of much of our internal experiences and mental images. We return to this issue later, when we treat images.

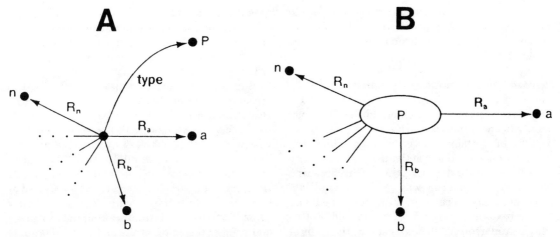

**Figure 8.8.** The basic scheme for representing an $n$-place predicate (a predicate with $n$ arguments). The central node in $A$ represents an instance or token of the predicate $P$, the labels on the relations represent the roles played by the various arguments in the predicate, and the relation labeled *type* shows that this central node is a token of type $P$. An abbreviated notation is shown in $B$. When this notation is used, the connection between the node and the name of the predicate is not always shown. From EXPLORATIONS IN COGNITION by D.A. Norman and D.E. Rumelhart, and the LNR Research Group, 1975, p. 36. W.H. Freeman and Company. Copyright (c) 1975. Reprinted by permission.

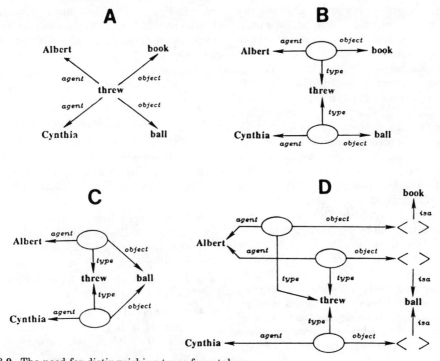

**Figure 8.9.** The need for distinguishing types from tokens.

A. Who threw the ball and who threw the book?

B. Token nodes for "threw" solve the problem shown in $A$.

C. Did both Albert and Cynthia throw the same ball?

D. Token nodes for "ball" solve the problem in $C$.

relations are not shown, but the use of angle brackets and ovals indicates that the nodes are tokens and that type relations exist, but are not shown.)[5]

### Spreading Activation in Semantic Networks

One important processing method that has commonly been associated with semantic networks is that of spreading activation, in which the network itself conducts activation values among its links. The first description of a spreading activation mechanism was made by Quillian, and the ideas were most fully described and elaborated in a paper by Collins and Loftus (1975). Anderson (1976) has used it as the basis of his modeling of human memory, both for guiding psychological predictions and experimentation and also for the construction of his computer simulation.

The basic idea of spreading activation is rather simple. The semantic network is a highly interconnected structure, with relations connecting together nodes very much as highways and airline routes interlink cities of the world. Much as motor vehicles and aircraft travel the routes between cities, activation is thought to travel the routes between nodes. The concept of activation is a general one. If the model is thought of as only a functional description, not necessarily dictating a physical system within which it is embedded, then the nodes can be thought of as data structures and the relations as pointers between structures. In these cases, activation is an abstract quantity, usually represented by a real number that represents how much information processing activity is taking place on a structure. This is the interpretation usually given by psychologists (Anderson, 1976; Collins & Loftus, 1975) and by those who work with computer representations of spreading activation (Fahlman, 1981; McClelland & Rumelhart, 1981; Rumelhart & McClelland, 1982). In some cases, the network is interpreted more literally as being constructed out of physical nodes and interlinking relations (wires if the data base is an electronic circuit, or neu-

rons if it is thought of as a neural network). In this case, activation is thought to be the actual electrical or chemical activity through the interconnections (e.g., see Feldman & Ballard, 1982).

Suppose one had a network representing the structure of animals (much as in Figure 8.7). How would a question such as, "Does a shark have mass?" get answered? The spreading activation algorithm operates by starting at both "shark" and "mass" simultaneously. This activates the nodes for "shark" and "mass," which then, simultaneously, activate all of the relations that leave these two nodes. Activation spreads down the relations, taking time to do so, and reaches the nodes at the end of the relations. These nodes get activated and, in turn, spread activation down all the relations that lead from them. Imagine spreading rings of activation, each ring originating from one of the starting points. Eventually these expanding rings will coincide. When that happens, we know there is a path between the nodes that have originated the colliding rings of activation. That path can then be readily found by following the activation traces, and, depending upon the nature of the path, the question can then be answered.

There are many details left out of this story, and there are a number of possible questions:

- How is the fact that two expanding rings of activation have intersected actually detected?
- How can the resulting path be followed?
- If there are $N$ relations leaving a node, does the amount of activation depend upon $N$?
- Do the expanding rings of activation trace out all of the possible relations, or can they be restricted to a subset of the class of relations?
- For how long a period of time does activation leave a trace?
- Are there different kinds of activations? That is, is it possible to distinguish the activation left by one process from the activation left by another?
- What is the best possible way to model this process?
- What is the best possible way to construct a working simulation model of this process?

[5] Actually, even the diagram illustrated in Figure 8.9D is not quite accurate, for it shows the English names for the nodes and relations on the diagram. In fact, the names of the node and the relations do appear within the network itself, but instead exist outside the network in what might be called the vocabulary.

These are the kinds of questions that have guided the research in this area. One of the major psychological issues addressed by activation studies has been the time course of activation (e.g., Maclean & Schulman, 1978; Neely, 1976). A second use of activation has been as a tool to examine the nature of the representation: if activation of one node will activate another, then the secondary activation primes any information processing that must make use of that other, thereby speeding its operation. Priming, therefore, is a technique that allows one to study the manner by which the interconnections are constructed. The basic priming study goes like this (after Meyer & Schvaneveldt, 1971): Subjects are asked to read two strings of letters and to decide as rapidly as possible whether each is a word or nonword. Thus, a typical pair of items might be "nurse plame." If the two words are related (as in "bread butter"), the judgment that both are words is considerably faster than if the two are not related (as in "bread nurse"). The interpretation is that reading of the first word sends activation to words related to it, thus priming the other words and making their detection and judgment easier and faster. Clearly, this kind of result can be used to study the interrelationships of items within memory by examining the amount of priming effect.

In a similar way, Collins and Quillian (1970) argued for support of their hierarchical organization of memory by demonstrating that prior exposure to the statement *A canary is a bird* reduced the amount of time that it took a person to determine whether it was true that *A canary can fly* more than it reduced the time to decide whether it was true that *A canary can sing.* They argued that to answer the question about flying, the node for bird had to be examined, and this was primed by the prior exposure, whereas to answer the question about singing, only the canary node was involved, and this was only minimally primed by the prior exposure.

Neely (1976, 1977) used priming as a technique to study Posner and Snyder's (1975) view of spreading activation. Posner and Snyder suggested that a visually presented word will automatically activate its representation, with the activation then spreading to the representations for other related words. This automatic activation is rapid, it occurs without attention or conscious awareness, and it has no effect upon

unrelated items. Conscious activation can also occur, through the limited capacity of the conscious-attention mechanism. This type of activation is slow, it requires attention and conscious awareness, and it can be applied to information unrelated to the item upon which it is focused (usually by inhibiting these other items). The experimental procedure followed by Neely was to prime the subject by the presentation of a word, then, after a delay, to present a target item consisting of a letter string to the subject. The subject had to decide as quickly as possible whether or not the target item was a word. In some cases, the prime and the target were related, in other cases unrelated. In some cases the subject was told the relationship the target item would have to the prime, and in other cases the subject was not told. The critical test concerns what happens when the prime is a word like "building" and the test item a word like "door" or "arm." When the subject thought that the word "building" would usually be followed by words that were parts of buildings, a facilitation on those words occurred, with no decrement in the ability to determine whether unrelated words, such as "arm," were words or not. Now suppose that the subject were told that whenever "building" occurred as the prime, the test word was likely to be a part of a body. In this case, the subject should activate "body" upon seeing the word "building." In fact, when the delay between the prime and the test item was short (less than 250 ms), the results were essentially the same as in the first case, when the subject expected the prime of "building" to be followed by words that referred to parts of a building. However, when the delay was long (greater than 700 ms), the speed to respond to body parts was increased and the speed to building parts decreased. Thus, it appears that spreading activation can be initiated either automatically, in which case it serves primarily to activate related concepts, or consciously, in which case it takes some time to be initiated, but it can both increase and inhibit the activation levels.

A third issue that has been widely investigated is whether or not the number of relations that leave a node affect the speed or amount of activation that does down the interconnecting links. This is called the fan effect, and it has most widely been studied by Anderson and his collaborators. Anderson's model of cognition

(ACT: Anderson, 1976) uses activation as one of its central themes, and so in addition to describing the fan effect that he has studied so extensively, let us also review the basic model.

## ACT and the Fan Effect

ACT makes a set of processing assumptions that are used in conjunction with its representational assumptions (which are of the standard form we described for propositional representation) to make predictions about specific experiments. In particular, ACT consists of the following assumptions about memory structure.

1. *Representation*. Information in memory is stored in network structures.
2. *Activation*. Each node and each link in memory can be in one of two states, either active or not. The links connecting active nodes need not be active. If a link is active, the nodes it connects with become active; activation spreads from one node to the next through the active interconnecting links.
3. *Strength of links*. Each link has a strength associated with it.
4. *Spread of activation: The fan effect*. The probability that activation will spread through a link is a function of the ratio of the strength of the particular link to the sum of the strengths of all of the links emanating from the node.
5. *Active lists*. Active nodes may be on an active list. The number of nodes that can be on the active list at one time is limited, but unless a node is on this list, its activity cannot be sustained for more than a short period.

Anderson assumes that the actual processing and interpretation is performed by an external interpreter in the form of a production system (more on this in a later section). The processor can put nodes on the active list (or remove them) and carry out the specific tasks required of the cognitive system as a whole.

One major set of investigations motivated by the ACT system has been studies of the fan effect. The fan experiments are strong tests of assumption 4 and weaker tests of the other assumptions. In the fan effect, the activation

that goes across a link is inversely proportional to the number of links that fan out from or leave the node. This results in the somewhat nonintuitive prediction that the more one knows about something, the longer it takes to retrieve that information: the more links emanating from a particular node, the longer, on average, it should take the activation to spread to adjacent nodes. Because the major mechanism for retrieving information uses the activation spreading along links, it should be possible to get information on the pattern of links from observations on retrieval time. The typical procedure for these experiments involves teaching subjects a set of facts arranged so that different number of facts apply to different concepts. The subjects may be shown a number of sentences to learn and then tested on their ability to recognize test sentences. Results indicate that subjects are slower to recognize a sentence of the form "The doctor hated the lawyer" if they had learned other facts about the lawyer and the doctor than if they had not. Thus, the more sentences of the form "The doctor loved the actor" and "The lawyer owned a Cadillac," the slower the recognition of the test sentence. The basic result is as predicted: the more facts, the slower the recognition time.

The basic fan effect might also be called the paradox of the expert; the theory appears to say that the more one knows about a topic, the slower will be the access to material about that topic. This flies in the face of common wisdom. Could common wisdom be wrong? Smith, Adams, and Schorr (1978) challenged the result, pointing out that one difference between the knowledge structures of experts and the knowledge structures studied in these experiments is that we would expect the knowledge of experts to consist of a large number of tightly interrelated structures, not just random facts like those in the basic fan experiment. Smith et al. tested this hypothesis by presenting their subjects with interrelated materials in which the facts about a specific topic formed thematic units. Indeed, they found that, with these materials, the fan effect was greatly diminished, and possibly reversed. In further studies, Reder and Anderson (1980) and Reder and Ross (1983) have shown that whether or not one gets a fan effect depends upon the exact question that must be answered by the subjects. When the subject must retrieve a particular proposition, the fan effect does indeed occur. However, when the same subject is asked to make a consistency judgment on the same information, the fan effect is reversed—the more the subject knows about the item, the faster the response. Thus, there must be multiple processes acting upon the information within memory that yield different results for different tasks. Reder and Ross (1983) proposed that when subjects learn a consistent set of facts about a concept in memory, they generate subnodes upon which to attach the information. Without going into the details at this point, note that the theory makes a counterintuitive prediction that appears to hold in appropriate circumstances, but that requires different processes to operate upon the same data structures within memory. The results again emphasize that, in studies of representation, it is not possible to separate the effects of the processes that operate upon the data structures from the data structures; the two must be considered together.

### Schank's Conceptual Dependency

One of the more important applications of the semantic network has been the work of Schank and his colleagues on the representation of concepts (Schank, 1975, 1981; Schank & Abelson, 1977). Schank took seriously the task of creating a plausible representation of the kind of knowledge that underlies language use. He wanted a representation that was unambiguous and unique. He wished to be able to express the meaning of any sentence in any language. The representations were intended to be language independent; if two sentences had the same meaning, they should have the same representation whether they were paraphrases within a given language or translations between languages. Moreover, Schank wished concepts that were similar to have representations that were likewise similar. In order to carry out this process he proposed that all incoming information be stored in terms of a set of conceptual primitives. Conceptual dependency theory was designed to interrelate these conceptual primitives in order to represent a wide range of different meanings. The first job with such an enterprise is to be very specific about what the representational primitives are, and Schank, more than anyone, has taken this task seriously. He has proposed a list of eleven primitive acts which he believes underlie the representation of all concepts. These include

five basic physical actions of people:

- **PROPEL**, which means to apply force to;
- **MOVE**, which means to move a body part;
- **INGEST**, which means to take something inside of an animate object;
- **EXPEL**, which means to take something that is inside an animate object and force it out;
- **GRASP**, which means to grasp an object physically.

There are also two basic change of state acts:

- **PTRANS** (for physical transition), which means to change the location of something;
- **ATRANS** (for abstract transition), which means to change some abstract relationship (usually ownership) of an object.

Schank lists two instrumental acts:

- **SPEAK**, which means to produce a sound;
- **ATTEND**, which means to direct a sense organ towards some particular stimulus.

Finally, there are two basic mental acts:

- **MTRANS** (for mental transition), which means to transfer information such as from one person to another or from one part of the memory, say LTM (long term memory) to STM (short term memory);
- **MBUILD** (for mental build), which means to create or combine thoughts. This is involved in such concepts as thinking, deciding, and so on.

In addition to these primitive acts, there are a number of other primitive elements that are combined to represent meanings. For example, there are **PP**s (picture producers) underlying the meanings of concrete nouns, and there are sets of primitive states, such as **HEALTH, FEAR, ANGER, HUNGER, DISGUST, SURPRISE**, and so on. There is also a set of conceptual roles that these various primitive elements can play, such as **ACTOR, OBJECT, INSTRUMENT, RECIPIENT, DIRECTION**, and so on. A simple example will suffice to illustrate how the various basic elements combine in Schank's

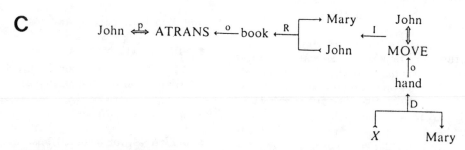

**Figure 8.10.** The conceptual dependency representation underlying three interpretations of "John gave Mary a book." *A* shows the most basic interpretation of the sentence, *B* is the case in which John did something that allowed Mary to take the book, and *C* shows the representation for John handing Mary the book. From *Conceptual Information Processing* (pp. 31, 32) by R.C. Schank, 1975. New York: North-Holland. Copyright 1975 by North-Holland Publishing Co. Reprinted by permission.

representational system. Figure 8.10A shows the conceptual dependency representation for the sentence *John gave Mary a book*. In this case, the verb "to give" has been represented as the primitive **ATRANS**, the **ACTOR** (illustrated by the double arrow) is "John," the time is the past (illustrated by the **p** labeling the double arrow), the **OBJECT** is "book," and the **RECIPIENT** goes from "John" to "Mary." Note that the representation is not for the particular words of a sentence, but rather for the intended meanings. Thus, the figure represents only one interpretation of the sentence. The point is that in Schank's system, it is not sentences that have representations, rather it is meanings that are represented. Figure 8.10A represents the case in which John physically gave Mary the book. The

same sentence could have been used for the case in which John had carried out some other action that let Mary take the book for herself. In this case, the correct representation would be the one illustrated in Figure 8.10B. Here, we see that "Mary" is now the **ACTOR** of the **ATRANS** and the action of "John" is the non-specific **DO**. Figure 8.10C illustrates the conceptual dependency underlying the case in which the same sentence means that John handed the book to Mary. In this case we see that "John" is again the **ACTOR** of the **ATRANS**, and that there is now an **INSTRUMENT** of the **ATRANS** specified. Note that the **INSTRU-MENT** is an entire conceptualization that involves "John" **MOVE**ing his hand from some location "X" to "Mary."

## KL-ONE

In spite of their empirical successes, all of the various semantic network models have received criticisms. In particular, Woods (1975) challenged the consistency and adequacy of these models to represent many of the distinctions of meaning that can be expressed in the predicate calculus and other logical formalisms. More recently, Brachman (1979) has furthered Woods' critique and proposed a new semantic network formalism, called KL-ONE (for Knowledge Language One and pronounced "clone"), that is intended to overcome the inadequacy of the previous models.

Woods and Brachman pointed out that the concepts of nodes and relations were imprecisely specified and inconsistently used. What exactly does it mean to connect one node to another with a labeled relation? What does a node or relation really stand for? Sometimes a node or a relation would stand for one kind of thing, other times for another. To begin, consider the nature of relations. Sometimes, as in Quillian's early work, a relation is treated as an attribute and the thing it points to as a value. Thus, a relation labeled COLOR might point from the node APPLE to the node RED. Other times, the relations might be labeled with transitive verbs and point from the subject to the object. Thus, the sentence *The ball is on the table* is, according to some semantic network representations, characterized as a link labeled ON pointing from BALL to TABLE. More complex cases occur when three place predicate must be represented. Thus, the sentence *The ball is between the table and the chair* simply doesn't fit into the same format. Other semantic networks have links stand for still other things. In this case, some links, such as *type*, point from a token to a type. Other links, such as *agent* or *recipient*, do not stand on their own, but are only interpretable in the context of all of the other links on the node. Still other links, such as *iswhen*, have still other special functions. The complaint is not so much that links are not used consistently but that so many different kinds of links are used to mean so many different kinds of things. Without a good deal of explication, it is easy to be confused about the meaning of a link. In particular, although all semantic network representations look superficially similar, a careful analysis of what the relations are actually used for and how they actually work shows that the similarity

between systems and the homogeneity within systems is, at best, only superficial and, at worst, misleading.

Similar arguments apply to nodes. In particular, Woods argued that semantic network structures must represent the intensions of concepts. The term "intension" contrasts with the term "extension." The extension of a concept is the set of things that it denotes, whereas the intension of a concept is its internal structure, by virtue of which it denotes what it does. These correspond to what Frege (1892) called *Sinn* (sense) and *Bedeutung* (reference). Concepts both refer to things (extensions) and have a sense (intension). Two concepts could both refer to the same thing in the world, but have different senses or intensions. A famous example of this is the contrast between Morning Star and Evening Star, both having the same extension (because they both refer to the planet Venus), but with each having a different intension.

Consider, as an example, the network structure illustrated in Figure 8.11A. Various semantic network theorists might wish to say that it represents the fact "John sees an airplane." Figure 8.11B might be said to represent the fact "John wants to see an airplane." Notice that the shaded part of Figure 8.11B is identical to the structure for Figure 8.11A, but the meaning of these two structures is different in the two cases. In the first case, we can conclude that there was an airplane that John saw: this would be an extensional interpretation. In the second, we can make no such interpretation. The node *airplane represents a real airplane in Figure 8.11A, but only a hypothetical one in Figure 8.11B. Representational systems must distinguish between these two meanings of nodes, the extensional and the intensional.

Brachman (1979) developed a semantic network type of representational system designed to be very clear about the semantics of the networks. In particular, Brachman developed a system in which distinctions among the type classes of links were clearly marked and in which concepts were always intensional. Brachman called his kind of network a structured inheritance net (SI-Nets) and called his implementation of the idea KL-ONE.

There are two kinds of concepts in KL-ONE: generic and individual. Generic concepts represent classes of individuals; individual concepts represent particular individuals. Generic concepts

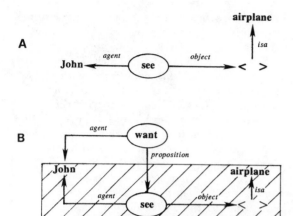

**Figure 8.11.** The representational formalism adopted by KL-ONE (Brachman, 1979). *A:* "Johns sees an airplane." *B:* "John wants to see an airplane." The shaded portion of *B* is identical to *A*. The node ⟨*airplane⟩ represents a real airplane in *A*, but a hypothetical one in *B*.

represent classes by describing a prototype class member, organized in an inheritance hierarchy. Thus, as in traditional semantic networks, the concept for a term like "dog" might be repre-

sented as a specialization of the concept for a term like "animal."

Concepts themselves have an internal structure. The meaning of a given concept is determined jointly by its superconcept and its own internal structure. Internally, concepts consist of two major types of entities: Role/Filler Descriptions (roles) and Structural Descriptions (SDs). Every concept has a set of superconcepts, a set of roles that represents the components of the concept, and a set of SDs that describes the relationships among the various roles.

Roles, too, have an internal structure. A given role has a Modality, (is it an obligatory, optional, inherent, or a derivable part?), a Value Restriction (V/R) (what kind of thing fills this slot?), a Role Name (an arbitrary name for internal reference only), and a Number (the number of such parts allowed for the particular concept). Figure 8.12 illustrates a KL-ONE representation of the concept *arch*. Arches have three roles, designated R1, R2, and R3. R1 represents the lintel or top of the arch. It is *obligatory*, in the network, it is locally called a "lintel," it must be a kind of wedge-brick, and there can only be one of them in an arch. R2 represents the sides of the

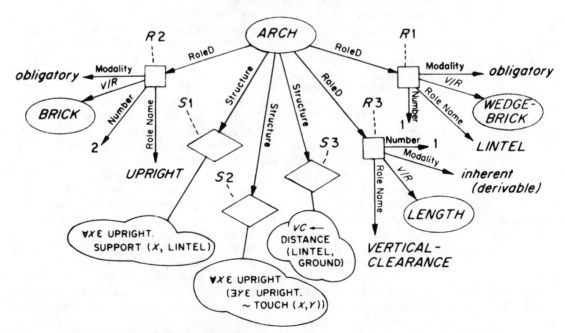

**Figure 8.12.** A schematic representation of the KL-ONE representation for the concept ARCH. From "On the Epistemological Status of Semantic Networks" by R.J. Brachman in *Associative Networks: Representation and Use of Knowledge by Computers* (p. 37), N.V. Findler (Ed.), 1979. New York: Academic Press. Copyright 1979 by Academic Press. Reprinted by permission.

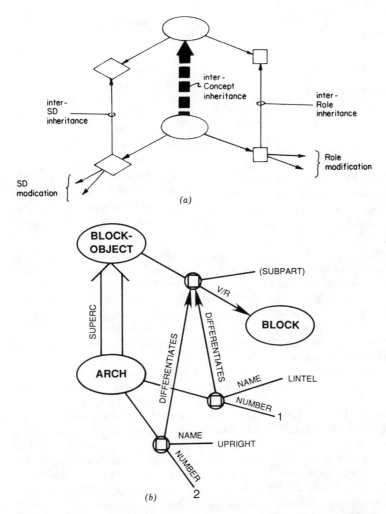

**Figure 8.13.** *A*: The relationship between a concept and its superconcept in KL-ONE (shown in schematic form). From "On the Epistemological Status of Semantic Networks" by R.J. Brachman in *Associative Networks: Representation and Use of Knowledge by Computers* (p. 41), N.V. Findler (Ed.), 1979. New York: Academic Press. Copyright 1979 by Academic Press. Reprinted by permission. *B*: The relationship for the case of ARCH.

arch, it is also obligatory, it is a kind of brick, it is locally called an "upright," and there are two of them. R3 represents the height of the arch. This is an *inherent* or *derivable* part: "vertical-clearance." The structural descriptions are the essential part of the concept: they indicate how the various parts are interconnected. Thus, for example, S1 gives the essential relationship between the UPRIGHTs and the LINTEL.

Knowledge in KL-ONE is stored in strictly hierarchical structures. Thus, each KL-ONE concept is defined as a specialization of some higher level concept. In this definition, the rela-

tions between the roles of the concept and the superconcept must be specified, as must the relationship among the SDs of the concept and superconcept. Figure 8.13A illustrates the relationship between a concept and its superconcept. Figure 8.13B shows that relationship for the case of an arch. In addition to the aspects of KL-ONE already discussed, KL-ONE has mechanisms for representing individual concepts and associated procedures.

In KL-ONE we have the latest and most sophisticated of the semantic network type representations. KL-ONE contains mechanisms for representing virtually all of the kinds of knowledge we have thus far described. It is, however, much farther from the empirical base than any of the other models.

## Schemata and Frames

So far, we have covered a variety of representational schemes that focus on the basic, elementary levels of representation. The semantic feature approaches focused almost exclusively on the representation of word meanings, the predicate calculus focused on the kind of knowledge that could be expressed in a single sentence, and the semantic network and the conceptual dependency formalisms strived to include both lexical level and sentence level knowledge. The one thing that all these systems have in common is that they each represent all knowledge in a single, uniform format. What is needed is the ability to introduce higher levels of structure and to represent suprasentential knowledge. In this case the goal is not to remedy the expressive problems of other representational methods, but to change the level of discourse.

The movement towards systems that focused on higher units of knowledge was signaled by the publication, in 1975, of four papers: "A framework for representing knowledge" by Minsky, "Notes on a schema for stories" by Rumelhart, "The structure of episodes in memory" by Schank, and "Concepts for representing mundane reality in plans" by Abelson. Over the next several years, these papers led to the development of a number of related knowledge representation proposals, all aiming at the representation of suprasentential knowledge units. In his paper introducing the concept of the frame as a knowledge representation formalism, Minsky put the argument this way:

> It seems to me that the ingredients of most theories both in artificial intelligence and in psychology have been on the whole too minute, local, and unstructured to account—either practically or phenomenologically—for the effectiveness of common sense thought. The "chunks" of reasoning, language, memory, and "perception" ought to be larger and more structured, and their factual and procedural contents must be more intimately connected in order to explain the apparent power and speed of mental activities (Minsky, 1975, p. 211).

A number of theorists have developed representational systems based on these larger units. We will discuss three of them here:

- A theory of schemata as developed by Rumelhart and Ortony (1977) and extended by Rumelhart and Norman (1978) and Rumelhart (1981).
- A theory of scripts and plans developed by Schank and Abelson (1977) and further elaborated into **MOPS** by Schank (1980).
- KRL, the first of the knowledge representation languages, developed by D.G. Bobrow and Winograd (1977).

The basic assumption of these theories is that the earlier work was useful in providing a foundation for further work, but that it was focused on the wrong level to be useful in the understanding of understanding. The nodes and relations of semantic networks, the formulas of predicate calculus, and the feature lists of semantic concepts do have a place in the structure of representation, but they do not allow one to structure knowledge into higher order representational units. The major function of these new approaches is to add such a structure, using holistic units that allow for the encoding of more complex interrelationships among the lower level units. These higher order units were given different names by each of the theorists: frame (Minsky, 1975), schema (Rumelhart & Norman, 1978), script (Schank & Abelson, 1977), and unit (Bobrow & Winograd, 1977). Nonetheless, the motivating force and, in most cases, the underlying themes are similar. We now turn to examine these higher level structures.

### Summary of the Major Features of Schemata

The notion of the schema finds its way into modern cognitive psychology through the writings of Bartlett (1932) and from Piaget (1952). Throughout most of its history, the notion of the schema has been rejected by mainstream experimental psychologists as being too vague. Recently, however, as we have begun to see how such ideas might actually work, the notion has become increasingly popular. In this section, we sketch the basic ideas of the schema, particularly as developed in the papers by Rumelhart and Ortony (1977), D.G. Bobrow and Norman

(1975), Rumelhart and Norman (1978) and by Rumelhart (1981). For the most part, the characteristics of the schema as developed in these papers is consistent with the work of the other writers on the subject. However, as we will indicate below, there are features that differentiate the ideas as well.

Schemata are data structures for representing the generic concepts stored in memory. There are schemata for generalized concepts underlying objects, situations, events, sequences of events, actions, and sequences of actions. Roughly, schemata are like models of the outside world. To process information with the use of a schema is to determine which model best fits the incoming information. Ultimately, consistent configurations of schemata are discovered that, in concert, offer the best account for the input. This configuration of schemata constitutes the interpretation of the input. There appear to be a number of characteristics of schemata that are necessary (or at least useful) for developing a system that behaves in this way. Rumelhart (1981) and Rumelhart and Ortony (1977) listed several of the most important features of schemata. These include:

1. Schemata have variables;
2. Schemata can embed, one within another;
3. Schemata represent knowledge at all levels of abstraction;
4. Schemata represent encyclopedic knowledge rather than dictionary-like definitions;
5. Schemata are active recognition devices whose processing is aimed at evaluating how well they fit to the data being processed.

Perhaps the central feature of schemata is that they are packets of information that contain variables. Roughly, a schema for any concept contains a fixed part—those characteristics that are always (or nearly always) true of exemplars of the concept—and a variable part. Thus, for example, the schema for the concept **DOG** would contain constant fixed parts such as "a dog has four legs," and variable parts such as "a dog's color can be black, brown, white, and so on." Thus, **NUMBER-OF-LEGS** would be a constant in the schema, whereas **COLOR** and **SIZE** would be variables. Similarly, in the

**GIVE** schema the aspects involving a change of possession would be constants, and those aspects involving who the giver or the receiver is would be variables. There are two important aspects of variables for schema-based systems. In the first place, variables have default values. That is, the schema contains information about what values to assume for the variables when the incoming information is unspecified. Thus, consider as an example the following story sentences:

> Mary heard the ice cream truck coming down the street. She remembered her birthday money and rushed into the house.

In processing such a text, people usually invoke a schema for ice cream trucks going through a community selling ice cream to the children. In this schema there is a fixed part involving the relationships among the characters of the ice cream truck drama and a variable part concerning the particular individuals playing the particular roles in this drama. In this case, we tend to interpret Mary as the filler of the **BUYER** variable in the schema. Although the story tells us nothing about the age of Mary, we tend to think of her as a little girl. Thus, the default value of the age of the **BUYER** in this schema is childhood, and unless otherwise indicated, we tend to assume that this is the age of the **BUYER**. Default values can, of course, be overcome by explicit information in the incoming information. A second important aspect of variables is our knowledge of the plausible range over which the fillers of a particular variable might vary. Thus, consider for example, the following examples:

> The child broke the window (with a hammer).

and

> The hammer broke the window (with a crash).

In the first case, we are likely to assign "the child" to the **AGENT** variable of the **BREAK** schema and to assign "hammer" to the **INSTRUMENT** variable. We might naively be tempted to assign "the hammer" to the **AGENT** role in the second example (after all child and hammer are both subjects of the verb). However, we know that hammers lie outside of the class of possible **AGENT**s for the schema and a much better fit is attained with the mapping of "hammer" onto the **INSTRUMENT**al variable in the second sentence as well. Thus, the process of interpretation involves selecting appropriate schemata to account for the input and determining which aspects of the incoming information map onto which variables of the schema. We say that the variables are bound to various parts of the incoming array of information. Binding variable assigns an interpretation to that part of the situation.

A second important characteristic of schemata is that they can embed one within another. Thus, in general, a schema consists of a configuration of subschemata. Each subschema in turn consists of configuration of subschemata, and so on. Some schemata are assumed to be primitive and undecomposable. Thus, we might imagine that the schema for a human body consists, in part, of a particular configuration of a head, a trunk, two arms, and two legs. The schema for a head contains, among other things, a face and two ears. The schema for a face contains a particular configuration of two eyes, a nose, a mouth, and so on. The schema for an eye contains an iris, an upper lid, a lower lid, and so forth. The schemata at the various levels can offer each other mutual support. Thus, whenever we find evidence for a face, we thereby have evidence for two eyes, a nose, and a mouth. We also have evidence for a head and, thereby, perhaps for an entire body. Thus, unlike the attribute or featural representational systems in which features are generally viewed as unitary elements, the schema theories propose a whole hierarchy of additional levels.

The third characteristic of schemata is that they represent knowledge at all levels of abstraction. Just as theories can be about the grand and the small, so schemata can represent knowledge at all levels—from ideologies and cultural truths, to knowledge about what constitutes an appropriate sentence in our language, to knowledge about the meaning of a particular word, to knowledge about what patterns of excitations are associated with what letters of the alphabet. We have schemata to represent all levels of our experience, at all levels of abstraction. Thus, the schema theories suppose that the human memory system contains countless packets of knowledge. Each packet specifies a configuration of other packets (subschemata) that represent the constituents of the schema. Furthermore, these theories assume that these packets themselves vary in complexity and level of application.

The fourth characteristic involves the kinds of information that schemata are assumed to represent. We believe that schemata are our knowledge. All of our generic knowledge is embedded in schemata. When we think of representations for word meanings, we may wish to represent one of two kinds of information. On the one hand, it has been common for representational theorists to assume that word meanings are rather like what one might find in a dictionary—the essential aspects of the word meanings. On the other hand, one may assume that the meaning of a word is represented by something more like an encyclopedic article on the topic. In this case one would expect that in a schema for a concept like "bird," we would have, in addition to the dictionary knowledge, many facts and relationships about birds. A third kind of information needs to be represented: our experiences with birds. The first two kinds of knowledge about birds are referred to as semantic memory. The third kind of knowledge is referred to as episodic memory (the terms were invented by Tulving, 1972). It is generally assumed that schemata must exist for both semantic and episodic memory and that schemata for semantic memory contain a great deal of world knowledge and are much more encyclopedic than dictionary-like.

Finally, schemata should be envisioned as active processes[6] in which each schema is a process evaluating its fit, binding its variables, and sending messages to other schemata that indicate its current estimate of how well it accounts for the current data. It is useful to distinguish between two data sources that a schema can use in evaluating how well it fits:

1. Information provided by the schema's subschemata on how well they account for their parts of the input (bottom-up information);

2. Information from those schemata of which the schema is a constituent about their degree of certainty that they are relevant to the input (top-down information).

---

[6]Not all versions of schema theories emphasize this feature, but it is a useful conceptualization. See the discussion by Rumelhart (1981).

The process of interpretation can consist of repeated processing loops as various schemata interact with top-down and bottom-up information processing in an attempt to find the best overall fit. Eventually, the process settles down. The set of schemata that fits the input best constitutes the final interpretation of the input data.

### Scripts, Plans, and MOPS

According to schema theory the memory system consists of an enormous number of packets of knowledge. Schank, Abelson, and their colleagues (cf., Schank & Abelson, 1977) have developed specific examples of the knowledge one may have stored. These examples allow us to determine whether this memory system has practical value, that is, whether such knowledge really can serve as the basis for the way we interpret the stories we read. Schank and Abelson have developed a number of specific kinds of schemata, the simplest type being the script. A script can be thought of as a schema for a frequently occurring sequence of events. Schank and Abelson suggest that there are scripts for very common types of social events. For example, they suggest that there are scripts for a visit to a restaurant, for a visit to a doctor, for a trip on a train, and many other frequent event sequences. The script that has received the most attention is that for the restaurant. Figure 8.14 gives Schank and Abelson's proposal for the restaurant script. A script, like all schemata, has a number of variables. These can be divided roughly into two categories, those that require a person to fill them (called roles) and those that must be filled by objects of a certain kind (called props). Each script contains a number of entry conditions, a sequence of scenes, and a set of results. Script processing, like schema processing in general, allows one to make inferences about aspects of the situation that were not explicitly mentioned. Consider the following example:

Mary went to a restaurant.

She ordered a quiche.

Finally, she paid the bill and left.

Once it is determined that the restaurant script is the proper account for this little story, it is possible to make a large number of inferences.

In the first place, we can assume that, when Mary started the episode, she was hungry. We also can assume that she had some money before she went into the restaurant and that she ate the quiche before she paid the bill. We further assume that there was a waiter or waitress who brought her a menu, that she waited for the food to be served, and so on. Thus, among other things, the script provides the structure necessary to understand the temporal order of events. In communicating, we need only provide enough information to be certain that our listener finds the correct script, and we assume the rest follows automatically. The script itself allows the listener to infer many of the details.

Bower, Black, and Turner (1979) carried out a number of experiments designed to evaluate the script as an explanation for how people actually understand and remember stories. Their first tack was to collect some direct evidence on the kinds of scripts that people in our culture actually have for such things as going to a restaurant, attending a lecture, going to a grocery store, getting up in the morning, and going to a physician. They then developed a composite script by assigning an importance to each action depending on how many students named that aspect. The results of this experiment are shown in Figure 8.15.

Bower, Black, and Turner also looked for the expected inferences to show up when their subjects recalled stories. The procedure was to present a story in which only some of the events in the script were explicitly mentioned, then to see whether, in a subsequent recall, subjects recalled events that were part of the script, but not part of the material actually mentioned in the story. The results indicated that, under some conditions, as many as 30 percent of the events subjects recall are events mentioned in the script, but not in the story itself. Clearly, the scripts are potent determiners of a subjects recall.

According to Schank and Abelson, the script is only the simplest of the schema-like knowledge structures. Clearly, not all situations that we wish to understand consist of a sequence of high frequency events. Often, the knowledge structures we have to bring to bear to get an interpretation must consist of more general and more abstract schemata. One important type of such an abstract schema is what Schank and Abelson have called the plan. Plans are

THEORETICAL RESTAURANT SCRIPT (ADAPTED FROM SCHANK & ABELSON, 1977)

*Name: Restaurant*

| | | | |
|---|---|---|---|
| *Props:* | Tables | *Roles:* | Customer |
| | Menu | | Waiter |
| | Food | | Cook |
| | Bill | | Cashier |
| | Money | | Owner |
| | Tip | | |

| | | | |
|---|---|---|---|
| *Entry Conditions:* | Customer hungry | *Results:* | Customer has less money |
| | Customer has money | | Owner has more money |
| | | | Customer is not hungry |

*Scene 1: Entering*
    Customer enters restaurant
    Customer looks for table
    Customer decides where to sit
    Customer goes to table
    Customer sits down

*Scene 2: Ordering*
    Customer picks up menu
    Customer looks at menu
    Customer decides on food
    Customer signals waitress
    Waitress comes to table
    Customer orders food
    Waitress goes to cook
    Waitress gives food order to cook
    Cook prepares food

*Scene 3: Eating*
    Cook gives food to waitress
    Waitress brings food to customer
    Customer eats food

*Scene 4: Exiting*
    Waitress writes bill
    Waitress goes over to customer
    Waitress gives bill to customer
    Customer gives tip to waitress
    Customer goes to cashier
    Customer gives money to cashier
    Customer leaves restaurant

*Note.* From "Scripts in Memory for Text" by G.H. Bower, J.B. Black, and T.J. Turner, 1979, *Cognitive Psychology, 11*, p. 179. Copyright 1979 by Academic Press. Reprinted by permission.

**Figure 8.14.** The restaurant script. (From Bower, Black, & Turner, 1979; adapted from Schank & Abelson, 1977.)

formulated to satisfy specific motivations and goals. Future actions can be expected to involve attempts to attain these goals. Consider the following example:

John knew that his wife's operation would be very expensive.
There was always Uncle Harry . . . .
He reached for the suburban phone book.

Many people, when they encounter this story, assume that John wants to borrow money from Uncle Harry and that he is reaching for the phone book to find Uncle Harry's phone number to ask for the money. Now, we probably don't have a specific script for this particular activity. We do, however, probably know that when people are presented with problems, they attempt to solve them. Thus, having identified the problem in the story (the cost of the wife's

EMPIRICAL SCRIPT NORMS AT THREE AGREEMENT LEVELS

| GOING TO A RESTAURANT | ATTENDING A LECTURE | GETTING UP | GROCERY SHOPPING | VISITING A DOCTOR |
|---|---|---|---|---|
| Open door | ENTER ROOM | *Wake up* | ENTER STORE | *Enter office* |
| *Enter* | *Look for friends* | Turn off alarm | GET CART | CHECK IN WITH RECEPTIONIST |
| *Give reservation name* | FIND SEAT | Lie in bed | Take out list | SIT DOWN |
| Wait to be seated | SIT DOWN | Stretch | Look at list | Wait |
| Go to table | Settle belongings | GET UP | Go to first aisle | Look at other people |
| BE SEATED | TAKE OUT NOTEBOOK | Make bed | *Go up and down aisles* | READ MAGAZINE |
| *Order Drinks* | *Look at other students* | *Go to bathroom* | PICK OUT ITEMS | *Name called* |
| Put napkins on lap | *Talk* | Use toilet | Compare prices | Follow nurse |
| LOOK AT MENU | Look at professor | *Take shower* | Put items in cart | *Enter exam room* |
| *Discuss menu* | LISTEN TO PROFESSOR | *Wash face* | Get meat | Undress |
| ORDER MEAL | TAKE NOTES | Shave | Look for items forgotten | *Sit on table* |
| *Talk* | CHECK TIME | DRESS | Talk to other shoppers | Talk to nurse |
| Drink water | Ask questions | Go to kitchen | Go to checkout counters | NURSE TESTS |
| *Eat salad or soup* | Change position in seat | Fix breakfast | *Find fastest line* | Wait |
| Meal arrives | Daydream | EAT BREAKFAST | WAIT IN LINE | Doctor enters |
| EAT FOOD | Look at other students | BRUSH TEETH | *Put food on belt* | Doctor greets |
| Finish meal | Take more notes | Read paper | Read magazines | Talk to doctor about problem |
| *Order Desert* | *Close notebook* | *Comb hair* | WATCH CASHIER RING UP | Doctor asks questions |
| *Eat Desert* | *Gather belongings* | *Get books* | PAY CASHIER | DOCTOR EXAMINES |
| Ask for bill | Stand up | Look in mirror | *Watch bag boy* | Get dressed |
| Bill arrives | Talk | Get coat | Cart bags out | Get medicine |
| PAY BILL | LEAVE | LEAVE HOUSE | Load bags into car | Make another appointment |
| *Leave Tip* | | | LEAVE STORE | LEAVE OFFICE |
| Get Coats | | | | |
| LEAVE | | | | |

Items in all capital letters were mentioned by the most subjects, items in italics by fewer subjects, and items in small case letters by the fewest subjects

*Note.* From "Scripts in Memory for Text" by G.H. Bower, J.B. Black, and T.J. Turner, 1979, *Cognitive Psychology, 11,* p. 182. Copyright 1979 by Academic Press. Reprinted by permission.

**Figure 8.15.** Empirically determined scripts at three different levels of agreement. The events listed in all capital letters were the most frequently mentioned, those in italics the next most frequently mentioned, and those in lowercase letters were less frequently mentioned. (From Bower, Black, & Turner, 1979.)

operation), we expect to see some problem-solving behavior on the part of the protagonist, so that we interpret further activity as an attempt to solve the problem. Moreover, we can assume that subgoals will be generated along the way and that further activities will be generated toward the solution of the subgoal. In this case, the primary goal is to pay for the operation; the plan is to borrow money from Uncle Harry. Borrowing money involves contacting Uncle Harry, which in turn leads to the subgoal of calling on the telephone, which involves the further subgoal of discovering his phone number, and so on. Rumelhart (1975, 1977) and Wilensky (1978) have shown that many stories can be analyzed by means of problem solving.

In one of their experiments Bower, Black, and Turner (1979) found that subjects sometimes confused events that were part of one script with events that were part of other, similar, scripts. Thus, events that took place during a visit to a dentist might be confused with events that took place in a visit to a physician. But if different scripts are distinctly separate data structures, there is no reason to suppose that events from

similar scripts would be more often confused than events from quite different scripts. This result prompted Schank to revise the notion of the script so that scripts are not stored in memory as a simple sequence of events, but are derived at the time they are used from smaller, more fundamental data elements (Schank, 1980). Those elements combine to form scripts that Schank calls **MOPS**. Thus, the doctor script is not a unitary element. Rather, it is derived from the interrelationship of such **MOPS** as the **fix-problem-MOP**, the **health-care-MOP**, the **professional-office-visit-MOP**, and many other **MOPS**. Figure 8.16 illustrates the configuration of **MOPS** that Schank assumes might underlie the doctor script.

## KRL: A Knowledge Representation Language

D.G. Bobrow and Winograd (1977) developed a formal computational language for dealing with representational issues that they call KRL (for Knowledge Representation Language). Their goals were slightly different from those that led to the systems we have already described, for in

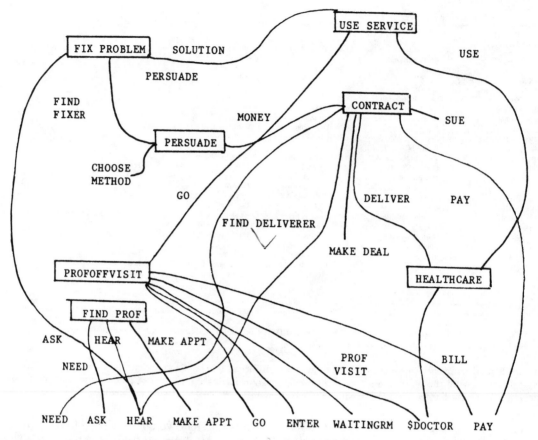

**Figure 8.16.** The configuration of **MOPS** that are assumed to underlie our knowledge of a doctors visit. From "Language and Memory" by R.C. Schank, 1980, *Cognitive Science, 4*, p. 275. Copyright 1980 by ABLEX Publishing. Reprinted by permission.

addition to their interest in expanding our understanding of representational issues, they also wished to emphasize the utility of developing a computational tool for those interested in the construction of computer models. Thus, they emphasized control processes and computational issues as well as representational issues. In addition, they developed several important concepts, including descriptions, perspectives, and procedural attachment. Bobrow and Winograd described their goals this way:

> Much of the work in Artificial Intelligence has involved fleshing in bits and pieces of human knowledge structures, and we would like to provide a systematic framework in which they can be assembled. Someone who wishes to build a system for a particular task, or who wishes to develop theories of specific linguistic phenomena should be able to build on a base that

includes well thought out structures at all levels. In providing a framework, we impose a kind of uniformity (at least in style) which is based upon our own intuitions about how knowledge is organized. We state our major intuitions here as a set of aphorisms . . . .

1. Knowledge should be organized around conceptual entities with associated descriptions and procedures.

2. A description must be able to represent partial knowledge about an entity and accommodate multiple descriptors which can describe the associated entity from different viewpoints.

3. An important method of description is comparison with a known entity, with further specification of the desired instance with respect to the prototype.

4. Reasoning is dominated by a process of

recognition in which new objects and events are compared to stored sets of expected prototypes, and in which specialized reasoning strategies are keyed to these prototypes.

5. Intelligent programs will require multiple active processes with explicit user-provided scheduling and resource allocation heuristics.

6. Information should be clustered to reflect use in processes whose results are affected by resource limitation and differences in information accessibility.

7. A knowledge representation language must provide a flexible set of underlying tools, rather than embody specific commitments about either processing strategies or the representation of specific areas of knowledge. (Numbering of the seven aphorisms was not done in the original.)[7]

The list of aphorisms reveal much of the common agreement about properties of higher order structures, by whatever name. Thus, aphorisms 1, 3, and 4 reflect general properties of schemata, things that we have already discussed. Aphorisms 2 and 3 introduce the notion of description. Aphorism 2 is of special interest, for it introduces the notion of perspectives, an important concept, one that we will elaborate in a moment. Aphorisms 5, 6, and 7 reflect processing considerations, important for any usable system (including biological systems), but not relevant to the discussions of this chapter, so we will not elaborate upon them except to note that even when processing issues are not of prime concern, the tight relationship between representational structure and processing is evident in these three aphorisms: in general, one cannot ignore the processing structure when dealing with the knowledge structure. To translate this into psychological terms: psychologists interested in psychological mechanisms and knowledge structures cannot ignore the issues and constraints placed upon the human system by neurological structures.

Descriptions were introduced into KRL both as an important processing and representational structure and as a response to processes that might actually operate within human memory (D.G. Bobrow & Norman, 1975; Norman & D.G.

Bobrow, 1979). The major issue is just how one should refer to a concept or record in memory. There are only a few possibilities:

- Give each record a unique name, and refer to the record by that name. This corresponds to the use of proper names in language and such unique identifiers as catalog numbers, part numbers, employee numbers, or Social Security numbers.

- Put each record in a unique place, and refer to the record by referring to the place. This corresponds to the use of street addresses, telephone numbers, and memory addresses in computer systems.

- Point at the desired record, much the way arrows in a semantic network point to the nodes to which the relations refer. This corresponds to the use of wires in electronic circuits to interconnect the parts of the circuit, or the wires in a telephone switchboard, through which one physically makes the desired connection.

Further discussion of these issues takes us away from our topic (but see Norman & D.G. Bobrow, 1979; Norman, 1982, pp. 37–44). Note that all of the representational systems we have examined so far use the methods of either unique names or pointers to refer to their items. But what if you know neither the name nor the location (address) of the item to which you wish to refer? What if the memory structure does not make available unique addresses or pointers, nor readily makes available unique names (which is what we suspect is true of human memory)? How then does one describe the item one is seeking? For KRL, Bobrow and Winograd suggest the use of descriptions (much as Norman and Bobrow suggest for human memory in general). Descriptions offer an alternative method of referring to the desired record by describing the item being sought.

Descriptions have several virtues aside from their ability to refer to other items. Perhaps the most important is that of partial specification in which it is possible to describe the characteristics that one knows of an item without fully specifying the item. Essentially, this is what one requests from an eye witness to a crime, for example:

**Query:** *What did the criminal look like?*

**Reply:** *It was a woman, very tall, with red hair.*

[7] From "An Overview of KRL, A Knowledge Representation" by D.G. Bobrow and T.J. Winograd, 1977, *Cognitive Science, 1*, pp. 4–5. Copyright 1977 by ABLEX Publishing. Reprinted by permission.

The reply in this example is a description that partially specifies the person. It is not enough to identify the person uniquely, but it goes a long way to constrain the set of possibilities. In many cases, it might even be sufficient to yield a unique identification. Examples of the use of descriptors of this sort from KRL include:

- The specification for the last name of a person as:

  {(a ForeignName)

  (a String with firstCharacter = "M")}

- The specification for the husband of Mary as:

  (the maleParent from

  (a Family with femaleParent = Mary))

Descriptions are quite useful in specifying default values. In our earlier examinations of default values, we only looked at simple values. Consider, though, a default value constructed of a description of the sort used above: "a person with red hair, whose height is more than 6 feet." This kind of description clearly increases the power of the defaults, for it allows them to use a variable amount of power, sometimes specifying what exact thing is to serve as the default and sometimes being able to specify the characteristic only loosely and imprecisely.

The second major innovation of KRL was the development of perspectives. The basic notion is that the very same concept or event can often be viewed for different purposes, with different information desired from each view. Each of these views is called a perspective. Thus, a restaurant may be viewed as a place to eat, in which case the type, quality, and cost of the food are important. But a restaurant might also be viewed as a business (by a potential investor, for example), in which case it is the location, size, clientele, and balance sheet that are important. Which of these views the system provides to the user depends on which perspective is requested.

The mechanism for handling perspectives is always to describe an entity by comparing it with some other entity in the memory: this is aphorism 3 of KRL, from the above list. Bobrow and Winograd describe this property this way:

The object being used as a basis for comparison (which we call the *prototype*) provides a *perspec-*

*tive* from which to view the object being described. The details of the comparison can be thought of as *further specification* of the prototype. Viewed very abstractly, this is a commitment to a *holistic* as opposed to a *reductionistic* view of representation. It is quite possible (and we believe natural) for an object to be represented in a knowledge system only through a set of such comparisons. There would be no simple sense in which the system contained a "definition" of the object, or a complete description in terms of its structure . . . . This represents a fundamental difference in spirit between the KRL notion of representation, and standard logical representation based on formulas built out of primitive predicates.

In describing an object by comparison, the standard for reference is often not a specific individual, but a stereotypical individual which represents the *typical* member of a class. Such a prototype has a description which may be true of no one member of the class, but combines the *default* knowledge applied to members of the class in the absence of specific information. The default knowledge can itself be in the form of *intensional* description (for example, the prototypical family has "two or three" children) and can be stated in terms of other prototypes.[8]

Procedural attachments provide a means for the knowledge structures to trigger the active processes (D.G. Bobrow & Winograd, 1977; Winograd, 1975). Procedures can be attached to KRL structures in much the same way that general information about an object is attached to them (e.g., that Mary is a person). Procedures are of two forms: servants or demons. Servants are called when needed to perform some particular action. A typical servant resides on a slot labeled with a particular action, and when there is a desire for that action, then the servant procedure that resides there is the relevant one to use. Demons, when activated, await some special condition that causes them to perform their functions. Thus, if a set of units about a person is being established, several demons may be activated, each looking for information relevent to the slot from which it was invoked. Suppose we have established a unit for a person but

[8]From "An Overview of KRL, A Knowledge Representation" by D.G. Bobrow and T.J. Winograd, 1977, *Cognitive Science, 1,* pp. 7–8. Copyright 1977 by ABLEX Publishing. Reprinted by permission.

do not know the person's name. If in the course of the ensuing interaction the person's name is mentioned, the name demon would immediately see it and place a copy on the relevant structure within the relevant unit. Demons provide a powerful tool, for they allow general processing to continue while they sit alert for information relevant to themselves.

Although KRL represents an important contribution to the development of knowledge representation systems, in fact, KRL itself has not been used much. Rather, its importance has been in the exploration of a variety of specific representational issues. Most of the innovations of KRL such as descriptions, perspectives, and procedural attachments are now considered standard tools.

## The Relationship of these Representations to Classical Associations

Before we leave the discussion of propositional representation, it is useful to note the relationship between the representational systems described here and classical association theory. After all, are not these systems simply systematic presentations of the associations that everyone has long believed must exist among different items within memory? The answer is yes, but no. Current representational models do indeed represent a formalization of associations. However, this is a new association theory: a neo-associationism. The basic propositional and procedural representation system contains pointers from one item within memory to another; these pointers correspond to the associations of the classical theory. However, these modern theories of representation—especially propositional and procedural representations—differ from classic associations in four ways:

1. The relations are directed. This means that the direction of the association matters, so that the association from A to B is not necessarily the same as that from B to A (and in general, is not the same). Some classical theories of association had this property.
2. The associations are labeled. This means that two items A and B can be associated in many different ways, and in following these associations heavy use is made of the differences among labels. The labels are meaningful, and different labels imply different logical relationships.
3. A distinction is made between types and tokens. This overcomes one of the major problems of association theory in allowing a particular instance of an item to be activated without confusing it with all instances of the same item or with the generic item itself.
4. There is a distinction made among levels of representation. This allows for processing of higher order structures. Classical association theory (as well as the early semantic networks and the predicate-calculus and set-theoretic representations) suffered from a homogeneity of representational levels, thus considerably weakening their power and inferential ability.

These four properties yield several important benefits, including enhanced powers of logical inference, including inheritance properties and a natural representation for default values. The distinction among levels of representation allows for the use of prototypical or generic units that can guide in the construction of new units or in the interpretation of existing ones. All in all, these properties enhance the powers of these neo-associational representations sufficiently well to overcome all the classic objections to them, as well as to solve some issues that were not even considered earlier. An excellent treatment of the relationship of semantic networks to association theory is given in the first section of the book by Anderson and Bower (1973).

## ANALOGICAL REPRESENTATIONS

Most of the representational systems we have discussed this far were designed to represent information stored in long-term memory. In particular, their focus was meanings, which led naturally to propositional representations. But other considerations have led to other classes of representational ideas. Consider the representation of an image; how would one represent objects undergoing various transformations? A number of researchers, especially Shepard, Kosslyn, and their colleagues (cf. Shepard &

Cooper, 1982; Kosslyn, 1980), have proposed that the knowledge underlying images is analogical rather than propositional. There has been a good deal of debate concerning the nature of analog representations and how they differ from propositional ones. In this section, we proceed by summarizing the work carried out under the rubric of analogical representations. We enter into the debate only after we have presented both points of view.

## Shepard

Shepard and his co-workers have focused primarily on a set of simple mental transformations of mental images. Most of their work has focused on a study of mental rotations. The general procedure is to present a picture of a pair of objects that are either similar or mirror images of one another, but that differ in orientation (see Figure 8.17). The subject's task is to decide, as quickly as possible, whether the objects can be rotated into congruence. Typical data from these experiments are illustrated in Figure 8.18: the time to respond increases linearly and continuously as the angular difference between the two objects increase, whether they differ in picture plane orientation or in orientation in depth. Subjects often report that they do the task by imagining one of the objects being rotated into congruence with the other.

Based on their experimental findings, Metzler and Shepard (1974) argued that the process of mentally rotating an object requires a mental analog of a physical rotation. There are, they argue, two characteristics of such an analog process. First, an analog process

> has something important in common with the internal process that would go on if the subject were actually to perceive the one external object physically rotating into congruence with the other.

Second, in an analog process,

> the internal representation passes through a certain trajectory of intermediate states each of which has a one-to-one correspondence to an intermediate stage of an external physical rotation of the object . . . . To speak of it [a process] as an analog type of process is . . . to contrast it with any other type of process (such as feature search, symbol manipulation, verbal analysis,

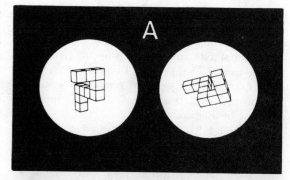

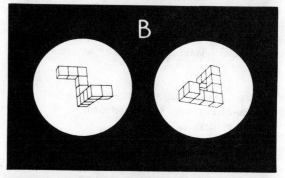

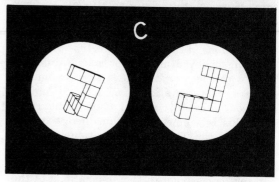

**Figure 8.17.** Illustrative pairs of perspective views, including a pair differing by an 80° rotation in the picture plane (*A*), a pair differing by an 80° rotation in depth (*B*), and a pair differing by a reflection as well as rotation (*C*). From "Transformation Studies of the Internal Representation of Three-Dimensional Objects" by J. Metzler and R.N. Shepard in *Theories in Cognitive Psychology: The Loyola Symposium* (p. 35), R. Solso (Ed.), 1974. Hillsdale, NJ: Erlbaum. Copyright 1974 by Lawrence Erlbaum Associates, Inc. Reprinted by permission.

or other "digital computation") in which the intermediate stages of the process have no sort of one-to-one correspondence to intermediate situations in the external world. (Metzler & Shepard, 1974, pp. 150–151.)

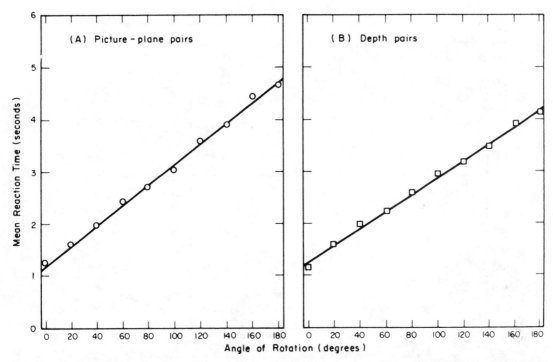

**Figure 8.18.** Mean time to determine that two objects have the same three-dimensional shape as a function of the angular difference in their portrayed orientations. From "Transformational Studies of the Internal Representation of Three-Dimensional Objects" by J. Metzler and R.N. Shepard in *Theories in Cognitive Psychology: The Loyola Symposium* (p. 36), R. Solso (Ed.), 1974. Hillsdale, NJ: Erlbaum. Copyright 1974 by Lawrence Erlbaum Associates, Inc. Reprinted by permission.

In addition to the claim that the processes are analog, Shepard and his colleagues have argued that the representations themselves are analog: "The internal representation undergoing the rotation is viewed as preserving some degree of the spatial structure of its corresponding external object" (Cooper & Podgorny, 1976) and in this sense is an analog to the object itself (see also Shepard & Cooper, 1982, pp. 12–13).

That the time to rotate something mentally grows linearly with angular difference does not, of course, mean that the process of mental rotation passes through the intermediate states. This datum by itself merely indicates that it takes longer to make the judgments the greater the angular disparity. In a very clever and important experiment, Cooper (1976) demonstrated that during mental rotation the internal representations do indeed pass through intermediate points and are, in that sense, analog. Subjects were to imagine an object rotating on a blank circular field. While they were doing this, a test object was presented in one of twelve orientations. The subject was to decide as quickly as possible whether it was the same as or a mirror image of the object being imagined. The critical feature of this experiment is that Cooper had previously determined the rate of mental rotation for her subjects, and therefore, depending on the initial orientation of the object being mentally rotated and on the time since the subject began, she could calculate the current orientation of the imagined object. Thus, she knew the angular difference of the test object and the imagined rotating object. The results, illustrated in Figure 8.19, showed that the greater the angular departure of the test stimulus from the orientation of the imagined stimulus, the longer it took the subjects to respond. It appears that subjects indeed form images of the object and that rotation involves the representation passing through intermediate orientations.

Despite the clarity of the empirical results, not everyone has been convinced of the need for an analog as opposed to a propositional

DATA FOR INDIVIDUAL SUBJECTS

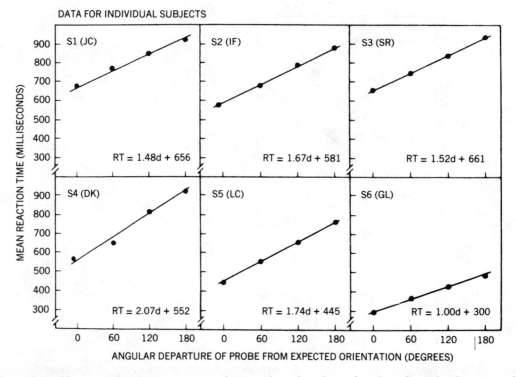

**Figure 8.19.** Mean reaction time to unexpected test probes, plotted as a function of angular departure of the test probe from the expected orientation, for each of the six individual subjects. From "Demonstration of a Mental Analog of an External Rotation" by L.A. Cooper, 1976, *Perception and Psychophysics, 19,* p. 300. Copyright 1976 by the Psychonomic Society. Reprinted by permission.

representational system. There are three reasons for this. First, it is possible that a propositional system could be constructed that would produce the same results. Second, the kind of analog system envisioned by Shepard and his colleagues is clearly a special case system: it is not at all clear how it might interface with the kinds of propositional representational systems that have been so powerful in other domains. Third, it is not at all clear what the analogical system would look like in detail. How should these analog systems be represented in our theories? What would such a system actually look like? In what ways would it really be different from the representational systems we have discussed thus far? These questions have been addressed, and tentative answers have been proposed by Kosslyn and his colleagues, and so we turn now to a discussion of that work.

## Kosslyn

The best articulated theory of image representation was put forth by Kosslyn and Schwartz (1978) and refined in Kosslyn (1980). Kosslyn's theory was built around what he called the Cathode Ray Tube (CRT) metaphor for visual imagery. Figure 8.20 illustrates the basic aspects of the metaphor. The basic idea is that there are two fundamental kinds of representations of imaginal information. First, there is the surface representation corresponding to the visual image itself. This representation is assumed to occur in a spatial medium, which imposes a number of characteristics on the image:

- Parts of the image represent corresponding parts of the imaged object in such a way that, for example, distance between parts

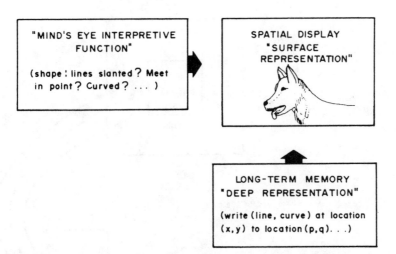

**Figure 8.20.** A schematic representation of the cathode-ray-tube (CRT) metaphor. From *Image and Mind* (p. 6) by S.M. Kosslyn, 1980. Cambridge, MA: Harvard University Press. Copyright 1980 by Harvard University Press. Reprinted by permission.

of the representation correspond to distance between parts of the imaged object.

- Just as a CRT has a limited spatial extent, so an image should have a limited spatial extent: images that are too large cannot be represented without overflowing.
- Surface representations of images, like those of CRTs, are assumed to have a grain size, so that there is a loss of detail when an object is imaged too small.
- Images, like CRT screens, require a periodic refreshing without which they will fade away.

In addition to the surface representation, the CRT metaphor suggests that there is a deep representation from which the image is being generated. Kosslyn (1980) suggested that images are generated from some sort of propositional representation, so that the underlying memory representation may not have the same spatial properties as the surface image. The third suggestive aspect of the CRT metaphor is the existence of an interpreter or mind's eye that processes the surface image and serves as an interface between the surface image and a more abstract semantic interpretation of the constructed image. The interpretive processes may use some of the same processing mechanisms as general visual processing.

Kosslyn has constructed a computer simulation model that offers plausible accounts of a variety of data on visual imagery. In his model, Kosslyn proposes that the surface representation consists of a matrix of points. An image is represented in the matrix by filling in the cells of the matrix.[9] The matrix is of limited extent, thus limiting how large an image can be; it has a particular grain size, thus limiting how small an image can be and still be seen clearly; and it is organized so that the grain of the central region is smaller than the grain of the peripheral region (the cells in the outer region of the matrix are not all used). Further, Kosslyn assumes that the representations in the visual matrix fade unless the old material is refreshed periodically. This is implemented by having the magnitude of the value within each cell of the matrix decrease with time after it is written into the matrix.

As with the CRT model, the images in the computer model are not long-term representations, but simply temporary representations that are constructed to aid in the solution of particular problems. The long-term representations or deep representations contain the knowledge that allows the construction of the images.

[9] In computer graphics, this is known as a bit map representation.

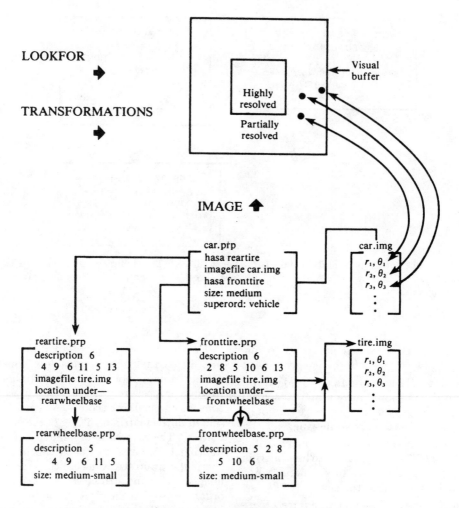

**Figure 8.21.** A schematic representation of the structures posited by Kosslyn. The major processes of the model **LOOKFOR** things in the image, perform **TRANSFORMATIONS** on the images, and create an **IMAGE** from a long-term memory representation. From *Image and Mind* (p. 147) by S.M. Kosslyn, 1980. Cambridge, MA: Harvard University Press. Copyright 1980 by Harvard University Press. Reprinted by permission.

Consequently, Kosslyn has two kinds of long-term representations. He uses a relatively standard propositional representation for storing general knowledge and also what he calls literal representations for storing the data necessary to create an image. These literal images are themselves stored as a set of polar coordinates $(r, \Theta$ pairs) with respect to an origin. The polar coordinates allow easy change of size (by multiplying the values of $r$ by a constant) and easy rotation (around its origin) although they present some difficulty in translation of an image. Figure 8.21 shows the long-term memory

representations and the major processes of the theory.

There are three major classes of processes proposed by Kosslyn. These are **IMAGE**, **LOOKFOR** and various **TRANSFORMATIONS**. **IMAGE** is a procedure for generating an image from the stored representation. It constructs a whole image out of the literal representations of their parts and their descriptions. **LOOKFOR** scans the image, using the surface representation along with the long-term memory description of the object, and it finds the location of the object in the image—if it is indeed in the image. There are also four image transformation operations: **SCAN**, **ZOOM**, **PAN**, and **ROTATE**. **SCAN** moves the image within the matrix. **ZOOM** moves all points out from the center, leaving a larger image. **PAN** moves all of the points toward the center, creating a smaller image. **ROTATE** moves all points of an image around a pivot, thus rotating the surface image. All of these transformations operate in small steps so that the surface matrix goes through intermediate points as it processes. Thus, in Shepard's sense, Kosslyn's system is truly an analogical system.

Kosslyn has arrayed an impressive amount of evidence for many of the detailed assumptions of his theory. In sone such experiment, Kosslyn, Ball, and Reiser (1978) showed that the time to scan between two points on an image was proportional to the distance between those two points on the object being imaged. Thus, subjects were presented with a picture of a map (Figure 8.22A) and were asked to memorize it, particularly noticing the seven $X$'s on the seven key locations of the map. The subjects continued to study the map until they could reproduce it with great accuracy. They were then instructed to image the map and told to mentally stare at a named location. They were then given another location name and told to mentally scan to that location and press a button when they reached it. Figure 8.22B shows the results. Clearly, mental scanning depends on the mental distance over which the scan takes place.

In another experiment, Kosslyn (1975) showed that the time that it takes to verify that an image of an animal has a particular property depends on the imaged size of the animal. Thus, subjects were told to image a particular animal in one of four relative sizes. The largest size was as large as they could imagine without overflowing their image, the others to be scaled down by a factor of six in each case. Subjects were then asked whether the image of the animal had a particular property (i.e., they were asked to image a rabbit and then asked whether a rabbit has claws). The time to answer the question depended strongly on the size of the image and not on the size of the animal. The larger the image the faster the decision (small images involve loss of detail, due to Kosslyn's grain size, making the identification of a feature more difficult). Figure 8.23 shows the results of this experiment.

One of the important assumptions of Kosslyn's model is that the medium in which images are created has size limitations such that it will hold only a certain amount of material. Kosslyn wished to get an empirical measure of the size of the visual image or, as he called it, "the visual angle of the mind's eye." To do this, Kosslyn devised a mental walk task to measure the visual image. In these experiments people were asked to image particular objects as if the object were at some distance. They were then asked to mentally walk toward the object until it completely filled their mental image and to estimate the mental distance to the object. Using a variety of imaged objects, Kosslyn found that the estimated distance at which a particular object was imaged to overflow the image was linearly related to the size of the object. Figure 8.24 shows the results for imagined line drawings of animals. These results suggest that the visual angle of the mental image subtends about 20°. Similar results were found for several other sets of imagined stimuli. Clearly, a visual image has a definite perceived size, and there is substantial agreement about what that size is.

In addition to these results, Kosslyn has found that the time to create an image depends on the number of objects in the image, that an image of a large object takes longer to create than an image of a smaller object, that the fields on which visual images occur are roughly circular, and other similar results. Based on these results, Kosslyn argues that the key features of the CRT model and its computer simulation are confirmed. In particular, Kosslyn (1980) argues that:

1. Images occur in a spatial medium in which locations are accessed in such a way that the interval properties of physical space are preserved, and they are preserved in such a way that each portion of the image corresponds to a portion of the object being imaged. Evidence for this comes from introspection and from the results of the scanning experiments. Since the time to scan an image from one point to another is proportional to the actual distance between the points on the physical object being imaged, the image must be preserving the distance relations of the object.

2. Images have a finite grain size. Evidence for this assumption comes from the experiments

(a)

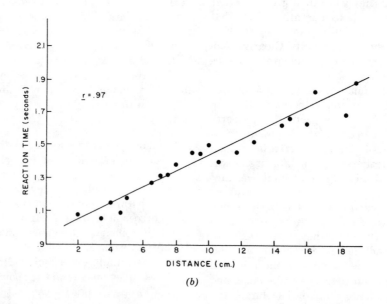

(b)

**Figure 8.22.** *A*: A fictional map subjects memorized and later imaged and scanned across. (From Kosslyn, 1980.) *B*: The time to scan between all pairs of locations on an image of the map illustrated in *A*. From *Image and Mind* (pp. 43, 44) by S.M. Kosslyn, 1980. Cambridge, MA: Harvard University Press. Copyright 1980 by Harvard University Press. Reprinted by permission.

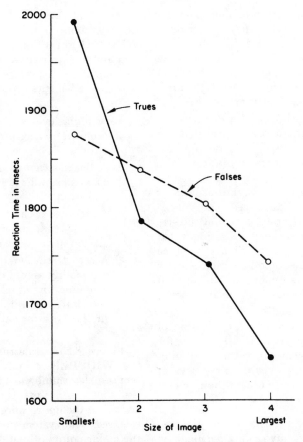

**Figure 8.23.** The time required to evaluate properties of animals imaged at one of four relative sizes. The largest size was to be as large as possible without overflowing, and the rest were scaled down according to a training procedure. From *Image and Mind* (p. 59) by S.M. Kosslyn, 1980. Cambridge, MA: Harvard University Press. Copyright 1980 by Harvard University Press. Reprinted by permission.

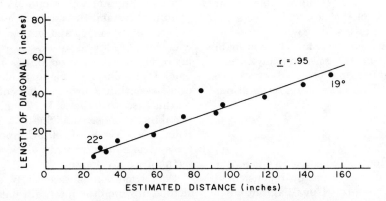

**Figure 8.24.** The average distance at which imaged objects seemed to overflow when subjects imaged line drawings of animals. From *Image and Mind* (p. 78) by S.M. Kosslyn, 1980. Cambridge, MA: Harvard University Press. Copyright 1980 by Harvard University Press. Reprinted by permission.

on judging the properties of objects imaged at different sizes. The fact that parts of smaller objects are more difficult to see, implies that things lose precision when they get too small in an image. This precision is presumably determined by the grain size of the imaginal medium.

3. The imaginal medium has a definite size and shape that limits the amount that can be imaged at one time. Evidence for this comes from experiments on the size of the visual angle of the mind's eye. Since images of large objects overflow the medium at greater subjective distances than images of smaller objects, it appears that the size of the imaginal medium is a limiting factor on the size of the image. Similarly, since the subjective distance at which a ruler overflows is independent of the imaged orientation of the ruler, the medium must be roughly circular.

4. Images are constructed over a period of time on a part by part basis. Evidence for this conclusion comes from the result indicating that images containing several objects take longer to create than images containing fewer objects.

In Kosslyn, then, we have a detailed model of an analogical representation and a substantial amount of evidence illustrating many important features of images. Perhaps the strongest single conclusion to be drawn is that people can create images that are surprisingly veridical and that can be processed in the way that an actual picture would be processed. Imagined objects are certainly analogs of the physical objects that they represent. As we will see later, however, the matrix representational format is probably not sufficiently general for use in many cases in which we use our imagination to solve problems. It seems likely that a richer representational format is necessary.

## Funt

Diagrams are often valuable aids to our reasoning. We very often find it useful to construct a diagram and reason through our diagram. Given our ability to construct relatively reliable mental images, it should not be surprising that we can solve problems by constructing mental diagrams. Funt (1980) has developed a representational system (and a computer program called **WHISPER**) in which it is convenient to represent and to manipulate mental diagrams for the solution of simple problems. **WHISPER** contains four basic elements:

1. A high level reasoner that guides the problem-solving process and produces an answer,

2. A diagram that is represented by values in a matrix similar to Kosslyn's surface representation,

3. A retina that can inspect the diagram and provide the high level reasoner with information about a transformed diagram,

4. A set of redrawing transformations that can modify an old diagram and produce a new one in which certain objects are translated or rotated or undergo other similar transformation.

Figure 8.25A illustrates a typical problem that **WHISPER** can solve. In this case, the system is to determine the nature of the chain reaction that will occur if the system of blocks illustrated in the figure were to be constructed and released. The system proceeds by first finding the major points of instability in the system. It then finds the pivot of rotation for the most unstable object. The object is then rotated about its pivot point until either the conditions for a collision are met or until the conditions for the object falling free are met. In this case, the system detects a collision (i.e., points of two different objects falling on top of one another). At this point new instabilities might be added, so a new evaluation is made, and a new instability is chosen and followed. In the case shown in the figure, block $D$ (the one on top of small triangular block $C$) is chosen as the unstable one and the process continues until another collision occurs (in this case, with the table). Then, still another instability is chosen, and finally, no instabilities remain. Figures 8.25B, 8.25C, and 8.25D show the system at the critical points at which new instabilities are sought.

Funt's method is essentially a simulation method in which the internal relationships of a complex system are found through the simulation of a process. It is very often the case for complex problems that simulation is the most

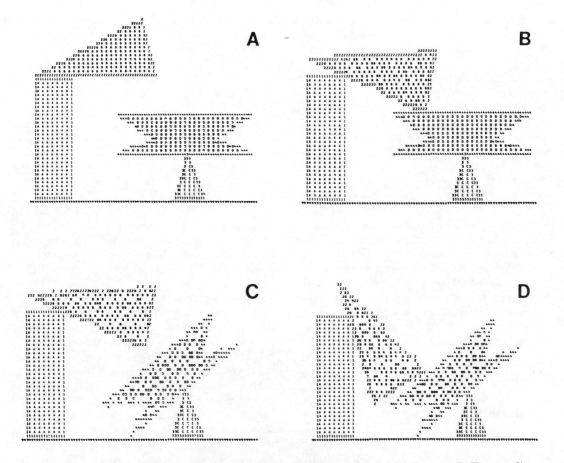

**Figure 8.25.** The chain reaction problem as solved by **WHISPER**. *A*: The initial diagram. *B*: The new diagram at the point of the first collision. *C*: The diagram at the point of the second collision. *D*: The diagram at its final state. From "Problem Solving with Diagrammatic Representations" by B.V. Funt, 1980, *Artificial Intelligence*, *13*, pp. 214, 215, 218. Copyright 1980 by North-Holland Publishing Co. Reprinted by permission.

effective solution method. In fact, it may very well be that the essential characteristic of reasoning through imagery is that imagination is a mechanism for performing mental simulations. We turn now to a general discussion of the notion of a mental simulation and the more general notion of the mental model.

## Constraint Based Representation of Images

It is important to distinguish the views of an image that is created when it is needed in short-term memory from the views of an image as a format in which information is stored in long-term memory. It is quite possible that the knowledge stored in long-term memory is best charac-terized propositionally and then somehow con-verted into an image when it is needed. This seems to be the view of Kosslyn, but this distinc-tion is not always made. So-called dual code theorists suppose that long-term memory itself consists, in part, of images. In Kosslyn's scheme, the long-term information itself is not imaginal in format, but it contains explicit instructions on how to construct an image. It is possible to have a model in which the long-term representa-tion consists of merely qualitative statements similar to Clark and Chase's ABOVE(STAR, PLUS), from which detailed images can be regenerated through a process known as con-straint satisfaction. The idea is very similar to multidimensional scaling. In multidimensional scaling, a series of similarity judgments are collected. A program then tries to find the euclidean space that is most consistent with the observed judgments. It can be shown that although the original judgments are ordinal only as the number of judgments increases, the reconstructed space can contain accurate interval representations. The set of similarity data constitutes a set of constraints, and the multidimensional scaling programs find the euclidean space that best satisfies them. The same process can be used to reconstruct map information from a set of simple constraints concerning the directions from one object on a map to another. As the number of such constraints increases, the reconstructed map becomes more and more accurate. The map is distorted in those regions where there are few constraints and more accurate in those regions where the constraints are richer. Images can be shown to contain many similar distortions. It is possible that there is no special long-term representation specifically for imaginal information, but that images are simply the product of using propositional information as constraints on a euclidean embedding of stored spatial relations.

# Mental Models and Mental Simulations

So far, we have restricted our discussion of analogical representations to cases of imagining. We can imagine two objects rotating, and this helps us decide whether the objects are congruent. We can imagine a paper cutout being folded into a cube and answer questions about which sides fit together (Shepard & Feng, 1972). We can imagine an animal (such as a German shepherd) and use our image to verify characteristics of it (does it have pointed ears?). We can imagine diagrams similar to those used by Funt (1980) and predict the outcome of a chain reaction. We can imagine a ball rolling down a mental roller coaster and predict where it might end up (de Kleer, 1975). We can imagine walking through our house and counting how many windows it has. We can imagine a person pole vaulting over a high bar and just barely knocking the bar off (or just barely making it). We can imagine waking up to the smell of bacon and eggs. We can imagine the sounds of a symphony orchestra and hear a friend's reponse to our questions.

It is clear that our ability to imagine a wide range of activities is a very useful mechanism in our ability to reason about our world. It is not so clear, however, that a matrix representation is a very useful representational format for most of the cases of imagining just mentioned. In particular, we believe that rather than the mental image we should think of the mental model, and rather than the mental transformation we should think of mental simulations. It seems that humans have the remarkable ability to construct a representation of an object or situation that is a kind of model of the object or situation, where the model is manipulable as a mental simulation. As is usual, the question of the kind of representation most suited to these mental models is a notational issue. How best can we express our theories about what these mental models are like, and how best can we characterize their important features?

## Mental Simulation

One of the most important phenomena that drives the study of mental models is that of mental simulation. This is essentially what a billiard player must do in lining up a new shot, or, for that matter, what any skilled athlete or performer must do in determining the best course of action, be it for golf, tennis, chess, or bridge. In these situations, people act as if they were running a mental simulation and observing its behavior. The chain reaction problem of Funt (1980) illustrated in Figure 8.25 is a good example, both of a problem that a person might solve by running a mental simulation and also of a representational system that solves the problem in much the spirit that we imagine a person would.

Consider how we might determine the functional properties of an object. It may be argued that an essential property of chairs is their sit-on-able-ness. That is, among other things, for something to be a chair, it must be possible to sit on it. How do we determine whether it is possible to sit on something? Mental simulation often appears to be a method. Consider, for example, whether a salt shaker is sit-on-able. Many people, when considering this example, report mentally simulating such an event, giggling at the expected outcome, but reaching an affirmative outcome when they mentally simulate either a six-inch tall human or a two foot tall salt shaker.

Mental simulations appear to be useful devices for discovering factual knowledge buried in our tacit or procedural representations. Thus, for example, when asked a question such as "How many windows are there in your home?" people often report mentally simulating a walk through their house counting the windows.

An interesting example of the use of mental simulation in a computer system to facilitate the answering of questions is provided by the work of Brown and Burton (1975) and Brown, Burton, and de Kleer (1982). In particular, Sophie (the computer system) could answer hypothetical questions about what would happen if a particular circuit component were changed or damaged. Sophie had two distinct knowledge representations about circuits. It had a traditional propositional representation about the causal relationships among the components, as well as principles of circuit design. In addition, Sophie had a mathematical model of the circuit. Some questions were best answered by inferences in the the semantic network, whereas other questions were best answered by having the system set up the model of the circuit and run it, using the results of the simulation to determine the answer. The Sophie system captures most of the important features of mental models and mental simulations and illustrates the power and utility of a system that has multiple representations of the same represented world. Even though a mathematical model may not be the best representation of the human capacity for creating mental models, the system serves as a powerful example of how one may combine multiple representations, including one that can be executed to determine the results.

## The Essential Features of Mental Models

A detailed description of the state of the art on work in mental models is presented in Gentner and Stevens (1983). Although the work reported in this book is just the beginning of the field and the approach (consider it a report of work in progress), we believe that it is an important beginning for two reasons: (1) as a practical aid in the design of applied systems that must reason about complex physical systems; and (2), in providing a considerably richer framework than now exists for the study of mental imagery and mental transformations. These new approaches allow us to examine images by means of methods that do not view them as purely two-dimensional visual phenomena in which a quasipictorial representation seems appropriate, but rather as part of a much broader and more important human capacity. In general, the studies of mental models reveal a number of features that characterize the approach (see Gentner & Stevens, 1983 for expansion of these ideas):

- Data and process are closely bound. Procedural information plays a critical role in mental models, although, as the work on the Sophie system shows, there may be both procedural and propositional representations intermixed. However, much of the power of mental models comes from their ability to simulate the represented world (by running the model), with the results available only by inspecting the outcome of that simulation.

- Mental models are likely to use qualitative reasoning. A person's ability to reason often seems quite good qualitatively, but when the answers depend on a quantitative relation, abilities deteriorate (in the absence of external aids). (See Forbus, 1983.)

- Mental models are often causal models. That is, they are models that embody the causal features of the domain that they model. Thus, for example, in solving physics problems, experts often develop mental models of the physical systems discussed in the problems. These systems are abstract (in that they contain frictionless planes and other similar idealized objects), they embody the causal laws of physics in a qualitative fashion (cf. de Kleer & Brown, 1983), and they can be run to make predictions.

- Introspection reveals that mental models contain a strong experiential component. Thus, the phenomenology of imagery is also the phenomenology of mental models. It is, of course, not clear how much one should rely on introspective evidence, but it is also clear that one should not ignore it. It should be noted that the experiential component need not be visual, and if it is visual, it need not be (and probably isn't) merely two dimensional. Our imagination and mental transformations appear to contain visual, auditory, kinesthetic, and emotive components, in addition to the more abstract components necessary for the kinds of causal reasoning processes that seem to be such a fundamental part of mental simulations.

## Propositional and Analogical Representation

Much has been made of the supposed fundamental differences between analogical and propositional systems of representation. We believe that these differences are overstated and overemphasized. There are indeed different methods of representation, each with its own virtues and deficits, each good for a particular set of circumstances. Clearly, however, the notion of analogical representation conjures up a particular form of representation. Let us examine these aspects of representation so that we can understand how they fit into the entire spectrum of representational systems.

What does it mean for a representation to be analogical? In one sense, the question is meaningless, for the whole point of any representational system is that the representing world be similar or analogous to the represented world. Perhaps the best way to examine this issue is to examine the major points made in two prescient analyses of representational systems: the point made by D.G. Bobrow (1975) that there are numerous, separable dimensions of representation and the distinction raised by Palmer (1978) between intrinsic and extrinsic aspects of representation.

Representation is (purely) intrinsic whenever a representing relation has the same inherent constraints as its represented relation. That is, the logical structure of the representing relation is intrinsic to the relation itself rather than imposed from outside. Representation is purely arbitrary whenever the inherent structure of a representing relation is totally arbitrary and that of its represented relation is not. Whatever structure such a representing relation has, then, is imposed on it by the relation it represents. It is typical of analogical representational systems that the crucial relations of the system tend to be intrinsic in their representational format. It is typical of propositional representations that the inherent characteristics of the representing relations are not characteristics of the objects being represented and thus must be added to the representation as additional, extrinsic, constraints. It should be emphasized, however, that whether a set of constraints is intrinsic or extrinsic makes no difference in the operation of the representational system. The essential feature is that representational systems have the power to express those relationships of the represented world that are being represented.

As we have already seen, the critical requirement of a representation is that it map some selected aspects of the represented world into a representing world. There are two keys to understanding the differences among representations:

1. The selection of which dimensions of the represented world are to be captured within the representing world,
2. The determination of how the selected dimensions shall be represented.

These two aspects of the decision—the which and the how—then govern the properties of the representational system. Note that even in the mapping of a single represented world, the questions may have to be answered several times. For each dimension of the represented world that is selected, there may very well be a different determination of how that dimension is to be represented. In some cases, the very choice of a dimension tightly constrains the set of possible ways to do the representation. In other cases, having made the one decision, there are a number of possibilities remaining for the second.

Suppose we wished to represent the star above the plus of Clark and Chase (1972), the figures that so perplexed our undergraduate students (Figure 8.26A). If we wished to represent all the spatial details of the figure, then an appropriate representational scheme might be to map spatial dimensions in the represented world into spatial dimensions in the representing world. In this case, we might set up an array of elements, letting each element in the representing world take on a value of 1 wherever the corresponding spatial location in the representing world has a light intensity less than some critical value, and 0 otherwise: the result is shown in Figure 8.26B. For many people, this result captures the essence of an analogical representation, for the representing world looks like an image of the represented world (and this is basically the representational format used by Kosslyn, 1980, and Funt, 1980). Presumably, this representation would have satisfied our students.

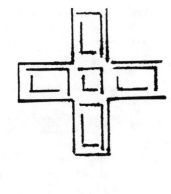

```
0000000000000000000
0000000000000000000
0000000001100000000
0000000001100000000
0000000001100000000
0000111111111111000
0000111111111111000
0000000001100000000
0000000001100000000
0000000001100000000
0000000000000000000
0000000000000000000
```

```
0000000000000000000
0000000000000000000
0000000001000000000
0000000011100000000
0000000111110000000
0011111111111111100
0000111111111110000
0000011110111100000
0000111100011110000
0001100000000011000
0000000000000000000
0000000000000000000
```

**Figure 8.26.** *A* shows an elaboration of the illustration used in the experiments of Clark and Chase (1972) in which subjects were asked to answer TRUE or FALSE to the question of whether or not the figure shows a PLUS above a STAR. In the original experiment, the stars and pluses were simple line drawings. This figure shows much more elaborate detail, intended to make the point that the characteristics of a representation are determined to a large extent by which aspects of the represented world are selected to be represented within the representing world. *B* shows a possible representation of *A*, in which spatial dimensions of *A* have been mapped into spatial dimensions of *B*.

However, looks are not important; what matters is what can be done with the representation.

Suppose we wished to judge the relative areas of the two figures, or compare the lengths of the vertical heights, or horizontal widths, or diagonal lengths. This representation, a spatial matrix, would indeed be appropriate, for having mapped spatial attributes into spatial attributes, the relative lengths of the various dimensions are automatically (intrinsically) captured by the representation.[10] Suppose we wanted to

answer Clark and Chase's question? Is the PLUS above the STAR? To do this, we would have to examine the representation, determine which set of darkened squares corresponds to the plus, which to the star, and which direction corresponds to up, then make a judgment. The representation is of no particular help. That is, it is no easier to make this judgment from the representing world than from the original, represented world. Once having made that judgment, how might we record the resulting fact, namely that the star is above the plus? Well, such a fact is a proposition about the represented world, and an appropriate representation for it would be a proposition something of the form:

ABOVE (PLUS, STAR).

Note that this propositional representation, if

[10]There are still some assumptions that must be met. Thus, we have depicted the different elements in the representing world adjacent to one another, with the coordinate systems parallel, linearly related, and with the same scaling factor. In other situations, it might be advisable to choose otherwise, in which case the intrinsic relations that we have just relied on for the various comparisons among dimensions might not still hold.

we were asked the question a second time, would indeed help us get to the answer. However, if we were asked to judge the relative dimensions of the two figures, the proposition would be of no use whatsoever. Different representations have different virtues and should be used for different purposes. In general, a representation is best for purposes in which the information desired is captured in its intrinsic properties.

Note that we represented intensity in the original world by 1s and in the depicting world by 0s. That is obviously an arbitrary, discrete representation for what could be a rich, continually varying dimension. That we chose to map spatial properties into spatial representations leaves completely open the issue of how to map other dimensions, such as intensity, color, weight, odor, monetary value, and so on. Again, for the purposes of this particular set of tasks, it was sufficient to represent intensity in this binary-valued, discrete fashion. Indeed, it is superior, for it means that subtle differences in intensity do not confuse our comparisons. For other purposes, such a representational choice might not be adequate.

### Analogical Does Not Mean Continuous

One common misconception of the meaning of analog representation is that it is continuous, whereas propositional representation is digital, or discrete. This can't really be true, for although the matrix representation of Figure 8.26B would be classified as an image or analog representation, it clearly is composed of finite, discrete cells. The distinction is a result of the choice of dimensions from the represented world that are to be represented, not from any inherent property of the representational system itself. If we map spatial information into spatial form, then we are apt to use a continuous method of representation. If we map a number of objects into either the number system or a one-to-one map of object to representational symbol, then the most reasonable analogical representation is discrete nonnegative integers or finite symbols. That is, if the dimension in the represented world is continuous, then it makes sense for the representing world to be continuous. If the represented dimension is discrete—or if the continuity of the dimension is of no particular interest—then the best analog in the representing world would be a finite representational format. Whether or not we wish to characterize the representation as

analogous depends on how well we have captured the critical features of the represented world.

A discrete representation of a continuous dimension may still be characterized as analogical. Take the mental rotation phenomenon of two-dimensional figures as an example. First, we separate consideration of the representation of the figures from the representation of the rotation: either one may be analogical or propositional, regardless of the other. Consider the four possibilities this gives rise to. If the figure is propositionally represented (by statements of the form ONTOPOF(cube1, cube2)),[11] then angular position may be represented either by discrete position (POSITION-OF(main-axis, horizontal)) or by continuous position (POSITION-OF(main-axis, 30.267...°)), the difference being whether the position is selected from a finite set of descriptions (such as the integers) or from the real numbers. (Levin [cited in Shepard & Cooper, 1982, pp. 141, 144] described how this form of representation might work for mental rotation.) If the figure is analogically represented, perhaps as in the spatial matrix form of Figure 8.26B, we still need to determine how to represent the rotation. It is easy to see how we might represent rotation in nonanalogical form: we simply jump from the current position to the new position, traversing few or none of the intermediate states. If there is a matrix representation, it is not simple to actually do the rotation: the contents of each cell of the matrix would have to be moved to an appropriate new cell, and the algorithm that might accomplish this move in a continuous way is not at all obvious. Yes, one could do the appropriate matrix multiplication, but then, why not just compute the desired end point? Then there would be no need to actually rotate the representation. Moreover, if the representation is a matrix, continuity is not possible in principle, for the same angular rotation covers different numbers of matrix cells at the periphery of the figure than near the center: at some point, intervening cells must be either repeated or skipped. If we try angular rotation on a cartesian grid, the grain size problem is a fundamental limitation. As solution to this problem, Funt (1983) proposed using a spherical

---

[11] Presumably the representation would be based upon the relationships of the component parts to some canonical position determined by the axes and centroids of the figures—an aspect that is critical for all the representational forms.

coordinate system for the representation. Funt shows that continuous rotation can be performed if a large number of processing mechanisms are packed into a spherical array, each processor communicating only with its neighbors, each containing the relevant segments of the represented figure. To perform rotation, each processor passes the relevant segments to the appropriate neighboring processor. This is true rotation, for the representation truly rotates through the spherical array. Note, however, that because the number of processors is finite, the rotation still takes place in discrete steps.

The critical feature that identifies a representation of rotation as analogous to physical rotation is that the rotation passes through intermediate values. Indeed, this is why Shepard and Cooper (1982) place so much stress on the demonstration that their subjects did appear to rotate the test figures through the intermediate states. Their findings allow us to conclude that people do represent rotation in a manner analogous to physical rotation. We can make this statement with confidence, regardless of whether human rotation actually is smooth and continuous, or whether it might be by discrete rotational jumps, perhaps—as has been suggested by Just and Carpenter (1976)—rotating in steps of 50°. As Shepard and Cooper (1982, p. 175) put it: "Just and Carpenter (1976) acknowledge that their model of mental rotation fulfills our criterion for an analog process in that during rotation of, for example, 150°, the internal process passes through intermediate stages corresponding to intermediate external orientations of 50° and 100°." The point is that we can separate the determination of something's being continuous from the determination of its being analogical.

## PROCEDURAL REPRESENTATIONS

There is a classic distinction in representational systems between knowledge about something (called knowledge of, or declarative knowledge) and knowledge about how to do something (knowledge how, or procedural knowledge). Some of our knowledge is declarative, in the sense of making a statement about some property of the world. Thus, a statement of the form "George Washington was the first president of the United States" is a prototypical declarative statement. Knowledge of how to kick a football is a prototypical piece of procedural knowledge. Declarative knowledge tends to be accessible; it can easily be examined and combined with other declarative statements to form an inference. Procedural knowledge tends to be inaccessible, being used to guide our actions, but often offering remarkably little access for examination. Thus, although we can pronounce a word like "serendipitous," most of us cannot say what movements our tongue takes during the pronunciation without actually doing the task and noting the tongue movements. We seem to have conscious access to declarative knowledge; but we do not have this access to procedural knowledge.

So far in this chapter we have only discussed declarative systems of representations, systems in which the manner by which knowledge is represented is the critical concern. Procedural representational systems comprise a contrasting class of systems in which the concern is what they do, not how they do it. Note, however, that the discussion of procedural representation has intermixed two different, but related, concepts. One concern is with how we should represent the knowledge of how to do things: knowledge of how to perform actions upon the world and knowledge of mental strategies that allows us to perform actions upon the representational structures of the mind. The other concern is why there is this apparent difference between the accessibility of declarative and procedural knowledge. The two issues need not be related, although in practice, they are. The first issue is actually concerned with the representation of procedures. The second issue is concerned with procedural representation. To understand the differences between these two concepts, we must first look at some of the properties of an information processing system.

## The Human Information Processing System

The human organism can be viewed from many perspectives, each offering different and valuable insights into our overall understanding. One important viewpoint is that of a symbol processing system, capable of manipulating, interpreting, and generating symbols to aid in its processing and understanding of itself, others, the local environment, and the world. (See Newell, 1981, for a thorough treatment of the basic components of a symbol processing system.) The concept of a symbol is, of course, critical, although precise formal definition is difficult. We define a symbol to be an arbitrary entity that stands for or represents something else. By entity we mean anything that can be manipulated and examined. Thus, a symbol is a physical thing as opposed to an imaginary or hypothetical concept. In mammals, symbols are realized by neural signals: chemical or ionic and electrical potentials. Humans also use external devices as symbols, such as the symbols of writing and printing, electronic displays, or speech waves.

Note that the entity that is the signal is arbitrary. The marks on this page are symbols, but only because our culture has agreed upon how they shall be interpreted. Thus, not all the marks are symbols: some are not interpretable, and thus can be dismissed as noise. Symbols alone do not suffice, for if they are to symbolize or stand for something, there must be an agreed upon convention between the symbol maker and the symbol user as to their interpretation. This, in turn, requires that there be some mechanism that can interpret symbols, manipulate them, and perform actions based upon them: we call this mechanism an interpreter.

Any information processing system can be conceptualized as containing a number of distinct components. There must be a system of sensors that is responsive to variations of energy flux in the environment (a sensory apparatus). There must be a system of effectors through which the system can affect the external environment (a motor system). There must be a way of storing information so that the past can affect the present (a memory system). There must be a set of processes that use both information that has been stored in memory and information that is arriving currently via the sensors to determine what kinds of responses to generate and what aspects of the current state of the system will be preserved by the memory system (a processing mechanism and an interpreter). Overall, an information processing system must have five separately identifiable components:

- A sensory apparatus,
- A motor system,
- A memory,
- A processing mechanism, and
- An interpreter.

Note that these five components need not be physically distinct. The processor, the memory, and the interpreter may use the same physical mechanisms. The sensory and motor apparatuses may share mechanisms. The distinctions among these five are conceptual, not physical.

Our interest here is in the interpreter and the symbol system upon which it operates. An interpreter acts as a translator, going from symbols to actions. An interpreter, therefore, must be capable of examining symbols and executing the actions that they specify. This means that the interpreter itself is composed of procedures. It can perform operations upon the symbols, including getting access to them, comparing them with others, and initiating actions that depend upon the results of the comparisons. Interpreters therefore use symbols in the declarative sense, for they must be able to examine the symbols and perform the operations that they specify.

## The Representation of Procedures

When we represent procedures in a form that is to be interpreted, then we are representing procedures in a declarative format. Consider the procedure for answering the question, "Can X fly?":[12]

*Procedure*: "Can X fly?"

*If there exists a relation* can fly *leading from X,*

 *then answer "Yes, X can fly" and stop.*

*If there is no Y such that*
(*X isa Y or X subset Y*),

  *then answer "As far as I can tell,*
   *X does not fly" and stop,*

*otherwise, for each Y such that*
(*X isa Y or X subset Y*),

  *do the procedure "Can Y fly?"*

---

[12]This is a basic recursive procedure for following a semantic network hierarchy to answer a question about a property. Note that it is not a good model of human behavior: it will always take longest to answer that "X does not fly," which is not consistent with the observed data. Moreover, its representation of the property "can fly" is not consistent with modern systems. The procedure is being presented in order to demonstrate its format and how it gets interpreted.

Note that this procedure can be represented in propositional representational systems. If such a representational system has an appropriate interpreter, it can then execute the procedure to produce the desired result. Moreover, it would even be possible to modify the representational structure according to the results found by the procedure. As now described, the procedure can answer simple questions. But if it were modified slightly, it could do simple learning, modifying the representational structure according to the information found. One way to do this is to change the procedure as follows (the new material is printed in **boldface**):

*If there exists a relation* **can fly** *leading from X,*

*then answer "Yes, X can fly"*

**and if there exists a relation** *can fly* **leading from X,**

**then stop,**

**otherwise, connect** *can fly* **to X and stop.**

*If there is no Y such that*
*(X isa Y or X subset Y),*

*then answer "As far as I can tell,*
*X does not fly" and stop,*

*otherwise, for each Y such that*
*(X isa Y or X subset Y),*

*do the procedure "Can Y fly?"*

In this method of embedding procedures within the representation, the representational format for the knowledge (the data) and for the procedures that operate upon the knowledge (the programs) both have the same format. This was a major insight of computer science in the 1940s: that it was possible to have information structures within the computer memory that could be interpreted as either data or program, whichever was relevant for the moment. Thus, the same information structure can be viewed as either data (declarative) or program (procedural), and that duality is the key to this method of procedural representation. The power of this system is the ability of the interpreter to access procedural information as data, and thus describe it, alter it, and even simulate what would happen if the procedure were actually invoked to do the operations. Similarly, the interpreter can simply follow the procedure, thus doing the operations in the manner specified.

The kind of accessibility provided by embedding procedures within their own representational structure, accessible to an interpreter, seems critical for many aspects of learning. Indeed, this is what verbal or written instructions consist of: descriptions of procedures that are to be followed in performing the task being learned. The learner is expected to understand the instructions, to convert them into knowledge structures within the representational system, and then to follow them at the appropriate times in the performance of the task.

Modern algebraic computer languages (such as ALGOL, FORTRAN, Pascal, and Ada) do not allow for this kind of embedding, for they rigidly separate the data structures and the procedures that operate upon them. (Of course, the compilers for these languages do treat the procedural statements of the language, the programs, as data and transform them from a format readable and interpretable by humans into the machine language specifications necessary for the computer hardware.) Many research languages, especially interpretive languages such as LISP, are self-embedded. In LISP, the data structures and the procedures that operate upon them are all written in LISP, except for a few basic primitives. The LISP interpreter is capable of understanding the procedural information, which is stated in the formalism of LISP. The schemes used in representational systems are closely related to the methods used within LISP.

One representational system to use this approach of self-embedding the procedures within the representational structures is the active network structures of the LNR research group (Norman & Rumelhart, 1975; hence the word "active" that modifies the term "network"). The definitions, although appearing as ordinary semantic networks, are actually procedures that, when interpreted, carry out the necessary structure building and structure matching processes to check newly asserted information against the data base, fill unspecified variables from the context, and, when needed, build pieces of semantic network to represent the facts being asserted. (For a more complete discussion, see Rumelhart & Levin, 1975.) Note that it is not enough to represent the sequences of arguments that are to be applied. Rather, one must eventually turn to some primitives, information about the actions themselves that cannot be represented at the same level as the rest of the representation (and must therefore be inaccessible to the interpreter). These primitives control the actual motor system (at least in a human: in a computer the equivalent would be the basic machine operations). Therefore, even in self-embedded representations in which the procedural information is available for inspection, there is at least one kernel that is procedural in the second sense of the term: inaccessible to inspection, the view of procedures to which we now turn.

## Procedural Representation

In one important class of representational systems, data are stored in a procedural representation of the second sense: inaccessible to inspection. This form of representational system has certain efficiencies and other virtues. Suppose we wished a representational system to be able to answer queries of the form *Do birds fly?* In the representational systems that we have studied so far, that questions would be answered by seeking an explicit declaration of the knowledge, perhaps in the form of the predicate

$$Vx(bird(x) \rightarrow fly(x))$$

or the equivalent semantic network structure. In the preceding section we illustrated how one might search for such information within an interpreted, declarative system of representation. In a procedural representational system, the details of how the information is stored would not be visible. Instead, there would simply be a procedure available that would yield the appropriate response. Thus suppose that "bird" were a procedure (which could be thought of as a program) that could answer questions about itself. When the questions "Do birds fly?" is asked, the procedure for "bird" would supply the answer "yes" (or perhaps, "usually"). The rest of the system would have no access to the knowledge structures except through the outputs of procedures: the representational system is opaque in the sense that its contents are not visible.

There are several important distinctions between declarative and procedural systems, most dealing with problems of efficiency and the control processes that are invoked in the use of the system, as well as with issues of modularity

and accessibility of knowledge. For psychologists, it is these last issues that are of most concern —modularity and accessibility. In a declarative system, the manner in which information is represented is of critical importance, and it is essential that the data structures be available for interpretation by other processes. In procedural representations, the data format is hidden away, inaccessible to procedures other than the one in which the knowledge is contained. All one knows is the output of the operations themselves. These differences have led to considerable argument and speculation about the most appropriate form of representation (see Hewitt, 1975; Winograd, 1972, 1975).[13]

Benefits of procedural representation include efficiency of operation and the abilities to encode heuristics and to readily incorporate both knowledge processing considerations within the same structure (see Winograd, 1975, for a good discussion of these issues). Thus, many things we know seem difficult to describe in declarative fashion: we know them by the way in which we do the task. Good examples come from our skilled behavior, whether it be speech, motor control, or thought. Procedural representation allows one to tailor the way that knowledge is represented in the manner best suited for the particular task in which it will be needed. Knowledge in a declarative system must, in general, be usable for a variety of purposes, and it is not apt to be maximally efficient for any particular use. To many people, procedural representations seem appropriate for the knowledge used in skilled human performance; declarative forms seem more appropriate for less skilled performance. The efficiency of procedural representations must be contrasted with the ease of inspection and modification (and thereby the ease of learning) of declarative representations. It is clear that the two different forms of representation each have their strengths and weaknesses, so that any sufficiently general system is apt to contain aspects of both.

The major point of the procedural-declarative distinction is to emphasize the level of analysis. Any computational system—and this includes the human information processing system—consists of mechanisms that actually perform

---

[13] Hewitt (1975) points out that these two different methods of invoking procedures are really completely equivalent. Nonetheless, the distinction is useful.

operations and symbols or information that specifies the nature of those operations. In some sense, all knowledge is declarative up to the point where the final machinery that actually performs the physical actions is reached. Any information processing system can be thought of as being composed of a number of levels: the representation of procedural information is in declarative form at one level, and the mechanisms that serve as the interpreter translate it into the procedural form—which is thereby a declarative form for the next lower level. Thus, in writing a computer program in LISP, for example, the symbols that comprise the program are declarative, being interpreted at what might be called level 1 by the LISP interpreter into some primitive assembler commands for the machine. These assembler commands, in turn, are treated as data by the interpreter at level 2, which translates them into machine language level commands. These commands must then be interpreted by an interpreter at level 3 into appropriate electrical signals that get sent to the processing unit of the computer. The processing unit, in turn, acts as a level 4 interpreter, matching appropriate patterns of voltage levels with its stored repertoire of actions, and translating the command signals into signals to the specific elements of the machine that are to do the tasks (and which might be considered to be level 5 interpreters). The difference between knowledge that is declarative and knowledge that is procedural simply depends upon one's viewpoint.

### Psychological Implications

In computer systems, the act of assembling or compiling translates a declarative representation at one level of operation to a procedural representation at another level, thereby making the operations more efficient, and at the same time, less accessible from the original level. Probably from the day that an assembler or compiler was first invented, people have suggested that a major difference between skilled and less skilled human behavior is that knowledge in the skilled case has been compiled. This notion has not been pursued extensively in the psychological literature, probably because skills themselves have not been studied as heavily as other topics. The idea has recently surfaced again in a proposal by Anderson (1982).

In a series of studies, Cohen has shown that amnesiac patients can suffer severe impairments in their ability to learn new declarative knowledge while retaining considerable learning capabilities of procedural skills (N. Cohen, 1981, 1983; N. Cohen & Squire, 1980; N. Cohen & Corkin, 1981). Thus, studies of two of the better studied (and most cleanly impaired) amnesiac patients, N.A. and H.M., show that although they have great difficulty in learning new declarative material, they seem to perform at an almost normal level with procedural material. For example, when N.A. was given the Tower of Hanoi puzzle to solve,[14] on successive days he would deny ever having experienced it before, he would complain that it was clearly a memory task that exceeded his abilities, and he would have to be talked into doing it. Yet his performance would be excellent, reaching perfect scores at about the same rate as unimpaired subjects, all while he would be stating that he did not remember how to do it. It must clearly be an oversimplification to say this, but the performance looks like a perfect example for a handbook chapter on representation: the declarative knowledge is deficient, but the procedural knowledge is normal. Because N.A. is only aware of his declarative knowledge, he denies being able to do the task, but because his procedural knowledge is normal, he can in fact do it. He can only demonstrate his knowledge by performing it. Normal people overcome these difficulties by having metaknowledge of the contents and abilities of our knowledge structures. That is, we know what it is we know and do not know, and so we can answer questions about the competency levels of our procedures.

### Actor and Object Based Systems

Hewitt (1975) developed a computational system using procedures he has called actors that are triggered by appropriate data conditions and that communicate by sending one another messages. Actors are closely related to the general concept of object-oriented programming (as developed in Smalltalk: Kay, 1977; and now,

---

[14]Three pegs are placed side by side: name them **A**, **B**, and **C**. Five rings ordered in size are placed on **A**, biggest ring on the bottom. The task is to get all the rings to peg **C**, with the restriction that only one ring may be moved at a time, that a ring can be placed on any of the three pegs, but that a bigger ring can never be placed on top of a smaller one. (The number of rings can be varied.)

most commonly found in LISP machines as flavors). Object-oriented programs represent an interesting class of representational structures in which procedures act as representational objects, each an expert about a domain. Each object has a set of allowable operations that can be requested by things outside the object, usually by sending messages to the object and getting an answering message in reply. Thus, the representation of "plus," "rocket-ship," or "Henry" would be handled by making them objects, each of which has an internal state that only it knows about (or cares about). Thus, "plus" is an object that, when sent two numbers, responds by producing the sum of the numbers. In similar fashion "rocket-ship" can respond to messages about its velocity, direction, mass, and destination. "Henry" can respond to questions about "spouse," "children," "parents," "occupation," "height," and so on. How the internal variables are represented is of no particular interest. To the outside user, the meanings of these data structures are given only by their actions.

Because objects serve both as data structures and as procedures that operate upon them, they can serve both as data (declarative structures) and as programs (procedures). Hewitt (1975) discusses the relevance of his actor system to the declarative-procedural controversy this way:

> Actors make a contribution to the "declarative-procedure" controversy in that they subsume both the behavior of pure procedures (functions) and pure declaratives (data structures) as special cases. Discussions of the controversy that do not explicitly recognize the ability of actors to serve both functions are doomed to sterility. (Hewitt, 1975, p. 189.)

In an actor or object-oriented system, all data structures are objects, as are all procedures. To understand such a system, then, one has to know the following things (taken from Hewitt, 1975):

- What constitutes the natural choice of objects,
- The kinds of messages that the various objects can receive, and
- The kinds of operations that each particular object can perform for each kind of message that it can receive.

One important innovation in object-based programming is offered in the flavors package, available on a number of LISP systems: inheritance of procedures. Much as we defined inheritance of properties (and default values) in propositional representational systems, one can define procedures (objects) whose basic kinds of operation are inherited from its parents (procedures higher than it in the procedure network) and that get transmitted to its descendants (procedures lower than it in the network). This is quite analogous to inheritance in the declarative systems we have already described, and it further strengthens the close relationship between these objects and both procedural and declarative representations.

Although object-oriented representations offer some important properties that might well be suggestive of human representational issues, to date, there have not been any investigations of these ideas from a psychological point of view. We thus cannot yet comment upon their strengths and weaknesses for psychological theory. However, there is much to commend them, and as we shall see in a minute, some of their properties have been incorporated into production systems.

## Demons and Production Systems

One important question about procedures is how they are to get triggered: what makes them do their actions? There are basically two ways that have been suggested for invoked procedures. One is by direct invocation: some other procedure (or the interpreter) determines just which procedure it should call for the need at hand and causes it to be brought into action. The second is by a triggering mechanism: the procedure itself watches over an appropriate data base of information for data structures that are relevant to it; when the appropriate data structures exist, the procedure is triggered. (These two methods correspond to the two methods of procedural attachment used by KRL: servants—the first method—and demons—the second method.)[FN]

### Demons

An attractive processing strategy for modern representational systems is that conceptualized by demons. It is as if there were a group of active processing structures all sitting above a data base, looking for patterns relevant to themselves. Whenever a relevant pattern occurs, the demon is triggered, going into action and performing its activities. The results of those activities can

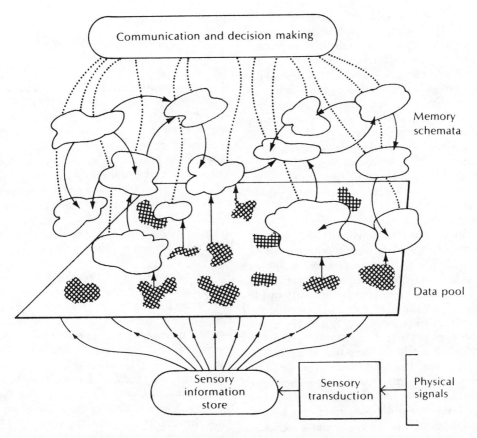

**Figure 8.27.** The memory schemata view of the human information processing system. Incoming data and higher order conceptual structures all operate together to activate memory schemata. Short-term memory consists of those schemata that are undergoing active processing. There is no set of sequential stages; the limits on processing capability are set by the total amount of processing resources available to the system. From "On the Role of Active Memory Processes in Perception and Cognition" by D.A. Norman and D.G. Bobrow, in THE STRUCTURE OF HUMAN MEMORY, ed. C.N. Cofer, W.H. Freeman and Company. Copyright 1976. Reprinted by permission.

then cause new data structures to appear in the data base, possibly causing other demons to be triggered. Alternatively, demons may pass messages among one another, or they may directly lead to sensory or motor activity.[15]

[15] It is not clear exactly when these structures first appeared. The predecessor for much of the work is the demons of Neisser and Selfridge's Pandemonium model of perception (1959: see the presentation in Lindsay & Norman, 1972). Not much actual work was done on these systems until recently, when the development of actor based systems, demons, the blackboard processor for speech recognition, and production systems all adapted various aspects of these fully or partially autonomous processing structures. Without following the history exactly, it is still clear that they are today an important conceptual tool, both for psychology and for computer science.

These processing structures are relevant to our discussion of representation because they combine representational information with control structures. Norman and D.G. Bobrow (1976) suggested that these processing structures could be used to direct processing in such tasks as perceptual recognition, problem solving, and memory retrieval (Figure 8.27), and Rumelhart (1977) demonstrated how such combined processing-representational systems could lead to an interactive system for word recognition (Figure 8.27). These processing schemes are called interactive because they combined both data-driven (bottom-up) and conceptually driven (top-down) processing with the appropriate representational systems. The representational systems that they use are not new; what is new is the combination of processing structures. Each schema detects arriving data that are relevant to it, processes them, and then communicates what it has found to other, higher level schemata. This represents the bottom-up, or data-driven processing. In addition, higher level schemata can direct queries to lower level ones, shaping the course of processing, seeking evidence that would confirm their relevance. (In the work of McClelland and Rumelhart, 1981, schemata also could inhibit their neighbors, so that positive evidence for one schema would also decrease the relevance of competing methods.)

Suppose that a group of schemata were attempting to recognize a printed word that had been presented to them: let the target word be *mate* (which has as neighbors such words as *date, fate, gate, late, rate, mite, mote, mute, made, make, male, mane, mare,* and *maze*—all words that differ from the target by only one letter). The letter schemata for **M, A, T,** and **E** will all be active, each saying, "I have a −, in position −." Then, schemata for the possible words are activated. Thus, the schemata for **MATE, MALE,** and **LATE** may each see evidence that supports them, and therefore direct messages down to the lower order schemata: the **LATE** schema will enquire of the **L** schema whether it has evidence for an "L" in the first position, the **MALE** schema will ask of "L" whether it has evidence for an "L" in the third position, and the **MATE** schema will make similar enquiries. Data-driven processing takes place when a schema observes data of relevance to itself and sends messages to others telling them what it has. Conceptually driven processing takes place when a schema seeks evidence that would confirm its own relevance.

### Production Systems

Production systems are a form of demon system in which all the communication among schemata takes place through a common data structure, usually called the Working Memory (WM). A production consists of an "if → then" or "con-

dition → action" statement:

IF (*condition-for-triggering*) →

THEN (*do-these-actions*)

If the conditions described on the left-hand side of the arrow are found in WM, then do the actions described on the right-hand side of the arrow. Production systems represent a form of processing called pattern directed processing, because the processing actions associated with a production (the procedures) are triggered into action whenever the pattern of data represented by the condition side of the production appears within WM. In general, in a production system, the actions operate upon the structures within WM, which triggers other productions to operate.

Because of the way they have been used in representational systems, production systems provide an interesting merger of active processes and control structure with representational issues. The modern use of production systems in psychology and artificial intelligence is largely due to the work of Newell (1973: the basic concept is due to Post, 1943, although it will also be recognizable as classic S-R psychology). Perhaps the easiest way to understand productions is to work through an example. Consider the productions system necessary to solve a problem in addition, such as:[16]

$$614$$
$$438$$
$$\underline{683}$$

The productions necessary to solve any problem in addition of this type are given in Figure 8.28. The system works this way. First, we put the problem plus the data structure representing the goal into WM:

**goal:** do an addition problem.

This data structure matches only one production: P1. P1 is therefore activated, and it adds a new

[16]This example is taken from Anderson (1982).

**Figure 8.28.** A production system for performing addition, consisting of 12 productions. Part A represents the flow of control of the productions. The boxes correspond to goal states, and the arrows correspond to the productions that change these states. Control starts with the top goal. Part B shows the structure of the 12 productions. From "Acquisition of Cognitive Skill" by J.R. Anderson, 1982, *Psychological Review, 89,* pp. 370, 371. Copyright 1982 by the American Psychological Association. Reprinted by permission.

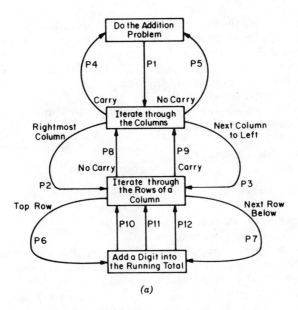

(a)

*A Production System for Performing Addition*

| | | |
|---|---|---|
| P1. | IF | the goal is to do an addition problem, |
| | THEN | the subgoal is to iterate through the columns of the problem. |

P2.  IF  the goal is to iterate through the columns of an addition problem and the rightmost column has not been processed,
THEN  the subgoal is to iterate through the rows of that rightmost column and set the running total to zero.

P3.  IF  the goal is to iterate through the columns of an addition problem and a column has just been processed and another column is to the left of this column,
THEN  the subgoal is to iterate through the rows of this column to the left and set the running total to the carry.

P4.  IF  the goal is to iterate through the columns of an addition problem and the last column has been processed and there is a carry,
THEN  write out the carry and POP the goal.

P5.  IF  the goal is to iterate through the columns of an addition problem and the last column has been processed and there is no carry,
THEN  POP the goal.

P6.  IF  the goal is to iterate through the rows of a column and the top row has not been processed,
THEN  the subgoal is to add the digit of the top row into the running total.

P7.  IF  the goal is to iterate through the rows of a column and a row has just been processed and another row is below it,
THEN  the subgoal is to add the digit of the lower row to the running total.

P8.  IF  the goal is to iterate through the rows of a column and the last row has been processed and the running total is a digit,
THEN  write the digit and delete the carry and mark the column as processed and POP the goal.

P9.  IF  the goal is to iterate through the rows of a column and the last row has been processed and the running total is of the form "string + digit,"
THEN  write the digit and set carry to the string and mark the column as processed and POP the goal.

P10.  IF  the goal is to add a digit to a number and the number is a digit and a sum is the sum of the two digits,
THEN  the result is the sum and mark the digit as processed and POP the goal.

P11.  IF  the goal is to add a digit to a number and the number is of the form "string + digit" and a sum is the sum of the two digits and the sum is less than 10,
THEN  the result is "string + sum" and mark the digit as processed and POP the goal.

P12.  IF  the goal is to add a digit to a number and the number is of the form "string + digit" and a sum is the sum of the two digits and the sum is of the form "1 + digit*" and another number sum* is the sum of 1 plus string,
THEN  the result is "sum* + digit*" and mark the digit as processed and POP the goal.

(b)

goal to WM. Note that P1 adds the new goal to the previous one. In particular, it creates a list of goals, with the new goal on top. When productions scan WM, they only see the top-level goal. This type of list is called a push-down stack; putting a new item on the list is called PUSHing and taking an item off the top is called POPping. Thus, the goal stack in WM now looks like this:

**goal**: iterate through the columns of an addition problem.

**goal**: do an addition problem.

Note that only the top goal of the stack is accessible in WM. The top goal matches the condition side of production P2, and because no columns of the problem have yet been processed, P2 is invoked, PUSHing a new goal onto the stack and setting the variable running total to 0. Conditions are now proper for production P6 to fire, which PUSHes the goal "add the digit of the top row into the running total." Production P1, P2, and P6 have now all executed, each of them really acting to set-up the structure of the problem. Working memory looks like this:

**goal**: add the digit of the top row into the running total.

**goal**: iterate through the rows of the right most column.

**goal**: iterate through the columns of an addition problem.

**goal**: do an addition problem.

running total = 0

Finally, the system now does something with the problem, for the top-level goal matches the condition of production P10, which not only does an addition, but for the first time, POPs the goal stack, thus removing a goal. Working memory now looks like this:

**goal**: iterate through the rows of the right most column.

**goal**: iterate through the columns of an addition problem.

**goal**: do an addition problem.

running total = 4

marked as processed: "4"

The operations continue, with productions P7, P10, P7, P11, and P9 operating in that order to complete the processing of the right most column, leaving the working memory in this state:

**goal**: iterate through the columns of an addition problem.

**goal**: do an addition problem.

running total = "1" + 5

marked as processed: "4" "8" "3" "right most column"

carry = 1

Moreover, P9 puts out the partial answer: "5." The process continues until the problem is completed.

One important property of production systems is modularity. That is, because each production is a self-contained entity, it is possible to add or subtract productions at will, without worrying about the structure of the system. As a result, new learning is readily incorporated into the system, at least in principle; as new productions are learned, they can simply be added to the existing base of productions. In practice, however, such additions are not so straightforward, and as the system gets too large, strange behavior can result from too many new additions. It seems clear that a good theory of learning is going to be required before production systems (or any other formalisms) will be able to meet their promise.

Production systems are destined to play an increasingly important role in the development of psychological theory, for they combine a formal processing structure of the sort that is consistent with psychological theory, plus ready implementation via a number of readily available computer programs.[17] Production systems have now been widely used in a variety of tasks, in both psychology and artificial intelligence. They form the basis for much work in artificial intelligence on expert systems, and they play a major role in such psychological work as Anderson's (1976) ACT system. A good review of production systems can be found in Waterman and Hayes-

---

[17]The cost of the computers required to implement such systems is rapidly dropping; home computers will soon have this capability.

Roth (1978) and in the volumes of the *Handbook of Artificial Intelligence* (Barr & Feigenbaum, 1981, 1982; P.R. Cohen & Feigenbaum, 1982).

# SUPERPOSITIONAL MEMORIES

## Local and Superpositional Memory Systems

One fundamental question that has major implications for theories of representation is "How is knowledge stored in memory?" Most views of memory either explicitly or implicitly assume a localized memory storage system. That is, they assume that different memories are stored in different places. Nearly all information processing systems that we understand very well have been constructed with localized memories, and it is quite plausible to assume that human memories are organized along similar lines. Thus, knowledge could be represented in the brain by local changes to individual neurons or groups of neurons. There is another possibility, however. It is possible that a given memory is distributed over many memory storage elements so that each storage element contains information from many different memories superimposed upon one another. This is a distributed or superpositional memory and it contrasts with localized or place storage systems. Thus, knowledge could be distributed in millions of neuron structures throughout the brain with different data structures stored in the same brain structures.

Superpositional memory systems have quite different basic characteristics. In this system, different memories are not stored in separate places. Rather, they are placed on top of one another, superimposed, if you will. These systems of memory storage and retrieval offer very different solutions to some of the major issues of memory and representation. Consider the properties of the two memory systems. In localized memory systems:

- Different memories occupy different brain structures.
- There is a unique path or address that specifies how to retrieve the contents of any particular memory structure. Retrieving information, in part, consists of recovering this path information and then applying it.

- Different memory structures are stored quite independently of one another. Therefore, the physical integrity of the information within memory is not affected by what else is in memory. Of course, memory structures refer to one another by means of pointers or associations, and so they affect one another through this route. In addition, recovery of the appropriate path to a particular memory structure is made more difficult when there are many related items within the memory. But the physical integrity of the memory structures are independent of one another.

In superpositonal memory systems:

- Different memory structures are superimposed upon one another.
- The memory structures are distributed: that is, any given memory structure must be represented across a large number of storage elements (in place memories, this is possible, but not required).
- Superpositional memories are very robust and are resistant to damage of part of their memory structures. This follows from the distributed property of these memories.
- Information within the memory system is directly affected by other material. In a superpositional memory system, items are stored on top of one another so that storage interference is a common source of error. As a result, one cannot guarantee error-free retrieval of information.
- Retrieving information from a superpositional memory is like detecting a signal in noise. The particular item desired is the signal, and the noise is contributed by all the other memory structures that have been superimposed on the desired one. Sometimes the signal-to-noise ratio will be high, sometimes it will be low, hampering the retrieval efforts.
- When a known signal is presented, the system responds by amplifying the signal.
- When an unknown signal is presented, the system responds by damping the signal.
- When part of a known signal is presented, the system responds by filling in the missing parts of the signal.

- When a signal similar to a known signal is presented, the system responds by distorting the presented signal toward the known signal.
- When a number of similar signals have been stored, the system will respond strongly to the central tendency of those signals—whether or not the signal corresponding to the central tendency has been presented.

For the most part, our ways of thinking about memory have been conditioned by our use of the local metaphor. Our language is permeated by the local view of memory. We talk about memory search, which suggests that the memories are someplace, if only we could find them. We talk about memories as if they were things, suggesting a localist view of memory. For the most part, we simply adopt this view without thought. It is useful, therefore, to consider the alternative and to show how this alternative can carry out the essential tasks of a memory system.

## Associative Memories

One major form of superpositional memory structure, called an associative memory, has been summarized in the book edited by Hinton and Anderson (1981). The studies reported in this book focus on the ways in which a superpositional memory might actually be realized within the brain, and so the memory structures that were examined tended to consist of a large set of simple, homogeneous, neuron-like units. A memory, in these systems, consists of a pattern of activation across the entire set of units. Knowledge is stored in the pattern of interconnections among the units. Whenever new information is encoded in the system, those links between units whose activity patterns are similar are strengthened, and those links between units whose activity patterns are different are reduced in strength. Whenever the links between two units have a positive strength, we say that the two units excite one another. Whenever the link has a negative strength, we say that the two units inhibit one another. In an associative memory system, knowledge is both distributed and superimposed (additive). To say that knowledge is distributed is to say that a given concept is represented by a pattern of activity distributed over a large number of

units. To say that knowledge is superimposed or additive is to say that a given unit participates in the representation of many different knowledge structures. In the simplest cases, all units are involved in the representation of all knowledge.

Perhaps the simplest way to explain these superpositional memories is by example. Figure 8.29A shows a simple ten-unit associative memory system. Each unit in the system is connected to an input line and also to each other unit in the system. It is useful to imagine that each input line corresponds to a feature, perhaps one of the semantic features that we discussed earlier. Input lines 1 through 4 represent the category of thing being represented. Lines 5 and 6 indicate the particular class member, and 7 through 10 represent the color of the object being represented. The specific representations we are using for *elephants, gray things, Fido, black things, tweety bird, yellow things, dogs,* and *Clyde the elephant* are illustrated in Figure 8.29B. Note that a plus on one input line indicates that that particular feature is present, a minus indicates that it is absent, and a zero indicates that the presence or absence of the feature is not specified in the input. In associative memory systems such as the one illustrated here, the input that a given unit receives is determined by the activity of units to which it is connected and by the nature of the interconnection between the units. If two units are connected by a positive strength, then the one unit tends to increase the activation level of the other. If two units are connected by a negative strength, then activation in one unit tends to decrease the activation of the other. Each unit responds in proportion to its total inputs and is assumed to affect other units at a rate determined by their strength of association. When a particular input is presented to the system, it causes each unit of the system to achieve an activation level that depends upon both the input signal and the interconnections among the units. In a system with $N$ units, the activity of the system can be characterized as a vector of length $N$ in which the value of each element of the vector represents the activity of the corresponding unit of the system. The pattern of interconnections of such a system can be represented by an $N \times N$ matrix, in which the $i$-$j$th cell of the matrix represents the degree to which unit $i$ excites or inhibits unit $j$.

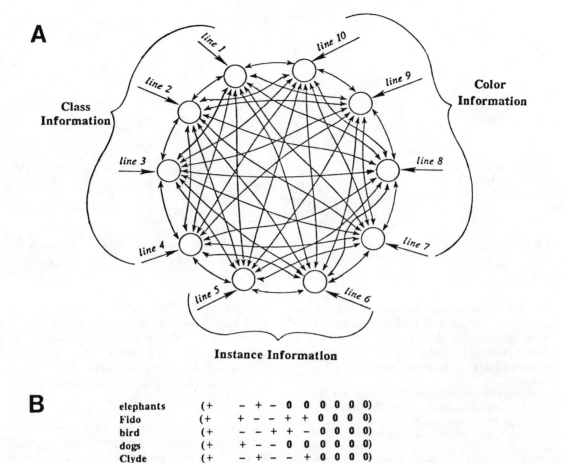

**B**

| | | | | | | | | | | | |
|---|---|---|---|---|---|---|---|---|---|---|---|
| elephants | (+ | | – | + | – | 0 | 0 | 0 | 0 | 0 | 0) |
| Fido | (+ | | + | – | – | + | + | 0 | 0 | 0 | 0) |
| bird | (+ | | – | – | + | + | – | 0 | 0 | 0 | 0) |
| dogs | (+ | | + | – | – | 0 | 0 | 0 | 0 | 0 | 0) |
| Clyde | (+ | | – | + | – | – | + | 0 | 0 | 0 | 0) |
| grey-things | (0 | | 0 | 0 | 0 | 0 | 0 | + | – | + | –) |
| black-things | (0 | | 0 | 0 | 0 | 0 | 0 | + | + | – | –) |
| yellow-things | (0 | | 0 | 0 | 0 | 0 | 0 | + | – | – | +) |

**Figure 8.29.** An associative memory structure consisting of 10 units, each connected to an input line and to each other units. *B*: The activity patterns associated with the concepts of *elephants, gray things, Fido, black things, tweety bird, yellow things, dogs,* and *Clyde the elephant.* Note that colors are indicated by input lines 7 through 10, and the kinds of things are indicated by input lines 1 through 6. Representations of specific individuals have nonzero values on lines 4 and 5.

Information is retrieved from an associative memory in essentially two ways:

1. A weak pattern may be presented to the system and the system allowed to respond. If the pattern has already been stored in the system, then it will amplify the pattern, and the final state of activation of the system will look just like the input, except each unit will be more extreme than the input pattern. If the pattern has not yet been stored, then the final state of the system will be weak and different from the input pattern. This is a kind of recognition, in which the magnitude of the response of the system can be taken as a measure of familiarity.

2. A type of recall procedure can be use in which a part of the signal can be presented and the system can reconstruct the original pattern from the partial cue.

One might suppose that it would be difficult to set the interconnections so that they generate

**Connection Matrix**

| Unit Number | 1 | 2 | 3 | 4 | 5 | 6 | 7 | 8 | 9 | 10 |
|---|---|---|---|---|---|---|---|---|---|---|
| 1 | 2 | 0 | 0 | -2 | 1 | 1 | 2 | 0 | 0 | -2 |
| 2 | 0 | 2 | -2 | 0 | 1 | 1 | 0 | 2 | -2 | 0 |
| 3 | 0 | -2 | 2 | 0 | -1 | -1 | 0 | -2 | 2 | 0 |
| 4 | -2 | 0 | 0 | 2 | -1 | -1 | -2 | 0 | 0 | 2 |
| 5 | 1 | 1 | -1 | -1 | 1 | 1 | 1 | 1 | -1 | -1 |
| 6 | 1 | 1 | -1 | -1 | 1 | 1 | 1 | 1 | -1 | -1 |
| 7 | 2 | 0 | 0 | -2 | 1 | 1 | 2 | 0 | 0 | -2 |
| 8 | 0 | 2 | -2 | 0 | 1 | 1 | 0 | 2 | -2 | 0 |
| 9 | 0 | -2 | 2 | 0 | -1 | -1 | 0 | -2 | 2 | 0 |
| 10 | -2 | 0 | 0 | 2 | -1 | -1 | -2 | 0 | 0 | 2 |

**Figure 8.30.** The connectivity matrix (set of strengths) generated by storing the patterns for "elephants are gray" (+ − + − 00 + − + −) and "Fido is black" (+ + − − + + + + − −).

this kind of behavior. However, a very simple storage procedure will lead to this pattern of behavior under rather general conditions. A simple storage procedure of this type uses the so-called Hebbian learning rule:

> If two units both respond the same way (i.e., both respond positively or both respond negatively) to a given input, then the connection between the two units should be strengthened (i.e., made more positive). If two units respond differently to a given input, then the connection between the two should be weakened (i.e., made more negative).

Figure 8.30 shows the connectivity matrix (set of strengths) generated by storing the patterns for "elephants are gray" (+ − + − 00 + − + −) and "Fido is black" (+ + − − + + + + − −). Note that the connection between unit 1 and unit 4 is negative (−2). This is because in both patterns, the first feature and the fourth feature have opposite polarity. The connection between the second unit and the eighth unit is positive because, in both patterns, features 2 and 8 have the same polarity (in "elephants are gray" both are negative, while in "Fido is black" both are positive).

Now, to a first order of approximation, the output of the system to a probe can be given by taking the matrix product of the vector representing the test stimulus with the connectivity matrix. Thus, when we present the pattern for "elephants are gray" we multiply the vector (1, −1, 1, −1, 0, 0, 1, −1, 1, −1) by the connectivity matrix. In this case we get, (8, −8, 8, −8, 0, 0, 8, −8, 8, −8)—an amplified version of the input vector. If, on the other hand, we present a pattern that is very different from any presented we get no response. Thus, if we present "tweety bird is yellow", (1, −1, −1, 1, 1, −1, 1, −1, −1, 1), we get (0, 0, 0, 0, 0, 0, 0, 0, 0, 0). Of course, this is an extreme case, because the probed item is entirely orthogonal to any presented target. If we had presented a probe more similar to one of the stored items, we would have gotten some response out of the system.

Suppose we present the partial probe "Fido is ????." In this case we expect the system to fill in the color of Fido. Thus, we present the input (1, 1, −1, −1, 1, 1, 0, 0, 0, 0), and we get out (6, 6, −6, −6, 6, 6, 6, 6, −6, −6). We see that the response of the system is somewhat less than for the intact pattern, but that the system correctly fills in the pattern (+ + − −) for the color—that is, the color "black" for "Fido."

Suppose we probe with the pattern for "Clyde the elephant." What color would we get back? "Clyde" was never presented, but since "Clyde" is very similar to "elephant," we would expect the system to respond rather strongly to this input. Thus, if we probe with (1, −1, 1, −1, −1, 1, 0, 0, 0, 0) we get (4, −4, 4, −4, 0, 0, 4, −4, 4, −4)—that is, we get back a version of the pattern "elephants are gray." Thus, we might be able to conclude that "Clyde is gray" even though we were never presented with this input.

Superpositional memory systems seem promising models of human memories, but their potential has not yet been fully explored. It is not yet clear whether such superpositional models will displace the more traditional local view of memory in our conception of how the human memory system works.

# GENERAL ISSUES IN THE STUDY OF REPRESENTATION

## Cognition and Categorization

Now that we have considered a range of representational formats, it is time to think of how the things that are represented might be organized within human memory. It is easy to view the organizational problems of representation in one of two ways; we have taken both views within this chapter. One view is that the world contains objects and events, and so a major representational issue becomes how each is to be represented, perhaps by determining what features and relations are attended to and encoded by the human, perhaps by determining what primitive representational elements might be involved, and in all cases, by attempting to determine which representational format might be used. Another view is that the object and events of the world can be classified into categories, and the representations should therefore reflect these categories so that one item might be an instance of another (hence the development of the relation *isa*), one item might be a subset of another (hence the relation *subset*), and so on. But in neither view is the emphasis on the categories themselves and just how they might be represented or related to one another. Yes, the formal tools for doing the representations of relations were discussed; but not the manner in which the human relationships might actually exist. The study of categories play an especially important role in theories of representation and, indeed, in theories of cognition. Hence the title of this section—"Cognition and Categorization" —borrowed from the seminal book by that title edited by Rosch and Lloyd (1978).

Categories are neither fully artificial nor fully natural. Were they artificial, then they would be arbitrary, and the shape of existing categories would reflect the perceiver's organizational processes, driven by various internal processing matters, strategies, and communication (social) considerations. Were they fully natural, then they would exist in the world, with people acting only to perceive and thereby to encode them appropriately. The view given by Rosch and Lloyd (1978), one that we support, is that categories are neither fully natural nor fully artificial, but that they represent an interplay among (1) the structured nature of items and events in the world, (2) the processing that takes place by the perceiver, and (3) cultural and social factors that help shape and govern a person's knowledge.

### Cognitive Economy and Perceived World Structure

Rosch (1978) suggests that there are two basic principles that govern the formation of categories. One has to do with cognitive economy, minimizing cognitive processing (mental work) by taking advantage of structure in the world. Thus, by recognizing that living creatures that fly all have some common features (such as wings), it becomes easier to perceive, think about, and discuss these commonalities, even though they may actually look and function quite differently from one another. Compare the wings of a mosquito with those of an eagle; the task is aided considerably by the fact that both structures are classified within the same category—wings. The second principle asserts that the world as it is perceived already comes with structure. Some of this is a result of correlations among the objects of the world: wings concur with feathers more than with fur. Objects that are perceived to be sit-on-able will share more things in common than an arbitrary collection of objects. Some of the perceived structure is internal, a result of the structure of the human processing system. Thus, we can only perceive certain physical inputs, and we often add structure to the perceptions. The separate bands of the rainbow that divide it up into distinct stripes are perceived, not real: the physical structure of the rainbow is of a continually varying spectrum of electromagnetic radiation, with no breaks, discontinuities, or other boundaries. In a similar way, we perceive the hues of the spectrum as a color circle, whereas in nature, it is linear.

### Shareability Constraints

To these two basic principles of Rosch, Freyd (1983) suggests we must add a third: shareability constraints. Freyd points out that regardless of how we might be capable of organizing things within our minds, the necessity to share these structures with other people will necessitate a common, simplifying structure. Thus, in determining of kinship relations, the concepts of uncle, cousin, mother, son, brother, or sister are both easily represented and easily communicated; they pass the shareability test. Different cultures share different agreed upon structures, and so what is natural and easily categorized for one culture may not be for another. Thus, the Lapps have a term (*akke*) that means "father's older brother or father's older male blood relative in his generation," a categorization that does not exist in our culture. Because new concepts are described to people who do not have them in terms of concepts that they already know and understand, the concepts that already exist within a culture (and for which words already exist within their language) place strong constraints on what new concepts can be transmitted among members of that culture. Moreover, Freyd suggests that "the attempt to introduce a new term that *almost* neatly fits into the pre-existing structure of the semantic domain will probably result in a distorted meaning that nearly fits into the pre-existing structure."

Freyd's hypothesis provides some interesting suggestions for a theory of knowledge representation. She points out that

> it might be that the structural properties of the knowledge domain came about because such structural properties provide for the most efficient sharing of concepts. That is, we cannot be sure that the regularities tell us anything about how the brain can represent things or would even "prefer" to, if it didn't have to share concepts with other brains. (Freyd, 1983.)

These three basic principles of categorization, then, to a large extent control the sorts of knowledge structures people develop. However, there are still a number of issues that need to be resolved. One interesting way to divide up the remaining issues is to examine separately what Rosch calls the vertical dimension of categories from the horizontal dimension. The vertical dimension reflects the *isa-superset* hierarchy, the reflection of what items belong to what other items. The horizontal dimension tells us how things at the same level of vertical organization vary. Thus, vertically, we might go from "rock-

ing chair" to "chair" to "furniture" and to "household goods"; here, we are concerned with the features that these items have in common, or how one category is included in another. Horizontally (within the domain of furniture) we might go from "chair" to "table" to "bookcase"; here we are concerned with just how all these furniture categories differ from one another. Through a number of studies, Rosch and her colleagues have demonstrated that there are differences in the utility of the different levels of vertical structure, and that there is one level, the basic level, that tends to capture some important properties of representation.

### Basic-level Categorization

We have yet to discuss how categories are formed and how they are represented. Let us briefly return to the formalization provided by Tversky earlier in this chapter (Tversky, 1977; Tversky & Gati, 1978). We can state the measure of similarity between two sets, A and B, by an expression of the form:

$$f(A \cap B) - [\alpha f(A - B) + \beta f(B - A)]$$

where $f(X)$ is a measure of the salience of the features in set $X$, and $\alpha$ and $\beta$ are constants. This expression states that the similarity is a function of what the two sets have in common ($f(A \cap B)$) minus the ways in which they differ (the features in $A$ but not in $B$, $A - B$, and the features in $B$ not in $A$, $B - A$). Rosch proposes that basic-level categories are those that maximize the similarity of things within the category and that have minimized the similarity of things between categories.

Consider the categorization of furniture. The category "furniture" is not at the basic level: things within the category (chair, table, bookcase, picture, clock) do not share many features in common. The basic level is one level down. Thus, "chair," "table," and "bookcase" are basic-level items. Consider chairs: they share much in common with one another; they tend to look the same, have the same function, similar size, and so on. Moreover, chairs are quite distinct from the other members of the furniture category; chairs don't look the same or function the same as tables, pictures, or clocks. At a lower level, different categories such as "armchairs" or "rocking chairs," are quite similar: there is not much distinction between categories. Thus, all rocking chairs may tend to look and act in a similar way, but they are also similar in appearance and function to armchairs, dining-room chairs, and office chairs. It is only at the basic level that we simultaneously maximize similarity within and differences between category members. Rosch argues that basic categories can be determined by examining the attributes that items have in common (or in distinction), differences and similarities in motor movements when using the items, and in their shapes.

Rosch suggests that basic-level categories play major roles in processing and organizing knowledge. One role they play is that of prototypes, helping to classify new experiences, and then helping to form a new encoding. Rosch argues that the basic level has at least four different implications:

Images. The basic level is the highest level for which a person can form an image of the class. That is, it is possible to form an image of your favorite living-room chair, or of living-room chairs in general, or even of chairs in general, but it is not possible to form an image of one piece of furniture that is not also a basic-level (or lower) exemplar of furniture. Basic and lower level categories can have images that represent the entire class: higher levels cannot.

Perception. Consider the perception of an object at a distance: small, fuzzy, not readily identifiable. Suppose the object is in the distance coming toward you, on the ground. At first it is unidentifiable, although the fact that it is visible traveling on the ground at a certain distance and speed restricts the set of possibilities. Rosch argues that the first identifiable level at which an object can be identified is the basic level (see Smith, Balzano, & Walker, 1978).

Development. Because perception, motor movements, functions, and images all lead to the same level of categorization, Rosch argues that "basic objects should be the first categorizations of concrete objects made by children" (Rosch, 1978, p. 38).

Language. Finally, basic-level items tend to have single-word names and tend to be the level at which something is described (unless there is a communicative need to be more specific or more general), so that in describing a general object, such as an animal in the park, one is apt to call it a dog rather than an animal or, more specifically, a yellow labrador retriever. In American Sign Language (Newport & Bellugi, 1978), it is basic-level categories that are most often coded by single signs, and super- and subordinate categories that are likely not to have any sign encoding.

Despite these processing implications, Rosch argues that the notion of basic-level categories is most important for the culture, not necessarily so important for a particular individual's processing and representational structures. That is, individuals develop their internal representational structures as a result of the particular experiences that they have had. Basic-level structures are of more importance to the culture and the language. Freyd's shareability notion suggests how the transfer between the concepts acquired by an individual and the concepts held by the culture may take place.

### How Are Categories Defined?

Recent advances in our understanding of categorization have made it clear that we cannot expect most natural categories to have clear, rigid definitions. That is, we should not expect that we can always find clear, definite rules that allow us to determine exactly what the members of any particular category are. Yes, some categories are well defined, such as the concept of a square. In general, however, we find that category members include some clear exemplars—things that nobody would dispute are members of the category—and some marginal exemplars—things that are disputed and for which even one person may vacilitate from moment to moment. Determining category membership is much like determining whether a particular sample of time should be defined as night or day: we think we understand the difference, and the instances are clear cut, as long as we stick to instances near midday or midnight and do not have to consider the boundaries at dusk and dawn. Matters are even less clear if we are asked to define the categories dusk and dawn.

It is, of course, not a new finding that category membership can be an ill-defined concept. Within philosophy, the point has long been made, Wittgenstein (1953) being perhaps the prototypical example. Given that firm boundaries cannot be established to define category membership, how then is membership to be defined? There are numerous possibilities. One point of view is that the classical definition should be the starting point: all instances of a concept share common properties—call these the defining properties—and category membership is simply determined by whether or not any particular instance has all of the defining properties. From this starting point, one can then argue that the concept of membership in the category should not be determined by classical logic, but rather by alternative rules. One major alternative is to use the mathematics of fuzzy set theory or fuzzy logic to define the degree of category membership of any particular instance (Zadeh, 1965; Oden, 1977). One approach is to assume that each category has some general, prototypical member, and category membership is determined by how well any particular instance matches the prototype. Another approach is to argue that there is neither a set of defining features nor a prototype, simply examples of category members. Overall, there are numerous approaches, and perhaps numerous solutions, but as yet, no common agreement exists on the appropriate methods for representing human categorization. (Smith & Medin, 1981, offer a good review of many of the approaches.)

### Prototypes

Rosch (1978) and Rosch and Mervis (1975) define prototypes to be "the clearest cases of category membership defined operationally by people's judgments of goodness of membership in that category." The prototype of a category does not really have to exist. Thus, the prototypical animal for American university students may be a four-legged animal with fur, a tail, size somewhere between a large dog and a cow, and other features borrowed or adapted from a variety of actual animals. No single existing animal may match the prototype. Rosch believes that the prototype probably develops in much the same way as the basic-level category develops: the prototype is formed so as to maximize its similarity to the other members of the category while also maximizing its difference from the prototypes of other, contrasting categories.

The notion of prototype has important implications. People do not act equally toward all members of a category. Robins are more typical birds than are chickens, ducks, or penguins. Murder is a typical crime, whereas vagrancy is not. People are much faster at determining category membership for typical members than for nontypical members. Rips, Shoben, and Smith (1973) found that to American college students, "mammal" and "animal" meant almost the same thing, that typical animals were thought of as having four legs and being warm-blooded. Not only does this make a person a nontypical animal, but insects, lizards, and other such creatures are far from the central prototype animal. As a result, when one thinks of a category, one thinks of the things like the prototype. One is therefore apt to attribute characteristics to the entire category that actually apply only to things like the prototype. This is an obvious source of error.

Prototypes can aid in determining category membership. One processing rule that captures much of the flavor of prototypes is to determine the similarity of the instance that is to be judged to all possible prototypes; the prototype that is most similar to the instance determines its categorization. This is a version of the nearest neighbor rule; if you imagine the prototypes as points in a multidimensional space, where the dimensions are the possible features, then the instance to be judged can also be represented by a point, and its categorization is determined by which prototypical point is closest to it. The rule of similarity, however, is richer than the multidimensional nearest neighbor rule because it allows for nondimensional considerations such as fuzziness or probabilistic characterization of the variables. Note too that the rule of similarity allows for the various features and aspects of similarity to be weighted differently at different types, so that depending upon the circumstances (that is, the context in which the judgment is being made), the same instance can be categorized differently.

## Generalization

A pervasive tendency of human thought is to generalize, to act as if general truths exist on the basis of experiences with a limited number of examples. The tendency is strong enough that we can believe that we have been given specific evidence for the generalization, even though we have not. Posner and Keele (1968) demonstrated that when subjects are shown dot patterns that are distorted versions of a prototype, they learn to classify them quite well, generalizing across the various presentations. More importantly, the subjects judged the actual prototype to be the best exemplar of the category and believed that they had been presented with it, even though they were never shown the prototype during the training trials. A similar finding has been reported for people's memory for sentences (Bransford & Franks, 1971) and for the characteristics of members of social clubs (Hayes-Roth & Hayes-Roth, 1977).

Two important by-products of generalization are overgeneralization and overdiscrimination. In overgeneralization, too many things are classified as instances of the category; in overdiscrimination, not all members of the category are properly classified. Thus, if we were to classify all animals that fly as birds we would overgeneralize, for we would falsely include bats and flying fish. If we were to believe that all chairs have legs, we would overdiscriminate, for we would thereby exclude chairs that hung from the ceiling, chairs on pedestals, and beanbag chairs. Perhaps the most famous cases of overgeneralization and overdiscrimination occur in the study of the categories of developing children who have been reported to do such things as call all men "daddy" or use the term "doggie" only to refer to the family dog. In the learning of the inflections of language, we can find overgeneralization and sometimes oscillation. Thus, a child may first learn the proper past tense of a particular verb, thereby using verbs like "give" and "gave" properly. Then the child learns that past tenses are formed by adding "ed" to the verb, leading to overgeneralization; the past tense of "give" is spoken as "gived." Eventually, the child learns not to apply the generalization to all possible instances. The pattern of responses therefore oscillates:

$$\text{give} \rightarrow \text{gave}$$

$$\text{give} \rightarrow \text{gived}$$

$$\text{give} \rightarrow \text{gave}$$

In part because of the general importance of the phenomena, the issues of generalization are important testing grounds for theories. In this section we demonstrate the differences among representational theories by discussing three different ways of handling generalization.

### Generalization Through the Formation of Generalized Schemata

Perhaps the easiest way to begin is to consider how one of the standard schema-based theories handles generalization. The basic principles are fairly straightforward and have even been incorporated into introductory textbooks (Lindsay & Norman, 1972). The essence is that concepts are generalized whenever a number of different concepts share a sufficient number of attributes. The generalization takes place by forming a new schema, the generalized schema, that acts as a superset of the instances to be generalized. This forms a new class of elements, a category, and through the principle of inheritance of properties, from then on all instances of the class inherit the appropriate generalized properties. Thus, whenever a new instance is added to the category, it automatically inherits the generalized properties by default unless specific information is available to indicate otherwise.

Note that this model can easily lead to the phenomena of overgeneralization and overdiscrimination. Thus, if the generalized schema is not sufficiently specific, it will match a large number of instances, thereby leading to the inclusion of too many things into its class (giving the wrong default values). This is overgeneralization: applying the concept to too broad a range of exemplars. If the generalized schema is too specific, having too many restrictions on what it requires of its exemplars, it will not match a sufficient number of instances, thus leading to overdiscrimination.

This model is, in many ways, the prototypical model of generalization. It is difficult to get data that would discriminate between this model and others, but because this is such a natural way to handle generalization, it is the natural starting place, the model against which all others must compete.

### Generalization Without Specific Generalized Concepts

There is no real need to form a specific generalized schema to represent the generalization of a concept. The issue here really is the relationship between the information within memory and the information implicit within the procedures that operate upon the memory structures.

Representational issues really require consideration of the doublet of representational structure and procedure; information can be traded between the explicit structure and the procedures that operate upon the structures. So it is with generalization. If the procedures contain the proper mechanisms, the generalizations can always be performed on the fly, when needed, from whatever information is already present in the data base. Thus, suppose we have four specific exemplars of something: call them **A**, **B**, **C**, and **D**. We could generalize these four exemplars by forming a specific generalized schema, **G**. But suppose, instead, that we simply keep the specific examples. Whenever we need information about things with attributes of these schemata, we could procedurally operate upon the memory structures, and compute the desired information. In this way, generalization would occur without any need for an explicit generalized schema to be formed. Moreover, the outside observer could not distinguish this schema from the one in which a particular generalized node existed. Basically, the difference between this method of forming generalizations and the preceding method is exactly the difference between declarative and procedural representations: the difference is solely in the availability of the information and the efficiency of the operation; to the observer, the two processes cannot be distinguished.

### Superpositional Models of Generalization

The difference between place and superpositional memory storage also leads to a difference in how generalization may be made. Generalization falls readily out of superpositional representational models. Thus, McClelland (1981) has shown how it is possible for a superpositional model to generalize the general attributes of class members without having any explicit generalized schema. This model differs from the procedural model just discussed only in that the distinction between the memory representations and the procedures are not clearly marked, for in the superpositional model, the procedures act on the representations through activation.

McClelland's model can be considered a cross between the normal schema-based models and the full superpositional memory system. The most serious problem with this model is its lack of a type-token distinction. Thus, it is difficult to prevent generalized values from being associated with instances even where it is clearly known that the normal default does not apply. McClelland examined the distribution of members in two different hypothetical social clubs (this is similar to the situation studied by Hayes-Roth & Hayes-Roth, 1977). Thus, if most members of the Jets wear glasses, but one member (Helen) does not, it is difficult to prevent this model from asserting that even Helen wears glasses. This overgeneralization is actually reasonable, for we would expect people to have problems with this fact, but of course, they would eventually be able to learn the actual situation. In McClelland's model, this ability requires the development of more distinguishing features so that Helen would be different enough from the other members of the group to stand out as a distinct individual.

## CONCLUSION

The problem of representation is one of determining a mapping between the concepts and relations of the represented world and the concepts and relations of the representing world. The problem for the psychologist, of course, is to find those representational systems that cause the behavior of our theories to correspond to the behavior of humans. In developing a theory of representation, it is important to be aware of exactly what it is that is being represented: in particular, much of cognitive psychology and artificial intelligence is concerned with attempts to represent the mental activity of the human. To quote an earlier portion of this chapter: "within the brain, there exist brain states that are the representation of the environment. The environment is the represented world, the brain states are the representing world. Our theories of representation are in actuality representations of the brain states, not representations of the world."

In many ways, the representation problem is, in truth, a notation problem. That is, in establishing a representation for our theories, we wish to discover a notation

1. That is rich enough to represent all of the relevant data structures and processes;
2. In which those processes that we wish to assume are natural (i.e., are easily carried out) are, in fact, easily carried out.

## Three Major Controversies

Traditionally, the problem of representation has had a number of different components that have led to long debate. Three major debates have arisen over the distinctions between representational formats: propositional versus analogical, continuous versus discrete, and declarative versus procedural. The position that we have taken in this chapter is that these debates do not reflect fundamental distinctions about representational systems, but rather reflect differences in the way that representational systems meet the two criteria for such systems stated above. Let us review each issue briefly.

### The Propositional-analogical Controversy

Propositional representations are ones that consist of formal statements that reflect the represented world, either in the form of networks, schema-based structures, or logical formulas. Analogical representations attempt a direct mapping between the important characteristics of the represented world and the representing world. Thus, spatial or temporal properties of the represented world might be mapped onto spatial properties of the representing world, and ordered properties of the represented world are mapped onto ordered properties of the number system in the representing world. All representational systems are, of course, to some extent analogs of the represented world; after all, that is what a representation is all about—to capture the essence of the represented world. Whatever the mapping, a key feature of representations that we are willing to call analogical is that if the thing being represented undergoes change or modification, then the structure in the representing world should undergo the corresponding change or modification, passing through the same intermediate states as the original. Thus, if we have a picture of a star above a cross and move the star closer to or further from the cross, an analogical representation of that movement will have to represent the same set of intermediate states as the physical movement. This could be accomplished with a representation that consisted of a manipulable picture of the star and cross, perhaps in a matrix or bit map, or it could be represented by using a two-dimensional coordinate system within a set of propositions, specifying location by values on the real numbers.

A useful way to view the differences between analogical and propositional representation is to map it into the distinction raised by Palmer (1978) between information that is intrinsic to the representation and that which is extrinsic. We say that a representation is an analog of the represented world when the relations of interest to us are intrinsic to the representation.

### The Continuous-discrete Controversy

Often, continuous representations are confused with analogical, and discrete with propositional representations. However, the two distinctions are actually independent of one another. What is involved here is the grain size or acuity that one wishes to have in the represented world. Thus, if the things to be represented are discrete, then even the most analogical representation in the representing world is likely to be discrete. Alternatively, one might choose a continuous (real-number) representation within a propositional structure. The real point is that one is attempting to capture aspects and relations that are considered important in the represented world within the structures of the representing world, and the choice of a discrete or continuous representation simply reflects the choice of which features are important. Thus, if one represented a moving object by a matrix representation of the object, where the movement was represented by small, discrete changes in the representing location, this matrix would qualify as an analogical representation as long as the discrete steps within the representing movement were small relative to the step size of interest. In this case, a discrete representation of a continuous event would still be considered analogical.

### The Declarative-procedural Controversy

The difference between representations called declarative and representations called procedural really reflects differences in the accessibility of the information to the interpretive structures. In the case of declarative representations, the information is represented in a format that can be examined and manipulated directly by the interpretive processes. Thus, the information is accessible for inspection, for use by multiple processes, and for that matter, for the interpreter simply to announce whether or not the information is known to be present within the representational system. In the case of procedural representations, the information is not available in a form that can be accessed by the interpreter. Rather, one must execute the procedure and examine the results. Information that is procedural is therefore encapsulated for this level of representation, not available for inspection, and not easily available for multiple processes (unless their use has been explicitly provided for), and it is not possible for the interpreter to make announcements regarding the presence or absence of information that is procedurally encoded. Declarative information is explicit in that it is directly encoded. Procedural information is implicit in that the procedure has to be executed in order to get the information.

In this chapter, we have argued that what is declarative and what is procedural information is context dependent. That is, any realistic information processing system has several levels of processing and interpretation, and what is procedural at one level of interpretation is most likely declarative at a different level—indeed, at the level where some interpretive process operates upon the procedure in order to execute it. The system is eventually grounded in the primitives of the system and in actual physical actions. And at this level, all the actions of the system are procedural.

## Data Structure and Process

Representational systems consist of at least two parts:

- The data structures, which are stored according to some representational format; and
- The processes that operate upon the data structures.

Much confusion has arisen in the comparison of representational systems because of a lack of recognition that both data and process are essential; one cannot be understood without reference to and understanding of the other. Note that the distinction between data structures and interpretive processes varies with different modes of representation. Thus, one difference between declarative and procedural representations is in the relative tradeoff between, on one hand, the division of the knowledge among the data structures and, on the other, the interpretive system. In the superpositional structures, the two different aspects are merged into the same structures, so that the interpretive structures are the data structures. In all cases, both need to be considered in order to understand the representational system. Data structures and their interpretive processes are intrinsically intertwined; the two must be considered as an inseparable pair in determining the properties and powers of the representation.

## Multiple Representations

There is no single answer to the question "How is information represented in the human?"; many different representational formats may function within the human representational system. Thus, within the representing world, different aspects of the represented world may be represented through different representational formats. This allows each dimension to be represented by the system that maps best into the sets of operations that one wishes to perform. Different representational systems have different powers, and the choice of which one is used reflects those powers.[18]

Like every other representational decision, the decision to use multiple representations of the same information has its tradeoffs. The extra powers must be traded off against the problem of coordinating the information in the separate representations so that, when a change is made, all structures are properly synchronized so as to reflect the same represented world.

### Virtual Knowledge

Procedural, declarative, analogical, propositional—these different terms refer to different choices in the representational format, different decisions as to which information is to be represented intrinsically and which extrinsically, which is to be explicit, and which implicit. Analogical systems are those in which the mapping of the intermediate states of the representing world correspond to the intermediate states

---

[18]See the discussions by R.J. Bobrow & Brown (1975). D.G. Bobrow (1975) emphasizes the differences among the different dimensions of a representation. And note the mixed mode format that Kosslyn (1980) uses to represent mental images.

of the represented world. Procedural systems are those in which the interpretive processes have access only to the products (results) of running the representation.

One of the problems in attempting to assess a person's knowledge structure is that some of that knowledge may be directly represented, and some may be indirectly coded, inferred, or otherwise generated at the time of test. Modern representational theory, as represented by the discussions in this chapter, provides a rich set of possibilities for the possessor of knowledge. The research recognizes that people have the capability of making new inferences even as they answer a query, that much of what is reported may be generated, on-line, in real time, at the time of answering the questions put to them, using the representational properties of inheritance and logical inference, and using prototypical schemata to structure the organization of what is being generated, complete with default values. The possessor of the knowledge itself cannot distinguish between memory retrievals that are regenerated on the spot according to some generic properties and memory retrievals that are accurate reflections of the actual events. Finally, the problem of determining a person's memory structures is amplified by the fact that much knowledge may be represented procedurally, and procedural knowledge—by definition—is inaccessible to its possessor.

## GENERAL REFERENCES AND SOURCES

There are a number of good general sources for more thorough treatment of the issues discussed in this chapter. We recommend two handbooks:

- *The Handbook of Learning and Cognitive Processes*, especially Volumes 4 and 6 (Estes, 1976, 1978).
- *The Handbook of Artificial Intelligence*, Volumes 1, 2, and 3 (Barr & Feigenbaum, 1981, 1982; Cohen & Feigenbaum, 1982).

In addition, see the book that started much of the work on representation in memory: Tulving and Donaldson's *Organization and Memory* (1972). Two important collections of papers are D.G. Bobrow and Collins's *Representation and Understanding* (1975), and Rosch and Lloyd's *Cognition and Categorization* (1978).

## REFERENCES

Abelson, R. (1975). Concepts for representing mundane reality in plans. In D.G. Bobrow & A.M. Collins (Eds.), *Representation and understanding: Studies in cognitive science* (pp. 273–309). New York: Academic Press.

Anderson, J.R. (1976). *Language, memory, and thought.* Hillsdale, NJ: Erlbaum.

Anderson, J.R. (1982). Acquisition of cognitive skill. *Psychological Review, 89*, 369–406.

Anderson, J.R. & Bower, G.H. (1973). *Human associative memory.* Washington, DC: Winston.

Barr, A. & Feigenbaum, E.A. (Eds.). (1981–1982). *The handbook of artificial intelligence* (Vols. 1–2). Los Altos, CA: William Kaufman.

Bartlett, F.C. (1932). *Remembering.* Cambridge: Cambridge University Press.

Bobrow, D.G. (1975). Dimensions of representation. In D.G. Bobrow & A.M. Collins (Eds.), *Representation and understanding: Studies in cognitive science* (pp. 1–34). New York: Academic Press.

Bobrow, D.G. & Collins, A.M. (Eds.). (1975). *Representation and understanding: Studies in cognitive science.* New York: Academic Press.

Bobrow, D.G. & Norman, D.A. (1975). Some principles of memory schemata. In D.G. Bobrow & A.M. Collins (Eds.), *Representation and understanding: Studies in cognitive science* (pp. 131–149). New York: Academic Press.

Bobrow, D.G. & Winograd, T. (1977). An overview of KRL, a knowledge representation language. *Cognitive Science, 1*, 3–46.

Bobrow, R.J. & Brown, J.S. (1975). Systematic understanding: Synthesis, analysis, and contingent knowledge in specialized understanding systems. In D.G. Bobrow & A.M. Collins (Eds.), *Representation and understanding: Studies in cognitive science* (pp. 103–129). New York: Academic Press.

Bower, G.H., Black, J.B., & Turner, T.J. (1979). Scripts in memory for text. *Cognitive Psychology, 11*, 177–220.

Brachman, R.J. (1979). On the epistemological status of semantic networks. In N.V. Findler (Ed.), *Associative networks: Representation and use of knowledge by computers* (pp. 3–50). New York: Academic Press.

Bransford, J.D. & Franks, J.J. (1971). The abstraction of linguistic ideas. *Cognitive Psychology, 2*, 331–350.

Brown, J.S. & Burton, R.R. (1975). Multiple representations of knowledge for tutorial reasoning. In D.G. Bobrow & A.M. Collins (Eds.), *Representation and understanding: Studies in cognitive science* (pp. 311–349). New York: Academic Press.

Brown, J.S., Burton, R.R., & de Kleer, J. (1982). Knowledge engineering and pedagogical techniques in SOPHIE I, II, and III. In D. Sleeman & J.S. Brown (Eds.), *Intelligent tutoring systems*. London: Academic Press.

Clark, H.H. & Chase, W.G. (1972). On the process of comparing sentences against pictures. *Cognitive Psychology, 3,* 472–517.

Cohen, N. (1981). *Neuropsychological evidence for distinction between procedural and declarative knowledge in human memory and amnesia.* Unpublished doctoral dissertation, University of California, San Diego.

Cohen, N.J. (1983). Amnesia and the distinction between procedural and declarative knowledge. In N. Butters & L.R. Squire (Eds.), *The neuropsychology of memory*. New York: Guilford Press.

Cohen, N. & Corkin, S. (1981). The amnesic patient, H.M.: Learning and retention of a cognitive skill. *Society for Neuroscience Abstracts, 7,* 235.

Cohen, N.J. & Squire, L.R. (1980). Preserved learning and retention of pattern analyzing skill in amnesia: Dissociation of knowing how and knowing that. *Science, 210,* 207–209.

Cohen, NP.R. & Feigenbaum, E.A. (Eds.). (1982). *The handbook of artificial intelligence: Vol. 3.* Los Altos, CA: William Kaufman.

Collins, A.M. & Loftus, E.F. (1975). A spreading activation theory of semantic processing. *Psychological Review, 82,* 407–428.

Collins, A.M. & Quillian, M.R. (1969). Retrieval time from semantic memory. *Journal of Verbal Learning and Verbal Behavior, 8,* 240–247.

Collins, A.M. & Quillian, M.R. (1970). Facilitating retrieval from semantic memory: The effect of repeating part of an inference. In A.F. Sanders (Ed.), *Attention and performance III* (pp. 304–314). Amsterdam: North Holland. (Also published in *Acta Psychologica, 33,* 304–314.)

Cooper, L.A. (1976). Demonstration of a mental analog of an external rotation. *Perception & Psychophysics, 19,* 296–302.

Cooper, L.A. & Podgorny, P. (1976). Mental transformations and visual comparison processes. *Journal of Experimental Psychology: Human Perception and Performance, 2,* 503–514.

De Kleer, J. (1975). *Qualitative and quantitative knowledge in classical mechanics.* Unpublished master's thesis, MIT, Cambridge, MA.

De Kleer, J. & Brown, J.S. (1983). Assumptions and ambiguities in mechanistic mental models. In D. Gentner & A.L. Stevens (Eds.), *Mental models* (pp. 155–190). Hillsdale, NJ: Erlbaum.

Estes, W.K. (Ed.). (1976). *Handbook of learning and cognitive processes: Vol. 4. Attention and memory.* Hillsdale, NJ: Erlbaum.

Estes, W.K. (Ed.). (1978). *Handbook of learning and cognitive processes: Vol. 6. Linguistic functions in cognitive theory.* Hillsdale, NJ: Erlbaum.

Fahlman, S.E. (1981). Representing implicit knowledge. In G.E. Hinton & J.A. Anderson (Eds.), *Parallel models of associative memory* (pp. 145–159). Hillsdale, NJ: Erlbaum.

Feldman, J.A. & Ballard, D.H. (1982). Connectionist models and their properties. *Cognitive Science, 6,* 205–254.

Fillmore, C.J. (1968). The case for case. In E. Bach & R.T. Harms (Eds.), *Universals in linguistic theory*. New York: Holt, Rinehart, & Winston.

Forbus, K. (1983). Qualitative reasoning about space and motion. In D. Gentner & A.L. Stevens (Eds.), *Mental models* (pp. 53–73). Hillsdale, NJ: Erlbaum.

Frege, G. (1892). Uber Sinn und Bedeutung [On sense and reference]. *Zeitschrift fur Philosophie und philosophiche Kritik, 100* (Complete issue). (Also see P. Geach & M. Black, (Eds.). (1960). *Translations from the philosophical writings of Gottlob Frege*. Oxford: Basil Blackwell.)

Freyd, J.J. (1983). Shareability: The social psychology of epistemology. *Cognitive Science, 7,* 191–210.

Funt, B.V. (1980). Problem solving with diagrammatic representations. *Artificial Intelligence, 13,* 201–230.

Funt, B.V. (1983). A parallel-process model of mental rotation. *Cognitive Science, 7,* 67–93.

Gentner, D. & Stevens, A. (Eds.). (1983). *Mental models*. Hillsdale, NJ: Erlbaum.

Hayes-Roth, B. & Hayes-Roth, F. (1977). Concept learning and the recognition and classification of exemplars. *Journal of Verbal Learning and Verbal Behavior, 16,* 321–338.

Hewitt, C. (1975). How to use what you know. *Proceedings of the Fourth International Joint Conference on Artificial Intelligence, 4,* 189–198.

Hinton, G.E. & Anderson, J.A. (Eds.). (1981). *Parallel models of associative memory*. Hillsdale, NJ: Erlbaum.

Just, M.A. & Carpenter, P.A. (1976). Eye fixations and cognitive processes. *Cognitive Psychology, 8,* 441–480.

Kay, A.C. (1977). Microelectronics and the personal computer. *Scientific American, 237,* 231–244.

Kintsch, W. (1972). Notes on the structure of semantic memory. In E. Tulving & W. Donaldson (Eds.), *Organization and memory* (pp. 249–308). New York: Academic Press.

Kintsch, W. (1978). Comprehension and memory of text. In W.K. Estes (Ed.), *Handbook of learning and cognitive processes: Vol. 6.* Hillsdale, NJ: Erlbaum.

Kosslyn, S.M. (1975). Information representation in visual images. *Cognitive Psychology, 7,* 341–370.

Kosslyn, S.M. (1980). *Image and mind.* Cambridge, MA: Harvard University Press.

Kosslyn, S.M., Ball, T.M., & Reiser, B.J. (1978). Visual images preserve metric spatial information: Evidence from studies of image scanning. *Journal of Experimental Psychology: Human Perception and Performance, 4,* 47–60.

Kosslyn, S.M. & Schwartz, S.P. (1978). Visual images as spatial representations in active memory. In E.M. Riseman & A.R. Hanson (Eds.), *Computer vision systems.* New York: Academic Press.

Lindsey, P.H. & Norman, D.A. (1972). *Human information processing.* New York: Academic Press.

MacLean, J. & Schulman, G. (1978). The construction and maintenance of expectancies. *Quarterly Journal of Experimental Psychology, 30,* 441–454.

McClelland, J.L. (1981). Retrieving general and specific information from stored knowledge of specifics. *Proceedings of the Third Annual Conference of the Cognitive Science Society, 3,* 170–172.

McClelland, J.L. & Rumelhart, D.E. (1981). An interactive activation model of context effects in letter perception: Part 1. An account of basic findings. *Psychological Review, 88,* 375–407.

McCloskey, M.E. & Glucksberg, S. (1978). Natural categories: Well defined or fuzzy sets? *Memory or Cognition, 6,* 462–472.

Metzler, J. & Shepard, R.N. (1974). Transformational studies of the internal representation of three-dimensional objects. In R. Solso (Ed.), *Theories in cognitive psychology: The Loyola Symposium,* Hillsdale, NJ: Erlbaum.

Meyer, D.E. (1970). On the representation and retrieval of stored semantic information. *Cognitive Psychology, 1,* 242–299.

Meyer, D.E. & Schvaneveldt, R.W. (1971). Facilitation in recognizing pairs of words: Evidence of a dependence between retrieval operations. *Journal of Experimental Psychology, 90,* 227–234.

Minsky, M. (1975). A framework for representing knowledge. In Winston, P. (Ed.), *The psychology of computer vision* (pp. 211–277). New York: McGraw-Hill.

Neely, J.H. (1976). Semantic priming and retrieval from lexical memory: Evidence for facilitory and inhibitory processes. *Memory & cognition, 4,* 648–654.

Neely, J.H. (1977). Semantic priming and retrieval from lexical memory: Roles of inhibitionless spreading activation and limited-capacity attention. *Journal of Experimental Psychology: General, 106,* 226–254.

Newell, A. (1973). Production systems: Models of control structure. In W. Chase (Ed.), *Visual information processing.* New York: Academic Press.

Newell, A. (1981). Physical symbol systems. In D.A. Norman (Ed.), *Perspectives on cognitive science* (pp. 37–85). Norwood, NJ: Ablex.

Newell, A. & Simon, H. (1963). GPS, a program that simulates human thought. In E.A. Feigenbaum & J. Feldman (Eds.), *Computers and thought* (pp. 279–293). New York: McGraw-Hill.

Newell, A. & Simon, H. (1972). *Human problem solving.* Englewood Cliffs, NJ: Prentice-Hall.

Newport, E.L. & Bellugi, U. (1978). Linguistic expression of category levels in a visual-gestural language: A flower is a flower is a flower. In E. Rosch & B.B. Lloyd (Eds.), *Cognition and categorization* (pp. 49–71). Hillsdale, NJ: Erlbaum.

Nilsson, N.J. (1980). *Principles of artificial intelligence.* Palo Alto, CA: Tioga.

Norman, D.A. & Bobrow, D.G. (1976). On the role of active memory processes in perception and cognition. In C.N. Cofer (Ed.), *The structure of human memory* (pp. 114–132). San Francisco: Freeman.

Norman, D.A. & Bobrow, D.G. (1979). Descriptions: An intermediate stage in memory retrieval. *Cognitive Psychology, 11,* 107–123.

Norman, D.A. & Rumelhart, D.E. (1975). *Explorations in cognition.* San Francisco: Freeman.

Norman, D.A. (1982). *Learning and memory.* San Francisco: Freeman.

Oden, G.C. (1977). Integration of fuzzy logical information. *Journal of Experimental Psychology: Human Perception and Performance, 3,* 565–575.

Ortony, A. (1979). Beyond literal similarity. *Psychological Review, 86,* 161–180.

Palmer, S.E. (1978). Fundamental aspects of cognitive representation. In E. Rosch & B.B. Lloyd (Eds.), *Cognition and categorization* (pp. 259–303). Hillsdale, NJ: Erlbaum.

Piaget, J. (1952). *The origins of intelligence in children* (M. Cook, Trans.). New York: International Universities Press.

Posner, M.I. & Keele, S.W. (1968). On the genesis of abstract ideas. *Journal of Experimental Psychology, 77,* 353–363.

Posner, M.I. & Snyder, C.R.R. (1975). Attention and cognitive control. In R. Solso (Ed.), *Information processing and cognition: The Loyola symposium* (pp. 55–85). Hillsdale, NJ: Erlbaum.

Post, E. (1943). Formal reductions of the general combinatorial problem. *American Journal of Mathematics, 65,* 197–268.

Quillian, M.R. (1968). Semantic memory. In M. Minsky (Ed.), *Semantic information processing* (pp. 227–270). Cambridge, MA: MIT Press.

Reder, L.M. & Anderson, J.R. (1980). A partial resolution of the paradox of interference: The role of integrating knowledge. *Cognitive Psychology, 12,* 447–472.

Reder, L.M. & Ross, B.H. (1983). Integrated knowledge in different tasks: The role of retrieval strategy on fan effects. *Journal of Experimental Psychology: Learning, Memory and Cognition, 9,* 55–72.

Rips, L.J., Shoben, E.J., & Smith, E.E. (1973). Semantic distance and the verification of semantic relations. *Journal of Verbal Learning and Verbal Behavior, 12,* 1–20.

Rosch, E. (1978). Principles of categorization. In E. Rosch & B.B. Lloyd (Eds.), *Cognition and categorization* (pp. 27–48). Hillsdale, NJ: Erlbaum.

Rosch, E. & Lloyd, B.B. (Eds.). (1978). *Cognitive and categorization.* Hillsdale, NJ: Erlbaum.

Rosch, E. & Mervis, C.B. (1975). Family resemblance: Studies in the internal structure of categories. *Cognitive Psychology, 7,* 573–605.

Rumelhart, D.E. (1975). Notes on a schema for stories. In D.G. Bobrow & A.M. Collins (Eds.), *Representation and understanding: Studies in cognitive science* (pp. 211–236). New York: Academic Press.

Rumelhart, D.E. (1977). Toward an interactive model of reading. In S. Dornic (Ed.), *Attention and performance VI.* Hillsdale, NJ: Erlbaum.

Rumelhart, D.E. (1981). *Understanding understanding* (Tech. Rep. CHIP 100). La Jolla, CA: University of California, San Diego, Center for Human Information Processing.

Rumelhart, D.E. & Levin, J.A. (1975). A language comprehension system. In D.A. Norman & D.E. Rumelhart, *Explorations in cognition* (pp. 179–208). San Francisco: Freeman.

Rumelhart, D.E. & McClelland, J.L. (1982). An interactive activation model of context effects in letter perception: Part 2. The contextual enhancement effect and some tests and extensions of the model. *Psychological Review, 89,* 60–94.

Rumelhart, D.E. & Norman, D.A. (1978). Accretion, tuning, and restructuring: Three modes of learning. In J.W. Cotton & R.L. Klatzky (Eds.), *Semantic factors in cognition* (pp. 37–53). Hillsdale, NJ: Erlbaum.

Rumelhart, D.E. & Ortony, A. (1977). The representation of knowledge in memory. In R.C. Anderson, R.J. Spiro, & W.E. Montague (Eds.), *Schooling and the acquisition of knowledge* (pp. 99–135). Hillsdale, NJ: Erlbaum.

Schank, R.C. (1975). *Conceptual information processing.* New York: North-Holland.

Schank, R.C. (1975). The structure of episodes in memory. In D.G. Bobrow & A. Collins (Eds.), *Representation and understanding: Studies in cog-*

*nitive science* (pp. 237–272). New York: Academic Press.

Schank, R.C. (1980). Language and memory. *Cognitive Science, 4,* 243–284.

Schank, R.C. (1981). Language and memory. In D.A. Norman (Ed.), *Perspectives on cognitive science* (pp. 105–146). Norwood, NJ: Ablex. Hillsdale, NJ: Erlbaum.

Schank, R. & Abelson, R. (1977). *Scripts, plans, goals, and understanding.* Hillsdale, NJ: Erlbaum.

Selfridge, O. (1959). Pandemonium: A paradigm for learning. In *Symposium on the Mechanisation of thought processes*: Proceedings of a Symposium held at the National Physical Laboratory, November 1958, Vol. 1. London: HM Stationery Office.

Shepard, R.N. & Cooper, L.A. (1982). *Mental images and their transformations.* Cambridge, MA: MIT Press.

Shepard, R.N. & Feng, C. (1972). A chronometric study of mental paper folding. *Cognitive Psychology, 3,* 228–243.

Smith, E.E., Adams, N., & Schorr, D. (1978). Fact retrieval and the paradox of interference. *Cognitive Psychology, 10,* 438–464.

Smith, E.E., Balzano, G.J., & Walker, J.H. (1978). Nominal, perceptual, and semantic codes in picture categorization. In J. Cotton & R. Klatzky (Eds.), *Semantic factors in cognition* (pp. 137–168). Hillsdale, NJ: Erlbaum.

Smith, E.E. & Medin, D.L. (1981). *Categories and concepts.* Cambridge, MA: Harvard University Press.

Smith, E.E., Shoben, E.J., & Rips, L.J. (1974). Structure and process in semantic memory: A feature model for semantic decisions. *Psychological Review, 81,* 214–241.

Tulving, E. (1972). Episodic and semantic memory. In E. Tulving & W. Donaldson (Eds.), *Organization of memory* (pp. 381–403). New York: Academic Press.

Tversky, A. (1977). Features of similarity. *Psychological Review, 84,* 327–352.

Tversky, A. & Gati, I. (1978). Studies of similarity. In E. Rosch & B.B. Lloyd (Eds.), *Cognition and categorization* (pp. 79–98). Hillsdale, NJ: Erlbaum.

Waterman, D.A. & Hayes-Roth, F. (Eds.). (1978). *Pattern-directed inference systems.* New York: Academic Press.

Wilensky, R. (1978). *Understanding goal-based stories* (Research Report 140), New Haven, CT: Yale University, Computer Science Dept.

Winograd, T. (1972). *Understanding natural language.* New York: Academic Press.

Winograd, T. (1975). Frame representations and the declarative-procedural controversy. In D.G. Bobrow & A.M. Collins (Eds.), *Representation and understanding: Studies in cognitive science* (pp. 185–210). New York: Academic Press.

Wittgenstein, L. (1953). *Philosophical investigations.* Oxford: Blackwell.

Woods, W.A. (1975). What's in a link: Foundations for semantic networks. In D.G. Bobrow & A. Collins (Eds.), *Representation and understanding: Studies in cognitive science* (pp. 35–82). New York: Academic Press.

Zadeh, L. (1965). Fuzzy sets. *Information and Control, 8,* 338–353.

# Chapter 9

# PROBLEM SOLVING AND REASONING

**James G. Greeno,** *Stanford University*

**Herbert A. Simon,** *Carnegie-Mellon University*

## INTRODUCTION

Important advances were made in the 1960s and 1970s in the scientific study of thinking. They have resulted from new methods for formulating models of the cognitive processes and structures underlying performance in complex tasks, and the development of experimental methods to test such models. A major accomplishment was the discovery of general forms of cognitive activity and knowledge that underlie human problem solving and reasoning. This chapter surveys the major theoretical concepts and principles that have been developed, presents some of the evidence that supports these principles, and discusses the empirical and theoretical methods

[1]Now at Stanford University.

Preparation of this chapter was supported by the Personnel and Training Programs, Office of Naval Research, under Contract Number N00014-79-C-0215, Contract Identification Number NR 667-430 (JGG), and by grants from the National Institute of Mental Health and the Alfred P. Sloan Foundation (HAS).

that are used in this domain of scientific study. This introductory section gives an overview of the major concepts that will be described in the chapter. We discuss relations between these concepts and issues that have been investigated in experimental psychology as well as some general methodological issues.

### Overview of Concepts

The concepts that have been developed can be placed in two groups: hypotheses about the form of cognitive action and hypotheses about the form of cognitive representation. The hypotheses about cognitive action extend analyses of behavior that were developed in general behavior theory by investigators such as Thorndike (1923), Tolman (1928); Skinner (1938), and Hull (1943). The hypotheses about representation extend analyses that were developed by Gestalt psychologists such as Köhler (1929), Duncker (1935/1945), Katona (1940), and Wertheimer (1945/1959). One of the important insights reached in the analysis of problem solving is that hypotheses about these issues of action and representation are complementary; both are necessary components of a theory of human thought.

### Form of Cognitive Action

Hypotheses about cognitive action can be considered at two levels: basic action knowledge and strategic knowledge.

A consensus has developed that human knowledge underlying cognitive action can be represented in the form of *production rules*, a formalism introduced by Post (1943) to represent reasoning in mathematics, and adapted for application to psychology by Newell and Simon (1972). Models in which knowledge for action is represented as a set of production rules are referred to as *production systems*.

Any theory of performance must include hypotheses about the process of choice whereby individuals select the actions that they perform. A production system provides a framework for expressing hypotheses about this process in specific detail. A production rule (or, more simply, a *production*) consists of a condition and an action. The *condition* specifies a pattern of information that may or may not be present in the situation. The *action* specifies something that can be performed. The general form of action based on productions is simply: If the condition is true, perform the action.

In a production system, the basic problem of choice among actions is solved by specifying conditions that lead to the selection of each action that can be performed. The condition of each production rule is a *pattern of information* that the system can recognize. These patterns include features of the external problem situation (the stimulus). They also include information that is generated internally by the problem solver and held in short-term memory. The internal information includes *goals* that are set during problem solving. It also can include information in memory, such as past attempts to achieve specific goals. Thus, production rules, which represent basic action knowledge, consist of associations between patterns of information and actions. An action is chosen when the individual has a goal with which the action is associated, and the external stimulus situation as well as information in memory include features associated with the action.

An important component of a model of cog-

nitive activity is its representation of *strategic knowledge*. This includes processes for setting goals and adopting general plans or methods in working on a problem. Models of general problem-solving strategies have been developed to simulate performance in novel problem situations where the individual has little or no experience. One important model is based on a process of means–ends analysis (Newell & Simon, 1972) in which goals are compared with current states, and actions are selected to reduce differences that are identified. General strategies also include processes for setting subgoals when the current goal cannot be achieved directly. Analyses of strategic knowledge in specific domains also have been developed to simulate performance by problem solvers who have received special training (e.g. Greeno, 1978). Strategic knowledge of experienced problem solvers includes global plans for solving classes of problems and knowledge of subgoals that are useful in classes of problem situations.

The general ideas used in formulating hypotheses about cognitive activity in production systems build upon the concepts developed and used in general behavior theory, particularly the formulations of Tolman (1928) and the later forms of Hull's (1952) theory. Early expositions of behavior theory emphasized the direct relations between stimuli and responses, with rather deliberate inattention to intervening events in the brain. Thorndike (1923) emphasized that actions are chosen because of their associations with stimulus conditions. In Skinner's (1938) formulation, actions are performed under the 'control' of external stimulus features. Tolman (1928), on the other hand, emphasized internal goals and information stored in memory in the determination of response selection. Tolman used such terms as '*means–end expectation*' and '*means–end readiness*' in referring to these factors. In Hull's theory, concepts of covert anticipatory responses (1930) and incentive motivation (1952) were used. In discussions of problem solving, Maltzman (1955) and Staats (1966) postulated stimulus–response units at different levels of generality. The idea of knowledge about action at different levels is used in more recent formulations of strategic knowledge, especially in hypotheses about planning, some of which we discuss in the sections on well specified problems and on problems of design and arrangement.

The concept of a production rule is consistent with these formulations; and behavior theory, even in the terms used by Watson and Skinner, can be expressed as a system of productions (Millenson, 1967). However, as production rules are used in contemporary information processing theory, they more explicitly emphasize the motivational states and memories of prior experiences that combine with external stimulus conditions to determine response choice. Modern production system models of problem solving and similar cognitive processes may be viewed as an (lengthy) extrapolation of Tolman's research program whereby the roles of external environment (stimulus) and inner environment (motivational states and memory contents) as determinants of respose are symmetrical. It also makes exactly how those two sources of information control responses much more explicit. We characterize the extrapolation as lengthy because it postulates not only that many of the essential components of the stimulus lie in the brain, but also that a large part of the response to a production (or all of it) may be internal—consisting, for example, of a change in content of short-term (STM) or long-term memory (LTM). We do not want to underestimate the magnitude of the shift in viewpoint, but we do emphasize that it is a continuous development from the experimental psychology that preceded it. That is presumably what Miller, Galanter, and Pribram (1960) meant when they described the new approach (half jokingly) as 'subjective behaviorism.' Subjective, of course, referred to the minds of the subjects, not to the scientific methods of the investigators.

One major difference between recent hypotheses about cognitive activity and those developed in general behavior theory (in addition to the shift to internal events in behavior) is that recent formulations are much more definite and specific. Models have been formulated as production systems with sufficient specificity to be expressed as computer programs that simulate actual performance of solving specific problems. It is not sufficient to postulate the existence of stimulus–response associations and goals, even at differing levels of generality, to do this. It is necessary also to formulate hypotheses about just what the stimuli, responses, and goals are. Hypotheses about specific structures of knowledge concerning actions and goals in the problem domain must be constructed, and

processes must be designed to recognize specific, relevant patterns of information in the task situation. Hypotheses about strategic knowledge have to specify the conditions in which goals will be set and plans adopted.

Again, we prefer to emphasize continuity in this development. Nothing in the new fine-grained mechanisms is antithetical to the grosser level of description of the earlier theories. In fact, important progress has been made in explaining in detail (sometimes quantitatively) the rich body of experimental data provided within the behavioral framework (Simon & Feigenbaum, 1964; Gregg & Simon, 1967). The impact from achieving this higher level of resolution in our theoretical models and their predictions has led to significantly greater understanding of the psychological processes involved in problem solving and reasoning.

### Hypotheses about Representation

Hypotheses about cognitive representations of problems are formulated using the idea of a *problem space*. The problem space includes an individual's representation of the *objects* in the problem situation, the *goal* of the problem, and the *actions* (operators) that can be performed as well as strategies that can be used in working on the problem. It also includes a knowledge of *constraints* in the problem situation—restrictions on what can be done, as well as limits on the ways in which objects or features of objects can be combined.

In developing hypotheses about the representation of problems, much use has been made of concepts developed in analyses of language understanding, including networks of propositions (Anderson, 1976; Kintsch, 1974; Quillian, 1968), procedural representation of concepts (Feigenbaum, 1963; Hunt, Marin, & Stone, 1966; Winograd, 1972), and schemata (Hayes & Simon, 1974; Norman & Rumelhart, 1975; Schank, 1972; Schank & Abelson, 1978). Representations of problems differ from those usually postulated for the understanding of language in that they are constrained to provide information needed for solving the problem. Hypotheses about knowledge used in representing problems include processes for recognizing features that are relevant to actions, strategies, and constraints of the problem domain, and for constructing representations with information that can be used in the cognitive processes of problem solving.

Hypotheses about problem representations address some of the issues of understanding principles and structure in problem solving that were emphasized by some educational, developmental, and Gestalt psychologists (Brownell, 1935; Duncker, 1945; Judd, 1908; Katona, 1940; Köhler, 1929; Piaget, 1952; Wertheimer, 1959). As with hypotheses about cognitive activity, current hypotheses about representation are more definite and specific than those of previous discussions. The hypotheses specify cognitive processes and structures that actually construct representations from texts or other presentations of problem information (Hayes & Simon, 1974; Larkin, McDermott, Simon, & Simon, 1980; Riley, Greeno, & Heller, 1983). Hypotheses about understanding of problem structure and general principles include cognitive structures that specify just what is understood about the problem and how the understanding is achieved (Greeno, 1983; Greeno, Riley, & Gelman, 1984). Another characteristic of recent discussions is that hypotheses about understanding are coordinated with hypotheses about cognitive activity in problem solving, so the significance of understanding, as well as the specific information that it provides for the problem solver, is made clear.

## Methodology

The use of computer programming languages as formal systems for psychological theory has been a major factor in the development of the concepts and empirical results discussed in this chapter. The standards that are now common for adequacy of a hypothesis include its expression in a computer program that simulates actual solution of problems—that is, a description of the problem can be given as input for the program, and the program carries out steps that result in the problem's solution. To meet this standard, the theorist must develop specific hypotheses about many aspects of the psychological process that had been unspecified. Representations of specific stimulus situations must be postulated, including relations among cues that are assumed to provide important information for the subject. Knowledge structures and processes required for comprehension of stimulus situations must also be specified, leading to specific forms of information that are assumed to constitute the subject's cognitive representations of the stimuli. Assumptions about knowl-

edge in the subject's memory are specified in detail, including associative structures of information and production rules in which specific actions are associated with specific stimulus conditions. The actions include overt responses and internal actions such as setting goals and choosing plans.

To provide evidence to evaluate these more detailed hypotheses, more detailed data are required. A major source of these data has been the increased use of thinking-aloud protocols. These protocols provide a more detailed description of behavior, enabling inferences about intermediate steps such as subgoals and attention to specific aspects of the problem. Protocol statements are treated not as introspective descriptions of psychological processes, but rather as overt reports of mental activity that the subject would be aware of in any case, but usually would not announce. Indeed, subjects are instructed to avoid trying to explain their behavior, but only to give reports of things they notice or think about as they are working (Ericsson & Simon, 1980). Statements in protocols provide data to be explained by models that constitute hypotheses about the process. Thus, protocol statements have the same status as other detailed observations, such as specific patterns of error by individuals on sets of problems, latencies of response when information for problems is presented sequentially, or eye fixations during processing of problem information.

The remainder of this chapter is organized in five sections. "Well-Specified Problems" deals with problems in which a definite goal or solution procedure is specified. "Problems of Design and Arrangement" considers problems in which goals are specified in terms of general criteria, rather than as definite states or procedures. In "Induction" and "Evaluation of Deductive Arguments" we consider tasks that are often called reasoning, rather than problem solving. Finally, we present conclusions and unifying concepts.

## WELL-SPECIFIED PROBLEMS

This section concerns problem solving in relatively well structured situations in which a definite goal is specified. The problem solver is given an initial situation or problem state, a set of operators that can be used to change the situation, and a goal state. The task is to find a sequence of actions, restricted to use of the permitted operators, that results in the goal state. Problems discussed here include (1) goal-directed problems for which the problem solver has little or no specific knowledge or experience and must resort to what are sometimes called 'weak methods,' (2) solution of problems of the same structure for which individuals have received special training or experience, (3) problems that specify a procedure rather than a goal, and, (4) the representation of problems for which the individual has received special training.

## General Knowledge for Novel Problems with Specific Goals

A substantial body of research has been conducted on the solution of well-structured puzzle-like problems that require relatively little domain-specific knowledge. The research strategy of focusing on such problems has some advantages beyond those of making the experiments simpler and the data easier to interpret. In difficult problem domains requiring special knowledge, we are likely to learn from our subjects principally what they know and how they have organized and represented their knowledge in memory, because much of an individual's success depends on whether he or she knows the specific principles and procedures of the domain.

In experiments in domains that are relatively free of specialized content and where subjects are relatively naive, we may still find significant differences in behavior from subject to subject and from domain to domain, but we are also likely to discover some of the commonalities of behavior that characterize problem solving, at least by novices, over a wide range of domains. We are also likely to detect the flexible, general-purpose techniques that people fall back on when they do not have special knowledge or methods adapted specifically to the task at hand. These fallback techniques, often called *weak methods,* are the only weapons that are available for attacking truly novel problems. Hence, understanding them should contribute to an understanding of discovery processes and creative problem solving.

The *problem space* consists of the problem solver's representation of the materials of the problem, along with knowledge that is relevant to the task. This includes a representation of the problem goal and operators that can be used. These may be specified in the problem description or supplied by the problem solver's knowledge. The operators include actions that can be performed and conditions that are required for performance of the actions. The problem space also includes the problem solver's strategic knowledge, which may include methods previously acquired through experience in the domain, as well as general problem-solving methods.

The tasks discussed in this section have definite goals specified in the problem instructions. Subjects solving these problems are usually not experienced in the tasks. The problem-solving operators also are specified in the problem instructions, rather than being known in advance by the problem solvers, and the problem solvers must rely on general problem-solving strategies—that is, on weak methods. The principal methods of this kind employ a general problem-solving heuristic called *means–ends analysis,* in which the current state is compared with the goal of the problem or a subgoal that the problem solver is trying to achieve, and an operator is selected that can reduce differences between the current state and the goal.

Research has been conducted on several tasks of this general kind, two of which we discuss here: proof discovery exercises in logic (Newell & Simon, 1972), and water-jar problems (Atwood & Polson, 1976). These studies illustrate two empirical methods. Newell and Simon's study of logic-proof discovery used detailed analyses of thinking-aloud protocols obtained from a few subjects, with data from a larger group of subjects to check the representativeness of some general features of performance. Atwood and Polson's study of water-jar problems used frequencies of responses that occurred during problem solving to evaluate a model of problem solving expressed in quantitative form.

### Discovering Proofs in Logic
Discovering proofs for mathematical theorems of one kind or another is a task all of us have faced. One domain in which theorem proving has been studied extensively is elementary symbolic logic (Moore & Anderson, 1954; Newell, Shaw, & Simon, 1957; Newell & Simon, 1972). The propositional calculus is defined by

only two rules of inference and a dozen axioms. In the studies discussed here the task was presented as a syntactic game of transforming strings of uninterpreted symbols according to rules given as symbolic formulas. This ensured that subjects could not draw readily on common-sense knowledge they may have had of the laws of reasoning. (The studies of syllogistic reasoning discussed later directly address the question of subjects' knowledge of formal logical rules.)

## DEDUCTION AND INDUCTION IN PROBLEM SOLVING

At the outset we must deal with one common misconception about proof-finding tasks. Logic is the science of deductive reasoning from premises to conclusions. A proof is a sequence of expressions starting with axioms (or previously proved expressions) and terminating with the desired theorem; each step of the proof must satisfy the laws of deduction. Its validity can be checked, step by step, by applying those laws systematically.

*Finding* the proof of a theorem is another matter. We have a known starting point, the axioms, and a known goal, the theorem. However, in most mathematical domains there is no systematic rule for constructing a path from axioms to theorem. That path must be discovered, and the method usually used is to search for it; the amount of trial and error required depending on how selectively the search is carried out. Hence, while a *proof* is an example of a logical deduction, the problem-solving activity involved in searching for a proof is an inductive search.

## THE MOORE–ANDERSON LOGIC PROBLEMS

In the logic task designed by Moore and Anderson (1954), subjects were not told that they were discovering proofs in symbolic logic, but were simply instructed to 'recode' certain strings of symbols into other specified strings, using a given set of transformation rules. The rules were displayed on a sheet of paper that was available to the subjects at all times. A typical rule (there were twelve, some with subparts) was:

$$A \lor B \to B \lor A,$$

which was to be interpreted: The expression $A \lor B$ may be transformed into the expression $B \lor A$, where $A$ and $B$ are variables for which any parts of an expression can be substituted. The connectives in such expressions were referred

to by the experimenter as *wedge* ($\lor$), *dot* ($\cdot$), *horseshoe* ($\supset$), and *tilde* ($\sim$), instead of being given their usual interpretations in logic of *or*, *and*, *implies*, and *not*. Subjects were run on this task by Carpenter, Moore, Snyder, and Lysansky (1961) at Yale, and by Newell and Simon (1972) at Carnegie Institute of Technology.

Several kinds of data can be obtained in problem-solving tasks of this kind. The times to solution can be recorded, as well as the times for making each successive transformation of an expression. Numbers of correct solutions can be counted, and errors can be classified and analyzed.

## THINKING-ALOUD PROTOCOLS

The richest data, however, are obtained by instructing subjects to think aloud while solving the problem. The verbal protocols provide a higher temporal density of data than is usually obtained by other methods (except perhaps from records of eye movements). Typically, subjects speak at an average rate of about two words per second, although there are substantial differences among subjects and from one part of a task to another.

In order for thinking-aloud data to be used correctly and effectively to help understand subjects' cognitive processes, answers are needed to several questions, especially: (1) which processes, or what parts of the processes, are verbalized, and (2) to what extent does verbalization alter or in any way affect the problem-solving process itself? A recent extensive review of relevant literature (Ericsson & Simon, 1980) supports three general conclusions. First, subjects mainly verbalize a subset of the symbols that pass through the STM as the task is being performed. The verbalizations are more complete (i.e., give a fuller record of successive STM contents) when the problem is solved in terms of verbal symbols than when the STM contents have to be translated from some other modality (i.e., visual image). Second, the *process* of recognizing some familiar visual or auditory stimulus does not produce any intermediate symbols in STM that can be reported; only the *result* of the recognition process can be reported. Third, in most problem-solving tasks, the cognitive processes are the same in the thinking-aloud as in the silent condition. Moreover, the speed of task performance is generally neither increased nor decreased by the instruction to think aloud.

The protocols under discussion here are those produced by subjects while they are performing the cognitive task. In using retrospective protocols as data, additional factors must be taken into consideration. First, only such information can be reported retrospectively as has been transferred to LTM and retained there. Second, unless the instructions call for recall of specific events, subjects may engage, in a variety of ways, in active reconstruction of the event or process that is being probed. Hence, retrospective protocols must be interpreted in the light of what we know about the laws of memory and forgetting (Bartlett, 1932; Nisbett & Wilson, 1977).

The most detailed analysis of problem-solving protocols calls for reconstructing from them the successive cognitive states of subjects as they work toward solution of the problem. 'Cognitive state' means what the subject knows or has found out about the problem up to the time of the protocol fragment being examined, along with information, such as subgoals and evaluations, that has been generated by the subject from decisions and judgments. Typically, in tasks like the logic-theorem proving task, subjects verbalize the symbolic expressions they produce and those they are actively considering, the operators they are applying to transform expressions, and often the goals they are trying to attain—such as the final theorem or expressions they think would bring them closer to it (Newell & Simon, 1972). As they proceed, subjects often evaluate their progress and the suitability of steps they have just taken.

From such protocol statements we can usually reconstruct the problem space in which a subject is operating. Formally, a *problem space* is defined by a set of symbol structures, corresponding to the cognitive states that can be generated as the subject works on the task, and a set of cognitive operators, or information processes that produce new cognitive states from existing ones. The problem-solving efforts of a subject may be described as searches through a problem space from one cognitive state to another until the solution (a particular cognitive state) is found or the search is abandoned.

Given a description of the problem space inferred from a protocol, a search tree called a *Problem Behavior Graph* (PBG) can be constructed to represent the course of the subject's search. The size and shape of the PBG discloses the extent of the subject's skill and knowledge and the consequent selectivity he is able to achieve. With the PBG, the experimenter can construct a simulation program for a computer which, if given the same problem, would generate the same PBG as that generated by the subject.

The accuracy of fit of the simulation program to the strategy that guides a subject's behavior can be judged by comparing the program's trace step-by-step with the problem-solving protocol. Formal methods for judging goodness of fit in a statistical sense are not available, but departures of trace from protocol are easy to detect. These discrepancies form the basis for modifying the simulation program to fit the protocol more closely. Except for the fact that the data in this case are not numerical, the process of fitting a computer program to protocol data is identical in principle to the process of fitting a system of differential equations to time series data.

A *basic problem space* for the logic task is one in which the subject's cognitive state is defined by the logic expressions thus far derived from the initial given expression, and by the legal operators for generating new expressions from these. Since the protocol normally discloses both what operators are being applied and what expressions are obtained from the application, a great deal of redundancy is contained in the available information, with which the consistency of the interpretation is tested. Many protocols allow a richer problem space to be inferred—one in which the subject notes similarities and differences among logic expressions, and chooses the next step in those terms. When the subject's choice of actions is also guided by goals and subgoals, these are added to the description of the problem space.

SOLUTION PROCESSES

No single strategy, or simulation program based on such a strategy, can be expected to describe the problem-solving behavior of all subjects. However, the behavior of many subjects in tasks like the proving of logic-theorems reveals that a small number of common mechanisms are central features of the problem-solving process. One of the most important of these is means–ends analysis, first introduced into the problem-solving literature by Duncker (1935/1945). Means–ends analysis requires a problem space rich enough to contain not only logic expressions and operators, but also symbol structures describing differences between pairs of logic expressions and other symbol structures that describe goals. Thus, a subject operating in such a problem space might say, "I have an expression whose main connective is a horseshoe, and my goal expression has a wedge. Let me look for an operator that will change horseshoe to wedge."

In broadest outline, means–ends analysis can be described by the following set of productions, where $S$ is the present state or expression, $G$ is the goal expression, $D$ is a difference between two expressions, and $O$ is an operator:

If the goal is to remove difference $D$ between $S$ and $G$ → find a relevant operator $O$ and set the goal of applying it.

If the goal is to apply $O$ to $S$, and condition $C$ for applying $O$ is unsatisfied → set the goal of satisfying $C$ by modifying $S$.

If the goal is to apply $O$ to $S$ → make application

If there is a difference $D$ between $S$ and $G$ → set the goal of removing it.

If there is no difference between $S$ and $G$ → halt and report problem solved.

While the production system displayed here does not describe all the details of the control of search, it provides the main outlines of means–ends analysis. The system seeks to detect a difference between the present position in the problem space and the goal position. Given such a difference, it searches memory for an operator that is relevant for removing the difference and attempts to apply it. If all the conditions for operator application are not satisfied, it expresses the discrepancy as a new difference and establishes the goal of reducing it. The scheme operates recursively, and when one difference has been removed it looks for another. An important component of the strategy not represented in the productions is the use of memory to store goals that have been tried, so the problem solver can avoid looping through the same cycle of repeated unsuccessful attempts of a goal that cannot be achieved.

A clear distinction can be made between the general strategy of means–ends analysis and domain-specific knowledge that is required for the strategy to be used in solving any particular problem. The general strategy is represented in the productions shown above. To use these productions, a problem solver must be able to represent the state, $S$, and the goal, $G$ and identify differences between them. In the domain of logic, states correspond to expressions, and differences involve different letters, different connectives, and different arrangements of letters and connectives. The problem solver also must know what operators can be used, what conditions permit each operator to be applied, and what kinds of difference are removed by use of each operator. In logic, the operators are the rules for transforming expressions. The conditions are patterns that are specified in the rules, and the relevant differences for a rule can be inferred by comparing the two sides of the rule. For example, $A \cdot B \rightarrow A$ requires a pattern in which two subexpressions are connected by a dot, and has the effect of removing a letter or a subexpression, as well as removing the dot. $A \supset B \leftrightarrow \sim A \vee B$ does not remove or add any letters, it can be applied to a pattern with a horseshoe to change the horseshoe to a wedge or vice versa, and it changes the sign of one of the letter or subexpressions.

The general strategy of means–ends analysis has been implemented in a program called the *General Problem Solver* (GPS) and shown to be sufficient for providing solutions in over a dozen problem domains, including puzzles such as the Tower of Hanoi and tasks such as integral calculus, given appropriate representations of the states, operators, and connections between operators and differences in the specific domains (Ernst & Newell, 1969).

In the experiments conducted with the logic task, subjects were not experienced in the domain. The operators were presented as part of the task instructions, and it is reasonable to presume that subjects relied primarily on general problem-solving strategies, rather than on knowledge that was specific to that task. If that is correct, and if the subjects' general problem-solving strategies have the properties of GPS, then their performance in the logic task should be similar to that of the program when it is run on the task. The results supported this hypothesis.

## KINDS OF EVIDENCE

The hypothesis was evaluated at three levels. First, specific protocols were examined that compared the statements made by subjects with the steps in solutions by specific versions of GPS. For these simulations, GPS was varied by supplying it with differing priorities of differences. Second, a set of protocols [all those obtained by Newell and Simon (1972) on one moderately difficult problem] were coded, and each was translated into a *problem behavior graph* (PBG) showing a succession of cognitive states that was inferred from the statements and problem-solving operators to account for the transitions between states. The state-to-state transitions were classified and the categories were compared with categories of activity performed by GPS. Third, some summary statistics were compiled for Newell and Simon's subjects and for the subjects run at Yale, involving the frequencies of occurrence of several intermediate steps in solutions of the problems. These statistics were compared in order to detect any gross abnormalities in Newell and Simon's data, with the results from a larger group of subjects at Yale who solved the problem with pencil and paper and without the requirement of thinking aloud.

As Table 9.1 illustrates, individual protocols can often be simulated in great detail, but there will undoubtedly be differences among individuals in their problem solving methods, and hence in the production systems that would describe them. For purposes of psychological theory, we are often less interested in the details of a particular simulation (except as a strong test of the theory) than we are in the structure of a program that simulates the main mechanisms revealed in a set of protocols. The problem of averaging over groups of subjects can also be handled formally by comparing the statistics of the behavior of a program with the statistics of the human subjects as a group. This section examines comparisons of programs in detail with individual protocols, and the statistical approach is described in the next section.

## INDIVIDUAL PROTOCOLS

Newell and Simon have presented several protocols in which activities of subjects reflect processes similar to those in GPS. The illustration in Table 9.1 shows a segment of one subject's protocol along with a trace of a version

of GPS working on the same problem. In the protocol and the GPS trace, L0 refers to the goal expression and L1 refers to the initial expressions of the problem. The expressions L2, L3, and so on refer to additional expressions that are generated by the problem solver by applying operators to L1 and other previously generated expressions. The operators that are referred to in this segment are

$$R6: A \supset B \leftrightarrow \sim A \lor B$$

$$R7: A \lor (B \cdot C) \leftrightarrow (A \lor B) \cdot (A \lor C)$$

$$A \cdot (B \lor C) \leftrightarrow (A \cdot B) \lor (A \cdot C)$$

The protocal segment in Table 9.1 began near the end of the first minute of work on the problem and lasted slightly more than three minutes.

In this segment, the goal of both the subject and GPS was to delete the letter R from the initial expression. Both problem solvers considered rule R7 as a possible way to do so. The rule R7 cannot be applied to L1 because its connectives are wrong, so a subgoal was set to change the connective of L1. This led to use of R6, but the two occurrences of R in the transformed expression have opposite signs. When attempts were made to change one of the signs, the horseshoe was returned to the subexpression. At this point the subject and the specific version of GPS that produced this run were unable to continue on this line of work.

This protocol and GPS trace are alike in an impressive degree of detail. However, the important finding is not that the subject and GPS tried to use the same rules in the same sequence. The precise sequence of rules used by GPS can be tailored fairly arbitrarily, and other versions of GPS would not try to use R6 and R7 in this situation. The important finding involves the general character of the subject's performance, involving goals related to differences between the current expression and the problem goal and subgoals to make operators applicable. The protocol provides several clear illustrations of activities that are consistent with the hypothesis of a GPS-like problem-solving process.

## PROBLEM BEHAVIOR GRAPHS

It is important to consider whether activities like those in Table 9.1 are typical of problem solvers or are relatively rare. Newell and Simon addressed this question by examining Problem

**Table 9.1. Comparison of GPS with protocol data**
*Source*: (Newell & Simon, 1972)

| GPS trace | Subject protocol |
|---|---|
| L0: $\sim (\sim Q \cdot P)$ | |
| L1: $(R \supset \sim P) \cdot (\sim R \supset Q)$ | |
| Goal 1: Transform L1 into L0 | |
| Goal 2: Delete R from L1 | |
| . | |
| . | |
| . | |
| . | |
| Goal 2: (reinstated) | Now I'm looking for a way to get rid |
| Goal 9: Apply R7 to L1 | of the horseshoe inside the two |
| Goal 10: Change connective to $\vee$ | brackets that appear on the left |
| in left (L1) | and right sides of the equation. |
| Goal 11: Apply R6 to left (L1) | And I don't see it. |
| Produce L4: | Yeh, if you apply R6 to both sides |
| $(\sim R \vee \sim P) \cdot (\sim R \supset Q)$ | of the equation, |
| | From there I'm going to see if I can |
| | apply R7. |
| | [E writes L2: $(\sim R \vee \sim P) \cdot (R \vee Q)$] |
| Goal 12: Apply R7 to L4 | I can almost apply R7, but one R needs |
| Goal 13: Change connective to $\vee$ | a tilde. So I'll have to look for |
| in right (L4) | another rule. |
| Goal 14: Apply R6 to | I'm going to see if I can change that R to |
| right (L4) | a tilde R. As a matter of fact, I should |
| Produce L5: | have used R6 on only the left hand side |
| $(\sim R \vee \sim P) \cdot (R \vee Q)$ | of the equation. So use R6, but only on |
| | the left hand side. |
| | [E writes L3: $(\sim R \vee \sim P) \cdot (\sim R \supset Q)$] |
| Goal 15: Apply R7 to L5 | Now I'll apply R7 as it is expressed. |
| Goal 16: Change sign of | Both... excuse me, excuse me, it can't be |
| left (right (L4)) | done because of the horseshoe. So... |
| Goal 17: Apply R6 to | now I'm looking... scanning the rules |
| right (L5) | here for a second, and seeing if I |
| Produce L6: | can change the R to a $\sim$ R in the second |
| $(\sim R \vee \sim P) \cdot (\sim R \supset Q)$ | equation, but I don't see any way of |
| | doing it. |
| | (Sigh) I'm just sort of lost for a second. |
| Goal 18: Apply R7 to L6 | |
| Goal 19: Change connective to | |
| $\vee$ in right (L6) | |
| Reject | |
| Goal 16: (reinstated) | |
| Nothing more | |
| Goal 13: (reinstated) | |
| Nothing more | |
| Goal 10: (reinstated) | |
| Nothing more | |

*Note.* From Allen Newell, Herbert A. Simon, HUMAN PROBLEM SOLVING, (c) 1972, p. 482. Adapted by permission of Prentice-Hall, Inc., Englewood Cliffs, NJ.

Behavior Graphs (PBGs) obtained from the protocols of several subjects working on a moderately difficult problem.

An example of a PBG is shown in Figure 9.1. The numbers prefixed by B on the left, correspond to lines of the transcribed protocol. This PBG was obtained from the protocol that includes the segment given in Table 9.1, which corresponds to the section of the PBG starting at B10 and ending just before B29. Information included in the cognitive states is in the rectangles; operators are shown on the lines that connect

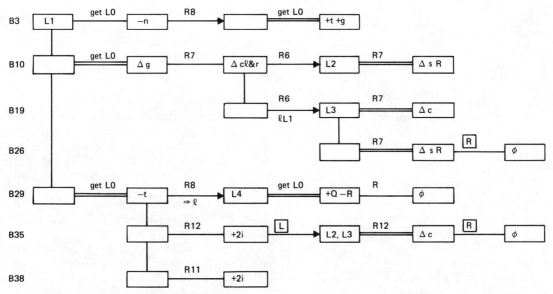

**Figure 9.1.** Problem behavior graph for a protocol, including the segment in Table 9.1. From Allen Newell, Herbert A. Simon, HUMAN PROBLEM SOLVING, (c) 1972, p. 468. Adapted by permission of Prentice-Hall, Inc., Englewood Cliffs, NJ.

the rectangles. Information in the rectangles refers to new expressions that were written (e.g., L2 or L3 in the protocol), or differences between a current expression and the goal that the subject was considering. For example '$\Delta$g' refers to a difference in grouping of terms and '$\Delta$c $\ell$ & r' refers to the differences between connectives in the given expression and the goal of applying R7 (horseshoes in both the left and right sides of L1 and wedges or dots needed to apply R7).

Most of the operators refer to the rules; we mentioned R6 and R7 earlier. When a rule is applied successfully, there is an arrowhead on the line between rectangles. A rule shown with a line but no arrowhead indicates that there was a goal of applying the rule but it was not achieved. Double lines indicate repeated attempts to apply rules.

The relation between the protocol and the PBG can be illustrated by examining the first few lines of Table 9.1 and the PBG starting at B10. The instruction "get L0" refers to consideration of the goal; this led to recognition of the difference in grouping between L0 and L1 ($\Delta$g). The subject then attempted to apply R7; this led to identifying the differences in connectives noted in the third rectangle ($\Delta$c $\ell$ & r). An attempt to apply R6 was then successful, resulting in line L2. The subject attempted to apply R7

a second time and noticed that there was a difference in the signs of the R terms in the two subexpressions ($\Delta$sR). From time to time, the subject returned to an earlier state, as when he decided that R6 should be applied only to the left side of L1. This is indicated by a vertical line drawn down from the cognitive state that the subject returned to. The rule R6 was applied to the left subexpression of L1, giving line L3; then R7 was attempted again, but the subject noticed the horseshoe, an incorrect connective for R7. The subject returned to the goal of changing the sign of R in expression L2, but the search for an appropriate rule (indicated by R in a box) failed to produce anything helpful.

PBGs were compiled from protocols of seven subjects working on the problem in Table 9.1. The transitions between states were classified, and the categories were compared with activities that occur when GPS works on a problem. The categories, and their frequencies in the seven PBGs, are shown in Table 9.2. Frequencies in the second and third columns of Table 9.2 are for subcategories of the categories in columns to the left. For example, the 258 occurrences of means–ends analysis consisted of 89 steps toward goal objects, 151 steps involving operator applicability, and 18 steps to avoid consequences.

Most of the categories shown in the table

**Table 9.2. Total frequencies of occurrences of GPS-like mechanisms in seven protocols**
*Source*: (Newell & Simon, 1972).

| Category | Frequency | | |
|---|---|---|---|
| Means–ends analysis | 258 | | |
| towards goal object | | 89 | |
| operator applicability | | 151 | |
| overcome difficulty | | | 143 |
| further specify | | | 5 |
| resolve uncertainty | | | 3 |
| *avoid consequences | | 18 | |
| avoid difficulty | | | 17 |
| prepare desired result | | | 1 |
| Working forward | 41 | | |
| systematic scan and evaluate | | 37 | |
| input form similarity | | 3 | |
| do something different | | 1 | |
| Working backward | 2 | | |
| output form similarity | | 2 | |
| Repeated application | 230 | | |
| after subgoal | | 93 | |
| to overcome difficulty | | | 58 |
| to further specify | | | 11 |
| to resolve uncertainty | | | 2 |
| to avoid consequences | | | 12 |
| to correct error | | | 8 |
| to process interruption | | | 2 |
| implementation | | 97 | |
| for plan | | | 84 |
| *to command experimenter | | | 13 |
| *review | | 40 | |
| Other | 27 | | |
| *noticing | | 6 | |
| *repeated application | | 11 | |
| *new application | | 10 | |
| Total | 558 | | |

*Note.* From Allen Newell, Herbert A. Simon, HUMAN PROBLEM SOLVING, (c) 1972, p. 493. Adapted by permission of Prentice-Hall, Inc., Englewood Cliffs, NJ.

correspond to GPS-like activities. Those that do not are marked with asterisks, accounting for about 18 percent of the transitions in the PBGs. The most interesting discrepancies involved choice of operators to avoid undesirable consequences ('*avoid consequences*'), and the noticing of features of the problem not related to the present goal ('*noticing*'). Simulation of these would require significant additions to the problem-solving processes of GPS. The remaining discrepancies involve activities that relate to the requirement of giving protocols ('*command*

*experimenter*' and '*review*') or points in the protocol where there was insufficient information to determine whether the transition was related to one of the GPS-like categories ('*other*,' except for those in the subcategory *noticing*).

AGGREGATE FREQUENCIES

The data in Table 9.2 were obtained from a small group of subjects who were required to think aloud as they worked. It is possible that the subjects were atypical, or that the instruction to think aloud caused major distortions in the problem-solving method.

Newell and Simon compared some summary statistics from their subjects with data obtained by Carpenter et al. (1961) at Yale University. The larger number of subjects run at Yale (64) solved the problems with pencil and paper, without thinking aloud. If the data for the Carnegie subjects do not differ from the Yale data in significant ways, then there is evidence that the general characteristics of their problem solving were not caused by individual idiosyncracies, or by the requirement of verbalizing protocols while working on the problems.

The summary statistics involved a division of expressions into categories. Each category consists of an expression from the problem, such as the left subexpression of expression L1, and other expressions that can be formed from it by making minor transformations. Minor transformations for this purpose are those involving rules that change the order of terms, the connectives, or the signs, but do not change the terms in an expression. The data for each group of subjects are the proportions of all the expressions written that fall into the categories. The categories of expressions are listed in the left column. For example, expressions in Class L1 are those that can be formed by applying one of the minor transformations to expression L1 as shown in Table 9.1. The categories used are not arbitrary; they are motivated by the observation that differences that depend on changing the terms in expressions are more difficult to remove, and thus, require higher priority in solving the problems.

Data for the problem in Table 9.1 are shown in Table 9.3. The comparison of the two groups of subjects does not show exact agreement but indicates no major differences in their problem-solving processes. A statistical test shows that the difference between the category frequencies

**Table 9.3.   Proportions of expressions**

| Class of expressions | Carnegie (78 expressions) | Yale (519 expressions) |
|---|---|---|
| L1 | .37 | .29 |
| Left of L1 | .14 | .16 |
| Right of L1 | .12 | .22 |
| L0 | .24 | .17 |
| Other | .13 | .16 |

in the two groups was not significant $[\chi^2(4) = 8.86; p > .05]$. (The independence assumption of the chi-square test was not met in these data, since several expressions were written by each subject. However, this would generally make it more likely that a significant difference would be obtained, so the conclusion seems warranted.)

Data are shown in Table 9.4 for a somewhat harder problem, in which the given expression was L1 = $(P \vee Q) \cdot (Q \supset R)$, and the goal was L0 = $P \vee (Q \cdot R)$. Again, the agreement is not exact, but the difference is not large enough to reject the hypothesis that the two sets of responses were produced by a single underlying process $[\chi^2(8) = 15.27, p > .05]$.

PLANNING STRATEGY

A second strategy of broad applicability and wide use that was identified in the logic protocols is *planning*. Its underlying idea is that some gaps between the initial situation and the goal are more important and potentially harder to remove than others. If the problem space is simplified by abstracting the problem expressions—removing from them the less important features—the

**Table 9.4.   Proportions of expressions**

| Class of expressions | Carnegie (97 expressions) | Yale (487 expressions) |
|---|---|---|
| L1 | .33 | .28 |
| Extended L1 | .02 | .04 |
| Left of L1 | .14 | .19 |
| Right of L1 | .14 | .15 |
| $(R \vee P)$ | .13 | .07 |
| $(P \vee Q) \cdot (P \vee R)$ | .03 | .01 |
| L0 | .03 | .01 |
| Rule 9 | .16 | .18 |
| Other | .01 | .07 |

simplified expressions will define a much smaller space through which the search can be conducted expeditiously. If a solution can be found to the simplified problem, the omitted details can be restored and this solution is used as a guide for searching in the original problem space.

To use the planning strategy subjects not only must be able to apply means–ends analysis, but must have enough knowledge of the problem space to be able to distinguish important from unimportant differences between expressions. For example, in the domain of logic, subjects gradually learn that it is easier to change the connectives in logic expressions than to change the letters. The planning space is then a space in which expressions like $(R \supset \sim P) \cdot (\sim R \supset Q)$ are replaced by $(RP)(RQ)$. The sequences of proof steps in the original space, $R \supset \sim P$, $\sim R \supset Q$, $\sim Q \supset R$, $\sim Q \supset \sim P$, $Q \vee \sim P$, $\sim (\sim Q \cdot P)$, becomes the simpler sequence in the planning space, $RP, RQ, PQ$. The second step of the search in the planning space corresponds to two separate steps in the original space, and the third step in the planning space corresponds to three steps in the original space—a reduction of one-half in the length of the derivation, and of a much larger factor in the amount of search required to find it.

Evidence for planning was obtained in protocols like the following, obtained in a problem with four given expressions: L1 = $P \vee Q$; L2 = $\sim R \supset \sim Q$; L3 = $S$; L4 = $R \supset \sim S$; and the goal: L0 = $P \vee T$. Rule R9, mentioned in the protocol, is $A \rightarrow A \vee X$, a rule for adding a term to an expression.

Well, one possibility right off the bat is when you have just a $P \vee T$ like that the last thing you might use is that R9. I can get everything down to a $P$ and just add a $\vee T$. So that's the one thing to keep in mind.

Well, maybe right off the bat, I'm kinda jumping into it, I maybe can work everything down to just a $P$; I dunno if that's possible. But I think it is, because I see that steps 2 and 4 are somewhat similar; if I can cancel out the $R$s, that would leave me with just an $S$ and $Q$; and if I have just an $S$ and $Q$, I can eventually get step 3, get the $S$s to cancel out and end up with just a $Q$; and if I end up with just a $Q$, maybe the $Q$s will cancel out; so you see, all the way down the line. I dunno, it looks too good to be true, but I think I see it already.

## Water-Jar Problems

Water-jar problems, studied extensively by Luchins (1942), are transformation problems with definite goals, involving a set of three jars of different capacities. In the form studied by Atwood and Polson (1976), the largest jar is full in the initial state, and the goal is for the water to be divided equally between two jars. For example, the capacities may be: jar A, 8 oz; jar B, 5 oz; jar C, 3 oz. Then in the initial state, jar A contains 8 oz of water, and jars B and C are empty. The goal is to have 4 oz of water each, in jars A and B. The problem-solving operators involve pouring water from a source jar into a target jar. Water can be poured into the target jar until it is full if there is enough water in the source jar; water can be poured out of the source jar until it is empty if there is enough room in the target jar. Intermediate actions are not possible.

In the water-jar task, differences between any state and the problem goal consist of discrepancies between the contents of the three jars in that state and the contents that are specified in the goal. Atwood and Polson hypothesized that subjects would judge their progress by combining the discrepancies, forming an overall *evaluation function* for the current state, and would try to select moves that would improve the value of this function. They assumed that the evaluation of a specific state $i$ was

$$e_i = |C_i(A) - G(A)| + |C_i(B) - G(B)|,$$

where $C_i(A)$ and $C_i(B)$ are the actual contents of jar A and jar B in state $i$ and $G(A)$ and $G(B)$ are the contents of jar A and jar B in the goal state. (The contents of jar C are redundant with those of A and B.)

Atwood and Polson formulated a process model, based on the means–ends strategy of attempting to reduce the evaluation to zero. They assumed that at each move, subjects would consider various pouring operations that could be made legally and would try to choose one that would make the evaluation function smaller, or at least would not increase its current value by more than a threshold amount. This strategy differs from the means–ends strategy of GPS in one significant respect: GPS considers all the ways in which the current state and the goal differ and selects a move to reduce the most important of these qualitative differences. Atwood and Polson's model combines the dif-

ferences into a single numerical index—the value of the evaluation function—and tries to reduce that difference by at least a threshold amount. This difference probably does not have a significant effect on predictions of performance in the water-jar task, but there are situations in which strategies based on global evaluations and on individual qualitative differences would lead to significantly different performance.

Atwood and Polson also made specific assumptions about memory capacity; they assumed that a limited short-term memory would hold information about states that would be produced by alternative moves, and that each state reached in solving the problem would be stored in long-term memory with a fixed probability.

The model also specifies a sequence of processes for selecting a move. The sequence includes calculating the evaluation function for alternative moves, storing information about alternatives in STM, recognizing states that have occurred before on the basis of information in LTM, and deciding whether to make a given move under consideration. The assumptions of the model allow for several possibilities: (1) A move may be selected if it leads to an acceptable state (this was assumed to be less likely if the state was recognized as having occurred before); (2) the moves stored in STM may be examined, with a selection of those stored in LTM from previous occurrences; (3) a move may be chosen at random from the set of possible moves; or (4) the subject may decide to return to the initial state of the problem.

Atwood and Polson tested their model with data from human subjects who solved different versions of the problem. Problems were presented at computer terminals, and the moves made by each subject were recorded. The model was implemented as a computer program which was run with various values of the parameters, but because it contains probabilistic processes, it does not produce a single sequence of moves in solving a problem. The model was run many times with each set of parameter values, and its performance was summarized by the average frequency of each of the possible problem states. The parameter values were chosen for which the set of frequencies for two problems (jar sizes of 8, 5, 3 oz. and of 24, 21, 3 oz.) that approximated the frequencies obtained from the human subjects. These parameter values seem quite reasonable. The size of STM was set at three alternative moves; states reached in the problem were stored in LTM with a probability of .90; and the threshold of acceptability for a new state was set at 1.0 above the value of the current state.

Results of the simulation are shown in Figure 9.2. Each set of predictions was based on running the model 250 times. The data for each problem came from a group of about 40 subjects and were different from the data used to estimate the parameters, for which only one problem (8, 5, 3) was used. The model correctly predicted the order of difficulty of the four problems. For two problems, Figure 9.2a and 9.2b, the detailed predictions of response frequency were not significantly different from the data by a statistical test. In the two harder problems, Figure 2c and 2d, the general shapes of the frequency distributions agreed with the data, but the model erred by predicting too many returns to states at the beginning of a path that led to the goal. As Atwood and Polson noted, this defect could be corrected by assuming that the probability of recognizing a previous state depends on the number of times it has been encountered.

### Conclusions

Problem solving in situations that are novel to the problem solver, in which a definite goal and a set of legal problem-solving operators are described by the instructions, requires some general problem-solving strategy. In situations of this kind the strategy of means–ends analysis represents the major feature of human problem-solving performance. The evidence discussed in this section consists of individual thinking-aloud protocols and aggregate response frequencies in two tasks. Findings that fit this general pattern have been obtained in a wide range of problem-solving tasks, including puzzles such as the Tower of Hanoi (Anzai & Simon, 1979) and physics textbook problems (Simon & Simon, 1978), which are discussed below in "Problems with Specified Procedures."

Means–ends analysis is perhaps the single most important strategy that people employ to search selectively through large problem spaces. The selectivity is powerful because it points search in the direction of the goal, selecting operators on the basis of their relevance to reducing the distance from that goal. Use of means–ends analysis requires some domain-specific knowledge; for example, it can be employed efficiently only if the subject has learned enough about the problem domain to associate particular differences with particular operators that remove them. However, it is basically a weak method, applicable in situations where the problem solver has little specific knowledge based on experience in the problem domain.

## Domain-Specific Knowledge for Familiar Problems with Specified Goals

We now turn to problems solved by individuals who have specialized knowledge, acquired either through instruction or practice. The first subsection concerns problem solving in a domain of school mathematics—high school geometry. We will then discuss problem-solving set or Einstellung, which we interpret as resulting from domain-specific knowledge structures.

### Geometry Exercises

In school subjects such as geometry, the knowledge for solving problems is imparted intentionally, through instruction. Research conducted by Greeno (1978) had the goal of investigating and characterizing the knowledge that is acquired by students who learn successfully in the course.

The main data were obtained in a series of interviews conducted weekly with six students who were taking a standard high school geometry course. In each interview, an individual student worked for about 20 minutes to solve three or four problems. Most of the problems were typical of homework or test problems that the class was working on at the time. Students were asked to think aloud as they worked, and their protocols were recorded and transcribed.

One of the problems solved in an early session (during the second month of the course) is shown in Figure 9.3. The problem as it was presented is shown in Figure 3a. The upper right diagram (in Figure 3b) provides notation for referring to the various angles in diagram (3a). The seven steps shown below the diagrams are a formal solution with inferences and justifying reasons. The students were not required to write the solution steps of this problem formally but they were required to state aloud the intermediate inferences they made. Most of the students solved the problem in Figure 9.3 correctly. Specific aspects of their solutions are discussed

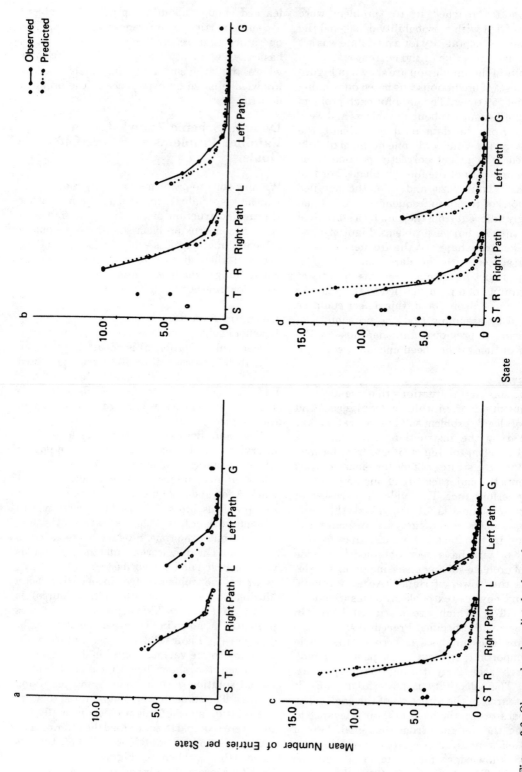

**Figure 9.2.** Observed and predicted values of mean visits per state for four water-jar problems. (a) problems 8, 5, 3; (b) 12, 7, 4; (c) 14, 9, 5; (d) 16, 10, 3. From "A Process Model for Water Jug Problems" by M.E. Atwood and P.G. Polsen, 1976, *Cognitive Psychology*, 8, pp. 206–207. Copyright 1976 by Academic Press. Adapted by permmission.

604

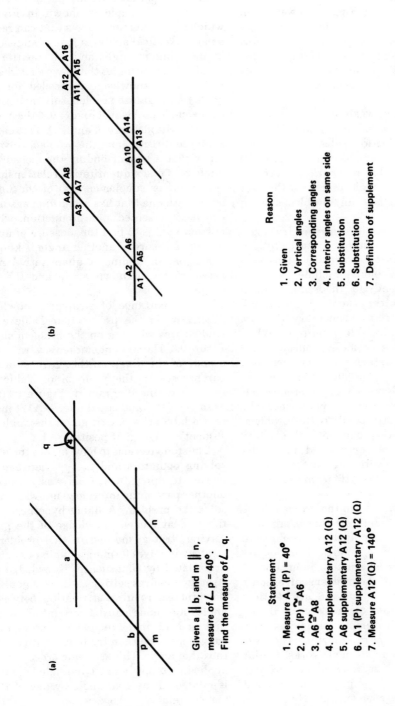

(a)

(b)

Given a ∥ b, and m ∥ n,
measure of ∠ p = 40°.
Find the measure of ∠ q.

**Statement**

1. Measure A1 (P) = 40°
2. A1 (P) ≅ A6
3. A6 ≅ A8
4. A8 supplementary A12 (Q)
5. A6 supplementary A12 (Q)
6. A1 (P) supplementary A12 (Q)
7. Measure A12 (Q) = 140°

**Reason**

1. Given
2. Vertical angles
3. Corresponding angles
4. Interior angles on same side
5. Substitution
6. Substitution
7. Definition of supplement

**Figure 9.3.** A solved problem in geometry. A1, A6, etc., in the solution refer to the positions of angles in the upper right diagram.

below. They are generally similar to the solution shown in Figure 9.3.

The solution shown in Figure 9.3 was given by a computational model called Perdix that was formulated to simulate the students' performance. The structures and processes represented in Perdix are hypotheses about the knowledge that students acquire in a geometry course.

PROBLEM-SOLVING KNOWLEDGE

Perdix contains three kinds of knowledge, all represented as production rules: (1) problem-solving operators that make inferences, (2) perceptual concepts that recognize patterns in diagrams, and (3) strategic processes that set goals and select plans for problem-solving activities.

Problem-solving operators in geometry correspond to the theorems, postulates, and definitions that are used as reasons to justify steps in a problem solution. Examples include "Vertical angles are congruent" (a theorem), "Corresponding angles are congruent" (a postulate), and "If two angles are supplementary, the sum of their measures is 180°" (a definition). When the antecedent of one of these propositions is satisfied in a problem, then the consequent can be inferred. For example, because $A1$ and $A6$ are vertical angles in Figure 9.3, the inference that $A1$ and $A6$ are congruent is permitted. The propositions that correspond to the problem-solving operators are prominent in geometry instruction. They are represented in Perdix as production rules, with the antecedents as conditions and the relations that can be inferred as actions.

Patterns of information in the problem have to be recognized to determine that a problem-solving operator can be applied. For example, to apply the inference rule, "Vertical angles are congruent," in Figure 9.3 and thus infer that $A1$ and $A6$ are congruent, the problem solver must first recognize that $A1$ and $A6$ are vertical angles. In the geometry course, perceptual concepts are taught with examples using diagrams. In Perdix, knowledge for recognizing patterns is represented by discrimination networks, similar to the structures in the *Elementary Perceiver and Memorizer*, EPAM (Feigenbaum, 1963) and the *Concept Learning System*, CLS (Hunt et al., 1966). Perdix's recognition system is based on features of a diagram, such as sides of two angles that are collinear, along with other

information that may be given or inferred, such as statements that lines are parallel or perpendicular. An example is shown in Figure 9.4 which represents the process that can recognize a pair of vertical angles, a pair of angles formed by bisecting an angle, and other patterns that involve pairs of angles that have a single vertex.

Strategic knowledge is needed for setting goals that organize problem-solving activity. In the example problem of Figure 9.3, the main goal is to find the measure of angle Q. This cannot be achieved directly, and the problem solver must know that a way of finding the measure of an angle is to find a quantitative relationship (e.g., congruent or supplementary) of the unknown angle with one that has a known measure. This can be represented as a production: when the current goal is to find the measure of an angle, and the measure of another angle is known, set a subgoal of finding a quantitative relation between the unknown angle and the known angle.

The importance of strategic knowledge is illustrated in the protocol in Table 9.5. The student was working on the problem shown in Figure 9.3. The student marked several angles in a copy of the diagram; these are indicated in parentheses in the protocol of Table 9.5 in relation to the diagram in Figure 9.3(b). For example, "$P$ would equal one ($\rightarrow A1$)" indicates that a label '1' was written on the angle in the student's diagram at position $A1$.

The student seems to have known the problem-solving operators and the geometric patterns needed to apply them (this was confirmed in another part of the interview) but was unable to solve the problem. A likely hypothesis is that the student lacked knowledge of the problem-solving strategy needed in this problem. The strategy involves forming a chain of angles that are related by congruence. Knowledge of this strategy involves setting a series of goals; when the problem requires a relation between two angles and none can be recognized, one must first find an angle related to one of them by congruence and then try to relate that angle to the other angle. This strategic procedure can be applied recursively until an angle is found that is related to the goal angle by one of the geometric relations from which a quantitative relation can be inferred.

Four of the six students who were interviewed in Greeno's study solved the problem in

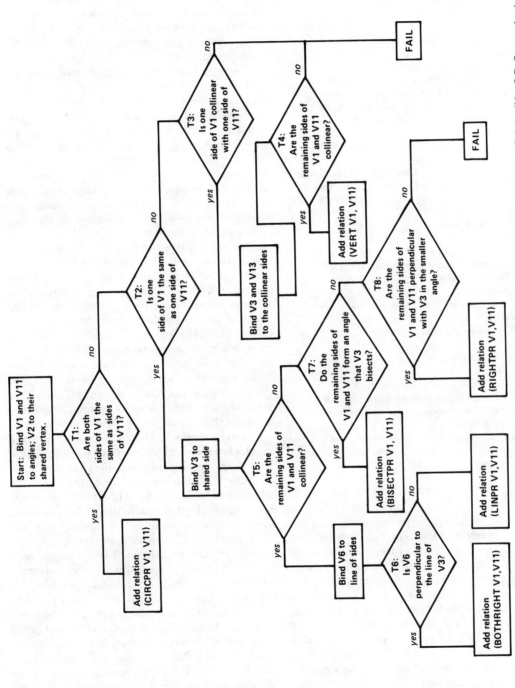

**Figure 9.4.** Pattern recognizing system in Perdix for analyzing angles with a shared vertex. From "A Study of Problem Solving" by J.G. Greeno in *Advances in Instructional Psychology: Vol. 1* (p. 21), R. Glaser (Ed.), 1978. Hillsdale, NJ: Erlbaum. Copyright 1978 by Lawrence Erlbaum Associates. Reprinted by permission.

**Table 9.5. Protocol of an attempt to solve Figure 9.3**

S:  All right, I would put, like, P would equal one (→A1).
E:  Okay.
S:  And then, two (→A6).
E:  Put in two there, right.
S:  And then three (→A15); no, wait—three (→A15) and four (→A12), I guess.
E:  Okay. Now, why did you put two there?
S:  Well, I don't know. It could have something to do with vertical angles.
E:  Okay.

...

S:  All right, the first thing I guess I should try to do, I would try to find if there were any alternate interior or corresponding angles?
E:  Okay.
S:  Or any of those.
E:  Mm-hm.
S:  I guess I would say that . . . well, wait a minute. I guess maybe I would put five there (→A16).
E:  Okay.
S:  I don't know if I would need this.
E:  Okay.
S:  These two are supplementary.
E:  Right.
S:  That doesn't help much. And then, the measure of angle five . . . would it equal the measure of angle one?
E:  Well, you might have to work that out.
S:  How . . . if this equals . . . this equals forty.
E:  That's right.
S:  Oh, all right. Wait, the measure . . . I can't, I don't know. I don't know how to do these.
E:  Okay.

Figure 9.3 successfully, apparently applying the strategy of forming a chain of congruent angles. The students used different specific sequences of angles, which could result from differences in the way they scanned the diagram looking for angles to add to the chain, or differences in the ease with which they recognized various geometric patterns. About a week after one unsuccessful student gave the protocol in Table 9.5, that student successfully solved a different problem that also required the chaining strategy.

In geometry instruction, very little strategic knowledge is taught explicitly; it has to be inferred by the students from example problems. Inference appears to be a common feature of

instruction in domains requiring acquisition of knowledge for problem solving, and, in the light of results of basic research on cognitive processes in problem solving, we consider the explicit teaching of problem-solving strategies to be a potentially productive development for instruction.

Strategic knowledge is represented in Perdix by productions that select plans for work on problems. A *plan* is a general approach to the problem, based on information in the problem situation. GPS forms such plans using its general planning strategy, described on page 601. Perdix has specific cognitive structures for plans that are used frequently for geometry problems. Forming a chain of congruent angles is one such plan. Another is using congruent triangles to prove that two angles or two line segments are congruent.

The organization of planning knowledge in Perdix is similar to that developed by Sacerdoti (1977), called a *procedural network*. In a procedural network, there are units of knowledge corresponding to actions at different levels. Each of these knowledge units includes information about the prerequisites and consequences of an action that can be performed. In Perdix, knowledge of each plan includes information about goals that can be achieved using the plan (its consequences), conditions in problems that make the plan promising (its prerequisites), and subgoals that should be set if the plan is adopted.

Perdix's strategic knowledge constitutes the main way in which it differs from GPS. Strategic knowledge in GPS is the general means–ends strategy that can be used in any domain for which the problem solver is taught the operators together with the productions that connect operators with differences, and is given the goal of a problem. The hypothesis represented in Perdix is that instruction in a domain such as geometry leads to acquisition of strategic knowledge specific to that domain, such as the schematic knowledge that represents plans to use chains of congruent angles or congruent triangles. Both GPS and Perdix construct plans that are more general than the actions that must be performed in solving the problem. The difference is that GPS forms plans using its general means–ends strategy, whereas Perdix's plans are based on knowledge of specific geometry strategies.

When GPS plans, it uses the strategic process

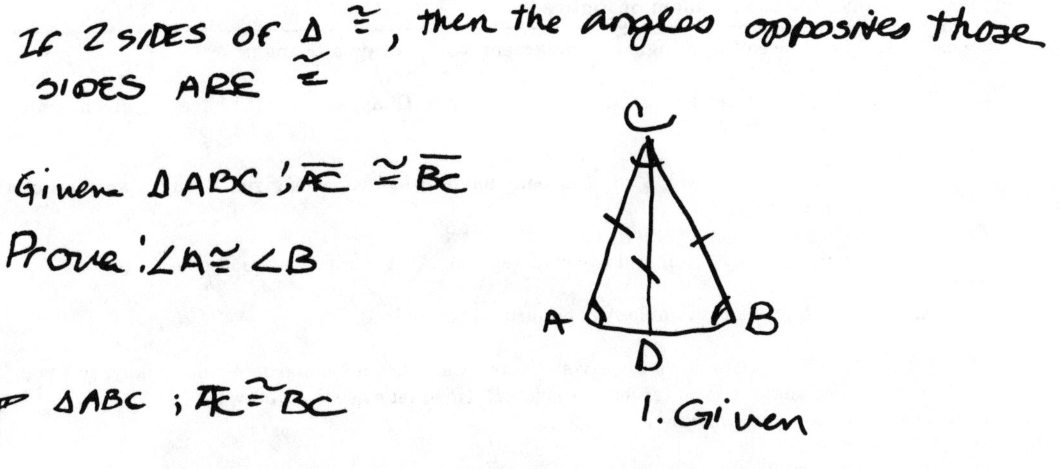

*If 2 SIDES OF Δ ≅, then the angles opposite those SIDES ARE ≅*

*Given ΔABC; AC̅ ≅ BC̅*

*Prove: ∠A ≅ ∠B*

*1. ΔABC ; AC̅ ≅ BC̅*
*2.*

*1. Given*

**Figure 9.5.** Written work and drawing by a student on the problem, "Prove that if two sides of a triangle are congruent then the angles opposite those sides are congruent. From "Theory of Constructions and Set in Problem Solving" by J.G. Greeno, M.E. Magone, and S. Chaiklin, 1979, *Memory and Cognition*, 7, p. 447. Copyright 1979 by the Psychonomic Society. Reprinted by permission.

of means–ends analysis in a problem space that contains features taken directly from the basic representation of the problem. The planning space of GPS can be acquired by learning which features of objects should be given first priority. In Perdix, planning uses schematic knowledge of specific methods applicable to problems in the domain of geometry. These schemata include general subgoals, such as proving that triangles are congruent or finding an angle with a relation based on parallel sides, that can be used as intermediate steps. The associations of these subgoals with the goals they help to achieve have to be acquired by students; they are not explicitly given as goals of problems in which they are used.

SOLUTION OF ILL-STRUCTURED PROBLEMS
A hypothesis that is consistent with the analysis of geometry problem solving is that domain-specific strategic knowledge may provide the main basis for solving ill-structured problems. Problems may lack definite structure for many reasons. One important source of indefinite structure is that a problem may require knowledge from several different sources, with the result that its solution requires coordinated work in several disparate problem spaces (Simon, 1973).

A modest form of this kind of problem arises in geometry, involving problems that require

construction of auxiliary lines. The problem space that is presented, including a diagram, given information, and a goal to be proved, must be augmented in order for the problem to be solved. Greeno, Magone, and Chaiklin (1979) proposed that the solutions of such problems can be based on an individual's knowledge of plan schemata. In the Perdix model the need for an auxiliary line is recognized when a plan's prerequisites are partly satisfied in the problem situation. This leads to the definition of a subproblem; the goal is to complete the pattern of features that constitute the prerequisites, which is achieved in a problem space with operators appropriate to that goal.

An example is shown in Figure 9.5, the drawing and written work of a student on the following problem: Prove that if two sides of a triangle are congruent, then the angles opposite those sides are congruent. The protocol given by this student is in Table 9.6. After drawing the triangle ABC, the student added the line CD, which is not specified in the initial problem space. The student's comments at *1 and *2, along with the retrospective comment at *3, provide evidence that construction of the auxiliary line was related to a plan of proof involving congruent triangles, and the construction completed a pattern that is required for that plan to be applied—that is, the presence of two triangles in the diagram. Perdix simulates solutions like

**Table 9.6.    Protocol for the problem of Figure 9.4**

|  |  |  |
|---|---|---|
|  | S: | Okay, if two sides of a triangle are congruent, so . . . draw a triangle. |
|  | E: | Okay. |
|  | S: | Then the angles opposite those sides are congruent. Okay, so, like, if I have . . . given: triangle ABC—I'll letter it ABC. |
|  | E: | Right. |
|  | S: | And then I have . . . prove: . . . do I already have these two sides given? Okay. Two sides of a triangle are given. |
|  | E: | Mmm-hmm. |
|  | S: | Let me go back to my given and say that segment AC is congruent to segment BC. |
|  | E: | Okay. |
|  | S: | And I want to prove that angle A is congruent to angle B. |
|  | E: | Good. |
|  | S: | All right. Let me write down my given. Okay. And mark my congruent sides. Okay, so I want to prove that angle A is congruent to angle B. Now, let's see. Do you want . . . ? |
|  | E: | Yeah. Why are you drawing a line there? |
| *1 | S: | I don't know yet. |
|  | E: | Oh, that's okay. Don't erase it. |
|  | S: | I'm going to do it, no, I just . . . |
|  | E: | Oh, okay, fine. |
|  | S: | Okay . . . okay, then I could . . . if I drew a line . . . |
|  | E: | Mmm-hmm. |
| *2 | S: | That would be the bisector of angle ACB, and that would give me . . . those congruent angles . . . no. (Pause.) Yeah, well, that would give me those congruent angles, but I could have the reflexive property, so this would be equal to that. Okay, I've got it. |
|  | E: | Okay. |
|  | S: | Okay. |
|  | E: | Now, before you go ahead and write it all down, when you said you were going to draw the line . . . |
|  | S: | Yeah. |
|  | E: | And I said why are you doing that, and you said you didn't know yet, what do you think happened to give you the idea of making it the bisector? |
| *3 | S: | Okay, well, I have to try to get this . . . I have to try to get triangle ACD congruent to BCD. Because, if I do that, then angle A is congruent to angle B because corresponding parts of congruent triangles are congruent. |
|  | E: | So you were drawing the line to give yourself triangles, is that the idea? |
| *4 | S: | No, to . . . to get a side that was in both triangles. |
|  | E: | Okay. |
|  | S: | And to get congruent angles. |
|  | E: | So that's why you drew it as the bisector. |
|  | S: | Yeah. |

this with a process of pattern recognition that identifies partial patterns of two triangles missing a line, and uses special problem-solving operators to complete the patterns.

Another way in which problems can be ill structured involves the way in which goals are formulated. Goals in well-structured problems are presented as specific objects (e.g., a specific logic expression to be derived or a specific distribution of water among some jars). In ill-structured problems, goals are often underdetermined, with several alternative ways in which they might be satisfied. Examples are frequently cited from art or science, such as the goal of composing a fugue, or of designing an interesting experiment. In school geometry, the goals of problems are usually well specified, but a subgoal that arises in many problems functions as an indefinite goal for experienced problem solvers. This is the goal of proving that two triangles are congruent. There are several ways in which congruence of triangles can be proved, involving different patterns of congruent components such as side–side–side, side–angle–side, and so on. Beginning learners treat these as definite subgoals, trying one after another until one works (Anderson, Greeno, Kline, & Neves, 1981). More experienced students do not mention specific patterns in their protocols, and appear to engage in a relatively diffuse search for congruent components of triangles with a kind of monitor that identifies whatever pattern of congruent components happens to emerge. Greeno (1976) hypothesized that experienced students acquire an integrated structure of knowledge in the form of a pattern-recognizing system that represents the goal of proving that triangles are congruent. A version of this that was implemented in Perdix is shown in Figure 9.6.

### ACQUISITION OF PROBLEM-SOLVING SKILL

An important question is how the knowledge that is needed for solving problems in a domain such as geometry is acquired. Studies of learning involving the three kinds of knowledge needed for problem solving have been undertaken: these are problem-solving operators, perceptual concepts for pattern recognition, and strategic knowledge.

Anderson (1982) based an analysis of problem-solving operators on observations of three students as they studied and worked problems in the early sections of a geometry text. He simulated processes of acquiring problem-solving skill in a version of his ACT model (cf. Anderson, 1983).

A major aspect of Anderson's model is a process that acquires cognitive procedures from declarative information. This model learns new procedures by working on problems. When ACT encounters a problem for which it has not learned a procedure, it uses general problem-solving methods along with information that is available. For example, a geometry problem may require finding a theorem that can justify a step in a proof. The ACT model has a general procedure for searching in a list of theorems and for matching features of theorems to the information in a problem. When an applicable theorem is found, ACT asserts that theorem to solve that part of the problem.

ACT has a learning process called *procedur-alization*, which forms new production rules that are added to ACT's procedural knowledge. A new production can be formed when a theorem has been found and applied successfully in problem solving. The new production has conditions corresponding to selected features in the problem situation, and an action that asserts

the theorem. The production is a new problem-solving operator; ACT has acquired a new ability to assert a theorem in appropriate conditions without having to search through the list of theorems in the text. It has learned the theorem, not in the sense of having memorized it, but in the sense of being able to recognize when it is applicable, and to apply it.

Acquisition of perceptual concepts for pattern recognition in problem solving was studied by Simon and Gilmartin (1973) in the domain of chess. The learning mechanism used was adapted from the EPAM model (Feigenbaum, 1963), which simulates acquisition of discrimination networks like that in Figure 9.4. Simon and Gilmartin developed an EPAM-type model that acquired knowledge of patterns of chess pieces from presentations of board positions. This knowledge was used to simulate performance in a task of reconstructing positions after brief presentations, a task known to differentiate among players according to their level of skill (Chase & Simon, 1973; deGroot, 1965; also see "Chess and Go").

Acquisition of strategic knowledge for solving problems has been studied empirically by Schoenfeld (1979). Four students in upper-division college mathematics courses were given special instruction in the use of five heuristic strategies for working on problems: drawing a diagram, arguing by induction, arguing by contradiction or contraposition, considering a simpler problem with fewer variables, and establishing subgoals. Each strategy was presented in a training session, lasting about one hour, including an explanation of conditions in which the strategy is useful as well as practice in using the strategy. Students took a pretest and a posttest with problems not included in the training. These students had a list of the strategies available during the posttest and were reminded from time to time to try one of the strategies if they were not progressing well on a problem. Performance of these students was superior to that of another group of students who had worked on the same training problems as the instructed group, but without explanation of the strategies. Thinking-aloud protocols confirmed that students considered and used strategies that they had been trained to use. The training was especially effective with strategies that have clear cues for their application: the fewer-variables strategy, cued by the presence of many variables;

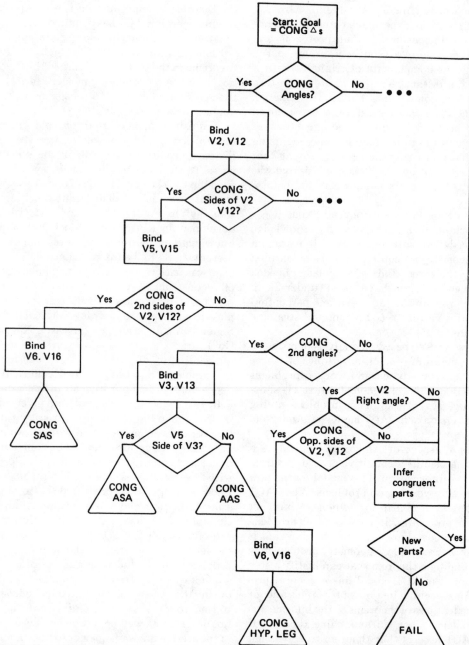

**Figure 9.6.** Part of Perdix's goal structure for proving congruence of triangles, represented as a pattern-recognizing system. Cong = congruent; SAS = side–angle–side; ASA = angle–side–angle; AAS = angle–angle–side; HYP, LEG = hypotenuse–leg. From "Indefinite Goals in Well-Structured Problems" by J.G. Greeno, 1976, *Psychological Review, 83,* p. 486. Copyright 1976 by the American Psychological Association. Adapted by permission of the author.

and arguing by induction, cued by an integer argument.

Processes of acquiring strategic knowledge have been addressed in theoretical analyses by Anzai and Simon (1979) and by Anderson, Farrell, and Sauers (1984). Anzai and Simon observed and simulated acquisition of a strategic concept in the Tower of Hanoi puzzle. The concept involves movement of a set of disks requiring a sequence of individual moves, with the sequence considered as a global action. Anderson et al. simulated the acquisition of knowledge for applying techniques in learning the programming language LISP. In both theoretical analyses, important factors in acquiring strategic knowledge are the activation of a problem goal that can be achieved by a sequence of actions and the acquisitions of a production in which the action of setting the goal is associated with appropriate conditions in the problem situation.

### Einstellung (Set)

The context in which problem solving occurs may have an important influence on the process. As a consequence of previous tasks that a subject has engaged in or previous stimuli that have been presented, certain responses may become more readily and speedily available and others less readily available. The subject has acquired a 'set' for the familiar stimuli and responses.

One experimental design that has often been used to demonstrate the effects of set is to present subjects with a sequence of tasks that induce set, then a new sequence of tasks in which this set either facilitates or impedes performance relative to that of control subjects who were not exposed to the first sequence. Luchins (1942) conducted a well-known set of experiments using this design, with water-jar tasks.

In Luchins's version of the water-jar task, subjects must measure a specified amount of water, using a given set of ungraduated measuring jars. A source of water is assumed to be available, so that any of the jars can be filled to its capacity if the subject so chooses. Water can be poured from one jar to another, until the target jar is filled or the source jar is empty. Also, the contents of the jar can be discarded.

The series of problems that Luchins used is shown in Table 9.7. All the problems except the first and the ninth can be solved by filling jar $B$, then pouring from it to fill $A$, and then filling $C$ twice ($X = B - A - 2C$). But problems 5, and 7 through 11, can also be solved using only jars $A$ and $C$—by either adding the contents of $C$ to the contents of $A$, or subtracting the contents of $C$ from $A$, and for problem 9, the $B - A - 2C$ procedure does not work.

Table 9.7. Problems used by Luchins (1942)

| Problem Number | Measuring Jugs | | | Required Amount |
|---|---|---|---|---|
| | A | B | C | |
| 1 | 29 | 3 | | 20 |
| 2 | 21 | 127 | 3 | 100 |
| 3 | 14 | 163 | 25 | 99 |
| 4 | 18 | 43 | 10 | 5 |
| 5 | 9 | 42 | 6 | 21 |
| 6 | 20 | 59 | 4 | 31 |
| 7 | 23 | 49 | 3 | 20 |
| 8 | 15 | 39 | 3 | 18 |
| 9 | 28 | 76 | 3 | 25 |
| 10 | 18 | 48 | 4 | 22 |
| 11 | 14 | 36 | 8 | 6 |

Subjects given problems 7 through 11 immediately after solving problem 1 generally use the two-jar procedure just described. Subjects who are first given problems 1 through 6 generally use the $B - A - 2C$ procedure, which is more complex than necessary for problems 7 through 11, and they have considerable difficulty with problem 9.

Set effects can be the result of several cognitive processes of which three that have been put forward will be discussed.

First, set may be the result of a bias in retrieving knowledge structures from memory. A standard assumption is that the alternative concepts or cognitive procedures that might be retrieved have varying strengths or levels of activation which determine the probabilities of their retrieval. If a cognitive unit has been used successfully several times in the immediate past, a relatively high level of activation for that unit results.

Schemata used in planning provide one kind of structure that can account for set. An example is in the domain of geometry, where Greeno et al. (1979) developed a simulation model with planning schemata, described above in "Geometry Exercises." Luchins (1942) included a study of geometry problem solving in his investigations of Einstellung. Figure 9.7 shows the kind of problem used as a test. The proof can be obtained in one step; $\angle AMC$ and $\angle BMD$ are vertical angles. However, if subjects were first given a series of problems where they used congruent triangles in proofs, they were likely to construct the more complex proof for Figure 9.7 in which triangles $AMC$ and $BMD$ are proved congruent by side–side–side. An explanation is provided if

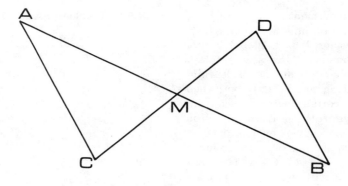

Given:   M is the midpoint of $\overline{AB}$ and $\overline{CD}$;
         $\overline{AC} \cong \overline{BD}$.

Prove:   $\angle AMC \cong \angle BMD$

**Figure 9.7.** An einstellung problem in geometry.

we assume that students have a schema corresponding to the plan of using congruent triangles for a proof, and that this schema has a high level of activation because of its use in the initial series of problems. Greeno et al. (1979) reported an experiment with a test problem that could be solved by using either congruent triangles or angles formed by a transversal with parallel lines, but either method required construction of an auxiliary line. Subjects were given series of problems to solve before the test problem, involving either congruent triangles or parallel lines. They were strongly biased toward solving the test problem in the same way that they had solved the trial problems.

Set based on activation may either facilitate task performance or impede it, depending on whether the memory elements that are activated contain the information that is needed for performance. Sweller and Gee (1978) showed that the tendency to use a previously successful rule can greatly facilitate solution of a relatively complex problem, presumably by eliminating the need to search in a large space of possibilities, even when in the same situation it prevents subjects from noticing a simpler solution method. Such situations are common, since set is bound to arise wherever memory organization is not neutral with respect to the problem-solving process—that is, wherever there are alternative ways of storing information in memory, one of which may be more conducive

to retrieval in a given problem context than another.

A second possible explanation of Einstellung is provided by composition of productions, investigated first by Lewis (1978). *Composition* is a process in which a newly acquired production performs actions that required two or more productions in the previous knowledge structure. Composition generally makes performance more efficient by providing a way to act directly rather than requiring several steps to achieve a goal. The new productions created by composition usually have conditions that are relatively specific, and in some production systems (including ACT) this leads to their being preferred to productions with less specific conditions. Anderson (1982) noted that this would simulate the performance observed by Luchins (1942) on problems like Figure 9.7.

Third, some setlike phenomena could also be produced by the basic problem-solving procedure that a subject uses. We have already noted that subjects frequently use the heuristic of means–ends analysis—that is, comparing situation with goal and taking an action that seems to reduce the difference between them. In their analysis of behavior of subjects solving water-jar problems, Atwood and Polson (1976) showed that where alternative actions could be taken, most subjects selected the one that led to a situation that most resembled the goal situation. As with the more specific sets induced by

Luchins's manipulation, this general set to pick paths that lead toward the desired goal can sometimes interfere with problem solution. Where memory limitations prevent subjects from looking far ahead, this goal-oriented strategy may sometimes produce a myopic preoccupation with immediate progress and the avoidance of paths that lead to the goal only indirectly. Jeffries, Polson, Razran, and Atwood (1977) showed that, without looking ahead, subjects solving the Missionaries and Cannibals puzzle would have difficulty (as, in fact, they do) on the step where they were required to bring two persons back from the farther bank of the river to which they were trying ultimately to transport them all.

## Problems with Specified Procedures

The present section examines tasks in which the problem presents material for a procedure, and the task is to apply the procedure to find the result. While the tasks discussed in "General Knowledge for Novel Problems with Specific Goals" and "Domain-Specific Knowledge for Familiar Problems with Specified Goals" specify a goal and require finding a method to get there, the tasks in this section specify a method and ask where the method leads.

The tasks chosen for discussion come from arithmetic. Many tasks in mathematics involve applying procedures, for example, finding a derivative in calculus or the product of two expressions in algebra. Such tasks may not be thought to involve problem solving, since they require knowledge of a procedure rather than search in a space of possible solutions. However, students who receive these tasks as homework assignments and presumably the teachers who assign them consider them to be problems.

More significantly, the knowledge required for these procedure-based tasks is similar to the knowledge that students acquire when they learn to solve problems that do not specify solution methods, such as geometry proof exercises or water-jar problems. Knowledge for planning in geometry consists of a set of procedures that the student has acquired for solving various kinds of problems. In geometry use of these procedures requires recognition of their applicability, which is not required if the problem calls for the operators *subtract* or *differentiate*. Nevertheless, characteristics of

the procedural knowledge that have been identified by theoretical analyses of the various tasks are more notable for their similarities than for their differences.

This section focuses on empirical methods that have been used to infer the nature of procedural knowledge, on inferences based on patterns of errors that occur in elementary arithmetic and on inferences from latency data.

### Diagnosis of Cognitive Procedures from Patterns of Errors

Brown and Burton (1980) analyzed children's knowledge for solving subtraction problems with multidigit numbers. Their data were obtained in an arithmetic achievement test taken by 1325 school children. Although performance on tests is ordinarily used to assign a simple score for each student, thus allowing judgments of which students have learned a satisfactory amount, Brown and Burton's analysis showed that test data are potentially much richer and can be used to make stronger inferences about the nature of children's knowledge.

The more powerful theoretical use of test data depends on two conditions. First, performance on the test is not characterized simply by the number of problems correct, but by the specific answers given to all the problems, with particular attention to the incorrect answers. Second, the analysis of each student's test performance consists of a model of a procedure for solving the problems.

The idea of using patterns of errors to infer underlying psychological processes is not new, either in the psychological or the educational literature. Earlier psychological models were simpler, and the inferences about processes were correspondingly less powerful; an example is Polson, Restle, and Polson's (1965) use of errors to identify a stage of learning in which similar stimuli have not yet been discriminated. In the educational literature more complex psychological distinctions have been made, for example by Brownell in 1941. However, analyses of underlying psychological processes was informal in that work, consisting of verbal descriptions of procedures hypothesized to produce observed error patterns, and, as Brown and Burton documented, verbal descriptions of procedures turn out to be ambiguous in important ways.

An example of an individual student's

Table 9.8.   One student's performance on subtraction problems
Source: (Brown & Burton, 1978)

| 8 | 99 | 353 | 633 | 81 |
|---|---|---|---|---|
| 3 | 79 | 342 | 221 | 17 |
| 5 | 20 | 11 | 412 | 64 |
| 4769 | 257 | 6523 | 103 | 7315 |
| 0 | 161 | 1280 | 64 | 6536 |
| 4769 | 96 | 5243 | 139 | 779 |
| 1039 | 705 | 10038 | 10060 | 7001 |
| 44 | 9 | 4319 | 98 | 94 |
| 1995 | 76 | 15719 | 10962 | 7007 |

Note. From "Diagnostic Models for Procedural Bugs in Basic
Mathematical Skills" by J.S. Brown and R.R. Burton, 1978,
Cognitive Science, 4, p. 178. Copyright 1978 by the ABLEX
Publishing Co. Reprinted by permission.

performance is shown in Table 9.8. This table
contains six errors (the fourth problem in the
second row, and all the problems in the third
row), not a very good score. However, all but
one of the errors were apparently caused by a
single flaw in the student's procedure. When the
subtraction required borrowing and the numeral
to be decreased was zero, the student replaced
the zero by a nine, but did not take the further
step of subtracting one from the preceding digit.

Brown and Burton developed a general model
of subtraction for which various flawed versions
can be represented as variants. The desired
outcome was that the performance of each
individual child, like the one shown in Table 9.8,
should correspond as closely as possible to one
of the variants of the general model. The general
model has the form of a procedural network, the
formalism developed by Sacerdoti (1977) and
used by Greeno et al. (1979) to explain constructions and set in geometry problem solving.
The main features of a procedural network are
that units of knowledge correspond to actions at
differing levels of generality, and each action
unit includes information about conditions
for performing the action, and the action's
consequences.

Figure 9.8 shows the action components
in Brown and Burton's procedural network for
subtraction. The diagram shows component
procedures and their subprocedures, but does
not show the control information that is also
required. For example, the diagram includes
a procedure Subtract-Column, and three subprocedures, Borrow-Needed, Do-Borrow, and

Complete-Column. Control knowledge involving
these subprocedures includes the information
that Borrow-Needed is a test that determines
whether it is necessary to borrow before finding
the difference in the column, and the outcome of
that test determines whether Do-Borrow will be
called.

Brown and Burton formulated models of
faulty performance by varying components of
the procedural network for correct subtraction.
For example, the flaw of borrowing from zero is
modeled by removing some of the control processing from the procedure Borrow-Ten in the
Do-Borrow subprocedure. The change involves
removing the decision Find-Next-Column if a
zero is found, resulting in a procedure that just
changes zero to nine and adds ten to the original
column.

The family of models that Brown and Burton
arrived at included 60 procedural flaws of the
kind described above. They provide explanations
for many of the patterns of performance found in
the test data, and more students' performance is
explained if combinations of elementary flaws
are included in the analysis. About 40 percent of
the students' error patterns were explained
reasonably well by single flaws or combinations
of two elementary flaws. In examining additional
sets of data, more elementary flaws have been
identified (115 were in the data base in 1982), and
adequate explanations are typically provided
for about 40 percent of students who make
errors (VanLehn, 1982).

An alternative analysis of subtraction errors
was provided by Young and O'Shea (1981), who
developed a relatively simple production system
that simulates correct subtraction performance
and, by deleting individual productions, simulates faulty performance. Young and O'Shea's
analysis provides explanations for about the
same proportion of students as Brown and
Burton's model. On the other hand, it provides
explanations for only a small proportion of
the patterns of performance that have been
observed. While many patterns occur rarely,
their existence provides evidence for a relatively
complex generative system.

Another significant development was an effort
by Brown and VanLehn (1980) and VanLehn
(1983) to formulate a system that explains the
production of flawed procedures. These formulations distinguish between a cognitive structure
of partial knowledge of subtraction, and a fall-

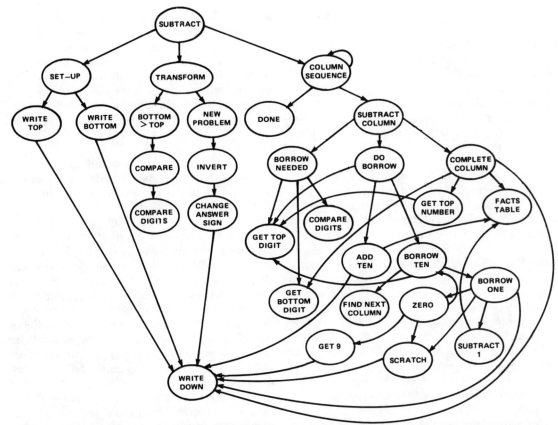

**Figure 9.8.** A procedural network for subtraction. From "Diagnostic Models for Procedural Bugs in Basic Mathematical Skills" by J.S. Brown and R.R. Burton,, 1978, *Cognitive Science, 4*, p. 162. Copyright 1978 by the ABLEX Publishing Co. Reprinted by permission.

back process of problem solving that is used when a situation is encountered for which the partial knowledge is not adequate. In Van-Lehn's (1983) version, the underlying cognitive structures (core procedures) result from a combination of partial learning and deletion of components of procedural knowledge. A core procedure might, for example, lack a component for dealing with a zero during borrowing. When such as impasse occurs it is assumed that the problem solver applies a general problem-solving method in order to continue. Methods available include skipping an operation, applying the operation to a different problem element, and using an alternative operation that is applicable in a similar problem situation. One form of evidence that supports the theory comes from data obtained by giving students repeated tests. Many students perform differently on two tests separated by two or three days, but the performance can be explained by assuming

a single core procedure for which different problem-solving methods have been used.

VanLehn (1983) conducted theoretical investigations in which a small set of problem-solving methods is combined with a plausible set of core procedures to generate flawed subtraction procedures. The generative system that has been developed can account for about half of the flawed procedures that have been observed; amendments that would increase the theory's empirical adequacy could easily be devised but would not have strong theoretical motivation. Part of the progress that has been made involves identifying some general features of the system. It can be argued, on the basis of general properties of flaws, that the system has a push-down memory for recalling past goals, that goals are organized hierarchically, and that the representation of a goal includes the problem components to which the goal applies.

Another line of analysis that has developed

from the study of subtraction flaws involves analysis of cognitive structures for understanding general arithmetic principles that underlie correct subtraction procedures. See "Problem Representation in Mathematics and Physics."

### Inferences Based on Latencies

An arithmetic task that is even simpler than multidigit calculation is the solution of basic addition problems such as 3 + 5. The main data used in the analyses of this task are latencies. Patterns of latencies of individual subjects are used to diagnose their solution processes.

In an empirical study by Groen and Resnick (1977), five preschool children who knew how to count and could recognize the numerals 1 to 9, but who did not know about addition were used as subjects. These children were taught a method for addition using blocks. The procedure was to count out two piles, each having one of the numbers in it, and then count how many were in the two piles together. For example, for 3 + 5, the child could count out a pile of three, then a pile of five, and then count the complete set to find eight as the answer. In showing the child the method, the experimenter sometimes started with the number on the left of the problem, and sometimes with the number on the right.

The problems used were basic addition facts involving the digits 1 to 5, omitting 5 + 5. After a child could solve all 24 of the problems correctly using blocks, a new apparatus was introduced. The blocks were no longer provided, and the child answered problems by pressing buttons labeled 1 to 9. Children were shown how to count out answers on their fingers if it was necessary. Children received from four to seven sets of problems with this apparatus, with about 25 problems per set.

The latency data were analyzed with regression techniques; models of cognitive processes were employed to determine the values of independent variables. Two models were used. According to one, the process of finding the answer to each problem was much like the procedure that the children were taught. In that procedure, a number of sets must be counted; in fact, the total number of counts equals double the number of the answer. If we assume that a fairly uniform amount of time is used each time something is counted, the total amount of time needed is

$$T = A + B(2S),$$

where $S$ is the sum of the two numbers (i.e., the answer), and A and B are constants. In the second model, the process is considerably simpler. The sum can also be found by starting with the larger of the two addends and counting up the number of the smaller addend. According to this model, the time it takes to find the answer is

$$T = A + B(M),$$

where $M$ is the minimum addend, and A and B are constants. These two models are called the *sum model* and the *min model*, respectively.

Comparison of these two models with the data of children's performance is interesting primarily because of the possibility that children spontaneously change their procedure for solving addition problems. If they use the procedure they were taught, their performance should agree with the sum model. However, performance consistent with the min model would reflect a more efficient procedure, and would indicate that children had spontaneously modified their problem-solving procedures. It would thus indicate a significant capability for discovery or invention.

To apply either the sum or the min model to the data, problems are grouped according to the number of counting operations they require. Because the models specify different counting operations, they imply different groupings of items. For example, according to the sum model, the problems 6 + 1, 5 + 2, and 4 + 3 all require the same number of operations, but these problems require different numbers of counts according to the min model. On the other hand, the problems 4 + 3 and 3 + 5 require the same number of counts by the min model, but are different according to the sum model.

If a model is approximately correct, the regression based on it should give accurate predictions of problem latency. The criterion of fit used by Groen and Resnick was the proportion of variance $R^2$ accounted for by the regression. Higher values of $R^2$ indicate better agreement between the latency data and the theoretical function.

Table 9.9 shows that about half the subjects were fitted better by the min model than by the sum model. Values of $R^2$ are shown for latency data from each block of problems except the first, in which the children were getting used to the new apparatus. Subjects 2 and 4 were fitted

**Table 9.9. Results of applying regression models to latency data**
*Source*: (Groen & Resnick, 1977)

| Subject | Block | Proportion errors | Proportion covert | $R^2$ Sum | Min | Slope of best fitting line (seconds) |
|---------|-------|-------------------|-------------------|-----|-----|------------------------|
| 1 | 2 | .15 | .02 | *.78** | .65* | .92 |
|   | 3 | .09 | .00 | *.45** | .16 | .60 |
|   | 4 | .03 | .04 | *.79** | .38 | .67 |
|   | 5 | .03 | .08 | *.69** | .57* | .91 |
|   | 6 | .06 | .33 | .50* | *.59** | 1.66 |
|   | 7 | .05 | .34 | .40* | *.63** | 1.90 |
| 2 | 2 | .18 | .40 | .44* | *.65** | 2.82 |
|   | 3 | .14 | .57 | .51* | *.88** | 2.30 |
|   | 4 | .11 | .57 | .51* | *.69** | 2.06 |
|   | 5 | .06 | .76 | .22 | *.38** | 1.40 |
|   | 6 | .06 | .99 | .23 | *.54** | .40 |
|   | 7 | .11 | 1.00 | .17 | *.43** | .26 |
| 3 | 2 | .04 | .00 | .14 | .00 | – |
|   | 3 | .03 | .09 | *.71** | .57* | .99 |
|   | 4 | .05 | .05 | .50* | .27 | .73 |
|   | 5 | .11 | .30 | .06 | .13 | – |
|   | 6 | .12 | .92 | .05 | .30 | – |
|   | 7 | .07 | .83 | .03 | .10 | – |
| 4 | 2 | .25 | .73 | .23 | *.54** | 1.77 |
|   | 3 | .12 | .61 | *.38** | .41* | 1.60 |
|   | 4 | .06 | .94 | .32 | *.65** | 1.38 |
| 5 | 2 | .04 | .94 | *.47** | .43* | 1.30 |
|   | 3 | .09 | 1.00 | *.55** | .49* | 1.66 |
|   | 4 | .02 | 1.00 | .25 | .12 | – |
|   | 5 | .01 | .99 | .21 | .17 | – |
|   | 6 | .06 | 1.00 | *.52** | .20 | .64 |

*Note*. Asterisks denote slope significantly different from zero at .01 level. Italics denote maximum $R^2$.
*Note*. From "Can Preschool Children Invent Algorithms?" by G. Groen and L.B. Resnick, 1977, *Journal of Educational Psychology*, 69, p. 648. Copyright 1977 by the Ammerican Psychological Association. Reprinted by permission of the author.

better by the min model, subject 5 by the sum model, and subject 1 underwent a transition, being fitted better by the sum model in blocks 2 through 5, but by the min model in blocks 6 and 7. Another experiment, in which practice problems were presented in a systematic order, had similar results.

The important conclusion from these data is that the children must have discovered the procedure represented by the min model, since they were not taught how to add in that way. Neches (1981) developed an analysis of learning mechanisms that can produce modified procedures, and he used that system to simulate changes in counting procedures for addition problems. The main ideas in the Neches model are that redundant components of the procedure can be removed, and when there are alternative ways of reaching the same result, the easier

method can be chosen. For example, in the sum procedure, the first addend is counted, and then later the process of counting the combined set includes counting the first addend as a part. Noticing this redundancy leads to removal of the initial count of the first addend from the procedure. Choice of the larger addend to initialize the procedure can be made if the subject notices that the same result is obtained with either addend, but that less effort is required when the larger addend is chosen. To produce modifications in its procedures, the Neches system requires a trace of its activity, including the goals that are active during the various stages of its performance.

The regression method has also been used in analyzing performance of adults in simple arithmetic tasks. Groen and Parkman (1972) found that college students' performance is quite consistent with the min model. The slope of the best-fitting regression equation is far too small to correspond to verbal counting, but an analogue of a counting procedure might account for the result.

Performance in mental arithmetic has been studied recently by Ashcraft and his associates. Using a task in which subjects are shown a problem with a possible answer and are asked whether it is correct, Ashcraft and Battaglia (1978) found longer latencies for problems involving larger numbers, but this effect was not linear in the smaller addend, as required by the min model. A better predictor of latency was the square of the problem sum, an effect that seems inconsistent with a simple process of counting. Ashcraft and Battaglia also found shorter latencies for the rejection of wrong answers that differed more from the correct answer, than for wrong answers close to the correct answer. Another relevant finding by Winkelman and Schmidt (1974) was that latency increased for a false answer that could be correct for a different operation; for example $3 \times 4 = 7$. As Ashcraft and Stazyk (1981) have argued, these findings suggest a process of retrieval from memory, rather than a counting procedure, with effects on latency that result from the way in which information is stored and from processes of activation and search.

## Problem Understanding; Representation

Before a problem can be solved, it must be understood. Many problems used in education are presented as natural-language texts that describe situations and ask questions, usually the values of some quantities. In laboratory studies, problems are often presented in the form of instructions that specify the goals and problem-solving operators that can be used in working on the problems. These texts or instructions must be interpreted, and some kind of representation of the problem must be generated before problem-solving processes can be put to work in seeking a solution.

The same problem may be represented in radically different ways, as is illustrated by the 'mutilated checkerboard' problem. The subject is given an ordinary $8 \times 8$ checkerboard, with alternating black and red squares, and a set of dominoes, each of which covers two squares. The entire board can be covered by 32 dominoes, with no square left uncovered, and no domino hanging over the edge of the board. Suppose now that the northeast square and the southwest square of the checkerboard are cut off, leaving 62 squares. Can the mutilated board now be covered neatly by 31 dominoes?

It is impossible for a human being or a computer to answer this question by exhaustive search in the obvious but enormous problem space in which the squares and dominoes are represented directly. Consider, however, an abstract problem space in which we represent only the number of dominoes that have been laid down, and the numbers of both black and red squares that remain uncovered. At the outset, because of the mutilation, there are 32 red squares, but only 30 black squares (or vice versa). Each domino covers exactly one red and one black square. Hence, no matter how the dominoes are placed on the board, after 30 have been placed, if that is possible, two red squares and no black squares will remain uncovered. But the final domino cannot cover two red squares, hence there is no way to complete the covering. Here, a change in problem representation changes the problem from one that is practically unsolvable to one that is quite easily solvable.

Another famous example of problem understanding, discussed by Wertheimer (1959), arises in finding the area of a parallelogram. Students are taught that the area of a parallelogram can be calculated with a formula $A = b \times h$, where $b$ and $h$ are the base and height, respectively. Wertheimer described two ways in which the formula may be understood. In one representation, $b$ is the length of a horizontal side of the parallelogram, and $h$ is the length of a vertical line drawn from a corner at the top of the figure to its base, as shown on the upper part of Figure 9.9. Many students, apparently using that representation, become confused if they are then asked to find the area of a parallelogram oriented differently, as in the lower part of Figure 9.9. Another way to understand the formula includes a relation between parallelograms and rectangles. A parallelogram can be transformed into a rectangle by removing a triangular piece from one end and attaching it to the other end. Then $b$ and $h$ are equal to the length and width, respectively, of the rectangle that the parallelogram can be transformed into. Children who

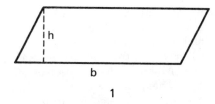

1

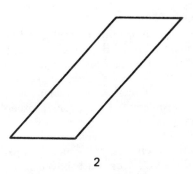

2

**Figure 9.9.** Parallelograms in two orientations. Some students who learn the formula $A = b \times h$ have difficulty applying it to a figure like the lower one (Wertheimer, 1945–1959).

understand the parallelogram problem in this way have no difficulty in solving problems where the figure is oriented differently and can frequently transfer their knowledge to solve more complex problems, such as finding the area of a trapezoid. The two representations involve different features of specific problems, one with $b$ and $h$ identified with specific locations in the figure, and the other with $b$ and $h$ defined in more general terms.

### Understanding Problem Instructions

In most studies, consideration of subjects' behaviors in problem-solving tasks is begun after the subjects have received the definition of the problem with appropriate instructions, and have been tested by the experimenter for their understanding of the problem. A few studies investigate the processes required for assimilating the problem before attempting to solve it.

In the situations already studied, solution of the problem is likely to proceed by a form of means–ends analysis. Therefore, the information that subjects extract from instructions is probably similar to the information needed by the General Problem Solver. When GPS is given a problem, it is provided with a list of the objects involved in the problem, the relevant properties of these objects, operators for legal moves, a description of the starting situation, and a set of tests to determine when the final goal has been reached. GPS may be provided with, or otherwise must acquire by learning, a set of tests for differences between situations and a set of productions that evoke, with certain differences, operators that are relevant to reducing these differences.

For example, in the Tower of Hanoi problem, the objects consist of $N$ disks (where $N$ = number) and three pegs. A legal move consists of transferring the smallest disk on one peg to another peg that holds no smaller disk. Hence, the size of a disk is its relevant property. Situations differ as to which disks are on a particular peg, or on which peg a particular disk is located. In one starting situation, all the disks are held on a single peg; the goal is to move the entire set of disks to another particular peg. The problem description must provide this information in English, and the subject (or computer program) must convert this English prose into an internal representation that permits situations, moves, and their consequences to be modeled. A disk, for instance, may be represented as a schema, one of whose attributes is its size, and a peg by a schema, one of whose attributes is the list of disks currently on that peg. A move operator is a process that changes a pair of the latter lists by moving the name of a particular disk from one list to the other.

Two central problems for psychological research on the understanding of problem instructions are: (1) how the verbal instructions are converted to an internal representation, and (2) what characteristics of the instructions cause the problem to be represented in one way, rather than other possible ways. The second question is especially important when alternative representations result in problem difficulty differences (as with the mutilated checkerboard example), or provide differing degrees of generality (as with the parallelogram problem). These questions have been addressed by Hayes and Simon (1974), who obtained information about internal representations by collecting extensive verbal protocols of problem-understanding processes. By using problems in which alternative representations were available, Hayes and

Simon also cast light on the question of which representations are formed.

The Understand program (Hayes & Simon, 1974) is a computer simulation of the problem-understanding process for puzzlelike problems like the Tower of Hanoi or Missionaries and Cannibals—that is, for problems that do not assume that the subject has any prior knowledge of the problem domain. The program matches human thinking-aloud protocols sufficiently well to lay claim to being a good first-approximation model of the process.

Understand operates in two principal phases. In the first, a language-parsing program extracts the deep structure from the language of the instructions. In the second phase, another set of processes constructs from this information a problem representation that is suitable as input to a GPS-like problem-solving program. This is accomplished by (1) identifying the objects and sets of objects that are mentioned in the parsed text, (2) identifying the descriptors of those objects and the relations among them, (3) identifying the descriptions of legal moves and constructing move operators that fit those descriptions, (4) identifying the description of the solution and constructing a test for attainment of the solution, and (5) constructing an organization of schemata that describes the initial problem situation.

For example, after parsing the written description of the Tower of Hanoi problem, Understand would identify pegs and disks as the relevant sets of objects, and would notice that disks are on pegs and that they move from one peg to another. It would extract the information that only the smallest disk on a peg may be moved, and only to a peg on which there is no smaller disk, and it would construct a test process for checking these conditions. It would determine that the problem is solved when all the disks are on, for example, the third peg, and would construct a test to determine when that condition is satisfied. Finally, it would generate a list structure showing that all the disks initially are on the first peg. From the evidence of protocols, and of subjects' subsequent problem-solving behavior, this is also the method that human solvers use.

## Problem Isomorphs

A powerful experimental manipulation for studying problem understanding is to use variant problem instructions, all of which describe *isomorphs* of a single problem. Two problems are isomorphic if the legal problem situations and the legal moves of the one can be mapped in one-to-one fashion on the situations and moves of the other. Then, if situation $S'$ is the isomorph of $S$, and moves $A'$, $B'$, etc., are the isomorphs of $A$, $B$, etc., and if the succession of moves $A$, $B$, ... takes the one system from $S$ to $T$, then the succession of moves $A'$, $B'$, ... will take the other system from $S'$ to $T'$, where $T'$ is the isomorph of $T$.

Using a number of isomorphs of the Tower of Hanoi problem, Hayes and Simon (1977) demonstrated that problem difficulty varied by a factor of two to one from one class of problem descriptions (transfer problems) to another (change problems). Moreover, protocols and diagrams produced by subjects showed that they consistently used different representations for the different classes of isomorphic problems. The Understand program behaved in the same way, constructing different representations for both the transfer and change problems. In only one case out of the nearly 100 that have been examined did a subject shift from the more difficult 'change' representation to the easier 'transfer' representation.

The reasons that the change problems take twice as long to solve as the isomorphic transfer problems are not yet fully elucidated. It can be shown, however, that the tests for legality of moves are a little more complex for change than for transfer and this complexity may increase the short-term memory load for the subject who is seeking to understand the problem instructions.

Problem isomorphs can be used to study transfer of training, as in the study conducted by Reed, Ernst, and Banerji (1974). They devised a variant of the Missionaries and Cannibals problem, called the Jealous Husbands problem. It differs from the Missionary–Cannibal problem in that specific husbands are paired with specific wives, and no woman may be left in the company of men unless her husband is present. Experimental results showed that subjects were not better at solving one of these problems if they had previously solved the other. We must conclude that, although subjects may use analogies to help solve problems, there is nothing automatic about the availability of an analogy, and subjects may fail to take advantage of analogies unless their attention is drawn to them or they are made salient in some other way. Positive transfer between isomorphs in a different type of problem is discussed below in "Construction tasks and other insight problems."

## Problem Representation in Mathematics and Physics

Typically a problem given in a mathematics or physics text describes a situation, including quantitative values of some variables, and asks for the value of another variable. The given quantities correspond to the initial state of a problem and the unknown quantity provides the goal. The problem is presented in a natural-language text, as are the instructions for novel problems discussed in the previous section. A physics or mathematics problem differs from a puzzle in that the instructions for the problem, do not provide a description of the problem-solving operators that can be used. It is assumed that the student already knows the operators, from class instruction or from reading the text. The interpretation of puzzle instructions is a representation that can be used by a general problem-solving system such as GPS, whereas the interpretation of a text problem in mathematics or physics is a representation that can be used only by domain-specific problem-solving procedures.

### ALGEBRA WORD PROBLEMS

Word problems in algebra describe situations that can be translated into equations, which are then solved to find the values of unknown variables. An early model of solution to word problems, called Student (Bobrow, 1968), showed that the translation can be accomplished mainly by using the forms of sentences in the problem text, and the numerical quantities, with very little knowledge about the objects that are described. For example, in the sentence, "The number of customers Tom gets is twice the square of the number of advertisements he runs," Student does not need to know anything about what customers or advertisements are, but can form the equation $X = 2Y^2$ using the function words *is* and *of* in critical ways.

In an empirical study of the solving of algebra word problems, Paige and Simon (1966) found great similarities between human solutions and those given by Bobrow's Student program. Their more skillful subjects, however, used an intermediate semantic representation in the translation of the English-language problem statements into algebraic equations. Some problems presented descriptions of situations that were contradicted implicitly by real-world knowledge (boards of negative length, nickels worth more than quarters, and so on). The weaker subjects often made accurate syntactic translations of English into equations, as Student does, even though the equations represented nonsense situations. The abler subjects either noticed the contradictions between the statements and their knowledge or translated the statements into equations that were not quite equivalent syntactically, but that represented physically realizable situations.

Another difference between subjects was that those who were more able, unlike the less able, generally drew diagrams of the problem situation that contained all the essential relations from which the equations could be derived.

Both kinds of evidence—the response to 'impossible' situations and the nature of the problem diagrams produced—indicate that the more competent subjects used an intermediate semantic representation of problem situations, rather than a direct translation from English to algebra.

### ARITHMETIC WORD PROBLEMS

Detailed analyses of intermediate representations have been worked out for a class of word problems in elementary arithmetic. Riley et al. (1983) and Briars and Larkin (1984) have developed models of representation and solution of word problems that are solved by a single operation of addition or subtraction. Examples of the problems studied are: "Jay had eight books; he lost five of them; how many books does Jay have now?" or "Jay has some books; Kay has seven more books than Jay; Kay has eleven books; how many books does Jay have?"

In the Riley et al. (1983) model, problems are represented by three schemata that provide knowledge of basic quantitative relationships. One schema represents problems involving events that change the value of a quantity, either by increasing or decreasing it, as in the loss of five books; in the problems of the second schema two separate quantities are considered in combination; and in the third schema the problems involve comparison between two separate quantities. (This classification of problems is not unique; Carpenter and Moser, 1982, Nesher, 1982, and Vergnaud, 1982, have offered similar, though distinct, characterizations.)

Arithmetic word problems are usually classified according to the operations used in their solution, and children are often taught to look for certain key words to decide how to solve the problems. This is inadequate, because choice of the correct operation depends on understanding the structure of quantities in the problem, rather than on a single feature corresponding to a key word. For example, 'altogether' is sometimes suggested as a key word for addition, but this is not a reliable cue, as in the problem, "Jay and Kay have nine books altogether; Jay has seven books; how many books does Kay have?"

The model by Riley et al. simulates children's solutions of word problems when small blocks are available for the children to use in solving the problems. The model forms representations of problem texts using the schemata of change, combination, and comparison. Based on the representation that is formed for a problem, the model performs quantitative actions, such as joining two sets of objects together or removing a specified number of objects from a set and counting how many remain. Different versions of the model were formed to correspond to different levels of skill that were observed in a study of children from kindergarten through third grade. The versions differ in the detail with which internal representations are formed (which affects their ability to retrieve information from earlier steps), and in their ability to perform transformations that provide information in a form needed to make inferences. The patterns of correct responses and errors observed in the performance of most of the children were consistent with the patterns obtained in the simulation models.

Briars and Larkin's (1984) model constructs less elaborate intermediate representations of problems, and thus relies more on procedures for inferences. Their model uses a schema for representing part–whole relations among sets for some relatively difficult problems.

## Physics Problems

The knowledge structures used in simulating solutions to arithmetic word problems are quite general, involving relation between quantities that children probably learn about in their ordinary experience. In technical domains such as physics, specific instruction is given to teach students the nature of theoretical quantities and the ways in which they combine.

Novak (1976) constructed a program called Isaac that builds problem representations in a domain of physics (simple statics) from problem descriptions in English. Isaac uses schemata of physical subsystems (levers, masses, etc.), assumed to be understood already by the solver in order to build a compound schema to fit the problem at hand. Thus, it may assemble a wall schema (surface), a floor schema (surface), a ladder schema (lever), and a man schema (mass) to represent a situation in which a man stands on a ladder that is leaning against a wall, assigning to each component appropriate numerical quantities and appropriate connections to the others.

Models such as Riley's for arithmetic word problems and Novak's for physics problems are based on the idea that understanding a problem requires schematic knowledge of the quantities in problem situations. The schemata provide knowledge of ways in which quantities are related to one another. These quantitative relations are not expressed adequately in the algebraic formulas that are taught in physics and other quantitative sciences, even though the formulas are based on quantitative relations and students must be able to choose formulas and assign values to variables correctly on the basis of the problem representations that they construct.

The distinction between knowledge of a formula and knowledge of quantities and their relations is illustrated in experiments conducted by Mayer (1974). The experiments were instructional studies, concerned with different methods of teaching the formula for binomial probability. One group of subjects received instruction that emphasized calculation, presenting components of the formula with explanations of the calculation steps, some practice exercises, and relatively brief explanations of the referents of terms in the formula. Another condition emphasized the information needed in order for students to acquire schematic knowledge. In it, definitions of terms and explanations of relevant concepts, such as the number of combinations and the probability of a single sequence of outcomes, were presented before calculation exercises were given. Tests given following instruction contained a variety of problems, including some that involved direct application of the formula, and others that required more interpretation. The latter group included word problems, problems that could not be solved because of inconsistent or insufficient information, and problems requiring use of a component of the formula rather than the whole formula. The subjects whose instruction emphasized the formula excelled on the problems involving direct use of the formula, but the subjects given more conceptual instruction were more successful on the problems requiring more interpretation.

Several studies have compared the performance of physics students with that of expert physicists to identify some of the components of knowledge that characterize more advanced problem solvers. Three of the characteristics that differentiated the physicists were identified as (1) their use of abstract physics principles in representing problems as well as in providing methods of solution; (2) the strong organization of their knowledge of physics, including relations among principles and recognition of complex patterns of problem features; and (3) the integration of their physics knowledge with general concepts and reasoning processes.

The use of abstract physics concepts by experts was shown in experiments by Chi, Feltovich, and Glaser (1981), who gave subjects a set of 24 physics textbook problems and asked them to sort the problems into groups. Groupings formed by advanced graduate students were based primarily on abstract principles, such as conservation of energy, whereas subjects who had completed a single course in mechanics were much more likely to base their groupings on superficial features such as the kinds of objects (pulleys, levers, etc) that were mentioned in the problems. Chi et al. (1981) also found that experts used abstract physics principles in studies where they reported their thoughts and hunches while deciding on a 'basic approach' to solving the problem. Use of abstract principles as included in a computational model developed by McDermott and Larkin (1978) that simulates the representation of textbook problems by an expert. The representation of a problem included a diagram with major components and relations, followed by an abstract description of the theoretical entities such as forces and energies and their interrelations, based on general principles.

Instructional materials designed by Reif and Heller (1981) provide training for beginning students in a procedure for constructing abstract representations of problems. Reif and Heller provided an explicit method for arriving at the kind of problem representation used by experts (although their method was not patterned after the experts' performance, since experts form a representation rapidly and apparently automatically, without easily discerned intermediate steps).

Larkin and Reif (1979) also designed instruction to strengthen students' knowledge of relations among physics principles and their ability to apply principles in solving problems. The instruction grouped principles on a chart and suggested to students that, in applying certain principles it was generally useful to consider the application of other related principles. Qualitative analogies were also used, such as a fluid–current analogy for electric current and a height analogy for potential. Students who received this instruction solved test problems more successfully than students who received instruction in the principles only, without the organization and qualitative analogies.

Experts in various domains have been shown to have superior skill in recognizing complex patterns of information in the domain of their expertise. This phenomenon has been demonstrated in chess (Chase & Simon, 1973), go (Reitman, 1976), electronics (Egan & Schwartz, 1979), computer programming (McKeithen, Reitman, Rueter, & Hirtle, 1981), and radiology (Lesgold, Feltovich, Glaser, & Wang, 1981). A highly developed skill in pattern recognition may provide an explanation for the finding obtained in several studies that expert problem solvers tend to work forward from the given information to the unknown, whereas novices work backward from the unknown, searching through a series of subgoals for formulas that can provide the needed quantities (e.g., Simon & Simon, 1978). Applying formulas involves using more complex patterns of known values of variables, which experts have probably learned to recognize directly, thus avoiding the more laborious searches that novices conduct (Larkin, 1981). This view is supported by Malin (1979), who found that subjects were more likely to adopt a forward-search strategy to solve problems if the formulas they were using had an obvious organization than if the formulas did not fit together in any evident way.

A third characteristic of experts' knowledge is that their domain-specific knowledge (e.g., in physics) is integrated with powerful general concepts and procedures for making inferences. An example comes from Simon and Simon (1978) who obtained protocols from a novice and an expert on problems from a high school physics text. One problem was: "An object dropped from a balloon descending at four meters per second lands on the ground 10 seconds later. What was the altitude of the balloon at the moment the object was dropped?" The novice subject's solution had the properties of means–ends analysis, using the formula $s = v_0 t + .5at^2$. In contrast, the expert calculated a quantity that he called the total additional velocity by multiplying the time by the gravitational constant (i.e., $10 \times 9.8 = 98$); he then added that to the initial velocity to obtain the final velocity ($98 + 4 = 102$), took the average velocity [$(4 + 102)/2 = 53$], and found the distance by multiplying the average velocity by the time of 10 seconds ($53 \times 10 = 530$ meters). The expert apparently had a representation of the problem in terms of physical quantities that enabled him to apply general procedures, such as computing components of velocity and taking an average, whereas the novice was restricted to using the formulas that were provided in the text. Relations between technical knowledge and general concepts have been investigated theoretically by deKleer (1975) and Bundy (1978), who developed models of physics problem-solving that combine general knowledge about the motion of objects on surfaces with knowledge of formulas in kinematics, and by Larkin (1982) who studied the use of spatial information in the solving of hydrostatics problems.

## UNDERSTANDING OF STRUCTURE AND PRINCIPLES

The integration of problem-solving knowledge with general conceptual structures has also been used to characterize structural understanding as discussed by Wertheimer (1945/1959), and the understanding of general principles, including the relation of abstract properties of number (cardinality, order, one-to-one correspondence) to children's cognitive procedures for counting.

The understanding of structure has been investigated theoretically by Greeno (1983) on a problem, discussed by Wertheimer (1945/1959),

of proving the congruence of vertical angles. Wertheimer distinguished between a relatively mechanical process for generating the proof, involving the use of algebra without cognizance of spatial relations in the problem, and a more meaningful process based on part–whole relations between pairs of angles and operations to remove a part that is included in each of two whole angles. Greeno's model simulates the more meaningful process by using a schema that represents part–whole relations in a general way and applying problem-solving operators that make inferences based on the part–whole structure. Data were available in the form of protocols from students working on the vertical-angle problem after they had learned to solve other problems with similar part–whole structure involving line segments. The model simulates learning in the line-segment situation. Once the learned problem-solving operators are integrated into the part–whole schema, the model can apply this knowledge when it encounters the vertical-angle problem. The model thus provides an explanation for transfer that occurs between problems in different domains, with a characterization of structural understanding based on schematic representation. An account of transfer based on acquisition of a schema in a different problem domain is discussed below in "Construction tasks and other insight problems."

A similar idea was used by Resnick, Greeno, and Rowland (described by Resnick, 1983) in analyzing children's understanding of a procedure for subtraction with multidigit numbers. According to their analysis, children who understand the procedure have a representation that includes general relations—such as part–whole relations between quantities represented by individual digits and the quantities represented by combinations of digits and constraints such as the requirement that the total value of a number remain unchanged when borrowing is used. The analysis focused on knowledge acquired in meaningful instruction (cf. Brownell, 1935), in which children were shown the correspondence between subtraction with numerals and an analogous subtraction procedure using blocks. Resnick et al. (in Resnick, 1983) hypothesized that the understanding was achieved through acquisition of a schema, involving part–whole relations, that was general enough to apply to both—the numerals and the blocks.

Efforts are being made to develop rigorous and explicit characterizations of knowledge that includes implicit understanding of general principles (cf. Judd, 1908; Piaget, 1941/1952). A representation of preschool children's understanding of the principles of counting has been formulated by Greeno et al. (1984). Their analysis was based on evidence presented by Gelman and Gallistel (1978) that young children have significant understanding of principles such as cardinality, order, and one-to-one correspondence, rather than a simple 'mechanical' knowledge of counting procedures. The evidence includes their performance in novel situations, such as being asked to evaluate counting performance by a puppet that sometimes makes errors, or counting with the novel constraint of associating a specified numeral with a particular object. Greeno et al. (1984) also proposed an analysis of conceptual competence to represent children's implicit understanding of principles. Conceptual principles are represented as schemata that incorporate constraints on correct counting and express general properties, such as the part–whole relation between the counted objects and the whole set. The conceptual principles are related to procedures of counting by a set of planning rules, which permit derivation of procedures from the schematic representations of the principles.

## PROBLEMS OF DESIGN AND ARRANGEMENT

Problems discussed in this section require finding an arrangement of some objects that satisfies a problem criterion. Simple examples include puzzles in which the objects are given in the problem situation. For example, an anagram presents some letters, and the task is to find a sequence of those letters that forms a word. In more complex cases, the problem solvers must provide the materials based on their own knowledge. Examples are writing an essay or a computer program.

The problem space in a problem of design includes the objects that are given to or are known by the problem solver. The space of possible solutions is the set of arrangements that can be formed with the available objects. The problem goal is to construct an arrangement that meets a criterion, which may be either specific or nonspecific. An anagram problem has a specific criterion: the sequence of letters should form a word. A written composition has several less specific criteria, such as clear exposition, persuasive argument, and an entertaining style. Many problems of design have a mixture of specific and nonspecific criteria. For example, a problem in computer programming may combine a criterion of a specific function to be computed with less specific criteria, such as efficient computation and clarity of structure.

Satisfying constraints is an important factor in solving problems of design. The metaphor that best characterizes typical solution processes is 'narrowing the set of possibilities' rather than 'searching through the set of possibilities.' Although it is entirely possible to describe the solution process as a search, the main steps in this search lead to the acquisition of new knowledge that rules out a whole set of problem states as potential solutions—a wholesale approach to the reduction of uncertainty. The use of constraints is important because the set of possible arrangements is usually very large, compared to those that satisfy the problem criterion.

Problems of design are differentiated from the transformation problems discussed above in "Well-Specified Problems," in both the nature of the goal and the set of alternatives that are considered. In a transformation problem such as the Tower of Hanoi or in finding a proof for a theorem, the goal is a specific arrangement of the problem objects, such as a specific location of all the disks in the Tower of Hanoi or a specific expression to be proved in logic. Thus, the question is not what to construct, as it is in a design problem, but how the goal can be constructed with the limited set of operators that are available. The search for the solution of a transformation problem often examines one problem situation after another, uncovering knowledge that helps point the direction of the search toward the goal situation.

Viewed in another way, however, transformation problems and problems of design are very similar in structure. The solution of a transformation problem is a sequence of actions that changes the initial problem situation into the goal. The solution process can be considered as the construction of an appropriate sequence of actions, involving search in the very large space of possible sequences. This view emphasizes similarities between problems of transformation and of design, which are especially apparent when the solution of transformation problems includes planning.

Problem solving in design is discussed in four parts: (1) Two simple problems of forming arrangements—cryptarithmetic and anagrams—provide paradigms for analyzing search among sets of possible arrangements; (2) problems in which an arrangement of objects is already presented, and the task is to modify the arrangement according to some criterion (e.g., Katona, 1940); (3) 'insight' problems that depend on finding a successful formulation or representation of the problem; and (4) more complex problems of composition and design, including the composition of essays and musical pieces, the design of procedures, and the formation of administrative policies.

## Simple Problems of Forming Arrangements

### Cryptarithmetic Problems
In cryptarithmetic problems, digits are arranged to form a correct addition problem, constrained by a set of letters for which the digits are to be substituted (Newell & Simon, 1972). One of the best known examples follows:

$$DONALD$$
$$+ GERALD$$
$$= ROBERT$$

The task is to replace each letter in the array with a distinct digit, from 0 to 9, the same digit replacing a given letter in all its occurrences (no digit being used for more than one letter). To make the problem easier, the solver is usually told that D = 5.

The cryptarithmetic task was apparently first studied by Bartlett (1958), who reported some retrospective protocols of subjects in his book on thinking. Subsequently, Newell and Simon (1972) carried out extensive analyses of thinking-aloud protocols for cryptarithmetic problems. From this work, we now have quite a clear picture of how human subjects approach such problems.

There are 10! = 3,628,800 ways of assigning ten digits to ten letters. Most subjects, without calculating this number, realize that it is very large, and do not even attempt to solve the problem by making random assignments and testing them. Instead, they look for information in the form of constraints that permit values to be assigned to particular letters at once. If that can be done, the number of possibilities declines rapidly. Simply giving the information that D = 5 already reduces the possible solutions by a factor of 10, that is, to 362,880—still a large number!

The constraints in cryptarithmetic problems that sometimes make systematic elimination possible derive from the fact that each column of the literal array must be translated into a correct example of addition (subject to carrying into and out of the column). Thus, as soon as it is known that D = 5, the sixth column can be processed to produce the inference that T necessarily equals 0, and that 1 is carried into the fifth column. This single inference reduces the remaining set of possible assignments by a factor of nine to 40,320.

Next, consideration of the second column allows the subject to infer that E is equal to 0 or 9. Since 0 has already been preempted by T, we have E = 9, reducing the possible assignments to 5,040. A few more steps of reasoning, based on information contained in columns 1 and 5, allow the subject to infer that R = 7, reducing the possible assignments to 720. An inference in column 4 gives A = 4 (120 possibilities remain); and an inference on column 5 gives L = 8 (leaving only 24 possibilities). From column 1, G = 1 (leaving 6 possibilities), and now the remaining digits must be assigned to N, O, and B, a task easily carried out by trial and error.

Newell and Simon (1972) obtained thinking-aloud protocols of subjects solving cryptarithmetic problems. Problem behavior graphs were constructed based on the protocols, and a detailed model of one subject's problem-solving processes was developed in the form of a production system. (This methodology is discussed above in "Discovering Proofs in Logic.") In the model several productions represent a problem-solving strategy. These productions set goals of examining a column or the occurrences of a variable; they make decisions on the assignment of a value to a variable or the testing of a candidate value, and they perform other general functions. There are also a few dozen productions that represent the operation of specific processes. One, called *Process Column*, contains 26 productions; others are considerably simpler.

The productions in this process examine the letters in a column and use any information that has been gathered about them to make further inferences. The subject's performance, recorded in a problem behavior graph, was compared in detail with the model, and approximately 80 percent of the protocol units were explained by processes in the model.

Protocols obtained from five subjects were consistent in their general characteristics of problem-solving processes. They also revealed significant individual differences, and these can be interpreted as differences between the problem spaces of the individual problem solvers. All the subjects made use of their knowledge of arithmetic in order to make inferences, and all subdivided the problems into subproblems involving the columns. There were important differences among subjects in their strategies for selecting columns to work on and in their use of specific constraints for making inferences.

For an efficient solution of this problem, subjects must use the search heuristic of attacking the most constrained columns first, since most information can be extracted from a column in which the assignment of one or more letters has already been made, or in which the same letter occurs twice. Some subjects used this selection heuristic immediately; others began by attacking the columns systematically, from right to left, and only later abandoned that strategy for the more powerful one. Subjects who did not use the heuristic usually failed to solve the problem.

Another factor that influenced success was the use of specific constraints. The problem spaces of some subjects included rules of parity. For example, one of the inferences needed in order to conclude that R = 7 is that, whatever R's exact value, it must be an odd number. This is inferred by processing column 5, containing two Ls whose sum must be even, and the carrying of 1, making the total an odd number. Subjects whose problem spaces did not include the parity constraints were generally unable to solve their problems.

Even subjects who used the available heuristics and constraints for efficient elimination found the DONALD + GERALD problem difficult. Most of their difficulties arose from one or both of two sources. One such source is the making of conditional assignments (e.g., "suppose that L = 1"). Then, if the assignment was wrong and they arrived at a contradiction, they may have been unable to remember which prior number assignments they had inferred definitely and which they had postulated conditionally. Another source of difficulty involved errors of inference, resulting in incorrect assignments. For example, from the fact that R = 7 some subjects concluded that L = 3 (with a carry from the sixth column), ignoring the possibility that L might be 8, with a carry into the fourth column. When L = 3 led to a contradiction, they found it difficult to discover the cause.

Errors of inference are forms of the errors of syllogistic reasoning discussed below in "Propositional and categorical syllogisms." In the example just cited, subjects appeared to infer from the premise, "if L = 3 then R = 7" and the premise "R = 7," the conclusion "L = 3," an example of the classical fallacy of inferring the antecedent from the consequent. They did not notice that L = 8 also implies R = 7. Thus, the cryptarithmetic task draws on reasoning processes as well as search processes.

Nothing in the behavior of subjects solving cryptarithmetic problems suggests that they decide consciously to treat it as a constraint problem rather than a search problem. In fact, their behavior can be described as a search through the space of possible assignments, and Newell and Simon's analysis took this point of view. What distinguishes it from search in many other problem spaces is that the problem is factored into 10 separate but interdependent searches for the individual assignments. Success in each of these searches constrains the problem space by reducing the number of alternative possibilities for the remaining assignments, and by providing additional information about some of the columns. Hence, it is not unlike an ordinary search in which each step of progress provides clear feedback of information that the right track is being followed.

### Anagrams

Anagrams are strings of letters that can be rearranged to form words, for example, *thgli* → *light*. The problem space of an *N*-letter anagram contains *N*! possibilities, and therefore, increases rapidly with *N*. The solution process can be viewed as a search through this space of permutations of the letters, but most persons presented with an anagram use various heuristics to speed up the search. One of these is to pick out initial combinations of letters that are pronounceable (e.g., *ti* or *li* in the example above), and then try to complete a word with the remaining letters. Imposing the condition of pronounceability on solution attempts may restrict the search space considerably.

The course of the search is also much influenced by the structure of long-term memory. For example, if there are two possible solutions to an anagram, the one corresponding to the more frequent and familiar word is likely to be found by most of the subjects. Moreover, the solution can be primed by presenting the word to the subject, or a semantically related word, some time before the anagram task is taken up (Dominoswski & Ekstrand, 1967).

Perceptual factors may affect performance on anagram tasks. Anagrams that are already words (e.g., *forth → froth*) or are easily pronounced (e.g., *obave → above*) take longer to solve than those without such properties (Beilin & Horn, 1962). This finding is consistent with Gestalt principles that meaningful forms resist restructuring. Gavurin (1967) found a correlation of .54 between success in solving anagrams and scores on a standard test of spatial abilities. When the subject was provided with tiles that could be rearranged physically, the correlation disappeared, indicating that the original relation had to do with the perceptual ability to operate on visual or auditory images.

It is easy to induce a problem-solving set in anagram solving by presenting subjects with several anagrams that call for the same permutation (say, 5 4 1 2 3) of the letters. If an ambiguous anagram (one with several possible solutions) is then presented, most subjects will find the solution requiring the same permutation rather than the alternative solution (Rees & Israel, 1935).

Thus, subjects' behaviors on the anagram task combines search (generating possible solutions) with constraint satisfaction (rejecting unpronounceable initial segments). The process of alternative generation, in turn, is influenced by long-term memory organization and priming, and by the subject's skill in forming and holding in short-term memory the permutations of the stimulus.

## Problems of Modifying Arrangements

Unlike the problems just discussed in which arrangements are formed from materials pro-

vided that the problem solver must put together to satisfy a specified criterion, we now turn to problems in which an arrangement of objects is presented, and the task is to modify the arrangement. Perceptual processes important to the solution of these problems involve recognition of general features and complex patterns.

These problems combine features of the transformation problems discussed above in "Well-Specified Problems" with features of design problems. Like design problems, a goal is specified as a general criterion rather than as a specific state that the problem solver tries to produce. At the same time, in these problems significant restrictions on the operators can be used to change the situation. Therefore, the problems can be conceptualized as search either in a space of possible arrangements or in a space of possible sequences of moves.

### Matchstick Problems

Figure 9.10 shows a matchstick problem used by Katona (1940). The 16 matches form five squares; the task is to move exactly three matches in such a way that the matches form only four

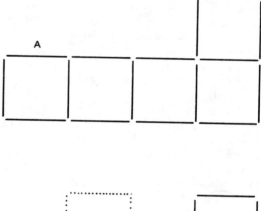

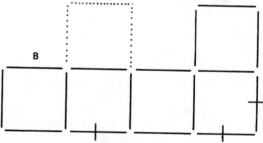

**Figure 9.10.** A matchstick problem used by Katona (1940).

squares, and all the matches serve as sides of squares. Katona tested subjects under three conditions: (1) in rote learning (subjects were shown and required to learn a specific solution), (2) with a logical condition for the solution (subjects were taught that in the solution, each match formed a side of one and only one square), and (3) with a heuristic for solving the problem (subjects were told "you need to open up the figure").

The subjects learned the solutions and then were tested on transfer tasks (different initial arrangements of the matches and different numbers of squares). Differences in the ease of learning the solution were minimal, with the rote solution being learned most rapidly. Two weeks later they were invited back and tested for their memory of the solution. In the test of transfer and retention, the logical and heuristic solutions far outshone the rote solution, and the heuristic solution scored slightly better than the logical. From this evidence Katona concluded that problem-solving knowledge and skills are better transferred and retained when the learning is meaningful than when it is rote.

The experimental manipulations leave implicit, however, the theoretical import of the term 'meaningful'. Why does meaningful learning facilitate retention and transfer, and why is the heuristic form of the instruction superior to the logical form?

With respect to transfer and retention, meaningful learning involves the same issues as structural understanding (discussed above in "Problem Representation in Mathematics and Physics"). Transfer is facilitated because, with more meaningful instruction, subjects acquire knowledge that can be applied more generally —in particular, to the new problems presented in the test as well as the problems used in training. It is easy to see why this occurs; the meaningful instruction can be applied to matchstick problems generally, while a specific solution sequence applies only to a single problem.

As for retention, meaningful forms of instruction may provide more redundancy, and hence, more opportunity to recover from partial forgetting. The general principles of single versus double function and of loosening or condensing the figure are constraints that can be used to limit search for information in memory, or to reconstruct solutions that are only partly remembered.

The difference between the two meaningful procedures appears to derive from the distinction between generators and tests. The instruction to 'open up the figure' provides a constraint on the selection of an operator—it suggests something to do, however vague, relative to a general property of the figure that can be perceived. The rule, 'each match must form a side of one and only one square,' constrains solution arrangements. It provides a test that can be applied to an attempted solution, but does not suggest what to move to produce the solution in the first place. In fact, the matches that have to be moved to solve the problem are not those with double function but rather those that already lie on the side of only one square. In this situation, at least, the knowledge that facilitates a solution most effectively increases the selectivity of the move generator rather than of the candidate solution states.

Katona noted that the heuristic of opening the figure or closing gaps uses a feature that is important in the perception of form, the Gestalt principle of good continuation. Attending to that feature and considering moves to adapt an arrangement to it constitutes a general strategy for solving matchstick problems.

### Chess and Go

Board games offer problems of the same general form as matchstick problems. An arrangement of objects is presented—the current situation in the game—and a player has the task of selecting a move or move sequence. Some criteria for a good solution are quite specific (e.g., white to mate in four moves); more often they are general, involving a goal to achieve a stronger position. Recent experiments comparing the performances of individuals who differ in skill show the importance of knowledge in the recognition of large numbers of complex patterns that occur during games.

In complex games, as in other domains in which some people become expert, problems that would be difficult or impossible for novices are often solved 'instantly' by experts—that is, in a few seconds. For example, a chess grand master, who is presented with a position from an actual but unfamiliar game and asked to recommend a move, will usually be able to report a good move, often the best move, in five seconds or less (deGroot, 1965). In a 'blitz' game, the same player, required to move within 10 seconds, will probably be unable to play at the grand master level but will achieve master level. Players at this level will be able to play 50 or more opponents simultaneously, with a high level of success, taking only a few seconds for each move. When experts are asked how they solve problems so rapidly, they may reply, "I use intuition," or, "I use my judgment."

The nature of this intuition or judgment has been clarified by experiments on skill in chess by deGroot (1965) and Jongman (1968) and repeated and extended by Chase and Simon (1973), and on skill in the game Go by Reitman (1976). In the experiments on chess skill, a chessboard with a position from a game (containing perhaps 25 pieces) is shown to a subject for 5 to 10 sec. The subject is then asked to reconstruct the position. Chess grand masters and masters can perform this task with 90 percent accuracy. Ordinary players can replace only five or six pieces correctly (20 to 25 percent accuracy). In a second condition the task is the same, except that the pieces are now arranged on the chessboard at random, rather than in a pattern that could have arisen in a game. In this condition, the performance of masters falls to the level of ordinary players—both can replace, on average, only about six pieces. This second part of the experiment demonstrates that the chess masters do not have any special powers of visual imagery.

Reitman's (1976) study of skill in Go had similar results. Go is a game of territory played on a 19 × 19 grid. The pieces are round 'stones' differing only in color for the two players, black and white. An experienced subject (not as strong as a professional player), was able to reproduce 66 percent of the pieces of meaningful patterns, compared to 39 percent for a beginner who had played about 50 games. On random patterns the players replaced 30 percent and 25 percent, respectively or an average of five to seven stones.

This experimental procedure has been applied to the pattern-recognition abilities of experts in several other domains; see "More Complex Tasks of Composition and Design" and "Diagnostic Problem Solving," below.

The behavior of the chess and Go experts in the perception and memory task can best be explained as a function of their chess and Go experience. As a result of thousands of hours spent at game boards, they become familiar with many configurations of three, four, or more pieces that recur again and again in games. For example, a configuration known as a 'fianchettoed castled Black King's position' occurs in perhaps one in ten games between expert chess players. This configuration is defined by the positions of six pieces. It has been estimated that a chess master has stored in long-term memory not fewer than 50,000 familiar patterns of this kind (Simon & Barenfeld, 1969; Simon & Gilmartin, 1973). This number is comparable to the 50,000 words in the vocabulary of a typical college graduate, or perhaps the total number of human faces a gregarious person learns to recognize over a lifetime.

When a chess master is confronted with a chessboard on which the pieces are arrayed in a 'reasonable' way, he can store this information in short-term memory in a half dozen or fewer 'chunks'—familiar configurations. The ordinary player, or the chess master confronted with a randomly arrayed chessboard, must store the information piece by piece, and hence, can hold the positions of only half a dozen or so pieces in short-term memory.

The skill that the expert acquires does not consist simply of being able to recognize familiar stimuli or configurations of stimuli. As deGroot showed, the recognition of perceptual features on the chessboard reminds the grand master of moves that are potentially good when those features are present. Indeed, we should expect the expert's knowledge for pattern recognition to be integrated with strategic knowledge so that the patterns the expert has learned to recognize are those relevant to the choices of moves and plans encountered in games.

The importance of game strategy in perception and representation of complex patterns was shown in an experiment by Eisenstadt and Kareev (1975). The games Go and Gomoku are played with entirely different rules, though on the same board and with the same kinds of pieces. Two groups of subjects, who knew how to play both games, were shown the same patterns of stones on boards. One group was told that the patterns were from a game of Go, and the other from a game of Gomoku. When they were subsequently asked to recall the patterns, the subjects in the first condition better recalled the pieces that were critical to selecting the correct move in the Go position, whereas the others recalled better those pieces that were critical to selecting a move in the Gomoku position. Thus, in the face of a complex stimulus situation, attention to a particular task determines the sequence in which information is extracted from the stimulus and the patterns in which it is organized.

Studies of specific knowledge structures that integrate strategic knowledge and knowledge for recognizing patterns have been carried out by Wilkins (1980) in a model of choosing moves in chess, and by Reitman and Wilcox (1978) in a model of playing Go.

Wilkins's (1980) model represents board positions by recognizing concepts, such as Attack and Safe, based on relations among pieces. The model uses schemata that correspond to the concepts in proposing and evaluating plans. In formulating a plan, a concept such as Safe or Defend-Threat can be set as a goal; the schema for each concept includes conditions that are required to satisfy the goal. The model's strategy of using proposed plans to guide its search restricts the set of moves it considers, enabling relatively thorough evaluations. The model is successful in solving problems of choosing moves in middle game positions that are sufficiently difficult to be used in a standard chess textbook.

Reitman and Wilcox's (1978) model simulates representation of board positions and changes of board positions in Go. The model forms a multilevel representation with low-level units such as strings and chains of stones, and higher-level units called groups and fields involving collections of points and their surrounding stones. The representations include features that are relevant to Go tactics, such as the stability of a group of stones. Perceptual activity is organized according to several structures including lenses, which monitor changes on the board relevant to relations between groups of stones, and webs, which monitor changes on radii and circumferences around groups. The model's capabilities for representation, combined with some relatively low-level processes for selecting moves, is similar to a human player with the experience of playing 40 or 50 games.

The ability of experts to recognize complex patterns of information related to a highly integrated structure of actions has been found in other domains in which expertise has been analyzed. The importance of knowledge for representing problems in physics was discussed above in "Problem Understanding; Represen-

tation," and similar conclusions were found for medical diagnosis and electronic troubleshooting ("Diagnostic Problem Solving," below). It is reasonable to conjecture on present evidence that high levels of expertise generally require tens of thousands of perceptual 'chunks' relevant to the domain. In domains where the minimal time required to become a world-class master has been measured, the estimate turns out to be about a decade (Hayes, 1981; this finding is discussed below for musical composition in "Problems of Composition").

## Construction Tasks and Other Insight Problems

Much attention in research has been given to problems in which some physical device or arrangement is required, often to satisfy a functional criterion. An example is Duncker's (1935/1945) famous 'tumor' problem in which a patient has a stomach tumor that is to be destroyed by radiation without damaging the surrounding healthy tissue. How is it to be done?

The source of difficulty in construction problems differs from the problems discussed above in "Simple Problems of Forming Arrangements" and "Problems of Modifying Arrangements" where difficulty arises from the large number of possible solutions. The tumor problem and other 'insight' problems are difficult, primarily because most of the candidate solutions considered are ruled out by the constraints of the problem. In the tumor problem, for example, simply directing the rays to the tumor would destroy all the tissue along their path; to open a path to the tumor by surgical procedures would cause intolerable damage, and so on. The 'textbook' solution to the tumor problem calls for irradiating the tumor from many different angles, and hence, via many different paths through the surrounding tissue. By this means a large quantity of radiation is concentrated on the tumor, while each path of surrounding tissue is subjected to only a small fraction of that amount.

Solving the tumor problems and similar insight problems often depends on finding a way to represent the problem so that the solution becomes obvious. Achievement of such a representation, corresponding to a moment of insight, is a phenomenon of great interest, especially in relation to issues of cognitive organization in Gestalt psychology. In problems such as cryptarithmetic and anagrams, the problem space is easily constructed, and problem-solving activity consists of searching in the set of possibilities that arise in that space. On the other hand, in insight problems such as the tumor problem, the problem solver's initial representation usually provides an inadequate problem space, one in which a solution will not be found. Problem solving involves a construction of several problem spaces—only to be discarded as factors are discovered that make each of them inadequate—until a successful representation is found. Processes of problem representation thus play a central role in the solution of these problems of construction. The process can be characterized as a search for alternative ways to represent the problem. However, the usefulness of such a characterization is limited unless the set of alternative representations can be specified more definitely than we are at present able to do.

Duncker (1935/1945) emphasized the *demand*, the condition to be met by the problem solution, as the chief source of solution proposals. The initial proposals are not unmotivated, but they are faulty in not attending to all the conditions a solution must meet. False analogies may produce inadequate solutions because of their failure to match the actual situation in crucial dimensions. At the same time, Duncker stressed that the proposals are not produced by simple association:

In short, it is evident that such proposals are anything but completely meaningless associations. Merely in the factual situation, they are wrecked on certain components of the situation not yet known or not yet considered by the subject.

Occasionally it is not so much the situation as the demand, whose distortion or simplification makes the proposal practically useless (p. 3).

By constructing a taxonomy of correct and inadequate solutions to the tumor problem, Duncker showed how the solution-generating process can be understood as a process of means–ends analysis. His taxonomy can be depicted in outline form:

Treat tumor by rays without destroying healthy tissue

Avoid contact between rays and healthy tissue
    Use free path to stomach
      Use esophagus
    Remove healthy tissue from path of rays
      Insert a cannula
    Insert protective wall between rays and tissue
      Feed substance that protects
    Displace tumor toward surface
      Apply pressure
Desensitize the healthy tissue
    Inject desensitizing chemical
    Immunize by adaptation to weak rays
Lower intensity of rays through healthy tissue
    Postpone full intensity until tumor is reached
    Use weak intensity in periphery, strong near tumor
      Use a lens

Duncker described the solution process as the successive development or reformulation of the problem. Working both forward and backward may contribute to the process. Seeing a stick may give a chimpanzee the clue to obtaining a banana that is out of reach. Alternatively, the banana's being out of reach may lead the chimpanzee to look for an object that could be used to reach it (cf. Köhler, 1929). Mistakes may also call attention to features of the problem situation that must be incorporated in the solution, and hence, may lead to new solution attempts.

From the idea that the solution of a problem depends on an appropriate formulation, it would be expected that hints could be used to make problems significantly easier. One experiment on the effects of hints used a problem of constructing a hat rack, invented by Maier (1945). Two sticks and a clamp were given. The hat rack could be constructed by clamping the sticks together so that the assemblage was long enough to be wedged between the floor and the ceiling. Subjects usually began by either laying one stick on the floor and clamping the other stick to it vertically, or standing both sticks on the floor in an $X$ or inverted $V$ shape. Neither of these structures is stable. If the experimenter said, "In the correct solution, the clamp is used as a hanger," the solution was facilitated somewhat, mainly by reducing attempts made with one stick lying on the floor. If the experimenter said, "In the correct solution the ceiling is part of the construction," the solution was facilitated even more forcefully, by reducing attempts that used only the floor as support (Burke, Maier, & Hoffman, 1966).

A potential source of problem solutions is analogy with similar problems. Gick and Holyoak (1980) gave Duncker's tumor problem to subjects, some of whom had studied a story in which a fortress was taken by a converging attack. The subjects who were familiar with the military problem were more successful than control subjects in solving the tumor problem. An important factor was the inclusion of an instruction that the fortress story might provide a useful hint for solving the problem. With the hint, most subjects found the convergence solution to the tumor problem, but without the hint only about half as many subjects found that solution, even though they had read the story and recalled it in a test.

In a subsequent study, Gick and Holyoak (1983) examined conditions favoring the spontaneous use of an analogy. Asking the subjects to summarize the military story, rather than recall it, had little effect, and giving them a verbal statement or diagram showing the convergence principle did not noticeably increase their use of the analogy. However, more solutions were proposed by subjects who read two stories involving convergence, summarized both of them, and discussed ways in which the stories were similar. Gick and Holyoak concluded that those subjects acquired a schema with the idea of convergence represented in a general way, and that such a schema is more likely to be used than is a specific analogous problem. (In "Problem Representation in Mathematics and Physics," above, a similar hypothesis was offered.)

Duncker (1935/1945) also studied problems that required subjects to construct some item out of potential components, including some inessential components, that were provided. He showed that the problems could be made difficult by presenting one of the components in such a way that it was conceptually 'unavailable' for its required function. For example, in one problem the building materials were a candle, matches, and a box full of thumbtacks. The task was to mount the candle on a wall so that it could burn without dripping wax on the floor. The problem could be solved by thumbtacking the box to the wall, then mounting the candle in it.

This problem was so difficult that fewer than half the subjects in one experiment were able to solve it in 20 minutes (Adamson, 1952). When the problem was presented to another group of subjects with the thumbtacks lying on a table, and the box empty, 86 percent solved it in less than 20 minutes. The phenomenon underlying this finding has been labeled 'functional fixity.' When an object is performing, or has recently been used to perform some function, subjects are less likely to recognize its potential use for another function.

Birch & Rabinowitz (1951) demonstrated a similar phenomenon, using another problem originally studied by Maier (1931). In a room where two strings were hanging from a ceiling, too far apart to be reached simultaneously, the task was to tie them together. This could be accomplished if a heavy object was tied to one string and the string was swung as a pendulum. This string could be grasped as it swung toward the subject, who meanwhile had the other string in hand. Two objects, an electric switch and a relay, were available for constructing the pendulum. The subjects had used either the switch or the relay (but not both) in a previous task. Of ten subjects who had used the relay previously, all used the switch to construct the pendulum; of nine who had used the switch, seven used the relay to construct the pendulum. Of six subjects who had used neither object previously, three used the switch and three the relay to construct the pendulum.

Several findings support a hypothesis that functional fixity results from a decrease in the likelihood of noticing certain critical features of objects in the situation, such as the flatness of a box (in use as a container), or the heaviness of a switch (after use in a circuit), or the features in functional fixity may be quite different in different situations, involving restrictive hypotheses about general classes of solutions in some cases, and simple competition between feature-recognition processes in others.

Some of the findings that support this explanation involve demonstrations that the solution of problems can be influenced even by very low-level perceptual factors. For example, in the pendulum task, the idea of making one string swing so that it would be reachable by someone holding the other one does not occur readily to most subjects, even in the presence of one or more heavy objects. Maier (1931) showed that this idea occurred immediately to many subjects who had not previously thought of it, when the experimenter casually brushed against the string and set it swinging. Glucksberg and Weisberg (1966) presented pictures of the materials available for use in solving Duncker's candle problem, and found that solutions were markedly increased when the label 'Box' was included in the picture. A process of noticing features of objects that can be related to the problem goal (Duncker's 'suggestions from below') probably plays a significant role in the solution of construction problems, as Weisberg and Suls (1973) concluded in their theoretical analysis of solution processes for the candle problem. Results consistent with that idea were obtained by Magone (1977), whose subjects produced a greater variety of solutions to Maier's two-string problem if they were initially prompted to consider features of objects than if they were prompted to seek a solution of a specified kind, such as extending one of the strings or causing a string to swing back and forth.

The Einstellung effect discussed above in "Einstellung" is similar in character to functional fixity in that in both effects, previous experience influences the availability of alternative steps toward solution. The processes responsible for the two effects are probably analogous in a subtle but significant way since in both, a form of search is made less likely than it would normally have been. With Einstellung, the previous use of a solution path suppresses a search for problem-solving operators. With functional fixity, the search for features of objects that could be useful to a solution is suppressed.

Another 'insight' problem that has been studied is the nine-dot problem. A three-by-three matrix of dots is given, and the task is to connect all the dots with four straight lines without any retracing. Several lines may pass through the same dot. The problem is difficult; most subjects do not think of drawing lines outside the space defined by the matrix of dots, as is required for the solution. The difficulty is apparently another instance of a restricted domain of search, but the obvious hypothesis of a restriction based on the spatial arrangement is not supported by data. Weisberg and Alba (1981) instructed their subjects to draw lines outside the square of dots, but that had little effect. However, when they

gave an easier problem requiring drawing lines beyond the region that contained dots to other subjects, subsequent solution of the nine-dot problem was facilitated. A reasonable interpretation is that the easier problem led the subjects to consider problem-solving operators that were not in the problem space of subjects who had not solved the simpler problem first. This finding involves the same principles as the finding of Katona (1940; see "Matchstick Problems") that a heuristic for choosing operators is more effective than a test applicable to the results of operators.

## More Complex Tasks of Composition and Design

### Problems of Composition

Flower and Hayes (1980), who studied the task of writing an essay, noted that successful writing requires simultaneous compliance with a large number of constraints, operating at different levels. One set of constraints requires the selection and organization of ideas from the writer's knowledge into a coherent network of concepts and information for inclusion in the essay. Another involves the linguistic and discourse conventions of written language. A third is rhetorical, involving the need to arrange the essay so as to accomplish the writer's purpose for the intended audience.

Using protocols obtained from subjects working on writing tasks, Hayes and Flower (1980) found three general processes: planning, translating, and reviewing. These three processes allow the writer to attend to a subset of the constraints at any time. In planning, information relevant to the topic is generated from the problem solver's memory, and decisions are made about what to include. In translating, a text is produced using information that has been retrieved, consistent with a writing plan that has been formed. In reviewing, the generated text is evaluated and revised in accord with the constraints of rhetoric, text structure, and such detailed linguistic concerns as correct grammar. Hayes and Flower found that writing involves a combination of these processes and postulated that the writing process includes a monitor that determines the sequence of subprocesses, depending on the nature of difficulties that arise.

To write successfully, an individual must

understand the constraints that apply at various levels to the text, must have effective methods for generating or revising text to conform to those constraints, and must actively engage in evaluation in light of the constraints. In studies of young writers, Bereiter and Scardamalia (1982) noted that inattention to constraints, especially global rhetorical concerns, characterizes the writing of many children. When they revise a text that have produced, most children attend exclusively to low-level constraints, usually changing only single words or small phrases, rather than attempting to improve more significant general features of their essays. Bereiter and Scardamalia hypothesized that the difficulty lies in the process of evaluating the text, rather than in a failure to understand rhetorical goals or the lack of effective means to produce an improved text. They gave students a set of cue cards with evaluative comments, such as "I need another example here," "The reader won't be convinced by this," "Even I seem to be confused here," and "This is a good sentence." The children's task was to choose a card that seemed appropriate for each sentence in their texts and to make appropriate changes. The technique was effective and consistent with the idea that the children's problem lay in the difficulty of evaluating their texts and applying global constraints, rather than in ignorance of the constraints or methods for complying with them.

Multiple interacting constraints also characterize composition of music, as Reitman (1965) showed in an analysis based on a protocol obtained from a professional composer as he wrote a fugue. Reitman noted that schematic structures that he called transformational formulas played an important role; these included knowledge of the main components of the musical form being composed (exposition, development, and conclusion) as well as subcomponents of those units (exposition → thematic material + countermaterial; thematic material → motive + development, etc.). Reitman found that much problem-solving activity was concerned with constraints. Some constraints were generated by properties of the instrument (piano) chosen for the piece, requiring musical material suited to the instrument. Other constraints were produced by material already included in the piece, such as a requirement that countermaterial should be compatible with thematic

material, but sufficiently different to elicit interest. The composer characterized patterns that he developed as conventions, producing melodic, rhythmic, and instrumental properties that were then "used to carry on the movement of the music" (Reitman, 1965, p. 169), with variations introduced to maintain interest.

A substantial knowledge base is required to solve problems of composition, and an important question is how much experience and training a person needs to make substantial creative contributions to a field such as musical composition. Using data from biographies and a standard catalogue of recordings, Hayes (1981) determined the time between a composer's beginning serious musical training and the first composition that had five independent recordings in the catalogue. In almost every case, at least ten years of virtually full-time training occurred before a composer produced a work of sufficient quality to appear commonly in the recorded repertoire.

### Recognition and Knowledge of Constraints

In problems that impose constraints, a problem solver must recognize the constraints in order to perform successfully. "Cryptarithmetic Problems" discussed Newell and Simon's (1972) finding that individual differences in cryptarithmetic depended on inclusion in the subjects' problem spaces of significant constraints, such as odd–even parity. Two studies have investigated this factor, one on examination questions by Bloom and Broder (1950) and one on administrative policy by Voss, Greene, Post, and Penner (1983).

In comprehensive college examination questions studied by Bloom and Broder (1950), students were often required to make inferences or deal with information presented in an unusual form. For students who performed poorly, a significant factor was their inattention to constraints in the statements of some questions. For example, when the task was to choose the best explanation for a situation, some students would ignore the relation of alternative answers to the situation and would pick the answers that seemed most nearly true in itself. For such students, the activity of problem solving occurred in a problem space that lacked some of the information that was required for good performance. Bloom and Broder developed an instructional method in which students compared their own problem-solving process, recorded in a thinking-aloud protocol, with the process of another student whose performance was more successful. This training was effective for many students, teaching them to attend more carefully to constraints in questions as well as such other helpful strategies as increasing their efforts to infer plausible answers from information they could retrieve from memory.

Voss et al. (1983) obtained thinking-aloud protocols on problems involving the design of an administrative policy. For example, problem solvers were asked to develop a policy for improving agricultural productivity in a region of the Soviet Union. Subjects with different amounts of knowledge about Soviet government and history worked on the problem, including students in an introductory course in Soviet politics, experts in political science (some of whom specialized in the Soviet Union and some with other specialties), and experts in another field altogether (chemistry). The solving process of experts was primarily to formulate the problem, and then, after a long initial period devoted to considering historical and political factors, to make successive reformulations based on evaluations of proposed solutions against known constraints. The inexpert student subjects offered problem formulations that failed to include important constraints. Experts in chemistry worked more systematically than the political science students, sometimes using general knowledge about administrative systems to provide useful conjectures, but they too lacked the rich formulations that characterized the problem solver with specialized knowledge.

### Design of Procedures

Another type of problem involves tasks in which the materials consist of a set of actions that can be performed, and the problem solver constructs a procedure from these components. These problems are similar to problems of transformation, discussed in "Well-Specified Problems" especially when planning is used to construct a sequence of actions to reach the problem goal.

Hayes-Roth and Hayes-Roth (1978) gave subjects a map of a fictitious town, showing the locations of several stores and other businesses. The subjects were also given a list of errands, such as buying fresh vegetables at the grocery, picking up medicine for a dog at the vet, and seeing a movie. The subjects' task was to plan a schedule that included as many of the errands

as possible. The task presented some general constraints, in particular, a limit on the amount of time available. It also presented local constraints and interactions. For example, it is better to buy groceries late in the day, so they will still be fresh when the shopper returns home; and it is best to go to the movie at one of the times when the feature is starting. Interactions include the proximity of shops, making it more efficient to group together in the sequence errands that involve shops that are near one another.

The Hayes-Roth's simulated performance on their planning task with a model that contained several planning specialists and a blackboard control structure, a design similar to one used earlier in a speech understanding system called Hearsay (Reddy, Erman, Fennell, & Neely, 1973). The specialists are designed to make suggestions about different kinds of planning decisions: They all have access to inferences, suggestions, and other information, which is located in the system's blackboard. This system design supports a feature called opportunistic planning, which has been found in the performance of human problem solvers. Opportunities arise in the form of conditions that make it easy to include an errand, such as the proximity of a store to a place that is already included in the plan, and an appropriate specialist can be activated by that condition.

In the writing of a computer program, the procedure is designed to perform a designated function. Studies of computer programmers and designers have revealed important characteristics of the knowledge required for the solution of these design problems.

Soloway, Ehrlich, Bonar, and Greenspan (1982) gave three problems, typical of elementary programming courses, to students in the first and second introductory courses in programming. They identified schematic cognitive structures that they called plans, needed for successful problem solving. The required schemata are quite basic, involving the construction of iterative loops and the use of variables. The schemata provide knowledge of requirements for performing significant program functions, such as the interactions between processing and testing a variable within a loop and between the loop processing and initialization. Students who lacked adequate versions of these schemata made significant errors, for example, by failing to recognize distinctions between different looping structures. Experiments on memory for program texts have shown that experienced programmers can recall more successfully than beginners (Adelson, 1981; McKeithen et al., 1981; see also "Einstellung"). The acquisition of plan schemata as hypothesized by Soloway et al. (1982) provides a natural explanation of this finding.

More advanced problems, involving software design, were studied by Polson, Atwood, Jeffries, and Turner (1981). A task in software design involves planning a complex program; actual writing of the program is performed separately. Polson et al. studied the design of a program for compiling an index for a text, given a set of key words to be included in the index. Both professional software designers and students gave solutions with thinking-aloud protocols. The experts recognized functions that had to be included in the solution, such as defining a data structure for the text and searching the key word set for a word that would match each word encountered in the text. Polson et al. concluded that experts' knowledge includes general design schemata that enable decomposition of problems and the progressive forming of more well-defined subproblems, with specific techniques available for some of the subproblems encountered. These schemata provide another example of knowledge for action organized hierarchically like that developed by Sacerdoti (1977; see "Domain Specific Knowledge for Familiar Problems with Specified Goals.")

In the domain of microbiology, two versions of a program that solves problems of experimental design, called Molgen, have been developed. One program by Stefik (1981) designs procedures for modifying the genetic structure of microorganisms. An important issue considered by Stefik is the handling of constraints that arise from interactions between components of a procedure. Molgen designs procedures in a top-down manner, in which abstract plan schemata are gradually made more specific. A method of constraint posting was developed in which requirements for one of the design components could be taken into account in the decisions made about other components.

The second version of Molgen, by Friedland (1979), designs analytic experiments, such as the determination of the sequence of base molecules in a DNA strand or the location of a set of restriction sites on a molecule. In this model schemata called skeletal plans incorporate information about experimental procedures that, through a process of filling in details, develop specific experimental plans based on the specific problem requirements.

# INDUCTION

In a problem of induction, some material is presented and the problem solver tries to find a general principle or structure that is consistent with the material. Important examples include (1) scientific induction, including situations in which the material is a set of numerical data and the task is to induce a formula or a molecular structure, (2) language acquisition, where the material is a set of sentences and the task is to induce the rules of grammar for the language, and (3) diagnosis, in which the material is a set of symptoms and the task is to induce the cause of the symptoms. Problems of analogy and extrapolating sequences are inductive tasks that are widely used in intelligence tests. The task of inducing a rule for classifying stimuli into categories has been used in a larger and significant body of experimental study.

An induction problem presents a dual problem space that includes a space of stimuli or data and a space of possible structures, such as rules, principles, or patterns of relations (cf. Simon & Lea, 1974). The task can be conceptualized as a search, within the space of structures, to find a structure that satisfies a criterion of agreement with the stimuli or data. An experimental subject can be tested by being required to use the structure for stimuli that have not yet been shown. When the task is to induce a rule for classifying stimuli, new stimuli may be presented to test whether the subject can classify them correctly. When the task is to induce a pattern in a sequence, the subject may be required to extend the sequence by producing additional elements that fit the same pattern as those that are given.

Solving an induction problem can proceed in two ways, and most tasks use a combination of the methods. The first, a top-down method, involves generating hypotheses about the structure and evaluating them with information about the stimulus instances. The second, a bottom-up method, involves storing information about the individual stimuli and making judgments about new stimuli on the basis of similarity or analogy to the stored information. Use of the top-down method requires a procedure for generating or selecting hypotheses, a procedure for evaluating hypotheses, and then a way of using the hypothesis generator to modify or replace hypotheses that are found to be incorrect. Use of the bottom-up method requires a method of extrapolating from stored information, either by judging the similarity of new stimuli to stimuli stored in memory, or by forming analogical correspondences with stored information.

Induction involves a form of understanding in which a representation is found that provides an integrated structure for diverse stimuli. This general feature also characterizes processes of representing problems such as the textbook physics problems discussed above in "Problem Understanding; Representation." There the space of stimuli is the information in the problem situation—often a problem text or instructions—and the space of structures is a set of possible representations that can be constructed. To be successful, a problem representation must provide the information needed to achieve the problem goal. Thus, in representing transformation problems, the inductive search is constrained by the requirements of problem-solving operators that are available. In some problems of induction, such constraints are not present, and one does not have to do anything with the pattern that is found in the information. However, in some inductive problems, such as medical diagnosis, there are strong constraints related to available operators. The goal is to restore the ailing person to proper functioning, and the effort to induce a cause serves the goal of determining an effective remedy.

In some task domains, the possible structures are represented explicitly as formulae. Examples include induction of quantitative formulas from numerical data in physics, or induction of the molecular structure of a chemical compound. Patterns induced in letter-sequence problems also consist of explicit formula-like rules. These tasks share important properties with problems of design and arrangement (discussed above in "Problems of Design and Arrangement"). The goals of these induction tasks can be considered as the design of a formula that agrees with the data. The solution of design problems generally requires use of strong constraints to limit the space of possibilities for search and this important property is also found in tasks that involve induction of formulas.

The discussion of inductive problem solving will cover: (1) induction of categorical concepts, (2) induction of more complex concepts involving sequential stimuli, (3) induction of relational structure, and (4) diagnostic problem solving.

## Categorical Concepts

Of the various inductive tasks that have been studied, by far the most attention has been given to the induction of categorical concepts. This is partly in recognition of their practical importance. Our human capability of organizing experience using conceptual categories undoubtedly contributes much to making our cognitive lives manageable.

In an experiment on concept induction, the experimenter constructs a set of stimuli (e.g., diagrams with figures that vary in shape, size, color, and other attributes) and decides on a rule to classify the stimuli (e.g., "the red circles are positive, all other stimuli are negative"). The subjects are given information about several individual stimuli—that is, they are told whether each stimulus is positive or negative. The subject's task is to induce the rule of classification. Usually, the experimenter tests whether the subjects have induced the concept by presenting new stimuli to determine whether they can classify them correctly.

In an early discussion, Woodworth (1938) distinguished between processes of concept induction involving bottom-up and top-down methods. In a bottom-up process, knowledge of the concept is analogous to a composite photograph, consisting of an impression summed over the various stimuli in the category, with the common features emphasized and the variable characteristics 'washed out.' In a top-down process, the problem-solver actively constructs hypotheses about features that define the concept and tests these hypotheses with additional information about examples.

The following discussion deals first with two studies of top-down processes, and then with studies of bottom-up processes of inducing concepts.

### Multifeature Concepts

When two or more stimulus features are

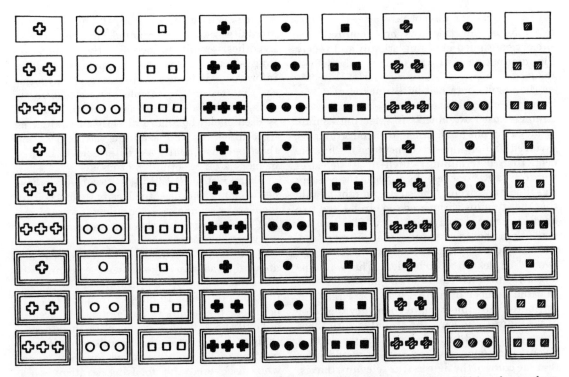

**Figure 9.11** An array of instances comprising combinations of four attributes, each exhibiting three values. Open figures are in green, striped figures in red, solid figures in black. From *A Study of Thinking* (p. 42) by J.S. Bruner, J.J. Goodnow, and G.A. Austin, 1956. New York: Wiley. Copyright 1956 by Jerome Bruner. Reprinted by permission.

combined to form a categorical concept, they are combined in some logical formula, such as 'A and B,' or 'If A, then B.' A stimulus is a positive example of the concept if the formula truly describes the stimulus. In the set of stimuli shown in Figure 9.11 the concept 'Green and Circle' specifies the stimuli in column 2; the concept 'Green or Circle' specifies the stimuli in columns 1, 2, 3, 5, and 8.

Consider the requirements for performance of this task, assuming that it is done in a top-down, hypothesis-testing manner. First, the stimulus features must be discriminated; the problem solver must have processes for *recognition* of the features that are used to define concepts. Second, there must be a process for *hypothesis formation*, which constructs candidate hypotheses to be considered. Third, a process of *hypothesis evaluation* is needed to test the hypotheses that have been formed. Fourth, a process for *hypothesis modification* is required in order to use the results of the tests to elimi-

nate incorrect hypothesis, to change existing hypotheses, or to form new ones.

In a landmark study of multifeature concept induction, Bruner, Goodnow, and Austin (1956) observed subjects who, as they worked on concept induction problems, made oral reports about their hypotheses. In certain of these experiments subjects were instructed that concepts were conjunctions of features, and that their task was to induce how many features were relevant and what the features were. Two experiments are considered here.

In one experiment subjects were required to solve two problems with the array shown in Figure 9.11 and a third problem of the same kind from memory—that is, with the stimuli not available. Each of the problems began with the experimenter providing a positive instance—a stimulus that was a member of the concept category. The subject could then choose any stimulus in the display and ask whether it was a positive or negative instance of the concept. The subject could offer a hypothesis after the choice of stimulus, but this was not required. The subject continued choosing stimuli and receiving information until the correct concept was induced.

The results obtained by Bruner et al. (1956) included characterizations of a variety of strategies used by subjects in selecting stimuli. Strategies of one kind, called focusing strategies, involved finding a positive instance of the concept, then determining which of its features were relevant. For example, suppose the concept was 'Red and Circle.' The subject might be told that the stimulus with three red circles and two borders was a positive instance. The subject could then choose a stimulus that differed from the focal stimulus in the number of circles, say, two red circles with two borders. This would be a positive instance, and the subject would infer that the number of figures was not a relevant attribute. The subject might then vary the color of the figures, choosing the stimulus with three green circles and two borders. This would be a negative instance, and the subject would infer that the color of the figures was relevant, that is, that 'Red' was part of the definition of the concept. With further choices and information, the concept's definition would be inferred.

Other strategies called scanning strategies, involve consideration of specific hypotheses and the use of information to narrow down the set of possible hypotheses. For example, a subject might consider as distinct possibilities the hypotheses 'three figures,' 'red,' 'three and red,' 'circle,' 'three circles,' and 'red circles.' Then finding that a stimulus with two red circles and two borders is a positive instance, all the hypotheses with the property 'three' could be eliminated. Use of a scanning strategy places severe demands on memory. It is impossible to consider all the possible hypotheses simultaneously (there are 255 of them), but it is desirable to consider as many as one can, since information can be used to evaluate hypotheses only in the sample being considered.

The focusing strategies and the scanning strategies differ primarily in the processes they use to form hypotheses. In the focusing strategies, information about instances is used to constrain hypothesis formation. Tests are performed to see whether an attribute is relevant, and when the attribute is eliminated, no hypothesis using it will be formed. If the focusing

strategy is used successfully, all but the correct attributes can be eliminated, and the correct hypothesis can be formed directly. In the scanning strategies, less use is made of problem information in forming hypotheses, and hypotheses that are in the sample are tested directly with information about instances. Information is used somewhat more directly in evaluating hypotheses in the scanning strategies, but there is consequently a greater need to keep in memory a large set of hypotheses.

Bruner et al. (1956) used 12 subjects whose performance was used to classify them as either focusers or scanners. Seven subjects were classified as focusers and the rest were treated as scanners. The focusing strategy was advantageous for the subjects who used it. They required about half as many choices as the scanners to solve a problem with the stimulus array present (medians of 5 and 10 choices, respectively). In addition, the scanners had noticeably greater difficulty in solving a problem 'in their heads' than they did when the stimuli were present (median of 13 choices), except for one scanner who discovered the focusing strategy while working on the third problem. The focusers' performance without stimuli present did not differ from their performance on the second problem with stimuli present.

Bruner et al. (1956) conducted two experiments to investigate situational factors that influenced subjects' choices of strategies. One experiment compared the effect of an orderly arrangement of stimuli with the same stimuli presented haphazardly. The stimuli used abstract forms, differing on six dimensions, with two values on each dimension. With the 64 stimuli arranged systematically, similar to the arrangement in Figure 9.11, almost all subjects used focusing strategies. When stimuli were not arranged systematically, subjects typically used scanning strategies. There was also a tendency to use scanning strategies when concrete stimuli were used, such as drawings of persons who varied in sex, size, and clothing.

Analyses by Hunt (1962) and Hunt et al. (1966) provided a hypothesis on how to represent categorical concepts in cognitive structure. Hunt proposed that the knowledge of a categorical concept is a cognitive procedure for deciding whether a stimulus is a member of the category. The form of the procedure that Hunt investigated was a decision network, a structure of perceptual tests organized in a way that reflected the logical structure of the concept. (This same form was used by Feigenbaum, 1963, for the Elementary Perceiver and Memorizer, used in simulations of rote verbal memorizing. Examples of such decision networks, for recognizing some concepts in geometry problems, were shown in Figures 9.5 and 9.6.) Experiments conducted by Trabasso, Rollins, and Schaughnessy (1971) provided evidence that supports Hunt's characterization. Trabasso et al. measured latencies for categorical decisions about stimuli and obtained results that agreed with Hunt's model: Longer times were required for decisions in which the model specified a larger number of perceptual tests. A model that simulates acquisition of conjunctive concepts was developed by Williams (1971) who used Hunt's representational hypothesis together with assumptions about limited short-term memory capacity and changes in the salience of dimensions.

An important aspect of the acquisition of complex concepts is induction of the logical relation between the stimulus features in the definition. This has been studied by Bourne and his associates in experiments in which subjects are informed of the features that the rules include. For example, a subject may be told that the rule includes 'Red' and 'Circle,' but the subject would then have to discover from examples whether the combination is conjunctive, disjunctive, conditional, or biconditional. When subjects are not experienced in this rule-learning task, there are substantial differences in the difficulty of inducing the various kinds of rules, and these correspond to differences among the types of rules found in standard concept induction tasks (Haygood & Bourne, 1965).

One possible explanation for differences in difficulty is that the rules differ in familiarity to the subjects, with conjunction being the most familiar way to combine features. Overuse of conjunction would lead to a bias in the process of forming hypotheses, with the less familiar forms of hypothesis generated later, if at all, and consequent delays in problem solutions. Evidence in support of this interpretation was obtained by Bourne (1970), who found that differences among the rule forms decreased when subjects were given a series of rule-induction problems. A more specific hypothesis, proposed by Bourne (1974), is that, with experience, subjects acquire a strategy for representing information about

stimuli in terms of truth-table values based on the features known to be relevant. For example, if 'Red' and 'Circle' are the features, then a red circle has the value T–T (true on both attributes), a green circle has the value F–T, and so on. This is an efficient representation for solving concept-induction problems, because each of the alternative rule forms corresponds to a distinctive subset of truth-table values. A conjunctive rule is satisfied only by T–T; a disjunctive rule is satisfied by T–F, F–T, and T–T; a conditional rule is satisfied by T–T, F–T, and F–F; and a biconditional rule is satisfied by T–T and F–F. The truth-table hypothesis is supported by Dodd, Kinsman, Klipp, and Bourne's finding (1971), that training on a task of sorting stimuli into the four categories of the truth table facilitated subsequent performance on rule-induction problems.

### Single-Feature Concepts

Induction of conceptual rules may also consist of single features, such as 'all the red pictures,' or, 'the circles.' The task of inducing such a concept is simpler, of course, than inducing a multifeature concept.

#### EVIDENCE FOR TOP-DOWN INDUCTION

Single-feature concept induction has been studied extensively by H.H. and T.S. Kendler and their associates. One question addressed in their experiments is whether concepts are acquired in the form of a verbalized rule or in the form of an aggregation of individual stimulus–response connections. It is likely that a verbalized rule would result from a top-down hypothesis-testing process of induction, and an aggregation of stimulus-response connections from a bottom-up process.

Evidence has been obtained in experiments in which the conceptual category is changed without informing the subject. A subject is given an initial concept-induction problem involving a single stimulus feature (e.g., "respond positively to red stimuli"). After the subject meets a criterion of correct responses, the rule is changed, either by changing the positive value of the same attribute (e.g., from red to green), called a reversal shift, or by changing to a different attribute (e.g., from red color to large size), a nonreversal shift. It was found that both adult human subjects, and kindergarten children who solved the initial problem quickly, adjusted more easily to the reversal than to the nonreversal shift (Buss, 1953; Kendler & D'Amato, 1955; Kendler & Kendler, 1959), whereas rats and slower-learning kindergarten children adjusted more quickly to the nonreversal shift (Kelleher, 1956). An interpretation is that adults and school-aged children use a hypothesis such as 'it depends on color,' which does not have to be changed to adjust to the reversal shift, while nonhuman subjects and preschool children learn specific stimulus–response associations, for which the reversal shift requires a greater change. In a later study, Erickson (1971) found that college students adjusted more rapidly to nonreversal shifts if they had been carefully instructed about the nature of the concept induction task, suggesting that when subjects have more complete information about the task they tend to remove stimulus attributes from consideration when their hypotheses are not confirmed.

Further evidence that adult human performance in concept induction is based on definite hypotheses was obtained by Levine (1963) who showed that on a series of test trials with no feedback given, nearly all the sequences of responses given by college students were consistent with a systematic hypothesis about the conceptual rule.

## Processes of Sampling Hypotheses

The processes of forming and evaluating hypotheses in single-feature concept induction are quite straightforward. Any stimulus feature that is noticed can be the basis of a rule, and a rule that links a feature with a response is confirmed or refuted directly by information about the category of any example. Because the hypotheses are simple, and many hypotheses are possible, it is efficient for subjects to consider samples of hypotheses rather than one hypothesis at a time. When a sample of hypotheses is considered, the subject can on each trial eliminate hypotheses that are inconsistent with the information given about that trial's stimulus. If the sample includes the correct hypothesis, the process of elimination can narrow the sample down to that hypothesis, which solves the problem. If the sample does not include the correct hypothesis, all the hypotheses in the sample will eventually be eliminated and the subject will have to generate another sample. Note that this method is similar to the strategies that Bruner et al.

(1956) called scanning. Like the scanning strategies, the strategy of testing samples of hypotheses is demanding on memory.

Proposals about the processes of choosing hypotheses to be considered, the eliminating of hypotheses on the basis of stimulus information, and the recall of previously eliminated hypotheses have been discussed in theoretical papers by Gregg and Simon (1967) and by Millward and Wickens (1974).

Wickens and Millward (1971) provided support for the assumption that experienced subjects remember stimulus attributes after eliminating them. According to their model, if the sample of hypotheses is exhausted, the attributes of eliminated hypotheses may still be stored in memory. Limitations of memory apply to both the size of the sample that can be considered and the number of previously eliminated attributes that can be remembered. In Wickens and Millward's experiment, subjects received extensive training in concept induction, solving many problems with the same set of stimuli, with different attributes used to define the concept in the successive problems. Performance improved sharply after the first problem or two, and stabilized within 10 to 20 problems. The model of attribute elimination was supported by statistical data as well as by the subjects' responses to a retrospective questionnaire. Differences in performance among the individual subjects can be explained by assuming that they all performed in accord with the model's assumptions, but that they differed in the size of hypothesis sample that they considered and in their capacity to remember previously eliminated hypotheses.

When performance of inexperienced subjects has been analyzed using stochastic models, the results have revealed a problem-solving process of suprisingly simple structure. Restle (1962) investigated the mathematical properties of a process in which a subject considered a sample of hypotheses and on each trial chose a response based on one of the hypotheses. In Restle's model it is assumed that the way subjects process information differs, depending on whether the response on a trial happens to be correct. After each correct response, hypotheses that are inconsistent with the information about that trial's stimulus are eliminated from the sample. After an error, the subject considers a new sample of hypotheses. A simple stochastic process results if it is assumed that sampling occurs with replacement. If this assumption is correct, solution of the problem is an all-or-none event; the probability of solving the problem with no more errors after a new sample is taken is a constant, independent of the number of trials or errors that have occurred previously. This implication is counterintuitive. If we assume that the subject is sampling and testing hypotheses, the assumption of sampling with replacement says that there is no accumulation of information over trials that makes sampling of the correct hypothesis more likely. The all-or-none property is also incompatible with almost any assumption that learned stimulus–response associations are strengthened gradually over trials, or that there is a summative or 'composite photograph' process as Woodworth (1938) proposed.

The counterintuitive all-or-none property of Restle's model received strong empirical support in experiments by Bower and Trabasso (1964). Their experiments with college students as subjects included conditions in which the categorical rule was changed before the subject solved the problem, using either a reversal or a nonreversal shift. The assumption of resampling with replacement after errors predicts that shifts prior to solution should not delay the solution of the problem, and this surprising result was obtained.

Computer simulation models of the concept-induction task, using different hypothesis-generating strategies, have been proposed by Gregg and Simon (1967). They showed that when these process models are aggregated (approximately) into simple stochastic models like Restle's (1962), they provide an information-processing explanation for the simple statistical regularities implied by the stochastic models and found in Bower and Trabasso's (1964) data. Gregg and Simon found that a range of different models is required to account for the set of experiments reported by Bower and Trabasso. According to these models, the nature of sampling depends primarily on how much information the subjects can retain about the classification of previous instances and about which hypotheses have already been refuted by the evidence. In general, the process models that fitted the data best were those that implied severe restrictions on short-term memory for previous instances and their classification. Given this retriction on memory, the models are consistent with the all-or-none property—that is, the expected number of trials to solve the problem is independent of the time the subject has already spent on it.

## Bottom-Up Induction of Concepts

In addition to inducing categorical concepts in a top-down, hypothesis-based manner, induction also can be a bottom-up process, involving gradual emergence of the concept from the features of individual stimuli. This idea has received less attention in psychological research, but it has not been totally missing from the discussion.

Hull (1920) conducted a study of learning in which the materials were pseudo-Chinese ideograms paired with nonsense syllables. The stimuli paired with the same response syllable from list to list all shared a stimulus component, a radical that was part of each of the stimuli. Hull's subjects showed positive transfer on the later lists in the experiment, indicating that they had induced the concepts to some extent. However, most of them were not aware of the feature or features that were shared, indicating that they were not actively testing hypotheses about the categorical rules. It seems likely that the subjects stored information about the individual stimulus–response pairs and gradually built up impressions that included the shared components.

A result similar to Hull's was obtained by Reber (1967), who studied induction of rules for an artificial language. Reber constructed sequences of letters using a set of grammatical rules: for example, "Start with a T or a V," or "After an initial T, use a P or another T," or "After a V that is not at the beginning, use a P or end the sequence." The sequences, from six to eight letters long, were used in a learning task in which subjects were shown the sequence and had to recall them. Subjects working on the grammatical sequences learned faster than subjects who worked on a comparable set of random letter sequences. After learning a set of grammatical sequences, subjects were able to discriminate, with greater than 75 percent accuracy, between new grammatical sequences and sequences that violated the grammar. Even so, subjects were not aware of the rules that were used to form the grammatical sequences, and showed little awareness of their shared features.

Rosch (1978) recently argued persuasively that little of our conceptual knowledge is organized on the basis of definite feature structures, like those used in most experiments on induction of categorical rules. First, Rosch, Mervis, Gray, Johnson, and Boyes-Braem (1976) proposed, with empirical support, that concepts at different levels of generality are not equally salient, but that there are basic categories whose members share features that are not shared by members of other categories, including characteristic patterns by which we interact with them physically. For example, chair, table, and hammer refer to basic categories, while their superordinates, furniture and tool, and their subordinates, such as picnic table and claw hammer, are less fundamental. Data supporting this distinction were obtained by Rosch et al., whose subjects were given a series of 90 terms and were asked to write all the attributes that came to mind. Another group of subjects was given the same terms and were asked to write descriptions of muscle movements that they would make in interacting with the objects. Many more attributes and movements were associated with the basic terms than with their superordinates, and few additional attributes beyond those for the basic terms were given for the subordinate terms.

Rosch (1973, 1975) has also contended that natural concepts are represented as prototypes, rather than as sets of features. A prototype may be thought of as a kind of schema for recognition of members of a category, which is activated more readily by typical representatives than by atypical ones. For example, in the category of birds, robins and canaries are judged to be more typical than penguins or peacocks; in the category of tools, hammers and saws are judged more typical than anvils or scissors. Rosch (1975) found that there is firm agreement among subjects in ratings of typicality. Evidence that typicality influences cognitive processes has been obtained when subjects are asked to judge whether statements such as "A robin is a bird" or "An anvil is a tool" are true. In these experiments, judgments are made more quickly for the statements involving more typical examples (Rosch, 1973; Rips, Shoben, & Smith, 1973).

Acquisition of prototypical concepts has been studied experimentally (Posner, Goldsmith, & Welton, 1967; Franks & Bransford, 1971; Reed (1972); and others). For these experiments, a set of stimuli is constructed by varying a single stimulus, the prototype. The stimuli, which may be geometric forms, patterns of dots, or schematic faces, are shown to subjects, after which a recognition test is given. Subjects' confidence in recognition is a function of the similarity of stimuli to the prototype. When the prototype itself is shown, subjects respond positively and confidently, even if the prototype was not included in the set of stimuli they saw. Several investigators have shown that this performance can be explained by considering the frequencies with which various stimulus features occur during the learning trials; for example, the features of the prototype appear with great frequency, even if the prototype itself is not presented (Reitman & Bower, 1973; Neumann, 1974).

A model that simulates bottom-up acquisition of a prototypical concept has been formulated by Anderson, Kline, and Beasley (1979), using general principles of learning in the context of a production-system model of performance. The Anderson et al. system stores cognitive representations of the patterns seen in individual stimuli, and additional representations are stored by processes of generalization and discrimination. Representations are strengthened when they provide a basis for recognizing stimuli that are presented. The Anderson et al. simulation accurately mimics subjects' performance on recognition tests, including false recognition of prototypes that have not been presented during learning.

A reasonable expectation is that many learning processes are not strictly top-down or bottom-up, but a combination of the two. Such combinations were analyzed by Greeno and Scandura (1966) and by Polson (1972) in studies of concept induction involving verbal items. In an experimental setup like that used by Hull (1920), lists of paired associates were presented to be memorized, and in successive lists the same response term was paired with different but interrelated stimuli. Greeno and Scandura found that transfer to individual items occurred in an all-or-none manner; different sets of items had differing proportions of items with no errors, but for items with any errors performances in the transfer conditions could not be distinguished from each other or from performance on control items. The finding of all-or-none transfer suggests a top-down conceptual process in which any individual item either is or is not recognized as a member of a definite category. Polson (1972) studied acquisition of the conceptual categories and found that it was not an all-or-none process. His findings suggest a two-stage process. For some subjects, there is an initial stage of bottom-up learning, in which associations of responses with patterns of features are stored, with transfer depending on features that are shared by similar items. In the initial phase, the subject may notice by chance the shared features of members of a concept category. Once the shared feature of a category is recognized, the second stage of learning occurs, involving an active, top-down process in which the subject searches actively for features to use in classifying the stimuli.

It is likely that both the top-down and the bottom-up methods of learning about categories are available to human learners, and the question arises as to what circumstances make it more likely for one rather than the other to occur. Brooks (1978) compared a condition in which subjects were asked to learn names for individual stimuli with one in which subjects induced a rule for classifying stimuli. Explicit rule induction led to better knowledge of relevant features, reflected in better performance on classification of new stimuli, as would be expected from learning by top-down induction. Subjects who learned individual names showed superior performance in recognition of specific stimuli from the learning set, but also recognized new stimuli at an above-chance level, as would be expected from bottom-up acquisition of a concept involving a summation of instances.

## Sequential Concepts

We now turn to two more complex tasks involving induction of concepts, in which the materials are sequences of elements organized in patterns, and the subject's task is to induce the patterns. In the first task which concerns extrapolating sequences of letters, the subject's task is to identify patterns in the sequences presented and to use the patterns to extend the sequences. The second task concerns induction of grammatical rules of a language from example sentences that are consistent with the grammar.

In these tasks the problem space includes a set of stimuli and a space of possible structures, as in all induction problems. However, compared to the space of possible rules for classifying stimuli, the spaces of possible pattern descriptions for sequences and of possible grammatical rules are extremely large. To solve these problems, substantial reductions of the search spaces are required. These reductions are accomplished by constraints on the generation of hypotheses. In sequence extrapolation, a limited set of relations and sequence forms are considered; in grammar induction, hypotheses about the structures of sentences are constrained by the structures of situations that the sentences describe.

### Sequence Extrapolation

An example of a sequence extrapolation problem follows: *mabmbcmcdm* . . . , where the task is to extend the sequence. In a model of sequence extrapolation formulated by Simon and Kotovsky (1963), a pattern is induced from basic relations between the letters in the problem string. The pattern is a kind of formula for producing the sequence; once discovered, the formula can be used to extend the sequence, as required.

For example, for the problem *mabmbcmcdm* . . . , the formula that is induced is the following: $[s_1 : m; s_2 : a], [s_1, s_2, (N(s_2)), s_2]$. The first part of the formula is initialization. There are two subsequences, denoted $s_1$ and $s_2$. $S_1$ starts with $m$, and $s_2$ starts with $a$. The second part of the formula gives instructions for producing the sequence. The instructions are interpreted as follows: $s_1$—write the current symbol of $s_1$; $s_2$—write the current symbol of $s_2$; $(N(s_2))$— change the symbol in $s_2$ to the successor ($N$ for next) of the current symbol; finally, $s_2$—write the (new) current symbol of $s_2$. The entire sequence is generated by repeating this routine as many times as necessary.

The problem solver constructs a formula as a hypothesis, based on the first letters of the given sequence, and tests the hypothesis with more letters. Since there are many different ways to form a sequence of letters, the number of possible formulas is, in principle, extremely large. To make the task manageable, some constraints have to be imposed. In Simon and Kotovsky's (1963) model, constraints are imposed on the generation of hypotheses. As in the focusing strategies about the structure of a pattern are based on features of the stimulus, rather than being generated a priori. Furthermore, only a few of the possible hypotheses are ever generated, because the model considers only a small set of relations between elements and it is assumed that the sequence fits a specific form.

The model knows the alphabet of letters, both forward and backward. The relations that are recognized are identity, $I$, and successor $N$. The problem solver assumes that the sequence is periodic, an important structural characteristic.

The model begins by determining the period of the sequence. Periodicity can be discovered either by noting that a relation is repeated every $n$th symbol, or noting that a relation is interrupted at every $n$th position. In the problem *mabmbcmcdm* . . . the periodicity is identified by noting that the relation $I$ occurs at every third symbol. Then the problem solver produces a description of the symbols that occur within the periods and relations between corresponding symbols in successive periods. For *mabmbcmcdm* . . . the description requires two subsequences, one of which is just repetition of $m$; the other starts with $a$ and moves incrementally to produce the final term in the set of three symbols. The result of the process is a formula for producing the sequence, such as the one described earlier for the example problem.

Because the product of the inductive process is an explicit formula, sequence extrapolation can be considered as a problem of design as well as of induction. Viewed in this way, the problem solver has available a set of symbols—$s_1$, $s_2$, $s_3$, (perhaps more), $N$, and the letters of the alphabet—and has the task of constructing from these symbols. The feature of sequence extrapolation that makes it an inductive task is the criterion that the construction must satisfy, the criterion that the formula should produce the sequence of letters that is given in the problem. In ordinary problems of design, such as anagram or cryptarithmetic, the criterion is a general property rather than agreement with an arrangement of stimuli.

Simon and Kotovsky (1963) reported data on the difficulty of solving 15 different sequence-extrapolation problems by two groups of subjects and found that the solvers agreed fairly well with their program on the relative difficulty of the 15 problems. In a more thorough empirical study, Kotovsky and Simon (1973) collected thinking-aloud protocols on problems with sequences so presented that the subjects had to lift a panel to see the individual letters. The data were consistent with the model in important

respects. Like the model, the subjects determined the periodicity of sequences and looked for relations between successive elements or between elements separated by a regular period. Representations of sequences induced by the subjects agreed with those induced by the model in a majority of cases.

There were also discrepancies, some of which involved relatively minor details of programming, but two of which revealed significant processes in humans not represented in the model. First, the subjects' performance showed closer integration than did the program between discovery of the period of the sequence and induction of the pattern description. These are distinct phases in the model, whereas the human problem solvers used information in forming the pattern description that they had picked up during the phase of finding the period. Another discrepancy between human data and Simon and Kotovsky's simplest model was that in some problems, human solvers induced patterns with hierarchical structure, involving a single low-level description and a higher-level switch that transited between versions of the low-level structure. A hierarchical relation between levels of pattern description is a basic structural feature of sequential patterns that can play a dominant role in the induction process, as Restle (1970) has shown.

### Grammatical Rules

In considering the induction of the grammar of a language we limit the discussion to those aspects of language acquisition that relate directly to general issues in the theory of problem solving.

In acquiring the grammar of a language, learners are presented materials that include sentences in the language. Their task is to infer a set of rules that can be used to parse sentences they hear and to produce sentences that are grammatical in the language. Thus, the problem solving involves a search in a space of possible syntactic rules. The space of stimuli includes the grammatical sentences that the learners hear and the task is to induce the rules that characterize the structure of those sentences.

Human knowledge of the rules of grammar is *implicit*, in contrast to the explicit formulas that are induced in the sequence extrapolation task. This can be seen in the fact that very young children have a significant knowledge of grammar (e.g., Brown, 1973), whereas adults know grammatical rules explicitly only if they have had special training. Because of the implicit nature of grammatical knowledge, the product of language learning is characterized as a set of *procedures*, rather than explicit formulas or other descriptions of structure. The procedures acquired by learners of a language enable them to produce and understand sentences that are in accord with the grammar of the language, and to distinguish between grammatical and ungrammatical sequences of words. Such a set of procedures is referred to as knowledge of the grammatical rules, because the rules are built into the procedures. As with much procedural knowledge, an individual's knowledge of the rules in the form of procedures does not imply the ability to state what the rules are.

There is evidence from both empirical studies (e.g., Moeser & Bregman, 1972) and theoretical analyses (e.g., Wexler & Cullicover, 1980) that grammatical rules are learned more easily if reference is provided for terms in the language. This indicates that, in the space of stimuli for inducing a grammar, each sentence is paired with a situation that the sentence describes. The functions of situations in facilitating induction of grammatical rules probably include assisting in determining which words belong together in constituent units (cf. Morgan & Newport, 1981).

An analysis of language acquisition by Anderson (1975, 1977) serves as an example of a definite information-processing mechanism for acquiring knowledge of grammatical rules in the form of procedures. Anderson's system includes learning processes that show how semantic reference can facilitate the acquisition of grammar. His learning program called LAS for *Language Acquisition System*, induces rules of grammar when it is given sentences in a language accompanied by the semantic objects to which the sentences refer. For example, if the sentence, "The red square is above the small circle," was presented to LAS, there would also be a semantic network that represented an object with the properties *red* and *square*, and another with the properties *small* and *circle*, and the relation *above* between the two objects.

LAS has a procedure, used in its learning of grammar, that identifies the objects in the semantic network that correspond to words in the sentence and forms a structure showing the relations among those concepts. This structure is used to determine constituent units of the sentence. In the example sentence, the words *red* and *square* are bracketed together, because they are properties of the same object, as are *small* and *circle*. The relational term *above* is at a higher level in the bracketing formed by LAS. The procedures that LAS acquires include rules for parsing noun phrases (NP) such as *the red square* and *the small circle*, and sentences of the form NP Relation NP. There is also a mechanism for generalization in LAS that makes it eventually parse similar structures with a single rule, and some of these generalizations produce recursive parsing rules. The generalization process sometimes produces incorrect rules that are too general, and LAS also includes a discrimination mechanism that restricts the application of its language-processing procedures.

Viewed as a problem-solving system, LAS conducts search in a space of procedures for producing and understanding sentences. Note that LAS can also be viewed as designing or constructing these procedures. The system's use of the structure of situations provides significant constraints that are needed for the search. As in Simon and Kotovsky's (1963) model of sequence extrapolation, the constraints are applied to the generation of hypotheses. Processes for modifying the induced procedures are available; LAS can generalize its procedures, which makes its performance more efficient, and it can add restrictions to the application of procedures when it is informed that the use of a procedure has produced an error.

## Nonsequential Patterns

Our discussion of induction of patterns that are not sequential in character begins with a simple case; an analogy problem in which one or two pairs of items are presented that are related in some way. The task is to form another pair with the same relation. The solving of simple analogy problems has been analyzed both empirically and theoretically. For more complicated problems, involving induction of concepts in mathematics and of quantitative regularities and structures in scientific domains, the available analyses are primarily theoretical.

### *Analogy Problems*
The form of an analogy problem is A : B :: C : D, where D is often a set of alternative items that

can complete the analogy, with the subject required to choose one from the set. A and B are related in some way, and the correct choice is a D item with the same relation to C as B has to A. Solution of an analogy problem involves search in a space of relations for a relation that can be applied to both the A : B and the C : D pairs, or to one of the C : Di alternatives more successfully than any of the others. Analogy problems are commonly used in tests of intellectual ability. In factor-analytic studies, analogy problems contribute most to the factor of induction, the single best predictor of academic achievement (Snow, 1980).

Solutions of analogy problems requires (1) a process for recognizing or analyzing relations between pairs of stimuli—that is, between the A and B stimuli and between C and each of the Di alternatives; and (2) a process that compares relations found for the A : B pair with relations found for the various C : Di alternatives and chooses the C : Di relation that best matches an A : B relation. In the simplest case, the relation for A and B that comes to mind first also applies to one and only one of the C : Di pairs. When this does not occur—because the relations found for A : B apply either to more than one C : Di pair or to none of them—some further analysis of the A : B pair is required. In such cases, other A : B relations may be suggested by relations that are found in considering the C : Di pairs.

Two processes for solving analogy problems have been described. In one, relations between pairs of items are based on information stored in the problem solver's memory. Memory-based analogy problems include most verbal analogies, where solutions use relations between words that are stored in memory or are inferred from word meanings. In the other process, relations are determined by analysis of features of stimuli. For example, in analogy problems composed of geometric diagrams, the relations between pairs of terms are found by comparing pairs of diagrams and identifying differences between the members of each pair.

## Relations Based on Semantic Memory

Solutions to many verbal analogies are based on their meanings stored in semantic memory. Reitman (1965) formulated a model for verbal analogies based on the activation of concepts in a semantic network. Reitman's model, called Argus, solves problems such as bear : pig : : chair : (foot, table, coffee, strawberry). Argus has knowledge of words in a network of relational connections; for example, bear and pig are both connected to animal through the relation *superordinate*. Activation and inhibition are transmitted through connections between units.

Argus can perform according to different strategies. In one strategy, the A and B terms are activated, and relations that become active are noted; then C becomes active, and the Di alternatives are activated in turn. A goal is set for relations that are the same as the ones activated by the A : B pair. When a C : Di pair activates those relations, that Di alternative is chosen. In the example, after bear and pig are activated, their superordinate relations to animal become active, because these relations lie on a path between the activated terms. Then chair is activated along with the Di alternatives taken in turn, with the goal of finding active superordinate relations. This goal is achieved when table is activated, because both chair and table are connected by superordinate relations to furniture.

Strategic factors in analogy problems were demonstrated in an experiment by Grudin (1980). Grudin presented two kinds of analogy items: standard items, where a salient relation between A and B can be matched with one of the C : Di pairs; and nonstandard items, where there is no salient relation between A and B, but a relation between A and C matches one between B and a Di alternative. An example is the item bird : air : : fish : (breath, water, swim) in standard form, which in its nonstandard version is bird : fish : : air : (breathe, water, swim). The nonstandard problems are more difficult, as measured by the time required for a solution. However, if subjects can adapt their strategies to look for relations between A : C and B : Di pairs, the difficulty of nonstandard problems may be reduced. Grudin's sequence of problems included five-item sets that were either all standard or all nonstandard, followed by either a standard or a nonstandard problem. During solution of a set of nonstandard items, a shift in strategy could occur, involving more attention to the A : C and B : Di pairs. This produced shorter times for nonstandard problems following nonstandard sets than for nonstandard problems following standard sets, and that result was obtained.

Thinking-aloud protocols in solution of verbal

analogies were obtained in a study by Heller (1979) and were also described by Pellegrino and Glaser (1982). Heller first presented the three terms of an analogy stem and asked the subject to think aloud and to include a statement of any A : B relations and expectations about the answer that came to mind. Then four alternative answers were presented individually and the subject judged whether each alternative was an acceptable answer, and why. The complete problem was then presented for a final choice.

Heller's findings were consistent with the general features of Reitman's (1965) hypotheses of solution strategies and of finding relations by the activation of a semantic network. In Heller's experiment strategic factors provide an interpretation of individual differences in performance, and the activation hypothesis is supported by the variability in solution sequences.

Heller's major finding was a striking difference between the degree to which groups of subjects adhered to the task constraints of analogy problems. The main constraint of an analogy is the requirement that the relation A : B and C : Di correspond. If a subject chooses a Di response on the basis of a relation to C without regard to whether that relation corresponds to the A : B relation, then the analogy constraint has not been applied. Subjects who had good overall performance mentioned the similarity or difference between an A : B relation and at least one of the C : Di relations on nearly all the problems. In contrast, subjects with poorer overall performance were inconsistent in applying the constraint of matching the A : B and C : Di relations and frequently accepted answers based on a vague relation between Di and C, or with other terms in the analogy. To account for the differences among subjects in this adherence to the task constraints, Heller proposed that individuals differ in the strengths of the goals that require different solution strategies. In Reitman's model, this would be analogous to the better subjects' having more strongly activated strategic goals or to differences in the degree to which other processes interfered with goals.

Heller's protocols also revealed considerable variability in the sequence of steps taken to solve the problems. In most cases, subjects identified an A : B relation and then thought about C : Di alternatives in the context of that relation. There were also cases in which a relation between A and B came to mind as a subject thought about one or more of the C : Di relations. Such solution sequences occurred in about 20 percent of the problems on which subjects adhered to the analogical constraints. Reitman's assumption that relations are found by activation of a semantic network provides an interpretation of the variability of solution sequences, since activation of a relation in the context of a C : Di pair would facilitate its recognition for A : B in some cases where A : B did not elicit it.

Further information relevant to individual differences was obtained in a study by Pellegrino and Glaser (1982). Analogy items with single D alternatives were presented and subjects judged the items as true or false. Pellegrino and Glaser used an experimental and statistical method introduced by Sternberg (1977), in which the four terms are presented in sequence, with the subject making a response to request presentation of the each succeeding term. The latencies of the responses are used to estimate the time for various components of the solution process, according to a general model. Each latency includes time to encode the new item. When B is presented, the latency includes time to infer one or more relations between A and B. When C is presented, the latency includes time to map A : B relations onto the C term. When D is presented, C : D relations are inferred and compared with the A : B relations. It was assumed that the comparison process could have three outcomes. The relations could correspond well, leading to a response of *true*. The lack of correspondence could be so great that the subject would immediately reject the analogy and respond *false*. The subject could also judge that the correspondence was indeterminate and requires a more extended analysis, possibly including review of the A and B terms to find new relations.

Pellegrino and Glaser used four sets of items in this study; positive items, which were judged to be appropriate analogies, and negative items, which were judged to be inappropriate. Within each of these sets, there were items in which the C and D terms were closely associated and other items in which they were not associated. A weak C–D association for a positive item, or a strong C–D association for a negative item, was expected to make the item more ambiguous and increase the frequency of extended analyses in the final component of the solution process. The results supported this expectation; estimates of the proportion of problems with extended analyses were higher for weakly associated than for strongly associated positive items (.55 and .23, respectively), and also higher for strongly associated than for weakly associated negative items (.19 and .07, respectively). A similar correlation of item difficulty with time spent in the final stage of solution was obtained by Barnes and Whitely (1981).

Pellegrino and Glaser's major finding was that the frequencies of an extended analysis were correlated with the subject's overall ability in the analogies task. The subjects were college students divided into two groups on the basis of their scores on a standard analogies test. The estimates of time for the various information-processing components were generally longer for the low than for the high-ability subjects. But the most striking difference was in the frequency of engaging in an extended analysis, which was more than twice as high for the low- than for the high-ability subjects. Pellegrino and Glaser concluded that, since the low-ability subjects often arrived at the final stage of processing an analogy with an inadequate representation of the relations among the other terms, they had to reconsider the A, B, and C terms more frequently than the high-ability subjects. A similar difference in the solution process was found by Snow (1980), for spatial reasoning tasks in which the items are diagrams, and the subjects' reexaminations of terms could be observed by recording eye movements. In verbal analogies, this difference in processing could be due to differences in the information in semantic memory, differences in the activation process, or differences in strategy, with the low-ability subjects more likely to want to see the final term to facilitate recognition of A:B relations. This conclusion is consistent with Heller's finding that students with low ability in analogies often choose responses that violate the constraint of an analogy problem. When they lack a response that satisfies the constraints, they are likely to choose a response on some other basis.

In Reitman's (1965) model of verbal analogy solution, relations are relatively discrete components of semantic memory. This characterization is probably correct for most verbal analogies, though not for all. An example is provided by Rumelhart and Abrahamson (1973), who studied the solution of verbal analogy problems in a single semantic domain, the names of animals.

Analogies composed of animal names have two properties that are different from most verbal analogies: first, they depend on more than one relation, and the relations are combined somehow in solving the problem; and second, the relations differ in degree, rather than just being present or absent.

An example that illustrates multiple relations is the following: rabbit : sheep :: beaver : (tiger, donkey). Donkey seems the better answer, perhaps because while a relation involving size is similar for beaver : tiger and beaver : donkey, and both are similar to the size relation for rabbit : sheep, there also is an additional difference for beaver : tiger—tigers are ferocious while beavers are not, and thus the beaver : donkey pair matches the rabbit : sheep pair better, which also lacks a difference in ferocity. The graded nature of relations is illustrated by rabbit : beaver :: sheep : (donkey, elephant). Donkey seems the better answer. The judgment seems to depend mainly on the sizes of the animals, and beavers are larger than rabbits, but the difference is not large enough to make sheep : elephant seem appropriate.

It is convenient to use a spatial representation to represent differences of graded magnitudes that can be combined easily. In such a representation, the dimensions of the space correspond to salient ways in which items differ from each other. Each item is located at a point in the space. The coordinates of the point correspond to the values that the item has on each of the dimensions.

A spatial representation of a set of items can be obtained by presenting pairs of the items to subjects and asking them to judge how similar the members of each pair are to each other. These judgments of similarity are used as estimates of the distances between pairs of items, and items are located in the space so that the distances between points are as close as possible to the estimates obtained in the experiment. In the method of choosing the spatial representation, called *multidimensional scaling*, an attempt is made to represent the items in one dimension; if that is unsuccessful two dimensions are used, and so on until a space is found in which the points are located so that interpoint distances agree satisfactorily with the similarity judgments given by subjects.

Henley (1969) obtained judgments of similarity for pairs of animal names, and obtained a spatial representation with three dimensions: size, ferocity, and a third dimension that probably involves a mixture of attributes, including similarity to humans. These results were used by Rumelhart and Abrahamson (1973) in their study of analogy problem solving. The relation between two items A and B corresponds to the vector that connects the points for A and B in the spatial representation. The vector represents the combination of differences in the three dimensions between the two items; for example, the vector from *beaver* to *tiger* represents a moderate increase in ferocity, a large increase in size, and very little difference in 'humanness.' In Rumelhart and Abrahamson's model, to solve an analogy A : B :: C : (D1, D2, D3, D4), the A → B vector is translated to C, and the probability of choosing each of the Di alternatives is a function of its distance from the ideal point defined by the end of the vector. In one experiment, the model provided accurate predictions of the frequencies of subjects' rankings of the various response alternatives in analogy problems. In another experiment, fictitious animal names were assigned to locations in the spatial representation. These fictitious names were used in analogy problems for which subjects received feedback, and the subjects induced features of the fictitious animals, responding appropriately to new analogies involving their names.

## RELATIONS BASED ON FEATURE ANALYSIS

In a geometric analogy problem, the terms are diagrams that differ in various ways. In the example given in Figure 9.12, the best answer is apparently D2. Diagrams A and B are related by deletion of the dot and moving the rectangle from inside the triangle to a position at the left of the triangle. Diagrams C and D2 are related similarly: the dot in C is also deleted, and the Z is moved from inside the segment of the circle to the left of the segment.

As Figure 9.12 illustrates, the relation between two diagrams can involve several aspects, corresponding to components of the diagrams that differ. Some of the differences may be quantitative, for example, the amount of rotation of a component or the amount by which the size of a component is increased or decreased. In analogy problems involving animal names, these characteristics of composite and quantitative

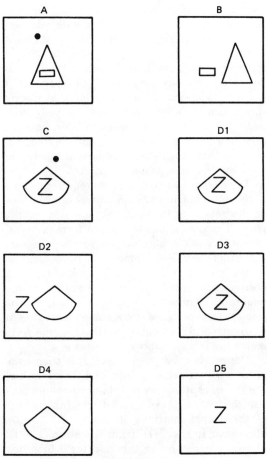

**Figure 9.12.** A geometric analogy problem. From "A Program for the Solution of Geometric-Analogy Intelligence Test Questions" by T.G. Evans in *Semantic Information Processing* (p. 273), M. Minsky (Ed.), 1968. Cambridge, MA: MIT Press. Copyright 1968 by the MIT Press. Reprinted by permission.

relations make a spatial representation of items a reasonable one. On the other hand, spatial representation is not economical for geometric analogies, because there are too many ways in which diagrams can differ. For animal names, a satisfactory approximation can be reached by characterizing all pairwise relations by differences on three dimensions, but geometric diagrams do not have so simple a structure.

In geometric analogies, relations are found by examining features of the diagrams, rather than by retrieving information from memory, as with verbal analogies. Therefore, a model for solving geometric analogy problems has two components: one that analyzes diagrams and identifies relations between them, and another that compares the relation of A : B with relations of the C : Di alternatives and chooses the best match.

Evans (1968) developed a model that solves geometric analogy problems. The program is given descriptions of some diagrams that specify the locations of straight lines, curved lines, and closed figures. From these descriptions, relations among components are derived: for example, that one figural component lies inside another, or above it in a diagram.

The model then compares its representations of the diagrams in pairs and forms descriptions of the relations between the members of the pairs. These relations are in the form of transformations—that is, changes in one diagram that would make it the same as the other diagram in the pair. For example, in one diagram a component might be removed or added, or one might be changed in size or rotated, or the relative positions of two components might be changed, for example, by moving one from inside the other to above the other.

The relation between A and B is then compared with the relations between C and each of the Di alternatives, by matching components of A with components of C and determining which of the transformations in the A : B relation also occur in the C : Di transformation. The Di alternative chosen is the one for which the greatest number of transformations can be made to correspond.

Evans (1968) developed his model as a project in artificial intelligence, rather than as a simulation of human problem solving, but the model nevertheless has features that seem plausible as psychological hypotheses. One such feature is a suggestion that problems with more complex diagrams or relations between diagrams should be more difficult for human subjects to solve. In the model, diagrams are more complex if they have more components, and relations are more complex if there are more transformations— that is, if there are more changes in components between related diagrams. These two factors were varied in an experiment by Mulholland, Pellegrino, and Glaser (1980), and both had significant effects. Problems whose diagrams had more components and problems with more transformations both required longer times for solution.

In the human solution of geometric analogy problems, we should expect some of the same characteristics of performance that have been observed in the solution of other analogy problems. In verbal analogy problems when the subject's representation of the A : B relation and the C : Di relations are not sufficient to provide a determinate answer, additional further processing is necessary. Findings by Sternberg (1977) show that this factor is important in geometric analogy problems as well. Sternberg measured the time to solve problems presented after part of the problem had been shown, enabling part of the processing to occur. He used the differences between conditions as estimates of the times for components of the solution process. In comparing subjects with differing levels of general reasoning ability, Sternberg found a large difference in the time required to process the C : Di alternatives in geometric analogy problems, with much of the difference attributable to a process of comparing alternatives when prior processing had not provided a unique solution.

## Inductive Problems in Mathematics and Science

Cognitive analyses have been developed in the form of computer programs that invent new mathematical concepts, based on properties of examples, and that induce formulae and structures from data in scientific domains. Three models are discussed: one that invents new mathematical concepts, one that induces formulae from sets of quantitative data, and one that induces molecular structure from data of mass spectroscopy.

### INVENTION OF CONCEPTS IN MATHEMATICS

A program called AM (Lenat, 1982) generates examples of concepts that it knows, and develops new concepts based on properties of the examples. The main domain in which AM was run was elementary mathematics. The AM program was given initial concepts involving sets and developed a variety of concepts involving numbers. For example, AM developed concepts of addition and multiplication, developed the concept of primes, and arrived at a conjecture that every number is the product of a unique combination of prime numbers.

It is useful to compare AM's task to the standard experimental task of concept induction, for example, that of Bruner et al. (1956). In standard concept induction, a set of examples is provided by the experimenter, with some positive examples and some negative examples determined by a rule, and the subject's task is to induce the rule. Hypotheses are generated by the subject and tested with information about further examples until the correct concept has been found. Each hypothesis that is generated is itself a concept, in the sense that it provides a rule for classifying the stimuli. The main problem-solving work is to determine which rule is correct.

The task of AM is not defined as well, in two respects. First, the examples are not provided by an experimenter, but rather are produced by AM. Second, AM does not have a specified criterion of correctness for the concepts that it generates. Instead, AM evaluates its concepts by some criteria of importance, based in part on how easy it is to generate examples.

In AM the knowledge of concepts is organized as a set of *facets*, including some that are standard for semantic networks, such as generalizations, specializations, and examples, and others that are especially useful in mathematics, such as objects that are in the domain or range of a function. Facets also hold procedural information, such as ways to test whether an object is an example of the concept. Reasoning activity in AM is organized as a set of tasks, each involving a concept and one of its facets. Examples of tasks include filling in examples of a concept or forming a generalization or a canonical representation of a concept. Tasks that are proposed are placed on an agenda, and the choice of a task to perform is based on an evaluation of the reasons for the task, including the importance of concepts for which the task would contribute new information. Heuristics that contribute to the developments of new concepts include efforts to form a more general concept if an existing concept has very few examples, and to form new representations that clarify the relations between concepts.

Table 9.10. **Data for a simple induction problem**

| Time | Distance |
|------|----------|
| 1 | 0.98 |
| 2 | 3.92 |
| 3 | 8.82 |
| 4 | 15.68 |
| 5 | 24.50 |

We note that AM does not really do mathematics in the usual sense. It has no concept of deductive consequence and thus, does not develop a body of concepts and principles with a formal structure. Even so, it provides an example of a system that goes well beyond the knowledge that it is given initially, moving into a conceptual domain that is quite different from that of its initial concepts.

INDUCING QUANTITATIVE REGULARITIES

A system called Bacon induces formulas from numerical data (Langley, 1981; Langley, Bradshaw, & Simon, 1983). The data are values of some variables that are controlled and other variables that are measured; a simple example is in Table 9.10. The goal is to find a formula that describes the relation between the variables, in this case distance and time. The two components of the problem space are the subspace of stimuli (the set of data) and the space of structures (the set of formulas constructable with the variables that are included in the data).

A simpler approach than Bacon's is adequate for relatively simple induction problems. This simpler approach tries to fit alternative formulas that are known in advance. For example, for Table 9.10, a linear function can be tried, and the discrepancy that is noted shows that there is positive acceleration. This suggests trying a quadratic formula, which fits the data. Generate-and-test methods of this kind have been analyzed by Huesmann and Cheng (1973) and by Gerwin (1974), with supporting experimental data.

The task of inducing formulas can become unmanageable for a simple generate-and-test method if there are several variables that can be related in complex ways. For example, Bacon is able to induce Coulomb's Law, $f = q_1 q_2 / d^2$, which relates electrical force to the charges on two bodies and the distance between them; and a formula for the electrical current in a wire connected to a battery and a metal rod, $I = T/(R + L/D^2)$ which depends on the temperature differential of the bar, and the internal resistance of the battery, and the length and diameter of the wire. The set of formulae that includes these is extremely large, and it seems unlikely that simple equation fitting would be an effective method for inducing formulae of this complexity.

Bacon's search method uses properties of the data to guide the formation of hypotheses. Other induction systems have this capability including the concept-induction strategy of focusing described by Bruner et al. (1956), the method for inducing patterns in letter sequences studied by Simon and Kotovsky (1963), and AM's heuristics for generating new concepts based on properties of examples. Bacon's heuristics involve properties of quantitative data and thus differ, as one would expect, from the heuristics of other systems such as AM, where the data involve categories of examples and sets of defining features. Bacon's use of data has the further interesting feature of creating new data in the process of evaluation hypotheses. In evaluating a hypothesis, Bacon calculates values of a new function of available data, and if the hypothesis does not succeed, those values become part of the data available to Bacon for further problem solving. Thus, though an attempt to solve the problem may fail, it leaves new results that may be instrumental in a later successful attempt.

Bacon's basic method is to search for a function of data that gives constant values across experimental conditions. As an example, the formula for the data in Table 9.10 is $d = kt^2$, where $k$ is a constant; the form in which Bacon discovers the law is $d/t^2 = k$.

Bacon uses heuristic rules to form hypotheses, consisting of functions of variables in its data base that might give constant values. For example, if two quantities increase or decrease together, Bacon forms their ratio as a new quantity to be considered. If one variable decreases as another increases, Bacon forms their product as a new quantity. These heuristics, and another that forms linear functions of variables, enable Bacon to induce relatively complex functions. The first two are sufficient for the problem in Table 9.10. First, note that $t$ and $d$ increase together, and form the ratio $t/d$. Since this ratio decreases with $t$, Bacon forms the product $t^2/d$, which quantity is constant across the observations.

Some other heuristic methods are also used, including the definition of 'intrinsic variables' as properties of objects that are associated with constant values of quantities, and attempts to find a common divisor for values of intrinsic variables that have been induced. These heuristics enable induction of properties such as the resistances of different wires from measurements of current, and the atomic and molecular weights of chemical elements from data about the weights and volumes of elements and compounds involved in chemical reactions.

As previously noted, induction problems can also be understood as problems of design, especially when the structures that are induced are expressed explicitly as formulae. This view is particularly appropriate to Bacon's induction of formulae. Consider the task as the construction of a formula using symbols for the variables in the problem. Bacon's heuristics then are rules for forming combinations of the symbols that may satisfy the problem criterion. Even if a formula does not solve the problem, it may provide part of the formula that is needed. Thus, the process of search through the construction of partial solutions, which is characteristic of design problems, provides an appropriate characterization of Bacon's process of induction.

Bacon is not intended as a complete simulation of cognitive processes in scientific research, where hypotheses about causal mechanisms often play a critical role in the decision to measure variables or to examine quantitative relation. Even so, it demonstrates that quite simple heuristics are sufficient to produce quite complex inductive conclusions from quantitative data, and it is reasonable to suppose that these heuristics correspond to significant components of complex scientific reasoning.

### INDUCING MOLECULAR STRUCTURE

Another scientific task that has been investigated is induction of the molecular structure of organic compounds. A system called Dendral induces molecular structure from data in the form of mass spectra (Lindsay, Buchanan, Feigenbaum, & Lederberg, 1980). A mass spectrum is a set of quantities of the fragments of various sizes that are produced when molecules of a substance are bombarded by electrons.

Like AM and Bacon, Dendral performs induction using heuristic search. An important difference is that Dendral uses search heuristics that are based on principles that are specific to organic chemistry, whereas AM's methods apply to any structure of categorical concepts, and Bacon's methods can be applied to any quantitative data.

Dendral's method of induction has three main stages. First, the chemical formula of the compound is inferred from features of the mass spectrum. Then hypotheses about molecular structures are generated with constraints based on knowledge of the class of compounds that the substance belongs to. Finally, the hypotheses are tested by comparing their implications with the quantitative details of the mass spectrum, and the hypothesis that fits the data best is chosen.

The data used to infer the chemical formula are the peaks in the mass spectrum. The largest mass represented is probably either the mass of the molecular ion or a mass smaller than the molecular ion by one fragment. Differences between peaks usually correspond to the masses of fragments that are broken off in the bombardment. Dendral uses the value of the largest peak and the interpeak distances, along with knowledge of chemistry, to infer one or more chemical formulas that are consistent with the spectrum.

Dendral's next task is to generate possible molecular structures, with the ions in the formula arranged in ways consistent with known possible arrangements. There are many millions of possibilities for most problems, so Dendral formulates constraints based on knowledge of the class of compounds that the sample belongs to. With the constraints, Dendral constructs hypotheses about molecular structure with a method that first determines the maximum number of rings in the structure, then constructs the possible partitions of ions into rings and remaining components, and finally constructs the possible structures for each possible partition.

Dendral now tests its many hypotheses, using the quantitative details of the mass spectra. In the different hypothesized structures, since different components are separated by different numbers of bonds, there are differences in the likelihood of this occurring together in a fragment. Assuming that fragments are produced by breaking one or two bonds at once, predictions are made about the relative amounts of material to be found at each peak in the spectrum, and the structure that fits the data best is chosen.

Note that Dendral's task, like Bacon's, involves constructing an explicit formula to represent the structure it induces. Thus, its method can also be considered to solve problems of design, where the materials for the construction are symbols that represent the atomic components of chemical compounds, and the chemical knowledge that it uses constrains the search to arrangements of those materials that agrees with the mass spectra.

## Diagnostic Problem Solving

In the problem solving tasks of troubleshooting in electronics and diagnosis in medicine, the problem solver has a space of stimuli consisting of one or more symptons and further information that can be obtained by performing tests. The space of structures is a set of possible causes of the symptoms—faulty components in electrical circuits or disease states in medical diagnoses.

In addition to its characteristics of inductive problem solving, diagnostic problem solving also has components of operational thinking, because it is based on the goal of curing a patient's illness or repairing a device. Thus the information and conclusions in the diagnosis are directed toward making a decision about a remedial treatment that should be applied.

### Troubleshooting

The task in troubleshooting is to determine which of the many components of an electronic system is causing the system to function improperly. There may be more than one fault, but it simplifies the problem greatly to assume that there is only a single fault in the system.

In a general way, troubleshooting resembles the task of inducing categorical concepts when the subject chooses the stimuli for which information is given. In concept induction the problem solver obtains information by asking whether a specific stimulus is positive or negative. In troubleshooting, information is obtained by taking readings of voltage or current at specific locations in the circuit. In both tasks there are many possible hypotheses to be considered, but the set of possibilities can be specified: in concept induction it is the set of logical combinations of the stimulus attributes, and in troubleshooting it is the set of possible faults of components. These similarities in the tasks are correlated with an important resemblance in effective methods for working on the problems. The focusing strategy in concept induction uses information obtained about instances in order to eliminate classes of hypotheses, rather than considering each hypothesis individually as is done in the less effective scanning strategy (Bruner et al., 1956). Similarly, in troubleshooting an important component of strategy is to conduct tests that permit elimination of sets of possible faults from consideration. Use of this strategy is made possible by both a general knowledge of electronic components and a knowledge of the specific circuit in the problem. This requirement of knowledge to support the process of induction is analogous to the role played in concept induction by knowledge of the alternative logical forms (conjunction, disjunction, etc.) and the truth-table combinations that correspond to them (Dodd et al., 1971), although the knowledge required in troubleshooting is considerably more elaborate.

A model of troubleshooting is included in a system called Sophie that provides computer-based instruction for trainees in electronics maintenance (Brown, Burton, & deKleer, 1983). The troubleshooting system provides a model for the student to observe in learning how to diagnose faults in a circuit. If the student specifies a fault in the circuit, Sophie can diagnose the fault, perform a series of tests to obtain readings of current or voltage at various points in the circuit, form hypotheses about the fault, and eventually arrive at a decision about it. Sophie has a store of general knowledge about electronics and an explicit representation of strategy that enables it to provide explanations of both the principles of electronics and the strategic purposes of its activity for tests that it is performing. Sophie's troubleshooting knowledge is also used to evaluate the problem-solving performance of students, by providing a series of problem-solving steps that can be compared with the steps taken by students.

Sophie's knowledge for troubleshooting has four main components: two components of electronics knowledge, a component of knowledge for making specific inferences, and a component of strategic knowledge. The component for specific inferences includes general knowledge in the form of 'experts' that have information about characteristics of different kinds of electronic components such as resistors and diodes. These experts can use data obtained from readings to calculate values for other variables, assuming normal functioning of components of the circuit; the inferred values can then be compared with actual readings of those variables.

A second component of Sophie's knowledge is information about the specific circuit that is used for instruction. The circuit is represented hierarchically as a set of modules with sub-modules and components. Possible functional states of each module and component are represented, including normal functioning and possible fault states. Experimental evidence obtained by Egan and Schwartz (1979) is consistent with a hypothesis that human electronics experts represent circuits in ways similar to Sophie's. Egan and Schwartz showed that experts encode information from circuit diagrams rapidly, much the way experts perform in other domains such as chess (see "Problems of Modifying Arrangements"), and that functional modules made up of components that are spatially contiguous in the diagram play an important role in the performance.

A third part of Sophie's knowledge involves specific actions that occur during troubleshooting. This knowledge is in the form of rules for making inferences about the states of modules and components of the circuit. Readings are used to eliminate hypotheses about faults by showing that a module is functioning normally, and for propagating inferences in the hierarchical representation; for example, if a component is faulted, then all the modules that contain that component must also be faulted.

The fourth component of knowledge is Sophie's strategy, a breadth-first search method with backtracking. Sophie considers all the possible states that can occur, according to its representation of the circuit, and eliminates possible faulty states on the basis of readings that are consistent with normal functioning. It assumes normal functioning of components until there is a reading that conflicts with that assumption; however, it keeps a record of the assumptions used in its inferences, and if information contradicts an assumption made earlier, inferences based on that assumption are revised.

### Medical Diagnosis

In medical diagnosis, as in troubleshooting, a system—in this case, a human body—is functioning improperly, and the inductive task is to infer the cause of the malfunction. Also, as in troubleshooting, the purpose of the diagnosis is to determine a treatment that can remedy the malfunction, and the diagnostic activity is conducted in a way that provides information relevant to choosing a treatment.

Several systems have been developed that solve diagnostic problems in various domains of medicine, including diagnosis of infectious agents and prescription of antibiotics (Shortliffe, 1976), prescription of digitalis therapy for cardiac patients (Silverman, 1975), and diagnosing and prescribing treatment for varieties of glaucoma (Weiss, Kulikowski, & Safir, 1977). (For a review, see Ciesielski, Bennett, & Cohen, 1977.) One system, Caduceus, which performs general diagnosis, is discussed here, along with empirical studies of diagnostic problem solving by physicians with varying amounts of training and experience.

## A MODEL OF KNOWLEDGE FOR GENERAL DIAGNOSIS

Knowledge used in general medical diagnosis has been investigated in the context of a model named Caduceus (Miller, Pople, & Myers, 1982; Pople, 1982). The knowledge with which Caduceus diagnoses diseases is similar in important ways to the knowledge used by Sophie for diagnosing faults in electronic circuits. Its hierarchical form enables systematic search in the space of hypotheses. The Caduceus system also has rules that infer hypotheses from symptoms and test results, and that propagate the inferred information using the hierarchical structure of its knowledge.

Caduceus's knowledge about diseases is of two kinds, organized in separate but related graph structures. One of these, called a nosological graph, provides a taxonomy of diseases based on the organs of the body involved and on etiological factors. This graph groups diseases according to their manifestations. The other knowledge structure, called a causal graph, contains information about disease states and processes. The causal graph contains technical concepts of pathology that refer to states of disease, such as cardiogenic shock.

Caduceus has the goal of identifying one or more disease entities that provide a complete explanation of a set of symptoms and findings in the case. Subproblems are formulated from findings that are not yet integrated into an explanatory network; these constitute diagnostic tasks that are generated by the system. Identification of the disease depends mainly on the nosological graph; this hierarchical structure is used in a top-down search to narrow the possible disease entities. The information about the states and processes of disease in the causal graph provides links between hypothesized disease entities and the specific symptoms and test results that are available. Caduceus concludes its diagnostic analysis when an explanatory network has been developed that includes all the available symptoms and findings.

## EMPIRICAL STUDIES OF DIAGNOSTIC PERFORMANCE

An extensive study of performance in diagnostic problems was conducted by Feltovich (1981, also described in Johnson, Duran, Hassebrock, Moller, Prietula, Feltovich, & Swanson, 1981). The results were consistent with the general properties of the Caduceus model. They also provide information about characteristics of knowledge for diagnosis at different levels of experience and expertise. Feltovich obtained problem-solving protocols for cases in pediatric cardiology from individuals varying in experience from fourth-year medical students who had just completed a six-week course in pediatric cardiology to two professors who had more than 20 years of experience in that subspecialty. Information from five cases was presented serially and the physicians gave their hypotheses and other thoughts about the cases, attempting to arrive at a correct diagnosis.

The performance of experts indicated that their knowledge differed from that of novices in several ways, consistent with the general features of expert knowledge in chess and Go discussed above in "Problems of Modifying Arrangements." The major difference was that experts had more integrated knowledge about diseases —more detailed knowledge of variation in disease states and more precise knowledge of relation between diseases and symptoms. For example, one advanced expert mentioned groups of hypotheses that were supported by the findings presented first and then used later information to narrow the range of possibilities. The other advanced expert used more of a depth-first strategy—proposing a likely hypothesis based on preliminary findings, but modifying the hypothesis in a flexible way when later evidence provided counterindications. The knowledge of novices was primarily in the form of a few specific disease forms used in textbook cases. The novices responded to early evidence by proposing reasonable hypotheses but were less likely to recognize the significance of later evidence and change their hypotheses when necessary. The sets of hypotheses mentioned by novices during problem solving were significantly smaller than those of the experts.In a study of expert and novice radiologists, Lesgold et al. (1981) came to similar conclusions regarding expert knowledge for diagnosis. They found that in reading x-ray films experts generated representations in a three-dimensional system and used salient features to generate initial hypotheses that were refined or modified on the basis of more detailed features. The knowledge necessary for recognizing features associated with abnormalities appeared to be well integrated with a general knowledge of anatomy. The integration of experts' knowledge was indicated by their ability to use features noted early as constraints on later interpretations (cf. Stefik, 1981). Novices—in this case, first-year residents in radiology—depended more on finding an explanation for a few features and to let other details be assimilated to the initial hypothesis rather than used to generate alternative hypotheses or modifications.

Conclusions from these studies of expert diagnosticians in medicine show close similarity to the studies of expert performance in other problem-solving domains, especially physics and chess. According to current findings, a major source of expert performance is the expert's ability to represent problems successfully. This results from the expert's having a well integrated structure of knowledge in which patterns of features in the problem are associated with concepts at varying levels of generality, enabling efficient search for hypotheses about the salient features of the problem that cannot be observed directly, as well as for methods and operations to be used in solving the problem.

# EVALUATION OF DEDUCTIVE ARGUMENTS

The relation between human reasoning and formal logic has long been a subject of discussion and debate and, for some decades, a subject for experiment as well. It is generally agreed that human 'logical reasoning' does not always conform to the laws of formal logic. Formal logic is a normative theory of how people ought to reason, rather than a description of how they do reason. It is important, then, to develop a descriptive theory of human reasoning to compare and contrast with the logic norms.

Experiments aimed at developing a theory of human reasoning have mostly set tasks of judging the correctness or incorrectness of formal syllogisms. These tasks require application of the rules of deductive argument that are special in some ways, and correct performance depends on the subject's knowledge and use of the technical rules of formal deductive inference. However, the processes used in these tasks do not differ in any fundamental way from those involved in problem solving in other domains. Psychological analyses provide no basis for a belief in deductive reasoning as a category of thinking processes different from other thinking processes, other than in the special set of operators that are permitted in rigorous deductive arguments. As Woodworth put the matter, "Induction and deduction . . . are distinguished as problems rather than processes" (1938, p. 801).

Two tasks are discussed: First, we discuss propositional and categorical syllogisms, which present arguments in the sentential and predicate calculus; subjects frequently make errors in evaluating these syllogisms, and research has focused on why the reasoning process differs from correct logical inference. Second, we discuss linear syllogisms, which present arguments that depend on transitivity of order relations. Subjects make the transitive inferences in these tasks without difficulty, and psychological analyses have focused on the cognitive representation of information in the syllogisms.

## Propositional and Categorical Syllogisms

Subjects in experiments on propositional or categorical syllogisms are asked to judge the validity of arguments such as the following (invalid) propositional syllogism:

> If I push the left-hand button, the letter T appears.
> I did not push the left-hand button.
> Therefore, the letter T did not appear.

The major premise states what will happen if the button is pushed. It says nothing about what will or will not happen if the button is not pushed. Hence the conclusion does not follow from the premises. Yet in a typical experiment (Rips & Marcus, 1977) a fifth of the subjects accepted this as a valid syllogism.

Categorical syllogisms in the predicate

calculus involve statements containing the terms *some*, *all*, and *no*. An example of a (valid) categorical syllogism is

> Some jewels are diamonds.
> All diamonds are valuable.
> Therefore, some jewels are valuable.

Again, human subjects make frequent mistakes in judging whether certain kinds of categorical syllogisms are valid. For example, many subjects judge mistakenly that the following argument is a valid syllogism (Johnson-Laird & Steedman, 1978):

> Some As are Bs.
> Some Bs are Cs.
> Therefore, some As are Cs.

In experiments on syllogistic reasoning, the type of syllogism presented is most commonly taken as the independent variable, and the numbers of subjects that make errors on syllogisms of different kinds are measured. By comparing the error rates for different kinds of syllogisms, the experimenter seeks to formulate and test hypotheses about the cognitive processes that subjects use to make such syllogistic judgments.

For example, though many subjects will accept, "No As are Bs and no Bs are Cs, therefore no As are Cs," almost all will reject, "No As are Bs and no Bs are Cs, therefore all As are Cs." Yet both syllogisms are equally invalid. Such errors of reasoning have sometimes been attributed to an 'atmosphere effect.' In the example above, since *no* is present in both premises, it appears to be more acceptable than *all* in the conclusion (Woodworth & Sells, 1935). Alternatively, some investigators have claimed that the reason for these errors is that the quantifiers and connectives, *all*, *some*, *no*, *if . . . then*, *and*, *or*, do not have the same meanings in natural language as they do in formal logic (Braine, 1978). According to this hypothesis, since the experimenter judges the correctness of answers by their conformity to the rules of formal logic, whereas the subjects use the natural language meanings, errors follow when the two kinds of meaning diverge.

Errors and latencies in reasoning tasks depend not only on the form of the syllogism, but also on whether it has meaningful content (Wilkins, 1928). Thus, subjects may respond differently to the syllogism, "If some As are Bs and some Bs are Cs, then some As are Cs," and the syllogism "If some birds have blue eyes and some blue-eyed creatures are human, then some birds are human."

In general, subjects' error rates are lower when syllogisms have meaningful content, but there is an important class of exceptions. Subjects often reject valid syllogisms when the conclusions are contrary to facts known to them. "If all horses have four feet and all fish are horses, then all fish have four feet," may be rejected by subjects who know that fish are footless. The rate of rejection rises when subjects react emotionally to the conclusion. "If drug addiction is a disease and diseases should not be punished, then drug addiction should not be punished," is more likely to be rejected by subjects who support strong measures against drug usage then by those who do not (Janis & Frick, 1943; Lefford, 1946). Conversely, subjects often accept invalid syllogisms when the conclusions are consistent with their knowledge about the world or their preferences.

All these findings must be stated as 'tendencies,' since many subjects who make errors on some syllogisms of a certain form do not make such errors consistently. Moreover, there are large individual differences among subjects. For example, subjects trained in formal logic generally make fewer errors—not surprisingly—than do subjects without such training.

While human syllogistic reasoning conforms to some broad generalizations of the sorts that have been mentioned already, the findings derived from experiments are complex and confusing. In recent years, a few investigators have sought to cut through the confusion by creating models of the inference process or some components of it. The attempt to create such models has revealed features of the reasoning task that had not been entirely obvious.

Subjects may use any one of a wide range of strategies to solve the problems, and there is no reason to believe that all subjects use the same strategies. Subjects who reason by vague verbal analogies may succumb to the atmosphere effect, whereas subjects who create semantic images of the propositions and reason by operating on those images may make quite different errors. (Certain syllogisms may require the creation of images more complex than a subject can handle in memory.) Subjects' knowledge of logical inference can be embedded in formal axioms or in inference rules, with different consequences for the likelihood of error. The axioms that define connectives or the inference rules may conform to some natural logic that deviates from the formal logic of the textbooks.

Several quite successful recent efforts at modeling have used the idea that evaluation of syllogisms is a form of problem solving similar to that discussed above in "General Knowledge for Novel Problems with Specific Goals." Using a set of inferential operators, the subject attempts to confirm the conclusion working from the premises, and accepts the conclusion if this problem-solving effort succeeds. The process typically used by subjects differs from the task of finding explicit proofs in that the inferential operators are not expressed overtly and need not, of course, correspond completely to the rules of formal logic.

Models of evaluating propositional syllogisms have been formulated by Osherson (1975), Braine (1978), and Rips (1983). These models are based on the concept of natural deduction, discussed by Gentzen (1935/1969). A system of natural deduction is a form of production system. Rules for making inferences specify conditions in the form of patterns of propositions, and when a pattern is matched in premises the inference is made. The models account for performance by postulating sets of inference rules assumed to be used implicitly by subjects. Rips also formulated a specific process of applying the rules and forming representations of the derivation. An interesting feature of Rips's formulation is the inclusion of suppositions that provide a backward-chaining component in the search process. A syllogism is judged valid if the system can generate a derivation of the conclusion from its inference rules.

The idea that sentential syllogisms are evaluated by natural deduction provides an interpretation of many of the kinds of errors that occur in syllogistic reasoning. Because it is an informal reasoning system, it is not surprising that it is susceptible to influence by general knowledge and affect. Performance would be expected to improve if subjects were taught a more explicit procedure for verifying the applica-bility of inference rules in evaluating syllogisms, and this result was obtained in the domain of geometry proofs in a study by Greeno and Magone (described in Greeno, 1983).

Models of reasoning for categorical syllogisms have been formulated by Guyote and Sternberg (1981) and by Johnson-Laird and Steedman (1978). These models use the idea that the information in premises is represented in the form of examples; for example, "Some jewels are diamonds" might be represented by a symbol for a jewel that is a diamond and another symbol for a jewel that is not a diamond. A representation based on the premises is formed and is used to evaluate the conclusion. Errors occur because the representations are incomplete; the examples generated by the system often fail to exhaust the possibilities, leading to incorrect conclusions.

## Linear Syllogisms

In a linear syllogism, premises specify ordered relations between pairs of objects, and questions are asked about pairs for which the order was not specified. An example from Egan and Grimes-Farrow (1982) is:

> Circle is darker than square.
> Square is darker than triangle.
> Is triangle darker than circle?

(An alternative is to ask, "Which is darkest?" or, "Which is lightest?") Problems are presented with relations expressed differently, such as "Triangle is lighter than square," or "Triangle is not as dark as square," with the premise information given in different orders, and with different questions.

To answer the question, the information in the premises must be encoded in some represen-tation that enables the answer to be derived. Three hypotheses about representation have been considered.

According to a spatial hypothesis (DeSoto, London, & Handel, 1965; Huttenlocher, 1968) information in the premises is integrated into an ordered list, possibly using an image in which symbols are spatially aligned. A representation for the example would be an ordering with circle first, square second, and triangle third, perhaps imagined in a vertical line with the circle at the top. Then a question such as, "Is circle darker than triangle?" would be answered by comparing the positions of the circle and the triangle in the ordered representation.

A second hypothesis (Clark, 1969) is that the representation consists of propositions in which individual objects are associated with values of attributes. For the example, circle would be associated with a large degree of darkness, square with a medium degree, and triangle with a small degree. A question would be answered by retrieving representations of the objects in the question and comparing the properties associated with them.

The third hypothesis is that representation of binary relations are stored in memory. This hypothesis assumes the simplest process of representation, since information in memory corresponds directly to the information in the premises. To answer a question, however, a sequence of propositions has to be retrieved; for example, to answer "Is circle darker than triangle?" both "Circle darker than square" and "Square darker than triangle" have to be retrieved.

The hypothesis that binary relations are represented is ruled out by data obtained by Potts (1974), who had subjects study paragraphs containing series with six terms and asked questions (e.g., "Does B precede D?") involving pairs that varied in their separation: with the ordering A > B > C > D > E > F, the pair C > D has a separation of 0; the pair B > D has a separation of 1; the pair B > E has a separation of 2, and so on. If binary relations are represented in memory, questions about pairs with greater separation should take longer, since answers to these questions require more inferential steps. The finding was the opposite: it took less time to respond to items with greater separation. This finding has also been obtained with comparisons involving general knowledge, such as the relative sizes of animals (Banks, 1977).

The question whether premises are represented by an integrated spatial array or by propositions associating properties with individual objects has been harder to resolve. Huttenlocher (1968) provided an argument for the spatial hypothesis, including the finding that latency is shorter when the second premise has the third individual as the subject of the sentence (e.g., A > B, C < B rather than A > B, B > C). The interpretation is that the subject imagines placement of the new object in a spatial array, and this is easier if the object is mentioned as the sentence subject than the sentence object. Clark (1969) argued for a propositional representation, presenting evidence that performance is influenced

by linguistic factors such as the congruence of questions with premises (e.g., "A > B; which is greater?" is easier than "B < A; which is greater?").

Sternberg (1980) formulated models that specify stages of processing based on assumptions of a spatial or a propositional representation of premises. He also formulated a model that combines those assumptions, so that linguistic factors influence an initial encoding of premises, and relations among propositions influence conversion of the information into an integrated spatial array. The combined linguistic-spatial model provided a more accurate account of latency data than did either of the simpler models.

Several investigators have provided evidence that subjects do not all solve linear syllogisms in one way; rather, different subjects use different representations (Mayer, 1979; Sternberg & Weil, 1980). Egan and Grimes-Farrow's (1982) evidence was particularly direct. They used retrospective protocols obtained after solutions of individual problems. The protocols indicated that some subjects used spatial representations consistently, and others sometimes formed representations by associating certain objects in the problem with different quantitative values of attributes. The protocol evidence was substantiated by analyses showing that subjects differed in their performance, according to the representations they reported using. The order in which objects were mentioned was significant for subjects who used spatial representations, and the linguistic factor of consistency of the relational term used was significant for those subjects who sometimes used individual object propositions.

## Conclusions

Until recently, little attempt has been made to establish a relation between research on reasoning and research on problem solving of the sorts discussed earlier in this chapter. Sometimes this separation has been justified on the grounds that syllogistic reasoning is 'deductive' whereas problem solving is 'inductive,' but we have seen that this distinction does not hold. Although a syllogism is a deductive structure, neither finding valid steps nor testing whether proposed steps are valid is a deductive process. Indeed, the major process in the evaluation of a propositional or categorical syllogism is to seek a proof of the conclusion, the process discussed above in "General Knowledge for Novel Problems with Specific Goals" as the prototypical example of goal-based problem solving. For linear syllogism problems, the major process is an example of inductive problem solving, as defined in "Induction," in which the subject forms an integrated representation of the premises using the structure of an ordered list induced from the order relations that the premises state.

Although all reasoning involves problem solving, it does not follow that there is no need for a special theory of syllogistic reasoning. To understand human reasoning, we must understand the meanings that people attach to words and the rules of inference that constitute their systems of 'natural logic' as well as the structure of the control system that guides their problem-solving search. Recent investigations show progress on these questions.

## CONCLUSIONS

The literature reviewed in this chapter includes analyses of problem solving on a few dozen tasks. One way to express the important general characteristics that have emerged here is to apply problem-solving analyses to a new domain. The analyses shown have provided strong guidance about the kinds of processes and knowledge structures that one should look for in an investigation of problem solving.

First, it is important to investigate the subjects' knowledge and processes for representing the problem. If the subjects do not have special training in the problem domain, they must construct a problem space that includes representations of the problem materials, the goal, operators, and constraints. If subjects have special training or experience in the domain, their prior knowledge includes general characteristics of the problem space, and their representations of individual problems are based on that general knowledge. Experts in various domains are cognizant of the general methods that can be used for solving problems, and their representations include use of problem information relevant to the choice of a solution method.

A second major task is to characterize the problem representations that subjects form in their understanding of the problem. In relatively unfamiliar domains, the problem solving is primarily a process of search, and the problem representation determines the space of possibilities in which the search will occur. Some basic features of the problem space depend on the problem itself. A problem may present constraints on the operators that the subjects are permitted to use in trying to achieve a goal, or on the arrangement of materials that is acceptable as a solution. The problem may also require induction of a pattern or rule from materials presented. These alternatives lead to differences in the problem space: a space of possible sequences of actions, of possible solution arrangements, of possible structures, or some combination of these.

The problem space constructed by an individual subject is also determined by the method of search that the subject uses, the features of the problem that are used, and the general knowledge that is applied. In a problem of transforming a situation by a sequence of actions, subjects typically use some form of means–ends analysis. They may distinguish between features of the situation that are more-or-less essential for the solution, and they may organize their search by a process of planning that focuses on the more essential features. Searching in a space of possible solution arrangements typically involves generating partial solutions on a trial basis, and the search is influenced by the subjects' knowledge of constraints that can be used to limit the candidate arrangements that are considered. Similarly, solution of induction problems is influenced by the subjects' knowledge of general constraints on possible solutions, which may be used in generating and testing hypotheses, or in synthesizing or abstracting structures from the features of individual objects that are provided.

In solving problems for which subjects have special training or experience, the problem space of operators and constraints is provided by the subjects' existing knowledge. Experts have highly organized knowledge that includes solution methods and concepts for representing problems at varying degrees of generality and abstraction. For simple problems, experts' knowledge often provides a basis for immediate recognition of methods as well as detailed features relevant to the solution. Their knowledge of relations among methods and operators and of constraints in the domain enables them to solve problems in a highly organized and planned manner.

The study of problem solving and reasoning has progressed to a substantial level of knowledge and theory, however, several questions remain unanswered.

First, while we are beginning to understand the performance of experts on simple problems, little is known about their performance on problems that are difficult and deep. When confronted by problems for which their knowledge does not provide a ready method of solution, do experts resort to weak methods of search and analysis fundamentally similar to those used by novices? Or do experts who have acquired powerful processes of reasoning in one domain apply those processes to solving problems in areas where specific solution methods have not been worked out and stored in memory?

A second question, closely related to the first, involves the general nature of problem solving in its more powerful and productive forms. In their discussions of productive thinking, Duncker (1935, 1945) and Wertheimer (1945, 1959) raised a critical issue that has not been dealt with in the recent literature, namely, the process of constructing more powerful representations of problems by analysis of problem components. The initial representation of a problem frequently fails to include important relations that are required for meaningful solution, although the problem solver is able to construct a reformulation that includes its important structural features.

A third question concerns learning. How is problem-solving skill learned? To analyze acquisition requires an understanding of the skills and knowledge to be acquired, and promising results in characterizing skill and knowledge in problem solving could provide a basis for the investigation of learning. New approaches to the acquisition of cognitive skill such as those of Anderson (1982), Anzai and Simon (1979), Neches (1981), and Neves (1981), may provide some keys to the analysis of learning processes.

A fourth question concerns the theoretical power of general principles in the analysis of problem solving and reasoning. The literature discussed in this chapter offers detailed hypotheses about performance on specific tasks that are testable at the level of their assumptions about specific processes. The more general assump-

tions are more heuristic. These general concepts and principles provide guidance in constructing hypotheses about specific cognitive structures and processes, but they rarely constrain those hypotheses in wholly specifiable ways. It is an open question whether complex processes of problem solving and reasoning can be defined solely by underlying formal principles. Some investigators (Keil, 1981; VanLehn, Brown, & Greeno, 1984) have urged that research should seek general principles with deductive power that would determine characteristics of process models. Others (e.g., Newell & Simon, 1976) assert that there are good reasons for expecting that complex cognition is constrained only by relatively weak structural principles, of the kind that are characteristic of current theoretical analyses.

A review of any body of scientific research can be closed with the remark that much has been accomplished, and more remains to be done, and the psychology of problem solving and reasoning is no exception. The progress of the 1960s and 1970s has provided concepts and methods that future investigators may use as the basis for further advances.

# REFERENCES

Adamson, R.E. (1952). Functional fixedness as related to problem solving: A repetition of three experiments. *Journal of Experimental Psychology, 44,* 288–291.

Adelson, B. (1981). Problem solving and the development of abstract categories in programming languages. *Memory and Cognition, 9,* 422–433.

Anderson, J.R. (1975). Computer simulation of a language acquisition system: A first report. In R.L. Solso (Ed.), *Information processing and cognition: The Loyola symposium.* Hillsdale, NJ: Erlbaum.

Anderson, J.R. (1976). *Language, memory, and thought.* Hillsdale, NJ: Erlbaum.

Anderson, J.R. (1977). Computer simulation of a language acquisition system: A second report. In D. LaBerge & S.J. Samuels (Eds.), *Perception and comprehension.* Hillsdale, NJ: Erlbaum.

Anderson, J.R. (1982). Acquisition of cognitive skill. *Psychological Review, 89*(4), 396–406.

Anderson, J.R. (1983). *The architecture of cognition.* Cambridge, MA: Harvard University Press.

Anderson, J.R., Farrell, R., & Sauers, R. (1984).

Learning to program in LISP. *Cognitive Science, 8,* 87–129.

Anderson, J.R., Greeno, J.G., Kline, P.J., & Neves, D.M. (1981). Acquisition of problem-solving skill. In J.R. Anderson (Ed.), *Cognitive skills and their acquisition.* Hillsdale, NJ: Erlbaum.

Anderson, J.R., Kline, P.J., & Beasley, C.M. (1979). A general learning theory and its application to schema abstraction. In G.H. Bower (Ed.), *The psychology of learning and motivation* (Vol. 13, pp. 277–318). New York: Academic Press.

Anzai, Y. & Simon, H.A. (1979). The theory of learning by doing. *Psychological Review, 86,* 124–140.

Ashcraft, M.H. & Battaglia, J. (1978). Cognitive arithmetic: Evidence for retrieval and decision processes in mental addition. *Journal of Experimental Psychology: Human Learning and Memory, 5,* 527–538.

Ashcraft, M.H. & Stazyk, E.H. (1981). Mental addition: A test of three verification models. *Memory and Cognition, 9,* 185–196.

Atwood, M.E. & Polson, P.G. (1976). A process model for water jug problems. *Cognitive Psychology, 8,* 191–216.

Banks, W.P. (1977). Encoding and processing of semantic information in comparative judgments. In G.H. Bower (Ed.), *The psychology of learning and motivation: Advances in research and theory*: Vol. 11. New York: Academic Press.

Barnes, G.M. & Whitely, S.E. (1981). Problem restructuring processes for ill-structured verbal analogies. *Memory and Cognition, 9,* 411–421.

Bartlett, F.C. (1932). *Remembering: A study in experimental and social psychology.* Cambridge, England: Cambridge University Press.

Bartlett, F.C. (1958). *Thinking.* New York: Basic Books.

Beilin, H. & Horn, R. (1962). Transition probability effects in anagram problem solving. *Journal of Experimental Psychology, 63,* 514–518.

Bereiter, C. & Scardamalia, M. (1982). From conversation to compositions: The role of instruction in a developmental process. In R. Glaser (Ed.), *Advances in instructional psychology*: Vol. 2. Hillsdale, NJ: Erlbaum.

Birch, H.G. & Rabinowitz, H.S. (1951). The negative effect of previous experience on productive thinking. *Journal of Experimental Psychology, 41,* 121–125.

Bloom, B.S. & Broder, L.J. (1950). *Problem solving processes of college students.* Chicago: University of Chicago Press.

Bobrow, D.G. (1968). Natural language input for a computer problem-solving system. In M. Minsky (Ed.), *Semantic information processing.* Cambridge, MA: MIT Press.

Bourne, L.E., Jr. (1970). Knowing and using concepts. *Psychological Review, 77,* 546–556.

Bourne, L.E., Jr. (1974). An inference model of conceptual rule learning. In R. Solso (Ed.), *Theories in cognitive psychology.* Washington DC: Erlbaum.

Bower, G.H. & Trabasso, T.R. (1964). Concept identification. In R.C. Atkinson (Ed.), *Studies in mathematical psychology* (pp. 32–94). Stanford, CA: Stanford University Press.

Braine, M.D.S. (1978). On the relation between the natural logic of reasoning and standard logic. *Psychological Review, 85,* 1–21.

Briars, D.J. & Larkin, J.H. (1984). An integrated model of skill in solving elementary word problems. *Cognition and Instruction, 1,* 245–296.

Brooks, L. (1978). Nonanalytic concept formation and memory for instances. In E. Rosch & B.B. Lloyd (Eds.), *Cognition and categorization.* Hillsdale, NJ: Erlbaum.

Brown, J.S. & Burton, R.B. (1980). Diagnostic models for procedural bugs in basic mathematical skills. *Cognitive Science, 4,* 379–426.

Brown, J.S., Burton, R.R., & de Kleer, J. (1983). Pedagogical, natural language and knowledge engineering techniques in SOPHIE I, II, and III. In D. Sleeman & J.S. Brown (Eds.), *Intelligent tutoring systems.* New York: Academic Press.

Brown, J.S. & VanLehn, K. (1980). Repair theory: A generative theory of bugs in procedural skills. *Cognitive Science, 4,* 379–426.

Brown, R. (1973). *A first language: The early stages.* Cambridge, MA: Harvard University Press.

Brownell, W.A. (1935). Psychological considerations in the learning and teaching of arithmetic. In *The teaching of arithmetic: Tenth yearbook of the National Council of Teachers of Mathematics.* New York: Columbia University Press.

Brownell, W.A. (1941). *Arithmetic in grades I and II: A critical summary of new and previously reported research.* (Duke University Research Studies in Education, No. 6). Durham, NC: Duke University Press.

Bruner, J.S., Goodnow, J.J., & Austin, G.A. (1956). *A study of thinking.* New York: Wiley.

Bundy, A. (1978). Will it reach the top? Prediction in the mechanics world. *Artificial Intelligence, 10,* 129–146.

Burke, R.J., Maier, N.R.F., & Hoffman, L.R. (1966). Function of hints in individual problem solving. *American Journal of Psychology, 79,* 389–399.

Buss, A.H. (1953). Rigidity as a function of reversal and nonreversal shifts in the learning of successive discriminations. *Journal of Experimental Psychology, 45,* 75–81.

Carpenter, J.A., Moore, O.K., Snyder, C.R., & Lisansky, E.S. (1961). Alcohol and higher-order problem solving. *Quarterly Journal of Studies on Alcohol, 22,* 183–222.

Carpenter, T.P. & Moser, J.M. (1982). The development of addition and subtraction problem-solving skills. In T.P. Carpenter, J.M. Moser & T. Romberg (Eds.), *Addition and subtraction: A cognitive perspective.* Hillsdale, NJ: Erlbaum.

Chase, W.G. & Simon, H.A. (1973). Perception in chess. *Cognitive Psychology, 4,* 55–81.

Chi, M.T.H., Feltovich, P., & Glaser, R. (1981). Categorization and representation of physics problems by experts and novices. *Cognitive Science, 5,* 121–152.

Ciesielski, V.B., Bennett, J.S., & Cohen, P.R. (1977). Applications-oriented AI research: Medicine. In A. Barr and E.A. Feigenbaum (Eds.), *The handbook of artificial intelligence*: Vol. 2. Stanford, CA: Heuristech Press.

Clark, H.H. (1969). Linguistic processes in deductive reasoning. *Psychological Review, 76,* 387–404.

deGroot, A.D. (1965). *Thought and choice in chess.* The Hague: Mouton.

deKleer, J. (1975). *Qualitative and quantitative knowledge in classical mechanics.* (AI Lab Tech. Rep. No. AI-TR-352). Cambridge, MA: Massachusetts Institute of Technology.

DeSoto, C.B., London, M., & Handel, S. (1965). Social reasoning and spatial paralogic. *Journal of Personality and Social Psychology, 2,* 513–521.

Dodd, D.H., Kinsman, R., Klipp, R., & Bourne, L.E., Jr. (1971). Effects of logic pretraining on conceptual rule learning. *Journal of Experimental Psychology, 88,* 119–122.

Dominowski, R.L. & Ekstrand, B.R. (1967). Direct and associative priming in anagram solving. *Journal of Experimental Psychology, 74,* 84–86.

Duncker, K. (1945). On problem solving. *Psychological Monographs, 58*:5 (Whole No. 270). (Original version published in 1935, in German.)

Egan, D.E. & Grimes-Farrow, D.D. (1982). Differences in mental representations spontaneously adopted for reasoning. *Memory and Cognition, 10,* 297–307.

Egan, D.E. & Schwartz, B.J. (1979). Chunking in recall of symbolic drawings. *Memory and Cognition, 7,* 149–158.

Eisenstadt, M. & Kareev, Y. (1975). Aspects of human problem solving: The use of internal representations. In D.A. Norman & D.E. Rumelhart (Eds.), *Exploration in cognition* (pp. 308–346). San Francisco: Freeman.

Erickson, J. (1971). Problem shifts and hypothesis behavior in concept identification. *American Journal of Psychology, 84*(1), 101–111.

Ericsson, K.A. & Simon, H.A. (1980). Verbal reports as data. *Psychological Review, 87,* 255–251.

Ernst, G.W. & Newell, A. (1969). *GPS: A case study in generality and problem solving.* New York: Academic Press.

Evans, T.G. (1968). A program for the solution of geometric-analogy intelligence test questions. In M. Minsky (Ed.), *Semantic information processing* (pp. 271–353). Cambridge, MA: MIT Press.

Feigenbaum, E.A. (1963). The simulation of verbal learning behavior. In E.A. Feigenbaum & J. Feldman (Eds.), *Computers and thought.* New York: McGraw-Hill.

Feltovich, P.J. (1981). *Knowledge based components of expertise in medical diagnosis.* (Report No. PDS-2). Pittsburgh: University of Pittsburgh, Learning Research and Development Center.

Flower, L.S. & Hayes, J.R. (1980). The dynamics of composing: Making plans and juggling constraints. In L.W. Gregg & E.R. Steinberg (Eds.), *Cognitive processes in writing.* Hillsdale, NJ: Erlbaum.

Franks, J.J. & Bransford, J.D. (1971). Abstraction of visual patterns. *Journal of Experimental Psychology, 90,* 65–74.

Friedland, P.E. (1979). *Knowledge-based experiment design in molecular genetics.* (Report No. 79-771). Stanford, CA: Stanford University, Computer Science Dept.

Gavurin, E.I. (1967). Anagram solution and spatial aptitude. *Journal of Psychology, 65,* 65–68.

Gelman, R. & Gallistel, C.R. (1978). *The child's understanding of number.* Cambridge, MA: Harvard University Press.

Gentzen, G. (1969). Investigations into logical deduction. In M.E. Szabo (Ed. and Trans.), *The collected papers of Gerhard Gentzen.* Amsterdam: North-Holland. (Original work published 1935.)

Gerwin, D. (1974). Information processing, data inferences, and scientific generalization. *Behavioral Science, 19,* 314–325.

Gick, M.L. & Holyoak, K.J. (1980). Analogical problem solving. *Cognitive Psychology, 12,* 306–355.

Gick, M.L. & Holyoak, K.J. (1983). Schema induction and analogical transfer. *Cognitive Psychology, 15,* 1–38.

Glucksberg, S. & Weisberg, R.W. (1966). Verbal behavior and problem solving: Some effects of labeling in a functional fixedness problem. *Journal of Experimental Psychology, 71,* 659–664.

Greeno, J.G. (1976). Indefinite goals in well-structured problems. *Psychological Review, 83,* 479–491.

Greeno, J.G. (1978). A study of problem solving. In R. Glaser (Ed.), *Advances in instructional psychology*: Vol. 1. Hillsdale, NJ: Erlbaum.

Greeno, J.G. (1983). Forms of understanding in mathematical problem solving. In S.G. Paris, G.M. Olson, & H.W. Stevenson (Eds.), *Learning and motivation in the classroom.* Hillsdale, NJ: Erlbaum.

Greeno, J.G., Magone, M.E., & Chaiklin, S. (1979). Theory of constructions and set in problem solving. *Memory and Cognition, 7,* 445–461.

Greeno, J.G., Riley, M.S., & Gelman, R. (1984). Conceptual competence and young children's counting. *Cognitive Psychology, 16,* 44–143.

Greeno, J.G. & Scandura, J.M. (1966). All-or-none transfer based on verbally mediated concepts. *Journal of Mathematical Psychology, 3,* 388–411.

Gregg, L.W. & Simon, H.A. (1967). Process models and stochastic theories of simple concept formation. *Journal of Mathematical Psychology, 4,* 246–276.

Groen, G.J. & Parkman, J.M. (1972). A chronometric analysis of simple addition. *Psychological Review, 79,* 329–343.

Groen, G.J. & Resnick, L.B. (1977). Can preschool children invent addition algorithms? *Journal of Educational Psychology, 69,* 645–652.

Grudin, J. (1980). Processes in verbal analogy solution. *Journal of Experimental Psychology: Human Perception and Performance, 6,* 67–74.

Guyote, M.J. & Sternberg, R.J. (1981). A transitive-chain theory of syllogistic reasoning. *Cognitive Psychology, 13,* 461–525.

Hayes, J.R. (1981). *The complete problem solver.* Philadelphia: Franklin Institute Press.

Hayes, J.R. & Flower, L.S. (1980). Identifying the organization of writing processes. In L.W. Gregg & E.R. Steinberg (Eds.), *Cognitive processes in writing.* Hillsdale, NJ: Erlbaum.

Hayes, J.R. & Simon, H.A. (1974). Understanding problem instructions. In L.W. Gregg (Ed.), *Knowledge and cognition.* Hillsdale, NJ: Erlbaum.

Hayes, J.R. & Simon, H.A. (1977). Psychological differences among problem isomorphs. In N.J. Castellan, P.B. Pisoni, & G.R. Potts (Eds.), *Cognitive theory*: Vol. 2. Hillsdale, NJ: Erlbaum.

Hayes-Roth, B. & Hayes-Roth, F. (1978). *Cognitive processes in planning.* (Report No. R-2366-ONR). Santa Monica, CA: Rand Corporation.

Haygood, R.C. & Bourne, L.E., Jr. (1965). Attribute- and rule-learning aspects of conceptual behavior. *Psychological Review, 72,* 175–195.

Heller, J.I. (1979). *Cognitive processing in verbal analogy solution.* Unpublished doctoral dissertation, University of Pittsburgh.

Henley, N.M. (1969). A psychological study of the semantics of animal terms. *Journal of Verbal Learning and Verbal Behavior, 8,* 176–184.

Huesmann, L.R. & Cheng, C. (1973). A theory for the induction of mathematical functions. *Psychological Review, 80,* 126–138.

Hull, C.L. (1920). Quantitative aspects of the evolution of concepts. *Psychological Monographs, 28* (Whole No. 20).

Hull, C.L. (1930). Knowledge and purpose as habit mechanisms. *Psychological Review, 37,* 241–256.

Hull, C.L. (1943). *Principles of behavior: An introduction to behavior theory.* New York: Appleton-Century-Crofts.

Hull, C.L. (1952). *A behavior system.* New Haven: Yale University Press.

Hunt, E.B. (1962). *Concept learning: An information processing problem.* New York: Wiley.

Hunt, E.B., Martin, J., & Stone, P.I. (1966). *Experiments in induction.* New York: Academic Press.

Huttenlocher, J. (1968). Constructing spatial images: A strategy in reasoning. *Psychological Review, 75,* 550–560.

Janis, I.L. & Frick, F. (1943). The relationship between attitudes toward conclusions and errors in judging logical validity of syllogisms. *Journal of Experimental Psychology, 33,* 73–77.

Jeffries, R., Polson, P.G., Razran, L., & Atwood, M.E. (1977). A process model for missionaries–cannibals and other river crossing problems. *Cognitive Psychology, 9,* 412–440.

Jongman, R.W. (1968). *Het oog van de Meester.* Amsterdam: van Gorcum.

Johnson, P.E., Duran, A.S., Hassebrock, F., Moller, J., Prietula, M., Feltovich, P.J., & Swanson, D.B. (1981). Expertise and error in diagnostic reasoning. *Cognitive Science, 5,* 235–283.

Johnson-Laird, P.N. & Steedman, M. (1978). The psychology of syllogisms. *Cognitive Psychology, 10,* 64–99.

Judd, C.M. (1908). The relation of special training to general intelligence. *Educational Review, 36,* 28–42.

Katona, G. (1940). *Organizing and memorizing.* New York: Columbia University Press.

Keil, F.C. (1981). Constraints on knowledge and cognitive development. *Psychological Review, 88,* 197–227.

Kelleher, R.T. (1956). Discrimination learning as a function of reversal and nonreversal shifts. *Journal of Experimental Psychology, 51,* 379–384.

Kendler, H.H. & D'Amato, M.F. (1955). A comparison of reversal and nonreversal shifts in human concept formation behavior. *Journal of Experimental Psychology, 49,* 165–174.

Kendler, H.H. & Kendler, T.S. (1959). Reversal and nonreversal shifts in kindergarten children. *Journal of Experimental Psychology, 58,* 56–60.

Kintsch, W. (1974). *The representation of meaning in memory.* Hillsdale, NJ: Erlbaum.

Köhler, W. (1929). *The mentality of apes.* New York: Harcourt Brace.

Kotovsky, K. & Simon, H.A. (1973). Empirical tests of a theory of human acquisition of concepts for sequential events. *Cognitive Psychology, 4,* 399–424.

Langley, P. (1981). Data-driven discovery of physical laws. *Cognitive Science, 5*(1), 31–54.

Langley, P., Bradshaw, G.L., & Simon, H.A. (1983). Rediscovering chemistry with the BACON system. In R. Michalski, J. Carbonell, & T. Mitchell (Eds.), *Machine learning: An artificial intelligence approach.* Palo Alto, CA: Tioga Press.

Larkin, J.H. (1981). Enriching formal knowledge: A model for learning to solve problems in physics. In J.R. Anderson (Ed.), *Cognitive skills and their acquisition.* Hillsdale, NJ: Erlbaum.

Larkin, J.H. (1982). *Spatial knowledge in solving physics problems.* (C.I.P.434). Carnegie-Mellon University, Department of Psychology.

Larkin, J.H., McDermott, J., Simon, D.P., & Simon, H.A. (1979). Models of competence in solving physics problems. *Cognitive Sciences, 4,* 317–345.

Larkin, J.H. & Reif, F. (1979). Understanding and teaching problem-solving in physics. *Journal of Science Education, 1*(2), 191–203.

Lefford, A. (1946). The influence of emotional subject matter on logical reasoning. *Journal of Genetic Psychology, 34,* 127–151.

Lenat, D.B. (1982). *AM: Discovery in mathematics and heuristic search.* Stanford, CA: Stanford University Press.

Lesgold, A.M., Feltovich, P.J., Glaser, R., & Wang, Y. (1981). *The acquisition of perceptual diagnostic skill in radiology.* (Report No. PDS-1). University of Pittsburgh, Learning Research and Development Center.

Levine, M. (1963). Mediating processes in humans at the outset of discrimination learning. *Psychological Review, 70,* 254–276.

Lewis, C.H. (1978). *Problem system models of practice effects.* Unpublished doctoral dissertation, University of Michigan, Ann Arbor.

Lindsay, R.K., Buchanan, B.G., Feigenbaum, E.A., & Lederberg, J. (1980). *Applications of artificial intelligence for organic chemistry.* New York: McGraw Hill.

Luchins, A.S. (1942). Mechanization in problem solving. *Psychological Monographs, 54*: 6 (Whole No. 248).

Magone, M.E. (1977). *Goal analysis and feature detection as processes in the solution of an insight problem.* Unpublished master's thesis, University of Pittsburgh.

Maier, N.R.F. (1931). Reasoning and learning. *Psychological Review, 38,* 332–346.

Maier, N.R.F. (1945). Reasoning in humans: III. The mechanisms of equivalent stimuli and of reasoning. *Journal of Experimental Psychology, 35,* 349–360.

Malin, J.T. (1979). Information-processing load in problem solving by network search. *Journal of Experimental Psychology: Human Perception and Performance, 5,* 379–390.

Maltzman, I. (1955). Thinking: From a behavioristic point of view. *Psychological Review, 62,* 275–286.

Mayer, R.E. (1974). Acquisition processes and resilience under varying testing conditions for structurally different problem-solving procedures. *Journal of Educational Psychology, 66,* 644–656.

Mayer, R.E. (1979). Qualitatively different encoding strategies for linear reasoning premises: Evidence for single association and distance theories. *Journal of Experimental Psychology: Human Learning and Memory, 5,* 1–10.

McDermott, J. & Larkin, J.H. (1978). Representing textbook physics problems. In *Proceedings of the Second National Conference, Canadian Society for Computational Studies of Intelligence.* Toronto, Canada: University of Toronto.

McKeithen, K.B., Reitman, J.R., Rueter, H.H., & Hirtle, S.C. (1981). Knowledge organization and skill differences in computer programmers. *Cognitive Psychology, 13,* 307–325.

Millenson, J.R. (1967). *Principles of behavioral analysis.* New York: MacMillan.

Miller, G.A., Galanter, E.H., & Pribram, K.H. (1960). *Plans and the structure of behavior.* New York: Holt, Rinehart, & Winston.

Miller, R.A., Pople, H.E., & Myers, M.D. (1982). Internist-1, An experimental computer-based diagnostic consultant for general medicine. *New England Journal of Medicine, 307,* 468–476.

Millward, R.B. & Wickens, T.D. (1974). Concept-identification models. In D.H. Krantz, R.C. Atkinson, R. D. Luce, & P. Suppes (Eds.), *Contemporary developments in mathematical psychology*: Vol. 1. (pp. 45–100). San Francisco: W.H. Freeman and Company.

Moeser, S.D. & Bregman, A.S. (1972). The role of reference in the acquisition of a miniature artificial language. *Journal of Verbal Learning and Verbal Behavior, 11,* 759–769.

Moore, O.K. & Anderson, S.B. (1954). Modern logic and tasks for experiments on problem solving behavior. *Journal of Psychology, 38,* 151–160.

Morgan, J.L. & Newport, E.L. (1981). The role of constituent structure in the induction of artificial language. *Journal of Learning and Verbal Behavior, 20,* 67–85.

Mulholland, T.M., Pellegrino, J.W., & Glaser, R. (1980). Components of geometric analogy solution. *Cognitive Psychology, 12,* 252–284.

Neches, R. (1981). *Models of heuristic procedure modification.* Unpublished doctoral dissertation, Carnegie-Mellon University, Pittsburgh.

Nesher, P. (1982). Levels of description in the analysis of addition and subtraction. In T.P. Carpenter, J.M. Moser, & T. Romberg (Eds.), *Addition and subtraction: A cognitive perspective.* Hillsdale, NJ: Erlbaum.

Neumann, P.G. (1974). An attribute frequency model for the abstraction of prototypes. *Memory and Cognition, 2,* 241–248.

Neves, D.M. (1981). *Learning procedures from examples.* Unpublished doctoral dissertation, Carnegie-Mellon University, Pittsburgh.

Newell, A., Shaw, J.C., & Simon, H.A. (1957). Preliminary description of the general problem solving program I (GPS I). CIP Working Paper 7. Carnegie-Mellon University, Pittsburgh.

Newell, A. & Simon, H.A. (1972). *Human problem solving.* Englewood Cliffs, NJ: Prentice–Hall.

Newell, A. & Simon, H.A. (1976). Computer science as empirical inquiry: Symbols and search. *Communications of the Association for Computing Machinery, 19,* 11–126.

Nisbett, R.E. & Wilson, T.D. (1977). Telling more than we know: Verbal reports on mental processes. *Psychological Review, 84,* 231–259.

Norman, D.A. & Rumelhart, D.E. (1975). *Explorations in cognition.* San Francisco: Freeman.

Novak, G.S. (1976). Computer understanding of physics problems stated in natural language. *American Journal of Computational Linguistics,* Microfiche 53.

Osherson, D.N. (1975). *Logical abilities in children*: Vol. 3. Hillsdale, NJ: Erlbaum.

Paige, J.M. & Simon, H.A. (1966). Cognitive processes in solving algebra word problems. In B. Kleinmuntz (Ed.), *Problem solving.* New York: Wiley.

Pellegrino, J.W. & Glaser, R. (1982). Analyzing aptitudes for learning: Inductive reasoning. In R. Glaser (Ed.), *Advances in Instructional Psychology*: Vol. 2. (pp. 269–345). Hillsdale, NJ: Erlbaum.

Piaget, J. (1952). *The child's conception of number.* New York: Norton. (Original work published, 1941, in French.)

Polson, M.C., Restle, F., & Polson, P.G. (1965). Association and discrimination in paired-associates learning. *Journal of Experimental Psychology, 69,* 47–55.

Polson, P.G. (1972). A quantitative analysis of the conceptual processes in the Hull paradigm. *Journal of Mathematical Psychology, 9,* 141–167.

Polson, P.G., Atwood, M.E., Jeffries, R., & Turner, A. (1981). The processes involved in designing software. In J.R. Anderson (Ed.), *Cognitive skills and their acquisition.* Hillsdale, NJ: Erlbaum.

Pople, H.E. (1982). Heuristic methods for imposing structure on ill-structured problems: The structuring of medical diagnostics. In P. Szolovits (Ed.), *Artificial intelligence in medicine* (pp. 119–185). AAAS Symposium Series. Boulder, CO: Westview Press.

Posner, M.I., Goldsmith, R., & Welton, K.E., Jr. (1967). Perceived distance and the classification of distorted patterns. *Journal of Experimental Psychology, 73,* 28–38.

Post, E.L. (1943). Formal reductions of the general combinatorial decision problem. *American Journal of Mathematics, 65,* 197–268.

Potts, G.R. (1974). Storing and retrieving information about ordered relationships. *Journal of Experimental Psychology, 103,* 431–439.

Quillian, M.R. (1968). Semantic memory. In M. Minsky, (Ed.), *Semantic information processing* (pp. 216–270). Cambridge, MA: MIT Press.

Reber, A.S. (1967). Implicit learning of artificial grammars. *Journal of Verbal Learning and Verbal Behavior, 6,* 855–863.

Reddy, D.R., Erman, L.D., Fennell, R.D., & Neely, R.B. (1973). The HEARSAY speech understanding system: An example of the recognition process. *3rd International Joint Conference on Artificial Intelligence.* Stanford, CA.

Reed, S.K. (1972). Pattern recognition and categorization. *Cognitive Psychology, 3,* 383–407.

Reed, S.K., Ernst, G.W., & Banerji, R. (1974). The role of analogy in transfer between similar problem states. *Cognitive Psychology, 6,* 435–450.

Rees, H.J. & Israel, H.C. (1935). An investigation of the establishment and operation of mental sets. *Psychological Monographs, 46,* Whole No. 210.

Reif, F. & Heller, J.I. (1981). *Knowledge structure and problem solving in physics.* (Educational Science Paper 12.) University of California, Berkeley, Physics Department and Group in Science and Mathematics Education.

Reitman, J.S. (1976). Skilled perception in GO: Deducing memory structures from inter-response times. *Cognitive Psychology, 8,* 336–356.

Reitman, J.S. & Bower, G.H. (1973). Storage and later recognition of exemplars of concepts. *Cognitive Psychology, 4,* 194–206.

Reitman, W.R. (1965). *Cognition and thought.* New York: Wiley.

Reitman, W.R. & Wilcox, B. (1978). Pattern recognition and pattern-directed inference in a program. In

D.A. Waterman & F. Hayes-Roth (Eds.), *Pattern-directed inference systems*. New York: Academic Press.

Resnick, L.B. (1983). A developmental theory of number understanding. In H.P. Ginsburg (Ed.), *The development of mathematical thinking*. New York: Academic Press.

Restle, F. (1962). The selection of strategies in cue learning. *Psychological Review, 69*, 329–343.

Restle, F. (1970). Theory of serial pattern learning: Structural trees. *Psychological Review, 77*, 481–495.

Riley, M.S., Greeno, J.G., & Heller, J.I. (1983). Development of children's problem-solving ability in arithmetic. In H.P. Ginsburg (Ed.), *The development of mathematical thinking*. New York: Academic Press.

Rips, L.J. (1983). Cognitive processes in propositional reasoning. *Psychological Review, 90*, 38–71.

Rips, L.J. & Marcus, S.L. (1977). Suppositions and the analysis of conditional sentences. In M.A. Just & P.A. Carpenter (Eds.), *Cognitive processes in comprehension*. Hillsdale, NJ: Erlbaum.

Rips, L.J., Shoben, E.J., & Smith, E.E. (1973). Semantic distance and the verification of semantic relations. *Journal of Verbal Learning and Verbal Behavior, 12*, 1–20.

Rosch, E.H. (1973). On the internal structure of perceptual and semantic categories. In T.E. Moore (Ed.), *Cognitive development and acquisition of language*. New York: Academic Press.

Rosch, E.H. (1975). Cognitive representations of semantic categories. *Journal of Experimental Psychology: General, 104*, 192–233.

Rosch, E.H. (1978). Principles of categorization. In E. Rosch & B.B. Lloyd (Eds.), *Cognition and categorization*. Hillsdale, NJ: Erlbaum.

Rosch, E.H., Mervis, C.B., Gray, W.D., Johnson, D.J., & Boyes-Braem, P. (1976). Basic objects in natural categories. *Cognitive Psychology, 8*, 382–439.

Rumelhart, D.E. & Abrahamson, A.A. (1973). A model for analogical reasoning. *Cognitive Psychology, 5*, 1–28.

Sacerdoti, E.D. (1977). *A structure for plans and behavior*. New York: Elsevier–North Holland.

Schank, R.C. (1972). Conceptual dependency: A theory of natural language understanding. *Cognitive Psychology, 3*, 552–631.

Schank, R.C. & Abelson, R.P. (1978). *Scripts, plans, goals, and understanding: An inquiry into human knowledge structures*. Hillsdale, NJ: Erlbaum.

Schoenfeld, A.H. (1979). Explicit heuristic training as a variable in problem-solving performance. *Journal of Research in Mathematics Education, 10*, 173–187.

Shortliffe, E.H. (1976). *Computer-based medical consultations: Mycin*. New York: American Elsevier.

Silverman, H. (1975). A digitalis therapy advisor. (Rep. No. MACTR-143.) Cambridge, MA: MIT, Computer Science Dept.

Simon, D.P. & Simon, H.A. (1978). Individual differences in solving physics problems. In R. Siegler (Ed.), *Children's thinking: What develops?* Hillsdale, NJ: Erlbaum.

Simon, H.A. (1973). The structure of ill structured problems. *Artificial Intelligence, 4*, 181–201.

Simon, H.A. & Barenfeld, M. (1969). Information processing analysis of perceptual processes in problem solving. *Psychological Review, 76*, 473–483.

Simon, H.A. & Feigenbaum, E.A. (1964). An information-processing theory of some effects of similarity, familiarization, and meaningfulness in verbal learning. *Journal of Verbal Learning and Verbal Behavior, 3*, 385–396.

Simon, H.A. & Gilmartin, K. (1973). A simulation of memory for chess positions. *Cognitive Psychology, 2*, 29–46.

Simon, H.A. & Kotovsky, K. (1963). Human acquisition of concepts for sequential patterns. *Psychological Review, 70*, 534–546.

Simon, H.A. & Lea, G. (1974). Problem solving and rule induction: A unified view. In L.W. Gregg (Ed.), *Knowledge and cognition*. Potomac, MD: Erlbaum.

Skinner, B.F. (1938). *The behavior of organisms: An experimental analysis*. New York: Appleton-Century-Crofts.

Smith, E.E., Shoben, E.J., & Rips, L.J. (1974). Structure and process in semantic memory: A featured model for semantic decisions. *Psychological Review, 81*, 214–241.

Snow, R.E. (1980) Aptitude processes. In R.E. Snow, P.A. Federico, & W.E. Montague (Eds.), *Aptitude, learning, and instruction: Cognitive process analysis analyses of aptitude*: Vol. 1. Hillsdale, NJ: Erlbaum.

Soloway, E., Ehrlich, K., Bonar, J., & Greenspan, J. (1982). What do novices know about programming? In B. Schneiderman & A. Bodre (Eds.), *Directions in human-computer interactions*. Norwood, NJ: Ablex.

Staats, A.W. (1966). An integrated-functional learning approach to complex human behavior. In B. Kleinmuntz (Ed.), *Problem solving: Research, method, and theory*. New York: Wiley.

Stefik, M. (1981). Planning with constraints (MOLGEN: Part 1). *Artificial Intelligence, 16*, 111–140.

Sternberg, R.J. (1977). Component processes in analogical reasoning. *Psychological Review, 84*, 353–378.

Sternberg, R.J. (1980). Representation and process in linear syllogistic reasoning. *Journal of Experimental Psychology: General, 109*, 119–159.

Sternberg, R.J. & Weil, E.M. (1980). An aptitude-strategy interaction in linear syllogistic reasoning. *Journal of Educational Psychology, 72,* 226–239.

Sweller, J. & Gee, W. (1978). Einstellung, the sequence effect, and hypothesis theory. *Journal of Experimental Psychology: Human Learning and Memory, 4,* 513–526.

Thorndike, E.L. (1923). *The psychology of learning.* New York: Teachers College, Columbia University.

Tolman, I. (1928). *Purposive behavior in animals and men.* New York: Century.

Trabasso, T.R., Rollins, H., & Schaughnessy, E. (1971). Storage and verification states in processing concepts. *Cognitive Psychology, 2,* 239–289.

VanLehn, K. (1982). *Bugs are not enough: Empirical studies of bugs, impasses, and repairs in procedural skills.* Palo Alto: Xerox PARC.

VanLehn, K. (1983). On the representation of procedures in repair theory. In H.P. Ginsburg (Ed.), *The development of mathematical thinking.* New York: Academic Press.

VanLehn, K., Brown, J.S., & Greeno, J.G. (1984). Competitive argumentation in computational theories of cognition. In W. Kintsch, J. Miller, & P. Polson (Eds.), *Methods and tactics in cognitive science.* Hillsdale, NJ: Erlbaum.

Vergnaud, G. (1982). A classification of cognitive tasks and operations of thought involved in addition and subtraction problems. In T.P. Carpenter, J.M. Moser, & T. Romberg (Eds.), *Addition and subtraction: A cognitive perspective.* Hillsdale, NJ: Erlbaum.

Voss, J.F., Greene, T.R., Post, T.A., & Penner, B.C. (1983). Problem solving skill in the social sciences. In G.H. Bower (Ed.), *The psychology of learning and motivation: Advances in research theory*: Vol. 17. (pp. 165–213). New York: Academic Press.

Weisberg, R. & Suls, J.M. (1973). An information-processing model of Duncker's candle problem. *Cognitive Psychology, 4,* 255–276.

Weisberg, R.W. & Alba, J.W. (1981). Gestalt theory, insight, and past experience: Reply to Dominowski. *Journal of Experimental Psychology: General, 110,* 193–203.

Weiss, S., Kulikowski, C., & Safir, A. (1977). A model-based consultation system for the long-term management of glaucoma. IJCAI5, 826–832.

Wertheimer, M. (1959). *Productive thinking* (enlarged ed.). New York: Harper. (Original version published in 1945.)

Wexler, K. & Cullicover, P.W. (1980). *Formal principles of language acquisition.* Cambridge, MA: MIT Press.

Wicken, T.D. & Millward, R.B. (1971). Attribute elimination strategies for concept identification with practiced subjects. *Journal of Mathematical Psychology, 8,* 453–480.

Wilkins, D. (1980). Using patterns and plans in chess. *Artificial Intelligence, 14,* 165–203.

Wilkins, M.C. (1928). The effect of changed material on ability to do formal syllogistic reasoning. *Archives of Psychology,* No. 102.

Williams, G. (1971). A model of memory in concept learning. *Cognitive Psychology, 2,* 158–184.

Winkleman, J.H. & Schmidt, J. (1974). Associative confusions in mental arithmetic. *Journal of Experimental Psychology, 102,* 734–736.

Winograd, T. (1972). Understanding natural language. *Cognitive Psychology, 3,* 1–191.

Woodworth, R.S. (1938). *Experimental psychology.* New York: Holt.

Woodworth, R.S. & Sells, S.B. (1935). An atmosphere effect in formal syllogistic reasoning. *Journal of Experimental Psychology, 18,* 451–460.

Young, R.M. & O'Shea, T. (1981). Errors in children's subtraction. *Cognitive Science, 6,* 153–178.

# Chapter 10

# DECISION MAKING

**Paul Slovic and Sarah Lichtenstein,** *Decision Research*

**Baruch Fischhoff,** *Carnegie-Mellon University*

## INTRODUCTION

Although decision making has been studied for centuries by philosophers, mathematicians, economists, and statisticians, it has a relatively short history in experimental psychology. The first extensive review of the theory of decision making was published in the *Psychological Bulletin* by Edwards (1954c). This paper introduced psychologists to the "exceedingly elaborate, mathematical and voluminous" (p. 380) economic literature on risky and riskless choice, utility, and game theory and reviewed the handful of relevant experimental studies then in existence.

Edwards' review was followed by a rapid proliferation of theories of choice and decision making, along with carefully controlled experi-

This research was supported by the Office of Naval Research under Contracts N014-80-C-0150 and N0014-82-C-0643 to Perceptronics, Inc.

Discussions with Ward Edwards, Ola Svenson, and Amos Tversky helped us greatly with organizing this chapter. Tversky, along with Duncan Luce, Don MacGregor, Maya Bar-Hillel, and Nils-Eric Sahlin, gave us very helpful comments on an early draft. Nancy Collins, Leisha Sanders, and Geri Hanson provided invaluable secretarial and technical assistance. We thank them all.

ments designed to test these theories. This work followed two parallel streams. One of these streams, the theory of riskless choice, had its origins in the notions of utility maximization put forth by Jeremy Bentham and James Mill. The first formal economic theories based on these notions assumed that decision makers are (1) completely informed about the possible courses of action and their consequences, (2) infinitely sensitive to differences in alternatives, and (3) rational in the sense that they can weakly order the possible courses of actions and make choices so as to maximize something—usually designated by the term *utility*. This stream of thought began to be interesting from the point of view of experimental psychology when theorists such as Thurstone (1927), Luce (1959), and Restle (1961) introduced modifications designed to capture the fact that decisions are characterized by inconsistency. Recognition of this fact has led to the development of stochastic theories of choice and a rich body of experiments designed to test those theories.

The second stream, the theory of risky choice, deals with decisions made in the face of uncertainty about the events that will determine the outcomes of one's actions. Maximization also

673

plays a key role in these theories, but the quantity to be maximized becomes, due to the uncertainty involved, *expected utility*. Tests of the theory that individuals behave so as to maximize expected utility have been the topic of hundreds of studies, most of which studied reactions to well-defined manipulations of simple gambles as the basic experimental paradigm.

During the period between 1955 and 1960, another development was taking place that was to have a profound influence on the study of decision making. This was the work of Simon (1956), who sharply criticized the notion of maximization as used in expected utility theory. Simon argued that actual decision-making behavior is better described in terms of *bounded rationality*. A boundedly rational decision maker attempts to attain some satisfactory, if not maximal, level of achievement—a goal that was labeled *satisficing*. Simon's conceptualization highlighted the role of perception, cognition, and learning in decision making and directed researchers to examine the psychological processes by which decision problems are represented and information is used in action selection.

In recent years, the information-processing view has dominated the empirical study of decision making. Both streams of research, on risky and riskless choice, have been merged in a torrent of studies aimed at understanding the mental operations associated with judgment and decision making. The result has been a far more complicated portrayal of decision making than that provided by the utility-maximization theory. It is now generally recognized that, although utility maximization can predict the outcomes of some decision-making processes, it provides only limited insight into how decisions are made. This descriptive limitation does not necessarily mean that utility maximization is not a valid principle for indicating how decisions should be made. Indeed, utility theory still forms the basis for the analysis of many applied decision problems. Increasingly, though, empirical evidence has prompted questioning of previously accepted tenets of rationality.

The theoretical status of the field of decision making is undergoing a period of reexamination and criticism. Nevertheless, a coherent body of empirical findings exists and is beginning to be applied toward the solution of important practical problems faced by individuals, organizations, and societies, in the world outside of the labora-tory. The path leading to this state of affairs is described in this chapter.

The chapter begins with a review of research describing the decision maker's subjective representation of the problem—the available alternatives, the possible outcomes of the decision, the environmental states that determine those outcomes, and the uncertainties surrounding those states and outcomes. Following this, we examine theories of the decision-making process, starting with models for deciding among simple, single-attribute alternatives and proceeding to models for handling more complex options. Some of these models are prescriptive, concerned with identifying courses of action that are logically consistent with the decision maker's expectations and values, whereas other models attempt to describe how people incorporate these expectations and values into their decisions. Some of these descriptive models closely resemble their normative counterparts. Others describe in detail the mental operations occurring during the decision-making process and thus look quite different. The chapter concludes with some speculations about a new view of preference emerging from empirical observations of decision making. This view poses a challenge to existing theories and to the decision–aiding technologies that have been derived from these theories.

## COMPREHENDING THE DECISION ENVIRONMENT

This section presents research describing people's comphehension of the world in which a decision is being made. It focuses on predecisional activities. Perhaps the most important of these activities is problem structuring, in which the decision maker specifies the possible actions, the states of the world relevant to the decision, and the outcomes contingent on both the chosen action and the states of the world that can occur. After structuring the problem, decision makers must consider the probabilities of the possible states of the world and the subjective values associated with the potential outcomes. To do this, they must infer the causes, effects, and overall predictability of probabilistic phenomena. These inferences are partly generated by deduction and partly induced from experience. These various aspects of the decision environment are considered below.

## Problem Structuring

A full description of a decision maker's intuitive problem structure would consist of all the options, consequences, and uncertainties considered in the course of reaching a decision. Although structuring is a key problem for decision makers, it has been less of a problem for decision researchers. In many experiments, subjects are presented with a predetermined problem, explicitly specifying all structural elements. This strategy allows researchers to focus on how people evaluate and integrate those components, at the expense of shedding light on how they identify them in less structured situations.

Gettys and his colleagues have undertaken an extensive research program on problem structuring. To look at hypothesis generation, Gettys, Manning, Mehle, and Fisher (1980) asked subjects to list all possible hypotheses about the cause of a problem, such as an automobile malfunction. The subjects then estimated the probability that the actual cause of the problem was included in the list of generated hypotheses. Other tasks asked for hypotheses about students' undergraduate majors, workers' occupations, animals, and geographical areas. In all of these studies, subjects consistently generated hypothesis sets that lacked important hypotheses. However, they also regarded these impoverished sets as far more complete than they actually were. These general conclusions held for experts as well as lay subjects. Gettys et al. (1980) suggested using reference lists to facilitate the structuring process.

Not only do subjects fail to generate important hypotheses, they fail to recognize such omissions in lists generated by others. Fischhoff, Slovic, and Lichtenstein (1978) asked people to evaluate the completeness of an experimenter-generated hierarchical list of hypotheses (i.e., fault tree) describing why a car might fail to start (see Figure 10.1). Some subjects were given pruned trees in which half the major components were omitted. Subjects were asked to assess the probability that each of the presented components, including one called "all other problems," would prove to be the cause of car-starting failure. For both naive subjects and experienced auto mechanics, what was out of sight was largely out of mind: the probability assigned to the "all other problems" branch was not much larger for severely pruned trees (e.g., those lacking "battery charge insufficient," "fuel system deffective," and "other engine problems") than for the full tree.

Action generation has been found to be as impoverished as hypothesis formation. Pitz, Sachs, and Heerboth's (1980) subjects generated, on average, less than one third of the actions the experimenters judged worth considering in the context of solving a personal problem (e.g., dealing with an obnoxious roommate). Gettys, Manning, and Casey (1981) also gave subjects realistic dilemmas (e.g., solving a university's parking problem) and asked them to respond with possible actions. Performance was evaluated by constructing a group decision tree, combining all the acts suggested by the subjects into a hierarchical structure (as in Figure 10.1). The major ideas (e.g., increase available space for parking) formed the limbs of the tree and the variations of these ideas (e.g., build parking structures) formed the branches and twigs (e.g., build underground structures). It was found that individual subjects failed to generate many limbs and branches of the group decision tree, all of which they could, in principle, have thought of.

Gettys, et al. (1981) also evaluated the quality of act-generation. A separate group of subjects estimated the utility of the acts generated by subjects in the act-generation experiment. These utility estimates were used to calculate the potential cost of failing to generate important limbs and branches. This analysis indicated that omissions were not only numerous, but also quite serious. In a follow-up study, Pliske, Gettys, Manning, and Casey (1982) found that monetary incentives for quantity and quality of action produced did not improve performance.

Inability to conceive of important courses of actions has been found to degrade decision making in important settings outside of the laboratory. For example, field studies have shown that residents of flood plains are typically unaware of the range of actions that could be taken to reduce the risk of flood damage or insure against it (Kunreuther et al. 1978; White, 1964).

## Uncertainty

Because many decisions involve uncertainty, a large literature exists on assessing and using probabilities (see, e.g., Kahneman, Slovic, & Tversky, 1982). Two views of probability under-

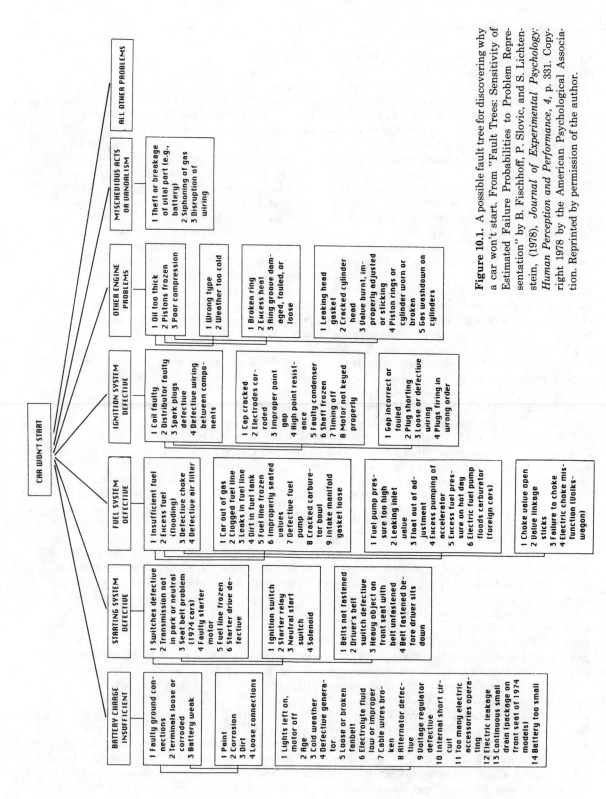

**Figure 10.1.** A possible fault tree for discovering why a car won't start. From "Fault Trees: Sensitivity of Estimated Failure Probabilities to Problem Representation," by B. Fischhoff, P. Slovic, and S. Lichtenstein, (1978), *Journal of Experimental Psychology: Human Perception and Performance, 4,* p. 331. Copyright 1978 by the American Psychological Association. Reprinted by permission of the author.

lie this work. In the first, probability is defined as the limit of relative frequency. In the second, all probabilities are subjective. They are degrees of belief that are coherent—that is, they obey the probability laws. This view has been championed by de Finetti (1937/1980a; 1980b) and Savage (1954), who incorporated it into utility theory. This subjectivist (also called personalistic or Bayesian) approach was introduced to psychologists by Edwards, Lindman, and Savage (1963).

Although the battle between frequentists and subjectivists has raged for years among mathematicians and statisticians (e.g., de Finetti, 1980b), its effect upon experimental psychology has been limited. Researchers have elicited probabilities for a variety of decision problems. Some of these allow an objective definition of probability whereas others deal with unique events for which only subjective probabilities are meaningful. Edwards and his associates used a core principle in the subjectivist theory, Bayes' Theorem, as the basis for an optimal model of information processing (Slovic & Lichtenstein, 1971). Outside of that research tradition, it is rarely clear which meaning of probability is held by an experimenter. In most cases, the distinction is immaterial. For example, if you know that an urn contains 4 red balls and 6 white balls, both camps would agree that there is a probability of .4 that a ball blindly drawn from the urn will be red. One hint regarding the experimenter's view of probability is sometimes found: subjectivists are more likely to refer to the subjects *assessing* a probability (implying an internal search), while frequentists refer to subjects *estimating* the probability (implying the existence of an external answer).

### Eliciting Probabilities

In everyday speech, people often use verbal phrases, such as likely or improbable, to express their degree of uncertainty. Attempts to discover the numerical equivalents of these labels have shown great variability across people (Lichtenstein & Newman, 1967). The problem that this causes for communication, even among experienced forecasters, points to the need to use numbers or to develop consensual verbal labels (Beyth-Marom, 1982a).

A variety of approaches to elicit numerical probabilities are possible. These include a simple probability scale between 0 and 1, an unlabeled rod with a moveable pointer, a logarithmically-spaced probability scale, verbally given odds, and a logarithmically-spaced odds scale (DuCharme & Donnell, 1973). There are also indirect methods such as response time (Geller & Pitz, 1968), choices among bets (Jensen & Peterson, 1973), or strength of a handgrip squeeze (Shapira, 1975). A moderate level of agreement has typically been found in studies comparing these direct and indirect methods (Wallsten & Budescu, 1983).

One theoretically based way to infer probabilities from bets is by means of *proper scoring rules*. These are functions that evaluate assessed probabilities according to both the degree of confidence and the outcome of the event being assessed. A scoring rule is proper if the only strategy for maximizing one's expected score is to state one's true belief (Shuford, Albert, & Massengill, 1966). Proper scoring rules can be used to construct a list of payoffs for two-outcome bets. Each pair of payoffs is the pair of scores corresponding to a particular probability. The list is presented to subjects who are asked, for each event of interest, to pick the pair of scores they most prefer as outcomes for a bet, with the payoffs to be determined by the occurrence or nonoccurrence of the event. If the assumption is made that subjects choose in such a way as to maximize their expected earnings, then their subjective probabilities for events can be inferred from their choices (Jensen & Peterson, 1973).

An elicitation technique frequently used by decision analysts is a probability wheel (Spetzler & Staël von Holstein, 1975). This small device is a disc with two sectors of different colors, such that the relative proportion of the colors is easily changed. To assess the probability of an event, E, the wheel is adjusted until the assessor is indifferent between two (imaginary) bets, for example:

Win $100 if *E* occurs; otherwise win nothing.

Win $100 if a spinner, spun on the wheel, lands in the red sector; otherwise win nothing.

The probability inferred from this operation is equal to the proportion of red in the circle. This technique and others that similarly emphasize the relationship between probabilities and bets are the methods preferred by subjectivists. Their practical advantage has yet to be demonstrated.

The simplest method is to ask subjects to produce numerical probabilities after minimal instruction in the meaning of probability (e.g., "a response of .6 means that there's a 60 percent chance . . . a response of 1.0 means you're completely sure . . .") or no instruction at all ("what's the probability that . . ."). Surprisingly, the amount of instruction appears to make little difference (Lichtenstein & Fischhoff, 1980).

Variants on these methods are available for expressing uncertainty about the value of an uncertain quantity (e.g., next year's interest rates, tomorrow's temperature). Ideally, subjects would draw subjective probability density or cumulative density functions. A less demanding approach, called the *fractile* method, has the experimenter specify several probabilities (e.g., .05, .25, .50, .75, and .95). For each probability, the subject then names a value of the uncertain quantity, such that the specified probability is the probability that the true value of the uncertain quantity is less than the subject's named value. Thus, for example, to elicit the .25 fractile for the population of the United States, the instructions might say "Write a population value such that there's a 25 percent chance that the true population is smaller than the one you write."

In the *fixed interval* method, the experimenter specifies several ranges of the uncertain quantity and asks the subject to assign a probability to each range. This method cannot easily be compared with the fractile method because the experimenter's choice of segments may provide information to the subject. For example, the following two partitions give quite different hints regarding the population of the United States:

__ less than 100 million
__ 100 to 200 million
__ 200 to 300 million
__ 300 to 400 million
__ more than 400 million

__ less than 1 million
__ 1 to 10 million
__ 10 to 100 million
__ 100 million to 1 billion
__ more than 1 billion

## Evaluating Probabilities

A large number of experimental studies have examined how and how well people assess proba-

bilities for tasks involving single and multiple events, uncertain quantities, and compound and conditional probabilities.

### FREQUENCY-BASED PROBABILITIES

Several studies (e.g., Robinson, 1964; Shuford, 1961) have found that people are quite good at estimating the relative proportions of binary events, displayed either sequentially (e.g., sequences of two rapidly flashing lights) or simultaneously (e.g., brief presentations of 400-element matrices of horizontal and vertical lines). To the extent that a probability is viewed as the limit of a relative frequency, these results suggest that within a reasonable range, say, .05 to .95, people are adept at assessing probabilities when the events are unambiguously presented in a short span of time. Estes (1976) and Whitlow and Estes (1979) have proposed a limited-capacity, multiple-trace model of memory to account for such findings.

When the relative frequencies are not presented directly, people must search their memories for instances. For such cases, Tversky and Kahneman (1973) have proposed that frequency and probability assessments are based on the ease by which instances come to mind. They called this process the *availability heuristic*. In addition to being easy to apply, this heuristic is usually valid, because frequent events typically come more easily to mind. However, because availability is also affected by subtle factors unrelated to likelihood, such as familiarity, recency, and emotional salience, reliance on it may result in biased assessments. For example, Lichtenstein, Slovic, Fischhoff, Layman, and Combs (1978) found that the frequencies of dramatic, well-publicized causes of death such as accidents, natural disasters, fires, and homicides were overestimated and the frequencies of less-dramatic causes of death such as stroke, diabetes, emphysema, and asthma were underestimated.

### PROBABILITY AS CONFIDENCE

Some events seem unique, or so nearly unique that it is difficult to conceptualize them as arising from a set of events with relative frequencies. For example, what is the probability that in 1997 the President of the United States will be a Republican? Probabilities for such events can be interpreted as degrees of belief or degrees of confidence. For such probabilities, there is no right answer; different people can

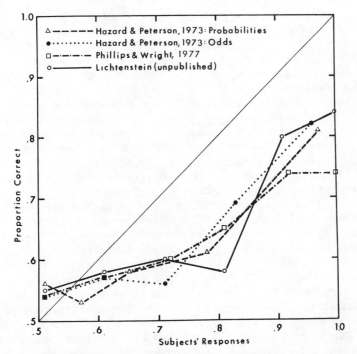

**Figure 10.2.** Calibration curves showing overconfidence. From "Calibration of Probabilities: The State of the Art" by S. Lichtenstein, B. Fischoff, and L. Phillips in *Decision Making and Change in Human Affairs* (p. 292), H. Jungermann and G. de Zeeuw (Eds.), 1977. Copyright 1977 by D. Reidel Publishing Company, Dordrecht, Holland. Reprinted by permission.

justifiably hold different degrees of confidence in the same proposition. However, a kind of validity, called *calibration*, can be examined in a large collection of probability assessments. A set of probability assessments is said to be well calibrated if, in the long run, for all the events to which a probability of .XX was assigned, XX percent of the events occur.

A large literature exists on calibration (for a review, see Lichtenstein, Fischhoff, & Phillips, 1982). In a typical calibration experiment, subjects are given two-alternative general-knowledge questions (e.g., Which is longer, the Suez Canal or the Panama Canal? Are cabbage butterflies white or yellow?). For each question, they first select the alternative they believe to be the correct answer and then assess the probability that their chosen answer is, in fact, correct. These data are analyzed by computing the proportion correct for each probability value (or range of probabilities, such as .60 to .69). The most common finding is that people's confidence in their knowledge is somewhat related to the accuracy of that knowledge. As confidence

increases so does accuracy. However, the relationship is imperfect, with increases in confidence being accompanied by smaller increases in proportion of correct responses. In the typical study, this insensitivity leads to overconfidence. For all but guesses ($p = .5$), the proportions correct are notably smaller than the assessed probabilities (see Figure 10.2). This overconfidence is related to the difficulty of the items; it decreases as the difficulty of the items decreases until, for very easy items, underconfidence occurs.

The certainty response, $p = 1.0$, is particularly misused by subjects. Even when they are instructed that 1.0 means "you are absolutely sure . . .," 10 to 30 percent of the answers to which certainty is attached are incorrect. Concerned that this result reflected only an insensitivity of the response scale—subjects who use only one-digit probabilities may use the response of 1.0 to mean more than .95—Fischhoff, Slovic, and Lichtenstein (1977) studied the calibration of subjects who responded with odds (e.g., 9 : 1, 10,000 : 1) rather than probabilities. This change did not eliminate the overconfidence observed with extreme responses. Subjects often used high odds (about one quarter of all responses were odds of 1000:1 or greater), that were too often wrong. For example, when using odds of 100:1, subjects were right only 80 percent of the time; for odds of 10,000:1, they were 89 percent correct.

Overconfidence in probability assessments has been remarkably robust in the face of other manipulations as well (Fischhoff, 1982a; Lichtenstein et al., 1982). It has been found with both men and women and with people more or less expert in the content of the items (when task difficulty is controlled). Variations in instructions, response mode, and item content seem to make little difference. Efforts to eliminate overconfidence with monetary incentives, through training, or by requiring subjects to list reasons why they might be wrong have led to no improvement, improvement with limited generalization, and modest improvement, respectively.

The major exception to overconfidence is the performance of weather forecasters making probabilistic forecasts of precipitation (Murphy & Winkler, 1977). As a group, they are magnificently well calibrated. This superiority might be attributed to their years of experience in giving probabilistic forecasts, the homogeneous content area, and the unambiguous and rapid outcome feedback they receive.

Although calibration appears to be a universally desirable quality for probability assessments, that is not true when the set of items are not independent and the assessor receives no outcome feedback (Kadane & Lichtenstein, 1982). As an extreme (and artificial) example, suppose there are two urns, one containing 80 percent red balls, the other 20 percent red balls. One urn is chosen at random and one ball at a time is sampled from it (with replacement). You are not told which urn was chosen, nor the color of any of the sampled balls, yet you are asked, for each ball sampled, to assess the probability that the ball is red. Many people would find it appropriate to assess $p = .5$ for every ball, even though this string of .5 assessments will surely not be well calibrated, since, in the long run, the proportion of red balls will be either .8 or .2.

Why are people overconfident when assessing the extent of their own knowledge? Three possible explanations link this phenomenon to findings or theories in the domain of cognitive psychology:

(1) Fischhoff et al. (1977) noted the tendency for people to believe that their memories are faithful (if faded) copies of their experiences, whereas evidence suggests that memory is a reconstructive process in which errors are sometimes incorporated as facts. (2) Pitz (1974) suggested that in a series of inferences the uncertainty in the earlier stages may not be carried over into the later stages. (3) Koriat, Lichtenstein, and Fischhoff (1980) emphasized the degree to which people search their memory only for confirming, not disconfirming, evidence concerning an initially favored answer.

Having arrived at a degree of confidence, how is that feeling translated into a numerical response? Ferrell and McGoey (1980) proposed a signal detection model (Luce & Krumhansl, Chapter 1, Vol. I) for this process. They assumed that, in the absence of feedback about the difficulty of the items, people will not change the set of cutoff values that determine the translation of certainty feelings into probabilities. This model predicts overconfidence with hard items and underconfidence with easy items.

Calibration may also be studied in the assessment of probability density functions for uncertain quantities. Here, calibration refers to the correspondence between the fractiles of the distribution and the proportions of true values falling below or between the fractiles. For example, good calibration implies that, in the long run, just 25 percent of the true values should fall below the .25 fractile, whereas 98 percent should fall between the .01 and .99 fractiles. Many experiments (reviewed by Lichtenstein et al., 1982) show that here, too, assessors are overconfident, in that they tend to report overly tight distributions. In a typical study, 30 to 40 percent of the true values of general-knowledge uncertain quantities (e.g., how many foreign cars were imported into the U.S. last year?) fall outside the .01 to .99 interval of the assessed distribution, rather than the appropriate 2 percent.

The three explanations offered for overconfidence apply here as well, as does an explanation based on the *anchoring and adjustment* heuristic (Slovic, 1972). Having decided there were, say, one million foreign cars imported, you may take that initial estimate as an anchor and adjust it up and down to arrive at the higher and lower fractiles. These adjustments are likely to be insufficient, failing to account for the many ways the initial estimate could be in error.

## Hindsight Bias

Another form of overconfidence emerges in experimental studies of retrospective judgment. Studies by Fischhoff (1975, 1982b) have shown that reporting the outcome of an event increases the perceived likelihood of that outcome. Moreover, it does so in such a way that people underestimate the effect of outcome knowledge on their beliefs. As a result, people believe that they would have seen in foresight the relative inevitability of the reported outcome which, in fact, was only apparent in hindsight. Thus, they exaggerate the predictability of reported outcomes. Slovic and Fischhoff (1977) showed similar effects in evaluations of scientific research; once people hear the results of an experiment, they tend to believe that they knew all along what the findings would be. Apparently, outcome information is assimilated with whatever else is known about the event in question in a way that makes it impossible to retrieve the perspective once held in foresight. Hindsight bias seems to be as hard to reduce as other forms of overconfidence (Fischhoff, 1982a). Education or warnings have little effect. However, forcing people to think about how they could have explained the event that did *not* happen reduces the bias somewhat.

## Judging Probability by Representativeness

When an uncertain event or sample is generated from a parent population by some process (such as randomly drawing a sample from a population), studies have shown that people judge its probability "by the degree to which it: (i) is similar in essential properties to its parent population; and (ii) reflects the salient features of the process by which it is generated" (Kahneman & Tversky, 1972a, p. 431). Kahneman and Tversky have labeled this strategy for assessing probabilities the *representativeness* heuristic.

People using the representativeness heuristic can be led astray either by attending to characteristics that are normatively irrelevant or by disregarding characteristics that are normatively important. As an example of the first type of error, people judging possible outcomes of tosses of a fair coin consider HTTHTH to be more likely than the outcome HHHTTT, because the lack of apparent order in the former seems more representative of a random process. They also find HTTHTH to be more likely than HHHHTH, because the latter does not represent the fair-

ness of the coin (Kahneman & Tversky, 1972a). The second type of error is exemplified by people's disregard of sample size, a characteristic of a sample that has no parallel in the population. Thus, people consider that a large hospital (in which about 45 babies are born each day) will be as likely as a small hospital (in which about 15 babies are born each day) to experience a day on which more than 60 percent of the babies born are male.

### Combining Probabilities

## Conservatism

In the 1960s a much-researched topic was the question of how well people use the information from data to update the probability that a hypothesis is true. This research (reviewed by Slovic & Lichtenstein, 1971) was based on a strong normative model, Bayes' theorem. Given several mutually exclusive and exhaustive hypotheses, $H_i$, and a datum, $D$, Bayes' theorem states that

$$P(H_i|D) = \frac{P(D|H_i)\,P(H_i)}{\Sigma_i P(D|H_i)\,P(H_i)}$$

$P(H_i|D)$ is the posterior probability that $H_i$ is true, taking into account the new datum, $D$, as well as all previous data. $P(D|H_i)$ is the conditional probability that the datum $D$ would be observed if hypothesis $H_i$ were true. For a set of mutually exclusive and exhaustive hypotheses, $H_i$, the values of $P(D|H_i)$ represent the impact of the datum $D$ on each of the hypotheses. The value $P(H_i)$ is the prior probability of hypothesis $H_i$. It, too, is a conditional probability, representing the probability of $H_i$ conditional on all information available prior to the receipt of $D$. The denominator serves as a normalizing constant.

The following hypothetical experiment, similar to one actually performed by Phillips and Edwards (1966), illustrates the Bayesian paradigm. Subjects see two bookbags, one containing 70 red poker chips and 30 blue poker chips, the other containing 30 red chips and 70 blue chips. The experimenter flips a coin to choose one of the bags and then begins to draw chips from the chosen bag, with replacement. After each chip is drawn, the subject assesses the probability that the predominantly red bag is the one being sampled. The optimal responses are computed from Bayes' theorem and are compared with the subjects' responses. The most frequently documented result is that subjects' assessments are conservative, in the sense that the optimal posterior probability of the most likely hypothesis is far larger than subjects' assessment. In the example just described, a sample of eight red chips and four blue chips produces, from Bayes' theorem, a posterior probability of .97. Most subjects give an assessment between .7 and .8 (Edwards, 1968).

Early explanations attributed conservatism to subjects' (1) misunderstanding of the data-generating process and, thus, of the diagnostic impact of the data, $P(D|H_i)$; (2) inability to aggregate the information received; and (3) unwillingness to use up the bounded probability response scale, knowing that more data were forthcoming. Each of these explanations received some empirical support.

Later explanations have rejected the view that the normative model provides a good first approximation to a descriptive model, arguing that subjects rely on simple rules arrived at through "groping attempts to ease cognitive strain and to pull a number out of the air" (Slovic & Lichtenstein, 1971, p. 714). For example, when the data are presented sequentially, one simple strategy is to revise the estimate by a constant amount, upwards for confirming data or downwards for disconfirming. When simultaneous (aggregate) samples are presented, subjects appear to employ the representativeness heuristic, judging the similarity between the sample and the two possible populations (Kahneman & Tversky, 1972). The most notable feature of the populations is the ratio of red to blue chips in each; the representativeness heuristic, therefore, puts heavy emphasis on the ratio of red to blue chips in the sample. However, in such cases it is the difference, rather than the ratio, between the frequencies of the two colors in the sample which determines the posterior probability.

A variant of the bookbag and poker chip task presents inconclusive evidence drawn from uncertain sources. For example, Gettys, Kelly, and Peterson (1973) sampled a single chip (one of four possible colors) from a small container (one of four kinds of containers) that itself had been drawn from one of two bookbags. They then asked subjects to assess the probability that the chip was drawn from each bookbag, given the color of the sampled chip. Fifteen of

25 subjects followed a best-guess strategy that ignores the probabilities of all but the most likely hypothesis. Such simplification is a typical response to multistage inference tasks, and one that supports Pitz's (1974) attribution of overconfidence to the failure to carry forward uncertainty from earlier stages. Schum (1980) gave a detailed discussion of the logical structure of more complex inference tasks.

## THE BASE-RATE FALLACY

Bayes' theorem combines base-rate information (prior probabilities) with indicator information (conditional probabilities). Meehl and Rosen (1955) noted that clinical psychologists often disregard base-rate information when making predictions of rare events (like suicide), but only recently has the problem received experimental attention.

Kahneman and Tversky (1973) had subjects assess the likelihood that an individual described in a brief personality description was an engineer or a lawyer. The individual was allegedly sampled at random from a group consisting of 70 enineers and 30 lawyers, or from a group consisting of 30 engineers and 70 lawyers. The odds that any particular description belongs to an engineer rather than to a lawyer should be higher in the first condition, where there is a majority of engineers, than in the second condition, where there is a majority of lawyers. In violation of Bayes' theorem, subjects in the two conditions produced essentially the same probability judgments.

Kahneman and Tversky attributed this neglect of base-rate information to a reliance on representativeness, expressed as the similarity of the descriptions to one's mental image of an engineer or a lawyer. Their subjects did use prior probabilities correctly, however, when they had no other information. In the absence of a personality sketch, they judged the probability that an unknown individual is an engineer to be .7 and .3, respectively, in the two base-rate conditions. This pattern of reliance on representativeness whenever possible has been verified in subsequent studies (reviewed by Bar-Hillel & Fischhoff, 1981).

Neglect of base-rate information has also emerged in studies of the cab problem by Kahneman and Tversky (1972b) and others:

Two cab companies operate in a given city, the Blue and the Green (according to the color of cab they run). Eighty-five percent of the cabs in the city are Blue, and the remaining 15 percent are Green.

A cab was involved in a hit-and-run accident at night.

A witness later identified the cab as a Green cab.

The court tested the witness' ability to distinguish between Blue and Green cabs under nighttime visibility conditions. It found that the witness was able to identifv each color correctly about 80 percent of the time, but confused it with the other color about 20 percent of the time. What do you think are the chances that the errant cab was indeed Green, as the witness claimed?

Using Bayes' theorem, one finds that effect of the prior probabilities (.85, .15) slightly outweighs the effect of the conditional probabilities (.8, .2); the normatively correct answer is:

$$P(\text{Green}|\text{Data}) = \frac{.8(.15)}{.8(.15) + .2(.85)} = .41$$

However, in several studies (e.g., Bar-Hillel, 1980), the median and modal answer to the cab problem was 80 percent, showing a disregard of the base rates.

Bar-Hillel (1980) offered the most encompassing explanation of the base-rate fallacy, proposing that ". . . subjects ignore base rate information, when they do, because they feel that it *should* be ignored—put plainly, because the base rates seem to them *irrelevant* to the judgment that they are making" (p. 216). According to Bar-Hillel, apparent relevance can be produced not only by saliency, as in the engineer/lawyer problem above, but also by casual links among the data. For example, the cab problem can be modified to create a causal link with the base rate by replacing the sentence "Eighty-five percent of the cabs in the city are Blue, and the remaining 15 percent are Green" with the sentence "Although the two companies are roughly equal in size, 85 percent of cab accidents involve Green cabs and 15 percent involve Blue cabs" (Tversky & Kahneman, 1982). The problem now suggests that Green drivers are more reckless or incompetent than Blue drivers. Although answers to this version were still highly variable, the median response was 60 percent, indicating that the base rate was less often ignored.

## CONJUNCTION PROBLEMS

One of the simplest and most basic laws of probability is the conjunction rule: the probability of a conjunction, $P(A \cap B)$, cannot exceed the probabilities of its constituents, $P(A)$ and $P(B)$. Tversky and Kahneman (1983) have shown that people's intuitive judgments of probability violate the conjunction rule when the conjunction is more representative of the underlying process than is one of the two constituent events. For example, most subjects violated the conjuncton rule in the following problem.

Linda is 31 years old, single, outspoken, and very bright. She majored in philosophy. As a student, she was deeply concerned with issues of discrimination and social justice, and also participated in anti-nuclear demonstrations.

Which of the following statements is more likely?

Linda is a bank teller.

Linda is a bank teller and is active in the feminist movement.

The first of these answers seems to fit the description of Linda so poorly that is was deemed less likely than the conjunction in the second answer, which added a detail fitting her description. Tversky and Kahneman argued that it is hard to advance any normative theory of inference that would view such behavior as acceptable. Earlier studies (e.g., Bar-Hillel, 1973; Beyth-Marom, 1981) have shown, either using direct estimates or choices among bets, that the probabilities of conjunctions (i.e., the probability that all of several uncertain events will occur) are overestimated and the probabilities of disjunctions (at least one event will occur) are underestimated. These violations, too, were traced to reliance on the representativeness heuristic.

### Debiasing

A number of studies have attempted to eliminate judgmental biases in probability assessment. There are two possible goals for such studies: (1) to find practical ways to improve performance and (2) to test the robustness of the bias and thereby reveal something about the processes that produced it. These debiasing manipulations can be categorized according to whether they attribute the source of the bias to the task (for failing to elicit the subjects' extant knowledge), to the subjects (for lacking the requisite skills),

**Table 10.1. Debiasing methods**

| Assumption | Strategies |
| --- | --- |
| *Faulty tasks*<br>Unfair tasks | Raise stakes<br>Clarify instructions/stimuli<br>Discourage second-guessing<br>Use better response modes<br>Ask fewer questions |
| Misunderstood tasks | Demonstrate alternative goal<br>Demonstrate semantic disagreement<br>Demonstrate impossibility of task<br>Demonstrate overlooked distinction |
| *Faulty judges*<br>Perfectible individuals | Warn of problem<br>Describe problem<br>Provide personalized feedback<br>Train extensively |
| Incorrigible individuals | Replace them<br>Recalibrate their responses<br>Plan on error |
| *Mismatch between judges and task*<br>Restructuring | Make knowledge explicit<br>Search for discrepant information<br>Decompose problem<br>Consider alternative situations<br>Offer alternative formulations |
| Education | Rely on substantive experts<br>Educate from childhood |

*Note.* From "Debiasing" in *Judgment under Uncertainty: Heuristics and Biases* (p. 424) by D. Kahneman, P. Slovic, and A. Tversky, 1982. New York: Cambridge University Press. Copyright 1982 by Cambridge University Press. Reprinted by permission.

or to a mismatch between subject and task (meaning that the subject cannot manage the task as presented, but could do better with a restructured version). These categories can be subdivided further into the set of debiasing categories described in Table 10.1.

The list in Table 10.1 provides a way to generate experiments as well as a way to categorize debiasing studies that have already been conducted. A review of all published studies attempting to eliminate two biases (overconfidence and hindsight) revealed some consistent patterns (Fischhoff, 1982a). Manipulations that treat the bias as an experimental artifact have had little effect. Thus, for example, it does not help to raise the stakes, exhort subjects to work harder, or rework the instructions (providing they were already clear and fair). Nor is there any consistent improvement when the stimuli come from people's areas of expertise. Thus, although substantive expertise gives people

many answers and tools with which to seek answers, it is not clear that it improves their judgment. On this important question, further research is needed.

It is, however, possible to improve performance somewhat through training that includes personalized feedback. Merely warning subjects about the problems that others experienced makes no difference (unless it is so directive as to tell subjects what to do). There has been some success with manipulations based on theories of the cognitive processes leading to the biases. For example, the belief that subjects are overconfident because they naturally tend to think of reasons justifying their answers led to a manipulation that required them to list reasons why they might be wrong (Koriat et al., 1980). Similarly, Lopes (1987) reported success in debiasing judgments in a Bayesian inference task by analyzing the procedures used by untutored subjects, warning subjects about the procedures they use that are inappropriate, and providing information about appropriate procedures.

In debiasing research, an important distinction is between producing better judgments and producing better judges. One could produce better probability judgments on a calibration task with items of moderate difficulty by telling subjects to lower their responses. Unfortunately, that same advice might increase the underconfidence found with tasks having easy items. By contrast, training or looking for contradictory reasons offers some hope of improving the judgment process and being broadly useful.

## Relatedness

### Correlations

A key intellectual skill and the basis for a causal understanding of the world is the ability to assess the interrelatedness of two variables. Jennings, Amabile, and Ross (1982) distinguished between two versions of this skill. *Data-based* assessment concerns the ability to detect covariation in novel data, about which one has no expectations. *Theory-based* assessment concerns covariation estimates that are derived from one's a priori expectations or theories, rather than from any immediately available data.

DATA-BASED ASSESSMENT
In order to avoid the influence of prior expectations, studies of relatedness have typically presented subjects with data concerning two hypothetical dichotomous variables, such as could be represented in a four-fold table. The correct interpretation of correlation involves all four cells. When the cells are labeled $a$, $b$, $c$, $d$ in the conventional way, the correlation is the difference between two conditional probabilities:

$$\frac{a}{a + c} - \frac{b}{b + d}$$

Oft-cited studies have indicated that subjects base their judgments of relatedness on only one cell (the "yes/yes" cell; Jenkins & Ward, 1965; Smedslund, 1963) or on two cells (the "yes/yes" and "no/no" cells; Ward & Jenkins, 1965). Beyth-Marom (1982b) noted that the instructions to the subjects in the earlier studies may have accounted for these results. For example, Smedslund's instructions included the statement, "You are to concentrate entirely on symptom A and diagnosis F," which could be interpreted as telling the

subjects to focus on only one cell, which most did. Instructions given by Ward and Jenkins included the sentence "Complete control means that whenever you seed, it rains, and whenever you don't seed, it doesn't rain," thus focusing on the $a$ and $d$ cells.

Shaklee and Tucker (1980) devised a series of four-fold tables and used more neutral instructions that enabled them to infer the rule subjects were using. Subjects' accuracy in judging whether the variables were correlated was improved by instruction in the concept of covariation and by use of a response format that highlighted the conditional probabilities of events. Beyth-Marom (1982b) presented subjects with a list of explicit rules and asked subjects to choose the one that best fit their interpretation of a statement such as, "A paper published in a major biological journal reported that for one species of widely distributed animals a strong relationship was found between the animal's skin color and the mean temperature in its territory." Beyth-Marom's study, like that of Shaklee and Tucker, found that subjects exhibited or chose rules involving all four cells, either the correct rule or a rule contrasting the sums of the two diagonals. Beyth-Marom further showed that the simpler incorrect rules were chosen more often with asymmetric variables, for which the name of one pole of the variable is the name of the variable (e.g., a disease is present or absent), than with symmetric variables (e.g., skin color is dark or light).

*Multiple-cue probability learning* (MCPL) studies have examined people's understanding of interconnectedness in tasks that involve continuous or many-valued variables in an environment that provides an opportunity for learning. In the typical study, subjects predict a numerical criterion on the basis of sets of numerical cues. The cues are related to the criterion probabilistically by adding an error term to the functional relationship between the cues and the criterion. Blocks of training trials, during which the criterion number is shown to the subject after each prediction, are alternated with test blocks, during which the subject makes predictions without receiving feedback. Results of MCPL studies show that: (1) subjects can learn to use linear cues appropriately; (2) learning of nonlinear functions is slow, especially when subjects are not forewarned that relations may be nonlinear; (3) subjects are inconsistent, particularly when task predictability is low; and (4) subjects fail to take proper account of cue intercorrelations. For a review of MCPL studies, see Brehmer (1979).

### THEORY-BASED ASSESSMENT

The distinction between data-based and theory-based assessment is not always a firm one. Brehmer (1980a) showed that subjects in MCPL tasks are guided by specific hypotheses about the functional rule relating cues and criterion. These hypotheses appear to be sampled from a set based on previous experience and dominated by the positive linear rule. Testing of these rules shows inadequate appreciation of the probabilistic nature of the task. Subjects keep searching for deterministic rules that will account for the randomness in the task. Because there are none, they change rules frequently (i.e., become inconsistent) and eventually resample rules they had previously disgarded.

The MCPL studies typically use artificial tasks, for which people have no firm expectations regarding the kinds of results that might be found. Chapman and Chapman (1967) hypothesized that when people have strong expectations they tend to find confirmation of their beliefs in settings that show quite the opposite. To demonstrate this, they created a set of 45 drawings from the Draw-A-Person test, a common diagnostic tool in clinical psychology. Each drawing was labeled with two symptom statements (e.g., "He is suspicious of other people") in such a way that each symptom statement appeared once with each drawing, producing zero correlation between any drawing characteristic and any symptom. The statements were collected from practicing clinicians regarding characteristics of drawings that they believed to be associated with the symptoms (e.g., "eyes atypical"). When the subjects (students in an introductory psychology class) listed characteristics that were associated with each symptom, they reported the same symptom-characteristic correlations as had the clinical psychologists. For example, the majority of both clinicians and naive subjects reported atypical eyes being associated with suspiciousness. This phenomenon, which the Chapmans labeled "illusory correlation," persisted even when the subjects were given more study time, were rewarded for accuracy, or were shown negative correlations between symptoms and diagnoses.

The shaping effect of preconceptions on the processing of subsequent data has been shown in a variety of other settings (Nisbett & Ross, 1980). It stands in sharp contrast to the neglect of base rates discussed earlier. The key difference between those two settings seems to be whether subjects create those prior beliefs themselves or receive them in the experiments.

Once people believe in the existence of a relationship, they may use it in prediction tasks. When the relationship is between continuous variables, statistical theory requires that the prediction be regressed to the mean to the extent that the relationship is not perfect. In practice, though, such regression is often absent. Subjects predicting variable $Y$ from variable $X$ tend to make their prediction of $Y$ as extreme as that of $X$. For example, Kahneman and Tversky (1973) found that two groups of subjects gave virtually identical predictions of 10 students' GPAs (grade point averages), although one group was given each student's percentile score on GPA (which is perfectly correlated with GPA), while the other group was given percentile scores of a test of mental concentration that was described as quite unreliable (". . . when tested repeatedly, the same person could obtain quite different scores, depending on the amount of sleep he had the night before or how well he felt that day"). A third group, given percentile scores for a test of sense of humor, showed only a slight regression in the prediction of GPA. Tversky and Kahneman (1974) linked nonregressive prediction to the representativeness heuristic, which leads people to predict outcomes that are maximally representative of (similar to) the input.

Failure to appreciate the workings of regression effects is not limited to naive subjects working on unfamiliar tasks in psychological experiments. Several articles have taken statistically trained researchers to task for failing to recognize possible regression artifacts in their data (e.g., Campbell & Boruch, 1975; Furby, 1973).

### The Lens Model

The philosophy of *probabilistic functionalism* put forth by Brunswik (1952, 1956) has played an important role in conceptualizing how people attempt to understand and cope with uncertainty in the decision environment. Brunswik's main interest was the adaptive interrelationship between the person (judge or decision maker) and the decision situation. He developed the

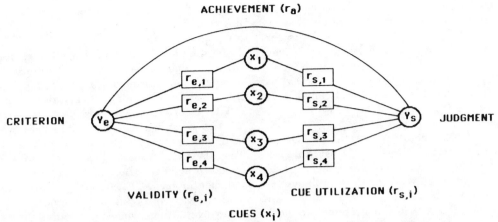

**Figure 10.3.** The lens model. From "Social Judgement Theory: Applications in Policy Formation" by K.R. Hammond, J. Rohrbaugh, J. Mumpower, and L. Adelman in *Human Judgment and Decision Processes in Applied Settings* (p. 3), M.F. Kaplan and S. Schwartz (Eds.), 1977. New York: Academic Press. Copyright 1977 by Academic Press. Reprinted by permission.

*lens model* to study simultaneously the uncertain, interdependent structure of the world and the judgments that people make about that structure.

The lens model, shown in Figure 10.3, gets its name from the symmetry between the environmental system and the organismic system. In the center are the cues: the proximal variables available as information for the judge. The cues are related to the criterion variable in the environmental half of the lens and to judgments in the other half of the lens.

The first step in applying the lens model is to develop sets of stimuli that match, in their structure, the structure of the environment. For example, in such a *representative design*, cues that are interrelated in the world are similarly correlated across the stimulus set. These stimuli are presented to subjects whose task is to make wholistic judgments (estimates) of the criterion value for each stimulus profile of cue values. These judgments are then analyzed in terms of a model; the linear additive model is most commonly used. The analysis produces statistical measures of the key concepts: *achievement* ($r_a$, the correlation between the judgments and criterion values), *ecological validity* ($r_{e,i}$, the correlation between the cue values and the criterion), and *cue utilization* ($r_{s,i}$, the correlation between the cue values and the judgments). Further measures based on mulitple regression analysis have been developed by Hursch,

Hammond, and Hursch (1964), Tucker (1964), and Dudycha and Naylor (1966).

The relationships studied within the lens model can be either data-based (as with the MCPL studies described above) or theory-based. Numerous studies have shown that the lens model in its simplest, additive linear form is remarkably sucessful in fitting such diverse judgments as psychiatric and medical diagnoses, judicial decisions in workers' compensation and civil liberties cases, and roll-call votes of U.S. Senators, as well as judgmental evaluations of job performance, graduate-school applicants, suicide risk, financial status, stock prices, theatrical plays, and trout streams (Slovic et al., 1977; Slovic & Lichtenstein, 1971). The variety of ways in which the model can be used to understand and improve judgments has been summarized by Hammond, Stewart, Brehmer, and Steinmann (1975).

### Randomness

An understanding of probabilistic relationships requires understanding of randomness. When people judge the randomness in a sequence of dichotomous events or attempt to create random sequences, they demonstrate a consistent bias in believing that random sequences have more alternations than they actually do have (Evans & Pollard, 1982; Wagenaar, 1972).

A related expression of these same intuitions is the gambler's fallacy: the belief that following a period in which one possible outcome of a random sequence occurs less often than its expected frequency, its future occurrence is more likely. Also known as the "negative recency effect" (Jarvik, 1951), this belief has been frequently reported: "Of course, after the red has come up ten times in a row, hardly anyone will persist in betting on it" (Dostoevsky, 1866/1964, p. 146).

Lopes (1982a) pointed out some problems in the design and interpretation of psychological studies of subjective randomness. She criticized the relatively narrow conception of randomness that underlies these experimental studies, and contrasted this with the conceptions found in pholosophical and mathematical treatments.

## The Place of Bias in Judgment

### Defining Optimality
Optimality must be well defined in order to claim that responses are biased, with a normative theory of how probabilistic judgments should be made and a substantive theory specifying how a particular problem is interpreted in terms of the normative theory. In many studies the rules of Bayesian inference have been used to define optimality. However, the normative status of Bayesian inference is not unquestioned. Some philosophers (e.g., Cohen, 1981) have offered alternative formulations and even those who accept the Bayesian framework (e.g., Diaconis & Zabel, 1982) acknowledge certain limitations. An emerging compromise position (Shafer & Tversky, 1985) is that a normative theory should not be treated as an absolute standard, valid in all situations. Rather, there are alternative theories, each suited for particular situations, with the choice between them determined on grounds of practicality.

More serious questions have been raised about whether specific instances of observed behavior can be properly described as suboptimal, under the assumption that the decision maker is attempting to follow an optimal model. To make an unambiguous interpretation of an act, one needs to know how the decision maker construed the model for that situation. Inferences that appear to be biased may prove to be legitimate given a better understanding of how the decision maker's hypotheses were formulated or of what actions hinged on those inferences. Moreover, a full account of suboptimal judg-

ment must consider each component of the model, lest a difficulty with one component be misattributed to another.

Fischhoff and Beyth-Marom (1983) examined the components of Bayesian inference (e.g., hypothesis formation, assessing prior odds, and likelihood ratios), calling into question a number of attributions of judgmental bias. In some cases, the bias was other than had been claimed, whereas in others there may have been no bias at all. They also found cases in which apparently diverse effects proved to be special cases of a single judgmental bias. The most powerful of these metabiases is the tendency to ignore $P(D|H)$ when evaluating evidence. Finally, they suggested that the confirmation bias (Doherty, Mynatt, Tweney, & Schiavo, 1979; Synder & Swann, 1978; Wason, 1960, 1968) should not be viewed as a single bias towards seeking confirmation of an hypothesis but as several different patterns of information search and evaluation grouped under a common label.

### Learning From Experience
In probabilistic tasks for which optimal responses have been satisfactorily defined, research has shown that people often lack or fail to exhibit the cognitive skills required for optimal performance. Moreover, people do not seem to realize their inabilities, exhibiting what Dawes (1976) called "cognitive conceit." In part, these failings may be traced to a lack of formal schooling in probabilistic inference (Beyth-Marom, Gombo, Dekel, & Shaked, 1985). However, Brehmer (1980b) and Einhorn and Hogarth (1978) have attributed cognitive conceit to difficulties inherent in learning from an uncertain environment.

First, learning requires the formation of concepts or hypotheses about what is to be learned. In the laboratory such concepts are made evident by the experimenter. In the real world, instances are multidimensional and the concepts are not manifest. Concepts about uncertainty may be particularly slow to form. We could not function in our environment without searching for regularities and finding deterministic rules. The attention given to regularity may cause us to overlook or even deny the existence of unpredictability.

Once generated, hypotheses must be evaluated. Even in laboratory studies, hypothesis evaluation has been found to be flawed (Evans, 1982; Fischhoff & Beyth-Marom, 1983). When deterministic prediction rules are used in uncertain environments, an inaccurate prediction may be interpreted as evidence that the rule is wrong, rather than as an acceptable and expected error in a world that is only partially predictable. When probability assessment is flawed, a few surprising outcomes cannot pinpoint the error. Even in ideal circumstances, an evaluation of the hypothesis of overconfidence in probability assessment requires a great amount of data.

The feedback necessary for learning may be unavailable or distorted. Some outcomes are never known. Others are so delayed that they have little impact. Whenever memory is required to compare outcomes against predictions, inaccuracies may arise. For example, memory of one's prediction may be biased by knowledge of subsequent events (Fischhoff, 1975). Moreover, outcomes may be stored in memory according to their content rather than as examples of inferential rules, making their recall difficult when evaluating one's predictive skills (Tversky & Kahneman, 1974).

Futher complications arise when judgment leads to action, such as selecting applicants for a job. Einhorn and Hogarth (1978) showed how such choices bias the feedback received, as a function of four variables: (1) judgmental validity (how good the judgments are), (2) selection ratio (what proportion of cases are selected), (3) base rate (what proportion of cases meet the criterion), and (4) treatment effects (what effect selection has on the success rates for selected cases).

When the base rate of success is high, one will observe a high proportion of successes (positive hit rate), almost regardless of the selection ratio or the validity of the judgments. When the selection ratio is low (few applicants are accepted), the improvement in proportion of successes is a steep function of judgment validity. For example, if the selection ratio is .1, the base rate is .5, and judgmental ability is zero (judgments uncorrelated with the success criterion), only 50 percent of those accepted will succeed. But if the judgments correlate .4 with the criterion, over 75 percent of the selections will succeed, and if judgmental validity is .6 (i.e., only 36 percent of the variance associated with the success variable is explained by the judgments), 90 percent of the selections will succeed.

The positive hit rate is biased further when the act of selection improves the selected object

or individual, as when new employees are trained to make them more capable at the job or when research grants improve both the quality and the quantity of the recipients' research. Einhorn and Hogarth (1978) showed that the effect of such enhancement is largest when the positive hit rate is otherwise low.

In sum, the world does not work in a way that helps us recognize our deficiencies in probabilistic judgment. As a result, we maintain an exaggerated sense of our judgmental prowess.

# THEORIES OF DECISION MAKING

## Single Attribute Risky Models

Decision problems under conditions of risk can be conveniently represented by means of decision matrices and decision trees. In the decision matrix, the rows correspond to alternative acts that the decision maker can select and the columns correspond to possible states of nature. The cells of the matrix describe the consequences contingent upon the joint occurrence of a decision and a state of nature. A simple illustration for a traveler is given in Table 10.2. An analogous pictorial representation takes the form of a decision tree (Figure 10.4). Trees have the advantage of being better able to represent complex problems involving sequences of decisions over time (Figure 10.5).

### Early Theories

Because it is not always possible to make a decision that will turn out best in any eventuality, decision theorists view choice alternatives as gambles and try to determine the best bet. With the development of probability theory during the seventeenth century, the best bet came to be defined as the alternative that maximizes the *expected value* of the decision—that is, it maximizes the quantity

$$EV(A) = \sum_{i=1}^{n} P(E_i)V(x_i)$$

where $EV(A)$ represents the expected value of a course of action that has consequences $x_1, \ldots x_i, \ldots x_n$ depending on events $E_1, \ldots E_i, \ldots E_n$, $P(E_i)$ represents the probability of the $i$-th outcome of that action, and $V(x_i)$ represents the stated value of that outcome (e.g., the monetary gain or loss). The expected value of a gamble can

**Table 10.2. Matrix form of a simple decision problem**

|  |  |  | *State of nature* | |
|---|---|---|---|---|
|  |  |  | sun ($E_1$) | rain ($E_2$) |
| *Alternatives* | $A_1$ | carry umbrella | stay dry carrying umbrella | stay dry carrying umbrella |
|  | $A_2$ | leave umbrella | dry and unburdened | wet and unburdened |

be viewed as the average outcome resulting from playing it a large number of times. Gambles are often labeled as favorable, unfavorable, or fair depending on whether their expected values are positive, negative, or zero.

A little reflection shows that maximization of expected value is an inadequate model for describing people's behavior. People gamble in casinos even though the expected value of playing the games there is less than that of not playing. People buy insurance even though the premium costs more than the expected value of the undesirable risk that the insurance covers. Nor are people indifferent in their evaluation of fair bets. For example, most would reject the opportunity to toss a fair coin offering the possibility of either winning or losing $100.

Related observations led mathematician Daniel Bernoulli (1738/1954) to propose that people's actions are governed by the expected utility, rather than the expected value, of a gamble. Expected utility is determined by substituting the subjective worth or utility of each outcome in place of the values $V(x_i)$. Bernoulli went on to propose a specific logarithmic func-

tion to represent his notion that the more money one has, the less each additional increment is valued.

Given the selection of an appropriate utility function, substitution of utilities for actual monetary values can account for gambling and insurance decisions that fail to maximize expected value. This does not mean that people gamble or insure their property in order to maximize some utility function, only that their choices are consistent with utility maximization.

### Modern Utility Theory

A major deficiency of Bernoulli's principle is that it provides no normative justification for maximizing expected utility on a single choice as well as on a long-run series of decisions. Modern utility theory, as formulated by von Neumann and Morgenstern (1947), provides such a justification. Von Neumann and Morgenstern showed that if people's preferences among gambles satisfied certain axioms, then their behavior could be described as the maximization of expected utility. Because the axioms embody basic principles of rational behavior, they

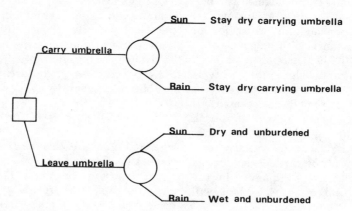

**Figure 10.4** Tree representation of a simple decision problem. Circles represent uncertain events: The square represents the decision point.

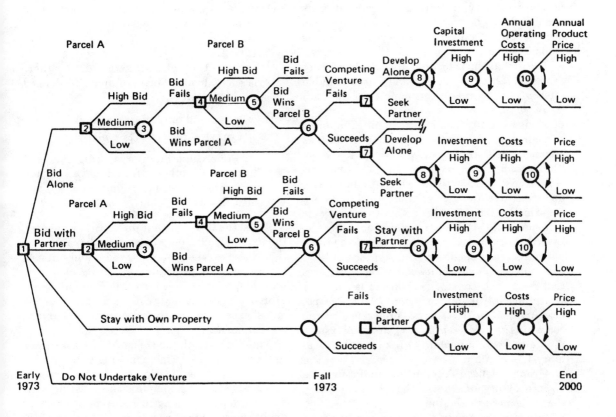

**Figure 10.5.** Decision tree representing the problem faced by a mining company in determining bids for two parcels of land with extensive ore deposits. Circles represent uncertain events: squares represent decision alternatives. From "The Use of Decision Analysis in Capital Investment Problems" by A.C. Hax and K.M. Wiig in *Conflicting Objectives in Decisions* (p. 286), D.E. Bell, R.L. Keeney, and H. Raiffa (Eds.), 1977. Reprinted by permission of John Wiley & Sons, Ltd.

provide a normative basis for the expected-utility principle.

The von Neumann and Morgenstern axioms will be presented in the form given by Coombs, Dawes, and Tversky (1970). The axioms are formulated in terms of a preference-or-indifference relation, denoted $\succsim$, defined on a set of outcomes, denoted $A$. This set is enriched to include gambles, or probability mixtures, of the form $(x, p, y)$, where outcome $x$ is obtained with probability $p$ and outcome $y$ is obtained with probability $1 - p$. Given the primitives $\succsim$ and $A$, the following axioms are assumed to hold for all outcomes $x$, $y$, $z$ in $A$ and for all probabilities $p$, $q$ that are different from zero or one.

Axiom 1: $(x, p, y)$ is in $A$.

Axiom 2: $\succsim$ is a weak ordering of $A$, where

$\succ$ denotes strict preference, $\sim$ denotes indifference, and for all outcomes $x$, $y$, $z$, the relation satisfies:

1. Reflexivity: $x \succsim x$.
2. Connectivity: Either $x \succsim y$ or $y \succsim x$, or both.
3. Transitivity: $x \succsim y$ and $y \succsim z$ imply $x \succsim z$.

Axiom 3: $[(x, p, y), q, y] \sim (x, pq, y)$.

Axiom 4: If $x \sim y$, then $(x, p, z) \sim (y, p, z)$.

Axiom 5: If $x \succ y$, then $x \succ (x, p, y) \succ y$.

Axiom 6: If $x \succ y \succ z$, then there exists a probability $p$ such that $y \sim (x, p, z)$.

Utility theory can be viewed either as a

normative theory, justified by the appeal of its axioms as ways in which one should make decisions, or as a descriptive theory. Hence, the axioms can be examined from both perspectives.

The first axiom is technically called a closure property. It asserts that if $x$ and $y$ are available alternatives, so are all the gambles of the form $(x, p, y)$ that can be formed with $x$ and $y$ as outcomes. Because gambles are defined in terms of their outcomes and their probabilities, it is assumed implicitly that $(x, p, y) = (y, 1 - p, x)$. The second axiom requires the preference-or-indifference relation to be reflexive, connective, and transitive. Reflexivity and connectivity are empirically trivial. Although transitivity is systematically violated in certain contexts, it is, nevertheless, a very compelling normative principle and a plausible descriptive hypothesis.[1]

Axiom 3 is a reducibility condition. It requires that the gamble $(x, pq, y)$, in which $x$ is obtained with probability $pq$, and $y$ with probability $1 - pq$, be equivalent (with respect to preference) to the compound gamble $[(x, p, y), q, y]$, in which $(x, p, y)$ is obtained with probability $q$, and $y$ with probability $1 - q$. Axiom 3 asserts, in effect, that the preferences depend only on the final outcomes and probabilities and not on the process by which the outcomes are obtained.

Axiom 4 is a substitutability condition. It states that if $x$ and $y$ are equivalent, then they can be substituted for one another in any gamble.

The fifth axiom asserts that if $x$ is preferred to $y$, then it must be preferred to any probability mixture of $x$ and $y$, which, in turn, must be preferred to $y$.

The sixth axiom embodies a continuity or a solvability property. It asserts that if $y$ is between $x$ and $z$ in the preference order (i.e., $x \succ y \succ z$) then there exists a probability $p$ such that the gamble $(x, p, z)$ is equivalent to $y$. This axiom excludes the possibility that one alternative is infinitely better than another one.

Axiom 6 captures the relationships between probabilities and values and the form in which they compensate for each other. This form

becomes transparent in the following theorem of von Neumann and Morgenstern.

### THEOREM

If axioms 1 through 6 are satisfied, then there exists a real-valued utility function $u$ defined on $A$, such that

1. $x \succsim y$ if and only if $u(x) \geqslant u(y)$.
2. $u(x, p, y) = pu(x) + (1 - p)u(y)$.

Furthermore, $u$ is an interval scale; that is, if $v$ is any other function satisfying 1 and 2, then there exist numbers $a > 0$ and $b$ such that $v(x) = au(x) + b$.

Thus, the theorem guarantees that whenever the axioms hold, there exists a utility function that preserves the preference order and satisfies the expectation principle: the utility of a gamble equals the expected utility of its outcomes. Moreover, this utility scale is uniquely determined except for an arbitrary origin and unit of measurement.

The main contribution of modern utility theory to the analysis of decision making under risk is in providing a justification for the Bernoullian expected utility principle. This justification does not depend on long-run considerations; it is applicable to unique choice situations. Furthermore, the axiomatic structure highlights those aspects of the theory that are critical for both normative and descriptive applications.

### SUBJECTIVE EXPECTED UTILITY

One limitation of the von Neumann and Morgenstern theory is its treatment of probability. Although Ramsey (1931) and de Finetti (1937/1980) had laid the groundwork for a subjective theory based on the concept of probability as a degree of belief about the likelihood of an event, von Neumann and Morgenstern assumed the existence of known numerical probabilities for all events. A major advance occurred when Savage (1954) developed an axiomatic theory allowing simultaneous measurement of utility and subjective probability. By means of several powerful axioms, Savage proved the existence of a unique subjective probability function, $S$, which obeys all the usual laws of probability, and an interval scale utility function, $u$, such that

1. $x \succsim y$ if and only if $u(x) \geqslant u(y)$ and
2. $u(x, E, y) = S(E)u(x) + [1 - S(E)]u(y)$

---

1. The compelling nature of transitivity as a rational principle is illustrated by the fact that those who violate transitivity are behaving in effect as money pumps. Suppose an individual prefers $y$ to $x$, $z$ to $y$, and $x$ to $z$. It is reasonable to assume that he or she will pay some amount of money to replace $x$ by $y$, a second amount to replace $y$ by $z$ and a third amount to replace $z$ by $x$. Thus, the individual ends up with the original alternative and less money.

where $(x, E, y)$ denotes the gamble where $x$ is obtained if $E$ occurs and $y$ otherwise. Edwards (1955) labeled this the subjective expected utility (SEU) model. Excellent discussions and critiques of Savage's theory are provided by Krantz, Luce, Suppes, and Tversky (1971) and Fishburn (1982a).

## RISK AVERSION

Although the utility function under either the von Neumann-Morgenstern formulation or the Savage formulation can take on any shape, utility functions are often characterized as risk averse, risk prone, or risk neutral. A risk-averse function is one such that, for probability $p$,

$$U(px) > pU(x)$$

A risk-prone function reverses this preference,

$$pU(x) > U(px)$$

whereas risk neutrality means indifference between the two quantities. A risk-averse utility function is concave, a risk-prone function is convex, and a risk-neutral function is linear with value. There is nothing in the theory to bar a person's utility function from being risk prone in some regions and risk averse in others.

A risk-averse person—that is, a person whose utility function is concave in the region of interest—will prefer, for example, to receive $50 for sure over a 50–50 chance of receiving either $100 or nothing; a risk-prone person will prefer the gamble, and the risk-neutral person will be indifferent between the two options.

## MEASUREMENT METHODS

Farquhar (1982) has discussed more than two dozen techniques for measuring utility based on variations of a few general methods. The *standard gamble* contrasts a bet $(x, p, y)$ with a sure outcome, $w$, called the *certainty equivalent*. One of the four elements, $w, x, y,$ or $p$, is omitted and the decision maker is asked to specify it so as to create indifference between the bet and the sure outcome. For example, consider a bet paying either $0 or $10 and a sure outcome of $5. What probability of winning $10 would make you indifferent between playing the bet and receiving $5? A bit of algebra shows that if $u(\$0) = 0$ and $u(\$10) = 1$, the answer, $p$, to this question is equal to the utility of the sure outcome. For example, if you answered .8, then $u(\$5) = .8$ (thus exhibiting risk aversion). Because of this directness, standard gambles are often construc-

ted with $x$ being the best possible outcome and $y$ being the worst possible outcome. The assessor is asked to supply $p$ values for enough $w$ values to reveal the utility curve, scaled from 0 to 1, to any desired degree of precision.

Alternatively, a series of bets paired with sure outcomes is presented and the decision maker indicates for each pairing, preference for the bet, preference for the sure outcome, or indifference. Each such comparison provides a constraint that the utility function must satisfy. With a well chosen set, sufficiently tight bounds on the utility function can be found.

Finally, all the above variations can be used with pairs of gambles rather than pairs consisting of a gamble and a sure outcome.

With the use of computers, multiple methods can be employed, in which sequences of comparisons are used to generate systems of equations whose solutions provide the utility function (Novick, Dekeyrel, & Chuang, 1981). Built-in consistency checks show the decision maker the implications of previous choices and allow adjustments to be made to achieve consistency.

## Tests of Utility Theory

Following the development of an axiomatic justification leading to measurable probability and utility functions, expected-utility maximization gained great popularity, not only as a model of how people should behave, but also as a psychological or descriptive theory about how they actually do behave. The model's normative and descriptive properties have steadily infiltrated theories in such diverse disciplines as economics, philosophy, finance, psychology, political science, and management science and have formed the basis of a new discipline, *decision analysis*, designed to help people make optimal decisions in situations of risk. Coombs (1975) observed that the fundamental role played by utility maximization demands that the theory be "probed relentlessly" (p. 65), and so it has been.

## PREDICTIVE TESTS

Early empirical studies based on the von Neumann-Morgenstern and Savage formulations attempted to determine whether people's decisions were consistent enough that utility functions could actually be constructed and used to predict other decisions. The first such study was conducted by Mosteller and Nogee (1951), who presented subjects with gambles constructed from possible hands of a poker game played with dice. If subjects rejected a gamble, no money changed hands; if a gamble was accepted, subjects won $x$ if they beat the hand but lost a nickel otherwise. The actuarial probability of beating each hand was made available to the subjects. By varying the payoffs, the experimenter determined the value of $x$ for which the subject was indifferent between the two alternatives. These indifference amounts were used to construct utility functions, with $u(0)$ set equal to 0 and $u(\text{lose } 5\cancel{c})$ set equal to $-1$. These utility functions predicted subjects' choices among new bets more accurately than did predictions based on the maximization of expected monetary value.

Whereas Mosteller and Nogee assumed that their subjects used the stated actuarial probabilities, Davidson, Suppes, and Siegel (1957) attempted to measure both utility and subjective probability. Their approach followed Ramsey's (1931) procedure for finding events whose subjective probability equals one half. After much experimentation, Davidson et al. selected a six-sided die with the nonsense syllable ZEJ printed on three of its sides and ZOJ on the other three. Subjects didn't seem to care which syllable was associated with the more favorable outcome of a two-outcome bet. Assuming the subjective expected-utility model, these equiprobable events were used to construct a utility scale, which in turn was used to measure the subjective probabilities of another event. The results of this experiment showed that utility functions and subjective probabilities could be produced for most subjects. Moreover, the resulting SEU values predicted subjects' choices better than did the expected value model.

Later studies by Tversky (1967a) and others have measured utilities and subjective probabilities simultaneously and used them to predict responses to gambles. Although these studies showed that single-attribute utility functions for money could be measured and used to predict people's preferences, this by no means validates expected-utility theory. It is difficult to establish that subjects are using a particular model simply on the basis of that model's ability to predict the outcome of their decision-making process (Birnbaum, 1973; Fischhoff, Goitein, & Shapira, 1982; Hoffmann, 1960). In this case, moderately good predictability would be guaranteed by the mere fact that people prefer more money to less or higher probabilities of gain to lesser proba-

bilities (Dawes & Corrigan, 1974). Any model capturing this aspect of preference would predict well even if it was seriously deficient on other grounds. Furthermore, subsequent research has shown that the various methods used to determine utility functions may induce substantial biases in those functions, a topic that will be discussed later in this chapter.

TESTS OF THE AXIOMS
Many studies have tested utility theory by examining the validity of its axioms. One of the key principles in Savage's axiomatization of subjective expected utility is the *extended sure-thing principle* which, in one form or another, is crucial to all expected-utility theories. This axiom asserts that if two alternatives have a common outcome under a particular state of nature, then the ordering of the alternatives shall be independent of the value of that common outcome. According to Savage (1954): ". . . except, possibly, for the assumption of simple ordering, I know of no other extralogical principle governing decisions that finds such ready acceptance" (p. 21).

Despite its intuitive appeal, several robust violations of the extended sure-thing principle have been demonstrated. One is the paradox put forth by Allais (1953), which contrasts two hypothetical decision situations, each involving a pair of gambles (expressed in units of one million dollars):

---

*Situation 1. Choose between*

Gamble 1: 1/2 with probability 1

Gamble 2: 2-1/2 with probability .10
         1/2 with probability .89
         0 with probability .01

*Situation 2. Choose between*

Gamble 3: 1/2 with probability .11
         0 with probability .89

Gamble 4: 2-1/2 with probability .10
         0 with probability .90

---

Most people prefer gamble 1 to gamble 2, presumably because the small probability of missing the chance of a lifetime to become rich seems very unattractive. At the same time, most people also prefer gamble 4 to gamble 3, presumably because the large difference between the payoffs dominates the small difference between the chances of winning. However, this seemingly innocent pair of preferences is incompatible with utility theory. The first preference implies that

$$.11u(1/2) > .10u(2\text{-}1/2) + .01u(0)$$

whereas the second preference implies the opposite

$$.10u(2\text{-}1/2) + .01u(0) > .11u(1/2)$$

Another well-known violation of the extended sure-thing principle occurs in the following problem, created by Ellsberg (1961):

Imagine an urn known to contain 90 balls. Thirty of the balls are red; the remaining 60 are black and yellow in unknown proportion. One ball is to be drawn at random from the urn. Consider the following actions and payoffs:

| Situation X | 30<br>Red | 60<br>Black | Yellow |
|---|---|---|---|
| Act 1: Bet on red | $100 | $ 0 | $0 |
| Act 2: Bet on black | $ 0 | $100 | $0 |

If you bet on red, Act 1, you will win $100 if a red ball is drawn and nothing if a black or yellow ball is drawn.

If you bet on black, Act 2, you will win $100 if a black ball is drawn and nothing if a red or yellow ball is drawn.

Now consider the following two actions, under the same circumstances:

| Situation Y | 30<br>Red | 60<br>Black | Yellow |
|---|---|---|---|
| Act 3: Bet on red or yellow | $100 | $ 0 | $100 |
| Act 4: Bet on black or yellow | $ 0 | $100 | $100 |

In this problem, the extended sure-thing principle implies that one must choose either 1 and 3 or 2 and 4 in the two situations. Most people select Acts 1 and 4, thus violating the principle. Presumably, they prefer to bet on payoffs whose probabilities are known precisely rather than on payoffs with ambiguous probabilities.

When confronted with such inconsistencies between their intuitions and expected-utility theory, some people reject the theory. Or, to use Samuelson's (1950) phrase, they prefer to "satisfy their preferences and let the axioms satisfy themselves." Others reexamine their preferences in the light of the axioms and revise their initial choices.

Savage (1954) offered an illuminating introspective discussion of Allais' example. He admitted that he intuitively preferred gamble 1 to gamble 2 and gamble 4 to gamble 3. Then he adopted another way of looking at the problem: the gambles can be operationalized by a lottery with 100 numbered tickets, one of which is drawn at random to determine the outcome according to the payoff matrix presented in Figure 10.6. If one of the tickets numbered 12 to 100 is drawn, it does not matter, in either situation, which gamble is chosen. Hence, one should consider only the possibility that one of the tickets numbered 1 to 11 is drawn, in which case the two choice situations are identical. Limiting our attention to tickets 1 to 11, the problem in both situations is whether a 10 : 1 chance to win 1.5 million dollars is preferred to .5 million dollars with certainty. If one prefers gamble 1 to gamble 2, therefore, one should also prefer gamble 3 to gamble 4 in order to be consistent. In concluding his discussion, Savage (1954) wrote:

It seems to me that in reversing my preference between gamble 3 and 4 I have corrected an error. There is, of course, an important sense in which preferences, being entirely subjective, cannot be in error; but in a different, more subtle sense they can be. Let me illustrate by a simple example containing no reference to uncertainty. A man buying a car for $10,138 is tempted to order it with a radio installed, which will bring the total price to $10,476, feeling that the difference is trifling. But, when he reflects that, if he already had the car, he certainly would not spend $338 for a radio for it, he realizes that he has made an error (p. 103) [prices revised to reflect inflation since 1954].

Here, Savage used utility theory as a prescriptive framework for ordering his preferences, rather than as a descriptive model of his nonreflective choices. In this spirit, MacCrimmon (1968) presented Allais-type problems to upper-middle-level executives. Although they initially showed the usual inconsistencies, most eventually came to regard their deviations from utility theory as mistakes and desired to correct them. However, Slovic and Tversky (1974) challenged MacCrimmon's procedure for discussing violations on the grounds that it may have pressured the subjects to accept the axioms. Slovic and

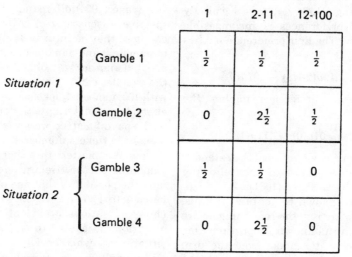

**Figure 10.6.** Matrix representation of the Allais problem. From "Who Accepts Savage's Axiom?" by P. Slovic and A. Tversky, 1974, *Behavioral Science, 19,* p. 370. Copyright 1974 General Systems Science Foundation. Reprinted by permission.

Tversky presented subjects with arguments for and against the extended sure-thing principle and found persistent violations, even after the axiom was presented in a clear and presumably compelling fashion. Moskowitz (1974) used a variety of problem representations (matrix formats, trees, and verbal presentations) to clarify the principle and still found that it was consistently rejected. MacCrimmon and Larsson (1976) later reevaluated the evidence and suggested that revision of the theory might indeed be in order.

Transitivity of preferences is another key principle of expected-utility theory, due to its strong normative appeal and its status as a prerequisite for the existence of any order-preserving utility scale. Transitivity has both a deterministic and a stochastic (probabilistic) form. The latter takes three levels. Let $p(a, b)$ denote the probability that $a$ is preferred to $b$. If $p(a, b) > 1/2$ and $p(b, c) > 1/2$ then

strong stochastic transitivity →

$$p(a, c) > \max[p(a, b), p(b, c)];$$

moderate stochastic transitivity →

$$p(a, c) > \min[p(a, b), p(b, c)];$$

and weak stochastic transitivity →

$$p(a, c) > 1/2.$$

Tversky (1969) demonstrated violations of weak stochastic transitivity in a situation in which gambles varied in probability and payoff as shown in Table 10.3. The gambles were constructed so that adjacent gambles had small differences in probability, which subjects tended to ignore when making choices. However, for comparisons between gambles lying far apart in the chain, the cumulative difference in probability of winning (or expected value) dominated the decision. Thus, subjects preferred $a$ to $b$, $b$ to $c$, $c$ to $d$, and $d$ to $e$, but $e$ to $a$, thereby violating transitivity. Tversky's subjects did not realize their preferences were intransitive and some even denied this possibility emphatically.

**Table 10.3 Gambles used as stimuli by Tversky (1969)**

| Gamble | Probability of Winning | Payoff (in $) | Expected Value |
|--------|------------------------|---------------|----------------|
| $a$    | 7/24                   | 5.00          | 1.46           |
| $b$    | 8/24                   | 4.75          | 1.58           |
| $c$    | 9/24                   | 4.50          | 1.69           |
| $d$    | 10/24                  | 4.25          | 1.77           |
| $e$    | 11/24                  | 4.00          | 1.83           |

*Note.* From "Transitivity of Preferences" by A. Tversky, 1969, *Psychological Review, 76,* p. 33. Copyright 1969 by the American Psychological Association. Reprinted by permission of the author.

According to Axiom 5 of expected-utility theory, any probability mixture of two gambles will always lie between them in the preference order—that is, a mixture can never be better or worse than both the components. Coombs and Huang (1976) tested this betweenness property by asking subjects to rank three gambles, $a$, $b$, and $c$ in order of attractiveness. Gamble $b$ was a probability mixture of $a$ and $c$. For example, if $a$ and $c$ represent gambles offering a 50/50 chance to win or lose $1 (for $a$) or $5 (for $c$), $b$ would be a four-outcome gamble ($-$$5, $-$$1, $1, $5), each outcome having probability .25. Studying decisions among 20 different triples of gambles, Coombs and Huang observed that in a substantial number (about 27 percent) of the response patterns, the mixture, $b$, was the most preferred gamble. Coombs and Huang attributed such patterns to subjects' preference for the level of risk embodied in the mixture over the level of risk in the component gambles.

In sum, many of the axioms of utility theory are systematically and consciously violated. These violations have led to a great deal of theoretical activity, both normative and descriptive. On the normative side, a number of decision theorists have proposed revised sets of axioms designed to be consistent with observed behavior without giving up too much of the mathematical convenience and normative value of the earlier models. Thus, Chew and MacCrimmon (1979) weakened the substitution axiom in a way that enabled the Allais paradox to be accommodated within the normative theory. Munera and de Neufville (1982) eliminated the substitution principle and Fishburn (1982b) proposed eliminating the transitivity axiom. A review of these and other attempts to revise the von Neumann and Morgenstern axioms is provided by Fishburn (1983).

On the empirical side, the inadequacies of utility theory have stimulated the development of alternative descriptive theories, to which we now turn.

### Other Descriptive Theories

#### MOMENT THEORIES
Any gamble can be viewed as a probability density distribution over the possible outcomes. The distribution's mean is the gamble's expected value. An early alternative to SEU as a descriptive theory proposed that people base their decisions on the shape of the gamble's distribution as characterized by its first three moments: expected value, variance, and skewness. Fisher (1906) first brought up the potential importance of variance and Allais (1953) used it to criticize expected-utility theory, which assumes that variance preferences can be subsumed under the utility function for money.

For the gamble $(x, p, y)$

$$\text{variance} = p(1 - p)(x - y)^2$$

and

$$\text{skewness} = \frac{1 - 2p}{\sqrt{p(1 - p)}}$$

When probabilities are held constant in two-outcome bets, variance is synonymous with the range of outcomes. Preference for an intermediate level of variance is difficult to account for within utility theory: it suggests a utility curve with several inflection points (alternating regions of risk aversion and risk proneness). Because skewness is monotone with probability in two-outcome bets, preference for a specific skewness level suggests preference for betting at specific probabilities to win and lose.

Edwards (1953, 1954a, 1954b) was the first to study probability and variance preferences. Using two-outcome gambles of equal expected value, he found that 50/50 bets were generally the most preferred and bets with .75 probability of winning were avoided. However, this experiment confounded probability differences with variance differences. To remove this confounding, Coombs and Pruitt (1960) constructed a set of two-outcome gambles, all of zero expected value, varying skewness and variance independently. Their subjects exhibited stable probability preferences (usually favoring the highest or lowest probabilities) and variance preferences that interacted with these probability preferences. Specifically, subjects preferred greater variance for gambles containing their preferred probabilities. Although these findings could be explained by an SEU model, Coombs and Pruitt argued that a moment model provided a more parsimonious explanation.

For two-outcome gambles, variance preferences are necessarily confounded with utility and skewness preferences with probability. To break this confounding, Lichtenstein (1965) constructed three-outcome bets that permitted independent variation of probabilities, expected

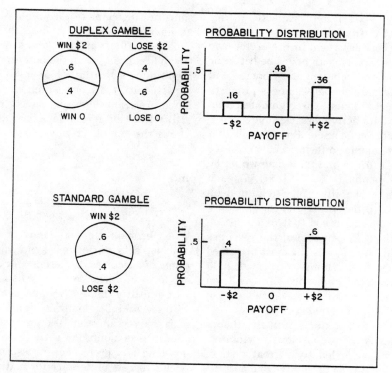

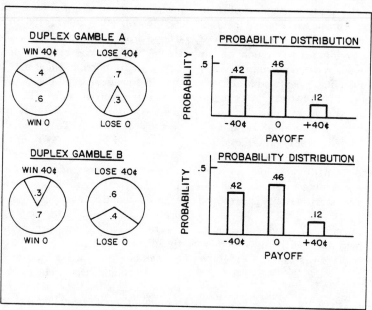

**Figure 10.7.** Duplex and standard gambles used to study moment effects. (a) From "Importance of Variance Preferences in Gambling Decisions" by P. Slovic and S. Lichtenstein, 1968, *Journal of Experimental Psychology, 78,* p. 648. Copyright 1968 by the American Psychological Association. Reprinted by permission of the author. (b) Adapted from "Preferences Among Gambles with Equal Underlying Distributions" by J.W. Payne and M.L. Braunstein, 1971, *Journal of Experimental Psychology, 87,* p. 14. Copyright 1971 by the American Psychological Association. Reprinted by permission of the author.

value, variance, and skewness. To assess preferences, she used a bidding method in which subjects stated the largest amount they would pay to play an attractive bet or the largest amount they would pay the experimenter in order to avoid playing an unattractive bet. The results indicated a strong influence of expected value on the amount bid, a slight preference for low variance, and no influence of skewness or probability. The variance effect could be accounted for by a simple utility function.

Another aspect of Lichtenstein's results cast doubt upon the validity of moment theories. This was the finding of large variations in bids within a set of gambles whose first three moment functions were all equal. The case against moment theories was strengthened in subsequent studies by Slovic and Lichtenstein (1968a) and Payne and Braunstein (1971). Slovic and Lichtenstein used specially constructed gambles to manipulate variance without changing the probabilities and payoffs that were explicitly displayed to the subject. The upper half of Figure 10.7 shows two such bets: a duplex bet and a standard bet, which were termed *parallel* because both have the same stated probabilities and the same payoffs, namely, .6 chance to win $2 and .4 chance to lose $2. Imagine that the bets can be played by spinning pointers on the circular discs shown in Figure 10.7 such that one wins or loses the amount indicated by the final position of the pointer. To play a duplex bet, one must spin the pointer on both discs. Thus, one can win and not lose, lose and not win, both win and lose, or neither win nor lose. As a consequence, the duplex bet has much less variance than its parallel standard bet. That is, the standard bet leads either to a gain or loss of $2; however, by playing the duplex bet, one has a fairly high probability of breaking even. Most subjects perceived duplex bets and their parallel standard bets as equally attractive, indicating that they were responding to the explicitly stated probabilities and payoffs of the duplex bet and not to its underlying distribution.

Payne and Braunstein used pairs of duplex gambles with equal underlying distributions but different explicit probability values, as illustrated in the lower half of Figure 10.7. Subjects showed strong preferences for one member of such pairs over the other, which further demonstrates the dominance of explicit or surface information. Taken together, these two studies imply

that what passed for probability and variance preferences in earlier studies were byproducts of decision rules applied to the stated probabilities and payoffs. These results helped prompt the study of information processing in decision making, which will be described later.

PORTFOLIO THEORY

The failures of the SEU model led Coombs (1969, 1975) to develop an alternative descriptive model called *portfolio theory*, which highlights risk preference as a determinant of choices among gambles. One assumption of the theory is that preferences among risky alternatives are a function of only two variables, *EV* and perceived risk (the concept of risk is left undefined, to be inferred from the choice behavior). A second assumption is that the preference function over a set of gambles equal in *EV* is a single-peaked function of risk.[2] Tests of the theory require additional *ad hoc* assumptions about the subjective definition of risk. For example, Coombs and Meyer (1969) assumed that the perceived risk of a coin-tossing game increases with the denomination of the coin and with the number of tosses one is committed to playing; that is, tossing a coin for a dollar seems at least as risky as tossing for a dime, and tossing for a dollar 10 times seems at least as risky as tossing for a dollar once. Their subjects chose among gambles arranged in sets, with each set having either a fixed monetary denomination or a fixed number of tosses. The results supported the hypothesis that risk, as defined above, was a determinant of subjects' preference.

In another attempt to infer the meaning of risk and validate portfolio theory, Coombs and Huang (1970a) assumed that a probability mixture of two gambles, each with the same expected value, will have a level of risk intermediate between the two. They hypothesized that individuals with single-peaked preference functions over risk would, for some mixtures, violate the betweenness principle of utility theory. The data confirmed their hypothesis.

Portfolio theory has stimulated a number of empirical and theoretical studies of the perceived

2. The property of single-peakedness means here that, for any three gambles with the same EU and ordered in risk, the intermediate one cannot be the least preferred. Psychologically, this implies that, for a fixed expected value, an individual has an optimum level of risk and that preference declines as risk increases or decreases from this optimum.

risk of a gamble. Coombs and Huang (1970b) examined the effects on risk judgments of various transformations of probabilities and payoffs, and Coombs and Bowen (1971) examined the effects of variance and skewness. The results suggested that risk could be predicted by a simple polynomial model incorporating variables such as expectation and skewness. Luce (1980, 1981) suggested four specific models of a gamble's risk, depending upon how risk changes given a change of scale and how a probability density distribution aggregates into a single value for risk. Weber (1984) found that multiplying all outcomes by a scale factor had an additive effect on perceived risk, thus supporting one of Luce's models. Coombs and Lehner (1981) argued that models involving moments of distributions and functions of the moments imply a symmetry that does not correspond with people's perceptions of risk. For example, adding $10 to the positive outcome of a gamble has less effect on perceived risk than a symmetric addition of $10 to the negative outcome. They proposed separating the good and bad outcomes by means of a model that does not include moments. If $g$ is a gamble with a winning and a losing outcome, $W$ and $L$, having probabilities of $p$ and $q$, respectively, and the residual probability $(1 - p - q)$ is associated with a zero outcome, the Coombs and Lehner model for the riskiness of $g$ is

$$R(g) = \theta_1(p)\, \theta_2(W) + \theta_3(q)\, \theta_4(L)$$

where the $\theta_i$ are real-valued monotone functions.

## PROSPECT THEORY

Kahneman and Tversky (1979) also developed an algebraic model that was designed to remedy the descriptive failures of utility theory. Referring to gambles as risky prospects, they named their approach *prospect theory*. They demonstrated three pervasive phenomena, labeled the certainty effect, the reflection effect, and the isolation effect, that were used to determine the structure of prospect theory.

The *certainty effect* is the tendency to overweight outcomes that are considered certain, relative to outcomes that are merely probable. For example, most subjects preferred option $B$ over option $A$ in the following choice (outcomes were Israeli pounds)

A: Win 4,000 with probability .80

B: Win 3,000 with certainty

However, the majority of subjects also preferred $C$ over $D$

C: Win 4,000 with probability .20

D: Win 3,000 with probability .25

This pattern of preferences, $B$ over $A$ and $C$ over $D$, violates a lemma of utility theory's substitutability axiom. Option $C$ is a probability mixture of $A$ (i.e., $C$ can be seen as a .25 chance to win $A$) and $D$ is the same probability mixture of $B$. Thus, if $B$ is preferred over $A$, $D$ must be preferred over $C$. Kahneman and Tversky explained the violation as a result of the certainty effect; the reduction in probability has greater impact when it alters the character of the prospect from a sure gain ($B$) to a probable one ($D$) than when both the original and the reduced prospects ($A$ and $C$) are uncertain.

The *reflection effect* is the tendency for preferences between positive prospects to be reversed when the gains are replaced by losses. For example, when options $A$, $B$, $C$ and $D$, above, are changed to losses (e.g., $A'$: lose 4,000 with probability .80), the majority of subjects prefer $A'$ over $B'$ and $D'$ over $C'$. The reflection effect implies risk aversion in the positive domain and risk proneness in the negative domain.

The *isolation effect* is the tendency to simplify choices between alternatives by disregarding components that the alternatives share and focusing on the components that differentiate them (Tversky, 1972b). This tendency can produce inconsistent preferences when a pair of prospects are decomposed into common and distinctive components in different ways. For example:

Consider a two-stage game in which stage 1 offers a probability of .75 to end the game without winning anything and a probability of .25 to move to the second stage. The second stage offers a choice between

E: Win 4,000 with probability .8, and

F: Win 3,000 with certainty

One's choice for the second stage must be made before the game starts.

In terms of the final outcomes, the real choice in this game is between a .25 × .80 = .20 chance to win 4,000 and a .25 × 1.0 = .25 chance to win 3,000, as with options $C$ and $D$ above. There most subjects chose option $C$. However, the isolation effect leads subjects to disregard the common first stage and treat the game as if it were composed only of the second stage: 78 percent of the subjects chose option $F$.

The preceding two-stage game shows that preferences can be changed by different representations of probabilities. The following pairs of choices show the isolation effect with varying representations of outcomes:

Pair 1: In addition to whatever you own, you have been given 1,000. You are now asked to choose between:

$G$: Win 1,000 with probability .50, and

$H$: Win 500 with certainty.

Pair 2: In addition to whatever you own, you have been given 2,000. You are now asked to choose between:

$I$: lose 1,000 with probability .50, and

$J$: lose 500 with certainty.

The majority of subjects chose $H$ in Pair 1 and $I$ in Pair 2. However, the final states are the same in the two pairs; $G = (2,000, .50, 1,000) = I$ and $H = 1,500 = J$. Evidently, subjects did not integrate the bonuses with the respective prospects. These results are inconsistent with utility theory, which assigns the same utility to a final outcome regardless of how that outcome was obtained.

Prospect theory was designed to accommodate these various behavioral phenomena. The theory distinguishes two phases in the choice process. An editing phase organizes and reformulates the options so as to simplify subsequent evaluation and choice. The major operations of editing include (1) coding of outcomes as gains or losses around some neutral reference point, (2) combination of probabilities associated with identical outcomes, (3) separation of risky from riskless components, and (4) cancellation of components shared by all offered prospects.

Following editing, the decision maker is assumed to evaluate each of the edited prospects and to choose the prospect with the highest value. The overall value of an edited prospect, denoted $V$, is expressed in terms of a value function $v(x)$, which attaches a subjective worth to each outcome, and a weighting function, $\pi(p)$, which expresses the subjective importance attached to the probability of obtaining a particular outcome. The attractiveness of a gamble that offers a chance of $p$ to gain $x$ and a chance

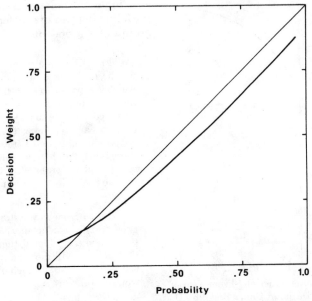

**Figure 10.8.** A hypothetical weighting function. From "Prospect Theory: An Analysis of Decision Under Risk" by D. Kahneman and A. Tversky, 1979, *Econometrica, 47*, p. 279. Copyright 1979 by the Econometric Society. Reprinted by permission.

of $q$ to lose $y$ is:

$$V = \pi(p)v(x) + \pi(q)v(y)$$

A slightly different equation is applied if both outcomes are on the same side of the zero point.

The decision weight $\pi(p)$ is a monotonic function of $p$ but is not a probability. Although $\pi(0) = 0$ and $\pi(1) = 1$, the function is not well behaved near the end points. In addition, for low probabilities, $\pi(p) > p$ but $\pi(p) + \pi(1 - p) < 1$. Also, $\pi(pq)/\pi(p) < \pi(pqr)/\pi(pr)$ for all $0 < p, q, r < 1$. That is, for any fixed probability ratio, $q$, the ratio of decision weights is closer to unity when the probabilities are lower than when they are high. For example, $\pi(.4)/\pi(.8) > \pi(.1)/\pi(.2)$. An illustrative weighting function that satisfies these properties is shown in Figure 10.8.

The general form of the value function is shown in Figure 10.9. It is defined on gains and losses relative to some psychologically neutral reference point. The function is steeper for losses than for gains, implying that a given change in one's status hurts more as a loss than it pleases as a gain. A third feature is that it is concave above the reference point and convex below it, meaning, for example, that the subjective difference between gaining (or losing) $10 and $20

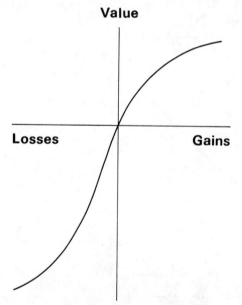

**Value**

**Losses**  **Gains**

**Figure 10.9.** S-shaped value function. From "Prospect Theory: Analysis of Decision Under Risk" by D. Kahneman and A. Tversky, 1979, *Econometrica, 47,* p. 283. Copyright 1979 by the Econometric Society. Reprinted by permission.

is greater than the difference between gaining (or losing) $110 and $120.

Payne, Laughhunn, and Crum (1980, 1981) treated the reference point as a level of aspiration. They showed how equal additions or subtractions to all outcomes in a gamble, by changing the relation of the outcomes to the level of aspiration, could markedly affect an individual's preferences.

## FRAMING

The editing phase of prospect theory was subsequently labeled *framing* by Tversky and Kahneman (1981). Much as changes in vantage point induce alternative perspectives on a visual scene, the same decision problem can be viewed in alternative frames. The frame that is adopted is determined in part by the external formulation of the problem and in part by the standards, habits, and idiosyncratic perspectives of the decision maker.

If $\pi$ and $v$ were linear functions, preferences among risky prospects would be independent of the problem frame. However, because of the nonlinearity of these functions, normatively inconsequential changes in the problem frame can have profound effects on preferences. This was illustrated in several of the examples described above. Tversky and Kahneman (1981) provided additional examples of framing effects, such as the following pair of problems, given to separate groups of respondents.

> *Problem 1.* Imagine that the U.S. is preparing for the outbreak of an unusual Asian disease, which is expected to kill 600 people. Two alternative programs to combat the disease have been proposed. Assume that the consequences of the programs are as follows: If Program $A$ is adopted, 200 people will be saved. If Program $B$ is adopted, there is a 1/3 probability that 600 people will be saved, and 2/3 probability that no people will be saved. Which of the two programs would you favor?

> *Problem 2.* (Same cover story as Problem 1). If Program $C$ is adopted, 400 people will die. If Program $D$ is adopted, there is 1/3 probability that nobody will die, and 2/3 probability that 600 people will die. Which of the two programs would you favor?

Although the two problems are formally identical, the preferences tend to be quite different. In a study of college students, 72 percent of the respondents chose Program *A* over Program *B*, whereas 78 percent chose Program *D* over Program *C*. A framing interpretation of this inconsistency is that the "save lives" wording of the first problem induces a reference point of 600 lives lost, whereas the "people will die" wording of Problem 2 induces a reference point of no lives lost. Thus, Problem 1 falls in the concave gain region of the value function, whereas Problem 2 is in the convex loss region. In another study, physicians and patients reversed their choice between radiation versus surgical treatments for lung cancer when the relevant statistics were changed from probabilities of surviving for various lengths of time after treatment to probabilities of not surviving (McNeil, Pauker, Sox, & Tversky, 1982).

One class of framing effects, called *pseudocertainty* by Tversky and Kahneman (1981), converts uncertainty about an outcome to certainty about a subset of that outcome. Protective actions, for example, may be easily manipulated so as to vary the apparent certainty with which they prevent harm. Thus, an insurance policy that covers fire but not flood could be presented either as a reduction in the overall probability of property loss or as full protection against the specific risk of fire. Because possible outcomes are undervalued in comparison with certain outcomes, Tversky and Kahneman hypothesized that such an insurance policy would appear more attractive in the context that offers unconditional protection against a restricted set of problems.

Slovic, Fischhoff, and Lichtenstein (1982) found empirical support for this conjecture in the context of one particular kind of insurance, vaccination. Two forms of a vaccination questionnaire were created. Form I (probabilistic protection) described a disease expected to afflict 20 percent of the population and asked people whether they would volunteer to receive a vaccine that protects half of the people receiving it. In Form II (pseudocertainty), there were two mutually exclusive and equiprobable strains of the disease, each likely to afflict 10 percent of the population; the vaccination was said to give complete protection against one strain and no protection against the other. More people were willing to be vaccinated with Form II than with Form I.

In order to use prospect theory predictively, one must be able to discern the frames that subjects adopt. In the examples given above, investigators were successful in inducing subjects to adopt frames whose interpretation was clear to other investigators. Using similar kinds of problems, however, Fischhoff (1983) was less successful. Each problem offered a choice between a sure loss (e.g., $50) and a gamble with two negative outcomes (e.g., a 50/50 chance to lose $40 or $60). Three possible frames were identified, two of which would, according to prospect theory, lead to the choice of the gamble, whereas the third would lead to choice of the sure thing. Most subjects preferred the gamble, an example of risk seeking in the domain of losses that prospect theory would predict. Most subjects also indicated that they found the frames leading to the gamble (assuming the truth of prospect theory) to be most natural and that they had, in fact, used those frames. However, there was no relationship between individual subjects' choices and their frame preferences. Nor was it possible to alter the choice patterns by changing the wording of the problems to highlight particular frames. These results suggest (1) that people may not be able to introspect well regarding the judgmental processes involved in framing and (2) that some natural frames may be so robust that it is difficult to dislodge them by experimental manipulation. The study points out the need for a substantive theory showing how framing works in particular situations.

REGRET THEORIES

The demonstrated violations of utility theory that prompted prospect theory have also led to the development of other theories of decision making under risk. Bell (1982), Loomes and Sugden (1982), and Sage and White (1983) have developed highly similar theories based on regret. In these theories, the utility of a risk prospect depends not only on the choiceless or inherent utility of each possible outcome but also on the regret or rejoicing one might experience upon making a choice, receiving an outcome, and comparing the actual outcome with the outcome that would have obtained had some other choice been made. Thus, a preference for *A* over *B* really means that choosing *A* and rejecting *B* is preferable to choosing *B* and rejecting *A*.

Since every choice depends on the regret/rejoicing involved in the particular pair of options being considered, transitivity of choice is not ensured in regret theories. Indeed, Loomes and

Sugden (1982) argued against transitivity as an appropriate prescriptive goal.

Another principle of utility theory that is rejected by regret theories is that options with identical probability distributions of outcomes are equivalent. Consider the following two formally identical gambles. The chosen gamble will be decided by blindly drawing a ball from an urn containing one red, one white, and one black ball.

|           | Red      | White    | Black    |
|-----------|----------|----------|----------|
| Option A  | Win $8   | Win $2   | Win $1   |
| Option B  | Win $1   | Win $8   | Win $2   |

The regret/rejoicing function is not linear with differences in outcomes (if it were, regret theories would be identical to utility theory). Thus, a person may have a strong preference for one of the two options, since if A is chosen the rejoicing resulting from drawing the red ball and winning $8 rather than $1 would not necessarily balance the sum of the regrets felt from drawing the white ($2 − $8) or black ($1 − $2) ball.

With suitable assumptions about the shapes of the choiceless utility and regret functions, regret theories can explain many, but not all, of the best-known violations of utility theory.

### Expected Utility Theory: An Assessment

Experimental psychology has played a key role in testing the descriptive validity of utility theory. The insights gained from empirical studies have been synthesized in descriptive theories in ways that dramatize the major differences between the normative postulates of the theory and the behaviors that people exhibit when making decisions among risky alternatives.

Examination of trends across thirty years of empirical research shows an increasing sensitivity to psychological considerations. The regret theories certainly fit this pattern, as does prospect theory with its emphasis on problem representations, reference points, and editing operations designed to simplify information processing. The increasing prominence of information-processing considerations is a theme we shall return to later in this chapter. In fact, the impact of information-processing considerations appears so great that even the proponents of prospect theory and regret theory see their models as approximate, incomplete, and much too simplified descriptions of behavior.

These descriptive considerations have also affected the normative theory. From Bernoulli to Savage, the history of utility theory is one of successive adjustments, incorporating increasing subjectivity into the theory, in order to accommodate observed behavior. The new descriptive theories are likely to leave their mark on normative theory, too, although the nature of that mark remains to be seen. More thought is needed regarding whether the effects of regret, decision weights, reference points, and framing should be treated as errors of judgment or as valid elements of human experience whose appeal remains after thoughtful deliberation. In time, some of the established axioms may lose some of their normative status because of their descriptive shortcomings. What is evident, however, is that the field of risky decision making, so simple, orderly, and "wrapped up" two decades ago, has been shaken into an exciting state of turmoil by recent experimental results.

Although utility theory is obviously an incorrect descriptive model, it continues to play a central role in many important practical problems ranging from counseling individuals on family-planning decisions to guiding government policies (Feather, 1982; Fischhoff, Lichtenstein, Slovic, Derby, & Keeney, 1981). Coombs (1980) observed that "the vitality of [utility] theory in the face of criticism is astounding" (pp. 346–347). One reason for the theory's staying power is that it provides an excellent approximation to many judgments and decisions. Goodman, Saltzman, Edwards, and Krantz (1979) found that even the simple expected-value model accounted for 88 percent of the variance of maximum buying prices for gambles in a study conducted in a Las Vegas casino. Coombs and Huang (1976), using gambles specially constructed to induce violations of the betweenness principle, found that utility theory still accounted for 86 percent of the preference orderings. As Coombs (1980) concluded, "A theory that provides good approximations, even though it is wrong in principle, is going to be used until a more useful theory comes along" (p. 348).

The problem, of course, is that effective personal and social decisions often require more than approximate understanding of behavior. For example, Kunreuther et al. (1978) showed that flood-insurance programs, designed under the assumption that people maximize expected utility when buying insurance, failed because those decisions were actually made on other grounds.

## Single-Attribute Probabilistic Choice Models[3]

Consider a decision situation in which there is no uncertainty about the outcomes; you get what you choose. An intriguing characteristic of choices in such situations is their inconsistency. People do not always make the same choice when faced with the same alternatives under seemingly identical conditions. Inconsistency remains even after controlling for factors such as learning, satiation, or changes in taste over time.

One way of accounting for inconsistency is by postulating a random element in choice, replacing the deterministic notion of preference with a probabilistic one. In modeling such choices, the (absolute) preference of $x$ over $y$ is replaced by the probability of choosing $x$ over $y$, denoted $p(x, y)$. This probability can be estimated from the relative frequency with which $x$ is chosen over $y$. It is commonly viewed as a measure of the degree to which $x$ is preferred over $y$. If an individual strongly prefers $x$ to $y$, one would expect $p(x, y)$ to be close to unity and hence, $p(y, x)$ to be close to zero. If the individual is indifferent between $x$ and $y$, one would expect $p(x, y)$ to be close to one half. The deterministic notion of preference is viewed, in this framework, as a special case where all pairwise choice probabilities are either zero, one, or one half.

Probabilistic decision theories can be divided into two types: constant utility models and random utility models. *Constant utility models* assume that each alternative has a fixed utility value and that the probability of choosing one alternative over another is a function of the distance between their utilities. The decision task is viewed as a discrimination problem in which the individual is trying to determine which alternative would be more satisfying. The greater the distance between the utilities, the easier the discrimination. *Constant utility models* resemble psychophysical theories in which, for example, the probability of judging one object as heavier than another is expressed as a monotonic function of the difference between their weights.

3. The reader is referred to Chapter 1 in Vol. I by Luce and Krumhansl who discuss these issues from a measurement perspective.

Random utility models assume that decision makers always choose the alternative that has the highest utility, but the utilities themselves are random variables rather than constants. The actual choice mechanism, therefore, is purely deterministic, but the utility of each alternative varies from moment to moment.

### Thurstone's Random Utility Model

One of the first to recognize the probabilistic nature of choice behavior was Thurstone (1927):

> An observer is not consistent in his comparative judgments from one occasion to the next. He gives different comparative judgments on successive occasions about the same pair of stimuli. Hence we conclude that the discriminal process corresponding to a given stimulus is not fixed. It fluctuates (p. 271).

To explain these fluctuations, Thurstone introduced the law of comparative judgment. This model represents stimuli as distributions, or random variables, reflecting the momentary fluctuations of their perceived values. The probability of choosing one alternative over another is the probability that the first random variable exceeds the second. Thurstone proposed several alternative sets of assumptions about the form and the interrelations among the stimulus distributions. In the simplest case, called Case V, all the distributions are independent and normal, with equal variance. In this case, the means of the distributions can be easily calculated from the observed choice probabilities. Thurstone used his model to scale preferences among foods, potential birthday gifts, and other riskless options.

### Coombs' Random Utility Model

Coombs (1958) proposed that both the choice alternatives and the decision maker's ideal point could be represented as random variables along a common underlying dimension. As in the Thurstonian model, the distributions are independent of each other and unimodal. Because both the alternatives and the ideal point are random variables, so is the distance between them. The probability of preferring one alternative over another, therefore, equals the probability that the distance between one alternative and the ideal is less than that between the other alternative and the ideal.

Preference for room temperature may illustrate the model. One has an ideal temperature level that fluctuates over time. One's perception of any given temperature also fluctuates randomly. In comparing two temperature conditions, one chooses the temperature that appears closer to the ideal point at the moment of comparison.

Coombs tested his model via its implications for transitivity. The model implies that the kind of transitivity that will be observed depends on the position of the alternatives relative to the ideal point. Strong stochastic transitivity is expected to be satisfied when all three alternatives are on the same side of the ideal. When the ideal point is between the stimulus points, its variability should combine with variability of the stimuli to produce inconsistency and a greater amount of intransitivity. These predictions about transitivity were supported in a study using as stimuli 12 shades of gray varying only in brightness (Coombs, 1958). The subjects, given all possible sets of four stimuli, were asked to choose among them according to how well each represented the notion of an ideal gray. Further support for the model's transitivity predictions was described by Coombs (1964).

Coomb's work is significant because it demonstrates that choice probabilities cannot be converted into differences along a single dimension without considering the relationships between the alternatives and the ideal point. Thus, it points to the importance of option comparability in determining preference.

### Luce's Constant Utility Model

Instead of making assumptions about the form of the value distribution (which are typically hard to justify), Luce (1959) assumed that choice probabilities satisfy one simple but powerful axiom. Despite the different conceptualization of choice embodied in Luce's model and Case V of Thurstone, the two models have been shown to be closely related (e.g., see Block & Marschak, 1960, and the chapter by Luce and Krumhansl in this volume).

Suppose that all choice probabilities are neither zero nor one. Let $T$ be a finite set of alternatives and $R$ be any subset of $T$. Luce's choice axiom asserts that the probability of choosing an element $x$ of $R$, from the entire set $T$, $p(x; T)$, equals the probability that the selected alternative will be in the subset $R$, $p(R; T)$, multiplied by the probability of choosing

$x$ from $R$, $p(x; R)$. That is,

$$p(x; T) = p(x; R)\, p(R; T) \text{ for } R \subset T$$

For example, the probability of selecting roast beef $(x)$ from an entire menu $(T)$ equals the probability of selecting roast beef from the meat entrees $(R)$ times the probability of choosing a meat entree.

Let $p(x, y)$ be the probability of choosing $x$ over $y$. If $p(x, y) = 0$ for some $x, y$ in $T$, it is further assumed that $x$ can be deleted from any choice set containing $y$ without affecting the choice probabilities. Doing this allows one to reduce all choice problems to the imperfect discrimination case where all probabilities differ from zero or one.

Using the choice axiom and the laws of probability theory, Luce derived a number of testable consequences. One is the constant ratio rule

$$\frac{p(x; T)}{p(y; T)} = \frac{p(x; R)}{p(y; R)} = \frac{p(x, y)}{p(y, x)}$$

That is, ratios of the form $p(x; R)/p(y; R)$ are independent of $R$. Thus, the odds of choosing steak rather than roast beef for dinner are the same for all menus containing both entrees.

The probability of choosing any item $x$ from $T$ can be found from the pairwise choice probabilities via the relationship

$$p(x; T) = \frac{1}{\Sigma_y\, [p(y, x)/p(x, y)]}$$

Luce's model implies the existence of a ratio scale of preference. To construct such a scale, select one element, $a$, and set its value at one

$$v(a) = 1$$

Then for any other member, $x$, of the choice set

$$v(x) = \frac{p(x, a)}{p(a, x)} = \frac{p(x; T)}{p(a; T)}$$

Although the choice axiom is directly testable, many observations are needed in order to obtain stable estimates of choice probabilities. Consequently, most studies combine the choices of several individuals in estimating the probabilities. Unfortunately, the model cannot be unambiguously tested with group data, because each individual in the group may satisfy the axiom, yet the average probabilities violate it, or vice versa.

Within the constraints of these methodological difficulties, the choice axiom has been tested in a wide variety of settings ranging from consumer and political choices to studies of learning and psychophysics, with animals as subjects as well as humans. After a comprehensive review of these studies, Luce (1977) reached a conclusion similar to that given above for expected-utility theory. The choice axiom is surely incorrect in many settings, yet it often provides a reasonable approximation. Moreover, the choice axiom embodies, in probabilistic form, an important principle of rational choice put forth by Arrow (1951): Decisions should be independent of irrelevant alternatives. Hence, the axiom often serves as a basis for rational, probabilistic theories of economic and social behavior.

The inadequacies of the choice axiom are most clearly seen in violations of simple scalability (Luce & Suppes, 1965). This property, which holds for all constant utility models, requires the alternatives to be scaled so that each choice probability is expressable as a monotonic function of the scale values of the respective alternatives. Coombs' (1958) data on preferences among shades of gray (discussed above) violate simple scalability. Another violation of this principle comes from Debreu (1960a). Suppose you are offered a choice among three records: a suite by Debussy, denoted $D$, and two different recordings of the same Beethoven symphony, denoted $B_1$ and $B_2$. Assume that the two Beethoven recordings are of equal quality and that you are indifferent between adding a Debussy or a Beethoven to your record collection. Hence

$$p(B_1; B_1, B_2) = p(D; D, B_1)$$
$$= p(D; D, B_2) = 1/2$$

It follows from Luce's model that

$$p(D; D, B_1, B_2) = 1/3$$

Intuitively, however, the basic conflict between Debussy and Beethoven is not likely to be affected by adding another Beethoven recording. Instead, Debreu suggested that $B_1$ and $B_2$ be treated as one alternative to be compared with $D$. Consequently, one would expect $p(D; D, B_1, B_2)$ to be close to .5, whereas $p(B_1; D, B_1, B_2) = p(B_2; D, B_1, B_2)$ will be close to .25, contrary to simple scalability. Empirical support for Debreu's hypothesis was presented by Becker, DeGroot, and Marschak (1963) in a study of choice among gambles. Although offered as a criticism of

Luce's model, Debreu's example applies to any model based on simple scalability.

A minor modification of an example due to L.J. Savage (see Tversky, 1972b) illustrates yet another difficulty encountered by simple scalability. Imagine a person who is indifferent between a trip to Paris and a trip to Rome, So that $p(\text{Paris}, \text{Rome}) = .5$. When the person is offered a new alternative consisting of the trip to Paris plus a \$1 bonus, denoted Paris +, this option will certainly be preferred to the original trip to Paris, so $p(\text{Paris} +, \text{Paris}) = 1$. Simple scalability predicts that $p(\text{Paris} +, \text{Rome}) = 1$, which is counterintuitive. It is unlikely that a relatively small bonus would resolve the conflict so completely. Rather, $p(\text{Paris} +, \text{Rome})$ should remain close to .5. Experimental data (e.g., Tversky & Russo, 1969) support this intuition. Choice probabilities, therefore, reflect not only the utilities of the alternatives in question, but also the difficulty of comparing them. Thus, an extreme choice probability (i.e., close to 0 or 1) can result from either a large discrepancy in value or from an easy comparison, as in the case of the added bonus. The comparability of the alternatives, however, cannot be captured by their scale values; hence simple scalability is violated.

## Multi-Attribute Probabilistic Choice Models

We turn now to decision-making models that consider the more complex situation in which the objects or actions have several aspects, attributes, or dimensions. For the sake of continuity, we begin with *probabilistic choice models*.

### Choice and Similarity

As the preceding example suggests, simple scalability seems particularly unlikely to hold when the choice set contains similar outcomes. As a consequence, choice models may be restricted to sets of dissimilar alternatives or elaborated to incorporate the structure of the choice set. Two theorists, Restle (1961) and Tversky (1972a, 1972b; Tversky & Sattath, 1979) have followed this latter course.

Restle proposed a variation of Luce's theory that assumed choices depend on the elements that differentiate the alternatives, rather than on those common to them. Each alternative is viewed as a set of objects or outcomes, as

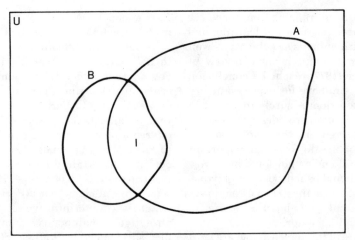

**Figure 10.10.** Value sets in choice between A and B. From *Psychology of Judgment and Choice: A Theoretical Essay* by F. Restle, 1961. New York: Wiley. Copyright 1971 by John Wiley & Sons, Inc. Reprinted by permission of John Wiley & Sons, Inc.

schematized in Figure 10.10. The set actually contributing to the choice of $A$ is the set difference, $A \cup \bar{B}$, denoted $A-B$. The set contributing to the choice of $B$ is $B-A$. The intersection of $A$ and $B$, marked $I$, is assumed not to affect the response probabilities. In Restle's theory,

$$P(A, B) = \frac{V(A-B)}{V[(A-B) \cup (B-A)]}$$

where $V$ is a value measure across all the elements of the set. If the sets $A$ and $B$ have no overlap, then Restle's and Luce's theories make equivalent predictions about choice probabilities.

Rumelhart and Greeno (1971) compared the Luce and Restle models. Their stimuli were nine famous people of the era, including three political leaders, three athletes, and three film stars. Subjects were presented with pairs of these people and were asked to choose the one with whom they would prefer to spend an hour. It was assumed that there were important overlaps or similarities within but not across categories. The Restle model, with parameters that took similarity into account, predicted the choices between similar pairs much better than did the Luce model.

### Elimination by Aspects

Tversky (1972a, 1972b) developed a context-dependent probabilistic model that generalized both the Luce and Restle theories. Tversky's model, called elimination by aspects (EBA), views each alternative as a collection of measurable (i.e.,

scalable) aspects and describes choice as a covert process of successive elimination. At each stage in the process, one selects an aspect of the available alternatives with probability proportional to its value. Any alternative that does not include the chosen aspect is eliminated and the process continues until a single alternative remains. Consider, for example, the choice of a restaurant for dinner. The first aspect selected may be seafood, thus eliminating all restaurants that do not serve seafood. Another aspect, say a price range, is then selected and alternatives failing to meet this criterion are eliminated. The process continues until only one restaurant, which includes all the selected aspects, remains.

Formally, the EBA model is represented by a recursive formula, which expresses the probability of choosing option $x$ from set $A$ as a weighted sum of the probabilities of choosing $x$ from proper subsets of $A$. For binary choices, EBA coincides with Restle's model (and hence with Luce's if the aspects for each alternative are disjoint). EBA predicts violations of simple scalability for overlapping alternatives and makes sensible predictions for the choice problems posed by Debreu and Savage. Moreover, it has several testable consequences that considerably constrain the observed choice probabilities and permit a measurement-free test of the model.

The EBA model is an appealing way to make decisions because it is easy to apply and is easy to explain and justify to others. There is no guarantee, however, that the model will lead to normatively defensible decisions. That is, the EBA process cannot ensure that the alternatives retained are superior to those that are eliminated.

### Preference Trees

The EBA model imposes no restrictions on the structure of the choice aspects. As a result, for a choice set of $n$ alternatives, a large number of scale values ($2^n - 2$, corresponding to the number of proper subsets of the total set) are required to fit the model. Thus, the model cannot be estimated from binary choice probabilities because the number of parameters exceeds the number of data points. Tversky and Sattath (1979) simplified the EBA model by imposing structure on the set of aspects in a way that reduced the number of parameters to $2n - 2$. They represented choice alternatives by a tree-like graph in which each terminal node is associated with a single alternative and each link between nodes is associated with the set of aspects that are shared by all the alternatives that include or follow from that link and are not shared by any of the alternatives that do not include that link. The length of each link in the tree represents the value measure of the respective set of aspects. Hence, the set of all aspects that belong to a given alternative is represented by the path from the root of the tree to the terminal node represented by the alternative and the length of the path represents the overall measure of the alternative.

Figure 10.11 illustrates a tree representation of a menu. The set of alternatives consists of five entrees, which appear as the terminal nodes of the tree. Thus, the link labelled $\lambda$ represents the aspects shared by all meat entrees but not by fish, $\theta$ represents the aspects shared by steak and roast beef but not by lamb or fish, and $\gamma$ represents the unique aspects of lamb. The suggested labels of the clusters (defined by the links) are displayed horizontally. When choices are represented in this way, elimination by aspects reduces to elimination by tree (EBT). That is, one selects a link from the tree (with probability proportional to its length) and then eliminates all alternatives that do not include the selected link. This process is then applied to the selected branch until only one alternative remains. Tree models have provided excellent representations for a wide variety of data, including choices among the nine celebrities studied by Rumelhart and Greeno (1971) and preferences among political parties and among academic disciplines collected by Sjöberg (1977).

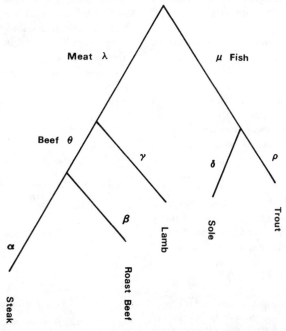

**Figure 10.11.** Tree representation of the choice among entrees. From "Preference Trees" by A. Tversky and S. Sattath, 1979, *Psychological Review, 86,* p. 545. Copyright 1979 by the American Psychological Association. Reprinted by permission of the author.

### Probabilistic Theories of Choice: An Assessment

The development of probabilistic theories of choice shows some remarkable parallels with the development of risky decision models. Both lines of research show a progression from simple conceptions to more complex psychological models. Early models, such as SEU and the constant ratio rule, ignored framing or contextual manipulations; later models, such as prospect theory and preference trees, did not. The introduction of psychological complications such as reference points and regret into theories of decision making under risk are paralleled by the introduction of comparability and similarity parameters in theories of riskless choice. Nonetheless, even the most elaborate descriptive theories in each domain are viewed by their creators as useful approximations, but incomplete and not fully adequate.

## Multi-Attribute Value Models

There are several models for preference among multi-attribute objects that entirely disregard both uncertainty about the state of the world and uncertainty about one's preferences. Following Keeny and Raiffa (1976), we call these risk-less algebraic utility models *value* models, saving the term *utility* for the risky models.[4] In these models, all objects are assumed to be described by a common set of dimensions or attributes.

### Axiomatized Models

The axioms for these models, like the axioms for Expected Utility Theory, specify the conditions under which a value function exists and point to the measurement procedures by which the value functions may be found.

#### WEAK ORDER

The simplest model, with the fewest assumptions, leads to a value function that is only ordinally scaled. The key axiom for this *weak order model* (Krantz et al., 1971) is transitivity. The model states that

$$A \succsim B \text{ iff } v(A) \geq v(B)$$

4. This distinction is not often made. The acronym MAUT (for multiattribute utility theory) is often used to describe the models discussed here. Unfortunately, it is also sometimes used to describe the risky multiattribute models covered in the next section.

where $v$ is an ordinal function. One measurement procedure for implementing this model is ranking, with the ranks constituting the value function. A second method is indifference curve construction, which places the objects in an $n$-dimensional indifference map (where $n$ is the number of attributes that describe each object). Figure 10.12 shows a prototypical indifference map for two unspecified attributes, 1 and 2. Each object is represented by a point in the space. Indifference curves connect points that are equal in value. Every point above and to the right of a given indifference curve is preferred to any point on the curve, whereas any point to the left and below the indifference curve has less value. Although indifference maps can, in theory, be derived for objects with more than two attributes, the judgments become so difficult that the procedure is rarely undertaken. Consider, for example, filling in the blank in dinner $B$, shown in Table 10.4, so that you are indifferent between dinner $A$ and dinner $B$.

#### STRONGER MODELS

In order to facilitate measurement, additional assumptions are made, creating stronger models. Some additional axioms ensure interval scaling for the overall value; others, called *decomposition models*, yield interval scales of value for each of the attributes and a rule for combining the separate values into an overall value for each object (von Winterfeldt, 1975; von Winterfeldt & Edwards, 1986).

One of the strongest value models is the

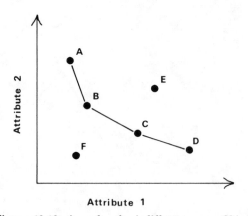

**Figure 10.12.** A weak-order indifference map. Objects $A$, $B$, $C$, and $D$ are equal in utility. $E$ is better than all of them, and $F$ is worse.

Table 10.4. An exemplar indifference task: Choose a desert for dinner $B$ that makes you indifferent between dinners $A$ and $B$

|  | Dinner $A$ | Dinner $B$ |
|---|---|---|
| Soup | Chicken Gumbo | Cream of Asparagus |
| Salad | Tossed Greens | Spinach |
| Entree | Steak | Lobster |
| Vegetable | Baked Potato | Rice Pilaf |
| Dessert | Chocolate Cake | ? |

additive conjoint model

$$A \gtrsim B \text{ iff}$$

$$v(A) \geqslant v(B) \text{ where}$$

$$v(A) = \sum_{i=1}^{n} v_i(A_i)$$

That is, under the axioms (not given here; see Debreu, 1960b and Keeney & Raiffa, 1976), the desirability of an object is determined by the sum of the values of its attributes. One of the strong assumptions made by this model is that the attributes are *pairwise preferentially independent*, which means that the tradeoff between any two attributes does not depend on the levels of any other attribute.

In order to find the value functions, $v_i$, the decision maker must make several direct tradeoffs between every pair of attributes. These tradeoff questions are called *dual standard sequences*. For example:

Holding constant all other attributes, suppose an apartment has a rent of $420 and distance to work of 5 miles. How many more miles would you be willing to drive to work if the rent decreased to $400?

The test for pairwise preferential independence requires several more such trade-offs as the levels of all the other attributes are systematically varied.

### Non-axiomatized Value Models

Axiomatized value models have no error component. People are assumed to have stable preferences they can reliably report. However, for complex problems, common sense (as well as much of the research reviewed elsewhere in this chapter) suggests that the axiomatically justified measurement techniques may generate enough cognitive strain to cause serious errors. Thus, several authors (e.g., von Winterfeldt, 1975) have argued that more accurate representations of people's preferences may be obtained with very simple assessment procedures even if these procedures lack axiomatic justification.

### SMART

One such simplified multiattribute value model, proposed by Edwards (1977), is called SMART (**S**imple **M**ultiattribute **R**ating **T**echnique). Edwards defended SMART by arguing

... While it lacks ... theoretical elegance ..., it has the great advantage of being easily taught to and used by a busy decision maker ....

Moreover, it requires no judgments of preference or indifference among hypothetical entities. My experience with elicitation procedures suggests that such hypothetical judgments are unreliable and unrepresentative of real preferences; worse, they bore untutored decision makers into either rejection of the whole process or acceptance of answers suggested by the sequence of questions rather than answers that reflect their real values. (p. 327)

SMART reduces the elicitation procedure to ten relatively easy steps, the most significant of which follow:

1. Rate the attributes by assigning the number 10 to the least important attribute and assigning numbers to the others that preserve the ratio of importance to the least important (and, as a check, preserve the ratios of all pairs of attributes).
2. Normalize these importance weights by dividing each by the sum of the weights. Call these normalized weights $w_j$.
3. Rate the value of each object, $i$, on each attribute, $j$, using a scale from 0 to 100, with 0 defined as the worst plausible value and 100 defined as the best plausible value. Call these ratings $v_{ij}$.
4. Calculate $V_i = \sum_j w_j v_{ij}$ for each object.
5. Choose the object with the largest $V_i$.

With this model, the resultant values are scaled in a common range and the weights reflect the relative importance of the attribute dimensions. In contrast, axiomatically-based value models either (1) do not elicit weights directly because the tradeoffs across attribute dimensions emerge from the value scaling procedures (as with dual standard sequences for the additive conjoint model) or (2) have indirectly assessed weights that are uninterpreted (as with the multiplicative model not described here: see Keeney & Raiffa, 1976; von Winterfeldt & Edwards, 1986).

## SOCIAL JUDGMENT THEORY

Social judgment theory is a set of techniques, based on the previously described lens model, designed to aid societal decision making (see Hammond & Adelman, 1976; Hammond, Rohrbaugh, Mumpower, & Adelman, 1977; and Hammond, Stewart, Brehmer, & Steinmann, 1975). Unlike decision theories, social judgment theory does not prescribe a course of action. Instead, it is used to externalize decision makers' implicit policies (i.e., their preferences and beliefs). In applications of the theory, the judgments of another person or another social group replace the criterion on the other side of the lens. Thus, the technique is useful for locating sources of conflict. The art of the social judgment theorist lies in designing stimulus profiles that appropriately represent the configurations of possible alternatives. An armamentarium of on-line computer programs enables decision makers to respond to stimulus profiles designed by the analysts and to receive feedback about the weights and the functional relationships implied by their judgments.

The application of social judgment theory is illustrated by a study designed to help the Denver Police Department select the best bullet to use (Hammond, Stewart, Adelman, & Wascoe, 1975). The analysts asked ballistics experts to rate available bullets on the dimensions deemed important by the decision makers: stopping power, injury potential, and danger to bystanders. The analysts then asked the decision makers for holistic judgments of preference for bullet profiles drawn from the experts' ratings. Correlational analyses based on the lens model were used to infer the importance weights for each of the attribute dimensions. The analysis revealed a bullet that had greater stopping power (which the police wanted) yet no greater potential for injury and less danger to bystanders than the bullet the police were then using. This bullet was subsequently adopted for use. Social judgment theory has also been used to facilitate public input into regional planning, to structure faculty participation in university policy decisions, and to reduce conflict in labor-management negotiations (Hammond et al., 1977).

## Validating Value Models

In a sense, the results from axiomatized value models are automatically valid. If you accept the axioms and are satisfied with your judgments, then the resulting evaluations follow logically, as reflections of your values. Furthermore, the consistency checks (e.g., transitivity) built into some of the elicitation procedures allow you to identify and correct errors. But you may not be fully satisfied with your judgments. How good, then, is the model based on them? In the realm of values, there is no public right answer against which to compare a model's output. Nonaxiomatic models face the same problem, without the partial reassurance of asking normatively justified questions.

The validity of the lens model that underlies social judgment theory has been tested in settings in which some criterion exists. Linear additive models derived from subjects' responses typically predict the criterion values better than do the judgments on which the models were based (Goldberg, 1970). Dawes (1971) called this effect "bootstrapping." Such models are particularly effective when there is error in the judgments and when the attributes are positively intercorrelated. Indeed, Dawes and Corrigan (1974) and Wainer (1976) have shown that in such situations even equal-weight models predict the criterion well. Equal-weight models disregard all aspects of judgment except the judgment of whether the criterion tends to increase or decrease with an increase in each attribute. Given this judgment of sign, the equal-weight model is a simple summation of the standardized attribute values.

The predictive accuracy of linear additive models depends in part upon the options or items in the judgment set. The condition of positive intercorrelations among attributes is most likely to be met across a large heterogeneous set of options (e.g., better-furnished apartments are usually found in nicer neighborhoods). Thus, the model will do a good job of ordering such options. However, it will be less helpful in identifying the best option from the subset of top contenders. The set of serious contenders is the subset of options that lie on the *Pareto Frontier*. This is the subset of options that are not dominated by some other option. An option is dominated if at least one other option is at least as good as it on all attribute dimensions. By definition, the options on the Pareto Frontier are better than one another in some respects and worse in others, so the attributes are negatively correlated across the subset (even if they are highly correlated across the entire domain). Such negative correlations weaken the predictive power of linear additive models (Stillwell, Seaver, & Edwards, 1981).

Validation of both axiomatized and nonaxiomatized value models has also been attempted in situations in which no criterion value is known. Of the several approaches to validation, the most unsatisfactory is to compare the output of a decomposition model with unmodeled holistic value judgments (e.g., Fischer, 1977; Huber, Daneshgar, & Ford, 1971). High correlations may mask important deviations from the model or reflect the use of a very heterogeneous set of options for which all plausible procedures will produce similar orderings of the options. Furthermore, whenever people have difficulty integrating many items of information, holistic judgments are an error-prone, flawed criterion. Thus, methods yielding low correlations with holistic evaluations may be preferable to those that correlate highly with them.

A more sophisticated procedure is *convergent validation*, used by Fischer (1975) in comparing two holistic methods and two methods based on additive value models in preference judgments for compact cars described by three or nine attributes. The overall values produced by the two additive value models were in greater agreement than were those for the two holistic methods. Eckenrode (1965), using experts as subjects, showed high convergent validity across six weight estimation procedures.

Short of entirely rejecting holistic judgments, some researchers have argued that a small number of paired-comparison, holistic choices might be a relatively trustworthy expression of people's values. Thus, Schoemaker and Waid (1982) used 20 such binary choices as a criterion for evaluating 14 different value models. The task involved judging the suitability for college admission of high school graduates described on four attributes. The predictive accuracy of the different models did not vary much, except that linear value functions performed better than nonlinear functions and unit weighting did poorly. MacCrimmon and Siu (1974) had subjects generate two indifference curves, one using paired-comparison choices and the other based on equivalence judgments like the following:

... The current [fiscal] policy [of an unspecified country] leads to an inflation rate of 8 percent and an unemployment rate of 8 percent. At what new inflation rate, paired with a new unemployment rate of 6 percent, would you feel indifferent toward the new policy and the one currently in effect (p. 683)?

The resultant curves were never identical, although in some cases they were very close. After both curves were elicited, a computer generated one critical pair of stimuli that would lead to different choices under the two indifference curves. In all cases, the choice made for the critical pair was consistent with the tradeoff curve generated by the paired-comparison choices.

One way of circumventing the privateness of people's values is by teaching subjects artificially designed real values. These values can then be compared with those derived from different assessment methods. Using the multiple-cue probability learning paradigm, John and Edwards (1978) taught their subjects the worth of diamonds described by four attributes (cut, color, clarity, and carat). They found that the values derived from several weight-estimation methods closely matched the true values and that most subjects' weights provided a great improvement over equal weights. Whether these results can be generalized to situations in which values are private depends, in part, upon how explicit instruction affects values. Stillwell, Barron, and Edwards (1983) asked experienced bankers to use several different decomposition methods for evaluating the acceptability of loan applications. Several of the methods produced evaluations similar to those produced by the bankers' usual computational procedure.

Dawes (1977) noted the success of simple models in prediction situations and the difficulty people experience in performing complicated mental computations. He proposed that these constitute theoretical grounds for trusting values produced by decomposition procedures more than values produced by holistic judgment. Assuming that people can think clearly about what attributes should be important to them and how well each option rates on each attribute, then the model can hardly help but produce better summaries than the individuals themselves.

## Riskless Value Models: An Assessment

Much of the interest in value models has centered around applications. Keeney and Raiffa (1976) wanted to help decision makers who were willing to spend the time and energy to think through their complex problems thoroughly. Edwards (1977) wanted an easy decision-making tool that could be widely used. Hammond and his colleagues focused on methods for resolving policy conflicts. Therefore, the literature has emphasized the development of decision aids rather than the descriptive adequacy of the models. Indeed, the justification for decision aids is that people do not usually make good decisions.

The strength of riskless value models rests on their ability to capture simpler component values and combine them to identify the overall evaluations that people would have if they had unlimited, errorless computational capacity and time for rumination. But what if people do not have consistent values or do not have any directly relevant values at all until asked? Then the method of asking may shape or create the values. A further concern is that the elicitation methods prescribed by the models are vulnerable to the potential sources of bias identified in the psychophysical literature, such as anchoring, recency, range, and other contextual effects (Poulton, 1982).

## Multiattribute Utility Models

Risky utility theories will now be examined in their multiattribute forms. Either the von Neumann-Morgenstern or the Savage formulation can be expanded to treat multiattribute risky situations. Two general approaches may be taken (von Winterfeldt, 1975). Under the first, one starts with a riskless value model, $v(a) = f[v_i(a_i)]$, where $i$ indexes the $n$ attributes of an object, $a$. Then a function $h$ is constructed that transforms the overall value function, $v$, into a risky utility function, $u$:

$$u(a) = h[v(a)]$$

The methods used to measure $v(a)$ depend upon the particular value model used, but the stimuli presented to the assessor will always be riskless. For example, one might use dual standard sequences ("How many more miles would you be willing to drive to work for a rent decrease of . . ?"). Only in the final step, that of transforming the overall value function into an overall

utility function, is uncertainty introduced. The transformation function $h$, is found by using standard gambles—that is, finding indifference between a sure thing, $w$, and a gamble $(x, p, y)$, where the outcomes $w$, $x$, and $y$ are all multi-attributed objects.

The second general approach is to assess the utilities directly, bypassing value functions (Keeney & Raiffa, 1976). A variety of models are available, each specifying a different combination rule by which the utilities of the attributes, $u_i(a_i)$, are combined into an overall utility for the object, $u(a)$. Here all the elicitation procedures involve gambles.

Among multiattribute utility models, the stronger the assumptions, the simpler the elicitation methods. Attributes are *mutually utility independent* if preference orderings over two gambles that vary in one or more attributes but are constant for the remaining attributes do not change as a function of the particular levels of the attributes held constant. For example, consider possible job offers varying in salary, location, and commuting time. Suppose you would prefer a sure job paying $25,000 in San Francisco with a 10-minute commuting time ($25,000, S.F., 10) to a 50/50 gamble yielding either ($15,000, S.F., 10) or ($35,000, S.F., 10). To satisfy utility independence of the attribute salary, you should also prefer a sure job of ($25,000, Denver, 60) over a 50/50 chance of either ($15,000, Denver, 60) or ($35,000, Denver, 60). Mutual utility independence requires this sort of consistency for each attribute and all subsets of attributes.

If mutual utility independence holds, then either the additive or the multiplicative model is satisfied. In the multiplicative model, the overall utility is the weighted sum of all the single attribute utilities and all possible cross-products of attribute utilities. A bit of algebra simplifies this to the following form:

$$1 + ku(a) = \prod_{i=1}^{n} [1 + kk_i u_i(a_i)]$$

The overall utility and all the attribute utilities are scales from 0 (the worst level) to 1 (the best level). The $k_i$ and $k$ are scaling parameters; the $k_i$ cannot be interpreted as importance weights because they depend on the relative ranges of the attributes. Thus, for example, if all job offers had approximately the same salary, $k_i$ for salary would be small, even if money is very important to the decision maker. The other parameter, $k$, is a measure of multiattribute risk aversion (when $k < 1$) or risk proneness (when $k > 1$). It is a function of the other scaling parameters, $k_i$, and need not be assessed directly.

The additive model

$$u(a) = \sum_{i=1}^{n} k_i u_i(a_i)$$

is a special case of the multiplicative model and requires an additional assumption called *additive independence:* Attributes are additive independent if preferences over gambles depend only on the marginal probability distributions of the attributes and not on their joint probability distribution. One test for additive independence is that the $k_i$ sum to 1. Another test is that you should be indifferent between two gambles, one of which offers a 50/50 chance of getting either (1) the best object or (2) the worst object and the other of which offers a 50/50 chance of getting either (3) an object for which some attributes are at their best level and the rest are at their worst level or (4) an object for which those attributes that were at their best level in (3) are here at their worst level and vice versa. For example, (1) might be your favorite phonograph record and $10; (2) your least favorite record and $.10; (3) your favorite record and $.10; (4) your least favorite record and $10.

For either the multiplicative or the additive model, each single-attribute utility function can be elicited using standard gambles, holding constant (at any convenient level) the levels of all but one attribute. The scaling parameters, $k_i$, may be found by eliciting, for each attribute in turn, a probability, $p_i$, that makes you indifferent between receiving the object having the best level of attribute $i$ and the worst level of all other attributes versus a gamble that pays the best object with probability $p_i$ and the worst object with probability $(1 - p_i)$. Then $p_i = k_i$. When the so-called "corner" objects, all of whose attribute levels are either the worst or the best, seem unrealistic, other, more lengthy, elicitation techniques may be used.

Fischer (1977) devised a cover story to facilitate use of the standard gamble techniques. The stimuli were multiattribute job descriptions. Subjects identified the worst job, $J_*$, and the best job, $J^*$. They were told to imagine that they had been firmly offered $J_*$ and that they might also be offered $J^*$ some time from now. For each intermediate job, $J'$, they were to imagine that they had just received a job offer, which they must accept or reject immediately:

> Clearly your decision in this matter will depend upon how likely you think you are to receive the $J^*$ offer. Your task . . . is to specify for each offer $J'$ a probability $p$ of receiving the $J^*$ offer such that you would be indifferent between accepting or rejecting the $J'$ offer (p. 308).

These multiattribute risky models are intended for practical application. However, they are so complicated that they require an extended interaction between the decision maker and an analyst. The decision maker should be an expert in the problem area; the analyst, an expert in the methodology. Keeney (1977) has published his elicitation of an energy expert's utility model and functions over 11 attributes, including deaths, pollution, nuclear safeguards, and electricity generated. The model was designed for evaluating energy policies differing in type of fuel (fossil or nuclear) and degree of conservation. The dialogue between Keeney and the energy expert shows the intense cognitive effort required of both individuals.

## INFORMATION PROCESSING IN DECISION MAKING

The experimental study of decision making has paralleled the emergence of the field of cognitive psychology. This field, with its emphasis on internal processes, mental limitations, and the way in which the processing of information is shaped by these limitations, has come to have a profound influence on decision theory and research. Examples of this influence include prospect theory, with its emphasis on the decision frame, and the EBA model, which is essentially a strategy for reducing the strain of choosing among many complex alternatives.

This section examines the information-processing approach to decision making. Although we shall continue to distinguish between risky and riskless choice studies, this distinction is less relevant than in the theories of choice described earlier. The information-processing paradigm represents alternatives as multidimensional stimuli, with outcome probability as just another, albeit somewhat special, dimension. Many of the same cognitive processes can be observed in both risky and riskless settings.

## Confronting Human Limitations: Bounded Rationality

The traditional view of human beings' higher mental processes assumes that we are, in Shakespeare's words, "noble in reason, infinite in faculties." A twentieth century expression of this esteem was provided by a well-known economist who asserted, "we are so built that what seems reasonable to us is likely to be confirmed by experience or we could not live in the world at all" (Knight, 1921, p. 227).

Research in cognitive psychology has painted a much more modest picture of human capabilities. In his influential study of classification and coding, Miller (1956) demonstrated the limitations of people's ability to attend to and process sensory signals. About the same time, Bruner, Goodnow, and Austin (1956) concluded that subjects in their concept formation tasks were experiencing a condition of cognitive strain, which they attempted to reduce by simplification strategies.

In the study of decision making, too, the classic view of behavioral adequacy was being challenged on psychological grounds. A leading critic of utility maximization was Simon (1959), who observed:

> The classical theory is a theory of a man choosing among fixed and known alternatives, to each of which is attached known consequences. But when perception and cognition intervene between the decision-maker and his objective environment, this model no longer proves adequate. We need a description of the choice process that recognizes that alternatives are not given but must be sought; and a description that takes into account the arduous task of determining what consequences will follow on each alternative (p. 272).

As an alternative to the maximization hypothesis, Simon introduced the notion of *bounded rationality*, which asserts that cognitive limitations force decision makers to construct simplified models of their problems. Simon argued that the decision maker behaves rationally with respect to this simplified model. To predict decisions, we must understand how this simpli-

fied model is constructed through processes of perception, thinking, and learning.

According to Simon, the key to simplification was the replacement of the maximization goal by the *satisficing* principle: outcomes are first classified as satisfactory or unsatisfactory with respect to each of the relevant attributes; the first alternative that satisfies this level of aspiration for every attribute is selected. In evaluating investment plans, for example, one may select the first plan that provides satisfactory profit as well as adequate security. What is considered to be a satisfactory profit may change with time and experience as one's aspiration level increases or decreases.

Satisficing is simpler than utility maximization in several important respects. It bypasses the problems of evaluating the overall utility of each outcome or of comparing diverse attributes. It does not call for detailed exploration of all the available alternatives and it requires only limited computational capacity.

Like other models of decision making, bounded rationality has predictive power only if its primitives can be specified. That is, one must be able to tell, independently of people's choices, what attributes they consider and what their levels of aspiration are on each. Information-processing studies have been used to provide such evidence (see, e.g., Payne et al., 1980).

## Methods for Studying Information Processing

There are three major categories of experimental methods used to provide insight into decision processes: (1) inference from stimulus/response studies, (2) algebraic modeling of holistic judgments, and (3) process-tracing methods.

### Inference Studies

Inferences about mental strategies can often be derived from responses made to specifically constructed stimuli. Shaklee and Tucker's (1980) investigation of the strategies used in assessing degree of relatedness follows this pattern as does the use of duplex gambles to determine the relative attention paid to surface characteristics and underlying probability distributions (Payne & Braunstein, 1971; Slovic & Lichtenstein, 1968a). Another example of this approach is a study by Huber (1983), who constructed pairs of alternatives, $x$ and $y$, such that the application of one choice rule led to selection of $x$, the application of a second rule led to selection of $y$, and use of any other rule (from a set of five possibilities) led to no decision. Choices among a set of such pairs ordered the rules in terms of popularity.

### Algebraic Models

The lens model, previously discussed, is one of several algebraic models used to study how decision makers weigh and combine information from multiple sources (Slovic & Lichtenstein, 1971). The multiple regression analysis used in the lens model produces an equation

$$\hat{Y} = \sum_{i=1}^{n} b_i X_i$$

where $\hat{Y}$ is the predicted judgment and the $b_i$ are interpreted as the weights given to the cue dimensions, $X_i$. The equation can be expanded by adding exponential terms to model nonlinear use of the cues, or cross-product terms to model nonadditive combination rules (Einhorn, 1970).

Evidence about information processing has been obtained by studying changes in lens model measures as the task or stimulus set is changed. For example, Hoffman (1968) reported data showing that the relative weights of two cues changed as a function of cue consistency. For stimulus sets in which the two cues tended to have similar values (the cues were congruent in their implications for the criterion value), the judges weighted the two cues approximately equally. However, in repsonse to stimulus sets in which the cues were incongruent, judges weighed one cue more heavily than the other.

Whereas the lens model assumes that the decision maker operates on the cue dimensions as given, Anderson (1970, 1974, 1981) has developed methods for simultaneously scaling the subjective stimulus values and determining the weighting parameters. The resulting models are used to test theories about the information integration rules used by subjects. Particular attention has been given to tasks in which a simple algebraic model, involving adding, averaging, subtracting, or multiplying the informational inputs, serves as the substantive theory of judgment that is being tested.

Anderson's approach, called *information integration theory*, uses stimuli created by factorial combinations of information dimensions. The subjects' holistic judgments are analyzed with an analysis-of-variance model. The model incorporates both a theory (the form of the model) and a goodness-of-fit test for the data. An invalid response scale could cause a valid model to fail the test of fit. Therefore, Anderson's approach performs a monotone rescaling of the response variable. Failure to find any rescaling that will make the data fit some version of the basic model argues against the model, and success argues for it. Once the model and response scale are established, the subjective values of the stimuli can be derived. Anderson uses the term *functional measurement* to describe this interplay between theory and scaling.

Another method that assumes the form of a model and then attempts to fit data to it is *conjoint measurement* (Debreu, 1960b; Krantz & Tversky, 1971; Luce & Tukey, 1964; Tversky, 1967b). Here, the ordinal properties of the judgments are used to test proposed rules for integrating items of information. The simple algebraic theories tested by functional measurement and conjoint measurement methods have been found to provide excellent fits to data in such diverse domains as social cognition, developmental psychology, psychophysics, and linguistics, as well as decision making.

Despite their successes, these algebraic modeling techniques have serious limitations. First, they require many judgments. Judges facing a long, perhaps boring, task may resort to simplifying strategies that do not represent their usual ways of thinking (Slovic, Lichtenstein & Edwards, 1965). In order to mitigate this problem, Barron and Person (1979) have proposed a method (called HOPE), based on a highly fractionated orthogonal design, that requires many fewer judgments.

Additional problems arise from the deficiencies of representative and orthogonal designs. Orthogonal designs may include stimulus profiles that are so peculiar and so unlikely to occur that the judge cannot reasonably evaluate them. In representative designs, the stimulus dimensions are typically intercorrelated. As a result, the derived weights are nonunique and difficult, if not impossible, to interpret (Darlington, 1968).

Finally, an algebraic model's ability to model a set of responses is no guarantee that it captures the psychological processes that produced those responses. As Hoffman (1960, 1968) noted, two or more models may be algebraically different yet equally predictive, given fallible data.

Furthermore, two or more models may be algebraically equivalent yet suggest radically different processes. Drawing an analogy to problems of classification in mineralogy, Hoffman introduced the term *paramorphic representation* to remind researchers that "the mathematical description of judgment is inevitably incomplete . . .and it is not known how completely or how accurately the underlying process has been represented" (1960, p. 125).

Lopes (1982b) recognized the need to go beyond mathematical equations to understand the fine structure of the cognitive mechanisms involved when people produce averages, products, or other algebraic forms. Noting that judges are typically not conscious of these computations or of the equations they represent, she asked: "What psychological processes give rise to this algebra-less algebra?" (p. 1). To answer this question, she proposed a procedural theory in which judgments are produced by a serial process whereby an initial quantity or anchor is adjusted one or more times in accordance with other available information. Lopes argued that this process can plausibly account for a wide variety of judgments that have been modeled by algebraic functions. A thorough test of Lopes' theory requires use of special experimental methods, such as those that we describe next.

### Process-tracing Methods

In contrast to methods that make inferences about unseen processes intervening between stimulus and response, process-tracing techniques (Raaij, 1983; Svenson, 1979) attempt to make these processing strategies directly observable. There are three main process-tracing methods: verbal protocols, information monitoring, and eye-movement analysis. Response time analysis has also been used, but to a lesser extent.

Verbal protocols require subjects to think aloud as they perform their decision tasks. This approach differs from the introspective methods employed in the early days of experimental psychology (Titchener, 1910). Introspection used retrospective reports by highly trained subjects, whereas verbal protocols attempt to capture thoughts as they occur, using subjects who are relatively naive about the researcher's theories. For example, subjects might be instructed to report what information they consider as they examine an alternative, to describe each thought

they have about it, and to verbalize the reasoning that leads them from observation to decision. Typically, the protocol is partitioned into short phrases corresponding to single cognitive operations. These are then coded and analyzed to test or design process models (Newell & Simon, 1972).

Several concerns have been raised regarding the validity of verbal protocols. One is that subjects cannot report accurately on their own mental processes. Nisbett and Wilson (1977) reviewed the literature and concluded that subjects tend to describe what they believe their mental states should have been, not what they actually were. A second concern is that the act of reporting and the instructions regarding what to report may distort the processes (Flaherty, 1975; Lichtenstein, 1982; Posner, 1982). In addition, people may not be able to articulate all their internal states (Lindsay & Norman, 1972). In fact, some hold that this is a hallmark of substantive expertise (Polanyi, 1958). Ericsson and Simon (1980) have rebutted many of these criticisms, noting, in particular, that many of Nisbett and Wilson's observations pertained to retrospective rather than concurrent protocols. In defending verbal protocols, Hayes (1982) concluded:

> Analysing a protocol is like following the tracks of a porpoise. Occasionally, the porpoise reveals itself by breaking the surface of the sea. Its brief surfacings are like glimpses which the protocol affords us of underlying mental process. Between surfacings, the mental process, like the porpoise, runs deep and silent. Our task is to infer the course of the process from these brief traces (p. 77).

An eye-movement protocol records where the subjects fix their gaze as they perform a decision task (Russo & Rosen, 1975; Russo & Dosher, 1983). The sequence of fixations produces a detailed trace that may be harder for subjects to censor and better suited for rapid processes than are verbal protocols. On the negative side, the measurement apparatus is quite obtrusive and often restricts the stimuli to simplistic displays. To obtain an accurate record, the subject's head must be immobilized and the items widely separated. In addition, eye fixations reflect information-seeking responses and, hence, cannot reveal all details of internal processing.

For both verbal protocols and eye-movement protocols, data collection is time consuming, producing masses of data requiring detailed analysis. Information-monitoring methods restrict the data to a simpler type, suitable for testing hypotheses regarding information search (Jacoby, 1975, 1977; Payne, 1976). The typical study presents information on a display board, a matrix array with alternatives as rows and attributes as columns. Information is available in each cell of the matrix, giving the value for the particular attribute and alternative. Subjects choose an option after selecting as much information as desired. The sequence of selections can reveal, for example, whether people first examine the value of all alternatives on a given attribute (as might be predicted by the EBA model) or try to get a fuller picture of individual alternatives. The disadvantages of this method are its obtrusiveness, its inability to provide insight regarding the use of information stored in memory, and its lack of informativeness regarding how acquired information is processed.

Results from any of these process-tracing methods can be represented in terms of a *flow diagram* (e.g., Newell, 1980) or *decision net* (Bettman, 1979). An early example was produced by Clarkson (1962), who attempted to simulate a trust investment officer's portfolio selection process (see Figure 10.13). To evaluate his model, Clarkson fed the relevant information about various stocks into a computer model analogous to the net. The model matched 24 of the officer's 29 stock selections. Decision nets have been used to model medical and psychiatric diagnoses (Kleinmuntz, 1963), accounting decisions (Bouwman, 1982), and consumer product choices (Bettman, 1979). Bettman (1979) described a variety of methods for analyzing and characterizing the structure, reliability, and efficiency of these nets.

### Integration of Methods

Advocates of process tracing have expressed serious reservations about the ability of algebraic models to represent mental operations. For example, Simon (1976) stated that:

> The variance analysis paradigm. . .is largely useless for discovering and testing process models to explain what goes on between the appearance of stimulus and performance of response (p. 261).

Einhorn, Kleinmuntz, and Kleinmuntz (1979) defended the algebraic models by arguing, theoretically and empirically, that both process tracing and algebraic methods can provide valid descriptions of the same processes, although at different levels of detail. Further, they advocated employing the two techniques together in a multimethod approach to take advantage of their complementary strengths and offset their respective weaknesses. A similar recommendation was been put forth by Payne, Braunstein, and Carroll (1978). The procedural theory of judgment proposed by Lopes (1982b) provides a nice illustration of how process tracing studies might usefully complement algebraic modeling.

## Information-Processing Findings

The methods described above have been used by researchers with two general objectives in mind. The first is to discover the elementary operations and rules that are employed in decision making. The second is to determine how features of the decision task govern the selection and use of these rules.

### Basic Rules

The decision rules that have been observed can be categorized in a number of ways. Some, like the linear additive model, are *compensatory*, meaning that a high score on one dimension can offset a low score on another dimension. In contrast, *non-compensatory* processes do not permit trade-offs among dimensions. For example, a *conjunctive* rule eliminates any alternative that fails to surpass a criterion value on any dimension. It is the basic rule of satisficing. A *disjunctive* rule selects any alternative that surpasses the criterion for at least one dimension. A *lexicographic* process chooses the alternative that is superior on the most important dimension. If more than one alternative has top ratings on this dimension, then the next most important dimension is considered, and so forth. Tversky's EBA model is a probabilistic version of this rule.

Another way of categorizing an information-processing pattern is according to whether it focuses on alternatives or on attributes. *Intra-alternative* rules consider all the attributes of each alternative before going on to the next alternative. Compensatory and conjunctive rules are instances of intra-alternative processing. *Dimensional* rules compare all alternatives

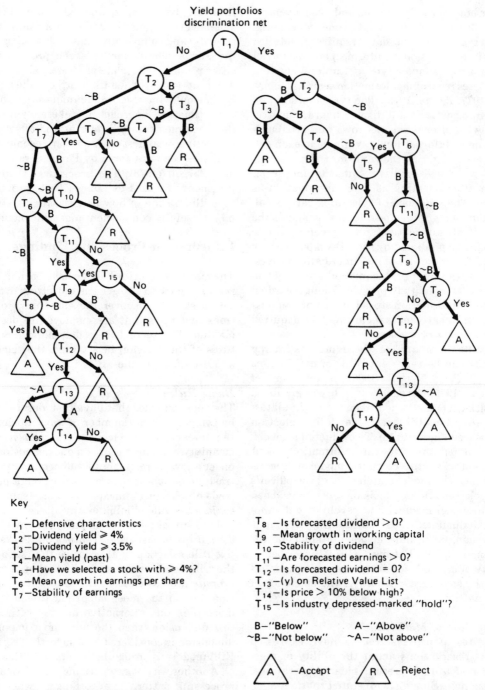

**Figure 10.13.** Clarkson's yield portfolio stock selection model. From *Portfolio Selection: A Simulation of Trust Investment* (p. 110), by G.P.E. Clarkson, 1962. Englewood Cliffs, NJ: Prentice-Hall. Copyright 1962 by G.P.E. Clarkson. Reprinted by permission.

on one dimension at a time. The lexicographic and disjunctive rules involve dimensional processing.

### Effects of Task Difficulty and Context

Pure reliance on any one strategy is uncommon in information-search tasks; subjects typically alternate between intra-alternative and dimensional processing (Bettman & Jacoby, 1976). In decision-making tasks, the strategy used seems to depend upon task characteristics such as difficulty, context, and familiarity. Task difficulty has been studied by varying the number of alternatives, the number and relevance of dimensions or attributes, and the information display.

Svenson (1979) manipulated difficulty by varying the number of attributes (from 2 to 12) and number of alternatives (from 2 to 13). His subjects examined less information as both alternatives and attributes increased, with increases in the number of attributes having the greater effect. As the number of alternatives increased, there was a shift from dimensional to intra-alternative processing along with increased use of absolute statements (e.g., "this apartment is big") relative to comparative statements (e.g., "that apartment is bigger").

Wright (1974a, 1974b) found that making the task more difficult by including incomplete or irrelevant data, noncomparable scaling across dimensions, and time pressure increased the use of elimination strategies such as the conjunctive and lexicographic rules. Because negative (unfavorable) data are conducive to elimination strategies, such data tend to be used more as task difficulty increases. Gaeth and Shanteau (1984) demonstrated that presence of irrelevant information impaired performance in an applied setting (soil judgment). However, this impairment was reduced by training.

Tyszka (1983) observed strong effects of context in choices among multiattribute alternatives. Introduction of an alternative C, which was dominated by alternative B, enhanced B's chances to be chosen over a third alternative, A, in violation of the principle of independence from irrelevant alternatives.

Another contextual effect is that dimensional processing generally occurs more often when the alternatives have dimensions or attributes in common (Capon & Burke, 1977; Russ, 1971; Russo & Dosher, 1975). The attractiveness of performing dimensional comparisons can give an otherwise secondary dimension greater importance if all alternatives are characterized on it (Slovic & MacPhillamy, 1974). Tversky (1969) noted that processing by dimensions is often more efficient, in the sense of requiring fewer operations, allowing small differences to be ignored, and facilitating the use of the dominance rule to eliminate inferior alternatives.

### Effects of Display

Numerous studies have found that decisions can be sensitive to how information is displayed. Friedman (1966) and Branscombe (1975) found that few consumers could perform the mental calculations needed to select the most economical products in the marketplace. Unit pricing is a remedy for this problem. However, Russo (1977) found that consumers failed to use unit prices when they were displayed under each brand. Only if the unit prices were displayed in a simple organized list was this information used. Huber (1980) showed that decision processes were influenced by whether information was described in numerical or verbal form. Numerical presentation led to more dimensional comparisons and fewer comparisons against a criterion.

Display effects highlight the difficulties that decision makers have in making tradeoffs and performing even simple mental calculations. Such difficulties led Slovic (1972) to observe:

> . . . that a judge or decision maker tends to use only the information that is explicitly displayed in the stimulus object and will use it only in the form in which it is displayed. Information that has to be stored in memory, inferred from the explicit display, or transformed tends to be discounted or ignored (p. 14).

### Phased Strategies

Many studies have found evidence for phased strategies, in which an initial set of rules, designed to eliminate alternatives, is followed by more detailed evaluation of the surviving options (Wright & Barbour, 1977). Phased strategies seem particularly likely when the number of alternatives is large (Sheridan, Richards, & Slocum, 1975; Svenson, 1974). A verbal protocol illustrating a multiple-rule sequence is shown in Table 10.5. The subject used an elimination-by-aspects process to reduce the choice problem from 12 to eight, and eventually to just two alternatives.

**Table 10.5. Protocol for a subject selecting among 12 apartments**

| (A)<br>Protocol | (A)<br>Protocol (continued) |
|---|---|
| Let's just see what the rents are in all the apartments first. | Kitchen facilities in *A* are poor. |
| The rent of *A* is $140. | In *A*, poor. |
| The rent of *B* is $110. | In *B*, poor. |
| The rent of *C* is $170. | In *J*, fair. |
| . . . | In *H*, they're good. |
| Um, $170 is too much. | Oh, *J* and *H* have better kitchen facilities than *A* and *B*. |
| But, if the other ones aren't good, I'll look at them later. | And everything else is about the same. |
| But, right now I'll look at the other ones. | So eliminate those two. |
| . . . | And, decide between these two. |
| I'm going to look at landlord attitude. | . . . |
| In *H*, it's fair. | Let's see furniture quality. |
| In *D*, it's poor. | In *H*, it is below average. |
| *B*, it's fair, and | In *J*, it's below average, so that's about the same there. |
| *A*, it's good. | . . . |
| So, one of them. . .is poor. | Landlord attitude in *J* is better than in *H*. |
| So that's important to me. | . . . |
| . . . | In *J*, the rooms are larger, so, I guess, *J* will be better. |
| So, I'm not going to live any place where it's poor. | |
| . . . | |

*Note.* From "Task Complexity and Contingent Processing in Decision Making: An Information Search and Protocol Analysis" by J.W. Payne, 1976. *Organizational Behavior and Human Performance, 16*, pp. 374–380. Copyright 1976 by Academic Press. Reprinted by permission.

At that point, an additive-difference strategy was used.

Although intuitively appealing, the application of an initial screening phase can lead to suboptimal decisions. Removal of dominated alternatives is certainly defensible. However, other elimination strategies may lead to rejection of options that would, under more thorough scrutiny, prove to be quite attractive.

### Selection of Decision Rules

Payne (1982) has offered an account of how people choose decision rules. He points to three rule-selection processes: cost/benefit principles, perceptual processes, and adaptive production systems. *Cost/benefit principles* involve a trade-off between optimality and simplicity in choosing a way to process information. They are similar to the economists' notion of transaction costs, which determines how hard people will work at making decisions and can be used to explain away apparent instances of suboptimality (by saying that it was not worth the added effort to identify the very best alternative). The most elaborate model of this sort is that of Beach and Mitchell (1978; see also Christensen-Szalanski, 1978). In order to have any empirical content, such models need an independent measure of mental effort. Shugan (1980) proposed measuring the cost of thinking in terms of the number of single-attribute comparisons needed to discriminate between two alternatives. Johnson (1979) developed a measure of effort based on the number of elementary operations (e.g., multiplication, addition, subtraction, and comparison) required to apply a rule in a given situation.

*Perceptual processes* are involved when the selection of decision rules is done in a non-deliberative manner. For example, Tversky and Kahneman (1981) proposed that decision frames shape the choice of decision rules in as automatic a way as different spatial perspectives shape visual perceptions. In contrast to the cost/benefit theory, the perceptual analogy implies that subjects will typically be unaware of the effects of alternative frames, consistent with the findings of Fischhoff (1983).

The *production-systems* approach was adapted by Pitz (1977) from information-processing theory (Newell & Simon, 1972). A production system is a condition-action pairing such as, "If you have the values of two alternatives on the same attribute, then compare the values and note which alternative is better." Newell (1980, p. 704) called such a system "a species of pattern-directed rule-oriented program system" that is an active candidate "for the underlying architecture of human cognition."

## Justification and Choice

One appealing aspect of relying on a series of deliberative rules is that it produces a set of reasons for justifying the alternative that is eventually selected. Tversky (1972b) invoked justifiability as a reason why people might use elimination by aspects. That process leads to a clear-cut choice without recourse to relative weights, tradeoff functions, or other numerical computations that are hard to describe to those not versed in decision theory.

The importance of justification processes can be seen in a study of difficult choices (Slovic, 1975). Each of two options was defined by two dimensions differing in importance. To maximize the difficulty of choice, the paired options were designed to have equal worth by making the option that was superior on the more important dimension so inferior on the lesser dimension that its advantage was cancelled. For example, one pair of options involved gift packages with two components, cash and a coupon book offering miscellaneous products and services with a stated monetary value. The subject was shown two such gift packages with one component missing, for example:

|  | Cash | Coupon Book Worth |
| --- | --- | --- |
| Gift package A | $10 | – |
| Gift package B | $20 | $18 |

The subject supplied a value for the missing component such that the two options would be equally attractive. After equating various pairs of options, subjects made choices from the equated pairs. Contrary to most choice theories, decisions regarding these equally attractive alternatives were not made randomly. Rather, most subjects consistently selected the option that was superior on the more important dimension. Apparently, reliance on the more important

dimension makes a better justification ("I chose this gift package because it provided more cash") than random selection ("They looked about equally attractive, so I flipped a coin"). Tversky, Sattath and Slovic (in press) showed that the findings by Slovic (1975) stemmed from a general tendency for the more important dimension to be weighted more heavily in choice than in the mode where a subject makes the two options match in value.

Tyszka (1981) and Montogmery (1983) have both advocated theories based on the concept of justification. Montgomery proposed a model that describes the decision process as a search for a dominance structure, whereby decision makers restructure decision problems until they find a perspective that shows a (relatively) conflict-free way to make a choice. This search may involve bolstering or deemphasizing the importance of certain attributes or collapsing two or more attributes into a more comprehensive one.

## Script Processing

Abelson (1976) has criticized traditional theories of decision making as being "overly elementaristic, stilted, and static" (p. 33). He proposed an alternative theory, based on the concept of a *script*, defined as a coherent sequence of events expected by an individual. Scripts are learned throughout one's lifetime, by experiencing and observing event sequences. A restaurant script, for example, involves a set of expectations about food prepared and served, about menus, waiters, tips, and checks.

Abelson (1981) noted that scripts can provide guides or strategies for decision making. Abelson (1976, p. 37) described several scripts that might influence decisions about graduate school applicants made by a member of an admissions committee. For example, in an *episodic* script, a past single case would be recalled, similar to the applicant under consideration, "Mr. X reminds me very much of Mr. Y, who hung around for eight years, never writing his dissertation. Let's not get into that again." A *categorical* script assimilates the applicant to a category, "He's one of those guys who writes about all this existential stuff and ends up wanting to go into clinical psych." Although many behaviors observed in studies of decision making can be interpreted in terms of scripts, Abelson admits

that the theory needs much more precise specification.

## Information Processing in Risky Choice

### Gambles as Multidimensional Stimuli

Slovic and Lichtenstein (1968b) proposed that
gambles could be characterized in terms of four
basic dimensions—probability of winning ($P_W$),
amount to win ($\$_W$), probability of losing ($P_L$), and
amount to lose ($\$_L$). They argued that an ade-
quate descriptive theory of risk taking required
an understanding of how people integrated these
dimensions when evaluating gambles.

In attempting to understand the relative
influence of these risk dimensions, Slovic and
Lichtenstein hypothesized that an individual
assigns weight to a particular risk dimension
according to its perceived importance. However,
information-processing limitations may restrict
the individual's ability to act on the basis of
those importance beliefs when evaluating a
gamble.

To test their hypotheses, Slovic and Lichtenstein (1968b) presented several groups of subjects with duplex gambles (see Figure 10.7) that
allowed all four risk dimensions to vary independently. Several groups of subjects expressed
their attitudes toward playing these gambles,
but did so using different response modes. One
group rated the attractiveness of each gamble,
whereas each of three other groups used a bidding method in which the gamble was equated
with an amount of money (either the maximum
buying price, the minimum selling price, or the
monetary equivalent). A regression analysis
indicated large differences in the relative
weights of the various risk dimensions. On
the average, the highest correlation between a
subject's evaluations and one of the four risk
dimensions was twice the size of the lowest correlation. Attractiveness ratings correlated more
highly with $P_W$ than with any other dimension,
whereas the bidding responses correlated most
highly with the payoff dimensions, particularly
$\$_L$. Slovic and Lichtenstein (1968b) suggested
that the reference to money in a bid focused
attention on the monetary aspects of the gamble,
whereas the rating focused attention on the
probabilities.

Although not designed specifically to test
the SEU model, these results cast doubt on its

adequacy. According to the model, all risk dimensions should have equal influence and evaluations
of gambles should be invariant across response
modes. The Slovic and Lichtenstein results
are, however, compatible with an information-
processing perspective.

### Integration Rules

Slovic and Lichtenstein showed that an additive
model, with each risk dimension weighted by its
correlation with the responses, fit their data
well (Slovic & Lichtenstein, 1968b). However,
Anderson and Shanteau (1970) found a better fit
with a modified SEU model

$$R = W_W S_W + W_L S_L$$

where $S_W$ and $S_L$ corresponded to subjective versions of $\$_W$ and $\$_L$ and the $W_W$ and $W_L$ were subjective functions of the probabilities of winning
and losing. Unlike subjective probabilities, however, these weights do not have to sum to 1.0.[5]

Payne (1980; Payne & Braunstein, 1978) elaborated the Anderson and Shanteau model by proposing that it implied (1) intra-alternative
processing of alternatives, involving many
probability-amount comparisons (as opposed
to probability-probability or amount-amount
comparisons); and (2) a compensatory process in
which equal amounts of information are sought
for each alternative. He noted that these implications were not confirmed by the results of
several process-tracing studies. These studies
showed that the amount of information searched
varied from one gamble to another. Furthermore, this variation increased with the number
of gambles in the choice set, many gambles
being eliminated after only a limited amount of
search. As the number of gambles increased, the
proportion of available information searched
decreased. There was more intra-dimensional
search as the number of gambles increased.
Payne concluded that, with more gambles to
consider, subjects are less likely to use strategies consistent with a compensatory algebraic
model. Payne has proposed a contingent, multi-
stage model to account for these and other
choice data.

---

5. The form of this model is similar to prospect theory
(Kahneman & Tversky, 1979), although the underlying rationale and primitives are different.

## Response Mode Effects

Individuals can express their preferences in many different ways. Although the decision maker is sometimes free to determine the mode of response, more often some external source defines it. A common (and critical) distinction is whether the task is presented as one of judgment (evaluating individual options) or as one of choice among two or more options. Most theories of decision making view judgment and choice as equivalent. However, numerous empirical studies have found that information-processing strategies used in making choices are quite different from the strategies employed in judging single alternatives. As a result, choices and evaluative judgments of the same options often differ, sometimes dramatically.

An early demonstration of response-mode effects in risky choice was the finding by Slovic and Lichtenstein (1968b) that ratings of a gamble's attractiveness and choices among pairs of gambles were influenced primarily by the probabilities of winning and losing, whereas buying and selling prices were primarily determined by the dollar amounts that could be won or lost. When subjects found a bet attractive, their prices correlated predominantly with the amount to win; when they disliked a bet, their prices correlated primarily with the amount that could be lost. This pattern of correlations was explained as the result of a starting point (anchoring) and adjustment procedure used when setting prices. Subjects setting a price on an attractive gamble appeared to start with the amount to win and adjust it downward to take into account the probability of winning, the possibility of losing and the amount that could be lost. However, the adjustment process was typically inadequate, leaving the price response unduly influenced by the starting point payoff. Choices, on the other hand, appeared to be governed by different rules, such as dimensional comparisons of the gamble's probabilities.

Lichtenstein and Slovic (1971) hypothesized that, if people process information differently when making choices and setting prices, it should be possible to construct pairs of gambles such that the same individual would choose one member of the pair but set a higher price on the other. They demonstrated this predicted effect in several studies, including one conducted on the floor of the Four Queens Casino in Las Vegas (Lichtenstein & Slovic, 1973). A typical pair of gambles in that study consisted of:

Bet $A$: 11/12 chance to win 12 chips
1/12 chance to lose 24 chips

Bet $B$: 2/12 chance to win 79 chips
10/12 chance to lose 5 chips

where each chip was worth 25 cents. Each subject first made a simple choice, $A$ or $B$. Later, the subject indicated a minimum selling price for each bet. For this pair of gambles, Bets $A$ and $B$ were chosen about equally often, across subjects. However, Bet $B$ received a higher selling price about 88 percent of the time. Of the subjects who chose Bet $A$, 87 percent gave a higher selling price to $B$, thus exhibiting a preference pattern inconsistent with almost every normative and descriptive theory of preference.[6]

These response-mode induced reversals of preference have been replicated in numerous other studies (reviewed by Slovic & Lichtenstein, 1983). Of particular interest is a study performed by Grether and Plott (1979), two skeptical economists concerned about the challenge that preference reversals pose for theories of choice. They conducted a series of experiments "to discredit the psychologists' works as applied to economics" (p. 623). Their design was based on thirteen criticisms or explanations that would render the preference-reversal phenomenon irrelevant to economic theory, including the fact that the experimenters were psychologists, which might have led the subjects to behave peculiarly. Their manipulations included using special incentive systems to heighten motivation, controlling for income and order effects, testing the influence of strategic or bargaining biases, and having economists conduct the study. To their surprise, preference reversals remained much in evidence despite their careful attempts to eradicate them. Not all economists have been so skeptical. Arrow (1982) has pointed out a number of failures of utility theory in nonexperimental contexts such as insurance, securities, and futures markets, which he feels are directly interpretable in terms of information-processing factors.

---

6. Subsequently, a number of normative and descriptive theories have been proposed to account for preference reversals (see, e.g., Fishburn, 1982b; Goldstein & Einhorn 1981; and Loomes & Sugden, 1982).

*Implications for Utility Theory*

Hershey, Kunreuther, and Schoemaker (1982) have applied the findings from information processing studies to the problem of measuring utility curves. They identified five choices that must be made in order to select a method for eliciting a utility curve. They then showed that each of these choices can affect the shape of the curve elicited, although none of these factors is incorporated into utility theory.

First, what response mode is used? Hershey et al. demonstrated that the use of the certainty-equivalence method for eliciting utilities, in which the subject specifies the value of a sure outcome, $w$, such that the subject is indifferent between $w$ and a given gamble, $(x, p, y)$, leads to more risk-prone utility functions than the use of the probability-equivalence method, in which $x$, $y$, and $w$ are given and the subject specifies the value of $p$. Second, what values are used in the standard gamble and the sure outcome? Variations in the experimenters' choice of values for $x$, $y$, $w$ and $p$ led to sytematic changes in the proportion of risk-averse responses, changes that could not be explained by utility theory. Third, what is the domain of the standard gamble? Subjects showed significantly more risk aversion for gambles containing both wins and losses than for gambles offering no possibility of winning. Fourth, who gets the risk? Subjects who were offered the opportunity to receive a gamble to play were more risk averse than those who were told they were already in the risky situation and were asked if they wished to transfer the risk to someone else. Fifth, what is the decision context? Subjects were more risk averse when gambles were presented with an insurance frame than when presented with a gamble frame.

Taken together, these results, along with other, related findings previously discussed, show that risk attitudes as defined in utility theory are easily manipulated, perhaps indeterminate. Thus, the very concept of a utility function is in doubt.

# PREFERENCE MANAGEMENT

## Applications of Decision Theories

The study of decision making is an applied science as well as a theoretical one. Its aim is to help individuals make better decisions in their personal lives and in their jobs as managers, physicians, policy makers, etc. The studies described in this chapter have been scrutinized by those concerned with improving the practice of decision making. For example, the field of behavioral accounting applies the information-processing approach to financial analysis (Ashton, 1982). Market researchers have adopted expected utility and probabilistic choice theories as models of consumer decision making (Bettman, 1979; Jacoby, 1975). *Medical Decision Making, The New England Journal of Medicine,* and related publications report numerous applications of utility theory to medical diagnosis and treatment (Krischer, 1980).

The dominant methodology for aiding decision making is a blend of systems analysis, operations research, and utility theory called *decision analysis* (Howard, 1968; Keeney, 1982; Raiffa, 1968; von Winterfeldt & Edwards, 1986). It assumes that decision makers wish to select actions with the highest expected utility, based on their preferences and beliefs. The tools it offers are methods for structuring the decision problem and eliciting the decision maker's subjective utilities and probabilities. For example, when outcomes have many components, multi-attribute techniques can help assess and integrate the various utilities. Decision analysis has been applied to such diverse problems as hurricane seeding (Howard, Matheson, & North, 1972), selecting experiments for a Mars space mission (Matheson & Roths, 1967), coronary artery surgery (Pauker, 1976), cancer chemotherapy (McNeil, Weichselbaum, & Pauker, 1981), and family planning (Beach, Townes, Campbell, & Keating, 1976).

Psychological studies have had a substantial effect on decision-aiding methods. The heuristics and biases observed by Tversky and Kahneman (1974) and others have changed how decision analysts elicit probabilities (Spetzler & Staël von Holstein, 1975). The work by Gettys et al. (1980) points toward improved methods for structuring event hypotheses and decision alternatives. Psychological considerations are increasingly incorporated in the design of decision support and management information systems (Benbasat & Taylor, 1982; National Academy of Sciences, 1983).

In considering the influence of behavioral research on choice theories, March (1978, 1982) noted that theories of rational choice presume two improbably precise guesses about the future. One guess concerns the future consequences of current actions. The other guess concerns future preferences among those consequences. March (1978) argued that behavioral research has already shaped the rational theory's treatment of the first guess. For example, economic theories now place considerable emphasis on ideas of search, attention, and information costs. Aspiration levels and satisficing have been described as sensible in many settings. The future may see similar progress devoted to the second guess.

## Labile Values

Regarding the second guess, March (1978) argued that the same limited cognitive capacity that affects information processing about facts also affects information processing about values: "Human beings have unstable, inconsistent, incompletely evoked, and imprecise goals at least in part because human abilities limit preference orderliness (p. 598)." March drew upon a rich and diverse array of observations to argue that, contrary to normative theory, preferences are neither absolute, stable, consistent, precise, nor unaffected by the choices they are presumed to control. The framing and response-mode effects described above represent a few pertinent examples of this fact.

Even when cognitive capacity is not strained, preferences may be labile because we do not really know what we want or how we will experience certain outcomes. When considering simple, familiar decision consequences, one's preferences may be well articulated. But the most interesting and important decisions, such as medical treatments, marriage, and career choice, tend to have novel, unfamiliar, and complex outcomes. In such circumstances our values may be incoherent, not sufficiently thought through (Fischhoff, Slovic, & Lichtenstein, 1980). When we think about societal risks, for example, we may have contradictory values (e.g., a strong aversion to catastrophic losses of life, but an awareness that we are no more moved by a plane crash with 500 fatalities than one with 300). We may occupy different roles in life (parents, workers, children), each of which produces clear-cut but inconsistent values. We may vacillate between incompatible but strongly held positions (e.g. freedom of speech is invio-

late, but it should be denied authoritarian movements). We may not even know how to begin thinking about some issues (e.g., the appropriate tradeoffs between the outcomes of surgery for cancer vs. the very different outcomes from radiation therapy). We may underestimate our ability to adapt to extremely good or extremely bad circumstances (Brickman, Coates, & Janoff-Bulman, 1978; Cameron, Titus, Kostin, & Kostin, 1973). Our views may change so much over time (say, as we near the hour of decision or of experiencing the consequences) that we become disoriented as to what we really think.

At times, it seems as though there are rival selves within the same individual, each vying for legitimacy. Schelling (1982) pointed to people who set alarm clocks but do not respond to them, who want to quit smoking but cannot. Noting that robot chess players can be programmed to play at different levels of skill, he asked whether analogous signals in humans might tune in and tune out particular qualities of memory, perceptual acuity, motivation, and value, thereby selecting the individual who is to act in a particular setting. Thaler and Shefrin (1981) modeled self-control as a balancing of the interests of a doer and planner within each individual (with the former acting like an id and the latter like a superego). A striking empirical demonstration of multiple selves is provided by Christensen-Szalanski (1984), who recorded the changes in attitudes of pregnant women toward anesthesia before, during, and after labor.

Fischhoff et al. (1980) noted the problems that labile preferences pose for the measurement of values. Although some practitioners have been sensitive to the possibility that complex elicitation methods may induce errors of assessment (e.g., Bursztajn & Hamm, 1982; Edwards, 1977; Llewellyn-Thomas, Sutherland, Tibshirani, Ciampi, Till, & Boyd, 1982; von Winterfeldt, 1975), most applications of multiattribute models or decision analysis assume that people know their own values and that the methods are unbiased channels for translating subjective feelings into analytically usable expressions. Fischhoff et al. (1980) argued that the strong effects of framing and information-processing considerations, acting upon inchoate preferences, can make elicitation procedures major forces in shaping the expression of values. In such cases, the method becomes the message. As shown above, subtle aspects of how problems are posed, questions are phrased, and responses are elicited can have a substantial effect on people's expressed preferences.

## Managing Preferences

There are two potential reactions to the problems posed by labile values, one conservative and one radical. The conservative (decision theoretic) response assumes that true expressions of value are possible and attempts to clarify them through education (to reduce the uncertainty surrounding preferences) and the use of sophisticated elicitation techniques (to reduce biases). Consider, for example, a physician attempting to help a patient with cancer of the larynx choose between surgery and radiation therapy. Surgery produces longer life expectancy, but carries wih it the loss of normal speech. Radiation therapy creates nausea and hair loss, but entails a much lower risk of serious long-term side effects (for those who survive the cancer). The conservative approach attempts to assess utility functions for varying lengths of survival with and without normal speech— perhaps by asking the patient to assign certainty equivalents to gambles involving death and non-normal speech as outcomes. The patient's difficulty in forecasting how he or she would adapt to artificial speech or radiation therapy means that some education would have to take place prior to the value assessment procedure. That education might include contact with persons who did and did not choose surgery. How did these people react to the consequences of their decision? Did they correctly anticipate what it would be like to live without normal speech? Would they make the same decision again? After the education is completed, multiple assessment techniques would be employed to ensure that the patient's utility functions were faithfully captured.

The radical reaction to lability is to abandon the decision analytic approach on the grounds that it seeks to determine utility functions that do not exist and, as a result, has false pretensions about being able to identify the optimal decision. In the example of laryngeal cancer, decision analysis could produce utility functions that do not truly represent the patient's concerns, leading to recommendations of actions that are not in the patient's best interests.

Furthermore, the very analytical process might raise the patient's anxiety about doing the right thing and increase the chances for strong post-decision regret. One possible alternative approach begins with the same educational effort, but then asks directly, "which option do you prefer?" Patient and physician would then sift and weigh alternative reasons (or justifications), trying to develop a rationale for action. A strong rationale might buffer the patient from post-decision regret and make it easier to accept the consequences of the decision. If the patient is an intuitive decision theorist, this process could involve utility functions and maximization rules. However, quite different justifications could be equally legitimate if they have been thoughtfully derived.

Both education to inform preference and justification structuring to define it are forms of deliberate preference management. We manage our preferences in many ways. Aware, to some extent, of our multiple selves and changing tastes, we do such things as join Christmas clubs which bind us to our current preferences (Thaler & Shefrin, 1981), much as Ulysses forced his crew to tie him to the mast so that he might withstand the lure of the Sirens.

Deeper understanding of framing effects, which used car salespeople have had for a long time and psychologists are beginning to acquire, could help us manage our own preferences more effectively (Thaler, 1985). Suppose, for example, that a person with $5,500 in a bank account misplaces a $100 bill. Rather than isolating and dwelling on this painful loss, assimilating it into one's total account may ease the sting by exploiting the perception that $5,500 is not that different from $5,600. Because neither perspective on the loss is inherently the right one, the choice between them could be a strategic decision, dependent upon the circumstances. If it is important to ensure that the mistake does not recur, then it might be best to isolate the loss, so as to maximize its impact. If the loss could not have been prevented, or if its impact has been traumatic, then one might well assimilate it, thus reducing the distress it is causing.

The concept of preference management reflects the deep interplay between descriptive phenomena and normative principles. Experimental study of decision processes appears to be forging a new conception of preference, one that may require serious restructuring of normative theories and approaches toward improving decision making.

# REFERENCES

Abelson, R.P. (1976). Script processing in attitude formation and decision making. In J.S. Carroll & J.W. Payne (Eds.), *Cognition and social behavior.* Hillsdale, NJ: Erlbaum.

Abelson, R. P. (1981). Psychological status of the script concept. *American Psychologist, 36,* 715–729.

Allais, M. (1953). Le comportement de l'homme rationnel devant le risque: critique des postulats et axiomes de l'ecole americaine. *Econometrica, 21,* 503–546.

Anderson, N.H. (1970). Functional measurement and psychophysical judgment. *Psychological Review, 77,* 153–170.

Anderson, N.H. (1974). Algebraic models in perception. In E.C. Carterette & M.P. Friedman (Eds.), *Handbook of perception:* Vol. 2. New York: Academic Press.

Anderson, N.H. (1981). *Foundations of information integration theory.* New York: Academic Press.

Anderson, N.H. & Shanteau, J.C. (1970). Information integration in risky decision making. *Journal of Experimental Psychology, 84,* 441–451.

Arrow, K. J. (1951). *Social choice and individual values.* New York: Wiley.

Arrow, K.J. (1982). Risk perception in psychology and economics. *Economic Inquiry, 20,* 1–9.

Ashton, R.H. (1982). *Human information processing in accounting.* Sarasota, FL: American Accounting Association.

Bar-Hillel, M. (1973). On the subjective probability of compound events. *Organizational Behavior and Human Performance, 9,* 396–406.

Bar-Hillel, M. (1980). The base-rate fallacy in probability judgments. *Acta Psychologica, 44,* 211–233.

Bar-Hillel, M. & Fischhoff, B. (1981). When do base rates affect predictions? *Journal of Personality and Social Psychology, 41,* 671–680.

Barron, F. H. & Person, H.B. (1979). Assessment of multiplicative utility functions via holistic judgments. *Organizational Behavior and Human Performance, 24,* 147–166.

Beach, L.R. & Mitchell, T.R. (1978). A contingency model for the selection of decision strategies. *Academy of Management Review, 3,* 439–449.

Beach, L.R., Townes, B.D., Campbell, F.L., & Keating, G.W. (1976). Developing and testing a decision aid for birth planning decisions. *Organizational Behavior and Human Performance, 15,* 99–116.

Becker, G.M., DeGroot, M.H., & Marschak, J. (1963). Probabilities of choices among very similar objects. *Behavioral Science, 8,* 306–311.

Bell, D. (1982). Regret in decision making under uncertainty. *Operations Research, 30,* 961–981.

Benbasat, I. & Taylor, R.N. (1982). Behavioral aspects of information processing for the design of management information systems. *IEEE Transactions on Systems, Man and Cybernetics, SMC-12,* 439–450.

Bernoulli, D. (1738/1954). Specimen theoriae novae de mensura sortis. *Commentarii Academiae Scientiarum Imperiales Petropolitanae,* 1738, *5,* 175–192. (Transl. by L. Sommer in *Econometrica,* 1954, *22,* 23–36.)

Bettman, J.R. (1979). *An information processing theory of consumer choice.* Reading, MA: Addison–Wesley.

Bettman, J.R. & Jacoby, J. (1976). Patterns of processing in consumer information acquisition. In B.B. Anderson (Ed.), *Advances in consumer research.* Chicago: Association for Consumer Research.

Beyth-Marom, R. (1981). *The subjective probability of conjunctions* (Report No. 81–12). Eugene, OR: Decision Research.

Beyth-Marom, R. (1982a). How probable is probable? Numerical translation of verbal probability expressions. *Journal of Forecasting, 1,* 257–269.

Beyth-Marom, R. (1982b). Perception of correlation reexamined. *Memory and Cognition, 10*(6), 511–519.

Beyth-Marom, R., Dekel, S., Gombo, R., & Shaked, M. (1985). *An elementary approach to thinking under uncertainty* (S. Lichtenstein, B. Marom, & R. Beyth-Marom, Trans.) Hillsdale, NJ: Erlbaum.

Birnbaum, M.H. (1973). The devil rides again: Correlation as an index of fit. *Psychological Bulletin, 79,* 239–242.

Block, H.D. & Marschak, J. (1960). Random orderings and stochastic theories of responses. In I. Olkin et al. (Eds.), *Contributions to probability and statistics.* Stanford, CA: Stanford University Press.

Bouwman, M.J. (1982). The use of accounting information: Expert vs. novice behavior. In G.R. Ungson & D.N. Braunstein (Eds.), *Decision making: An interdisciplinary inquiry.* Boston: Kent.

Branscombe, A. (1975). Checkout on consumer math. *American Education, 11* (Oct.), 21–24.

Brehmer, B. (1979). Preliminaries to a psychology of inference. *Scandinavian Journal of Psychology, 20,* 193–210.

Brehmer, B. (1980a). Effect of cue validity on learning of complex rules in probabilistic inference tasks. *Acta Psychologica, 44,* 201–210.

Brehmer, B. (1980b). In one word: Not from experience. *Acta Psychologica, 45,* 223–241.

Brickman, P., Coates, D., & Janoff-Bulman, R. (1978). Lottery winners and accident victims: Is happiness relative? *Journal of Personality and Social Psychology, 36,* 917–927.

Bruner, J.S., Goodnow, J.J., & Austin, G.A. (1956). *A study of thinking.* New York: Wiley.

Brunswik, E. (1952). *The conceptual framework of psychology.* Chicago: University of Chicago Press.

Brunswik, E. (1956). *Perception and the representative design of experiments.* Berkeley: University of California Press.

Bursztajn, H. & Hamm, R.M. (1982). The clinical utility of utility assessment. *Medical Decision Making, 2,* 161–165.

Cameron, P., Titus, D.G., Kostin, J., & Kostin, M. (1973). The life satisfaction of nonnormal persons. *Journal of Counseling and Clinical Psychology, 41,* 207–214.

Campbell, D.T. & Boruch, R.F. (1975). Making the case for randomized assignment to treatments by considering the alternatives: Six ways in which quasi-experimental evaluations in compensatory education tend to underestimate effects. In C.A. Bennett & A.A. Lumsdaine (Eds.), *Evaluation and experiment: Some critical issues in assessing social progams.* New York: Academic Press.

Capon, N. & Burke, M. (1977). Information seeking behavior in consumer durable purchase. In B.A. Greenberg & D.M. Bellenger (Eds.), *Contemporary marketing thought.* Chicago: American Marketing Association.

Chapman, L.J. & Chapman, J.P. (1967). Genesis of popular but erroneous psychodiagnostic observations. *Journal of Abnormal Psychology, 73,* 193–204.

Chew, S.H. & MacCrimmon, K. (1979). *Alpha utility theory, lottery composition, and the Allais Paradox.* Working Paper #686, University of British Columbia.

Christensen-Szalanski, J.J.J. (1978). Problem-solving strategies: A selection mechanism, some implications, and some data. *Organizational Behavior and Human Performance, 22,* 307–323.

Christensen-Szalanski, J.J.J. (1984). Discount functions and the measurement of patients' values: Womens' decisions during childbirth. *Medical Decision Making, 4,* 47–58.

Clarkson, G.P.E. (1962). *Portfolio selection: A simulation of trust investment.* Englewood Cliffs, NJ: Prentice–Hall.

Cohen, J. (1981). Can human irrationality be experimentally demonstrated? *The Behavioral and Brain Sciences, 4,* 317–331.

Coombs, C.H. (1958). On the use of inconsistency of preferences in psychological measurement. *Journal of Experimental Psychology, 55,* 1–7.

Coombs, C.H. (1964). *A theory of data.* New York: Wiley.

Coombs, C.H. (1969). Portfolio theory: A theory of risky decision making. *La Decision,* Paris: Centre National de la Recherche Scientifique.

Coombs, C.H. (1975). Portfolio theory and the measurement of risk. In M. Kaplan & S. Schwartz (Eds.), *Human judgment and decision processes.* New York: Acdemic Press.

Coombs, C.H. (1980). Risk preference and the theory of risk. In E. Lantermann & H. Feger (Eds.), *Similarity and choice* (pp. 346–364). Bern, Switzerland: Hans Huber.

Coombs, C.H. & Bowen, J. (1971). Additivity of risk and portfolios. *Perception and Psychophysics, 10,* 43–46.

Coombs, C.H., Dawes, R.M., & Tversky, A. (1970). *Mathematical psychology: An elementary introduction.* Englewood Cliffs, NJ: Prentice–Hall.

Coombs, C.H. & Huang, L.C. (1970a). Polynomial psychophysics of risk. *Journal of Mathematical Psychology, 7,* 317–338.

Coombs, C.H. & Huang, L.C. (1970b). Tests of a portfolio theory of risk preference. *Journal of Experimental Psychology, 85,* 23–29.

Coombs, C.H. & Huang, L.C. (1976). Tests of the betweenness property of expected utility. *Journal of Mathematical Psychology, 13,* 323–337.

Coombs, C.H. & Lehner, P.E. (1981). Evaluation of two alternative models for a theory of risk: I. Are moments of distributions useful in assessing risk? *Journal of Experimental Psychology: Human Perception and Performance, 7,* 1110–1123.

Coombs, C.H. & Meyer, D.E. (1969). Risk-preference in coin-toss games. *Journal of Mathematical Psychology, 6,* 514–527.

Coombs, C.H. & Pruitt, D.G. (1960). Components of risk in decision making: Probability and variance preferences. *Journal of Experimental Psychology, 60,* 265–277.

Darlington, R.B. (1968). Multiple regression in psychological research and practice. *Psychological Bulletin, 69,* 161–182.

Davidson, D., Suppes, P., & Seigel, S. (1957), *Decision making: An experimental approach.* Stanford, CA: Stanford University.

Dawes, R.M. (1971). A case study of graduate admissions: Applications of three principles of human decision making. *American Psychologist, 26,* 180–188.

Dawes, R.M. (1976). Shallow psychology. In J.S. Carroll & J.W. Payne (Eds.), *Cognition and social behavior.* Potomac, MD: Erlbaum.

Dawes, R.M. (1977). Predictive models as a guide to preference. *IEEE Transactions on Systems, Man and Cybernetics, SMC-7,* 355–358.

Dawes, R.M. & Corrigan, B. (1974). Linear models

in decision making. *Psychological Bulletin, 81,* 95–106.

Debreu, G. (1960a). Review of R.D. Luce. *American Economic Review, 50,* 186–188.

Debreu, G. (1960b). Topological methods in cardinal utility theory. In K.J. Arrow, S. Karlin, & P. Suppes (Eds.), *Mathematical methods in the social sciences, 1959.* Stanford, CA: Stanford University Press.

de Finetti, B. (1980a). Foresight: Its logical laws, its subjective sources. In H.E. Kyburg, Jr. & H.E. Smokler (Eds.), *Studies in subjective probability.* Huntington, NY: Krieger. (Originally published, 1937.)

de Finetti, B. (1980b). Probability: Beware of falsifications. In H.E. Kyburg, Jr. & H.E. Smokler (Eds.), *Studies in subjective probability.* Huntington, NY: Krieger.

Diaconis, P. & Zabel, S.L. (1982). Updating subjective probability. *Journal of the American Statistical Association, 77,* 822–829.

Doherty, M.E., Mynatt, C.R. Tweney, R.D., & Schiavo, M.D. (1979). Pseudodiagnosticity. *Acta Psychologica, 43,* 111–121.

Dostoevsky, F. (1964). *The gambler* (A.R. MacAndrew, trans.). New York: Bantam Books. (Original work published 1866)

DuCharme, W.M. & Donnell, M.L. (1973). Intrasubject comparison of four response modes for "subjective probability" assessment. *Organizational Behavior and Human Performance, 10,* 108–117.

Dudycha, A.L. & Naylor, J.C. (1966). Characteristics of the human inference process in complex choice behavior situations. *Organizational Behavior and Human Performance, 1,* 110–128.

Eckenrode, R.T. (1965). Weighting multiple criteria. *Management Science, 12,* 180–192.

Edwards, W. (1953). Probability-preferences in gambling. *American Journal of Psychology, 66,* 349–364.

Edwards, W. (1954a). Probability preferences among bets with differing expected values. *American Journal of Psychology, 67,* 56–67.

Edwards, W. (1954b). The reliability of probability preferences. *American Journal of Psychology, 67,* 68–95.

Edwards, W. (1954c). The theory of decision making. *Psychological Bulletin, 51,* 380–417.

Edwards, W. (1955). The prediction of decisions among bets. *Journal of Experimental Psychology, 51,* 201–214.

Edwards, W. (1968). Conservatism in human information processing. In B. Kleinmuntz (Ed.), *Formal representation of human judgment* (pp. 17–52). New York: Wiley.

Edwards, W. (1977). How to use multiattribute utility measurement for social decision making. *IEEE Transactions on Systems, Man, and Cybernetics, SMC-7,* 326–340.

Edwards, W., Lindman, H., & Savage, L.J. (1963), Bayesian statistical inference for psychological research. *Psychological Review 70,* 193–242.

Einhorn, H.J. (1970). The use of nonlinear, noncompensatory models in decision making. *Psychological Bulletin, 73,* 211–230.

Einhorn, H.J. & Hogarth, R.M. (1978). Confidence in judgment: Persistence of the illusion of validity. *Psychological Review, 85,* 395–416.

Einhorn, H.J., Kleinmuntz, D.N., & Kleinmuntz, B. (1979). Linear regression and process tracing models of judgment. *Psychological Review, 86,* 465–485.

Ellsberg, D. (1961). Risk, ambiguity, and the Savage axioms. *Quarterly Journal of Economics, 75,* 643–669.

Ericsson, K.A. & Simon, H.A. (1980). Verbal reports as data. *Psychological Review, 87,* 215–251.

Estes, W.K. (1976). The cognitive side of probability learning. *Psychological Review, 83,* 37–64.

Evans, J.St.B.T. (1982). *The psychology of deductive reasoning.* London: Routledge & Kegan Paul.

Evans, J.St.B.T. & Pollard, P. (1982). Statistical judgment: A further test of the representativeness construct. *Acta Psychologica, 51,* 91–103.

Farquhar, P.H. (1982) *Utility assessment methods.* Working Paper 81–5, Graduate School of Administration, Davis, CA: University of California.

Feather, N. (Ed.). (1982). *Expectations and actions: Expectancy-value models in psychology.* Hillsdale, NJ: Erlbaum.

Ferrell, W.R. & McGoey, P.J.A. (1980). A model of calibration for subjective probabilities. *Organizational Behavior and Human Performance, 26,* 32–53.

Fischer, G.W. (1975). Experimental applications of multi-attribute utility models. In D. Wendt & C. Vlek (Eds.), *Utility, probability, and human decision making.* Dordrecht, The Netherlands: D. Reidel.

Fischer, G.W. (1977). Convergent validation of decomposed multiattribute utility assessment procedures for risky and riskless decisions. *Organizational Behavior and Human Performance, 18,* 295–315.

Fischhoff, B. (1975). Hindsight ≠ foresight: The effect of outcome knowledge on judgment under uncertainty. *Journal of Experimental Psychology: Human Perception and Performance, 1,* 288–299.

Fischhoff, B. (1982a). Debiasing. In D. Kahneman, P. Slovic, & A. Tversky (Eds.), *Judgment under uncertainty: Heuristics and biases.* New York: Cambridge University Press.

Fischhoff, B. (1982b). For those condemned to study

the past. In D. Kahneman, P. Slovic, & A. Tversky (Eds.), *Judgment under uncertainty: Heuristics and biases*. New York: Cambridge University Press.

Fischhoff, B. (1983). Predicting frames. *Journal of Experimental Psychology: Learning, Memory and Cognition, 9,* 103–116.

Fischhoff, B. & Beyth-Marom, R. (1983). Hypothesis evaluation from a Bayesian perspective. *Psychological Review, 90,* 239–260.

Fischhoff, B., Goitein, B., & Shapira, Z. (1982). The experienced utility of expected utility approaches. In N. Feather (Ed.), *Expectancy, incentive, and action*. Hillsdale, NJ: Erlbaum.

Fischhoff, B., Lichtenstein, S., Slovic, P., Derby, S.L., & Keeney, R.L. (1981). *Acceptable risk*. New York: Cambridge University Press.

Fischhoff, B., Slovic, P., & Lichtenstein, S. (1977). Knowing with certainty: The appropriateness of extreme confidence. *Journal of Experimental Psychology: Human Perception and Performance, 3,* 552–564.

Fischhoff, B., Slovic, P., & Lichtenstein, S. (1978). Fault trees: Sensitivity of estimated failure probabilities to problem representation. *Journal of Experimental Psychology: Human Perception and Performance, 4,* 330–344.

Fischhoff, B., Slovic, P., & Lichtenstein, S. (1980). Knowing what you want: Measuring labile values. in T. Wallsten (Ed.), *Cognitive processes in choice and decision behavior*. Hillsdale, NJ: Erlbaum.

Fishburn, P.C. (1982a). *The foundations of expected utility theory*. Dordrecht, Holland: D. Reidel.

Fishburn, P.C. (1982b). Nontransitive measurable utility. *Journal of Mathematical Psychology, 26,* 31–67.

Fishburn, P.C. (1983). *Normative theories of decision making under risk and under uncertainty*. Research paper, 75th Anniversary Colloquium Series, Harvard Business School, Cambridge, MA.

Fisher, I. (1906). *The nature of capital and income*. New York: Macmillan.

Flaherty, E.G. (1975). The thinking aloud technique and problem solving ability. *Journal of Educational Research, 68,* 223–225.

Friedman, M.P. (1966). Consumer confusion in the selection of supermarket products. *Journal of Applied Psychology, 50,* 529–534.

Furby, L. (1973). Interpreting regression toward the mean in developmental research. *Developmental Psychology, 8,* 172–179.

Gaeth, G.J. & Shanteau, J. (1984). Reducing the influence of irrelevant information on experienced decision makers. *Organizational Behavior and Human Performance. 33,* 263–282.

Geller, E.S. & Pitz, G.F. (1968). Confidence and decision speed in the revision of opinion. *Organizational Behavior and Human Performance, 3,* 190–201.

Gettys, C.F., Kelly, C. III., & Peterson, C.R. (1973). The best-guess hypothesis in multistage inference. *Organizational Behavior and Human Performance, 10,* 364–373.

Gettys, C.F., Manning, C.A., & Casey, J.T. (1981). *An evaluation of human act generation performance*. (Report No. TR 15-8-81). Decision Processes Laboratory, University of Oklahoma, Norman, OK.

Gettys, C.F., Manning, C., Mehle, T., & Fisher, S. (1980). *Hypothesis generation: A final report of three years of research*. (Report No. TR-15-10-80). Decision Processes Laboratory, Dept. of Psychology, University of Oklahoma, Norman, OK.

Goldberg, L.R. (1970). Man vs. model of man: A rationale, plus some evidence, for a method of improving on clinical inferences. *Psychological Bulletin, 73,* 422–432.

Goldstein, W.M. & Einhorn, H.J. (1987). Expression theory and the preference reversal phenomena. *Psychological Review, 94,* 236–254.

Goodman, B., Saltzman, M., Edwards, W., & Krantz, D.H. (1979). Prediction of bids for two-outcome gambles in a casino setting. *Organizational Behavior and Human Performance, 24,* 382–399.

Grether, D.M. & Plott, C.R. (1979). Economic theory of choice and the preference reversal phenomenon. *American Economic Review, 69,* 623–638.

Hammond, K.R., & Adelman, L. (1976). Science, values, and human judgment. *Science, 194,* 389–396.

Hammond, K.R., Rohrbaugh, J., Mumpower, J., & Adelman, L. (1977). Social judgment theory: Applications in policy formation. In M.F. Kaplan & S. Schwartz (Eds.), *Human judgment and decision processes in applied settings*. New York: Academic Press.

Hammond, K.R., Stewart, T.R., Adelman, L., & Wascoe, N.E. (1975). *Report to the Denver City Council and Mayor regarding the choice of handgun ammunition for the Denver Police Department*. (Report No. 179). Program of Research on Human Judgment and Social Interaction. Boulder: University of Colorado, Institute of Behavioral Science.

Hammond, K.R., Stewart, T.R., Brehmer, B., & Steinmann, D.O. (1975). Social judgment theory. In M.F. Kaplan & S. Schwartz (Eds.), *Human judgment and decision processes*. New York: Academic Press.

Hax, A.C. & Wiig, K.M. (1977). The use of decision analysis in capital investment problems. In D.E. Bell, R.L. Keeney & H. Raiffa (Eds.), *Conflicting objectives in decisions*. New York: Wiley.

Hayes, J.R. (1982). Issues in protocol analysis. In G. Ungson & D. Braunstein (Eds.), *Decision making: An interdisciplinary inquiry.* Boston: Kent.

Hershey, J.C., Kunreuther, H.C., & Schoemaker, P.J.H. (1982). Sources of bias in assessment procedures for utility functions. *Management Science, 28,* 936–954.

Hoffman, P.J. (1960). The paramorphic representation of clinical judgment. *Psychological Bulletin, 47,* 116–131.

Hoffman, P.J. (1968). Cue-consistency and configurality in human judgment. In B. Kleinmuntz (Ed.), *Formal representation of human judgment.* New York: Wiley.

Howard, R.A. (1968). The foundation of decision analysis. *IEEE Transactions on Systems, Science and Cybernetics, SSC-4,* 393–401.

Howard, R.A., Matheson, J.E., & North, D.W. (1972). The decision to seed hurricanes. *Science, 176,* 1191–1202.

Huber, G.P., Daneshgar, R., & Ford, D.L. (1971). An empirical comparison of five utility models for predicting job preferences. *Organizational Behavior and Human Performance, 6,* 267–282.

Huber, O. (1980). The influence of some task variables on cognitive operations in an information-processing decision model. *Acta Psychologica, 45,* 187–196.

Huber, O. (1983). Dominance among some cognitive strategies for multidimensional decisions. In L. Sjöberg, T. Tyszka, & J. Wise (Eds.), *Human decision making.* Bodafors, Sweden: Doxa.

Hursch, C., Hammond, K.R., & Hursch, J.L. (1964). Some methodological considerations in multiple cue probability studies. *Psychological Review, 71,* 42–60.

Jacoby, J. (1975). Perspectives on a consumer information processing research program. *Communication Research, 2,* 203–215.

Jacoby, J. (1977). The emerging behavioral process technology in consumer decision-making research. In W.D. Perreault (Ed.), *Advances in consumer research.* Chicago: Association for Consumer Research.

Jarvik, M.E. (1951). Probability learning and a negative recency effect in the serial anticipation of alternative symbols. *Journal of Experimental Psychology, 41,* 291–297.

Jenkins, H. & Ward, W. (1965). Judgment of contingency between responses and outcomes. *Psychological Monographs, 79,* 1–17.

Jennings, D.L., Amabile, T.M., & Ross, L. (1982). Informal covariation assessment: Data-based versus theory-based judgments. In D. Kahneman, P. Slovic, & A. Tversky (Eds.), *Judgment under uncertainty: Heuristics and biases.* New York: Cambridge University Press.

Jensen, F.A. & Peterson, C.R. (1973). Psychological effects of proper scoring rules. *Organizational Behavior and Human Performance, 9,* 307–317.

John, R.S. & Edwards, W. (1978). *Importance weight assessment for additive, riskless preference functions: A review.* (SSRI Technical Research Report 78-5). Los Angeles: University of Southern California.

Johnson, E. (1979). *Deciding how to decide: The effort of making a decision.* Unpublished manuscript, University of Chicago.

Kadane, J. & Lichtenstein, S. (1982). *A subjectivist view of calibration.* Decision Research Report 82-6.

Kahneman, D., Slovic, P., & Tversky, A. (Eds.) (1982). *Judgment under uncertainty: Heuristics and biases.* New York: Cambridge University Press.

Kahneman, D. & Tversky, A. (1972a). Subjective probability: A judgment of representativeness. *Cognitive Psychology, 3,* 430–454.

Kahneman, D. & Tversky, A. (1972b). On the psychology of prediction. *Oregon Research Institute Research Monograph, 12,* No. 4.

Kahneman, D. & Tversky, A. (1973). On the psychology of prediction. *Psychological Review, 80,* 237–251.

Kahneman, D. & Tversky, A. (1979). Prospect theory. *Econometrica, 47,* 263–292.

Keeney, R.L. (1977). The art of assessing multiattribute utility functions. *Organizational Behavior and Human Performance, 19,* 267–310.

Keeney, R.L. (1982). Decision analysis: An overview. *Operations Research, 30,* 803–838.

Keeney, R.L., & Raiffa, H. (1976). *Decisions with multiple objectives: Preferences and value tradeoffs.* New York: Wiley.

Kleinmuntz, B. (1963). MMPI decision rules for the identification of college maladjustment: A digital computer approach. *Psychological Monographs, 77,* No. 14 (Whole No. 577).

Knight, F.H. (1921). *Risk, uncertainty, and profit.* Boston: Houghton Mifflin.

Koriat, A., Lichtenstein, W., & Fischhoff, B. (1980). Reasons for confidence. *Journal of Experimental Psychology: Human Learning and Memory, 6,* 107–118.

Krantz, D.H., Luce, R.D., Suppes, P., & Tversky, A. (1971). *Foundations of measurement: Vol. 1.* New York: Academic Press.

Krantz, D.H. & Tversky, A. (1971). Measurement analysis of composition rules in psychology. *Psychological Review, 78,* 151–169.

Krischer, J.P. (1980). An annotated bibliography of decision analytic applications to health care. *Operations Research, 28,* 97–113.

Kunreuther, H., Ginsberg, R., Miller, L., Sagi, P., Slovic, P., Borkan, B., & Katz, N. (1978). *Disaster insurance protection: Public policy lessons.* New York: Wiley.

Lichtenstein, S. (1965). Bases for preference among three-outcome bets. *Journal of Experimental Psychology, 69*, 162–169.

Lichtenstein, S. (1982). Commentary on Hayes's paper. In G. Ungson & D. Braunstein (Eds.), *Decision making: An interdisciplinary inquiry.* Boston: Kent.

Lichtenstein, S. & Fischhoff, B. (1980). Training for calibration. *Organizational Behavior and Human Performance, 26*, 149–171.

Lichtenstein, S., Fischhoff, B., & Phillips, L.D. (1982). Calibration of probabilities: State of the art to 1980. In D. Kahneman, P. Slovic, & A. Tversky (Eds.), *Judgment under uncertainty: Heuristics and biases.* New York: Cambridge University Press.

Lichtenstein, S. & Newman, J.R. (1967). Empirical scaling of common verbal phrases associated with numerical probabilities. *Psychonomic Science, 9*, 563–564.

Lichtenstein, S. & Slovic, P. (1971). Reversals of preference between bids and choices in gambling decisions. *Journal of Experimental Psychology, 89*, 46–55.

Lichtenstein, S. & Slovic, P. (1973). Response-induced reversals of preference in gambling: An extended replication in Las Vegas. *Journal of Experimental Psychology, 101*, 16–20.

Lichtenstein, S., Slovic, P., Fischhoff, B., Layman, M., & Combs, B. (1978). Judged frequency of lethal events. *Journal of Experimental Psychology: Human Learning and Memory, 4*, 551–578.

Lindsay, P.H. & Norman, D.A. (1972). *Human information processing: An introduction to psychology.* New York: Academic Press.

Llewellyn-Thomas, M., Sutherland, H.J., Tibshirani, R., Ciampi, A., Till, J.E., & Boyd, N.F. (1982). The measurement of patients' values in medicine. *Medical Decision Making, 2*, 449–462.

Loomes, G. & Sugden, R. (1982). Regret theory: An alternative theory of rational choice under uncertainty. *Economic Journal, 92*, 805–824.

Lopes, L.L. (1982a). Doing the impossible: A note on induction and the experience of randomness. *Journal of Experimental Psychology: Learning, Memory, and Cognition, 8*, 626–636.

Lopes, L.L. (1987). Procedural debiasing. *Acta Psychologica, 64*, 167–185.

Lopes, L.L. (1982b). *Toward a procedural theory of judgment.* (Report WHIPP 17). Wisconsin Human Information Processing Program, Dept. of Psychology, Madison, WI.

Luce, R.D. (1959). *Individual choice behavior.* New York: Wiley.

Luce, R.D. (1977). The choice axiom after twenty years. *Journal of Mathematical Psychology, 15*, 215–233.

Luce, R.D. (1980). Several possible measures of risk. *Theory and Decision, 12*, 217–228.

Luce, R.D. (1981). Correction to "Several possible measures of risk." *Theory and Decision, 13*, 381.

Luce, R.D. & Suppes, P. (1965). Preference, utility, and subjective probability. In R.D. Luce, R.R. Bush, & E. Galanter (Eds.), *Handbook of mathematical psychology: Vol. 3.* New York: Wiley.

Luce, R.D. & Tukey, J.W. (1964). Simultaneous conjoint measurement: A new type of fundamental measurement. *Journal of Mathematical Psychology, 1*, 1–27.

MacCrimmon, K.R. (1968). Descriptive and normative implications of the decision-theory postulates. In K. Borch & J. Mossin (Eds.), *Risk and uncertainty.* New York: St. Martins Press.

MacCrimmon, K.R. & Larsson, S. (1976). Utility theory: Axioms versus "paradoxes." In M. Allais & O. Hagen (Eds.), *Rational decisions under uncertainty,* special volume of *Theory and Decision.*

MacCrimmon, K.R. & Siu, J.K. (1974). Making tradeoffs. *Decision Sciences, 5*, 680–704.

March, J.G. (1978). Bounded rationality, ambiguity, and the engineering of choice. *Bell Journal of Economics, 9*, 587–608.

March, J.G. (1982, January). *Theories of choice and the making of decisions.* Paper presented at the American Association of the Advancement of Science, Washington, DC.

Matheson, J.E. & Roths, W.J. (1967). Decision analysis of space projects: Voyager Mars. In R. Howard, J.E. Matheson, & K.L. Miller (Eds.), *Readings in decision analysis.* Palo Alto, CA: Stanford Research Institute.

McNeil, B.J., Pauker, S.G., Sox, H.C. Jr., & Tversky, A. (1982). On the elicitation of preferences for alternative therapies. *New England Journal of Medicine, 306*, 1259–1262.

McNeil, B.J., Weichselbaum, R., & Pauker, S.G. (1981). Speech and survival: Tradeoffs between quality and quantity of life in laryngeal cancer. *New England Journal of Medicine, 305*, 982–987.

Meehl, P.E. & Rosen, A. (1955). Antecedent probability and the efficacy of psychometric signs, patterns or cutting scores. *Psychological Bulletin, 52*, 194–216.

Miller, G.A. (1956). The magical number seven, plus or minus two: Some limits on our capacity for processing information. *Psychological Review, 63*, 81–97.

Montgomery, H. (1983). Decision rules and the search for a dominance structure: Towards a process model of decision making. In P. Humphreys, O.

Svenson, & A. Vari (Eds.), *Analyzing and aiding decision processes*. Amsterdam: North Holland.

Moskowitz, H. (1974). Effects of problem representation and feedback on rational behavior in Allais and Morlat-type problems. *Decision Sciences, 3,* 225–241.

Mosteller, F. & Nogee, P. (1951). An experimental measurement of utility. *Journal of Political Economics, 59,* 371–404.

Munera, H.A. & de Neufville, R. (1982, July). *A decision analysis model when the substitution principle is not acceptable*. Paper presented to the First International Conference on Foundations of Utility and Risk Theory, Oslo, Norway.

Murphy, A.H. & Winkler, R.C. (1977). Can weather forecasters formulate reliable probability forecasts of precipitation and temperature? *National Weather Digest, 2*(2), 2–9.

National Academy of Sciences. (1983). *Research needs in human factors*. Washington, DC: The Academy.

Newell, A. (1980). Reasoning, problem solving and decision processes: The problem space as a fundamental category. In R.S. Nickerson (Ed.), *Attention and Performance, VIII*. Hillsdale, NJ: Erlbaum.

Newell, A. & Simon, H.A. (1972). *Human problem solving*. Englewood Cliffs, NJ: Prentice–Hall.

Nisbett, R.E. & Ross, L. (1980). *Human inference: Strategies and shortcomings of social judgment*. Englewood Cliffs, NJ: Prentice–Hall.

Nisbett, R.E. & Wilson, T.D. (1977). Telling more than we can know: Verbal reports on mental processes. *Psychological Review, 84,* 231–259.

Novick, M.R., Dekeyrel, D.F., & Chuang, D.T. (1979). *Local and regional coherence utility procedures*. Technical Report 79-7. College of Education, Univ. of Iowa, Iowa City.

Pauker, S. G. (1976). Coronary artery surgery: The use of decision analysis. *Annals of Internal Medicine, 85,* 8–18.

Payne, J.W. (1976). Task complexity and contingent processing in decision making: An information search and protocol analysis. *Organizational Behavior and Human Performance, 16,* 36–387.

Payne, J.W. (1980). Information processing theory: Some concepts applied to decision research. In T. Wallsten (Ed.), *Cognitive processes in choice and decision behavior*. Hillsdale, NJ: Erlbaum.

Payne, J.W. (1982). Contingent decision behavior. *Psychological Bulletin, 92,* 382–401.

Payne, J.W. & Braunstein, M.L. (1971). Preferences among gambles with equal underlying distributions. *Journal of Experimental Psychology, 87,* 13–18.

Payne, J.W. & Braunstein, M.L. (1978). Risky choice: An examination of information acquisition behavior. *Memory and Cognition, 6,* 554–561.

Payne, J.W., Braunstein, M.L., & Carroll, J.S. (1978). Exploring predecisional behavior: An alternative approach to decision research. *Organizational Behavior and Human Performance, 22,* 17–44.

Payne, J.W., Laughhunn, D.J., & Crum, R. (1980). Translation of gambles and aspiration level effects in risky choice behavior. *Management Science, 26,* 1039–1060.

Payne, J.W., Laughhunn, D.J., & Crum, R. (1981). Further tests of aspiration level effects in risky choice behavior. *Management Science, 27,* 953–958.

Phillips, L.D. & Edwards, W. (1966). Conservatism in a simple probability inference task. *Journal of Experimental Psychology, 72,* 346–354.

Pitz, G.F. (1974). Subjective probability distributions for imperfectly known quantities. In L.W. Gregg (Ed.), *Knowledge and cognition*. Potomac MD: Erlbaum.

Pitz, G.F. (1977). Decision making and cognition. In H. Jungermann & G. de Zeeuw (Eds.), *Decision making and change in human affairs*. Dordrecht, Holland: D. Reidel.

Pitz, G.F., Sachs, N.J., & Heerboth, J. (1980). Procedures for eliciting choices in the analysis of individual decisions. *Organizational Behavior and Human Performance, 26,* 396–408.

Pliske, R.M., Gettys, C.F., Manning, L., & Casey, J.T. (1982). *Act generation performance: The effects of incentive*. (TR 15-8-82). Decision Processes Laboratory, University of Oklahoma, Norman, OK.

Polanyi, M. (1958). *Personal knowledge*. London: Routledge & Kegan Paul.

Posner, M.I. (1982). Protocol analysis and human cognition. In G. Ungson & K. Braunstein (Eds.), *Decision making: An interdisciplinary inquiry*. Boston: Kent.

Poulton, E.C. (1982). Biases in quantitiative judgments. *Applied Ergonomics, 13,* 31–42.

Raaij, W.F. van. (1983). Techniques for process training in decision making. In L. Sjöberg, T. Tyszka, & J. Wise (Eds.), *Human decision making*. Bodafors, Sweden: Doxa.

Raiffa, H. (1968). *Decision analysis*. Reading, MA: Addison–Wesley.

Ramsey, F.P. (1931). Truth and probability. In F.P. Ramsey, *The foundations of mathematics and other logical essays*. New York: Harcourt Brace.

Restle, F. (1961). *Psychology of judgment and choice: A theoretical essay*. New York: Wiley.

Robinson, G.H. (1964). Continuous estimation of a time-varying probability. *Ergonomics, 7,* 7–21.

Rumelhart, D.L. & Greeno, J.G. (1971). Similarity between stimuli: An experimental test of the Luce and Restle choice models. *Journal of Mathematical Psychology, 8,* 370–381.

Russ, F.A. (1971). Consumer evaluation of alternative product models. Unpublished doctoral dissertation, Carnegie-Mellon University, Pittsburgh, PA.

Russo, J.E. (1977). The value of unit-price information. *Journal of Marketing Research, 14,* 193–201.

Russo, J.E. & Dosher, B.A. (1983). Strategies for multiattribute binary choice. *Journal of Experimental Psychology: Learning, Memory, and Cognition, 9,* 676–696.

Russo, J.E. & Rosen, L.D. (1975). An eye-fixation analysis of multialternative choice. *Memory and Cognition, 3,* 267–276.

Sage, A.P. & White, E.B. (1983). Decision and information structures in regret models of judgment and choice. *IEEE Transactions on Systems, Man and Cybernetics, SMC-13,* 136–145.

Samuelson, P.A. (1950). Probability and the attempts to measure utility. *Economic Review* (Toyko), *1,* 167–173.

Savage, L.J. (1954). *The foundations of statistics.* New York: Wiley.

Schelling, T.C. (1982, January). *Identifying that authentic self.* Paper presented at the meeting of the working group on rationality. Paris.

Schoemaker, P.J.H. & Waid, C.C. (1982). An experimental comparison of different approaches to determining weights in additive utility models. *Management Science, 28,* 182–196.

Schum, D. (1980). Current developments in research on cascaded inference processes. In T. Wallsten (Ed.), *Cognitive processes in choice and decision behavior.* Hillsdale, NJ: Erlbaum.

Shafer, G. & Tversky, A. (1985). Languages and designs for probability judgment. *Cognitive Science, 9,* 309–339.

Shaklee, H. & Tucker, D. (1980). A rule analysis of judgments of covariation between events. *Memory and Cognition, 8,* 459–467.

Shapira, Z. (1975). Measuring subjective probabilities by the magnitude production method. *Organizational Behavior and Human Performance, 14,* 314–320.

Sheridan, J.E., Richards, M.D., & Slocum, J.W. (1975). Comparative analysis of expectancy and heuristic models of decision behavior. *Journal of Applied Psychology, 60,* 361–368.

Shuford, E.H., Jr. (1961). Percentage estimation of proportion as a function of element type, exposure type, and task. *Journal of Experimental Psychology, 61,* 430–436.

Shuford, E.H., Jr., Albert, A., & Massengill, H.E. (1966). Admissible probability measurement procedures. *Psychometrika, 31,* 125–145.

Shugan, S.M. (1980). The cost of thinking. *Journal of Consumer Research, 7,* 99–111.

Simon, H.A. (1956). Rational choice and the structure of the environment. *Psychological Review, 63,* 129–138.

Simon, H.A. (1959). Theories of decision making in economics and behavioral science. *American Economic Review, 49,* 253–283.

Simon, H.A. (1976). Discussion: Cognition and social behavior. In J.S. Carroll & J.W. Payne (Eds.), *Cognition and social behavior.* Hillsdale, NJ: Erlbaum.

Sjöberg, L. (1977). Choice frequency and similarity. *Scandinavian Journal of Psychology, 18,* 103–115.

Slovic, P. (1972). From Shakespeare to Simon: Speculation—and some evidence—about man's ability to process information. *Oregon Research Institute Research Monograph, 12*(2).

Slovic, P. (1975). Choice between equally valued alternatives. *Journal of Experimental Psychology: Human Perception and Performance, 1,* 280–287.

Slovic, P. & Fischhoff, B. (1977). On the psychology of experimental surprises. *Journal of Experimental Psychology: Human Perception and Performance, 3,* 544–551.

Slovic, P., Fischhoff, B., & Lichtenstein, S. (1977). Behavioral decision theory. *Annual Review of Psychology, 28,* 1–39.

Slovic, P., Fischhoff, B., & Lichtenstein, S. (1982). Response mode, framing, and information processing effects in risk assessment. In R.M. Hogarth (Ed.), *New directions for methodology of social and behavioral science: The framing of questions and the consistency of response.* San Francisco: Jossey-Bass.

Slovic, P. & Lichtenstein, S. (1968a). The importance of variance preferences in gambling decisions. *Journal of Experimental Psychology, 78,* 646–654.

Slovic, P. & Lichtenstein, S. (1968b). The relative importance of probabilities and payoffs in risk-taking. *Journal of Experimental Psychology Monograph Supplement, 78*(3), part 2.

Slovic, P. & Lichtenstein, S. (1971). Comparison of Bayesian and regression approaches to the study of information processing in judgment. *Organizational Behavior and Human Performance, 6,* 649–744.

Slovic, P. & Lichtenstein, S. (1983). Preference reversals: A broader perspective. *American Economic Review, 73,* 596–605.

Slovic, P., Lichtenstein, S., & Edwards, W. (1965). Boredom-induced changes in preferences among bets. *American Journal of Psychology, 78,* 208–217.

Slovic, P. & MacPhillamy, D.J. (1974). Dimensional commensurability and cue utilization in comparative judgment. *Organizational Behavior and Human Performance, 11,* 172–194.

Slovic, P. & Tversky, A. (1974). Who accepts Savage's axiom? *Behavioral Science, 19,* 368–373.

Smedslund, J. (1963). The concept of correlation in adults. *Scandinavian Journal of Psychology, 4*, 165–173.

Synder, M. & Swann, W.B. (1978). Hypothesis testing procedures in social interaction. *Journal of Personality and Social Psychology, 36*, 1202–1212.

Spetzler, C.S. & Staël von Holstein, C.A.S. (1975). Probability encoding in decision analysis. *Management Science, 22*, 340–358.

Stillwell, W.G., Barron, F.H., & Edwards, W. (1983). Evaluating credit applications: A valuation of multiattribute utility techniques against a real world criterion. *Organizational Behavior and Human Performance, 32*, 87–108.

Stillwell, W.G., Seaver, D.A., & Edwards, W. (1981). A comparison of weight approximation techniques in multiattribute utility decision making. *Organizational Behavior and Human Performance, 28*, 62–77.

Svenson, O. (1974). Coded think-aloud protocols obtained when making a choice to purchase one of seven hypothetically offered houses. Unpublished manuscript, University of Stockholm.

Svenson, O. (1979). Process descriptions of decision making. *Organizational Behavior and Human Performance, 23*, 86–112.

Thaler, R.H. (1985). Mental accounting and consumer choice. *Marketing Science, 4*, 199–214.

Thaler, R.H. & Shefrin, H.M. (1981). An economic theory of self control. *Journal of Political Economy, 89*, 392–406.

Thurstone, L.L. (1927). A law of comparative judgment. *Psychological Review, 34*, 273–286.

Titchener, E.B. (1910). *A textbook of psychology*. New York: MacMillian.

Tucker, L.R. (1964). A suggested alternative formulation in the development of Hursch, Hammond, and Hursch, and by Hammond, Hursch, and Todd. *Psychological Review, 71*, 528–530.

Tversky, A. (1967a). Additivity, utility and subjective probability. *Journal of Mathematical Psychology, 4*, 175–202.

Tversky, A. (1967b). Utility theory and additivity analysis of risky choices. *Journal of Experimental Psychology, 75*, 27–36.

Tversky, A. (1969). Intransitivity of preferences. *Psychological Review, 76*, 31–48.

Tversky, A. (1972a). Choice by elimination. *Journal of Mathematical Psychology, 9*, 341–367.

Tversky, A. (1972b). Elimination by aspects: A theory of choice. *Psychological Review, 79*, 281–299.

Tversky, A. & Kahneman, D. (1973). Availability: A heuristic for judging frequency and probability. *Cognitive Psychology, 4*, 207–232.

Tversky, A. & Kahneman, D. (1974). Judgment under uncertainty: Heuristics and biases. *Science, 185*, 1124–1131.

Tversky, A. & Kahneman, D. (1981). The framing of decisions and the psychology of choice. *Science, 211*, 453–458.

Tversky, A. & Kahneman, D. (1982). Evidential impact of base rates. In D. Kahneman, P. Slovic, & A. Tversky (Eds.), *Judgment under uncertainty: Heuristics and biases*. New York: Cambridge University Press.

Tversky, A. & Kahneman, D. (1983). Extensional vs. intuitive reasoning: The conjunction fallacy in probability judgment. *Psychological Review, 91*, 293–315.

Tversky, A. & Russo, J.E. (1969). Similarity and substitutability in binary choices. *Journal of Mathematical Psychology, 6*, 1–12.

Tversky, A. & Sattath, S. (1979). Preference trees. *Psychological Review, 86*, 542–573.

Tversky, A., Sattath, S., & Slovic, P. (in press). Contingent weighting in judgment and choice. *Psychological Review*.

Tyszka, T. (1981). Simple decision strategies vs. multiattribute utility theory approach to complex decision problems. *Praxiology Yearbook, No. 2*.

Tyszka, T. (1983). Contextual multiattribute decision rules. In L. Sjöberg, T. Tyszka, & J. Wise (Eds.), *Human decision making*. Bodafors, Sweden: Doxa.

von Neumann, J. & Morgenstern, O. (1947). *Theory of games and economic behavior*. Princeton, NJ: Princeton University Press.

von Winterfeldt, D. (1975). An overview, integration, and evaluation of utility theory for decision analysis. (SSRI Technical Research Report 75-9). Los Angeles: University of Southern California.

von Winterfeldt, D. & Edwards, W. (1986). Decision analysis and behavioural research. Cambridge, Cambridge University Press.

Wagenaar, W.A. (1972). Generation of random sequences by human subjects: A critical survey of literature. *Psychological Bulletin, 77*, 65–72.

Wainer, H. (1976). Estimating coefficients in linear models: It don't make no never mind. *Psychological Bulletin, 83*, 213–217.

Wallsten, T. & Budescu, D. (1983). Encoding subjective probabilities: A psychological and psychometric review. *Management Science, 29*, 151–173.

Ward, W. & Jenkins, H. (1965). The display of information and the judgment of contingency. *Canadian Journal of Psychology, 19*, 231–241.

Wason, P.C. (1960). On the failure to eliminate hypotheses in a perceptual task. *Quarterly Journal of Experimental Psychology, 12*, 129–140.

Wason, P.C. (1968). Reasoning about a rule. *Quarterly Journal of Experimental Psychology, 23,* 273–281.

Weber, E.U. (1984). Combine and conquer: A joint application of conjoint and functional approaches to the problem of risk measurement. *Journal of Experimental Psychology: Human Perception and Performance, 10,* 179–194.

White, G.F. (1964). Choice of adjustment to floods. (Research Paper No. 93). Chicago: University of Chicago, Dept. of Geography.

Whitlow, J.W., Jr. & Estes, W.K. (1979). Judgments of relative frequency in relation to shifts of event frequencies: Evidence for a limited-capacity model. *Journal of Experimental Psychology: Human Learning and Memory, 5,* 395–408.

Wright, P.L. (1974a). The harassed decision maker: Time pressures, distraction, and the use of evidence. *Journal of Applied Psychology, 59,* 555–561.

Wright, P.L. (1974b). The use of phased, noncompensatory strategies in decisions between multi-attribute products. (Research Paper 223). Graduate School of Business, Stanford University.

Wright, P.L. & Barbour, F. (1977). Phased decision strategies: Sequels to an initial screening. In M.K. Starr & M. Zeleny (Eds.), *North-Holland/ TIMS studies in the management sciences: Multiple criteria decision making.* Amsterdam: North Holland.

# Chapter 11

# ATTENTION

**Richard M. Shiffrin,** *Indiana University*

Concepts, theories, and research concerning attention have come to play a major role in almost every subfield within psychology. Contributing to this prominence is the generality of the construct. *Attention* has been used to refer to all those aspects of human cognition that the subject can control (like those aspects that Atkinson and Shiffrin, 1968, termed *control processes*), and to all aspects of cognition having to do with limited resources or capacity, and methods of dealing with such constraints.

The pervasiveness of attention in cognition was accepted from the earliest days of psychology, and the term was used almost synonymously with cognition and consciousness (e.g. James, 1890; Pillsbury, 1908). Although attentional research has continued throughout the intervening years, the central status of the concept was lost with the rise of behaviorism (circa 1920), probably because most prior research had been based on introspective methods. The modern upsurge in attentional research and theory began about 1950 among applied psychologists and engineers concerned with man-machine interactions and communication and information theory. The field grew rapidly following publication of Broadbent's book in 1958.

The coverage in this chapter will be quite limited, focusing upon a few of the important themes that have motivated the greatest theoretical interest and empirical study: These include automatism and control, dividing and focusing of resources during perception, locus and generality of capacity limitations, and stimulus and task characteristics important for the understanding of these issues. The reader interested in more comprehensive coverage within the cognitive, perceptual, and performance areas is referred to the continuing series of edited volumes titled Attention and Performance (12 volumes thus far), a volume entitled Varieties of Attention edited by Parasuraman and Davies (1984), and books by Broadbent (1958, 1971), Kahneman (1973), Keele (1973), Moray, (1969a,b), Posner (1978), Underwood (1976), Norman (1969), and Neisser (1967, 1976). These sources refer to most of the important studies, though they themselves represent only a small sample of the extant literature.

Everyone who has worked in the field of attention has made note of the organism's limited ability to process information and carry out actions. These are usually termed *capacity limitations* or *resource limitations*. At times there appears to be a pure trading relationship in force, such that extra resources devoted to one task or process need to be borrowed (at a cost) from some other task or process. Furthermore, attention is often conceived as a relatively slow and serial activity, the focus of attention being in one place at one time. It had been equally clear to workers in the field that normal human behavior could not take place if all activity had to be governed by attentive processes operating in such a limited fashion. Almost any skilled activity, whether involving actions (e.g. sports, music performance, typing, automobile driving) or mental operations (e.g. reading, retrieving information from memory, perceiving) is carried out with such a complex set of operations operating in concert (in parallel) that much of the behavior must be occurring outside the normal focus of attention. Partly for this reason, all researchers have incorporated various types of *automatic processes* into their theories. Much of the research and theory testing in the field has been directed toward understanding the roles of automatic and attentive processes. A common theoretical view of perceptual processing places automatic processes (often termed *preattentive*) at an early stage, followed by limited attentive processes. An alternative theoretical view, to be explored in this chapter, assumes automatic and attentive processes operate interactively and concurrently, at most stages of processing.

Regardless of one's theoretical perspective, it is clear that automatic processes and attention go hand in hand, an understanding of one requiring an understanding of the other. We shall therefore begin this chapter by assessing the characteristics of automatism and attentive processes. Such distinctions date back to the beginning of psychology, and it is useful to start by reviewing some research carried out around the turn of the century.

## EARLY STUDIES CONCERNING AUTOMATIZATION

### Skill Development

Skill acquisition is one of the most fundamental topics in psychology. One of the best known and earliest studies of the relationship of skill acquisi-

tion to attention and automatism[1] was carried out by Bryan and Harter (1899). They studied the development of ability to send and receive telegraph messages (short and long pulses arranged in coded groups). Figure 11.1 shows representative learning curves for two subjects. *Sending* exhibits a relatively smooth improvement to an asymptote. *Receiving* exhibits two phases: a growth to a first asymptote, and then, for connected discourse, another rise to a second asymptote.

Subjective reports by expert telegraph receivers suggested a gradual shift in focus of attention during learning, from letters, to words, to phrases or groups, and then to meaning. At the same time the attention demands drop, so that the expert can take the message and yet think about the sense of the message or even about other matters entirely. Expert testimony and evidence suggested it may take ten years of practice to reach the point where the receiver finds the task to become relatively free of effort, so asymptotic automatization is no easy matter to achieve in this fairly complex task.

Bryan and Harter (1899) concluded that the receiver learns by acquiring a hierarchy of habits, from letters to syllables, to words, to phrases, to higher language habits. These are acquired simultaneously, but not equally. Movements to higher stages of expertise must await sufficient automatization of the elements lower in the hierarchy of habits. The length of any plateau in development is a measure of the difficulty of making the lower-order habits sufficiently automatic. The rapid rise afterward represents a "quick realization of powers potentially present by reason of preceding gradual and unconscious habituation." (*Sending* presumably shows no plateaus because finger movements limit performance starting at an early stage of learning.)

Bryan and Harter suggested that the rate of processes in consciousness does not increase with practice so much as the amount included in each process, consistent with their hierarchical view. They concluded that "There is no freedom except through automatism." That is, automatism

---

[1]The noun representing a state of automatic processing has traditionally been "automatism" (stress on the second syllable). In recent years, the term "automaticity" (stress on the fourth sylable) has become quite prevalent. The traditional usage will be followed in this chapter.

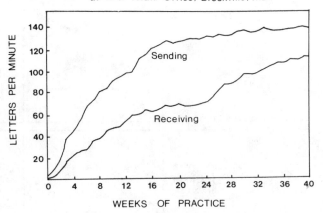

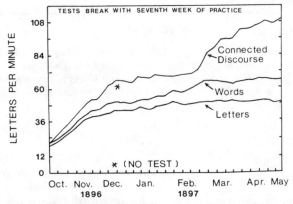

**Figure 11.1.** Telegraph learning performance for two subjects tested by Bryan and Harter (1899). Top panel shows learning to send and receive messages. Bottom panel shows receiving data only, for three types of material. From "Studies on the Telegraphic Language: The Acquisition of a Hierarchy of Habits" by W.L. Bryan and N. Harter, 1899, *Psychological Review, 6*, p. 350.

frees attention for other uses. This hypothesis, and indeed most of the suggestions of Bryan and Harter (and other early psychologists) are still an important part of present-day distinctions between automatic and attentive processes.

It should be noted that the plateaus observed by Bryan and Harter (and shown in Figure 11.1) are observable only rarely, possibly because successive stages of skill acquisition tend to merge smoothly into one another. Keller (1958) reviewed other studies of telegraphy learning (receiving) and noted that learning proceeded smoothly and regularly, without plateaus (and indeed took place far more quickly than indicated in Figure 11.1). On the basis of these

observations Keller suggested additional and different mechanisms involved in telegraphy (phonological recoding and other similar processes). Although the alternative proposals are also compatible with Bryan and Harter's views concerning automatization, they do suggest that the telegraph receiver could receive automatically, could utilize attentive resources, or both. Thus more stringent tests of automatism are needed. In one such test the subject would carry out a second attention-demanding task concurrently with the telegraphy task. As telegraphy becomes increasingly automatized, it should become possible to carry out both tasks together with increasing efficiency. Dual task

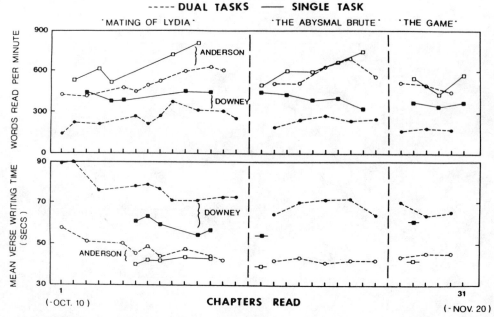

**Figure 11.2.** Performance of Downey and Anderson (1915) at reading chapters from books and at writing memorized verses, when each task is carried out alone (single task) and when both are carried out together (dual tasks). 31 chapters from three books were read over a period of about 40 days. The verses were short and did not vary during the course of the study. From "Automatic Writing" by J. Downey and J. Anderson, 1915, *American Journal of Psychology*, 26, p. 167.

studies of this sort (though not involving telegraphy) are discussed next.

## Dual Task Studies

Solomons and Stein (1896) set out to demonstrate that fairly complex tasks could be automatized. They used a dual task technique because they wished awareness to be removed from one task, and the presence of another task seemed a plausible way to accomplish this goal. In one task, one of the authors silently read an interesting story while writing down an occasional word dictated by the other (the reader scribbling continuously between dictations). Introspections revealed several stages of learning: (1) Generalized difficulty with both tasks; (2) Rapid attention switching from the story to dictation and back when necessary; (3) Less and less effort needed for dictation: (4) Dictation occurred without volition, though awareness of writing something remained; (5) Writing occurred entirely without awareness (this occurred only occasionally). With enough practice, the loudness of the dictated word could drop close to the threshold of easy hearing without affecting the automatism. Finally, the authors noted that memory for

the written words disappeared rather early in training.

In another study Solomons and Stein found it easy to learn to read in a low voice something uninteresting while listening with full attention to an interesting story read aloud at normal loudness. Quite a different situation occurred when the two subjects each read aloud something different at equal loudness, each trying to attend to the other. In this situation each was aware of hearing both voices, although grasping the meaning of one only (normally the one to be attended).

Although these introspections were useful, Downey and Anderson (1915) were motivated to obtain objective data in a similar paradigm. In the second of their five studies, the subjects (Downey and Anderson) continuously wrote perfectly memorized verses, while silently reading chapters of a novel. (The same verses were written over and over throughout the study.) Figure 11.2 gives the control ("normal") reading and writing times when only one task is carried out, and the corresponding times when both tasks are carried out together. Anderson came close to being able to carry out both tasks together at rates comparable to those holding for single tasks, possibly because he reported a tendency to read visually, a whole paragraph at a time (reading aloud caused greater deficits). Attempts to introspect tended to interfere with dual task performance and hence introspections were not reported. Retrospections revealed for both subjects an increasing tendency to lose awareness of the writing, especially when an exciting chapter was read (although writing was not greatly affected).

Downey and Anderson's fifth task was similar to that used by Solomons and Stein: Reading was done aloud and dictation consisted of continuous writing of dictated stories. The task seemed relatively easy to the subjects but a dual task deficit in performance was observed even after considerable practice. Both subjects remembered the reading material well; Anderson remembered as well much of what was dictated, although Downey had little consciousness of writing and recalled very little of the dictation.

Downey and Anderson concluded that in most of their tasks, true simultaneity of operations, without cost, could not be achieved. At least one of the tasks usually showed some deficit (although dual task performance was nonetheless impressive). They suggested the deficit could be explained not by a failure to develop some type of automatism, but by an increased effort needed to keep two processes going together, or by a specific interference with either of the operations (these ideas are reflected in recent proposals, e.g., Navon and Gopher, 1979). Finally, Downey and Anderson interpreted their lapses of awareness of dictation as lapses of memory rather than failures of perception (ideas reflected in recent proposals, e.g., Deutsch and Deutsch, 1963; Shiffrin, 1975a).

A few modern dual task studies related to these are worthy of mention in this section. Allport, Antonis, and Reynolds (1972) used students who were skilled enough to play the piano by sight-reading. These students took part in two sessions of training in which they attempted to sight-read piano pieces of differing difficulty and also shadow (repeat word for word) auditory prose passages of differing difficulty. By session two, both sight-reading and shadowing could be carried out together as well as either alone. Furthermore, memory for the prose material was as good in the dual task conditions as in the single task control conditions. The authors argued that the results could not be explained by rapid and continuous attention shifts between the two tasks, and hence argued against a single, central attention bottleneck. They suggested the existence of a number of independent, special-purpose processors and stores operating in parallel. Bottlenecks of attention are in this view due to tasks requiring use of the same processors. The authors did not give much consideration to automatization as a basis for, or as an alternative to, the development of special processors. If either or both tasks had become automatized (probably sight reading, since this skill had been practiced pre-experimentally), then the notion of a central attention bottleneck could have been retained.

Shaffer (1975) tested a skilled typist in various conditions. She could (1) Type visually presented material and simultaneously recite nursery rhymes fluently, with a cost of only about 10 percent in typing speed and errors; (2) Type and simultaneously shadow (repeat aloud) prose dictated at 140 words per minute, with only a 10 percent cost; (3) Type and simultaneously shadow random letters dictated once per second, with only a 10 percent cost (but shadowing exhibited a 20 percent performance drop). In other conditions the typing was done from auditory dictation. While typing dictation from a male voice in one ear, shadowing dictation from a female voice in the other ear proved difficult—typing speed and accuracy were poor, and shadowing was very error prone. Similarly poor results were obtained when the typing was done from auditory dictation, and the shadowing from visual input. Shaffer concluded that "attention is a control process which directs translation processing to an orderly (intended) completion." Presumably attention is needed more in the unpracticed typing from dictation tasks. Shaffer argued that all stimuli impinging on the senses are brought into contact automatically with a richly connected semantic memory, but that attention is needed to prevent the information from being dissipated in nonsystematic processing. The possibility of explaining the dual task results on the basis of automatism of certain types of typing was not considered because Shaffer felt that automatization "begs the question of what is attention."

Hirst, Spelke, Reaves, Caharack, and Neisser (1980) had subjects read stories (easy) or encyclopedia articles (hard), while writing down dictated material simultaneously. The dictation consisted of isolated words presented at a rate of about 10 per minute. As opposed to Downey and Anderson (1915) or Solomons and Stein (1896), the emphasis was on the reading, and the speed of dictation was not stressed (subjects were tested in a group and all had to finish writing a word before the next was presented). In such conditions all subjects eventually (over 50 sessions) came to read about as rapidly and comprehend the read material about as well in the dual task conditions as in the read-only control conditions. Furthermore, subjects trained to read material of one difficulty could be switched to the other material without affecting the results (except for one subject who needed additional practice). Hirst et al. (1980) argued against the possibility of rapid attention switching between tasks to explain the results, although they allow that this strategy could have been used early in training. (The argument was based on the results for tasks of differing difficulty, but is not entirely convincing because the subjects were not pushed to the limits of their dictation ability.)

In a second task, Hirst et al. (1980) trained two subjects (others could not manage to learn) to read stories while simultaneously writing down short dictated sentences (three or five words in length). The rate of dictation was determined by the subject and averaged about 20–30 words per minute. (This method was similar to that used by Downey and Anderson, 1915, who dictated whole stories.) After considerable training, dual task reading rate and comprehension of read material were comparable to those in control conditions.

The memory and understanding of the dictated sentences were also tested. When one word from a sentence was given as a cue, there was much better recall of the other words in that sentence than was the case on control trials where the "sentences" consisted of random word combinations. The dictated sentences were made up in groups such that an implication could be drawn from several successive sentences (e.g., "Their house burned. Everything was destroyed." The implication was "Everything was burned.") Subjects rated test sentences as to their likelihood of being "old." They gave slightly higher confidence ratings to "old" sentences than to "implications" which in turn were rated slightly higher than "unrelated" new sentences (made up of old words). Clearly some semantic analysis

of the dictated material was being carried out and remembered, even though little awareness of the dictated material was reported.

Hirst et al. (1980) used these results to argue against the notion that dictation had become "automatic," on the basis that automatic processing must surely be too simple to encompass the observed degree of semantic analysis. The authors argued that the development of skill results from a qualitative change involving the development of new action patterns and processing modes, not just a learning to do old things unconsciously. (They do not discuss the possibility that the newly developed processes may be automatic, nor do they justify the assertion that automatic processes must be simple, an assertion that Bryan and Harter, for example, would have found very strange.)

A comparison with Downey and Anderson's results is useful here. Downey and Anderson were able to take story dictation at about 20 words per minute while coming close to, but not quite attaining, the control reading speed. This dictation rate is quite good for story material, even though slightly less than those obtained by Hirst et al., since the sentences were of random length and read continuously. When Hirst et al. tried to dictate sentences of variable length, their subjects experienced great difficulty. Anderson's memory for dictated material was quite good, since he was able to recall freely about half of the dictated words in a one minute period. Both Anderson and Downey (who did not recall very well) reported a feeling that the meaning of the dictation had been available at the time of writing, but was then forgotten at the time of test. This observation may explain the recognition results obtained by Hirst et al. in the face of "unawareness."

## Assessment

The skill acquisition and dual task studies raise many more questions than they answer. At least one thing is clear: extended practice of the kind reported thus far leads simultaneously to improved performance and a lessening of attention demands, measured by any or all of a decrease in effort, an ability to carry on multiple tasks, a decrease in awareness, or other factors. Hirst et al. (1980; also Spelke, Hirst, & Neisser, 1976) were so impressed by such results they rejected the idea of fixed attentional capacity and argued for the "attention-is-a-skill" hypothesis, by which all attentional limitations may be removed by practice. As we shall see in the next section, this hypothesis is incorrect (though in the colloquial sense, attention is indeed a "skill").

Perhaps most striking is the contrast between the conclusions reached by the early and recent psychologists. Bryan and Harter (1899), Solomons and Stein (1896), and Downey and Anderson (1915) attributed the training effects and dual task ability to automatization; on the basis of much the same data, recent investigators such as Allport et al. (1972), Shaffer (1975), and Hirst et al. (1980) postulated alternative mechanisms (even though their alternative proposals are hard to differentiate from those positing automatization).

Although the dual task studies raise interesting questions concerning automatism and attention, and suggest some plausible hypotheses, they do not provide definitive answers. To some degree, such answers may be found in a well-studied paradigm known as *search*. This paradigm has been explored systematically and parametrically, and within the paradigm critical contrasts between automatic and attentive processes have been carried out. Furthermore, the results have suggested detailed theoretical accounts of automatic and attentive processes; the relative precision of these accounts may help resolve the worries of the recent dual task researchers who have been reluctant to invoke automatism as an explanatory construct.

For all these reasons, results from search paradigms will be treated in detail in the next section. Lest the reader be misled, it should be noted at the outset that the simple picture of automatism suggested by dual task studies must be amended in fundamental fashion. That is, the dual task results suggest that automatization is accompanied by removal of attention and consciousness. Although this may be true in some settings, the search results demonstrate that attention itself can be automatized (stimuli can be trained to attract attention automatically), a fact with important ramifications that will be covered in the next section.

## SEARCH PARADIGMS

The core area of selective attention research in the modern era is concerned with the detection or location of signals. Stimuli are presented and the subject tries to detect or locate the presence of target stimuli at least some of whose characteristics are defined in advance. The findings of greatest interest from an attentional viewpoint are the decreases in performance that occur when the number of sources of stimuli increases, when stimulus uncertainty increases, when the number of stimuli increases, or when the number of targets increases. In the following we shall focus upon paradigms in which the stimuli are presented visually, termed *visual search*. (Somewhat greater power is available in the visual modality than, say, the auditory modality because of the relative ease with which many stimuli may be presented simultaneously.)

## Terminology

The set of stimuli that the subject is instructed to detect on a trial is called the *memory set*. Sometimes there is a larger group of stimuli from which the memory set is chosen on successive trials. If so, this set is called the *memory ensemble*. The set of stimuli presented on a trial is called the *display set* (whether presented simultaneously or successively). The display set includes targets, distractors, or both. The *distractor set* is the group of stimuli presented on a trial that are *not* in the memory set. When the distractor sets on successive trials are chosen from a larger group of stimuli, the larger group is called the *distractor ensemble*. The stimuli from the memory set that are presented (in the display set) on a trial are called *targets*.

When the display set contains just one item, and memory set size varies, then the paradigm is called *memory search*. When the display set size varies, the paradigm is called *visual search*.

When the display set is presented simultaneously, the paradigm is called a *single frame* task. When the display set is presented successively (regardless of the number of stimuli in a single frame, or the overlap between frames), the paradigm is termed a *multiple frame* task. *Threshold detection* tasks involve displays presented so briefly that significant numbers of errors would be made even were the memory set size and display set size both equal to one. Thus, in threshold tasks errors and performance levels will be a mixture of attention effects and sensory failures. Since our interest is primarily in attention, rather than in structural limitations of the peripheral sensory system, we will focus discussion upon above-threshold tasks. These are usually divided into two classes: (1) Those in which the set sizes are small enough that errors are very few, called *reaction time* tasks; (2) Those in which the set sizes are large enough and the search time available small enough that many errors are made, called *accuracy* tasks.

The potential difficulty of a given task is often indexed by the *load*, defined as the product of memory set size and display set size. However, when the display consists of a series of separated, successive frames, the load is instead defined as the product of memory set size and *frame size*: frame size is the number of stimuli presented in a given frame. Which meaning of load is meant will always be clear in context, since all the multiple-frame tasks we will discuss will utilize nonoverlapping frames of constant size.

Two basic paradigms will be considered. *Consistent mapping* (CM) refers to tasks in which the memory ensemble and the distractor ensemble do not overlap; hence, targets from one trial are never distractors on another, and vice versa. *Varied mapping* (VM) refers to tasks in which consistent mapping is not maintained. In most such tasks, targets on one trial are distractors on others, and vice versa.

In many studies, targets appear only on some trials (usually 50 percent). The subject attempts to identify the presence or absence of targets as quickly or accurately as possible. Target-present trials are termed *positive*, and target-absent trials *negative*.

## Memory Search

The prototype for memory search studies was carried out by Sternberg (1966). Digits were used as stimuli, and targets were present on 50 percent of the trials. Memory set size varied from one to six, across trials. The results from the varied mapping study are shown in Figure 11.3. Reaction time is slightly slower for negative responses, and rises as a linear function of load (memory set size), with about equal slopes for negative and positive functions.

### Serial-Exhaustive Comparisons
Sternberg (1966) proposed a *serial-exhaustive* comparison model to account for the results. The visual display item is compared to each memory set item in turn (hence the term *serial*).

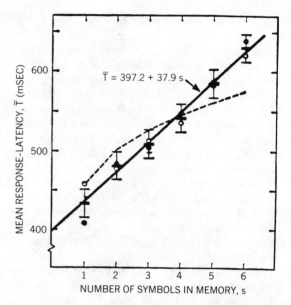

**Figure 11.3.** Relation between response latency and the number of symbols in memory, s, from Sternberg (1966). Mean latencies, over eight subjects, of positive responses (filled circles) and negative responses (open circles). About 95 observations per point. For each s, overall mean (heavy bar) and estimates of $\pm \sigma$ are indicated. Solid line was fitted by least squares to overall means. Upper bound for parallel process (broken curve).

The successive comparison times have identical distributions. The comparisons continue until the memory set is exhausted (hence the term *exhaustive*), regardless of whether a match is encountered before all comparisons are complete.

Response time in this model consists of a base term representing all processes not involved in comparisons (such as perception, encoding, deciding, and motor-responding), plus the sum of times for the various comparisons. The base time has its own distribution, but is independent of the memory set size. The base time has a slightly larger mean for the negatives, possibly reflecting a difference in the decision component or the motor component. The base time is given by the zero intercept of the functions, and the slope of the functions gives the mean comparison time. Linearity of mean reaction time is predicted because the time is a sum of the base time and the times for each of the comparisons.

If the comparison process would terminate when a match is reached, then on the average only one-half as many comparisons would take place on positive trials as negative ones. This is so because on negative trials no matches occur, but on positive trials, the match is equally likely to occur on any of the $m$ comparisons. This *terminating* model therefore predicts a slope one-half as great on positive trials. Most people find terminating models more intuitively plausible, but the rapid rate of comparisons (about 40 msec) may not allow time for decisions to be made en route, especially if the decision time would apply after each comparison, and could not operate in parallel with the comparisons. In such a case, greater efficiency can be obtained by finishing all comparisons and then making a single decision.

### Potential Problems

The basic memory search findings (i.e., linear, parallel set-size functions) have been replicated in endless variations. However, certain data seem to raise problems for the serial-exhaustive comparison model. The first set of problems concern the existence of errors and the possibility that the shape of the set-size functions could be affected by a trade-off of accuracy for speed. In fact errors virtually always increase with set size (see Sternberg, 1975; also see Figure 11.3). If a trade-off were operating, then an inducement for the subjects to equate errors at all set sizes would produce steeper slopes than those observed. When error rates rise above about 10 percent, it is difficult to discuss slopes because the basic linearity of the set-size functions is usually lost (e.g., Reed, 1976). However at rates below 10 percent the slopes and shapes of the functions change very little, even when subjects are instructed to increase speed at the cost of accuracy (see Sternberg, 1975). Thus for typical memory search studies worries about the form of the data caused by differential error rates are probably unfounded.

A second class of findings from varied-mapping memory search studies have also produced problems for the serial-exhaustive model. An item that is a target much more often than others, that is peculiarly salient, that is especially marked, that appears more than once in a given memory set, or that the subject predicts to occur as a test item, will produce an especially fast response when tested (for a summary see Shiffrin & Schneider, 1973, or Sternberg, 1975). The set size functions are shifted downward for such items, but the slope remains largely unchanged. Possibly related to such findings are the observations of serial position effects: Reaction time is dependent upon the presentation position of the test item within the memory set, especially when the time interval between study and test is short (see Sternberg, 1975, for a review).

These findings are not easy to reconcile with an exhaustive serial search, if the source of the effects is in the comparison process. In a terminating search, the order of the search determines reaction time for positive responses. In an exhaustive search, order is irrelevant since all memory set items are compared. Also arguing against the source of the effect being in the comparison process is the fact that distractors that are salient also show intercept changes rather than slope changes (Shiffrin & Schneider, 1973). Therefore, the serial exhaustive model can be salvaged only if such effects take place in stages of the process other than the comparison stage: the encoding, decision, or motor response stages (a not unreasonable assumption: see Miller and Pachella, 1973).

### Alternative Models

Although the effects just discussed may be consistent with the serial-exhaustive model, they have encouraged the development of alternative models. Most of these involve some form of parallel, concurrent comparisons. We must distinguish between two kinds of models. In one, all memory set items are compared to the test item simultaneously, with distributions of completion times *that do not depend upon the size of the memory set*. When this is true, the time to complete the slowest of the comparisons rises with memory set size. Nevertheless, it can be shown that such models cannot predict the observed data (see Sternberg, 1966, and the dashed line in Figure 11.3). On the other hand, if one allows comparison time to depend on memory set size (i.e., a limited capacity approach), then it can be shown that there almost always exist parallel models that will match the predictions of a given serial model (e.g., Townsend, 1976). For present purposes, it is important to note that all the alternative models proposed for memory search data have been based upon limited capacity in some form: when the comparisons are assumed to be concurrent, the rate at which each is completed is assumed to go down as memory set-size goes up.

### Training Effects in Varied Mapping Tasks

Given the dramatic effects of extended training that were reviewed in the first section, it is important to examine the effects of practice upon memory search. Kristofferson (1972a) trained subjects for 30 days in a varied mapping memory search study similar to that used by Sternberg (1966). The results are shown in Figure 11.4. The slope remained constant (at 36 msec per comparison) during the entire course of training, but the intercept decreased from 350 to 299 msec. The intercept, of course, reflects components of the search task that are not changed over trials, components that are practiced in consistent fashion (such as, say, the motor response). The fact that the slope does not change suggests a rather fixed attentional or capacity limitation that cannot be removed by practice (a conclusion to be contrasted with that drawn by Hirst et al., 1980).

### Attentional Implications

There are important attentional features to the varied-mapping memory search results. First, there is a strict capacity limit: each comparison takes about 40 additional msec; thus memory search is an example of time sharing of attentive processes. Second, there is great effort associated with the task, according to subjective reports. Third, the task occupies attention to the extent that it is difficult, if not impossible, to carry out any other attention demanding task simultaneously (we will present the evidence shortly). Fourth, the attentional limitations in varied-mapping settings do not change with practice. (But note that "awareness" of the comparison process seems to be lacking in detail, possibly because it occurs so quickly, and evidence that the subject can control the process, say, by switching from an exhaustive to a terminating search mode, is not available.)

### Training Effects in Consistent Mapping Tasks

When consistent mapping is used during memory search, practice produces marked slope reductions. In consistent mapping the memory ensemble and the distractor ensemble remained fixed over trials: No memory set item is ever a distractor and vice versa. The memory set on a given trial consists of a choice of items from the memory ensemble, so it is still possible to vary memory set size. Kristofferson (1972b) trained

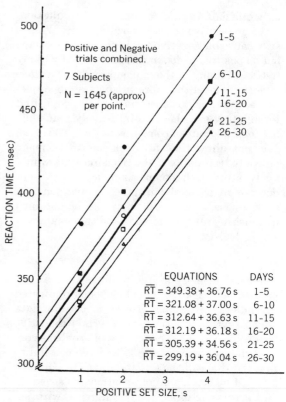

**Figure 11.4.** Mean response latency as a function of size of positive set with lines fitted by least squares, as a function of days of training, from varied mapping search. From "Effects of Practice on Character-Classification" by M. Kristofferson, 1972, *Canadian Journal of Psychology*, 26, p. 57.

subjects in memory search using consistent mapping for 36 days. The results are shown in Figure 11.5. The set-size functions are nonlinear from the first few sessions onward. The nonlinearity makes slope analysis problematic, but however one defines it, the slope does drop consistently with training. These changes certainly imply that the serial exhaustive comparison model is inappropriate. It would not be sensible to argue, for example, that the subject increasingly ignores the presented memory set (since the memory set is well learned), thereby flattening the slope. Such an argument would imply that practice leads the subject to operate less efficiently, since attention to the memory set would improve performance. Furthermore, as we shall see in the section on visual search, consistent practice leads to reduced reaction times at large set sizes (compared with varied

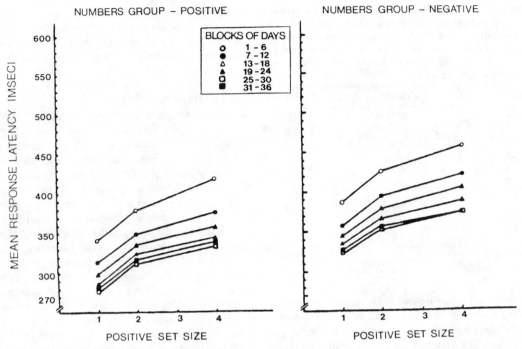

**Figure 11.5.** Mean response latency, calculated separately for trials requiring positive and negative responses, shown as a function of set size for each successive 6-day block, where numbers were the stimuli. Data from a consistent mapping search task. From "When Item Recognition and Visual Search Functions are Similar" by M. Kristofferson. Reprinted with permission from *Perception and Psychophysics, 12*, p. 381. Copyright 1972 by the Psychonomic Society, Inc.

conditions), rather than increased reaction times at small set sizes. It is more likely that some sort of automatic detection process has developed, a process that is increasingly insensitive to load. We will return to this hypothesis, and other alternatives, after considering results from visual search tasks.

## Visual Search

In this section are considered search studies in which (most of) the trials have a display set greater than one.

### Stimulus Factors

Perhaps the single most prominent factor in visual search is related to the similarity and confusability of the items. By now, hundreds of studies testify to the positive relationship between speed of search and the similarity difference between targets and distractors, and this relationship transcends considerations of type of training and other factors. (One example of the large perfor-

mance differences that can arise due to physical differences among targets is seen in Table 11.1, from a study to be described shortly). Anne Treisman and her colleagues have argued in a number of recent papers that many of these effects are due to the need to use limited attentive resources to integrate features that are processed automatically and separately by the perceptual system (e.g., Treisman & Gelade, 1980). John Duncan, Glynn Humphreys and colleagues have suggested that feature conjunction effects are subsumed under more general considerations of stimulus similarity, with search being speeded by dissimilarity of targets to distractors, and by similarity of distractors to each other (e.g., Quinlan & Humphreys, in press; Duncan, 1985, in press). Whatever the basis for similarity effects, they are powerful enough in some cases to take precedence over effects of training.

There are two situations in which stimulus factors can eliminate differences normally seen between consistent and varied training. The first occurs when target-distractor confusability is

Table 11.1. Comparison of the estimated probability $\hat{p}$ of correctly detecting the location of (i) a known numeral and of (ii) an unknown one-of-ten numerals. Nine-letter arrays were presented at ISI's of 60 msec; approximately 100 trials were used to estimate each $\hat{p}$.

| Numeral | Known | Unknown |
|---------|-------|---------|
| 0 | .019 | .011 |
| 1 | .344 | .296 |
| 2 | .572 | .636 |
| 3 | .642 | .691 |
| 4 | .206 | .293 |
| 5 | .479 | .449 |
| 6 | .662 | .646 |
| 7 | .429 | .406 |
| 8 | .719 | .648 |
| 9 | .572 | .633 |
| Mean | .464 | .469 |

extremely high. For example, in my laboratory Mary Czerwinski has examined visual search with memory set size of one. When the target is a four letter word and distractors are four letter words sharing a random three letters with the target, even 24 sessions of training failed to produce differences between consistent and varied conditions (and search rates were high: about 150 msec per word). Such results point to limits on the ability of consistent training to produce automatic detection in visual search.

The second situation occurs when target-distractor confusability is extremely low, and stimuli are not very complex. In many such situations search shows no effect of load regardless of the consistency of training, and indeed the load independent processing is seen at the onset of the experiment, before training has taken place. Simple examples would include detecting a target of one color among distractors of a clearly different color, or detecting an X among O's or an O among X's. To take just one case, Donderi (1983, Experiment 1) demonstrated no effect of display size in a varied mapping study in which subjects were to say whether a display contained all identical letters, or one discrepant letter (see also Treisman & Souther, 1985, for some examples). In such situations it is clear that a feature(s) capable of leading directly to a correct response is extracted automatically from the display, even without training.

Despite the existence of visual search cases in which training has little effect, there are many

cases where training effects are large, and these cases can provide important evidence concerning differences between automatic and attentive processes. Studies of this type are considered next.

### Varied-Mapping Studies

In varied-mapping paradigms, search time is usually a linear function of load (in situations where eye movements are not a contaminating source of performance variation). Atkinson, Holmgren and Juola (1969) utilized memory set-size of one and varied display size. They obtained linear functions that were parallel for negative and positive responses. (Reaction time was notably affected by display position of a target.) However, more often than not in visual search studies, the slopes of the negative responses are twice that for positive responses. One example of such data, from Hockley (1984), is shown in Figure 11.6. Also shown are the effects of visual display position for each frame size. The strong display position effects may have been induced by the procedure: The memory set item was presented at the center of fixation. The test stimuli were then presented two seconds later, in a vertical array, with the topmost item in the same position as the previous memory set item.

As noted earlier, set size functions that are linear, with negative slopes twice positive slopes, are consistent with a serial, terminating, comparison process. It is not clear what experimental conditions produce two-to-one slope ratios, but a rule of thumb seems to be the following: The more complex the search task, the greater the load, and the slower the average response time, the more likely are two-to-one slope ratios.

Increases in complexity can be achieved by varying both memory-set size and display set size. Examples of such paradigms are provided by Schneider and Shiffrin (1977) and Briggs and Johnsen (1973). The results were quite similar, and those from Schneider and Shiffrin (1977, Experiment 2) are presented in Figure 11.7. The memory set size and frame size both ranged from one to four (all conditions blocked). The predicted functions are generated from a type of serial, terminating model: A memory set item is chosen and compared with each displayed item in turn, with a mean time of 42 msec per comparison; then a new memory set item is chosen, and the comparisons continue; the mean time needed to choose each new memory set item is

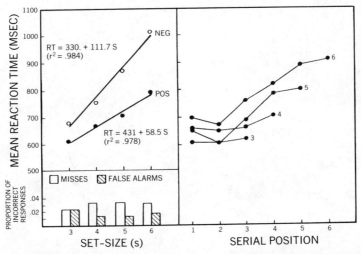

**Figure 11.6.** Response latency and best fit linear function, error rates, and serial position functions (top to bottom of display) for a varied mapping visual search task. From "The Analysis of Response Time Distributions in the Study of Cognitive Processes" by W.E. Hockley, 1984, *Journal of Experimental Psychology: Learning, Memory, and Cognition, 10*, p. 601. Copyright 1984 by the American Psychological Association. Reprinted by permission of the publisher and author.

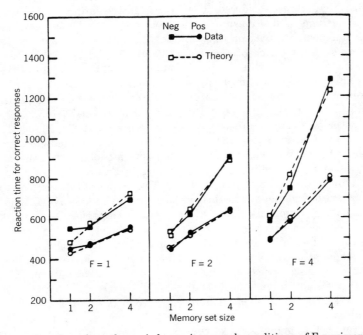

**Figure 11.7.** Mean reaction times from the varied-mapping search conditions of Experiment 2 from Schneider and Shiffrin (1977). (F = frame size). Predictions derived from the theory described in the text. From "Controlled and Automatic Human Information Processing: I. Detection, Search, and Attention" by W. Schneider and R. Shiffrin, 1977, *Psychological Review, 84*, p. 24. Copyright 1977 by the American Psychological Association. Reprinted by permission of the publisher and author.

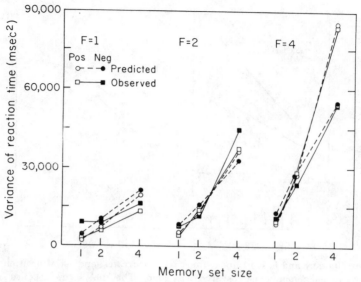

**Figure 11.8.** Variance of the reaction times from the varied-mapping conditions from Experiment 2 from Shiffrin and Schneider (1977). (F = frame size). Predictions from the model described in the text. From "Controlled and Automatic Human Information Processing: I. Detection, Search and Attention" by W. Schneider and R. Shiffrin, 1977, *Psychological Review, 84*, p. 25. Copyright 1977 by the American Psychological Association. Reprinted by permission of the publisher and author.

40 msec. This model was superior to other serial terminating models that were considered. The same model fit the Briggs and Johnson data quite well, but with a mean comparison time of 57 msec and a mean switching time of 27 msec.

The results we have presented thus far have been concerned with mean reaction times. However, examination of other characteristics of the reaction time distributions proves quite informative. The variance estimates are particularly revealing when the means show linearity with two-to-one slope ratios. When comparisons are independent, variance according to serial models should be a linear, increasing function of the number of comparisons made. For negative responses, the number of comparisons equals the load; variance is indeed observed to be a linear increasing function (see Figure 11.8). On the other hand, when positive responses are determined by a terminating process there are two components making up the variance: (1) a component growing linearly with load, at half the rate of the negative function; (2) a component representing the random stopping point of the comparison process. As the load rises, the second of these components becomes increasingly important. Thus the variances of positive responses are predicted to rise in a curvilinear

fashion, the positive variance being less than the negative variance when the load is small but crossing over and becoming greater than negative variance when the load is high (even though the mean positive reaction time remains at one half of the mean negative reaction time at all loads).

Results showing this pattern, from Schneider and Shiffrin (1977), for the same data giving rise to the results in Figure 11.7, are shown in Figure 11.8. The predicted functions are from the same model used to generate the predictions shown in Figure 11.7.

The shapes of the reaction time distributions may also be informative. Distributions for correct negative responses, for each set size, for one of the subjects in Hockley's study (1984) are depicted in Figure 11.9. In the case of memory search the modes of the distributions remain fixed, but the skewness increases. In the case of visual search, the distributions tend to shift upward by constant amounts. Each of these patterns is consistent with serial comparison processes; however, the distribution of a comparison would have to differ considerably in the two cases, with a much larger variance and skewness in the case of memory search. It is not known whether the difference in the distributional

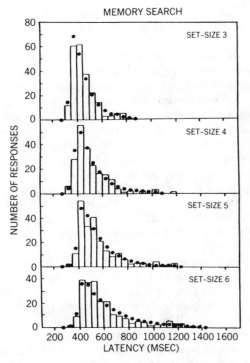
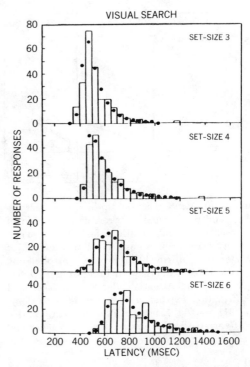

**Figure 11.9.** Distributions of reaction times for negative responses for each set size for one subject in each of two varied mapping search tasks. Dots give best fitting convolution of an exponential and gaussian distribution. From "The Analysis of Response Time Distributions in the Study of Cognitive Processes" by W.E. Hockley, 1984, *Journal of Experimental Psychology: Learning, Memory, and Cognition, 10*, p. 604. Copyright 1984 by the American Psychological Association. Reprinted by permission of the publisher and author.

patterns for visual and memory search shown in Figure 11.9 generalizes to other studies. Nonetheless it should be kept in mind that comparison operations might be different in memory search (with one display item) and visual search (with one memory set item). Other evidence suggesting differences between memory search and visual search may be found in Flach (1986).

In summary, there are some important differences between memory search and visual search involving slope ratios of positive to negative responses and the nature of the respective comparison processes. Nevertheless, the use of varied mapping often shows that reaction time is a linear function of load, and the results are consistent with a serial comparison process. Such results indicate a limited attentional capacity.

### Consistent Mapping Studies

In visual search with consistent mapping, early results were obtained by Neisser (1963) who showed that the rate of search became much faster with practice. Furthermore, in one study, search for 10 items in the memory set could be carried out as rapidly as for one (Neisser, Novick, & Lazar, 1963). The technique used by Neisser involved many lines of characters presented on a printed sheet. The subject scanned down the sheet until locating the target. The problem with this technique (and with related techniques using card-sorting) is that eye movements (and/or hand movements) are needed to bring successive groups of items into foveal vision. Eye movements are relatively slow (4 or 5 per second) and could be establishing a mechanical limit on search speed. Kristofferson (1972c) used a similar technique, but with varied mapping, and argued that eye movements were not hindering the search rate. If she was correct in this assertion, it may be that serial search continues during eye movements so that no comparison time is lost. The same is not true when consistent mapping is used, as demonstrated by Sperling,

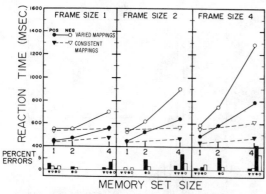

**Figure 11.10.** Mean reaction times for correct responses, and percentages of error, as a function of memory-set size, for all conditions, for both varied and consistent search conditions from Experiment 2 of Schneider and Shiffrin (1977). From "Controlled and Automatic Human Information Processing: I. Detection, Search, and Attention" by W. Schneider and R. Shiffrin, 1977, *Psychological Review, 84*, p. 19. Copyright 1977 by the American Psychological Association. Reprinted by permission of the publisher and author.

Budiansky, Spivak, and Johnson (1971). They used a method in which accuracy was the dependent measure: Displays of items were presented in rapid succession on each trial, each display in foveal vision so that eye movements were not needed. In this study much faster rates were attained that would be possible were eye movements used. Thus, we will focus our discussion upon studies not dependent on eye movements.

Studies by Schneider and Shiffrin (1977) and Briggs and Johnson (1973) used a reaction time measure, consistent mapping, and varied both memory set size and frame size from one to four. We will present the Schneider and Shiffrin (1977) data because their subjects trained much longer. The data from well practiced subjects are shown in Figure 11.10, along with data from the varied mapping conditions on the same subjects at comparable levels of practice (repeated from Figure 11.7). The notable characteristic of these data is the relative flatness of the set size functions: The load has very little effect, whether defined by memory set size or display size. The contrast with the varied mapping results is particularly striking. It should be pointed out that these functions are not completely flat. Most consistent mapping studies produce substantially larger effects of load than are seen here

(sometimes nonlinear), though still much smaller than the load effects seen in varied mapping conditions.

In summary, when targets and distractors are not too easily discriminable, varied-mapping search studies produce linear search functions with substantial slopes, consistent with serial comparison processes (exhaustive or terminating in different studies). Extended practice lowers reaction times, but the rate of search remains constant. When targets and distractors are not too confusable, consistent mapping leads to a flattening of the reaction time function of load, which most researchers have interpreted as a switch from serial to parallel search, or from limited parallel to partially unlimited parallel search.

It is tempting to suggest, as did Shiffrin and Schneider (1977), that search becomes increasingly automatized in consistent paradigms. (Tests of this hypothesis involve variants of the paradigm that will be discussed in the next section.) Increasing automatization could, of course, produce increasingly flat set size functions. At first glance, such a prediction appears consistent with the data. However, in many cases the degree of flattening seems to cease at some point in training (e.g. the data from Kristofferson, 1972b; Figure 11.5). One could assume that automatic detection is only partially unlimited, even after asymptotic training in consistent paradigms (e.g. Fisher, 1982, 1984). Alternatively, performance may represent a mixture of (almost) unlimited automatic detection and a concurrent serial search. This would be possible because automatic processes might be able to occur concurrently with attentive processes. Both processes could operate in parallel with the first to finish triggering the response. If the automatic process is independent of load, then the serial process will tend to finish first much more often when the load is small, producing faster responses only at small set sizes. According to this account curvilinear set size functions could be seen even after considerable consistent practice has produced (almost) complete automatization. Data suggesting such an analysis were collected by Ellis and Chase (1971), whose distractors differed from targets in size or color, and by Jones and Anderson (1982), whose distractors differed from targets in category membership. Evidence that performance in visual search is governed jointly by a parallel detection system and a

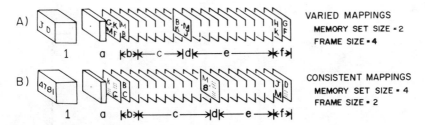

**Figure 11.11.** Two examples of a positive trial in the multiple-frame search paradigm of Experiment 1 from Schneider and Shiffrin (1977). (A) varied mapping with memory set = (J, D), and (B) consistent mapping with memory set = (4, 7, 8, 1). (1: presentation of memory set; a fixation dot goes on for .5 sec when subject starts trial; b: three dummy frames that never contain target; c: distractor frames; d: target frame; e: distractor frames; f: dummy frames that never contain target. Frame time is varied across conditions.) From "Controlled and Automatic Human Information Processing: I. Detection, Search, and Attention" by W. Schneider and R. Shiffrin, 1977, *Psychological Review*, *84*, p. 11. Copyright 1977 by the American Psychological Association. Reprinted by permission of the publisher and author.

system that depends on a gradually moving focus of attention is reported by Jonides (1980a,b; 1983) and Eriksen and Yeh (1985).

### Visual Search with Accuracy Measures

Accuracy and reaction time measures of search performance ought to be related in lawful ways. Sperling et al. (1971) used a consistent mapping task with a digit target contained in a long sequence of letter displays. The time per display was varied between trials and the subject attempted to identify the location of the target within the display. A certain degree of automatism seemed to develop, since subjects were able to search for any one of ten digits about as rigidly as for an average, single, known digit. The relevant performance levels are given in Table 11.1. Note that there is enormous variation in detection accuracy over the set of targets (presumably based on the visual similarity of the target to the distractors), but the size of the memory set makes very little difference. Such a result mimics those we have presented in the reaction-time domain.

Schneider and Shiffrin (1977) used a technique based on that of Sperling et al. (1971). They used both varied and consistent mapping. The subjects were those that produced the reaction time data shown in Figure 11.7. A trial consisted of 20 consecutive four-item frames arranged as a square, each presented for t msec. Display positions not used for characters were filled with random dot masks. A target occurred in a random position on a random frame (except the first three and last two), on half the trials; the other

trials contained no target. An example of a varied and consistent trial are depicted in Figure 11.11. (For this subject the varied items were all letters; these letters were also the consistent distractors; the consistent targets were digits.) For every condition, the time per display was varied across trials, so as to produce psychometric functions. The accuracy results as a function of frame time, for each load condition and each type of mapping, are shown in Figure 11.12.

In varied mapping the task was enormously difficult, especially at high loads. When the load was 16, even 800 msec per display only allowed 70 percent accuracy of detection. In the varied condition almost all errors were omissions, or misses; there were few false alarms. This would be expected if a serial comparison process were operating, one that would switch to the next items as each new frame was presented. Schneider and Shiffrin (1977) were able to predict rather roughly the performance in these conditions by utilizing the comparison time distributions that fit the reaction time data (Figure 11.7) and assuming a serial comparison process.

The consistent mapping data are quite different. The task can be carried out at much faster display rates. Accuracy is relatively little affected by load, and false alarms occur about as often as misses. This latter result suggests that the source of error is not in the limited attentional system; instead the errors may arise in the peripheral sensory system. Presumably the characters are presented so briefly they cannot be identified clearly even at the lowest load (of one per display). Norman and Bobrow (1975)

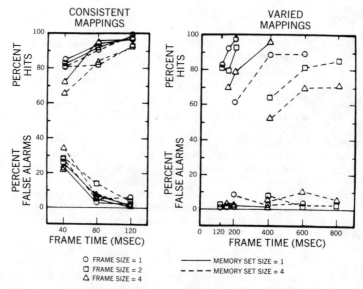

**Figure 11.12.** Data from Experiment 1 from Schneider and Shiffrin (1977). Hits and false alarms as a function of frame time for each of the 12 conditions in the multiple frame search task illustrated in Figure 11.11, for consistent and varied training. From "Controlled and Automatic Human Information Processing: I. Detection, Search, and Attention" by W. Schneider and R. Shiffrin, 1977, *Psychological Review, 84,* p. 12. Copyright 1977 by the American Psychological Association. Reprinted by permission of the publisher and author.

have called this case a "data limitation," as opposed to a "process limitation," since the data provided to the processing system is impoverished and no attentional allocation can improve matters (a related distinction is that between *state* and *process* limitation; Garner, 1974). Note that even at the smallest load, the varied conditions are inferior to the consistent conditions. This is to be expected, since the successive frames must be dealt with serially in the varied conditions, but may be dealt with in parallel in the consistent conditions. In summary, then, the multiple frame search paradigm, using accuracy as a dependent measure, produces results that are comparable to those in single frame tasks using reaction time as a measure.

Despite the enormous differences between the consistent and varied conditions illustrated in Figure 11.12, a careful look reveals differences as a function of load within the consistent conditions. This point was made even more clearly in studies carried out by Fisher (1984). Analysis of data from his study using consistent mapping and a multiple frame technique suggested that subjects performed about equally well when twice as many items were presented

at one half the presentation rate. Fisher proposed a model (1982, 1984) in which consistent training leads to only partially unlimited processing. He suggested that a maximum of about four simultaneous, unlimited comparisons from a visual display could be carried out together. Alternatively, one could argue that load effects in consistent mapping are due to concurrent use of attentive serial search along with automatic, unlimited detection. (In the previous section, this argument was used to explain load effects in consistent mapping when reaction time was the dependent measure.) Further research will be needed to discriminate these competing explanations.

Whether consistent training produces unlimited or partially unlimited automatic detection, the training effects that are observed may be related to the training effects obtained by the earliest psychologists. It seems natural to suggest that the serial search seen in varied mapping paradigms is identified with an attention-demanding control process, and that the gradual improvement seen in consistent mapping may track the development of automatic processes that carry out detection in parallel.

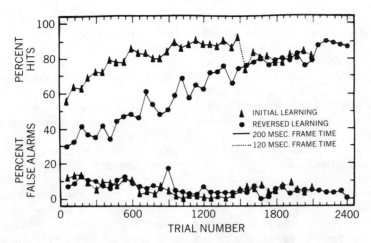

**Figure 11.13.** Data from Experiment 1 of Shiffrin and Schneider (1977). Initial consistent-mapping learning and reversed consistent-mapping learning for target and distractor sets taken from the first and second halves of the alphabet in a multiple frame search task. Memory set size = 4, frame size = 2, frame times are shown. Percentage of hits and percentage of false alarms are graphed as a function of trial number. After 2,100 trials the target and distractor sets were switched with each other. From "Controlled and Automatic Human Information Processing: II. Perceptual Learning, Automatic Attending, and a General Theory" by R. M. Shiffrin and W. Schneider, 1977, *Psychological Review, 84*, p. 132. Copyright 1977 by the American Psychological Association. Reprinted by permission of the author.

## Automatization in Consistent Search

The studies in the previous section point to the development of automatic detection during consistent training, but provide little information concerning its characteristics. The experiments in this section are aimed at the question of what is learned.

### The Effects of Task Reversal

It is conceivable that consistent training simply causes the discriminability of targets and distractors to increase. If so, one might expect that after training the roles of targets and distractors could be reversed without loss of performance. Reversal of roles is not merely a matter of saying "yes" where formerly one said "no" and vice versa. Instead, the roles are reversed so that in memory search (some of) the former distractors are presented as memory set items, and in visual search all but at most one of the displayed items are the former targets. Regardless, the superior discrimination mechanisms that have presumably been learned should operate in this new task.

Shiffrin and Schneider (1977) carried out several tests of this kind, with similar results. In one task, subjects were consistently trained to detect consonants from one half of the alphabet in distractors consisting of consonants from the other half of the alphabet. They used a multiple frame paradigm similar to that depicted in Figure 11.11, with accuracy as the dependent measure. Memory set size was four, and each of the 20 displays contained two letters and was presented for 200 msec.

The results of the initial training are shown as the triangles in Figure 11.13. Performance improved rapidly, seen primarily as an increase in the hit rate (detection of targets). After 1500 trials, the display duration was reduced to 120 msec for the next 600 trials. Performance seemed fairly stable at this point, so a *reversal* was now undertaken. Display time was returned to 200 msec and the targets and distractors exchanged roles. (The subjects were told this would occur; they predicted they would perform well after reversal.)

The reversal results are shown in Figure 11.13 as circles. Performance not only did not remain stable, but dropped well below the level seen at the start of original training. Almost 900 trials were needed to return to that initial performance level and gradual relearning occurred thereafter. A clearer result could hardly be imagined: certainly the hypothesis of increased discriminability of memory set items and distractors may be ruled out as an explanation for the consistent training effects. (For completeness, it should be noted that similar reversal results are obtainable using reaction time tasks; Dumais, 1979; Shiffrin, Dumais, & Schneider, 1981; Schneider, Dumais, & Shiffrin, 1984). What the reversal results do suggest is an automatization of attention itself.

### Automatization of Attention

Shiffrin and Schneider (1977) suggested that the tendency for particular stimuli to attract attention is altered by consistent training: targets come to attract attention more and distractors less as training proceeds, independently of the subject's own attempts to allocate attention through active control on a trial by trial basis. The hypothesis holds that stimuli have a normal automatic tendency to attract attention when presented. If more than one item occurs at a time, then the items will compete against each other for attention. If no item is much better at attracting attention than another, then attention will either drift randomly to some item or, more likely, go to an item selected by the subject using momentary attentional control. Presumably this situation holds at the start of training, and throughout varied mapping practice. On the other hand, when one stimulus attracts attention preferentially, then this item will tend to be checked first in any comparison process. This process presumably operates in consistent tasks after training is well along, and explains the independence of performance from visual display size.

The reversal findings of the preceding section are explicable according to this hypothesis: After reversal, attention is attracted to the former targets which are now distractors; since distractors are checked first, performance is worse than in the varied mapping case or the case holding at the start of practice in which attention is given to items in effectively random order.

However, additional mechanisms are needed to explain the independence of performance from memory set size. For example, when there is only one display item, it will be attended regardless of type of training. Thus automatic attention attraction must be augmented by additional automatic processes before an adequate model is reached. It is possible that the fact that

a test item calls strongly for attention is in and of itself sufficient to identify it as a target, regardless of the number of memory set items. Alternatively, a target response separate from the attention response could be learned.

### Automatic Categorization

Both of these suggestions may well be correct, but there is little if any data that bear on their validity. On the other hand, a categorization hypothesis can explain the lessening of the memory-set-size slope, and much evidence supports this view. The categorization hypothesis has two parts: (1) all the targets in consistent training are learned as a category; (2) when a target item appears for test, the category "label" is extracted automatically (in the same fashion that the item's "name" is extracted). When this hypothesis holds, then a test item need only have its category checked, effectively making the memory set size one. A number of results in the literature are consistent with this view (see Shiffrin and Schneider, 1977, for a review).

Shiffrin and Schneider (1977) experimentally separated the process of category automatization from the development of an automatic attention response. They used a special type of varied training: The stimuli consisted of eight characters divided into two sets of four so that there was maximum visual confusability between the two sets [e.g., (GMFP, CNHD)]. The memory set items were chosen from one of these sets and the distractors from the other, but the roles were random from trial to trial. Thus, although the mapping was varied, the four-item sets stayed together throughout training, allowing each to be learned as a "category." Memory set size was varied (two or four) and a multiple frame technique was used with two items per frame. If the four item sets became learned as categories, and if after that point the category membership was extracted automatically for each test item, then each test item need only have its category checked in order to come to a correct decision. In effect, the memory set size would become "one." This condition was contrasted with a normal varied search procedure using eight other characters, with random selections on every trial so no categorical structure could be learned.

The results are shown in Figure 11.14. At first performance is better for the smaller memory set sizes in both conditions. However, as would be

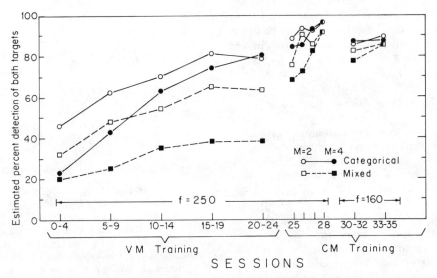

**Figure 11.14.** Data from Experiment 3 of Shiffrin and Schneider (1977). Estimated percentage of detection of both targets, as a function of session number for each of the four main conditions (see text). At Session 25 training was switched to a CM procedure. At Session 30, the frame time was reduced to 160 msec. (VM = varied mapping; CM = consistent mapping; M = memory-set size; f = frame time, in msec). From "Controlled and Automatic Human Information Processing: II. Perceptual Learning, Automatic Attending, and a General Theory" by R. M. Shiffrin and W. Schneider, 1977, *Psychological Review, 84*, p. 139. Copyright 1977 by the American Psychological Association. Reprinted by permission of the author.

expected if categories are learned, the "category" conditions improve with training until they are equal, and superior to the control conditions (which still differ with memory set size). It appears as if the memory set size in the categorical condition is effectively one. However, automatic detection was not yet operating. At that point, all conditions were switched to completely consistent training (one of the learned categories forming the target ensemble in the experimental condition, and four randomly chosen items forming the target ensemble in the control condition). Performance rose considerably and rapidly and all conditions became equal, indicating automatic detection had been learned.

The results of this study and the reversal study suggest some sources of automatization. At least two factors operate: (1) targets come to attract attention automatically (and distractors repel it); (2) automatic categorization develops for the memory ensemble (and possibly for the distractor ensemble). These two factors can explain the independence of performance from memory set size and display size in consistently mapped search.

Are these in fact the mechanisms that produce the consistent mapping results? It is possible that the same mechanisms that produce automatic categorization will simultaneously produce automatic responses of other sorts, such as a response of "target." That is, when the displayed item is presented it may lead automatically to an internal response such as "category 1," another internal response such as "target," and other relevant responses that have been consistently trained. Thus although the memory-set-size independence could be due to automatic categorization, it could be due as well to an automatic "target" response. These factors could be operating together and further research would be necessary to isolate them.

Although automatic categorization may underlie automatic detection in memory search, it is an open question whether it underlies automatic detection in visual search when memory set size is one. If an item's category is encoded automatically, an automatic attention response to that encoding could be learned. However, in most cases either a feature of an item, the item's identity, or the item's category could serve as a basis for response. All of these could be encoded automatically; if so, which would be used to govern the response would presumably be determined by which encoding is more readily achieved (see Cardosi, 1986, for evidence and discussion concerning this point.)

### The Relationship of Automatism to Attention

The hypothesis that an automatic attention response is learned provides quite a contrast with the automatization that was studied by investigators such as Solomons and Stein (1896), Downey and Anderson (1915), Shaffer (1975), Allport et al. (1972), Spelke et al. (1976), and Hirst et al. (1980). In those dual task studies, especially the earliest ones, the object was to produce an automatic process that would operate *without* attention. To a certain degree, these investigators succeeded: Stimuli were presented, processed, and responded to with little conscious awareness, and little interference with a concurrent task was observed. A key difference between the dual-task and the search studies may be the presence of an attention demanding primary task in the dual task paradigm; perhaps under these circumstances the subject learns to direct attention away from the secondary task that is becoming automatized. This redirection is apparently possible without significantly harming the performance of the secondary task. It would be interesting to learn whether automatic detection in search tasks could be learned without concomitant attention attraction, but the data are not available.

There is little question that an automatic attention response is learned in consistent search tasks. Although the reversal results shown in Figure 11.13 suggest such a conclusion, a study by Shiffrin and Schneider (1977) addressed this point directly. They first consistently trained a set of characters as targets until automatic detection was well established (slopes of search functions were near zero). Then a new task was used in which subjects searched a series of rapidly presented four-item frames for memory set items. Although each frame contained four items arranged in a square, only the items on one diagonal, the same for all frames, were relevant for the task. The memory set items and distractors on this relevant diagonal were all items that had been used in *varied mapping* search previously, and the search in the present task also used varied mapping. On one third of

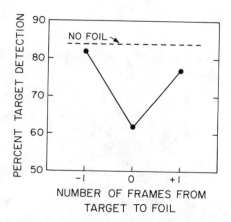

**Figure 11.15.** Data from Experiment 4d of Shiffrin and Schneider (1977). Percentage of target detection in a varied-mapping multiple frame task, as a function of the temporal spacing between the target and an automatically trained distractor in an irrelevant display position. Frame time was 200 msec. From "Controlled and Automatic Human Information Processing: II. Perceptual Learning, Automatic Attending, and a General Theory" by R.M. Shiffrin and W. Schneider, 1977, *Psychological Review, 84,* p. 111. Copyright 1977 by the American Psychological Association. Reprinted by permission of the author.

the trials, one target was present on the relevant diagonal of one of the 20 frames that made up a trial.

Almost all the stimuli that appeared on the irrelevant diagonal were chosen from the same item pool that was used for the relevant diagonal. However, on two thirds of the trials, one stimulus that appeared on the irrelevant diagonal of one of the frames had previously been given consistent training as a target. If the stimulus had developed the ability to attract attention automatically, then it should have continued to do so in the study described. To see whether this was the case, Shiffrin and Schneider (1977) examined performance on the relevant, varied diagonal as a function of the number of displays between the relevant target and the irrelevant, presumably automatic, target, on trials when both were present. In particular, when the two targets were in the same display, attention attraction to the irrelevant automatic item should cause attention removal from the relevant target. The results are given in Figure 11.15. The dashed line represents detection probability when the "automatic" item is not present. Note that there is a 22 percent drop in the probability of relevant target detection when an automatic item in a known to-be-irrelevant location occurs in the same display. This occurred even though the subjects knew that such automatic items would occur only in irrelevant locations, and were told to ignore them completely.

When no automatic items are presented, then performance on the relevant diagonal is identical to that when only two items are presented per frame. Thus in the absence of automatic items attention can be focused entirely upon the relevant diagonal. The fact that subjects could not maintain their attention focus in the presence of "automatic" irrelevant items suggests that the consistent training of items as targets causes a training of the attention system itself. When an automatic target appears, it attracts attention, albeit briefly, causing a relevant target somewhere else to be missed. This attention attraction occurs despite all attempts by the subject to force attention to relevant locations and items. (This result is related to a number of findings in search tasks showing that two simultaneous targets can interfere with each other; e.g., see Schneider & Shiffrin, 1977, Experiments 3 a,b,c; and Duncan, 1980.)

The time course of attention attraction and its rebound can be estimated, very roughly, from the results in Figure 11.15. The displays in a trial occurred every 200 msec. A slight drop in performance occurs even when the automatic item is on the display *subsequent* to the target. Thus the attention attraction must occur quite rapidly. Possibly controlled serial search from one display overlaps the physical presentation of the next display. If so, a rapid withdrawal of attention caused by an item in that second display could cause some performance loss due to premature interruption of the controlled search of the preceding display. On the other hand, attention rebounds quickly—when the target is in the display following the automatic item, a negligible performance drop takes place. It seems plausible to interpret these findings in terms of an attention shift away from the relevant diagonal, and back again, within a total of 200 msec (and probably less). As we shall see, there are longer switching time estimates from other studies, but the described study has an unusual feature—the subject is attempting throughout to fix attention on the relevant diagonal, and the temporary shift is automatically

driven. Were this not the case, shifts of attention could be slower.

Although these results suggest that targets attract attention automatically, they leave open an important question: Does consistent training cause distractors to repulse attention? A study by Dumais (1979; Shiffrin & Dumais, 1981) answered this question. Original training was carried out in a consistently mapped reaction time search task, with controls utilizing variable mapping. The automatism measure was the difference between reaction times to displays of 4 and 16 items.

After consistent training had produced considerable automatism (a small difference between display sizes of 4 and 16), a variety of transfer conditions were tested. The targets could be retrained, and the distractors replaced by items that had received (1) varied training or (2) no training. Alternatively, the distractors could be retained, and the targets replaced by items that had received (1) varied training or (2) no training.

All these conditions resulted in considerable (almost complete) transfer of training. The fact that the retention of trained distractors produces good transfer suggests that these items had developed a tendency to attract attention that was *lower* than for the varied or new items that were used as targets. The fact that new items and varied items differed little in any of these conditions suggests the varied mapping training leaves unchanged the "normal" tendency for an item to attract attention.

Examples of automatic attraction of attention can also be found in paradigms quite different than visual search. For example, Flowers, Polansky, and Kerl (1981) used a variant of the partial report paradigm of Sperling (1960). A display of multiletter items was presented to the subject very briefly. Shortly after display offset, a cue was given to report one of the letter strings. When one of the non-cued strings was a word, the report of the cued string was harmed, possibly because the word tended to "pop out" and call attention to itself.

### Interference and its Absence

If targets come to attract attention (and distractors the reverse) then it is clear that such an automatic process *must interfere* with other ongoing attentive processing. This is clearly demonstrated in Figure 11.15. On the other hand,

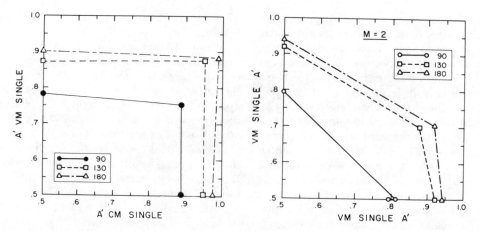

**Figure 11.16.** Data from Schneider and Fisk (1982). Performance in a multiple frame search task, either when one task is to be carried out alone (SINGLE) or two tasks are to be carried out together. The joint task performance levels are given in the interior of the panels, and the single task levels on the margins. Memory set size was two, and three frame times were utilized (90, 130, and 180 msec). Left panel: consistent and varied search tasks to be carried out together, with instructions to emphasize VM performance in the joint task setting. Right panel: two varied tasks to be carried out together. A is a measure of detection sensitivity. From "Concurrent Automatic and Controlled Visual Search" by W. Schneider and A.D. Fisk, 1982, *Journal of Experimental Psychology: Learning, Memory, and Cognition, 8*, p. 270. Copyright 1982 by the American Psychological Association. Reprinted by permission of the author.

such interference ought to occur only when a target is presented. At other times interference with other processes ought not to occur, even though the requirement to respond to trained targets is in force at all times.

Schneider and Fisk (1982a) tested this possibility in a dual task experiment. The subjects searched through multiple frames. Each frame contained four characters arranged in a square. Subjects carried out two search tasks simultaneously. On one diagonal varied mapping search was required (digits among digits, with the memory set of two items presented before each trial). On the other diagonal, a consistent search was required (letters among digits, any letter constituting a target). In single task control conditions, the displays were unchanged, but only one diagonal was relevant and only one task was required (no targets occurred on the irrelevant diagonal). In all conditions the subject pressed a key after the sequence of 12 displays to indicate the presence of a target. On any trial at most one target could occur. Subjects were well practiced so that in the consistent conditions automatic detection was well developed.

In one version of this study subjects were told to attempt to perform well in both tasks when both were required. Under these conditions, automatic detection was equal in both single and dual task conditions, but controlled search (the varied diagonal) was much worse in the dual task setting. This was true even though no automatic target occurred on the same trial as a varied target. Schneider and Fisk (1982a) hypothesized that subjects might have been allocating some attention to the consistent diagonal even though it was not needed there. They therefore instructed subjects to give primary attention to the varied diagonal, responding to targets on the other diagonal only if one happened to be noticed.

The results are given in the left hand panel of Figure 11.16, in terms of the A' performance measure which takes into account both hits and false alarms. On the boundaries of the square are plotted the single task results; in the interior are plotted the dual task results. The three conditions plotted come from three replications using different times per frame. Clearly, both tasks could be accomplished together about as well as when each task was carried out alone. The automatic performance showed what is termed a bias shift: Both hits and false alarms dropped when subjects were told to attend almost fully to the varied diagonal. However, sensitivity, as measured by A', did not change, and was not lower than the single task control.

These results stand in sharp contrast to those

in the right panel of the figure, in which the subject carried out two varied mapping searches concurrently. Here limited attentional capacity came into play (even though any trial contained at most one target, just as was true in the left hand panel). It seems clear that the subject was actively checking (comparing) the test items in the varied conditions, but was not doing so in the consistent conditions—instead the automatic target called attention to itself.

### The Causes of Automatization

Although it is clear that consistent training facilitates automatization, there are a good many questions left unanswered by the studies described thus far. For example, how consistent must training be? Schneider and Fisk (1982b) held constant across trials the number of times various items appeared as targets, and varied the number of times these items appeared as distractors (the stimuli were nine consonants and a multiple frame search task was utilized). Five degrees of consistency were used: (1) always target, never distractor (consistent control); (2) target twice as often as distractor; (3) target and distractor equally often; (4) target half as often as distractor; (5) target about one seventh as often as distractor (varied control). After training, performance was a monotonic function of consistency. Conditions (1), (2) and (3) were all much better than (5), but (4) and (5) did not differ statistically. Examination of the training data suggested that inconsistency both slowed the rate of automatization and limited the asymptotic degree of automatism that could be reached (when an item was used as a distractor two times or more often than as a target, detection of that item could not be automatized).

An interesting variant on the usual search task may also provide evidence concerning automatization based on partial consistency: Durso, Cooke, Breen, and Schvaneveldt (1987) had subjects search displays of digits for the largest. When 9 was present, it was always largest; when 1, 2, or 3 were present they were never largest; when intermediate digits were present, the probability they were largest was proportional to their size. Shiffrin and Czerwinski (in press) proposed that digits came to attract attention based on their relative frequency of being largest. The time for attention to settle on the actual largest digit in a display was assumed to be a function of the difference in attention attract-

ing tendencies for the two largest digits in a display (nicely predicting the fact that observed reaction times were faster, the larger was the numerical difference between the two largest digits). This model did a good job of predicting most of the findings, including some that appeared puzzling at first glance. For example, the model correctly predicted targets 4 and 9 to be fastest. Target 4 was predicted to be fast because it was guaranteed to have the low strength digits 1, 2, and/or 3 as competitors, whereas target 5, say, would often have the higher strength digit 4 as a competitor.

What is it about a trial that produces automatization? Searching for and finding an item produces automatization; however, searching for and not finding an item is somewhat harmful compared with not searching for it at all. Other factors affecting rate of automatization include: (1) Learning is faster the less the feature overlap between target and distractor items. (2) Massing or distribution of practice makes little difference. (3) Prior varied training may slow the subsequent rate of consistent learning. (4) Multiple display tasks may lead to faster learning, in terms of trials of practice, than single frame tasks. These matters are discussed by Shiffrin, Dumais, and Schneider (1981).

Finally, it may be asked how the development of automatic detection is affected by contextual conditions. For example, can both a consistent task and its reversal be automatized if the environmental, task-irrelevant context changes sufficiently between the two situations? Relatively little is known yet about contextual control of automatism (or even about generalizability of automatic detection to related stimuli). Shiffrin and Dumais (1981) obtained one negative result: Three consistent visual search tasks were trained in successive blocks in repeating fashion for many days. In one task, items denoted by A were targets with B distractors; in the second task, B were targets with C distractors; in the third task, C were targets with A distractors. All three of these did not become automatized. The data suggested that one task became automatized, one was entirely non-automatic, and the third a mixture of these two. This is a rather weak manipulation of context (and perhaps should not even be called a context manipulation); common sense suggests that different types of automatism (perhaps even incompatible types) could be learned in substantially different contexts, but the relevant research has yet to be carried out.

### Theoretical Interpretation

The data from consistently mapped search studies can be interpreted within the following model of automatic detection and automatization. When any item or items are presented in a display, each is processed with two sets of complementary processes, one a group of automatic processes, and the other a group of attentive mechanisms. The attentive and automatic processes may trade information at various levels, but it can be useful to conceptualize any local process as either automatic or attentive. The automatic processes are either innate or have been learned, and do not much partake of capacity limitations: They can operate in parallel with certain other automatic and attentive processes without loss and without interference with those other processes. The attentive processes are limited in capacity and tend to interfere with one another, often leading them to be used successively.

Examples of internal responses that may be produced largely by automatic processes if, say, an alphabetic character is presented include the following: brightness contours, contrast, color, spatial frequency analyses, and other primitive sensory analyses. In addition, well learned responses that are more central such as the "name" of the letter or the "category" of the character may be determined in largely automatic fashion. An internal attention response (perhaps a call to the attention system) will also be produced automatically, though the automatic calls to the attention system will certainly have to compete with the calls produced by other impinging stimuli, external or internal, and the calls produced electively by the subject.

In varied mapping paradigms none of the automatic responses prove effective in generating correct responses independent of load. Instead the memory set items and display items must be compared with the use of a limited, perhaps serial, comparison process. The varied practice does not lead to the development of helpful automatic responses because what may be learned and helpful on one trial is harmful on the next. For example, an increased tendency to attract attention for a target from one trial will harm performance on other trials when that item becomes a distractor.

On the other hand, when the mapping is con-

sistent, a number of new and helpful automatic responses can and will be learned. For example, target stimuli can develop strong calls to the attention system (and distractor stimuli can develop less strong than normal calls to the attention system); target stimuli can come to elicit category responses; targets can come to elicit internal "target" responses; target stimuli can even come to elicit automatic overt responses (e.g., a particular button press). It should also be emphasized that such automatic responses can be learned not only to the nominal stimuli themselves, but also to the features of those stimuli that are consistently related to target status. Thus if some aspect of the targets as a group distinguishes the targets from the distractors (for example, vertical line segments in all targets but in no distractors) then automatic responses can be attached to those features in addition to, or as an alternative to, the responses to the targets themselves. Whichever types of automatic responses are learned, traditional associative learning mechanisms are capable of subserving this new learning.

A model of automatization based on these principles (or similar ones) seems capable of handling the findings from search paradigms (see Shiffrin and Schneider, 1984, for some mild constraints). Within this experimental context, the distinctions between automatic and attentive processes are well defined in both theoretical and empirical terms. To what extent can the approach be generalized to other settings? A partial answer can be found in auditory search tasks, in which similar findings are obtained (Poltrock, Lansman, & Hunt, 1982). However, a switch from the visual to the auditory modality in the same task environment is not a very substantial test of generalization.

The dual task paradigms discussed in the first section provide a stronger generalization test. It appears that certain characteristics of automatization that apply to search can be carried over. For example, consistent practice of a task could lead to the development of (partly) automatic sequences of overt and covert responses, reducing the attentive demands of that task, and allowing an attention demanding primary task to be carried out at near optimal levels of performance. Nonetheless, there are important differences: Attention itself seems to be automatized in the consistent search task, so that an irrelevant automatically trained target causes interference with a simultaneous task (see the section on automatization of attention). Why attention can be removed from a secondary task in some settings but not in the search task is a research issue yet to be explored.

A more general issue concerns the existence of characteristics that can be used to discriminate automatic and attentive processes in all task settings. Many such characteristics have been proposed and a number of these will be reviewed in the next section.

## CHARACTERISTICS OF AUTOMATIC AND ATTENTIVE PROCESSES

We shall see in this section that there do not seem to be any simple defining features of automatic and attentive processes that can be applied in complete generality. Nevertheless, the search for such characteristics has generated some of the most valuable and interesting research in the attention area. In this section we shall review a number of defining characteristics that have been proposed over the years. This review is meant to provide a vehicle by which many important research findings and issues can be organized and presented in coherent fashion. Many of the criteria discussed below overlap or are correlated with one another, so certain groups of criteria are discussed together.

### Capacity/Resource Use and Interference

The fact that attention itself can be automatized raises some problems for criteria based on capacity/resource use, and interference. Because attention is *called* by targets, the presentation of targets will interfere with other ongoing processes requiring that attention; similarly resources will be utilized since attention to the target will occur. The problem here is locating necessary and sufficient conditions for automatism, or for attentive processes. A process that does not use resources, or does not interfere with other attentive processes, is certainly automatic. Hence such criteria are sufficient, but not necessary. Conversely, attentive processes must use central capacity and must interfere with other attentive processes; hence such criteria are necessary but not sufficient.

The interference criterion is an interesting

one: Attentive processes must interfere with other attentive processes if they are used, but the interference can be eliminated because the subject can choose not to use the process in question (although performance may drop if this is done). On the other hand, if a process produces interference with attentive processes despite the subject's attempts to eliminate the interference, then the process in question is surely automatic (as was the case in the study whose results are shown in Figure 11.15).

Although we have focused our discussion upon search paradigms, the most well known task used to study "automatic" interference is known as the *Stroop* task (Stroop, 1935; see Dyer, 1973, for one review). The standard task requires the subject to name the ink colors in which a series of words are printed. In one control condition, the words are random, and do not contain any color names. In the interference condition the letters spell a color that is different than the ink color in which the word is printed (e.g., RED printed in blue ink). In the facilitation condition, the printed word names a color matching the color of ink in which the word is printed (e.g., RED printed in red ink). There are many variants of this task: For example, one might have to name the number of digits in a region, when the digits themselves are consistent with, or inconsistent with, the number present (Morton, 1969); name pictures representing words, with printed words as interfering stimuli (e.g., Lupker & Katz, 1981); name letters which in outline, form a larger, different letter (e.g., Hoffman, 1980); identify letters (or words) flanked by different letters (or words) (e.g., Eriksen & Schulz, 1979; Shaffer & LaBerge, 1979).

The standard result is that the time to name the color of ink is slowed by inconsistency (and somewhat helped by consistency), with errors showing a similar pattern. The standard interpretation of the interference is that the printed name is encoded automatically, despite the subject's attempt to ignore the printing, producing a response tendency that conflicts with the different response required to name the ink color.

Researchers have questioned this interpretation on several grounds. For example, the entire process by which the interference occurs can hardly be automatic, else normal reading would be virtually impossible: The several words in the field of vision would interfere with one another. Perhaps more to the point, the fact that neutral words produce less interference than color words suggests that the subject's *intent* to emit color names primes these responses and accounts for the interference they produce. Evidence supporting this view comes from a study in which the subject must emit digit names as well as color names; in such a case printed names of digits produce as much interference with the ink color naming as does printed color words (Neumann, 1984). The idea that attentional control interacts with automatic feature extraction to produce the Stroop effect (see Logan, 1980) is supported on several grounds. For example, matching the ink color to a colored patch does not show the interference from the printed color name, presumably because the translation of the written code to a perceptual one is not as automatic as the transmission of the written code to a verbal one (unless attention is used to facilitate the translation; see Virzi & Egeth, 1985).

It also appears that the spatial distribution of attention affects the amount of interference. To take one of many examples, Goolkasian (1981) presented a word printed in black at the fovea, and a color patch as a target (whose color was to be spoken) either in the fovea, or at seven degrees from the fovea. The target was presented briefly and the distractor's onset was varied systematically with respect to target onset. Regardless of stimulus onset asynchrony, foveal presentation of the target produced large Stroop effects, but parafoveal target presentation produced rather small and irregular effects, primarily facilitating. Apparently the directing of attention to a spatially distant location from the distractor eliminates most of the Stroop interference. Somewhat different studies leading to similar conclusions were carried out by Kahneman and Henik (1981).

Thus there are certainly automatic aspects to the Stroop situation (such as the encoding of the name represented by the printed word, and the inevitable interference that occurs in certain situations), but the magnitude of inhibitory and facilitory effects are determined by certain attentive effects as well. Among these are requirements that the subject intend to emit responses of the type represented by the distractor, and that the distractor appears near the region where the subject is placing his visual attention.

Although much more can be said about the Stroop effect, these results serve to illustrate an important point: certain component processes used to accomplish tasks can be automatic or attentive, but tasks as a whole are accomplished by complex mixtures of automatic and attentive processes operating in concert. Finally, the recent findings concerning the Stroop effect demonstrate an important point. A finding of mandatory interference implies that certain automatic processes are taking place, but not that entire tasks are automatic. The existence of altered conditions in which the interference is eliminated does not imply that automatic processes are not present. The implication is instead that in the new task a crucial link in the sequence of attentive and automatic processes learning to the interference must have been eliminated.

## Preparation

In an effort to find a necessary and sufficient criterion one might propose that an automatic process is one that requires no preparation for its operation. In this context, preparation refers to processes carried out before the stimuli requiring a response are presented. For an automatic process, preparation should use no resources, should not interfere with other activities and should require no effort or awareness, primarily because active processes in advance of stimulus presentation should not be needed. This definition may be adequate for many automatic processes, including many of those in the search domain, but has difficulty with automatic processes that are initiated by an attentive process. For example, a tennis player might have a choice of two backhands to hit: slice and topspin. Once a shot is chosen, a whole set of (partly) automatic processes might carry the action to its completion, but the actions would not occur without the original choice. If the units of analysis in question were large enough, then the entire sequence including and ensuing from an attentive act might be considered an attentive process. This would strike most researchers as an overly restrictive view.

At a more molecular level of analysis, a long sequence of processes begun by an attentive choice could be broken into component parts, only the first necessarily being attentive. The preparation criterion would not be useful in such a case. Furthermore, a basic issue must be faced: What status should a process have when among its necessary triggering stimuli are one or more attentive processes or choices? An answer to this question is not available.

## Rate of Learning

A somewhat different approach to a criterion involves the speed of learning and unlearning. Automatic processes are generally learned gradually, or if they are already learned, they are difficult to unlearn. Attentive processes can be "turned on" or "turned off" at the momentary whim of the subject. James (1890) conceived of attention in the immediate sense as something "to make us: (a) perceive, (b) conceive, (c) distinguish, (d) remember better than otherwise we could." The "otherwise" refers to the normal automatic processes that would operate without attention. It is interesting that automatization can serve these same functions in the long run, given an appropriate training regimen. Unfortunately, a criterion based on speed of learning is almost impossible to apply in practice: Certain automatic processes may come close to asymptotic learning in as little as a single trial (for example, aversion caused by strong negative reinforcements such as strong shocks or negative agents producing taste aversion). Even in the search domain, evidence for automatization has been seen in as few as eight trials (Schneider, 1985).

## Depth of Automatic Processing

### Preattentive Processes

Many modern attention theorists beginning with Broadbent (1958), and including Treisman (1969), Kahneman (1973), and Neisser (1967) among others, have accepted the need for automatic processes but have tended to relegate them to peripheral mechanisms early in the processing stream. These have sometimes been called "preattentive" processes, and often are said to be based on analyzers tuned to sensory features on primitive dimensions. No one would disagree that such processes are automatic (in some cases chemical or neural substrates for the analyses have been identified). However, much deeper analysis can also be automatic, as discussed next.

### Automatic Processing Based on Semantic Factors

One of the strongest and clearest demonstra-

tions of automatic processing at a "deep" level has been provided by Schneider and Fisk (1984) in the search domain. Subjects were trained in a consistent paradigm to pick out and indicate the position of a target within a display of three words. Before each trial the subject was given a category of words to search for (e.g., *weapons*). Over trials the number of exemplars seen as targets was limited; for different categories, the number was either 4, 8, or 12. Distractors were words from four other categories. All three categories improved with practice at similar rates and automatic detection of either the category, the members (4, 8, or 12), or both, appeared to have developed. The fact that improvement with training took place at similar rates for the categories represented by different number of exemplars suggested that the performance was mainly governed by category detection, rather than exemplar detection.

A stronger test of the hypothesis that the category was being detected automatically came from a transfer test: New exemplars from the previously trained categories were introduced. Positive transfer to these new items was high (about 92 percent). The most plausible hypothesis is clear: When a new item was presented in a display its category was generated automatically (as would normally be the case even without training in this task). The category response in turn generated another response, one learned during consistent training, probably a response causing attraction of attention (as in the case with item automatization). In the control conditions using varied mapping (in which performance was much worse) each test item presumably also had its category extracted automatically, but these category names then had to be compared serially to the target category.

An even stronger demonstration of detection based on automatic category extraction came from a condition using multiple frames and two simultaneous tasks. In the center of each display a word appeared and in the periphery, digits appeared. For word detection, the category name was specified before each trial in a consistently mapped fashion. Simultaneously the subjects searched for target digits specified before each trial in a variably mapped fashion. After training, subjects appeared capable of carrying out both searches simultaneously, presumably because the word task was automatized. Then new exemplars from the trained categories were introduced. Even though the subjects were carrying out an attention-demanding search for digits simultaneously, the new examplars were detected almost 82 percent of the time. Comparison with various control conditions confirmed the conclusion that the items presented for test had their category membership extracted automatically, and that the category label then attracted attention automatically, on at least a large proportion of the trials.

Such results imply that depth of processing is not a criterial difference between attentive and automatic processing. Indeed, there is reason to believe that at least some processes at almost any depth can be automatized, given appropriate consistent training. Nonetheless, as Bryan and Harter (1899) suggested, later developing automatic processes probably build on a base of already developed automatic processes, so the *likelihood* of automatism is probably less the deeper is the process in question. Furthermore, there is every reason to believe that certain types of peripheral mechanisms are structurally predisposed to be automatic even at birth or shortly thereafter, regardless of learning.

### Control of Processing Depth

Given that relatively late and central stages of processing can be automatized, two related questions arise: Can processing be made more deep, or more shallow, through application or attentive resources? That processing can be extended through application of attentive resources has never been in doubt (e.g., the extraction of meaning from poetry). However, a distinction must be made between a direct application of attentive resources (e.g., serial comparisons during search tasks), and modification of automatic processing through attentive control, which is an indirect application of attentive resources. This latter issue has undergone considerable scrutiny, perhaps because some theorists feel that automatic processes ought *not* to be modifiable. The question of modifiability will be discussed in the next section (and also later in the paper during sections on locus of control and locus of limited capacity). For present purposes, it should be noted that processing depth would not be a suitable criterion for discriminating automatic and attentive processes, whether depth of processing is modifiable or not.

## Modifiability of Automatic Processing

Automatic processes may sometimes have consequences that are impossible to eliminate through attentional control (e.g., the interference seen in Figure 11.15; see also the section above on the Stroop effect). Nonetheless, most automatic processes may be partially controllable and some automatic processes may be highly controllable through attentive means, especially when such attentive processing provides some of the contextual stimuli that trigger the operation of the automatic process. That is, the subject can through attentive means control the input to an automatic process, thereby exerting control over the process itself. An extreme example would be an eye movement to move a character in the visual field to a region of different acuity, thereby controlling the automatic processing it is given. (Related to this notion is the possibility that some automatic processes might usually or always be initiated by attentive processes.) One might think it would be useful to draw a distinction between indirect control of an automatic process through the inputs it receives in advance, and more direct control of an ongoing automatic process, but such a distinction is too subtle at the present theoretical and empirical development of the field.

Given that the possibility of direct or indirect modifiability of automatic processing is accepted, it is still useful to cite instances in which attention can influence processes that appear on the face of things to be quite peripheral and automatic. Consider, for example, the eyeblink reflex studied by Graham and her colleagues (e.g., Graham, 1975; Bohlin & Graham, 1977; Silverstein, Graham, & Bohlin, 1981; Bohlin, Graham, Silverstein, & Hackley, 1981). The blink reflex is a startle response to sudden auditory or visual stimuli that is governed by the brainstem (e.g., occurs in decorticate animals). This response seems to be a good candidate for an automatic process. Nevertheless a number of studies in animals and adult humans have shown this reflex is modifiable by attentive control. A representative study using infants (16 weeks) was published by Anthony and Graham (1983). The infant was given a foreground stimulus for five seconds to attract attention to a sensory modality. The foreground stimulus was either interesting (a face or a tune) or dull (a blank side or a tone). Then a sudden light flash or noise was introduced. Blinks were larger when the modalities of foreground and stimulus matched when they mismatched. This effect was larger for interesting foregrounds. The conclusion reached by Anthony and Graham seems reasonable: The attention to modality produced by the foregrounds was causing a modification of a relatively peripheral and low level automatic process. It seems highly likely in this case that the movement of attention to the appropriate modality was an automatic response to the foreground stimuli (as, for example, the attention shift to an irrelevant automatic target was involuntary in the study of Figure 11.5), but this reasoning only confirms that an attentional shift produces the changes observed in the blink reflex. Indeed, in other studies using adults, similar changes were induced by instructions and other means.

Results like these suggest that there can be some degree of attentive control of automatic processes. However, they leave open the degree to which most automatic processes are attentively modifiable. Johnston and Dark (1982) contrast two views: (1) *Extraperceptual*: perceptual processing is automatic and unmodifiable by attention; attention acts directly by supplementing automatic processing. (2) *Intraperceptual*: automatic perceptual processing is modifiable by attention; the more attention directed to an item the more perceptual processing occurs. Convincing evidence distinguishing these views is very hard to find.

Consider the study reported by Johnston and Dark (1982): Subjects listened to lists of pairs of different words presented dichotically, one pair every 1.5 seconds. The subject's main task was to detect names of states. In the *focused* condition 67 state names were presented to a known, designated, ear. In the *divided* condition, these targets were divided 33 and 34 between the two ears. Simultaneously with this task, the subjects viewed a screen: whenever a word was presented visually, the subjects named a free associate and then returned to their auditory task.

The visual words were homographs (two meanings). Just before the visual word test, and just after, two of the nontarget auditory words were primes that biased the subject toward perceiving one of the two meanings of the visual homograph (e.g., the visual test word *bark* would be paired with successive auditory words, either *wood* and *chips*, or *growl* and *noise*). The two primes occurred successively on one of the two ears.

The results showed the usual effect of focusing attention: Target detection (states) was superior in the focused attention condition (in visual search terms, the task varied "display" size). It is unclear to what extent this primary auditory detection task was accomplished by automatic detection. In any event, the question of present interest concerns processing of the nontargets, as assessed by responses to the visual probes: In fact, a meaning consistent with the biasing words was obtained most often when these biasing words were on the attended ear in the focused condition and least often when these words on the unattended ear in the focused condition; the divided condition was intermediate. Johnston and Dark (1982) argued that automatic perceptual processing of the auditory words was directly affected by the degree of attention paid to the ear containing them (as assessed by the effects produced by the biasing words). Unfortunately, as the authors admit, the same results would be predicted if the biasing effect was caused by the amount of direct, attentive processing given to the biasing words. This problem (or similar ones) afflicts most of the studies in this area, so at the present time, the degree to which automatic processing is affected by attention is an unsettled issue.

## Effort

Effort has long been thought related to attention, the term "effortful processing" being used by Hasher and Zacks (e.g., 1979) to refer to attentive processing. If effort is defined only subjectively, then this definition is unlikely to be of much help. If effort is defined in terms of objective measures, these measures may lead to empirical tests; indeed many of these are discussed in this section. It must be admitted that differential effort is the most introspectively obvious difference between processes researchers would like to call automatic and attentive. Nevertheless, some nagging problems remain: (1) How does one deal with "automatic" processes that require an attentive process to trigger? (2) If attention is called automatically, some effort might be engaged. (3) When attentive processes become very easy, effort might tend to drop below noticeable threshold.

In an effort to assess the effort required of

processing, Posner and his colleagues developed what is known as the "probe" technique (e.g., Posner and Boies, 1971). The subject is asked to carry out a primary task, such as visual letter matching, and at various times after task onset is occasionally interrupted by presentation of a probe stimulus, such as a brief tone. Whenever the probe occurs, the subject attempts to respond to it as quickly as possible. It is reasoned that responding to the probe should utilize at least some capacity and therefore that speed of responding to the probe should be inversely related to the momentary effort being required by the primary task. Posner and Boies (1971) used this approach when the primary task was the matching of sequentially, visually presented letters. They concluded that encoding of at least the first letter was automatic and effortless because probes just after the onset of the first letter were responded to quite quickly relative to, say, probes during the intertrial interval. Posner and Klein (1973) extended these findings and came to similar conclusions (see also Posner, 1978, 1982). The conclusion that letter encoding is effortless, however, was a bit premature. Ogden, Martin, and Paap (1980), Paap and Ogden (1981), and Johnson, Forester, Calderwood, and Weisgerber (1983) utilized improved methodology with better controls and come to the opposite conclusion. Probe times were indeed increased by encoding demands, and this interference was present even when letters were presented that were to be ignored. Thus these authors concluded that encoding of letters utilized capacity and did so in obligatory fashion.

Several issues of present importance are raised by these results. The finding of interference caused by a presented stimulus is not necessarily evidence against automatism (we saw interference in a search task, in Figure 11.15, when the stimulus causing the interference had been trained to attract attention). Indeed, the obligatory nature of the interference suggests that processing was automatic. One possibility is that presentation of a letter engages the attention system, and calls for attention, thereby producing the observed interference. Do the results imply that *effort* was required for encoding? Probably not, unless a call for attention caused by presentation is interpreted as a source of effort. Thus even though attentive processes may be characterized by an output of effort, the tasks used to assess effort (such as the probe technique) may give misleading results. They may give the appearance of effortful processing, through automatic activation of the attention system itself, in cases that most people would prefer to classify automatic.

## Precedence and Speed

It is sometimes thought that automatic processes should *precede* attentive processes in any processing sequence, and should operate more quickly than attentive processes. Neither of these criteria are essential, as we have indicated in earlier sections, but evidence that bears on the issue comes from what has been an important paradigm in the study of attention and automatism: the *priming paradigm*.

There are many variants of priming tasks. Usually some decision (e.g., Is the stimulus a word? Was the stimulus on a recent list? Is the stimulus an animal?) is to be made as well or as quickly as possible about a target stimulus. Shortly before the target is presented, a *prime* is presented. The prime may occasionally be informative concerning the decision to be made but often is completely irrelevant. However, unbeknownst to the subject, the prime is semantically related to the target in the key experimental conditions.

Consider tasks with words and nonwords as stimuli: the subject is asked to decide whether the target is a word (i.e., lexical decision). The key result is as follows: when the prime is semantically related to the target (e.g., *water*–ICE) then the response to the target is facilitated, compared with controls using "neutral" primes consisting of a row of Xs. Sometimes there is also interference: The neutral primes lead to better performance than an "unrelated" word prime. It is usually assumed that relatedness information is automatically activated and resides in short-term memory until it affects the target decision, or that the prime begins a process of automatic spreading activation that pre-activates the target, thereby affecting the decision. Whether the activation is truly automatic is a question that arises in many of these paradigms.

Posner and Snyder (1975a, b) proposed a theory and collected certain data suggesting that a prime leads to automatic, fast, activation of related items, thereby producing better processing of these related items when they are targets. In addition, a prime may lead to conscious, attentive processing which is slow and produces both costs and benefits, depending on task details.

One of the best studies supporting such a view was carried out by Neely (1977). Each target item was to be judged word or nonword: Shortly before, a prime appeared, at stimulus onset asynchronies of 250–2000 msec. Neutral primes were strings of Xs. The word "bird" as a prime was usually followed by a name of a bird. However, the word "body" was usually followed by a part of a building, and the word "building" was usually followed by a part of a body. One might expect that at small stimulus onset asynchronies each word prime would automatically activate related words, producing speeded responses whenever the tested word was a member of the category named. On the other hand, at longer stimulus onset asynchronies, the subject would have time to invoke an attentive process and translate the "body" and "building" primes into the other term, activating the other set of related words, and speeding responses to them. In addition, according to the Posner and Snyder (1975a, b) theory, at the longer delays one should expect inhibition whenever the category expected does not match the test word category. Just these effects were observed, including the somewhat startling finding that at long delays, a building prime *slowed* responses to a building part (and similarly for a body prime), just as a bird prime slowed responses if a body or building part was tested. This was true even though *speeding* of responses to a building part was produced by a building prime at short delays (and similarly for body primes and parts).

Such results seem best interpreted as evidence for fast automatic activation of words related to the prime or of semantic features of the prime, producing speeded target processing, followed by slower, attentively governed processing that produces both costs and benefits, depending on the relationship between what is expected, and what is tested. It should be noted, however, that this conclusion applies to this particular paradigm, or others like it. It is perfectly possible for an inhibitory effect to be produced rapidly and automatically in other types of paradigms (as was seen in Figure 11.15). Also, there is no reason in principle why certain types of attentive processes (in other tasks) could not be as fast or faster than certain types of automatic activation.

## Awareness and Consciousness

Some investigators have tried to equate attentive processes with "awareness" or "consciousness" (e.g., Posner & Klein, 1973). This idea was discussed by the early investigators mentioned in the first section (e.g., Solomons & Stein, 1896; Downey & Anderson, 1915—though these researchers eventually decided against using such a criterion).

The awareness criterion has been used in several interesting studies to infer the existence of automatic processing. An item is presented very briefly and then followed by a masking stimulus. The conditions are such that the subject cannot report the item presented even though attention is focused upon it. This stimulus is called the prime, and is followed within a few seconds by a target that is not masked. The target item is classified in some fashion, perhaps as a word or nonword. In some studies the masked prime that cannot be reported affects processing of the target. For example a word prime may speed a decision about a word that is semantically related to the prime (e.g., Marcel, 1978, 1980; Fowler, Wolford, Slade, & Tassinary, 1981). Such effects must be automatic if "awareness" is used as a criterion for automatism. Nonetheless, attention is certainly focused on the prime that is masked, and in many studies, subjects report an impression that the prime is perceived but then lost from memory when the mask occurs. Thus it would be premature to assume that attentive processing plays no role in the observed priming effects. (A related effect occurs when the prime is not masked, but presented several times at durations such that later yes-no recognition judgments are at chance levels. In these cases the prime itself is then used as a target and subjects like it more than a control word, as reported by Kunst-Wilson & Zajonc, 1980, or think it brighter than a control word, as reported by Mandler, Nakamura, & Van Zandt, 1987).

The priming effects in these situations are often interpreted in terms of *automatic spreading activation* and are generally thought to be quite transient. However, even though a lexical decision may not be speeded by an "unaware" word presented several items earlier, the possibility exists that a more sensitive test could show relatively long lasting changes in memory as a result of an "unaware" prime. Such effects have been reported and are reviewed by Bargh (1984; see also the first section).

Despite the attractiveness of the "awareness" criterion, it has a number of problems. Awareness is defined by the subject's memory. Something may be "aware" at one time and then forgotten within a few hundred milliseconds (as suggested by the rapid sensory forgetting seen in studies like those of Sperling, 1960). Related to this is the possibility that some attentive processes operate so quickly that awareness of the components of the process is low (e.g., the comparisons used in varied-mapping search tasks). Conversely, because at least some automatic processes attract attention, they can produce awareness (at least shortly after the fact). For these and related reasons, the consciousness criterion is at best of very limited usefulness and generality.

## Control, Intentionality, and Parameter Specification

Shiffrin and Schneider (1977) called attentive processes "control processes." This seems a crucial characteristic, but there are a few problems: (1) Some automatic processes may be triggered directly or indirectly by attentive processes, thereby requiring control and intentionality. (2) Some automatic processes may trigger attentive processes (such as automatic calls to the attention system). (3) Some attentive processes (such as the comparison process in search tasks using varied mapping) operate so quickly that the moment-to-moment details may be difficult to control.

Neumann (1984) has proposed a definition for automatism based on *parameter specification*. A process is automatic if its parameters (process variables whose values must be specified for the process to operate) are specified by (1) skill and (2) input information. When this is not possible then attention comes into play to specify the remaining needed parameters. In this view, control of automatic processing is vested in incoming environmental information and prior learning (or genetically predisposed structures), a view basically consistent with the *control* criterion, and sharing its problems. Perhaps most crucial is the definition of input: if internal

states produced by attentive processes are allowed to be part of the contextual stimulus environment that triggers an automatic process, then the parameter specification criterion (and the control criterion, as well) does not provide a useful distinction in all settings.

## Level of Performance and Parallel Processing

Although automatic processing is often thought of as unlimited, there are many limitations on both the performance level that is reachable, and the ability to carry out automatic processes simultaneously without cost. Clearly, whenever two automatic processes share some subprocesses or component in incompatible fashion, there *must* be interference. For example, if one automatic process involves an eye movement to the right, and another an eye movement to the left, both cannot occur together. More subtle examples occur as well. Shiffrin and Schneider (1977, Experiment 4c) carried out a search study using a multiple frame design. On each four item display one diagonal was relevant and one irrelevant. Consistent mapping occurred on the relevant diagonal. When a (automatic) target occurred on the relevant diagonal, an identical (albeit irrelevant) target on the irrelevant diagonal in the same frame cause a small drop in detection. A similar result occurred in a task in which all four locations in each display were relevant, but two identical targets would occur together in the same display. In both cases, there may have been a competition between two items both demanding attention, but this is an unlikely explanation, because two *nonidentical* automatic targets do not lead to a similar performance deficit. Schneider and Shiffrin (1977) suggested that both items tend to be attended and accentuated in short-term memory, but that in a multiple frame task the only lasting and useful memory representation is a positionless central one. When two targets are different, the central representations are different; when they are identical, there may be only one central representation, leading to difficulty in judging either the number presented or the position of origin. (See also Eriksen & Eriksen, 1974, and the section on the *Stroop* effect, for related research).

Automatic processing in parallel may be limited by demands for common pathways or physical structures. In other cases, parallel operation is impossible because automatic processes occur in chains, the output of one providing some of the necessary input for the next. Thus while the observation of parallel, independent processing may allow an attentive processing hypothesis to be ruled out, the failure of this criterion to hold does not rule out automatic processes.

Level of performance of automatic processes is limited by what Norman and Bobrow (1975) have termed a *data limitation* (as opposed to a *process limitation*). When the inputs to an automatic process are too weak or impoverished to trigger the process fully or correctly, then poor performance will result. An example is seen in Figure 11.12 in the left hand panel: At brief display times, false alarms begin to arise, presumably because the features extracted from the display are improverished.

Of course, data limitations should apply equally whether the subsequent processing is automatic or attentive, so it is sometimes thought that appropriately trained automatic processing must be superior to attentive processing. However, the advantage of automatic processing lies in the relative independence from effects of load. When the load is small, there is no reason to expect an inherent advantage for automatic processing, and the opposite may be true. For example, in many consistent search tasks, the set size function shows superior performance at small loads even after extensive training (e.g., Kristofferson, 1972b; Shiffrin & Dumais, 1981). This result may be obtained because attentive processing is used at small loads in parallel with automatic detection: The attentive processing might be often enough superior at small loads to produce the observed advantage.

## Memory Effects

Awareness and retention are related criteria. As Downey and Anderson (1915) noted, their retrospections sometimes showed no awareness, but they felt this was often due to forgetting of an original awareness. The memory criterion is based on the assumption that attentive processing should lead to observable retention, whereas automatic processing may sometimes lead to no retention.

Fisk and Schneider (1984) provided evidence from a multiple-frame search task. Each display consisted of a word presented at the point of fixation, and digits presented in a square surrounding the word. In various conditions, subjects were induced to attend to the words to varying degrees. On a later recognition test subjects were asked to give frequency estimates for test words; these had been presented either 0, 1, 5, 10, or 20 times. Estimation was worse, the less attention was given to the words. In fact when subjects were told to ignore the words and carry out a digit detection task only, they remembered nothing about the words even though they appeared at the center of fixation.

In a second study, subjects carried out digit detection, but simultaneously picked out words of a given category that appeared in the displays. After much training the category task became substantially automatic. Then new members of the trained category were introduced, as well as new distractors (from other categories). Substantial numbers of the new targets were detected, even though an attention demanding digit search was being carried out simultaneously. Thus the subjects were analyzing words automatically up to the category level, at least on most trials. Then recognition and frequency judgments were obtained for the new distractor words used in the transfer session. These judgments were not dependent on the frequency of presentation over a range of 1 to 20. Furthermore, the presented items were only slightly discriminable from not presented items (forced choice recognition probability was .55, where .50 is chance, and $d'$ was equal to .19). These small effects could have been due to some attention given inadvertently to the words, even though it was not necessary. Thus recognition of unattended words seems to be at least poor and possibly missing, even when those words are being analyzed automatically to the category level.[2]

It may be that a different and/or more sensitive test could bring to light some modifications of memory produced by automatic processing of the type studied by Fisk and Schneider.

[2]The present results have another implication that bears on claims for automatic processing. Hasher and Zacks (1979) and Zacks, Hasher, and Sanft (1982) have argued that encoding of frequency is automatic. Although their results demonstrated that encoding of the frequency variable is somewhat different than for many other variables, the Fisk and Schneider (1984) results make it unlikely that frequency is encoded automatically according to the criteria we have been discussing.

Eich (1984) demonstrated this point. Subjects listened to an interesting story presented to one ear, and shadowed it (repeated it aloud). During this shadowing, pairs of successive words were presented to the other ear (at a somewhat lower loudness). Each pair consisted of a modifier and a homophone, the modifier biasing the less common interpretation of the homophone (e.g., taxi-FARE). Subsequently subjects were tested for their ability to recognize (pick out the presented homophones from new ones), and also for their ability to spell auditorily presented homophones.

The recognition results confirmed the findings of Fisk and Schneider (1984): The probability of judging a homophone to have been presented was .398 when the tested homophone had been presented and .383 when it had not; the homophones could not be recognized. Nonetheless, the spelling chosen for a presented homophone was more often in line with the less common interpretation than was true for nonpresented homophones (.348 vs. .235). Thus even though recognition was at chance, presumably because attention had not been given to the nonshadowed items, automatic semantic processing took place to some degree for those same items, causing (automatically) the interpretation of the homophone to be affected. (See also results by Lewis, 1970; Treisman, Squire, & Green, 1974; Johnston & Heinz, 1979; MacKay, 1973; Newstead & Dennis, 1979; Corteen & Wood, 1972). It should be noted that the biasing effect on spelling can be greatly enhanced by application of attention (Eich, 1984; see also Jacoby & Witherspoon, 1982).

As interesting as are these various memory findings, memory effects do not appear to lead to a useful criterion. It is far from clear that attentive processing must lead to observable retention, and, on the other hand, automatic processing may have some effects on memory, depending on the type of test that is used.

## Partial Automatism

In most cases, processes will not be practiced to the point of reaching their maximum degree of automatism (or performance, if these are not equivalent). The status of processes before asymptotic levels are reached is not clear. It is possible that a process is either automatic or not, and that practice merely increases the probability of the former. Perhaps this view could be defended if the units of analysis are extremely small, but it seems more likely that performance and automatism both improve gradually with consistent practice.

Certain data support the gradual view. For example, in search tasks, the probabilistic mixture model predicts that at any stage of training the set size function should be linear (with a slope that decreases with practice). This prediction is based on the assumption that whenever the automatic process is triggered, the set-size function will be flat, and fast. On the other hand, one version of the gradual model assumes that the automatic process always operates in parallel with the serial comparison process, and is a flat function of set size, but with a speed that gradually improves with practice. If so, the set size function should have two limbs: one with normal slope at small set sizes (due to serial comparisons finishing first), and then a flat portion at larger set sizes (due to automatic detection finishing first). The break point should move to smaller set sizes as automatic detection becomes faster. In practice, such a two limbed function might well appear curvilinear, due to "noise" affecting the predictions. The data does seem consistent with this version of the gradual model, since the consistently mapped set size functions typically become curvilinear with decreasing "slope" (e.g., Kristofferson, 1972b) or exhibit two limbs with a decreasing break point (e.g., Ellis & Chase, 1971). It should be emphasized, however, that this reasoning applies only to these versions of the gradual and all-or-none models; distinguishing between more general classes of these models would be much more difficult.

## Overview: Criteria for Automatic and Attentive Processing

Most researchers and theorists agree that a distinction between automatic and attentive processes is useful, necessary, and valid, notwithstanding a good deal of controversy concerning the characteristics and roles of these processes. In the domain of search tasks, a breakdown of processes into automatic and controlled components is well advanced, and a good deal is understood concerning the properties of these processes and the nature of their development. However, automatic and attentive processes in search are at most only occasionally used in other tasks. Attempts to define necessary and sufficient criteria to distinguish automatic and attentive processes in complete generality have not yet proven successful. Certain sufficient criteria appear at first glance to be available for automatic and attentive processes; if so, some processes and task components could be identified unambiguously. However, even in these cases, different answers may be obtained when the size of the unit of analysis is changed. Furthermore, in practice, many processes that have the potential to become fully automatic will have been trained only to some degree of partial automatism.

It seems likely that future progress will take place on two fronts: (1) The concepts of automatism and attentive processing will be further refined and broken down into subcategories, each of which can be defined more generally and rigorously than is possible globally. (2) Formal, quantitive, or simulation models will be developed for particular classes of tasks, the roles of automatic and attentive processes being precisely defined within the model. Developments of this second kind are currently taking place, and as they continue we can expect to learn a good deal about the roles of automatism and attentive processing within certain restricted task domains. An example in the search domain is the recent simulation model by Schneider (1985).

## SELECTIVE ATTENTION

In the following sections, we shall deal with the nature of attentive processes when automatic processing is not playing an important (or differential) role. There are many important questions. For example: What are the limitations of attention? How widely can attention be spread? How finely can attention be focused? What is the nature of attentional bottlenecks and where in the processing system are they to be found? On what may attention be focused? How does attention help stimulus features cohere into organized entities? What are the different roles of attentional processes? A variety of theoretical disputes have arisen concerning these questions and their answers. In the remainder of this chapter we shall attempt to present some of

the more important issues and data bearing on them.

## Limitations of Attention

In varied mapping search tasks we have seen a strict limit upon attentional resources: Single frame tasks show that each additional comparison requires on the average a fixed amount of time to be accomplished (about 40 msec in the case of simple memory search). This limitation may explain performance in multiple frame tasks as well. Since the frame time is fixed, the average number of comparisons that can be accomplished per frame is fixed; thus the chance of completing the key comparison that produces a match decreases as load increases. It may well be the case that a mechanism like this produces limitations of attention in a much wider class of target detection paradigms, as well. Before considering the possible bases for attentional limitations, however, a certain amount of terminology is needed.

Limitations of attention are conveniently classified in two forms: *divided* and *focused*. In *divided attention paradigms* the subject is asked to spread attention over as many stimuli, or potential stimuli, or sources of stimuli, as possible. Limits are seen because not many things can be attended at once. The analogy of a cocktail party is often used by way of example: one can attempt to listen to multiple conversations simultaneously, but attentional limitations strictly limit one's ability to do so. In *focused attention paradigms*, the subject attempts to place all available attention on just one stimulus, type of stimuli, or source of stimuli, ignoring and/or excluding all other inputs. In the cocktail party analogy, one attempts to attend to just one conversation, but may find it difficult to do so because of distraction from other conversations. There are, of course, a variety of paradigms lying somewhere between these two extremes. For example, in many *shadowing* studies, the subject attempts to repeat aloud stimuli presented to one ear, presumably focusing attention on that ear, but nevertheless tries to detect signals on either or both ears, providing some incentive to spread attention. In the cocktail party analogy, one might be attending to one conversation but trying to remain alert to the mention of some important matter in another conversation. These issues and many related ones will be the topics of the following sections.

## Dividing Attention

As a general rule, subjects find it extremely difficult to divide attention. When there are more tasks to be carried out, more stimuli to be attended, more potential stimuli to be monitored, or more attributes to be attended, performance is reduced. There are exceptions, of course, as indicated earlier in this chapter, but many, and possibly all, of the exceptions may be due to the operation of automatic processes.

Kahneman (1973) has suggested that the exceptions may be related to *effort*. Dividing becomes easy when the total effort required and/ or expended becomes low. If effort is determined by task demands and difficulty then this view is virtually correct by definition. Furthermore, although differential allocation of effort across conditions or tasks might account for changing performance levels, such a possibility seems rather more likely in uncontrolled natural settings. In the laboratory, the experimenter generally attempts to see that the subject is performing at the highest possible level in each condition. Finally, it should be noted that automatization will usually not only improve performance, but also lead to a lessening of effort, defined by either objective or subjective measures. Thus automatization could well explain much of the phenomena that the effort hypothesis was designed to handle. For these reasons we shall not discuss the effort hypothesis in any detail in this chapter.

We shall not try in this section to review studies purporting to show an ability to divide attention successfully, since many if not all the traditional studies of this sort can be reinterpreted in terms of automatization. Examples were discussed in the preceding sections. Very recently, studies purporting to show multiple central resource pools have begun to appear. These will be discussed in a later section.

Automatization aside, there are situations where attention may be divided more easily than others, and situations in which competing demands are allocated resources differentially. Proper measuring of attention demands, and attention sharing, requires fairly sophisticated techniques of data collection and analysis. These methods are becoming an important part of

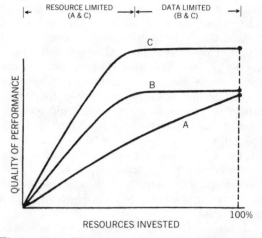

**Figure 11.17.** *Performance-Resource-Functions* adapted from Wickens (1984). Quality of performance as a function of resources invested, for three hypothetical situations (see text). From "Processing Resources in Attention" by C.D. Wickens in *Varieties of Attention* (p. 68). R. Parassuraman and D.R. Davies (Eds.), 1984. Orlando, FL: Academic Press. Copyright 1984 by Academic Press. Reprinted by permission.

modern attentional research and are reviewed next.

### Performance-Resource Functions

Norman and Bobrow (1975) introduced the notion of a *performance-resource function* (PRF). It is a hypothetical function giving performance as a function of resources invested in the task. Presumably the remaining resources are either withheld by the subject, or are used to carry out some other task and to manage the carrying out of the two tasks together. The demands of managing two or more tasks together are termed a *concurrence cost* by Navon and Gopher (1979). Figure 11.17 illustrates some PRFs. For the sake of this example, we assume that the other tasks, if any, do not affect the PRF for the task in question, except by determining the proportion of resources given on the horizontal axis. It is also assumed in this example that there is just one pool of resources. (If there were more than one, the PRF would be multidimensional, one dimension for each resource; the PRF would give performance for each combination of resource values.) Figure 11.17 gives three possible PRFs: Performance in curves B and C improves with resources up to a point, but then reaches asymptote. The asymptote is a *data limited* region, where the information provided to the decision system from automatic perceptual mechanisms is impoverished; in this region extra resources do not help because the system is acting optimally on the provided data. The PRF C shows that better data is being provided to the system than is the case in B. Since the B and C asymptotes are reached at the same investment of resources, it could be argued that both processes utilize resources in similar fashion. The PRF A never does reach asymptote. The data provided in this case may or may not be impoverished, but in either event, the process in question is so difficult that the best level of performance potentially available is not reached even when 100 percent resources are invested. It is possible that some automatization could occur with practice, and alter a PRF like A into one like B or C.

These functions are hypothetical because, in practice, they are produced by experimentally varying the investment of resources in some other task, a task that could interact with the first in ways other than diversion of attentional resources. (Wickens, 1984, reports that a subject simply instructed to utilize different degrees of resources in a task can produce PRFs like those depicted in Figure 11.17. However, there are obviously other ways than resource limitations to explain such a finding, such as compliance with demand characteristics after decision making has made full use of resources.)

### Attention Operating Characteristics

Again hypothetically, suppose there are performance resource functions for two tasks, as illustrated in Figure 11.18a. Suppose these tasks are carried out together and do not interfere or interact other than through sharing of resources; assume, furthermore, that there are no concurrence costs. Then one can plot Task 1 performance against Task 2 performance when there are differing degrees of allocation of resources to the two tasks (e.g., a condition might cause 70 percent resources to be given to Task 1 and the remainder, 30 percent to be given to Task 2). The results are given in Figure 11.18b, curve I.

The figure illustrates how a joint performance graph can be constructed in theory from PRFs if these are available. In practice, the PRFs are not available, and the joint performance function is plotted directly from the data; it is the PRFs that must be inferred.

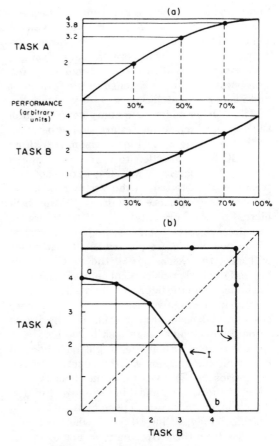

**Figure 11.18.** Performance of two tasks under different resource allocation policies, (a) as represented on two PRFs, and (b) the same points represented in The Performance Operating Characteristic (POC; Curve I). The performance measures 1–4 in arbitrary units are those from the PRFs in (a). Single-task performance indicated by points a and b. Curve II shows what may be expected if the two tasks do not interfere with one another. From "Processing Resources in Attention" by C.D. Wickens in *Varieties of Attention* (p. 69), R. Parasuraman and D.R. Davies (Eds.), 1984. Orlando, FL: Academic Press. Copyright 1984 by Academic Press. Reprinted by permission.

The joint performance function is known as an *attention operating characteristic* (*AOC*; Kinchla, 1969, 1980; Sperling, 1975) or equivalently as a *performance operating characteristic* (*POC*; Norman and Bobrow, 1975; Navon and Gopher, 1979). Curve II in the lower panel of Figure 11.18 illustrates what sort of AOC could be expected if neither task utilizes resources needed by the other. An empirical example of this type from Schneider and Fisk (1982a), indicating that automatic detection and controlled search could be carried out together, was given in Figure 11.16. The place where the joint performance matches the performance in both single task controls is called the *independence point*. This point was almost reached in the Schneider and Fisk (1982a) study.

The AOC provides a summary description of the way in which resources are shared between two tasks. In Figure 11.18b, as one moves along the AOC from upper left to lower right, one is tracing the progressive withdrawal of resources from the task plotted on the vertical axis, and the addition of those resources to the task plotted on the horizontal axis. If there are no concurrence costs, then the single task control conditions, which are plotted on the margins, will meet the extensions of the AOC interior curve. The single task control points in this case are indicated in the figure by a and b. If there are costs to managing two tasks together, and these costs are independent of the relative sharing of resources (as long as each task is given at least some resources), then the single task control points on the margins will be superior to the extensions of the AOC function. This is indicated by the points c and d in the figure. Finally, if the concurrence costs depend on the degree of sharing, it may be difficult to tell whether this is the case from the AOC function. For example, suppose that concurrence costs are largest when each task is given equal resources, but drop to zero when the resources devoted to one of the tasks drops to zero. Then the AOC function will meet the single task control points, but will be depressed in the central region relative to the theoretical case where there are no concurrence costs.

It should be noted that subjects generally have a variety of strategies that can be adopted in dual task situations. It is possible to share resources in the usual sense, doing some of each task on a given trial (possibly even simultaneously), but is also possible to use a mixture strategy. The simplest mixture strategy would involve devoting all resources to just one task on a given trial, but varying over trials the particular task that is given those resources. If the performance on the margins is graphed in linear fashion, then such a mixture strategy will produce a point somewhere on the straight line connecting the two control points on the margin. "True" sharing could produce an AOC that lies

outside this line, inside this line, or crossing this line, depending on the nature of the (unknown) PRFs and the nature of concurrence costs.

It is generally the case that the performance on the joint task can be compared to performance on another (or performance can be compared between different subjects, or conditions) by examining the AOCs. When the AOC lies entirely outside another, it is safe to conclude that joint performance is better. Furthermore, if the single task controls are identical in two cases, but one AOC curve is bowed more than another, and therefore lies outside, it can be considered that sharing is more efficient for the dominating AOC.

Two points are important to note. (1) It is generally useless to compare two situations if only *one* point on each of two AOCs is available. This is illustrated in Figure 11.19, Panels a, b, and c. Panels b and c show that either of the points in Panel a could lie on an AOC that is dominant. (2) Although an AOC is useful in many respects, it is basically a descriptive device, and provides relatively little information about the underlying mechanisms that are operating in the two tasks. For this reason, it is generally desirable to construct performance models for each task and their combination. With the use of models it may be possible to make inferences about concurrence costs, mixing of strategies, the effects of decision factors, the nature of the mechanisms underlying performance, and other matters. (In this respect and others, an analogy can be drawn between AOCs and the *receiver operating characteristic* of signal detection theory). Examples of the use of models in conjunction with AOCs can be found in Kinchla (1980) and Sperling (1984). Discussions of inferences that can and cannot be drawn without models is found in Navon and Gopher (1979) and Navon (1984).

### Sharing of Attention

An example of the use of AOCs to assess the sharing of attention in the domain of visual search comes from Sperling and Melchner (1978b). Subjects were asked to search a series of visual frames presented for 250 msec each. Each frame consisted of an outer region of large letters, and an interior region that in different conditions contained (a) small letters, (b) large but degraded letters, and (c) large numbers. One frame in the sequence contained two targets to be reported,

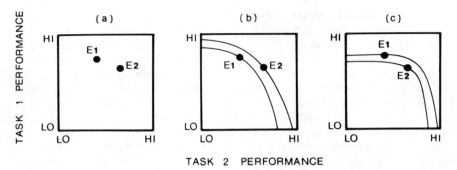

**Figure 11.19.** Potential performance operating characteristics. (a) Two observed data points. (b) Two POCs with E2 on the superior function. (c) Two POCs with E1 on the superior function. In all three graphs, E1 and E2 are the same data points.

one in the outer region, one in the inner region. The outer target was a randomly chosen digit; the inner target was a randomly chosen digit in conditions (a) and (b) but a randomly chosen letter in condition (c). See Figure 11.20, top, for illustrations (from Sperling & Melchner, 1978a). The subject attempted to report both the inner

and outer targets; in each condition three different attention allocation instructions were used: 90 percent to outer; 50 percent to outer; 10 percent to outer. Control conditions required report of just the outer, or inner, target.

The results for one subject are given in Figure 11.20. The condition in which attention

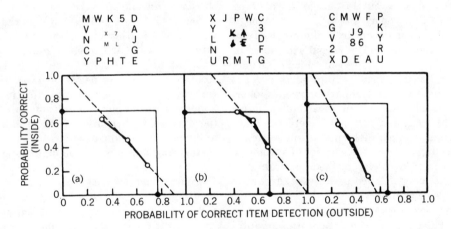

**Figure 11.20.** Attention operating characteristics for three pairs of concurrent tasks. In (a), concurrent detection of large and small numeral targets is shown. The abscissa indicates the percentage of correct identifications of the outside target; the ordinate indicates the percentage of correct identifications of the inside target. Isolated control conditions are indicated by darkened circles on coordinate axes; the independence point is defined by the meeting of the perpendiculars drawn through these control points. Concurrent performance is indicated by open circles. Attention conditions, ordered from upper left to lower right, respectively, are 90% to the inside, equal, and 90% to the outside. The heavy line connecting the data points is the AOC. The broken line represents the best-fitting straight line to the data. In (b), coordinates are the same as in (a), the outside task is the same as in (a). The inside task is detection of a noise-obscured numeral target of the same size as the outside target. In (c), the coordinates and the outside task are the same as in (a). The concurrent inside task is detection of a letter target among three numeral distractors, instead of vice versa as in (a) and (b). (Subject MJM, from Sperling and Melchner, 1978a). From "The Attention Operating Characteristic: Examples from Visual Search" by G. Sperling and M.J. Melchner, 1978, *Science, 202*, p. 316. Copyright 1978 by the AAAS. Redrawn with permission.

sharing is easiest is (b), since the AOC is closest to the independence point (at the corner of the square); the hardest condition by this criterion is (c), in which letters and numbers are both to be detected.

These findings may be related to the search results discussed earlier. Training in conditions (a) and (b) was consistent so digit detection in these conditions may have been at least partially automatized. It is unlikely that automatization was operating fully, since the frame presentations were so rapid that even one task was producing only 70 percent correct responses. A data limitation was unlikely since replacement of distractors with dots led to perfect performance. On the other hand, serial search at a mean rate of 40 msec per comparison is also unlikely since load in each frame was 9 (number of digits in memory set) × 20 (display size) = 180. Performance could not have been as high as 70 percent if anything close to 180 normal comparisons were needed on each 250 msec frame. Very possibly the digits were automatically being treated as a single category, reducing the load to the display size of 20. However, a very rough extrapolation from the results from Schneider and Shiffrin (1977) that are shown in Figure 11.12 suggests that even a load of 20 may have made performance as high as 70 percent unlikely, were a serial comparison process operating. Probably the best guess is that in Tasks (a) and (b) occasional automatic detection may have been used in parallel with a serial comparison of the digit category.[3] Occasional automatic detection would have pushed performance toward the independence point, away from the diagonal, as was observed.

In the case of task (c), inconsistent responses probably ruled out the use or operation of automatic detection. In this case, serial comparisons were probably utilized (albeit with digits and possibly letters treated as one category) and something very close to a pure trading of performance between tasks should have occurred, as was observed. (Better performance than pure trading would be predicted because on frames where, say, the "outer" search was completed early, the extra time would be wasted in the single task control, but could be used for "inner" search in the dual task.)

Although this general model may provide a plausible explanation, additional hypotheses are needed to explain why condition (b) should be superior to (a). A contingency analysis helps to clarify matters somewhat. Contingency analyses are used to assess the use of strategy mixtures. The idea is simple: If on a given trial only outer search, or only inner search, is carried out (called a *switching* model), then the subject should often detect one or the other target, but seldom both. On the other hand, if sharing occurs within a trial (whether simultaneously or successively, called a *sharing* model) then one might expect something like independence: The product of the marginal probabilities of detecting targets separately might equal the joint probability of detecting both. Sperling and Melchner's contingency data in (a) and (c) were more consistent with a *switching* model, and a pure *sharing* model could be ruled out. However, the data were not powerful enough to rule out either model for condition (b). Perhaps there was a time cost associated with switching from large to small characters, or from one category to another, that did not appear in switching from large letters to degraded large letters, so that within-trial sharing was effective only in condition (b). Other explanations are possible (perhaps related to differences in efficiency of automatic detection between (a) and (b)), but further discussion would be highly speculative.

### Compound vs. Concurrent Tasks

Sperling (1984) calls attention to an important distinction that has appeared in many guises in the literature. He classifies joint task studies as either *concurrent* or *compound*. Concurrent tasks are basically separate, have their own stimuli and responses, and do not have to interact other than through competition for attentive resources. Thus an "ideal subject" not subject to resource limitations would operate at the independence point (each joint task equal to its single task control). The "outer" and "inner" tasks used by Sperling and Melchner in the preceding section provides an example of concurrent tasks. On the other hand, compound tasks are inherently interactive: What is presented on one task affects performance on the other, even for an "ideal subject" not subject to resource

---

[3]Note that even were automatic detection operating on every trial, joint performance would have shown a decrement due to the presence of two simultaneous targets: we saw in the section on the relationship of automatism to attention that simultaneous targets did require resources even in fully automatized settings; also see Duncan, 1980.

limitations. The interaction usually is caused by decision factors. For example, a single response might be required, based on the inputs to both tasks.

Suppose the Sperling and Melchner task were altered so that on each trial the subject was given two potential target stimuli, one from the display, and one not from the display, and asked to choose which had been presented. On joint trials the outer or inner target would be chosen randomly for testing; on single task trials, only a target from the relevant region would be tested. One might think that in the absence of attentive limitations, control performance would be equal to that on the subset of tests of that same region from the joint condition. This would be incorrect in the cases where the outer and inner targets are both numbers. In a joint test, choosing between, say, a 5 (target from outside) and a 3 (not in the display) would require consideration of stimuli everywhere in the display, not just in the outer region. Occasionally a 3 could be seen mistakenly in the inner region (i.e., a data limitation) reducing the probability of a correct choice. This could not happen in the control condition because only the outer region would be considered; a 3 seen in the inner region would be ignored. Thus the extra locations to be considered in the joint task would lower joint performance relative to the control conditions, even in the absence of attention limitations, and the independence point would not be reached. This would be an example of a compound task.

The allocation of resources determines which of several concurrent tasks are performed more or less well. In compound tasks, an additional factor must be considered: the effect of decision uncertainty. Thus in compound tasks an attentional allocation must be viewed first as a decision manipulation (as in signal detection or decision theory). Only after decision factors are properly taken into account can inferences concerning resources be made. Of course, when *no* loss due to sharing is observed, inferences are easy, but such an outcome is atypical. Furthermore, while process models are very helpful for understanding the mechanisms at work in concurrent tasks, they are essential for understanding mechanisms operating in compound tasks. If a trading membership in the AOC is observed for concurrent tasks then some sort of resource sharing seems likely (even if the resources are

uninteresting such as "left arm movements"). On the other hand, an apparent trading relationship can appear in compound tasks purely on the basis of decision factors, even if no resource sharing is required (see Kinchla, 1980). Sperling (1984) provides a useful analysis of this issue and many related ones.

The importance of taking decision factors into account has been noted by a variety of researchers. Eriksen and Spencer (1969) and Shiffrin and Gardner (1972) varied the number of simultaneous stimuli presented, thereby changing the decision components as display size changed. In an effort to control this problem, they used another condition in which the same stimuli were presented successively, rather than simultaneously (these results are discussed in a later section). In attention studies concerned with threshold stimuli, models incorporating decision theory are the norm (although perhaps the applications have not always been correct—see Swets, 1984; Sperling, 1984). To the reader unfamiliar with signal detection methodology and models of decision factors in attention studies, the present discussion of compound and concurrent tasks must appear quite esoteric. Nonetheless, the distinctions are of crucial importance both in designing interpretable studies and in analyzing the data: There are many examples in the literature of conclusions whose validity cannot be assessed because decision factors vary across conditions, but are not properly taken into account by the authors.

## Focusing of Attention

On what can attention be focused, and how successful can the focusing be? Consider tasks in which attention is to be directed toward some type of stimuli, and all others are to be strictly ignored. Probably the best examples of focusing involve signal location or signal modality. We shall see that signals occupying a given location in visual (or auditory) space (or a given sensory modality) can be given priority in processing, and signals in reasonably distant locations (or other modalities) can be ignored. We shall adopt the terminology of a *region of focus* to refer to all the types of stimuli that are to be attended, even when location is not involved.

There are several plausible ways to assess the degree of successful focusing. First, performance in a region should rise as focusing on that region increases, and fall as focusing decreases. Second, it might be required that signals in a region of maximum focus should be processed as well when there are signals outside this region as when there are not. This criterion should hold if the signals outside the region of focus do not interfere automatically (as they do when they attract attention automatically—see Figure 11.15—or as they do when they produce responses antagonistic to the responses required for signals in the region of focus—see the discussion of the Stroop effect on pages 765–766). Third, it might be required that the signals outside the region of focus should not be processed at all beyond the degree accomplished automatically. Other possible criteria involve effects upon automatic processing. The focusing upon one region might (a) increase the degree of automatic processing of signals in that region and/or (b) decrease the degree of depth of processing of signals outside that region.

Before turning to the data, it should be kept in mind that other criteria might be appropriate for attention tasks not requiring strict focusing. For example, in some tasks attention is to be given primarily to one region (e.g., one ear in a shadowing task) but signals are nonetheless to be detected both in and out of the region of focus (e.g., in both ears). In such tasks there is obviously an inducement to attend to both regions, so that processing of signals not in the primary region of focus would be expected to increase, perhaps due to some slippage of attention to the other regions.

### Focusing upon Location

In search tasks, focusing upon location is fairly successful. For example, Shiffrin and Schneider (1977) had subjects search a series of four-item square displays for targets in a varied mapping paradigm. When attention was focused on a specified diagonal of each four-character frame, detection probability was identical to the case when the frame size was two (two stimuli and two masks randomly positioned in the four positions of each frame or two stimuli on the relevant diagonal and two masks on the other), and much superior to the case when frame size was four. Thus attention focusing on a given diagonal produced optimal performance for targets on that diagonal, in the sense that the comparisons could be restricted to those locations.

This leaves open the possibility that items on the other diagonal are processed in some fashion. Shiffrin and Schneider used another condition in which items from the memory set were included on the irrelevant diagonal. When such an irrelevant memory set item occurred on the frame preceding the real target, it caused about a 10 percent performance drop. It is possible that irrelevant diagonal memory set items, but not distractors, occasionally attract attention automatically, but this hypothesis seems unlikely since such a mechanism would produce improved target detection in normal visual search using varied mapping: For example, terminating search would show a greater than two-to-one slope ratio for negative to positive reaction times. More likely is the possibility that attention wanders occasionally from the relevant diagonal when processing is completed on that diagonal before the next frame arrives. When a memory set item happens to be noticed, it produces interference. Perhaps such wandering of attention would have been reduced if the frame speeds had been higher, so that less "spare time" would have been available.

In the visual modality, it has always been evident that attention and the direction of gaze are highly correlated. A region the subject decides needs attention and a position containing stimuli that attract attention automatically are generally the recipient of saccadic eye movements designed to bring the region into the fovea. However, the relationship is far from immutable. For example, Klein (1979) reported that a readiness to move one's eyes does not necessarily induce an attentional shift, and that an attentional shift does not necessarily result in oculomotor readiness; Remington (1980) noted that voluntary eye movements did not have to be associated with attention shifts.

A number of researchers have studied the degree to which attention can be assigned to one or more spatial locations away from the fovea in the absence of eye movements. Shaw and Shaw (1977) presented a letter in one of eight locations arranged in a circle. The subject was required to judge which of three possible targets was presented. In one condition, the probabilities of a target were varied across the eight positions in such a way that highly likely locations were opposite on the circle, and in general, the likelihoods varied considerably along the circumference of the circle. Performance varied across locations in a manner matching the probabilities of presentation. Shaw and Shaw (1977) proposed a model in which a limited total attentional capacity was distributed across locations in such a way as to maximize performance, and this model fit the data quite well. It is tempting to conclude that attention is simultaneously allocatable to disparate locations, but Shaw and Shaw were careful to point out that the basis for the attentional allocations was not ascertainable from the data. For example, subjects could have attended to different locations with different probabilities across trials. We shall return to this issue in the next section.

Results analogous to those in vision also obtain for auditory inputs. Whether location is defined by actual physical location or, more often, by ear of input, focusing is usually quite effective (e.g. Cherry, 1953; Cherry & Taylor, 1954; Poulton, 1953; Spieth, Curtis, & Webster, 1954). Thus information in the region of focus is processed about as well with or without information present in other regions. On the other hand, the messages arriving in nonattended locations are given a certain amount of analysis. It is not clear how much of this analysis is generated by automatic mechanisms, and how much is due to a wandering or subsidiary allotment of attention. This issue will be dealt with shortly.

### Attentional Spotlights

Posner, Snyder, and Davidson (1980) were able to disentangle the hypothesis of a distributed spatial attention from a moving focus of attention. The subject responded as quickly as possible to the presence of a simple above-threshold stimulus. The probability that the stimulus was presented in a location was varied experimentally across several locations, in a manner known to the subject. The responses were faster to more probable locations. In the condition relevant to the Shaw and Shaw (1977) study, two locations were designated: a most probable and a second most probable. When these two locations were adjacent, both were about equal and much faster than unlikely locations. When these two locations were separated, the second most likely location was about as slow as unlikely locations. These results suggested a "spotlight" model of visual-spatial attentional focus: Attention can be placed more or less at will in the visual field, but only in a contiguous spatial region (the "spotlight") at any given time. According to this hypothesis, enhanced performance in nonadja-

cent likely locations would be due to factors such as (1) mixing of attention focus across trials (e.g., Shaw and Shaw, 1977) or (2) movement of the attention focus from one location to another within a trial (e.g., in a search task, serial comparisons along a diagonal of a display; Shiffrin and Schneider, 1977).

This "spotlight" view has achieved some support, and some extensions. For example, LaBerge (1983) had subjects categorize five-letter words, or categorize the central letter of (a) five-letter words or (b) five-letter nonwords. This manipulation was used to focus attention broadly on a word as a whole (condition a), or sharply on the central letter (condition b). Attentional focusing was assessed with a probe task: The digit 7 occasionally appeared instead of a word at what would have been word onset, in one of the five letter positions, and required a speeded response. In the other condition, the word did appear, and was followed 500 msec later by the probe digit. The results are shown in Figure 11.21.

Reaction times are flat in the word categorization conditions, but are V-shaped in the letter conditions, suggesting that a narrow spotlight of attention is centered in the letter conditions (and may move to the sides at some rate), but that a wide spotlight of attention is spread across all positions in the word condition. In this model, the wide spotlight would have to be uniform across an extent of at least five letters. Although the letter conditions are consistent with a narrow moving spotlight, the data would also be consistent with a spotlight that is most bright in the central region, with brightness falling off to either side, or with a probabilistic placement of a narrow spotlight across trials, with central positions having the highest probability.

In a subsequent study LaBerge and Brown (1986) had subjects focus attention narrowly at a fixation point and then collected reaction times for an identification response to a single object presented somewhere along a horizontal range centered at fixation. As in Figure 11.21 reaction times showed a V shape. In this study, subjects were told in advance the extent of the range that applied on that trial, and this extent was varied widely. The results showed that the slopes of the V shape were lower, the wider was the range (and the reaction time at fixation was, if anything, faster for wider ranges). If one assumes a gradient theory for a spotlight of

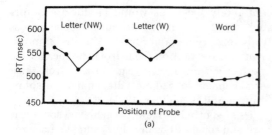

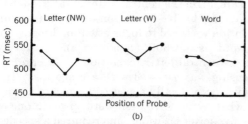

**Figure 11.21.** Data from LaBerge (1983). (a): Mean reaction time to the probe stimulus as a function of probe position. (The probe was presented at the time that a letter string would have been displayed. W and NW refer to word and nonword, respectively.) From "Spatial Extent of Attention to Letters and Words" by D. LaBerge, 1983, *Journal of Experimental Psychology: Human Perception and Performance, 9*, p. 373. Copyright 1983 by the American Psychological Association. Reprinted by permission of the publisher and author. (b): Mean reaction time to the probe stimulus as a function of probe position. (The probe was presented 500 msec after the letter string was displayed. W and NW refer to word and nonword, respectively.) From "Spatial Extent of Attention to Letters and Words" by D. LaBerge, 1983, *Journal of Experimental Psychology: Human Perception and Performance, 9*, p. 374. Copyright 1983 by the American Psychological Association. Reprinted by permission of the publisher and author.

attention, the gradient seems to gain in capacity for wider ranges. Alternatively, if one assumes that an attentional focus moves from fixation to the object, then the velocity of movement seems to increase for wider ranges (a conclusion to be contrasted with that of Tsal, 1983; see Figure 11.22). Interestingly, the present results suggest that subjects would do best by setting their expectancies as if targets might arrive in as wide a range as possible; in this case, focusing of attention to an appropriately narrow range appears harmful (a conclusion also supported by the results in the top panel of Figure 11.21.)

Despite the evidence consistent with the spotlight view, some studies may point toward a model in which attention can be spread more flexibly across the visual field. For example, Podgorny and Shepard (1983) had subjects either view a 3 × 3 group of squares shaded white and black, or imagine such a group of shaded squares. One region was designated "figure" and the subject responded "on figure" or "off figure" to a probe dot presented in the position of one of the squares. Reaction time turned out to be determined not by the number of squares in the "figure" but by *compactness* of the regions containing the squares in the figure. In another condition, all the squares in the figure contained dots (or an equal number of dots would appear off the figure). The results were similar to the one-dot condition, suggesting the subject was not moving an attention spotlight across the figure. Instead, Podgorny and Shepard (1983) suggest that each square in the figure gets some "attention" that spreads to nearby regions as well. Attention accumulates in regions of overlap, explaining the advantage when regions are compact (note that this is a rather liberal reinterpretation of the authors' model in attentional terminology; see also Crassini, 1986; Shepard & Podgorny, 1986).

A number of other recent studies also suggest that a visual focusing mechanism must be quite flexible, even if characterizable as a "spotlight." For example, Lambert and Hockey (1986) manipulated subjects' attention to two dimensions at once: an object's spatial position and form. They found that focusing was sensitive to precise combinations of location and form: At a cued location, subjects showed an advantage for the form that was probable there; at the uncued location the advantage was seen for the other form, the one most probable at that location. This may suggest a somewhat more selective and complex spotlight than discussed thus far.

### Focusing upon Size and/or Globality

In recent years, considerable research has been directed toward the hypothesis that attention may be focusable upon size, or "globability," and that a switch to other sizes or "globalness" may take time. We have seen one example of this already in the paper: In the Sperling and Melchner study in the section on sharing, subjects shared attention less successfully between large exterior characters and small interior ones, than between large exterior letters and large, degraded, interior letters (see Figure 11.20).

One possibility is that attention was focused on one size (or the other) and needed to be switched to the other size (see below), costing time that need not be spent for same size letters.

Many of the recent studies utilize a paradigm in which a large character or stimulus is made up in outline form of many smaller characters or stimuli. The subject could be asked to respond on the basis of the large character, the small characters, or both, and the responses to the two sizes could be compatible, incompatible, or neutral with respect to each other.

Navon (1977) found that when large letters are to be decided about, the small letters of which it is made up are effectively ignored. However, when small letters were to be focused upon for the decision, Stroop-like effects were caused by the large letters: When the identities of large and small letters matched, their responses were faster than when they mismatched (and indicated incompatible responses). Navon (1977) suggested a principle of *global precedence*, according to which information at the global level is invariably available prior to information at the local level.

Many researchers noted that perceptual factors were uncontrolled in such a study. Experiments were carried out to show that: (1) Large letters covering more than about 6–10 degrees of visual angle caused the global precedence effect to reverse, suggesting that speed of processing of either level was determined by ease of perceptual processing (Kinchla & Wolf, 1979). (2) Distortions of the large letters to lower perceptibility led to local precedence, while distortion of small letters led to global precedence (Hoffman, 1980). Hoffman's data suggested that subjects focused upon one level (global or local), searched it and if no target was found switched to the other level and searched it. Automatic processing of the unattended level occurred in parallel with this serial terminating process and produced facilitation or inhibition if perceptibility allowed it to take place quickly enough. (3) If the local elements were fewer in number and somewhat larger than in Navon's study, local precedence occurred (Martin, 1979). (4) Focusing initial attention upon a given level (local or global) had at least as large an effect upon the direction of precedence as perceptibility factors (attention tended to be given to the level that was relevant for the preceding trial; Ward, 1982). (5) Under conditions that produce

global precedence, an analysis of the response time distributions rules out a strict precedence model in which global analysis precedes local analysis. The data were consistent with parallel extraction of information from both levels, with speeds determined by perceptability (Miller, 1981).

There is perhaps evidence for some advantage of the global level in certain cases where perceptibility is better controlled (e.g., Navon & Norman, 1983; Hughes, Layton, Baird, & Lester, 1984), but other studies controlling perceptibility show either local precedence or no precedence (e.g., Pomerantz & Sager, 1975; Pomerantz, 1983). Thus the studies to date do not suggest any inherent precedence of processing of a feature of a particular size or globality. In general, both levels are processed in parallel at rates determined by experimental conditions of presentation. The data do show a strong effect of attention focusing upon a given level of size or globality. The result of focusing may have several effects, including (1) causing a search order in accord with the focus; (2) possibly improving perceptibility at the focused level, and (3) causing focusing on the next trial in accord with the level of the preceding trial. At the same time automatic processing of the unattended level occurs and can facilitate or inhibit responding depending on the compatibility of the response assignments. Presumably the automatic effects are akin to the Stroop effects seen in other settings.

## Inhibition of Objects in Nonfocused Regions

It may be that objects presented in regions of nonfocus will be processed automatically and hence will generate encodings that must be inhibited in order to carry out the requirements of the main task. Tipper (1985) and Tipper and Cranston (1985) presented two objects, each in a different color. The object of a given color was to be reported. A second later a test might require report to the object previously ignored. When this subsequent test also involved color selection, responses were slowed to the ignored object (and slowed to an associate of the ignored object). In these circumstances, objects in regions of nonfocus are not treated purely passively, solely through removal of attentive resources. Apparently the automatic responses that these objects produce require inhibition.

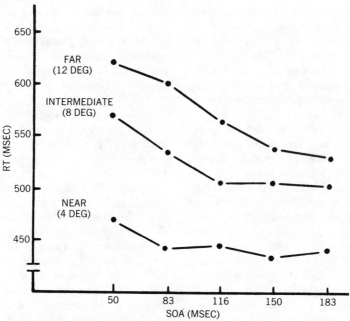

**Figure 11.22.** Data from Experiment 1 from Tsal (1983). Mean reaction time (RT) to vocalize the target letter as a function of the stimulus-onset asynchrony (SOA) between the onset of the cue and the onset of the letter, as a function of three different distances of the target letter (and cue) from the fixation point. From "Movements of Attention Across the Visual Field" by Y. Tsal, 1983, *Journal of Experimental Psychology: Human Perception and Performance, 9*, p. 525. Copyright 1983 by the American Psychological Association. Reprinted by permission of the publisher and author.

## Attention Switching Time

Given that attentive resources tend to be applied serially, it is important to determine how quickly the focus of attention can shift. As we shall see, an upper limit of about 500 msec (or less) can be set with some confidence. Many different estimates have been obtained, depending on the type of attentional shift being studied.

Perhaps the simplest attention shift is one requiring movement of attention across the visual field (in the absence of eye movements, of course, since attention shifts indexed by eye movements are limited by muscular constraints). Shulman, Remington, and McLean (1979) had subjects shift attention from a central cue to a peripheral target. Stimuli located at a point along the path between these two points received maximal facilitation at a time prior to maximal facilitation at the target. Such a result suggests a gradual movement of a limited region of maximum attention along a path from fixation to target. Tsal (1983) extended these results. Subjects fixated centrally and then received a brief

dot in the periphery near the position where a target letter (O or X) would appear. The dot was designed to attract attention. After a delay that was experimentally varied, the target letter was presented for vocalization. Dots (and hence targets) were presented 4, 8, and 12 degrees to right and left of fixation. The results are shown in Figure 11.22. The farther is the target position from fixation, the later is the SOA at which the curves reach asymptote. Various calculations on these data and the results of several control conditions suggested that when summoned by a cue in the periphery, attention moves toward the cue at a constant velocity of 1 degree per 8 msec. Further analyses suggested that the time to decide to move and to initiate the movement was 50 msec. In this case, total attention switching time obviously depends on "distance" to be moved (see also Eriksen & Hoffman, 1972; Posner, 1980). It should be noted that this model of continuous and regular movement of attention focus is consistent with the data, but models in which movement is probabilistic and discrete cannot be ruled out. It should be pointed out that the various results on moving attentional spotlights are rather preliminary and fraught with interpretational difficulties, as discussed by Eriksen and Murphy (1987).

A somewhat different approach to the switching of visual attention was taken by Sperling and Reeves (1980). Two streams of characters were presented, one to the right and one to the left of fixation. On one side digits occurred successively at a rapid rate (e.g., 109 msec each); on the other side letters occurred somewhat less rapidly (e.g., 218 msec each). The subjects carried out a search task amongst the letters for the appearance of a critical target letter. Mapping was consistent and amount of training was sufficient that search was probably automatic. In any event targets were seldom missed. Upon detection of a target, the subject attempted to switch attention to the digits and report the "next" four digits starting with the one appearing simultaneously with the target. The results suggested that a "window" of digit attention opens briefly about 400 msec after target detection. The 400 msec estimate of switching time includes any time to detect the target letter, overcome any automatic tendency there may have developed to attend to the target, switch to the digit locations and open the "gate."

Weichselgartner and Sperling (in press) used a variant of this paradigm in which only a string of successive digits was presented. The cue to respond with the next four digits was an outline square around one digit, or a brightening of one digit. In this case responses were clearly bimodal. The cue numeral was always reported (and occasionally the following numeral); there was then a gap and the remaining numerals reported are from a temporal region about 400 msec after the cue. The authors proposed that the initially reported numerals represent an automatic detection process, and the subsequent ones a controlled process of attention switching (this distinction being supported by demonstrations that these two regions of report could be separately manipulated by different variables). The similarity of the controlled attention shift data to those of Sperling and Reeves (1980) suggests that the requirement to move attention *spatially* in the earlier study was much less important than the time needed to open a window of attention temporally.

It is interesting to contrast these results with those discussed on pages 760–761. In that case attention was to be focused continuously on one

diagonal of a four item display. An "automatic" distractor on the irrelevant diagonal pulled attention away briefly (and automatically), but it apparently moved away and "snapped back" within no more than 200 msec. It seems natural that attention switching would be much faster in those circumstances. The movement of attention away may have been automatic, and attention may have been "pulled back" by a force that stayed in operation throughout the trial, since attention was supposed to have been fixed at all times on the relevant diagonal.

Visual search results provide other means of assessing attention switching. The cases in which serial terminating search is indicated by the means and variances of reaction times (i.e., varied mapping tasks) suggest an interpretation in terms of attention switching. If so, both the switching and the comparison together must take an average of 40 msec. Of course, visual attention need be switched only a small distance since the displays fall within several degrees of fixation. It is less clear whether or how far attention must be switched among memory set items. For both types of search, the sequence of switches could be "preplanned" (although the subject may be unaware of the planning).

If we move from the visual modality, yet other methods are used to estimate switching times. The original studies on switching of auditory attention between ears were carried out by Broadbent (1954). In one type of study, six auditory digits are presented to the subject in three groups of two, each simultaneous pair consisting of a digit to one ear and another digit to the other ear. The rate of presentation of the three pairs was varied. At two pairs per second, subjects asked to report the digits report them most often first from one ear and then the other. It is very difficult to report the digits in order of presentation, pair by pair. When presentation rate was slowed down to one pair each two seconds, then report in temporal order could be carried out as well as in order of location. Broadbent (1954) argued that attention could not be switched well between ears at fast rates, but could be switched at 2 seconds per pair; thus two shifts of attention and two perceptions of digits could occur in 1 to 2 seconds. Subtracting about one-half second for perception gives 1/6 to 1/2 second as a rough estimate of switching time.

A large number of studies in subsequent years was aimed at the validity of Broadbent's conclusion from this paradigm (for one summary, see Broadbent, 1971). One main line of attack involved studies utilizing items of different types (e.g., digits and letters, words forming meaningful phrases and digits, etc.). If digits and letters, for example, alternate between ears then there is at least as strong a tendency to report by item type as by ear. Yntema and Trask (1963) suggested that information is tagged during storage and the tags later enable selection of items during retrieval. Broadbent and Gregory (1964) showed that at fast rates, report of items by alternating type is more difficult than by same type (e.g., A6J4L9 harder than AJL649), even when all items are presented to one ear. They concluded that a second type of selection was occurring in these situations, selection by type, rather than by ear (whether type selection is "early" or at retrieval, and how much time is needed for switching such selection, is unclear).

We shall not attempt to discuss in this chapter the extensive series of studies on the topic of auditory switching. To the extent that attention can be focused in auditory situations, attentional focus can be switched and the switch takes some time. No very precise estimates of switching times seem to be available, but at least one type of switching between ears may take from 1/6 to 1/2 second.

## Bottlenecks of Attention

As we have seen, attention cannot be divided easily. Why is this the case? Broadbent (1957, 1958) proposed a *filter theory*, based on the results of auditory detection and shadowing studies. There were three stages to the theory: (1) a short-term system; (2) a selective filter; (3) a limited capacity processing channel. The short-term system analyzes information in parallel, and stores it briefly. This system is similar to that described as "pre-attentive" by other authors and the processing is what we have termed automatic. Most of the examples utilized by Broadbent suggested that this system is restricted to analysis of primitive physical features, but it is not clear whether such a restriction is a necessary part of the theory.

The second phase of the system was a rather strict filter that allows only those stimuli on a designated "channel" to pass through for further processing. What a channel is has never

been entirely clear, but probably corresponds to those attributes and features that lead to effective focusing of attention, such as those discussed in the section on focusing. Attributes based on simple physical features define a channel in most applications (e.g., location, color) and stimuli sharing that attribute are allowed to pass the filter.

There are two characteristics of such a model that have led to a great deal of research: (1) Is the filter completely selective, or does it allow information to be passed on nonattended channels? (2) Whatever the nature of the filter, how deep in the processing system is it placed?

The initial position by Broadbent stipulated a completely selective filter, with no passage of information on other channels. It soon became clear that this simple view needed modification. In many studies by Treisman and others (e.g., Treisman, 1969 for a summary) it became clear that various types of information about stimuli on unattended channels were sometimes available to subjects. Many of the initial studies utilized auditory shadowing; for example, repeating aloud a message in one ear while detecting occasional signals presented to either ear (e.g. Treisman & Riley, 1969). The results are clear: Signals are better detected on the attended ear, but are also detected to some degree on the unattended ear. Such results led Treisman (1960) to modify the filter model, to allow the possibility of less than complete selectivity. The *attenuation* model posited that the attended channel would receive "complete" processing but the other channels would receive an attenuated degree of processing.

There are many conceivable variants of attenuation models. The particular model proposed by Treisman (1960) supposed detection occurs when "dictionary" units are activated beyond threshold. The items on the attended channel are transmitted "normally," but all stimuli on the unattended channel have their transmission efficiency reduced: The "signal-to-noise" ratio is reduced, and the threshold is presumably raised concurrently. In our present terminology, Treisman's (1960) attenuation mechanism acts by reducing the effectiveness of automatic processing on unattended channels. Because certain thresholds on unattended channels can be much higher than others (either permanently or temporarily), the model can explain why "unattended" items such as the subject's own name are sometimes detected (e.g., Moray, 1959), or why semantic relatedness effects take place (e.g., while shadowing one ear, subjects follow connected discourse to the other ear for a word or two when a switch occurs; see Treisman, 1960). Thresholds vary on both attended and unattended channels for individual stimuli for a variety of reasons: long-term importance (e.g., prior learning), contextual priming (e.g., spreading activation from recent related inputs), and expectancy (in our terms, attentive mechanisms).

This model seems reasonable, but one interesting possibility should be noted. If automatic detection is accepted as a mechanism, then it may be possible to salvage the original form of filter theory. A certain amount of processing and detection may occur automatically regardless of the channel attended. This automatic detection could account for detection of "unattended" stimuli, and could be similar in character to the notion of a dictionary unit exceeding threshold. The advantage of stimuli on the attended channel would derive from a different source: an attentive mechanism such as a serial comparison process. If this approach is taken, it leads to a certain reinterpretation of the data, and it may even be possible for filter theory to be resurrected (as long as the filter refers to the non-automatic part of the processing system). Whether the resultant filter theory would in fact be much different in substance from Treisman's attenuation theory is a debatable point.

To reassess filter theory it helps to distinguish weak and strong versions of the model. The strong version postulates that the filter can be set to a channel and remain there until a conscious decision to switch is made. Shiffrin and Schneider (1977) carried out a relevant study. Subjects were instructed to attend to one diagonal of a four item square display in a multiple frame, varied-mapping search task. Although distractor items on the irrelevant diagonal had no effect, target items on the irrelevant diagonal (which should have been ignored) were sometimes processed and hindered processing on the relevant diagonal. These targets were the same items that were given varied training, and hence were unlikely to have attracted attention automatically. Thus a strong version of filter theory is difficult to defend.

The weak version of filter theory posits that the filter is all-or-none at any moment, but occasionally wanders from the channel of focus, either accidentally or by intent of the subject. Distinguishing such a model from an attenuation model would at the least be extremely difficult.

The problem in more general terms is one of distinguishing two approaches in cases where attention is apparently being shared: (1) Attention is given in some measure to several sources at once (a type of attenuation theory). (2) Attention is given to one source at one time, but is switched between sources, either within a trial or between trials. The switching model is discussed in the section on sharing. In general, subtle techniques are needed to disentangle these models. If switching occurs only between trials then contingency analyses may help provide a check of the model's validity, otherwise the application of quantitative models to the data would probably be needed. (See the discussions on pages 778–781, and discussions by Kinchla, 1980 and Sperling, 1984).

In 1969 Treisman modified her version of attenuation theory, partly to account for cases in which aspects of messages on an unattended channel are invariably noticed. For example, major changes of attributes on simple basic dimensions are easy to note (Lawson, 1966; Treisman & Riley, 1969). The new theory proposed a bank of analyzers operating in parallel. Several analyzers operate on a "single" input in parallel, explaining such effects as the Stroop effect (e.g., outputs of color analyzers may compete with the outputs of some sort of "reading" analyzers). Two or more inputs can be handled in parallel, but only if they don't contact the same analyzers. Any one analyzer must handle inputs serially. Such an account can explain a result such as that of Rollins and Hendricks (1980) who showed that auditory shadowing and visual search would operate together somewhat independently, but shadowing and rhyme judgments for visual inputs could not be handled in parallel.

The multiple analyzer approach is consistent with much of the data concerning automatic processing. On the other hand, the notion that different inputs requiring one analyzer *must* be treated serially is very likely wrong. We have seen in numerous examples from memory search and visual search studies that automatic processing can occur in parallel at virtually any depth of analysis, from peripheral to central, given suitable consistent training. For example, numerous words and digits can be processed in parallel up to the level of category knowledge (Schneider and Fisk, 1984), even though various analyzers such as shape and modality (visual) must be utilized numerous times. Nonetheless, it should be noted that the idea of multiple analyzers went a good way toward a theory of automatic processes, even though the Treisman (1969) version seems to have stopped a bit short of the views suggested in this chapter.

The Treisman (1969) approach in effect introduced multiple bottlenecks or filters in the place of one. A related hypothesis holds that there are multiple resource pools rather than a single unitary central resource. This issue will be taken up in a later section.

## Depth of the Attentional Bottleneck

Perhaps more than any other issue in the study of attention, research and controversy have been associated with a single question: the placement in the processing system of the attentional bottleneck(s). The approaches of Broadbent (1957, 1958) and Treisman (1960, 1964, 1969) seemed to suggest a relatively peripheral placement, shortly after certain physical attributes have been extracted automatically (preattentively). Deutsch and Deutsch (1963) and Norman (1968) proposed quite different models. A somewhat free interpretation of their views goes as follows: All processing occurs automatically until the results are placed in short-term memory; the bottlenecks of attention then become the limitations of short-term memory (see also Shiffrin, 1975b).

One way these views were contrasted concerned the issue of depth or degree of processing of "unattended" inputs. As we have seen, even when unattended inputs are apparently having no effect on behavior, other types of tests usually show that many of those same inputs had been analyzed to at least the level of meaning (e.g., category membership; see page 771). Of course, such analysis is most likely to be automatic, but many of the studies in this area have been carried out without much thought to the possible role of automatism.

In this chapter it is possible only to touch upon some of the different approaches to this issue. Consider two visual search studies by Francolini and Egeth (1979, 1980). In both studies, subjects viewed letters and/or digits randomly positioned around the circumference of an imaginary circle. In the 1979 study, red and black letters were presented; subjects searched for a target letter and were told that if one was present, it would be red. In this case, reaction time increased not only with the number of relevant, red, letters, but also with the number of irrelevant, black, letters. On the other hand, when subjects were asked to count the number of red letters present, the number of irrelevant black letters had no effect. Francolini and Egeth (1979) concluded that an early selectivity based on color (process red items, but not black) occurred in the counting task, but not the detection task. In one sense of the term "selectivity" this conclusion is certainly correct, but it should not be concluded that the "unattended" black items did not have their names processed automatically in the counting task.

It would be more parsimonious to assume that in both these tasks the automatic processing system provided "character name" information, but that this information was not involved in the counting task. Also, the counting is much slower than detecting, so a fast process (perhaps even serial in nature) could be locating red items for a much slower counting system to process. On the other hand, detecting operates very quickly, so that there is a tendency to check all items, regardless of color. (A similar analysis explains results by Green & Anderson, 1956, and Smith, 1962; these studies used detection of two digit numbers, producing slower comparisons, and hence greater benefits of selectivity by color. Also Egeth, Virzi, & Garbart, 1984, showed color selectivity *does* occur in a harder detection task involving search for conjunctions of features—see page 799). A related finding by Dumais (Shiffrin, Dumais, & Schneider, 1981) showed subjects could not selectively count the numbers in a display of numbers and letters. However, if the subjects had been consistently trained to detect automatically number targets in letter distractors, then when transferred to the counting task, selection on the basis of character type (number vs. letter) became possible.

Francolini and Egeth (1980) utilized the Stroop effect in a task requiring counting of the red characters and not the black. Either the red items or the black consisted of digits different from the required counting response. The Stroop effect (interference with the counting response) occurred when the interfering digits were red, but not black. The authors concluded the irrelevant black items were not processed to the level of character name, since interference did not occur. However, we have seen that the Stroop effect is often diluted or eliminated when attention is directed to locations different from the focus of attention (e.g. Goolkasian, 1981; Kahneman and Henik, 1981). Thus the Francolini and Egeth failure to obtain an interference effect does not imply that the black items were not given deeper processing. One way to settle this issue within this type of paradigm would involve showing that an item that does not produce a Stroop effect (due to attention focused elsewhere) nevertheless is processed to the level of meaning (perhaps using a method like that of Eich, 1984; see the section on memory effects). Since deep processing has been shown to occur for unattended items in other paradigms, it seems likely that it occurs also in these paradigms involving the Stroop effect.

### Threshold Detection Tasks

A rather different approach to the early or late selection issue involves threshold detection studies. In many detection tasks, performance drops as the number of presented stimuli rises. One hypothesis explains the drop as a result of limited (or fixed) processing resources being spread over the various inputs. For example, Rumelhart (1970) explained the set size effect in threshold detection situations by assuming a fixed processing capacity, c, was available. If n inputs are presented, each is processed at a rate c/n (on the average—the capacity must be divided up among the inputs). Since in threshold tasks the elements being processed are likely to be features below the level of the name of the presented items (such as line segments when letters are presented), the bottleneck of attention in models such as that of Rumelhart appears to be somewhat peripheral.

Tests of models like that of Rumelhart will be discussed shortly, but we consider first some of the difficulties that arise during attempts to assess the presence of attentional limitations in threshold tasks. In particular, consider whether attentional limitations (such as serial search or the like) can explain performance decrements as set size increases. This turns out to be a very intricate question to answer, based on analyses carried out within the context of signal detection theory. Experience has shown that firm answers almost certainly

require detailed mathematical models of processes underlying task performance (see Sperling, 1984; Swets, 1984).

A few examples help to clarify some of the problems. First, all conclusions must take into account performance levels that could be achieved by an "ideal detector" that has no attention limitations. Most theories assume that degraded stimuli are "noisy." Targets and distractors will sometimes be perceived incompletely and sometimes completely but incorrectly. In cases of incomplete processing, the features that are perceived are sometimes consistent and sometimes inconsistent with targets or distractors. Under these circumstances, correct decisions are inevitably more difficult when more distractors are presented. For example, the probability that some distractor will be misperceived as a target rises as the number of distractors rises.

In order to control for *decision effects* of this kind, Eriksen and Spencer (1969), and Shiffrin and Gardner (1972), contrasted two basic conditions: In one, all the stimuli are presented together; in the other, all the stimuli are presented successively. The detection decision that is made at the end of either of these types of trials should involve similar decision factors since the presented stimuli are identical in the two cases. An ideal detector would exhibit equal performance in these cases. On the other hand, attentional limitations should cause poorer processing when stimuli are simultaneous, since attention must be divided among multiple inputs; when stimuli are presented successively at a slow enough rate, attention could be switched to each in turn.

Shiffrin and Gardner (1972) carried out several variants of this paradigm. Four characters were presented at threshold. A trial contained three distractors and one of two possible targets. The subject attempted to determine which of the two targets was presented. In the *simultaneous* condition, all four stimuli occurred together for t msec each. In the *successive* condition, each stimulus followed upon the previous, each presented for t msec. In both conditions, masking patterns preceded and followed each stimulus to control the effective duration of the stimuli. Surprisingly, performance was, if anything, better in the simultaneous condition. This result was replicated in a long series of studies by Shiffrin and his colleagues (summarized in Shiffrin, 1975a), and many other researchers, studies varying time between successive stimuli, modality of presentation, type of stimuli, and type of task.

Since the results showed no successive advantage, Shiffrin (1975a) concluded that there could have been no peripheral bottleneck. This may be true, but left unexplained was the failure to have found any attentional effect of dividing attention: There was no bottleneck at all. Lupker and Massaro (1979) suggested that the use of identical distractors may have provided an "oddity" cue for the target location, thereby eliminating the necessity both for spreading attention to distractor locations and for taking distractor information into account in the decision. When distractors are very dissimilar to targets, this hypothesis may be correct. When distractors are confusable with targets, it seems unlikely that any very discernable cue "pointing" to target location would be available under threshold conditions (also see Burns, 1979). Foyle (1981) collected evidence for another factor explaining the failure to find limitations. Since all the *successive-simultaneous* studies had used a consistent mapping paradigm, automatic target detection may have developed, drawing attention to the target location. Foyle repeated the Shiffrin and Gardner (1972) task, but added a variably mapped condition; in this extra condition an advantage for successive presentation appeared. Foyle concluded that oddity alone could not account for the results since the oddity factor was present in both mapping conditions. Thus either automatic detection or a combination of the factors of oddity and automatic detection probably account for the failure to find a divided attention deficit in the successive-simultaneous experiments.

The hypothesis that automatic detection can develop in threshold conditions is problematic. If threshold conditions produce "noisy" stimuli, then targets and distractors will be confused with each other on occasion, and the consistency of training will be reduced, if not eliminated. Thus only in very special conditions with limited confusability can one expect automatic detection to develop. Foyle (1981) found that increasing the confusability, the number of stimuli, or the diversity of distractors all produced a successive advantage even when "consistent" training was used. This result suggests that only in very limited conditions with low confusability can automatic detection be expected to develop in threshold tasks, and

otherwise a successive advantage should be seen.

The implications of these various findings for early or late selection are somewhat different than was originally thought. If automatic detection is operating, then attentional bottlenecks become an orthogonal issue: The whole attentional system, is in effect, bypassed. On the other hand, when varied mapping is used, or when confusability is high, automatic detection does not operate effectively and the successive stimuli are better processed. As usual in such cases, the locus of the bottleneck is unclear: (1) Processing of features could be less efficient when more stimuli are present. (2) All features could be processed equally regardless of load and entered briefly into a very short-term memory, but forgotten more often before they can be utilized when presentation is simultaneous.

Finally, it should be noted that it is possible to assess threshold processing in tasks other than those using the successive-simultaneous technique. This could even be desirable since there is the possibility that extra forgetting could occur in the successive condition by the time the decision is made. In these other tasks, it is essential to have a model for the decision processes at work. A good example comes from Kinchla (1977) who showed that subjects can process two adjacent stimuli without perceptual limitations, once decision factors are taken into account.

The importance of utilizing decision models to analyze threshold tasks is illustrated by results such as those of Bashinski and Bacharach (1980). They demonstrated that a threshold signal was better processed in a location whose expectation of containing a signal was high (and worse processed in an unlikely location), a result similar to many others (see the focusing section). A receiver operating characteristic (ROC) was used to demontrate this point. However, as is true for AOC's, an ROC curve is a summary measure that tells little of underlying mechanisms. In the case of the present study, the subject carried out a compound task (see the section on dividing attention) in which *both* locations contribute to a single decision about target presence. As demonstrated by Kinchla, when several locations may contribute to a decision, ROC curves computed by standard methods can be moved inward or outward by decision factors, weighting schemes and biases, and thus tell us very little about the source of a performance deficit.

It should be noted that even were an analysis carried out that properly took into account decision factors, or instead a concurrent task procedure utilized, and the results demonstrated that better information is obtained under threshold conditions from attended locations, such a finding would not have much bearing on the location of the attentional bottleneck. Believers in "late" limitations could argue that the information from all locations was processed and placed in short-term memory where attention began to operate upon it in an order determined by signal probability. Information dealt with later in the decision sequence could be impoverished due to rapid forgetting of sensory features (especially in threshold tasks in which the sensory features may have been emplaced in memory very weakly). Finally, as pointed out in the section on modifiability, automatic processes may sometimes be modifiable by allocation of attentional resources; if so, information transmission may be affected by the probability, say, of location, but this fact would not establish a mandatory early focus for an attentional bottleneck. Shortly we shall assess the current status on the locus of the bottleneck.

### Perceptual Set and Response Set

Broadbent (1971), Kahneman (1973), and others have argued for a rather fundamental distinction between what Broadbent (1971) has termed *stimulus set* and *response set* (or alternatively *filtering* and *pigeonholing*). Broadbent viewed these as two fundamentally different selection processes that the subject could adopt as needed. Stimulus set refers to selection of certain items to pass the filter on the basis of some common characteristic possessed by the stimuli (usually a simple, physical, peripheral characteristic such as modality, location, color, etc.). Response set is the selection of certain classes of responses to output, based on the available evidence, however strong. Thus attending to items on one ear (e.g. repeating them) is an example of stimulus set; attending to digits (e.g. repeating them) regardless of ear is an example of response set.

At first glance this distinction seems compelling and fundamental. For example, as Broadbent (1971) pointed out, response set produces no instrusions from the wrong set: Subjects attempting to report items from one ear occa-sionally report items from the other, whereas subjects attempting to report digits do not report letters. Indeed, within this task setting, there is an important difference between the two report conditions; the tasks impose markedly different decision structures in the two cases. It would be quite misleading, however, to suggest that this argument implies anything about the differential nature of attending to locations vs. character category, or about the depth of attentional selection.

The easiest way to demonstrate this fact is through an example. One can change the task in such a way that the roles of character category and location are exactly reversed. Let the new task consist of the visual presentation of 20 characters, 10 to the right side of the visual field, and 10 to the left. On each side, 5 of the characters will be the digit "6," and 5 of the characters will be the letter "A." The instruction "report locations of all letters" in the new task corresponds to the instruction "report names of all left ear items" in the original task. Intrusions of locations of 5s in the new task corresponds to intrusions of names of right ear items in the original task. Furthermore, it would be possible to apply the traditional two-stage argument in both cases: One property is identified (letter, or location of ear) and used to identify a subset of items to be analyzed further for other properties (location, or category of character). Similarly, the instruction "report all *left* field locations" in the new task corresponds to the instruction "report all digits" in the original task. In the new task no *right* locations will be reported, and in the original task, no letters will be reported. This example shows that there is no logically necessary relationship between response set and stimulus set and particular stimulus characteristics and/or depth of processing.

In practice, however, especially in auditory settings, tasks are usually designed so that stimulus set refers to selection on the basis of simple, physical, peripheral features such as location, and response set refers to selection on the basis of more central, derived, categorical features, such as "letter vs. digit." Thus in practice there is a strong correlation between the two kinds of sets and the type of attentional selection that proves possible. The correlation occurs because, in the absence of special training, selection is far easier on the basis of simple physical features. Very likely, the persistence of the "stimulus set"—"response set" distinction lies in the fact that the task assignments have usually equated stimulus set with physical feature selection.

Selection on the basis of more central, categorical features (which in the usual tasks is equated with "response set") is possible after consistent training produces automatic responses. These studies were reported earlier in the paper: Selection on the basis of symbol name, or even category name (e.g., Schneider & Fisk, 1984) is not hard to demonstrate. One should not be misled, however, into thinking these two situations, physical feature selection and trained feature selection, are identical. At least in the studies that have been carried out thus far, one set of items, or feature(s), is trained to attract attention, while the remaining item(s) or feature(s) do not attract attention and may repulse it. Thus the subject cannot shift the basis of selection once it has been established through training (see Figure 11.15). In the case of physical features such as location, effective selection can occur even if the feature (location) is shifted from one trial to the next. It is not yet known whether a different kind of training procedure (perhaps one that would not produce an automatic attention response) would allow selection to occur on a trial by trial basis for "deeper" features. In any event, at the present time, it is clear that the simpler, more primitive, and more "physical" a feature is, the more effective it will be as a cue for selection (a conclusion reflecting those in the section on *focused attention*).

It can be concluded, then, that "early" selection on the basis of primitive physical features is indeed easier than "late" selection on the basis of learned, complex, features. This does not imply that there is an early attentional bottleneck, however; it implies, rather, that perceptual space divides up (or can be divided up through application of attention) into regions on the basis of simple, salient features (see the next section). Early selection and an early bottleneck are not equivalent concepts, because early selection does not prohibit very deep processing of items that are not selected, whereas an early bottleneck (in, say, the sense of Broadbent's filter theory) does.

### Assessment of Bottleneck Depth
The field of attention owes a good deal of its technical development to research aimed at deter-

mining the locus of the attentional bottleneck. However, if one accepts the view that a good deal of processing occurs automatically, that automatic processing is not restricted to any particular stage of the processing system, and that attention can be applied at most or all stages of processing, then there is no one stage at which a bottleneck appears. Instead, whatever information extraction is carried out by attentive processes rather than automatic ones is subject to limitations, and these limitations will appear at whatever processing stages are being improved by attention.

A geometric interpretation of these views might run as follows. The early theories tended to construe processing as consisting of automatic processing in parallel followed by limited attentive processing (see Figure 11.23, Panel A). The view suggested in the preceding paragraph would have both automatic and attentive processing operating side by side at each stage of processing, with the attentive resources limited (see Figure 11.23, Panel B). According to this view, in the typical task, most "early" processing tends to be automatic, and the least attentive processing occurs at early stages, while less "late" processing is automatic and more attentive processing occurs at late stages. In Panel B of the figure this concept is illustrated by the widths of the wedge shaped regions. The attentive wedge is smaller to indicate that attentive processing is limited in capacity or resources. (This view is similar in some ways to that proposed by Johnston & Heinz, 1978, and related to the model of Schneider, 1985).

## Features, Dimensions, and Objects

Throughout this chapter, we have used rather imprecise terminology when referring to stimuli, lumping together features, attributes, and dimensions rather loosely, and not attempting to draw any hard and fast line between simple, physical, peripheral features, and more derived features. Many researchers have attempted to draw these sorts of distinctions quite precisely and relate them to attentional phenomena. Some of the key ideas are treated in this section, but the discussion will be brief since extensive coverage is available elsewhere (e.g. see Treisman, in press) and detailed coverage would take us far afield into areas of perception and perceptual development. The discussion will be limited to visual

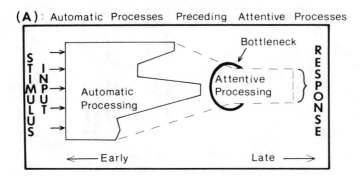

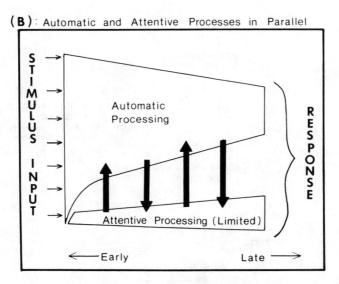

**Figure 11.23.** Two depictions of models of the interaction of automatic and attentive processes. (A): Traditional model in which attentive processes follow automatic ones. (B): Model in which automatic and attentive processes co-occur at all levels of processing.

stimuli, though similar issues and results occur for other types of stimuli.

### Perceptual Organization

As a conceptual starting point, we might consider the process of *perceptual organization*. When a visual presentation occurs, a good deal of organization takes place, including division into *figure* and *ground*, and a breakdown into *objects*. A good deal of this organization may take place automatically, based in part on detection of homogenous regions, graded changes, and discontinuities in the visual field, but there is ample evidence that these processes are affected strongly by attentive processes as well (e.g., see Neisser, 1967; Kubovy & Pomerantz, 1981; Spoehr & Lehmkuhle, 1982). One of many examples

comes from Kinchla (1980). Figure 11.24 illustrates the type of stimuli. A letter was presented as zeros in a background of Xs, or vice versa. Before each trial a three letter memory set was presented and the subject stated as quickly as possible whether one of these was present in the display. The probability of the letter being made of zeros was varied in different conditions. The results in Figure 11.24 gives the response latencies for letters in zeros graphed against the latency for letters in Xs, for each probability condition. The latencies show a trading relationship between the two types of figure-ground organization. Apparently the subjects choose an initial organization (i.e., "figure" in zeros or Xs) with probabilities determined by the likelihoods, respond quickly if the letter is in accord with

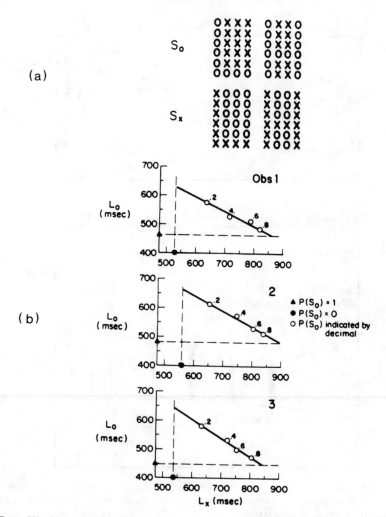

**Figure 11.24.** From Kinchla (1980). (a) Illustrative stimulus patterns from the "figure ground" experiment, which can be seen as a large L or H with Xs defining the "figure" ($S_x$) or Os defining the figure ($S_0$). (b) Empirical and theoretical organizational operating characteristic (OOC) functions. From "The Measurement of Attention" by R.A. Kinchla in *Attention and Performance VIII* (p. 232), R.S. Nickerson (Ed.), 1980. Hillsdale, NJ: Erlbaum. Copyright 1980 by the International Association for the Study of Attention and Performance. Reprinted by permission.

that organization, but otherwise must switch organizations, and respond more slowly as a result. Apparently both organizations are not seen at once, so the initial organization is a crucial determinant of subsequent processing.

An example of organizational effects on attention in the search domain comes from Prinzmetal and Banks (1977). Subjects attempted to say as rapidly as possible whether displays contained a T or F. Distractors were non-letter stimuli similar to both T and F. The displays were constructed to be non-regular in their spatial distribution. For example, one type of display would have five items arranged linearly along a diagonal, with a single extra item off to one side. When the target was in the perceptually "odd" position, responses were faster than when on the diagonal. Similar results were obtained with other spatial configurations. Perhaps the perceptual organization of the displays takes place early and automatically and guides the search process. Either the smaller distinct regions call for attention automatically, or the subject directs attention to the smaller of the perceptually distinct regions; in either case the search would be faster if it tended to begin with the item in the "odd" position in the display. (Similar results were obtained by Brown & Monk, 1975, and Carter, 1982. Carter showed that perceptual grouping by color played the same role as grouping by spatial arrangement.)

**Integrality, Separability, and Configurality**
The organization of a visual presentation into separate objects, or into attributes of single objects, is an important determinant of processing. Although sometimes the organization is modifiable by attention, other times it seems to be immutable. Consider a case where two distinct objects are presented side by side. One might expect that these objects would be *separable* (Garner, 1974), so that one could be attended and the other ignored. This quite often turns out to be the case, and is in fact one of the defining characteristics of separable dimensions, even when the dimensions are part of what we would think of as a single object. An example from Garner and Felfoldy (1970) consisted of circles of two sizes containing a radius pointing in one of two directions. Subjects sorted stimuli as rapidly as possible. In *control* sorts two stimuli are used, and the irrelevant dimension does not vary (e.g., two large circles to be classified on the basis of differing angles). In *correlated* sorts both dimensions are redundant in the two stimuli to be sorted (e.g., a large circle with one angle vs a small circle with the other angle). In *orthogonal* sorts, all four stimuli are used, but classification is based on only one dimension; hence, there is variation on the irrelevant dimension (e.g., classify on the basis of angle, but all four stimuli appear). All three types of sorts take equal time for these stimuli, verifying that the dimensions are separable.

Other types of stimuli are made of *integral* dimensions because correlated tests lead to improved speed and orthogonal tests lead to reduced speed. Felfoldy (1974) showed this to be the case for rectangles made from two heights and two widths. In these cases perception of one characteristic of the stimulus is affected by the other, as if both *had* to be attended to some degree (at least both influenced the decision, so focusing was not completely successful).

Garner originally tried on logical grounds to divide stimulus dimensions into separable and integral pairs, but a number of findings have shown this to be difficult if not impossible (e.g., Garner, 1978; Pomerantz, 1983). One problem arose when Pomerantz and Garner (1973) used parenthesis pairs as stimuli: ((, (), )), )(. The direction of the parenthesis is one dimension, and left or right location is the other. In this case redundancy provided no gain, but orthogonality had a cost. Most important, )( vs. () provided the fastest discrimination of any pair, while (( vs. )) was slowest. Thus the two redundant pairs were the fastest and slowest. These combinations of dimensions were called *configural* because they seemed to produce performance dependent on *emergent* features that arose from the particular arrangements.

As cases began to accumulate that did not seem to be consistent with even this three way classification scheme (integral, separable, configural), and as other classification tasks were added to those given above, more and more refined and complex classification schemes for stimulus arrangements began to be developed (e.g., Pomerantz, 1981, 1983; Garner, 1978). These will not be described here, because it seems clear that the process of determining the stimulus features that produce different sorts of attentional effects is still evolving rapidly. Furthermore, the classification schemes are becoming so complex that it is difficult to say a priori which stimuli will fall into which categories. Stimuli can be found for which focusing, dividing, and conjoining are possible or impossible, but these stimuli do not map easily onto a "simplicity" scale (Garner, 1978).

The reader will no doubt notice that the features, dimensions, and attributes we have discussed are defined physically and are just one choice of many possible descriptions of stimuli. Thus height and width may be sufficient to describe any rectangle stimulus, but height and width do not have to be the psychological dimensions by which rectangles are seen. A plausible alternative might be shape (height to width ratio) and area (height times width). Such an alternative has empirical support (e.g., Weintraub, 1971).

Cheng and Pachella (1984) generalize this view and question whether integral psychological dimensions exist. The findings of gains due to correlated dimensional cues and losses due to variation of irrelevant, orthogonal, dimensional values, may be due to a choice of dimensions for analysis that does not correspond to the underlying psychological dimensions. Cheng and Pachella used isoceles triangles as stimuli; the four stimuli vary in ways that can be described along different pairs of dimensions. The psychological dimensions were "shape" and something else that could be described as size, or height or width. The non-psychological dimensions were lengths of particular sides. For the psychological dimensions, separability was observed: Variation of the irrelevant dimension produced no cost. However, cost was observed for the non-psychological dimensions. Instead of concluding that these dimensions are integral, Cheng and Pachella suggest that they are not true dimensions at all. Furthermore, they raise the possibility that other problems with dimensional analysis (e.g., configurality, non-symmetric integrality) may be due to the choice of dimensions that do not correspond to psychological ones.

Although the Cheng and Pachella (1984) view is worthy of consideration, even psychologically separable dimensions such as color and size do not always produce data consistent with the view that they are attended and dealt with separately. For example, Smith and Kemler Nelson (1984) show that color and size are dealt with in separable fashion when responses may be made relatively slowly, but are dealt with in apparently integral fashion when greatly speeded responses are required (or in certain cases involving sufficiently young children). Such data certainly raise the possibility that a primitive integral analysis of stimuli tends to occur in addition to analysis along separable dimensions.

One way to think about such findings is to assume that prior learning as well as innate stimulus properties produce automatic perceptual encoding. This automatic encoding can be affected by attentive mechanisms in many cases, especially when the stimuli allow multiple interpretations. Nonetheless, automatic analysis proceeds at many levels in parallel and produces a perceptual organization. This organization then becomes a crucial determinant of the subsequent attentional processing that can take place. This view is seen in models by Neisser (1976), Lockhead (1972), Monahan and Lockhead (1977) and others. It differs in some ways from another recent view of attentional processing suggested by Treisman and her colleagues, reviewed in the next section.

## Feature Integration

The data mentioned in the preceding section concerning configurability, the Smith and (Kemler) Nelson data, and the (rather weak) data in the focusing section concerning the "global precedence" hypothesis suggest an initial stage of processing at a global level of analysis, followed by an analysis of parts, the second analysis being attentionally driven. This view may be contrasted with the recent theories of Treisman and her colleagues (e.g., Treisman, Sykes, & Gelade, 1977; Treisman & Gelade, 1980; Treisman, in press). The *feature integration* model assumes *features* comes first in perception. Features are assumed to be registered automatically and in parallel, and to consist of values on primitive dimensions such as color, orientation, spatial frequency, brightness, and direction of movement. *Objects*, consisting of collections of features, are not encoded automatically and must be constructed by use of the "glue" of focal attention. Once attention is used to form objects, these objects enter (short-term) memory where they might eventually decay into component features again before being lost.

In this simple form, the theory is quite incapable of explaining very much perception or behavior. For example, as Treisman and Gelade (1980) point out, we seldom see a blue sun in a yellow sky, even if our attention is directed elsewhere. Thus our knowledge, learning, and experience must also act to conjoin features into objects. Presumably the top-down effects of prior knowledge occur automatically in relevant cases.[4] The theory has been tested thus far primarily in situations where the conjoined features do not form a particular, well-learned combination. Under such circumstances, when attention is not focused upon groups of features, objects should not be seen in an automatic, preattentive manner, and features will be relatively free to recombine in illusory ways.

---

[4]The theory does not yet have well worked out mechanisms to detect unusual objects when the features of those objects can be recombined to form common objects. A superficial application of the theory would suggest that top-down mechanisms would cause the features to recombine in a way consistent with past knowledge, and a realization that something is amiss would have to await the application of focal attention; e.g. a blue sun and yellow sky would be seen normally until focal attention is applied. Presumably the theory will be extended to incorporate "error correction" mechanisms.

There are two types of feature pairs that need to be distinguished: *separable* and *integral* (the definitions and empirical tests do not correspond exactly to those of Garner, 1974, but the idea is related). Integral feature pairs conjoin automatically, while separable pairs need attention to be conjoined. Which feature pairs are which is an empirical question (and little if any research directed toward "integral" pairs has been carried out).

Treisman and Gelade (1980) carried out several empirical tests (using what are concluded to be separable features) that supported and illustrated the main points. (1) Visual search for single features (or integral conjunctions, but this has not been tested) should be insensitive to load, but search for conjunctions of two features should be serial in nature, as attention is shifted from item to item in turn. (2) A discontinuity in texture between two regions of stimuli should be easy to find for a single feature discontinuity, but difficult for a conjunction. (3) In the absence of attention, (separable) features should be free floating and sometimes recombine into *illusory conjunctions* (Treisman and Schmidt, 1982). (4) When single feature targets are found in visual search, their spatial position might be inaccurate since detection need not require focal attention; conjunction targets require attention and should be well localized. (5) Grouping of identical items together in a display should allow search for conjunctions to proceed group by group, while search for single feature targets should remain unaffected by display size (Treisman, 1982).

Each of these predictions was given empirical support, (1), (2), and (4) by Treisman and Gelade (1980), (3) by Treisman and Schmidt (1982), and (5) by Treisman (1982). Certain additional results should be mentioned that amend and extend these predictions and findings. First, Egeth, Virzi, and Garbart (1984) showed that search for conjunctions is not really serial. Instead, the subject chooses one feature (presumably the easiest) to segregate the display into two regions and then serially searches the items within the relevant region for the other feature. Treisman and Gelade (1980) and Treisman et al. (1977) had subjects search for conjunctions (e.g., red O) in distractors each of which contained one of these values (e.g., black Os and red Ns). The number of each type of distractor was highly correlated with the

display size. Egeth et al. (1984) covaried the numbers of each type of distractor and also instructed subjects to attempt to search just within the relevant color, or the relevant letter. The results are given in Figure 11.25. The curve labeled "confounded" had equal numbers of distractors of both types. The unconfounded cases always had just three letters of the type to be attended, regardless of display size (e.g., "Attend-to-red" cases had three red letters, possibly including the target). Attending to red was easier than attending to O, but clearly search could be limited to the relevant subset to a large extent. In fact, the "attend-to-color" findings are very much like the *single feature* findings of Treisman and Gelade (1980).

These search results are like those of Green and Anderson (1956), Smith (1962), and Carter (1982), in showing that search could be restricted to the relevant color subset. However, Carter (1982) showed that the background elements did begin to have an effect when color discriminability was reduced, findings that may be analogous to the letter discrimination results in Figure 11.25. The very flat slopes for "attend-to-color" seen in the figure, and also found by Carter (1982) show that restriction to the stimuli of the relevant color takes a time that does not depend on the number of distractors, and suggest that automatic perceptual grouping might precede the search. However, it is also possible that a rapid serial search for color operates in parallel with a slower comparison process, providing candidates for the slower process to evaluate. Finally, it should be noted that these results are not opposed to feature integration theory in general, merely to the particular assumptions concerning search processes. In fact, the results are similar in many ways to those obtained by Treisman (1982) concerning the relationship between spatial grouping and conjunction search.

The findings of "illusory conjunctions" by Treisman and her colleagues have sparked a good deal of research, partly intended to test various aspects of the theory. An interesting study supporting the theory was carried out by Prinzmetal (1981). He used stimuli like those shown in Figure 11.26. Subjects searched for a plus sign in a circle. Examples of the target absence trials are given in the figure. Illusory conjunctions were seen as an excess of false alarms in A and B relative to C and D. However,

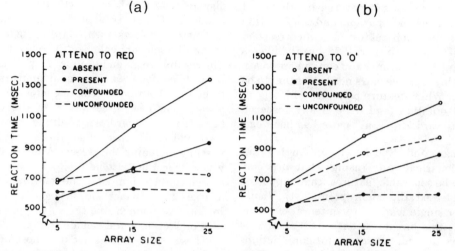

**Figure 11.25.** Data from Experiment 1 of Egeth et al. (1984). (a): Mean reaction time as a function of display size for the attend-to-red conditions. (b): Mean reaction time as a function of display size for the attend-to-0 conditions. From "Searching for Conjunctively Defined Targets" by H.E. Egeth, R.A. Virzi, and H. Garbart, 1984, *Journal of Experimental Psychology: Human Perception and Performance, 10*, p. 35. Copyright 1984 by the American Psychological Association. Reprinted by permission of the author.

more false alarms occurred in A than B, showing that features were not conjoined as often across the evident perceptual groups. There are many possible interpretations of these findings, but they suggest that perceptual grouping can be at least as primitive and early a process as feature extraction, a prediction of the theory (Treisman, 1982). It is likely that automatic encoding of displays goes on in parallel at several levels at once, without the necessity of focal attention, but that focal attention is sometimes needed to "glue" together the low level features and

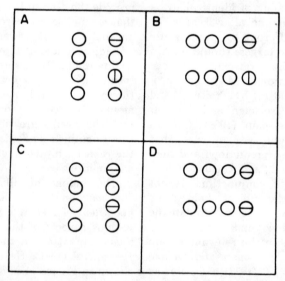

**Figure 11.26.** Displays from Prinzmetal (1981): Examples of the target-absent stimuli in an "illusory conjunction" detection study. The fixation point is the exact center of each panel. From "Principles of Feature Integration in Visual Perception" by W. Prinzmetal, 1981, *Perception and Psychophysics, 30*, p. 332. Copyright 1981 by the Psychonomic Society. Reprinted by permission.

preserve them better for accurate future report. This notion is supported by findings of Prinzmetal and Millis-Wright (1984) showing that report of the color of a predesignated letter is affected by the word-like qualities of the letter strings containing the target.

A related but somewhat different finding concerning illusory conjunctions was reported by Virzi and Egeth (1984). They showed that illusory conjunctions occur not just for unattended "simple" features, but even for meaning. For example, subjects presented with the word BROWN in red ink, and the word HEAVY in green ink, both in unattended locations, would sometimes report, incorrectly, that the word RED, or the ink color brown, had appeared in the display. It may be that these are "memory" rather than "perception" errors, but memory and perception can be notoriously difficult to disentangle, so that at the least illusory conjunction errors should be interpreted with some caution. If the Virzi and Egeth data are accepted as demonstrating perceptual illusory conjunctions, then the features of the system must in this case be quite "deep," and in fact be a conjunction of elementary features. This could be consistent with the Treisman approach, since a word is part of general knowledge, which can serve to conjoin its features automatically.

It is still somewhat early to assess feature integration theory. When applied to explain the slopes of visual search functions the theory may have some difficulties. As discussed earlier in this chapter, in the section on stimulus factors in visual search, Duncan, Humphreys, and their colleagues have argued the theory has trouble accounting for certain results, for any simple choice or features. They also suggest that factors of similarity between sets of targets and distractors can handle the search findings that seem to support the theory. Further research is needed to explore these issues.

### Some Observations about Features

Obviously much research is being carried out to explore the relation of stimulus attributes and combinations to perceptual organization and selective attention. At this writing it would be premature to try to draw general conclusions, since the issues and results are changing and evolving. A few observations are worth making, however. First, despite a century of research aimed at establishing the features and dimen-

sions that make up stimuli, we are still a long way from firm answers. At present it is not possible to predict a priori what are the stimuli in a given setting, what will be their salient features, and how the features will affect attention or perception. Instead, studies using attentional and perceptual tests are carried out on such stimuli and the results used to infer the features that must have been present and their nature. Second, there is no good reason to think that the results used to support global processing, global feature precedence, automatic conjoining of features, and automatic perception of complex objects are inconsistent with the results used to support feature integration theory. Since prior knowledge can act to conjoin features in the theory, these results may well be consistent with the theory. Third, feature integration theory may have some difficulties explaining the slopes of visual search functions unless other mechanisms are posited. Finally, it is safe to conclude that, however we ascertain the nature of the features in a given task, those features that are automatically extracted (or otherwise extracted) by the perceptual system and made especially salient to the decision system have enormous effects upon both performance and subsequent attentive processing.

### Multiple Resource Pools

Much of the research discussed in this chapter has been predicated upon the assumption, explicit or implicit, that there is a single pool of central resources that is allocated to or shared among the processing needs of the system. Nonetheless, there may be reasons to think that different tasks or task components may require different resources. The basic idea is that different resources (if these exist) are not always *substitutable*. When Resource A is in short supply, the deficit cannot necessarily be made up by Resource B, even if Resource B is underutilized.

Demonstrating the existence of multiple resource is not very easy, but is possible if one is not concerned with the nature of the resources in question. Some "resources" are not very interesting. For example "right arm movement" could be viewed as a resource if needed for several tasks requiring such movements; "left leg movements" could be another resource. Even if left leg movement is not needed in a particular experiment, the availability of this resource would not much help a subject faced with the need to make three different, incompatible, right arm movements simultaneously. These sort of motor response constraints could be ruled out of consideration, but automatic responses and processes could exhibit similar patterns of independence and incompatibility, making interpretations in terms of *attentive* processing problematic. Such considerations must be kept firmly in mind.

How may one assess the existence of multiple resource pools? This is a most subtle research issue. Consider one proposal: "The central capacity notion cannot withstand the finding that when the performance of a certain task is disrupted more than the performance of another one by pairing either of them with a third one, it is nevertheless disrupted *less* by a fourth one" (Navon & Gopher, 1979, pg. 232). This may be restated as follows. Let $P(Ti)$ be the performance of task i alone, and $P(Ti|Ti + Tj)$ be the performance of task i when it is paired with task j. Then,

$$P(T1) - P(T1|T1 + T3) < P(T2)$$

$$- P(T2|T2 + T3) \qquad (1)$$

$$P(T1) - P(T1|T1 + T4) > P(T2)$$

$$- P(T2|T2 + T4) \qquad (2)$$

How can such a pattern occur? One possibility is that T3 is at least partially incompatible with T1, but not T2, and that T4 is at least partially incompatible with T2, but not T1. If T1 and T3 must share one central resource, and T2 and T4 some other central resource, the above outcome would occur. Unfortunately T1 and T3 could share a resource as uninteresting as muscle availability (e.g. T1 and T3 require left and right eye movements, respectively), and the same could be true for T2 and T4.

This problem is pretty much universal. One can establish, using the above criteria or others, that multiple resources are required, but separate means must be used to establish the nature of those resources. The difficulty of this latter task must not be underestimated.

We shall return to the question of tests for multiple resources after considering an empirical study. Friedman, Polson, Dafoe, and Gaskill (1982) tested the hypothesis that the left and right hemispheres have separate, limited-capacity resource pools that are not mutually accessible, so that different tasks can overlap in their resource demands either completely, partially, or not at all.

We shall present a simplified description of their Experiment 2 in the hope that clarification will be gained without much loss of accuracy. Subjects were chosen on the basis of pretests (e.g., righthandedness) to insure they processed verbal material in their left hemisphere. Presentation of material to their right fields produces initial processing in the left hemisphere, and vice versa, though the other hemisphere could eventually carry out processing after information is transmitted from one hemisphere to the other. Two tasks were to be carried out together: (1) Three five-letter nonsense words were presented to the right visual field (i.e., left hemisphere). These were to be studied and held in memory while a second task was carried out. (2) Two three-letter nonsense words were presented very briefly for a same-different judgment, in which accuracy of response was measured. The pair of words was presented either to the right or left visual field, and the judgment required was "name" or "physical" identity (e.g., name match: DAP—dap; physical match: DAP—DAP). Finally, subjects were told to emphasize either the memory task or the matching task.

Some results are given in Figure 11.27, in terms of the loss or decrement from the single task control conditions to the dual task conditions. Note that when the *same* hemisphere must carry out both tasks (left panel) there were clear indications of resource sharing: As emphasis is shifted to the memory task, memory performance went up and matching performance went down. On the other hand, emphasis made no difference when *different* hemispheres were presumed to be carrying out the tasks (right panel). One could interpret these findings in terms of different resource pools: Sharing is necessary when both tasks require the left hemisphere, but not when each task can be carried out by a separate hemisphere. Of course, even when different hemispheres are utilized, dual task performance is worse than single task performance (right panel), so at the least there is a *concurrence cost*.

There have been quite a few other attempts to establish the nature and number of multiple

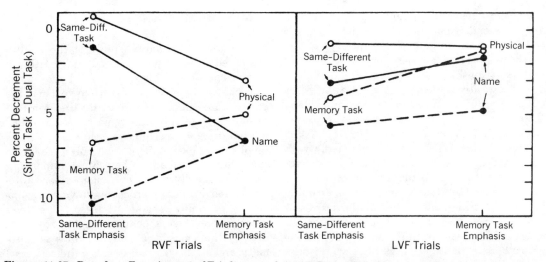

**Figure 11.27.** Data from Experiment 2 of Friedman et al. (1982). Percentage decrements from single to dual task conditions. (RVF = right visual field; LVF = left visual field.) (See text for details.) From "Dividing Attention Within and Between Hemispheres: Testing a Multiple Resources Approach to Limited-Capacity Information Processing" by A. Friedman, M. Polson, C. Cameron, and S. Gaskill, 1982, *Journal of Experimental Psychology: Human Perception and Performance, 8,* p. 645. Copyright 1982 by the American Psychological Association. Reprinted by permission of the author.

resources (e.g. Hirst & Kalmar, 1987). Wickens (1980) and his colleagues have tried to argue that different resources exist for different modalities, because auditory and visual tasks can be carried out more easily together than auditory and auditory or visual and visual tasks. Some studies show this to be the case but others do not; the exceptions might be due to other factors that help when both tasks are in one modality. For example, when both tasks are in one modality attention switching between modalities is not needed. Another possibility is that some sort of helpful integration of two tasks can occur when they are in the same modality (Wickens, Fracker, & Webb, 1987).

It seems likely that the establishment of multiple resources in particular studies will not prove too useful for theorists of attention until general models are developed that will specify the nature of the resources, that will explain the way in which they will be used in carrying out specific tasks, and that will allow predictions of multiple task performance in new situations. It would be useful for the development of such a model if evidence could be found allowing a choice to be made between a view like that of Kahneman (1973), in which there is one central resource and many "satellite" resources (like those concerned with motor movements, or

automatic perceptual mechanisms), and a view like that of Wickens (1980) in which there are multiple central resource pools (possibly overlapping partially). An example of the latter might be found in the theory of Friedman et al. (1982). Wickens (1984) concludes that a decision between between such views is most difficult if not impossible, but any discussion is beyond the scope of this chapter (see also Navon & Gopher, 1980; Navon, 1984). It is certainly safe to conclude that multiple resources exist, but whether more than one of these could properly be viewed as a central resource is presently an open question.

## VARIETIES OF ATTENTION

The topics touched upon in this chapter represent an extremely limited selection from the field, both in terms of depth and breadth of coverage. Even within the classic domain of attention, a great deal of the traditional research in the auditory modality has been omitted, or given very brief mention. Part of the reason lies in the extensive coverage of auditory studies already in the literature, and part of the reason lies in personal preferences of the author. In any event, the presentation of the key issues, and the conclusions reached, would not be different in any important way were the auditory studies added to the coverage in the chapter.

The most significant omission in the chapter is the relationship between attention and memory. These are as inextricably intertwined as automatic and attentive processes, and many theorists have treated them as a single topic (cf. Norman, 1968, 1969; Underwood, 1976). Atkinson and Shiffrin (1968) dealt extensively with "control processes," which was another term for attentive processes, in the domain of memory. Since decisions, retrieval mechanisms, coding processes, rehearsal and other similar processes represent the use of attention, virtually the entire field of memory falls in principle into the proper domain of attention. Studies whose main import lies in memory have been excluded for the most part from this chapter, primarily in consideration of space limitations, but also because other chapters in the handbook deal with various manifestations of memory.

Many other topics have been excluded as well. A nonexhaustive list of these includes: (1) The *intensive* aspects of attention, including *arousal*, roughly revolve around the possibility that attentional capacity can be raised or lowered by the subject (in accord with environmental demands) or will be raised or lowered by influences not under the control of the subject (e.g., Kahneman, 1973). We have tried to discuss tasks for which it is not unreasonable to assume that attentional resources are being utilized at, or close to, their maximum level. (2) *Vigilance* or *sustained attention* tasks require the subject to continue to perform (or detect) over long periods of time. Much research has been carried out to study decrements in performance that take place over time (e.g., Broadbent, 1971; Parasuraman, 1984). (3) Physiological and psychophysiological correlates of attention. (4) Effects of *environmental stress* on attention and performance. (5) Automatism and performance in *motor skill acquisition* and performance. (6) *Individual differences* in attentional selectivity and sustained attention. (7) Attention in nonhuman organisms and *animal learning*. (8) Attentional *aberrations* as a factor in mental disease. (9) Attention and automatism in *social* perception, judgment and memory. Introductions to these topics can be found in the references given at the outset of this chapter.

## FINAL REMARKS

Throughout this chapter, most of the studies presented in detail (and cited) have utilized search paradigms. There is a good reason for this choice. Search paradigms have been the most studied in the experimental literature on attention; although there remain many perplexing questions concerning search, the processes involved in this paradigm are better understood than those from any other. Most important, search is one of the few paradigms where automatic and attentive processes have been disentangled to any substantial degree. The treatment in the present chapter emphasizes more heavily than most the separate roles of automatic and attentive processes, and their interaction. It is this author's firm opinion that little empirical or theoretical sense can be made of attentional phenomena without a firm grasp of the symbiotic roles played by automatism and attention. This opinion would hardly have been a surprise to the pioneering psychologists concerned with attention near the turn of the century. Perhaps the point has not received the prominence it merits in some modern treatments, but the field seems to be moving in this direction in recent years (see Kahneman & Treisman, 1984, for a different perspective on the same topic). In an effort to pinpoint the actions of automatic and attentive processes, search paradigms have probably been covered in more detail than anyone finds congenial for easy reading, but no convincing case could have been made by a superficial summary.

Even within search tasks, there is a good way to go before a satisfactory understanding of processes and mechanisms is reached; in the field as a whole, understanding is a much more distant goal. Thus, although the distinction between automatic and attentive processes in search is fairly well defined, both in theory and in terms of experimental operations, as seen in the section on process characteristics, these distinctions are not universal. It is even possible that no simple operational distinction may ever be found that will apply to all tasks. This possibility is a bit troublesome from the global point of view, but considering the scope of the field, it may not be too disturbing to have to settle for a high degree of understanding of particular task domains.

Are there any global conclusions that can be reached concerning some of the traditional issues that have driven modern attentional theory? At the cost of vast oversimplification, matters might be summarized as follows: Performance, but not attention, may be divided successfully through the use of development of automatic processes, and successful focusing takes place through the application of limited attentive resources. Failures to focus at all are due to an inability to select inputs at "late" levels of processing (at least without special training), but momentary interruptions of focusing are due to automatic mechanisms involving and interfering with the attentive system itself. Selection of inputs to process is easiest when the selection is based on simple, primitive features of the type that are closely related to the operations of the peripheral sensory systems. The limitations of the attentive system, however, are not restricted to any particular locus in the processing system, and appear whenever and wherever attentive resources are used to facilitate performance. Behavior in general is accomplished by limited, perhaps serial, attentive processes operating in parallel with numerous automatic processes, with the two systems passing information back and forth at all levels of analysis.

# REFERENCES

Allport, D.A., Antonis, B., & Reynolds, P. (1972). On the division of attention: A disproof of the single channel hypothesis. *Quarterly Journal of Experimental Psychology*, *24*, 225–235.

Anthony, B.J., & Graham, F.K. (1983). Evidence for sensory-selective set in young infants. *Science*, *220*, 742–744.

Atkinson, R.C., Holmgren, J.E., & Juola, J.F. (1969). Processing time as influenced by the number of elements in visual display. *Perception & Psychophysics*, *6*, 321–326.

Atkinson, R.C., & Shiffrin, R.M. (1968). Human memory: A proposed system and its control processes. In K.W. Spence & J.T. Spence (Eds.), *The psychology of learning and motivation: Advances in research and theory* (Vol. 2). New York: Academic Press.

Bargh, J.A. (1984). Automatic and conscious processing of social information. In R.S. Wyer, Jr. & T.K. Srull (Eds.), *Handbook of social cognition* (Vol. 3). Hillsdale, NJ: Erlbaum, pp. 1–43.

Bashinski, H.S., & Bacharach, V.R. (1980). Enhancement of perceptual sensitivity as the result of selectively attending to spatial locations. *Perception & Psychophysics*, *28*, 241–248.

Bohlin, G., & Graham, F.K. (1977). Cardiac deceleration and reflex blink facilitation. *Psychophysiology*, *14*, 423–430.

Bohlin, G., Graham, F.K., Silverstein, L.D., & Hackley, S.A. (1981). Cardiac orienting and startle blink modification in novel and signal situations. *Psychophysiology*, *18*, 603–611.

Briggs, G.E., & Johnsen, A.M. (1973). On the nature of central processes in choice reactions. *Memory & Cognition*, *1*, 91–100.

Broadbent, D.E. (1954). The role of auditory localization in attention and memory span. *Journal of Experimental Psychology*, *47*, 191–196.

Broadbent, D.E. (1957). A mechanical model for human attention and immediate memory. *Psychological Review*, *64*, 205–215.

Broadbent, D.E. (1958). *Perception and communication*. London: Pergamon Press Ltd.

Broadbent, D.E. (1971). *Decision and stress*. London: Academic Press.

Broadbent, D.E., & Gregory, M. (1964). Stimulus set and response set: The alternation of attention. *Quarterly Journal of Experimental Psychology*, *16*, 309–317.

Brown, B., & Monk, T.M. (1975). The effect of local target surround and whole background constraint on visual search times. *Human Factors*, *17*, 81–88.

Bryan, W.L., & Harter, N. (1899). Studies on the telegraphic language. The acquisition of a hierarchy of habits. *Psychological Review*, *6*, 345–375.

Burns, D. (1979). A dual task analysis of detection accuracy for the case of high target-distractor similarity: Further evidence for independent processing. *Perception & Psychophysics*, *25*, 185–196.

Cardosi, K.M. (1986). Some determining factors of the alphanumeric category effect. *Perception & Psychophysics*, *40*, 317–330.

Carter, R.C. (1982). Visual search with color. *Journal of Experimental Psychology: Human Perception and Performance*, *8*, 127–136.

Cheng, P.W., & Pachella, R.G. (1984). A psychophysical approach to dimensional separability. *Cognitive Psychology*, *16*, 279–304.

Cherry, E.C. (1953). Some experiments on the recognition of speech, with one and two ears. *Journal of the Acoustical Society of America*, *25*, 975–979.

Cherry, E.C., & Taylor, W.K. (1954). Some further experiments upon the recognition of speech with one and two ears. *Journal of the Acoustical Society of America, 26*, 554–559.

Corteen, R.S., Wood, B. (1972). Autonomous responses to shock associated words in an unattended channel. *Journal of Experimental Psychology, 94*, 308–313.

Crassini, B. (1986). On the spatial distribution of visual attention. *Journal of Experimental Psychology: Human Perception and Performance, 12*, 380–382.

Deutsch, J.A., & Deutsch, D. (1963). Attention: Some theoretical considerations. *Psychological Review, 70*, 80–90.

Donderi, D.C. (1983). Acquisition and decision in visual same-different search of letter displays. *Perception & Psychophysics, 33*, 271–282.

Downey, J.E., & Anderson, J.E. (1915). Automatic writing. *The American Journal of Psychology, 26*, 161–195.

Dumais, S.T. (1979). *Perceptual learning in automatic detection: Processes and mechanism.* Unpublished doctoral dissertation, Indiana University, Bloomington, IN.

Duncan, J. (1980). The locus of interference in the perception of simultaneous stimuli. *Psychological Review, 87*, 272–300.

Duncan, J. (1985). Visual search and visual attention. In M.I. Posner and O.S.M. Marin (Eds.), *Attention and performance XI.* Hillsdale, NJ: Erlbaum, pp. 85–105.

Duncan, J. (In press). Attention and reading: Wholes and parts in shape recognition. In M. Coltheart (Ed.), *Attention and performance XII.* Hillsdale, NJ: Erlbaum.

Durso, F.T., Cooke, N.M., Breen, T.J., & Schvaneveldt, R.W. (1987). Is consistent mapping necessary for high-speed search? *Journal of Experimental Psychology: Learning, Memory, and Cognition, 13*, 223–229.

Dyer, F.N. (1973). The Stroop phenomenon and its use in the study of perceptual, cognitive and response processes. *Memory & Cognition, 1*, 106–120.

Egeth, H.E., Virzi, R.A., & Garbart, H. (1984). Searching for conjunctively defined targets. *Journal of Experimental Psychology: Human Perception and Performance, 10*, 32–39.

Eich, E. (1984). Memory for unattended events: Remembering with and without awareness. *Memory & Cognition, 12*, 105–111.

Ellis, S.H., & Chase, W.G. (1971). Parallel processing in item recognition. *Perception & Psychophysics, 10*, 379–384.

Eriksen, B.A., & Eriksen, C.W. (1974). Effects of noise letters upon identification of target in nonsearch task. *Perception & Psychophysics, 16*, 143–149.

Eriksen, C.W., & Hoffman, J.E. (1972). Temporal and spatial characteristics of selective encoding from visual displays. *Perception & Psychophysics, 12*, 201–204.

Eriksen, C.W., & Murphy, T.D. (1987). Movement of attentional focus across the visual field: A critical look at the evidence. *Perception & Psychophysics, 42*, 299–305.

Eriksen, C.W., & Schultz, D.W. (1979). Information processing in visual search: A continuous flow conception and experimental results. *Perception & Psychophysics, 25*, 249–263.

Eriksen, C.W., & Spencer, T. (1969). Rate of information processing in visual perception: Some results and methodological considerations. *Journal of Experimental Psychology Monograph, 79* (2, Part 2).

Eriksen, C.W., & Yeh, Y. (1985). Allocation of attention in the visual field. *Journal of Experimental Psychology: Human Perception and Performance, 11*, 583–597.

Felfoldy, G.L. (1974). Repetition effects in choice reaction time to multidimensional stimuli. *Perception & Psychophysics, 15*, 453–459.

Fisher, D.L. (1982). Limited channel models of automatic detection: Capacity and scanning in visual search. *Psychological Review, 89*, 662–692.

Fisher, D.L. (1984). Central capacity limits in consistent mapping, visual search tasks: Four channels or more? *Cognitive Psychology, 16*, 449–484.

Fisk, A.D., & Schneider, W. (1984). Memory as a function of attention, level of processing, and automatization. *Journal of Experimental Psychology: Learning, Memory, and Cognition, 10*, 181–197.

Flach, J.M. (1986). Within-set discriminations in a consistent mapping search task. *Perception & Psychophysics, 39*, 397–406.

Flowers, J.H., Polansky, M.L., & Kerl, S. (1981). Familiarity, redundancy, and the spatial control of visual attention. *Journal of Experimental Psychology: Human Perception and Performance, 7*, 157–166.

Fowler, C.A., Wolford, G., Slade, R., & Tassinary, L. (1981). Lexical access with and without awareness. *Journal of Experimental Psychology: General, 110*, 341–362.

Foyle, D.C. (1981). *Automatic processing and selective attention.* Unpublished doctoral dissertation, Indiana Univeristy.

Francolini, C.M., & Egeth, H.A. (1979). Perceptual selectivity is task dependent: The pop-out effect poops out. *Perception & Psychophysics, 25*, 99–110.

Francolini, C.M., & Egeth, H.A. (1980). On the nonautomaticity of "automatic" activation: Evidence of selective seeing. *Perception & Psychophysics, 27*, 331–342.

Friedman, A., Polson, M.C., Dafoe, C.G., & Gaskill,

S.J. (1982). Dividing attention within and between hemispheres: Testing a multiple resources approach to limited-capacity information processing. *Journal of Experimental Psychology: Human Perception and Performance, 8,* 625–650.

Garner, W.R. (1974). *The processing of information and structure.* Potomac, MD: Erlbaum.

Garner, W.R. (1978). Selective attention to attributes and to stimuli. *Journal of Experimental Psychology: General, 107,* 287–308.

Garner, W.R., & Felfoldy, G.L. (1970). Integrality of stimulus dimensions in various types of information processing. *Cognitive Psychology, 1,* 225–241.

Goolkasian, P. (1981). Retinal location and its effect on the processing of target and distractor information. *Journal of Experimental Psychology: Human Perception and Performance, 7,* 1247–1257.

Graham, F.R. (1975). The more or less startling effects of weak prestimulation. *Psychophysiology, 12,* 238–248.

Green, B.F., & Anderson, L.K. (1956). Color coding in a visual search task. *Journal of Experimental Psychology, 51,* 19–24.

Hasher, L., & Zacks, R.T. (1979). Automatic and effortful processes in memory. *Journal of Experimental Psychology: General, 108,* 356–388.

Hirst, W., & Kalmar, D. (1987). Characterizing attentional resources. *Journal of Experimental Psychology: General, 116,* 68–81.

Hirst, W., Spelke, E.S., Reaves, C.C., Caharack, G., & Neisser, U. (1980). Dividing attention without alternation or automaticity. *Journal of Experimental Psychology: General, 109,* 98–117.

Hockley, W.E. (1984). Analysis of response time distributions in the study of cognitive processes. *Journal of Experimental Psychology: Learning, Memory, and Cognition, 10,* 598–615.

Hoffman, J.E. (1980). Interaction between global and local levels of a form. *Journal of Experimental Psychology: Human Perception and Performance, 6,* 222–234.

Hughes, H.C., Layton, W.M., Baird, J.C., & Lester, L.S. (1984). Global precedence in visual pattern recognition. *Perception & Psychophysics, 35,* 361–371.

Jacoby, L.L., & Witherspoon, D. (1982). Remembering without awareness. *Canadian Journal of Psychology, 36,* 300–324.

James, W. (1890). *The principles of psychology.* New York: Holt.

Johnson, P.J., Forester, J.A., Calderwood, R., & Weisgerber, S.A. (1983). Resource allocation and the attentional demands of letter encoding. *Journal of Experimental Psychology: General, 112,* 616–638.

Johnston, W.A., & Dark, V.J. (1982). In defense of

intraperceptual theories of attention. *Journal of Experimental Psychology: Human Perception and Performance, 8,* 407–421.

Johnston, W.A., & Heinz, S.P. (1978). Flexibility and capacity demands of attention. *Journal of Experimental Psychology: General, 107,* 420–435.

Johnston, W.A., & Heinz, S.P. (1979). Depth of nontarget processing in an attention task. *Journal of Experimental Psychology, 5,* 168–175.

Jones, W.P., & Anderson, J.R. (1982). Semantic categorization and high-speed scanning. *Journal of Experimental Psychology: Learning, Memory, and Cognition, 8,* 237–242.

Jonides, J. (1980a). Toward a model of the mind's eye. *Canadian Journal of Psychology, 34,* 103–112.

Jonides, J. (1980b). Voluntary versus automatic control over the mind's eye's movement. In J.B. Long & A.D. Baddeley (Eds.), *Attention and Performance IX.* Hillsdale, NJ: Erlbaum, pp. 187–203.

Jonides, J. (1983). Further toward a model of the mind's eye's movement. *Bulletin of the Psychonomic Society, 21,* 247–250.

Kahneman, D. (1973). *Attention and effort.* Englewood Cliffs, NJ: Prentice-Hall.

Kahneman, D., & Henik, A. (1981). Perceptual organization and attention. In M. Kubovy & J.R. Pomerantz (Eds.), *Perceptual organization.* Hillsdale, Erlbaum.

Kahneman, D., & Treisman, A. (1984). Changing views of attention and automaticity. In R. Parasuraman & D.R. Davies (Eds.), *Varieties of attention.* Orlando, FL: Academic Press, pp. 29–61.

Keele, S.W. (1973). *Attention and human performance.* Pacific Palisades, CA: Goodyear.

Keller, F.S. (1958). The phantom plateau. *Journal of the Experimental Analysis of Behavior, 1,* 1–13.

Kinchla, R. (1969). *An attention operating characteristic in vision. Technical Report.* Department of Psychology, McMaster University, Hamilton, Ont.

Kinchla, R.A. (1977). The role of structural redundancy in the detection of visual targets. *Perception & Psychophysics, 22,* 19–30.

Kinchla, R.A. (1980). The measurement of attention. In R.S. Nickerson (Ed.), *Attention and performance VIII.* Hillsdale, NJ: Erlbaum.

Kinchla, R.A., & Wolf, J.M. (1979). The order of visual processing: "Top-down," "bottom-up," or "middle-out." *Perception & Psychophysics, 25,* 225–231.

Klein, R. (1979). Does oculomotor readiness mediate cognitive control of visual attention? *Attention and performance VIII.* Hillsdale, NJ: Erlbaum.

Kristofferson, M.W. (1972a). Effects of practice on character classification performance. *Canadian Journal of Psychology, 26,* 54–60.

Kristofferson, M.W. (1972b). When item recognition and visual search functions are similar. *Perception & Psychophysics, 12*, 379–384.

Kristofferson, M.W. (1972c). Types and frequency of errors in visual search. *Perception & Psychophysics, 11*, 325–328.

Kubovy, M., & Pomerantz, J. (Eds.). (1981). *Perceptual organization.* Hillsdale, NJ: Erlbaum.

Kunst-Wilson, W.R., & Zajonc, R.B. (1980). Affective discrimination of stimuli that cannot be recognized. *Science, 207*, 557–558.

LaBerge, D. (1983). Spatial extent of attention to letters and words. *Journal of Experimental Psychology: Human Perception and Performance, 9*, 371–379.

LaBerge, D., & Brown, V. (1986). Variations in size of the visual field in which targets are presented: An attentional range effect. *Perception & Psychophysics, 40*, 188–200.

Lambert, A., & Hockey, R. (1986). Selective attention and performance with a multidimensional visual display. *Journal of Experimental Psychology: Human Perception and Performance, 12*, 484–495.

Lawson, E.A. (1966). Decisions concerning the rejected channel. *Quarterly Journal of Experimental Psychology, 18*, 260–265.

Lewis, J.L. (1970). Semantic processing of unattended messages using dichotic listening. *Journal of Experimental Psychology, 85*, 225–228.

Lockhead, G.R. (1972). Processing dimensional stimuli: A note. *Psychological Review, 79*, 410–419.

Logan, G.D. (1980). Attention and automaticity in Stroop and priming tasks: Theory and data. *Cognitive Psychology, 12*, 523–553.

Lupker, S.J., & Katz, A.N. (1981). Input, decision and response factors in picture-word interference. *Journal of Experimental Psychology: Human Learning and Memory, 7*, 269–282.

Lupker, S.J., & Massaro, D.W. (1979). Selective perceptive without confounding contributions of decision and memory. *Perception & Psychophysics, 25*, 60–69.

MacKay, D.G. (1973). Aspects of the theory of comprehension, memory and attention. *Quarterly Journal of Experimental Psychology, 25*, 22–40.

Mandler, G., Nakamura, Y., & Van Zandt, B.J.S. (1987). Nonspecific effects of exposure on stimuli that cannot be recognized. *Journal of Experimental Psychology: Learning, Memory, and Cognition, 13*, 646–648.

Marcel, A.J. (1978). Unconscious reading: Experiments on people who do not know they are reading. *Visible Language, 12*, 392–404.

Marcel, A.J. (1980). Conscious and preconscious recognition of polysemous words: Locating selective effects of prior verbal context. In R.S. Nickerson (Ed.), *Attention and performance VII.* Hillsdale, NJ: Erlbaum.

Martin, M. (1979). Local and global processing: The role of sparsity. *Memory & Cognition, 7*, 479–484.

Miller, J. (1981). Global precedence in attention and decision. *Journal of Experimental Psychology: Human Perception and Performance, 7*, 1161–1174.

Miller, J.O., & Pachella, R.G. (1973). Locus of the stimulus probability effect. *Journal of Experimental Psychology, 101*, 227–231.

Monahan, J.S., & Lockhead, G.R. (1977). Identification of integral stimuli. *Journal of Experimental Psychology: General, 106*, 94–110.

Moray, N. (1959). Attention in dichotic listening: Affective cues and the influence of instructions. *Quarterly Journal of Experimental Psychology, 11*, 56–60.

Moray, N. (1969a). *Listening and attention.* Baltimore: Penguin Books.

Moray, N. (1969b). *Attention: Selective processes in vision and hearing.* London: Hutchinson Educational Ltd.

Morton, J. (1969). Categories of interference: Verbal mediation and conflict in card sorting. *British Journal of Psychology, 60*, 329–346.

Navon, D. (1977). Forest before trees: The precedence of global features in visual perception. *Cognitive Psychology, 9*, 353–383.

Navon, D. (1984). Resources—a theoretical soup stone? *Psychological Review, 91*, 216–234.

Navon, D., & Gopher, D. (1979). On the economy of the human processing system. *Psychological Review, 86*, 214–255.

Navon, D., & Gopher, D. (1980). Interpretations of task difficulty. In R. Nickerson (Ed.), *Attention and performance VIII.* Hillsdale, NJ: Erlbaum.

Navon, D., & Norman, J. (1983). Does global precedence really depend on visual angle? *Journal of Experimental Psychology: Human Perception and Performance, 9*, 955–965.

Neely, J.H. (1977). Semantic priming and retrieval from lexical memory: Roles of inhibitionless spreading activation and limited-capacity attention. *Journal of Experimental Psychology: General, 106*, 226–254.

Neisser, U. (1963). Decision time without reaction time: Experiments in visual scanning. *American Journal of Psychology.* New York: Appleton-Century-Crofts.

Neisser, U. (1967). *Cognitive Psychology.* New York: Appleton-Century-Crofts.

Neisser, U. (1976). *Cognition and reality.* San Francisco: W.H. Freeman and Company.

Neisser, U., Novick, R., & Lazar, R. (1963). Searching for ten targets simultaneously. *Perceptual and Motor Skills, 17*, 955–961.

Neumann, O. (1984). Automatic processing: A review of recent findings and a plea for an old theory. In W. Prinz & A.F. Sanders (Eds.), *Cognition and motor processes*. Berlin, Heildelberg: Springer-Verlag.

Newstead, S.E., & Dennis, I. (1979). Lexical and grammatical processing of unshadowed messages: A re-examination of the MacKay effect. *Quarterly Journal of Experimental Psychology, 31,* 477–488.

Norman, D.A. (1968). Towards a theory of memory and attention. *Psychological Review, 75,* 522–536.

Norman, D.A. (1969). *Memory and attention: An introduction to human information processing.* New York: John Wiley.

Norman, D.A., & Bobrow, D.G. (1975). On data-limited and resource-limited processes. *Cognitive Psychology, 7,* 44–64.

Ogden, W.C., Martin, D.W., & Paap, K.R. (1986). Processing demands of encoding: What does secondary task performance reflect? *Journal of Experimental Psychology: Human Perception and Performance, 6,* 355–367.

Paap, K.R., & Ogden, W.G. (1981). Letter encoding is an obligatory but capacity-demanding operation. *Journal of Experimental Psychology: Human Perception and Performance, 7,* 518–528.

Parasuraman, R. (1984). Sustained attention in detection and discrimination. In R. Parasuraman & D.R. Davies (Eds.), *Varieties of attention*. Orlando, FL: Academic Press, pp. 243–271.

Parasuraman, R. & Davies, D.R. (Eds.). (1984). *Varieties of attention.* Orlando, FL: Academic Press.

Pillsbury, W.B. (1908). *Attention.* New York: Macmillan.

Podgorny, P., & Shepard, R.N. (1983). Distribution of visual attention over space. *Journal of Experimental Psychology: Human Perception and Performance, 9,* 380–393.

Poltrock, S.E., Lansman, M., & Hunt, E. (1982). Automatic and controlled attention processes in auditory target deteection. *Journal of Experimental Psychology: Human Perception and Performance, 8,* 37–45.

Pomerantz, J.R. (1981). Perceptual organization in information processing. In M. Kubovy & J.R. Pomerantz (Eds.), *Perceptual organization*. Hillsdale, NJ: Erlbaum.

Pomerantz, J.R. (1983). Global and local precedence: Selective attention in form and motion perception. *Journal of Experimental Psychology: General, 112,* 516–540.

Pomerantz, J.R., & Garner, W.R. (1973). Stimulus configuration in selective attention tasks. *Perception & Psychophysics, 14,* 565–569.

Pomerantz, J.R., & Sager, L.C. (1975). Asymmetric integrality with dimensions of visual pattern. *Perception & Psychophysics, 18,* 460–466.

Posner, M.I. (1978). *Chronometric explorations of mind.* Hillsdale, NJ: Erlbaum.

Posner, M.I. (1980). Orienting of attention. *Quarterly Journal of Experimental Psychology, 32,* 3–25.

Posner, M.I. (1982). Cumulative development of attentional theory. *American Psychologist, 37,* 168–179.

Posner, M.I., & Boies, S.J. (1971). Components of attention. *Psychological Review, 78,* 391–408.

Posner, M.I., & Klein, R.M. (1973). On the functions of consciousness. In S. Kornblum (Ed.), *Attention and performance IV*. New York: Academic Press.

Posner, M.I., & Snyder, C.R.R. (1975a). Attention and cognitive control. In R. Solso (Ed.), *Information processing and cognition: The Loyola symposium*. Potomac, MD: Erlbaum.

Posner, M.I., & Snyder, C.R.R. (1975b). Facilitation and inhibition in the processing of signals. In P.M.A. Rabbit & S. Dornic (Eds.), *Attention and performance V*. New York: Academic Press.

Posner, M.I., Snyder, C.R.R., & Davidson, B.J. (1980). Attention and the detection of signals. *Journal of Experimental Psychology: General, 109,* 160–174.

Poulton, E.C. (1953). Two-channel listening. *Journal of Experimental Psychology, 46,* 91–96.

Prinzmetal, W. (1981). Principles of feature integration in visual perception. *Perception & Psychophysics, 30,* 330–340.

Prinzmetal, W., & Banks, W.P. (1977). Good continuation affects visual detection. *Perception & Psychophysics, 21,* 389–395.

Prinzmetal, W., & Millis-Wright, M. (1984). Cognitive and linguistic factors affect visual feature integration. *Cognitive Psychology, 16,* 305–340.

Quinlan, P.T., & Humphreys, G.W. (In press). Visual search for targets defined by combinations of color, shape, and size: An examination of the task constraints on feature and conjunction searches. *Perception & Psychophysics*.

Reed, A.V. (1976). List length and the time course of recognition in immediate memory. *Memory & Cognition, 4,* 16–30.

Remington, R.W. (1980). Attention and saccadic eye movements. *Journal of Experimental Psychology: Human Perception and Performance, 6,* 726–744.

Rollins, H.A., Jr., & Hendricks, R. (1980). Processing of words presented simultaneously to eye and ear. *Journal of Experimental Psychology: Human Perception and Performance, 6,* 99–109.

Rumelhart, D.E. (1970). A multicomponent theory of the perception of briefly exposed visual displays. *Journal of Mathematical Psychology, 7,* 191–218.

Schneider, W. (1985). Toward a model of attention and the development of automatic processing. In

M.I. Pasner and O.S.M. Marin (Eds.), *Attention and performance XI*, Hillsdale, N.J.: Erlbaum.

Schneider, W., Dumais, S.T., & Shiffrin, R.M. (1984). Automatic and control processing and attention. In R. Parasuraman & D.R. Davies (Eds.), *Varieties of attention*. Orlando, FL: Academic Press, pp. 1–27.

Schneider, W., & Fisk, A.D. (1982a). Concurrent automatic and controlled visual search: Can processing occur without resource cost? *Journal of Experimental Psychology: Learning, Memory, and Cognition, 8,* 261–278.

Schneider, W., & Fisk, A.D. (1982b). Degree of consistent training: Improvements in search performance and automatic process development. *Perception & Psychophysics, 31,* 160–168.

Schneider, W., & Fisk, A.D. (1984). Automatic category search and its transfer. *Journal of Experimental Psychology: Learning, Memory, and Cognition, 10,* 1–15.

Schneider, W., & Shiffrin, R.M. (1977). Controlled and automatic human information processing: I. Detection, search, and attention. *Psychological Review, 84,* 1–66.

Shaffer, L.H. (1975). Multiple attention in continuous verbal tasks. In P.M.A. Rabbitt & S. Dornic (Eds.), *Attention and performance V*. New York: Academic Press.

Shaffer, W.O., & LaBerge, D. (1979). Automatic semantic processing of unattended words. *Journal of Verbal Learning and Verbal Behavior, 18,* 413–426.

Shaw, M., & Shaw, P. (1977). Optimal allocation of cognitive resources to spatial location. *Journal of Experimental Psychology: Human Perception and Performance, 3,* 201–211.

Shepard, R.N., & Podgorny, D. (1986). Spatial factors in visual attention: A reply to Crassini. *Journal of Experimental Psychology: Human Perception and Performance, 12,* 383–387.

Shiffrin, R.M. (1975a). The locus and role of attention in memory systems. In P.M.A. Rabbit & S. Dornic (Eds.), *Attention and performance V*. New York: Academic Press.

Shiffrin, R.M. (1975b). Short-term store: The basis for a memory search. In F. Restle, R. Shiffrin, J. Castellan, H. Lindman, & D. Pisoni (Eds.), *Cognitive theory* (Vol. 1). Hillsdale, NJ: Erlbaum.

Shiffrin, R.M., & Czerwinski, M.P. (In press). A model of automatic attention attraction when mapping is partially consistent. *Journal of Experimental Psychology: Learning, Memory, and Cognition.*

Shiffrin, R.M., & Dumais, S.T. (1981). The development of automatism. In John Anderson (Ed.), *Cognitive skills and their acquisition*. Hillsdale, NJ: Erlbaum.

Shiffrin, R.M., Dumais, S.T., & Schneider, W. (1981). Characteristics of automatism. In J.B. Long &

A.D. Baddeley (Eds.), *Attention and performance IX*. Hillsdale, NJ: Erlbaum.

Shiffrin, R.M., & Gardner, G.T. (1972). Visual processing capacity and attentional control. *Journal of Experimental Psychology, 93,* 72–83.

Shiffrin, R.M., & Schneider, W. (1973). An expectancy model for memory search. *Memory & Cognition, 2,* 616–628.

Shiffrin, R.M., & Schneider, W. (1977). Controlled and automatic human information processing: II. Perceptual learning, automatic attending, and a general theory. *Psychological Review, 84,* 127–190.

Shiffrin, R.M., & Schneider, W. (1984). Theoretical note. Automatic and controlled processing revisited. *Psychological Review, 91,* 269–276.

Shulman, G.L., Remington, R.W., & McLean, J.P. (1979). Moving attention through visual space. *Journal of Experimental Psychology: Human Perception and Performance, 5,* 522–526.

Silverstein, L.D., Graham, F.K., & Bohlin, G. (1981). Selective attention effects on the reflex blink. *Psychophysiology, 18,* 240–247.

Smith, J.D., & Kemler Nelson, D.G. (1984). Overall similarity in adults' classification: The child in all of us. *Journal of Experimental Psychology: General, 113,* 137–159.

Smith, S.L. (1962). Color coding and visual search. *Journal of Experimental Psychology, 64,* 434–440.

Solomons, L., & Stein, G. (1896). Normal motor automatism. *Psychological Review, 3,* 492–512.

Spelke, E., Hirst, W., & Neisser, U. (1976). Skills of divided attention. *Cognition, 4,* 215–230.

Sperling, G. (1960). The information available in brief visual presentations. *Psychological Monographs, 74* (Whole No. 498).

Sperling, G. (1975). Multiple detections in a brief stimulus: The sharing and switching of attention. *Bulletin of the Psychonomic Society, 9,* 427. (Abstract)

Sperling, G. (1984). A unified theory of attention and signal detection. In R. Parasuraman & D.R. Davies (Eds.), *Varieties of attention*. Orlando, FL: Academic Press. pp. 103–181.

Sperling, G., Budiansky, J., Spivak, J.G., & Johnson, M.C. (1971). Extremely rapid visual search: The maximum rate of scanning letters for the presence of a numeral. *Science, 174,* 307–311.

Sperling, G., & Melchner, M.J. (1978a). The attention operating characteristic: Some examples from visual search. *Science, 202,* 315–318.

Sperling, G., & Melchner, M.J. (1978b). Visual search, visual attention, and the attention operating characteristic. In J. Requin (Ed.), *Attention and performance VII*. Hillsdale, NJ: Erlbaum, 675–686.

Sperling, G., & Reeves, A. (1980). Measuring the reaction time of an unobserved response: A shift of visual attention. In R. Nickerson (Ed.), *Attention and performance VIII.* Hillsdale, NJ: Erlbaum, 347–360.

Spieth, W., Curtis, J.F., & Webster, J.C. (1954). Responding to one of two simultaneous messages. *Journal of the Acoustical Society of America, 26,* 390–396.

Spoehr, K.T., & Lehmkuhle, S.W. (1982). *Visual information processing.* San Francisco: W.H. Freeman and Company.

Sternberg, S. (1966). High-speed scanning in human memory. *Science, 153,* 652–654.

Sternberg, S. (1975). Memory scanning: New findings and current controversies. *Quarterly Journal of Experimental Psychology, 27,* 1–32.

Stroop, J.R. (1935). Studies of interference in serial verbal reactions. *Journal of Experimental Psychology, 18,* 643–662.

Swets, J.A. (1984). Mathematical models of attention. In R. Parasuraman & D.R. Davies (Eds.), *Varieties of attention.* Orlando, FL: Academic Press, pp. 183–242.

Tipper, S.P. (1985). The negative priming effect: Inhibitory priming by ignored objects. *Quarterly Journal of Experimental Psychology, 37A,* 571–590.

Tipper, S.P., & Cranston, M. (1985). Selective attention and priming: Inhibitory and facilitatory effects of ignored primes. *Quarterly Journal of Experimental Psychology, 37A,* 591–612.

Townsend, J.T. (1976). Serial and within-stage independent parallel model equivalence on the minimum completion time. *Journal of Mathematical Psychology, 14,* 219–238.

Treisman, A.M. (1960). Contextual cues in selective listening. *Quarterly Journal of Experimental Psychology, 12,* 242–248.

Treisman, A.M. (1964). Effect of irrelevant material on the efficiency of selective listening. *American Journal of Psychology, 77,* 533–546.

Treisman, A.M. (1969). Strategies and models of selective attention. *Psychological Review, 76,* 282–299.

Treisman, A. (1982). Perceptual grouping and attention in visual search for features and for objects. *Journal of Experimental Psychology: Human Perception and Performance, 8,* 194–214.

Treisman, A. (in press). Properties, parts, and objects. In K. Boff, L. Kaufman, & J. Thomas (Eds.), *Handbook of perception and human performance.*

Treisman, A.M., & Gelade, G. (1980). A feature integration theory of attention. *Cognitive Psychology, 12,* 97–136.

Treisman, A.M., & Riley, J.G.A. (1969). Is selective attention selective perception or selective response? A further test. *Journal of Experimental Psychology, 79,* 27–34.

Treisman, A.M., & Schmidt, H. (1982). Illusory conjunctions in the perception of objects. *Cognitive Psychology, 14,* 107–141.

Treisman, A. & Souther, J. (1985). Search asymmetry: A diagnostic for preattentive processing of separable features. *Journal of Experimental Psychology: General, 114,* 285–310.

Treisman, A., Squire, R., & Green, J. (1974). Semantic processing in dichotic listening? A replication. *Memory & Cognition, 2,* 641–646.

Treisman, A.M., Sykes, M., & Gelade, G. (1977). Selective attention and stimulus integration. In S. Dornic (Ed.), *Attention and performance VI.* Hillsdale, NJ: Erlbaum, pp. 333–361.

Tsal, Y. (1983). Movements of attention across the visual field. *Journal of Experimental Psychology: Human Perception and Performance, 9,* 523–530.

Underwood, G. (1976). *Attention and memory.* Oxford, England: Pergamon.

Virzi, R.A. & Egeth, H.E. (1984). Is meaning implicated in illusory conjunctions? *Journal of Experimental Psychology: Human Perception and Performance, 10,* 573–580.

Virzi, R.A. & Egeth, H.E. (1985). Toward a translational model of Stroop interference. *Memory & Cognition, 13,* 304–319.

Ward, L.M. (1982). Determinants of attention to local and global features of visual forms. *Journal of Experimental Psychology: Human Perception and Performance, 8,* 562–581.

Weichselgartner, E. & Sperling, G. (In press). Dynamics of automatic and controlled visual attention. *Science.*

Weintraub, D.J. (1971). Rectangle discriminability: Perceptual relativity and the law of Pragnanz. *Journal of Experimental Psychology, 88,* 1–11.

Wickens, C.D. (1980). The structure of attentional resources. In R. Nickerson (Ed.), *Attention and performance VIII.* Hillsdale, NJ: Erlbaum.

Wickens, C.D. (1984). Processing resources in attention. In R. Parassuraman & D.R. Davies (Eds.), *Varieties of attention.* Orlando, FL: Academic Press, pp. 63–102.

Wickens, C.D., Fracker, L., & Webb, J. (1987). Cross-modal interference and task integration: Resources or preemption switching? *Proceedings of the 31st Annual Meeting of the Human Factors Society.*

Yntema, D.C. & Trask, F.P. (1963). Recall as a search process. *Journal of Verbal Learning and Verbal Behavior, 2,* 65–74.

Zacks, R.T., Hasher, L., & Sanft, H. (1982). Automatic encoding of event frequency: Further findings. *Journal of Experimental Psychology: Learning, Memory, and Cognition, 8,* 106–116.

# Chapter 12

# INDIVIDUAL DIFFERENCES IN COGNITIVE FUNCTIONING

**John B. Carroll,** *University of North Carolina at Chapel Hill*

This chapter is intended to enhance experimental psychologists' awareness of the relevance of individual differences (IDs) to their work. These IDs, which appear in nearly every phase of behavior and performance, have been treated mainly in a branch of psychology known as psychometrics. Psychometrics has dealt with numerous phenomena that are also of interest in experimental psychology. It is necessary for experimentalists to understand the relevance of IDs because it is important to establish interrelations between IDs and experimentally described phenomena and to uncover any interactions that require nomothetic interpretations. In recent years there have been many calls for establishing closer links between experimental psychology and ID research (Cronbach, 1957, 1975; Estes, 1974; Hunt & Lansman, 1975; Neisser, 1976; Underwood, 1975). Partly as a result of these calls for action, it is now possible to indicate in considerable detail how such links can be forged.

The canonical approach to problems in experimental psychology has been to subject a group or groups of individuals to varied, manipulable experimental conditions, to observe and measure one or more dependent variables of interest, and then through statistical analyses to draw conclusions on the effects of the experimental conditions, either singly or in interaction. In the more sophisticated investigations, experimental conditions are selected, designed, or programmed to test hypotheses or models concerning the laws or processes underlying the observed behavior. Often a central feature of the statistical analysis is the use of an error term, representing variance across individuals, as a baseline value for assessing variance across experimental conditions or their interactions, as in F-ratio tests. Currently, space constraints in journals encourage authors simply to report F-ratios for treatments and interactions, but the error terms themselves, from which some information about individual variation might be derived, are seldom reported, as they were in the 1950s and 1960s when complete ANOVA tables were published more often than now.

Perusal of a sample of recent literature suggests that the role of IDs is generally neglected in experimental psychology. Although new data and models concerning a variety of behaviors are being offered, it would seem that there is a studied neglect of IDs in these behaviors—IDs that are patently obvious in the psychometric literature.

To be sure, many instances of experimental psychologists' concern with IDs can be found. Hasher and Zacks (1979), for example, state their assumption that attentional capacity varies both within and among individuals, and they investigate the extent to which depression, high arousal levels, and old age might reduce such capacity. Di Lollo (1980) shows plots of individual data in a study of iconic memory. Revelle, Humphreys, Simon and Gilliland (1980) consider interaction between a personality trait (introversion-extraversion), time of day, and caffeine on performance in a verbal reasoning task. R.J. Sternberg (1980b) reports correlations between parameters of a model of linear syllogistic reasoning and scores on verbal and spatial ability tests. It remains generally the case, however, that while experimentalists are aware of IDs in performance, these IDs serve mainly as leverage for establishing the statistical significance of effects associated with experimental conditions.

If psychology is to be a complete science of behavior, IDs must be taken into account in explaining that behavior. Furthermore, if significant interactions between IDs and other types of variables are found, as it appears they frequently are or can be, one has to conclude that characteristics of individual organisms must function as terms in any general laws or functional analyses of behavior. One of the major goals of ID research, therefore, is to identify the varieties and dimensions of individual characteristics that might serve in discovering the regularities of behavior. (Other goals of ID research, not featured in this chapter, are to investigate causes of IDs and their relations to such variables as sex, age, health status, training and education, and so forth, but these goals cannot be satisfactorily achieved without adequate identification and characterization of ID variables.)

The kinds of individual characteristics that will probably be most relevant to establishing regularities of behavior are those that are relatively stable over time and occasions, or, in psychometric terms, are reliable. In experimental literature it has been relatively uncommon to find assessments of the reliability of any IDs that are observed, although the magnitudes of group differences or the dispersions of individual regression lines may be such as to lend intuitive credibility to their reliabilities. Whenever such IDs appear to be either intuitively or demon-strably reliable, it becomes of interest to consider their possible relations to the substantial number of individual difference dimensions that have been established in psychometric research, particularly those that factor-analytic research has identified as having at least a fair degree of generality over types of psychometric tasks, samples of persons, and testing conditions.

This chapter presents an overview of methodologies for establishing individual differences in both psychometric and experimental research for using ID variables in experimental designs, and for determining links between psychometrically and experimentally observed dimensions of behavior. The chapter also assesses the present state of knowledge concerning such dimensions, at least in the domain of what may be called cognitive tasks. It also considers the possibilities of relating ID dimensions to psychological theory.

The focus on cognitive tasks comes about not only because a large amount of psychometric research concerns ID variables that pertain to individual subjects' abilities to perform such tasks successfully, but also because present-day trends in experimental psychology emphasize the analysis of the knowledge, skills, strategies, and basic information-handling processes involved in the performance of such tasks, that is, the analysis of such higher cognitive functions as perception, learning, memory, thinking, and the use of symbolic systems such as language and mathematics.

The concept of cognitive task defies clear and easy definition. Most generally, a cognitive task may be defined as one that is designed to provide information on subjects' repertoires of cognitive responses and their modes of cognitive functioning. It may be a task that taps the individual's knowledge or skill in some domain, or it may be one that has promise of revealing how the individual processes information in order to arrive at a response. A cognitive task usually involves the subjects' understanding the task in terms of its intended end results or final state. One possible criterion for considering a task cognitive is the extent to which, given the same stimulus conditions and context in which to perform, a subject might respond and perform differently as a function either of being given or of adopting different instructions. For example, given a series of digits to repeat (as in the traditional digit span test), a subject would be expected to respond differently depending on whether the instruction was to repeat the digits in the order presented or in reverse order, or with the addition of a constant to each digit. In this case, the cognitive phenomena revealed by the task would be a function of the subjects' mental set, program or strategy for performance. Another possible criterion is the extent to which variations in stimulus attributes make for consistent variations in subject performances. An example is the Stroop color-naming task, in which words naming colors may be printed either in black and white or in colors different from the colors they name. The cognitive phenomena revealed by the task are taken to be a function of the subject's cognitive processing of stimulus attributes that may or may not be conflicting. For some purposes it may be useful to restrict attention to elementary cognitive tasks that would appear to require, in their performance, a relatively small number of mental processes acting either sequentially or simultaneously. Obviously it is difficult to specify exactly what cognitive processes are involved in any given task, but in certain experimental settings it may be possible to give operational meaning to the measurement of certain processes or components (R.J. Sternberg, 1977, 1980a).

## INDIVIDUAL DIFFERENCE METHODOLOGY IN EXPERIMENTAL SETTINGS

### The Creation of Individual Difference Variables

The term testing can refer either to the administration of a psychometric instrument (e.g., an aptitude test) or to the conduct of an experiment, because both psychometric tests and psychological experiments are normally conducted with conditions held as constant (in some sense) as possible over individuals, occasions, or both. In conducting a psychometric test, the dependent variable is the individual's score or performance measurement; this is often true also in a psychological experiment, but in addition there is usually some kind of designed experimental variation of conditions. Nevertheless, for any given experimental condition one seeks to ensure that stimulus conditions (including any verbal instructions), instrumentation, and response

modes do not vary in significant ways from subject to subject. Constancy of conditions is of course a relative matter. Testing conditions can never be exactly the same for all possible administrations of a test or an experiment; in psychometric testing there is often a deliberate looseness of control, as when, even with constant testing time, there is leeway for variation in the number of items or test tasks that different individuals attempt.

Whether the concern is with formal experiments or with psychometric instruments, the assumption is that, with conditions held in some sense constant, any reliable variance in response measurements that cannot be attributed to different treatments or to different task reflects characteristic differences among individuals. This assumption can possibly be extended even to the case of what Battig (1979) called intraindividual differences, that is, differences in the strategies of information processing or modes of performance that are adopted by an individual on a particular occasion or trial, if one also assumes that individuals characteristically adopt different strategies or performance modes in response to particular experimental conditions or settings, or that, as Battig sugggests, individuals differ in their cognitive flexibility or ability to select the strategies most effective for performing a given task.

The number of ID variables that might be created is practically infinite, like the number of 20-word grammatical English sentences that might be generated. In other words, a practically infinite number of experimental settings (or test items) could be devised to measure IDs. In this embarrassment of potentialities, it is a problem to know where to start. One might be tempted to go on a sort of hunting expedition, creating ID variables somewhat haphazardly from almost any task that seemed to merit study. Essentially this was the strategy employed by investigators in the late 19th century, in their relatively primitive researches with stock paradigms like sensory discrimination, simple and choice reaction time, object naming, word reading, and digit span. In fairness it should be said that these investigators had reasonable intuitions about profitable directions of research. When it appeared that individual difference variables created in this way had little practical significance for prediction of educational or occupational success, this approach was virtually abandoned. In the last few years some of these paradigms have been taken down from the shelf and attacked anew (Hunt, Frost & Lunneborg, 1973; Hunt, Lunneborg & Lewis, 1975; Jensen, 1980), and in the attempt to test new theories of cognitive psychology and information processing a number of new paradigms have been devised (Atkinson & Shiffrin, 1968; Posner & Mitchell, 1967; S. Sternberg, 1966). While it is not yet clear whether the individual difference variables that might be created within such paradigms will have any more practical significance than those investigated in the early years of psychological research, advances in experimental and statistical methodology give this work promise of important theoretical contribution. We may remind ourselves that theoretical developments can have long-range practical significance.

### Deriving ID Variables from Experimental Paradigms

In recent years, there has been increased appreciation for the potential complexity of even quite elementary cognitive tasks such as that of the choice reaction-time experiment. The stages by which performances in such tasks take place are apparently more numerous and varied than may appear at first sight (Posner & McLeod, 1982; Sanders, 1980), and the types of information processing that can occur in any given stage can vary considerably over subjects, occasions, and conditions. Moreover, different dimensions of IDs may be involved in different stages or aspects of such tasks, and even within a given stage, it is often useful to consider the subject's speed or latency of response separately from the accuracy or appropriateness of the response. For this reason, in using experimental paradigms to generate ID variables it is desirable to conduct experiments with greater precision and articulation of response measurement techniques than may ordinarily be the case if there is no interest in IDs. It is conceivable, of course, that separate stages are not truly independent, and that certain information processing operations carry over several stages. Pachella (1974) has discussed such problems in connection with reaction time data, concluding that while various methods (the additive factor method, the subtraction method, etc.) all have certain defects, the method of "converging operations", that is, the accumulation of evidence from a variety of related

studies, can be expected eventually to produce scientifically valid results and interpretations. This is the stance adopted here; indeed, it can further be argued that the use of the statistical technology associated with ID research has potential for helping to resolve difficulties that cannot otherwise be dealt with readily.

In order to analyze experimental paradigms into stages of information processing in which IDs might be discovered, it is useful to adopt a tentative list of behavioral processes, some or all of which may be called cognitive. The list offered here, bearing some similarity to those suggested by Newell and Simon (1972) and Chase (1978), includes the following:

1. *Monitoring behavior.* This is the set of instructions, rules, and guidelines that a subject maintains (presumably in memory) throughout the performance of a task. It corresponds to the production system postulated by Newell (1973) to describe the sequence of mental operations in computer terms. It may be analyzed into smaller component processes, including those listed below, but for purposes of clear exposition of task analyses it seems wise to retain the concept of a single process or program that an individual is caused to have in mind (by instructions or other means) while responding in any particular experimental or task setting. Normally it has a hierarchical structure in the sense that it contains major, minor, and subsidiary goals (Miller, Galanter & Pribram, 1960). It also contains a series of expectations as to what kinds of stimulus and other events may be anticipated, as may be verified by suddenly changing the structure of an experiment (without warning to subject) and noting abnormal responses. The monitoring process may vary over individuals or replicate tasks; subjects may differ in the way they understand or interpret instructions, and they may adopt different strategies for dealing with the separate tasks in a series of apparently similar tasks. In the analysis of experimental data, it is desirable to detect and take account of such variations. (Here I adopt the term "monitoring behavior" to denote a process that is more general than strategy or performance component.)

2. *Attention.* The process whereby the subject's conscious, focal attention is directed toward some potential stimulus source and modality, with an expectation of, and concentration on, the potential nature of, the stimulus to be presented.

For example, in Sperling's (1960) iconic memory task, a differential signal directs the subject to read out either the top or the bottom row of stimuli formed in a visual memory buffer. In the auditory modality, the process may consist of tuning attention to a particular type of range of potential stimuli (e.g., high tones as opposed to low tones and noises) or to stimuli received in one ear rather than the other. To the extent that subjects can program conscious attention to stimuli (Posner & Snyder, 1975), there may be characteristic IDs in their ability to do so (Hasher & Zacks, 1979).

3. *Stimulus apprehension*. The process of receiving stimulus energy in a sensory buffer to a degree sufficient for the subject to become aware of the stimulus. Individual differences in stimulus apprehension processes can be assessed by experimental paradigms in which stimulus duration and intensity are varied systematically, usually by a method of ascending limits with no poststimulus masking, the subjects being asked merely to report apprehension of the stimulus.

4. *Perceptual integration of the stimulus*. The process whereby sensory buffer information is referred to memory stores so as to find a match with a previously formed memory representation. Normally this match is found rapidly, but if the stimulus is ambiguous or otherwise not easily recognizable, the speed of perceptual integration may be slower. There is reason to believe that the speed of perceptual integration may be measured by a paradigm experiment on visual or auditory duration with poststimulus masking, but as yet there is little information on IDs in such measurements.

5. *Encoding*. The process of forming in memory a representation of a stimulus or some derivative of it such as an attribute (color, form, etc.) or associated class concept. There are IDs in both the speed and veridicality of this process. Encoding is one of the components assumed in R.J. Sternberg's (1977) system of analyzing experimental data; it is measured by obtaining a regression coefficient for the number of stimuli encoded (this number being varied over experimental conditions). In this system, however, the encoding speed component score would also include times for apprehension and integration of stimuli.

6. *Stimulus comparison*. The process of comparing two stimuli for sameness or similarity, assuming that they have already been separately encoded. One or both of the stimuli may be in memory rather than physically present. The outcome of the comparison is usually either same or different. (This process does not include finding in what respect two items are similar or different, or finding which of two stimuli is greater or smaller on a specified dimension; such operations would involve other processes.)

7. *Formation of corepresentation with a stimulus*. The process of establishing, in memory, the association between two representations in terms of some rule that specifies the basis on which the association is formed. For example, "French translation" is the basis on which the representation *"chaise"* is assciated with "chair"; "square root" is the basis for associating 7 with 49; "arbitrary sequence" is the basis on which the sequence [5, 7] might be established in serial learning.

8. *Retrieval of a corepresentation with a stimulus*. The process of finding, from memory, the corepresentation associated with a particular stimulus on the basis of the rule governing the association. Thus, given the rule "French translation" one would find *"chaise"* for the stimulus "chair," or given the rule "square root" one would find 7 for the stimulus 49.

9. *Transformation of a stimulus*. The process of mentally transforming a stimulus representation to some form other than its original, for example, mentally rotating a visual stimulus through a required rotation angle, or (in the auditory modality) changing a melody to a different key. Individual and group differences have been observed in the speed of mental rotation (Pellegrino & Kail, 1982; Shepard & Feng, 1972; Tapley & Bryden, 1977).

10. *Response execution*. The process of operating on a mental representation that specifies a target response in such a way as to plan and produce the actual response, be it overt (such as the pressing of a button) or covert (as in rehearsal of memory items). Response execution is thought of primarily as a cognitive process that involves planning the required movement, utterance, or whatever; the process is mainly what precedes the actual response. Speed or latency measurements are usually best made by observing the time (decision time) taken to begin the response,

from some prior point in the task, rather than the time taken to complete it, since completion time also includes a component of movement time (Fitts, 1954; Fitts & Peterson, 1964) or articulation time. Decision times are apparently regular functions of various experimental conditions. Movement times can be taken to reflect a second stage of the response execution process and are worthy of investigation, though differences in subject strategies may block attempts to separate decision and movement times (Smith & Stanley, 1980).

Doubtless a number of other elementary cognitive operations could be identified; some of these, like eduction of correlates and eduction of relations, have played an important role in psychometric theories of intelligence (Spearman, 1927). Carroll (1976) suggested ways in which such elementary operations might be interpreted as functioning in the performance of tasks studied in psychometric research.

A heuristic strategy for forming ID variables is to use experimental and other paradigms to obtain measurements, in the framework of these postulated processes or information-processing operations, that will reflect different aspects of them: (1) probabilities that the process will occur, (2) times taken by the process, (3) probabilities that the outcome response will be correct or appropriate according to a specified rule or criterion, and (4) parameters of functional relations. Because many if not all psychometric tasks may be considered exemplars of experimental tasks or paradigms, ID variables may be formed from psychometric tasks in almost precisely the way they are formed from experimental paradigms.

## Types of ID Variables

### PROBABILITIES OF PROCESS OCCURRENCE

The idea that tasks may be performed or learned in different ways by different subjects is the notion of "strategy" (Newell & Simon, 1972; O'Neil, 1978). In terms of the list of cognitive processes proposed here, such variations might well be conceived of as variations in the monitor process. Numerous examples could be given of attempts to control and manipulate subjects' strategies. (Some of this work is reviewed by Masters, 1981, pp. 129–131.) Sometimes experimental data can be analyzed *post hoc* to reveal the operation of different strategies. A striking

example comes from the work of MacLeod, Hunt, and Mathews (1978; see also Mathews, Hunt & MacLeod, 1980), who were able to show that IDs in spatial ability were related to individual subject strategies in performing the Clark and Chase (1972) sentence verification task. For the majority of subjects, Clark and Chase's model fitted the data well. In their model, when a sentence such as "Star is not below cross" is presented, the truth of which is to be verified from a picture (a display in which the star may appear either above or below the cross), the subjects wait until the actual presentation of the display before finding a semantic representation of the sentence. This model, however, gave a poor fit to data of some subjects with high test scores for spatial ability. The data of those subjects provided a better fit if it was assumed that they found a semantic representation of the sentence and predicted the nature of the visual display before it was actually presented. From the vantage of the present discussion, the monitoring processes of the two groups of subjects contained different sequences and probabilities of cognitive operations—probabilities that were related to external measures of verbal and spatial ability. Further studies by Glushko and Cooper (1978) of the sentence verification task indicated that task-specific factors often control the patterning and durations of verification processes. Similarly, Cooper (1976, 1982; Cooper & Podgorny, 1976) found that subjects could be classified into two groups according to the pattern of their performance data in a certain visual comparison task. However, Cooper's studies employed no external measures of ability.

### PROCESS TIMES

Each of the processes listed has certain temporal aspects. The monitor process may require a certain amount of time to take form and be learned or altered. The remaining processes can also be assumed to take certain amounts of time to perform and it is useful to try to measure or estimate those times with the object of discovering IDs and their statistical characteristics (central tendencies and variances). While it is not always possible to measure the time for a given process directly or to separate it completely from times of other processes, experimental and task design can often be manipulated so as to narrow the range of operations encompassed in a given measurement procedure. It is also possible to derive ID measurements by comparing data from contrasting tasks or experimental settings. Several widely applicable illustrations of these points can be given.

ILLUSTRATION 1. Many choice-reaction experiments involve a setting in which the subject must move a finger from some initial position to a button or other response device that corresponds to the stimulus. The choice-reaction time is then taken as the time from initiation of the stimulus to the time of button pressing. In the standard arrangement, this time actually includes two phases: (1) a decision time that may include apprehension, perceptual integration, encoding, and retrieval (in the sense that the representation of the response position that corresponds to the stimulus must be found), and (2) response execution, that is, the planning and execution of the movement to the selected response button. Jensen (1980, pp. 688ff.) reports an experimental arrangement that permits at least a partial separation of these two phases. The response apparatus consists of a panel as illustrated in Figure 12.1; before any given stimulus is presented, the subject rests a finger on the button at the bottom center. On presentation of a stimulus (a light at one of the eight positions), the subject moves the finger to press the button next to the light. Decision time is measured as the time from initiation of the stimulus to the time when the subject's finger leaves the home position; movement time is the additional time taken between leaving the home position and pressing a response button. Jensen reports that decision times have fairly low correlations with movement times; these two measurements may therefore be taken to index different ID dimensions. In accordance with Hick's (1952) law, decision times are mainly a function of the stimulus set size, which can be varied from one to eight by superimposing appropriate masks on the apparatus. Presumably movement times are in large part a function of IDs since the distances from the rest position to the response buttons are uniform.

In cognitive tasks involving a choice-reaction feature, the experimental arrangement should permit separate determinations of decision and movement times when IDs in these measures are of interest.

ILLUSTRATION 2. In a choice-reaction experiment used by Keating and Bobbitt (1978) to

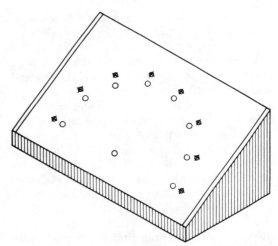

**Figure 12.1.** Subject's console of the reaction time–movement time apparatus. Red push buttons are indicated by circles, faceted green lights by crossed circles. From *Bias in Mental Testing* (p. 689) by A.R. Jensen, 1980. New York: Free Press. Copyright 1980 by the Macmillan Publishing Co. Reprinted by permission.

study IDs developmentally, the setting was such that, if the stimulus light was green, the response was to be made by pushing a button with, say, the left hand, and if the light was red, by responding with the right hand. In this case, one may assume that it was necessary for the subject to perform a relatively difficult corepresentation retrieval process, namely, finding the representation (right or left) that corresponded to the stimulus light color. The total response time would therefore include time for this retrieval process, even though it could be very short and could be minimized by practice. Because the process of translating a color to a corresponding left or right position may depend on a different ID characteristic from those underlying the other processes involved in this experiment, one could recommend that a parallel experimental variation be used in this paradigm to detect the variance associated with this retrieval process.

Both Illustrations 1 and 2 suggest the question, asked by Smith and Stanley (1980), whether the home-button arrangement actually makes possible a clear separation of decision and movement times, since some subjects may respond immediately to the stimulus before actually making a decision, even when carefully instructed not to do so. In this case, model-fitting procedures may be used to detect different subject strategies.

ILLUSTRATION 3. In the stimulus matching paradigm originally employed by Posner and Mitchell (1967), two stimuli—for example, a capital letter such as *A* and a lower-case letter such as *a*—are to be compared for either physical or name identity. (*A* and *a* are not physically identical but they are identical in name.) Posner and Mitchell presented the stimuli simultaneously, closely juxtaposed, but the stimuli may also be presented successively, as in an experiment of Hunt, Frost, and Lunneborg (1973). In simultaneous presentation, the response time would include encoding time for both stimuli, whereas in successive presentation it would include encoding time only for the second stimulus (if response time is measured from initiation of the second stimulus), and possibly a short-term memory component. If encoding and stimulus comparison times depended on different traits of IDs, one might expect somewhat different results from simultaneous versus successive presentations. To be sure, in a study of a word-matching task, Hunt, Davidson, and Lansman (1981) found no differences in correlations for simultaneous and successive presentations with certain reading scores, but this does not exclude the possibility of finding differences in other contexts.

ILLUSTRATION 4. R.J. Sternberg (1977) developed models for assessing component processes in analogical reasoning tasks. In brief, the models involve the computation of regression coefficients to be attached to stimulus values and task characteristics that depend on particular experimental settings. For example, a measurement may reflect the encoding of either one, two, three, or four terms of an analogy of the form $A : B :: C : D$; thus the raw regression coefficient associated with the number of stimulus terms to be encoded is an estimate of the amount of time required for one encoding (on the implicit assumption, probably false in general, that all encodings take the same amount of time). The regression coefficients are computed by placing all the data obtained—whether for a single subject or aggregated over subjects—in a multiple regression system for predicting total response time, and treating the coefficients as ID variables. Sternberg's techniques of componential analy-

sis may be regarded as an elegant elaboration of the subtraction method.

MEASURES OF RESPONSE ACCURACY OR APPROPRIATENESS

Many ID traits reflect the overall accuracy or appropriateness (by some given standard) of the performances of subjects in a given class of settings, or with a given class of stimuli. Many types of cognitive tasks (e.g., free recall tasks) yield data that are scored for overall correctness, and of course most psychometric tests are scored for the number of items correctly answered by an examinee (sometimes with corrections for chance guessing). Forming an ID variable in this way is based on assumptions that the resulting scale represents an appropriate metric for measuring an ability, and that the scale reflects IDs in an ability that can be regarded as unitary (single factored) for some theoretical or practical purpose. The scale may indeed be regarded as having at least ordinal properties (Stevens, 1951), but the likelihood that the scale reflects differences in a single underlying ability is often less than certain. Nevertheless, total number correct scores are customarily employed in various statistical manipulations such as variance ratio tests, correlations, and factor analysis, and if adequate precautions are taken regarding their distributional characteristics (possibly with appropriate scale transformations, as discussed on p. 830, such use is generally safe (Gaito, 1980).

The relations between item responses and abilities can be explored in more detail through techniques available from psychometric test theory, which is concerned mainly with binary response data (e.g., 1 for correct, 0 for incorrect) from a series of items or tasks of a generally similar nature.

In the general case, the items vary in easiness or difficulty, as customarily indexed by the proportions $p$ of subjects that pass them. It is generally assumed that there is a strongly nonlinear relation between $p$ and ability. This assumption is reasonable since an easy item with $p = 1$ could have been passed by subjects whose true ability levels extend over a considerable range; similarly, the true ability levels of subjects failing a hard item (with $p = 0$) could range widely. A simple and customary transformation of item $p$ values to an item difficulty measure referenced to ability levels assumes that abilities are normally distributed and uses the inverse normal probability function. This transformation requires consideration of whether an item can be passed by chance guessing. When the probability $c$ that a subject can pass an item by chance is zero, the ability level of an item is assigned as the normal deviate corresponding to $p$ taken as the cumulative probability in the upper portion of the normal distribution. For example, the ability level of an item with $p = .8$ would be $-.842$. Subjects with that ability level would be expected to have a probability of .5 of passing the item. For items with $a$ alternative choices, the probability of chance success may often be assumed to be $c = 1/a$, and $p$ is rescaled to $p' = (p - c)/(1 - c)$ before taking the inverse probability function. Thus, for a two-choice item with $p = .8$, the adjusted difficulty is $p' = .6$, and the normal deviate value is $-.253$; at that ability level, a subject may be expected to have a .75 probability of passing, or a .5 probability of passing, corrected for chance guessing. This procedure provides at least a scaling of task difficulty whose units and distances are more reasonable than those of raw probabilities. It has the drawback that items with $p = 0$ and 1 must be assigned ability levels of $+\infty$ and $-\infty$, respectively, or arbitrary values of, say, $+3$ and $-3$. It also depends on the possibly questionable assumption of normality of ability distributions. Nevertheless, this assumption has been found to be generally reasonable, and even the most advanced formulations of test theory have difficulty dealing with $p$ values equal or close to 0 or 1.

This procedure, while useful in many circumstances, is concerned only with the ability levels of a group in relation to item difficulties. Also, it considers only one item at a time. The more advanced models of test theory pertain to such relations for individuals over sets of items. The simplest of these models is the so-called Guttman scale (Guttman, 1941, but noted earlier by Walker, 1931), whereby an individual's passing of an item of a given difficulty implies passing all items of lesser difficulty, and failing an item of a given difficulty implies failing all items of greater difficulty. The Guttman scale, which is rarely if ever approximated in practice, can be regarded as a special case of the more general latent-trait model, one version of which—the three parameter logistic model (Lord & Novick, 1968; Lord, 1980)—specifies that the probability

of an individual's passing an item is a function of:

$\theta$ = a parameter specifying the individual's position on the latent ability trait (in the population, mean = 0, standard deviation = 1, but not necessarily normally distributed);

$a$ = a parameter specifying the slope of the function relating probability of passing to $\theta$ and in effect specifying also the degree to which the task performance reflects the ability or abilities measured by an ensemble of items analyzed by this model;

$b$ = a parameter specifying the difficulty of the item, equal to the value of $\theta$ at which $(p - c)/(1 - c) = .5$, i.e., at the inflection point of the function relating probability of passing to $\theta$;

$c$ = a parameter specifying the lower asymptote value of the function, that is, the probability of passing (presumably by guessing or chance) for an individual with infinitely low ability.

In this model, for individual $i$ and item $j$,

$$p_{ij} = c_j + \frac{1 - c_j}{1 + \exp\left[-1.7a_j(\theta_i - b_j)\right]}.$$

The shape of this function, which specifies what is called the item characteristic curve, is very like that of the cumulative normal probability function from $p = c$ to $p = 1$. (It uses the logistic function, which is a mathematically tractable approximation to the normal probability function.) Figure 12.2 depicts, for three items with different parameters, the function relating individuals' probabilities of passing to their ability levels. For comparison, it depicts in item 4 the function implied by the Guttman scale model for an item with $b = .5$, $c = 0$; in the Guttman scale the parameter $a$ becomes infinity.

The popular one-parameter model of Rasch (1980) assumes that the parameter $a$ is uniform for all items and that $c = 0$. In computation, it is somewhat simpler to use than the three-parameter model, but like the three-parameter model it assumes that all items measure the same ability or complex of abilities. In practice, the Rasch model is useful for identifying items that do not fit this model satisfactorily (and thus do not measure the same ability or abilities as the generality of items); it is also useful for scaling item

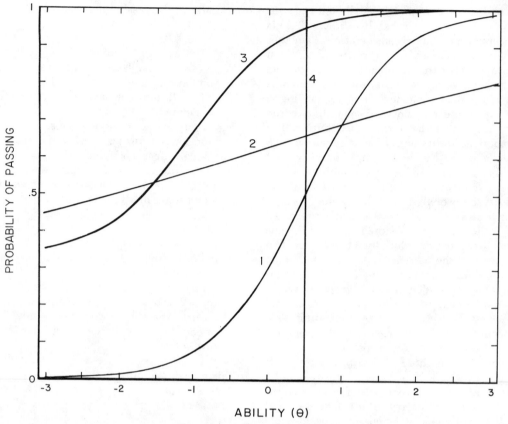

**Figure 12.2.** Item characteristic curves (ICC's) for four items. Parameters are: item 1: $a = 1, b = .5, c = 0$; item 2: $a = .2, b = 0, c = .25$; item 3: $a = 1, b = -1, c = .333$; item 4: $a = \infty, b = .5, c = 0$.

difficulties in a somewhat more elegant and valid fashion than the normal approximation procedure explained at the outset of this section. (For details, see Wright & Stone, 1979; or Thorndike, 1982, pp. 96–104.) All these model-fitting procedures, especially the three-parameter model, appear to require fairly large data sets. Unfortunately, the assumptions of the Rasch model are often too strong to be safely acceptable.

Lord and Novick (1968) and Lord (1980) show that for typical psychometric tests the theoretical relation between $\theta$ (ability) and the number of correct scores, though monotonic, is generally nonlinear; the departures from linearity are generally not marked, however, and become pronounced mainly toward the tails of the distribution.

Recent advances have made it possible to examine the important question of what makes an item or a task difficult, in terms of the cog-

nitive processes that contribute to its performance.

ILLUSTRATION 1. Whitely (1980a, 1980b) has developed models by which one can attempt to predict or fit ability test performances by estimating item and person parameters of information-processing components. She calls these models multicomponent latent trait models. In one application of her procedure, she gave verbal analogy items to subjects under two conditions: (1) regular test administration with no time limit, and (2) administration of three subtasks of the same items, (a) image construction (finding and stating the rule governing the item), (b) event recovery (verification or modification of the rule, given the five item alternatives), and (c) response evaluation (choice of correct answer, given both the correct rule and the five alternatives). Table 12.1 illustrates these tasks. Correctness of each

**Table 12.1.   Examples of experimental component tasks for verbal analogies**

| | |
|---|---|
| *Subtask 1*<br>Image construction | Blue:_____ ::Yellow:Orange<br>Rule?_____ |
| *Subtask 2*<br>Event recovery | Blue:_____ ::Yellow:Orange<br>(1) Purple (2) Red (3) Green (4) Brown (5) Gold<br>New Rule?_____ |
| *Subtask 3*<br>Response evaluation | Blue:_____ ::Yellow:Orange<br>Rule: Color obtained when red is added to blue<br>(1) Purple (2) Red (3) Green (4) Brown (5) Gold<br>Circle answer that best fulfills the given rule. |

*Note.* From "Multicomponent Latent Trait Models for Ability Tests" by S.E. Whitely, 1980, *Psychometrika*, 45, p. 489. Copyright 1980 by Psychometrika. Reprinted by permission.

task was assessed separately, and the data were found to give good multiple-regression predictions of item difficulties and total scores, suggesting that solution of verbal analogy items depends on the two separate abilities of image construction and response evaluation. Whitely does not give the correlation between these abilities, and it is not clear what cognitive processes they tap. Nevertheless, Whitely's techniques have promise for further use.

ILLUSTRATION 2. Mulholland, Pellegrino, and Glaser (1980) examined performance on a geometric analogy task in 28 adults and found that solution errors were highly predictable from the number of elements in the stimulus materials, the number of transformations involved, and their product. Whitely and Schneider (1981) used a linear logistic model (Fischer, 1973) to analyze item-difficulty (error) data from 211 undergraduates who were administered geometric analogy items. They tested the Mulholland et al. model and then two more elaborated models. For the first model, number of elements was a significant variable but number of transformations was not. The second model used number of elements, but transformations were classed separately as either distortions or displacements. In this model, in which item difficulties (as scaled by the Rasch model) were predicted with $r = .68$, number of elements was not significantly related to item difficulty, but increased displacements made items harder, while increased number of distortions slightly decreased item difficulty. With further subdivisions of displacements and distortions, a third model produced slightly better predictions ($r = .73$). According to Whitely and Schneider, all the items were found to be homo-

geneous in the sense of testing a common ability or abilities. It is perhaps too generous to assert that these findings reveal cognitive processes, but the data on what elements of tasks contribute to task difficulty have at least the potential of leading to interpretations of cognitive processes.

ILLUSTRATION 3. The previous illustrations pertain to relations between items (tasks) and subjects' probabilities of passing those items, as a function of the subjects' abilities. It is also possible to model these relations as a function of item difficulty, yielding what has been called the person characteristic function. This function is best depicted when probabilities of passing are plotted for groups of individuals with similar score levels for groups of items with similar difficulties. Figure 12.3 depicts such data for the Seashore Sense of Pitch test, a test of pitch discrimination ability. These data were collected by the writer and analyzed in another publication (Carroll, 1983a). The test contains ten groups of two-choice items, each group consisting of 10 pairs of tones that differ by a given number of hertz. The subject is asked to indicate whether the second tone is higher or lower than the first. The probability of chance success, $c$, is taken to be .5. The figure shows that subjects differ systematically in their person characteristic functions, with the probabilities of responding to items correctly being a function of item difficulty as indexed by pitch difference. Pitch discrimination ability is thus shown to be defined in terms of a special relation between individual characteristics and attributes of pitch discrimination tasks.

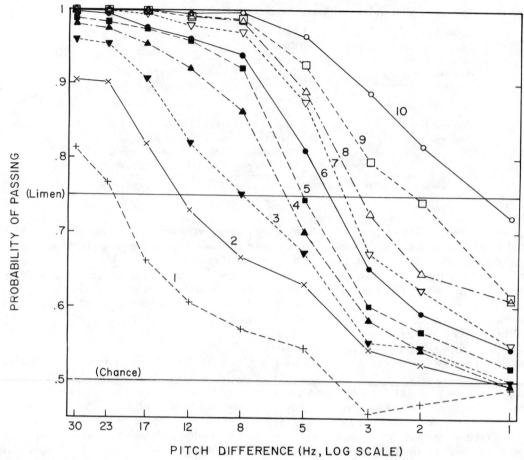

**Figure 12.3.** Mean person characteristic functions for deciles of total scores of 1,080 individuals on nine subtests of the Seashore Sense of Pitch test (1919 edition). Between 90 and 130 cases contributed to the curves, with an average of 108.

ILLUSTRATION 4. Figure 12.4 shows similar data for 119 10th-grade children given a block-counting test that appears to measure some kind of spatial ability and, more weakly, numerical ability. (The data were collected by E.S. Johnson and A. Meade, personal communication). As in Figure 12.3 items are grouped by item difficulty, and person characteristic curves are shown for groups of subjects of approximately similar total scores. Since the items required free responses, $c$ may be regarded as equal to zero. What is of particular interest is that the difficulties of the 32 items (as scaled in normal deviate values) could be predicted with multiple $R = .66$ ($p < .001$) from certain characteristics of the items, namely, the number of non-visible (hidden) blocks, and the judged symmetry of the

figure—that is, the degree to which the item could be solved by such simple arithmetic operations as multiplying the number of blocks in one dimension by the number of blocks in another dimension. Figure 12.5 gives examples of items varying in these characteristics. From this, it can be inferred that high scores on block counting are achieved by subjects who can visualize the hidden blocks accurately and can use simple arithmetical processes, when that is feasible, to compute answers.

PARAMETERS OF FUNCTIONAL RELATIONS

It is increasingly possible to describe psychological phenomena in terms of mathematical models and functional relations. Insofar as such models provide satisfactory fits to data from individual

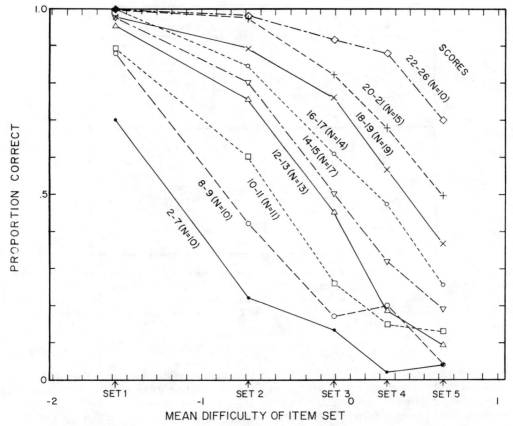

**Figure 12.4.** Mean person characteristic functions for nine total score groups on 26 items of a block-counting test given to 10th-grade students. The curves are plotted as a function of probabilities of correct scores for five item sets ranging in mean difficulty. All sets contain five items except set 3, which contains six items.

subjects, certain parameters of such functional relations may be considered as measures of IDs. Some examples of these possibilities have already been alluded to, for example, Jensen's (1980) application of Hick's (1952) law to determine for each subject the slope and intercept of the (linear) relation between choice reaction time and number of alternatives, expressed in bits, $\log_2 n$. Similarly, slope and intercept parameters can be computed (Chiang & Atkinson, 1976) for individuals' performances in S. Sternberg's (1966) short-term memory task and in the visual search task (Atkinson, Holmgren & Juola, 1969); in these paradigms, latency is related linearly, not with the logarithm of the number of elements in the display, but simply with that number itself. Rose and Fernandes

(1977) determined the parameters $A$ and $B$ from individual subjects' data for the equation $y = AX^B$ (or in its logarithmic form, $\log y = \log A + B \log X$) describing the probability of correct response as a function of lag in Shepard and Teghtsoonian's (1961) running memory recognition task. One of the most elaborate models was proposed by Atkinson and Shiffrin (1968) for performance in a continuous paired-associate task. Hunt, Frost, and Lunneborg (1973; Hunt & Lansman, 1975) estimated for each individual in their sample the four parameters postulated by this model and found certain relations of these parameters with scores on a scholastic aptitude test. It should be pointed out, however, that estimates of these parameters for individuals may contain a considerable amount of error unless

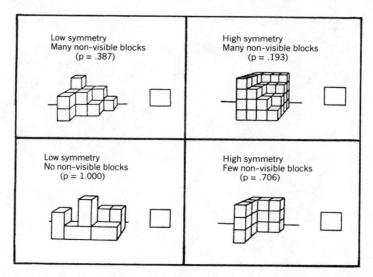

**Figure 12.5.** Sample block-counting items, arranged to suggest the effect of symmetry and of the number of non-visible blocks on item difficulty ($p$ = proportion of 10th-grade students giving correct answer). Subjects are instructed that all blocks in a given picture are of the same shape. Test items copyright 1986 by Industrial Psychology Inc., 515 Madison Avenue, New York, NY 10022. All rights reserved. Permission granted for limited reproduction in this instance only.

there is a very large number of trials. In fact, Atkinson and Shiffrin estimated these parameters only for data aggregated over subjects. Simpler scores (e.g., total number correct, or number correct over certain ranges of lags) seem to be more satisfactory and reliable for scoring individuals' performances on the Atkinson–Shiffrin task, even though they may not faithfully reflect the processes postulated by Atkinson and Shiffrin.

### Problems in Separating Temporal and Accuracy Parameters

Most mental ability tests can be viewed as collections of cognitive tasks (Carroll, 1976). Such tests are often administered with a time limit such that not all examinees are able to attempt all items. When these same tests are given without a time limit, the scores are usually quite highly correlated with time limit scores. For this reason, it is often asserted that speeded and unspeeded tests yield approximately similar information about examinees. Such an assertion neglects the fact that the high correlations are largely due to a part-whole relation: unspeeded scores contain the speeded scores plus whatever additional items the examinee is able to answer correctly in additional time. Davidson and Carroll (1945) found that for most subtests of a typical

intelligence test—the Army Alpha—time-limit scores could be interpreted as functions of two largely independent components—speed (rate at which items are attempted) and level of mastery. Their method was to administer a test first with a prescribed time limit, noting numbers of items attempted as a measure of rate of performance, and then allowing examinees to try all items, in essentially unlimited time, using a differently colored pencil, with number correct in the unlimited time as the level score. Davidson and Carroll found level scores essentially uncorrelated with speed or rate-of-performance scores; speed and level scores were correlated only for tasks in which a problem-solving feature enabled subjects to detect when they had arrived at a correct solution. Time-limit scores could generally be well predicted from speed and level scores with multiple-regression equations. This method of separating speed and level components of ability is not totally satisfactory, however, as Lohman (1979) and Rindler (1979) have noted. To make a series of spatial ability tests more amenable to analysis of speed versus level of ability effects, Egan (1978) converted them to a two-choice format and presented individual items in an experimental setting that permitted accuracy and latency of response to be measured separately. Although the finding is limited by the fact that the sample was to some extent preselected on spatial ability, Egan found essentially zero correlations between scores for speed and for level of accuracy. Nevertheless, scores for both latency and level of accuracy were related to identifiable item (task) characteristics. It would be profitable to apply Egan's procedure of presenting individual items to psychometric tests in other ability domains.

### Abilities and Processes

Illustrations in the immediately preceding sections have given concrete examples of relations between processes and abilities. There seems to be no formally and widely accepted definition of the phrase psychological process. (In many discussions this phrase is replaced by such terms as operation or component.) Loosely, the phrase refers to any action or event (or sequence of such actions or events) in covert or overt behavior that can be demonstrated to take place in a lawful manner. The goals of cognitive psychology are to determine what psychological processes can be demonstrated and to specify the laws governing them. The cognitive operations listed earlier are examples of such presumed processes, but investigators are far from demonstrating these processes satisfactorily or from fully specifying their laws.

We assume that psychological processes occur in the performance of cognitive tasks—indeed, that they are necessary and sufficient causes of whatever performance occurs, whether it is evaluated as successful or unsuccessful, or correct or incorrect. Nonetheless, an ability can be defined in terms of a special relation between a characteristic of an individual and whatever psychological processes are needed to increase the likelihood that a task will be performed to satisfy some criterion of success.

Consider, for example, the pitch discrimination ability whose person characteristic functions are depicted in Figure 12.3. The essential psychological process that must occur in order to increase the likelihood of correct performance in a pitch discrimination task is that a pitch difference must be perceived and used as the basis of a response. Individuals with superior pitch discrimination ability are more likely to perceive a given difference in pitch, and respond accordingly, than individuals with lower pitch discrimination ability. In other words, the

psychological processes that eventuate in correct responses are more likely to occur in individuals with superior ability. Exactly what processes are necessary for correct performance of a task is to be inferred from consideration of task characteristics. For pitch discrimination, many of the processes listed earlier can be involved, but the essential process appears to be stimulus comparison—comparison of tonal stimuli. The individual's pitch-discriminating ability is defined in terms of the psychometric function relating magnitude of pitch differences and likelihood of correct performance for that individual.

Similar lines of reasoning can be invoked to characterize relations between processes and other categories of ability. For example, abilities measured by the block counting test (see Figures 12.4 and 12.5) pertain to the processes of visualizing blocks that are not visible in the pictorial representation of a pile of blocks and using arithmetical operations to compute numbers of blocks; abilities in the Sternberg short-term memory task, as measured by intercept and slope parameters, are related to the times of processes involved in perceiving stimuli and scanning for memory matches; and so on.

It would be a mistake to identify an ability with a process, even though the logical relation is close. An ability is a characteristic of an individual; a process is an event or a series of events. The relation between process and ability has to do with how individual characteristics govern the probability, speed, or accuracy of the process.

## Use of Individual Difference Variables in Experimental Design

In much experimental research, ID variables function as nuisance variables—"undesired sources of variation in an experiment that may affect the dependent variable," according to Kirk (1982, p. 6). They are present because conditions must normally be replicated over subjects in order for findings to be generalizable. This is not the place to set out the various types of experimental designs that are available to control the possible effects and biases introduced by nuisance variables. According to several writers, these designs utilize various strategies to control experimental bias (Anderson, Auquier, Hauck, Oakes, Vandaele & Weisberg, 1980; Kirk, 1982;

and Winer, 1971). The most generally recommended strategy is random assignment of subjects to conditions or treatments. The advantage of randomization is that all possible nuisance variables (including ID variables) enter the treatment groups and affect the dependent variable or variables with the same a priori likelihood. With random assignment, it is not in principle necessary to take or use any measurements of ID variables that are not themselves dependent variables in the design. However, unless the treatment groups are of substantial size, uncontrolled though relevant variation among groups can introduce biases that, though statistically significant, may be, at least in part, artifactual. Even when subjects have been randomly assigned to treatments, measurements of possibly relevant ID variables should be taken and used as covariates to adjust results by statistical means, as in ANCOVA designs. This makes possible an estimate of the amount of bias that may be due to the covariates. At the same time, in making statistical adjustments, experimenters must keep in mind that they may not have measured all the relevant ID variables. The selecting of appropriate ID variables as covariates needs to be done with an awareness of relevant research literature on what kinds of ID variables may be sources of bias in a particular setting. Only with evidence from successive experiments that converge on a particular conclusion, using different types of ID variables, can one attain reasonable confidence that all relevant sources of ID bias have been adequately controlled.

Many experimental designs are available in which ID variation is controlled experimentally rather than statistically. Simple designs of this type use the technique of blocking, that is, using an ID variable to assign subjects to groups that are crossed with a treatment variable. For example, in an experiment on the effect of three different presentation times on paired-associate learning, one might have two groups for each presentation time condition, one from above-average and the other from below-average IQ ranges. (The groups would still be randomly assigned to conditions, from the above-average and below-average IQ pools.) This assignment would be done on the assumption that IQ is a variable that is relevant to whatever effect is represented in the dependent variable. It would probably be more useful to employ an ID variable more directly relevant to the phenomenon

being observed, for example, paired-associate learning ability as measured by a pretest. More complicated designs, generally using the Latin-square principle, attempt to control two or more ID variables simultaneously. The advantage claimed for blocking and Latin-square designs that use ID variables as a basis for classification is that they reduce the size of the error term and increase statistical power, and when relevant ID variables are employed, this is indeed the case.

Several cautions should be borne in mind in such use of ID variables, however. For one, the use of a small number of discrete categories of an ID variable is likely to involve a serious loss of information when the ID variable is on a continuous scale, as is true of most test scores. Generally, use of statistical adjustment by ANCOVA procedures is preferable to either blocking or the classifications required by Latin-square designs. For another, the use of two or more ID variables in a design that requires them to be orthogonal may make the experiment unrealistic if the ID variables are significantly correlated in the population from which subjects are drawn. Again, statistical control of such variables is generally preferable to direct experimental control by means of classifications. The variables used in designs involving classifications should generally be restricted to those that can be meaningfully manipulated and expressed as treatment levels. ID variables are not such variables.

As was noted above, the use of ID variables in experimental designs, whether by experimental or statistical controls, requires a knowledge of the types of ID variables likely to be relevant in a particular setting. A later section of this chapter attempts a survey of the varieties of ID variables that can be identified; it cannot, of course, offer suggestions or details about which variables might be relevant in a particular experimental setting. It is the responsibility of the investigator to select the variables most appropriate to the problem under study. Sometimes one or more measures of broad factors of abilities may be appropriate; at other times, measures of narrower abilities may lead to more incisive results. This would be true whenever the phenomenon being studied is closely related to an ability factor. For example, in studying phenomena of spatial perception, it could be advisable to employ statistical controls that rely on measures of one or more spatial abilities.

When experiments address the effects of treatments (practice, training, drugs, etc.) on ID variables, it may be advisable to study more than one dependent variable. Although different ID dependent variables can be studied in a series of experiments or in a series of separate analyses of a data set, a more efficient and often more illuminating procedure is a MANOVA (multiple ANOVA) design (Cooley & Lohnes, 1971). This will be true even when the several dependent variables are largely unrelated. In some cases the ID dependent variables may be considered as functions of a series of hierarchically ordered latent variables. For example, in a study of training effects on Piagetian conservation performances, the total variance in a series of performance measures might include systematic uniqueness in each measure, conservation of, say, volume, general conservation ability, a broad reasoning or Gf factor (see p. 848), and general intelligence, along with random error. MANOVA and related designs could be set up to estimate which if any of these types of variance are affected by treatments.

Finally, experimentalists may find it useful to consider the possibility of aptitude-treatment interactions (ATI), that is, the possibility that experimental treatments have effects that are systematically dependent on individual's aptitudes and abilities. Techniques for studying such interactions have been reviewed by Cronbach and Snow (1977). Although these techniques have been used most extensively in research on instructional treatments, they are equally applicable to many other phases of experimental research in psychology.

## SELECTED ASPECTS OF PSYCHOMETRIC METHODOLOGY

### Measurements and Scales

Although it has been much discussed and refined (Roberts, 1979), Stevens's (1951) classification of measurement scales in the first edition of this *Handbook* is still useful and relevant (Nunnally, 1978, pp. 12–24). There is the danger, however, of taking some of Stevens's precepts too strictly. Some investigators have tended to reject or devalue any scale that cannot be clearly defended as better than ordinal, such as the scales on many psychometric tests scored in terms of number correct. Actually, there are good reasons for considering such scales as approximately of interval level; but even if they are not, they can be used in most statistical contexts without seriously violating the assumptions underlying the statistics (Gaito, 1980).

At the same time, the scientific status of psychology can be promoted most effectively if both experimental and differential psychologists attempt to use measurements whose units can be clearly defined. Often this can be accomplished by the use of ratio scales that refer to physical measurements. In certain areas of psychometrics, notably in educational measurements, the discomfort with purely normative measurements (referenced only to score distributions of presumably but questionably representative samples of examinees) has been expressed in the push toward so-called criterion-referenced measurements (Berk, 1980). These are basically measurements whose quantitative values can be referred to identifiable levels of performance, behavior, knowledge, and skill. Developments in cognitive psychology appear to be moving in somewhat the same direction, in that many of the measurements reported in that field refer to identifiable levels of performance, probabilities of response, and the like. Surely this is a promising trend, worthy of being encouraged and promoted.

Many of the free parameters of psychological laws are related to IDs. Until now, it has rarely been possible to express these parameters in absolute measurement or in terms of event probabilities that could be dealt with in appropriate nomothetic and mathematical networks. Psychologists have usually measured IDs on an arbitrary, relativistic, or norm-referenced basis. Measures of performance in cognitive tasks, however, offer the possibility of bringing ID data into the realm of absolute measurement. Latency measurements are normally expressed in milliseconds or seconds, whereas accuracy measures can be expressed in proportions or probabilities. The component scores of R.J. Sternberg's (1977) componential analysis can be treated as times or probabilities. Some stimulus characteristics can be expressed in physical units, and some of the attributes of words, for example, can be referred to frequencies and probabilities (Rubin, 1980).

From this perspective, it should be possible to express many ID parameters as measurements in a physical and real number system. For some time, digit-span performance has been stated in such a system (of course, with certain psychophysical assumptions concerning thresholds and gradients), but similar logic could be applied to performance in various other cognitive tasks. Further attention would need to be given to the nomothetic description of experimental conditions, stimuli, and performance relations. Research and development along such lines, together with further developments in latent trait theory (Lord & Novick, 1968; Whitely, 1980a) should make it possible, eventually, to reduce greatly the use of normative procedures of measurement.

## Scale Transformations

Experimentalists are accustomed to applying scale transformations to measurements in order to make them conform to the requirements of certain statistical methodologies, in particular to ANOVA's requirements for homogeneity of variance. For example, probabilities are often subjected to the arc-sine transformation; positively skewed distributions are subjected to a square-root transformation, and so on. For discussions of various problems of scale transformation, many of which may be pertinent to ID research, see Budescu and Wallsten (1979), Smith (1976), and Wainer (1977).

Scale transformations are also sometimes desirable to meet certain requirements of Pearsonian correlation coefficients—not a requirement that the distributions be approximately Gaussian, however (for this is not actually a requirement of the Pearsonian coefficient), but a requirement that the marginal distributions be approximately similar, even if not normal, when linear relations are to be measured (Carroll, 1961).

Scale transformations should not, of course, be applied merely to meet requirements of statistical techniques. For example, to achieve conformity with universal systems of measurement, there are reasons for recommending the conversion of time per unit of performance measurements to measurements of performance per unit of time (by the reciprocal transformation) and the use of logarithmic units in the measurement of certain frequency and probability phenomena, for example, of word frequency, where a convenient scale is provided by Carroll's Standard Frequency Index:

$$SFI = 10 \ (\log_{10} p + 10),$$

where $p$ = word probability (see Carroll, 1970; Carroll & White, 1973). The IDs in speed of performance are often more normally distributed if expressed in performance per unit of time than if expressed as time per unit of performance.

## Concepts of Measurement Precision, Reliability, and Stability

For various historical reasons, concepts of measurement precision, reliability, and stability have been surrounded by much confusion in logic and terminology. The following discussion attempts to clarify matters for experimental psychologists seeking to apply these concepts to measurements of IDs.

Start by considering a single observation, a reaction time of, say, 253 msec obtained in a particular experimental setting on a single individual. We may ask how precise, reliable, and stable this measurement is. Precision of measurement could pertain to the precision of the apparatus used in obtaining the value and whether the measurement is accurate to the nearest 10 msec, 1 msec, or 0.1 msec or to some form of systematic apparatus error whereby all measurements are actually, on the average, say, 5.3 msec greater than their true values. Stability of measurement would concern whether a similar measurement would be obtained on a quite different occasion, perhaps after the individual had practiced the task or had been subject to some physiological change such as fatigue or the effect of a toxic substance. Unfortunately, the concept of reliability embraces both precision of measurement and stability, though it is not usually concerned with systematic error, only with error that is in some sense random around some hypothetical true value. Essentially, the concept of reliability has to do with the extent to which measurements are free of random error. In classical measurement theory, our observed value, $X = 253$ msec, would be conceived of as the sum of a true value $T$ and an error $E$. Assessing the reliability of $X$ is tantamount to assessing the possible size of the error term $E$, because for a particular experimental setting and a particular occasion we may assume that $T$ has some unknown, constant value.

All assessments of reliability depend in some way on obtaining replicate measurements. The replicate measurements can be taken either close together in time or over varying periods of time. The longer the time interval between them, the greater is the possibility that the value of the true score $T$ changes as a function of some combination of causative variables. Thus, the concept of reliability shades into that of stability.

Suppose that a series of 10 replicate measurements are taken on a single subject in the course of 2 minutes, and that no systematic trend in the measurements is noted. Let us suppose that the standard deviation of the ten measures is 23.4 msec. In classical measurement theory, this value is an estimate of the standard error of measurement. It is almost solely a matter of judgment to decide whether this standard deviation is small—sufficiently small to indicate satisfactory reliability. One might seek to assess this value by obtaining another series of 10 measurements, perhaps on the next day. If the variance of measurements on another occasion is not significantly different from that on the first occasion, one could at least regard these values as estimates of the characteristic precision of the total measurement procedure, but there would remain the problem of assessing the magnitude of the value. Of course, in practice one may need only to assess whether the value is small enough to support some type of experimental finding, such as the effect of different delay intervals. This might be done by conventional ANOVA computations, in which variance due to different conditions is compared with variance within conditions. Such computations can be carried out even with data from a single subject, but greater generalizability of findings would result with the use of data from a number of subjects, regardless of whether any reliable IDs are noted in the data.

The psychometric concept of reliability has dealt mainly with the reliability of ID measurements. Lord and Novick (1968, p. 61) define the reliability of a test as the squared correlation between observed scores and true scores, and such a correlation is almost always regarded as being taken over individuals. Obviously, reliability cannot be assessed directly through this definition, because true scores cannot be observed. If it is assumed, however, that the variance of observed scores is equal to the variance of true scores plus the variance of errors (because errors are assumed to be uncorrelated with true scores), one can estimate reliability (rel) by estimating the error variance term in the

formula

$$rel = 1 - (error\ variance)/(observed\ variance),$$

which, it so happens, is algebraically equivalent to the correlation between observed score and true score. Since this correlation happens to equal the correlation between two parallel measurements, the latter correlation can be taken as equal to the reliability of either of the parallel measurements. This last equality is the basis for a variety of psychometric procedures for evaluating reliability, such as the split-half reliability (usually corrected for length by the Spearman-Brown formula), the alternate-form reliability, and the test-retest reliability. All these formulas yield only approximations, however, and their accuracy would depend on the parallelism of the measurements, the amount of extraneous influence from practice, learning, and so on.

The basic formula for reliability given above can also be expressed as:

$$rel = \frac{true\ variance}{true\ variance + error\ variance}.$$

Here, the true variance is normally variance of true scores over individuals, while error variance is variance of replicate measurements within individuals. From this, it can be seen that the psychometric concept of reliability concerns both what may be called the reliability of IDs and the precision of measurement. A measuring procedure cannot have a high reliability coefficient unless there is substantial variance of true scores over individuals compared to the variance of replicate measurements within individuals. It also follows that the reliability of a test or measuring procedure depends partly on the variability of true scores observed in a particular sample. If a particular sample happens to be relatively homogeneous in true scores, the measuring procedure may appear to be unreliable, when in fact it could have quite satisfactory reliability when applied to a heterogeneous sample.

Thus, the psychometric concept of reliability —even when carefully defined and treated in an axiomatic system—is at best ambiguous, because it depends on both the range of a trait or characteristic in a sample and the precision of the measurements taken. For this reason, the concept and its measurement must be handled with caution. It is preferable to concern oneself primarily with the separate variances that contribute to reliability—the estimated true score variance over individuals and, more important, the estimated variances of replicate measurements within individuals and over occasions. Generally, the goal should be to develop measurement procedures that minimize the variance of replicate measurements. One can do little about the distribution of true score variance except perhaps by controlling the sampling of individuals.

In an experimental context, one is likely to be concerned with the variance of multiple replicate measurements, rather than the paired scores usually treated in psychometric contexts. Associated with such variances are the standard errors of measurements averaged over replications, which are a function of the number of measurements averaged. In the relatively frequent case in which $n$ measurements are collected on each of $N$ individuals, the ANOVA procedures suggested by Ebel (1951) and Winer (1971, pp. 283–296) prove useful if the estimation of standard errors of measurement from within-individual error terms is stressed over the estimation of reliability itself. Winer provides adjustments for anchor points, that is, differential biases of particular series of measurements, say, from different raters or apparatus configurations, and Ebel provides for the case in which the number of measurements varies over individuals. In more complex situations, for example, in an experimental design that investigates a series of treatments and interactions, special steps may have to be taken to estimate measurement error. An example involving the assessment of IDs in learning is discussed by Leicht, Miller, and Ramseyer (1978). Another illustration is provided in Baxter's (1942) classic study of reaction time.

One of the standard formulas of classical test theory is the so-called Spearman-Brown equation, which gives the reliability of a test of length $k$ ($\text{rel}_k$) relative to that of a test of unit length ($\text{rel}_1$). The formula is:

$$\text{rel}_k = \frac{k(\text{rel}_1)}{1 + (k - 1)(\text{rel}_1)}.$$

Of possibly more use in experimental contexts is a formula that can be derived either from this equation or from conventional sampling theory, namely, the formula for the decrease of the standard error (se) of measurement when the number of equivalent measurements taken is multiplied by $k$. The formula is simply

$$(\text{se})^2_{nk} = \frac{(\text{se})^2_n}{k}.$$

For example, if the standard error of measurement for measurements averaged over 10 replications is 2, it could be reduced to 1 by averaging measurements over 40 replications.

As yet there is little information on the reliabilities and standard errors of measurement of cognitive tasks. Rose and Fernandes (1977) offer test-retest (day 1, day 2) reliability data on 40 variables from a variety of cognitive tasks such as the Posner stimulus matching paradigm, the S. Sternberg short-term memory paradigm, and the Clark and Chase sentence-verification paradigm. These reliabilities range from $-.06$ (a theoretically impossible value) to .90, with a median of .515. Rose and Fernandes point out, however, that many of these test-retest correlations (actually, largely measurements of stability) are sensitive to strategy changes on the part of the subject, as well as to substantial practice effects. Kennedy, Carter, and Bittner (1980) present data on the stability characteristics of a number of performance tasks being evaluated for use in the assessment of environmental effects on behavior. Of 60 tasks they studied, they state that "all tasks . . . exhibit stable means and variances after adequate practice but: (a) less than 30% meet minimal stability criteria for intertrial correlations, and (b) substantial practice (typically more than an hour over five days) is required to achieve stability."

The effect of practice on performing these tasks presents a dilemma: the tasks may not be stable until they are well practiced, but if the learning ability of the subject is in question, it is conceivable that the most important variance is precisely that observed during the early phases of practice. In several studies, Fleishman (Fleishman & Hempel, 1954, 1955; Fleishman & Fruchter, 1960) showed that the factorial composition of the early stages of a learning task appears to be different from that of the later stages. In the absence of studies of cognitive task performance that cover protracted periods of practice, what is measured in a single test at an early stage of practice may be quite inadequate for assessing what might be measured by the same task at later stages of practice.

Mention of practice effects may prompt the reader to question whether IDs are real in the

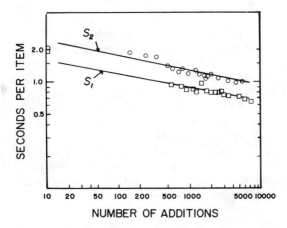

**Figure 12.6.** Gradual improvement in mental arithmetic with long continued practice. (From Fitts, 1964, p. 266, stated to be after Blackburn, 1936 though the figure is not found in that source.) From "Perceptual-Motor Skill Learning" by P.M. Fitts in *Categories of Human Learning* (p. 266), A.W. Melton (Ed.), 1964. New York: Academic Press. Copyright 1964 by Academic Press. Reprinted by permission.

**Table 12.2. Illustration of a simplex matrix: Intercorrelations of normalized scores on selected trials of a visual discrimination reaction task ($N = 264$)**

| Trial | 1 | 3 | 5 | 7 | 9 | 11 | 13 | 15 |
|-------|------|------|------|------|------|------|------|------|
| 1 | 1.00 | | | | | | | |
| 3 | .74 | 1.00 | | | | | | |
| 5 | .71 | .82 | 1.00 | | | | | |
| 7 | .69 | .78 | .83 | 1.00 | | | | |
| 9 | .62 | .74 | .79 | .80 | 1.00 | | | |
| 11 | .59 | .68 | .72 | .74 | .77 | 1.00 | | |
| 13 | .57 | .66 | .72 | .72 | .73 | .74 | 1.00 | |
| 15 | .56 | .64 | .71 | .74 | .77 | .80 | .79 | 1.00 |

*Note.* From "The Relation between Abilities and Improvement with Practice in a Visual Discrimination Task" by E.A. Fleishman and W.E. Hempel, Jr., 1955, *Journal of Experimental Psychology, 49*, p. 305.

sense of representing variance over and above any environmental and learning effects. An extreme environmentalist might claim, on the assumption that human beings are infinitely plastic, that all IDs represent nothing more than differential opportunities for learning and practice and differences in individuals' taking advantage of these opportunities. Although it is impossible to reject this argument completely, we may consider certain types of counterevidence. Examine, for example, Figure 12.6, presented by Fitts (1964, p. 266) from an earlier investigation by Blackburn (1936) of improvement in mental arithmetic with long-continued practice. The figure shows improvement curves for two subjects. Could it be said that the curve for subject 1 is essentially the same as that for subject 2, except that it begins at a later stage of practice? Since the improvement is a function of the logarithm of the number of mental additions, it can easily be seen that the curve for subject 1 could not be an extension of the curve for subject 2. An additional 5000 opportunities given to subject 2 for practice after a first 5000 trials did not result in as much improvement as subject 1 was able to achieve in the first 5000 trials. The parameters for the two subjects are different, and the differences between them are real. It seems reasonable to assume that similar findings would present themselves for many other types of cognitive tasks.

Intercorrelations of scores on successive stages of a learning task often take the form of what is called a simplex matrix. In the example given by Fleishman and Hempel (1955; Table 12.2 here), correlations between scores on trials near to each other in the series are distinctly higher than correlations between trials distant from each other, and in general the correlations decrease with their distance from the diagonal of the matrix. Such tables do not conform to the ordinary common factor model of factor analysis, to be discussed below (pp. 835ff.); Cureton and D'Agostino (1983, pp. 372–388) present the special techniques that can be used for analyzing them. Interpretation of such data usually appeals to the notion that, while the generally positive correlations indicate the operation of a general factor of learning ability over all stages of learning, the simplex form suggests that increments of learning at successive stages have low or zero correlations.

## Correlational and Factor Analysis

### Correlational Analysis

Since almost the beginning of the history of psychometrics (Spearman, 1904), the correlational method has been used to investigate ID variables and their relations. It has often been assumed that to the extent that two variables are intercorrelated, they measure the same thing. Even today, investigators frequently rely on single correlation coefficients between two variables to draw conclusions about the commonality of the processes measured by the variables. For example, Cohen and Sandberg (1977) reported correlations between an IQ measure and certain variables derived from a short-term memory task, in an effort to identify which aspects of the short-term memory task were loaded with intelligence. Similarly, Hock (1973), reporting a correlation of .6 between what he called a symmetry effect and a rotation effect in a study of reaction times on same-different comparison tasks involving dot patterns, claimed that the correlation represented presence or absence of structural processing in performing the tasks. (For further discussion of these examples, see Carroll, 1978). A single correlation coefficient, however, is seldom very informative. Instead of asserting that two highly correlated variables measure the same thing, it would be more accurate to conclude that they have in common one or more sources of variance. Only through the study of interrelationships with further variables can one begin to draw firmer conclusions about the identity of these sources of variance. The method of choice for these more detailed studies has been factor analysis.

Whether correlations are studied in an isolated way or through factor analysis, it is important first to consider the nature of the correlations themselves. The size of the sample is relevant, especially with certain types of correlation coefficients. The most frequently used is the Pearsonian product-moment correlation, tested for significance by standard statistical procedures. It is not always realized, however, that with a small $N$ even a single outlier case can make the difference between a highly significant and a nonsignificant coefficient. The jackknifing procedures recommended by Tukey (1977) provide a possible safeguard against drawing unwarranted conclusions from questionable data.

There are of course logistic difficulties in performing cognitive task research with large numbers of individually tested subjects. Many investigators have been satisfied with a fairly small sample of cases, for example, with $N < 50$. Results of such studies must be viewed with caution; while small samples could possibly give meaningful results, such results would need replication. Ideally $N$ becomes minimally acceptable for factor analytic studies only if it is around 100, and if the variables are dichotomous, somewhat larger $N$s are needed to achieve acceptable levels of interpretative significance, especially if tetrachoric correlations are used. A rule of thumb for deciding on sample size is to set $N$ equal to at least $2m + 2^m$, where $m$ is the anticipated number of factors, in order to make it likely that all regions of the factor space will be adequately filled by the sample of persons. (For small values of $m$, $N$ should be much larger than this quantity.)

The scaling of variables and the nature of their distributions are pertinent to correlational analysis. If the variables are measured on essentially continuous scales (divided, say, into at least five intervals), and show distributions of comparable shapes, the Pearsonian correlation coefficient can be used to investigate linear relations among variables. If the distributions are highly skewed, however, some type of scale transformation may be considered in order to make distributions more comparable (somewhere between Gaussian and rectangular, let us say). Although nonlinear relations are rarely encountered with cognitive ability variables when precautions have been taken to ensure comparable distribution shapes, it is recommended that checks for significant nonlinearity be made routinely. (Unfortunately, most standard computer packages make little provision for such checks.) If significant nonlinearity is discovered, consideration should be given to the possibility of further scale transformations to eliminate such nonlinearity. This recommendation applies especially if data are to be analyzed by factor analysis, because of the linear models assumed in factor analysis.

Dichotomous variables, or variables grouped into a small number of classes, present special problems in correlational and factor analysis. Often, it is not unreasonable to employ biserial and tetrachoric correlations, even though these techniques assume an underlying normal distribution of the variables. Phi coefficients (which are actually Pearsonian coefficients applied to dichotomous data) are subject to considerable distortion when marginal distributions differ in shape. Some investigators have attempted to adjust for this distortion by computing $\phi/\phi_{max}$, where $\phi_{max}$ is the maximal value (with the appropriate sign) for a given pair of marginal distributions. Even tetrachoric correlations are subject to similar distortions when correct responses can include responses made by guessing, and although possible corrections for these distortions have been proposed (Carroll, 1961) such corrections would require large $N$s and accurate estimates of the guessing parameters, and it is not known how effective they are.

Investigators need to be on guard for correlations involving part-to-whole or overlapping relations, or other types of artifactual dependence that can distort factor analytic results. Such dependence can spuriously increase the rank (number of common factors) of a correlation matrix. Common examples include the use of both time-limit scores and power scores, or both part scores and total scores, or both basic scores and derived difference scores, in a set of variables analyzed by factor analysis. Distortions can also arise from experimental dependence, that is, from artifactual dependence between pairs of variables derived from the same task or task setting. Nevertheless, no absolute prohibition can be given against including several variables from the same task or task setting; a good principle to follow would be to select variables that could be logically or conceivably independent. For example, speed and accuracy of performance of the same task could conceivably be independent and might have separate sources of variance. Difficulties can arise, however, when both the intercept and slope parameters of individuals' linear functions are included, as occurs in the function relating reaction time to set size in the S. Sternberg (1966) short-term memory paradigm; generally these parameters are found to be negatively correlated, and it is probable that such negative correlation is inevitable from the nature of the case. A possible solution is to partial out the influence of each variable from the other, or to place one of the variables in an extension analysis (see below, p. 841). Another solution would be to compute different types of variables (e.g., an intercept and a slope) from parallel halves of a task.

Whatever kind of correlation coefficient is computed, caution should be employed in interpreting its magnitude in terms of its squared value. It is true that the proportion of variance common to two variables is equal to the square of the correlation, but such a value can lead to underestimation of the interpretative or practical significance of the correlation. For example, with an $N$ large enough to make $r = .20$ statistically significant at some conventional alpha level, the proportion of variance common to a predictor variable and a criterion variable is .04,

to be sure, but from the standpoint of regression the correlation means that, for every standard unit of increase in the predictor variable, there is an increase of .2 standard units in the criterion variable. In personnel selection, this increase could make a practical difference, since there could be sizable differences in the probability that an individual would surpass a given level on the criterion variable, depending on whether that person was at a low or high level on the predictor variable. Figure 12.7 shows such probabilities for a correlation of .2.

### Factor Analysis

Many of the points made above have particular pertinence when correlations are used in factor analysis. Factor analysis can, in fact, be viewed as an especially searching and elegant way to analyze the intercorrelations among a set of variables. The technique has, however, been fraught with many difficulties, and over the years, some skepticism has been voiced about its usefulness in the behavioral sciences, particularly in the study of IDs. There have been almost endless debates about different factor models of intelligence (P.E. Vernon, 1961). From outside the field, it appears that factor analysts could not agree on methods and approaches, and factor analytic results have been looked on with considerable doubt. R.J. Sternberg (1977) devoted a chapter to what he regarded as unsatisfactory features of factor analysis. Estes made these comments:

The perennial efforts to analyze intelligence tests in terms of theoretically based ideas, and thus to arrive at purer measures of capacities, have never proved strikingly successful . . . . The almost ubiquitous occurrence of positive correlations among scores on various tests and scales led early to various conceptions of general ability, ranging from Spearman's $g$ to various systems of multiple factors. However, extensive and prolonged research efforts have not led to clear convergence on any one of these systems, and on the whole there seems to be increasing disillusion with the original idea that intercorrelations and factor analyses would lead to uncovering the basic structure of the mind as determined by the underlying neural organization (1976, pp. 295, 297).[1]

[1] From "Intelligence and Cognitive Psychology" by W.K. Estes in *The Nature of Intelligence* (pp. 295–297), L. Resnick (Ed.), 1976. Hillsdale, NJ: Erlbaum. Copyright 1976 by Lawrence Erlbaum Associates, Inc. Reprinted by permission.

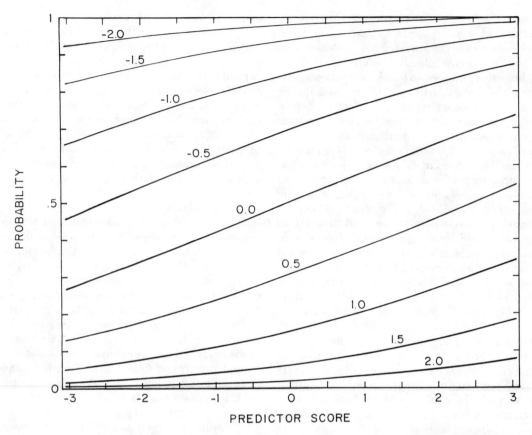

**Figure 12.7.** For a normal bivariate distribution with $r = .2$, probabilities of exceeding given standard score levels on a dependent variable, as a function of standard score on the predictor (independent) variable.

The stance adopted in the present chapter, however, is that factor analysis merits a prominent place in the toolkit of the ID researcher. Many of its past difficulties have now been resolved by methodological developments, and many of the discrepancies between different findings in the literature turn out to be only apparent if they are reinterpreted in terms of current methods or, in some cases, if the data are completely reanalyzed. Some of the bases for Estes' pessimism have largely evaporated.

An attempt will be made here to convey some current views on the possibilities and limitations of factor analysis. For more extended treatments, the reader is referred to works by Cattell (1978), Cureton and D'Agostino (1983), Gorsuch (1983), Harman (1976), Jöreskog and Sörbom (1979), Kim and Mueller (1978a, 1978b), and Mulaik (1972), as well as to articles in such journals as *Psychometrika* and *Multivariate*

*Behavioral Research.* Comrey (1978) presents useful advice on the conduct of factor analysis studies, and Carroll (1983b, 1985) gives further discussions of factor analytic methodology in ID research.

The basic purpose of factor analysis is to identify a small number of latent dimensions that can parsimoniously account for the intercorrelations of a set of variables, and to describe the composition of the variables in terms of those latent dimensions. When the variables are measures of IDs, the latent dimensions can be interpreted as individual traits or characteristics of potentially considerable generality. In the present chapter, where the focus is on cognitive abilities and performances, many of these abilities and performances can be profitably described in terms of dimensions identified through factor analysis; similar demonstrations could be made for variables more properly classified under the rubrics of personality and cognitive style (for reviews of these domains, see Cattell & Dreger, 1977).

Parsimony has long been recognized as one criterion for selecting and developing scientific models (Frank, 1957; Hempel, 1966; but see also Battig, 1962). The principle of parsimony dictates a number of guidelines for the conduct of factor analysis. Consider the equation that forms the basis for the so-called common factor model, according to which any variable $y$ is taken to be a linear composite of a series of latent factors:

$$y_{ji} = w_{j1}x_{1i} + w_{j2}x_{2i} + \ldots \; w_{jp}x_{pi} \ldots$$

$$+ \; w_{jm}x_{mi} + w_{js}x_{si} + w_{je}x_{ei}.$$

In this equation, $y_{ji}$ is the standard score of individual $i$ on variable $j$; $x_{pi}$ is the standard score of individual $i$ on factor $p$, and $w_{jp}$ is the weight of factor $p$ in producing the scores $y_{ji}$ on variable $j$. It is assumed that there are $m$ common factors; generally, $m$ is no greater than one-third to one-half the number of variables, and it is usually much smaller than that. In addition, the common factor model assumes that each variable can have a specific factor $s$ and an error factor $e$, independent of each other and the common factors. The specific factor $s$ refers to reliable variance that is unique to variable $j$; the error factor $e$ refers to unreliable variance in variable $j$. The reliable variance of variable $j$ is composed of all the common factor variances plus the variance specific to variable $j$. The sum of the common factor variances is called the communality of variable $j$ and is often denoted $h^2$.

The principle of parsimony applies to a number of aspects of this equation.

1. Parsimony constrains the equation to be linear, and this constraint requires that the correlations from which a factor analysis is derived describe linear rather than nonlinear relations. This is the reason for the attention devoted above to the kinds of correlation coefficients that are entered into a factor analysis.

2. Parsimony dictates that a clear distinction be maintained between common and unique variances. The common factor variance is the variance that is derived from the covariances of the variables, and covariance among variables is the primary concern of factor analysis. Specific variance is of interest only in the possibility of its being converted to common factor variance

in further studies by an appropriate selection of variables. The distinction between common and unique variance will be preserved by any method of factor analysis that analyzes estimated communalities. Such methods include principal axis factoring of a correlation matrix with iteration for communalities, image analysis, and maximum likelihood analysis. The all-too-frequently employed principal component analysis (principal axis analysis of a correlation matrix with unities in the diagonal) will not preserve this distinction properly and should generally be avoided except for certain special purposes, such as solving for factor scores. The preference of many factor analysts, including the writer, for the common factor model is based on its theoretical appeal in explaining common as distinct from unique variance. However, some writers argue that in most circumstances the choice of model makes little or no difference in the interpretation of the final factor pattern (Velicer, Peacock & Jackson, 1982). Indeed, the common factor model may introduce problems of mathematical indeterminacy and of improper solutions not involved in principal component solutions. Despite these considerations, the writer still prefers the common factor model, particularly for data sets with small numbers of variables.

3. Parsimony dictates that a minimum, yet sufficient, number of common factors be found to account, to a satisfactory approximation, for the covariances in a set of variables. In the initial stage of a factor analysis, this number refers to the number of primary factors; at later stages, the number may be increased to account for any correlations among primary or higher-order factors. Finding the appropriate number of initial common factors is one of the more difficult problems in factor analysis. A commonly used method, the Kaiser-Guttman unity-eigenvalue rule (Kaiser, 1960), may either underestimate or overestimate the appropriate value: underestimation may occur when primary factors are substantially correlated, and overestimation may occur when correlations are generally low and based on small $N$s. Cattell's (1966) scree test and the Montanelli and Humphreys (1976) parallel analysis criterion appear to be among the more reliable guides. Another guide is the patterning of salient loadings found in a varimax rotation of a common factor solution. If common factor

solutions are obtained and varimax-rotated for different values of $m$ (number of common factors), the number of common factors may be taken to be the largest value of $m$ such that each factor has at least two variables whose dominant loadings are on that factor. In this way each common factor accounts for at least some salient portion of covariance in the correlation matrix.

4. The principle of parsimony suggests that, for each variable, a minimum number of the weights be nonvanishing (i.e., be obviously different from zero). That is, one wants to describe each variable with a minimum number of factors; factors with essentially zero weights are regarded as not contributing to a description. This is essentially Thurstone's (1947) concept of simple structure. It justifies rotation of the frame of coordinate axes to positions—orthogonal or oblique—so that the equation for each variable will be as simple as possible. (The equation is the one embodied in the so-called pattern matrix, although to facilitate computations weights in the so-called reference vector matrix can be used.) Kaiser's (1958) varimax or a weighted varimax (see Cureton & D'Agostino, 1983) is normally the method of choice for an initial orthogonal rotation. Among the better objective methods of oblique rotation, when this is required by the structure, are the promax (Hendrickson & White, 1964) and the Harris and Kaiser (1964) orthoblique solutions; with experience, these solutions can be modified by the use of subjective graphical rotations that aim to maximize numbers of variables in hyperplanes, that is, numbers of variables that do not load on a given factor (Cattell, 1978).

5. If the criterion of simple structure is satisfied as well as can be and results in correlated primary factors, a further application of the principle of parsimony suggests that the number of common factors be expanded to make the final factors in the system uncorrelated (orthogonal), since orthogonality of factors contributes to both mathematical and psychological simplicity. This can be achieved by extracting higher-order factors from the correlations of primary or lower-order factors and using procedures developed by Schmid and Leiman (1957) to adjust the weights of lower- and higher-order factors to orthogonality. The final equation for any variable might then have the following form (for simplicity,

assume that there is one third-order general factor $g$, two second-order factors, $p$ and $q$, four first-order or primary factors, $a$, $b$, $c$, $d$, and a unique factor $u$ for each variable):

$$y_{ji} = w_{jg}x_{gi} \qquad \text{(general factor)}$$
$$+ w_{jp}x_{pi} + w_{jq}x_{qi}$$
$$\text{(second-order factors)}$$
$$+ w_{ja}x_{ai} + w_{jb}x_{bi} + w_{jc}x_{ci} + w_{jd}x_{di}$$
$$\text{(primary factors)}$$
$$+ w_{ju}x_{ui} \qquad \text{(unique factor)}$$

Over the whole of the resulting orthogonal factor matrix, nearly all variables could have salient weights on factor $g$, subsets of variables would have salient weights on each of factors $p$ and $q$, and still smaller subsets would have salient weights on each of the primary factors. The orthogonality of the matrix contributes to the parsimonious description of the variables, in the sense that each factor can be regarded as an independent source of variance.

6. A final application of the principle of parsimony to factor analysis specifies that the weights assigned to each variable in the factor matrix are the same for all individuals in the sample being studied. This assumption applies only to the interpretation of factor analysis results, not to the actual conduct of a factor analysis. It is a distinct limitation and constraint on factor analysis, early noticed by Wolfle (1940) and Jeffress (1948), and it is mentioned by R.J. Sternberg (1977, p. 33) in his critique of factor analysis. If it is believed that a given cognitive task may be attacked with different strategies by different individuals, and that the individuals' selections of strategies depend on their patterns of abilities, the weights solved for in factor analysis may in effect be averages of different weights for different individuals. No method of ordinary factor analysis can reveal differential patterns of weights for different individuals, unless samples can be divided in advance or post hoc according to strategies adopted for a given task variable, with separate factor analyses performed on the samples. Such a method was in fact explored by French (1965), who collected interview and questionnaire data from examinees concerning their strategies in taking each of a series of tests. He performed separate factor analyses for groups reporting different strategies. In some cases, factor patterns were dramatically

different. The results suggested that examinees' tendencies to approach a test systematically rather than unsystematically could radically change patterns of test intercorrelations.

Some points about factor analysis are illustrated in a further analysis of data reported by Underwood, Boruch, and Malmi (1978), who studied interrelations among scores on 22 episodic memory tasks performed by 200 undergraduates. These authors presented (in their Table 4, reproduced in a part of Table 12.3 here) an orthogonal maximum-likelihood factor solution for these variables, along with a useful discussion of the steps they took in deciding to accept only five factors. While this solution was certainly satisfactory for the authors' purposes, it seemed to this writer amenable to oblique rotation and Schmid-Leiman orthogonalization. A further analysis by this writer, achieved through graphical rotations to simple structure, is presented in Table 12.3, which includes the reference structure matrix for five primary factors, the primary factor correlations, and the Schmid-Leiman orthogonal loadings using the single second-order factor $g_m$ found to account quite well for the primary factor correlations.

The order of the variables has been arranged to clarify the alignment of variables with factors. Interpretations of the primary factors depart only slightly from those made by Underwood et al., but the factor pattern is somewhat simpler and cleaner, owing to the oblique rotations. What is interesting is that a general memory factor appears in varying degrees in all the primary factors; it is in effect partialed out in the Schmid-Leiman orthogonalization. This process does not change communalities and the orthogonal factor matrix reproduces the original correlation matrix exactly as is done by the maximum-likelihood solution presented by Underwood et al.

Thus far this section has presented mainly an exposition of what Tucker (1955) termed exploratory factor analysis, that is, factor analysis that, in contrast to confirmatory factor analysis, does not attempt to test statistical hypotheses concerning numbers of factors and factor loadings. Exploratory factor analysis procedures are the more popular and traditional and are for many reasons still widely and justifiably used, literally to explore interrelations among variables. In fact, beginning the analysis of a set of data with exploratory techniques aids in formulating any statistical hypotheses that might be tested through confirmatory techniques, exemplified, for example, in the COFAMM and LISREL programs now available (Jöreskog & Sörbom, 1983). In confirmatory factor analysis, certain statistical hypotheses are set up concerning the number of factors, their intercorrelations, and the loadings of variables on them; certain parameters are allowed to vary freely in an effort to attain best fit. The outcome yields statistical information on the degree of model fit. A problem with that technique, however, is that, although there may be an infinity of models that do not fit a set of data (at a certain level of confidence), there may also be an infinity of models that do fit. With some data sets, the investigator may have difficulty finding any model that gives a satisfactory fit. The temptation is to test a number of models and select the model that fits the data best; there is thus a degree of subjectivity in confirmatory factor analysis, just as there is in exploratory factor analysis. On the other hand, it can be reassuring to find that a particular set of model parameters fits data with a high degree of confidence.

Confirmatory factor analysis has been usefully applied in experimental psychology. Geiselman, Woodward, and Beatty (1982) found clear evidence for rejecting a uniprocess model of memory performances in verbal list learning and for supporting instead a model involving separate short-term and long-term memory processes. Their study provides an interesting case in which ID methodology and findings have contributed to psychological theory. Other examples, to be mentioned below, are studies by Frederiksen (1982) and by Lansman, Donaldson, Hunt, and Yantis (1982).

### The Design of Factor-Analytic Studies

In general it is unwise to apply factor analysis to any arbitrary set of ID (or other) variables. Ideally, even exploratory factor analysis studies should be designed to provide (nonstatistical) tests of a set of hypotheses concerning the identification and nature of factors or the factorial composition of variables. Tucker, Koopman, and Linn (1969) concluded that "the quality of factor analytic results depends greatly upon the quality of the design and conduct of the factor analytic experiment" and that "poorly designed

**Table 12.3. A Varimax factor matrix reported by Underwood, Boruch, and Malmi (1978) and its further analysis[a]**

| | No. | Varimax factor loadings | | | | | Oblique factor loadings | | | | | Gm | Orthogonalized factor loadings | | | | | $h^2$ |
|---|---|---|---|---|---|---|---|---|---|---|---|---|---|---|---|---|---|---|
| | | A | B | C | D | E | A | B | C | D | E | | a | b | c | d | e | |
| *Factor A: Paired associate learning (PA)* | | | | | | | | | | | | | | | | | | |
| PA-II: PA, Crossed associates | 11 | 80 | 29 | 10 | 13 | 11 | 65 | 02 | 03 | -01 | -04 | 76 | 50 | 02 | 03 | -01 | -04 | 82 |
| PA-CA: PA, Paired associates | 12 | 70 | 25 | 14 | 28 | 07 | 55 | -02 | 07 | 15 | -04 | 70 | 43 | -02 | 07 | 14 | -04 | 70 |
| PA-M: PA, Matching | 10 | 67 | 27 | 06 | 17 | 23 | 53 | 03 | 00 | 02 | 10 | 69 | 40 | 03 | 00 | 03 | 10 | 65 |
| PA-C: PA, Control | 9 | 66 | 38 | -02 | 09 | 18 | 49 | 16 | -09 | -02 | 03 | 69 | 38 | 14 | -08 | -02 | 03 | 65 |
| SL-M: Serial learning, matching | 14 | 50 | 35 | 11 | 35 | 12 | 33 | 12 | 04 | 25 | 03 | 63 | 25 | 10 | 04 | 24 | 03 | 53 |
| SL-C: Serial learning, control | 13 | 43 | 32 | 24 | 24 | 15 | 28 | 11 | 18 | 14 | 07 | 57 | 22 | 10 | 18 | 13 | 06 | 44 |
| *Factor B: Free recall (FR)* | | | | | | | | | | | | | | | | | | |
| FR-CO: FR, Concrete | 3 | 26 | 74 | 07 | 22 | 05 | -01 | 58 | -02 | 22 | -06 | 61 | -01 | 51 | -02 | 21 | -06 | 69 |
| FR-S: FR, Spaced/Massed | 2 | 24 | 70 | 08 | 14 | 40 | -02 | 55 | 01 | 07 | 28 | 64 | -01 | 49 | 01 | 06 | 27 | 73 |
| FR-C: FR, Control | 1 | 30 | 69 | 22 | 05 | 17 | 06 | 53 | 14 | 01 | 04 | 62 | 04 | 48 | 14 | 01 | 04 | 64 |
| FR-II: FR, Associated pairs | 5 | 32 | 60 | 06 | 35 | 10 | 08 | 41 | -03 | 31 | 01 | 62 | 06 | 36 | -02 | 30 | 01 | 61 |
| FR-CA: FR, Categorized lists | 6 | 29 | 55 | 07 | 32 | 09 | 07 | 37 | -01 | 29 | 01 | 57 | 05 | 33 | -01 | 27 | 01 | 51 |
| LD: List discrimination | 20 | 19 | 47 | 02 | 03 | 42 | 07 | 37 | -02 | -05 | 32 | 46 | 01 | 33 | -02 | -05 | 31 | 44 |
| SA-FR: Simul. acq., FR pairs | 25 | 18 | 39 | 11 | 06 | 15 | 04 | 29 | 07 | 02 | 08 | 38 | 03 | 26 | 07 | 02 | 07 | 22 |
| *Factor C: Memory span (Registration) (MS)* | | | | | | | | | | | | | | | | | | |
| MS-LL: MS, Low similarity letters | 22 | 06 | 09 | 90 | 10 | 04 | 03 | -03 | 88 | 01 | 04 | 25 | 02 | -03 | 90 | 01 | 04 | 84 |
| MS-D: MS, Digits | 21 | 01 | 11 | 77 | 02 | 06 | -02 | 03 | 75 | -05 | 06 | 19 | -02 | 02 | 75 | -05 | 06 | 61 |
| MS-HL: MS, High similarity letters | 23 | 16 | 11 | 67 | 10 | -06 | 12 | -02 | 64 | 04 | -08 | 27 | 09 | -02 | 64 | 04 | -07 | 50 |
| *Factor D: Memory for events (?)* | | | | | | | | | | | | | | | | | | |
| SF-Z: Situational freq. judgment | 19 | 11 | 20 | 10 | 67 | 28 | -03 | 02 | 05 | 57 | 31 | 40 | -02 | 02 | 05 | 54 | 30 | 54 |
| RR-D: Running recognition | 18 | 17 | 19 | 03 | 58 | 26 | 04 | 02 | -02 | 48 | 27 | 40 | 03 | 02 | -02 | 46 | 26 | 44 |
| FR-AB: Free recall, abstract | 4 | 24 | 61 | 17 | 43 | 03 | -01 | 41 | 08 | 41 | -04 | 59 | 00 | 37 | 08 | 39 | -04 | 64 |
| SA-D: Simul. acq., recog. pairs | 27 | 18 | 10 | 09 | 46 | 05 | 10 | -05 | 05 | 40 | 06 | 30 | 07 | -04 | 05 | 38 | 06 | 24 |
| *Factor E: Verbal discrimination (VD)* | | | | | | | | | | | | | | | | | | |
| VD-C: VD, Control | 15 | 18 | 10 | 01 | 23 | 63 | 10 | -01 | 00 | 06 | 60 | 37 | 08 | -01 | 00 | 06 | 58 | 48 |
| VD-A: VD, Affective | 16 | 10 | 21 | 01 | 22 | 63 | -01 | 12 | 00 | 07 | 59 | 36 | -01 | 10 | 00 | 07 | 58 | 48 |

*Factor correlations*

| | A | B | C | D | E | Gm |
|---|---|---|---|---|---|---|
| A | 100 | 62 | 16 | 39 | 30 | 83 |
| B | 62 | 100 | 22 | 28 | 28 | 73 |
| C | 16 | 22 | 100 | 19 | 02 | 24 |
| D | 39 | 28 | 19 | 100 | 20 | 46 |
| E | 30 | 28 | 02 | 20 | 100 | 37 |

[a]Entries have been multiplied by 100 to eliminate decimal points.

*Note.* Portions of this table come from "Composition of Episodic Memory" by B.J. Underwood, R.F. Boruch, and R.A. Malmi, 1978, *Journal of Experimental Psychology: General, 107*, p. 412. Copyright 1978 by the American Psychological Association. Reprinted by permission of the author.

and conducted research cannot be salvaged by efforts expended in data analysis" (p. 458).

Since the object of factor analysis is to explain the covariances among variables, variables must be so selected that there is promise of adequate covariances to be explained. If one postulates the existence of a certain latent variable or underlying factor, there must be a substantial number of variables (at least three, according to customary recommendations) that have promise of being loaded on or explained by that factor. At the same time it is recommended that the set of variables analyzed should contain a number of relevant marker or reference variables that one can be reasonably sure to define previously established factors. Such marker variables can be selected from relevant literature; marker tests from various psychometric domains have been published in the form of kits (French, Ekstrom & Price, 1963; Ekstrom, French & Harman, 1976). These kits contain series of tests that purport to define the various well-attested ability factors; they have been designed to facilitate comparisons among factor-analysis studies. The kits also contain scoring keys and extensive bibliographical references. Certain limitations in these kits must be recognized, however. Because the tests are relatively short, their reliabilities are limited and the standard errors of measurement may be somewhat larger than is desirable. Since nearly all are to be administered with strict time limits, speed and accuracy components in test scores and factors are not readily separable, except perhaps through the departure from conventional methods of test administration that was employed by Davidson and Carroll (1945) mentioned earlier.

There has been some confusion on the nature of the hypothesis-testing aspects of factor analysis. One kind of hypothesis testing concerns whether a certain postulated factor can be isolated and differentiated from other factors like it in its domain. It is certainly possible to test this type of hypothesis, either by exploratory or confirmatory techniques, by carefully selecting or constructing sets of variables that would, according to hypothesis, contrast in the extent to which they would measure the factor. The guideline in testing such a hypothesis would be to let the data speak for themselves, that is, to conduct a factor analysis in such a way as to allow the factor to appear if it indeed exists, but not to attempt to force it to appear. In

contrast, some investigators, notably Guilford (1967; Guilford & Hoepfner, 1971) have utilized certain "Procrustean" techniques whereby factor matrices are rotated to achieve the best fit to target matrices constructed on the basis of a set of hypotheses. Horn and Knapp (1973, 1974) have pointed out that such techniques run the danger of capitalizing on chance, thus appearing to confirm hypotheses that may in fact be false.

The variables to be studied in a factor analysis should be selected with as much knowledge as possible of their probable factorial composition. Planning a factor-analytic study therefore requires a knowledge of the literature. Some of the literature on IDs in psychometric tests and cognitive tasks is summarized or referenced later in this chapter.

In planning a factor analysis, it is wise to establish a hypothesized factor pattern matrix and be guided by it in selecting variables. This suggestion does not imply using the hypothesized pattern matrix as a target matrix in Procrustean rotations; the hypothesized matrix should in no way be used as a guide in arriving at the final solution. Generally variables with simple factor compositions are preferable. If variables with known complexity of factorial composition are to be used, they must be accompanied by variables that will adequately define, independently, the factors involved in such variables.

Certain types of variables—for example, highly complex variables, external criterion variables, and variables having suspected artifactual dependency relations with variables placed in an analysis—are best analyzed by extension analysis (see, for example, Gorsuch, 1983, pp. 236–238), in which these variables are defined in terms of the factorial space determined in the main analysis.

Planning a factor analytic study involves selecting an appropriate sample of subjects. If samples are used that are heterogeneous in age, educational status, or other characteristics, correlations among variables may be inflated by differential maturational, learning, and experiential effects. A correlation matrix based on a representative sample of children aged 6 to 18 years, say, would almost certainly reveal a powerful general factor that could best be interpreted as indicating level of maturity. With some justification, Guilford (1980) questioned whether the study by Horn and Cattell (1966), supporting a theory of fluid and crystallized intelligence, was based on too heterogeneous a sample, as it ranged in age from 14 to 61 years. In their reply, Horn and Cattell (1982) argued for the valid use of an age-heterogeneous population in view of the purpose of their study, and demonstrated that their results were not strikingly altered when age and education were partialed from the correlations. On the other hand, there are certainly circumstances in which heterogeneity could result in artifacts.

## Componential Analysis and Factor Analysis

In various domains of cognitive psychology, information processing models have been devised and tested to explore the proposition that overall performance on cognitive tasks can be explained in terms of the parameters of underlying processes and the influence on those parameters of various task conditions, such as stimulus values, instructions, and the like. For example, Trabasso, Rollins, and Shaughnessy (1971) postulated certain stages in the storage and verification of concepts; a similar model was presented by Clark and Chase (1972) for the verification of simple sentences against visual displays. As yet, few such models have been applied in ID research. One such application by MacLeod et al. (1978; see also Mathews et al., 1980), already mentioned, concerns strategy differences in the sentence verification task as related to verbal and spatial abilities.

What R.J. Sternberg (1977, 1980a) has called componential analysis is an elaboration of this approach applied specifically to IDs and the analysis and description of intellectual abilities. Essentially, Sternberg developed possible models for information flow through processing stages (components) and then designed experiments to test these models. By collecting substantial amounts of data from a single individual under various task conditions he determined the parameters of the several stages for that individual. The generality of the models can also be tested over individuals, and various types of component scores can be determined for these individuals and compared with scores on psychometric tests of abilities.

Carroll (1980) has suggested that it is possible to combine componential analysis with factor analysis by using the latter to analyze interrelations among component scores and, when available, scores on psychometric tests of ability. In such an analysis, the generality of components over experiments, cognitive tasks, and psychometric tests can be assessed. Factors determined by factor analysis become source traits of individual differences entering into the parameters for information-processing stages. Merely to illustrate this approach, Carroll performed factor analysis on intercorrelations reported by R.J. Sternberg (1977) for 17 variables on 16 individuals. Of course, the small size of the sample severely limits the possible significance of these results. Nevertheless, they suggest that scores on Sternberg's preparation and response component as well as his encoding component are intrinsically related to a reasoning or reasoning speed factor measured by several psychometric tests; scores on the remaining components show only sporadic relations with psychometric factors but appear to have some generality over experiments. Application of this approach is to be encouraged with larger samples and factor analysis designs better devised to investigate relations between component scores and psychometric abilities.

## INDIVIDUAL DIFFERENCES IN DOMAINS OF COGNITIVE FUNCTIONING

Differential psychologists have long been concerned with what is often called the structure of mental or cognitive abilities, that is, the identification and description of separate dimensions or sources of variance in IDs in these abilities and the specification of how these abilities are organized or otherwise interrelated in the total analysis of this domain of behavior. This section gives an overview of present knowledge of the structure of cognitive abilities insofar as it may be of use to experimental and cognitive psychologists interested in relating ID research to the detailed analysis of cognitive processes.

Evidence of the multifactorial character of human cognitive abilities has emerged gradually since Spearman (1904) first asserted that all abilities could be subsumed under a general factor that he called "$g$," a claim that was amplified in his major work on the subject (Spearman, 1927). It is of interest, incidentally, that the data on which Spearman based his assertion in 1904 included tests of several sensory and psychophysical judgment abilities. In the years immediately following the publication of Spearman's major treatise, however, there was increasing recognition of the existence of several narrower group factors of ability, such as verbal, number, rote memory, spatial, and speed factors (P.E. Vernon, 1961, pp. 14–17). During the 1930s, Thurstone (1938) developed multiple factor analysis methods and compiled data to support the identification of a number of "primary" mental abilities. By 1941 (Thurstone & Thurstone, 1941, p. 27), he regarded at least six such abilities as clearly established and reasonably invariant over samples of individuals and tests: Verbal Comprehension (V), Word Fluency (W), Number (N), Space (S), Rote Memory (M), and Induction (I). Factor P, Perception, he regarded as "quite certain," but its nature was unclear. Factor D, Deduction, was reported as not appearing consistently in different studies. Collating data from 69 studies that followed the Thurstonian model, French (1951) listed nearly 60 factors that he regarded as fairly well established; only about half of these, however, could be called "cognitive," the remainder being in psychomotor, personality, and affective domains.

Literally hundreds of factor-analytic studies of cognitive abilities have been published since the appearance of French's monograph. Summaries of the findings of these studies have been offered by Pawlik (1966), Royce (1973), Horn (1977, 1978), and Ekstrom, French, and Harman (1979). Useful bibliographical material is contained in publications by Bolton (Bolton & Hinman, 1981; Bolton, Hinman, & Tuft, 1973; Hinman & Bolton, 1979). Guilford (1967; Guilford & Hoepfner, 1971) also summarized and analyzed much of this literature in the course of developing his three-facet "Structure-of-Intellect" model, which postulates that any given cognitive factor can be described in terms of the particular type of operation, content and product involved in it (see also Guilford, 1979). He identified five operations, six types of products, and four types of content, and then postulated that each of the 120 combinations of facets could yield a cognitive factor, and by 1971 he claimed to have isolated nearly 100 of these factors.

Concerning the organization of mental abilities, however, there are fundamental differences between the views of Guilford and his followers, on the one hand, and those of most other factor analysts, on the other. It is beyond the scope of this chapter to discuss reasons for questioning Guilford's model; for critiques see Carroll (1972) and Horn and Knapp (1973, 1974), but Guilford (1982) now seems to have adjusted his model to admit higher-order factors. Rather, the present discussion gives credence to the view that mental ability factors are organized hierarchically—a view advanced by P.E. Vernon (1961), Cattell (1971), and Horn (1978), among others. Evidence for the hierarchical organization of mental ability factors is to be found in the correlations of primary factors that have been obliquely rotated to simple structure; Schmid and Leiman's (1957) orthogonalization procedures, mentioned above, can yield a hierarchical structure in such factors. This evidence is far from complete, but it permits the conclusion that primary factors of mental ability can be classified and organized into a number of clusters, including among others the fluid and crystallized intelligence clusters postulated by Cattell and Horn (1978), and that at least some of these clusters may be organized at a still higher level, possibly reflecting the operation of a very general factor of cognitive ability similar to the general factor originally set forth by Spearman.

Nearly all the literature on cognitive abilities is based on the analysis of data from psychological tests, administered either individually or to groups. Until recently, few studies were based at least partly on variables obtained in laboratory situations of the type traditionally employed in experimental psychology; a notable exception, however, is Thurstone's (1944) study of perceptual tasks, in which most of the variables were measured in individualized laboratory testing conditions. There is no essential difference between the tasks contained in psychometric tests and the tasks set in laboratory experiments; the differences are more of a situational character and reside in the types of controls exercised. While some types of ability factors are probably best revealed in the experimental laboratory and others in group testing situations, there is little point in attempting to create a principled difference between test- and laboratory-derived variables of IDs.

To offer a perspective on the diversity of abilities identified in the (largely psychometric) literature, Table 12.4 presents a concordance of selected cognitive and cognitive-related ability factors identified by French (1951) and represented in two successive kits of factor reference

**Table 12.4. Concordance of selected cognitive and cognitive-related factors.[a]**

| Factor code | Factor name | French (1951) code, name | 1963 ETS kit code, name | 1976 ETS kit code, name | Guilford factor[b] | Cattell universal index[c] |
|---|---|---|---|---|---|---|
| *Gf (Fluid intelligence) factors[d,e]* | | | | | | |
| I | Induction | I: Induction | I: Induction | I: Induction | (Several) | T5 |
| RL | Logical reasoning | D: Deduction | Rs: Syllogistic reasoning | RL: Logical reasoning | EMR? | T4 |
| RG | General reasoning | R: General reasoning | R: General reasoning | RG: General reasoning | CMS | T34 |
| IP | Integrative process | In: Integration | – | IP: Integrative process | – | – |
| J | Judgment | J: Judgment | – | – | – | – |
| PL | Planning | Pl: Planning | – | – | – | – |
| *Gc (Crystallized intelligence) factors* | | | | | | |
| V | Verbal knowledge | V: Verbal comprehension | V: Verbal comprehension | V: Verbal comprehension | CMU | T13 |
| N | Numerical facility | N: Number | N: Number facility | N: Number facility | NSI, MSI? | T10 |
| *Gv (General visual perception) factors* | | | | | | |
| | | S: Space | f | f | | |
| SO | Spatial orientation | SO: Spatial orientation | S: Spatial orientation | S: Spatial orientation | CFS | T11 |
| VZ | Spatial visualization | Vi: Visualization | Vs: Visualization | VZ: Visualization | CFT | T14 |
| CS | Speed of closure | GP: Gestalt perception | Cs: Speed of closure | CS: Speed of closure | CFU | T3 |
| CF | Flexibility of closure | GF: Gestalt flexibility | Cf: Flexibility of closure | CF: Flexibility of closure | NFT | T2 |
| SS | Spatial scanning | Sa: Spatial scanning | Sa: Spatial scanning | SS: Spatial scanning | CFI | – |
| LE | Length estimation | LE: Length estimation | Le: Length estimation | | | – |
| CV | Verbal closure | | | CV: Verbal closure | | – |
| P | Perceptual speed | P: Perceptual speed | P: Perceptual speed[g] | P: Perceptual speed | ESU, EFU | T12 |
| PA | Perceptual alternations | PA: Perceptual alternations | – | – | – | – |
| IL | Figure illusions | FI: Figure illusions | – | – | – | – |
| *Ga (General auditory perception) factors* | | | | | | |
| AUI | Auditory integration | AI: Auditory integration | – | – | – | – |
| AUR | Auditory resistance | AR: Auditory resistance | – | – | – | – |
| LO | Loudness | Lo: Loudness | – | – | – | – |
| PQ | Pitch quality | PQ: Pitch quality | – | – | – | – |

844

**Table 12.4. Continued.**

| Factor code | Factor name | French (1951) code, name | 1963 ETS kit code, name | 1976 ETS kit code, name | Guilford factor[b] | Cattell universal index[c] |
|---|---|---|---|---|---|---|
| *Gm (General memory) factors* | | | | | | |
| MA | Associative memory | M: Associative memory | Ma: Associative memory | MA: Associative memory | MSR | T7 |
| MS | Memory span | Sm: Span memory | Ms: Memory span | MS: Memory span | MSU, MSS? | — |
| MV | Visual memory | VM: Visual memory | — | MV: Visual memory | — | — |
| MMU | Musical memory | MM: Musical memory | — | — | — | — |
| *Fluency and production factors* | | | | | | |
| FA | Associational fluency | — | Fa: Associational fluency | FA: Associational fluency | DMR | — |
| FE | Expressional fluency | FE: Fluency of expression | Fe: Expressional fluency | FE: Expressional fluency | DMS | — |
| FI | Ideational fluency | IF: Ideational fluency | Fi: Ideational fluency | FI: Ideational fluency | DMU | T6 |
| FW | Word fluency | W: Word fluency | Fw: Word fluency | FW: Word fluency | DSU | T15 |
| XU | Flexibility of use | — | Xs: Semantic spontaneous flexibility | XU: Flexibility of use | DMC | — |
| XF | Figural flexibility | — | Xa: Figural adaptive flexibility | XF: Figural flexibility | DFT | — |
| NA | Naming speed | Na: Naming | — | — | — | — |
| FS | Speech fluency | PS: Public speaking | — | — | — | — |
| SA | Speed of association | SA: Speed of association | — | — | — | — |
| O | Originality | — | O: Originality | — | DMT | — |
| RE | Semantic redefinition | — | Re: Semantic redefinition | — | NMT | — |
| SEP | Sensitivity to problems | — | Sep: Sensitivity to problems | — | EMI | — |
| *Speed factors (not otherwise classified)* | | | | | | |
| SD | Speed | Sp: Speed | — | — | — | — |
| SDJ | Speed of judgment | SJ: Speed of judgment | — | — | — | — |
| *Selected psychomotor factors* | | | | | | |
| AIMG | Aiming | Ai: Aiming | — | — | — | — |
| AMB | Ambidexterity | Am: Ambidexterity | — | — | — | — |
| SDAR | Speed of articulation | Ar: Articulation | — | — | — | — |
| FD | Finger dexterity | FD: Finger dexterity | — | — | — | — |
| MD | Manual dexterity | MD: Manual dexterity | — | — | — | — |
| PC | Psychomotor coordination | PC: Psychomotor coordination | — | — | — | — |
| RT | Reaction time | RT: Reaction time | — | — | — | — |
| TA | Tapping | Ta: Tapping | — | — | — | — |

**Table 12.4. Continued.**

| Factor code | Factor name | French (1951) code, name | 1963 ETS kit code, name | Guilford factor[b] | Cattell universal index[c] |
|---|---|---|---|---|---|
| *Miscellaneous affective-cognitive factors* | | | | | |
| AT | Attention | At: Attention | — | — | — |
| CA | Carefulness | C: Carefulness | — | — | — |
| PE | Persistence | Pe: Persistence | — | — | — |
| PN | Perseveration | Ph: Perseveration | — | — | — |

[a] Identified by French (1951) and in the 1963 and 1976 ETS kits of factor reference tests (French, Ekstrom & Price, 1963; Ekstrom, French & Harman, 1976).

[b] Designations of Guilford factors are those shown in the 1963 ETS kit manual. A key to these designations is as follows:

First character: C, Cognition; D, Divergent production; E, Evaluation; M, Memory; N, Convergent production (Process)

Second character: F, Figural; M, Semantic; S, Symbolic (Content)

Third character: C, Classes; I, Implications; R, Relations; S, Systems; T, Transformations; U, Units (Products).

[c] Designations of Cattell (1957) Universal Index codes are those shown in the 1963 ETS kit manual.

[d] The classification of factors into higher-order groups is tentative; it generally follows the Cattell and Horn model (see Horn, 1978, pp. 211–256).

[e] The two ETS kits distinguish two factors (Rs, RL; R, RG) derived from French's (1951) Deduction.

[f] French's (1951) Space factor appears as two factors SO (Spatial orientation) and VZ (Visualization) in the ETS kits.

[g] The 1963 ETS kit notes that Perceptual speed may consist of several subfactors.

*Note.* From "Studying Individual Differences in Cognitive Abilities; Through and Beyond Factor Analysis" by J.B. Carroll in *Individual Differences in Cognition* (pp. 16–18), R.F. Dillon and R. Schmeck (Eds.), 1983. New York: Academic Press. Reprinted by permission.

tests assembled by groups organized at Educational Testing Service (ETS) (French et al., 1963; Ekstrom et al., 1976). Some factors defined by these kits may not actually be as distinct as is implied by the test designations. Their authors freely admit the inadequacies of the research evidence for some of the factors (Ekstrom et al., 1979). Nevertheless, the list of cognitive ability factors presumably defined by these tests represents a majority of the ability factors now recognized.

Each row of the table presents information, cross-identified over the three sources where possible, for a particular factor of IDs. Cross-identification was made by considering the nature of the tests and tasks subsumed by the factors in the several sources. To suggest some of the factors that may exist in domains other than those covered by the ETS kits (which are almost exclusively devoted to visually presented stimuli contained in paper-and-pencil tests), the table includes listings of certain factors identified by French (1951) in auditory, psychomotor, and affective-cognitive domains. The factor listings in some other domains have also been expanded to include types of abilities that may be of interest to experimental psychologists.

Some of the groupings of factors indicated in the table are based in part on tentative evidence for hierarchical classification, as assembled by Horn (1978), and in part on a more subjective, intuitive classification. On the whole, the list corresponds well with the lists of primary and higher-order factors presented by, for example, Royce (1973, Appendix A) and by Horn (1977, pp. 144–145).

A word is in order about designations of factors. Early in psychometric research, the tradition was established of designating factors with brief mnemonics using single alphabetic letters (in either upper or lower case), possibly with numerical suffixes. Thus Spearman (1927) designated factors $g$, $f$, $p$, etc.; Thurstone (1938, 1949) used designations such as V (Verbal Relations), Cl (Speed of Closure), and so on. As the number of factors proliferated, longer designations became necessary. In Guilford's (1967) system, three upper-case alphabetic characters designated the process, content, and product believed to be involved in a factor; thus factor EMS would presumably operate in tasks requiring the Evaluation of SeMantic Systems. Cattell (1957) proposed that each established factor be designated by a universal index number, together with prefixes and suffixes that would convey details on the types of measures employed, populations in which found, level of the factor in a hierarchical structure, and so on. There are problems with all these systems. Guilford's system prejudges the classification of the cognitive processes, contents, and products involved in a factor; indeed some designations have to be qualified to cover two or more distinct factors embraced by a given designation. Cattell's system does not facilitate reference and recall and has not been widely accepted. The system adopted here is an extension of the traditional one; the designation of each primary factor consists of one to four upper-case alphabetic characters that are intended to have mnemonic value. Designations starting with the letter G and followed by a lower-case letter are reserved for higher-order factors. It should be recognized, however, that factor designations are not intended to be static or unchangeable; as research refines the identification, cross-identification, and interpretation of factors, these designations may be allowed to keep pace.

There is no need to blanch at the thought of a rather substantial number of reliable dimensions of IDs in cognitive abilities. Human behavior and potentiality are widely diverse. A variety of stimuli can be received in several different sensory modalities; the information so received can be processed in many ways by neural and motor systems of high complexity. Indeed, the marvel is that a relatively small number of ID dimensions (ultimately, perhaps, no more than 40 or 50) appear to apply with much generality and organization over these complex systems.

## Cognitive Interpretation of Factors

A goal of cognitive research can be to characterize the several psychometrically defined factors in terms of the cognitive processes and functions that are involved, the types of tasks in which they appear, and the extent to which they reflect learned achievements. Many kinds of empirical evidence, as well as psychological theorizing, would need to be brought together to accomplish such a goal. The following summary reflects recent information and opinion concerning the more important and well-established factors. It draws on statements found in the ETS kit manuals, as well as in writings of French (1951),

Pawlik (1966), Royce (1973), Carroll (1976), and others. The data on which this summary is based come from numerous studies done in many countries—mostly studies of samples drawn from typical normal populations of children, high school students, university students, and adults. All such populations appear to vary widely in numerous abilities, although the samples may also vary in heterogeneity in such a way as to cause certain variations in findings. On the whole, the variations in findings are not so substantial as to make for drastic differences in conclusions. The factors of IDs described below tend to be universal over populations of different sex, age range, educational and mental status, ethnic composition, native language, and country of residence.

Space limitations preclude giving more than intimations of suggested relations between ability factors and psychological processes. It is hoped that the discussion given in the early part of this chapter may guide the reader in inferring the types of psychological processes, operations, or components that may play a role in the definition of an ability factor.

### Fluid Intelligence Factors (Gf)

This group of primary factors is loosely bound together (i.e., their factor scores tend to be somewhat correlated) by the fact that each of them involves what Cattell (1963, 1971) has called fluid intelligence, a kind of intelligence that can operate in any task requiring an ability to perceive or infer (or educe) similarities, differences, and relations among stimuli. (The adjective "fluid" is intended to connote that this kind of intelligence may be required in a wide variety of tasks that are met in the immediate environment and in the daily experience of people without the application of what Cattell called special aids that have been learned through special experience or schooling; tasks requiring such aids are thought to depend more on crystallized intelligence.)

Induction (I) is the somewhat special ability to perceive rules or principles that are implicit (and often not immediately obvious) in the organization or patterning of the task materials. Logical Reasoning (RL), sometimes called Deduction, is the ability to reason accurately from premises or given circumstances, often in a syllogistic manner. It can involve the ability to perform correct reasoning over a series of steps. General

Reasoning (RG) is the ability to understand and use a relatively complex system, often involving mathematically describable functional relations, in drawing necessary conclusions for a problem involving such a system. Integrative Processes (IP) is the ability to hold in mind and consider a number of relevant instructions, rules, or premises while solving problems or producing correct answers to questions. Judgment (J) is the ability to arrive at a sound solution to a somewhat ambiguous or underdetermined problem by making reasonable assumptions about its circumstances or the possible consequences of actions. Planning (PL) is the ability or predisposition to hold the requirements of future steps of a problem in mind while working on any particular step of the problem.

The loading of any test or variable on any one of these abilities will vary with, among other things, the degree to which the tasks are successfully contrived to emphasize one ability more than another. It is virtually impossible to make a task depend solely on one of these abilities, but some tasks emphasize certain abilities more than others. For example, tests of Induction (I) can make special demands on the ability to perceive nonobvious patternings, while tests of Logical Reasoning can deemphasize inductive ability by making patternings obvious, while putting special demands on the ability to carry through accurately a series of steps in reasoning. Similarly, the loading of any factor on the second-order Gf factor can vary with the degree to which the subsumed task variables focus on a consistent set of highly related abilities. Loadings of tests and factors can vary also with the degree to which the tasks call on learned abilities such as reading; tests of Gf factors are generally constructed to minimize the effect of such abilities by using stimuli (e.g., nonalphabetic visual patterns) that do not require reading skill for their interpretation. Factors in this domain are generally those most closely associated with problem-solving abilities (Greeno, 1978).

### Crystallized Intelligence Factors (Gc)

Cattell (1963) called this group of factors measures of crystallized intelligence because they are largely measures of learned, crystallized skills and knowledge. While factors in Gf and other classifications are often included in this group, the two factors that are most likely to call on concepts or skills that have been learned through special opportunities or experiences such as schooling are Verbal Comprehension (V) and Numerical Facility (N). Verbal Comprehension is a well attested factor that will appear in any task that calls on the subject's range of knowledge of, skill in using, the concepts, structures (lexical and grammatical), and even transitional probabilities embodied in the language in which the test is couched (usually a language that is either native or well known to the subjects). It is most often measured with tests of vocabulary meanings that are not likely to be readily familiar to all the persons in the sample, but it also appears in tests of listening or reading comprehension in which subjects must apprehend propositional meanings or implications from sentences or connected discourse. Marshalek (1981) has investigated trait and process aspects of verbal ability. Numerical Facility (N) is the ability to perform simple arithmetical operations (mainly the four basic operations of addition, subtraction, multiplication, and division) swiftly and accurately. Since in many samples most individuals can perform these operations with satisfactory accuracy if given enough time, the measurements of this factor tend to emphasize speed and hence probably degree of practice. The correlations between V and N depend on the degree to which the experiences of a sample of individuals have tended to make language and arithmetic operations learned and practiced together and to the same extent.

Relations between factors $Gf$ and $Gc$, their involvements in various primary factors, and the possible existence of a general factor similar to Spearman's (1927) $g$ are discussed by Pawlik (1966), with contributions by J. Horn. Summarizing intercorrelations among primary factors in a number of studies, Pawlik finds good evidence for Cattell's (1963) notion of a second-order factor of fluid general ability. According to these results, it appears that Spatial Relations (SR), Flexibility of Closure (CF), Induction (I), Logical Reasoning (RL), and Syllogistic Reasoning (RS) are among the better measures of $Gf$, whereas correlations among factors of Verbal Comprehension (V), Numerical Facility (N), and Word Fluency (FW) are supportive of $Gc$. Pawlik offered the opinion that the results he reviewed did not support the notion of a single general ability factor such as Spearman's $g$. He would have us view $g$ as simply a summation of a series

of largely independent factors; it would represent mere versatility. That is, a high score on $g$ would represent just the happy collocation of high scores on a variety of independent abilities. The evidence reviewed by Pawlik, however, arose mainly from studies of rather highly selected populations. Other writers such as Humphreys (1981) and Undheim (1981), citing numerous studies of relatively unselected populations, are more favorable to the notion of a third-order factor of general intelligence.

Horn (in Pawlik, 1966) argues that both $Gf$ and $Gc$, as manifested in test scores observed in later childhood and adulthood, stem from an original (historical) fluid intelligence that depends on constitutional (*Anlage*) attributes of the individual in early childhood; $Gf$ ability develops with experiences that are more or less common to all persons in a culture, while $Gc$ develops as the individual is able to invest original $Gf$ ability in learning through somewhat special cultural experiences such as schooling. Thus, many factors, particularly those subsumed under $Gc$, represent achievements, but they are achievements that are attained by the individuals that have sufficient levels of $Gf$ abilities.

### General Visual Perception Factors (Gv)

The higher-order structure of the factors included in this group is not as yet well defined, partly because of difficulties in defining and specifying some of the factors. In general, they pertain to abilities in perceiving and mentally dealing with visual forms and patterns and with the spatial environment. Originally, Thurstone (1938) identified a Space factor that appeared in a wide variety of tasks involving the perception of spatial relations and configurations, whether in rigid states or in situations requiring mental manipulation of these configurations, and regardless of whether the configurations involved two or (imaginally) three dimensions. French (1951) cited 44 studies that identified such a factor. More recent research has suggested that the Space factor can be decomposed into either two or three factors, a true Space Relations (SR) factor relating to "individual differences in correctly perceiving spatial relationships between rigid configurations," a Visualization (VZ) factor that requires "the imagining, in spatial terms, the end result of a certain displacement (movement or rotation) of a configuration"

(Pawlik, 1966, p. 543), and a Spatial Orientation (SO) factor involving "the ability to perceive spatial patterns or to maintain orientation with respect to objects in space" (Ekstrom et al., 1976, p. 149). The factors may be differentiated partly by the emphasis they put on speed. Tests of VZ are generally unspeeded, while those of SR and SO are generally speeded. Further, in tests of VZ, the subject "seems removed from the stimulus pattern in that he appears to alter and manipulate its image" (French et al., 1963, p. 38), while in tests of the other two factors the observer uses himself as a fixed reference point. Nevertheless, the 1976 ETS kit does not provide tests of the SR factor. In a review, Lohman (1979) concludes that evidence supports the identification of all three factors, but that it is difficult to separate processes involved in them. Lohman agrees that factor VZ is predominantly a power (level of ability) factor, whereas the others are chiefly matters of speed and facility. Recently, quite detailed process analyses of the SR and VZ factors have been published by Pellegrino and Kail (1982), tending to confirm Lohman's conclusions.

Spatial perceptual processes are undoubtedly involved in other factors in this group. Speed of Closure (CS) is reportedly "the ability to unite an apparently disparate perceptual field into a single percept" and to do so rapidly (Ekstrom et al., 1976, p. 25). It is usually measured by tests that require the subject to form a meaningful percept from a partially degraded or masked stimulus presentation (possibly involving, therefore, the process of "perceptual integration" mentioned earlier, p. 817). Flexibility of Closure (CF) is "the ability to hold a given visual percept or configuration in mind so as to disembed it from other well defined [and thus distracting] material" (Ekstrom et al., 1976, p. 19). A good marker test for this factor is the well-known Gottschaldt figures test (Gottschaldt, 1926); anyone administering this test to a group of subjects will be struck with the ease with which some subjects see the embedded figures and the enormous difficulty experienced by others, even given considerable time. Spatial Scanning (SS) is described as "speed in exploring visually a wide or complicated spatial field" such as a visual maze, circuit diagram, or map (Ekstrom et al., 1976, p. 155). It seems to depend on speed and control in directing gaze over a path on a printed page or similar visual display, guided by the total visual context. Length Estimation (LE) is the "ability to judge and compare visually perceived distances on paper" (French et al., 1963, p. 21). Verbal Closure (CV) is described as "the ability to solve problems requiring the identification of visually presented words when some of the letters are missing, scrambled, or embedded among other letters" (Ekstrom et al., 1976, p. 33). These authors claim to have demonstrated that this factor is distinct from CS; perhaps this is because the tests of CV always involve orthographic stimuli.

Perceptual Speed (P) is one of the best attested factors in this group, but it is possible that it should be considered a composite of several subfactors. Ekstrom et al. (1976, p. 123) describe it as follows: "Speed in comparing figures or symbols, scanning to find figures or symbols, or carrying out other very simple tasks involving visual perception. It may be a centroid of several subfactors (including form discrimination and symbol discrimination) which can be separated but are more usefully treated as a single concept for research purposes." It should be noted, however, that tests of perceptual speed always involve speed of mental comparisons, either between objectively presented stimuli or between a physical stimulus and a mental representation. Lansman et al. (1982) have confirmed a relation between psychometric P and an information-processing factor measured by the Posner and Mitchell (1967) letter-matching task.

Perceptual Alternations (PA) and Figure Illusions (IL) are not well attested, but are mentioned here for their possible interest to experimental psychologists. Thurstone (1944) identified PA as Rate of Alternations in viewing a Necker cube or being subjected to dioptic retinal rivalry of colors. In this same study, Thurstone identified a factor, here coded IL, in several tests of ability to resist such perceptual illusions as the Müller-Lyer, Sanders, and Poggendorf illusions. Additional information on factors in this domain can be found in work by Coren and Girgus (1978), Goldberg (1979), Künnapas (1969), and Taylor (1976).

### General Auditory Perception Factors (Ga)

The factors in this domain, listed in Table 12.4, are the four identified in a study by Karlin (1942), but they are not well defined, nor are they correlated in such a way as to suggest the operation of group factor in the auditory domain.

Auditory Integral (AUI) has mainly to do with the ability to judge time intervals and integrate auditory information over time. Auditory Resistance (AUR) is the ability to perceive sound patterns (spoken or sung words) against interfering or masking sounds. Loudness (LO) represents ability to make accurate judgments of differences in sound intensity. Pitch Quality (PQ) seems best described as ability to judge differences in pitch or make judgements about tonal complexes. Unfortunately, little factor-analytic work has been done on IDs in the auditory domain until recently. Horn (1973) concluded that many auditory tests tap factors also identified with the more usual visual tests, but that certain auditory factors can be regarded as measuring a broad auditory ability factor distinct from factors measured in visual tests. In a recent study, Stankov and Horn (1980) found four factors reasonably specific to the domain of auditory perception: Auditory Cognition of Relationships (designated ACoR by these authors), Discrimination among Sound Patterns (DASP), Speech Perception Under Distraction/Distortion (SPUD), and Maintaining and Judging Rhythm (MaJR). Of these, the factor SPUD seems similar to Karlin's AUR, and DASP to Karlin's PQ; Stankov and Horn consider these two factors sufficiently related to posit a "broad auditory function analogous to the Gv that has been found among visual-input variables" (1980, p. 42).

### General Memory Factors (Gm)

The evidence assembled from the study by Underwood et al. (1978; see also p. 839 and Table 12.3) may be offered as the principal basis for asserting the existence of a general memory factor, but evidence is also available from a study by Hakstian and Cattell (1978), who propose a General Memory Capacity factor loaded in tests of Associative Memory (MA), somewhat more weakly in tests of Meaningful Memory (MM) and Numerical Ability (N), but nonsignificantly in Memory Span (MS), contrary to results reported by Underwood et al. Meaningful Memory is not recognized as a distinct factor in the sources used to compile Table 12.4. According to Ekstrom et al. (1976, p. 93), Associative Memory (MA) is "the ability to recall one part of a previously learned but otherwise unrelated pair of items when the other part of the pair is pre-

sented."[2] It appears in tests of paired-associate memory recall constructed according to the study-test paradigm using different kinds of stimulus-response pairs (e.g., first and last names, object-number pairs). The data of Underwood et al. suggest that MA could be generalized to a variety of other paradigms of paired-associate learning. With reference to the list of elementary cognitive processes given earlier, this factor seems to tap abilities to form and retrieve corepresentations. Memory Span (MS) is described by Ekstrom et al. (1976, p. 101) as "the ability to recall a number of distinct elements for immediate reproduction"; it is measured by both auditory and visual memory-span tests using either digits or alphabetic letters. However, recent research (e.g., Berger & Goldberger, 1979; Martin, 1978) and theory (Bachelder & Denny, 1977a, 1977b; Drewnowski, 1980) suggest that memory-span performances reflect several different processes. Visual Memory is recognized as a distinct factor in the 1976 ETS kit, concerned with "the ability to remember the configuration, location, and orientation of figural material," and thus possibly with a type of iconic memory. It is measured by tasks requiring the subject to remember the positions of things on a map or to recognize shapes that have been studied earlier. Musical Memory (MMU) is not included in the ETS kits but was listed by French (1951) as having been identified by Woodrow (1939); the factor may possibly be cross-identified with the Nonsymbolic Recognition Memory ("Mr") factor described by Horn (1973).

### Production Factors

The ETS kits recognize six factors, all of which require the subject to produce, within a time limit, a large number of different responses—verbal or figural—that fit certain rules or constraints. The larger the number of acceptable responses produced, the higher the score. These factors are rather highly correlated, though they are apparently still distinct. They may be different subfactors of what Hakstian and Cattell (1978) called a second-order General Retrieval Capacity (Gr) factor. In tests of Associational

[2]From Ekstrom, R.B., French, J.W., Harman, H.H., *Manual for Kit of Factor-Referenced Cognitive Tests 1976*. Copyright (c) 1976 by Educational Testing Service. All rights reserved. Reprinted by permission.

Fluency (FA), subjects must produce rapidly a large number of words that share a given area of meaning or other semantic property, for example, synonyms for the word *short*. Expressional Fluency (FE) requires the subject to compose a variety of sentences using certain given words or other cues; the aspect of fluency appears to reside in the ability to manipulate syntax or sentence structure to conform to stated restrictions. In Ideational Fluency (FI), the task is to write a number of ideas about a given topic or to give instances of a given class of objects. In Word Fluency (FW) the task is to write a variety of words that "fit one or more structural, phonetic, or orthographic restrictions that are not relevant to the meaning of the words" (Ekstrom et al., 1976, p. 73), for example, words ending in certain letter groups. (The factor may be partly dependent on spelling ability but is probably distinct from spelling ability itself.) In Flexibility of Use (XU) the requirement is to think of a variety of ways of using or classifying objects. It is regarded as representing the ability to overcome what has been called functional fixedness (Duncker, 1945). In tests of Figural Flexibility (XF), subjects are required to generate a variety of novel or different solutions to problems involving visual figural material.

Naming Speed (NA) is not included in any ETS kit but receives support from several studies (Carroll, 1941; Kettner, Guilford & Christensen, 1959; Thurstone & Thurstone, 1941, factor X3). It is the ability to produce rapidly the conventional names for pictured objects. Speech Fluency (FS) was called Public Speaking by French (1951), but its measures do not require a public speaking context; rather, it appears to be the ability to produce a flow of well-formed spoken prose without undue lapses, hesitations, or disconnected syntax. It is quite different from the kinds of fluency measured by the other factors mentioned here.

Originality (O), Semantic Redefinition (RE), and Sensitivity to Problems (SEP) were recognized in the 1963 ETS kit, but a review of literature and certain studies conducted by Ekstrom et al. (1979) suggested that it was difficult to distinguish them from other factors already included. Originality (O), tests of which required subjects to give clever or unusual ideas in various situations, appeared to be quite similar to Ideational Fluency (FI). Semantic Redefinition (RE), described as "the ability to shift the function of an object or part of an object and use it in a new way" (French et al., 1963, p. 35), was found to be highly similar to Semantic Spontaneous Flexibility, later designated as Flexibility of Use (XU) in the 1976 kit. Sensitivity to Problems (SEP) was regarded as inadequately supported by evidence; this does not exclude the possibility that it could be successfully demonstrated with new evidence.

### Speed Factors

Factors pertaining to speed in cognitive performances have had an anomalous status in factor-analytic research. French (1951, p. 241) described a Speed factor as appearing to be "very general," covering "speed on everything from verbal tests to tapping speed and back again to reasoning tests . . . ." He noted that "it is a curious thing that a speed factor has not appeared in rather numerous analyses, since most analyses contain both speeded and unspeeded tests." He regarded Davidson and Carroll's (1945) study, in which rate of work and level of mastery scores were separately obtained for each of a series of Army Alpha intelligence tests, as yielding the most convincing evidence for one or more speed factors independent of power or level of accuracy factors in various domains. Lord's (1956) study later provided further evidence for this conclusion. The absence of separate factors for speed and level of mastery can be attributed to the fact that most factor-analytic investigations, even recent ones, have not obtained separate measurements of accuracy and rate of work; the time-limit score, according to Davidson and Carroll's findings, is usually factorially complex, having variance from factors for both rate of work and level of mastery. The problem of defining and separating speed and level, particularly in relation to the definition of spatial ability factors, has been comprehensively reviewed by Lohman (1979), who concludes that "speed-level and complexity differences are pervasive in the factor analytic literature on human abilities" (p. 151). We are therefore quite ignorant about the status of most of the factors listed in Table 12.4 with regard to the speed-level distinction. This conclusion applies not only to primary factors but also to higher-order factors; at least some of the covariance among primary factors that is cited to support their composition as second-order factors may be due partly to speed. On the other hand, logic and considerable evidence suggest that much of the differentiation among factors stems from differences in process and in content that are independent of speed or rate of work. Careful work on factor differentiation and interpretation requires as much control as possible on differential measurement of speed or rate of performance, on the one hand, and the level of accuracy or mastery that can be attained in relatively unlimited time, on the other. Rimoldi's (1951) work suggests the possibility of distinguishing speed from personal tempo by defining speed as the maximum rate at which satisfactory performance can be attained and personal tempo as the characteristic pace at which a person is inclined to work. Speed and accuracy tradeoffs would, of course, play some part in the relations discovered.

No attempt is made here to review the evidence for a variety of speed factors. Speed of Judgment (SDJ), a factor from Thurstone's (1944) study, was recognized by French (1951) and may be of interest to experimental psychologists since it loaded on several variables similar to those studied in experimental work: speed in sorting figures by color or form, speed in selecting trait names, and speed in comparing weights. Speed of Judgment was linearly independent of several other factors in the study that depended at least partly on speed.

### Psychomotor Factors

Eight psychomotor factors were listed by French (1951), all of which Pawlik (1966, pp. 539–541) mentioned in his review of psychometrically established factors. Aiming (AIMG) is the quickness and precision of hand and finger movements of comparatively small extent, requiring good eye-hand coordination. Ambidexterity (AMB), a factor not widely attested, is the skill in using the less preferred hand. Articulation Speed (SDAR), also not widely attested but apparently highly reliable, refers to the ability to read aloud or to utter consonant syllables repeatedly (diadochokinetically) at maximum rates. Finger Dexterity (FD) is the speed and accuracy of the fingers in manipulating small objects. Manual Dexterity (MD) is the speed and coordination of arm and hand movements in manipulating objects. Psychomotor Coordination (PC) is a factor of complex gross motor movements (sometimes involving the whole body) in certain types of tasks involving machines or apparatus in which there is continuous adjustment and kinesthetic feedback. Reaction Time (RT), as defined in a number of studies, is simple (as opposed to choice or disjunctive) reaction time. Tapping (TA), or as Pawlik prefers to call it, Wrist-Finger Speed, appears in tasks that make little demand on eye-hand coordination but that emphasize speed of repetitive wrist-hand movements.

Inclusion of this list of recognized psychomotor factors among factors of cognitive abilities may be justified by recalling Fitts's (1964) emphasis on the role of information processing in the formation and improvement of perceptual-motor skills. Moreover, since many psychological experiments entail the execution of some kind of response, IDs in psychomotor skills very likely contribute to the variance of response measurements, particularly if the apparatus involves any complexity of motor response.

### Miscellaneous Affective-Cognitive Factors

French (1951) recognized at least four factors that could be described as both affective and cognitive; in factorial studies, several factors were found associated with more clearly cognitive ability measures. While none of them is well defined or attested, they are mentioned here for their possible relevance. Attention (AT), as the name suggests, refers to variations in subjects' ability to maintain a focus of attention, or a constant and consistent set, in the performance of a protracted task such as a series of test items. Carefulness (CA) is the ability to perform a task (usually, a relatively easy one) accurately in spite of pressure for speed. Persistence (PE) is the ability to keep working at a protracted task in spite of its increasing mental or physical difficulty. As French remarks, however, "the factorial results yield no proof that this factor is persistence rather than motivation to get good test scores" (p. 230). Finally, Perseveration (PN) refers, apparently, to the tendency of a subject to persist in a particular set or state despite a change in instructions or, conversely, the ability to change set quickly. Its existence is not well supported in the literature, but it may be represented in the Einstellung effects demonstrated by Luchins and Luchins (1950).

## Individual Differences in Experimental Cognitive Tasks

Insofar as the tasks presented in psychometric tests exhibit similarities to those presented in experimental laboratory studies of cognition, there is every reason to predict that these two types of tasks tap similar or even identical dimensions of IDs, although minor differences may arise from differences in method—that is, differences may arise from psychometric paper-and-pencil methodologies as against controlled laboratory methods. A number of studies now available confirm this prediction.

An excellent example is a study by Lansman et al. (1982), who administered a series of psychometric tests and experimental information-processing tasks to 91 college students. The psychometric tests included measures of four factors recognized in the Cattell-Horn theory of intelligence (Cattell, 1963; Horn, 1978; Horn & Cattell, 1966): Gf, Gc, Gv, and Clerical and Perceptual Speed (CPS), identifiable with the factor P—Perceptual Speed of Table 12.4. Information-processing tasks studied were mental rotations (Shepard & Metzler, 1971), letter matching (Posner & Mitchell, 1967), and sentence verification (Clark & Chase, 1972). In order to investigate method factors, each task was presented in both a paper-and-pencil and a computerized laboratory version. Relations among all measures were examined by confirmatory factor analysis.

The four Cattell-Horn factors were confirmed and found to be largely independent in this college population. Speed of letter matching and of sentence verification were found to be highly correlated ($r = .59$ to $.77$ depending on the model tested), but both were nearly uncorrelated with mental rotation speed. These relations were found for both paper-and-pencil and computerized versions of the tasks. There was great correspondence between gross scores on the two versions, but not always between derived measures, such as the slopes and intercepts in the mental rotation task or the NI − PI (name identity minus physical identity) RTs in the letter-matching task.

Of most interest were the relations between psychometric factors and factors based on the information-processing tasks. As may be seen from Table 12.5, the mental rotation factor was strongly correlated with Gv and weakly with CPS. The letter-matching factor was strongly

**Table 12.5. Correlations between information processing factors and ability factors ($N = 91$)**

|  | Mental rotations | Letter matching | Sentence verification |
|---|---|---|---|
| Gc | .04 | .07 | .28 |
| Gf | − .10 | .02 | .00 |
| Gv | .78 | − .10 | − .07 |
| CPS | .21 | .69 | .38 |

*Note.* From "Ability Factors and Cognitive Processes" by M. Lansman, G. Donaldson, E. Hunt, and S. Yantis, 1982, *Intelligence, 6*, p. 376. Copyright 1982 by the ABLEX Publishing Corporation. Reprinted by permission.

correlated with CPS, a finding that supports the notion that a process of speed of mental comparisons is involved in CPS or Perceptual speed. The sentence-verification factor showed only weak relations with Gc and CPS. The psychometric factor Gf had no significant relation with any information-processing factor, a finding that the authors interpreted as indicating that the principal information-processing feature of Gf tests—inducing patterns and principles—was not called on in any of the three information-processing tasks they studied.

In another study relating information-processing parameters to psychometric test variables, Frederiksen (1982) obtained a series of theory-based information-processing measurements on 48 subjects of high school age chosen to represent a wide range of reading ability. Confirmatory factor analysis led to the isolation of eight components of reading skill, ranging from "letter encoding efficiency" to "semantic integration of antecedents with a discourse representation." Correlations of these components with five cognitive ability factors and with four conventional measures of reading skill show a number of strong relations. Scores on the Nelson-Denny reading comprehension test could be predicted from the eight components with a highly significant multiple R of .76.

Jensen (1982a, 1982b) has asserted that parameters derived from his choice-reaction test (described earlier) are related to the g factor of mental ability, and some of these claims appear to have been confirmed in further studies (P.A. Vernon, 1983), though Carroll (1981) reanalyzed Jensen's data and questioned some of his conclusions. Similarly, Hunt (1978) has assembled data suggesting that a variable measured by subtracting the average RT for physical matches from the average RT for name matches in the letter-matching task shows a consistent correlation of about $-.3$ with scores on scholastic aptitude tests. This finding is open to a number of interpretations because of the factorial complexity of scholastic aptitude measures. At this writing it is not possible to draw firm conclusions about the dimensional analysis of variables in the speed-of-information-processing domain. The next few years can be expected to witness thorough investigations of this domain. One of the chief issues to be resolved is the role of the range of talent in samples studied. Generally, relationships are much more striking in samples that range from mentally retarded to highly educated subjects than they are in, for example, the highly selected samples drawn from college populations.

## INDIVIDUAL DIFFERENCES AND PSYCHOLOGICAL THEORY

A major goal of psychological theory is to identify the processes that govern cognitive activity and to discover the laws relating such processes to behavior. The essential contribution of individual differences research to psychological theory is its delineation of the distinct ways in which individuals' performances vary consistently over different types of behavioral tasks. Information on the dimensions of such IDs becomes grist for the psychological theorist's mill, because these dimensions call for explanation in terms of fundamental processes, acquired skills and knowledges, and strategies of cognitive activity. Factor analysis and other psychometric procedures can yield information on independent sources of ID variance in task performance.

This chapter has emphasized methodologies and findings regarding dimensions of cognitive abilities. The strategy underlying this research has been to vary tasks with respect to hypothesized processes, types of stimuli and responses, and experimental conditions in such a way that IDs reliably identified in task performances can be assigned to different processes, skills, and strategies. It assumes that different processes, skills, and strategies will be reflected in different ID dimensions. For example, suppose it is hypothesized that memory span performances depend on two different processes—registration

of information concerning discrete stimuli and registration of information concerning the ordering of those stimuli. Such a hypothesis could be considered confirmed if the individual differences revealed in one of those processes proved to be independent of IDs in the other. Indeed, findings by Martin (1978) tend to confirm such a hypothesis. In this way IDs may become, as Underwood (1975) has pointed out, a crucible for theory construction. Underwood states what he calls the generalized case as follows:

> If we include in our nomothetic theories a process or mechanism that can be measured reliably outside of the situation for which it is serving its theoretical purpose, we have an immediate test of the validity of the theoretical formulation . . . . The assumed theoretical process will necessarily have a tie with performance which reflects (in theory) the magnitude of the process. Individuals will vary in the amount of this characteristic or skill they "possess." A prediction concerning differences in the performance of the individuals must follow. A test of this prediction can yield two outcomes. If the correlation is substantial, the theory has a go-ahead signal, that and no more; the usual positive correlations across subjects on various skills and aptitudes allow no conclusion concerning the theory per se. If the relationship between the individual difference measurements and the performance is essentially zero, there is no alternative but to drop the line of theoretical thinking (1975, p. 130).[3]

From Underwood's perspective, ID research appears to have a more negative than positive role in psychological theorizing. It assists in the rejection of theories, but it does not aid in their confirmation. From the perspective adopted here, however, it can have a positive role if it aids in the differentiation of psychological entities through associating them with different dimensions of IDs. Many hypotheses advanced in psychological theory deal with the differentiation of psychological concepts, and the mass of research evidence reviewed in this chapter suggests that psychological entities frequently show correspondences with ID phenomena.

---

[3]From "Individual differences as a crucible in theory construction," by B.J. Underwood. *American Psychologist*, 1975, *30*, 128–134. Copyright 1975 by The American Psychological Association. Reprinted by permission.

One can still agree with Underwood and other writers (e.g., Baron & Treiman, 1980) that a failure to differentiate psychological entities through ID research does not necessarily indicate that they cannot be differentiated by other means. The finding that two performances are correlated or are not correlated over individuals is always open to a number of possible interpretations. The methodology of IDs is only one of many avenues to elucidate such a finding. Nevertheless, if ID methodology is skillfully combined with such other methodologies as the experimental method, longitudinal and developmental research (Butterfield, Siladi & Belmont, 1980), and task analysis (McCormick, 1976), it can make a powerful contribution to psychological knowledge. Although it might approach the size of a Manhattan Project, it is not unreasonable to call for a research effort that would focus attention on each of the ID dimensions that might be identified, to investigate its genesis and the course of its development over the life span, its generality over ranges of behavior, and the extent to which the performances that manifest it are amenable to modification through learning and other experiences. The outcomes could hardly fail to make substantial contributions to psychological theory.

# REFERENCES

Anderson, S., Auquier, A., Hauck, W.W., Oakes, D., Vandaele, W., & Weisberg, H.I. (1980). *Statistical methods for comparative studies: Techniques for bias reduction.* New York: Wiley.

Atkinson, R.C., Holmgren, J.E., & Juola, J.F. (1969). Processing time as influenced by the number of elements in a visual display. *Perception & Psychophysics, 6,* 321–326.

Atkinson, R.C. & Shiffrin, R.M. (1968). Human memory: A proposed system and its control processes. In K.W. Spence & J.T. Spence (Eds.), *The psychology of learning and motivation: Advances in research and theory,* Vol. 2 (pp. 89–195). New York: Academic Press.

Bachelder, B.L. & Denny, M.R. (1977a). A theory of intelligence: I. Span and the complexity of stimulus control. *Intelligence, 1,* 127–150.

Bachelder, B.L. & Denny, M.R. (1977b). A theory of intelligence: II. The role of span in a variety of intellectual tasks. *Intelligence, 1,* 237–256.

Baron, J. & Treiman, R. (1980). Some problems in the study of differences in cognitive processes. *Memory & Cognition, 8,* 313–321.

Battig, W.F. (1962). Parsimony in psychology. *Psychological Reports, 11,* 555–572.

Battig, W.F. (1979). Are the important "individual differences" between or within individuals? *Journal of Research in Personality, 13,* 546–558.

Baxter, B. (1942). A study of reaction time using factorial design. *Journal of Experimental Psychology, 31,* 430–437.

Berger, E. & Goldberger, L. (1979). Field dependence and short-term memory. *Perceptual & Motor Skills, 49,* 87–96.

Berk, R.A. (Ed.). (1980). *Criterion-referenced measurement: The state of the art.* Baltimore: Johns Hopkins University Press.

Blackburn, J.M. (1936). *The acquisition of skill: An analysis of learning curves.* London: Medical Research Council, Industrial Health Research Board Report No. 73.

Bolton, B. & Hinman, S. (1981). Factor analytic studies: 1941–1970 (Ms. 2340). In *JSAS Catalog of selected documents in psychology,* pp. 11, 71.

Bolton, B., Hinman, S., & Tuft, S. (1973). *Annotated bibliography: Factor analytic studies 1941–1970,* Vols. 1–4. Fayetteville: Arkansas Rehabilitation Research and Training Center.

Budescu, D.V. & Wallsten, T.S. (1979). A note on monotonic transformations in the context of functional measurement and analysis of variance. *Bulletin of the Psychonomic Society, 14,* 307–310.

Butterfield, E.C., Siladi, D., & Belmont, J.M. (1980). Validating theories of intelligence. In H.W. Reese & L.P. Lipsitt (Eds.), *Advances in child development and behavior,* Vol. 15 (pp. 95–162). New York: Academic Press.

Carroll, J.B. (1941). A factor analysis of verbal abilities. *Psychometrika, 6,* 279–307.

Carroll, J.B. (1961). The nature of the data, or how to choose a correlation coefficient. *Psychometrika, 26,* 347–372.

Carroll, J.B. (1970). An alternative to Juilland's usage coefficient for lexical frequencies, and a proposal for a Standard Frequency Index (SFI). *Computer Studies in the Humanities and Verbal Behavior, 3,* 61–65.

Carroll, J.B. (1972). Stalking the wayward factors: Review of Guilford and Hoepfner's *The analysis of intelligence. Contemporary Psychology, 17,* 321–324.

Carroll, J.B. (1976). Psychometric tests as cognitive tasks: A new "Structure of Intellect." In L. Resnick (Ed.), *The nature of intelligence* (pp. 27–56). Hillsdale, NJ: Erlbaum.

Carroll, J.B. (1978). How shall we study individual differences in cognitive abilities?—Methodological and theoretical perspectives. *Intelligence, 2,* 87–115.

Carroll, J.B. (1980). Remarks on Sternberg's "Factor

theories of intelligence are all right almost." *Educational Researcher, 9*(8), 14–18.

Carroll, J.B. (1981). Ability and task difficulty in cognitive psychology. *Educational Researcher, 10*(1), 11–21.

Carroll, J.B. (1983a). The difficulty of a test and its factor composition revisited. In H. Wainer & S. Messick (Eds.), *Principals* [sic] *of modern psychological measurement: A Festschrift in honor of Frederic M. Lord* (pp. 257–283). Hillsdale, NJ: Erlbaum.

Carroll, J.B. (1983b). Studying individual differences in cognitive abilities: Through and beyond factor analysis. In R.F. Dillon & R.R. Schmeck (Eds.), *Individual differences in cognition*, Vol. 1 (pp. 1–33). New York: Academic Press.

Carroll, J.B. (1985). Exploratory factor analysis: A tutorial. In D.K. Detterman (Ed.), *Current topics in human intelligence*, Vol. 1 (pp. 25–58). Norwood, NJ: Ablex.

Carroll, J.B. & White, M.N. (1973). Word frequency and age of acquisition as determiners of picture-naming latency. *Quarterly Journal of Experimental Psychology, 25*, 85–95.

Cattell, R.B. (1957). A universal index for psychological factors. *Psychologia, 1*, 74–85.

Cattell, R.B. (1963). Theory of fluid and crystallized intelligence: A critical experiment. *Journal of Educational Psychology, 54*, 1–22.

Cattell, R.B. (1966). The scree test for the number of factors. *Multivariate Behavioral Research, 1*, 245–276.

Cattell, R.B. (1971). *Abilities: Their structure, growth and action.* Boston: Houghton Mifflin.

Cattell, R.B. (1978). *The scientific use of factor analysis in behavioral and life sciences.* New York: Plenum Press.

Cattell, R.B. & Dreger, R.M. (Eds.) (1977). *Handbook of modern personality theory.* Washington, DC: Hemisphere.

Cattell, R.B. & Horn, J.L. (1978). A check on the theory of fluid and crystallized intelligence with description of new subtest designs. *Journal of Educational Measurement, 15*, 139–164.

Chase, W.G. (1978). Elementary information processes. In W.K. Estes (Ed.), *Handbook of learning and cognitive processes: Vol. 5. Human information processing* (pp. 19–90). Hillsdale, NJ: Erlbaum.

Chiang, A. & Atkinson, R.C. (1976). Individual differences and interrelationships among a select set of cognitive skills. *Memory & Cognition, 4*, 661–672.

Clark, H.H. & Chase, W.G. (1972). On the process of comparing sentences against pictures. *Cognitive Psychology, 3*, 472–517.

Cohen, R.L. & Sandberg, T. (1977). Relation between intelligence and short-term memory. *Cognitive Psychology, 9*, 534–554.

Comrey, A.L. (1978). Common methodological problems in factor analytic studies. *Journal of Consulting & Clinical Psychology, 46*, 648–659.

Cooley, W.W. & Lohnes, P.R. (1971). *Multivariate data analysis.* New York: Wiley.

Cooper, L. A. (1976). Individual differences in visual comparison processes. *Perception & Psychophysics, 19*, 433–444.

Cooper, L.A. (1982). Strategies for visual comparison and representation: Individual differences. In R.J. Sternberg (Ed.), *Advances in the psychology of intelligence*, Vol. 1 (pp. 77–124). Hillsdale, NJ: Erlbaum.

Cooper, L.A. & Podgorny, P. (1976). Mental transformations and visual comparison processes: Effects of complexity and similarity. *Journal of Experimental Psychology: Human Perception and Performance, 2*, 503–514.

Coren, S. & Girgus, J.S. (1978). *Seeing is deceiving: The psychology of visual illusions.* Hillsdale, NJ: Erlbaum.

Cronbach, L.J. (1957). The two disciplines of scientific psychology. *American Psychologist, 12*, 671–684.

Cronbach, L.J. (1975). Beyond the two disciplines of scientific psychology. *American Psychologist, 30*, 116–127.

Cronbach, L.J. & Snow, R.E. (1977). *Aptitudes and instructional methods: A handbook for research on interactions.* New York: Irvington.

Cureton, E.E. & D'Agostino, R.B. (1983). *Factor analysis: An applied approach.* Hillsdale, NJ: Erlbaum.

Davidson, W.M. & Carroll, J.B. (1945). Speed and level components in time-limit scores: A factor analysis. *Educational & Psychological Measurement, 5*, 411–427.

Di Lollo, V. (1980). Temporal integration in visual memory. *Journal of Experimental Psychology: General, 109*, 75–97.

Drewnowski, A. (1980). Attributes and priorities in short-term recall: A new model of memory span. *Journal of Experimental Psychology: General, 109*, 208–250.

Duncker, K. (1945). On problem-solving. *Psychological Monographs, 58*(5, Whole No. 270).

Ebel, R.L. (1951). Estimation of the reliability of ratings. *Psychometrika, 16*, 407–424.

Egan, D.E. (1978). *Characterizing spatial ability: Different mental processes reflected in accuracy and latency scores.* (USN AMRL Technical Report, Aug. 1978, No. 1250). Murray Hill, NJ: Bell Laboratories.

Ekstrom, R.B., French, J.W., & Harman, H.H. (1976). *Manual for kit of factor-referenced cognitive tests, 1976.* Princeton, NJ: Educational Testing Service.

Ekstrom, R.B., French, J.W., & Harman, H.H. (1979). Cognitive factors: Their identification and replication. *Multivariate Behavioral Research Monographs* (No. 79-2).

Estes, W.K. (1974). Learning theory and intelligence. *American Psychologist, 29*, 740-749.

Estes, W.K. (1976). Intelligence and cognitive psychology. In L. Resnick (Ed.), *The nature of intelligence* (pp. 295-305). Hillsdale, NJ: Erlbaum.

Fischer, G.H. (1973). The linear logistic model as an instrument in educational research. *Acta Psychologica, 37*, 359-374.

Fitts, P.M. (1954). The information capacity of the human motor system in controlling the amplitude of movement. *Journal of Experimental Psychology, 47*, 381-391.

Fitts, P.M. (1964). Perceptual-motor skill learning. In A.W. Melton (Ed.), *Categories of human learning* (pp. 243-285). New York: Academic Press.

Fitts, P.M. & Peterson, J.R. (1964). The information capacity of discrete motor responses. *Journal of Experimental Psychology, 67*, 103-112.

Fleishman, E.A. & Fruchter, B. (1960). Factor structure and predictability of successive stages of learning Morse Code. *Journal of Applied Psychology, 44*, 97-101.

Fleishman, E.A. & Hempel, W.E., Jr. (1954). Changes in factor structure of a complex psychomotor test as a function of practice. *Psychometrika, 19*, 239-252.

Fleishman, E.A. & Hempel, W.E. Jr. (1955). The relation between abilities and improvement with practice in a visual discrimination task. *Journal of Experimental Psychology, 49*, 301-312.

Frank, P. (1957). *Philosophy of science: The link between science and philosophy.* Englewood Cliffs, NJ: Prentice-Hall.

Frederiksen, J.R. (1982). A componential theory of reading skills and their interactions. In R.J. Sternberg (Ed.), *Advances in the psychology of intelligence*, Vol. 1 (pp. 125-180). Hillsdale, NJ: Erlbaum.

French, J.W. (1951). The description of aptitude and achievement tests in terms of rotated factors. *Psychometric Monographs* (No. 5).

French, J.W. (1965). The relationship of problem-solving styles to the factor composition of tests. *Educational & Psychological Measurement, 25*, 9-28.

French, J.W., Ekstrom, R.B., & Price, L.A. (1963). *Manual and kit of reference tests for cognitive factors.* Princeton, NJ: Educational Testing Service.

Gaito, J. (1980). Measurement scales and statistics: Resurgence of an old misconception. *Psychological Bulletin, 87*, 564-567.

Geiselman, R.E., Woodward, J.A., & Beatty, J. (1982).

Individual differences in verbal memory performance: A test of alternative information-processing models. *Journal of Experimental Psychology: General, 111*, 109-134.

Glushko, R.J. & Cooper, L.A. (1978). Spatial comprehension and comparison processes in verification tasks. *Cognitive Psychology, 10*, 391-421.

Goldberg, L.R. (1979). A general scheme for the analytic decomposition of objective test scores: Illustrative demonstrations using the rod-and-frame test and the Müller-Lyer illusion. *Journal of Research in Personality, 13*, 245-265.

Gorsuch, R.L. *Factor analysis*, 2nd ed. (1983). Hillsdale, NJ: Erlbaum.

Gottschaldt, K. (1926). Ueber den Einfluss der Erfahrung auf die Wahrnehmung von Figuren. I. Ueber den Einfluss gehäufter Einprägung von Figuren auf ihre Sichtbarkeit in umfassenden Konfigurationen. [On the influence of experience on the perception of figures. I. On the influence of cumulated impression of figures on their perceptibility in enclosing configurations.] *Psychologische Forschung, 8*, 261-317.

Greeno, J.G. (1978). Natures of problem-solving abilities. In W.K. Estes (Ed.), *Handbook of learning and cognitive processes, Vol. 5: Human information processing* (pp. 239-270). Hillsdale, NJ: Erlbaum.

Guilford, J.P. (1967). *The nature of human intelligence.* New York: McGraw-Hill.

Guilford, J.P. (1979). *Cognitive psychology with a frame of reference.* San Diego: EdITS.

Guilford, J.P. (1980). Fluid and crystallized intelligences: Two fanciful concepts. *Psychological Bulletin, 88*, 406-412.

Guilford, J.P. (1982). Cognitive psychology's ambiguities: Some suggested remedies. *Psychological Review, 89*, 48-59.

Guilford, J.P. & Hoepfner, R. (1971). *The analysis of intelligence.* New York: McGraw-Hill.

Guttman, L. (1941). The quantification of a class of attributes: A theory and method for scale construction. In P. Horst, *The prediction of personal adjustment* (pp. 319-348). New York: Social Science Research Council.

Hakstian, A.R. & Cattell, R.B. (1978). Higher-stratum ability structures on a basis of twenty primary abilities. *Journal of Educational Psychology, 70*, 657-669.

Harman, H.H. (1976). *Modern factor analysis* (3rd ed.). Chicago: University of Chicago Press.

Harris, C.W. & Kaiser, H.F. (1964). Oblique factor analytic solutions by orthogonal transformations. *Psychometrika, 29*, 347-362.

Hasher, L. & Zacks, R.T. (1979). Automatic and effortful processes in memory. *Journal of Experimental Psychology: General, 108,* 356–388.

Hempel, C.G. (1966). *Philosophy of natural science.* Englewood Cliffs, NJ: Prentice-Hall.

Hendrickson, A.E. & White, P.O. (1964). PROMAX: A quick method for rotation to oblique simple structure. *British Journal of Statistical Psychology, 17,* 65–70.

Hick, W.E. (1952). On the rate of gain of information. *Quarterly Journal of Experimental Psychology, 4,* 11–26.

Hinman, S. & Bolton, B. (1979). *Factor analytic studies 1971–1975.* Troy, NY: Whitston.

Hock, H.S. (1973). The effects of stimulus structure and familiarity on same-different comparison. *Perception & Psychophysics, 14,* 413–420.

Horn, J.L. (1973). Theory of functions represented among auditory and visual test performances. In J.R. Royce (Ed.), *Multivariate analysis and psychological theory* (pp. 203–239). London: Academic Press.

Horn, J.L. (1977). Personality and ability theory. In R.B. Cattell & R.M. Dreger (Eds.), *Handbook of modern personality theory* (pp. 139–165). Washington, DC: Hemisphere.

Horn, J.L. (1978). Human ability systems. In P.B. Baltes (Ed.), *Life-span development and behavior,* Vol. 1 (pp. 211–256). New York: Academic Press.

Horn, J.L. & Cattell, R.B. (1966). Refinement of the theory of fluid and crystallized general intelligences. *Journal of Educational Psychology, 57,* 253–270.

Horn, J.L. & Cattell, R.B. (1982). Whimsy and misunderstandings of Gf-Gc theory: A comment on Guilford. *Psychological Bulletin, 91,* 623–633.

Horn, J.L. & Knapp, J.R. (1973). On the subjective character of the empirical base of Guilford's Structure-of-Intellect model. *Psychological Bulletin, 80,* 33–43.

Horn, J.L. & Knapp, J.R. (1974). Thirty wrongs do not make a right: A reply to Guilford. *Psychological Bulletin, 81,* 502–504.

Humphreys, L.G. (1981). The primary mental ability. In M.P. Friedman, J.P. Das & N. O'Connor (Eds.), *Intelligence and learning* (pp. 87–102). New York: Plenum Press.

Hunt, E. (1978). Mechanics of verbal ability. *Psychological Review, 85,* 109–130.

Hunt, E., Davidson, J., & Lansman, M. (1981). Individual differences in long-term memory access. *Memory & Cognition, 9,* 599–608.

Hunt, E., Frost, N., & Lunneborg, C. (1973). Individual differences in cognition: A new approach to intelligence. In G. Bower (Ed.), *The psychology of learning and motivation: Advances in research and*

*theory,* Vol. 7 (pp. 87–122). New York: Academic Press.

Hunt, E. & Lansman, M. (1975). Cognitive theory applied to individual differences. In W.K. Estes (Ed.), *Handbook of learning and cognitive processes, Vol. 1: Introduction to concepts and issues* (pp. 81–110). Hillsdale, NJ: Erlbaum.

Hunt, E., Lunneborg, C.E., & Lewis, J. (1975). What does it mean to be high verbal? *Cognitive Psychology, 7,* 194–227.

Jeffress, L.A. (1948). The nature of "primary abilities." *American Journal of Psychology, 61,* 107–111.

Jensen, A.R. (1980). *Bias in mental testing.* New York: Free Press.

Jensen, A.R. (1982a). The chronometry of intelligence. In R.J. Sternberg (Ed.), *Advances in the psychology of intelligence,* Vol. 1 (pp. 255–310). Hillsdale, NJ: Erlbaum.

Jensen, A.R. (1982b). Reaction time and psychometric *g.* In H.J. Eysenck (Ed.), *A model for intelligence* (pp. 93–132). Berlin: Springer-Verlag.

Jöreskog, K.G. & Sörbom, D. (1979). *Advances in factor analysis and structural equation models.* Cambridge, MA: Abt.

Jöreskog, K.G. & Sörbom, D. (1983). *LISREL V and LISREL VI: Analysis of linear structural relationships by the method of maximum likelihood and least square methods: User's guide* (2nd ed.) Mooresville, IN: International Educational Services.

Kaiser, H.F. (1958). The varimax criterion for analytic rotation in factor analysis. *Psychometrika, 23,* 187–200.

Kaiser, H.F. (1960). The application of electronic computers to factor analysis. *Educational & Psychological Measurement, 20,* 141–151.

Karlin, J.E. (1942). A factorial study of auditory function. *Psychometrika, 7,* 251–279.

Keating, D.P. & Bobbitt, B.L. (1978). Individual and developmental differences in cognitive-processing components of mental ability. *Child Development, 49,* 155–167.

Kennedy, R.S., Carter, R.C., & Bittner, A.C., Jr. (1980). A catalogue of performance evaluation tests for environmental research. *Proceedings of the Human Factors Society, 24,* 344–348.

Kettner, N.W., Guilford, J.P., & Christensen, P.R. (1959). A factor-analytic study across domains of reasoning, creativity, and evaluation. *Psychological Monographs: General & Applied, 73,* 1–31.

Kim, J-O. & Mueller, C.W. (1978a). *Introduction to factor analysis: What it is and how to do it.* Beverly Hills, CA: Sage.

Kim, J-O. & Mueller, C.W. (1978b). *Factor analysis: Statistical methods and practical issues.* Beverly Hills, CA: Sage.

Kirk, R.E. (1982). *Experimental design: Procedures for the behavioral sciences* (2nd ed.). Belmont, CA: Brooks/Cole.

Künnapas, T. (1969). Figural reversal rate and personal tempo. *Scandinavian Journal of Psychology, 10*, 27–32.

Lansman, M., Donaldson, G., Hunt, E., & Yantis, S. (1982). Ability factors and cognitive processes. *Intelligence, 6*, 347–386.

Leicht, K.L., Miller, R., & Ramseyer, G.C. (1978). Use of analysis of variance to assess individual differences in learning. *Psychological Reports, 42*, 487–491.

Lohman, D.F. (1979). *Spatial ability: A review and reanalysis of the correlational literature* (Technical Report No. 8). Stanford, CA: Aptitude Research Project, School of Education, Stanford University.

Lord, F.M. (1956). A study of speed factors in tests and academic grades. *Psychometrika, 21*, 31–50.

Lord, F.M. (1980). *Applications of item response theory to practical testing problems.* Hillsdale, NJ: Erlbaum.

Lord, F.M. & Novick, M.R. (1968). *Statistical theories of mental test scores.* Reading, MA: Addison-Wesley.

Luchins, A. & Luchins, E. (1950). New experimental attempts at preventing mechanization in problem solving. *Journal of General Psychology, 42*, 279–297.

MacLeod, C.M., Hunt, E.B., & Mathews, N.N. (1978). Individual differences in the verification of sentence-picture relationships. *Journal of Verbal Learning and Verbal Behavior, 17*, 493–507.

Marshalek, B. (1981). *Trait and process aspects of vocabulary knowledge and verbal ability* (Technical Report No. 15). Stanford, CA: Aptitude Research Project, School of Education, Stanford University.

Martin, M. (1978). Memory span as a measure of individual differences in memory capacity. *Memory & Cognition, 6*, 194–198.

Masters, J.C. (1981). Developmental psychology. *Annual Review of Psychology, 32*, 117–151.

Mathews, N.N., Hunt, E.B., & MacLeod, C.M. (1980). Strategy choice and strategy training in sentence-picture verification. *Journal of Verbal Learning and Verbal Behavior, 19*, 531–548.

McCormick, E.J. (1976). Job and task analysis. In M.D. Dunnette (Ed.), *Handbook of industrial and organizational psychology* (pp. 651–696). Chicago: Rand McNally.

Miller, G.A., Galanter, E., & Pribram, K. (1960). *Plans and the structure of behavior.* New York: Holt, Rinehart & Winston.

Montanelli, R.G., Jr. & Humphreys, L.G. (1976). Latent roots of random data correlation matrices with squared multiple correlations on the diagonal: A Monte Carlo study. *Psychometrika, 41*, 341–348.

Mulaik, S.A. (1972). *The foundations of factor analysis.* New York: McGraw-Hill.

Mulholland, T.M., Pellegrino, J.W., & Glaser, R. (1980). Components of geometric analogy solution. *Cognitive Psychology, 12*, 252–284.

Neisser, U. (1976). *Cognition and reality: Principles and implications of cognitive psychology.* San Francisco: Freeman.

Newell, A. (1973). Production systems of control processes. In W.G. Chase (Ed.), *Visual information processing* (pp. 463–526). New York: Academic Press.

Newell, A. & Simon, H.A. (1972). *Human problem solving.* Englewood Cliffs, NJ: Prentice-Hall.

Nunnally, J.C. (1978). *Psychometric theory* (2nd ed.). New York: McGraw-Hill.

O'Neil, H. F. (Ed.). (1978). *Learning strategies.* New York: Academic Press.

Pachella, R.G. (1974). The interpretation of reaction time in information processing research. In B.H. Kantowitz (Ed.), *Human information processing: Tutorials in performance and cognition* (pp. 83–132). Hillsdale, NJ: Erlbaum.

Pawlik, K. (1966). Concepts and calculations in human cognitive abilities. In R.B. Cattell (Ed.), *Handbook of multivariate experimental psychology* (pp. 535–562). Chicago: Rand McNally.

Pellegrino, J.W. & Kail, R. Jr. (1982). Process analyses of spatial aptitude. In R.J. Sternberg (Ed.), *Advances in the psychology of intelligence*, Vol. 1. Hillsdale, NJ: Erlbaum.

Posner, M.I. & McLeod, P. (1982). Information processing models—in search of elementary operations. *Annual Review of Psychology, 33*, 477–514.

Posner, M.I. & Mitchell, R. (1967). Chronometric analysis of classification. *Psychological Review, 74*, 392–409.

Posner, M.I. & Snyder, C.R.R. (1975). Attention and cognitive control. In R.L. Solso (Ed.), *Information processing and cognition* (pp. 55–85). Hillsdale, NJ: Erlbaum.

Rasch, G. (1980). *Probabilistic models for some intelligence and attainment tests* (expanded ed.). Chicago: University of Chicago Press.

Revelle, W., Humphreys, M.S., Simon, L., & Gilliland, K. (1980). The interactive effect of personality, time of day, and caffeine: A test of the arousal model. *Journal of Experimental Psychology: General, 109*, 1–31.

Rimoldi, H.J.A. (1951). Personal tempo. *Journal of Abnormal and Social Psychology, 46*, 283–303.

Rindler, S.E. (1979). Pitfalls in assessing test speediness. *Journal of Educational Measurement, 16*, 261–270.

Roberts, F.S. (1979). *Measurement theory: With applications to decision making, utility, and the social sciences.* Reading, MA: Addison-Wesley.

Rose, A.M. & Fernandes, K. (1977). *An information processing approach to performance assessment: I. Experimental investigation of an information processing performance battery* (Technical Report No. 1). Washington, DC: American Institutes for Research.

Royce, J.R. (1973). The conceptual framework for a multi-factor theory of individuality. In J.R. Royce (Ed.), *Multivariate analysis and psychological theory* (pp. 305–407). London: Academic Press.

Rubin, D.C. (1980). 51 properties of 125 words: A unit analysis of verbal behavior. *Journal of Verbal Learning and Verbal Behavior, 19,* 736–755.

Sanders, A.F. (1980). Stage analysis of reaction processes. In G.E. Stelmach & J. Requin (Eds.), *Tutorials in motor behavior* (pp. 331–354). Amsterdam: North Holland.

Schmid, J. & Leiman, J.M. (1957). The development of hierarchical factor solutions. *Psychometrika, 22,* 53–61.

Shepard, R.N. & Feng, C. (1972). A chronometric study of mental paper folding. *Cognitive Psychology, 3,* 228–243.

Shepard, R.N. & Metzler, J. (1971). Mental rotation of three-dimensional objects. *Science, 171,* 701–703.

Shepard, R.N. & Teghtsoonian, M. (1961). Retention of information under conditions approaching a steady state. *Journal of Experimental Psychology, 62,* 302–309.

Smith, G. & Stanley, G. (1980). Relationships between measures of intelligence and choice reaction time. *Bulletin of the Psychometric Society, 16,* 8–10.

Smith, J.E.K. (1976). Data transformations in analysis of variance. *Journal of Verbal Learning and Verbal Behavior, 15,* 339–346.

Spearman, C. (1904). "General intelligence," objectively determined and measured. *American Journal of Psychology, 15,* 201–293.

Spearman, C. (1927). *The abilities of man: Their nature and measurement.* New York: Macmillan.

Sperling, G. (1960). The information available in brief visual presentations. *Psychological Monographs, 74* (Whole No. 498).

Stankov, L. & Horn, J.L. (1980). Human abilities revealed through auditory tests. *Journal of Educational Psychology, 72,* 21–44.

Sternberg, R.J. (1977). *Intelligence, information processing, and analogical reasoning: The componential analysis of human abilities.* Hillsdale, NJ: Erlbaum.

Sternberg, R.J. (1980a). Sketch of a componential subtheory of human intelligence. *Behavioral & Brain Sciences, 3,* 573–614.

Sternberg, R.J. (1980b). Representation and process in linear syllogistic reasoning. *Journal of Experimental Psychology: General, 109,* 119–159.

Sternberg, S. (1966). High speed scanning in human memory. *Science, 153,* 652–654.

Stevens, S.S. (1951). Mathematics, measurement, and psychophysics. In S.S. Stevens (Ed.), *Handbook of experimental psychology* (pp. 1–49). New York: Wiley.

Tapley, S.M. & Bryden, M.P. (1977). An investigation of sex differences in spatial ability: Mental rotation of three-dimensional objects. *Canadian Journal of Psychology, 31,* 122–130.

Taylor, T.R. (1976). The factor structure of geometric illusions: A second study. *Psychologia Africana, 16,* 177–200.

Thorndike, R.L. (1982). *Applied psychometrics.* Boston: Houghton Mifflin.

Thurstone, L.L. (1938). Primary mental abilities. *Psychometric Monographs* (No. 1).

Thurstone, L.L. (1944). A factorial study of perception. *Psychometric Monographs* (No. 4).

Thurstone, L.L. (1947). *Multiple factor analysis: A development and expansion of "The vectors of mind."* Chicago: University of Chicago Press.

Thurstone, L.L. (1949). *Mechanical aptitude III: Analysis of group tests.* Chicago: University of Chicago, Psychometric Laboratory Research Reports (No. 55).

Thurstone, L.L. & Thurstone, T.G. (1941). Factorial studies of intelligence. *Psychometric Monographs* (No. 2).

Trabasso, T., Rollins, H., & Shaughnessy, E. (1971). Storage and verification stages in processing concepts. *Cognitive Psychology, 2,* 239–289.

Tucker, L.R. (1955). The objective definition of simple structure in linear factor analysis. *Psychometrika, 20,* 209–225.

Tucker, L.R., Koopman, R.F., & Linn, R.L. (1969). Evaluation of factor analytic research procedures by means of simulated correlation matrices. *Psychometrika, 34,* 421–459.

Tukey, J.W. (1977). *Exploratory data analysis.* Reading, MA: Addison-Wesley.

Underwood, B.J. (1975). Individual differences as a crucible in theory construction. *American Psychologist, 30,* 128–134.

Underwood, B.J., Boruch, R.F., & Malmi, R.A. (1978). Composition of episodic memory. *Journal of Experimental Psychology: General, 107,* 393–419.

Undheim, J.O. (1981). On intelligence II: A neo-Spearman model to replace Cattell's theory of fluid and crystallized intelligence. *Scandinavian Journal of Psychology, 22,* 181–187.

Velicer, W.F., Peacock, A.C., & Jackson, D.N. (1982). A comparison of component and factor patterns: A

Monte Carlo approach. *Multivariate Behavioral Research, 17,* 371–388.

Vernon, P.A. (1983). Speed of information processing and general intelligence. *Intelligence, 7,* 53–70.

Vernon, P.E. (1961). *The structure of human abilities* (2nd ed.). London: Methuen.

Wainer, H. (1977). Speed vs. reaction time as a measure of cognitive performance. *Memory & Cognition, 5,* 278–280.

Walker, D.A. (1931). Answer pattern and score scatter in tests and examinations. *British Journal of Psychology, 22,* 73–86.

Whitely, S.E. (1980a). Multicomponent latent trait models for ability tests. *Psychometrika, 45,* 479–494.

Whitely, S.E. (1980b). Latent trait models in the study of intelligence. *Intelligence, 4,* 97–132.

Whitely, S.E. & Schneider, L.M. (1981). Information structure for geometric analogies: A test theory approach. *Applied Psychological Measurement, 5,* 383–397.

Winer, B.J. (1971). *Statistical principles in experimental design* (2nd ed.). New York: McGraw-Hill.

Wolfle, D. (1940). Factor analysis to 1940. *Psychometric Monographs* (No. 3).

Woodrow, H. (1939). The common factors in fifty-two mental tests. *Psychometrika, 4,* 99–108.

Wright, B.D. & Stone, M.H. (1979). *Best test design.* Chicago: MESA Press.

# Chapter 13

# PSYCHOBIOLOGY OF COGNITIVE PROCESSES

**Harold Goodglass,** *Boston V.A. Medical Center and Boston University School of Medicine*

**Nelson Butters,** *University of California, San Diego and San Diego V.A. Medical Center*

The scientific study of brain-behavior relations is commonly regarded as beginning in the mid-nineteenth century with the discovery by Broca (1861, 1865) that the selective loss of language could be brought about by injury to a discrete zone in the left cerebral hemisphere. The intervening century has seen the recognition of an array of deficits in many additional aspects of cognitive functioning, usually associated with damage to particular sites in the brain. Dissociations of function brought about by brain injury have led to the formulation of new categories of analysis in a number of cognitive domains, and these in turn have been applied to taking a fresh look at cognitive processes in normal individuals.

The major areas of cognitive pathology that have been studied for their implications for normal function are memory and language, which are the subject matter of the first two sections of this chapter. The third section is devoted to the interaction of cerebral dominance with a variety of cognitive processes.

The writing of this chapter was supported in part by funds from the Medical Research Service of the Veterans Administration and by grants from the NIAAA (AA-00187) and the NINCDS (NS-16367, NS-06209, and NS-07615).

Current views on the neural basis of particular cognitive operations invariably have their origin in one or a series of clinical cases in which a particular deficit was observed by an examiner who made a first attempt to define its psychological dimensions. The psychological characterization was generally accompanied by an effort to explain the deficit in terms of existing notions of the functional anatomy of the brain or by suggesting new or elaborated models of brain function to account for it. In recent years models of cognition derived from experimental studies of normal subjects have been applied increasingly to brain-damaged patients with losses of memory and language functions.

An example of one of the most successful reconciliations of a dramatic dissociative symptom with existing concepts of brain function was Déjerine's (1892) explanation of pure alexia (loss of ability to read without impairment of writing or other language function). Déjerine proposed, on the basis of postmortem evidence, that the deficit was caused by an anatomical interruption (in the splenium of the corpus callosum) of the flow of information from the right visual cortex to the language zone of the left hemisphere, existing concurrently with destruction of the left visual cortex. Déjerine's insight was based on the then relatively recent demonstration that language processes were dependent on left brain function. In turn it was the forerunner (along with the clinical report by Liepmann & Maas, 1907) of the recent work on the cognitive function of isolated hemispheres in split-brain patients.

By now, there is hardly a reported symptom related to brain injury that has not passed through the filter of confirmation or refutation of its behavioral manifestations and its corresponding lesion site by many observers. Many of these aberrations of function have been subjected to probing analysis by experimental psychologists. Almost invariably, observations have led to the formulation of bridges between normal and organically disordered functions and to greatly increased understanding of the functional organization of the brain.

There is, however, an ever-present risk in using neuropathologically disordered behavior to interpret normal processes. The risk lies in assuming that pathology simply dissects away a portion of a complex normal process and reveals those of its components that have survived the damage. For example, the left brain-injured patient's frequent misnaming of objects, substituting words related by meaning or sound to the intended word, has led to the proposal that normal word retrieval involves scanning a pool of associated words and inhibiting the utterance of all but the best fitting candidate. Brain damage thus would have the effect of disabling this selection mechanism. The alternative, of course, is that the impairment of a normal process forces the individual to use alternative cognitive strategies, or removes the physiological inhibition on an alternative neural system for meeting a particular task demand in a different and less effective way. In either case, the alternative mode of function may undergo alteration with time, as a result of both practice and progressive neural changes.

From this introduction it is apparent that the methods used in investigations in neuropsychology cover a wide range of precision. They include clinical descriptions of single cases and of series of cases, controlled experiments carried out with individuals or groups of patients having similar deficits, and studies of normal subjects.

The treatment of each area of cognitive function will be introduced with an account of its organic psychopathology as observed clinically, followed by a consideration of the evidence bearing on the relation of symptoms of disordered function to normal function.

# NEUROPSYCHOLOGICAL STUDIES OF CHRONIC MEMORY DISORDERS

## Clinical Foundations

Memory disturbances are common consequences of brain damage. Cortical and subcortical lesions have been associated with various degrees and forms of retentive deficits, and the earliest signs of progressive dementing illnesses (e.g., senile dementia) are usually complaints about forgetfulness. Despite the ubiquity of memory deficits, most of the experimental research has focused on the relatively rare amnesic patients whose symptoms have been attributed to damage to the limbic structures. Difficulty in learning new materials and recalling past events occurs after hippocampal lesions (Milner, 1970), damage to medial diencephalic structures including n. medialis dorsalis and the mammillary bodies (Victor, Adams, & Collins, 1971), and lesions of the fornix (Heilman & Sypert, 1977). Figure 13.1 shows the location of these limbic structures in the human brain. The popularity of amnesic patients with experimenters is probably owing to the fact that although these patients have very severe and irreversible memory deficits their other intellectual functions remain relatively intact. Thus it is possible for the neuropsychologist and experimental psychologist to assess the nature of the amnesic patients' memory difficulties, unencumbered by the contaminating effects of aphasia, apraxia, and general dementia. This intactness is relative, however, since many amnesic patients evince some mild to moderate difficulties in other cognitive functions. Both Talland (1965) and Butters and Cermak (1980) have noted that amnesics with alcoholic Korsakoff's syndrome have significant visuoperceptual and conceptual impairments in addition to their severe memory deficits. Moreover, some amnesic patients have shown lowered levels of arousal and motivation (Talland, 1965; Oscar-Berman, 1980; Mayes, Boddy, & Meudell, 1980), two factors that can certainly influence learning and remembering.

Despite the locus of the lesions or the etiology

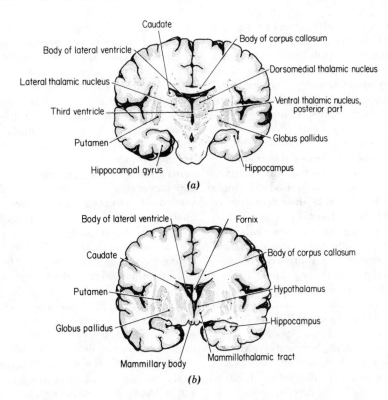

**Figure 13.1.** Two coronal sections through the human brain. The hippocampus (both sections), the dorsomedial nucleus of the thalamus (top section), the mammillary bodies (bottom section) and the fornix (bottom section) are structures often associated with amnesic syndromes. From *Alcoholic Korsakoff's Syndrome: An Information Processing Approach to Amnesia* (p. 12) by N. Butters and L.S. Cermak, 1980. New York: Academic Press. Copyright 1980 by Academic Press. Reprinted by permission.

of the disease, amnesic patients share two outstanding clinical symptoms. First, all amnesics have anterograde amnesia. This means that the patients, despite numerous repetitions, are unable to learn new verbal and nonverbal information from the time of onset of illness. They will not remember the names of their physician and nurses, and will even have difficulty learning the name of the hospital or nursing home in which they are being treated. Events that occurred hours or even minutes before will be forgotten by amnesic patients. Experimentally, this severe learning deficit can be demonstrated by the great difficulty they have in learning even short lists of five or six paired associates (Winocur & Weiskrantz, 1976; Ryan & Butters, 1980a). The acquisition of these associations may require 30 or 40 trials instead of the three or four presentations needed by intact subjects.

The second major symptom of amnesia is retrograde amnesia. The patient has trouble retriev-

ing from long-term memory events that occurred prior to the onset of the illness. When asked who was President of the United States before Mr. Nixon, the patient might answer "Truman" or "Eisenhower." One of Butters and Cermak's (1980) amnesic patients, who was asked if the United States was still at war, replied, "I think they have that war in Korea all wrapped up." In some instances, this difficulty in retrieving old memories is most pronounced for events just prior to the onset of the illness, whereas memories for events from the patient's childhood and early adulthood are relatively well preserved. Not only is this temporal gradient evident during a mental status examination, but it has also been demonstrated in numerous experimental studies (e.g., Seltzer & Benson, 1974; Marslen-Wilson & Teuber, 1975; Albert, Butters, & Levin, 1979; Squire & Cohen, 1982). Sanders and Warrington (1971) have challenged the validity of the temporal gradient on the grounds that the gradient may be artifactual owing to a failure to control for the difficulty of the questions representing different decades in the past. A thorough discussion of the issues raised by Sanders and Warrington and of the experimental studies that followed their critique will be pursued in a later section of this chapter.

## Methodological Issues in Neuropsychological Studies of Amnesia

Unfortunately for experimenters, brain damage in human populations is rarely limited to a single brain structure. Most patients' disorders involve a combination of lesions that may or may not be confined to a single region (e.g., the thalamus) of the brain. For example, alcoholic Korsakoff patients, whose amnesia is related to alcohol intoxication and malnutrition, have lesions involving n. medialis dorsalis, the mammillary bodies, the vermis of the cerebellum, the oculomotor nucleus, and in many cases the association cortex (for review, see Talland, 1965; Victor et al., 1971; Lishman, 1981). Similarly, patients with Alzheimer's disease, whose amnesic symptoms are part of a general intellectual decline, have progressive lesions of the hippocampus and of the posterior and anterior association cortex (Tomlinson, 1977). Even postencephalitic patients, whose amnesic symptoms are caused by a herpes virus that directly attacks the hippocampus, usually have considerable involvement of temporal and frontal neocortical areas (Drachman & Adams, 1962). When the multiplicity and variability of the patient's lesions are combined with a lack of postmortem verification of lesion sites, an assessment of what individual structures are contributing to a patient's amnesic symptomatology becomes nearly impossible.

In addition to problems with the localization of lesions, the scientific inquiry into the memory of brain-damaged patients is handicapped by the lack of specificity and definition of the terms psychologists use to study memory. Constructs like 'storage,' 'retrieval,' and 'encoding' are widely employed but poorly defined in the human memory literature. The havoc such lack of specificity produces for students of amnesia is easily exemplified. Some amnesic patients perform better with cued than with free recall. Though unable to recall the name of the doctor on direct inquiry, they may quickly supply the name when reminded that the physician's name begins with a 'B' or 'something associated with bread.' Such demon-

strations of cueing have led investigators to propose that amnesia represents a problem with retrieval, not storage (Warrington & Weiskrantz, 1970, 1973; Kinsbourne & Wood, 1975; McDowall, 1979). That is, the patient can and does store information normally but is impaired in the ability to retrieve the name. While this explanation seems plausible, it makes the implicit assumption that storage is all or none and not partial, an assumption that has little support in the literature on normal human memory. If in fact humans can store new information partially or in an inadequate form (e.g., poorly encoded), then the cueing phenomenon becomes equally consistent with a storage hypothesis. Retrieval processes may be quite normal even though some form of phonemic or semantic cue may be required to retrieve a partially or inadequately stored (i.e., degraded) engram. Of course, the point of this example is that, since storage is not fully understood in normal memory, attempts to separate storage and retrieval difficulties in amnesic patients have not been completely successful.

Meudell and Mayes (1981) have noted that many studies that attempt to apply the concepts and methods of cognitive psychology to amnesia are difficult, if not impossible, to interpret because of floor and ceiling effects. Since amnesic patients invariably remember much less than their controls at any fixed retention interval, experimental manipulations (e.g., supplying the first two letters of the words, phonemic cues, semantic cues) that appear to have a more beneficial effect on the performance of amnesics than of control subjects may in fact reflect a significant interaction between the manipulation and the initial level of performance. Various cues and orientation tasks may have a greater effect on amnesic patients, not because of some special deficit in the patients' information processing, but rather because any factor that aids retrieval may be more apparent, the worse the initial performance of the subjects. If the subjects perform initially at a fairly high level (e.g., 70% correct), the beneficial effects of any manipulation will be limited by a performance ceiling.

Despite the imprecision concerning lesions and memory concepts and the methodological problems just described, interest has increased in the study of organically based memory deficits during the past 15 years. Some neuropsychological studies have dealt with the localization and lateralization of memory functions, others with a description of the capacities and deficits of amnesic patients, and still others with the appliction of theories of information processing to the amnesic syndromes and milder forms of memory disturbances. The major findings of these studies will be reviewed in the following sections.

### Amnesia Following Bilateral Mesial Temporal-Lobe Lesions

Neuropsychological studies emanating from the Montreal Neurological Institute (McGill University) have left little doubt that the mesial region of the temporal lobes is directly associated with memory processes in man (Scoville & Milner, 1957; Penfield & Milner, 1958; Milner, 1966, 1970). Scoville and Milner described the severe memory disorder of a young man (HM) who had undergone bilateral ablations of the mesial temporal lobes to treat an uncontrolled form of epilepsy. This radical surgery was performed only after other more conservative therapies had failed to control HM's severe epileptic seizures. Upon recovering from surgery, HM manifested a severe inability to learn new information (i.e., anterograde amnesia) and was even unable to recall many events that had occurred prior to surgery (i.e., retrograde amnesia). Scoville and Milner also described the memory disturbances of eight psychotic patients who had received bilateral mesial temporal removals as a treatment for their psychotic thought disorders. Severe anterograde amnesia was noted in those cases in which the lesions included the anterior sector of the hippocampus but was not evident when the lesion was limited to the uncus and the amygdala, sparing the hippocampus. On the basis of these nine patients, the investigators concluded that an intact hippocampus was necessary for the acquisition of new memories and the maintenance or retrieval of old traces.

HM's surgery was successful in treating his seizures, but he was left with a permanent memory defect that has been studied extensively by Brenda Milner and her colleagues and students. HM continues to show a severe anterograde amnesia as evinced by his inability to learn the names of friends and his new address. He has difficulty recalling events that occurred just prior to the time of his operation but is able to remember events from his early childhood. His postoperative IQ is in the high-normal range and is somewhat better than his preoperative score. He is

reported to have been a placid person before surgery, and there has been no change in this personality evaluation in the years since surgery.

In addition to this general clinical evaluation, a large number of formal learning and cognitive tasks have been administered to HM. Two investigations (Prisko, 1963; Sidman, Stoddard, & Mohr, 1968) have found HM impaired on short-term memory tasks. In Prisko's study, HM was presented with two stimuli from the same modality, separated by intervals ranging from zero to 60 seconds; he was then asked to indicate whether the second stimulus was identical to or different from the first. The stimuli were either nonverbal visual stimuli, such as light flashes and shades of red, or nonverbal auditory material such as clicks and tones. The results were striking: while HM performed normally with very short delays between the two stimuli, his performance deteriorated as the delays increased. After a 60-sec delay his performance approached chance guessing. This short-term memory deficit stands in marked contrast to HM's normal immediate memory span. If seven single-digit numbers are presented in succession, HM can recall all numbers in order if recall is attempted immediately after presentation. When more than seven digits are presented, however, or when a delay intervenes between presentation and recall, HM is severely impaired on this task. HM's performance on the digit-span task is typical of all amnesic patients, regardless of the etiology of their disorder (Butters & Cermak, 1980).

HM's ability to learn and retain motor and maze tasks has been evaluated (Milner, 1962b; Milner, Corkin, & Teuber, 1968). Although HM could learn and retain for several days mirror-drawing and pursuit-rotor skills, his performance on visual and tactile mazes was grossly impaired. When Milner (1962a) attempted to train HM on a visual stylus maze (with 28 choice points), HM failed to show any progress in 215 trials. A subsequent study (Milner, 1968) indicated that HM failed on this test because the 28 rights and lefts were well beyond his immediate memory span. When tested on a shorter maze—with seven choice points—that was within his immediate span, he was able to attain criterion after 155 trials and 256 errors. What is most remarkable is that when HM was tested on this shortened version of the visual maze two years later, he showed 75-percent savings even though he did not remember the previous testing session.

Gardner (1975) and Cohen and Squire (1980) have noted similar phenomena in other amnesic patients. Gardner's patient, whose amnesia was traumatic in origin, had been taught to play a melody on the piano and retained this skill despite a total inability to remember the original learning sessions. Cohen and Squire have reported that amnesic patients of various etiologies can learn and retain the general rules needed to read mirror-reflected words. The patients acquired this mirror-reading skill despite a severe amnesia for the previous training sessions and for the specific words they had read. It appears then that HM, and other amnesics as well, usually have great difficulty in acquiring new information, but once some forms of material achieve long-term storage they can be retained fairly well.

Except for his severe and persistent memory defect, HM showed few other cognitive deficits. Although he was unable to use visual imagery as a mnemonic to improve his verbal paired-associate learning (Jones, 1974), HM performed normally on the Wisconsin Card Sorting Task and on a number of visuoperceptual tasks such as the Mooney face perception task. Since the Wisconson task has been shown to be sensitive to frontal cortical lesions (Milner, 1963, 1964) and the Mooney task to temporal-parietal lesions (Lansdell, 1968; Newcombe & Russell, 1969), HM's severe memory problems must be related to the mesial temporal ablations (probably the hippocampus) and not to any accessory cortical lesions.

## Memory Deficits after Unilateral Temporal Lobectomies

While the case of HM and other patients receiving bilateral mesial temporal lesions clearly established the importance of the mesial temporal region in memory, it has been the investigations of patients with unilateral temporal lobectomies that have pointed to the lateralized contributions to memory of the two temporal regions. Like HM, the patients with unilateral temporal lobectomies had surgical intervention to treat uncontrollable epileptic seizures. In most cases, the surgery dealt successfully with the seizure activity, and the patients returned to productive lives without any obvious amnesic symptoms. However, close examination of these patients has uncovered subtle memory defects that are dependent on whether the left or right temporal lobe was removed, and the severity of

the memory problem seems to depend on the amount of hippocampus ablated.

Removal of the left temporal lobe is followed by verbal memory deficits. Patients with left temporal lobectomies have more difficulty learning and retaining verbal materials (presented both visually and auditorily) than do patients with right temporal lobectomies. For example, patients with left temporal lobectomies have impaired recall for prose passages, in verbal paired-associate learning, and on Hebb's digit-sequence task, which assesses the patient's ability to learn a recurring sequence of numbers that exceeds the patient's digit span (Milner, 1971; Gerner, Ommaya, & Fedio, 1972). On a short-term memory task employing a distractor technique, left temporal lobectomy patients show faster decay of consonant trigrams than do those with right temporal lobectomies (Corsi, 1969). Some of these verbal learning deficits can be reduced by training patients with left temporal lesions to rehabilitate the function by substituting their intact right hemispheres. Jones (1974) has shown that patients with left temporal lobectomies can use visual imagery as a mnemonic to alleviate their deficits on a paired-associate task comprising 10 pairs of highly concrete words.

The results of these ablation studies have been supported and expanded by a study concerning the effects of electrical stimulation on language and memory processes (Fedio & Van Buren, 1974). The patients for this study were seven temporal-lobe epileptics who were candidates for unilateral temporal lobectomies. Before such patients undergo neurosurgery it is necessary to map via electrical stimulation the speech areas of their brain to avoid ablating tissue that is crucial for language capacities. In the Fedio and Van Buren study, the patients were given a naming and memory task as part of this mapping procedure. A series of pictures of common objects (e.g., hand, tree, clock) were presented with short delays between successive pictures. The patients were instructed first to name the object in the picture before them and then to recall the name of the object presented on the immediately preceding trial.

As expected, electrical stimulation of the left (but not the right) temporal lobe led to a variety of anomic (dysphasic) naming errors, but the new and important findings concerned the patients' memory (recall) performance during stimulation of the temporal lobes. Two distinct areas were found within the left temporal lobe: stimulation of the anterior sector of the left temporal lobe resulted in anterograde amnesia, whereas stimulation of the posterior (temporoparietal) region produced retrograde problems. If points in the anterior temporal region were stimulated while patients were correctly naming a presented picture, they were often unable to recall this picture on a later trial when no stimulation was present. Somehow stimulation of this anterior point had prevented the consolidation or acquisition of the picture's name. In contrast, electrical stimulation of points in the posterior left temporal region resulted in a failure to recall the picture exposed on the preceding trial, even though, at the time of original exposure and naming, no stimulation was being applied to the brain. That is, electrical stimulation of the posterior region made it difficult for patients to recall events that had occurred prior to the stimulation (i.e., retrograde amnesia). Fedio and Van Buren suggest that structures in the anterior portion of the left temporal lobe (e.g., the hippocampus) may play a role in the consolidation and storage of verbal materials, whereas structures in the posterior temporal region may be important in the retrieval of previously stored verbal stimuli.

While patients with right temporal lobectomies are unimpaired on verbal memory tasks, they have been found to be more impaired than those with left temporal lobectomies on tasks that require the processing of nonverbal patterned materials. The right-lobectomy patients have difficulty remembering whether they have previously seen an unfamiliar geometric pattern (Kimura, 1963a) and are impaired in the learning of visual and tactile mazes (Milner, 1965; Corkin, 1965). They have difficulty recognizing tonal patterns (Milner, 1967) and faces (Milner, 1968) after a short delay. Although patients with right temporal lobectomies have no difficulty learning to associate pairs of abstract nouns (e.g., advantage—occasion), they are significantly impaired in forming associations between pairs of concrete nouns (e.g., nail—salad) when visual imagery is encouraged for mnemonic purposes (Jones-Gotman & Milner, 1978).

The temporal lobectomies performed on the McGill patients have involved a number of neuroanatomical structures, such as the amygdala, uncus, hippocampus, anterior temporal neocortex, and parahippocampal gyrus, but there is now substantial evidence from Milner's laboratory that the ablation of the hippocampus is the critical factor in the patient's memory deficits. When the left and right temporal groups were divided according to the amount of hippocampal involvement, it was found that the degree of behavioral deficit correlated with the amount of hippocampus removed. Corsi (1969) found that patients having left temporal ablations with extensive hippocampal damage were more impaired on short-term memory tasks and in the learning of supraspan digit sequences (on Hebb's digit-sequence task) than were patients with little or no involvement of the hippocampus. On the other hand, only with extensive lesions of the right hippocampus was there impairment on maze learning (Milner, 1965: Corkin, 1965) or recognition of faces from photographs (Milner, 1968), or deficits on image-mediated verbal learning (Jones-Gotman & Milner, 1978). However, the impairments of right temporal patients on visual memory tasks involving unfamiliar geometric forms such as the Rey-Osterreith figure (Taylor, 1969) and recurring nonsense figures (Kimura, 1963a) have not been found to correlate with amount of hippocampal damage. Milner (1970) has suggested that such tasks involve extensive visuoperceptual analysis as well as memory and thus may depend on the integrity of both the temporal neocortex and the hippocampus.

For those studies that have shown a correlation between hippocampal damage and behavioral deficits, it should be stressed that temporal-lobe lesions that involved the amygdala, uncus, and cortex, but left the hippocampus relatively intact, produced no noticeable defects on the verbal and nonverbal memory tasks. Unfortunately, since all the patients with hippocampal damage also had extensive removals of the amygdala and uncus, the behavioral consequences of hippocampal lesions by themselves could not be evaluated in the McGill patient population.

## Experimental Studies of Anterograde Amnesia

While Milner and her colleagues have established the importance of an intact hippocampus for normal memory, the vast majority of studies of the information-processing deficits underlying anterograde amnesia have employed alcoholic Korsakoff patients whose severe memory disorders have been attributed to mesial diencephalic brain structures. The usefulness of this alcoholic population is owing primarily to their ubiquity as opposed to the rarity of patients with lesions limited to the hippocampus. The essential clinical symptoms of Korsakoff's syndrome have been known for about 100 years (for reviews, see Talland, 1965; Victor et al., 1971; Butters & Cermak, 1980). The patient's combination of chronic alcoholism and a specific nutritional deficiency (i.e., thiamine) has led to a neurological syndrome characterized by changes in motor, sensory, cognitive, and personality processes. In the acute stage the patient shows ataxia, nystagmus, confusions of both time and place, and various peripheral neuropathies (e.g., pain or loss of sensation in the extremities). A patient who is treated with large doses of thiamine may show a slow improvement in the motor and sensory abnormalities over a four- to eight-week period, but most such patients are left with a severe amnesia and striking personality alterations. Regardless of their premorbid personality, these patients are extremely passive, malleable, and emotionally flat in the chronic Korsakoff state. The memory disorder is severe and permanent and closely resembles that of HM.

Until recently, hippocampal lesions were believed to be responsible for the memory problems of Korsakoff patients (for reviews, see Talland, 1965; Victor et al., 1971; Mair, Warrington, & Weiskrantz, 1979), but the neuropathological analysis of an extensive series of alcoholic Korsakoff brains (Victor et al., 1971) has shown the critical lesions to involve mesial thalamic structures. In the study by Victor et al., every Korsakoff patient who had an amnesic syndrome also showed atrophy of the dorsal medial nucleus of the thalamus and of the mammillary bodies of the hypothalamus, but hippocampal lesions were not found consistently. Mair et al. (1979) examined the brains of two alcoholic Korsakoff patients whose memory disorders had been carefully documented. In both cases the most striking neuropathological findings were atrophy of the medial nuclei of the mammillary bodies and a thin band of gliosis between the wall of the third ventricle and the medial dorsal nucleus of the thalamus. Case studies demonstrating that tumors (Kahn & Crosby, 1972) and shrapnel wounds (Jarho, 1973) of the midline diencephalic region result in amnesic problems also point to thalamic and hypothalamic (mammillary bodies) involvement in memory. Teuber, Milner, and Vaughan (1968) have reported a single case (Case NA) of amnesia for verbal materials resulting from a stab wound that damaged sectors of the rostral midbrain. Squire and his collaborators (Squire & Slater, 1978; Squire & Moore, 1979) have confirmed NA's anterograde and retrograde verbal memory deficits and, with the use of sophisticated neuroradiological procedures (i.e., CT scans), have demonstrated that his brain damage is localized in n. medialis dorsalis of the left (dominant) hemisphere.

Coinciding with the recent neuropathological findings are a number of extensive experimental studies of the alcoholic Korsakoff patients' difficulties in acquiring new information (for reviews, see Cermak & Butters, 1973; Butters & Cermak, 1975, 1980; Piercy, 1977). These studies have focused on the patients' short-term memory (STM) capacities and the role of interference, encoding, and contextual analysis in storage and retrieval problems.

With two notable exceptions (Baddeley & Warrington, 1970; Mair et al., 1979), all the studies concerned with the STM of alcoholic Korsakoff patients have reported severe deficits for these patients (Samuels, Butters, & Goodglass, 1971; Cermak, Butters, & Goodglass, 1971; Goodglass & Peck, 1972; Butters, Lewis, Cermak, & Goodglass, 1973; Squire & Cohen, 1982). Most of these studies employed the Brown–Peterson distractor technique (Brown, 1958; Peterson & Peterson, 1959) with delays ranging between 0 and 18 seconds. With this procedure, the patients are shown or hear a stimulus (verbal or nonverbal) and immediately start to count backward by twos or threes. When the patient has counted for a predetermined interval, the examiner says "stop!" and the patient attempts to recall or recognize the stimulus previously presented. This counting procedure prevents the patients from rehearsing during the delay interval.

Figure 13.2 shows the performance of a group of alcoholic Korsakoff patients on the Brown–Peterson STM task with word triads (e.g., flower–ship–house) as the stimulus materials to be recalled. The Korsakoff patients show normal performance with zero-second delays, but their decay functions are much steeper than those of control subjects. This deficit is apparent

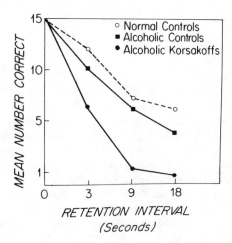

**Figure 13.2.** Number of words correctly recalled by alcoholic Korsakoffs, alcoholic controls and normal controls on the Brown-Peterson distractor task with word triads as the materials to be recalled. From "The Extent of Memory Loss in Korsakoff's Patients" by L.S. Cermak, N. Butters, and H. Goodglass, 1971, *Neuropsychologia, 9*, p. 310. Copyright 1971 by Pergamon Press, Ltd. Reprinted by permission.

regardless of the modality (visual, auditory, tactile) of presentation (Butters et al., 1973) and of whether the material to be retained can be verbalized (DeLuca, Cermak, & Butters, 1975).

In a recent report, Squire and Slater (1978) administered a Peterson distractor task to patient NA (described previously) and found severe impairments in his ability to retain verbal information for more than a few seconds. Since NA's lesions were localized to the n. medialis dorsalis in the left hemisphere, it would appear that damage to the midline diencephalic region is sufficient to produce significant impairments in STM. However, significant deficits on Brown–Peterson distractor tasks have also been reported in brain-damaged patients without amnesic syndromes. Patients with lesions involving the right parietal lobe show rapid loss of visually presented verbal and nonverbal materials (Samuels, Butters, Goodglass, & Brody, 1971; Samuels, Butters, & Goodglass, 1971), especially if the stimuli are exposed initially to the patients' left visual field. In another study, Samuels, Butters, and Fedio (1972) have reported that both right and left temporal lobectomies (with relatively little involvement of the hippocampus) are followed by deficits on Brown–Peterson tasks in which the verbal materials to be recalled are presented orally.

Warrington and her colleagues have described auditory verbal STM deficits in three nonamnesic patients with damage to the posterior parietal cortex of the left hemisphere (Warrington & Shallice, 1969; Shallice & Warrington, 1970; Warrington, Logue, & Pratt, 1972; Warrington & Shallice, 1972). These patients had a reduced auditory (but not visual) immediate memory span for letters and numbers, which could not be reduced to a motor-speech impairment or a problem with auditory perception. When the patients' STM was assessed with the Brown–Peterson technique, strings of one, two, or three letters were forgotten more rapidly after auditory than visual presentation. Despite this severe impairment in immediate memory and STM, these patients' long-term memory (LTM) appeared intact, as evinced by their normal performance on verbal paired-associate and recall tasks. In view of this evidence that cortical lesions can be associated with modality-specific STM deficits, the attribution of all the Korsakoff patients' problems on distractor tasks to diencephalic lesions remains problematical. This conservative position is reinforced by the mounting neuroradiological evidence (Lishman, 1981; Wilkinson & Carlen, 1981) that alcoholic Korsakoff patients, as well as nonamnesic long-term alcoholics, often have extensive anterior and posterior cortical atrophy.

The alcoholic Korsakoff patients' difficulties with the Brown–Peterson distractor task exemplify one of the most prominent features of their anterograde amnesia, that is, increased sensitivity to proactive interference (PI). Previously learned materials interfere with the patient's attempts to acquire new information. There are three sources of evidence for this interference phenomenon: (1) the type of errors made by Korsakoff patients on learning tasks (Meudell, Butters, & Montgomery, 1978), (2) demonstrations of normal performance when partial information is provided at the time of retrieval (Warrington & Weiskrantz, 1970, 1973), and (3) improved learning and retention when the experimental conditions are structured to reduce proactive interference (Cermak & Butters, 1972; Butters, Tarlow, Cermak, & Sax, 1976). Although the Korsakoff patients' overall performance on an STM distractor task is severely impaired, the deficit is not without variation during the tests session. On the first few trials of the test patients often perform within normal limits, but their performance may deteriorate rapidly on subsequent trials. Cermak, Butters, and Moreines (1974) noted that alcoholic Korsakoff patients may recall accurately as much as 90 percent of verbal materials presented on the first two trials, but may recall less than 50 percent of the materials shown on the fifth trial of the test session. On trial 5 the patient is still responding with material presented on trials 1 and 2.

Meudell et al. (1978) compared the types of errors compiled by alcoholic Korsakoff patients and patients with progressive dementia (Huntington's disease) on a Brown–Peterson distractor task. Though both groups were significantly impaired on this task, the types of errors they produced differentiated the two patient populations. The Korsakoff patients' errors were primarily intrusions from prior list items, whereas the demented patients made many omission errors (i.e., failure to make any response). These results suggested that PI may not be a crucial factor in the memory disorders of all brain-damaged patients.

With methods of retrieval that reduce interference, the performance of amnesic patients may not differ from that of intact normal controls. Warrington and Weiskrantz (1970) have shown that, although amnesics are severely impaired when unaided recall or recognition tests are employed, they retrieve normally when they are given partial information, such as the first two letters of the words to be remembered. Warrington and Weiskrantz (1973) suggest that the partial information method is more effective because it places limits on interference from previously learned information. According to Warrington and Weiskrantz (1973), free recall and recognition procedures do not limit proactive interference to the same degree.

The literature on normal human memory has long held that PI may be reduced by specific manipulations of the conditions under which learning is attempted. For example, distributed practice results in less interference than does massed practice. When the Peterson distractor task was administered with distributed (1-min rest between successive trials) rather than massed (6 sec between trials) presentation to alcoholic Korsakoff patients, demented patients (Huntington's disease), and alcoholic control subjects, the Korsakoff patients and the controls showed significant improvements in their performance (Butters et al., 1976). In fact, the

Korsakoff patients recalled as many items with distributed practice as the controls did with massed practice. However, this reduction in interference (via distribution of trials) had no effect on the memory deficits of the demented patients; they performed as poorly with distributed as with massed practice.

The amnesic patients' increased sensitivity to PI has led Warrington and Weiskrantz (1970, 1973) to propose a retrieval-interference theory of amnesia. According to this view, amnesic patients encode and store information in normal fashion but are unable to retrieve specific material from long-term memory because of interference. Although amnesics may employ normal retrieval strategies, they seem to be highly sensitive to interference from competing information and to have great difficulty in inhibiting the irrelevant material. Their theory proposes that items in storage are poorly insulated from one another and are in constant competition during the retrieval process. Thus, when alcoholic Korsakoffs or other amnesic patients are asked the name of their physician for the fifth or sixth time, they continue to answer incorrectly because they cannot differentiate the physician's name from all the other names held in LTM.

Despite the elegance of the retrieval-interference theory, a number of investigators (including Warrington and Weiskrantz themselves) have noted empirical and theoretical difficulties with that approach. Woods and Piercy (1974) reported that the partial information phenomenon was not peculiar to amnesics and actually characterized normal memory when traces were weak or poorly stored. They presented normal subjects with lists of words and tested for retention of one-half the material one minute later and the other half one week after original exposure. The major finding was that the differences between the one-minute and one-week retentions paralleled the differences between the normals and amnesics reported by Warrington and Weiskrantz (1970). Although yes–no recognition was significantly poorer after the one-week than after the one-minute delay interval, the partial information technique did not yield significantly different performances with the two delay intervals. It appears, then, that if intact subjects' memories are weakened by the passage of time, their retrieval can also be facilitated by the use of partial information. This finding questions whether partial-information experiments have uncovered any special processing problems of amnesic patients. As noted previously, this point has also been emphasized by Meudell and Mayes (1981).

Warrington and Weiskrantz (1978) have also reported a series of experiments that necessitate modification of their original retrieval-interference theory. In the main experiment of this series, the effect of prior-list learning on the learning of a second list was evaluated. High proactive interference was assured by having each word in list 1 matched in list 2 by a word that began with the same three letters; thus *cyclone* in list 1 was matched by *cycle* in list 2. Each word in list 1 was presented once visually, and retention was tested immediately by presenting the first three letters of each word on the list (i.e., cued recall). Immediately after the retention test for list 1, list 2 was presented and a cued retention test for list 2 followed without delay. In all, four presentation and cued retention trials of list 2 were administered.

The results indicated that, although the amnesic patients performed less well overall than did the normal control group, this difference became progressively greater as the testing proceeded. On list 1 retention and the first retention trial for list 2, no significant differences were noted between the two groups. Both groups performed less well on the first retention trial of list 2 than on the single list 1 retention trial, but the decrement was equal for the two groups. On the three subsequent retention trials of list 2, however, the differences between the amnesics and the normal subjects increased with each succeeding trial.

As the investigators note, list 1 words were expected to interfere with the learning of words on list 2, but the effect of this proactive interference should have been greater for the amnesic patients than for the normal subjects. Also, interference theory predicts that differences between amnesic and normal individuals should have been greatest on the first retention trial of list 2 and should have decreased with each successive presentation of list 2. As the results of this experiment are opposite to those predicted, Warrington and Weiskrantz seem justified in concluding that the amnesics' retrieval difficulties cannot be accounted for by a simple interference model.

In addition to the noted empirical problems, interference-retrieval theory has been viewed as primarily descriptive rather than explanatory (Piercy, 1977), and subsequently other hypotheses have been offered to account for the amnesic patients' retention and interference problems. Butters and Cermak (1974, 1975, 1980) have suggested that the alcoholic Korsakoff patient's verbal memory impairment is related to a failure to encode, at the time of storage, all the attributes of the stimulus. According to this hypothesis, Korsakoff patients may fully categorize verbal information according to its phonemic and associative attributes, but their analysis of the semantic features of the materials may be inadequate. Information that is not fully analyzed (encoded) may be stored in a degraded fashion and thus be more sensitive to interference. The initial evidence for this theory emanated from a series of cueing experiments in which phonemic (e.g., rhymes) and semantic (e.g., superordinate) cues were compared for their ability to facilitate recall (Cermak & Butters, 1972; Cermak, Butters, & Gerrein, 1973). In general, phonemic cues worked as well for Korsakoff patients as for controls, but semantic cues aided the recall only of the control subjects.

Cermak, Naus, and Reale's (1976) investigation of the rehearsal strategies manifested during list learning also provided evidence that Korsakoff patients do not facilitate their learning by making use of the semantic features of words. Alcoholic Korsakoff patients, alcoholic controls, and normal controls were asked to learn three 20-word lists. One list consisted of semantically unrelated words, one of related words presented in a random order, and one of related words presented in blocks. Each word in a given list was presented visually for 5 sec, and the subjects were instructed to rehearse aloud rather than in their usually covert manner. Two findings are of special relevance to the semantic encoding hypothesis. First, although recall improved as a function of the relatedness of the lists, normal and alcoholic controls were able to take more advantage of the increasing organization of the lists than were the amnesic Korsakoff patients. The Korsakoff patients' recall on the related-block list was not appreciably better than their performance on the unrelated list. Second, while the two control groups employed a semantic rehearsal strategy to aid their recall, the Korsakoff patients approached the rehearsal task in a concrete limited fashion.

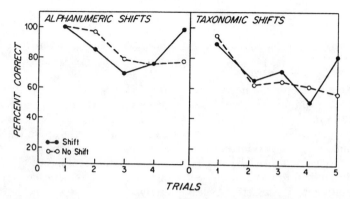

**Figure 13.3.** Release from PI. Percentage of words correctly recalled by alcoholic control subjects after alphanumeric and taxonomic shifts. From "Some Analyses of the Verbal Encoding Deficits of Alcoholic Korsakoff Patients" by L. Cermak, N. Butters, and J. Moreines, 1974, *Brain and Language, 1*, p. 145. Copyright 1974 by Academic Press. Reprinted by permission.

On the two organized lists, the control groups produced many words per rehearsal set belonging to the category (e.g., animals) of the presented word, whereas the Korsakoff patients simply repeated on each rehearsal set the single word that had just been presented. The authors concluded that the Korsakoff patients' inability to improve with lists organized for relatedness could be traced to their passive rehearsal strategy, which seemed to ignore the semantic associations among the words.

While many studies have shown that alcoholic Korsakoff patients are sensitive to proactive interference and engage in limited semantic encoding, there has been no convincing demonstration of a link between these two phenomena. Starting with the premise that deficits in semantic encoding lead to degraded engrams highly sensitive to proactive interference, Cermak et al. (1974) adapted Wickens's (1970) release from PI technique for use with alcoholic Korsakoff patients. With a modification of the Brown–Peterson distractor technique. Wickens had discovered that the PI generated by several consecutive trials with material from a single class of information can be released by introducing material from a new class of information. This finding was interpreted to mean that the extent of interference during STM recall is largely a function of the subject's ability to differentiate words in memory by their semantic features. When a subject encodes material differentially, the material is stored independently and does not interfere with the retrieval of other types of material. If the Korsakoff patients' increased

sensitivity to interference is related to their lack of semantic encoding, then the amount of PI release shown by these patients should vary with the encoding requirements of the verbal materials. Cermak et al. (1974) anticipated that alcoholic Korsakoff patients would demonstrate normal PI release when the verbal materials involved only rudimentary categorizations (e.g., letters versus numbers), but when the stimulus materials involved more abstract semantic differences (e.g., taxonomic differences such as animals versus vegetables) the Korsakoff patients could be expected to show far less PI release.

The Cermak et al. (1974) results are presented in Figures 13.3 and 13.4. The alcoholic control subjects (Figure 13.3) demonstrated release from PI for both alphanumeric (i.e., shifts from consonant trigrams to three-digit numbers or vice versa) and taxonomic (i.e., shifts from names of animals to names of vegetables or vice versa) materials, whereas the alcoholic Korsakoff patients (Figure 13.4) released only when the relatively simple alphanumeric materials were employed. The alcoholic Korsakoffs' failure to release with taxonomic materials was interpreted as reflecting inadequate semantic analyses. If the Korsakoff patients failed to encode along such semantic dimensions, then the PI accumulating during the block of five trials would probably not be specific to any one category (animals, vegetables), and a shift in categories would therefore have no effect.

Although the Cermak et al. (1974) findings seem to integrate the patients' retentive and encoding difficulties, Moscovitch (1982) has

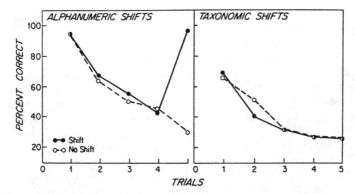

**Figure 13.4.** Release from PI. Percentage of words correctly recalled by alcoholic Korsakoff patients after alphanumeric and taxonomic shifts. From "Some Analyses of the Verbal Encoding Deficits of Alcoholic Korsakoff Patients" by L. Cermak, N. Butters, and J. Moreines, 1974, *Brain and Language, 1*, p. 146. Copyright 1974 by Academic Press. Reprinted by permission.

demonstrated that the failure to release from PI can occur in patients who are not clinically amnesic, and consequently that this deficiency is not inextricably tied to memory deficits. Patients with left-frontal, left-temporal (with and without hippocampal involvement), right-frontal, and right-temporal lesions participated in this study. Five different lists of 12 words each were read to subjects who were instructed to recall each list immediately after presentation. The words in the first four lists were all drawn from the same taxonomic category, the words in the fifth list from a different category. As anticipated, the buildup of PI, shown by a progressive decline in recall with each successive list, was apparent for all patient groups, but there were significant group differences in their tendency to release from PI when a taxonomic shift occurred on the fifth recall trial. Even though the left-temporal patients with hippocampal involvement had documented verbal learning deficits, these patients manifested normal release from PI. In contrast, the patients with left-frontal damage, whose learning capacities were not obviously compromised, performed like alcoholic Korsakoff patients in that many of them failed to release on the fifth (i.e., shift) trial. Of further interest was the finding that release from PI in the left-frontal group was positively correlated with performance on a concept-formation task (i.e., Wisconsin Card Sorting Test) known to be sensitive to long-term alcohol abuse (Tarter & Parsons, 1971; Tarter, 1973) as well as to damage to the dorsolateral surface of the frontal lobes (Milner, 1964). The

other patient groups, like the left-temporals with hippocampal damage, all showed normal release from PI.

In interpreting these results, Moscovitch (1982) suggests that amnesic patients of various etiologies may have numerous cognitive impairments that are independent of their anterograde memory problems. The evidence that nonamnesic frontal-lobe patients do not release when categories of words are shifted indicates that this failure and perhaps other encoding deficits as well, may not contribute to the Korsakoff patients' anterograde amnesia. As Moscovitch notes, the Korsakoff patients' failure to release from PI may be more a symptom of frontal-lobe damage than an indicator that a deficit in information processing is responsible for their inability to acquire new verbal materials. The neuroradiological evidence that long-term alcohol abuse is associated with extensive atrophy of the frontal lobes is consistent with this suggestion (Lishman, 1981; Wilkinson & Carlen, 1981).

In their search for evidence that deficits in semantic encoding play a vital role in the amnesic patients' amnesia, investigators have borrowed other experimental paradigms from the normal human learning literature. Cermak and Reale (1978), using a technique developed by Craik and Tulving (1975), attempted to ameliorate the alcoholic Korsakoff patients' verbal learning performance with orientation tasks that forced their subjects to analyze and judge the semantic attributes of words. Subjects were not told that they would have to remember anything; rather they were simply instructed to analyze each word on the basis of the particular characteristic suggested by the examiner's question. The basic premise is that, the higher the level of encoding that the subjects are required to perform on a word, the greater will be the probability that they will remember the word on a subsequent but unannounced recognition test. The questions were designed to necessitate processing on one of three levels: (1) a shallow orthographic level (e.g., "Is this [word] printed in upper case letters?"); (2) a phonemic level (e.g., "Does this [word] rhyme with *fat*?"); and (3) a semantic level (e.g., Does this [word] fit into the following sentence _____ _____ _____?"). For each question the subject had to make a yes or no response by pressing an appropriate response key. Following the presentation of the entire series of questions, the patients were administered a recognition test to determine how many of the exposed words they could identify correctly.

In an initial experiment, Cermak and Reale (1978) presented their alcoholic Korsakoff patients and alcoholic control subjects with 60 words and required them to answer one question about each word. Twenty of the questions dealt with the orthographic features of the words, 20 with the phonemic features, and 20 with the semantic characteristics. After presentation of the last word, the subjects were given a type-written sheet with 180 words (the 60 presented words and 120 filler nouns) and asked to circle those that had just been presented to them.

The results indicated that the alcoholic Korsakoff patients, unlike the control subjects, were unaffected by the level of processing performed upon the words. The alcoholic controls' recognition of semantic words was significantly better than their recognition of words analyzed orthographically or phonemically, and their recognition of orthographic words was the poorest of the three encoding conditions. The alcoholic Korsakoff patients, however, recognized few words overall, and there were no significant differences in their recognition of semantic, phonemic, and orthographic words.

In a second experiment, Cermak and Reale (1978) investigated the possibility that the previous failure of alcoholic Korsakoff patients to benefit from a semantic orientation task had been due to the magnitude of the word list and recognition task. They divided the 60-word stimulus list and the 180-word recognition test into a series of shorter encoding and recognition tasks. The patients were asked just 12 questions about 12 words, followed by a 36-word recognition test. This procedure was repeated five times until 60 words had been exposed and tested for recognition. Each of the 12-item lists contained four words that were analyzed orthographically, four that were analyzed phonemically, and four that were analyzed in terms of their semantic attributes.

The alcoholic Korsakoff patients' recognition performance with these abbreviated lists was at least partially consistent with the semantic encoding hypothesis. The Korsakoff patients were still impaired under all encoding conditions in comparison with the alcoholic controls, but they did benefit from the semantic orientation task. The Korsakoff patients' best recognition occurred for the semantic words, their poorest recognition for the words associated with orthographic questions. Although these results suggest that the Korsakoff patients' memory performance can be manipulated by orientation tasks that encourage or discourage semantic analysis, they provide no evidence that the patients' anterograde amnesia may be eliminated by semantic analysis. In fact, Cermak and Reale's experiments fail to demonstrate that semantic orientation tasks have a greater effect on Korsakoff patients than on control subjects. A greater effect would be necessary if one were to conclude that semantic encoding plays a special role in the memory disorders of amnesic patients.

McDowall (1979) has also assessed the semantic encoding hypothesis with orientation tasks and, ironically, he has found stronger evidence for this theoretical position than did Cermak and his colleagues. McDowall employed three conditions in his experiments: (1) a study (baseline) condition in which no specific instructions were provided, (2) a nonsemantic (phonemic) orientation task in which the subjects had to determine whether each word in a list contained the letter *e*, and (3) a semantic orientation task that required the subjects to assign each word in a list to the appropriate one of four taxonomic categories. For each condition, 20 words consisting of five nouns from each of four taxonomic categories (e.g., food, clothing) were presented to alcoholic Korsakoff patients and to alcoholic controls. Immediately after two presentations of

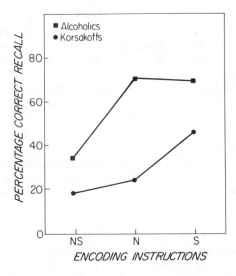

**Figure 13.5.** Percentage of words recalled by alcoholic Korsakoff patients and alcoholic control subjects after an undirected study (N) condition and nonsemantic (NS) and semantic (S) orientation tasks. From "Effects of Encoding Instructions Retrieval and Cueing on Recall in Korsakoff's Patients" by J. McDowell, 1979, *Memory and Cognition, 7,* p. 236, Copyright 1979 by the Psychonomic Society. Reprinted by permission.

the 20-word list, the subjects were asked to recall as many of the words as possible.

The results yielded a significant interaction of groups by conditions. The Korsakoff patients recalled many more words after the semantic orientation task than after the nonsemantic encoding or the baseline (no instruction) conditions, and their performance on the latter two conditions did not differ. In contrast, the alcoholic controls recalled more words after both the semantic and baseline conditions than after the nonsemantic orientation task, and their performance on the former two conditions could not be distinguished (Figure 13.5).

These results suggest that, whereas intact subjects encode the semantic features of words spontaneously, without formal instructions to do so, amnesic Korsakoff patients use and benefit from such an encoding strategy only when forced to analyze the semantic attributes. Left to their own devices, as in the baseline condition, the alcoholic Korsakoff patients tend to rely on superficial and ineffective encoding processes. This apparent support for the semantic encoding hypothesis is somewhat muted by

McDowall's (1979) additional finding that supplying taxonomic cues at the time of retrieval was sufficient to improve significantly the recall of words presented with no special encoding instructions. He concluded subsequently that Korsakoff patients may encode information normally at the time of storage but cannot generate the appropriate semantic retrieval strategies when attempting to recall previously presented verbal materials.

In recent years, Butters, Cermak and their colleagues have proposed that the alcoholic Korsakoff patients' deficiency in semantic encoding is only a single example of a general limitation in their ability to analyze all the dimensions of any complex stimulus, verbal and nonverbal. Glosser, Butters, and Samuels (1976) employed a modified version of the dichotic listening technique with alcoholic Korsakoff patients, chronic alcoholics, and normal controls. Their dichotic technique involved a simultaneous presentation of two single digits, one to the right ear of the patient and one to the left ear, at the rate of one pair every 1.2 sec. The patient was instructed to press a response key whenever the digit pairs had certain preselected spatial or identity features. Four conditions of dichotic presentation, each requiring a progressively more demanding stimulus analysis, were administered to each subject. For example, for the simplest condition the subjects had to determine whether the number *10* had been presented to their right or left ear. For the condition requiring the most extensive analysis of stimulus dimensions, the subjects were told to respond only when the digit *9* occurred in the right (left) ear and *10* in the left (right) ear.

The results showed that, as the stimulus analysis became more demanding the Korsakoff patients became increasingly impaired in comparison with the normal control group and made numerous errors of commission indicating an incomplete stimulus analysis. For instance, on the most complex condition, the Korsakoff patients performed normally when both dichotically presented digits were noncritical (e.g., *2* in the right ear, *7* in the left). However, when only one of the critical digits was present (e.g., *9* in the left ear, *2* in the right), or when the ear placement of the two critical digits was inverted (e.g., *10* in the left ear, *9* in the right), the alcoholic Korsakoff patients made many more errors of commission than did the normal controls. It appeared that, when conditions required complex decision processes, the alcoholic Korsakoff patients did not fully analyze all the incoming information. Glosser et al. (1976) provided some evidence that this deficit was time dependent. When the interpair interval was increased from 1.2 to 2.0 sec, the number of commission errors made by the Korsakoff patients was significantly reduced.

The limited encoding hypothesis has also been used to assess the alcoholic Korsakoff patients' difficulties in analyzing and retaining complex visuoperceptive materials. It has been shown that the STM of alcoholic Korsakoff patients is impaired for random geometric forms (DeLuca et al., 1975), on digit-symbol substitution tasks (Talland, 1965; Glosser, Butters, & Kaplan, 1977; Kapur & Butters, 1977), and on visual card-sorting tasks (Oscar-Berman, 1973; Oscar-Berman & Samuels, 1977). Oscar-Berman and Samuels reported that the Korsakoff patients' perceptual problems may be indicative of a limited partial analysis of all the attributes of visual stimuli. Their patients were trained to discriminate between complex visual stimuli differing on a number of relevant dimensions (e.g., color, form, size, position), and transfer tasks were then administered to assess which of the relevant stimulus dimensions had been noted. While the intact controls showed transfer to all relevant stimulus dimensions, the Korsakoff patients' discriminations were based on only one or two relevant features of the stimuli.

Dricker, Butters, Berman, Samuels, and Carey (1978) employed a series of facial-recognition and matching tasks to determine whether the alcoholic Korsakoff patients' amnesia for faces is attributable to a general limitation in their analyses of nonverbal stimuli. On an initial task, they found that the Korsakoff patients not only were unable to recognize 12 photographs of faces after a 90-sec delay but also made numerous errors on a simple facial matching task when a single target photograph and 25 comparison faces were exposed simultaneously. On a second test, the Korsakoff patients and control subjects were tested on a facial-matching task (developed by Diamond & Carey, 1977) that compared their tendency to use superficial piecemeal cues (e.g., paraphernalia and expression) with more advanced configurational cues (i.e., the spatial relation between the eyes, nose and mouth) in their analyses of faces. On each

trial, the subjects were presented simultaneously with a target face and two comparison faces, and their task was to indicate which of the two comparison faces was the same as the target. Under two conditions, paraphernalia were used to fool the subject; under two other conditions, facial expression was used for this purpose. For instance, the target face and the unmatching comparison face might be wearing the same hat or might be smiling in a similar manner. To select the matching comparison face on such trials, the subject had to reject superficial piecemeal similarities and extend the analysis to the configurational features of the three faces.

The Korsakoff patients were often fooled by both paraphernalia and expression in their matching of faces, with paraphernalia the more distracting of the two cues. Dricker et al. (1978) concluded that, just as Korsakoff patients fail to encode all the attributes of verbal material, they also perform incomplete, superficial analyses of nonverbal visual stimuli such as faces. If this limited perceptual analysis is a general cognitive characteristic of the amnesic Korsakoff patient, it could explain at least partially the patients' difficulties in learning, remembering, and perceiving nonverbal patterned materials.

With orientation tasks analogous to those employed by Cermak and Reale (1978) and McDowall (1979), two groups of investigators have evaluated the applicability of the limited analysis hypothesis to the Korsakoff patients' deficits in face perception. Mayes, Meudell, and Neary (1980) compared alcoholic Korsakoff patients and normal controls on a face-recognition task in which the subjects performed a 'high-level' or a 'low-level' orientation task, or examined the photographs of faces without specific instructions. The high-level task was chosen presumably to encourage configurational analyses of faces, whereas the low-level task focused the subjects' attention on the superficial features of faces. If the Korsakoff patients' impairments on face-recognition tests was due to their lack of configurational analysis, they would presumably benefit more than normal controls from the high-level orientation procedure. The results did not substantiate this prediction. While both the Korsakoff patients and the normal controls recognized more faces associated with the high-level instructions than with the other two experimental conditions, the two groups did not differ in the degree to which their

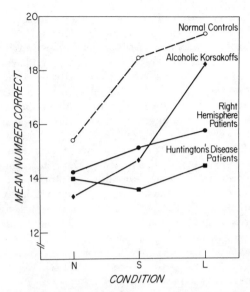

**Figure 13.6.** Number of faces correctly identified by four subject groups after free study (S), nose judgments (N), and likability judgments (L). From "Encoding Strategies and Recognition of Faces by Alcoholic Korsakoff and Other Brain-Damaged Patients" by C. Biber, N. Butters, J. Rosen, L. Gerstman, and S. Mattis, 1981, *Journal of Clinical Neuropsychology*, *3*, p. 322. Copyright 1981 by Swets Publishing Service. Reprinted by permission.

recognition was facilitated. In view of these results, Mayes, Meudell, and Neary (1980) dismissed deficiencies in perceptual encoding as the primary factor contributing to Korsakoff patients' nonverbal memory problems.

Another study, by Biber, Butters, Rosen, Gerstman, and Mattis (1981), used an orientation procedure in an attempt to improve face recognition and reported evidence that is consistent with the limited encoding hypothesis. A face recognition task—under three experimental conditions that presumably induced different levels of facial analysis—was administered to patients with alcoholic Korsakoff's syndrome, progressive dementia (Huntington's disease), and right hemisphere damage as well as to control subjects. The recognition scores of the Korsakoff patients, but not those of the other two patient groups, improved significantly after introduction of a high-level orientation task requiring the subjects to judge the likability of the faces to be remembered. Under baseline conditions (i.e., with no orientation task), normal controls appeared spontaneously to encode faces in a manner

induced by the high-level task, whereas the Korsakoff patients employed strategies consistent with the low-level orientation task (judgment of nose size). These findings, shown in Figure 13.6, closely parallel those of McDowall (1979), who used verbal material and a semantic orientation task (shown in Figure 13.5).

Although the results of Biber et al. (1981) suggest that faulty stimulus analysis plays an important and special role in the alcoholic Korsakoff patients' inability to recognize faces, their findings can also be explained by motivational-arousal concepts. Several investigators have remarked on the passivity and lack of initiative of alcoholic Korsakoff patients (Talland, 1965; Victor et al., 1971; Oscar-Berman, 1980) and have suggested that reduced motivation may contribute to the patients' severe learning and memory problems. Adapting methods borrowed from animal learning studies, Oscar-Berman and her collaborators (Oscar-Berman, Sahakian, & Wikmark, 1976; Oscar-Berman, Heyman, Bonner, & Ryder, 1980) have found that alcoholic Korsakoff patients show reduced responsiveness to the effects of positive reinforcement. When confronted with a two-choice test of spatial probability learning in which the two spatial alternatives were reinforced on a 70:30 or 30:70 ratio, normal controls altered their response to match the reinforcement contingencies. In marked contrast to the adaptability of the normals' behavior, the alcoholic Korsakoff patients continued to respond to each spatial alternative 50 percent of the time and seemed totally unaffected by the prevailing reinforcement contingencies (Oscar-Berman et al., 1976). In a second experiment (Oscar-Berman et al., 1980), Korsakoff patients and normal controls were placed on a complex concurrent variable schedule of reinforcement. As with the spatial probability learning test, the normal controls, but not the Korsakoff patients, responded by matching the reinforcement contingencies present in the experimental situation. In view of such demonstrations of motivational anomalies in Korsakoff patients, Oscar-Berman (1980) has urged caution in explaining all the memory deficits of Korsakoff patients from a strictly cognitive perspective. In the Biber et al. study (1981), the process of making a likability judgment (high-level orientation task) may have motivational as well as cognitive consequences, and the significant improvement in the memory of the alcoholic Korsakoff patients following these judgments may reflect some form of affec-tive-motivational arousal.

While theories of interference retrieval and stimulus encoding have dominated the amnesia literature during the past 12 years, some inves-tigators have suggested that amnesic memory deficits reflect a specific failure to retrieve the contextual attributes of verbal materials (Kins-bourne & Wood, 1975; Huppert & Piercy, 1976; Winocur & Kinsbourne, 1976, 1978; Winocur, Kinsbourne, & Moscovitch, 1981). That is, the Korsakoff patients may be able to encode many of the specific physical or semantic attributes of stimuli but fail to discriminate the unique spa-tial and temporal contexts in which the stimuli were encountered. Owing to this deficit, the patients may later recognize the stimulus as familiar without being able to 'recall' when or where they experienced the stimulus. It is impor-tant to note that these context theories focus on retrieval rather than on storage processes. Although the Korsakoff patients are viewed as having normal encoding processes, they are thought to be severely impaired in generating efficient temporal and spatial retrieval stra-tegies with which to search their memory stores. Kinsbourne and Wood (1975) have tied their context-retrieval theory to Tulving's (1972) dis-tinction between episodic and semantic memory and have suggested that the amnesic syndrome represents a loss of episodic memory. The fact that amnesics do not forget the meaning of words, the rules of syntax, or basic arithmetical procedures is considered by Kinsbourne and Wood as evidence of an intact semantic memory.

Empirical evidence supporting this context theory can be found in an experiment by Huppert and Piercy (1976). These investigators showed 80 pictures to alcoholic Korsakoff patients and normal controls on day 1 and 80 again on day 2. Day 2 pictures consisted of 40 new pictures and 40 repeats from day 1. Ten minutes after the exposure of the last picture on day 2, the sub-jects were presented with 160 pictures and asked to respond to the two questions: "Did you ever see this picture before?" "Was it presented today?" Of the 160 pictures, 120 had been exposed previously (on day 1, day 2, or both), and 40 were fillers that had not been used on either day. Of the 120 that had been exposed previously, 40 had been shown on day 1 only, 40 on day 2 only, and 40 on both days. The Korsakoff patients had no difficulty determining whether they had seen a given picture previously but made many false positive responses to the second question. In other words, they frequently said they had seen a picture on day 2 that had actually been pre-sented only on day 1. The patients recognized that they had viewed a picture but could not place the experience in a particular temporal context.

Two investigations by Winocur and Kins-bourne (1976, 1978) have shown that the verbal learning of alcoholic Korsakoff patients can be improved by increasing the saliency of contex-tual cues. In the first investigation, amnesic patients and controls were required to learn two lists of verbal paired associates under conditions that maximized the interference between the lists (i.e., the two lists contained the same stimuli but different response elements). In one condition, greater discriminability between the lists was achieved by printing the stimulus materials from list 1 and list 2 on different colored cards. In another procedure, the stimulus and response elements from list 1 were combined and then served as the stimulus elements for list 2. For example, *battle–soldier* in list 1 became *battle, soldier–army* in list 2. Winocur and Kinsbourne postulated that this manipulation would elimi-nate interference by circumventing any tendency to emit the list 1 response during list 2 learning. Both procedures led to a reduction in intrusion errors in the learning of list 2, and with that manipulation the Korsakoff patients' rate of learning was significantly improved. In their second study, Winocur and Kinsbourne (1978) introduced two additional methods for increas-ing the saliency of contextual cues for the alco-holic Korsakoff patients. Introducing a 3-min walk between the learning of the two lists and changing the room illumination for each paired-associate list were manipulations sufficient to reduce proactive interference from list 1 during the Korsakoff patients' attempts to learn list 2.

Winocur et al. (1981) have suggested that the Korsakoff patients' ability to discriminate con-texts also affects their performance on release from PI tasks. Korsakoff patients and normal subjects were asked to recall successive lists of nine nouns drawn from the same taxonomic cate-gory (e.g., sports, occupations, body parts). In the no-shift (i.e., control) condition, the same category of nouns was used for five successive lists; in the shift (i.e., experimental) condition, a new taxonomic category (e.g., sports) was introduced on the fifth list after a single category (e.g., body parts) had been employed on the first four lists. Both the alcoholic Korsakoff patients and the controls demonstrated progressive decrements in performance over the five lists in the no-shift condition. When no effort was made to increase the contextual saliency of the fourth and fifth lists in the shift condition, only the normal control subjects improved their performance significantly on the fifth (i.e., shift) list. However, when the subjects were provided with an instructional set warning them of the impending taxonomic change or when the words of the fourth and fifth lists were printed in inks of different color, the Korsakoff patients also recalled more words on the fifth than on the fourth list (i.e., release from PI). On the basis of these findings, Winocur et al. concluded that the alcoholic Korsakoff patients' failure to release from PI is owing not to a deficit in semantic encoding (Cermak et al., 1974), but rather to an inability to discriminate contextually the words that make up the fourth and fifth lists.

It is important to recall Moscovitch's (1982) finding that the alcoholic Korsakoff patients' failure to release from PI may be evidence of possible frontal lobe damage rather than a phenomenon linked to their amnesic syndromes. When that finding is combined with the demonstration by Winocur et al. (1981) of the importance of contextual factors in release from PI, it follows that impairments in the retrieval of contextual cues may be more characteristic of the cognitive problems of frontal lobe patients than of the amnesic syndromes of hippocampal or diencephalic patients. Milner (1971), describing an unpublished study by Corsi, has provided empirical evidence that the left and right frontal lobes are involved in the time-tagging (i.e., temporal ordering) of verbal and nonverbal materials, respectively. Patients with frontal, temporal, or combined frontotemporal lobectomies were presented with a series of 184 cards with two words (or two reproductions of abstract art for nonverbal test) printed on each card. On recognition test trials, the patients had to indicate which of the two words (or art works) had been presented previously during the test. On other test trials of recency, the patients had to judge which of the two stimuli had been exposed more recently (i.e., a contextual judgment). Whereas patients with combined frontotemporal lobectomies performed

poorly on both recognition and recency judgments (with left-hemisphere patients impaired on the verbal test and the right-hemisphere patients on the nonverbal task), the patients with lesions limited to one lobe or the other could be discriminated on the basis of their performance on the two judgment tasks: patients with left-temporal lobectomies were impaired only on verbal recognition judgments, whereas left-frontal patients performed at chance levels only on the verbal recency problems. A similar distinction between right-frontal and right-temporal patients was found with the nonverbal materials. Milner emphasizes that, despite their difficulty in making contextual (i.e., recency) judgments, none of her frontal-lobe patients were amnesic by conventional clinical criteria. It would appear then that the inability to retrieve the temporal and spatial contexts in which material is presented may be pronounced and enduring but still be unrelated causally to the anterograde memory deficits of amnesic patients.

Another weakness of context-retrieval theories of amnesia should be mentioned. Despite the emphasis some investigators have placed on the retrieval process (Kinsbourne & Wood, 1975), the patients' failures to discriminate contexts may have their origin during the storage stage. Context is just one of the many attributes intact people encode in the process of memorizing verbal and nonverbal materials. If alcoholic Korsakoff patients are generally limited in stimulus analysis (Butters & Cermak, 1980), then an impairment in contextual encoding, like the aforementioned problems in semantic analysis, may exemplify a more pervasive processing problem. The finding that enhancing the contextual cues reduced but did not eliminate the Korsakoff patients' impairment in verbal learning (Winocur & Kinsbourne, 1976, 1978) is consistent with the possibility that a combination of encoding deficiencies is involved.

Studies bearing directly on the nature of the amnesic patients' anterograde amnesias have focused on the forgetting of newly acquired pictorial information by patients with hippocampal (e.g., patient HM) or diencephalic (e.g., patient NA and the alcoholic Korsakoff patients) lesions. Huppert and Piercy (1977, 1978, 1979) have reported that when HM, alcoholic Korsakoff patients, and normal control subjects attain the same level of initial learning, important differences emerge in their rates of forgetting over a seven-day period. To ensure that all subjects attained approximately the same level of learning after a 10-min delay period, exposure time during the initial presentation of the slides was manipulated so that performance reached a level of at least 75 percent correct.

In Huppert and Piercy's studies, although patient HM, the normal subjects, and the alcoholic Korsakoff patients all performed worse on recognition tasks as the retention intervals increased (from one to seven days), patient HM's performance revealed a much steeper rate of forgetting than did the scores of the Korsakoff and control groups. Huppert and Piercy suggest that the anterograde amnesias of HM and the alcoholic Korsakoff patients involve different deficits in information processing. The difficulties of Korsakoff patients may emanate from a lack of stimulus analysis or encoding. When provided with sufficient time to analyze fully a complex stimulus, these patients are capable of learning, and they demonstrate normal recognition over an extended period of time. However, HM's rapid decline cannot be accounted for by such a cognitive deficit. Huppert and Piercy postulate that although HM's difficulty in learning new materials may also reflect a deficit in stimulus analysis, his inability to retain newly learned material suggests additional problem with consolidation and storage.

Squire (1981) evaluated patient NA, alcoholic Korsakoff patients, and depressed patients receiving bilateral electroconvulsive treatment (ECT) on pictorial (and verbal) forgetting tasks, in which recognition was assessed after delays of 10 min, 2 hours, and 32 hours. Squire's results are consistent with those of Huppert and Piercy. Patient NA and the alcoholic Korsakoff patients forgot at normal rates over the 32-hour period, whereas the patients receiving ECT evinced an accelerated decay rate for both pictorial and verbal material during the same period. On the basis of his data and those of Huppert and Piercy, Squire proposes that ECT affects memory by disrupting hippocampal mechanisms concerned with the consolidation process. He also concludes that amnesic symptoms associated with diencephalic and hippocampal dysfunction can be distinguished by the stage of information processing adversely affected.

In recent years interest has grown in those memory capacities that appear to be well pre-served even in severely amnesic patients (Brooks & Baddeley, 1976; Cohen & Squire, 1980). There have been numerous demonstrations of the amnesics' ability to acquire and retain a variety of perceptual-motor skills on mirror-tracing, bimanual tracking, and pursuit-rotor tasks (Corkin, 1965; Cermak, Lewis, Butters, & Goodglass, 1973) despite the failure of any patients to recall having performed the test previously. Amnesic patients have also performed well on tasks that are not primarily perceptual-motor in nature, such as rule-based paired-associate learning where word pairs are linked by a semantic or phonological rule (Winocur & Weiskrantz, 1976). Less formal demonstrations of preserved memory capacity have been reported by researchers who note that amnesic patients are often able to retain testing procedures across experimental sessions even when unable to recall the specific stimulus material (Corkin, 1965; Milner, Corkin, & Teuber, 1968). Such observations suggest that the acquisition and retention of at least some types of information are intact in patients with severe memory impairments.

A model to account for the pattern of preserved and impaired memory functions has recently been proposed (Cohen & Squire, 1980; Squire, 1984). It suggests that memory for information consisting of skills or procedures is spared in amnesia while memory for information that is data-based or declarative in nature (e.g., specific facts) becomes impaired. According to this view, amnesic patients are able to learn and retain mirror-tracing and pursuit-rotor tasks because successful performance on these tests depends on the ability to learn and retain the procedures involved, but not on the ability to recall the specific content of the tasks. This proposed dissociation between two types of memory in amnesia was demonstrated experimentally by Cohen and Squire (1980) with a pattern-analyzing task that involved both skill learning (procedural knowledge) and verbal recognition (declarative knowledge). Subjects were required to read blocks of word triads that appeared as mirror images of themselves. While half the words were unique to each block, half were repeated on every block during the three test sessions.

The results indicated that both the amnesic and normal control subjects showed significant and equivalent improvement in reading the unique, mirror-reflected triads over the three test days. Although the control subjects read the repeated words much faster than the unique words, the amnesic patients demonstrated only a slight improvement in reading speed for the repeated word triads. It seemed, then, that while amnesic patients were able to learn and retain the general skills underlying mirror reading, they, unlike the normal control subjects, did not recognize that specific word triads had been presented on numerous trials. A verbal recognition test administered following the skill-learning task confirmed that the Korsakoff patients could not identify the words employed on the mirror-reading task. Martone and her collaborators (Martone, Butters, Payne, Becker, & Sax, 1984) have replicated Cohen and Squire's findings with a mirror reading task, and Moscovitch (1984) has reported that amnesic patients learned to read sentences written in transformed script at the same rate as did intact control subjects.

## Experimental Studies of Retrograde Amnesia

Amnesic patients usually manifest some forgetting of events that occurred before the onset of their illness. For the alcoholic Korsakoff patient, this loss of remote memories is severe, extends over several decades (e.g., 1930s to 70s), and is characterized by a temporal gradient in which memories for very remote events (e.g., from the 1930s and 1940s) may be somewhat better (Seltzer & Benson, 1974; Marslen-Wilson & Teuber, 1975; Albert et al., 1979; Meudell, Northern, Snowden, & Neary, 1980; Cohen & Squire, 1981; Squire & Cohen, 1982). These features of the Korsakoff patients' retrograde amnesia have been noted consistently with a number of remote memory tests involving the identification of famous faces and voices and the recall and recognition of public events. In contrast to the extensive losses of the Korsakoff patients, systematic assessments of the retrograde amnesias of other patient populations have reported temporally limited (e.g., one to four years) forgetting of old memories. The well-studied patients HM (Marslen-Wilson & Teuber, 1975) and NA (Squire & Moore, 1979; Squire & Cohen, 1982), depressed patients receiving ECT (Squire, Slater, & Chace, 1975; Squire, Chace, & Slater, 1976), and traumatic amnesics (Russell & Nathan, 1946; Benson & Geschwind, 1967) all have losses of remote memories limited to the three or four years immediately preceding their illness or the beginning of shock treatment

(ECT). Recall of public events that occurred prior to this circumscribed retrograde amnesia is normal, a finding consistent with the notion that old, very remote memories are more resistant to forgetting than are newly acquired memories (Ribot, 1882).

Despite the consistency that investigators have noted for at least some sparing of very remote memories, Sanders and Warrington (1971) have raised a serious methodological issue concerning the validity of the temporal gradient in retrograde amnesia. They administered questionnaires on public events and a test of facial recognition to a group of amnesic patients of mixed etiology. On these tests, their amnesics showed severe impairment with little sparing of very remote events. The patients had as much difficulty recalling and recognizing public events from the 1930s as they did events from the 1960s. Sander and Warrington proposed that other demonstrations of a sparing of remote memories may have involved a failure to control for the difficulty and overexposure of the faces and events associated with the decades under study. That is, events and faces from the 1930s and 1940s are often easier to recall than those from the 1960s and 1970s because the earlier ones have been overlearned through overexposure in subsequent decades. Warrington and Weiskrantz (1973) interpret the demonstration of an extensive and flat retrograde amnesia as consistent with their interference-retrieval theory of amnesia. They believe that if all memory difficulties of amnesic patients are related to an inability to retrieve information from long-term memory, there is no reason to expect memories from childhood, adolescence, or young adulthood to be spared.

Although Sanders and Warrington's (1971) empirical data were flawed by 'floor' effects (i.e., their amnesics performed at chance levels on the recognition tests), their emphasis on the control of item difficulty and overlearning has face validity and has forced a reevaluation of retrograde amnesia with more carefully developed test instruments. Albert et al. (1979) constructed a test battery for retrograde amnesia, statistically controlled for item difficulty. Their battery included a famous-faces test, a recall questionnaire, and a multiple-choice recognition questionnaire. Each test consisted of items from the 1930s to the 1970s that had been assessed on a population of normal controls before their

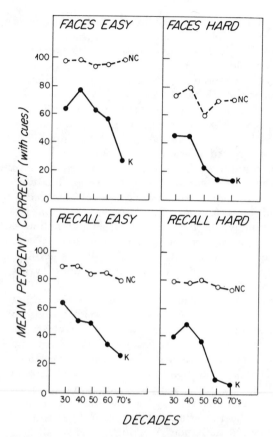

DECADES

**Figure 13.7.** Mean percent of easy and hard items correctly recalled by alcoholic Korsakoffs (K) and normal control (NC) subjects on the famous-faces test (top) and public-events recall questionnaire (bottom). From "Temporal Gradients in the Retrograde Amnesia of Patients with Alcoholic Korsakoff's Disease" by M. Albert, N. Butters, and J. Levin, 1979, *Archives of Neurology, 36*, pp. 213–214. Copyright 1979 by American Medical Association. Reprinted by permission.

inclusion in the final test battery. As judged by the performance of the standardization group, half the items were 'easy,' the other half 'hard.'

When this remote memory battery was administered to alcoholic Korsakoff patients and normal controls (Albert et al., 1979), little evidence was found supporting Sanders and Warrington's (1971) position. As shown in Figure 13.7 (upper graphs), the alcoholic Korsakoff patients identified more photographs from the 1930s and 1940s than from the 1960s. On the recall test of public events (lower graphs), the same pattern emerges.

Squire and Cohen (1982) have suggested that the statistical approach to item difficulty of Albert et al. (1979) may confound rather than

solve the equivalence and overlearning issue. If two public events (or faces), one from the 1930s and one from the 1970s, are both remembered by 80 percent of normal controls, can the two items be considered intrinsically equal in difficulty? Since the event that occurred 40 years earlier is remembered as well as the later event, it seems likely that the more remote event is in fact more famous and is thus overlearned compared with the more recent one. The passage of 30 years since original acquisition should have weakened the memory engram more than a five-year interval since original learning. From this point of view, statistical equality is simply a mask for an intrinsic inequality manifested by the temporal gradients of amnesic patients.

Butters and Albert (1982) have offered some additional empirical evidence for their statistical approach. They reanalyzed their original data on the famous-faces test so that easy items from the recent past could be compared with hard items from the remote past. Although, as expected, normal controls identified significantly fewer faces from the remote than from the recent past, the alcoholic Korsakoff patients showed the opposite trend. That is, the amnesic Korsakoff patients again correctly identified more hard faces from the remote past than easy faces from the recent past. Butters and Albert note that this relative preservation of remote memories under conditions of planned statistical inequality offers strong support that temporal gradients characterize the retrograde amnesia of alcoholic Korsakoff patients.

The findings of Albert, Butters, and Brandt's (1981) investigation of retrograde amnesia in demented patients (Huntington's disease) are also relevant with regard to the temporal gradient noted for amnesic patients. Unlike the amnesic Korsakoff patients, the demented patients showed equal forgetting of public events and famous faces across all decades from the 1930s to the 1970s. Figure 13.8 shows the demented patients' flat retrograde amnesia on the Albert et al. (1979) retrograde amnesia battery. Butters and Albert (1982) suggest that this equal loss of remote and recent memories weakens any criticisms of the statistical approach to item difficulty. If the temporal gradients of Korsakoff patients were owing to some intrinsic inequality in the difficulty of the faces and questions from the various decades, then the demented patients should have manifested a similar temporal

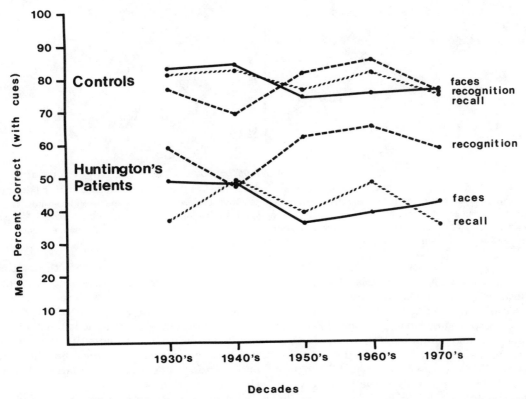

**Figure 13.8.** Performance of demented patients (Huntington's disease) and normal control subjects on the famous-faces test and the public-events recall and recognition questionnaires. From "Patterns of Remote Memory in Amnesic and Demented Patients" by M. Albert, N. Butters, and J. Brandt, 1981, *Archives of Neurology, 38*, p. 498. Copyright 1981 by American Medical Association. Reprinted by permission.

gradient. Like the amnesic Korsakoff patients, the demented patients should have identified more of the easy faces and public events from the 1930s and 1940s than the hard ones from the 1960s and 1970s. If one simultaneously accepts the flat gradients of the demented patients and dismisses the temporal gradients of the amnesic patients, one must explain why the items from the 1930s and 1940s of Albert et al. are not also intrinsically easy for demented patients.

Like Albert and Butters, Squire and his colleagues have attempted to develop a remote memory test that circumvents the overlearning and overexposure problems noted by Sanders and Warrington (1971). To ensure limited but equivalent public exposure, Squire and Slater (1975) used the titles of television programs that had been aired for one season or less in the construction of their recall and recognition tests. The individual items on these tests were matched for public exposure on the basis of their

known viewing histories, and since the items had a brief exposure period, the time of learning could be specified. The fact that normal subjects who resided out of the United States were unable to recognize the titles of the one-season programs that were aired during their absence provided strong support for the investigators' claim that the programs queried on the test were not overexposed or publicized in the years following their limited broadcast. The recognition form of the television program test requires the subjects to select from several alternatives the title of an aired program. On the recall test, the subjects are asked to supply details (e.g., names of characters and actors) about specified one-season television programs.

These tests of past television programs have been administered to depressed patients in the course of bilateral ECT. The results of these studies support Ribot's (1882) thesis that very remote memories are more resistant to

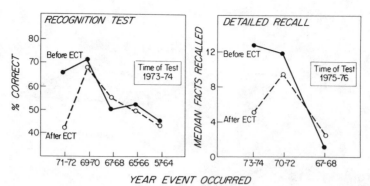

**Figure 13.9.** Retrograde amnesia following bilateral electroconvulsive therapy: (A) recognition of the titles of former one-season television programs: (B) recall of details about former one-season television programs. From "Remote Memory, Retrograde Amnesia, and Neuropsychology of Memory" by L. Squire and N. Cohen, pp. 282–283, in L. Cermak, *Human Memory and Amnesia*, Copyright 1979 by Lawrence Erlbaum Associates. Reprinted by permission.

forgetting than are recent memories. As Figure 13.9 shows, the retrograde amnesia following ECT is temporally limited. For both tests the patients served as their own controls, with testing occurring prior to the first administration of ECT and again one hour following its fifth administration. On the recognition form of the television test, the ECT patients were unable to recognize the titles of programs aired one to three years immediately prior to the ECT, but had no difficulty recognizing titles of programs broadcast 4 to 17 years prior to ECT (Squire et al., 1975). For the detailed recall task, the patients showed impairment in their recall of shows aired one to two years before ECT, but had no difficulty recalling programs broadcast prior to that time (Squire & Cohen, 1979).

While the majority of the published research with amnesic patients confirms the differential sparing of very remote memories, it also underscores the heterogeneity of the retrograde amnesias exhibited by different patient populations. Of the various amnesic patients that have been systematically studied, only the alcoholic Korsakoff patients, and possibly the postencephalitics have remote memory losses that extend back more than 10 years and involve all periods of their lives (see Butters & Cermak, 1980; Cermak, 1976; Cermak & O'Connor, 1983). The Korsakoff patients' memory of events that occurred during the 1940s is certainly superior to their recall of events in the 1960s, but their retention of information from the more remote decades is still significantly impaired in comparison with the recall of normal controls. As noted previously, this extensive graded loss of old memories is

much more evident and severe than the temporally limited retrograde amnesias of patients undergoing ECT, or patients with posttraumatic amnesia, or the well-studied patients HM and NA. In all these cases, the patients' inability to recall remote events is limited to the one- to four-year period immediately preceding the acute onset of their illness or the initiation of their shock treatments.

The difference between the retrograde amnesias of alcoholic Korsakoff patients and other amnesic populations has been addressed by Squire and Cohen (1982) and by Butters and Albert (1982). Both sets of investigators have suggested that the alcoholic Korsakoff patients' loss of remote memories may be secondary to a primary defect in establishing new memories (i.e., anterograde amnesia) during the 20 years of alcohol abuse that preceded the diagnosis of the amnesic syndrome. Although detoxified non-Korsakoff alcoholics have often been viewed as free of anterograde memory defects (for review, see Parsons & Prigatano, 1977), recent studies by Ryan and Butters (1980a, 1980b) using complex verbal and nonverbal stimuli, have shown that detoxified alcoholics are impaired on Brown–Peterson and paired-associate learning tasks, and that these deficits are positively correlated with years of alcohol abuse. Consequently, if chronic alcoholics acquire less information each year as a consequence of a progressive anterograde memory deficit, then at the time an alcoholic patient is diagnosed as having Korsakoff's syndrome one would expect to find a retrograde amnesia with a temporal gradient. In addition, the impairment of alcoholic

Korsakoff patients in searching their semantic memories (Cermak, Reale, & Baker, 1978) may exacerbate the temporal extent of their retrograde amnesias. From this standpoint, the Korsakoff patients' loss of remote memories would be considered an artifact related to a primary defect in establishing new memories and to a cognitive problem in locating memories that have been successfully stored. A corollary of this hypothesis is that true retrograde amnesias uncontaminated by deficiencies in original learning and cognitive retrieval strategies are temporally limited and are far less severe and devastating than the amnesic patient's anterograde memory problems (Squire & Cohen, 1982).

To evaluate this chronic explanation of the Korsakoffs' retrograde amnesia, Albert, Butters, and Brandt (1980) administered their remote-memory battery to detoxified long-term (non-Korsakoff) alcoholics and nonalcoholic control subjects. They noted that if the learning deficit related to alcoholism was responsible for the alcoholic Korsakoff patients' difficulties in recalled past events, two predictions could be made. First, the alcoholics should be impaired in their identification of famous faces and public events; and second, since the detrimental effects of alcohol on the learning of new materials are related to years of alcohol abuse, the alcoholics' deficits in recalling past events should be most apparent for the years immediately preceding testing. The results partially confirmed these expectations. Although the alcoholics' recall scores for hard famous faces from the 1960s and 1970s were lower than the scores of the nonalcoholic controls, the differences were not statistically significant. However, on the recall questionnaire the alcoholics had a significant but mild impairment in their recall of hard public events from the 1960s and 1970s, with the greatest loss associated with the immediately preceding decade. Cohen and Squire (1981) have reported similar evidence of mild remote memory deficits in non-Korsakoff alcoholics.

Although the results of the studies by Albert et al. (1980) and by Cohen and Squire (1981) are not of the magnitude to allow the alcoholic Korsakoff patients' retrograde amnesia to be reduced to an anterograde memory problem, they do suggest that two separate etiological factors may be involved. One factor is the impact of chronic alcohol abuse on anterograde memory processes. Since long-term alcoholics may retain somewhat

less information each year, owing to a progressive learning deficit (Brandt, Butters, Ryan, & Bayog, 1983), their store of remote memories for the recent past may be mildly or moderately deficient. The second factor may be a forgetting of —or loss of access to—old memories that appears acutely with the onset of the illness and results in a severe and equal loss for all time periods during the patients' lives. When this acute loss of remote memories is superimposed on the patients' already deficient store, a severe retrograde amnesia with a temporal gradient would be expected. Compared with controls, patients should be impaired across all time periods, but the memory for recent events should be most severely affected since less had been learned initially during this period.

The most convincing evidence for this two-factor model of the alcoholic Korsakoff patients' retrograde amnesia emanates from a single-case study of an amnesic patient's loss of autobiographical memory (Butters, 1984). This patient (with the fictitious initials PZ), an eminent scientist and university professor who developed alcoholic Korsakoff's syndrome at the age of 65, had written several hundred research papers and numerous books and book chapters, including an extensive autobiography two years prior to the acute onset of his amnesic condition in 1981. Like all alcoholics with Korsakoff's syndrome, PZ had severe anterograde and retrograde amnesia, as assessed by clinical and formal psychometric techniques. On Albert et al.'s (1979) famous-faces test, PZ's performance revealed a significant impairment across all time periods, but with some sparing of his ability to recognize famous faces from the 1930s and 1940s. To determine whether patient PZ had also lost access to autobiographical material well known to him before his illness, a retrograde amnesia test based on his autobiography was developed. The test consisted of questions about relatives, colleagues, collaborators, conferences, research assistants, research reports and books, all of which were prominently mentioned in his autobiography.

Patient PZ's recall of these autobiographical facts is shown in Figure 13.10. It is evident that PZ has a very severe retrograde amnesia for autobiographical events, with some sparing of information from the very remote past. These data also suggest that PZ's retrograde amnesia for autobiographical material cannot be

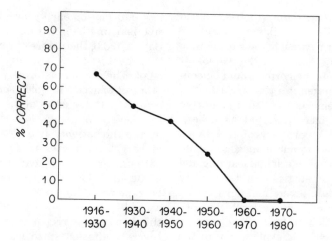

**Figure 13.10.** Patient PZ's retrograde amnesia for informaton from his published autobiography. From "Alcoholic Korsakoff's Syndrome: an Update" by N. Butters, 1984, *Seminars in Neurology, 4,* 236. Copyright 1984 by Thieme-Stratton, Inc. Reprinted by permission.

secondary to a deficiency in original learning. Since all the questions were drawn from his autobiography, PZ must have been aware of this information prior to the onset of Korsakoff's syndrome. Clearly, PZ's illness marked the acute onset of his inability to access information once readily available to him.

Patient PZ's total inability to retrieve information acquired during the past 20 years (Figure 13.10) indicates that this autobiographical information might not have been as stable (i.e., consolidated) as information acquired earlier in his lifetime. There are a number of plausible interpretations for this. One is that this instability represents a progressive loss of PZ's ability to acquire new information during his 35-year history of alcoholism (Albert et al., 1980; Cohen & Squire, 1981). Thus, PZ's memory for episodes and facts from the past 20 years may have been based on partial or degraded engrams. The more degraded or partial the memories, the more vulnerable they may have been to the acute brain damage that occurred in 1981.

Another plausible explanation for the temporal gradient that characterizes PZ's retrograde amnesia involves the notion that information acquired several decades previously might by necessity be retrieved from a more general knowledge system than would be used for recently acquired information. Cermak (1984) has suggested that newly acquired knowledge may be episodic in nature, but with time and continued rehearsal most memories become inde-

pendent of specific temporal and spatial contexts and are retained as general knowledge (i.e., semantic memory). From this point of view, the temporal gradient evinced by PZ (and other Korsakoff patients) might be caused by the greater vulnerability of episodic, than of semantic, memory to extensive damage to limbic-diencephalic regions of the brain. Information about the 1930s and 1940s may be part of everyone's semantic memory, whereas knowledge about the past decade may still be associated with specific temporal and spatial contexts (i.e., episodic memory). This application (Cermak, 1984) of Tulving's (1983) distinction between episodic and semantic memory to the amnesic condition is unique because it attempts to account for both anterograde and retrograde amnesia.

## NEUROPSYCHOLOGY OF LANGUAGE

### Clinical Foundations

Current views on the neural basis for language have developed largely from the observation of the selective deficits in language function that arise primarily from injury in the left perisylvian zone in previously normal adult speakers, and to which the general term *aphasia* is applied. Aphasia is a linguistic disorder in the sense that failures of visual or auditory processing of memory or of motor performance are specific to their use for language. Underlying these readily observable manifestations are impaired access to lexical and syntactic knowledge, and to the graphic code; the degree and nature of these impairments vary with lesion site.

Historically, a number of forms of aphasic language deficit were described in medical reports dating from the writings of the ancient Greeks (Benton & Joynt, 1960) to the modern period, but it was not until 1861 that the first of a series of cases was published by Broca, correlating the destruction of language production with a large lesion encompassing the lower posterior frontal lobe. By 1865 Broca could report that the lesions producing this disorder were virtually always in the left hemisphere, giving rise to the rule that the left hemisphere controlled language. Within a few years the association between left handedness and exceptions to left-hemisphere dominance became widely known.

While Broca's own descriptions of the linguistic and other cognitive defects of his patients were scanty by current standards, the configuration of deficits in what is now termed Broca's aphasia or motor aphasia has been well studied. The syndrome is produced by damage to the lower posterior portion of the left frontal lobe just anterior to the central (rolandic) fissure. Its dominant clinical feature is impaired voluntary production of articulatory gestures, ranging in severity from complete inability to form speech sounds to persistent clumsiness with consonant combinations. As with many aphasic features, articulation varies with the level to which the utterance is automatized. Even in the most severe case, memorized sequences (e.g., counting) and interjections may be well produced; at milder levels, high-frequency words and phrases are uttered with normal facility in a context of generally effortful articulation.

Of greater challenge to understanding, from the point of view of cognition, is the loss of access to the morphological and syntactic forms of language in a patient who has recovered some speech, resulting in a characteristic style of delivery that is called *agrammatic* because it is composed predominantly of substantives and uninflected verbs. Access to lexical elements —also reduced—outstrips the recovery of grammatical forms and may eventually approach the normal range. Auditory language comprehension, while grossly intact, usually breaks down when the unambiguous reception of a sentence depends critically on syntactic processing. Reading comprehension usually parallels auditory comprehension, while oral reading often parallels the agrammatism of the patient's oral conversation; that is, the patient reads the principal nouns and verbs but cannot verbalize the small grammatical words or the inflectional endings in the written sentence.

Occasionally, agrammatic oral reading is accompanied by semantic paralexia, that is, the misreading of lexical items with semantically related but perceptually and phonologically dissimilar words, betraying a loss of graphophonemic conversion rules. This feature, called *deep dyslexia* (Marshall & Newcombe, 1973; Shallice & Warrington, 1975; Saffran, Schwartz, & Marin, 1976), is not unique to Broca's aphasia; it will be discussed more fully in connection with reading processes.

Writing by Broca's aphasics is usually much more impaired than reading—often betraying difficulty even in the recalling of elementary letter forms. As writing recovers, the recall of written vocabulary and the grammatical form of sentences usually parallel the patient's oral language. Patients are commonly observed to recall the written form of an object name, relying purely on the visual and graphic structural features of the word, without being able to verbalize it (Friederici, Schoenle, & Goodglass, 1981).

The features of Wernicke's aphasia (Wernicke, 1874) are almost diametrically opposed to those of Broca's aphasia. This syndrome almost invariably involves injury to the posterior portion of the first temporal gyrus and is characterized by two dominant features. The first is the impairment of auditory language comprehension, primarily at the level of lexical comprehension, for example the patient may repeat a stimulus word perfectly without understanding it. Related auditory processing impairments play contributory roles—such as a reduced ability to discriminate similar speech sounds, unstable auditory verbal trace, impairment of syntactic decoding.

The second manifest feature is the intrusion of speech formulation errors (paraphasia) in an output that seems normal in articulatory facility, intonation, and rhythm, and that preserves elementary (and sometimes complex) syntactic forms and a generally appropriate use of grammatical morphemes. Errors of production may be at the level of phonology, so that sounds or syllables are transposed or substituted (phonemic paraphasia); they may be at the lexical level, in which case specific word substitutions are made (semantic or verbal paraphasia); or the errors may be at the level of the logical coherence of the semantic and grammatical structure (paragrammatism).

Voluntary access to the lexical store is impaired, sometimes impossible, probably accounting for the scant informational content of the speech of Wernicke's aphasics. Attempts to name objects on request reveal this deficit (anomia) directly, the failures taking the form of verbal or phonemic paraphasia or neologisms.

Reading comprehension of single words is often much better than auditory comprehension, though it breaks down at the sentence level; and writing may parallel speech as a paragrammatic and informationally empty production, despite preserving graphomotor skills and elementary syntax and morphology.

The distinguishing clinical features of the remaining aphasic syndromes can be summarized more briefly. Severely impaired access to substantives, with little impact on other aspects of language may be seen in anomic aphasia, which follows lesions of the temporoparietal junction but may also occur with diffuse brain injury. Severe impairment in reproducing a spoken model, in the presence of near perfect auditory comprehension and fairly fluent spontaneous speech, is found in conduction aphasia —usually associated with injury just superior to the sylvian fissure (supramarginal gyrus). The reverse pattern—that is, remarkable preservation of repetition of long sentences and even nonsense strings in the presence of severe language disorders—is seen in the transcortical aphasias (transcortical motor and transcortical sensory). These are usually produced by lesions in the zone concentric to or undercutting the immediate perisylvian gyri, but partly or totally sparing them. Figure 13.11 summarizes the major aphasic syndromes and their usual lesion sites.

The foregoing six syndromes, while distinctive in their profiles of relatively impaired and spared functions, all involve some degree of impairment in the use of linguistic knowledge via all modalities of sensory input and motor output. There are, however, a number of syndromes entailing language deficits that are pure in the sense that they may be confined to the

processing of input from a single sense modality. Pure alexia (Déjerine, 1892) has already been mentioned; it is paralleled by pure word deafness—loss of auditory language comprehension in the presence of adequate hearing and unimpaired speech and written language. Like pure alexia, pure word deafness is attributed to an anatomical interruption of sensory input to the language association area—specifically interruption of the fibres from both primary auditory cortices (Heschl's gyri) to the posterior portion of the left first temporal gyrus (Wernicke's area). At least one Heschl's gyrus must be intact to provide hearing. These are disconnection phenomena (Geschwind, 1965). Analogous disconnections that disable specific language operations are brought about by lesions of the corpus callosum, either through natural events (Liepmann & Maas, 1907; Geschwind & Kaplan, 1962; Poncet, AliCherif, Choux, Boudouresques, & Lhermitte, 1978) or by operative section (Gazzaniga, Bogen & Sperry, 1962). In these instances, patients are unable to name objects palpated by the left hand or presented visually to the left visual field, both deficits due to the "trapping" of sensory information in the right cerebral hemisphere.

The breakdown of function seen in aphasia and even in the disconnection phenomena is rarely a simple and complete deletion of function but rather entails errors betraying partial knowledge. It is the analysis of this partial knowledge that provides the clues to both the psychological nature of cognition and its relation to the functional organization of the brain.

## Experimental and Theoretical Approaches

### Phonological Processes

RECEPTIVE ASPECTS

We have seen that failures in the processing of auditory verbal input are most conspicuous in patients whose injuries are in the auditory association area of the temporal lobe (Wernicke's aphasics) or in the access to that area from the primary auditory centers (pure word deafness). To what extent are these impairments conditioned by difficulties at the level of speech-sound discrimination?

Luria (1970), while acknowledging the semantic character of the comprehension problems of

**TYPICAL LESION SITE**

**TYPICAL FEATURES OF SYNDROME**

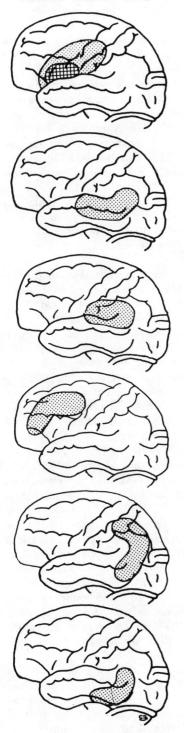

**BROCA'S APHASIA** Effortful articulation . Sparse agrammatic output and impaired wordfinding . Relatively spared auditory comprehension . SMALLER SHADED AREA ASSOCIATED WITH TRANSIENT DISORDER .

**WERNICKE'S APHASIA** Fluent paraphasic speech preserving articulatory and grammatical facility . Severely impaired auditory comprehension and severe wordfinding difficulty .

**CONDUCTION APHASIA** Predominantly fluent well articulated and grammatically organized speech with sporadic errors in selection and sequence of word-sounds . SEVERE DIFFICULTY IN REPEATING , in spite of good auditory comprehension .

**TRANSCORTICAL MOTOR APHASIA** Extreme difficulty in initiation and formulation of speech with preserved auditory comprehension . REMARKABLY PRESERVED REPETITION AND ABILITY TO RECITE MEMORIZED MATERIAL .

**TRANSCORTICAL SENSORY APHASIA** Fluent paraphasic speech , with impaired auditory comprehension and severe wordfinding difficulty . REMARKABLE PRESERVATION OF ACCURATE REPETITION AND OF ABILITY TO RECITE MEMORIZED MATERIAL .

**ANOMIC APHASIA** Fluent , well articulated grammatical speech with marked difficulty in retrieving the key nouns and verbs , compensated by circumlocution and occasional misnaming . Normal repetition and good auditory comprehension .

**Figure 13.11.** Typical lesion sites for six major syndromes of aphasia.

temporal lobe aphasics, made the strong claim that these impairments were secondary to a breakdown of discriminative phonemic audition. Luria's tasks required patients to distinguish between consonants that differed only in voicing (t–d, p–b) or only in place of articulation (k–t, b–g). He required patients either to repeat an alternating sequence of consonant–vowel (CV) syllables beginning with minimally differing consonants (e.g., ta da ta da) or to signal when they detected a target consonant occurring in a series of CV syllables, beginning with a minimally differing consonant.

Blumstein, Baker, and Goodglass (1977) questioned the grounds for attributing failures of word comprehension to phoneme-discrimination problems. They tested five diagnostic subtypes of aphasic patients, using a same-different sound discrimination paradigm. Contrasting phonemes were embedded both in real words (back-pack) and nonsense words (baf-paf). Wernicke's aphasics, although by far the more impaired on an independent measure of auditory comprehension, performed better than did patients with large anterior speech-zone lesions, who were at an intermediate level in auditory comprehension. Broca's aphasics made few sound-discrimination errors. All groups performed better on real words than on nonsense syllables, suggesting that, whenever possible, they coded the first stimulus word semantically and made a semantic comparison with the second word, rather than relying on a purely acoustic match, which they were compelled to do with the nonsense syllables.

Nevertheless, since this task could have been performed without semantic mediation, it was repeated (Baker, Blumstein, & Goodglass, 1981) in a form where all the words were names of picturable objects and the second member of the pair appeared as a picture to be matched against the immediately preceding spoken word. Another condition presented a four-way pictorial multiple choice, in which the spoken stimulus (e.g., bear) was to be selected from a set that included a phonologically similar distractor (pear), a semantically related one (wolf), and one semantically related to the phonological distractor, but unrelated to the stimulus (e.g., grapes). While Wernicke's aphasics again made more phonologically based confusions than Broca's aphasics, they made more semantically based errors than phonological ones. Errors in which there was a semantic misinterpretation of a phonologically misperceived word (e.g., pointing to grapes in response to bear) were very rare, although errors of the type pear-grapes occurred frequently when the same visual display was presented with 'pear' as the stimulus word.

The conclusion from this series of experiments was that, while sound-discrimination errors may well be a product of injury to the auditory association cortex suffered by Wernicke's aphasics, that does not explain their impaired language comprehension. This conclusion is in accord with the previously mentioned clinical observation that these patients often repeat a spoken stimulus word correctly without understanding it and also the fact that ambiguities in the perception of a sound in running speech are usually resolved by the context with little effect on comprehension.

Quite apart from the contribution of fine phonological discriminations to word comprehension, the perception and classification of speech sounds is, in itself a component of language knowledge and one for which refined experimental procedures have been developed. The methodology developed with normal listeners (Liberman, Harris, Hoffman, & Griffith, 1957) is based on the phenomenon of categorical perception of phonemes. In English, a major determinant for distinguishing voiced from unvoiced stop consonants (b versus p, d versus t) in an identification task is the interval between the release of the articulatory closure and the onset of phonation. This interval, the voice onset time (VOT), is shorter than 30 msec for voiced consonants, and over 30 msec for unvoiced consonants. The term categorical perception refers to the fact that, in same-different discrimination, normal listeners cannot distinguish well between differences in VOT of synthetic stop consonant-vowel syllables when both members of the test pair are on the same side of the boundary value of 30 msec. However, when the same physical differences in VOT are presented at values close to or straddling the boundary, discrimination is markedly enhanced. The same principle is observed in distinctions between stop consonants differing in place of articulation, although the continuum involved here is not the time interval but the frequency of the spectral components or formants of the consonant.

In a further inquiry into the relevance of fine sound discrimination to language comprehension,

Blumstein, Cooper, Zurif, and Caramazza (1977) applied the method of Liberman et al. to five groups of aphasic patients, including Broca's and Wernicke's aphasics. All four of their Wernicke's subjects and four of their five Broca's subjects had normal discrimination peaks at the boundary for the *t–d* distinction. However, only one of the Wernicke's subjects and three of the Broca's aphasics showed a clear boundary effect when required to identify single CVs at various positions on the VOT continuum by pointing to the written syllable *da* or *ta*. In particular, the one Wernicke's aphasic who succeeded in both the discrimination and identification tasks was the patient with the most profoundly impaired language comprehension. These results then provide evidence that the low-level speech perception process underlying categorical perception of VOT is unimpaired in most aphasics, regardless of their auditory comprehension level. The more demanding task of assigning a linguistic label to a perceived CV is taxing for all categories of aphasics, but is still poorly correlated with their auditory comprehension level.

The issue of an acoustic processing difficulty as the basis for impaired language comprehension has been pursued by Tallal and her co-workers (Tallal & Piercy, 1973, 1974, 1975; Tallal, Stark, & Curtiss, 1976; Tallal & Newcombe, 1978). Tallal and Piercy's original approach (1973) was to require subjects to reproduce the sequence of two brief complex tones, varying in both duration, from 75 to 250 msec each, and ISI, from 8 to 428 msec. Nine children with developmental aphasia involving both language comprehension and production were compared with 12 normal children, matched for age and nonverbal IQ. After training to criterion on associating each tone to a corresponding response panel, the subjects were required to reproduce the sequence of two paired stimuli, given in the four possible combinations 1-1, 2-2, 1-2, 2-1. Aphasic children were markedly impaired in perceiving auditory sequences of brief duration at all interstimulus intervals (ISIs) below 428 msec. Aphasic and control children performed alike in an analogous color-sequencing task.

Reasoning that the problem of the aphasics lay in the processing of rapid acoustic changes, Tallal and Piercy (1974, 1975) proposed that the source of the aphasics' comprehension disorder lay in the acoustic events that take place between the release of a stop consonant and the beginning of the following steady state vowel. This period, normally lasting about 40 msec, represents the formant transition, resulting from the change in the configuration of the articulators as they move into position for the vowel. The pattern of formant transitions is crucial for perceiving the place of articulation of the consonant. Synthetic CV syllables for *ba* and *da* were generated, in which the formant transition time was varied between 43 and 95 msec. In their 1974 study, Tallal and Piercy used combinations of *ba* and *da*, generated with fast (43-msec) transitions, presenting them in the same sequence-reproduction paradigm as for their 1973 experiment. Only five of 12 aphasic children ever learned to discriminate between the syllables and only two reached criterion on the experimental tasks. When these procedures were then repeated in a 1975 study, with the slow (95-msec) formant transition times all 12 aphasics reached criterion on the experimental tasks and matched the performance of controls.

These results indicate that stop-consonant discrimination may be dependent on the capacity for processing rapid acoustic events, which is deficient in some aphasic children. The effort to correlate this deficiency with the amount of functional impairment of language comprehension in adult aphasics produced less clear-cut results. Tallal and Newcombe (1958) compared ten left brain-injured subjects with varying degrees of comprehension impairment with ten right brain-injured subjects and six normal controls. Of the mildest aphasics three reached criterion for discriminating consistently between CVs at normal (short) transition times; four aphasics at widely varying levels of impairment succeeded only with the extended formant transitions, and three failed under both conditions.

Unlike patients with Wernicke's aphasia, those with pure word deafness appear to be free of impairment at the semantic level. To the extent that they can integrate their auditory input, sometimes with the assistance of lip-reading and sometimes with the aid of a slowed rate of speech, they may draw correct inferences from the words they have heard, or err only in terms of phonological similarity. Thus systematic study of their speech perception has addressed the question whether their disorder can be totally accounted for by elementary perceptual disorders or by reduced rate of processing.

Miceli (1982) reports the most extensive series of phonemic perception studies of a patient with pure word deafness who had suffered bilateral temporal-lobe damage. In addition to suffering severely impaired speech comprehension, she was no longer able to recognize familiar environmental sounds reliably (auditory agnosia), or to produce or recognize melody or tonal intervals. On testing for phoneme discrimination, the patient proved to be impaired only in the perception of differences between stop consonants; she performed almost perfectly in distinguishing vowel contrasts and contrasts between all types of continuant consonants, whether nasals, fricatives, sibilants, liquids, or affricates. Moreover, her errors on stop consonants were confined to distinguishing the place of articulation, whereas she distinguished voiced from unvoiced stop consonants almost flawlessly.

When tested with synthetic stop-consonant–vowel syllables, this word-deaf patient had a normal boundary for identifying CVs given singly, but a severely impaired discrimination pattern that showed no peak at the expected boundary value.

Auerbach, Allard, Naeser, Alexander, and Albert (1982) studied a word-deaf patient who had a similar configuration of clinical deficits in the recognition of speech, music, and environmental noises, and who also had lesions similar to those of Miceli's patient. As with Miceli's case, the ability to label a stimulus as *ta* or *da* (given only the two alternatives) was good and reflected a clear boundary effect, but discrimination between paired stimuli was only slightly more accurate at the boundary value.

An impaired rate of processing acoustic signals was implicated as a factor in pure word deafness by Albert and Bear (1974). The comprehension of one of their patients was markedly improved by slowing the rate of speech. That patient could count taps only at a slow rate of presentation. The patients of Auerbach, Allard et al. and of Miceli were similarly impaired in that they could count clicks only when they were slowed from the normal 9 to 11 to two or fewer per second.

Can the entire auditory comprehension defect of pure-word deafness be explained as an acoustic disorder affecting the perception of stop consonants and the rate at which auditory information is processed? There are too many inconsistencies for such a reductionist view. First, it is paradoxical that both the foregoing patients could correctly assign the linguistic label *ta* or *da* without being able to make a reliable same-different discrimination at the boundary between these categories. Second, given that both patients identified vowels and continuant consonants reliably and that, Miceli's patient, at least, could discriminate the voicing of stop consonants reliably, the impairment of speech comprehension appears disproportionately severe. Further, both patients (like most cases of pure word deafness) could grasp many individual words in which the succession of phonemes was far faster than the rate at which they could count clicks. Thus, even for pure word deafness, we must endorse Lesser's (1978) statement that, "From the linguistic perspective . . . , the weight of evidence suggests that a model of phonemic perception as the basic stage of a chain of events in language comprehension is too simple" (p. 174).

PRODUCTIVE ASPECTS

Listening to and watching the speech of a patient with Broca's aphasia suggests that difficulties in articulation lie in a motor-coordination problem and that, although an error analysis might reveal some relation to the complexity of the movements involved, it would have little bearing on the cognitive basis for articulation. Two clinical phenomena, however, belie such a view. The first is the previously noted variability in articulatory facility as a function of the automaticity of the utterance—as in recitation of overlearned series or the occasional facile production of words while singing. These dissociations may be so complete as to suggest that totally different neural systems are brought into play under the automatized or singing conditions from those engaged during efforts at discrete, voluntary speech acts.

The second clinical feature is that articulatory errors appear to fall into two different levels of linguistic organization: phonetic and phonemic. Phonetics is concerned with the relations between the sequence of configurations of the vocal tract during speech, the physical characteristics of the resulting acoustic waveforms, and the precise characterization of the sound that is perceived; phonemics is concerned with identifying the set of different sounds that determine the words of a given language (i.e., phonemes) and the perceptual features by which the speakers of the language distinguish one phoneme from another. Phonetic difficulties give the appearance of clumsiness of motor coordination in the execution of a target phoneme; phonemic errors seem to reflect the facile motor execution of incorrectly chosen targets—either by transposition of consonants within words or by intrusion of unintended sounds or syllables in a particular target word. While phonetic errors are particularly characteristic of the anterior speech-zone lesions of Broca's aphasia, phonemic errors occur with Broca's aphasics as well as with Wernicke's and conduction aphasics who have damage in the posterior speech zone.

Blumstein's (1973) study suggests that an underlying system of linguistic rules dictates the direction of phoneme substitutions in both phonetically and phonemically disordered articulation. She approached her analysis as a test of the linguist Jakobson's (1956) definition of the phoneme as a unique cluster of binary (present or absent) distinctive features. The presence of a particular feature (e.g., voicing, nasality) represented the marked form and its absence the unmarked form of the feature. Blumstein's hypothesis, following Jakobson, was that phoneme substitutions would most frequently diverge by only one distinctive feature from the target phoneme and that the direction of change would more often be from a marked to an unmarked form of a feature than the reverse.

She collected samples of 2000 words of conversation from each of 17 patients distributed among Broca's, Wernicke's and conduction aphasias and analyzed the phoneme substitutions in all cases where the target word was clearly identifiable. As predicted, 67 percent of substitutions represented shifts of only one distinctive feature, and substitution of unmarked for marked features outnumbered the reverse by 61 percent to 39 percent. Other investigators (Lecours & Lhermitte, 1969; Martin & Rigrodsky, 1974; Hatfield & Walton, 1975; Poncet, Degos, Deloche, & Lecours, 1972) have also observed regularities in the determination of phonological errors, although Blumstein's approach is the only one that was motivated by a theory of normal linguistic organization.

CENTRAL REPRESENTATION?
It seems intuitively obvious that native speakers of a language acquire their repertoire of spoken phonemes by hearing them from other speakers, and that early speech acquisition entails the development of a system for voluntarily bringing a produced sound into approximation with a perceived sound, as in mimicking or repeating. However, recent studies of child language (Barton, 1980) provide no support for the view that a common core of phonological rules governs both perception and production of speech sounds.

The availability of patients with an obvious organically based disability in the phonological aspects of their language has prompted several investigators to ask whether there are parallels between impairment of perception and impairment of production that might denote a common cerebral representation in both modes of performance. In general, the findings from these studies agree with the developmental data that phoneme production and phoneme perception are independently represented.

Blumstein, Cooper, Goodglass, Statlender, and Gottlieb (1980) mapped the distribution of VOTs produced by aphasics of five types (Broca's, mixed nonfluent, Wernicke's, anomic, and conduction) in a repetition task of words beginning with t or d. Figure 13.12 illustrates the clear boundary effect in sounds produced by a Wernicke's aphasic. All the sounds he produced fell clearly into the VOT range of either a voiced or an unvoiced alveolar stop. In contrast, the sounds produced by a Broca's aphasic showed no respect for the boundary value. Four of the nonfluent aphasics tested in this way were also among the subjects tested for their perceptual discrimination and labeling of sounds around the VOT boundary (p. 892). In spite of their poor production, all four had normal discrimination peaks, and three of the four had normal phoneme-labeling ability.

Thus production problems at the phonetic level imply no underlying disorder that would affect perception. The evidence supports the view that, while the productive and perceptual aspects of phonology are linked by a system that permits the modeling of output on perceived input, they are mediated by independent neural representations. The set of abstractly defined phonemes that is common to both modalities may then be regarded as a composite of an articulatory abstraction and a perceptual abstraction.

*Lexical Processes*
As noted in the clinical review, brain injury may produce a highly specific deficit for the recall of the lexical (or content) words of language, with little or no effect on phonology or production of

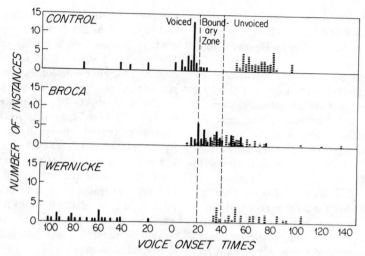

**Figure 13.12.** Distribution of voice onset times in repetition of words beginning with a voiced (*d*) or unvoiced (*t*) alveolar stop consonant. (Values to the left of zero indicate onset of phonation prior to release of stop.) From "Production Deficits in Aphasia: A Voice-Onset Time Analysis" by S.E. Blumstein, W.E. Cooper, H. Goodglass, S. Statlender, and J. Gottlieb, 1980, *Brain and Language, 9*, p. 158, Copyright 1980 by Academic Press. Reprinted by permission.

the grammatical background. Specifically, recalling for purposes of production words that have a semantic referent is a very different operation from producing the words that compose the grammatical matrix of sentences. While we have noted that the deficit of anomia may be produced by diffuse brain injury, it most regularly follows from lesions in the arc-shaped zone from the angular gyrus down, and forward into the middle temporal gyrus. Word-retrieval problems also appear, confounded with semantic and literal paraphasia, with lesions of the posterior perisylvian gyri. They are present in aphasias of the prerolandic speech zone—but now overshadowed by more prominent difficulties at the phonological and syntactic levels. Thus, while lexical production seems to be isolable by brain damage as a component of language, neither a psychological nor an anatomical flow diagram is easily generated by clinical and experimental data, because we are unable to discern, either behaviorally or anatomically, clearly segmented stages.

Research on naming is virtually limited to the act of producing a word on request, on being confronted with a visual stimulus or a stimulus in the form of a question requiring the target as a response. These are, of course, artificial situations, quite unlike inserting the word in its position in a sentence in the context of purposeful communication. In defense of these approaches, one can say, first, that naming to confrontation usually corresponds to the availability of words in conversation; second, that naming on request, though artificial, is a legitimate probe of the language mechanism through which normal and pathological function can be compared.

All approaches to the study of naming agree that performance depends on arousing a well-formed concept in the left hemisphere. The clearest evidence for this conclusion comes from cases in which a lesion of the corpus callosum acts to confine sensory information about the stimulus to the hemisphere contralateral to the side of stimulation. Geschwind and Kaplan's (1962) callosally damaged patient, when given objects for identification by touch in his left hand, called a ring an eraser, a padlock a book of matches and a screwdriver a piece of paper. The fact that his right hemisphere, but not his left hemisphere, knew what these objects were is attested by his ability to manipulate them appropriately with his left hand while blindfolded, and to draw them with his left hand but not his right. Naming upon palpation by the right hand was flawless, since for this task sensory information was accessible to the language system in the left hemisphere.

When the corpus callosum is sectioned along its entire length, as has been the practice in some of the operations for the relief of epilepsy (Sperry & Gazzaniga, 1967), even visual information is confined to the hemisphere opposite the visual hemifield in which a stimulus is exposed. Gazzaniga, Bogen, and Sperry (1965) have demonstrated that objects presented tachistoscopically to the left visual field are inaccessible for naming by the left or talking hemisphere, although they can be selected tactually from multiple choices with the left hand.

The foregoing instances of anomia based on interruption of particular sensory channels all relate to a condition that is relatively uncommon in nature—a lesion of the corpus callosum. These instances make it reasonable to ask to what extent the several sensory input channels through which an object may be experienced have autonomous associations to the name. When Spreen, Benton, and Van Allen (1966) compared naming of visually presented objects to the naming of the same objects by palpation in 21 patients considered to be anomic aphasics, they found that two were at least two standard deviations lower in tactile than in visual naming and three showed the reverse pattern. The remaining 16 were considered to have commensurate difficulties with both modalities. Goodglass, Barton, and Kaplan (1968) extended this approach to a comparison between naming on visual confrontation (pictures) and naming to auditory, tactile, and olfactory stimulation on the part of 27 aphasics, 12 nonaphasic, right brain-injured subjects, and 12 normal controls. Forty-eight pictures of objects or substances (e.g., coffee, mustard) were presented, of which 16 were also to be named through hearing a 5-sec tape recording of their characteristic sound, 16 by touch, and 16 by smelling a sample in a vial. While aphasics were slower and less successful than controls in naming via all four modalities, they did not differ, as a group, from control subjects in the ratios of response latencies for naming between visual presentation and each of the three nonvisual modalities. Of the 27 aphasic subjects, only two showed a marked discrepancy between their success in naming to visual presentation and their performance on one of the other modalities, one failing with auditory and one with olfactory stimuli.

Thus both the Spreen et al. and the Goodglass et al. studies emphasize the constancy of naming by most aphasics across modes of sensory stimulation. These results indicate that naming is mediated by a process that may be termed *concept arousal*, which may be set into motion through any sensory channel. The few discrepant cases could represent either disconnection or degradation of input to the language area from the deficient sense modality.

One of the incidental observations from the study of Goodglass et al. is that aphasic subjects had more difficulty in naming in response to auditory and olfactory than to visual and tactile stimuli. The authors suggested that the several sense modalities differ intrinsically in the redundancy of the information they provide: vision being the richest and olfaction the poorest in informational qualities. The hypothesis is proposed that the redundancy of sensory information affects the level of concept arousal, which in turn determines whether the threshold for retrieving the phonological form of the name is reached. This notion had already been expressed by Bisiach (1966) when he found that aphasics were more successful in naming realistic colored drawings than outlines or disfigured drawings of the same objects.

A study by North (1971) asked explicitly whether there was a level of reduced sensory information that was adequate for object recognition but was insufficient to bring about retrieval of the name of the object. She presented aphasic patients with a series of 16 objects under clear and degraded conditions in two modalities: visual and tactile. Visual blurring was obtained by defocusing projected color slides by amounts calibrated to produce seven correct identifications in a pilot group of eight subjects; tactile blurring was similarly achieved by determining the thickness of foam rubber wrapped around each actual object that would allow seven out of eight correct responses. North's results paralleled and extended those of Bisiach. Not only did degraded sensory input in either modality reduce the availability of names, but simultaneous presentation of reduced tactile and visual stimuli had an additive effect toward the facilitation of naming.

The foregoing studies at least support, if they do not establish, the view that retrieval of a name depends on the level of activation of a supramodal process in the left hemisphere—a process that is accessible via any sense modality. Indirect support for this position comes from studies (Zurif, Caramazza, Meyerson, & Galvin, 1974; Whithouse, Caramazza, & Zurif, 1978)

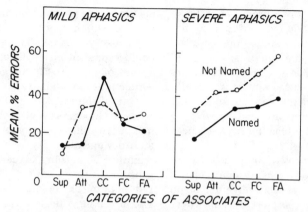

**Figure 13.13.** Relation between successful naming and detection of verbal associates to target words. Categories of associates along abscissa are Superordinate, Attribute, Contrast Coordinate, Functional Context, Function Associates. From "Semantic Field, Naming, and Auditory Comprehension in Aphasia" by H. Goodglass and E. Baker, 1976, *Brain and Language, 3,* p. 369. Copyright 1976 by Academic Press. Reprinted by permission.

reporting that aphasics with posterior speech-zone lesion and anomia have semantically disordered concepts.

Goodglass and Baker (1976) looked for a word-by-word relation between the accessibility of a word to an aphasic patient and the integrity of its conceptual representation, reasoning that not only the adequacy of sensory input, but also the availability of a network of verbal associations converged to trigger the retrieval of the name of the stimulus. Their operation for probing the integrity of the semantic field of each target picture was to require objects to react by squeezing a rubber bulb when they recognized a verbal associate to a pictured target in a tape-recorded list of associates interspersed among buffer items.

Associates were more often missed when targets were not named than when targets were successfully named. This finding was clear cut across the five categories of associates (Figure 13.13) for the more severely impaired subjects but was not significant for the 31 subjects with milder impairment. While the result supports the authors' hypothesis, it is limited by the fact that the probe of semantic fields depended on auditory comprehension, which was itself impaired in the subject population. A similar experiment that probed the semantic structure of the target concepts pictorially would be more convincing and remains to be carried out.

### From Concept to Sound Pattern

Given that a concept has been more-or-less well activated in the left hemisphere, what does pathology tell us about how its corresponding sound pattern achieves motor implementation?

There is intuitive appeal to the model of naming as an unfolding process, proceeding in real time from a stage of semantic representation to one of phonological retrieval and then to motor implementation. In fact, the form of aphasics' failures suggests that patients of different types may be derailed in their naming efforts at different points along this sequence. That is, patients with temporal lobe and temporoparietal lesions produce the largest proportion of errors, which may be considered prephonological in that they are semantically off target, circumlocutory, or grossly neologistic. Those with suprasylvian lesions (i.e., conduction aphasics) produce the largest proportion of phonemically altered near misses, and those with prerolandic lesions (i.e., Broca's aphasics) produce the largest proportion of motor errors. This pattern corresponds to a process beginning in the posterior (temporoparietal) speech zone and moving downstream to implementation via the motor cortex and the immediately adjacent motor association area.

Experimental efforts to distinguish between prephonological and postphonological stages of word-finding failure have attempted to determine how much tacit phonological information a patient has about a target he has failed to name. An obvious method uses an adaptation of the Brown and McNeill (1966) 'tip-of-the-tongue' experiment. Barton (1971) provided a series of unselected aphasics with an opportunity to demonstrate their knowledge of the number of syllables and the initial sounds of the words they failed to name. While many patients showed partial phonological retrieval, post-hoc categorization of subjects showed no relation between success and type of aphasia. Goodglass, Kaplan, Weintraub, and Ackerman (1976) applied this method to a series of 16 aphasic patients who had been preselected as typical instances of several aphasias—anomic, Wernicke's, conduction, or Broca's. The groups did not differ significantly in the number of pictures that they failed to name. Only conduction aphasics, with 33 percent correct, performed better than chance in identifying both initial sounds and syllabic count of the target word. Broca's aphasics performed better than chance for initial sounds but not for syllable count, while Wernicke's and anomic aphasics displayed no form of subvocal information about words that they did not name. Since conduction aphasics typically produce phonologically altered near misses in naming tasks, their demonstrations of partial phonological knowledge of failed words conforms to expectations. So does the poor performance of the Wernicke's and anomic aphasics, whose failures typically reflect no awareness of the sound structure of target words. The performance of the Broca's aphasics, however, does not conform to the anatomical model, which suggests that they should be impaired farthest downstream in the naming process and should, therefore, perform better than the conduction aphasics.

## Dissociations among Semantic Classes

Selective impairment and the selective sparing of naming or comprehending particular lexical categories occur regularly enough to deserve special mention. The relations between aphasic type and patterns of dissociation are so consistent as to point inescapably to anatomically based differences in the processing of particular symbolic categories for production rather than for auditory comprehension. The explanation for these differences is obscure; only for color aphasia has a reasonable hypothesis been proposed. The data available are in the form of case reports or retrospective tabulation of standard tests administered to patients of different types.

## Color-Name Aphasia

Geschwind and Fusillo (1966) described a patient who developed the syndrome of pure alexia, featuring impaired memory and the inability to read or to name colors or identify them on hearing their names. Speech and writing were not affected, nor was color perception. The disorder was caused by occlusion of the left-posterior cerebral artery, producing tissue damage to the left visual cortex, the splenium of the corpus callosum, and the left hippocampus. The authors argued that the loss of color names was owing to the disconnection between the source of visual color information in the right occipital lobe and the language area in the left hemisphere, that is, the same disconnection that accounts for loss of the ability to read. The preservation in these patients of the ability to name visual objects is attributed to the possibility that objects perceived in the right hemisphere arouse multimodal associations that can reach the left hemisphere through the intact, more anterior portions of the corpus callosum. Whether this explanation is valid or not, aphasia for color names is a regular (but not inevitable) feature of pure alexia and was present in 19 of a series of 27 such patients reported by Gloning, Gloning, and Hoff (1968).

## Dissociations of Letter and Number Naming

While privileged access to number words had been observed informally in certain patients, the first systematic comparison of the differential effects of contrasting types of aphasia on various semantic categories was reported by Goodglass, Klein, Carey, and Jones (1966), on the basis of a retrospective study of the performance of 135 aphasic subjects. They had been required to name on visual presentation, and to identify from auditory presentation, sets of numbers, letters, objects, actions, and colors. A fixed criterion was established to define a deviantly high or low score in any category, and Figure 13.14 shows the incidence of such deviant scores for each semantic class. Letters are the most frequently spared for naming; objects show the reverse of this pattern. Seventy-two of these subjects had been classified as either Broca's (37), Wernicke's (18), or anomic aphasics (17). A discriminant analysis, using all

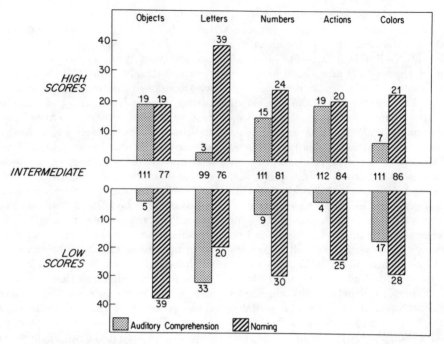

**Figure 13.14.** Dissociations between semantic word categories for naming and auditory comprehension. Bars represent numbers of subjects meeting criteria for deviantly high or low scores in each category.

naming and comprehension scores, correctly classified 75 percent of the subjects on the basis of the patterns of success and failure on the several semantic categories. Dissociations in naming were particularly striking in the patients with posterior speech-zone lesions (Wernicke's and anomic aphasics). These two groups made up the bulk of subjects with selective preservation of letter naming. Anomics, but not Wernicke's aphasics, were markedly better at naming numbers than all the other word categories.

It cannot be argued that differences between semantic categories are simply a function of word frequency or size of the set (e.g., 26 letters versus thousands of objects) because different, sometimes opposite, effects are obtained for comprehension and production of any given category. Patients who are severely impaired in comprehending letter or body-part names may be able to name the same items promptly upon request. These observations dictate the conclusion that, at least for certain word categories, the knowledge underlying production has a different anatomy from that serving comprehension.

## DISSOCIATIONS IN COMPREHENSION OF BODY PARTS AND GEOGRAPHIC PLACE NAMES

Body-part names and names of geographic features are similar in that their comprehension can be tested by having the patient point to the object—the patient's own body or a pictured mannequin for body parts, and an outline map for places. They differ, however, in word frequency and time of acquisition, since body-part names are high-frequency words learned in childhood, often in connection with pointing, and geographic place names are later acquisitions, less commonly used, and even more rarely used with actual reference to a map. Paradoxically, however, the auditory comprehension of body parts is the most fragile of semantic categories in aphasic patients, while that of place names is usually better preserved in the same individuals. Figure 13.15 summarizes the differences obtained from 121 consecutive aphasic patients in the authors' laboratory. These data indicate that anomic aphasics—generally patients with parietotemporal lesions—constitute the only patient group that follows the expected

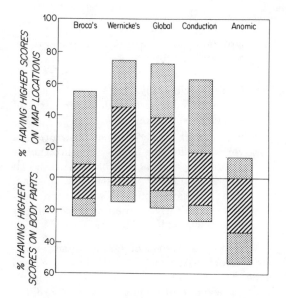

**Figure 13.15.** Comprehension of body parts versus comprehension of map locations. Dark portion of bar denotes proportion of subjects with 30 percent or greater difference between larger and smaller score.

pattern of a better response to body parts than to map locations. These data and those of Goodglass et al. (1966) both identify Wernicke's aphasics as showing the most marked selective impairment of body-part comprehension.

## LEVELS OF LEXICAL COMPREHENSION

It can easily be shown that brain injury does not ablate word knowledge in the sense that a concept either does or does not have a place in the lexicon. Partial knowledge of word meanings is usually demonstrable by the patient's success in selecting from multiple choices those items that are conceptually related to the target. The Boston Diagonstic Aphasia Examination (Goodglass & Kaplan, 1972) provides an opportunity for patients to point within either the correct semantic category or an unrelated one in response to the name of an object, color, letter, action, or number. In 10 successive patients whose records were examined, there were 120 correct identifications, 38 failures to respond, 99 within-category errors, and 95 out-of-category errors, where the chance of selecting an out-of-category error is twice that for a within-category error. Goodglass and Cohen (1954) found that 67 percent of errors made by aphasics in pointing to a body part named by the examiner were in the same area

(upper limb, lower limb, trunk, head) as the target.

Goodglass and Cohen's observations raise the possibility that these behaviors represent the operation of two parallel and autonomous neural systems. The first subserves one-to-one associations between word and referent. The second, which relates the word to a connotative or nonspecific association, appears to be more robust in the face of brain damage. As to the comprehension of body parts, a possible explanation is that the patient's gestural movement into the general area of the named target is mediated by motor pathways other than the contralateral pyramidal ones—pathways that receive input from the right hemisphere. The precise pointing response requires guidance by the contralateral pyramidal system acting on input provided by the language area of the left hemisphere. This explanation is consistent with the evidence for dissociation between the control of arm positions and distal hand movements described below in a case of callosal disconnection (Poncet et al., 1978).

## SELECTIVE SPARING OF AXIAL COMMANDS

The sparing of axial commands in patients with dense comprehension disorders is the most compelling evidence that performance may depend critically on access to a particular motor system. The clinical phenomenon pointed out by Geschwind (1965) is that severe Wernicke's or even global aphasics may promptly carry out, on verbal command, complex acts involving the body axis, for example, "Turn around twice, take a step backwards and bow," when they have failed by every other means to demonstrate comprehension of words or of limb commands. This is now recognized as a frequent and readily demonstrable clinical phenomenon, although it has not yet been studied experimentally. The one feature that these performances have in common is that bilateral, nonpyramidal motor pathways play a part in their innervation. It is not yet clear, however, where the auditory comprehension itself is mediated in these cases, since these patients may have massive destruction of the auditory language centers on the left. Geschwind (1975) suggests that the comprehension and innervation of axial movements may be a phylogenetically old capacity that is represented bilaterally and is therefore still available to an intact right hemisphere.

## Syntax

Unlike disorders in the selection, production, and comprehension of lexical elements, which were treated in the preceding section, syntactic disorders refer to the breakdown of the system of rules for organizing word strings into utterances recognized as grammatical by speakers of the language. These rules entail the use of word-order, inflections of nouns and verbs, and the appropriate use of a considerable set of grammatical words that carry little or no referential meaning in themselves, among them articles, auxiliary verbs, conjunctions, and prepositions.

Massive disintegration of syntax is seen in patients who have made partial recovery from global aphasia, to the point of being able to utter single words or short phrases. Since these individuals have usually suffered widespread destruction of the language zone of the left hemisphere, it is not clear to what extent their agrammatism can be separated from their minimal capacity to utter anything. At best it indicates that the recovery of expressive language in the right hemisphere begins with asyntactic words and phrases.

Agrammatism, as a selective disorder, requires that the patient have sufficient access to his lexicon to place at least two significant words in conjunction with each other, making it apparent that he lacks the rules for doing so grammatically. It is found in its clearest form in patients with lesions of the lower prerolandic zone (i.e., Broca's aphasics), who typically have good auditory comprehension, reduced and effortful speech output, but only fair-to-good recovery of naming ability. Agrammatism has been described in essentially the same terms by many behavioral neurologists since the nineteenth century, among them Kussmaul (1877) who introduced the term, Pitres (1898), Pick (1913), Goldstein (1913), Isserlin (1922), Bonhoeffer (1923), and Luria (1970). Pitres (1898), cited a case description published by Deleuze in 1817. The theoretical significance of agrammatism for cognitive neuropsychology is that its existence appears to suggest a common organic underpinning for a group of operations that have had only the linguistic definitions of being subsumed under morphology and syntax.

The features of agrammatism as summarized from the literature by Tissot, Mounin, and Lhermitte (1973) consist of the following universally accepted elements:

1. Dropping out of words that have purely grammatical functions (i.e., articles, conjunctions, prepositions, pronouns).
2. Disproportionately high frequency of nouns as compared with other parts of speech in verbal output.
3. Loss of verb inflection and substitution of verbs in infinitive form—a feature that is obvious in languages other than English where the infinitive is marked by a distinctive inflectional ending, whereas in English the infinitive cannot be distinguished from the uninflected verb stem.

Within the syndrome of agrammatism a number of efforts to distinguish subtypes have been made. Tissot et al. divided their agrammatics into a predominantly syntactically disordered subgroup and a predominantly morphologically disordered group. These two subtypes are best illustrated by a contrasting pair of Italian-speaking agrammatical aphasics studied by Miceli, Mazzucchi, Menn, and Goodglass (1983). Both patients used the infinitive rather than the appropriate inflected form for most of their verbs, and both omitted *have* and *be* as main verbs 50 percent of the time. The patients differed dramatically in that one (considered primarily syntactic) spoke in fragmented word groups, rarely completing the idea of a sentence, while the other, in spite of many more morphological omissions, maintained the general form of complex sentences, including subordinating constructions between clauses. Percentages of errors identified in obligatory contexts in free conversation were as follows:

| Omissions | Predominantly syntactic | Predominantly morphological |
|---|---|---|
| Prepositions | 10% | 26% |
| Main verb other than *have* or *be* | 18% | 2% |
| Object pronouns preceding verb | 15% | 100% |
| Auxiliary verb | 10% | 67% |

INTERPRETATIONS OF AGRAMMATISM

Two general directions are discernible in the interpretations of agrammatism. The first is to treat this symptom as specific to speech production. Pick (1913) suggested that the ability to evoke a sentence schema is defective, and that this defect in turn leads to an economy of effort —"an unconsciously active striving of the organism to function as easily and as parsimoniously as possible." He rejected the idea that the agrammatic patient has forgotten the grammatical morphemes, in favor of the view that all linguistic redundancy is eliminated from speech. Isserlin (1922) saw agrammatism as a form of economy of effort, in the sense that difficulties in word production lead patients to focus their effort on the major information-carrying (or lexical) elements, to the detriment of the nonrepresentational components of language (or grammatical morphemes). In a similar vein, Goldstein (1913) spoke of "the absence of all those words which are not completely indispensable to making oneself understood."

The alternative view is that agrammatism is a manifestation of a basic cognitive disorder in dealing with the relational aspects of language as contrasted with its lexical elements. This view was expressed by the linguist Jakobson (1956) who used the term *contiguity disorder* to describe a loss of those operations involved in placing linguistic elements in conjunction with each other. A contiguity disorder would abolish syntactic relations, along with the morphological elements that signaled these relations, and would reduce speech to "nouns and nominal forms of verbs." Similarly, Luria wrote (1970, p. 189): "The defect lies in the fact that the linguistic units innervated are not whole sentences but individual words. Its psychological nature goes even deeper. The word retains only its static nominative, designative function. The dynamic predicative function is completely destroyed." Luria's view, which implies manifestations of agrammatism in all language modalities, is endorsed by the approaches of Zurif, Caramazza, and Myerson (1972) and von Stockert (1972).

Clinical evidence can be marshaled to support both the speech-specific and the cognitive-linguistic interpretations of agrammatism. The speech-specific view is invoked when classical agrammatic features are observed in speech but not in oral reading, writing, or auditory syntac-

tic comprehension (Miceli, 1981; Miceli, Mazzucchi, Menn, & Goodglass, 1983). The economical view is not supported by these cases, since it would not explain the substitution of the longer infinitive verb forms (e.g., *cercare*—to look for) for the phonologically simpler forms (e.g., *cerco* —I am looking for) that are demanded by the contexts.

The cognitive-linguistic view is favored when agrammatism in speech is paralleled in repetition (e.g., Goodglass, Fodor, & Schulhoff, 1967), in oral reading (e.g., Andreewsky & Seron, 1975), and in writing (e.g., Goodglass & Hunter, 1970). Neither approach explains the double dissociations between the syntactic and morphological aspects of grammar that are documented in the case descriptions of Tissot et al. (1973) and of Miceli et al. (1983).

STUDIES OF THE HIERARCHY OF DIFFICULTY OF GRAMMATICAL OPERATIONS

A number of investigators, perceiving aphasia as fertile ground for testing linguistic theory, have focused on the order of difficulty of grammatical operations. A sentence-completion format was designed by Goodglass and Berko (1960) to determine the order of difficulty for aphasics of ten English morphological endings, and to compare this order with that previously observed by Berko (1958) in children between four and seven. They devised six items for each of the ten inflections, using the general form illustrated by the item:

My upstairs neighbor is a nurse and my downstairs neighbor is a nurse.

Both of my neighbors are _____ .

(This item is one of six for the /əz/ form of the plural.)

The orders of aphasics and children agreed only in that the simple, nonsyllabic form of the plural, as in *book*s (as opposed to *horse*s) was the easiest inflectional morpheme for both aphasics and children. While children aged four to seven had much greater difficulty with the syllabic than the nonsyllabic form of plural, possessive, present tense, and past tense, these phonological variants did not significantly affect performance of aphasics. Success with inflectional endings did not predict severity of aphasia, but the scores on the various inflectional endings were intercorrelated and correlated highly (.69) with

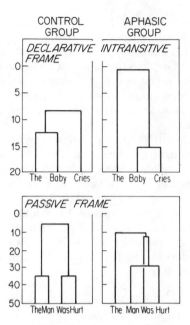

**Figure 13.16.** Word-relatedness within sentences based on hierarchical clustering procedure. Perceived strength of relationship between words is inversely related to height of cross bar. From "Grammatical Judgements of Agrammatic Aphasics" by E.B. Zurif, A. Caramazza, and R. Myerson, 1972, *Neuropsychologia*, *10*, pp. 411, 412. Copyright 1972 by Pergamon Press, Ltd. Reprinted by Permission.

subjects' articulatory agility. These correlations support the specificity of grammatical impairment as a disorder and its frequent association with the articulatory difficulty seen with anterior speech-zone lesions.

Another approach to comparing the order of children's acquisition of a specific set of grammatical morphemes with their disappearance in aphasia was taken by DeVilliers (1974), who tabulated the frequency of these morphemes in eight 5000-word samples of aphasic speech. Like Goodglass and Berko (1960), she found major discrepancies between developmental data on acquisition of the morphemes and their resistance in aphasia, confirming only that the plural is more robust in both aphasia and child language than the possessive.

STUDIES OF MULTIMODAL MANIFESTATIONS OF AGRAMMATISM

In spite of the conflicting clinical evidence concerning the modality-specific nature of agrammatism, the theoretical attractiveness of viewing

syntax as a central cognitive capacity has motivated a number of studies. Zurif et al. (1972) used a hierarchical-clustering design to test the appreciation of within-sentence word relations for lexical as opposed to grammatical words in a group of agrammatic Broca's aphasic patients and normal controls. A method of triadic comparisons was applied by displaying a short written sentence and, with it, cards bearing three of the words of the sentence. The patient's task was to choose the two words most closely related, in the context of the sentence. The hierarchy of word relations was displayed as in Figure 13.16, which shows that the agrammatics related both noun subjects to verbs and verbs to object nouns correctly but performed randomly with articles and auxiliary verbs. The absence of a control group of nonagrammatic patients of comparable severity, however, leaves in doubt the specificity of this finding to agrammatism (cf. Kurowski, 1981). This experiment and others by these authors (Caramazza & Zurif, 1976; Goodenough, Zurif, & Weintraub, 1977) provide convincing evidence, however, that the good comprehension of Broca's aphasics depends largely on their appreciation of the lexical items, on real world knowledge, and on word-order heuristics.

Another technique based on sentence reading —von Stockert's (1972) Sentence Order Test— was applied to an agrammatic patient who had demonstrated good comprehension of short written commands and a Wernicke's aphasic whose reading comprehension was virtually nil. They were given cut-up sentences written on three separate cards, following the form, "The girl / from Boston / is pretty," and were required to arrange the randomly ordered cards in correct sequence. The agrammatic patient, despite his ability to read, performed at chance level; the Wernicke's aphasic, despite his poor semantic comprehension, extracted sufficient syntactic information to succeed well above the chance level.

Another ingenious approach to syntactic competence in reading was applied to agrammatic aphasics by Bradley, Garrett, and Zurif (1980). Bradley and Garrett (1979) had previously used a lexical decision paradigm (latency for real word versus nonword decision for tachistoscopically presented letter strings) to show that recognition time for lexical words is linearly related to word frequency, whereas that for grammatical morphemes is flat, with respect to their frequency. This finding was interpreted as denoting a special access mechanism in the normal reader, enabling the rapid processing of the grammatical elements in a sentence. Unlike the performance of normal subjects, agrammatic patients showed the identical frequency-dependent relation for grammatical morphemes as for lexical words. A nonagrammatic (anomic) aphasic showed the normal pattern. The authors conclude that the agrammatic aphasic has lost the specialized access mechanism available to the normal reader for dealing with the grammatical features of a written sentence. While the experiment has yet to be carried out in the auditory modality, it illustrates the direction currently being explored to determine whether the linguistically defined rule systems of syntax and morphology have a common psychological basis, accounting for parallel deficits in all channels of language input and output.

## The Organic Foundations of Written Language

### Reading: Clinicopathological Clues to Cognitive Basis

The interdependence between the neural substrates of reading and of oral language is evident from the many references already made to particular aspects of reading deficits in the description of the aphasic syndromes and in the review of the linguistic levels of phonological, lexical, and syntactic processing. In general, some degree of impaired reading comprehension (dyslexia) is found with all forms of aphasia, and these disorders vary, not only in severity, but in the relative impairment of various aspects of the reading process, specifically in (1) appreciation of the semantic versus the grammatical content of the message; (2) the degree of preservation of letter-to-sound (or graphophonemic conversion) rules; (3) the degree of preservation of wholeword recognition skills; and (4) the degree of impaired visual recognition of letters and words as familiar units. The symptomatology of oral reading is affected not only by all the foregoing variables but by the tendency of some patients to make semantic substitutions (paralexias).

The characteristics of oral-reading deficits accompanying the major aphasic syndromes are less predictable than the features of oral language, and the regularities that have been noted

generally rest on the evidence of clinical description. The most challenging dissociations observed in reading follow.

### SELECTIVE PRESERVATION OF LEXICAL VERSUS GRAMMATICAL WORDS

This feature is most conspicuous in oral reading, where contentives may be read well, while grammatical words are either omitted or misread by substitution of another, quite unrelated word (e.g., *was* in place of *by*). Patients are often aware of their difficulty in reading the little words and comment that they see them as an undifferentiated class. Gardner and Zurif (1975) documented the patient's success in reading aloud a number of short content words that were homonyms of grammatical words on which the patient had just failed. Thus certain paitents could read aloud *bee* but not *be*; *oar* but not *or*; *buy* but not *by*, and so on. Andreewsky and Seron (1975) described a case (in French) in which the identical letter string *car* was correctly read aloud in its function as subject noun (meaning *bus*) but deleted later in the sentence in its function as a conjunction (meaning *because*). This selective difficulty in associating a sound to a nonreferential grammatical word is reminiscent of the problem of agrammatism. It is also related to a corresponding difficulty in inferring the syntactic relations denoted by these grammatical terms, even in silent reading comprehension, and has been shown to be particularly characteristic of patients with anterior speechzone lesions (Samuels & Benson, 1979). The nature of the selective reading deficit for grammatical morphemes will come up for discussion again in the context of deep dyslexia, below.

### PURE ALEXIA

The profound impairment of reading associated with interruption of all visual input to the language zone of the left hemisphere has already been described (p. 863). Patients with this disorder no longer recognize familiar letter strings as words through the visual channel, although they typically perform flawlessly in reporting words spelled out either orally or by having the letters traced tactually on their palm. Some patients with pure alexia can recognize letters and thus succeed in reading in a painstaking letter-by-letter fashion. Even when letter recognition is affected, number recognition is often preserved.

## DISSOCIATION OF SEMANTIC AND PHONOLOGICAL CHANNELS OF READING

Traditional views of the reading process for alphabetic languages have taken for granted that even in silent reading there is a subvocal conversion of letters or letter combinations to their corresponding sounds and that this process of inner phonological mediation is necessary for reading comprehension (cf. Bloomfield, 1942). Obviously phonological recoding by grapheme-phoneme correspondence rules is called on for the reading of nonsense words and of unfamiliar words such as uncommon proper names. Just as obviously, these rules are useless for reading such forms as *lb.*, *Mr.*, and other abbreviations. The status of irregularly spelled words (cough, though, weigh, etc.) also raises a question about the role of a grapheme–phoneme correspondence rule. The recent literature on reading by normals includes experimentally based arguments purporting to demonstrate that phonological recoding is an essential step (Rubenstein, Lewis, & Rubinstein, 1971; Gough, 1972); that fluent silent reading is purely a visual word-to-meaning process (Smith, 1971); and that both channels are used in parallel (Meyer, Schvaneveldt, & Ruddy, 1974). Coltheart (1980b) summarizes a body of experimental data that indicates that phonological recoding contributes minimally to fluent silent reading in normal English readers.

Two diametrically opposed varieties of reading disturbance have been described in aphasic patients that highlight the dual capacity of the normal reader; in patients with deep dyslexia, phonological mediation is lost, while semantic access is largely preserved; in the other form, semantic access is destroyed, but fluent oral reading through phonological recoding is maintained, though without comprehension.

## DEEP DYSLEXIA

Marshall and Newcombe (1966) described an oral reading disorder in an aphasic patient, which was characterized by a large number of semantic misreadings of lexical words (*play* for *act*; *food* for *dinner*; *long* for *tall*). There were also many misreadings in which the root of the target word was preserved but the derivational form changed (*wisdom* for *wise*; *stranger* for *strange*), as well as errors based on partial structural similarity (*sausage* for *saucer*; *crocodile* for *crocus*). Grammatical morphemes were usually totally rejected as unreadable ("Small words are the worst") but occasionally guessed at with a totally irrelevant grammatical word (*and* for *for*; *those* for *in*). Recognition or oral reading of pronounceable nonsense words was impossible. Additional cases of this type have been identified and studied by Shallice and Warrington (1975), Marin, Saffran, and Schwartz (1975), Schwartz, Saffran, and Marin (1977), Patterson and Marcel (1977). Probing for the conditions for success and failure has included presenting word lists of all parts of speech; comparing verbs in -ing that function as nouns (or gerunds), for example, *Fighting can be dangerous* with the identical word functioning as a verb in the progressive form, for example, *He is fighting for his life*; comparing identical words used as both common and proper nouns, for example, *robin* versus *my brother Robin*. These studies reviewed by Coltheart (1980a) reveal that nouns, particularly easily pictured nouns, are the most robust, that identical *-ing* verb forms are read better as gerunds than as verbs, and that contextual cues preserve the reading of words that are misread out of context.

Further dramatic evidence of reading without phonology is provided by studies of Japanese readers. The basis for the special status of the Japanese reading system is that it combines a phonological writing code of 69 characters (termed *Kana* characters) that denote all the possible consonant-vowel syllables of Japanese with an idiographic system of characters representing whole words (termed *Kanji* characters). While any word can be written and read correctly in Kana, normal Japanese text uses Kanji for all lexical terms in the language, reserving Kana for grammatical morphemes and for words borrowed from other languages.

Sasanuma (1980) describes four cases of deep dyslexia in Japanese speakers, including two of her own. These patients are severely impaired in their ability to read any real or nonsense words written in the Kana (phonetic syllabary), while their reading of Kanji idiographs includes many semantic misreadings unrelated to the visual configuration of the stimulus (e.g., *editorial* for *propaganda*; *enemy* for *evil*).

## ANATOMIC AND ORAL LANGUAGE CORRELATES OF DEEP DYSLEXIA

In spite of the marked deficit in the reading of grammatical morphemes that all these patients showed, only 12 of the 22 cases reviewed by

Coltheart (1980a) had a corresponding agrammatism in speech, the remaining 10 having preserved syntax and morphology. In a review of the anatomical lesions of five cases, Marin (1980) reports that all involved both prerolandic and suprasylvian speech areas with posterior extension to the angular gyrus. A sixth reported case (Shallice & Warrington, 1980) had extensive inferior parietal and temporo-occipital damage. Only the temporal lobe appears to be spared in these cases, and all have extensive subcortical damage. Marin (1980) comments that the extent of the lesions is striking, in view of the amount of residual language available to these patients.

## INTERPRETATIONS OF DEEP DYSLEXIA

All observers agree that the primary deficit in deep dyslexia is the inability to use the graphophonemic conversion rules of written language to arrive at the sound of a word. This defect applies equally to the consonant-vowel syllabary of Japanese and to the letter-by-letter code of alphabetic languages. The deep dyslexic patient's reading depends on direct extraction of meaning from the written word form. However, the success of this association depends on the semantic character of the stimulus, which is greatest for picturable nouns, less reliable for adjectives and verbs, and nil for grammatical morphemes. The nature of the semantic misreadings raises the question of whether the written stimulus elicits a poorly specified semantic field, or the errors occur at the level of word retrieval. The relatively good picture naming of deep dyslexics (Newcombe & Marshall, 1980) indicates that the semantic imprecision arises at the stage of interpreting the written word. Coltheart (1980b), and Saffran, Bogyo, Schwartz, and Marin (1980) marshall experimental and clinical evidence for the view that the reading performance of the deep dyslexic is mediated by the right hemisphere. Coltheart specifically rejects the notion that the direct graphic-to-semantic access of the deep dyslexic is what remains of normal reading when phonological decoding is destroyed. The direct visual reading of the normal reader is semantically precise and encompasses all linguistic features, lexical and morphological.

## PHONOLOGY WITHOUT SEMANTICS

In contrast with the deep dyslexics, some patients with transcortical sensory aphasia proved able to read English text orally without comprehension and perform well with pronounceable nonsense words. Sasanuma (1980) describes the Japanese counterpart of this disorder, which is called *Golgi aphasia* (word-meaning aphasia). Her patient could name only a few Kanji characters, but could read aloud connected text in the Kana (syllabary) script fluently though totally without comprehension.

### *Writing, Clinical Features*

Writing is more severely impaired than speech in most forms of aphasia and is rarely exempt from damage in any case of aphasia. The dimensions of writing impairments are roughly parallel to those of oral language, as indicated in the following table:

| Writing | Speech |
|---|---|
| Impaired recall of graphomotor movements for letter shapes | Impaired articulation at phonetic level |
| Impaired spelling | Impaired articulation at phonemic level |
| Impaired recall of written words as lexical units | Impaired word finding (anomia) |
| Fragmented syntax with omission of grammatical connectives | Agrammatism |
| Substitution of unintended words (paragraphia) | Semantic paraphasia |
| Logically disorganized sentence structure | Paragrammatism |

As is true for reading, the correspondence between lesion site and the configuration of defects is less consistent for writing than for oral language. However, there is a moderate correspondence between the form of the speech disorder and the form of the writing difficulties —particularly difficulties in word finding, syntax, and paragrammatism. These correspondences are reported in the clinical literature (e.g., Marcie & Hécaen, 1979) and are illustrated in a detailed comparison of speech and writing by Goodglass and Hunter (1970). Damage to the angular gyrus is associated with severe impairments of both reading and writing, but has little effect on oral language (Déjerine, 1891; Nielsen & Raney, 1938; Hécaen & Kremin, 1977). Some writers, therefore, consider the angular gyrus as the junction mediating associations between the auditory and visual aspects of language.

Isolated disturbance of writing from a focal lesion has been reported in rare instances, with little consensus on the precise lesion site. However, gross deterioration of elementary writing skills without impairment of oral language is seen in confusional states associated with metabolic disorders and not attributable to a known focal lesion (Chedru & Geschwind, 1972).

Writing has traditionally been regarded as dependent on speech in the sense that it is merely a transcription of oral language via a set of phonographemic conversion rules. The clinical evidence reviewed above contains both confirmatory and contradictory evidence for such dependency, but little formal experimental work has been done on the organic basis of writing.

Friederici et al. (1981) investigated the possibility that written word retrieval might bypass phonographemic recoding in some patients. Patients were required to name a set of pictures both orally and in writing, and an analysis of writing errors was carried out. Those who named better by writing than by talking made errors that were determined either by visual similarity (e.g., *affle* for *apple*) or by semantic substitutions (e.g., *page* for *book*). Those whose oral naming was superior to their written naming made spelling errors largely determined by misapplied phonographemic rules (e.g., *chare* for *chair*). These results were taken as supporting the view that there are two modes of access to written vocabulary: one originating with the phonological representation of the target and achieving written expression through phonographemic rules, and the other, a direct association from a semantic representation to a visually based image of the written word. As with deep dyslexia, brain damage may disable the phonologically mediated pathway, allowing some performance through the direct semantic route.

# CEREBRAL LATERALIZATION OF FUNCTION

## Clinical Basis

Broca (1865) was the first to report that loss of language results almost exclusively from left cerebral injury to previously normal adult speakers, and that the occasional exceptions to this association are usually left-handed. The doctrine that the hemisphere that is dominant for mediating language is contralateral to the preferred hand was taken for granted in the neurological literature until the mid-twentieth century. While exceptions were noted, they were rationalized on a case-by-case basis. However, Goodglass and Quadfasel (1954) surveyed 123 reported cases of left-handers who suffered injuries in the perisylvian zone of either cerebral hemisphere and found that fully 53 percent deviated from the supposed rule. Forty-three percent became aphasic from lesions of the left hemisphere, whereas 10 percent continued to speak normally after lesions of the right hemisphere. Many series of unselected cases, however, have supported the observation that, for right-handers, language deficit is tightly associated with damage to the left hemisphere, but for left-handers the side of injury seems to be indeterminate (Bingley, 1958; Penfield & Roberts, 1959; Gloning, Gloning, Haub, & Quatember, 1969; Luria, 1970).

While disorders of language use provided the first and clearest evidence of lateralization in the functional asymmetry of the cerebral hemispheres, the intervening years have disclosed further evidence of the lateralization of both perceptual and motor functions other than language—some dominated by the left, others by the right hemisphere in most people. For example, the major role of the left hemisphere in the planning and control of purposeful movements was first noted by Liepmann (1900); more recent are observations of its predominant role in the appreciation of arithmetical relations (Henschen, 1920–1922; Berger, 1926) and right–left awareness (Head, 1926; Gerstmann, 1930). The specialized capacities of the right hemisphere have also gained notice. Impaired perception of spatial configurations (Paterson & Zangwill, 1944), impaired bilateral distribution of attention resulting in neglect of the left perceptual space

(Brain, 1941), and dulling of emotional perceptiveness (Heilman, Scholes, & Watson, 1975) are now considered dependable clinical indicators of right-cerebral injury.

The systematic investigation of the many ramifications of brain laterality dates back less than twenty years. It has entailed the development of noninvasive techniques through which lateral asymmetry of function could be studied in the intact brain in large normal samples as well as the introduction of controlled studies of unilaterally brain-injured populations. Attention has been focused on the biological features of brain laterality, its heritability, its developmental course from birth to old age, and the appearance of sex differences. The major goals of experimental studies have been to define more precisely the operations for which the hemispheres have differing predilections, particularly to see whether they can be reduced to a basic dichotomy in modes of information processing, and to explore the interaction between the hemispheres in complex tasks. In the course of these investigations, the development of new experimental techniques has raised subsidiary questions as to why they work and how they can be improved.

Before reviewing the research data on the substantive theoretical issues, it appears most useful to outline the experimental techniques that will have to be cited.

## Methodology in the Investigation of Brain Laterality

### Clinical Methods

The comparison of right and left unilaterally brain-injured groups in controlled experimental tasks needs no special explanation. Pre- and postoperative comparisons of the same individuals have been possible when ablations of left or right temporal-lobe tissue are performed as treatment for epilepsy (Lansdell, 1962; Milner, 1962a; Shankweiler, 1966). These are instances in which the preoperative performance may be considered to approximate normal function, though with the reservation that the preexisting brain abnormality responsible for the epilepsy precludes the strict presumption of normality.

The Wada Test (Wada & Rasmussen, 1960) was introduced as a means of probing to determine language dominance in candidates for brain surgery who were at risk for inadvertent

injury to the language zones during operation. It consists in the injection of a measured dose of sodium amytal into the common carotid artery into one side of the neck at a time, a procedure that temporarily suppresses the activity in the corresponding side of the brain, during the period in which the drug spreads through the area of the brain irrigated by that artery and before it diffuses into the general circulation. Milner (1975) reported that injection of the left common carotid suppressed speech transiently in 87 percent of right-handers (N = 95) and 69 percent of left-handers (N = 74); 13 percent of the left-handers suffered speech suppression from injection on each side and 18 percent from injection in the right carotid only.

These percentages are in fairly close agreement with the experience for unilateral vascular lesions in right-handers, but indicate a smaller incidence of right-hemisphere-dependent language in the left-handed population.

A unique clinical population for study consists of patients whose two cerebral hemispheres have been partially or totally separated either by natural lesion of the corpus callosum (Liepmann & Maas, 1907; Geschwind & Kaplan, 1962; Poncet et al., 1978) or by surgical section (Gazzaniga et al., 1962) for the treatment of intractable epilepsy. In these patients either hemisphere can be challenged in isolation by means of tactile or visual presentation to the contralateral receptive field or by requiring fine motor output via the contralateral limb. While many of these patients (all the surgical cases) had preexisting brain abnormalities, studies of them here, for the most part, agreed with and added to the understanding gained from other clinical populations and from normal subjects.

### Noninvasive Experimental Methods

#### DICHOTIC LISTENING

The technique of presenting competing strings of digits to the right and left ears was used by Broadbent (1956) to study the processing of information received through parallel channels. Kimura (1961a) first demonstrated that when different lists of words (digit strings) were presented to both ears simultaneously, a greater proportion were correctly reported by the right ear than by the left ear. The relation of this effect to cerebral dominance for language was indicated by the total correspondence between right-ear advantage and left-sided aphasic response on the Wada Test and vice versa (Kimura, 1961b). Further evidence linking dichotic listening with cerebral dominance appeared in Kimura's (1964) findings of left-ear advantage for the recognition of dichotically presented melodies—a result in accord with other experimental evidence that tonal patterns are preferentially mediated in the right hemisphere (Milner, 1962a).

Requiring an oral report has been varied with (1) the technique of matching target stimuli presented dichotically to a series of binaurally presented multiple-choice stimuli (Kimura, 1964), (2) requiring a yes–no decision as to whether either of a pair of dichotic stimuli matches a single binaural stimulus that follows (Spellacy & Blumstein, 1970); and (3) requiring detection of a target, embedded in a dichotic series. All these techniques have figured among the hundreds of studies making up the dichotic listening literature.

The physiological mechanisms proposed by Kimura (1961b) for the dichotic listening effect is based on the hypothesis that, while the input to each auditory nerve reaches both auditory cortices, the signal to the contralateral hemisphere is more effective (Rosenzweig, 1951; Tunturi, 1946) and interferes with the competing signal from the ipsilateral ear. By this mechanism, the language-dominant left hemisphere would receive a stronger signal from the right ear than from the left, thus producing an advantage (typically 5 to 10 percent) to verbal stimuli presented to the right ear.

This model has been countered by one proposed by Sparks and Geschwind (1968) and Sparks, Goodglass, and Nickel (1970) on the basis of the observation (see also Milner, Taylor, & Sperry, 1968) that patients who have undergone transection of the corpus callosum show almost complete suppression of the signal to the left ear, a finding that Kimura's model does not account for. The Sparks–Geschwind model begins with the assumption that under competing binaural conditions the signal from the contralateral ear to each side of the brain suppresses the one from the ipsilateral ear. The signal from the right ear, then, arrives relatively undiminished in the language zone of the left hemisphere, while that from the left ear is first processed in the right auditory association cortex and relayed to the language area of the left hemisphere via

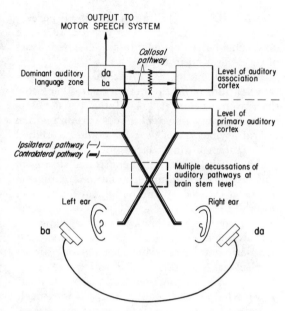

**Figure 13.17.** Model for dichotic listening effect with competing verbal inputs. Lesion at "X" would interrupt major pathway by which left ear input reaches language zone in left hemisphere.

the corpus callosum (Figure 13.17). It is this extra step of transmission that presumably attenuates the left-ear signal in comparison with the right.

While the dichotic listening paradigm has been widely used with replicable results in many subject groups, it is influenced by factors other than cerebral dominance. The proportion of right-handed persons with a right-ear advantage for verbal stimuli averages only about 80 percent across a group of representative studies (Blumstein, Goodglass, & Tartter, 1975). When the same subjects are retested, as many as 30 percent may show an ear advantage on the opposite side on retest, although the net percentage of individuals with right-ear advantage remains about the same (Blumstein et al., 1975; Pizzamiglio, DePascalis, & Vignati, 1974; Teng, 1981). Goldstein and Lackner (1974) showed that prismatic spectacles that shift the visual midline may have the effect of reversing the side of ear advantage. Thus applications of dichotic listening to the measurement of small differences in degree of lateralization of various types of auditory stimuli are suspect. Berlin (1977) reviews the many methodological variables that modify the magnitude of dichotic listening effects.

## VISUAL HALF-FIELD STIMULATION

The case for privileged access from each visual half-field to the contralateral visual cortex is more clear-cut than the corresponding claims (reviewed above) for audition. The decussation of the optic nerves at the chiasm is such that the left visual field, as perceived by each eye, is conveyed to the visual cortex of the right hemisphere and the right visual field to the left visual cortex. While visual information is shared promptly between the two visual association cortices, this sharing entails an extra synaptic step of information transmission via the splenium (posterior end) of the corpus callosum. The informational degradation produced by this transmission is presumed to confer an advantage in each cerebral hemisphere to the input that it receives directly from the contralateral visual field. As applied to the study of cerebral dominance, the visual half-field technique involves tachistoscopic presentations of a particular class of stimuli to each visual field, either to one field at a time or in simultaneous competition. The field that leads to greater perceptual efficiency (measured by correctness of identification, latency for decision, or exposure duration thresholds) is presumed to correspond to the hemisphere that is dominant for the class of material presented. Various techniques have been adopted for assuring fixation on a central point. They include simple randomization of left and right field stimuli, closed-circuit video monitoring of the gaze, and the inclusion of a digit at the central point that must be reported before the response to the lateral stimulus.

Mishkin and Forgays (1952) first used the visual half-field technique to show that words were more accurately read in the right than in the left visual field. They rejected the cerebral dominance interpretation on the grounds of evidence that the right-to-left direction of reading scan gave an advantage to the words that could be read in a direct scan from the fixation point over those whose beginning was remote from the fixation point. While the direction of scan was confirmed as an important factor in subsequent studies (Orbach, 1952; Harcum & Jones, 1962), the validity of the technique as an indicator of cerebral dominance was supported by the persistent advantage of the right visual field for words printed vertically (Goodglass & Barton, 1963) and even for Hebrew words presented vertically to native Hebrew readers, whose primary reading

habits are from right to left (Barton, Goodglass, & Shai, 1965). Further justification for using this technique as a probe for functional asymmetry in the brain was provided by findings of left visual-field (right hemisphere) advantage in visual perceptual tasks with nonverbalizable stimuli (Kimura, 1969; Benton, Hannay, & Varney, 1975) corresponding to evidence from unilateral brain pathology on visuospatial functions.

## ASYMMETRIES IN ORIENTATION

Kinsbourne (1973) challenged the foregoing accounts of the mechanism for both the dichotic listening and visual half-field effects. He rejected in particular the argument that they depend on superior informational access by each cerebral hemisphere to the contralateral receptive field rather than to the ipsilateral field. In place of this connectionist view, Kinsbourne proposed that the nature of the stimulus material (e.g., verbal versus visuospatial) activates an attentional mechanism in one hemisphere or the other that biases attention to the contralateral perceptual field.

One direct effect of such an attentional bias, according to Kinsbourne (1972), should be to mobilize the orienting response of the frontal eye fields so as to direct conjugate eye movements to the field opposite the hemisphere that is dominant for the material to be processed—for example, towards the right for verbal material. Kinsbourne (1972), Kocel, Galin, Ornstein, and Merin (1972), and Gur, Gur, and Harris (1975) carried out fairly similar experiments in which a hidden television camera recorded turning of the head and eye of normal subjects in response to questions requiring either verbal reasoning or spatial visualization. The former elicited right turning movements; the latter, leftward or upward turning of the gaze. The eye-gaze technique has served to support the notion of differential hemispheric activation as an attention-biasing mechanism, through the use of cognitive activities whose gross functional lateralization had already been established by other means. In addition to its intrinsic methodological limitations, however, it is confounded with habitual tendencies toward directional eye gaze that have been related to personality variables (Bakan, 1969; Gur & Gur, 1977). Eye gaze has therefore had limited value for probing the stimulus and organismic parameters that affect the laterality of cognitive operations.

ELECTROPHYSIOLOGICAL METHODS

The rhythmic electrical activity of the brain, recorded through electrodes as an electroencephalogram (EEG), provides several measures, all of which have been explored in an effort to find correlates of differential hemispheric activation in association with lateralized cognitive functions. One group of meaures, referred to as event-related potentials (ERPs) represent short-term electrical changes, time-locked to a stimulus or a response. Evoked cortical responses represent the electrical activity set off by a stimulus presentation and any immediately following decision process. They take the form of a train of alternating positive- and negative-going variations in potential, lasting about 500 msec. The ERPs, because of their small amplitude in comparison with ongoing electroencephalographic activity, are detected through computerized averaging of many repetitions of the same stimulus-response sequence, which has the effect of canceling out the background EEG activity and summing the repeated electrical responses that are time locked to the stimulus.

Studies of evoked responses have produced conflicting results. Buchsbaum and Fedio (1969, 1970) reported differences in the left-hemisphere waveforms for verbal and nonverbal stimuli presented visually. On the other hand, several authors failed to detect any hemispheric asymmetries in evoked cortical responses to visually presented words (Shelburne, 1972, 1973; Friedman, Simson, Ritter, & Rapin, 1975). Both language and nonlanguage stimuli have given more consistently positive results with auditory than with visual presentation. Morrell and Salamy (1971), on presenting nonsense words, observed greater amplitude in the negative wave at 100 msec poststimulus over the left language zone than the right. Wood, Goff, and Day (1971) required subjects to respond to either the linguistic or the tonal features of the same stimulus and found an increase in the amplitude of the left-hemisphere evoked response only during the linguistic response set. Neville (1974) found both latency and amplitude asymmetries between evoked responses to verbal stimuli but not to clicks, presented dichotically.

Another class of measurements derived from the EEG is based on the well-known observation (Adrian & Matthews, 1934) that the distribution of power in the frequency components of the EEG changes with mental effort. In particular,

the 8- to 12-Hz (alpha) frequency disappears during mental activity. Galin and Ornstein (1972) reported higher right-to-left EEG power ratios, indicating greater left-hemisphere activity during a verbal (letter-writing) task than during a spatial (block-design) task. Similar results have been obtained by Dumas and Morgan (1975), Butler and Glass (1974), and Doyle, Ornstein, and Galin (1974). Gardiner and Walter (1977) reported opposite hemispheric EEG power distributions during passive exposure to speech versus music in six-month-old infants. The relevance of the infant study to the aforementioned results is subject to the qualification that the discriminating frequency band in the Gardiner–Walter report centers about 4 Hz, because the 8- to 12-Hz alpha rhythm is not yet present in infants.

While some of the EEG-based approaches to the study of brain laterality still want confirmation of their sensitivity to gross differences in functional hemispheric asymmetry, power spectrum analysis has been found to be a useful tool. The EEG techniques have proved particularly valuable in the investigation of brain laterality in infants (Molfese, Freeman, & Palermo, 1975; Gardiner & Walter, 1977), since the EEG appears to be sensitive to passive exposure to stimulus.

## What is Lateralized?

From the time of the discovery of cerebral functional asymmetry for language and the subsequent discoveries of asymmetries for the control of purposeful movement, visuoperceptual and spatial skills, and aspects of nonverbal auditory perception, it was assumed that these hemispheric differences were based on specific capacities in the two hemispheres that predisposed each for dealing more effectively with particular types of material. This original assumption may be termed a *material-specific* theory of cerebral dominance. More recently, however, observations of split-brain patients by Levy-Agresti and Sperry (1968) and Nebes (1971) have led to the view that the operations controlled by the left hemisphere were those that required sequential processing of codable elements, referred to as analytic processing, whereas those controlled by the right hemisphere were holistic or configurational in nature. Other reductionist explanations have characterized the left hemisphere as a temporal sequential analyzer, and the right as a parallel processor. These attempts to reduce the basis for cerebral laterality to two opposing modes of information processing may be considered a hemisphere-strategy theory of cerebral dominance. The hemisphere-strategy concept has been studied extensively in normal subjects, particularly for visual perception and visuospatial tasks. The following review, organized by type of material, will consider the data supporting the material-specific and the hemisphere-strategy theories of cerebral dominance.

## Lateralization of Visual Perceptual and Spatial Processes, Clinical Evidence

Beginning in the 1880s a number of well-recognized selective disorders in nonverbal visually based functions have been identified in patients with lesions of the posterior cerebral cortex. Visual agnosia, first described by Lissauer (1889), denotes an inability to recognize objects visually, in spite of adequate visual sensory function and despite preservation of the ability to both recognize and name them through tactile or auditory input. A loss of visual recognition specific to familiar faces, termed *prosopagnosia* by Bodamer (1947), has been documented by many cases with autopsy findings (Benton, 1980). Spatial disorientation was first reported by Badal (1888) in a patient who could read and recognize objects but could not find her way in familiar surroundings. Impairment in the visually guided motor execution of spatial tasks (e.g., drawing, copying pictures and designs) was first noted as a specific deficit, referred to as *constructional apraxia* by Kleist (1923). Left hemispatial inattention following right-posterior brain damage was first described by Riddoch (1935) and Brain (1941). With the exception of left spatial inattention, initial clinical observations of the foregoing visual and visuospatial disorders did not suggest clear differences in the effects of right versus left cerebral damage (Benton, 1980). In constructional apraxia, for example, Kleist originally implicated the posterior left hemisphere. Paterson and Zangwill (1944), however, found that the most severe visuospatial disorders are associated with right-hemisphere pathology. Our concepts of lateral functional asymmetry in this group of operations have been refined only recently, and date to the introduction of the systematic study of patients with unilateral lesions, supplemented by visual half-field studies of normals.

## Experimental Studies of Laterality in Visual Perception

### LATERALITY IN VISUAL DISCRIMINATION AND PERCEPTION OF OBJECTS

Studies of functional brain asymmetry in the perception of elementary visual attributes of size, brightness, and curvature carried out on groups of unilaterally brain-damaged patients show only suggestive lateral effects at this level (Taylor & Warrington, 1973; Bisiach, Nichelli, & Spinnler, 1976; Kimura, 1973). As we progress up the scale of visual processing to the recognition and discrimination of complex configurations, the special role of the right hemisphere becomes more evident. However, in the task of assigning a specific identity to the percept, the left hemisphere is found to be dominant. This pattern appears consistently across studies of unilaterally brain-damaged groups and tachistoscopic studies of normal subjects.

Meier and French (1965) found that patients who had undergone right temporal-lobe resection for epilepsy were impaired in a visual pattern-discrimination task in comparison with left-resection patients. Using Mooney's test of faces (1957) for visual closure, Newcombe and Russell (1969) found that patients with focal lesions in the left hemisphere (N = 44) performed more successfully than those with right-hemisphere injuries (N = 37). The most impaired patients within the right brain-damaged group were those with temporal-lobe lesions. In contrast, patients with right parietal-lobe lesions were most impaired in a maze-learning task. That is, visual closure and visuospatial processes were independent and vulnerable to different sites in the right posterior quadrant.

Memory, as well as perception of form, is selectively vulnerable to damage in the right temporal lobe. Verbal codability, however, is a critical factor in determining whether left- or right-hemisphere processing dominates performance. Kimura (1963a) devised a recurring-figures test that consisted of a series of unverbalizable nonsense scrawls, some of which were repeated in the series as they were exposed one at a time. Patients who had undergone partial right temporal lobectomy for epilepsy were markedly deficient in this task, compared with those who had lost part of the left temporal lobe. Buffery (1974) obtained similar results in patients of the same types.

Tachistoscopic hemifield studies of normal subjects produce corresponding effects. Rizzolatti, Umilta, and Berlucchi (1971) required their subjects to memorize either two faces or two letters as positive or target items and to respond manually when a positive item, occurring randomly among buffer items of the same class, appeared in either the right or left visual field. Faces were reacted to more rapidly in the left visual field (implying more efficient right hemisphere processing) and letters more rapidly in the right visual field. Geffen, Bradshaw, and Wallace (1971) carried out a series of experiments on normal subjects in which the right-hemisphere biasing of perceptual matching was pitted against the left-hemisphere biasing of verbal identification. Like Rizzolatti et al., they first examined response latencies for the recognition of a particular target face among four other test faces, presented tachistoscopically to one or the other hemifield. They, too, observed a left-field (right hemisphere) advantage. This between-field difference disappeared when a vocal, rather than a manual, reaction time was measured. Similarly, no right–left difference was observed when the constant vocal response *bonk* was made in response to the appearance of any one of four possible digits in either field. However, reaction times were faster for the right visual field (left hemisphere) for both naming responses to digits presented unilaterally and manual responses to a designated digit.

The Geffen et al. study illustrates the principle that the nature of the physical stimulus alone does not determine which hemisphere will process it more efficiently, so much as does the operation to be performed on that stimulus. Thus, when identification by name is required, the advantage lies with the left hemisphere; when a perceptual match is required, the right hemisphere appears more efficient.

The opportunity to stimulate each hemisphere independently, afforded by the sectioning of the corpus callosum, has provided a number of dramatic confirmations of hemisphere differences as a function of the type of processing required, when stimulus materials are constant. The technique used was to present in a tachistoscope composite pictures, termed *chimeric stimuli*, consisting of the left side of one picture joined at the midline to the right side of another. It had previously been shown by C. Trevarthen and M. Kinsbourne (cited as a personal communication

by Levy, 1974) that the half of a visual stimulus presented to one half-field of a split-brain patients was perceived as a whole object, through a process of perceptual completion carried out by each hemisphere. The behavior of the split-brain patients with chimeric figures indicated that each hemisphere thought it had perceived the whole of the half-picture that fell in its side of the visual field in tachistoscopic presentation (see Figure 13.18 for examples of chimeric stimuli).

Levy, Trevarthen, and Sperry (1972) tested four such patients with a set of three male faces, for each of which the patients had first learned a name—Bob, Paul, Dick. The faces were then combined into the six possible chimeric stimuli and presented tachistoscopically under two conditions. The first condition required the subject to point on a multiple-choice display to the full face he thought he had seen. The second required the subject to name the faces he had seen. Regardless of the hand used, the subjects all pointed overwhelmingly to the face that had been seen by the right hemisphere (left visual field). Only 2.3 percent of responses identified both faces. In contrast, when required to name the face they had seen, 49 percent of responses named the left-hemisphere stimulus, 36 percent the right-hemisphere stimulus, and the remaining 15 percent were errors. An analogous procedure using familiar objects (rose, eye, and bee) gave even more one-sided results: visual match via a pointing response resulted in only 5 percent of identifications of the right-field (left hemisphere) stimulus, whereas naming elicited 63 percent right-field responses, 36 percent left-field responses, and only 1 percent errors. These results indicate that each hemisphere tends to preempt the execution of a task in the processing mode for which it is predisposed: verbal for the left and visual-perceptual for the right.

In a further experiment with one of these subjects, Levy (1974) demonstrated that the left hemisphere's valence cannot be categorized simply as verbal. Pictures of a hat, open shears, and spectacles were assembled into chimeric stimuli, and a corresponding set of multiple-choice response items (hat, spools of thread, crossed knife and fork) were drawn so that, while each of the response items was conceptually related to one of the three stimulus items, its external visual configuration was virtually identical with a different one of the stimuli. When the patient was asked to choose from a

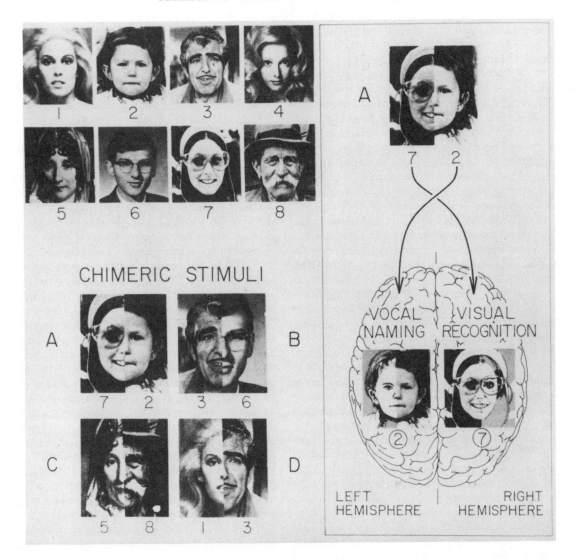

**Figure 13.18.** Illustration of chimeric figures of the type used by Levy, Trevarthen, and Sperry. From "Perception of Bilateral Chimeric Figures Following Hemispheric Disconnection" by J. Levy, C. Trevarthen, and R.W. Sperry, 1972, *Brain*, *95*, p. 68. Copyright 1972 by Oxford University Press. Reprinted by permission.

multiple choice one of the three pictures that matched what she had seen, her visually determined matches were always related to the left half of the chimeric stimulus, and her conceptual matches to the right half. Thus the right hemisphere never took the opportunity to direct a conceptual choice nor the left hemisphere to direct a visually determined choice.

### FACE RECOGNITION
The neuropsychology of face recognition has been a testing ground for two separate issues:

first, whether the recognition of faces is merely an instance of the recognition of any visual configuration and therefore preferentially carried out by the right hemisphere; second, whether alternative perceptual strategies may be used in face recognition by different individuals, some using a gestalt strategy, others noting particular features. The implication of the latter hypothesis is that the right hemisphere might control face recognition in the first group, the left in the second group.

There is strong clinical evidence that facial

recognition is a unique process. The phenomenon of prosopagnosia produces a disorder in which familiar faces can no longer be identified and even distinctions of age and sex may be lost, while the recognition of objects is unaffected. Further, as Tsavaras, Hécaen, and LeBras (1970) have shown, patients suffering from prosopagnosia may have no difficulty in matching photographs of unfamiliar faces. The difficulty would appear to be not at the level of perceptual discrimination, but in the process of attaching an identity to what is perceived. Another possible difference between prosopagnosia and impaired visual perception is in its organic basis. Every case that has come to autopsy to date has had bilateral lesions, usually involving both occipital lobes, with the major lesion on the right (Benton, 1980).

As already noted, perceptual matching of the human face has proved to be a reliable means of engaging the right hemisphere in normals. Correspondingly, patients with right cerebral lesions have invariably been found to perform less well than those with left cerebral lesions in tests of either immediate or delayed identification of sample faces (Benton & Van Allen, 1968; DeRenzi, Faglioni, & Spinnler, 1968). These deficits are usually worst in patients with retrorolandic lesions and visual field defects. However, unlike the case for prosopagnosia, perceptual defects for unfamiliar faces do not require involvement of the visual cortex, and in this respect they appear to share the same underlying lesion as nonfacial perceptual defects.

Two studies led Yin (1969, 1970) to conclude that face recognition entailed a special mechanism beyond that subserving the recognition of other classes of familiar objects. In an initial study with normal subjects Yin used faces and three other classes of objects: photos of houses sharing the same general architectural style, airplane silhouettes, and cartoon stick figures in various action poses. These classes of stimuli were chosen because all are normally recognized in an upright orientation. The pictures were divided into inspection sets containing 20 pictures of each class. Each inspection set had a corresponding recognition set containing 12 of the original items and 12 new items of the same class. After viewing one inspection set, subjects were required to identify the previously exposed pictures in the corresponding recognition set, the procedure being repeated for the second

inspection and recognition set. Either the first or second pair of sets was presented inverted, with the order counterbalanced across subjects. Yin found that, while upside-down learning and recognition were more difficult for all classes of items, the effect for faces was disproportionately severe. Moreover, those subjects who scored highest on upright faces had the most disruption on inverted faces. On applying this technique (for faces and houses only) to unilaterally brain-damaged patients (1970), he found that patients with right posterior damage were significantly worse on upright faces than patients with either right or left frontal damage or left posterior damage. On inverted faces, however, they were no worse than normal controls and significantly better than the patients with other unilateral lesions. All but the right posterior patients showed the same pattern as the earlier normal experimental group: faces were easier than houses for upright learning and recognition; faces were harder than houses in the inverted presentation. Yin's observations on subjects with unilateral lesions were confirmed for normal subjects in a tachistoscopic half-field study by Leehey, Carey, Diamond, and Cahn (1978).

The implication from all the foregoing studies is that face perception shares with the perception of other complex visual forms a vulnerability to lesions in the right posterior quadrant of the brain, but that face perception differs from other classes of material in that the right posterior zone is particularly vital for facial discrimination in the normal upright position. Moreover, the Tsavaras et al. (1970) data indicate that the loss of the ability to attribute identity to a previously familiar face involves a different lesion and is not merely a more severe form of the impairment of visual perception and delayed recognition of unfamiliar faces.

In the face of the consistent evidence for right cerebral control in the recognition of unfamiliar faces, Marzi and Berlucchi (1977) found that the recognition of familiar faces by normal subjects is dominated by the left hemisphere. When they presented a series of faces of celebrities to Italian university students, using the tachistoscopic half-field technique, they found a significant right-field advantage in correctness of reports.

Yin's observation that the best perceivers of upright faces are the poorest perceivers of inverted ones suggests that there may be two alternative perceptual strategies in face perception. Holistic or gestalt perception of the face could be expected to depend on its presentation in the familiar upright position, while registration of the face feature by feature should be about equally effective in either orientation. Experiments by Bradshaw and his collaborators (Patterson & Bradshaw, 1975; Bradshaw, Gates, & Patterson, 1976; Bradshaw, Taylor, Patterson, & Nettleton, 1980) indicate that holistic judgments of facelike drawings elicit a left-field (right hemisphere) advantage, whereas single feature differences in similar stimuli are detected more efficiently via the right visual field (left hemisphere). Patterson and Bradshaw (1975) devised two sets of four schematic facelike stimuli and chose one from each set as the target stimulus for that set. In one set, the nontarget stimuli differed from the target and from each other in the shape of all three features: eyes, nose, and mouth. It was presumed that in this condition, discriminating a target from a nontarget would occur holistically, at a glance. In the second set, each nontarget was identical to the target in two features, but differed in the shape of a third. It was presumed that discriminations in this condition would demand analytic, or feature-by-feature comparison. Twelve male and 12 female right-handed students were tested in a between-groups design for the two conditions. In each condition, after memorizing the target stimulus, the subjects viewed 128 stimulus presentations, randomized to the left or right visual field; half of these stimuli were the target and half were distributed among the three nontargets. Reaction times were recorded for same and different judgments. As expected, significantly shorter latencies for both same and different responses were elicited by left half-field presentations under the holistic conditions and by right-field presentations under analytic conditions.

The Patterson and Bradshaw study showed that subjects could be forced into a right- or a left-hemisphere-governed mode of information processing by the manipulation of highly contrived facelike stimuli. A more recent study by Ross and Turkewitz (1981) provides a more direct link to Yin's observations. They exposed faces tachistoscopically in the right or left visual field and required subjects to match each presented face to a multiple choice display of the four possible stimuli. They identified two subgroups of subjects—those who performed best with stimulus faces that appeared in the left visual field

and those who performed best with those that appeared on the right. Ross and Turkewitz hypothesized that left visual-field superiority might denote a holistic perceptual strategy and right-field superiority a feature-analytic one. They used two further procedures to test this hypothesis. One procedure required finding the match to a stimulus face presented upside down, a procedure presumed to be particularly disabling for the holistic strategy. The other procedure involved finding the match for stimuli in which one feature (e.g., nose, mouth, eye) was blocked out. This was presumed to create a greater handicap for subjects using a feature-analytic than a holistic strategy. As predicted, the subjects who showed left visual-field superiority in the original baseline procedure showed a greater decline from baseline in the inverted face condition than in the missing feature condition, suggesting a link between left visual-field (right hemisphere) superiority and a holistic perceptual strategy. The reverse was true for the subjects whose baseline performance showed a right visual-field advantage.

### Lateralization of Spatial Perception

Right-hemisphere dominance has been demonstrated for spatial localization, directional orientation, and depth perception through studies of unilaterally brain-damaged groups and of normals. This lateralization is reversed in conditions where the percept to be processed can be promptly coded into either a verbal or conceptual category.

#### SPATIAL LOCALIZATION

The prototype study of visuospatial localization was that of Kimura (1969), who used the tachistoscopic visual half-field technique on normal subjects. Her experiment, carried out with 19 male and 19 female subjects, entailed the presentation of a dot within a square frame in either the right or left visual field. After each 10-msec exposure, the subject identified the dot by its number in a 25-dot square multiple-choice matrix located above the eyepiece of the tachistoscope. A sex-by-field interaction was significant (p < .01) because men, but not women, were more accurate in the left visual field than the right. A modification of this procedure consisted of a single circular frame encompassing both visual fields, with 24 possible dot locations in each half of the circle. In this version of the experiment both men and women displayed a left-field advantage.

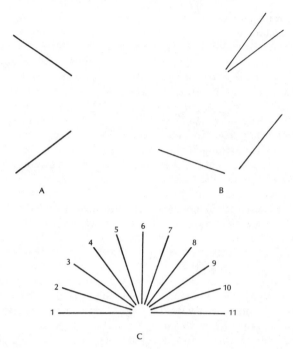

**Figure 13.19.** Line orientation task described by Benton, Hannay, and Varney. Either a single stimulus line, as in *A*, or two lines, as in *B*, are presented briefly and subject identifies them from immediate memory in display *C*. From "Visual Perception of Line Direction in Patients with Unilateral Brain Disease" by A.L. Benton, H.J. Hannay, and N.R. Varney, 1975, *Neurology, 25*, p. 908. Copyright 1975 by Harcourt Brace Jovanovich Publishers. Reprinted by permission.

A parallel study on brain-injured patients by Hannay, Varney, and Benton (1976) confirmed the right-hemisphere laterality for this operation but found that impaired performance was associated only with lesions posterior to the rolandic fissure on the right.

Discrimination of line orientation has also been studied in normal and brain-injured groups with the consistent findings that the right hemisphere is critically involved in this process. Benton, Hannay, and Varney (1975) used a group of normal controls to establish the lower limit of scores in a task of matching one or two tachistoscopically presented lines to a multiple-choice display of eleven lines, 18 degrees apart, arranged as radii of a semi-circle (Figure 13.19). Fifty-nine percent of right brain-damaged patients performed at a lower level than the poorest left brain-damaged or normal subject. A strikingly high correlation with the same patients' performance on the dot-location task suggests that the two tasks tap the same basic ability.

The critical importance of codability for the lateralization of line orientation was demon-

strated in a visual half-field study by Umilta et al. (1974). For a set of four easily codable orientations (vertical, horizontal, left diagonal, right diagonal), a right visual-field advantage was observed in normal subjects. For a set of intermediate slopes in the same direction, for which there is no readily available conceptual tag, a left-field advantage was obtained (see Figure 13.20).

Depth perception has also been shown to be preferentially processed in the right hemisphere, when information on binocular disparity is presented tachistoscopically to one hemisphere with either a standard depth-perception apparatus (Durnford & Kimura, 1971) or the Julesz random-dot stereogram (Kimura, 1973).

Observations of split-brain patients, operating under the control of each hemisphere separately, gave impetus to the view that the right hemisphere deals best with the relational aspect of spatial tasks and the left with the individual features. Separate access to each hemisphere was accomplished by having subjects identify stimuli with one hand at a time, behind a screen,

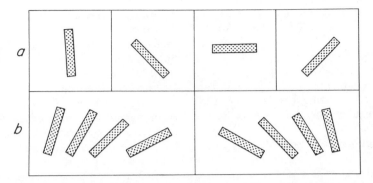

**Figure 13.20.** Codable (a) and non-codable (b) bar orientations used by Umilta et al. Two bars out of each set of four were designated as targets, to be responded to if they appeared in a visual hemifield. The two versions of set (b) were allocated to the left and right visual fields, for symmetry. From "Hemisphere Differences in the Discrimination of Line Orientations" by C. Umilta, G. Rizzolatti, C.A. Marzi, G. Zamboni, C. Franzini, R. Camarda, and G. Berlucchi, 1974, *Neuropsychologia, 12,* p. 167. Copyright 1974 by Pergamon Press, Ltd. Reprinted by permission.

with each hand providing input only to the contralateral hemisphere.

Levy-Agresti and Sperry (1968) gave six subjects a series of three-dimensional geometric forms, each with a distinctive shape and textural pattern. While palpating one of these forms, the subjects viewed a set of three drawings, one of which was an accurate representation of an unfolded version of the shape in his hand, laid out in two dimensions. Three subjects, all with preexisting right hemisphere damage, failed completely to match the object to its two-dimensional representation. The other three performed more accurately for stimuli felt in the left than in the right hand, only one of them performing above chance with the right hand. Examination of this subject's performance disclosed that items identified correctly with the right hand corresponded little with those done with the left. Objects identified best by the left hemisphere, using the right hand, contained manually discriminable details, though they were visually similar. Those identified best by the right hemisphere showed the reverse pattern. The authors proposed that the left-hand (right hemisphere) system solved these problems through its ability to reconstruct the solid form from its unfolded version, whereas the left hemisphere, via the right hand, solved its items by attention to particular features. A similar qualitative observation was made by Zaidel and Sperry (1973) in the administration of tactile adaptation of the Ravens Colored Progressive Matrices.

The poor performance of the left hemisphere on a spatial task with no isolable features to aid in its solution is demonstrated in a study by Nebes (1971). He required his split-brain subjects to palpate with one hand an arc of a circle of a given diameter and identify the corresponding circle in a visual display of three circles of different sizes. In alternative versions of the task, the arc was presented visually and the circles haptically, or both arcs and circles were presented haptically. Regardless of sensory modality, left-hand palpation led to accuracy scores ranging from 60 to 90 percent, while performance with the right hand was at chance levels. This pattern was consistent in five of his six patients.

Summarizing the experimental data from all sources on the lateralization of visual and visuospatial percepts, it appears that right cerebral control is maximum when a purely configurational task is presented, as in the experiment of Nebes (1971). The extreme case for left-hemisphere control is that of verbal or alphabetic material. To the extent that pictorial material can be dealt with in terms of either verbal coding or categorical properties, the left hemisphere appears to preempt its processing. For those pictorial or spatial stimuli that can be processed by both their configurational properties and their isolable features, alternative processing strategies are possible.

LATERALIZATION IN THE HAPTIC MODALITY
The investigation of form and space perception

has been less extensive in the haptic mode than in vision, partly because of the intrinsic limitations of the haptic channel. Studies of unilaterally brain-damaged and normal populations have generally followed the path of adapting to tactile presentations the methods used in visuoperceptual experiments. Results have indicated similar right-hemisphere dominance for most perceptual tasks.

DeRenzi, Faglioni, and Scotti (1968) found that patients with right posterior damage were more impaired in mastering a tactual form-board test than those with left-side injury. In a follow-up experiment DeRenzi and Scotti (1969) required 50 right brain-damaged and 71 left brain-damaged patients to identify visually a form whose outline they traced behind a screen. Again patients with right posterior lesions were most impaired.

Carmon and Benton (1969) tested right and left brain-damaged patients with a device that tested concurrently their tactile perception of number and their perception of spatial orientation. This was realized through configurations of one, two, or three rods, which contacted the hand in either a vertical, horizontal, or left or right diagonal alignment. The subjects' reports on the number of rods they could feel did not differ in accuracy between the two groups with hemisphere damage. However, the right brain-injured patients were significantly more impaired than the others in reporting the directional alignment of the rods. The same apparatus was used by Benton, Levin, and Varney (1973) to examine the manual lateralization of directional perception of normal subjects. Upon feeling one of the directional configurations in their palm, they were to point to the corresponding line in a multiple-choice display. Their left hands proved more sensitive than the right, suggesting that the right hemisphere is dominant for this task in the normal brain.

It is worth noting that the four directional choices in this task were the very ones with which Umilta et al. (1974) elicited a left-hemisphere advantage in the visual mode, offering the explanation that these directions were readily codable. While the fact of codability may be at work in the tactile task as well, it is probably overridden by the difficulty of the tactile perceptual-processing operation—producing the net effect of a right-hemisphere advantage. The issue of the balance of cognitive control between the hemispheres is discussed below (p. 929). Another

instance of preponderant right cerebral control for tactile perception of configuration is in the recognition of Braille letters, for which the left hand is also more adept than the right (Hermelin & O'Connor, 1971).

Two investigators have attempted to demonstrate an antithesis between spatial and linguistic processes in the haptic modality, using simultaneous competing stimulation. Witelson (1974) found that nonsense shapes, simultaneously palpated with both hands, were better identified by the left hand; but letter shapes tested in the same way led to no difference between the two sides. Oscar-Berman, Rehbein, Porfert, and Goodglass (1978) used the method of simultaneously tracing on the upturned palms two competing letters, two different line slopes, or two different digits. In addition, the order of the subjects' report from the two hands was randomized. The experimenters succeeded in obtaining a right-hand advantage for letters and a left-hand advantage for line slopes, but only in the comparisons between the second reported hands. The suggestion is made that the immediately reporting hand is using rapidly decaying iconic sensory information, whereas the hand giving the delayed report is relying on information that has undergone encoding for storage in memory. It is at the latter stage that lateralization may occur (see discussions on Levels of Processing, p. 928).

## MUSICAL PERCEPTION

The frequent preservation of melodic reproduction and musical appreciation in patients suffering from severe aphasia has led to the speculation that musical ability is controlled by the right hemisphere. However, clinical evidence based on many persons who have lost their ability to recognize or reproduce melody indicates that this disorder, termed *amusia* is not seen any more frequently after injury to the right than to the left hemisphere (Ustvedt, 1937; Wertheim, 1969; Gates & Bradshaw, 1977). Total amusia for both perception and reproduction of melody is the rule in cases of word deafness resulting from bilateral temporal lesions (e.g., cases of Miceli, 1982, and of Auerbach, Allard, Naeser, Alexander, & Albert, 1982). It was Milner's (1962a) experimental study of unilaterally brain-injured patients that disclosed the dominance of the right over the left cerebral hemisphere for melodic perception, a finding subsequently supported by dichotic listening studies of normal groups (Kimura, 1964).

Milner (1962a) used the six subtests of the Seashore Musical Aptitude Test to examine, both pre- and postoperatively, 16 subjects who underwent right temporal lobectomy and 22 with left temporal lobectomy, all for the relief of epilepsy. Only the right lobectomy group showed a postoperative decline in performance. These declines were most marked and were statistically significant for same-different judgments of Timbre and Tonal Memory. The tonal memory task required subjects to listen to successive pairs of tonal sequences of three, four, or five notes, in which one of the notes of the sequence was altered in the second member of the pair. The subject was required to identify the altered note by its position in the sequence. Nonsignificant declines in performance were also noted for tone duration and simple pitch discrimination, while a small but significant decline was found for loudness.

Parallel findings in normal subjects were first demonstrated by Kimura (1964) who presented melodies dichotically to 20 right-handed females. The melodies were all four-second segments of instrumental solo passages, of similar tonal range and tempo. After a pair had been played dichotically, four excerpts were played binaurally, two target melodies and two distractors. The subject reported the ordinal position of one or both excerpts she recognized. When 18 such sets were given, the left-ear advantage for melodies was significant (p < .01), and 16 of the 20 subjects showed this directional effect. A standard dichotic digits procedure produced a significant advantage for the right ear in 15 of the 20 subjects. The same experiment was administered by Shankweiler (1966) to patients undergoing right or left temporal lobectomies, again with the result that right cerebral damage produced more impairment than left.

A negative finding on dichotic ear differences for melodies was reported by Gordon (1978), who used melodies having identical rhythmic patterns. However, Gordon obtained a left-ear advantage for musical chords presented dichotically. Other studies using both complex melodies (e.g., Borod & Goodglass, 1980) and brief sequences of tones of equal durations (e.g., Spreen, Spellacy, & Reid, 1970) have shown left-ear advantages, with few exceptions (e.g., Johnson et al., 1977; Peretz & Morais, 1980).

The notion that music may be processed either holistically, by the right hemisphere, or analytically, by the left hemisphere, was proposed by Bever and Chiarello (1974). They argued that analytic processing or processing governed by the left hemisphere should be characteristic of people trained musically, because they would have learned to perceive the tonal components and their relations within a melody. Bever and Chiarello recruited 14 subjects who had taken music lessons for at least five years and were still either currently singing or playing an instrument nonprofessionally. These subjects were designated as musically experienced. A second group of 14 who had fewer than three years of music lessons and none within the previous five years were designated as musically naive. The task administered to all subjects was to listen to a series of 72 melodic sequences, each followed by a two-note sequence which either was or was not an excerpt of the preceding melody. Within the series of 72 melodies one-fourth were repetitions of a melody that had been previously heard no more than three trials earlier. The subjects were scored for their ability to judge whether the two-note sequences were in fact excerpts from the preceding melody and for their recognition of recurring melodies. Presentation was monaural, to either the left ear only or the right ear only, in a between-groups design, with seven subjects in each ear group. In the musically naive group, the left-ear listeners recognized more recurring melodies than the right-ear listeners, but neither subgroup performed above chance in recognizing two-note excerpts. In the musically experienced group, the right-ear listeners recognized more of the recurring melodies than the left-ear listeners. Both musically experienced subgroups were successful in identifying two-note excerpts, and they did not differ in their scores.

While this experiment has been widely cited as demonstrating that the holistic-analytic principal extends to musical perception, it must be viewed with caution. There were only seven subjects in each group and no independent control for preexisting group differences in lateralization. Moreover, the two-note excerpt task, which is clearly analytic in nature, showed no ear differences in the musically experienced subjects. The attribution of an analytic quality to the melodic recognition task is highly speculative. Since the Seashore Tonal Memory Test—an extremely analytic task—was sensitive only to right cerebral injury in Milner's (1962a) study, the Bever–Chiarello argument seems poorly justified.

Zatorre (1979) reexamined this issue with a more rigorous design, using dichotic listening and within-group comparisons. His 24 musically trained subjects had a mean of 11.8 years of instrumental experience and at least one course in music theory. His 24 nonmusicians had had no formal training in music. Musical segments were 18 six-tone sequences that had been preselected to provide varying degrees of melodic coherence and to sample the use of both whole-tone and chromatic scale in their composition. They were paired against each other in all possible combinations for a total of 90 trials. The format of the Kimura (1964) procedure was used, that is, after the dichotic presentations, the two members of the dichotic pair were heard along with two distractor melodies in a series of four binaural presentations. The subject was to indicate which two melodies he had heard. As a control condition, a verbal dichotic task composed of competing CV syllables was presented in the same multiple-choice response format.

Although musicians were more accurate in their identifications, both musicians and non-musicians showed significant left-ear advantages for melody, with no difference in degree of asymmetry between the groups. All variations in melodic construction showed identical effects. Right ear advantages of equal degree were observed for dichotic CV stimuli in both groups. Thus this experiment provides no support for a shift from a holistic to an analytic processing mode in musical perception as a result of musical training. In fact, of the eight subjects in Zatorre's study who had a right-ear advantage for melodies as well as for CV syllables, six were non-musicians.

Melody, of course, is only one component of music, and the predominance of the right hemisphere for musical perception does not mean that all aspects of music are lateralized in the same way. Indeed the ambiguous status of amusia as a lateralized disorder argues for bilateral distribution of its components. In fact, in an experiment by Shanon (1980) professional musicians showed left cerebral dominance in a task requiring difficult binary decisions about the structure of musical triads.

## Lateralization of Purposeful Movement

### CLINICAL BACKGROUND

The term *apraxia* refers to a disorder in the ability to carry out purposeful movements that cannot be accounted for by weakness or incoordination of the musculature involved in the action. The frequency of the association of this disorder with left cerebral lesions and aphasia was recognized in the neurological literature of the late nineteenth century, and a number of writers (e.g., Finkelnberg, 1870) considered it to be a symbolic disorder in the sphere of movements. Liepmann (1900, 1905, 1908) treated apraxia at length, noting that it was frequently observed in aphasic patients, less commonly observed in left brain-injured paitents without aphasia, and absent in right brain injury. A characteristic of apraxia, noted by Liepmann, was that a movement that could not be executed on request might be performed normally in an automatized context or in a situation with strong contextual support. For example, it can be readily demonstrated that patients who cannot pretend to blow out an imaginary match on request, or even in imitation of the examiner, usually blow promptly on being presented with a lighted match. Similarly patients who perform in a vague and amorphous manner when asked to pretend to use an implement (e.g., a comb or a hammer) use the object well or with only mild clumsiness when it is placed in their hands.

Liepmann proposed that this form of movement disorder, which he termed *ideomotor apraxia*, was caused by the isolation of the left parietal area from the motor execution centers in the left frontal lobe. He attributed the simultaneous involvement of the left hand (sympathetic apraxia) to the fact that the motor instructions for purposeful movement were relayed from the left to the right hemisphere via fibres passing through the corpus callosum. With left-handers, this relation might be reversed (Heilman, Coyle, Gonyea, & Geschwind, 1973). Support for the model was provided by a report by Liepmann and Maas (1907) of a patient who could not carry out movements with his left hand, either on request or in imitation, nor could he write with his left hand, although he was not otherwise aphasic. Liepmann predicted and verified at autopsy that the patient had a lesion of the corpus callosum that prevented the transmission of information originating in his left hemisphere to the motor systems of the right hemisphere. The fact that the patient failed not only with oral commands but also with visual demonstrations convinced Liepmann that both were mediated by a left-hemisphere system. However, Geschwind and Kaplan's (1962) callosally damaged patient, though similarly apraxic to command, was able to imitate a demonstrated movement.

A case of callosal disconnection in a left-handed patient described by Poncet et al. (1978) presents still another configuration of disorders related to praxis. This patient was unique in that, in addition to complete destruction of the corpus collosum, she had suffered destruction of her left visual cortex, so that she could see only in her left visual field, and visual information was confined to the right hemisphere. She could carry out gestures with either hand in response to oral command, showing that both hemispheres had auditory reception of language and that both could direct purposeful movements, a circumstance almost surely related to her left-handedness. Other tests of language confirmed the integrity of auditory comprehension in both hemispheres, although the right hemisphere was incapable of reading, writing, or naming visually presented objects. The one form of praxic disturbance that could be demonstrated was her inability to imitate either movements or static hand positions with the right hand. However, movements of the right upper arm were easily copied. All movements were perfectly imitated with the left hand. In this case, a simple anatomic explanation accounts for the dissociation between distal (hand) and proximal (upper arm) movements. Hand movements are under virtually exclusive contralateral pyramidal control, whereas proximal musculature is controlled partly by bilateral nonpyramidal motor systems. Thus visual input confined to the right hemisphere has access to motor systems controlling the right upper arm, but not the right hand. Dissociations in performance to command between body-axis movements and limb movements are similarly explained on the basis of the motor system involved in their control (Geschwind, 1975).

EXPERIMENTAL STUDIES OF CLINICAL GROUPS

Goodglass and Kaplan (1963) investigated the notion, first formulated by Finkelnberg (1870),

that the failure of many aphasics to use pantomime and gesture effectively was owing to the breakdown of a central symbolic capacity, encompassing speech and nonspeech activity. This contrasts with Liepmann's view that aphasia is merely a by-product of the same lesion that destroys the left-hemisphere motor-engram system or its connections to the frontal motor area. Goodglass and Kaplan present 20 aphasic and 19 nonaphasic brain-injured controls with a series of tasks ranging from conventional gestures through complex narrative pantomime, using oral commands, pictures, and imitation. They reported a low correlation between severity of aphasia and performance on these tasks and little improvement on imitation by those patients who failed on either verbal or pictorial request. However, failures were overwhelmingly more frequent in the aphasic group. The conclusion reached in their study was that the concept of asymbolia as the common basis for aphasia and impaired pantomime was not supported—that failure to use gesture and pantomime adequately represented a disorder specific to the execution of purposeful movements.

A diametrically contrary conclusion is reached in a report by Duffy and Duffy (1981). These authors made an a priori operational distinction between praxis and pantomime by defining praxis in terms of success in imitating a series of 80 manual movements graded in complexity, whereas pantomime was measured by success in demonstrating the use of 23 objects presented pictorially. Aphasics were inferior to right brain-injured and normal controls in pantomime production, pantomime comprehension, and praxis, but not in the Raven Matrices. Normal and right brain-injured controls did not differ on any of the measures. Within the aphasic group there were high intercorrelations between pantomime production, praxis, severity of aphasia, and nonverbal intelligence. However, a series of partial correlations indicated that the relation between pantomime production and severity of aphasia was the only one that persisted at a high level (0.80) when the other factors were partialed out. A significant but low correlation (0.38) remained between praxis and pantomime when severity of aphasia was partialed out. The Duffy and Duffy (1981) results must therefore be taken as a strong argument favoring the concept of a common factor of symbolic communicative competence underlying both aphasia and expression through gesture and pantomime. The one important discrepancy from clinical experience is the failure to account for those individuals with severe aphasia who pantomime flawlessly.

A series of studies by Kimura and co-workers places apraxia in the context of a general disorder in the execution of sequential movements, brought about by left-hemisphere injury. Kimura and Archibald (1974) reported that right and left brain-injured subjects were indistinguishable in their ability to copy static hand positions, but that left brain-injured patients were markedly inferior in imitating movements and in demonstrating the use of objects to oral command as well as to imitation. The degree of deficit for the aphasics was unrelated to the severity of aphasia and patients with no paralysis performed identically with both hands. In a subsequent study Kimura (1977) taught a meaningless sequential motor task to 28 left brain-injured (including 13 aphasics) and 16 right brain-injured subjects. Aphasics were significantly slower (14.5 sec) in learning the sequence than both the brain-injured nonaphasics (11.7 sec) and the right brain-injured patients (9.4 sec), while the difference between the latter two groups was short of significance (p < .10). Mateer and Kimura (1977) found that aphasics were impaired in the execution of serial oral nonspeech movements, whether their articulation was fluent or not. Nonaphasic patients with left-hemisphere injury performed as well as those with right-brain injury.

On the basis of all these observations, Kimura has discounted the factor of meaningfulness or communicative intent for the concept of apraxia. This position is congruent with that of Duffy and Duffy (1981) who separated motor imitation, or praxis, from representational pantomime. Kimura's results for manual movements agree with those of Goodglass and Kaplan (1963) and Duffy and Duffy in finding relative independence between impaired praxis and the severity of aphasia. Only the Duffy and Duffy approach separates the communicative from the motor aspect of organized movement.

The Kimura studies leave a number of loose ends in relation to the clinical phenomenon of ideomotor apraxia. One is the likelihood that assuming static positions (as in saluting, signaling to stop, etc.) may be affected in apraxic patients. A second is that a flawless movement may be released through the provision of con-textual support (cf. the example cited above of blowing out a match). Neither of these observations jibes readily with the reduction of apraxia to a deficit in the ordering of sequential movements. Finally, Mateer and Kimura report, but do not pursue, the paradoxical finding that serial oral nonspeech movements are impaired only in aphasic and not in nonaphasic patients with left-hemisphere damage, but that this impairment is unrelated to the presence of articulatory impairment in the aphasic group. Praxic disorders appear to be produced by left cerebral injury in the very zone where aphasia results and yet these disorders neither cause nor are caused by the aphasia.

### Lateralization of Emotion Related Percepts

Gainotti (1972), summarizing a large body of clinical observations, noted that, while left brain-injured subjects display appropriate or even heightened anxiety and depression in the face of their disabilities, right brain-injured patients are often indifferent or inappropriately jocular about their deficits. He confirmed this disparity between the two hemisphere-injured groups with a tabulation of the test behavior of 160 unilaterally damaged patients in his laboratory. Given these behavioral observations, it is not surprising to find experimental evidence of impaired emotional sensitivity.

Impaired perception of emotional vocal tone was demonstrated by Heilman et al. (1975). A neutrally worded sentence was tape recorded with vocal intonations corresponding to various emotional states. Patients with right brain injury proved inferior to those with left brain injury in interpreting mood from tone of voice. Cicone, Wapner, and Gardner (1980) compared 21 unilaterally right and 18 left brain-injured patients on two tasks of emotional perceptiveness: in one the subjects were required to select from a multiple choice a face expressing the same emotion as a given stimulus face; the second task required them to find, in an array of four pictured situations, one that implied the same emotional state as a simulus picture placed above them. In both tasks the right brain-damaged group peformed significantly worse than the left.

An interesting tachistoscopic study by Landis, Assal, and Perret (1979) showed that the categorizing of emotional expression was dominated by the right hemisphere, whereas categorizing objects was dominated by the left.

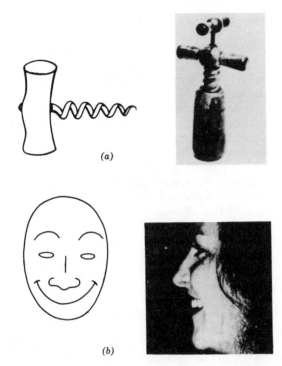

*(a)*

*(b)*

**Figure 13.21.** Examples of object and emotional expression stimuli used by Landis, Assal and Perret. Line drawing of prototype appeared in midfield and a matching or nonmatching photographic exemplar appeared in one lateral field. From "Opposite Cerebral Hemispheric Superiorities for Visual Associative Processing of Emotional Facial Expressions and Objects" by T. Landis, G. Assal, and E. Perret, 1979, *Nature, 278,* p. 739. Copyright by Macmillan Journals Ltd. Reprinted by permission.

Stimuli for categorizing objects were cards bearing a line drawing of a prototype exemplar of an object (e.g., a corkscrew or key or brush) in the center. A photograph, either of a real but different-looking example of the same object or of another object appeared in one of the lateral fields (Figure 13.21a). In this condition, only one subject failed to show right-field dominance for category matches. Stimuli for emotional categories were cards bearing a central full-face cartoon rendition of one of three emotions: happy, angry, or astonished. Displaced either to the right or left was a profile photograph of a male or female face displaying either the same or one of the other two emotional expressions (Figure 13.21b). Reaction times for matching emotions were faster in the left visual field for 23 of 24

subjects. Thus the finding by Cicone et al. on impaired recognition of facial emotion by right brain-injured patients is supported by results from normal subjects.

It would be difficult to fit affect into the mold of either holistic or analytic processing. The study of Landis et al. (1979) shows that categorizing emotions appears to activate a different hemispheric system from categorizing objects. Regardless of how we analyze the type of processing involved, affective content appears to dictate greater involvement of right- than of left-hemisphere function.

### Right- and Left-Hemisphere Components in the Processing of Language

The section on the Neuropsychology of Language, with its emphasis on aphasia, dwells largely on the effects of focal left-hemisphere damage. Further insight into the lateralization of language has been gained through the study of patients with transection of the corpus callosum and through the use of dichotic listening and visual half-field techniques in normal subjects.

Early reports (Sperry & Gazzaniga, 1967) showed that patients with callosal sectioning could read object names projected to their left visual field, finding them by palpation behind a screen with the left hand. They similarly demonstrated the auditory comprehension of object names and even the auditory comprehension of elaborate definitions of the object to be located. The right hemisphere, however, was unable to demonstrate its comprehension of written verbs. While some patients could do simple spelling with the left hand of objects presented pictorially to the left visual field, the right hemisphere had no useful access to language output by speech or writing. A notable deficit in the right hemisphere's language capacity is its total inability to retrieve the sound structure of either a picture or a written word so as to recognize rhyming words or homonyms (Zaidel & Peters, 1981).

Zaidel (1977) has succeeded in restricting prolonged visual presentations to either visual half-field, through the use of an ingenious optical arrangement. An auditory comprehension test, based on object manipulation (Token Test of DeRenzi & Vignolo, 1962) could thus be given under right-hemisphere control, with the left hand and under left-hemisphere control with the right hand. Zaidel found that the right hemisphere's overall performance was at about the level of a 4-year-old child. In this context, verbs were understood more frequently than the names of the shapes that constitute the objects for this test, but the comprehension of prepositions and conjunctions was severely impaired, as were references to size and color.

Since most split-brain patients had lived with brain abnormalities most of their lives prior to surgery, it is possible that the distribution of their language abilities is atypical, compared with normal speakers. Indeed great differences are reported in the extent of right-hemisphere language as a function of the age at which the original epileptogenic lesion was acquired (Gazzaniga & LeDoux, 1978). Consequently, rather than interpret the split-brain data as providing a view of normal right-brain language capacities, it is safer to regard it as reflecting the order of difficulty of various linguistic operations for the nondominant hemisphere.

### SEMANTIC FACTORS

Several tachistoscopic half-field studies with normal subjects (Ellis & Shepherd, 1974; Hines, 1976; Day, 1977) concur in finding that concrete nouns are about equally well identified in right and left visual fields, whereas abstract nouns are strongly lateralized to the right. These findings are consistent with observations from split-brain subjects. According to Graves, Landis, and Goodglass (1981), emotionally loaded words also have semantic properties that make them accessible to processing in either hemisphere.

### PHONOLOGICAL FACTORS

Liberman, Cooper, Shankweiler, and Studdert-Kennedy (1967) and Liberman (1975) have summarized the evidence for distinguishing between two modes of processing sounds—one auditory, the other phonetic—in which the phonetic mode involves the extraction of linguistically significant information from overlapping and rapidly changing acoustic signals. The rules for identifying a complex acoustic signal as a linguistic element are referred to as the speech code, which may be considered as that component of grammar that deals with phonology. In this view the most highly encoded sounds are stop consonants, because any given stop consonant has a number of different spectrographic representations—a different one for each following vowel. In spite of these differences, which are represented physically in the 40-msec duration of the

formant transition (p. 893) the listener decodes them all as the same phoneme. Continuant consonants and vowels, which are more invariant acoustically, are considered less highly encoded and may therefore be processed in the auditory mode.

A series of studies using dichotic listening have supported the concept of phonetic versus auditory processing by demonstrating that the highly encoded sounds are most strongly lateralized to the right ear, and that even continuants, such as vowels and fricatives, undergo a degree of coding in real speech contexts that calls on the specialized skills of the left hemisphere. Shankweiler and Studdert-Kennedy (1967) found that the stop consonants in competing dichotic CV syllables (*pa* versus *ta*, *ga* versus *da*, etc.) were better reported from the right ear, whereas steady-state vowels were equally well reported from both ears.

The presentation of steady-state vowels, whether synthetically generated or produced by a single speaker, omits a factor that is constantly present in real speech, namely, the difference in the physical acoustic signal for any speech sound from one speaker to another. Both the fundamental frequency and the overtones that determine the formants vary from individual to individual, as a function of each particular vocal tract.

Haggard (1971) found that, when vowels produced by different speakers were intermixed and presented dichotically, a right-ear advantage was obtained, presumably because the extraction of an invariant linguistic value entails a process of normalization of the acoustic parameters for each speaker (Ladefoged & Broadbent, 1957). C.J. Darwin (1971) showed that this normalization is a left-hemisphere function. He first used a dichotic series of competing synthetic steady-state vowels based on the parameters of a single (synthetic) vocal tract and showed (like Shankweiler & Studdert-Kennedy, 1967) that they were unlateralized—that is, they could be processed in the auditory mode. In a second dichotic series these vowels were intermixed with synthetic vowels based on the dimensions of a different vocal tract. This time all the vowels, including the original set, were better identified by the right ear, suggesting that the complex operation of normalizing entailed phonetic processing and engaged the left-hemisphere system.

Speech perception is based not only on the

identification of successive phonemes, but on intonational patterns that distinguish between commands, questions, and simple statements of fact. Blumstein and Cooper (1974) recorded sentences of similar length spoken with the intonation of commands, questions, and statements and passed them through low-pass filters so that the intonation pattern alone remained intelligible. When these were presented as dichotic stimuli, the sentence type was more accurately identified by the left-ear signal, indicating that the perception of speech prosody is predominantly a right-cerebral function.

## Language—Holistic or Analytic?

A review of the findings on the lateralization of language discloses no feature of language, whether perceptual or productive, that is not processed more efficiently by the left than the right hemisphere, with the exception of the intonation.

Any attempt to characterize the component processes of language as analytic as opposed to holistic seems rather futile. Some processes appear clearly holistic in nature, such as phonetic perception of vowels and consonants or appreciation of rhyming sounds; others such as syntax seem to demand sequential analysis. For still others—for example, sound-meaning association in either production or comprehension—the analytic-holistic dichotomy is irrelevant. The lateralization of language appears to be reflected in the lateralization of a variety of components at the auditory-perceptual, conceptual, and motor-control level, rathern than to be reducible to strategy of hemispheric processing.

## What is Lateralized? Summary

The data presented fail to make an airtight case for either an exclusively material-specific theory of laterality or a hemispheric cognitive-strategy theory. Each appears to play an exclusive role in some perceptual domains and to interact in others.

The interaction between material specificity and the cognitive strategy applicable to a task is best appreciated in visual perception. The right-cerebral predilection for dealing with complex visual percepts such as faces gives way to left-hemisphere control when such percepts can be labeled verbally, when they are to be categorized,

or when they can be dealt with on the basis of discrete codable features. Even greater malleability in response to the type of cognitive demand is seen in spatial perceptual tasks. Here, right-hemisphere control is the rule for problems that lack a codable element, whereas the left hemisphere takes charge when percepts are classifiable.

Emotional perceptiveness, on the other hand, appears to obey the rule of material specificity, since it is under right-hemisphere control regardless of the cognitive structure of the task—even when the task requires conceptual categorizing. A review of the data on melodic perception shows some conflicting interpretations, but the evidence for intrinsic right-hemisphere specialization is compelling.

Language, with its integration of elementary sensory and motor as well as central associative processes, appears to be rooted in special capacities, governed primarily by the left hemisphere. These processes vary in the degree to which they may be shared by the right hemisphere, or even taken over by that hemisphere, if there is injury to the left. Lexical comprehension for concrete nouns, both auditory and graphic, appears most readily shared by the right brain; control of syntactic and motor articulatory processes is almost exclusively under left-hemisphere control. Some of these lateralized processes are organized temporally; others, such as stop-consonant perception, need not be. It seems clear, however, that the capacity to assign a coded tag to an isolable conceptual unit is preferentially carried out by the left hemisphere, and this capacity, of course, underlies the naming function of language. It may also play a role in the use of pantomime. The active tendency of the left hemisphere to apply this capacity in nonlinguistic processes is seen most conspicuously in the visual perceptual and visuospatial domain, as previously noted.

## The Hemispheres as Information Processors

The versatility of the dichotic listening and visual half-field techniques has made it possible to use them as tools to probe the division of labor between the right and left hemisphere and the information-carrying capacity of a hemisphere. These studies, carried out on normal subjects, have no counterpart as yet in studies of laterally brain-injured populations.

## PRIMING AND OVERLOADING

Kinsbourne (1970) argued for differential hemispheric arousal as the basis for perceptual lateralization under conditions of either unilateral or competing bilateral stimulus presentation (see p. 911). On the basis of this postulate, he predicted that inducing a cognitive set that engaged one hemisphere should bias perception toward the contralateral field. Kinsbourne tested this hypothesis using a tachistoscopic perception task that was unlateralized under baseline conditions. With 32 right-handed adults as subjects, he presented a series of squares with the midpoint of one side at the fixation point, but so positioned that the critical side might be either the right or left vertical or the upper or lower horizontal side of the square. Half the squares had a small gap in one side, and half these gaps overlay the fixation point, whereas the others were located at the midpoint of the side opposite the fixation point. In a baseline condition there was no significant effect of laterality in detecting the gap.

As verbal priming condition, Kinsbourne required subjects to read and remember a list of six easy words before each exposure. They were to recite the first three if a gap was on the left side of the square, the last three if a gap was on the right side, but repeat no words if gaps were absent or were on the upper or lower sides. Under the verbal priming condition, a perceptual advantage appeared when the gap was on the side opposite the fixation point on the right but not on the left.

Hellige and Cox (1976) took into account the fact that using words to be remembered as a prime also imposed an information load on the language-dominant hemisphere. They investigated the relation between this memory load and the amount of right-field bias that it brought about. Using a visual perceptual half-field task —recognizing complex polygons—they found that the slight left-field advantage under baseline conditions shifted to a right-field advantage when a memory load of two or four words was introduced. The left-field advantage reappeared when the memory load was increased to six words. When the lateralized stimuli were words, the right-visual-field advantage of 23 percent, obtained as a baseline, was reduced to only 10 percent with memory loads of two, four, or six words. Hellige, Cox, and Litvac (1979) also

obtained a reversal of field advantage when a verbal memory load was added to a task that normally produced a right-visual-field (left hemisphere) advantage.

The effects reported by Kinsbourne and by Hellige and his associates demonstrated that unlateralized or weakly lateralized stimuli are susceptible to priming by introducing a low-level verbal memory load. When stimuli are already perceptually lateralized to the right, any memory load appears to overtax the left hemisphere and reduce or reverse the right-field advantage. The effects are easily modified by practice and order effects and have not been convincingly replicated (Boles, 1979).

Most reliable effects of intrahemispheric competition are observed when two left-hemisphere-controlled activities are required concurrently. Kinsbourne and Cook (1971) showed that balancing a dowel rod on the right index finger was more disrupted by concurrent speech than balancing it on the left. Similar effects have been found for tapping rate with each hand by Kinsbourne and McMurray (1975), Kinsbourne and Hiscock (1977) and Hellige and Longstreth (1981). Rizzolatti, Bertolini, and Buchtel (1979) found that simple motor reaction time to a light presented randomly to one half-field or the other was lengthened significantly more in the right visual field than the left during verbal activity and during a complexly sequenced finger-tapping test. This effect, which held whether the left hand reacted while the right hand tapped or the reverse, provides incidental support for the concept of left-hemisphere control of sequential movement of either hand. Hellige and Longstreth (1981) showed that cognitive activity in the right hemisphere interfered more with the tapping rate of the left than of the right hand. When one hand solved a block-design puzzle while the other tapped, the interference was greater when the right hand was engaged in solving the puzzle.

## LEVELS OF PROCESSING

It was observed earlier (p. 913) that elementary dimensions of form and shading show little if any lateralization, though right-hemisphere dominance appears in more complex operations. Moscovitch, Scullion, and Christie (1976) report that, during the time course of the development of a complex visual percept, lateralization arises relatively late in the process, whereas the initial extraction of elementary features is unlateralized. Moscovitch et al. presented a series of faces in midfield for 500 msec, that is, long enough for the face to establish full representation in both hemispheres. At various interstimulus intervals (ISIs) after offset, a matching or nonmatching face appeared in either the right or left visual field, and subjects were required to make a same–different response as quickly as possible. For ISIs of less than 100 msec, there were no lateral-field differences in the reaction time for correct judgments, but a left-field (right hemisphere) advantage appeared with longer ISIs. The authors reasoned that up to 100 msec decisions were based on iconic sensory information, which was equally available to both hemispheres. With the decay of the iconic trace, subjects made their judgments on the more stable, encoded representation, which was lateralized in the right hemisphere. This hypothesis was tested by interposing a visual mask almost immediately after the offset of the central face, on the presumption that it would disrupt the iconic trace but leave the longer-term representation intact. In fact, with the interposed mask, left-field (right hemisphere) advantages were obtained at all ISIs.

A somewhat analogous effect has been reported in the auditory sphere with the dichotic listening paradigm. Several investigators have found that the right-ear advantage for verbal material is greater for the stimulus sets reported second from the respective ears than for the sets reported first (Satz, Aschenbach, Pattishall, & Fennell, 1965; Goodglass & Peck, 1972). Oscar-Berman, Goodglass, and Donnenfeld (1974) observed a similar effect favoring the left ear for nonverbal pitch contours. In these instances, it may be that the verbal signal directed to the left hemisphere is encoded in more stable form than is the one to the right hemisphere and hence is more resistant to proactive interference when the left-ear signal is reported first. This differential susceptibility to decay is not manifest in comparisons of the scores for the two ears reported first (cf. Oscar-Berman et al., 1978; and above p. 920).

## COMPETITION BETWEEN RIGHT- AND LEFT-HEMISPHERE-GOVERNED COMPONENTS OF A PERCEPTUAL TASK

The same stimulus material may be operated on primarily by the right hemisphere when a visual perceptual decision is required, and by the left hemisphere when a verbal or categorical decision is required (see p. 914). What is the effect of complicating the perceptual operation that must be completed in order to give a verbal response? Bryden and Allard (1976) showed that letter naming, based on visual half-field presentation, could be shifted from right- to left-field dominance as a function of the perceptual clarity of the type font involved.

Capital letters in 10 different type fonts were presented in 10 blocks of 20 trials to each of 24 right-handed subjects. Within each block, each typeface and each letter appeared once in each visual field. The overall right-field advantage was not significant because of the interaction between visual field and typeface. The three typefaces that most nearly approached simple block letters gave significant right-field advantage. The most perceptually difficult gave left-field advantage. A correlation coefficient of 0.75 was obtained between accuracy of identification for a given typeface and its laterality index. These results suggest that the observed lateral-field advantage may result from contributions from both hemispheres. Varying the visual processing demands on the way to a verbal or categorical response may shift the net visual-field effect to the left.

Berlucchi, Brizzolara, Marzi, Rizzolati, and Umilta (1979) drew the same conclusions with a quite different task. Their visual half-field stimuli were clock faces without numbers and with the hands set to different positions around the dial. Subjects were required to name the time indicated by the hands. Presentation to the left visual field produced more accurate reports than to the right, presumably because the visuospatial component of the task involved a level of right-hemisphere activity that overrode the verbal components.

## PARALLEL PROCESSING

The lateralization indexes obtained in the two foregoing studies may be conceived as the algebraic sum of the left- and right-hemisphere components of a complex process, possibly carried out in sequential fashion (cf. Moscovitch et al., 1976, cited above). The single measure of net lateralization, however, does not permit conclusions on how the components are partitioned, particularly whether the activation of each hemsiphere counteracts the lateralizing influence of the other. The strong form of Kinsbourne's (1973) attentional orientation hypothesis (above, p. 928) predicts that equal activation of the two hemispheres by appropriate stimuli should neutralize laterality effects of both.

A study by Klein, Moscovitch, and Vigna (1976) showed that each hemisphere acted as an independent channel for the concurrent processing of the elements in a complex stimulus for which it was dominant, but that the degree of lateralization could be modified by strong priming procedures. Faces with unrelated concrete words printed above them were presented tachistoscopically in the two visual fields, and the subjects' task was to select both faces from a multiple-choice display and call out both words. However, half the subjects were told that the words were more important and should be reported first; the other half were given the reverse instructions. Overall field-by-stimulus effects were significant ($p < .001$) with a strong bias to the left field for faces and to the right for words. The subgroup subjected to verbal priming, however, showed no field advantage for faces; but the group primed for faces had both a marked left-field advantage for faces (19.9 versus 9.3) and a right-field advantage for words (21.9 versus 12.9) that was equal to that of the verbally primed groups (27.3 versus 17.8).

An analogous result in the dichotic listening mode was obtained by Goodglass and Calderon (1977). They required musically trained subjects to listen to sets of dichotic digits concurrently with dichotic piano notes, and to report both the verbal and tonal information from one ear, which was specified immediately after each presentation. In a second condition, the subjects heard dichotic digits sung in competing tonal patterns and were required to sing back both channels as they had heard them. Independent ear scores for verbal and tonal content were obtained for each condition, and each was converted to a laterality index. These indexes were compared to the laterality indexes for the baseline conditions of simple dichotic listening to digits and tonal patterns separately. Under all conditions, equally strong left-ear advantages were found for tones and right-ear advantages for digits. While no explicit effort was made to introduce an extra lateral bias by priming, it was clear that the concurrently activated hemispheres did not neutralize each other's laterality in any way.

## Biological Aspects of Cerebral Dominance

### Genetic Factors

#### HAND PREFERENCE

The investigation of genetic factors in cerebral dominance relies on familial patterns of hand preference, since direct evidence of familial patterns of language lateralization is unobtainable. The justification for treating hand preference as an index of functional brain laterality lies in the evidence cited that right-handedness in the individual predicts left-hemisphere language dominance with nearly 100-percent certainty, while left-handedness indicates a high probability of either bilateral or right-hemisphere language (Goodglass & Quadfasel, 1954; Gloning et al., 1969; Penfield & Roberts, 1959). Clinical data further indicate that the history of familial-handedness modifies the incidence and rate of recovery from aphasia over and above the manifest hand preference of the patient. Luria (1970) reports that, of 18 completely right-handed patients who had left-handed family members, none were left with a lasting severe aphasia following injury to the dominant language area; in contrast, 48 of 64 who had a purely right-handed family history remained permanently and severely aphasic. In a survey of left-handers who had suffered injury to the perisylvian zone of either hemisphere, Hécaen and Sauguet (1971) observed that while those from left-handed families were equally vulnerable to aphasia from injury to the right or left brain, those from completely right-handed stock were aphasic only after left-sided lesions.

Experimental data from normal subjects, using the dichotic listening paradigm, provide further evidence for the importance of genetic factors in the lateralization of cognitive functions. Zurif and Bryden (1969) found a greater incidence of left-ear advantage among familial than nonfamilial left-handers and Carter-Saltzman (1979) reported a significant left-ear advantage for familial left-handers while nonfamilial left-handers performed like right handers.

The basic fact to be accounted for by a theory on the inheritance of handedness is the incidence of left-handedness among the offspring of right–right, right–left, and left–left matings. Reports on large samples have been published by Chamberlain (1928), Rife (1940), and Annett (1978).

**Table 13.1. Summary of Chamberlain (1928) and Rife (1940) data on incidence of left-handedness in offspring, as a function of handedness of parents**

| | Type of mating Father × Mother | N | Lh boys N | Lh boys % | Lh girls N | Lh girls % | Total Lh N | Total Lh % |
|---|---|---|---|---|---|---|---|---|
| Chamberlain | R × R | 2031 | 223 | 5.1 | 84 | 3.1 | 307 | 3.9 |
| | L × R | 82 | 21 | 12.2 | 5 | 5.2 | 26 | 9.7 |
| | R × L | 55 | 18 | 14.0 | 9 | 13.0 | 27 | 13.7 |
| | L × L | 33 | 26 | 39.6 | 20 | 54.0 | 46 | 46.0 |
| Rife | R × R | 620 | 105 | 8.8 | 46 | 5.7 | 151 | 7.6 |
| | L × R | 32 | 9 | 18.4 | 9 | 18.0 | 18 | 18.2 |
| | R × L | 30 | 6 | 15.4 | 10 | 33.3 | 16 | 21.3 |
| | L × L | 5 | 3 | 60.0 | 3 | 50.0 | 6 | 54.5 |

However, the proportion of nonright-handers identified varies drastically with the criterion adopted for distinguishing right- from left-handers. The measures commonly used are inventories of 10 to 20 skilled unimanual actions, for each of which the subject indicates his preferred hand. Many such inventories have been developed, including recent articles by Oldfield (1971), Annett (1970), and Briggs and Nebes (1975). Trankell (1950), using a 15-item inventory in a survey of 10,000 students, noted that those identified by teachers as right-handers preferred the left hand for a mean of only 0.7 activities, while those considered to be left-handers gave a mean of 10 left-handed preferences out of the 15. This finding appears to indicate that right-handers are consistent in their hand preferences whereas left-handers represent a heterogeneous population and could be more accurately designated as nonright-handers (cf. Humphrey, 1951). This parallels the extremely strong left-brain language laterality of right-handers and the relatively indeterminate language laterality of nonright-handers. Annett (1980), however, points out that both the results of manual skill tests and handedness inventories indicate that hand preference really lies on a continuum, and that any dichotomy must be based on an arbitrary cutoff score on an inventory. Thus, various populations sampled with Annett's 12-item inventory yield 60 to 70 percent pure right-handers, 25 to 35 percent mixed-handers and 3 to 5 percent pure left-handers. Clearly, as the criteria for identifying left-handers become more liberal, the larger will be the proportion of persons performing from one to 11 of the 12 sampled activities with the right hand who are included on the left-hand side of the dichotomy.

Table 13.1, summarizing the results of the Chamberlain and Rife series, shows that the percentage of left-handed offspring increases to a maximum of about 50 percent when both parents are left-handed. Annett (1975, 1978, 1985) proposes to explain these and the associated statistical data by means of a simple Mendelian model, based on a single dominant gene, referred to as the right-shift factor. This factor, when present, interacts with random biological and experiential factors to bias the development of language control to the left hemisphere and of hand preference toward the right hand. Its absence (in L × L matings) leaves only random influences at work, explaining the even distribution of hand preferences among offspring of such matings. Levy and Nagylaki (1972) dispute the Annett model, with a more complex one involving two pairs of genes, one for language lateralization (left dominant, right recessive) and one for correspondence of hand preference to language laterality (contralateral dominant, ipsilateral recessive). For discussions on this controversy, see Levy and Nagylaki (1972), Levy (1976, 1977), Annett (1978), Hudson (1975), and Morgan (1977).

## WRITING POSTURE AND CEREBRAL ORGANIZATION

Levy and Reid (1976) investigated the common observation that many left-handed writers hold their writing hand above the line of writing, with the pen directed downwards, whereas others use the same posture that right-handers use. Rare right-handers also adopt the inverted writing posture. The explanation that the inverted posture is used to avoid covering the writing just completed is negated by the observation that Israelis, writing Hebrew from right to left, show the same distribution of writing posture as Americans, as a function of handedness. Levy and Reid administered two visual half-field tachistoscopic tests, one involving dot localization, the other involving the reading of consonant-vowel-consonant (CVC) syllables. Their subjects were 24 left-handers with inverted writing posture, 24 with non-inverted posture, 24 normal right-hand writers and one right-hander with inverted posture. With few exceptions, right-handers and left-handed inverters had right-field advantage for CVCs and a left-field advantage for dot localization. The noninverting left-handers showed the reverse pattern of lateralization, as did the one right-handed inverter. Levy and Reid propose that an inverted writing posture signals that language is mediated by the hemisphere ipsilateral to the writing hand and vice versa. Moscovitch and Smith (1979) succeeded in replicating some of Levy and Reid's results—though only with visual half-field techniques—but other investigators have failed to replicate the Levy and Reid findings, either with tachistoscopic half-field measures or with dichotic listening (McKeever & Van Deventer, 1980; M.C. Corballis, cited as a personal communication by Herron, Galin, Johnstone, & Ornstein, 1979). Herron et al. (1979) used both dichotic listening and EEG alpha asymmetry measures to compare right-handers with both inverting and non-inverting left-handers. The authors took EEG measures from three symmetrically paired locations on the scalp during four language activities and one visuospatial task. At the occipital EEG leads, the left-right alpha power ratios indicated greater right-sided activation during writing and reading for the noninverting left-handers than for the other left-handed group, a result that is in the direction of the Levy-Reid hypothesis. No differences were observed in other comparisons. The status of writing posture as a correlate of cerebral organization remains in doubt. If anything, it seems to be related to the lateralization of visual language processes, but there is no satisfactory account for this relation.

### Anatomical Factors

The long-standing assumption that the two cerebral hemispheres were morphologically symmetrical was shown to be unfounded when Geschwind and Levitsky (1968) reported an asymmetry that appeared to be closely related to language function. On exposing the superior surfaces of the two temporal lobes (planum temporale) in 100 brains, they found that the region posterior to the primary auditory areas was larger on the left than on the right in 65 percent of cases, smaller on the left in only 11 percent, and equal in 24. These proportions have subsequently been confirmed for both adults and infants and even for fetal brains (Teszner, Tsavaras, Gruner, & Hécaen, 1972; Wada, Clarke, & Hamm, 1975; Witelson & Pallie, 1973).

Corresponding to this asymmetry is one in the shape of the sylvian fissure, which curves upward more anteriorly in the right than in the left hemisphere. Rubens (1977) found this difference in 25 of 36 brains, the remaining 11 being equivocally different. Since the planum temporale corresponds to a major speech zone (Wernicke's area), it is tempting to relate the anatomical asymmetries to functional lateralization. While there is, as yet, no direct evidence of correlation at a behavioral level in individuals, there is some evidence relating the direction of brain asymmetries to handedness, with left-handers showing more nearly equal anatomic structures on the two sides (Galaburda, LeMay, Kemper, & Geschwind, 1978). The importance of the anatomic brain asymmetries is that they represent a difference between left and right brains that is clearly genetically based and present from birth. Correlations with behavioral indexes are still being awaited, but the relation to handedness suggests that there is a common genetic factor relating anatomic asymmetries to functional asymmetries.

### Developmental Aspects

#### CLINICAL EVIDENCE

Lenneberg (1967) proposed that the two cerebral hemispheres were equipotential for language at birth and that lateralization to the left hemisphere developed, with maturation, to completion at puberty. The clinical basis for this position appeared fairly convincing. Children born with one atrophic hemisphere, or who develop major unilateral brain damage before they have begun to talk, develop apparently similar language ability regardless of the side of lesion, often functioning within normal limits. For example, Basser (1962) reported that there were no differences in either level of language function or verbal IQ between 48 children with early left-hemisphere and 54 with early right-hemisphere lesions. Basser's data also indicated that unilateral lesions in children who had already begun to talk produced language disturbance after right-brain damage in 7 of 15 cases, that is, half as often as with left-brain damage, where the incidence was 13 of 15 cases. Woods and Teuber (1978), surveying the literature prior to 1927 on acquired aphasia in children, found similarly that over one-third of reported cases involved right-hemisphere lesions (172 right vs. 318 left). The final link in the chain of evidence motivating Lenneberg's position is the well-known fact that young children who develop aphasia after a unilateral lesion usually regain speech rapidly (Clarus, 1874) and that the degree of recovery decreases after puberty, so that permanent and severe aphasia is common in adults.

More recent clinical data argue more strongly for strong left cerebral lateralization from the time of beginning language acquisition. Woods and Teuber, in their own clinical material, found aphasia after right cerebral injury in only four of 31 children from two to 14, two of whom were left-handed. In contrast, 25 of 34 in the same age range developed aphasia from similar lesions on the left. Their 1978 survey of the literature since 1942 reveals only 21 cases (7 left-handed) of acquired childhood aphasia following right-hemisphere damage, as opposed to 249 (5 left-handed) following left-brain damage. Kinsbourne and Hiscock (1977) in a retrospective survey of all acquired childhood aphasias in the Hospital for Sick Children in Toronto found that, of 30 children under the age of 5, only four had right-hemisphere lesions.

Woods and Teuber (1978) suggested that the high incidence of aphasia reported in the earlier neurological literature for children with right-hemisphere involvement could be explained by the prevalence in these cases of systemic infections. A left-sided paralysis was taken as evidence of unilateral right cerebral involvement when, in fact, the brain may have had bilateral pathology. The introduction in about 1940 of antibiotics and other modern practices in medical management may have been responsible for eliminating most or all of these cases of undiagnosed left cerebral pathology.

To sum up, the clinical evidence indicates that the advantage to the left hemisphere for the mediation of language exists from the earliest time of language acquisition, but that the plasticity of the brain in the early years usually allows the right hemisphere to substitute quite efficiently for a damaged left hemisphere until early adolescence at least.

EXPERIMENTAL EVIDENCE

Electrophysiological techniques offer the easiest method of investigating the brain activity of the preverbal child. Molfese (1972) compared the evoked auditory potentials derived from left and right temporal electrodes in response to CV syllables (ba, da), words (boy, dog), a musical signal (C major chord on the piano), and a burst of noise. Ten infants (mean age 5.8 months), 11 children (mean age 6 years) and 10 young adults (mean age 24 years) served as subjects.

All but four of the 31 subjects showed greater peak-to-peak amplitudes from the left temporal than the right temporal leads in response to speech stimuli, and all but one showed the reverse asymmetry for the musical chord. In fact, the asymmetry was significantly greater in infants than in adults.

In a further study by Molfese et al. (1975), neonates less than a day old failed to show hemispheric asymmetries to acoustic parameters of speech stimuli on which adults showed the left hemisphere predominating over the right. In this experiment, the authors made use of the fact that the evoked response habituates with repeated presentation of the same signal but increases (dishabituates) when a change in the signal is perceived. Molfese et al. presented 15 repetitions of a given CV syllable and then shifted to another that differed in either consonant voicing (ba to pa) or place of articulation (ba to da). Dishabituation was measured by comparing the average of the last seven preshift responses with the average of the first seven postshift responses. The authors found that dishabituation occurred only in the left-hemisphere lead in adults, for both voicing and place of articulation. Neonates, on the other hand, showed dishabituation in both hemispheres to a change in voicing, but no reaction from either hemisphere to a change in place of articulation.

While the first and second Molfese experiments are not parallel, the results suggest that the selective sensitivity of the left hemisphere to the acoustic features of speech is present at six months but not at birth. The results of Molfese et al., which use evoked potentials, are entirely consistent with data of Gardiner and Walter (1977), cited earlier.

Infants' perceptual discrimination can also be studied by measuring their nonnutritive, high-amplitude sucking (Siqueland & DeLucia, 1969). In this technique a change in the sucking rate is used as an indicator that the infant has perceived a change in a recurring stimulus. Entus (1977) used this paradigm, in combination with dichotic stimulus presentation, to determine whether preverbal infants (mean age about 75 days) were differentially sensitive in the right and left ear to speech (CV syllables) and to musical quality. In the verbal experiment, Entus presented CV syllables (e.g., *da* vs. *ba*) dichotically until the sucking rate habituated to a rate two-thirds of the preceding maximum rate, at which point the stimulus in one ear was changed to another syllable (e.g., to *da* vs. *ma*). In the tonal experiment, the first series consisted of dichotic presentations of two different instruments (e.g., piano vs. viola or viola vs. bassoon) playing a 440 Hz, 500 msec tone). After habituation, the instrument was changed in either the left or right ear.

In 34 of 48 infants (71 percent) sensitivity to consonantal change in the CV condition was greater in the right ear, while in 38 of the infants (79 percent) sensitivity to changes in tonal quality was greater in the left ear. These proportions are not unlike those observed on adult samples, and they reinforce the conclusions of Molfese et al. (1975) and Gardiner and Walter (1977) that asymmetry of hemispheric function is operative a short time after birth.

Studies of brain laterality in later childhood have relied chiefly on dichotic listening, using competing strings of digits and requiring response by free report. This method has been found usable with children as young as three years, since the number of items presented can be reduced to one or two words in each ear. Kimura (1963b) tested 145 girls and boys from age four to nine and found right-ear advantage in all age groups. Of the studies that involved children as young as three all reported right-ear advantage at that age (Nagafuchi, 1970; Witelson, 1976; Hiscock & Kinsbourne, 1976; Peck, 1976; Kinsbourne & Hiscock, 1977). Most studies that explicitly tested for differences in degree of asymmetry with maturation failed to detect any change (Kinsbourne & Hiscock, 1977; Goodglass, 1973; Berlin, Hughes, Lowe-Bell, & Berlin, 1973). For a review of all published studies of laterality in children up to 1976, see Witelson (1977).

Investigations of lateralization of nonverbal auditory stimuli in children have used various adaptations of the dichotic listening paradigm. Knox and Kimura (1970) presented competing 4 sec segments of environmental sounds to the two ears of children aged five to eight and required them to make oral identification of the sounds. While an overall left-ear advantage was observed, this was not significant for 5-year-olds. Peck (1976) used a series of five hummed nursery tune segments recorded dichotically in their 10 possible combinations and trained his subjects to select from multiple choice the picture (three blind mice, birthday cake, etc.) corresponding to the name of the song. Consistent left-ear advantages were obtained at all ages from three to nine. A similar result was obtained with dichotically presented pairs of animal sounds, also involving responses by picture selection.

Several investigators have used the dichotic listening method to investigate changes in later maturity and old age. Clark and Knowles (1973), using competing three-digit sets as their stimuli, found a progressive decline in accuracy of report from the left ear, as compared with the right, in subjects in each age decade from the 40s to the 70s, which they attributed to a decline in information-processing capacity. Borod and Goodglass (1980), using a similar technique to examine 102 subjects whose ages ranged from 24 to 79, failed to replicate this finding, observing only a uniform decline in accuracy in both ears in subjects over 50, with a uniform right-ear advantage for digits across the entire age span. Borod and Goodglass also administered Peck's dichotic nursery-tune test to all their subjects and found a left-ear advantage that again did not interact with age. An absence of age differences in lateralization for verbal and visuospatial material was also reported by Nebes, Madden, and Berg (1980).

In summary, the weight of the clinical and experimental evidence supports the view that the left and right cerebral hemispheres differ in verbal and nonverbal processing from shortly after birth, and that, barring injury to the brain, the functional asymmetry remains consistent throughout life.

**Table 13.2. Sex-related differences in cognitive abilities and disabilities**

| Nature of ability or deficit | Sex-related finding | Source |
|---|---|---|
| Language skills | Females outscore males in most samples, from age 10 through college | Maccoby & Jacklin (1974) |
| Developmental reading disability | Male : female ratio greater than 2 : 1 | Eisenberg (1966) |
| Stuttering | Male : female ratio 2 : 1 | Ingram (1975) |
| Retarded speech development | Male : female ratio from 2 : 1 to 5 : 1 in various series | Ingram (1975) |
| Visuospatial skills | Males outscore females in almost all samples from age 10 through college level | Maccoby & Jacklin (1974) |
| Mathematics | Males outscore females in almost all samples from age 10 through college level | Maccoby & Jacklin (1974); Benbow & Stanley (1980) |

## Sex Differences in Cerebral Laterality

### CLINICAL BACKGROUND

There are well-established differences between males and females in a number of those cognitive abilities (language, visuospatial skills, calculation) that have been shown to be mediated preferentially by the left or right hemisphere. Some of these differences have been shown to persist into the adult years. Indeed a number of language-related disorders (developmental speech delay, developmental reading disability, stuttering) are universally recognized as several times more frequent in boys than in girls. The sex-linked disorder, Turner's syndrome, which is specific to females who lack one of their X-chromosomes, is marked by a severe deficit in visuospatial skills, in a context of delayed and incomplete sexual maturation. For economy, these sex-linked differences in cognitive skills are summarized in Table 13.2. For more complete reviews of the extensive literature, including the interaction between genetic and socio-cultural influences, see Maccoby and Jacklin (1974), Harris (1978), and McGlone (1980).

It must be stressed, however, that the differences in proficiency shown in Table 13.2 do not necessarily imply sex differences in their cerebral lateralization. In fact, there is no clinically observable difference between individual males and females in the behavioral consequences of unilateral brain lesions (Hier & Kaplan, 1980). The possibility that subtle quantitative differences do exist has emerged only since the application of statistical methods to groups of brain-injured male and female patients and the recent study of normal males and females by means of the noninvasive methods of dichotic listening and visual half-field stimulus presentation.

### STUDIES OF UNILATERALLY BRAIN-INJURED GROUPS

Several studies comparing groups of male and female patients who have suffered unilateral brain damage concur in finding that right-handed men are more vulnerable than women to selective cognitive deficits following damage to either hemisphere. Lansdell and Urbach (1965) reported on patients of both sexes who had undergone either a right or left temporal lobectomy for the relief of epilepsy. Using a verbal-nonverbal ratio derived from the Wechsler-Bellevue Intelligence Scale, they found that males showed selectively impaired verbal skills after left-temporal removal and nonverbal skills after right-temporal removal. Females in the two groups with lateral lesions did not differ in the verbal-nonverbal ratio.

A similar result was obtained by McGlone (1978) on a sample of 85 right-handed adults, using the verbal-performance IQ discrepancy on the Wechsler Adult Intelligence Scale. Males had a significant verbal IQ deficiency after left cerebral damage (N = 23) and a significant performance IQ deficiency after damage to the right brain (N = 17), whereas women showed no significant difference between verbal and performance IQ after either right (N = 17) or left (N = 20) brain damage. These findings might lead one to expect either a smaller incidence of aphasia in women following left-brain injury or more cases of aphasia following right-brain injury in women. As to the first of these expectations, McGlone (1977), in examining the incidence of language disorders in 35 men and 47 women who had suffered left brain damage, found aphasia in women only one-third as often as in men. However, only 16 patients were aphasic, and this finding has yet to be confirmed in a larger series. Hier and Kaplan (1980), citing the combined data in three series totaling 767 aphasic patients, found a ratio of 53 percent males to 47 percent females. As to the alternate possibility, the incidence of crossed aphasia (i.e., aphasia produced by right brain injury in a right-handed person) is so low that McGlone (1980) reveals only 21 reported cases since 1934, only nine of whom were women.

Little systematic research has been carried out on sex differences in the effect of brain lesions on visuospatial function, but the studies reported present a picture analogous to that for verbal abilities. Lansdell (1962) administered the Graves Design Judgment test both pre- and postoperatively to 22 men and women who underwent unilateral temporal lobectomy. In the right temporal group, men's scores declined while women's scores rose. The reverse pattern was observed in the left temporal group. The interaction between sex, side of operation, and change in score was significant and independent of the level of the preoperative score. McGlone and Kertesz (1973) compared males and females who had suffered unilateral injury to the left (35 males; 22 females) or right (13 males, 8 females) brain, using a visuospatial manipulative task (Wechsler-Bellevue Block Design), an intelligence test (Ravens Colored Progressive Matrices), and a set of language-skill tests. While male and female groups showed equal scores on the intelligence and language measures, there was a trend (p < .10) for males with right-brain damage to be more impaired on the block designs than any of the other groups.

STUDIES OF NORMAL GROUPS

Applications of dichotic listening and visual half-field studies to male and female groups have generally found a greater proportion of males than females displaying an advantage for verbal stimuli presented to the right ear. Lake and Bryden (1976) selected 144 subjects from a pool of over two thousand students who had been given a handedness inventory (Crovitz & Zener, 1962) and divided their subjects into predominantly right- and predominantly left-handed at the midpoint of the distribution of their scores on the inventory. These two groups were divided evenly into males and females and, in turn, into groups of 18 subjects each, those with and without a history of familial sinistrality (FS). Their dichotic stimuli were the CV syllables *ba, da, ga, pa, ta, ka,* presented one to each ear in all possible combinations for a total of 30 dichotic presentations. A right-left ear ratio (Halwes, 1969) was computed for each subject in which a positive value indicated right-ear superiority and a negative value left-ear superiority. Males had a greater mean right-ear advantage than did females. More striking, however, was the distribution of individuals by sex and ear laterality. Among right-handers, 30 of the 36 males but only 22 of the 36 females had a right-ear advantage. The corresponding figure for left-handers was 24 males and 20 females. History of FS showed opposite interactions with sex, in that the males with FS showed the strongest right-ear dominance, regardless of handedness, whereas females with FS were most likely to have left-ear dominance. Bryden (1979), reanalyzing earlier data of his own on dichotic digit presentation, found a right-ear advantage in 75 percent of 112 men but in only 58 percent of 60 women. Harshman and Remington (1974), combining three sets of data derived from administration of dichotic CV syllables to men and women, also report a higher incidence of right-ear advantage in men than in women. While a number of dichotic listening studies failed to obtain sex differences in mean right-ear advantage (Briggs & Nebes, 1975; Bryden, 1979; McGlone & Davidson, 1973), in no studies of normal subjects did females show either greater magnitude or greater frequency of right-ear advantage than male subjects.

Studies of visual half-field effects for verbal stimuli are more consistent in confirming that the strongest right-field (left hemisphere) effects are observed in right-handed males. Bradshaw, Gates, and Nettleton (1977) examined 24 males and 24 females, half of whom were right-handed and half left-handed. The subjects, who viewed a four-letter string presented tachistoscopically in either the left or right visual field, reported whether the stimulus was an English word or a nonword (lexical decision paradigm) by manually pressing a button. The principal finding was a sex-by-field interaction for right-handers: males had shorter latencies to presentation to the right than to left visual field, whereas females showed no significant differences between fields. Moreover, eleven of the twelve males showed the expected right-field (and presumed left hemisphere) advantage, while seven of the females showed a weak left-field advantage. Left-handed subjects showed a similar directional trend but half-field differences were smaller and short of significance. In a second experiment, Bradshaw and Gates (1978) replicated their earlier finding of a sex-by-field interaction in the lexical decision tasks, but found that their female subjects showed as much right-field dominance as males in latency for oral word reading.

Evidence of strong lateralization in right-handed males but not females is also reported by Graves et al. (1981). These authors, like Bradshaw et al., used a visual half-field lexical decision paradigm, with response latency as the dependent variable. Eleven of the 12 males, but only seven of the females, showed the right-field advantage. A few studies (Hannay & Boyer, 1978; Leehey et al., 1978) have failed to detect sex-by-field interactions. No studies have reported greater right-field (left hemisphere) asymmetries for women. All these studies are limited by the small numbers of subjects in each group, since none had more than 12 in each sex-by-handedness cell. The consistency of the findings of greater hemispheric disparity among males than females, however, must be taken seriously, even though there may be no corresponding difference in their susceptibility to aphasia. It should be noted, however, that the experimental tasks in which women have shown inconsistent lateralization involved language perception, rather than production. Bradshaw and Gates's (1978) report that latency for oral word reading was equally lateralized in their male and female subjects may indicate that language production in general is controlled as consistently by the left hemisphere in women as in men. If this result can be replicated, it would go far toward

reconciling experimental findings in normal subjects with clinical experience among the brain injured.

In the visual perceptual and visuospatial domains, tachistoscopic half-field studies have generally reported stronger and more consistent left visual field (right hemisphere) dominance in men than in women. Sasanuma and Kobayoshi (1978), using the line-orientation test of Benton et al. (1975), found a distinct left-field advantage in a group of 14 right-handed men, but no field difference at all among 14 women. Perez, Mazzucchi, and Rizzolatti (1975) found left-field advantages in latency for face recognition only for men. Rizzolatti and Buchtel (1977) conducted two successive experiments with two independent subject groups of eight men and eight women, varying only the stimulus duration from 100 msec in the first to 20 msec in the second. Again the men without exception had shorter latencies for face recognition in the left visual field, while the women showed no trend whatsoever toward difference between fields. The shorter exposure time markedly increased the disparity between fields for men without affecting that for women.

Noting that women as well as men have been shown to have a right-field advantage in other facial recognition studies (e.g., Young & Ellis, 1976), Rizzolatti and Buchtel point out that each of these studies has involved an extended exposure to a multiple-choice matching display. Women have failed to demonstrate a field advantage when a previously established target face was to be identified on a single exposure. Thus the possibility exists that this apparent disparity between the sexes may reflect either some difference in the strategies used or a sex difference in the conditions under which lateralization is activated.

## References

Adrian, E.D. & Matthews, B.H.C. (1934). The Berger rhythm: Potential changes from occipital lobes in man. *Brain, 57,* 355–385.

Albert, M.L. & Bear, D. (1974). Time to understand. A case study of pure word deafness with reference to the role of time in auditory comprehension. *Brain, 57,* 383–394.

Albert, M.S., Butters, N., & Brandt, J. (1980). Memory for remote events in alcoholics. *Journal of Studies on Alcohol, 41,* 1071–1081.

Albert, M.S., Butters, N., & Brandt, J. (1981). Patterns of remote memory in amnesic and demented patients. *Archives of Neurology, 38,* 495–500.

Albert, M.S., Butters, N., & Levin, J. (1979). Temporal gradients in the retrograde amnesia of patients with alcoholic Korsakoff's disease. *Archives of Neurology, 36,* 211–216.

Andreewsky, E. & Seron, X. (1975). Implicit processing of grammatical rules in a case of agrammatism. *Cortex, 11,* 379–390.

Annett, M. (1970). A classification of handedness by association analysis. *British Journal of Psychology, 61,* 303–321.

Annett, M. (1975). Hand preference and the laterality of cerebral speech. *Cortex, 11,* 305–328.

Annett, M. (1978). Genetic and nongenetic influences on handedness. *Behavior Genetics, 8,* 227–249.

Annett, M. (1985). *Left, right, hand and brain: the right shift theory.* London: Erlbaum.

Auerbach, S.H., Allard, T., Naeser, M., Alexander, M.P., & Albert, M.L. (1982). Pure word deafness: Analysis of a case with bilateral lesions and a defect at the prephonemic level. *Brain, 105,* 271–300.

Badal, J. (1888). Contribution à l'étude des cécités psychiques: Alexie agraphie, hémianopsie inférieure, trouble du sens de l'espace. *Archives d'Ophtalmologie, 8,* 97–117.

Baddeley, A.D. & Warrington, E.K. (1970). Amnesia and the distinction between long- and short-term memory. *Journal of Verbal Learning and Verbal Behavior, 9,* 176–189.

Bakan, P. (1969). Hypnotizability, laterality of eye movement, and functional brain asymmetry. *Perceptual and Motor Skills, 28,* 927–932.

Baker, E., Blumstein, S.E., & Goodglass, H. (1981). Interaction between phonological and semantic factors in auditory comprehension. *Neuropsychologia, 19,* 1–15.

Barton, D. (1980). Phonemic perception in children. In G.A. Yeni-Komshian, J.F. Kavanaugh, & C.A. Ferguson (Eds.), *Child phonology*: Vol. II. *Perception.* pp. 97–116. New York: Academic Press.

Barton, M.I. (1971). Recall of generic properties of words in aphasic patients. *Cortex, 7,* 73–82.

Barton, M.I., Goodglass, H., & Shai, A. (1965). Differential recognition of tachistoscopically presented English and Hebrew words in right and left visual fields. *Perceptual and Motor Skills, 21,* 431–437.

Basser, L. (1962). Hemiplegia of early onset and the faculty of speech with special reference to the effects of hemispherectomy. *Brain, 85,* 427–460.

Benbow, C.P. & Stanley, J.C. (1980). Sex differences in mathematical ability: Fact or artifact? *Science, 210,* 1262–1264.

Benson, D.F. & Geschwind, N. (1967). Shrinking retrograde amnesia. *Journal of Neurology, Neurosurgery and Psychiatry, 30,* 539–544.

Benton, A.L. (1980). Visuoperceptive, visuospatial, and visuoconstructive disorders. In K. Heilman & E. Valenstein (Eds.), *Clinical neuropsychology.* pp. 186–232. New York: Oxford University Press.

Benton, A.L., Hannay, H.J., & Varney, N.R. (1975). Visual perception of line direction in patients with unilateral brain disease. *Neurology, 25,* 907–910.

Benton, A.L. & Joynt, R.J. (1960). Early descriptions of aphasia. *Archives of Neurology, 3,* 205–222.

Benton, A.L., Levin, H.S., & Varney, N.R. (1973). Tactile perception of direction in normal subjects. *Neurology, 23,* 1248–1250.

Benton, A.L. & Van Allen, N.W. (1968). Impairment in facial recognition in patients with cerebral disease. *Cortex, 4,* 344–358.

Berger, H. (1926). Ueber Rechenstörungen bei herderkrankungen des Grosshirns. *Archiv für Psychiatrie, 78,* 238–263.

Berko, J. (1958). The child's learning of English morphology. *Word, 14,* 150–177.

Berlin, C.I. (1977). Hemispheric asymmetry in auditory tasks. In S. Harnad, R.W. Doty, L. Goldstein, J. Jaynes, & G. Krauthamer (Eds.), *Lateralization in the nervous system.* pp. 303–324. New York: Academic Press.

Berlin, C.I., Hughes, L.F., Lowe-Bell, S.S., & Berlin, H.L. (1973). Dichotic right ear advantage in children 5 to 13. *Cortex, 9,* 393–401.

Berlucchi, G., Brizzolara, D., Marzi, C.A., Rizzolati, G., & Umilta, C. (1979). The role of stimulus discriminability and verbal codability in hemispheric specialization for visuospatial tasks. *Neuropsychologia, 17,* 195–202.

Bever, T. & Chiarello, R. (1974). Cerebral dominance in musicians and nonmusicians. *Science, 185,* 537–539.

Biber, C., Butters, N., Rosen, J., Gerstman, L., & Mattis, S. (1981). Encoding strategies and recognition of faces by alcoholic Korsakoff and other brain-damaged patients. *Journal of Clinical Neuropsychology, 3,* 315–330.

Bingley, T. (1958). Mental symptoms in temporal lobe epilepsy. *Acta Psychiatrica et Neurologica,* Suppl. *120,* 33.

Bisiach, E. (1966). Perceptual factors in the pathogenesis of anomia. *Cortex, 2,* 90–95.

Bisiach, E., Nichelli, P., & Spinnler, H. (1976). Hemispheric functional asymmetry in visual discrimination between univariate stimuli: An analysis of sensitivity and response criteria. *Neuropsychologia, 14,* 335–342.

Bloomfield, L. (1942). Linguistics and reading. *Elementary English Review, 19*, 125–130.

Blumstein, S.E. (1973). *A phonological investigation of aphasic speech.* The Hague: Mouton.

Blumstein, S.E., Baker, E., & Goodglass, H. (1977). Phonological factors in auditory comprehension in aphasia. *Neuropsychologia, 15*, 19–30.

Blumstein, S.E. & Cooper, W.E. (1974). Hemispheric processing of intonation contours. *Cortex, 10*, 146–158.

Blumstein, S.E., Cooper, W.E., Goodglass, H., Statlender, S., & Gottlieb, J. (1980). Production deficits in aphasia: A voice-onset time analysis. *Brain and Language, 9*, 153–170.

Blumstein, S.E., Cooper, W.E., Zurif, E.B., & Caramazza, A. (1977). The perception and production of voice-onset time in aphasia. *Neuropsychologia, 15*, 371–383.

Blumstein, S.E., Goodglass, H., & Tartter, V. (1975). The reliability of ear advantage in dichotic listening. *Brain and Language, 2*, 226–236.

Bodamer, J. (1947). Die Prosop-Agnosie (die Agnosie des Physiognomieerkennens). *Archiv für Psychiatrie und Nervenkrankheit, 179*, 6–53.

Boles, D.B. (1979). Laterally biased attention with concurrent verbal load: Multiple failures to replicate. *Neuropsychologia, 17*, 353–362.

Bonhoeffer, K. (1923). Zur Klinik und Lokalisation des Agrammatismus und der rechts-links Desorientierung. *Monatschrift für Psychiatrie und Neurologie, 54*, 11–42.

Borod, J.C. & Goodglass, H. (1980). Lateralization of linguistic and melodic processing with age. *Neuropsychologia, 18*, 79–83.

Bradley, D. & Garrett, M. (1979). Effects of vocabulary type in word recognition. Working paper, Cognitive Science Center, MIT.

Bradley, D., Garrett, M., & Zurif, E.B. (1980). Syntactic deficits in Broca's aphasia. In D. Caplan (Ed.), *Biological studies of mental processes.* pp. 269–286. Cambridge, MA: MIT Press.

Bradshaw, J.L. & Gates, E.A. (1978). Visual field difference in verbal tasks: Effects of task familiarity and sex of subject. *Brain and Language, 5*, 166–187.

Bradshaw, J.L., Gates, E.A., & Nettleton, N.C. (1977). Bihemispheric involvement in lexical decisions: Handedness and a possible sex difference. *Neuropsychologia, 15*, 277–286.

Bradshaw, J.L., Gates, E.A., & Patterson, K.E. (1976). Hemispheric differences in processing visual patterns. *Quarterly Journal of Experimental Psychology, 28*, 667–681.

Bradshaw, J.L., Taylor, M.J., Patterson, K.E., & Nettleton, N.C. (1980). Upright and inverted faces and housefronts in the two visual fields. A right

and a left hemisphere contribution. *Journal of Clinical Neuropsychology, 2*, 245–258.

Brain, W.R. (1941). Visual disorientation with special reference to lesions of the right cerebral hemisphere. *Brain, 64*, 224–272.

Brandt, J., Butters, N., Ryan, C., & Bayog, R. (1983). Cognitive loss and recovery in chronic alcohol abusers. *Archives of General Psychiatry, 40*, 435–442.

Briggs, G.G. & Nebes, R.D. (1975). Patterns of hand preference in a student population. *Cortex, 11*, 230–238.

Broadbent, D.E. (1956). Successive responses to simultaneous stimuli. *Quarterly Journal of Experimental Psychology, 8*, 145–162.

Broca, P. (1861). Remarques sur le siège de la faculté du langage articulé suivie d'une observation d'aphémie. *Bulletin de la Société d'Anatomie* (Paris) *6*, 330–357.

Broca, P. (1865). Sur le siège de la faculté du langage articulé. *Bulletin de la Société d'Anthropologie, 6*, 337–393.

Brooks, N. & Baddeley, A. (1976). What can amnesic patients learn? *Neuropsychologia, 14*, 111–122.

Brown, J. (1958). Some tests of the decay theory of immediate memory. *Quarterly Journal of Experimental Psychology, 10*, 12–21.

Brown, R.W. & McNeill, D. (1966). The "tip-of-the-tongue" phenomenon. *Journal of Verbal Learning and Verbal Behavior, 5*, 325–337.

Bryden, M.P. (1979). Evidence for sex differences in cerebral organization. In M. Wittig & A. Peterson (Eds.), *Determinants of sex related differences in cognitive functioning.* pp. 121–144. New York: Academic Press.

Bryden, M.P. & Allard, F. (1976). Visual hemifield differences depend on typeface. *Brain and Language, 3*, 191–200.

Buchsbaum, M. & Fedio, P. (1969). Visual information and evoked responses from the left and right hemisphere. *Electroencephalography and Clinical Neurophysiology, 36*, 266–272.

Buchsbaum, M. & Fedio, P. (1970). Hemispheric differences in evoked potentials to verbal and non-verbal stimuli in the left and right visual fields. *Physiology and Behavior, 5*, 207–210.

Buffery, A.W.H. (1974). Asymmetrical lateralization of cerebral functions and the effects of unilateral brain surgery in epileptic patients. In S.J. Diamond & J.G. Beaumont (Eds.), *Hemispheric function in the human brain.* pp. 204–234. New York: Halstead.

Butler, S.R. & Glass, A. (1974). Asymmetries in the electroencephalogram associated with cerebral dominance. *Electroencephalography and Clinical Neurophysiology, 36*, 481–491.

Butters, N. (1984). Alcoholic Korsakoff's syndrome: An update. *Seminars in Neurology, 4,* 229–247.

Butters, N. & Albert, M.S. (1982). Processes underlying failures to recall remote events. In L.S. Cermak (Ed.), *Human memory and amnesia.* pp. 257–274. Hillsdale, NJ: Erlbaum.

Butters, N. & Cermak, L.S. (1974). The role of cognitive factors in the memory disorder of alcoholic patients with the Korsakoff syndrome. *Annals of the New York Academy of Sciences, 233,* 61–75.

Butters, N. & Cermak, L.S. (1975). Some analyses of amnesic syndromes in brain-damaged patients. In K. Pribram & R. Isaacson (Eds.), *The hippocampus.* pp. 377–409. New York: Plenum Press.

Butters, N. & Cermak, L.S. (1980). *Alcoholic Korsakoff's syndrome: An information processing approach to amnesia.* New York: Academic Press.

Butters, N., Lewis, R., Cermak, L.S., & Goodglass, H. (1973). Material-specific memory deficits in alcoholic Korsakoff patients. *Neuropsychologia, 11,* 291–299.

Butters, N., Tarlow, S., Cermak, L.S., & Sax, D. (1976). A comparison of the information processing deficits of patients with Huntington's chorea and Korsakoff's syndrome. *Cortex, 12,* 134–144.

Caramazza, A. & Zurif, E.B. (1976). Dissociation of algorithmic and heuristic processes in language comprehension: Evidence from aphasia. *Brain and Language, 3,* 572–582.

Carmon, A. & Benton, A.L. (1969). Tactile perception of direction and number in patients with unilateral cerebral disease. *Neurology, 19,* 525–532.

Carter-Saltzman, L. (1979). Patterns of cognitive abilities in relation to handedness and sex. In M. Wittig & A. Peterson (Eds.), *Determinants of sex related differences in cognitive functioning.* pp. 97–120. New York: Academic Press.

Cermak, L.S. (1976). The encoding capacity of a patient with amnesia due to encephalitis. *Neuropsychologia, 14,* 311–326.

Cermak, L.S. (1984). The episodic semantic distinction in amnesia. In L. Squire and N. Butters (Eds.), *The neuropsychology of memory.* (pp. 55–62). New York: Guilford Press.

Cermak, L.S. & Butters, N. (1972). The role of interference and encoding in the short-term memory deficits of Korsakoff patients. *Neuropsychologia, 10,* 89–96.

Cermak, L.S. & Butters, N. (1973). Information processing deficits of alcoholic Korsakoff patients. *Quarterly Journal of Studies on Alcoholism, 34,* 1110–1132.

Cermak, L.S., Butters, N., & Gerrein, J. (1973). The extent of the verbal encoding ability of Korsakoff patients. *Neuropsychologia, 11,* 85–94.

Cermak, L.S., Butters, N., & Goodglass, H. (1971). The extent of memory loss in Korsakoff patients. *Neuropsychologia, 9,* 307–315.

Cermak, L.S., Butters, N., & Moreines, J. (1974). Some analyses of the verbal encoding deficit of alcoholic Korsakoff patients. *Brain and Language, 1,* 141–150.

Cermak, L., Lewis, R., Butters, N., & Goodglass, H. (1973). Role of verbal mediation in performance of motor tasks by Korsakoff patients. *Perceptual and Motor Skills, 37,* 259–262.

Cermak, L.S., Naus, M.J., & Reale, L. (1976). Rehearsal and organizational strategies of alcoholic Korsakoff patients. *Brain and Language, 3,* 375–385.

Cermak, L.S. & O'Connor, M. (1983). The anterograde and retrograde retrieval ability of a patient with amnesia due to encephalitis. *Neuropsychologia, 21,* 213–234.

Cermak, L.S. & Reale, L. (1978). Depth of processing and retention of words by alcoholic Korsakoff patients. *Journal of Experimental Psychology: Human Learning and Memory, 4,* 165–174.

Cermak, L.S., Reale, L., & Baker, E. (1978). Alcoholic Korsakoff patients' retrieval from semantic memory. *Brain and Language, 5,* 215–226.

Chamberlain, H.D. (1928). The inheritance of left handedness. *Journal of Heredity, 19,* 557–559.

Chedru, F. & Geschwind, N. (1972). Writing disturbances in acute confusional states. *Neuropsychologia, 10,* 343–353.

Cicone, M., Wapner, W., & Gardner, H. (1980). Sensitivity to emotional expressions and situations in organic patients. *Cortex, 16,* 145–158.

Clark, L. & Knowles, J. (1973). Age differences in dichotic listening performance. *Journal of Gerontology, 28,* 173–178.

Clarus, A. (1874). Ueber Aphasie bei Kindern. *Jahresbuch der Kinderheilkunde, 7,* 369–400.

Cohen, G. (1972). Hemispheric differences in a letter classification task. *Perception and Psychophysics, 11,* 139–142.

Cohen, N.J. & Squire, L.R. (1980). Preserved learning and retention of pattern-analyzing skills in amnesia: Dissociation of knowing how and knowing that. *Science, 210,* 207–210.

Cohen, N.J. & Squire, L.R. (1981). Retrograde amnesia and remote memory impairment. *Neuropsychologia, 19,* 337–356.

Coltheart, M. (1980a). Deep dyslexia: A review of the syndrome. In M. Coltheart, K. Patterson, & J.C. Marshall (Eds.), *Deep dyslexia.* pp. 22–47. London: Routledge and Kegan Paul.

Coltheart, M. (1980b). Reading, phonological recoding, and deep dyslexia. In M. Coltheart, K. Patterson, & J.C. Marshall (Eds.), *Deep dyslexia.* pp. 197–226.

Corkin, S. (1965). Tactually-guided maze-learning in

man: Effects of unilateral cortical excisions and bilaterial hippocampal lesions. *Neuropsychologia, 3,* 339–351.

Corsi, P.M. (1969, April). Verbal memory impairment after unilateral hippocampal excisions. Paper presented at the 40th Annual Meeting of the Eastern Psychological Association, Philadelphia.

Craik, F.I.M. & Tulving, E. (1975). Depth of processing and retention of words in episodic memory. *Journal of Experimental Psychology, General, 104.* 268–294.

Crovitz, H.F. & Zener, K. (1962). A group test for assessing hand and eye dominance. *American Journal of Psychology, 75,* 271–276.

Darwin, C.J. (1971). Dichotic backward masking of complex sounds. *Quarterly Journal of Experimental Psychology, 23,* 386–392.

Day, J. (1977). Right-hemisphere language processing in normal right-handers. *Journal of Experimental Psychology: Human Perception and Performance, 3,* 518–528.

Déjerine, J. (1891). Sur un cas de cécité verbale avec agraphie, suivi d'autopsie. *Mémoires de la Societé de Biologie, 3,* 197–201.

Déjerine, J. (1892). Contribution à l'étude anatomo-pathologique et clinique des différentes varietés de cécité verbale. *Mémoires de la Société de Biologie, 4,* 61–90.

DeLuca, D., Cermak, L.S., & Butters, N. (1975). An analysis of Korsakoff patients' recall following varying types of distractor activity. *Neuropsychologia, 13,* 271–279.

DeRenzi, E., Faglioni, P., & Scotti, G. (1968). Tactile spatial impairment and unilateral cerebral damage. *Journal of Nervous and Mental Disease, 146,* 468–475.

DeRenzi, E., Faglioni, P., & Spinnler, H. (1968). The performance of patients with unilateral brain damage on face recognition tasks. *Cortex, 4,* 17–34.

DeRenzi, E. & Scotti, G. (1969). The influence of spatial disorders in impairing tactual discrimination of shapes. *Cortex, 5,* 53–62.

DeRenzi, E. & Vignolo, L.A. (1962). The token test: A sensitive test to detect receptive disturbances in aphasics. *Brain, 85,* 665–678.

DeVilliers, J. (1974). Quantitative aspects of agrammatism in aphasia. *Cortex, 10,* 36–54.

Diamond, R. & Carey, S. (1977). Developmental changes in the representation of faces. *Journal of Experimental Child Psychology, 23,* 1–22.

Donchin, E., Kutas, M., & McCarthy, G. (1977). Electrocortical indices of hemispheric utilization. In S. Harnad, R.W. Doty, L. Goldstein, J. Jaynes, & G. Krauthamer (Eds.), *Lateralization in the nervous system.* (pp. 339–384). New York: Academic Press.

Doyle, J.C., Ornstein, R., & Galin, D. (1974). Lateral specialization of cognitive mode: II. EEG frequency analysis. *Psychophysiology, 11,* 567–578.

Drachman, D.A. & Adams, R.D. (1962). Herpes simplex and acute inclusion body encephalitis. *Archives of Neurology, 7,* 45–63.

Dricker, J., Butters, N., Berman, G., Samuels, I., & Carey, S. (1978). Recognition and encoding of faces by alcoholic Korsakoff and right hemisphere patients. *Neuropsychologia, 16,* 683–695.

Duffy, R.J. & Duffy, J.R. (1981). Three studies of deficits in pantomimic expression and pantomimic recognition in aphasia. *Journal of Speech and Hearing Research, 23,* 70–84.

Dumas, R. & Morgan, A. (1975). EEG asymmetry as a function of occupation, task, and task difficulty. *Neuropsychologia, 13,* 219–228.

Durnford, M. & Kimura, D. (1971). Right hemisphere specialization for depth perception reflected in visual field differences. *Nature, 231,* 394–395.

Eisenberg, L. (1966). The epidemiology of reading retardation and a program for preventive intervention. In J. Money (Ed.), *The disabled reader.* pp. 3–20. Baltimore: Johns Hopkins Press.

Ellis, H.D. & Shepherd, J.W. (1974). Recognition of abstract and concrete words presented in the left and right visual fields. *Journal of Experimental Psychology, 103,* 1035–1036.

Entus, A.K. (1977). Hemispheric asymmetry in processing of dichotically presented speech and non-speech stimuli by infants. In S.J. Segalowitz & F.A. Gruber (Eds.), *Language development and neurological theory.* New York: Academic Press.

Fedio, P. & Van Buren, J.M. (1974). Memory deficits during electrical stimulation in the speech cortex of conscious man. *Brain and Language, 1,* 29–42.

Finkelnberg, R. (1870). Vortrag in der Niederrheinische, Gesellschaft der Aerzte. *Berline Klinische Wochenschrift, 7,* 449–450, 460–462.

Friederici, A., Schoenle, P.W., & Goodglass, H. (1981). Mechanisms underlying writing and speech in aphasia. *Brain and Language, 13,* 212–222.

Friedman, D., Simson, R., Ritter, W., & Rapin, I. (1975). Cortical evoked potentials elicited by real speech words and human sounds. *Electroencephalography and Clinical Neurophysiology, 38,* 13–19.

Gainotti, G. (1972). Emotional behavior and hemispheric side of lesion. *Cortex, 8,* 41–55.

Galaburda, A., LeMay, M., Kemper, T.L., & Geschwind, N. (1978). Right-left asymmetries in the brain. *Science, 205,* 852–856.

Galin, D. & Ornstein, R. (1972). Lateral specialization of cognitive mode: An EEG study. *Psychophysiology, 13,* 45–50.

Gardiner, M. & Walter, D.O. (1977). Evidence of hemispheric specialization from infant EEG. In

S. Harnad, R.W. Doty, L. Goldstein, J. Jaynes, & G. Krauthamer (Eds.), *Lateralization in the Nervous System.* (pp. 481–500). New York: Academic Press.

Gardner, H. (1975). *The shattered mind.* New York: Knopf.

Gardner, H. & Zurif. E.B. (1975). Bee but not be: Oral reading of single words in aphasia and alexia. *Neuropsychologia, 13,* 181–190.

Gates, A. & Bradshaw, J.L. (1977). The role of the cerebral hemispheres in music. *Brain and Language, 4,* 403–431.

Gazzaniga, M.S., Bogen, J.E., & Sperry, R.W. (1962). Some functional effects of sectioning the cerebral commissures in man. *Proceedings of the National Academy of Sciences, 48,* 1765.

Gazzaniga, M.S., Bogen, J.E., & Sperry, R.W. (1965). Observations on visual perception after disconnexion of the cerebral hemispheres in man. *Brain, 88,* 221–236.

Gazzaniga, M.S. & LeDoux, J.E. (1978). *The integrated mind.* New York: Plenum Press.

Geffen, G., Bradshaw, J.L., & Wallace, G. (1971). Interhemispheric effects on reaction time to verbal and nonverbal stimuli. *Journal of Experimental Psychology, 87,* 415–422.

Gerner, P., Ommaya, A., & Fedio, P. (1972). A study of visual memory: Verbal and nonverbal mechanisms in patients with unilateral lobectomy. *International Journal of Neurosciences, 4,* 231–238.

Gerstmann, J. (1930). Zur Symptomatologie der Hirnläsionen im Uebergangsgebiet der unteren parietal- und mittleren Occipitalwindung. *Nervenarzt, 3,* 691–695.

Geschwind, N. (1965). Disconnexion syndromes in animals and man: I, II. *Brain, 88,* 237–294, 585–644.

Geschwind, N. (1975). The apraxias: Neural mechanisms of learned movement. *American Scientist, 63,* 188–195.

Geschwind, N. & Fusillo, M. (1966). Color naming defects in association with alexia. *Archives of Neurology, 15,* 137–146.

Geschwind, N. & Kaplan, E. (1962). A human cerebral disconnection syndrome. *Neurology, 12,* 675–685.

Geschwind, N. & Levitsky, W. (1968). Human brain: Left-right asymmetries in temporal speech region. *Science, 161,* 186–187.

Gloning, I., Gloning, K., Haub, C., & Quatember, R. (1969). Comparison of verbal behavior in right-handed and non-right-handed patients with anatomically verified lesions of one hemisphere. *Cortex, 5,* 43–52.

Gloning, I., Gloning, K., & Hoff, H. (1968). *Neuropsychological symptoms and syndromes in lesions of the occipital lobe and the adjacent areas.* Paris: Gauthier-Villars.

Glosser, G., Butters, N., & Kaplan, E. (1977). Visuoperceptual processes in brain-damaged patients on the digit-symbol substitution test. *International Journal of Neurosciences, 7,* 59–66.

Glosser, G., Butters, N., & Samuels, I. (1976). Failures in information processing in patients with Korsakoff's syndrome. *Neuropsychologia, 14,* 327–334.

Goldstein, K. (1913). Ueber die Störungen der Grammatik bei Hirnkrankheiten. *Monatschrift für Psychologie and Neurologie, 36,* 540–580.

Goldstein, L. & Lackner, J.R. (1974). A sideways look at dichotic listening. *Journal of the Acoustical Society of America, 55,* 5a–10a.

Goodenough, C., Zurif, E.B., & Weintraub, S. (1977). Aphasics' attention to grammatical morphemes. *Language and Speech, 20,* 11–19.

Goodglass, H. (1973). Developmental comparison of vowels and consonants in dichotic listening. *Journal of Speech and Hearing Research, 16,* 744–752.

Goodglass, H. & Baker, E. (1976). Semantic field, naming, and auditory comprehension in aphasia. *Brain and Language, 3,* 359–374.

Goodglass, H. & Barton, M. (1963). Handedness and differential perception of verbal stimuli in left and right visual fields. *Perceptual and Motor Skills, 17,* 851–854.

Goodglass, H., Barton, M.I., & Kaplan, E. (1968). Sensory modality and object naming in aphasia. *Journal of Speech and Hearing Research, 11,* 488–491.

Goodglass, H. & Berko, J. (1960). Agrammatism and inflectional morphology in English. *Journal of Speech and Hearing Research, 3,* 257–267.

Goodglass, H. & Calderon, M.T. (1977). Parallel processing of verbal and musical stimuli in left and right hemispheres. *Neuropsychologia, 15,* 397–408.

Goodglass, H. & Cohen, M. (1954). Deterioration of word meanings in aphasia. Paper presented at American Psychological Association, Washington, D.C.

Goodglass, H., Fodor, I., & Schulhoff, C. (1967). Prosodic factors in grammar: Evidence from aphasia. *Journal of Speech and Hearing Research, 10,* 5–20.

Goodglass, H. & Hunter, M.A. (1970). Linguistic comparison of speech and writing in two types of aphasia. *Journal of Communication Disorders, 3,* 28–35.

Goodglass, H. & Kaplan, E. (1963). Disturbance of gesture and pantomime in aphasia. *Brain, 86,* 703–720.

Goodglass, H. & Kaplan, E. (1972). *The assessment of aphasia and related disorders.* Philadelphia: Lea and Febiger.

Goodglass, H., Kaplan, E., Weintraub, S., & Ackerman,

N. (1976). The tip-of-the-tongue phenomenon in aphasia. *Cortex*, *12*, 145–153.

Goodglass, H., Klein, B., Carey, P., & Jones, K.J. (1966). Specific semantic word categories in aphasia. *Cortex*, *2*, 74–89.

Goodglass, H. & Mayer, J. (1958). Agrammatism in aphasia. *Journal of Speech and Hearing Disorders*, *23*, 99–111.

Goodglass, H. & Peck, E.A. (1972). Dichotic ear-order effects in Korsakoff and normal subjects. *Neuropsychologia*, *10*, 211–217.

Goodglass, H. & Quadfasel, F.A. (1954). Language laterality in left-handed aphasics. *Brain*, *77*, 523–548.

Gordon, H. (1978). Left-hemisphere dominance for rhythmic elements in dichotically presented melodies. *Cortex*, *14*, 58–70.

Gough, P.B. (1972). One second of reading. In J.F. Kavanaugh & I.V. Mattingly (Eds.), *Language by ear and by eye*. pp. 331–358. Cambridge, MA: MIT Press.

Graves, R.E., Landis, T., & Goodglass, H. (1981). Laterality and sex differences for visual recognition of emotional and non-emotional words. *Neuropsychologia*, *19*, 95–102.

Gur, R.E. & Gur, R.C. (1977). Correlates of conjugate lateral eye movements in man. In S. Harnad, R.W. Doty, L. Goldstein, J. Jaynes, & G. Krauthamer (Eds.), *Lateralization in the nervous system*. pp. 261–281. New York: Academic Press.

Gur, R.E., Gur, R.C. & Harris, L.J. (1975). Cerebral activation, as measured by subjects' lateral eye movements, is influenced by experimenter location. *Neuropsychologia*, *13*, 35–44.

Haggard, M.P. (1971). Encoding and REA for speech signals. *Quarterly Journal of Experimental Psychology*, *23*, 34–45.

Halwes, T.G. (1969). Effects of dichotic fusion on the perception of speech. Supplement to Status Report on Speech Research, Haskins Laboratory, New Haven.

Hannay, H.J. & Boyer, C. (1978). Sex differences in hemispheric asymmetry revisited. *Perceptual and Motor Skills*, *47*, 317–321.

Hannay, H.J., Varney, N.R., & Benton, A.L. (1976). Visual localization in patients with unilateral brain disease. *Journal of Neurology, Neurosurgery and Psychiatry*, *39*, 307–313.

Harcum, E.R. & Jones, M.L. (1962). Letter recognition within words flashed left and right of fixation. *Science*, *138*, 444–445.

Harris, L.J. (1978). Sex differences in spatial ability: Possible environmental, genetic and neurological factors. In M. Kinsbourne (Ed.), *Asymmetrical function of the brain*. (pp. 405–522). London: Cambridge University Press.

Harshman, R. & Remington, R. (1974). Sex, language, and the brain: Part II. Evidence from dichotic listening for adult sex differences in verbal lateralization. Paper presented at UCLA Conference on human brain function, Los Angeles.

Hatfield, F.M. & Walton, K. (1975). Phonological patterns in a case of aphasia. *Language and Speech*, *18*, 341–357.

Head, H. (1926). *Aphasia and kindred disorders of speech* (2 volumes). London: Cambridge University Press.

Hécaen, H. & Kremin, H. (1977). Reading disorders resulting from left hemisphere lesions: Aphasic and "pure" alexia. In H. Whitaker & H.A. Whitaker (Eds.), *Studies in neurolinguistics*, Vol. 2. pp. 269–327. New York: Academic Press.

Hécaen, H. & Sauguet, J. (1971). Cerebral dominance in left-handed subjects. *Cortex*, *7*, 19–48.

Heilman, K.M. (1979). Apraxia. In K.M. Heilman & E. Valenstein (Eds.), *Clinical neuropsychology*. (pp. 159–185). New York: Oxford University Press.

Heilman, K.M., Coyle, J.M., Gonyea, E.F., & Geschwind, N. (1973). Apraxia and agraphia in a left-hander. *Brain*, *96*, 21–28.

Heilman, K.M., Scholes, R., & Watson, R.T. (1975). Auditory affective agnosia. *Journal of Neurology, Neurosurgery and Psychiatry*, *38*, 69–72.

Heilman, K.M. & Sypert, G.W. (1977). Korsakoff's syndrome resulting from bilateral fornix lesions. *Neurology*, *27*, 490–493.

Hellige, J.B. & Cox, P.J. (1976). Effects of concurrent verbal memory on recognition of stimuli from the left and right visual fields. *Journal of Experimental Psychology: Human Perception and Performance*, *2*, 210–221.

Hellige, J.B., Cox, P.J., & Litvac, L. (1979). Information processing in the cerebral hemispheres: Selective hemisphere activation and capacity limitations. *Journal of Experimental Psychology, General*, *108*, 251–279.

Hellige, J.B. & Longstreth, L.E. (1981). Effects of concurrent hemisphere-specific activity on unimanual tapping rate. *Neuropsychologia*, *19*, 395–406.

Henschen, S. (1920–1922). *Klinische und anatomische Beiträge zur Pathologie des Gehirns*. Stockholm: Nordiska Bokhandeln.

Hermelin, B. & O'Connor, N. (1971). Functional asymmetry in the reading of Braille. *Neuropsychologia*, *9*, 431–435.

Herron, J., Galin, D., Johnstone, J., & Ornstein, R.E. (1979). Cerebral specialization, writing posture, and motor control of writing in left handers. *Science*, *205*, 1285–1289.

Hier, D.B. & Kaplan, J. (1980). Are sex differences in

cerebral organization clinically significant? *The Behavioral and Brain Sciences, 3*, 238–239.

Hines, D. (1976). Recognition of verbs, abstract nouns and concrete nouns from the left and right visual half fields. *Neuropsychologia, 14*, 211–216.

Hiscock, M. & Kinsbourne, M. (1976). Perceptual and motor measures of cerebral lateralization in children. Paper presented at the 37th annual meeting of the Canadian Psychological Association, Toronto, June 9–11.

Hudson, P.T.W. (1975). The genetics of handedness—a reply to Levy and Nagylaki. *Neuropsychologia, 13*, 331–339.

Humphrey, M.E. (1951). Consistency of hand usage. *British Journal of Educational Psychology, 21*, 214–225.

Huppert, F.A. & Piercy, M. (1976). Recognition memory in amnesic patients: Effect of temporal context and familiarity of material. *Cortex, 12*, 3–20.

Huppert, F.A. & Piercy, M. (1977). Recognition in amnesic patients: A defect of acquisition? *Neuropsychologia, 15*, 643–652.

Huppert, F.A. & Piercy, M. (1978). Dissociation between learning and remembering in organic amnesia. *Nature, 275*, 317–318.

Huppert, F.A. & Piercy, M. (1979). Normal and abnormal forgetting in organic amnesia: Effect of locus of lesion. *Cortex, 15*, 385–390.

Ingram, T.T.S. (1975). Speech disorders in childhood. In E.H. Lenneberg & E. Lenneberg (Eds.), *Foundations of language development*, Volume 2. (pp. 195–261). New York: Academic Press.

Isserlin, M. (1922). Ueber Agrammatismus. *Zeitschrift für die gesamte Neurologie und Psychiatrie, 75*, 332–410.

Jakobson, R. (1956). *Fundamentals of language*. The Hague: Mouton.

Jarho, L. (1973). Korsakoff-like Amnesic Syndrome in Penetrating Brain Injury. Rehabilitation Institute for Brain Injured Veterans in Finland, Helsinki.

Johnson, R.C., Bowers, J.K., Gamble, M., Lyons, F.M., Presbey, T.W., & Vetter, R.A. (1977). Ability to transcribe music and ear superiority for tone sequences. *Cortex, 13*, 295–299.

Jones, M.K. (1974). Imagery as a mnemonic aid after left temporal lobectomy: contrast between material-specific and generalized memory disorders. *Neuropsychologia, 12*, 21–30.

Jones-Gotman, M. & Milner, B. (1978). Right temporal-lobe contribution to image-mediated verbal learning. *Neuropsychologia, 16*, 61–71.

Kahn, E. & Crosby, E. (1972). Korsakoff's syndrome associated with surgical lesions involving the mammillary bodies. *Neurology, 22*, 317–325.

Kapur, N. & Butters, N. (1977). An analysis of the visuoperceptual deficits in alcoholic Korsakoffs and long-term alcoholics. *Journal of Studies on Alcohol, 38*, 2025–2035.

Kimura, D. (1961a). Some effects of temporal lobe damage on auditory perception. *Canadian Journal of Psychology, 15*, 156–165

Kimura, D. (1961b). Cerebral dominance and the perception of verbal stimuli. *Canadian Journal of Psychology, 15*, 166–171.

Kimura, D. (1963a). Right temporal lobe damage: Perception of unfamiliar stimui after damage. *Archives of Neurology, 8*, 264–271.

Kimura, D. (1963b). Speech lateralization in young children as determined by an auditory test. *Journal of Comparative and Physiological Psychology, 56*, 899–902.

Kimura, D. (1964). Left-right differences in perception of melodies. *Quarterly Journal of Experimental Psychology, 16*, 355–358.

Kimura, D. (1969). Spatial localization in left and right visual fields. *Canadian Journal of Psychology, 23*, 445–458.

Kimura, D. (1973). The asymmetry of the human brain. *Scientific American, 228*, 70–78.

Kimura, D. (1977). Acquisition of a motor skill after left-hemisphere damage. *Brain, 100*, 527–542.

Kimura, D. & Archibald, Y. (1974). Motor functions of the left hemisphere. *Brain, 97*, 337–350.

Kinsbourne, M. (1970). The cerebral basis of lateral asymmetries in attention. *Acta Psychologica, 33*, 193–201.

Kinsbourne, M. (1972). Head and eye turning indicate cerebral lateralization. *Science, 176*, 539–541.

Kinsbourne, M. (1972). The control of attention by interaction betwen the cerebral hemispheres. In S. Kornblum (Ed.), *Attention and Performance: Vol. 4* (pp. 239–253). New York: Academic Press.

Kinsbourne, M. & Cook, J. (1971). Generalized and lateralized effects of concurrent verbalization on unimanual skill. *Quarterly Journal of Experimental Psychology, 23*, 341–345.

Kinsbourne, M. & Hiscock, M. (1977). Does cerebral dominance develop? In S.J. Segalowitz & F.A. Gruber (Eds.), *Language development and neurological theory*. pp. 172–191. New York: Academic Press.

Kinsbourne, M. & McMurray, J. (1975). The effect of cerebral dominance on time-sharing between speaking and tapping by pre-school children. *Child Development, 46*, 240–242.

Kinsbourne, M. & Wood, F. (1975). Short-term memory processes and the amnesic syndrome. In D. Deutsch & J.A. Deutsch (Eds.), *Short-term memory*. pp. 258–293. New York: Academic Press.

Klein, D., Moscovitch, M., & Vigna, C. (1976). Attention mechanisms and perceptual asymmetries in tachistoscopic recognition of words and faces. *Neuropsychologia*, *14*, 55–66.

Kleist, K. (1923). Kriegerletzungen des Gehirns in ihrer Bedeutung für die Hirnlokalisation und Hirnpathologie. In O. von Schjerning (Ed.), *Handbuch der ärztlichen Erfahrung-im Weltkriege, 1914/1918*, Vol. 4. pp. 343–1369. Leipzig: Barth.

Knox, C. & Kimura, D. (1970). Cerebral processing of nonverbal sounds in boys and girls. *Neuropsychologia*, *8*, 227–237.

Kocel, K., Galin, D., Ornstein, R., & Merin, E. (1972). Lateral eye movement and cognitive mode. *Psychonomic Science*, *27*, 223–224.

Kurowski, K. (1981). A contrastive analysis of the comprehension deficit in posterior and anterior aphasia. (Unpublished master's thesis, Brown University, Providence, RI.)

Kussmaul, A. (1877). *Die Störungen der Sprache*. Leipzig: Vogel.

Ladefoged, P. & Broadbent, D.E. (1957). Information conveyed by vowels. *Journal of the Acoustical Society of America*, *29*, 98–104.

Lake, D.A. & Bryden, M.P. (1976). Handedness and sex differences in hemispheric asymmetry. *Brain and Language*, *3*, 266–282.

Landis, T., Assal, G., & Perret, E. (1979). Opposite cerebral hemispheric superiorities for visual associative processing of emotional facial expressions and objects. *Nature*, *278*, 739–740.

Landis, T., Graves, R., & Goodglass, H. (1981). Dissociated verbal awareness vs. manual performance on two different visual associative tasks: A "split-brain" phenomenon in normal subjects? *Cortex*, *17*, 435–440.

Lansdell, H. (1962). A sex difference in effect of temporal-lobe neurosurgery on design preference. *Nature*, *194*, 852–854.

Lansdell, H. (1968). Effects of extent of temporal lobe ablations on two lateralized deficits. *Physiology of Behavior*, *3*, 271–273.

Lansdell, H. & Urbach, N. (1965). Sex differences in personality measures related to size and side of temporal lobe ablations. *Proceedings of the American Psychological Association*, 113–114.

Lecours, A.R. & Lhermitte, F. (1969). Phonemic paraphasias: Linguistic structures and tentative hypotheses. *Cortex*, *5*, 193–228.

Leehey, S., Carey, S., Diamond, R., & Cahn, A. (1978). Upright and inverted faces: The right hemisphere knows the difference. *Cortex*, *14*, 411–419.

Lenneberg, E.H. (1967). *Biological foundations of language*. New York: Wiley.

Lesser, R. (1978). *Linguistic investigations of aphasia*. London: Arnold.

Levy, J. (1974). Psychobiological implications of bilateral asymmetry. In S.J. Diamond & J.G. Beaumont (Eds.), *Hemisphere Function in the Human Brain*. pp. 121–183. New York: Halstead.

Levy, J. (1976). A review of evidence for a genetic component in the determination of handedness. *Behavioral Genetics*, *6*, 429–453.

Levy, J. (1977). A reply to Hudson regarding the Levy–Nagylaki model for the genetics of handedness. *Neuropsychologia*, *15*, 187–190.

Levy, J. & Nagylaki, J. (1972). A model for the genetics of handedness. *Genetics*, *72*, 117–128.

Levy, J. & Reid, M. (1976). Variations in writing posture and cerebral organization. *Science*, *195*, 337–339.

Levy, J., Trevarthen, C., & Sperry, R.W. (1972). Perception of bilateral chimeric figures following hemispheric disconnection. *Brain*, *95*, 61–78.

Levy-Agresti, J. & Sperry, R.W. (1968). Differential perceptual capacities in major and minor hemispheres. *Proceedings of the National Academy of Sciences*, *61*, 1151.

Liberman, A.M. (1975). The specialization of the language hemisphere. In B. Milner (Ed.), *Hemispheric specialization and interaction*. Cambridge, MA: MIT Press.

Liberman, A.M., Cooper, F.S., Shankweiler, D.P., & Studdert-Kennedy, M. (1967). Perception of the speech code. *Psychological Review*, *74*, 431–461.

Liberman, A.M., Harris, K.S., Hoffman, A.S., & Griffith, B.C. (1957). The discrimination of speech sounds within and across phoneme boundaries. *Journal of Experimental Psychology*, *54*, 358–368.

Liepmann, H. (1900). Das Krankheitsbild der Apraxie (Motorischen Asymbolie). *Monatschrift für Psychiatrie und Neurologie*, *8*, 15–44, 102–132.

Liepmann, H. (1905). Die Linke Hemisphäre und das Handeln. *Munchener Medizinische Wochenschrift*, *49*, 2375–2378.

Liepmann, H. (1908). *Drei Aufsätze aus dem Apraxiegebeit*. Berlin: Karger.

Liepmann, H. & Maas, O. (1907). Ein Fall von linksseitiger Agraphie und Apraxie bei rechtsseitiger Lähmung. *Zeitschrift für Psychologie und Neurologie*, *10*, 214–227.

Lishman, W.A. (1981). Cerebral disorder in alcoholism: Syndromes of impairment. *Brain*, *104*, 1–20.

Lissauer, H. (1889). Ein Fall von Seelenblindheit nebst Beitrage zur Theorie derselben. *Archiv für Psychiatrie und Nervenkrankheiten*, *21*, 222–270.

Low, M.D., Wada, J.A., & Fox, M. (1974). Hemispheric specialization of language production: Some electrophysical evidence. *Proceedings of the International Symposium on Cerebral Evoked Potentials in Man*, Brussels.

Luria, A.R. (1970). *Traumatic aphasia.* The Hague: Mouton.

Maccoby, E.E. & Jacklin, C.N. (1974). *The psychology of sex differences.* Stanford: Stanford University Press.

Mair, G.P., Warrington, E.K., & Weiskrantz, L. (1979). Memory disorder in Korsakoff's psychosis. A neurological and neuropsychological investigation of two cases. *Brain, 102,* 749–783.

Marcie, P. & Hécaen, H. (1979). Agraphia: Writing disorders associated with unilateral cortical lesions. In K.M. Heilman & E. Valenstein (Eds.), *Clinical neuropsychology.* pp. 92–127. New York: Oxford University Press.

Marin, O.S.M. (1980). CAT scans of five deep dyslexic patients. In M. Coltheart, K. Patterson, & J.C. Marshall (Eds.), *Deep dyslexia.* pp. 407–410. London: Routledge and Kegan Paul.

Marin, O.S.M., Saffran, E.M., & Schwartz, M.F. (1975). Dissociations of language in aphasia: Implications for normal function. *Annals of the New York Academy of Sciences, 280,* 868–884.

Marshall, J.C. & Newcombe, F. (1966). Syntactic and semantic errors in paralexia. *Neuropsychologia, 4,* 169–176.

Marshall, J.C. & Newcombe, F. (1973). Patterns of paralexia: A psycholinguistic approach. *Journal of Psycholinguistic Research, 2,* 175–199.

Marslen-Wilson, W.D. & Teuber, H.-L. (1975). Memory for remote events in anterograde amnesia: Recognition of public figures from news photographs. *Neuropsychologia, 13,* 347–352.

Martin, A.D. & Rigrodsky, S. (1974). An investigation of phonological impairment in aphasia: Part 2. Distinctive feature analysis of phonemic commutation errors on aphasia. *Cortex, 10,* 329–346.

Martone, M., Butters, N., Payne, M., Becker, J., & Sax, D. (1984). Dissociations between skill learning and verbal recognition in amnesia and dementia. *Archives of Neurology, 41.* 965–970.

Marzi, C.A. & Berlucchi, G. (1977). Right visual field superiority for accuracy of recognition of famous faces in normals. *Neuropsychologia, 15,* 751–756.

Mateer, C. & Kimura, D. (1977). Impairment of nonverbal oral movements in aphasia. *Brain and Language, 4,* 262–276.

Mayes, A., Boddy, J., & Meudell, P. (1980). Is amnesia caused by an activational deficit? A preliminary electrophysiological investigation of acquisition in amnesics. *Neuroscience Letters, 18,* 347–352.

Mayes, A., Meudell, P., & Neary, D. (1980). Do amnesics

adopt inefficient encoding strategies with faces and random shapes? *Neuropsychologia, 18,* 527–540.

McDowall, J. (1979). Effects of encoding instructions and retrieval cueing on recall in Korsakoff patients. *Memory and Cognition, 7,* 232–239.

McGlone, J. (1977). Sex differences in the cerebral organization of verbal functions in patients with unilateral brain lesions. *Brain, 100,* 775–793.

McGlone, J. (1978). Sex differences in functional brain asymmetry. *Cortex, 14,* 122–128.

McGlone, J. (1980). Sex differences in human brain asymmetry: A critical survey. *Behavioral and Brain Sciences, 3,* 215–263.

McGlone, J. & Davidson, W. (1973). The relation between cerebral speech laterality and spatial ability with special reference to sex and hand preference. *Neuropsychologia, 11,* 105–113.

McGlone, J. & Kertesz, A. (1973). Sex differences in cerebral processing of visuospatial tasks. *Cortex, 9,* 313–320.

McKeever, W.F. & Van Deventer, A.D. (1980). Inverted handwriting position, language laterality, and the Levy–Nagylaki genetic model of handedness and cerebral organization. *Neuropsychologia, 18,* 99–102.

Meier, M.J. & French, L.A. (1965). Lateralized deficits in complex visual discrimination and bilateral transfer of reminiscence following unilateral temporal lobectomy. *Neuropsychologia, 3,* 261–272.

Meudell, P., Butters, N., & Montgomery, K. (1978). Role of rehearsal in the short-term memory performance of patients with Korsakoff's and Huntington's disease. *Neuropsychologia, 16,* 507–510.

Meudell, P. & Mayes, A. (1981). Normal and abnormal forgetting: some comments on the human amnestic syndrome. In A. Ellis (Ed.), *Normality and pathology in cognitive function.* pp. 203–237. London: Academic Press.

Meudell, P., Northern, B., Snowden, J.S., & Neary, D. (1980). Long-term memory for famous voices in amnesic and normal subjects. *Neuropsychologia, 18,* 133–139.

Meyer, D.E., Schvaneveldt, R.W., & Ruddy, M.G. (1974). Function of graphemic and phonemic codes in visual word recognition. *Memory and Cognition, 2,* 309–332.

Miceli, G. (1981). Marked syntactic deficit; moderate morphological deficit. Paper presented at BABBLE Conference on Neuropsychology of Language, Niagara Falls, Canada.

Miceli, G. (1982). The processing of speech sounds in a patient with cortical auditory disorder. *Neuropsychologia, 20,* 5–20.

Miceli, G., Mazzucchi, A., Menn, L., & Goodglass, G.

(1983). Two contrasting cases of Italian agrammatic aphasia. *Brain and Language, 19*, 65–97.

Milner, B. (1962a). Laterality effects in audition. In V.B. Mountcastle (Ed.), *Interhemispheric relations and cerebral dominance.* (pp. 177–195). Baltimore: Johns Hopkins Press.

Milner, B. (1962b). Les troubles de le memorie accompagnant des lesions hipposcampiques bilaterales. In *Physiologie de l'hippocampe.* Paris: C.N.R.S. (English translation in P.M. Milner & S. Glickman (Eds.)), *Cognitive processes and the brain.* pp. 97–111. Princeton: Van Nostrand.

Milner, B. (1963). Effects of different brain lesions on card sorting. *Archives of Neurology, 9*, 90–100.

Milner, B. (1964). Some effects of frontal lobectomy in man. In J.M. Warren & K. Akert (Eds.), *The frontal granular cortex and behavior.* pp. 313–334. New York: McGraw-Hill.

Milner, B. (1965). Visually-guided maze learning in man: effects of bilateral hippocampal, bilateral frontal, and unilateral cerebral lesions. *Neuropsychologia, 3*, 317–338.

Milner, B. (1966). Amnesia following operation on the temporal lobes. In C.W.M. Whitty & O.L. Zangwill (Eds.), *Amnesia.* pp. 109–133. London: Butterworth.

Milner, B. (1967). Brain mechanisms suggested by studies of temporal lobes. In F.L. Darley (Ed.), *Brain mechanisms underlying speech and language.* pp. 122–145. New York: Grune and Stratton.

Milner, B. (1968). Visual recognition and recall after right temporal-lobe excisions in man. *Neuropsychologia, 6*, 191–210.

Milner, B. (1970). Memory and the medial temporal regions of the brain. In K.H. Pribram & D.E. Broadbent (Eds.), *Biology of memory.* pp. 29–50. New York: Academic Press.

Milner, B. (1971). Interhemispheric differences in the localization of psychological processes in man. *British Medical Bulletin, 27*, 272–275.

Milner, B. (Ed.) (1975). *Hemispheric specialization and interaction.* Cambridge, MA: MIT Press.

Milner, B., Corkin, S., & Teuber, H.-L. (1968). Further analysis of the hippocampal amnesic syndrome: 14-year follow-up study of H.M. *Neuropsychologia, 6*, 215–234.

Milner, B., Taylor, L., & Sperry, R.W. (1968). Lateralized suppresion of dichotically presented digits after commissural section in man. *Science, 161*, 184–185.

Mishkin, M., & Forgays, D.G. (1952). Word recognition as a function of retinal locus. *Journal of Experimental Psychology, 43*, 43–48.

Molfese, D.L. (1972). Cerebral asymmetry in infants, children, and adults: Auditory, evoked responses to speech and noise stimuli. (Unpublished doctoral dissertaion, Pennsylvania State University).

Molfese, D.L., Freeman, R.B., & Palermo, D.S. (1975). The ontogeny of brain lateralization for speech and non-speech stimuli. *Brain and Language, 2*, 356–368.

Mooney, C.M. (1957). Closure as affected by configural clarity and contextual consistency. *Canadian Journal of Psychology, 2*, 161–178.

Morgan, M. (1977). Embryology and inheritance of asymmetry. In S. Harnad, R.W. Doty, L. Goldstein, J. Jaynes, & G. Krauthamer (Eds.), *Lateralization in the nervous system.* (pp. 173–194). New York: Academic Press.

Morrell, L.K. & Salamy, J.G. (1971). Hemispheric asymmetry of electrocortical responses to speech stimuli. *Science, 174*, 164–166.

Moscovitch, M. (1982). Multiple dissociations of function in amnesia. In L.S. Cermak (Ed.), *Human memory and amnesia.* pp. 337–370. Hillsdale, NJ: Erlbaum.

Moscovitch, M. (1984). The sufficient conditions for demonstrating preserved memory in amnesia. In L. Squire & N. Butters (Eds.), *The neuropsychology of memory.* pp. 104–114. New York: Guilford Press.

Moscovitch, M., Scullion, D., & Christie, D. (1976). Early vs. late stages of processing and their relation to functional hemispheric asymmetries in face recognition. *Journal of Experimental Psychology: Human Perception and Performance, 2*, 401–416.

Moscovitch, M. & Smith, L.C. (1979). Differences in neural organization between individuals with inverted hand posture during writing. *Science, 205*, 710–713.

Nagafuchi, M. (1970). Development of click and monaural hearing abilities in very young children. *Acta Otolaryngologica, 69*, 409–415.

Nebes, R.D. (1971). Superiority of the minor hemisphere in commissurotomized man for the perception of part-whole relations. *Cortex, 7*, 333–347.

Nebes, R.D. (1974). Hemispheric specialization in commissurotomized man. *Psychological Bulletin, 81(1)*, 1–14.

Nebes, R.D., Madden, D.J., & Berg, W.D. (1980). The effect of age on hemispheric asymmetry in visual and auditory identification. Paper presented at the Gerontological Society, San Diego.

Neville, H. (1974). Electrographic correlates of lateral asymmetry in the processing of verbal and non-verbal auditory stimuli. *Journal of Psycholinguistic Research, 3*, 151–163.

Newcombe, F. & Marshall, J.C. (1980). Response monitoring and response blocking in deep dyslexia. In M. Coltheart, K. Patterson, & J.C. Marshall

(Eds.), *Deep dyslexia*. pp. 160–175. London: Routledge and Kegan Paul.

Newcombe, F. & Russell, W.R. (1969). Dissociated visual perceptual and spatial deficits in focal lesions of the right hemisphere. *Journal of Neurology, Neurosurgery and Psychiatry, 32,* 73–81.

Nielsen, J.M. & Raney, R.B. (1938). Symptoms following surgical removal of major (left) angular gyrus. *Bulletin of the Los Angeles Neurological Society, 3,* 42–46.

North, Elizabeth (1971). Effects of stimulus redundancy on naming disorders in aphasia (Unpublished doctoral dissertation, Boston University).

Oldfield, R.C. (1971). The assessment and analysis of handedness: The Edinburgh inventory. *Neuropsychologia, 9,* 97–113.

Orbach, J. (1952). Retinal locus as a factor in the perception of visually perceived words. *American Journal of Psychology, 65,* 555–562.

Oscar-Berman, M. (1973). Hypothesis testing and focusing behavior during concept formation by amnesic Korsakoff patients. *Neuropsychologia, 11,* 191–198.

Oscar-Berman, M. (1980). Neuropsychological consequences of long-term chronic alcoholism. *American Scientist, 68,* 410–419.

Oscar-Berman, M. Goodglass, H., & Donnenfeld, H. (1974). Dichotic ear-order effects with non-verbal stimuli. *Cortex, 10,* 270–277.

Oscar-Berman, M., Heyman, G.M., Bonner, R.T., & Ryder, J. (1980). Human neuropsychology: Some differences between Korsakoff and normal operant performance. *Psychological Research, 41,* 235–247.

Oscar-Berman, M., Rehbein, L., Porfert, A., & Goodglass, H. (1978). Dichhaptic hand-order effects with verbal and non-verbal stimuli. *Brain and Language, 6,* 323–333.

Oscar-Berman, M., Sahakian, B.J., & Wikmark, G. (1976). Spatial probability learning by alcoholic Korsakoff patients. *Journal of Experimental Psychology: Human Learning and Memory, 2,* 215–222.

Oscar-Berman, M. & Samuels, I. (1977). Stimulus preference and memory factors in Korsakoff's syndrome. *Neuropsychologia, 15,* 99–106.

Parsons, O.A. & Prigatano, G.P. (1977). Memory functioning in alcoholics. In I.M. Birnbaum & E.S. Parker (Eds.), *Alcohol and human memory*. Hillsdale, NJ: Erlbaum.

Paterson, A. & Zangwill, O.L. (1944). Disorders of visual space perception associated with lesions of the right cerebral hemisphere. *Brain, 67,* 331–358.

Patterson, K.E. & Bradshaw, J.L. (1975). Differential hemispheric mediation of non-verbal visual stimuli. *Journal of Experimental Psychology: Human Perception and Performance, 1,* 246–252.

Patterson, K.E. & Marcel, A.J. (1977). Aphasia, dyslexia, and the phonological coding of written words. *Quarterly Journal of Experimental Psychology, 29,* 307–318.

Peck, E.A. (1976). Dichotic ear asymmetries in children aged three to nine (Doctoral dissertation, Tufts University).

Penfield, W. & Milner, B. (1958). Memory deficit produced by bilateral lesions in the hippocampal zone. *A.M.A. Archives of Neurology and Psychiatry, 79,* 475–497.

Penfield, W. & Roberts, L. (1959). *Speech and brain mechanisms.* Princeton, NJ: Princeton University Press.

Peretz, I. & Morais, J. (1980). Modes of processing melodies and ear asymmetries in non-musicians. *Neuropsychologia, 18,* 477–490.

Perez, E., Mazzucchi, A., & Rizzolatti, G. (1975). Tempi di reazione discriminativi alla presentazione di materiale fisiognomico in soggetti maschili e femminili normali. *Bollettino della Società di Biologia Sperimentale, 51,* 1445–1450.

Peterson, L.R. & Peterson, M.J. (1959). Short-term retention of individual verbal items. *Journal of Experimental Psychology, 58,* 193–198.

Pick, A. (1913). *Die agrammatischen Sprachstörungen.* Berlin: Karger.

Piercy, M.F. (1977). Experimental studies of the organic amnesic syndrome. In C.W.M. Whitty & O.L. Zangwill (Eds.), *Amnesia* (2nd ed.). pp. 1–51. London: Butterworth.

Pitres, A. (1898). *L'aphasie amnésique et ses variétés cliniques.* Paris: Félix Alcan.

Pizzamiglio, L., DePascalis, C., & Vignati, A. (1974). Stability of dichotic listening test. *Cortex, 10,* 203–205.

Poncet, M., AliCherif, A., Choux, M., Boudouresques, J., & Lhermitte, F. (1978). Étude neuropsychologique d'un syndrome de déconnexion calleuse totale avec hémianopsie latérale homonyme droite. *Revue Neurologique, 134,* 633–653.

Poncet, M., Degos, C., Deloche, G., & Lecours, A.R. (1972). Phonetic and phonemic transformations in aphasia. *International Journal of Mental Health, 1,* 45–54.

Prisko, L. (1963). *Short-term memory in focal cerebral damage.* Unpublished doctoral dissertation, McGill University, Montreal.

Ribot, T. (1882). *Diseases of Memory.* New York: Appleton.

Riddoch, G. (1935). Visual disorientation in homonymous half-fields. *Brain, 58,* 376–382.

Rife, D.C. (1940). Handedness with special reference to twins. *Genetics, 25,* 178–186.

Rizzolatti, G., Bertolini, G., & Buchtel, H.A. (1979). Interference of concomitant motor and verbal tasks on simple reaction time: a hemispheric difference. *Neuropsychologia, 17*, 323–330.

Rizzolatti, G. & Buchtel, H.A. (1977). Hemispheric superiority in reaction time to faces: A sex difference. *Cortex, 13*, 300–305.

Rizzolatti, G., Umilta, C., & Berlucchi, G. (1971). Opposite superiorities of the left and right cerebral hemispheres in discriminative reaction times to physiognomic and alphabetic stimuli. *Brain, 94*, 431–442.

Rosenzweig, M.R. (1951). Representations of the two ears of the auditory cortex. *American Journal of Physiology, 167*, 147–158.

Ross, P. & Turkewitz, G. (1981). Individual differences in cerebral asymmetries for facial recognition. *Cortex, 17*, 199–214.

Rubens, A.B. (1977). Anatomical asymmetries of the human cerebral cortex. In S. Harnad, R.W. Doty, L. Goldstein, J. Jaynes, & R. Krauthamer (Eds.), *Lateralization in the nervous system.* pp. 503–516. New York: Academic Press.

Rubenstein, H., Lewis, S.S., & Rubenstein, M.A. (1971). Evidence for phonemic recoding in visual word recognition. *Journal of Verbal Learning and Verbal Behavior, 10*, 647–657.

Russell, W.R. & Nathan, P.W. (1946). Traumatic amnesia. *Brain, 69*, 280–300.

Ryan, C. & Butters, N. (1980a). Further evidence for a continuum-of-impairment encompassing male alcoholic Korsakoff patients and chronic alcoholic men. *Alcoholism: Clinical and Experimental Research, 4*, 190–197.

Ryan, C. & Butters, N. (1980b). Learning and memory impairments in young and old alcoholics: Evidence for the premature-aging hypothesis. *Alcoholism: Clinical and Experimental Research, 4*, 288–293.

Saffran, E.M., Bogyo, L.C., Schwartz, M.F., & Marin, O.S.M. (1980). Does deep dyslexia reflect right hemisphere reading? In M. Coltheart, K. Patterson, & J.C. Marshall (Eds.), *Deep dyslexia.* pp. 381–406. London: Routledge and Kegan Paul.

Saffran, E.M., Schwartz, M.F., & Marin, O.S.M. (1976). Semantic mechanisms in paralexia. *Brain and Language, 3*, 255–265.

Samuels, I., Butters, N., & Fedio, P. (1972). Short-term memory disorders following temporal lobe removals in humans. *Cortex, 8*, 283–298.

Samuels, I., Butters, N., & Goodglass, H. (1971). Visual memory deficits following cortical and limbic lesions: Effect of field of presentation. *Physiology and Behavior, 6*, 447–452.

Samuels, I., Butters, N., Goodglass, H., & Brody, B. (1971). A comparison of subcortical and cortical damage in short-term visual and auditory memory. *Neuropsychologia, 9*, 293–306.

Samuels, J.A. & Benson, D.F. (1979). Some aspects of language comprehension in anterior aphasia. *Brain and Language, 8*, 275–286.

Sanders, H.I. & Warrington, E.K. (1971). Memory for remote events in amnesic patients. *Brain, 94*, 661–668.

Sasanuma, S. (1980). Acquired dyslexia in Japanese: clinical features and underlying mechanisms. In M. Coltheart, K. Patterson, & J.C. Marshall (Eds.), *Deep dyslexia.* pp. 48–90. London: Routledge and Kegan Paul.

Sasanuma, S. & Kobayoshi, Y. (1978). Tachistoscopic recognition of line orientation. *Neuropsychologia, 16*, 239–242.

Satz, P., Aschenbach, K., Pattishall, E., & Fennell, E. (1965). Order of report, ear asymmetry, and handedness in dichotic listening. *Cortex, 1*, 377–396.

Schwartz, M.F., Saffran, E.M., & Marin, O.S.M. (1977). An analysis of agrammatic reading in aphasia. Paper presented at the International Neuropsychological Society, Santa Fe, NM.

Scoville, W.B. & Milner, B. (1957). Loss of recent memory after bilateral hippocampal lesions. *Journal of Neurology, Neurosurgery, and Psychiatry, 20*, 11–21.

Seltzer, B. & Benson, D.F. (1974). The temporal pattern of retrograde amnesia in Korsakoff's disease. *Neurology, 24*, 527–530.

Shallice, T. & Warrington, E.K. (1970). Independent functioning of verbal memory stores: A neuropsychological study. *Quarterly Journal of Experimental Psychology, 22*, 261–273.

Shallice, T. & Warrington, E.K. (1975). Word recognition in a phonemic dyslexic patient. *Quarterly Journal of Experimental Psychology, 27*, 187–199.

Shallice, T. & Warrington, E.K. (1980). Single and multiple component central dyslexic syndromes. In M. Colheart, K. Patterson & J.C. Marshall (Eds.), *Deep dyslexia.* pp. 119–145. London: Routledge and Kegan Paul.

Shankweiler, D. (1966). Effects of temporal lobe lesions on recognition of dichotically presented melodies. *Journal of Comparative and Physiological Psychology, 62*, 115–119.

Shankweiler, D. & Studdert-Kennedy, M. (1967). Identification of consonants and vowels presented to left and right ears. *Quarterly Journal of Experimental Psychology, 19*, 59–63.

Shanon, B. (1980). Lateralization effects in musical decision tasks. *Neuropsychologia, 18*, 21–32.

Shelbourne, S.A. (1972). Visual evoked responses to word and nonsense syllable stimuli. *Electroence-*

*phalography and Clinical Neurophysiology, 32,* 17–25.

Shelbourne, S.A. (1973). Visual evoked responses to language stimuli in normal children. *Electroencephalography and Clinical Neurophysiology, 33,* 135–143.

Sidman, M., Stoddard, L.T., & Mohr, J.P. (1968). Some additional quantitative observations of immediate memory in a patient with bilateral hippocampal lesions. *Neuropsychologia, 6,* 245–254.

Siqueland, E.R. & DeLucia, C.A. (1969). Visual reinforcement of non-nutritive sucking in human infants. *Science, 165,* 1144–1146.

Smith, F. (1971). *Understanding reading.* New York: Holt, Rinehart and Winston.

Smith, Lee C., & Moscovitch, M. (1979). Writing posture, hemispheric control of movement and cerebral dominance in individuals with inverted and noninverted hand postures during writing. *Neuropsychologia, 17,* 637–644.

Sparks, R. & Geschwind, N. (1968). Dichotic listening in man after section of neocortical commissures. *Cortex, 3,* 163–178.

Sparks, R., Goodglass, H., & Nickel, B. (1970). Ipsilateral versus contralateral extinction in dichotic listening, resulting from hemispheric lesions. *Cortex, 6,* 249–260.

Spellacy, F. & Blumstein, S. (1970). The influence of language set and ear preference in phoneme recognition. *Cortex, 6,* 430–439.

Sperry, R.W. & Gazzaniga, M.S. (1967). Language following surgical disconnection of the hemispheres. In C.H. Millikan & F.L. Darley (Eds.), *Brain mechanisms underlying speech and language.* pp. 108–121. New York: Grune and Stratton.

Spreen, O., Benton, A.L., & Van Allen, N.W. (1966). Dissociation of visual and tactile naming in amnesic aphasia. *Neurology, 16,* 807–814.

Spreen, O., Spellacy, F., & Reid, J.R. (1970). The effect of interstimulus interval and intensity on ear asymmetry for nonverbal stimuli in dichotic listening. *Neuropsychologia, 8,* 245–250.

Squire, L.R. (1981). Two forms of human amnesia: An anlysis of forgetting. *Journal of Neuroscience, 1,* 635–640.

Squire, L.R. (1984). The neuropsychology of memory. In P. Marler & H.S. Terrace (Eds.), *The Biology of Learning.* pp. 667–685. Berlin: Springer Verlag.

Squire, L.R., Chace, P.M., & Slater, P.C. (1976). Retrograde amnesia following electroconvulsive therapy. *Nature* (Lond.), *260,* 775–777.

Squire, L.R. & Cohen, N. (1979). Memory and amnesia: Resistance to disruption develops for years after learning. *Behavioral and Neural Biology, 25,* 115–125.

Squire, L.R. & Cohen, N. (1982). Remote memory, retrograde amnesia, and the neuropsychology of memory. In L.S. Cermak (Ed.), *Human memory and amnesia.* pp. 275–309. Hillsdale, NJ: Erlbaum.

Squire, L.R. & Moore, R.Y. (1979). Dorsal thalamic lesions in a noted case of chronic memory dysfunction. *Annals of Neurology, 6,* 503–506.

Squire, L.R. & Slater, P.C. (1975). Forgetting in very long-term memory as assessed by an improved questionnaire technique. *Journal of Experimental Psychology: Human Learning and Memory, 104,* 50–54.

Squire, L.R. & Slater, P.C. (1978). Anterograde and retrograde memory impairment in chronic amnesia. *Neuropsychologia, 16,* 313–322.

Squire, L.R., Slater, P.C., & Chace, P.M. (1975). Retrograde amnesia: Temporal gradient in very long-term memory following electroconvulsive therapy. *Science, 187,* 77–79.

Stockert, T.R. von. (1972). Recognition of syntactic structure in aphasic patients. *Cortex, 8,* 323–354.

Tallal, P. & Newcombe, F. (1978). Impairment of auditory perception and language comprehension in aphasia. *Brain and Language, 5,* 13–24.

Tallal, P. & Piercy, M. (1973). Developmental aphasia: impaired rate of stimulus processing as a function of stimulus modality. *Neuropsychologia, 11,* 389–398.

Tallal, P. & Piercy, M. (1974). Developmental aphasia: rate of auditory processing and selective impairment of consonant perception. *Neuropsychologia, 12,* 83–94.

Tallal, P. & Piercy, M. (1975). Developmental aphasia: the perception of brief vowels and extended stop consonants. *Neuropsychologia, 13,* 69–74.

Tallal, P., Stark, R.E., & Curtiss, B. (1976). Relation between speech perception and speech production impairment in children with developmental dysphasia. *Brain and Language, 3,* 305–317.

Talland, G. (1965). *Deranged memory.* New York: Academic Press.

Tarter, R.E. (1973). An analysis of cognitive deficits in chronic alcoholics. *Journal of Nervous and Mental Disease, 157,* 138–147.

Tarter, R.E. & Parsons, O.A. (1971). Conceptual shifting in chronic alcoholics. *Journal of Abnormal Psychology, 77,* 71–75.

Taylor, A.M. & Warrington, E.K. (1973). Visual discrimination in patients with localized brain lesions. *Cortex, 9,* 82–93.

Taylor, R.L. (1969). Comparison of short-term memory and visual sensory analysis as sources of information. *Journal of Experimental Psychology, 81,* 515–522.

Teng, E.L. (1981). Dichotic ear difference is a poor

index for the functional asymmetry between the hemispheres. *Neuropsychologia, 19,* 235–240.

Teszner, D., Tsavaras, A., Gruner, J., & Hécaen, H. (1972). L'asymétrie droite-gauche du planum temporale; à propos de l'étude anatomique de 100 cerveaux. *Revue Neurologique, 126,* 444.

Teuber, H.-L., Milner, B., & Vaughan, H. (1968). Persistent anterograde amnesia after stab wound of the basal brain. *Neuropsychologia, 6,* 267–282.

Tissot, R.J., Mounin, G., & Lhermitte, F. (1973). *L'Agrammatisme.* Brussels: Dessart.

Tomlinson, E. (1977). Pathology of dementia. In C. Wells (Ed.), *Dementia* (2nd ed.). pp. 113–153. Philadelphia: F.A. Davis.

Trankell, A. (1950). *Vansterhandhet hos barn i skolalderin.* Helsingfors, Finland: Forum.

Tsavaras, A., Hécaen, H., & LeBras, H. (1970). Le problème de la spécificité du déficit de la reconnaissance du visage humain lors des lésions hémisphériques unilaterales. *Neuropsychologia, 8,* 403–416.

Tulving, E. (1972). Episodic and semantic memory. In E. Tulving & W. Donaldson (Eds.), *Organization of memory.* pp. 381–403. New York: Academic Press.

Tulving, E. (1983). *Elements of episodic memory.* New York: Oxford University Press.

Tunturi, A.R. (1946). A study on the pathway from the medial geniculate body to the acoustic cortex in the dog. *American Journal of Physiology, 147,* 811–819.

Umilta, C., Rizzolatti, G., Marzi, C.A., Zamboni, G., Franzini, C., Camarda, R., & Berlucchi, G. (1974). Hemisphere differences in the discrimination of line orientations. *Neuropsychologia, 12,* 165–174.

Ustvedt, H. (1937). Ueber die Untersuchung der musikalischen Funktionen bei Patienten mit Gehirnleiden, besonders bei Patienten mit Aphasie. *Acta Medica Scandinavica, Suppl., 86,* 727.

Victor, M., Adams, R.D., & Collins, G.H. (1971). *The Wernicke-Korsakoff syndrome.* Philadelphia: F.A. Davis.

Wada, J., Clarke, R., & Hamm, A. (1975). Cerebral asymmetry in humans: Cortical speech zones in 100 adult and 100 infant brains. *Archives of Neurology, 32,* 239–246.

Wada, J. & Rasmussen, T. (1960). Intracarotid injection of sodium amytal for the lateralization of cerebral speech dominance: Experimental and clinical observations. *Journal of Neurosurgery, 17,* 266–282.

Walter, W.G., Cooper, R., Aldridge, V.J., McCallum, W.C., & Winter, A.L. (1964). Contingent negative variation: An electric sign of sensorimotor association and expectancy in the human brain. *Nature, 203,* 380–384.

Warrington, E.K., Logue, V., & Pratt, R.T.C. (1972). The anatomical localization of selective impairment of auditory verbal short-term memory. *Neuropsychologia, 9,* 377–387.

Warrington, E.K. & Shallice, T. (1969). The selective impairment of auditory verbal short-term memory. *Brain, 92,* 885–896.

Warrington, E.K. & Shallice, T. (1972). Neuropsychological evidence of visual storage in short-term memory tasks. *Quarterly Journal of Experimental Psychology, 24,* 30–40.

Warrington, E.K. & Weiskrantz, L. (1970). Amnesic syndrome: Consolidation or retrieval? *Nature, 228,* 628–630.

Warrington, E.K. & Weiskrantz, L. (1973). An analysis of short-term and long-term memory defects in man. In J.A. Deutsch (Ed.), *The physiological basis of memory.* pp. 365–395. New York: Academic Press.

Warrington, E.K. & Weiskrantz, L. (1978). Further analysis of the prior learning effect in amnesic patients. *Neuropsychologia, 16,* 169–177.

Wernicke, C. (1874). *Der aphasische Symptomenkomplex: Eine psychologische Studie auf anatomischer Basis.* Cohn und Weigert.

Wertheim, N. (1969). The Amusias. In P.J. Vinken & G.W. Bruyn (Eds.), *Handbook of clinical neurology,* Vol. 4. pp. 195–206. Amsterdam: North Holland.

Whitehouse, P.J., Caramazza, A., & Zurif, E.B. (1978). Naming in aphasia: Interacting effects of form and function. *Brain and Language, 6,* 63–74.

Wickens, D.D. (1970). Encoding categories of words: An empirical approach to meaning. *Psychological Review, 77,* 1–15.

Wilkinson, D.A. & Carlen, P.L. (1981). Chronic organic brain syndromes associated with alcoholism: Neuropsychological and other aspects. In Y. Israel, F. Glaser, H. Kalant, R. Popham, W. Schmidt, & R. Smart (Eds.), *Research advances in alcohol and drug problems,* Vol. 6. pp. 107–145. New York: Plenum Press.

Winocur, G. & Kinsbourne, M. (1976). Transfer of learning in brain-damaged patients. Paper presented at the International Neuropsychological Society Meeting, Toronto.

Winocur, G. & Kinsbourne, M. (1978). Contextual cueing as an aid to Korsakoff amnesics. *Neuropsychologia, 16,* 671–682.

Winocur, G., Kinsbourne, M., & Moscovitch, M. (1981). The effect of cueing on release from proactive interference in Korsakoff amnesic patients. *Journal of Experimental Psychology: Human Learning and Memory, 7,* 56–65.

Winocur, G. & Weiskrantz, L. (1976). An investigation of paired-associate learning in amnesic patients. *Neuropsychologia, 14,* 97–110.

Witelson, S.F. (1974). Hemispheric specialization for

linguistic and non-linguistic tactual perception, using a dichotomous stimulation technique. *Cortex*, *10*, 1–17.

Witelson, S.F. (1976). Sex and the single hemisphere: Right hemisphere specialization for spatial processing. *Science*, *193 (4251)*, 425–427.

Witelson, S.F. (1977). Early hemisphere specialization and interhemispheric plasticity: An empirical theoretical review. In S. Segalowitz & F.A. Gruber (Eds.), *Language development and neurological theory.* pp. 213–287. New York: Academic Press.

Witelson, S.F. & Pallie, W. (1973). Left hemisphere specialization for language in the newborn: Neuroanatomical evidence of asymmetry. *Brain*, *96*, 641–646.

Wood, C.C., Goff, W.R., & Day, R.S. (1971). Auditory evoked potentials during speech perception. *Science*, *173*, 1248–1251.

Woods, B.T. & Teuber, H.-L. (1978). Changing patterns of childhood aphasia. *Annals of Neurology*, *3*, 273–280.

Woods, R. & Piercy, M. (1974). A similarity between amnesic memory and normal forgetting. *Neuropsychologia*, *12*, 437.

Yin, R.K. (1969). Looking at upside-down faces. *Journal of Experimental Psychology*, *81*, 141–145.

Yin, R.K. (1970). Face recognition by brain injured patients: A dissociable ability? *Neuropsychologia*, *8*, 395–402.

Young, A.W. & Ellis, H.D. (1976). An experimental investigation of developmental differences in ability to recognize faces presented to the left and right cerebral hemispheres. *Neuropsychologia*, *14*, 495–498.

Zaidel, E. (1977). Unilateral auditory language comprehension on the Token Test following cerebral commissurotomy and hemispherectomy. *Neuropsychologia*, *15*, 1–18.

Zaidel, E. & Peters, A. (1981). Phonological encoding and ideographic reading by the disconnected right hemisphere: Two case studies. *Brain and Language*, *14*, 205–234.

Zaidel, E. & Sperry, R.W. (1973). Performance on the Raven's Colored Progressive Matrices by subjects with cerebral commissurotomy. *Cortex*, *9*, 34–39.

Zatorre, R. (1979). Recognition of dichotic melodies by musicians and non-musicians. *Neuropsychologia*, *17*, 607–618.

Zurif, E.B. & Bryden, M.P. (1969). Familial handedness and left-right differences in auditory and visual perception. *Neuropsychologia*, *7*, 179–187.

Zurif, E.B., Caramazza, A., & Myerson, R. (1972). Grammatical judgements of agrammatic aphasics. *Neuropsychologia*, *10*, 405–417.

Zurif, E.B., Caramazza, A., Myerson, R., & Galvin, J. (1974). Semantic feature representations for normal and aphasic language. *Brain and Language*, *1*, 167–187.

# AUTHOR INDEX

Entries for Volume 1 are in regular type; entries for Volume 2 are in **bold type**.

# SUBJECT INDEX

Entries for Volume 1 are in regular text type; entries for Volume 2 are in **bold type**.

Abilities, **827**, **851**
Absolute identification (AI), global
  experiments, 48, 50-52, 65
Absolute motion, 242
Absolute scales, 16
Absolute sensitivity, olfaction,
  416-419
Absolute threshold, 39, 40, 305
  of auditory signals, 331, 332-334
Absorption, quantum theory of, 76,
  78-79
Abstract attributes, **353**
Accessibility theory, 519
Accessory olfactory bulb, 415
Access time, **359**
Accommodation, of the eye, 209
Accumbens, nucleus, 604-605
  and stimulant abuse, 594-595
Accuracy, **826-827**, **835**
Accuracy measures, **755-756**
Accuracy tasks, **746**
Acetylcholine (ACh), 559, 647,
  **276**, **278**, **279**
Acetylcholine (ACh) pathways, 646
Acetylcholine esterase (ACh E),
  646
Achievement, **687**
Acoustic admittance, 280-282, 295
Acoustic compliance, 281
Acoustic impedance, 280-282, 294,
  308
Acoustic mass, 281
Acoustic phonetics, 395-397
Acoustic processing, **893**
Acoustic reflex, 308-310
Acoustic resistance, 281
Acoustics, 278-283
  fundamental equations of,
    278-279
Acoustic signals, 283-286, **894**
  deterministic nonrepeating
    (aperiodic), 284-285
  deterministic periodic, 284
  probabilistically definable (random),
    285
  spectrum of, 283
  spike trains as, 285-286
Acoustic startle reflex (see Startle
  response)
Acoustic striae, 288
Acoustic variables, measures of,
  282
Acquired distinctiveness, **139**
Acquisition
  defined, **475**
  retardation of, **303**
  of schemata, **501**
  theories of, **498-501**
Across-fiber pattern theory, 482
ACT, **529-530**
Action, **590**, **592**
Action generation, **590**, **592**, **675**
Action potential, **302**, **311**

Action spectrum, Scotopic Invari-
  ance Laws, 113
Activation, **528-530**
Active avoidance, **271**, **272**, **273**,
  **280**, **283**, **284**, **286**
Active network structures, **563**
Active short-term memory (see
  Working memory)
Active zones, **312**
ACT models, **400**, **402**, **403**,
  **405**, **611**
Actor based systems, **565-566**
Actors, **565**
Acuity
  alignment, 172
  stereoscopic, 174
  vernier, 172
  visual, 166, 169-171, 175
Acuity test, double bar, 170, 171
Adaptation, olfactory, 425-428, 449,
  450
  bilateral integration and localiza-
    tion in, 427-428, 450
Adaptation, taste, 471
Adaptational gain change, 143
Adaptation level theory, 54
Adaptive-evolutionary approach,
  503-537
Adaptive specializations, 518
Addition, Grassman's law of, 30
Additive clustering, 38
Additive conjoint models, **710-711**,
  **715**, **717**
Additive factor method, **816**
Additive independence, **715**
Additive models, **149**
Additive relationship, phenotype,
  681
Adjunctive behavior, 596, **79**
Adoption studies, 688, 748, 749
  on intellectual functioning,
    709-711
  on psychopathology, 712-715
Adrenalectomy, 484-486
Adrenal medulla, **277-278**, **281**
Adrenocorticotropic hormone
  (ACTH)
  and imprinting, 579
  and stress, 578-579
Adrenocorticotropin, 578
Aerial perspective, 199
Affective-cognitive factors, **846**,
  **853**
Afferent connections, **288**
Aftereffects
  contingent, 230
  figural, 176-179, 180, 181, 235
  perceptual adaptation and, 231,
    235
Afterimage, 204-205, 218, 230
Ageusia, 488
Aggregate frequencies, **600-601**
Aggression, **284**

Aggressive behavior, **220**
Agonist-antagonist muscles, **480**
Agrammatic speech, **889**
Agrammatism, **902**, **903**,
  **904-905**, **907**
Aiming, **845**, **853**
Airy disk, 90, 91
Akinesias, 562-563
Alanine, 477
Alcoholic Korsakoff's syndrome
  amnesia in, **865**, **866**,
    **869-870**, **875**, **877**, **879**,
    **880-882**, **883**, **884**,
    **886-887**, **888**
  commission errors in, **877**
  and context theories, **880**
  and contextual discrimination,
    **881**
  performance in, **870**, **872**
  and proactive interference, **875**
  and semantic encoding,
    **874-877**
  and verbal learning, **880**
  word recall in, **871**, **874**, **875**,
    **877**
Alcohol-related behaviors, genetic
  influence on, 732, 733
Aldosterone, 569, 572-574, 576,
  578
Alexia, **863**, **890**, **899**, **905**
Algebraic models, **716**, **717-718**,
  **719**
Algebra word problems, **623**
Algorithms, **474**
Alignment acuity, 172
Alkaloids, 468
Alkaptonuria, 729
Alleles, 681, 682
Alliesthesia, 434
Allochthonous activity, 781
All-or-none model, **377**, **403**,
  **645**, **646-647**
Alloxan, 467
All-*trans* retinal, 77, 78, 107, 111,
  150
Alpha conditioning, **255**
Alpha-neoendorphin, 579-580
Alpha response pathway, **257-258**
Alteration, **292**
Alternation, **284**, **285-286**, **289**
Alternative reinforcement, **201**
Altruistic behavior, 807, 808
  joy and sadness in, 660
Alzheimer's disease, 747, **866**
AM, **654-655**
Amacrine cells, 134, 135, 137
Ambergris odorants, 440
Ambidexterity, **845**, **853**
Ambiguity, **425**, **426**, **433**,
  **447-451**, **455**, **463**
Ames window, 245-248, 256
Amiloride, 466, 473
Amino acid uptake inhibitors, **275**

995